D1540964

Twentieth-Century
Literary Criticism

Guide to Gale Literary Criticism Series

For criticism on	Consult these Gale series
Authors now living or who died after December 31, 1999	*CONTEMPORARY LITERARY CRITICISM (CLC)*
Authors who died between 1900 and 1999	*TWENTIETH-CENTURY LITERARY CRITICISM (TCLC)*
Authors who died between 1800 and 1899	*NINETEENTH-CENTURY LITERATURE CRITICISM (NCLC)*
Authors who died between 1400 and 1799	*LITERATURE CRITICISM FROM 1400 TO 1800 (LC)* *SHAKESPEAREAN CRITICISM (SC)*
Authors who died before 1400	*CLASSICAL AND MEDIEVAL LITERATURE CRITICISM (CMLC)*
Authors of books for children and young adults	*CHILDREN'S LITERATURE REVIEW (CLR)*
Dramatists	*DRAMA CRITICISM (DC)*
Poets	*POETRY CRITICISM (PC)*
Short story writers	*SHORT STORY CRITICISM (SSC)*
Literary topics and movements	*HARLEM RENAISSANCE: A GALE CRITICAL COMPANION (HR)* *THE BEAT GENERATION: A GALE CRITICAL COMPANION (BG)*
Asian American writers of the last two hundred years	*ASIAN AMERICAN LITERATURE (AAL)*
Black writers of the past two hundred years	*BLACK LITERATURE CRITICISM (BLC)* *BLACK LITERATURE CRITICISM SUPPLEMENT (BLCS)*
Hispanic writers of the late nineteenth and twentieth centuries	*HISPANIC LITERATURE CRITICISM (HLC)* *HISPANIC LITERATURE CRITICISM SUPPLEMENT (HLCS)*
Native North American writers and orators of the eighteenth, nineteenth, and twentieth centuries	*NATIVE NORTH AMERICAN LITERATURE (NNAL)*
Major authors from the Renaissance to the present	*WORLD LITERATURE CRITICISM, 1500 TO THE PRESENT (WLC)* *WORLD LITERATURE CRITICISM SUPPLEMENT (WLCS)*

ISSN 0276-8178

Volume 171

Twentieth-Century Literary Criticism

**Criticism of the
Works of Novelists, Poets, Playwrights,
Short Story Writers, and Other Creative Writers
Who Lived between 1900 and 1999,
from the First Published Critical
Appraisals to Current Evaluations**

Thomas J. Schoenberg
Lawrence J. Trudeau
Project Editors

THOMSON
★ ™
GALE

Detroit • New York • San Francisco • San Diego • New Haven, Conn. • Waterville, Maine • London • Munich

THOMSON
GALE

Twentieth-Century Literary Criticism, Vol. 171

Project Editors
Thomas J. Schoenberg and Lawrence J. Trudeau

Editorial
Jessica Bomarito, Kathy D. Darrow, Jeffrey W. Hunter, Jelena O. Krstović Michelle Lee, Rachelle Mucha, Russel Whitaker

Data Capture
Francis Monroe, Gwen Tucker

Indexing Services
Factiva®, a Dow Jones and Reuters Company

Rights and Acquisitions
Margaret Abendroth, Margaret Chamberlain-Gaston, Edna Hedblad

Imaging and Multimedia
Dean Dauphinais, Robert Duncan, Leitha Etheridge-Sims, Mary Grimes, Lezlie Light, Michael Logusz, Dan Newell, Kelly A. Quin, Denay Wilding

Composition and Electronic Capture
Kathy Sauer

Manufacturing
Rhonda Dover

Associate Product Manager
Marc Cormier

LIBRARY OF CONGRESS CATALOG CARD NUMBER 76-46132

ISBN 0-7876-8925-4
ISSN 0276-8178

Printed in the United States of America
10 9 8 7 6 5 4 3 2 1

Contents

Preface

Since its inception more than fifteen years ago, *Twentieth-Century Literary Criticism* (*TCLC*) has been purchased and used by nearly 10,000 school, public, and college or university libraries. *TCLC* has covered more than 500 authors, representing 58 nationalities and over 25,000 titles. No other reference source has surveyed the critical response to twentieth-century authors and literature as thoroughly as *TCLC*. In the words of one reviewer, "there is nothing comparable available." *TCLC* "is a gold mine of information—dates, pseudonyms, biographical information, and criticism from books and periodicals—which many librarians would have difficulty assembling on their own."

Scope of the Series

TCLC is designed to serve as an introduction to authors who died between 1900 and 1999 and to the most significant interpretations of these author's works. Volumes published from 1978 through 1999 included authors who died between 1900 and 1960. The great poets, novelists, short story writers, playwrights, and philosophers of the period are frequently studied in high school and college literature courses. In organizing and reprinting the vast amount of critical material written on these authors, *TCLC* helps students develop valuable insight into literary history, promotes a better understanding of the texts, and sparks ideas for papers and assignments. Each entry in *TCLC*presents a comprehensive survey on an author's career or an individual work of literature and provides the user with a multiplicity of interpretations and assessments. Such variety allows students to pursue their own interests; furthermore, it fosters an awareness that literature is dynamic and responsive to many different opinions.

Every fourth volume of *TCLC* is devoted to literary topics. These topics widen the focus of the series from the individual authors to such broader subjects as literary movements, prominent themes in twentieth-century literature, literary reaction to political and historical events, significant eras in literary history, prominent literary anniversaries, and the literatures of cultures that are often overlooked by English-speaking readers.

TCLC is designed as a companion series to Thomson Gale's *Contemporary Literary Criticism,* (*CLC*) which reprints commentary on authors who died after 1999. Because of the different time periods under consideration, there is no duplication of material between *CLC* and *TCLC*.

Organization of the Book

A *TCLC* entry consists of the following elements:

- The **Author Heading** cites the name under which the author most commonly wrote, followed by birth and death dates. Also located here are any name variations under which an author wrote, including transliterated forms for authors whose native languages use nonroman alphabets. If the author wrote consistently under a pseudonym, the pseudonym will be listed in the author heading and the author's actual name given in parenthesis on the first line of the biographical and critical information. Uncertain birth or death dates are indicated by question marks. Single-work entries are preceded by a heading that consists of the most common form of the title in English translation (if applicable) and the original date of composition.

- A **Portrait of the Author** is included when available.

- The **Introduction** contains background information that introduces the reader to the author, work, or topic that is the subject of the entry.

- The list of **Principal Works** is ordered chronologically by date of first publication and lists the most important works by the author. The genre and publication date of each work is given. In the case of foreign authors whose works have been translated into English, the English-language version of the title follows in brackets. Unless otherwise indicated, dramas are dated by first performance, not first publication.

- Reprinted **Criticism** is arranged chronologically in each entry to provide a useful perspective on changes in critical evaluation over time. The critic's name and the date of composition or publication of the critical work are given at the beginning of each piece of criticism. Unsigned criticism is preceded by the title of the source in which it appeared. All titles by the author featured in the text are printed in boldface type. Footnotes are reprinted at the end of each essay or excerpt. In the case of excerpted criticism, only those footnotes that pertain to the excerpted texts are included.

- A complete **Bibliographical Citation** of the original essay or book precedes each piece of criticism. Source citations in the Literary Criticism Series follow University of Chicago Press style, as outlined in *The Chicago Manual of Style,* 14th ed. (Chicago: The University of Chicago Press, 1993).

- Critical essays are prefaced by brief **Annotations** explicating each piece.

- An annotated bibliography of **Further Reading** appears at the end of each entry and suggests resources for additional study. In some cases, significant essays for which the editors could not obtain reprint rights are included here. Boxed material following the further reading list provides references to other biographical and critical sources on the author in series published by Thomson Gale.

Indexes

A **Cumulative Author Index** lists all of the authors that appear in a wide variety of reference sources published by Thomson Gale, including *TCLC*. A complete list of these sources is found facing the first page of the Author Index. The index also includes birth and death dates and cross references between pseudonyms and actual names.

A **Cumulative Nationality Index** lists all authors featured in *TCLC* by nationality, followed by the number of the *TCLC* volume in which their entry appears.

A **Cumulative Topic Index** lists the literary themes and topics treated in the series as well as in *Classical and Medieval Literature Criticism, Literature Criticism from 1400 to 1800, Nineteenth-Century Literature Criticism,* and the *Contemporary Literary Criticism* Yearbook, which was discontinued in 1998.

An alphabetical **Title Index** accompanies each volume of *TCLC*. Listings of titles by authors covered in the given volume are followed by the author's name and the corresponding page numbers where the titles are discussed. English translations of foreign titles and variations of titles are cross-referenced to the title under which a work was originally published. Titles of novels, dramas, nonfiction books, and poetry, short story, or essay collections are printed in italics, while individual poems, short stories, and essays are printed in roman type within quotation marks.

In response to numerous suggestions from librarians, Thomson Gale also produces a paperbound edition of the *TCLC* cumulative title index. This annual cumulation, which alphabetically lists all titles reviewed in the series, is available to all customers. Additional copies of this index are available upon request. Librarians and patrons will welcome this separate index; it saves shelf space, is easy to use, and is recyclable upon receipt of the next edition.

Citing *Twentieth-Century Literary Criticism*

When citing criticism reprinted in the Literary Criticism Series, students should provide complete bibliographic information so that the cited essay can be located in the original print or electronic source. Students who quote directly from reprinted criticism may use any accepted bibliographic format, such as University of Chicago Press style or Modern Language Association (MLA) style. Both the MLA and the University of Chicago formats are acceptable and recognized as being the current standards for citations. It is important, however, to choose one format for all citations; do not mix the two formats within a list of citations.

The examples below follow recommendations for preparing a bibliography set forth in *The Chicago Manual of Style,* 14th ed. (Chicago: The University of Chicago Press, (1993); the first example pertains to material drawn from periodicals, the-second to material reprinted from books:

Morrison, Jago. "Narration and Unease in Ian McEwan's Later Fiction." *Critique* 42, no. 3 (spring 2001): 253-68. Reprinted in *Twentieth-Century Literary Criticism.* Vol. 127, edited by Janet Witalec, 212-20. Detroit: Gale, 2003.

Brossard, Nicole. "Poetic Politics." In *The Politics of Poetic Form: Poetry and Public Policy,* edited by Charles Bernstein, 73-82. New York: Roof Books, 1990. Reprinted in *Twentieth-Century Literary Criticism.* Vol. 127, edited by Janet Witalec, 3-8. Detroit: Gale, 2003.

The examples below follow recommendations for preparing a works cited list set forth in the *MLA Handbook for Writers of Research Papers,* 5th ed. (New York: The Modern Language Association of America, 1999); the first example pertains to material drawn from periodicals, the second to material reprinted from books:

Morrison, Jago. "Narration and Unease in Ian McEwan's Later Fiction." *Critique* 42.3 (spring 2001): 253-68. Reprinted in *Twentieth-Century Literary Criticism.* Ed. Janet Witalec. Vol. 127. Detroit: Gale, 2003. 212-20.

Brossard, Nicole. "Poetic Politics." *The Politics of Poetic Form: Poetry and Public Policy.* Ed. Charles Bernstein. New York: Roof Books, 1990. 73-82. Reprinted in *Twentieth-Century Literary Criticism.* Ed. Janet Witalec. Vol. 127. Detroit: Gale, 2003. 3-8.

Suggestions are Welcome

Readers who wish to suggest new features, topics, or authors to appear in future volumes, or who have other suggestions or comments are cordially invited to call, write, or fax the Associate Product Manager:

Associate Product Manager, Literary Criticism Series
Thomson Gale
27500 Drake Road
Farmington Hills, MI 48331-3535
1-800-347-4253 (GALE)
Fax: 248-699-8054

Acknowledgments

The editors wish to thank the copyright holders of the criticism included in this volume and the permissions managers of many book and magazine publishing companies for assisting us in securing reproduction rights. Following is a list of the copyright holders who have granted us permission to reproduce material in this volume of *TCLC*. Every effort has been made to trace copyright, but if omissions have been made, please let us know.

COPYRIGHTED MATERIAL IN *TCLC*, VOLUME 171, WAS REPRODUCED FROM THE FOLLOWING PERIODICALS:

African Literature Today: The Question of Language, v. 17, 1991. Jones, Palmer, and Jones, eds. James Currey, London & Africa World Press, Trenton, 1991. Copyright © 1991 by James Currey Ltd. Reproduced by permission.—*Cahiers du Monde Russe et Soviétique,* v. 26, April-June, 1985. © Editions de l'EHESS. Reproduced by permission.—*Canadian Slavonic Papers,* v. 36, March-June, 1994. Copyright © Canadian Slavonic Papers, Canada, 1994. Reproduced by permission of the publisher.—*Comparative Literature Studies,* v. 40, 2003. Copyright © 2003 by The Pennsylvania State University. Reproduced by permission of the publisher.—*Criticism: A Quarterly for Literature and the Arts,* v. 39, fall, 1997. Copyright © 1997 Wayne State University Press. Reproduced with permission of the Wayne State University Press.—*Essays in Poetics,* v. 14, September, 1989 for "'Spoil the Purest of Ladies': Male and Female in Isaac Babel's *Konarmiya*" by Joe Andrew. Copyright © 1989 by Joe Andrew. Reproduced by permission of the author.—*The Henry James Review,* v. 15, fall, 1994; v. 16, spring, 1995; v. 18, spring, 1997; v. 23, spring, 2002. Copyright © 1994, 1995, 1997, 2002 The Johns Hopkins University Press. All reproduced by permission.—*JNT: Journal of Narrative Theory,* v. 32, winter, 2002 for "Metafiction, Metadrama, and the God-Game in Murdoch's *The Unicorn*" by Jack Stewart. Copyright © 2002 by *The Journal of Narrative Theory*. Reproduced by permission.—*The Journal of Narrative Technique,* v. 26, spring, 1996. Copyright © 1996 by *The Journal of Narrative Technique*. Reproduced by permission.—*Modern Fiction Studies,* v. 47, fall, 2001; Copyright © 2001 by Purdue Research Foundation, West Lafayette, IN 47907. All rights reserved. Reproduced by permission of The Johns Hopkins University.—*Nineteenth-Century Literature,* v. 54, December, 1999 for "Rereading the Book in Henry James's *The Ambassadors*" by Kevin Kohan. Copyright © 1999, The Regents of the University of California. All rights reserved. Used by permission of the publisher and the author.—*Orbis Litterarum,* v. 52, 1997. Copyright © 1997 Munksgaard International Publishers Ltd. Reproduced by permission of Blackwell Publishing Ltd.—*The Russian Review: An American Quarterly Devoted to Russia Past and Present,* v. 59, July, 2000. Copyright © 2000 Russian Review. Reproduced by permission of Blackwell Publishing Ltd.—*Russian Studies in Literature: A Journal of Translations,* v. 37, winter, 2000-01. English translation copyright © 2001 by M. E. Sharpe, Inc. All rights reserved. Used with permission. Not for reproduction.—*Slavic Review: American Quarterly of Russian, Eurasian and East European Studies,* v. 53, fall, 1994. Copyright © 1994 by the American Association for the Advancement of Slavic Studies, Inc. Reproduced by permission.—*Studies in the Novel,* v. 29, spring, 1997; v. 36, spring, 2004. Copyright © 1997, 2004 by North Texas State University. Both reproduced by permission.

COPYRIGHTED MATERIAL IN *TCLC*, VOLUME 171, WAS REPRODUCED FROM THE FOLLOWING BOOKS:

Azuonye, Chukwuma. From "'I, Okigbo, Town-Crier': The Transition from Mythopoeic Symbolism to a Revolutionary Aesthetic in *Path of Thunder*," in *The Gong and the Flute: African Literary Development and Celebration.* Edited by Kalu Ogbaa. Greenwood Press, 1994. Copyright © 1994 by Kalu Ogbaa. All rights reserved. Reproduced by permission of Greenwood Publishing Group, Inc., Westport, CT.—Brooks-Davies, Douglas. From *Fielding, Dickens, Gosse, Iris Murdoch and Oedipal* **Hamlet**. Macmillan, 1989. Copyright © Douglas Brooks-Davies, 1989. Reproduced with permission of Palgrave Macmillan.—Dipple, Elizabeth. From "*The Green Knight* and Other Vagaries of the Spirit; or, Tricks and Images for the Human Soul; or, the Uses of Imaginative Literature," in *Iris Murdoch and the Search for Human Goodness.* Edited by Maria Antonaccio and William Schweiker. The University of Chicago Press, 1996. Methuen, 1996. Copyright © 1996 by The University of Chicago. All rights reserved. Reproduced by permission of Routledge/Taylor & Francis Books Ltd. In the U.S., Canada, and the Philippines by permission of The University of Chicago Press.—Erlich, Victor. From "Color and Line: Notes on the Art of Isaac Babel," in *Isaac Babel.* Edited by Harold Bloom. Chelsea House Publishers, 1987. Copyright © 1987 by Chelsea House Publishers. Chapter © 1987 by Victor Erlich. Reproduced by permission of the author.—Gordon, David J. From *Iris Murdoch's Fables of Unselfing.* University of Missouri Press, 1995. Copyright ©

Thomson Gale Literature Product Advisory Board

Isaak Babel
1894-1940

(Full name Isaak Emmanuilovich Babel; also transliterated as Isaac, Izaak; also Emanuilovich; also Babel'; also wrote under pseudonym of Kiril Liutov) Russian short story writer, playwright, screenwriter, essayist, journalist, editor, autobiographer, and translator.

The following entry presents an overview of Babel's life and works. For additional information on his career, see *TCLC*, Volumes 2 and 13.

INTRODUCTION

Isaak Babel is widely regarded as one of the most skillful short fiction writers of the twentieth century. Additionally, he stands out as an important and definitive figure in Soviet literature, despite the fact that the Soviet literary establishment disavowed both him and his work during his lifetime. Because his literary coming of age coincided closely with the transformation of Russia by the Bolshevik Revolution, his work provides a valuable account of that transformation, while it also stands out as a counterpoint to the development of the new Soviet aesthetic. As a writer Babel is praised as a brilliant stylist and a keen observer of human nature. He is best remembered for his short story cycle *Konarmiia* (1926; *Red Cavalry*) and the picaresque stories of *Odesskie rasskazy* (1931; *The Odessa Tales*). These two works use contrast and paradox to convey a number of themes, such as the conflict between violence and passivity, romanticism and primitivism, hero and antihero, and, most importantly, between a traditional Jewish ethos and a non-traditional Jewish environment.

BIOGRAPHICAL INFORMATION

Babel was born on June 30, 1894, to Emmanuel Isaakovich Babel and Fania Aronovna Shvevel Babel, in the port city of Odessa on the Black Sea. Babel's early development was shaped by the tension between the traditions of his Jewish heritage and Odessa's modern, cosmopolitan culture. Though his education was devoted to business and finance, Babel took a strong interest in literature after he was introduced to a number of French authors, most notably Guy de Maupassant and Gustave Flaubert. He soon began writing short stories in French. Babel moved to Petrograd in 1916, where he met the prominent author and editor Maxim Gorky. In addition

to publishing the first of Babel's stories in his magazine *Letopis'*, Gorky became a valued mentor and a lifelong proponent of the young author and his work. On Gorky's recommendation, Babel went off to expand the depth of his experience. He did so in a series of official and military posts, first in the Russian Army during World War I and then, purportedly, in a Bolshevist police force called the "Cheka." In 1919 Babel took a position as a newspaper correspondent with the Cossack Cavalry during their combat against the czarist White Army. In this capacity Babel encountered a range of astonishing events that profoundly influenced his life and work. Out of these experiences he wrote the stories in *Red Cavalry*, one of his best known and most deeply admired works.

Despite Babel's prominence in the Soviet literary scene during and immediately after the Revolution, his work began to lose favor with the Communist regime as early as the late 1920s. As the Communist Party began to control literary ideology more rigidly, Babel's writing was criticized heavily for its erotic nature and for its lack of socialist zeal. He lived and wrote abroad intermittently from 1928 to 1934, and this contributed to suspicions over his loyalty. When he returned home, his unwillingness to write convincing propaganda pieces further convinced the authorities that Babel was guilty of anti-Soviet sentiment. He was arrested in 1939 by the Soviet secret police and executed by firing squad in 1940.

MAJOR WORKS

Babel's importance to Soviet literature is based exclusively on the impressionistic and often ironic stories in *Red Cavalry* and *The Odessa Tales.* His most light-hearted and vibrantly drawn works are collected in *The Odessa Tales,* the characters and setting of which are depicted in an almost mythological style. Benia Krik, a central character of the story cycle, is a gangster of the Moldavanka underworld, the Jewish neighborhood in which Babel himself was born. Benia is a passionate and complicated hero, collecting protection money in one scene and falling madly in love in the next. The weddings, funerals, robberies, barn-burnings, and other events that animate the stories are larger than life, even carnivalesque. The colorful quality of these stories exemplifies the views expressed in an earlier essay Babel wrote in praise of Odessa. For Babel, Odessa symbolized life, exuberance, and rejuvenation. He believed that writers should look to Odessa for inspiration and the future of Soviet literature. Another striking feature of *The Odessa Tales* is Babel's unique and skillful writing style. Through his manipulation of syntax, grammar, and rhythmic phrasing, he captures the essence of the Odessan Jewish dialect. He shifts among various narrative forms, including the epic, the comic, the literary, and the colloquial, all to heighten or highlight the stories' desired effect.

Strikingly different in theme and tone is Babel's other major contribution to Soviet literature, *Red Cavalry.* Consisting of thirty-four stories in its first publication, the collection depicts the Polish-Soviet War between the spring and late summer of 1920. Although Babel manipulates facts for the sake of theme, the stories typically coincide both geographically and chronologically with the movements of Semyon Budyonny's cavalry during the conflict. While there are recurring characters and themes in *Red Cavalry,* the narrator of the stories, Kirill Vasil'evich Liutov, is the most significant unifying feature of the cycle. Liutov is a Jewish intellectual who joins Budyonny's cavalry after graduating from law school. His primary role in the war is to observe and report for the army newspaper, but he also explains and interprets events of the Revolution for the soldiers. Liutov expresses horror and anguish at the destruction

of human life and the natural world he observes. However, even though he laments the annihilation of his culture, he does not romanticize the past or forget its corrupt qualities. Liutov is unable to fully condone or condemn either side of the conflict he is observing. Formally, *Red Cavalry* blends striking, often brutal and violent, imagery with what has been called "ornamental" or poetic prose. This exemplifies Babel's participation in the modernist tradition of blurring the boundary between poetry and fiction, which can be seen in the writing of a number of Russian writers between 1890 and 1930. Assonance, alliteration, wordplay, onomatopoeia, and other poetic devices heighten the mood of his stories. Differing language styles also pervade the work; Babel shifts frequently between language registers in order to highlight the striking imagery for which he is so well known.

CRITICAL RECEPTION

During his lifetime, Babel's work received a wide range of responses, from high praise to harsh criticism. His writing was lauded frequently for its high artistic qualities: its rich imagery, emotional depth, and innovative style. In addition, Babel's proficient use of various language devices and registers earned him a reputation as an innovator in the development of Soviet literature. His popularity reached its peak in the early 1920s. After the publication of *Red Cavalry,* however, the praise gave way to an increasing amount of criticism and political suspicion. The same indirect and impassive style which some critics found masterful and subtle seemed too difficult and decadent to others. Officials identified him with the *poputchiki,* a group of writers who did not oppose the Revolution but did not necessarily share its central ideology. Although Babel's talent was generally acknowledged, he was censured for portraying the Revolution naturalistically, in all its chaos, rather than nationalistically, as a matter of cultural necessity. His erotic subject matter also drew increasing criticism as Soviet doctrine became more and more repressive. By the time of Babel's arrest and subsequent execution, his critical reputation had been destroyed.

With the loosening of control on artistic expression after Joseph Stalin's death in 1953, Babel's work was rediscovered and his reputation revived. Since then, his work has been admired widely for its formal skill, its structural intricacy, its powerful and creative use of language, and its complex use of perspective, much as it had been when it was first published. Recent criticism has been devoted to a number of central issues, including the formal architecture of Babel's stories and their depictions of the complex nature of human relations. Edyta Bojanowska has argued that rather than leading us to condemn evil and violence, "Babel aims at exposing the immense complexity of any moral action and, consequently, of any moral judgment. Instead of resolving a moral dilemma, he often chooses to dramatize it." Many critics have also been interested in explaining Babel's "preoccupations" in his tales, most notably with violence and sexuality, and theorizing about the mythological and social sources that inform his world. What has emerged is confirmation of Babel as a master of the short story form and one of the finest writers in Russian literature.

PRINCIPAL WORKS

Liubka Kazak: Rasskazy (short stories) 1925

Rasskazy (short stories) 1925

Benia Krik: Kino-Povest' [*Benya Krik, the Gangster, and Other Stories*] (short stories) 1926

Istoriia moei golubiatni (short stories) 1926

Konarmiia [*Red Cavalry*] (short stories) 1926

Korol' (novel) 1926

Zakat [*Sunset*] (play) 1927

Odesskie rasskazy [*The Odessa Tales*] (short stories) 1931

Mariia [*Marya*] (play) 1935

Collected Stories [edited by Walter Morison] (short stories) 1955

Liubka the Cossack and Other Stories (short stories) 1963

Isaac Babel: The Lonely Years, 1925-1939 [edited by by Nathalie Babel] (short stories, letters, essays, and speeches) 1964

Izbrannoe (short stories, letters, essays, and speeches) 1966

You Must Know Everything: Stories, 1915-1937 [edited by Nathalie Babel] (short stories) 1969

The Forgotten Prose [edited by Nicholas Stroud] (short stories and diary excerpts) 1978

Collected Stories (short stories) 1994

The Complete Works of Isaac Babel [edited by by Nathalie Babel] (short stories, plays, letters, essays, and speeches) 2002

Hamutal Bar-Yosef (essay date April-June 1985)

SOURCE: Bar-Yosef, Hamutal. "The Poetic Status of Direct Speech in the Stories of Isaak Babel'." *Cahiers du Monde Russe et Soviétique* 26, no. 2 (April-June 1985): 185-91.

[*In the following essay, Bar-Yosef argues that the moral center of Babel's work, considered by many critics to be absent or ambiguous, can best be discovered in re-curring epiphanic moments in which the narrators of the stories collide "with certain brutal, 'anti-poetic' facts, and this encounter is often accompanied by a direct statement," either by the narrator or another character. According to Bar-Yosef, these direct statements are a clue "to the conceptual and moral message" of Babel's stories.*]

1

Babel' assigned unlimited importance to the stylistic qualities of his stories, and indeed, his critics have often pointed out that the style is a central factor in the unique artistic achievement of his work. Nevertheless, the various elements of Babel''s style have only gradually penetrated critical and scholarly awareness. Contemporary criticism saw him chiefly as an ornamentalist, and attention was generally directed to passages of a poetic nature. "Style" was identified with poeticality. Today, however, it is generally accepted that the lyrical passages are only one component in the total stylistic texture of the stories, and what confers the uniqueness on Babel''style is precisely its heterogeneity. The stories are composed of elements belonging to various literary genres and to various linguistic registers: prose and poetry, journalism and folksong, political cliché and proverbs.

Various explanations have been given for the rapid stylistic switches in Babel''s stories: the aesthetic effect achieved by the combination or juxtaposition of opposites; or, the contribution made to the dynamics in stories where the dramatic situation is pushed off-stage. Some scholars have discussed the changing narrators, who supplant each other as the styles interchange. Other rhetorical aspects have also been noticed; the difference between Liutov and the "primary" narrator; the wide use of the *skaz* tradition, both by the anonymous narrator and by the fictional characters; and the repeated use of semi-documentary narrative—letter, diary, or the oral account given by one of the characters to the narrator. This variegated choir of voices suggests, according to most scholars, several simultaneous alternatives for the moral and emotional evaluation of the problematic historical and human reality depicted in the stories, especially in **Red Cavalry,** but also occurring in others. Hence the generally accepted conclusion, that Babel' does not assume a definite evaluatory attitude towards his events and characters. Kossacks, Jews and Poles, murderers and victims, on this view, are represented from the same ambivalent moral stance. Carol Luplow, in her excellent *Isaac Babel''s Red Cavalry* (1982), ascribes the moral "confusion" to the fictional narrator Liutov, and shows that his attitude and personality are not consistently represented in the different stories, or even within the same story. I would like to add two points to this discussion.

a. The reduced, even miniature, compass of Babel''s stories has induced a tendency to read them as if one were looking at a picture, that is, reacting to the paradigmatic level, while the dynamic process continuing throughout the sequence of the story has been neglected.

If one reads Babel''s stories not only in breadth but also in length, one may ask oneself: does what is represented at the beginning of the story have the same validity, the same authenticity, as what is represented as the story goes on and at the end? What emerges from the narrative voices: a static dynamics, as in a mobile, or is there some kind of development, in the course of which certain alternatives are rejected and others accepted in their place? The tendency to understand the significance of a story through an excessive reliance on the information presented in the earlier part, while ignoring the information accumulating as it progresses, is frequently found in the reading process.

b. The direct speech of Babel''s characters is a stylistic and thematic factor, that has not yet received due attention. Some critics have regarded it as a sign of aesthetic variation, meant to balance the poetic heights of other passages; others have seen in it a means of characterization, intended to give an authentic representation of the figures, while others again regard it as a factor in dynamization, adding dramatic body to the story.

In order to fill out the two points I have raised, I suggest to look at Babel''s stories not as at a well-tempered mobile, but as a gradual stripping of the consciousness, reaching a climax towards the end of the story in a moment of epiphany. The epiphany occurs in the collision of the narrator with certain brutal, "anti-poetic," facts, and this encounter is often accompanied by a direct statement in the voice of one of the characters, sometimes the narrator himself, not necessarily as part of a dialogue.

These direct statements are a clue to the conceptual and moral message of the story. In them is concealed the voice of the author, who is trying, as far as possible, to avoid a direct "telling." The statements are of two kinds: those that convey a harsh, callous attitude, of a speaker who identifies himself with the revolutionary cause, and those that convey tenderness, humanity and sensitivity to suffering, an attitude that belongs to the "old world." In many of the stories both kinds of statement appear, and it is important to note, that the statement of the first, "hard," kind appears first, and that of the second, softer, type—later, usually towards the end of the story.

2

Let us illustrate these remarks by means of two stories from *Red Cavalry*. **"Perekhod cherez Zbruch"** and **"Syn Rabbi."** In both the subject of Jewishness has a central importance, and their position at the beginning and end of the cycle (in the 1st edition, 1926) is not accidental.

The opening, very brief, paragraph of **"Syn Rabbi"** is written in the manner of news information, gliding into the style of the historical epic. The narrator appears as a collective voice, identifying himself with the Russian historical memory in the present and in the past. Next comes a long paragraph of nature depiction in a poetic style, moving from impressionism to expressionism. Aesthetic and sensual experience is here given a supreme value. In spite of hints of bloodshed the event is described as a celebratory pageant experience, filled with beauty. Notwithstanding the use of "we," the narrator observes all these details not from the human point of view, but from one that merges with nature (maybe from the point of view of the horses): "Zvuchnye potoki sochatsia mezhdu sotniami loshadnykh nog."

Only in the third paragraph, in the middle of the story, does the "we" turn into "I," and a human narrator appears, a Soviet officer who bivouacs in a Jewish lodging. We hear him saying just one sentence: "Uberite . . . kak vy griazno zhivete, khoziaeva . . ." This phrase expresses with trenchant cruelty Liutov's first reaction to the reality of Jewish life in the shtetl, from the point of view of one who has succeeded in emerging from it and considers himself to be a part of a higher, cleaner and more beautiful life. However, together with the feelings of disgust the description of the room contains hints of condemnation of the brutal sacrilege that has carelessly and indifferently been committed in it. The hints appear in a metonymic fashion: "fragments of the crockery the Jews use only once a year, at Passover" that are scattered on the floor together with "scraps of women's fur coats" . . . and "chelovecheskii kal." The hint is very well hidden and for the moment is presented as from an entirely external point of view. Liutov talks about the Jews as of an alien tribe with strange customs.

As the story goes on, the narrator falls asleep and dreams that the divisional commander, the Natch-Div, fires into the eyes of the Kom-Brig; the eyes fall to the ground, and the Natch-Div shouts: "Zachem ty povorotil brigadu?" The Natch-Div's indignant question echoes the narrator's indignation in his semi-question to the woman (kak vy griazno zhivete), both have the same harsh official tone, the same unrealistic exigence of some impossible "clean" behaviour, both ignore the suffering of common humanity in the name of the demands of the revolution.

The story concludes with the very simple words spoken by the Jewish woman, with a sudden and terrible violence: "I teper' Ia khochu znat' . . . Ia khochu znat', gde eshche na vsei zemle vy naidete takogo ottsa kak moi otets . . ."

This is also a question, a third one. It is the emotional and ideational gravity of the story. The woman's question is not equal in weight to those of the narrator and the Natch-Div, it does not merely counterbalance them. It overcomes them by its innate power. This is the thematic turning-point, the "pointe," that in retrospect illuminates the significance of the whole story. It also illuminates the identity of the narrator. The woman's words are heard at the moment when the narrator wakes from sleep and discovers that he is lying between the pregnant woman and the corpse of her murdered father. These bare facts, together with the simple, living, speech, of the woman, stir him through several layers of disguised identities.

The woman's speech is not part of a dialogue, it does not characterize her individual or social-cultural personality, it is not used in order to variegate the style. It appears as the voice of an old and ugly reality that cannot be cast aside.

The story **"Syn Rabbi"** begins with an invitation for the Sabbath eve in Zhitomir. The rhetorical address to some Vasilii (who appears in no other story) and the style, which is saturated with allusions to romantic Russian folksongs, establish a narrator whose consciousness is alien to Zhitomir and to the Sabbath eve, a consciousness possessing deep roots in Russian culture. Here too the narrator at the beginning of the story is a collective representative of Russia.

Then comes a reminiscent passage describing the narrator's visit to the house of Rabbi Motale Bratslavskii, still to the accompaniment of rhetorical addresses to Vasilii. The scene is described in a poetic style, and emerges as a theatrical tableau, exotic, grotesque, where against the dim background hovers the figure of Il'ia, the Rabbi's son, shining with magical holiness and beauty: "prekrasnoe litso Il'i, syna Rabbi, poslednego printsa v dinastii . . ."

Taking a sharp turn, the story leaps from this poetic, nostalgic picture, which belongs to the past, to the dreadful reality of the present narrative. Here we have a naturalistic passage describing the cruelty and ugliness of human conduct during the withdrawal from the front. The following part of this passage was deleted by the Russian censorship in the later editions of the collected stories (of 1957 and 1966): "I chudovishchnaia Rossiia, nepravdopodobnaia, kak stado platianykh vshei, zatopala laptiami po obe storony vagonov."

Il'ia, the Rabbi's son, suddenly appears before the narrator against a background of "typhus-ridden peasantry," who are trying to force their way on to the Political Section Train and are being thrown off it for lack of space. In the center of the story-sequence stands the description of Il'ia, dragged by Liutov on the wagon where he is dying naked in front of two staring girls. Il'ia's physical nakedness, which also reveals the sign of his Jewishness, is a projection of the exposure that the narrator's consciousness is also undergoing. The metonymic depiction of Il'ia's belongings represents the mixture of cultures and the contradictory, ridiculous, yearnings, that by analogy connect Il'ia and the narrator. From this point onwards the narrator's addresses to Vasilii disappear, and, for the first time in the story, towards the end, direct speech is used. Il'ia says with startling dogmatic firmness: "Mat' v revoliutsii—epizod." He concludes, however, the short talk with the narrator with another laconic sentence: "U menia ne khvatilo artillerii."

Here we have a close juxtaposition of the two contrasting voices: the bare harshness of the son of the revolution, and the helplessness and despair of the fighter who did not get enough arms to gain the battle, and became a victim of the revolution. In this short sentence—"I hadn't enough artillery"—Babel' communicates his own autobiographical despairing pessimism regarding the possibility of integrating into the new reality, being "insufficiently armed" as he was.

In this story, which was meant to close the whole cycle, Babel' added a sort of coda, a paragraph wending with the words: "Ia prinial poslednii vzdokh moego brata."

The narrator's self-identification with Il'ia, the uncovering of his own true identity, are rendered on the level of metaphoric language as an act of receiving a heritage, of dedication to the prophet, or even as an act of renewed creation. Il'ia's last sigh is the breath of life that enters into the narrator. In retrospect the appeals to Vasilii and the exotic coloring of the Jewish world appear as theatrical and superficial against the actual voice and image of Il'ia, a representative of the tragic situation of the young Jew in the new world of the revolution.

3

Attention to the bare, direct speech is not only useful in understanding the significance of Babel''s stories, but also in understanding his poetics. Switches of narrator and style are not only alternations of points of view and value attitudes, but also represent competing poetical alternatives.

The history of literature is, as we know, a history of changing norms. A set of stylistic means that is fresh and attractive at a certain time undergoes obsolescence and loses its force and poetical status in another period. Symbolism, even before formalism, emphasized the importance of the deautomatization of language. At the beginning of the twentieth century, poetry was seen as fulfilling a prime function in revitalizing contact with reality. The language of prose was seen as the result of the crystallization of thought in clichés, after the living contact had become fossilized. Musicality and rich figurativeness of language were hallmarks of a discourse possessing emotional force, and of epistemological authenticity. These theories, together with the achievements of poetry as compared with prose at the end of the nineteenth century and the beginning of the twentieth, conferred a preferential status on the language of poetry. It led to a poetic dynamic that caused the conventions of prose genres to approach those of poetry.

Babel' grew up in an atmosphere of strong consciousness of the rapid obsolescence of linguistic expression. He was very sensitive to the thinness of the clichés that depicted and explained contemporary events in the official means of communication. He aspired to illuminate reality afresh by means of stylistic innovations, writing explicitly on this subject in a letter to his mother from the 13th of June 1935:

> "In a country as united as ours, it is quite inevitable that a certain amount of thinking in clichés should appear, and I want to overcome this standardized way of thinking and introduce into our literature new ideas, new feelings and rhythms. This is what interests me and nothing else."
>
> **(The Lonely Years [Isaac Babel: The Lonely Years, 1925-1939]: 283)**

However, already in his early work Babel' shows signs that he was suspicious of poetic expression. The symbolist tradition of rejecting simple language seemed to him out of touch with real experience. In one of his first stories, **"Vdokhnovenie,"** Mishka, a novice author, explains his artistic intentions to his friend, the narrator, Sashka: "V etoi povesti [. . .] Ia khotel dat' novoe proizvedenie, okutannoe dalekoi mechty, nezhnost', poluteni i namek . . . Mne protivna, protivna grubost' nashei zhizni . . ."

Mist, half-shadows, suggestive language, these are echoes of symbolist poetry and narrative, dealing with vaporous situations and depicting characters in an over-refined style. The fictive materials and the human situations which Babel' confronted in his writing were, on the contrary, "low," violent and coarse, the kind of material that at that time was labelled "naturalistic." The representation of this kind of material in a poetic style drawn from the symbolistic tradition was in itself still innovatory. According to the formalist theories that considered de-automatization as the aesthetic purpose of literary creation, Babel' might have been satisfied with this one innovation. But he was aware of the fact that a poetical representation of "coarse" reality implies an attitude of estrangement and alienation towards the events and the characters, in fact, an attitude of hostility towards this "coarse" reality. Babel' refused to write like his Mishka who flees from facing what he finds disagreeable and wraps reality in a weak disguise of poetical beauty.

Babel' was suspicious and critical regarding that system of poetical means, which to symbolist poetics was an instrument for breaking down the screens set up by language and for touching "der Ding an sich."

When luxuriant poetical textures appear in Babel''s stories they are mostly found in the exposition, in the first part of the story, as a conceptual alternative to be rejected as the story proceeds. The exposition, which sometimes covers half the story, presents the possibility of absorbing crude reality without seeing its ugly sides, of wrapping it in an agreeable veil of tenderness and beauty, colourfulness and sensuousness, thus finding it nice and easy. However, as the story goes on, naked reality breaks into the narrator's consciousness, and forces him to face the inglorious and frightening truth that had been repressed. This move is carried out by abandoning the poetic style and by a transition of a style whose poetry belongs to other norms, to new ones. These are norms that in Russian poetry were represented chiefly by Akmeism. This tendency had an impressive continuation in Western poetry, European and American, in the first half of the twentieth century, poetry that rejected figurative excesses and over-rich musicality, and looked to plain, simple speech for new sources towards expressive revitalization and closer contact with reality. In the field of prose one can see a similar tendency in writers such as Hemingway or Camus, who transformed the "degré zéro de l'écriture" into a powerful stylistic instrument.

Babel' sensed the poetic force hidden in the lean and bare discourse of direct speech. Against a background of textures possessing "fat" poetic layers, these "lean" statements appear like holes in a theatre curtain, and like the seven cows that Pharoah saw in his dream, they swallow up the fat style and emphasize its illusory reality.

Efraim Sicher (essay date 1986)

SOURCE: Sicher, Efraim. "Sex and Violence: An Art of Contrasts." In *Style and Structure in the Prose of Isaak Babel'*, pp. 39-51. Columbus, Ohio: Slavica Publishers, Inc., 1986.

[*In the following essay, Sicher discusses the relationship of violence and sex in Babel's stories, stating that violence is artistically rendered "in the structuring of imagery and symbolism" of the narratives, and that it is "bound up with initiation rites through which the child and the intellectual must come to terms with cruelty, must know life in the sexual sense of the word."*]

Violence may appear gratuitous in Babel's stories, but artistically it is motivated in the structuring of imagery and symbolism as part of a deeply moral vision of the world. Babel's modernist prose shocks us into recognizing the primitive brutality of human beings, as well as the paradoxical violence of modernity. Violence is explicitly sexual, bound up with initiation rites, through which the child discovers he is a Jew in a world of pogroms and through which the intellectual must come to terms with cruelty, must know life in all senses of the word. For the narrator of Babel's early stories dealing with sex and prostitution, such as **"Doudou"** (**"Doudou,"** 1917) or **"Through the Fanlight"** (**"V shchelochku,"** 1923), curiosity embodies a kind of aesthetic voyeurism that searches for clues to the compelling complexity of human relations. Matvei Pavlichenko (the eponymous hero of one Red Cavalry story) kills his former master by stamping on him for an hour or more in order, he tells us, to know life fully for what it is.

The "saintly life" of Matvei (Matthew) Pavlichenko excels in its intense sexuality as much as the lives of the ecclesiastic saints excelled in asceticism. Summer and winter Matvei and Nastia go naked and tear off each other's skin. In the description of another Red Cavalry hero, Savitskii, sexuality and violence emphasize his physicality. The narrator of **"My First Goose"** (**"Moi pervyi gus"**) is astonished by the beauty of Savitskii's gigantic body which does not merely stand in the middle of the hut but slices it in two, "like a standard cuts the sky."[1] The narrator, whose own masculine prowess is questioned in the story, envies the violent sensuality of the mighty Cossack commander, a sensuality complicated by a femininity which strangely adds to his seductiveness and which, even more strangely, he shares with the Odessa gangsters in **"The Father"** (**"Otets,"** 1924) who walk past Baska "like girls who have known love" (*Detstvo* [*Detstvo i drugie rasskazy*], 271). Savitskii smells of scent and soap and his long legs are "like girls, clad to the shoulders in shining jackboots" (*Detstvo,* 129). There is gaiety in Savitskii's coarse brutality and he smiles at the narrator as he cracks his whip on the table. Living in disgrace with Pavla, Savitskii exudes an almost feminine perfume (*Detstvo,* 161) and he sees this world and the next as a whorehouse (*Detstvo,* 203). Russian literature has been more prurient than has been popularly suspected in the West, but Babel's Cossacks and Odessa gangsters exhibit an unusually uninhibited and frank libido. There is certainly a truth concerning Babel's portrayal of his characters in the view which the narrator of **"Story of a Horse"** (**"Istoriia odnoi loshadi"**) shares with Khlebnikov of the world as a field of women and horses in May (*Detstvo,* 164).

Babel's women are strong in physique and character; they are, moreover, also strangely sexed. Lyubka, nicknamed "The Cossack," boasts enormous breasts, yet she cannot give milk to her son (*Detstvo,* 266, 267) and she exhibits her masculinity by beating a drunken peasant "like a tambourine" (**"The Father,"** *Detstvo,* 275-6).

Baska in the same story parades in men's boots. With the sex drive of Babel's womenfolk, Cossacks and gangsters are associated the fertility symbols of blood, fire, and sweat. By contrast, the characters belonging to the old, spiritual world of Roman Catholic churches and the Jewish *shtetl* do not prove to be sexually reproductive. The Jewish hetman in **"Afonka Bida"** and Ilia Bratslavskii are impotent despite joining the Revolution; both doomed idealists are described as emaciated (*"chakhloe"*). Ilia has old women's knees, and two fat-breasted typists stare at the wasted virility of his stunted genitals (*Detstvo,* 299). Sexuality is reserved for the active heroes of the new age, not for the victims. Gregory Freiden has read castration and sterility complexes in Babel's portrayal of Jewish protagonists, particularly in his description of their thin necks.[2] One might add that the negation of the sexuality of Jewish protagonists is explicit in the image of the Jews in **"Crossing the Zbrucz"** as chimpanzees and Japs in a circus, or the association of Uncle Shoil in **"Story of My Dovecot"** with fish—he trades in fish in Fish Street and when he is killed in a pogrom he is left with a fish poking out of his open pants. However, such images are not negative in all respects and, needless to say, this does not apply to those Jews who have forcibly rejected the Gentiles' attempt to demean their sexuality, such as Benia Krik, who can sleep with a Russian woman and satisfy her (according to Arye-Leib in **"How It Was Done in Odessa"**).

That the revolutionary forces sweeping Russia were driven by primeval instincts was a motif of much fiction of the twenties and was not uncommonly illustrated by the infectious image of syphilis, from which a number of Babel's Cossacks suffer. Such sexual frankness bears no relation to the libertine *épater les bourgeois* but suggests that carnal passions rule human nature. The Jesus depicted in the Red Cavalry story **"Pan Apolek"** and **"The Sin of Jesus"** (**"Isusov grekh,"** 1922) is certainly more carnal than incarnate. Sex is essentially a bodily function in the Red Cavalry story **"The Widow"** (**"Vdova"**), where it is described in the same terms as eating: Levka chews meat and later has sex with Sashka "crunching and panting" (*"khrustia i zadykhaias"*)—the same noise made earlier by the fettered horses in the bushes (*Detstvo,* 204-206). The animalistic lust of Babel's women with their outsize busts and fleshy thighs is unmistakable. Take Pavla in the Red Cavalry story **"Story of a Horse"** (**"Istoriia odnoi loshadi"**), whose chest "moves like an animal in a sack" (*Detstvo,* 161). As the battle approaches in "Chesniki," two chubby medical sisters frolic in the grass, prodding each other's breasts, and lure on the narrator "like barelegged village girls" who "shriek like pampered puppies," while not far off a soldier lies wounded (*Detstvo,* 219). Then along comes Sashka, plump Sashka known to men in every division, to persuade Stepka Duplishchev to let his stallion mate with her mare. Whereas Sashka casts aspersions on the lad's manhood, her sexuality is typical of Babel's women:

> Шпоры на ее туфлях гремели, ажурные чулки были забрызганы грязью и убраны сеном, чудовищная грудь ее закидывалась за спину.
>
> *(Detstvo, 220)*

> The spurs jingled on her shoes, straw was stuck to her mud-splashed open-work stockings and her monstrous breasts swung round her back.

Animal love is substituted for that of the human couple and after the horses have copulated Sashka kisses her mare full on its moist lips.

The narrator grasps at some hidden secret in these voyeuristic scenes. In **"At Batko Makhno's"** (**"U bat'ki nashego Makhno,"** 1924), set against the bloody background of the Civil War, the narrator declares his curiosity about what a woman looks like after being raped six times in one night:

> Только неспешное существование на плодоносной украинской земле может налить еврейку такими коровьими соками. Ноги девушки жирные, кирпичные, раздутые, как шары, воняли приторно, как только что вырезанное мясо.[3]

> Only an unhurried existence on fertile Ukrainian soil could infuse a Jewess with such bovine juices. The girl's legs were fleshy, brick-red, inflated like balloons and gave off a sickly smell like freshly slaughtered meat.

In the mock rape scene in the Red Cavalry story **"At St. Valentine's Church"** (**"U sviatogo Valenta"**), Sashka's body similarly smells of a freshly slaughtered cow (**Detstvo**, 185). Cows' udders suggest promiscuity in Apolek's paintings as well as in **"The Life of Pavlichenko, Matvei Rodionych."** In **"The Father"** the "pink milk of spring" symbolizes that untiring life of sex and motherhood of the fat mamas of the Moldavanka coveted by Baska (**Detstvo**, 272). The pinkness of sweating flesh, rosy like blood or the foam of a mad dog (**Detstvo**, 239), emphasizes the overbearing physical presence of these Amazons. This evokes an exotic eroticism, but at the same time hints at a grotesque animal greed. At the end of **"The King"** forty-year-old Dvoira, disfigured by goiter, carries off her puny bridegroom, burning with lust for her prey:

> Двойра подталкивала мужа к двери их брачной комнаты и смотрела на него плотоядно, как кошка, которая, держа мышь во рту, легонько пробует ее зубами.
>
> *(Detstvo, 245)*

> Dvoira nudged her husband towards the door of their nuptial chamber and looked at him carnivorously, like a cat gently testing with its teeth the mouse it holds in its mouth.

By contrast, those unable to match the exploits of Cossacks and gangsters are likened to birds. Such are the idealist Kazantsev (in **"Guy de Maupassant"**) and the passive victims Gedali (in **"The Rebbe"**) or the poor sales clerk Muginshtein (in **"How It Was Done in Odessa"**). Not for nothing is Muginshtein's Aunt Pesia a chicken dealer. The Odessa gangsters described as birds in **"The Father,"** on the other hand, are of a different, more exotic feather. Pitiful are the Jewish "monkeys" in **"Crossing the Zbrucz"** and the "hungry donkeys" in **"End of the Old Folks' Home."** Yet beneath this apparent disdain lays a deep compassion for the narrator's brethren.

There is nothing more sensitive in Babel's imagery than a horse's lips, like the torn mouth of Jesus on the cross in **"At St. Valentine's Church"** (**Detstvo**, 187). Indeed, in the particularly inhuman world of war and pogroms horses are, by conrats, gifted with human qualities. The Cossacks, who at times behave in such a bestial fashion, treat their horses as more than friends, crediting them with more sense and intelligence than they display themselves. The "canine' understanding of the jade which Diakov forces to stand, or the kindness and tolerance perceived by the Jewish boy in the Cossack's horse during a pogrom in **"First Love"** speak for the ironic pity in the dumb beast that is absent in the human animal. Konkin (in the Red Cavalry story of that name) pities the Polish general's horse because he is sure it is a Bolshevik, being a beautiful copper red, and when he regretfully "liquidates" the animal it buckles under its rider "like a bride" (**Detstvo**, 165). The Cossack's passionate attachment to their mounts, the bane of the narrator's life in **"Argamak,"** of course, brings to mind Babel's own well-known devotion to the equine race.

Time and again one is struck by the affinity of Babel's heroes with beasts who know neither morality nor pity. People are dogs (*"psy"*), complains Levka when the crowds turn up to watch Mendel being beaten up by his own sons in the story **"Sunset"** (**Detstvo**, 284). The cat, tender and merciless, characterizes the spy Romuald (in the Red Cavalry story **"Church in Novograd,"** **Detstvo**, 104) and the future traitor Maslak (in **"Afon'ka Bida,"** **Detstvo**, 178). Nor is any creature more universally cunning than the serpent which slithers out of the treacherous Makhno's smiling mouth (**"The Sun of Italy,"** **Detstvo**, 122). Even before Romual'd is introduced the narrator hints at his viperous character:

> [. . .] где-то в змеином сумраке извивалась сутана монаха.
>
> (**"Church in Novograd,"** *Detstvo*, 103).

> [. . .] Somewhere in the twilight snaked a monk's soutan.

These iconic elements serve to *visualize* and *sensualize* Babel's imagery at the same time as stressing the paradoxical contrasts embodied in the protagonists, especially the bestial side of their nature. In addition, Babel's art of contrasts points allegorically to the protagonists' plot function, much as animal symbolism was used in Renaissance renderings of the Christian scriptures; indeed, the art of the heretical painter Pan Apolek owes much to Murillo and other masters whose work Babel saw in Polish churches in 1920.

It can thus be seen how important are the structural functions of imagery in Babel's prose; at the same time Babel's imagery plays on the unexpected, on the almost fantastic. Horses skip like calves (**"Story of My Dove-cot,"** *Detstvo,* 45); the narrator's dreams skip like kittens (**"The Sun of Italy,"** *Detstvo,* 121). Torches dance like black virgins (**"The King,"** *Detstvo,* 241), and the slant-eyed seeds of Kaplun's melon are likened to the eyes of stealthy Chinawomen (**"The Father,"** 273). The world comes alive, and this recreates the immediacy of visual and psychological impressions of metaphoric metamorphoses. Metaphor transplants human attributes to the animal kingdom, and it animates the inanimate. The effect is multi-sensory, kaleidoscopic. The ruined, burnt-out town of Novograd-Volynsk is alive, and yet unreal, appearing to the narrator to be hovering in the air as in a fabulous dream: blue roads flow past him "like streams of milk squirting out of many breasts" (**"Sun of Italy,"** *Detstvo,* 121). A similar dream-like vision suggesting actual decay and grotesque fantasy describes Nevsky Prospekt in **"The Journey"** (**"Doroga,"** 1920-1930), flowing like the Milky Way; dead horses' upturned hooves hold up the sky, like macabre milestones (*Detstvo,* 93). Imagination, dreamy, poetical, fantasizing, yet indicating essential if surprising truths, is a favorite medium of the intellectual narrator's vision. Typical is the personification of abstract concepts:

> Душа, налитая томительным хмелем мечты, улыбалась неведомо кому, и воображение, слепая счастливая баба, клубилось впереди июльским туманом.
>
> (**"Sun of Italy,"** *Detstvo,* 121)

> My soul was tipsy with heady daydreams and smiled at no one in particular, while my imagination, that blind, happy old hag, swirled before me like July mist.

In **"Story of My Dovecot"** misfortune rides a lame and high-spirited horse whose gallop the child can hear dying away in the distance (*Detstvo,* 46). In **"How It Was Done in Odessa"** misfortune takes the form of Savka Butsis, a noisy *deus ex machina* "as drunk as a water carrier," who—fatefully—brings fatal consequences to Benia's raid on **"Jew and a Half"** Tartakovskii (*Detstvo,* 250). And in **"Crossing the Zbrucz"** "timorous poverty" closes in over the narrator's bed to hint at an insight the narrator is slow to realize—his Jewish hosts are not themselves responsible for their despicable appearance (*Detstvo,* 102).

If abstract concepts are personified, by the principles of Babel's art of contrasts living beings are de-animated when Babel wishes to draw attention to their passivity or deadened awareness. Andrei grabs at the frightened prisoners in the Red Cavalry story **"Squadron Commander Trunov"** (**"Eskadronnyi Trunov"**) like reeds (*Detstvo,* 192). Battered and useless, drunkards clutter Lyubka's yard "like broken furniture" (*Detstvo,* 278).

Bullets have long whined and cannons have more often than not roared in most accounts of war, but the narrator conveys the unnatural tension of the death-bed scene in the Red Cavalry story **"The Widow"** (**"Vdova"**) as the battle approaches dangerously near the dying commander:

> [. . .] пули все тоскливее, все сильнее пели в густых просторах ночи.
>
> (*Detstvo,* 205)

> [. . .] the bullets sang even more loudly and mournfully in the thick expanse of night.

And in another Red Cavalry story, **"Death of Dolgushov"** (**"Smert' Dolgushova"**) the weaponry of war acquires a life of its own:

> Пули скулят и взвизчивают. Жалоба их нарастает невыносимо. Пули подстреливают землю и роются в ней, дрожа от нетерпения.
>
> (*Detstvo,* 141)

> The bullets whine and scream. Their moan grows unbearable. The bullets hit the earth and swarm in it, quivering with impatience.

The narrator focuses on the observer's sensory and sensual experience; the ground has an emotional smell for the child surrounded by death during a pogrom in **"Story of My Dovecot"**:

> земля моя пахла сырыми недрами, могилой и цветами. Я услышал ее запах и заплакал без всякого страха.
>
> (*Detstvo,* 46)

> My earth smelt of moist entrails, of the grave and of flowers. I sensed its smell and burst out crying without any fear.

Babel, incidentally, plays on the double meaning here of "entrails" (*nedra*) referring both to the boy's crushed pigeons and, figuratively, to the earth. In the Red Cavalry story **"Sashka the Christ"** (**"Sashka Khristos"**) the ground smells of sweat of a soldier's wife (*Detstvo,* 148). Froim Grach's supper in **"The Father"** smells like "a happy childhood" (*Detstvo,* 271) and the Bessarabian wine drunk by Lyubka and Trottyburn smells of "sun and bedbugs" (**"Lyubka the Cossack,"** *Detstvo,* 267). As these last stylized examples show, sensory, particularly olfactory, imagery evokes a sensuous local color, primarily, but not exclusively, in *skaz* and Odessa stories. Arye-Leib speaks of the smell of sea and milk coming from the wide hips of Odessa milkmaids (**"How It Was Done in Odessa,"** *Detstvo,* 253), but the device is also a mark of the intellectual-narrator's poetic imagination rendered with Babel's brilliant succinctness.

Babel's world is not only *seen* and *smelt,* but also *felt,* and felt uncomfortably closely, as when the narrator literally has a spine-chilling experience after antagonizing Afonka in **"Death of Dolgushov"**: he feels "cold and death" at his back as he steps away from Afonka's cocked gun (*Detstvo,* 144). Again, the icy stumps of the peasant's fingers poke into the narrator's body in **"The Journey"** and the sights of his gun light up on the narrator's back, penetrating his ribs (*Detstvo,* 91). Such immediacy is, of course, a distancing device which makes vivid the experience of the detached narrator and his alienation in a hostile environment (*Detstvo,* p. 157).

The sensory perception of the fictional world in Babel's prose conforms to a consistent pattern of symbolism. To take just the example of attributes denoting color, an example which also illustrates the visualizing function of Babel's imagery, it can be demonstrated how these organize a set of oppositions which structure, along with other lexical sets, the modeling system generated by the text. The structural function of a color word may coincide with its archetypal denotation in Jungian psychology or in the anthropological classifications, such as those of Lévi-Strauss in *La Pensée sauvage* or Turner in *The Forest of Symbols*; it may resemble the theosophical and mythological allusions exploited, for example, by Bely.[4] Yet without any attempt to prove a working analogy or correlation between the written word and the visual perception of colors, it has more than once been stated that color symbolism in Babel was influenced by Expressionism in painting,[5] despite the absence of any evidence that Babel had ever read Kandinsky's *Spiritual in Art* or that he was familiar with the work of Expressionists. However powerful color symbolism may be,[6] primarily emotional and subjective reader responses would not account for context or for variation of experiential associations among different readers. The following examples, on the contrary, demonstrate the structural function of color words in the Red Cavalry, Odessa, and Childhood stories by showing how each color word, like so many other images and details, is selected according to the context and structural function of the objects it defines.[7]

Red may be the color of the Revolution, but only in comparatively few cases in *Red Cavalry* do whites, reds, greens, and blacks designate the various political forces in the Russian Civil War. It is perhaps natural that red would be associated with the Cossacks in *Red Cavalry* since they have appropriated the Red Flag, but red signals particularly unbolshevik characteristics in the Cossack. Red is the color of flesh and blood, of the

sensual men of action—etymologically at least red (*krasnoe*) is beautiful,—but more often the Cossacks literally see red, as does Andrei after Trunov tries to shoot him (**"Squadron Commander Trunov,"** *Detstvo,* 192) or as does Afon'ka after his horse has been killed, his face red and raw "like meat cut into chunks" (**"Afon'ka Bida,"** *Detstvo,* 181). Like red, crimson (*bagrovoe*) colors the Cossacks' emotional blood, whether the drunken gaiety on Maslak's face in **"Afon'ka Bida"** when he sees the Cossacks mocking the infantry (*Detstvo,* 178), or despair on the face of the quartermaster in **"My First Goose"** when he leaves the narrator alone with the Cossacks (*Detstvo,* 130). Benia's car is red (**"How It Was Done in Odessa,"** *Detstvo,* 254, 255), and so is Liberman's jacket (**"Story of My Dovecot,"** *Detstvo,* 41), while Baska's cheecks are a brick color (**"The Father,"** *Detstvo,* 270). This red, however, is the healthy hue of Moldavanka women and wine, so unlike the passionate fury of the Cossacks or the despair of the war-torn Galician villages, whose wounds ooze crimson clay in the Red Cavalry story **"After the Battle"** (**"Posle boia,"** *Detstvo,* 224).

Babel seems to like bright pictures, and his fiery tableaux "shine," "shimmer," "glisten," "glimmer" and "burn," yet black scores the highest *relative frequency* of color words, perhaps because the author's view of the world is surprisingly gruesome.[8] Black often introduces death, evil and the grotesque. It is the color of the Zbrucz and the soldiers' carts during the crossing of the river which is also a crossing into a nocturnal world of death (*Detstvo,* 101). More significantly, black, green, yellow, and white are colors associated mostly with the non-Cossack world, with the decaying old order. Gedali, a blind old Jew in a dead world, wears a green coat and a black top hat, in which guise he is referred to twice in **"Gedali"** (*Detstvo,* 125-126, 127); he reappears in a green coat in **"The Rebbe"** (**"Rabbi,"** *Detstvo,* 134). Green betokens the mould of decay and putrefaction, as in the color of overgrown Jewish graves in **"Cemetery in Kozin"** (**"Kladbishche v Kozine,"** *Detstvo,* 158). Green is not the vegetation of living organisms, but of stagnation in **"Beresteczko"** (*Detstvo,* 168). The ancient and grotesque cupolas of the Polish church in Beresteczko are green, the walls white, with smoldering pink veins (**"At St. Valentine's Church,"** *Detstvo,* 184). The bell-ringer, like Gedali, wears a green coat (**"Afon'ka Bida,"** *Detstvo,* 182, and again in **"At St. Valentine's Church,"** *Detstvo,* 187), while his wife has yellow hair and her eyes are filled with the "white moisture of blindness" (*Detstvo,* 184). The blind Gottfried is associated with a yellow light (**"Pan Apolek,"** *Detstvo,* 119) and in **"Gedali"** the synagogue walls, as well as the beard of the narrator's pious grandfather, are yellow (*Detstvo,* 124, 125); the Zhitomir rebbe is likewise given a white kaftan and a yellow beard (**"The Rebbe,"** *Detstvo,* 133). These negatively evaluated colors bring together the inhabitants of the old world in *Red Cavalry,* who are blind physically and ideologically to the bright new age; their world is primarily spiritual, as opposed to the physical exuberance of the Cossacks, to their dynamism and sexuality. The old world is ascetic and unaesthetic.

In the Odessa stories key colors also perform valuable functions in plot structure. Among the pilgrims returning from Mecca in **"The Father,"** some of whom wear *white* towels draped round their heads, is an old man in a *green* turban who is "as green and light as a leaf." He is dying and wishes to be left alone, as it is considered a merit to end one's days on the way back from the holy city (***Detstvo,*** 275-6). After being shown this spectacle of death, Froim Grach next sees Mendel Krik relating how his own sons beat him up. As we know from the play and the story **"Sunset,"** this incident is the prelude to the fall of Mendel Krik. It should not escape attention that during this terrible tale Mendel is drinking his wine from a *green* glass (*ibid.,* 276).

The perception of the world in Babel's stories should not, however, be presented as a black and white division (or, in this case, red and white!) between "Cossack" and "victim" types.⁹ A color such as blue or pink can be ambiguous. While pink (*rozovoe*) is usually associated with the "lifeless" areas of the world in ***Red Cavalry,*** it adds a grotesque tinge to Afonka Bida's gouged-out eye (**"Afonka Bida,"** ***Detstvo,*** 183) or to the supernatural cradle in Sashka the Christ's dream (**"Sashka the Christ,"** ***Detstvo,*** 150). In nature descriptions it implies the ephemeral, as well as in Apolek's paintings and with reference to the painter himself.

In the Odessa stories, pink is sexy, while ginger red (*ryzhee*) implies a fiery physicality. Froim Grach's epithet is "red-headed robber" ("*ryzhii vor*"), a common Yiddish idiom being "red as a thief" . . . , and the narrator of **"How It Was Done in Odessa"** speaks of the "рыжая сталь его поступков" ("the ginger red steel of his actions," ***Detstvo,*** 246). Naftula, too, in **"Karl-Yankel"** is ginger (*ryzhii*), perhaps because blood and wine are the ruddy ritual circumciser's trade marks. Likewise, Mr. Trottyburn, the English seaman, is a "pillar of ginger red meat" (**"Lyubka the Cossack,"** ***Detstvo,*** 266).

In the tradition of Christian art, Jesus wore a purple garment to direct attention to the heavenly abode of the messianic bridegroom (cf. John, 19:2), but the curly-headed Jew on Apolek's crucifix in **"At St. Valentine's Church")** wears an orange (*oranzhevoe*) cloak and is remarkable for his ginger (*ryzhee*) eyebrows (***Detstvo,*** 187). Interestingly enough, the Jewish victims in ***Red Cavalry*** share their ginger hair with the coats of those sensitive creatures, the Cossacks' horses. Sky blue (*goluboe*) in ***Red Cavalry*** does suggest the expanse of the heavenly firmament; but Afon'ka too goes on the rampage in a jacket made from a blue carpet with a lily sewn on the back (***Detstvo,*** 183) and the holy Torah scrolls in **"The Rebbe's Son"** are wrapped in blue silk and purple velvet (***Detstvo,*** 228). The knights of the Modavanka, on the other hand, may be proud of their "blue blood."

Dark blue (*sinee*) in ***Red Cavalry,*** especially in the greenish shades of the spectrum, implies the bloodless lips or lifeless eyes of those about to die or suffer misfortune and can also discolor Jewish and Roman Catholic worlds. Generally speaking, blues and purples add a surreal note, as when the sky turns green and the earth blue in **"Beresteczko."**

Colors of precious metals usually symbolize the capitalist past, such as the gold and silver idols of icons and money found in **"Church in Novograd"** (***Detstvo,*** 104-105). But equally materialistic are the concerns of the Cossacks who set great store by personal belongings and have an eye on prisoners' clothing and valuables. In this respect the Cossacks are firmly rooted in the past: even their red uniforms have a silver stripe! The horse is, naturally, the Cossacks' dearest possession, after which come the saddlecloth and trappings. When Afonka's horse is felled, it is a *copper* finger he pokes into the wounds from which the blood flows like "two ruby breech bands" as the dying horse watches with a violet eye, the color of a frail flower (***Detstvo,*** 180).

Both minerals and materials are invariably contaminated with the corruption of the old order. Prior to the discovery of the church's hidden treasures, the narrator of **"Church in Novograd"** already senses an invisible, seductive order of things in the *satin* of women's letters which rot in the blue *silk* of waistcoats (***Detstvo,*** 104). The erotic but decadent luxury of silk drapes both Galina in **"First Love"** and the tsars' rooms in **"The Journey"**; the world of the lately departed imperial family is described in terms of rare valuables and jewels, right down to the sleeping lackey (who may well have slept through the Revolution) with his gold-braided livery and inky-deathly face (***Detstvo,*** 94-95). Mineral and material attributes, however, also characterize the earthy passion of the Odessa gangsters with their exotic costumes and contraband. Their silk, velvet, gold, silver, diamonds and steel prove an epic mettle.

As if to illustrate the maxim that you are what you eat, Babel has the gangsters consume fish soup in which *lemon* lakes shine like *mother-of-pearl* (**"The King,"** ***Detstvo,*** 242). In a hilarious feat of synaesthesia, the narrator interrupts Benia's speech in **"How It Was Done in Odessa"**:

> Тут Беня сделал паузу. На нем был шоколадный пиджак, кремовые штаны и малиновые штиблеты.

> (***Detstvo,*** 252)

Here Benia paused. He was wearing a chocolate jacket, cream trousers and raspberry boots.

Here taste also has color connotations, which, apart from amusing, remind us of the organizing function of sensory imagery. The Odessa gangsters wear raspberry waistcoats (**"The King,"** *Detstvo,* 243), but the gangsters of the Red Cavalry stories, the Cossacks, also don raspberry hats (Savitskii and Prishchepa) and raspberry riding breeches (Trunov's two machine-gunners). In all these cases they are men of action taking up heroic poses, but the playful raspberry image imparts a taste of irony.

There are thus two levels in the operation of the image in Babel's prose—the pictorial element and the structural function. Babel has an eye for the unexpected and the contradictory. He blithely switches from one sense to another, producing a collision of images which combine dissimilar and contrasting properties in a multisensory mosaic:

> Песня плыла, как дым. И мы двигались навстречу героическому закату.
>
> Его кипящие реки стекали по расшитым полотенцам крестьянских полей. Тишина розовела. Земля лежала, как кошачья спина, поросшая мерцающим мехом хлебов.
>
> **("The Road to Brody," *Detstvo,* 137)**

The song drifted like smoke. And we moved towards the heroic sunset.

Its seething rivers flowed across the embroidered towels of peasant fields. Silence grew roseate. The land lay like a cat's back, overgrown with a gleaming fur of wheat.

The association of earth with animal and animal with earth is, moreover, at once visual and associative. By way of contrast and more rarely, an object is reflected by an image of itself, as when Deborah, in **"Pan Apolek,"** comes out to the guests "like a woman who is proud of her fall" (**Detstvo,** 120), for that is exactly what she is.

"A smile must be as precise as a logarithm," Babel is reputed to have told his fellow Odessite, the Russian novelist Konstantin Paustovsky, "and must be as natural as the smell of fennel."[10] Babel tries for exact analogies which see into the mysteriously indefinable moments of existence and illuminate the startling paradoxes of human nature, at once animalistic, violent, warm, and loving. Babel did not radically reform his imagery in the thirties, but did introduce more sparsely and effectively his flamboyant metaphors, extravagant tropes, and colorful symbols. The contrasts became less violent, but Babel remained true to the principle of the world as a sense-experience, as a "field of women and horses in May." In **"My First Fee,"** a story which Babel was working on at the end of the twenties when he was searching for a new style, Vera's nipples open their moist eyelids and caress the narrator's cheeks like calves; but when the prostitute makes love the narrator euphemistically asks if the reader has ever seen the shavings fly gaily as a village carpenter planes down a plank for a friend's hut.

Notes

1. *Detstvo i drugie rasskazy,* ed. Efraim Sicher (Jerusalem: Biblioteka Aliya), p. 129. Further references will be to this edition and will be given in parenthesis [*Detstvo*].

2. "Fat Tuesday in Odessa: Isaak Babel's 'Di Grasso' as Testament and Manifesto," *Russian Review,* 2 (1981): 101-21.

3. Isaak Babel, *Peterburg 1918,* ed. Efraim Sicher (Ann Arbor: Ardis, 1979), p. 153.

4. See Ada Steinberg's incisive analysis of the function of color in the complex symbolist imagery of Bely's *Peterburg, Moskva* and *Maski* in "Color and the Embodiment of Theme in Bely's 'Urbanistic' Novels," *Slavonic and East European Review,* 57 (1979): 187-213. Babel was, of course, far from the complex metaphysics worked out by Bely in his 1903 essay *Sviastchennye tsveta* and in his later writings.

5. See T. Clyman, "Babel as Colorist," *Slavonic and East European Journal,* 21 (1977): 332-343. Clyman's count of color words unfortunately defines neither sample nor population, and gives only the number of occurences, not their frequency.

6. S. Solov'ev has proposed the intriguing thesis that color is a highly suitable indicator of a writer's style in a comparative study of Russian literature ("Tsvet, chislo i russkaia slovesnost'," *Znanie—sila,* 1 (1971): 54-56).

7. A pilot study by the Soviet scholar R. Nazar'ian demonstrates the structural function of color words in two stories, "Guy de Maupassant" and "Rue Dante" ("'Mopassanovskie' novelly I. Babelia: K voprosu ob assotsiativno—kontekstovoi koloristichnosti," *Trudy Samarkandskogo universiteta,* 320 (1977), pp. 51-62). Unfortunately, the structural function of connotative lexis in this analysis is not related to larger questions of Babel's style.

8. P. Novitskii sees red and pink as the basic color words, the colors of flesh and blood ("Babel'," in Yu. Tynianov and B. Kazanskii, eds., *I. E. Babel': Stat'i i materialy* [Leningrad, 1928], p. 51). This has been checked statistically by the present author and found not to be so, although the methodological question might be raised as to whether to

include in this category lexical items not directly denoting color but suggesting its effect, such as *krov', zakat, t'ma, noch'*: the play of light and shade might also be taken into account as a separate category in a lexical concordance of Babel's prose.

9. On the division of Babel's protagonists into "heroes" and "victims" see Patricia Carden, *The Art of Isaac Babel* (Ithaca, 1972), p. 107 ff.

10. Paustovsky, *Vremia bol'shikh ozhidanii* (Moscow, 1960), p. 153.

Victor Erlich (essay date 1987)

SOURCE: Erlich, Victor. "Color and Line: Notes on the Art of Isaac Babel." In *Isaac Babel,* edited by Harold Bloom, pp. 249-55. New York: Chelsea House Publishers, 1987.

[*In the following essay, Erlich argues that contrast, incompatibility, and incongruity are "the distinguishing characteristics of the Babelian universe" and the "shaping force" that works at all levels of his art, "from style through theme to narrative manner."*]

Western critics of Russian literature are fairly unanimous in hailing Isaac Babel as the finest early Soviet prose writer. Yet he remains to date one of the least deciphered modern Russian masters. His brilliantly idiosyncratic art eludes categories and subverts labels. Because of his proclivity for the hyperbole and his partiality for passion, he has been dubbed on occasion a romantic. Yet the stark and relentless naturalism of some of his scenes is not easily compatible with this designation. Even less illuminating, to be sure, is the "realistic" label pinned on Babel posthumously, in the process of his rehabilitation in the post-Stalin era, by Ilya Ehrenburg. This canny survivor knew only too well what he was doing: within the Soviet ambience to call a writer a realist is often simply an enabling act, a way of making him a safe topic of conversation or a legitimate subject of inquiry.

Clearly, in dealing with Babel "isms" will be of little avail. More helpful is the notion offered by some of the keenest commentators on Babel, notably that of contrast, incompatibility, incongruity as the distinguishing characteristic of the Babelian universe, as the organizing principle of his prose. N. Stepanov, an erstwhile fellow traveler of Russian Formalism, speaks of the "equalization of disparate and incommensurate entities." V. Shklovsky puts it more vividly: "Babel's principal device is to speak in the same tone of voice about the stars above and gonorrhea."

The tendency to bring together incompatibles, to juxtapose contraries, is a shaping force at all levels of Babel's art, from style through theme to narrative manner.

First, there is a use of the starting epithet, a tension between the adjective and the noun: in one of the key Odessa stories, **"The King,"** we read: "During the raid on the dreadful night when cows bellowed as they were slaughtered and calves slipped and slithered in the blood of their dams, when the torch flames danced like the dark village maidens, and the farm women lunged back in horror from the muzzles of amiable revolvers." The sample principle is operative here on the thematic level: the chief protagonist of the Odessa cycle, built around the exploits of the legendary Benya Krik, is a Jewish gangster, or even more paradoxically, an engaging and generous bandit. Incongruity is built into the structure of **Red Cavalry.** One of the major themes of this masterful cycle is the plight of the narrator, Lyutov, a dreamy, ineffectual Jewish *intelligent* in specs among Cossack roughnecks, who comprise the division to which, like Babel, he is assigned as a war correspondent.

Possibly the most quintessential Babelian contrast is that between manner and matter. Note the narrator's unruffled, businesslike tone as he relates in one of the **Red Cavalry** stories, **"Berestechko,"** the savage murder of an old Jew suspected of spying for the enemy: "Then Kudrya of the machine gun squad took a hold of his head and tucked it under his arm. The Jew stopped screaming and straddled his legs. Kudrya drew out his dagger with his right hand and carefully, without splashing himself, cut the old man's throat.

It would be naive and hopelessly literal-minded to construe the underlying authorial stance as actual detachment. In fact, there is good reason to view it not as absence of affect, but as flight from it, to posit a compelling need for "distancing" the nearly unbearable emotion, for keeping it at bay.

In her book *The Art of Isaac Babel*, Patricia Carden quotes a telling passage from a letter Babel wrote to his family from the Polish front in 1920: "I went through two weeks of utter despair here. That was because of the ferocious cruelty that never lets up for a moment, and because I clearly understand how unfit I am for the business of destruction, how difficult it is for me to break away from the past."

One of the strategies at Babel's disposal, serving to protect and conceal his emotional vulnerability, to distance his moral revulsion, is hiding behind the mask of a more or less crude rapporteur, clearly different from the primary narrator, be he a dull-clod Kurdyukov, who, in **"A Letter,"** relates stolidly and clumsily the murder by his brother of their Czarist policeman father, or—a somewhat more complex case!—a Bolshevik Cossack, Balmashev, not devoid of moral sensitivity and poetic flair, but all too ready to use his trusty rifle in order to rub off an "enemy of the people."

Where the voice of a Babel-like figure is unmistakably heard, the underlying disarray is often muted or deflected through a significant shift of emphasis or a displacement. An interesting case in point is provided by the double transformation in the **Red Cavalry** cycle of a 1923 reportage, **"And Then They Were None,"** which has never been published in the original. (its English translation appears in the volume edited by Nathalie Babel, *You Must Know Everything.*) I do not mean to suggest that the relationship between the sketch, a polished and well-rounded piece of writing, and the **Red Cavalry** stories is simply one between *Wahrheit* and *Dichtung.* But **"And Then They Were None"** seems to hew closer to Babel's actual experience as it is directly related to two August 1920 entries in his Polish campaign diary. The central event, in both the diary entries and the sketch, is a summary execution of nine prisoners of war, an execution which the narrator is powerless to prevent. The wanton savagery of this illegal act weighs heavily upon the speaker: "The prisoners are dead, all nine of them; I feel it in my bones." The one **Red Cavalry** story which bears visible resemblance to **"And Then They Were None," "The Squadron Commander Trunov,"** features a conflict between the narrator and Trunov over the handling of prisoners. Yet as the story progresses, Lyutov's rage over this wanton murder yields to the theme of the selfless heroism of Trunov's death. Interestingly enough, the rhythms of the speaker's anguish heard in **"And Then They Were None"** are echoed, though in a quite different context, in another **Red Cavalry** tale, **"The Road to Brody"**: "I felt sorry about the bees. The fighting armies treated them most brutally. There were no bees left in Volhynia." It is a curious and significant fact that in **Red Cavalry** the only explicit acknowledgment on the speaker's part of his guilt over what is being done to the ravaged, brutalized countryside, the only direct and personal statement about the "ferocious cruelty" of it all, is concerned with defiling the beehives, rather than destroying human lives.

It is at least arguable that these techniques of displacing and distancing affect, more broadly, this contrast between tone and subject bears some relation to what a number of Babel watchers assume to be a profound inner split in the author of **Red Cavalry.** Critics—both friendly and hostile—expatiated upon Babel's oscillation between two codes—the code of the humane old Jewish shopkeeper, Gedali, who dreams about the "International of good people," and that of the "soldier of the revolution," Balmashev. No less important, to my mind, is the hovering between the world which gave birth to Babel, the world he never fully repudiated or abandoned, one of dignified ritual, cozy family warmth, of strict discipline and sense of duty, and the lure of the disheveled, the unknown, the exotic, the forbidden, indeed, the hostile. In an interesting essay on Babel as a Russian-Jewish writer, Simon Markish states Babel's

central dilemma and major aspiration perceptively and eloquently: "Not to reject tradition, not to turn away from one's own history, but instead to leap into freedom, into open space, to burst free from one's chains, to know the taste, color, scent, texture of everything denied by the ghetto wall . . . And to find harmony in dichotomy."

To find harmony in dichotomy, to reconcile the unreconcilables, to square the circle, here is a paradoxical and gloriously unrealistic project. Markish is right in believing that Babel did crave "harmony in dichotomy" even as he must have felt in his bones that he would never achieve it. No wonder that in the story which concludes the first edition of **Red Cavalry, "The Rabbi's Son,"** the narrator's heart goes out to the Jewish outcast hero, Elijah Braclavskij, a "Jewish prince" and intrepid soldier of the revolution. Elijah Braclavskij, who served the cause until his dying breath, who incurs a fatal wound in trying to hold the enemy at bay in the face of a powerful Polish offensive, represents a triumph over incongruity, a successful, indeed a heroic synthesis of polarities: "His things were strewn about him pell mell—anecdotes of the propagandists and notebooks of the Jewish poet, the portraits of Lenin and Maimonides lay side-by-side, the knotted iron of Lenin's skull beside the dull silk of the portraits of Maimonides."

Lyutov's "spiritual brother" appears to have achieved what Markish has called harmony in dichotomy by forcing the disparate and seemingly incompatible beliefs and values into a life of total commitment, a life where the Bolshevik chieftain and the Jewish moralist merge in the consuming fire of passionate action.

It is fair to assume that for Babel, not unlike the narrator of **Red Cavalry,** "who can scarcely contain the tempests of his imagination within his age-old body," the conflict between Lenin and Maimonides remains unsolved. Not for the first time and not for the last time, what appears to have been in the writer's life a source of anguish or of a stalemate served to enrich and brilliantly complicate his art, to enhance the uniqueness and the keenness of his perception of the world.

II

Babel's *oeuvre* contains several remarkable narratives bearing directly on his concept of art and the artist, most notably, **"Guy de Maupassant," "Di Grasso,"** and, in part, **"In the Basement." "Line and Color"** (1923) lacks their power and poignancy, yet it can be seen as a telling commentary on the texture of Babel's imagination. This slender story is built around an encounter between the narrator and a man who was soon to become head of the ill-fated Provisional Government, A. F. Kerensky. The setting is provided by a Finnish sanitarium which bears the lilting name Olila; the time is December 1916. After a lyrical invocation of "Helsingfors, dream of my heart," and an olfactory recreation of the Olila dining room, which "smelled of pine trees, of the Countess Tyszkiewicz's fresh shoulders, and of the English officer's silk underwear," the narrator recounts a walk in the woods with the voluble, and, as it turns out, nearsighted luminary. As the evidence of Kerensky's myopia mounts—he is unable to recognize a single person he meets en route—the following exchange ensues:

> "Alexander Fyodorovich, you ought to wear glasses!"
>
> "Never!"
>
> Then bubbling over like a mere boy, I said to him: "Just think, you're not merely blind, you're practically dead. Line, . . . mistress of the world, eternally escapes you. Here we are, you and I, walking about in this magic garden, this Finnish forest that almost baffles description. All our lives we shall never see anything more beautiful. And you can't see the pink edges of the frozen waterfall over there by the stream! You're blind to the Japanese chiseling of the weeping willow leaning over the waterfall . . . The snow, shapeless when it fell, has draped itself along the branches lying under surfaces that undulate like a line drawn by Leonardo . . . And think what you'd have to say about Fröken Kirsti's silk stockings, about the line of her leg, that lovely line! I beseech you, Alexander Fyodorovich, buy a pair of glasses!"
>
> "My child," he replied, "don't waste your time. Forty kopecks for spectacles of only forty kopecks I've no wish to squander. I don't need your line, vulgar as the truth is vulgar. You live your life as though you were a teacher of trigonometry, while I for my part live in the world of miracles . . . What do I need Fröken Firsti's freckles for, if even when I can scarcely make her out, I can see in her all I wish to see? . . . What do I need line for when I have color? To me a whole universe is a gigantic theater and I am the only member of the audience who hasn't glued opera glasses to his eyes. The orchestra is playing the overture to the third act; the stage is far away, just as in a dream. My heart swells with ecstasy. I see Juliet's purple velvet, Romeo's lilac silk, and not a single false beard. And you want me to blind myself with the forty kopek spectacles."

When Kerensky reappears in the finale, he is at the peak of his short-lived power. This time he is cast in the role of a grandiloquent and somewhat maudlin orator, exhorting his audience to persevere in defending mother Russia against the German armies, and seemingly oblivious to the mounting hostility of the crowd:

> Six months later I saw Alexander Fyodorovich one more: it was June, 1917, and he was now supreme god of our army and arbiter of our destiny. . . . A rally had been called at a House of the People, and there Alexander Fyodorovich made a speech about Russia—Russia, mystic mother and spouse. The animal passion of the crowd stifled him. Could he, the only member of the audience without opera glasses, see how their hack-

les were rising? I don't know. But after him, Trotsky climbed to the rostrum, twisted his mouth and in an implacable voice began: "Comrades!" [Not surprisingly, the last words of the story as it appears in the 1966 Soviet edition of Babel's selected writings are "I don't know."]

Let us retrace our steps. One of the salient aspects of the dialogue quoted above is that the sense of color, which is, after all, a visual phenomenon, seems less affected by myopia, or near blindness, than that of the line, of the contours of reality. The narrator doesn't question, or to be exact, is not offered an opportunity to question, Kerensky's gesture of consigning color to the realm of imagination, the dreamer's "gigantic theater of the mind." I cannot help but be reminded of Babel's own use of color—of the extravagant, "theatrical" color themes of the ***Tales of Odessa***: "Aristocrats of Moldavanka, they [the bandits] were tightly encased in raspberry waistcoats. Russet jackets clasped their shoulders and on their fleshy feet the sky-blue leather cracked." Parenthetically, it is imagery such as this that moved V. Shklovsky to insist in his already quoted essay that Babel was good for Russian literature: "[Today's] Russian literature is as grey as a siskin: it needs crimson riding breeches and boots of sky-blue leather."

To be sure, one does not need to be Isaac Babel to appreciate the "Japanese chiseling of the frozen waterfall," or, for that matter, the line of *Fröken* Firsti's leg, more broadly, to insist that it is impossible to do justice to the world's beauty without being fully responsive to both the line and the color and the intricate interplay between them. Yet there is something unmistakably Babelian about making a myopic dreamer who is also a political sentimentalist and a rhetorician better attuned to the sound of his own voice than to the menacing growls of the people "out there," an impassioned champion of color, while exalting the "line," at once the principle of control, the form-giving, limit-setting artistic discipline, and the inexorable thrust of what Freud called "the reality principle." For the dichotomy which shapes the story can be shown to be operative on two distinct, but criss-crossing planes. In one sense "Color and Line" is a metaphor for Babel's own art, where the "orgy of color," the "tempests of the imagination," the richness and exuberance of imagery are disciplined, hemmed in, held in check by the "line," streamlined into unsurpassed concision and brevity. (Is there another prose writer within the Western tradition who makes one think at once of Nikolay Gogol and Guy de Maupassant?) Yet in a different context the metapoetic dialogue which ushers in the Kerensky-Trotsky antithesis may well suggest the conflict within the Babelian persona between daydreaming, which comes naturally to him, and the determination to face reality whatever the cost—especially if it means working against the grain—to confront the "implacable" exigencies of the life of action.

Through the 1930s Babel seems to have been oscillating between increasing dismay over the bleakness and sterility of accredited Soviet writing and, hoping against hope, between disenchantment and fierce loyalty to the revolutionary myth. Yet whatever his extraliterary delusions or confusions may have been, he never faltered in his commitment to what was for him the central and the least questionable value—exacting craftsmanship. It is this commitment which made it virtually impossible for him to produce dutiful socialist-realist fiction. It is said that when he was arrested in 1939, he was overheard by a witness to mutter "They didn't let me finish." Was he talking about the collectivization novel which he had been forcing himself to write for years or some other unfinished or unfinishable business? We may never know. What we have the right to assume is that when his turn came, the reality principle obtruded itself upon the stalemated master not in the guise of an implacable orator, but that of a silent executioner.

Joe Andrew (essay date September 1989)

SOURCE: Andrew, Joe. "'Spoil the Purest of Ladies': Male and Female in Isaac Babel's *Konarmiya*." *Essays in Poetics* 14, no. 2 (September 1989): 1-27.

[*In the following essay, Andrew examines the roles of men and women in Babel's* Red Cavalry, *arguing that the ways in which male characters defile and abuse women, both as characters and as archetypes, reflect Babel's indictment of patriarchy and the rituals of war.*]

The purpose of this article is to examine male and female characters in the thirty-five stories that comprise the final version of Babel's ***Konarmiya, or Red Cavalry,***[1] as well their interplay and what the masculine and feminine principles which are established signify. It may seem strange at first sight to consider female characters at all in these stories. No female character has the status of such as Savitsky, Gedali, or Afonka Bida and the rest, to say nothing of the almost ubiquitous Lyutov. Most are marginal, most are unnamed and women in the stories are generally passed over fleetingly in the critical literature, or else are seen merely as iconic, symbolic or emblematic of something in male destinies, especially Lyutov's.[2] However, as I will argue throughout this paper, an understanding of the female characters, their plot roles, the way they are depicted, and, indeed, what they symbolise, is critical in a broadly-based and systematic analysis of the world of war, Revolution and violence that constitutes ***Red Cavalry.***

That most critics tend to ignore or, rather, marginalise female characters in this work is not surprising. I have in mind not merely the male ethos of the work itself, but also the androcentric bias of most literary criticism.

Indeed, in order to appreciate the tenor of much of this paper it is necessary to make a brief excursus into the realms of feminist literary criticism.

Since it began to re-emerge as an important cultural and political force in the late 1960s, feminism has presented 'Incontestably the most important challenge'[3] in recent years to accepted academic approaches to literary studies. By now several 'feminisms' have emerged. Each in its own way may be said to have had the aim of radically reinterpreting established literary practices, strategies and analyses. As Carolyn Heilbrunn said of Kate Millett's *Sexual Politics*: 'for the first time we have been asked to look at literature as women; we, men, women, Ph.D.'s have always read it as men'.[4] Underlying this view are a number of assumptions, well summarised by Greene & Kahn:

> Feminist literary criticism is one branch of interdisciplinary enquiry which takes gender as a fundamental organizing category of experience. This enquiry holds two related premises about gender. One is that inequality of the sexes is neither a biological given nor a divine mandate, but a cultural construct, and therefore a proper study for any humanistic discipline. The second is that a male perspective, assumed to be 'universal', has dominated fields of knowledge, shaping their paradigms and methods. Feminist scholarship, then, . . . revises concepts previously thought universal but now seen as originating in particular cultures and serving particular purposes.[5]

The present paper will offer a reading, from a feminist perspective, of a cycle of stories produced in Soviet Russia of the 1920s with a view to understanding the 'particular purposes' of the way women were coded both in this particular work, and, at least by implication, in the culture more broadly. By rereading works, by reproducing meanings in this way, we achieve two things: we see the images of women in a particular culture (and we can assess the purposes of these images); and we derive a new perspective on the world of the work concerned.

It is important to re-evaluate works in this way, especially those which have been 'canonised' as having 'universal' significance.[6] This 'universality' is something of a myth as de Beauvoir maintains: 'Representation of the world, like the world itself, is the work of men; they describe it from their own point of view which they confuse with absolute truth'.[7] We may be trained to read the works of our cultural history as if they were of universal significance, whereas they are usually partial if not distorted representations of humanity.[8]

That ***Red Cavalry*** is primarily a world of men is no secret. It is equally no secret that it is also a world where violence, death and destruction predominate: these two propositions are closely interconnected, as we shall see.

Critic after critic rehearses the themes of morbidity. Murphy notes the common locus of the cycle, namely that of normal lives ruined by war,[9] while Hallett refers to the almost gratuitous blood-letting;[10] Falen talks of 'raging violence' always close to the surface.[11] At times the violence may be seen as merely the product of the particular situation, that is, the Revolutionary war.[12] However, others note that war and its accompanying violence seem to be endemic in this area: as Luplow puts it: 'there is a recurring sense of historical pessimism in ***Red Cavalry,*** a sense that the Revolution is neither new nor final, but one of an endless series of wars and oppressions.'[13] Lyutov himself makes the point when surveying a scene of particular devastation in **"Discourse on the Tachanka"**: 'I understood the painful history of this region'.[14]

Yet another aspect of this theme, and one that was common in the literature of the period,[15] was the way in which the Revolution, or war more generally, unleashed all that was worst in human (or rather *man's*) nature, the ferocious cruelty and other irrational forces. In particular, Luplow remarks upon the cycle's seeming 'obsession with violence, death and sex and their interrelationships.'[16] In Falen's view, sexual instincts and violent passions seem to originate in the same common source.[17] Despite these observations, however, few commentators make the simplest and most obvious of connections, namely that all the violence of the cycle is enacted by men. Usually this aggression is directed, frequently in the most ferocious of fashions, towards other men, but we also see instances of violence by men against women. This may be rather bathetic, as in the case of Lyutov's three-fold assaults on powerless old women, to which we shall return, or (literally) deadly earnest, as in **"Salt."** In these instances we see a tendency which is common in the literature of war more generally. As Judith Fetterley observes: 'War simplifies men's relations to women. It erases the distinctions among women that normally keep male hostility under some restraint and it legitimizes aggression against all women.'[18]

But it may be that this violence, aggression or, more particularly, this all-pervasive sadism can be explained not merely by the subject matter (war), but by something rather more fundamental to literature, namely the narrative process itself. Another theoretical digression is necessary at this point, to consider the views of Yury Lotman on plot typologies and, in particular, a feminist re-interpretation of them by Teresa de Lauretis.[19]

In Lotman's article "The Origin of Plot in the Light of Typology", first published in 1973, and translated in 1979, he proposes a number of basic plot types and character types. His study, in some senses an extension of Propp's work, has much that is relevant for our understanding of men and women in ***Red Cavalry,*** al-though Babel's work is not one of the very broadly-based works to which Lotman refers.

We must start, however, with an even more basic proposition, as formulated by Roland Barthes, for whom narrative is an absolutely universal phenomenon: 'Caring nothing for the division between good and bad literature, narrative is international, transhistorical, transcultural: it is simply there, like life itself.'[20] For Lotman, the universal phenomenon of story-telling has a particular relationship with reality: stories re-enact a disturbance: 'The fixing of unique and chance events, crimes, calamities—anything considered the violation of a certain primordial order—was the historical kernel of plot-narration'.[21] From this premise Lotman goes on to establish the basic chain of narrative, from which all stories can be said to be constructed, whether they be primitive anecdotes, nineteenth-century novels, or film:

> The elementary sequence of events in myth can be reduced to a chain: entry into closed space—emergence from it (this chain is open at both ends and can be endlessly multiplied). Inasmuch as closed space can be interpreted as "a cave", "the grave", "a house", "woman" (and correspondingly, be allotted the features of darkness, warmth, dampness), entry into it is interpreted on various levels as "death", "conception", "return home" and so on; moreover all these acts are thought of as mutually identical.[22]

Given this chain of events, narrative also presupposes types of characters, 'those who are mobile, who enjoy freedom with regard to plot-space, who can change their place in the structure of the artistic world and cross the frontier . . . and those who are immobile, who represent, in fact, a function of this space'. The mobile character may be a single individual, or may be 'a paradigm-cluster of different characters on the same plane'[23]. This possibility also applies to the immobile, obstacle, or antagonist character.

If we accept these propositions it is a short and simple step to argue, as Lotman never quite does, but as de Lauretis most definitely does, that all narrative is inherently male. After all, 'woman' is one possible variant of the closed space. In other words it is men who cross the frontier (as Lyutov, of course, does in ***Red Cavalry***) while women are merely a feature of the narrative topology, obstacles in the hero's quest. Indeed, the hero *must* be male, because the obstacle is morphologically female.[24] As de Lauretis goes on to argue

> the hero, the mythical subject is constructed as human being and as male; he is the active principle of culture, the establisher of dictinction, the creator of differences. Female is what is not susceptible to transformation, to life or death; she (it) is an element of plot-space, a topos, a resistance, matrix and matter.[25]

Furthermore, narrative is, therefore, essentially about a quest for human-becoming, a description of the process of becoming a *man.* Indeed, it can be argued, as we shall see in more detail later, that this is precisely what Lyutov is doing in **Red Cavalry,** and the women are, on the whole, mere elements of the spaces he enters and leaves, or else obstacles in his path, Propp's 'antagonists'.

From this perspective, we can see that **Red Cavalry,** or *any* narrative, is both universal, in the sense that it shares common typological features with other narratives, and not universal, in the more philosophical sense, in that it, like most fiction, fails to take account, or rather to *give an account* of female destinies. However, there is a rather more sinister side to **Red Cavalry,** as we have already briefly related, and to narrative more generally. Lotman's hero '*penetrates* into the other space and *overcomes* the obstacle'. Taking this, and other theories of narrative, de Lauretis comes to see narrative in a way which applies very well to the brutal world of **Red Cavalry**:

> Story demands sadism, depends on making something happen, forcing a change in another person, a battle of will and strength, victory/defeat, all occurring in a linear time with a beginning and an end.[26]

In **Red Cavalry,** as in most narratives, it is, indeed, men who force a change in others, and it is to a consideration of the types of men found in Babel's fiction that we now turn.

Red Cavalry, as we have already noted, is predominantly a man's world. In line with Lotman's theory the male character can be seen as a composite figure, what Lotman refers to as a 'paradigm-cluster', or what Carden calls more simply 'composite types'.[27] On the one hand are the heroic warriors, on the other is the saintly, but also weak, or maimed type. It is important to remember, however, that both are depicted as heroic. Amongst the first group may be numbered such recurrent characters as Savitsky, Afonka and Balmashev, while Trunov and Baulin (in *Argamak*) bear clear similarities. There are also important links made with real historical characters such as Lenin, Makhno and Budenny.[28] As such a multi-faceted male hero can be pieced together, part-fiction, part-fact and, linking the two worlds of history and literature, part-myth.

Lyutov, as we shall see, strives, and only partially succeeds in his attempts, to ally himself with this group.[29] Also vying for his affiliation is the cluster of saintly or intellectual figures, most notably Gedali, Pan Apolek and the recurrent Sashka Khristos. Not merely for reasons of verisimilitude, this type is rather less common in these tales of war. In other words, what Sinyavsky calls the 'ideal of virile humanism'[30] is given far more attention than those who aspire, like Gedali, to an International of 'Good People'. I too will devote the rest of this section primarily to man's men, while noting in passing that, as in Lotman's paradigm, there are no female heroes.

The group of heroic warriors has many characteristics. All *power,* whether in political or narrative terms, is invested in them. For example, the very opening words of the cycle inform us: 'The commander of the V1 Division [i.e. Savitsky] reported that Novograd-Volynsk was taken today at dawn' (27). Savitsky, like many other central male characters is given the power of the word, of organising the discourse. What he reports is also relevant: men acquire or retain power by violent aggression. This theme is immediately echoed by the reference to Nicholas I building the road 'on the bones of peasants' (27). Savitsky is also the central discursive referent in at least two stories which open with his name and rank, **"My First Goose,"**[31] and **"The Story of a Horse."** The nature of male power is particularly clearly illustrated in the latter story. Savitsky is able to dominate the hapless Khlebnikov by the capture of his horse, and, revealingly, by his equally ruthless and imperious possession of the woman, Pavia.[32] Indeed, his imperiousness is made explicit by the grandiose comparison with Peter the Great (84), and, in rather more bathetic terms, by his production of his 'cannon', that is the revolver, 'which was lying on his naked belly' (85).

In Oedipal terms these majestic figures may be interpreted as Father figures to whose stature Lyutov may only aspire.[33] In terms of literary tradition, as has been noted by numerous commentators, they inherit the Cossack tradition of Pushkin and, especially, Gogol and Tolstoy.[34] Lionel Trilling, in particular, comments upon the extent to which Babel's Cossacks echo Tolstoy's *Cossacks,* with the same 'primitive energy, passion and virtue'. For both writers, the Cossack is the man of the body and, significantly, of full sexuality.[35] The critical literature has tended to focus on this very masculine hero (Sinyavsky's 'virile humanism') and many striking phrases have been used to encapsulate the type, as we shall shortly see.

One obvious, and much remarked upon feature, is the close bond between Cossack and horse.[36] At times it seems that their equine companions are the *supreme* value signifying more even than their brothers in arms,—and certainly more than any woman, except the mother. Apart from the two sections relating the dispute between Savitsky and Khlebnikov, **"Afonika Bida"** is the story which most clearly highlights this theme. When Afonka's horse is shot its death is conveyed in terms of great elegiac pathos, which is reinforced by the depiction of Afonka subsequently asleep surrounded by magnificent equestrian trappings, which are itemised in loving detail. An interchange between two minor characters sums up the Cossack view:

> 'A horse is a friend', answered Orlov.
>
> 'A horse is a father', sighed Bitsenko . . .
>
> 'It's a disaster for Bida without a horse . . .'

(104)

Despite this eulogy, however, by the end of the cycle, even this highest value is to be desecrated by male violence.

If horses are the Cossacks' highest value, then they themselves are clearly valorised by the narrator and the text more generally. This at least is the common critical view. Particularly striking is their physical beauty. Viktor Shklovsky puts it, as always, pithily and wittily: 'Babel's Cossacks are all insufferably and ineffably handsome'.[37] Probably the most celebrated and oft-quoted instance is the opening paragraph of **"My First Goose,"** in which Savitsky rises before Lyutov's eyes with a peculiarly feminine kind of beauty:[38] in this particular story all Cossacks do indeed seem to be as Shklovsky depicts them. Here we are struck by what Hallett describes as 'the overwhelming feeling of physical strength and attractiveness of the Cossack male'.[39] Another Division Commander, Dyakov (who becomes yet one more member of the cluster-hero) has a no less awesome appearance: 'Dyakov, who used to be a circus athlete, and now the Remount Officer,—red-faced, with grey moustache, in a black cloak and with silver stripes along his red *sharovary*' (37). Rather more contentious, however, is Sinyavsky's assertion that Babel 'makes us see in his Red Cavalry the moral and aesthetic greatness of these men, even though they are stained with blood and mire'.[40] Sinyavsky goes on to term them 'figures in an epic', a view shared by other critics,[41] and one that is made explicit on several occasions within the text. For example, Makhno, by report is 'as various as nature' (62), while both Trunov and Savitsky are termed 'world-wide hero' (111 and 124), the repeated phrase (from different speakers) being a further instance of the text's reinforcing the similarities of all these heroes.

Although Sinyavsky, and Trilling who talks of the 'lyric joy' involved in the violence of **Red Cavalry**,[42] and grows enthusiastic about the 'ultimate psychic freedom [. . .] to be won through cruelty conceived of as a spiritual exercise',[43] may be able to admire the aesthetic dimensions of these heroes, serious doubts begin to arise when we look at what these 'heroes' actually do and why. In other words, the view of masculinity on offer must surely be seen as both damagingly one-sided, and ultimately dangerous and life-threatening. Thus, the violence may be sometimes for the sake of the Revolutionary cause (**"Salt," "Trunov"** [**"The Squadron Commander Trunov"**]), but it is no less commonly for motives of personal revenge (**"The Letter"**) or completely unmotivated, as Luplow has noted.[44]

Most worrying of all is the view that gradually emerges that to be a man is to kill, and to kill as sadistically as possible, 'to force a change in another person', of the most fundamental kind! In this sense, **Red Cavalry** takes the basic 'sadism 'of all stories to gruesome conclusions.

If any man in the stories can be seen as *primus inter pares*, it is Savitsky who appears to significant effect in four stories, including Lyutov's dream in the first of the cycle **"Crossing the Zbruch"**: indeed, he opens the cycle, as we have already noted. In the dream we meet the first of many gruesome killings. As in the later deaths it is not simple death, but extreme, overdetermined savagery.

> I dream of the Commander of the VI Division. On a heavy stallion he pursues the Brigade Commander and plants two bullets in his eyes. The bullets pierce the Brigade Commander's head and his eyes fall to the ground.
>
> (28)

Pavlichenko makes this kind of savagery explicit in his own *skaz* account of personal vengeance. Mere shooting, he asserts, is to let the other man off lightly. To really learn about life, he goes on, you have to trample a man to death for an hour and then you get through to his soul (80). In so doing, he echoes the words used at the end of **The Commander of II Brigade.** Lyutov sits and admires several of the members of the cluster-hero:

> That evening in Kolesnikov's quarters I saw the masterful indifference of a Tatar Khan and became aware of the schooling of the celebrated Kniga, the self-willed Pavlichenko, the captivating Savitsky.
>
> (70)

Over and over again Lyutov recounts, or we hear direct *skaz* reportage of quite ferocious, sadistic, overdetermined killings of men by other men. On two occasions at least, Lyutov makes more explicit the meaning of this theme. In a once more oft-quoted line he prays at the end of **"After the Battle"** 'for the simplest of skills—the ability to kill a man'(145), while in **"The Discourse on the Tachanka"** he remarks that 'I ceased being a pariah among the Cossacks'.(62) This is because he is the proud owner of a *tachanka*, which is the basis of the triangle 'to slash—*tachanka*—blood' (ibid.). Apart from the *tachanka* the main emblem of this kind of manhood is a suitably phallic one, namely the sabre, which Lyutov uses to pierce the dead goose (55), which is used to cull honey from the desecrated 'holy republics of bees' (60) in **"The Road to Brody,"** which is wielded by Pavlichenko who reappears in **"Berestechko"** (91), and which is later used by Trunov against the throat of an old man.(114)

More often than not, as I have already noted, men use this kind of extreme and sadistic violence against other men. Thereby, killing becomes an expression not only of manhood but of superiority over other men, a means of 'forcing a change in another person'. And, as I have also already noted, Lyutov prays for this very ability so that he too may be a true man. As Luplow puts it:

> The Cossacks often commit violence with such flair, in
> such a grand manner, that the narrator's fascination and
> even awe overshadows the horror and moral outrage he
> feels at their acts.[45]

Certainly I would agree that, although the violence is often gruesome—such as brains being splattered over Lyutov from a blown apart head (115)—it is valorised in a number of ways. Those such as Trunov who takes on the bombers single-handed are accorded the tribute of epic heroism: he is buried 'in a place of honour' (117) at the end of his own story. Moreover, he and others are specifically heroes of the Revolution, which, on the whole, receives a positive 'verdict' in the cycle. Not only does Trunov receive the epithet of 'world-wide hero', and the accolade of a posthumous 'laurel wreath' (112), he is also acclaimed as one of the 'dead warriors of the First Cavalry, this proud phalanx which beats the hammer of history on the anvil of future ages' (111). And after his death the Internationale is played. . . . This identification of male brutality with the progressive forces of history, the Revolution and the Communist Party is echoed and developed by Savitsky in **"The Continuation of the Story of a Horse,"** where he uses equally brutal/sadistic terms for the movement of history. He writes:

> Our Communist party is, comrade Khlebnikov, our iron
> rank of warriors who give their blood in the first order,
> and when blood flows from iron, then this is no joke
> for you, comrade, but victory or death.
>
> (125)[46]

This theme of Revolutionary glory being forged through blood and iron recurs and receives its final accreditation in the last story, in the last of the 'straight-line'[47] men, Baulin, who with thousands like him, we are told, played an important part in the victory of the Revolution.(152)

Whatever recurrent ambivalence there may be in Lyutov's heart as regards violence, it would seem to be ultimately vindicated by the text itself and, beyond that, by history. Yet we must also recognise what else the text tells us, namely that in this world of men, death, gruesome death is everywhere; that male violence (or, simply, masculinity so defined) is dangerous, particularly because, in the end, there is no value that these 'heroic warriors' respect. Male violence is, of course, dangerous to other men, and to women as we shall discuss in more detail. But it presents a very general threat to the world as it is depicted in ***Red Cavalry***: as already noted, this war is merely one of a succession throughout history, stretching right back into pre-history, as is suggested by the sentence near the opening of **"Berestechko"**: 'Monstrous corpses were littered on the thousand-year-old funeral mounds.' (91)[48] In the present, Gedali dreams of an International of 'good people': this must remain a fond hope. Lyutov tells him that 'it [the International] is eaten with gunpowder . . . and the best blood is used to season it' (52).

The cycle does, indeed, grow gradually darker with corpses piled on corpses, men fighting without ribs (*Chesniki*) and the fields littered with excrement, while dead mice float along the roads (*Zamost'ye*). Interestingly, it is one of the few recurrent women, Sashka, who conveys what the cycle as a whole suggests is the essence of maleness: '"Cocks only have one concern", said Sashka, "to smash each other in the face"'. (145) A matter of a few lines later, however, Lyutov prays to fate for the simplest of abilities—to kill another man. Earlier in this story the Cossacks' most sacred values have been harmed: they are now riding on 'utterly exhausted' horses (142) into battle against brother Cossacks who had joined the Poles.[49] This is merely the clearest illustration of internecine strife. If the simplest of abilities is to kill a fellow man, then to be a man is, *ipso facto,* to know how to kill. As a result this apparent paean to masculinity can equally be read as a savage indictment. A story, in de Lauretis's view may demand sadism. This particular cycle of stories suggests that masculinity equally demands sadism as well as desecration of the highest values.

To return briefly to a consideration of the plot typologies of this cycle we can see that many of them do involve precisely this kind of forced change in others' lives, often resulting in gruesome, prolonged violence.

The experience and causation of suffering are commonplaces in the critical literature of the cycle. Falen, for example, speaks of 'a Darwinian jungle in which the strong prevail while the weak are condemned to suffering and destruction'; it is a world, in his view 'of torturers . . . and passive sufferers.'[50] Grongaard, in turn, tells us of the two basic groups of characters, 'the perpetrators of violence and the victims'.[51] Luplow goes even nearer to the truth when she comments that 'the strong victimize the weak and even persecute them for their weakness'.[52] Yet none of the commentators quite catch the centrality of sadism as a plot device, nor, as I have already noted, do they make the obvious connection between masculinity and these plots.

Story after story tells of this sadism. Many are on an individual, man to man basis, as in **"The Letter"** where, in yet another echo of *Taras Bulba,* father kills son, only to be killed himself by another son. **"Pavlichenko"** [**"The Life and adventures of Matthew Pavlichenko"**], of course, enacts this plot while in the next story proper the eponymous Prishchepa destroys dogs, a cow, old women and defiles icons. As is often noted, even Lyutov attempts to join this plot by his three attacks on old women, thereby identifying himself with the aforementioned Prishchepa. The plot of sadism is extrapolated to a much more pandemic scale, as in the stealing of village horses (**"The Remount Officer"**), the destruction of the hives, in Trunov's battle and sadistic killing of prisoners. Indeed, it could be argued that the Revolution itself, or history more generally, is depicted in **Red Cavalry** as fitting this paradigm. History as well as a mere story, the view emerges, demands sadism.

If a story demands sadism and, going back one stage, if narrative in Lotman's model is inherently and *by definition* male, what role can women play in plots, and what role do they play in **Red Cavalry**? As we have already seen, following de Lauretis, who in turn develops Lotman and Propp, women are at best obstacles, 'antagonists' to the hero, or else merely a function of the space a hero crosses. De Lauretis develops this theme in her consideration of myth:

> Medusa and the Sphinx, like the other ancient monsters, have survived inscribed in hero narratives, in someone else's story, not their own; so they are figures or markers of positions—places and topoi—through which the hero and his story move to their destination and to accomplish meaning.[53]

With this in mind I will now move to a consideration of women in **Red Cavalry.** If men are heroic and, therefore, valorised by the text, women are almost uniformly denigrated, most usually in terms of their sexuality, although for many other reasons as well. **Red Cavalry** can be read as variations on very traditional stereotyped themes.

To return to some of my opening remarks, no female character has anything like the importance of Savitsky et. al., nor even of the 'artist' figures. Only two are recurrent, Pani Eliza and Sister Sashka to whom we will return. Most are marginal, and not even named, another link with Gogol's work.[54] Even such significant female characters as the Jewish daughter in **"Crossing the Zbruch,"** the treacherous woman in **"Salt"**, the beggar woman in **"Sashka Khristos"** or the old woman in **"The Song"** remain nameless, a fact which helps to reinforce their status as cyphers or symbolic presences. Women are often weak, and always powerless. The Jewish daughter has 'thin legs' (28), and although she may protest her fate with some dignity she remains impotent. Other instances of female weakness are the mother in **"The Letter"** who is described as a 'tiny peasant woman . . . with wasted, light and shy features' (36) and Pavlichenko's wife who goes mad.

Women are frequently characterised androcentically as daughters or mothers (to which we shall return) or as servants. Pani Eliza, as already noted appears in more than one of the early stories, but she is not given any distinct identity and remains locked in her role as housekeeper. As is traditional, women are associated with hospitality, that is, servicing men.

Another such is Braina, the wife of Schmerel who serves the guests raisin vodka and *zrazy* (40). While the men are warriors, saints or artists, and heroes all, the women wait dutifully to be part of some-one else's story. Nurses appear in a number of stories (**"Sun of Italy," "The Death of Dolgushov,"** for example) but are talked of merely as categories. Sashka again is a rare exception to this generic description.

Many of the women are characterised by their old-age, their widowhood or, yet another traditional stereotype, by their weeping and wailing. While men resist their cruel destinies (with some exceptions) women are passive sufferers. Pani Eliza is termed 'the old Polish woman' (29), while in **"Gedali"** we are told of the 'old woman' sitting in the background and 'sweetly sobbing' (50). The housekeeper in **"My First Goose"** is also *starukha*, while the other emblematic housekeeper (also pushed around by Lyutov) in **"The Song"** is described as an 'evil housekeeper. She was a widow, she was poor'. Evil, widow, poor—she becomes an overdetermined antagonist in Lyutov's path. Such piling of traditional image on traditional image can also be seen at the opening of **"Berestechko"**: Lyutov is billeted with 'a red-headed widow, who smelled of a widow's grief' (91): she is, of course, unnamed. We encounter another such emblematic figure in **"In St Valentine's Church,"** who also combines a number of traditional images. There appears in the church 'an old woman with loosened, yellow hair. She moved like a dog with a broken paw, reeling and falling to the ground'. (108) She is blind and begins kissing Lyutov's boots 'with tenderness, embracing them like a baby'. (108)

This *starukha* is old, blind, grotesque, mad, unnamed and mute. Occasionally the short step to becoming a witch is made,[55] as in the disgusting syphilitic beggar-woman who infects Sashka Khristos and his father, and who 'leaped into the room' (71) with remarkable agility for one so described. As well as the other connotations the two *starukha-khozyaka* figures of **"My First Goose"** and **"The Song"** clearly come close to the 'wierd sisters' of traditional folk-tales, and their role as antagonists, obstacles in Lyutov's path further endorses this view.

In more mundane terms women are not uncommonly shown to be treacherous, dangerous impediments to men's desires and destinies. Irina the washerwoman (another servant, albeit named) in **"Evening"** is faithless. Galin, weak, half-blind and ineffectual, worships her, but she goes off to make love with Vasily the cook, virtually in public. This story immediately follows, and provides a semi-comic variation on the theme of female duplicity as enacted in **"Salt"** by the false mother (unnamed) who is shot by Balmashev for smuggling salt under the guise of a baby. Balmashev, indeed, opens his *skaz* letter by declaring the theme of his story: 'Dear comrade editor. I want to describe to you about the un-consciousness of women who are harmful to us'. (94) Whereas men die and shed their blood for the Revolution, women—*as a group*—are politically unaroused and dangerous to the cause. Moreover, they betray their own sacred calling of motherhood, to which we shall return.

The danger that women present to men is taken one stage further by the several historical/literary references which characterise women as symbolic castrators. In **"Pan Apolek"** we are presented with a typically gruesome depiction of John the Baptist: 'John's head was jaggedly cut off, with a ragged neck' (39). This image is taken up in **"In St Valentine's Church"** where, lest we miss the point, we are told that other characters' hair shines 'like the beard of Holophernes' (109). The text then, in its usual mosaic way, establishes a series of plots and roles for women to show their danger to men, which is then subtly underscored by an apparently chance series of references.

Given, then, that many of the women are castrators, ugly old witches or merely faithless it is surprising to find at least one woman addressed as a pure love object, in **"The Sun of Italy."** However, here too, in a different way, a woman is objectified and presented as inscribed in someone else's story.

Sidorov 'an anguished murderer' (47) has written to Viktoria telling of the pain of being a man (a murderer) and imploring her assistance in securing his release from his torments. Her name, nearly rhyming with *Italia,* is repeated and repeated, almost like an incantation or talisman, representing an oasis amidst the death and destruction that Sidorov details. She becomes his Guardian Angel, almost his Muse. 'Save me, Viktoria' (47) he implores, echoing Gogol's Madman, as his letter builds to a lyric crescendo. Other notes are added: she is a fiancée who will never be a wife (an unsullied Virgin, a rarity in these stories). The concluding lines of the letter sum up her significance: 'Italy has entered my heart like an apparition. The thought of this country, which I have never seen, is sweet to me, like the name of a woman, like your name, Viktoria . . .' (48). Unlike many women in the cycle she is given a name. In the end, however, that is all she has, that is all she is, a romantic incantation to ward off the evil spirits of war and masculinity.

If Viktoria represents an oasis for Sidorov, then his love for her, if we can call it this, is a rarity in *Red Cavalry.* Much more commonly sexuality is represented as a 'mere bodily function'[56] and is usually depicted as particularly sordid. Furthermore, women are frequently defined in terms of their sexuality, either as whores, virgins, rape victims, pregnant or with 'monstrous breasts'.

Instances of sordid sexual relations are littered throughout the cycle.[57] The first and one of the most striking in-stances comes in **"Pan Apolek"** when Jesus and Deborah lie in her vomit. Sashka Khristos and his father both have sex with the disgusting beggar-woman (and, of course, contract syphilis), while later in the story Sashka watches his father and mother, just one of several such voyeuristic scenes. Later on, Sashka is to lie with the 'evil housekeeper' of **"The Song."** As Luplow has noted sex and death are linked in *Zamost'ye,* in Lyutov's dream.[58] Women are castrators, diseased and lead to death.

Particularly in the earlier stories, but later on as well, we encounter numerous whores. In **"Pan Apolek"** Lyutov tells us of Apolek's Mary Magdalene. The historical reference is not, however, sufficient to suggest female defilement. The model for the painting had been 'the Jewish girl El'ka, the daughter of unknown parents and the mother of many, illegitimate [lit. under-the-fence] children' (42). Shortly afterwards Lyutov tells us of other paintings by Apolek, including 'village Marys, who had many children, with knees apart'(43). He then returns to Mary Magdalene, to add other touches to the theme of endless generations of female depravity. We can still see in the Novograd church, *inter alia* 'her, the fornicatrix from Magdala, sickly and insane, with a contorted body and sunken cheeks'(43). Deborah, still in the same story, takes up this motif: after lying with Jesus in her own vomit she returns to the wedding-guests 'noisily triumphant, like a woman who is proud of her own fall'(45).

Other whores appear as characters in later stories. Savitsky's woman, the *kazachka* Pavla is apprehended by the narrative combing her luxurious hair, which she tosses over her back, before buttoning up Savitsky's shirt for him, making obvious references to what they have been up to. Sashka, in **"Chesniki"** is described as the 'lady of all the squadrons'(140), while the references to John the Baptist, and, therefore, implicitly, to Salome reinforce the historical dimension to this image. In literature, myth, holy writ, throughout history and in the diegetic present, whores abound and they, like Deborah, and Pavla are 'proud of their fall'.

Female virtue, then, is for sale, or else it is depicted as defiled. This image occurs, quite *en passant,* in the second story of the cycle, **"The Church at Novograd"** when Lyutov remarks in a striking image: 'I see the wounds of your God, oozing semen, a fragrant poison which intoxicates virgins' (30). In similarly casual fashion in **"Discourse on the Tachanka"** Lyutov ruminates on the history of this region, where there were stories 'of girls raped by Polish troopers and over whom Polish magnates shot each other'(64). There is a 'mock rape' of Sashka in **"In St Valentine's Church"** (108), while real, and multiple rape occurs throughout the night train of **"Salt."**[59] As Balmashev berates the false-mother he tells her 'Look at these two girls, who are crying at the present time, having suffered this night' (96). He then goes on to justify this course of events by suggesting that the woman remember the husbands 'also lonely who by evil necessity rape the girls who pass in their lives'(96).

Women are further defined by their sexuality in the frequent references to pregnant women. For Falen, this is a positive image:

> One of the great symbolic images woven through Babel's *oeuvre* is the heroic figure of the pregnant woman, and just as she is destined to give birth in pain and blood so too man, to create, must suffer and sacrifice.[60]

It is highly significant, given the androcentric bias of the text itself, that this critic does not see the women as self-determining, but merely as symbols of something in men's destinies. Certainly, it seems to me, the image of the pregnant woman in **Red Cavalry** is far from positive. For example, just after Lyutov has concluded his surreptitious reading of Sidorov's letter we return to the quotidian: 'On the other side of the wall a pregrant Jewess was sincerely weeping'(48). Here the woman provides a bathetic contrast to Sidorov's romanticism: equally, she, like all her weeping and widowed sisters is an emblem of female weakness and powerlessness, as too in **"Crossing the Zbruch"** where the bereft daughter is also pregnant. This theme is summed up by yet another man who is given a voice, Grishchuk in **"The Death of Dolgushov."** In this story of horrible suffering and Lyutov's fastidiousness, the soldier ruminates: 'Why do women labour . . . Why are there engagements, weddings, why do their friends make merry at weddings?' (67) Women, to interpret these lines, seem to be locked into an endless cycle of births, marriages— and deaths. They stand as an emblem for the futility of life.

Another aspect of female sexuality which has been noted in the critical literature is breasts. Luplow interprets this obsession quite positively: 'Lyutov also reveals his heightened sensuality in his fascination with large-breasted females, who embody for him human animality and sexuality'.[61] I take a rather different reading of some of the grotesquely atomised, indeed, fetishised descriptions of this part of the female anatomy with which Lyutov regales us. To return to Savitsky's Pavla. Tossing back her hair she walks over to her man 'carrying her breasts on high heels, her breasts which were moving like an animal in a bag'(85). Sashka is described in even more outlandish terms. During her 'mock rape' Lyutov offers the following: 'Sashka's body, flowering and strong-smelling like the meat of a newly slaughtered cow' (108). When she reappears in **"The Widow"** he refers to her 'excessive body' (127), while in *Chesniki* this 'lady of all the squadrons' is 'swollen' while her 'monstrous breasts swing behind

her back' (140). In the next story, **"After the Battle,"** these breasts are 'bouncing about' (145). Given these recurrent fetishistic references it is no surprise that a proferred breast plays a prominent part in one of Lyutov's dreams. He is lying asleep on hay in a barn, when the door opens:

> A woman, dressed for a ball, approached me. She took a breast out of the black lace of her corsage and raised it to me carefully like a wet-nurse offering food.
>
> (130)

However, as we have already noted, the seeming life-giving properties of the nurturing breast prove to be a cruel illusion as sexual ecstasy turns to death.

As we have seen on a number of occasions, the themes of the main body of the text are endorsed by intertextual references and casual remarks by the narrator or other characters. So too here: in **"Trunov,"** Lyutov observes some 'Jewish women, who looked like old negresses, Jewish women with excessive breasts' (112). Indeed, just as the depiction of women almost always denigrates them, so too does the narrator and the text as a whole, through the mechanism of casual, unmotivated misogynistic remarks which are scattered throughout it. For example, in **"The Church at Novograd,"** à propos of nothing in particular, Lyutov tells us of the 'bird-like madness in Pani Eliza's eyes' (31). Lyutov and Pan Apolek discuss, *inter alia* 'the ferocity of women's fanaticism' (43), while in the next story, **"The Sun of Italy"** he observes amidst the ruins of the town the 'crooks of evil old-women's little fingers dug into the ground'(46). In **"Sashka Khristos"** the natural scene is once more remarked upon by our narrator: 'And the earth gave off a sour smell, like from a soldier's wife at dawn' (72). Savitsky in **"The Story of a Horse"** lives in a town 'like a tattered old beggar-woman' (84). In **"In St Valentine's Church"** Lyutov describes the beauty of Apolek's John the Baptist, which is the kind 'for which the concubines of kings lose their already half lost honour' (109). And so it goes on. As a result, the text provides us with a series of demeaning images of women. Moreover, even when not talking of women directly, Lyutov, and other characters help to reinforce this view.

If it may be said that the text *as a whole* defiles femininity then this theme may be extended yet further. Remembering Lotman's basic chain of narrative, within which the hero enters an enclosed space and then leaves it, we may argue that **Red Cavalry** depicts males violating not only women, but space itself, which is often identified as female. The world itself is laid waste by men: space is entered and then left, destroyed.

The title of the opening story is significant in this context. **"Crossing the Zbruch"** implies in Russian the word *reka* (river) a feminine noun. The cycle begins, then, with an army of men crossing a female space. To emphasise the note of violation the river has to be forded, as the bridges are down. Another feminine noun *rodina,* the homeland has been violated throughout history as Lyutov learns in the second story when Romuald tells him in a graphic metaphor of the 'wounds of his homeland' (29), while the third story, **"The Letter"** recounts the violent destruction of yet another feminine entity the *sem'ya* (family).

As Falen has noted, the 'Mother' Church is violated on a number of occasions in the cycle.[62] **"The Church at Novograd"** details broken coffins while the parishioners brassieres have been hung by the priest 'on the nails of the Saviour' (31). The most noteworthy instance of this motif is in the two consecutive stories **"Afon'ka Bida"** and **"In St Valentine's Church"** where Afon'ka celebrates the acquisition of a new horse by desecrating the church dedicated to the patron saint of love, which is eventually closed down.

However, the most pointed and poignant desecration of an enclosed space occurs in the extended, lyrical account of the bee-hives, in **"The Road to Brody."** This story begins with a series of stark statements:

> I mourn the bees. They have been mutilated by warring armies. There are no longer any bees in Volhynia.
>
> We have defiled the hives. We exterminated them with sulphur and blew them up with gunpowder.
>
> (60)

In Russian bee (*pchela*) is also a feminine noun. These few lines can be read as a key-note section of the whole cycle. Warring armies (men) enter space, defile it, and then leave it, having exterminated all the (female) inhabitants. The desecration involved in these actions is made explicit in the next sentence when Lyutov remarks that 'Singed rags gave off a foul smell in the *sacred republics of the bees*'.(60-my italics). As noted elsewhere, the maleness of their destructive activity is signalled by the use of the phallic sabres to extract the honey, the property, as it were, of the Queen bee who must also have been exterminated.

There seems to be every justification in reading this extended metaphor as an allegory of the whole cycle, of what men do to their environment. This reading is, however, made absolutely explicit in a rather later story **"Two Ivans."** Surveying the grim landscape (fields strewn with excrement), an emblematic (Tolstoyan?) 'bearded peasant in copper-rimmed glasses'[63] remarks: 'We call ourselves men, but we foul things worse than jackals. You feel ashamed for the earth . . .'(122). In Russian *zemlya* (earth) is yet another feminine noun.

It seems clear, then, that *Red Cavalry* defiles women and femaleness more generally in a variety of ways. Moreover, it marginalises femaleness yet further in that the point of view in the cycle is almost exclusively male.

As Danuta Mendelson has noted, Babel, following Henry James, dispensed with the omniscient narrator, to replace him with a variety of 'truths'.: 'Thus the truth in *Red Cavalry* is always someone's truth'.[64] However, only very rarely is this 'someone' a woman. Moreover, as already seen, there is what might be called a 'masculinist collective' of voices which denies even the *possibility* of a woman's truth. This is comprised most notably of Balmashev, Pan Apolek as well as Lyutov himself. Most of the stories are about men, who are often valorised, as we have seen. This privileging of the male voice or, quite commonly the voice of violence, is achieved by the frequent use of the *skaz* technique. Because we hear of the acts of violence from the point of view of the men of violence themselves we are led to understand their motivation. Kurdyukov (**"The Letter"**), Pavlichenko and others speak directly to the reader. As Grongaard notes: 'one of Babel's basic principles was that his characters should have the opportunity to express themselves directly'.[65] Consequently, their voices are privileged and as Lermontov noted 'we almost always forgive what we understand'.[66]

Conversely no single story is exclusively or even primarily about a woman. Only one has a female title **"The Widow,"** but even this story deals mainly with male destinies. No women tell their own stories but remain 'inscribed in hero narratives'. For example, Pani Eliza or the old women in **"My First Goose,"** **"In St Valentine's Church"** and elsewhere could well have had fascinating narratives to relate. Instead, they flicker before us as emblematic presences in Lyutov's destiny.[67]

In fact, women hardly speak at all in *Red Cavalry.* On only three occasions do women have anything significant to say (excluding the duplicitous words of the unnamed woman in *Salt*). In the first story the Jewish daughter (unnamed) speaks words of eloquent and dignified protest. But this concerns the death of her father: it is not her *own* story. Sashka, as we have already seen, is allowed to sum up the danger that men's aggression causes (145), while in **"The Song"** the (unnamed) old woman makes similar remarks to Lyutov. Although these are important, if not crucial thematic statements, neither speaks *of herself.* Moreover, as we have also seen, both are profoundly denigrated by the way they are depicted. As a result, the point of view of *Red Cavalry* is almost always male and this aspect of the stories does more than any other to marginalise women.

Obviously the principal speaker and the 'sentient centre' of *Red Cavalry* is the Jewish intellectual and narrator, Lyutov. Most writers on *Red Cavalry* see his plot in terms of a quest. I would now like to examine his plot in these terms, with particular emphasis on his relations with other men, especially the Cossacks, and with women.

The opening story, and especially its title, **"Crossing the Zbruch,"** sets the scene. Lyutov is on a voyage into unknown territory, a voyage of discovery.[68] The 'crossing' of the title, with all its mythic connotations 'implies not only transition, but transformation', to which may be added the equally mythic theme of ritual re-birth.[69] As the cycle unfolds Lyutov 'literally and philosophically wanders'[70] through eastern Poland, the battlefields and mounting corpses.

As Trilling observes, Babel was 'captivated by the vision of two ways of being, the way of violence and the way of peace and he was torn between them'.[71] For Lyutov the central problem is his vacillation between the two, as well as his examination of why men kill violently and why the violated submit.[72] However, the cycle and its progression also mark Lyutov's attempts to become like the Cossacks, that is, to learn the simplest of abilities, how to kill. **"My First Goose,"** as I have noted elsewhere,[73] has as its central theme initiation into the group of Cossacks by means of an act of violence, the slaying of the goose. Other stories show a series of attempts on his part to become one of the boys, a series of temporary successes and then temporary set-backs. In **"The Road to Brody"** it is significant that he declares '*We* have defiled the hives' (60-my italics). But his lyricism, as at the end of **"My First Goose,"** indicates that he is still repelled by his own violence. *Tachanka* also marks assimilation ('I stopped being a pariah' (62)) which this time lacks the former ambivalence on his part: 'I experience the rapture of first possession' (63), a phrase of significantly distinct sexual overtones. However, the very next story **"The Death of Dolgushov"** brings renewed alienation following his inability to kill even out of pity. This is marked by the simple elegiac statement: 'Today I lost Afon'ka, my first friend' (68).

Roland Barthes has indicated the Oedipal nature of narrative texts:

> The pleasure of the text is . . . an Oedipal pleasure (to denude, to know, to learn the origin and the end), if it is true that every narrative (every unveiling of the truth) is a staging of the (absent, hidden or hypostatized) father.[74]

This typology tells us much about the nature of Lyutov's quest which is surely to learn how to become a man, and, *ipso facto,* to learn how to *be* the Father, whether he be incarnate in Savitsky (and the others who comprise the cluster-hero) or Makhno or Lenin.[75] (In this sense *Red Cavalry* can be seen as a disguised Russian *Ulysses*). But, as we have seen earlier, to become a man in this world means to be able to kill. As Lionel Trilling notes, Lyutov's initiation centres on the dilemma of 'whether he can endure killing'.[76]

In the text of *Red Cavalry* Lyutov does, indeed, learn how to kill, albeit only a goose and the bees. But he does, by the end of the cycle, learn two other important lessons of manhood as it is depicted here, namely, how to treat women and how to ride. On three occasions, **"My First Goose,"** **"Zamost'ye"** and **"The Song"** he stages attacks on powerless old women. Thereby he rejects the feminine principle so that he may aspire to be the Father.[77] **"The Song"** is the clearest enactment that Lyutov is, finally, learning the lessons of manhood. He presages his attack on the old woman by knocking the locks off her cupboards in the search of food: as in **"The Road to Brody"** he enters and defiles an enclosed space. He later claims: 'But nothing would have saved her, I'd have worn her out with my revolver, if Sashka Konyyaev or, alias, Sashka Khristos, hadn't stopped me' (146). Perhaps, in *Red Cavalry II,* if it had ever been written, Lyutov would have become fully a man, by killing and raping.

The last story, **"Argamak"** marks a beginning as well as an ending. Lyutov declares: 'I decided to transfer to the active forces' (152). The Russian verb *pereiti* (transfer) is exactly cognate with the 'crossing (*perekhod*)' of the opening story. A new story, a new quest begins. In this story Lyutov finally learns to ride properly. Falen sees this as a triumphant ending: 'the bespectacled narrator becomes fit at last to enter a sacred world. Lyutov . . . has triumphed in his quest.'[78] Yet, it must be remembered that he had to maim Argamak to learn this skill. His realisation of manhood reenacts the very plot typology of the cycle in that he desecrates one of the highest Cossack values and 'forces a change' in another being.

If any value may be said to stand higher than the horse in the world of *Red Cavalry* then it is the mother. It is with a consideration of women as mothers, as virgins and as the image which unites this seeming contradiction in terms, the Madonna, that I will conclude.

Although women characters are not especially important in the narratives that comprise *Red Cavalry,* the symbolism of women is, and mothers, particularly the Holy Mother, figure as a point of reference in many of the stories. This may be casual references, as in **"The Church at Novograd"** when the soldiers seem to be followed around the church by Mothers of God (30-1), or as in the discussion of Pan Apolek's heretical paintings. The mother emerges from these and the other references as a complex, indeed contradictory symbol. She is seen as a figure commanding respect. Several characters ask that their mother be contacted after their deaths, such as Dolgushov and Shevelyov in **"The Widow."** For Sashka Khristos his mother (the mother of Christ, of course) is an object almost of veneration in that he tells his father 'not to insult mother . . . you're tainted' (74). The clearest illustration of the Cossack view comes, admittedly in a somewhat paradoxical form, in **"Salt."** The woman is allowed to travel on the train of the Revolution, and to be protected by Balmashev, specifically because she is allegedly a mother. He addresses the troops: 'Remember, platoon, your life and how you yourselves were children with your mothers'.(95) He turns to the woman: 'We rely on your conscience that you will bring up others to replace us because the old are getting old and, as you see, there's few young ones'. (95) The mother is, then, an object of veneration, on this occasion because she will produce new fighting men. In these terms Balmashev feels entirely justified in wiping 'this disgrace' (97) from the face of the earth because she had betrayed her sacred calling.

The mother whether earthly or divine is also represented as the source of solace and potentially saving grace. Kurdyukov in **"The Letter"** writes to his mother, using the address 'Dear mother Yevdokiya Fyodorovna' over and over again almost as a ritual, prayer-like incantation, as if he were, indeed, beseeching the Holy Mother. In his own way, he allows her honour calling her a 'decent mother' (35). It is, however, the rather more elevated and intellectual Gedali who catches the divine significance of the mother in his remarks which open **"The Rabbi."**

> . . . . All is mortal. Only the mother is destined to eternal life. And when the mother is no more she leaves behind a memory which no-one has yet ventured *to defile.* The memory of the mother nurtures in us compassion.
>
> (57—my italics)

The very next story is **"The Road to Brody"** which uses precisely the same word *oskvernit'* (to defile) for the soldiers' destruction of the hives. Indeed, as we have already seen, nothing is sacred, everything may be, and is, defiled in this man's world, up to and including the Holy Mother of God. Compassion, which stems from the mother cannot be sustained.

Indeed, the Virgin Herself is defiled by the narrator's words on more than one occasion. Fusing the polarities of the traditional Virgin/Whore dichotomy, in *Red Cavalry* the Virgin is a Whore. Thus, as Lyutov thinks back on the events in **"The Church at Novograd"** he says to himself. 'Away from these winking Madonnas, deceived by soldiers'. (31) The Mother of God is defiled, but she behaves in distinctly whorish fashion! The Virgin Mother, in theological terms, is an attempt to deny sexuality.[79] In this metaphor the soldiers, and the narrator who creates the metaphor make her sexual once more. Furthermore the Virgin Mother stands beyond death and therefore time. Even eternity is defiled. **"Pan Apolek"**'s 'country Marys' (43) with their many children have a similar effect of re-sexualising the Holy Mother of God.

In the Russian language in general blasphemies often invoke the Mother of God and so too in *Red Cavalry.* On the very first page of the cycle this motif of des-ecration is established. Some-one is drowning in the Zbruch and 'loudly defames the Mother of God' (27). On the very last page Baulin berates Lyutov for trying to live without enemies and curses him: 'Clear off, to the demned [lit. dishevelled] mother . . .' (155). Throughout, anger and hatred are expressed in similarly blasphemous, defiling terms. The father of the writer of **"The Letter"** takes the name of the Holy Mother in vain (35), for example. In themselves these may be seen merely as reflections of the coarse colloquialisms to be heard in a war-zone. In the context of the cycle they take on rather greater significance.

As we saw earlier, women are raped and defiled. In this context it is interesting to re-examine Lyntov's initiation into the Cossack brotherhood in **"My First Goose."** When he is first rejected the quartermaster advises him: 'If you spoil a lady, the purest of ladies, then you'll be well treated by the lads . . .' (54). In the referential mosaic of *Red Cavalry,* as indeed in theology, the purest of ladies is the Virgin Mother of God. By attacking the old woman, and by his other attempts to achieve manhood Lyutov has to learn this particular lesson, namely, that even the 'purest of ladies', the Virgin, must be defiled.

In these terms one of the crucial stories of the cycle is the third last, **"The Song"** which is clearly linked to **"My First Goose"** by plot rhyme. The song of the title is one that Sashka Khristos has learned from a hunter and is of special significance to Lyutov. Indeed, Sashka sings it to him precisely to calm Lyutov's anger. Lyutov generalises the importance of such songs inasmuch as they, like the mother, serve as an oasis, a point of rest and respect amid the horrors of war:

> For this we forgave the cunning hunter because we needed his songs: at that time no-one could see an end to the war and Sashka alone could pave our wearisome paths with resonance and tears. Our bloody track went along this path. The song flew over our track.
>
> (147)

At least momentarily, then, this song can erase the bloody trace of men's killing. The refrain of the eponymous song is repeated. '"Star of the fields", he sang, "star of the fields above my father's house, and *the sad hand of my mother* . . ."' (146, 147-my italics). The song that soothes man's savage breast is of the mother. The mother grieves: indeed, she is the *Mater Dolorosa.*[80]

Shortly after the singing we see the old-woman with her strange child. She too is a mother, and with her wretched life and 'her dreary complaints' (148) a mother of sorrow. So, in attacking and threatening to kill this old woman Lyutov has desecrated the *Mater Dolorosa.* To him, as to other men, even the Holy Mother of God,

Our Lady of Sorrows is not sacred. Indeed, the very events of the cycle and the way in which they are related to us 'spoil the purest of ladies' over and over again.

Notes

1. All references to *Red Cavalry* are to the edition *Babel: Izbrannoye*, (Moscow, 1966), pp. 27-156.

2. See, *inter alia*, G. Williams, 'Two Leitmotifs in Babel's *Konarmiya*' in *Die Welt Der Slaven*, 17 (1972), pp. 308-17, especially 311-2; J. E. Falen, *Issac Babel, Russian Master of the Short Story*, (Knoxville: University of Tennessee Press, 1974), pp. 126, 166, 168 and 179; R. Grongaard, *I. Babel's Red Cavalry: An Investigation of Composition & Theme*, (Aarhus, 1979), p. 45; C. Luplow, *Isaac Babel's Red Cavalry*, (Ann Arbor, 1982), pp. 156 & 35; P. Carden, *The Art of Isaac Babel*, (Ithaca & London, 1972), p. 122; and A. Lee, 'Epiphany in Babel's *Red Cavalry*, in *Russian Literature Triquarterly*, 2 (1972) pp. 249-60, especially pp. 259-60.

3. See K. K. Ruthven, *Feminist Literary Studies. An Introduction*, (Cambridge, 1984), p. 7.

4. Quoted in J. Fetterley, *The Resisting Reader. A Feminist Approach to American Fiction*, (Bloomington & London, 1978), p. xviii.

5. See G. Greene & C. Kahn (eds.), *Making a Difference: Feminist Literary Criticism*, (London & New York, 1985), pp. 2-3.

6. Such claims are made for *Red Cavalry*. See, for example, Luplow, p. 6: the work is described as 'a lasting, universal vision of the paradoxical essence of reality and of human nature and the human condition'.

7. See S. de Beauvoir, *The Second Sex*, (London, 1972), p. 162.

8. For a discussion of this in earlier periods of Russian literature, see J. Andrew, *Women in Russian Literature: 1780-1863*, (London, 1988).

9. See A. B. Murphy 'The Style of Isaac Babel' in *Slavonic & East European Studies*, (1966), pp. 361-80, especially p. 371.

10. See R. Hallett, *Isaac Babel*, (Letchworth, 1972), p. 53.

11. See Falen, p. 122.

12. See Grongaard, pp. 63 & 68.

13. See Luplow, p. 58. Grongaard (p.64) makes similar remarks.

14. See *Konarmiya*, p. 64. All future references to this work will appear in the text. The translations are my own.

15. See Luplow, pp. 5 & 49.

16. ibid. p. 28.

17. See Falen, p. 121.

18. See Fetterley, p. 49. This remark arises from her discussion of *A Farewell to Arms*.

19. See J. Lotman, 'The Origin of Plot in the Light of Typology' in *Poetics Today*, Vol.1, Nos. 1-2, (Autumn, 1979), pp. 161-84 and T. de Lauretis, *Alice Doesn't: Feminism, Semiotics, Cinema*, (London, 1984) especially the section 'Desire in Narrative', pp. 103-57. I am much indebted to the latter work for the ensuing discussion.

20. Quoted in de Lauretis, p. 103.

21. See Lotman, p. 163.

22. See Lotman, p. 168. For de Lauretis's discussion of this passage, see de Lauretis, pp. 118ff.

23. See Lotman, p. 167.

24. See de Lauretis, pp. 118-19.

25. See de Lauretis, p. 119.

26. See de Lauretis, pp. 132-3.

27. See Carden, p. 111.

28. For the links established in *My First Goose* between Savitsky and Lenin, see J. Andrew, 'Babel's *My First Goose*' in J. Andrew (ed.), *The Structural Analysis of Russian Narrative Fiction*, (Keele, 1984), pp. 64-81, especially pp. 76-7.

29. See ibid.

30. See A. Sinyavsky, 'Isaac Babel', in E. J. Brown (ed.), *Major Soviet Writers*, (London, Oxford, New York), pp. 301-9, especially p. 302.

31. For a discussion of Savitsky's significance in this story, see Andrew (1984).

32. For a discussion of this, see Carden, p. 122.

33. See Andrew (1984).

34. For a discussion of these links, see L. Trilling 'Isaac Babel' in *Beyond Culture*, pp. 119-44, especially pp. 127-8; R. Hallett, pp. 50-1 and V. Shklovsky, 'Isaac Babel: A Critical Romance' in E. J. Brown, pp. 295-300, especially p. 299. Shklovsky, like other critics, notes parallels between *Red Cavalry* and Gogol's *Taras Bulba*. For a discussion of women in this latter work, see Andrew (1988) pp. 86-101.

35. See Trilling, p. 128.

36. See Hallett, p. 52 & Falen, p. 198. The latter sees the theme of the cavalry as such as an important dimension of the cycle's poetry:

As Babel well knew, the Revolution was to be the last great battle in which the cavalry would play an important role, and his nostalgic evocation of its ancient ethos imparts a lyrical tone to his book. The Cossack and his mount, forming a union that is at once both practical and mystic, create an image in which prosaic necessity and poetic form ride together in harmony.

37. See Shklovsky, p. 299.

38. See Andrew (1984) p. 74.

39. See Hallett, p. 55.

40. See Sinyavsky, p. 302.

41. ibid. See also Falen, p. 197.

42. See Trilling, pp. 120 & 126.

43. ibid, p. 138. For a discussion of Babel's Nietzscheanism, see Falen, pp. 160 ff.

44. See Luplow, p. 43.

45. ibid., p. 40.

46. See note 28 above.

47. ibid.

48. There are numerous historical references throughout the cycle including Napoleon, Bogdan Khmelnitsky & Nicholas I.

49. Internecine strife among the Cossacks is a further link with Gogol's *Taras Bulba.* See note 34 above.

50. See Falen, p. 133.

51. See Grongaard, p. 89.

52. See Luplow, p. 57.

53. See de Lauretis, p. 109.

54. See Andrew (1988), pp. 79-111.

55. ibid.

56. See Luplow, p. 16.

57. ibid.

58. ibid.

59. Multiple rape also occurs in Babel's *With Old Man Makhno.* The narrator of that story opens the story in the following chillingly clinical terms:

> Six of Makno's lads raped a servant-girl last night. When I got to know of this I decided to find out how a woman looks after a rape repeated six times.
>
> (Quoted in N. Stepanov, 'Novella Babelya' in *I. Babel: Mastera Sovremennoy Literatury, Stat'i i Materialy,* (Leningrad, 1928, reprint London, 1973), p. 21)

60. See Falen, p. 168.

61. See Luplow, p. 15.

62. See Falen, p. 166.

63. No reader of Babel will need reminding that spectacles, worn both by the narrator and the author themselves, are the sign of the intellectual.

64. See D. Mendelson, *Metaphor in Babel's Short Stories,* (Ann Arbor, 1982), p. 116.

65. See Grongaard, p. 62.

66. See M. Lermontov, *Sobraniye Sochineny v Chetyrekh Tomakh,* (Moscow—Leningrad, 1959-62), Vol. 4, p. 340. The remark is by the travelling narrator in his 'Foreword' to Pechorin's Journal.

67. Turgenev's eponymous heroine Asya can be said to fulfil a similar role in the story of N. N. For a discussion of *Asya* in these terms, see Andrew (1988), pp. 113-22, especially, pp. 120-2.

68. See M. Falchikov, 'Conflict & Contrast in Isaac Babel's *Konarmiya* in *Modern Languages Review,* (72), p. 125-33, especially, p. 125.

69. See Falen, p. 141.

70. See Luplow, p. 32.

71. See Trilling, p. 124, and Falchikov, p. 126.

72. See Carden, pp. 93-4.

73. See Andrew (1984).

74. Quoted in de Lauretis, pp. 107-8.

75. See Andrew (1984), pp. 76-7.

76. See Trilling, p. 134.

77. See Andrew (1984), pp. 75-7.

78. See Falen, p. 199.

79. For a discussion of this, see M. Warner, *Alone of All Her Sex. The Myth & Cult of the Virgin Mary,* (London, 1976), especially pp. 3-78.

80. For a discussion of this, see Warner, pp. 206-23.

Marc Schreurs (essay date 1989)

SOURCE: Schreurs, Marc. "Intertextual Montage." In *Procedures of Montage in Isaak Babel's* Red Cavalry, pp. 96-133. Amsterdam: Rodopi, 1989.

[In the following essay, Schreurs discusses the role and importance of "intertextual allusions" in Babel's Red Cavalry, *claiming that the stories in this collection involve the reader "in dialogical patterns not only with other literary texts, but often also with non-literary pretexts."]*

1. Introduction

The phenomenon of intertextuality in literary semantics may be approached in two different ways: in a general sense, as an inherent condition of the poetic word, and, in a more pragmatic sense, as a covert or overt allusion from one text to another. The first approach was launched by Julia Kristeva. She initiated the now widely used term as follows:

> Le mot (le texte) est un croisement de mots (de textes) ou on lit au moins un autre mot (texte).[1]

> Il se crée, ainsi, autour du signifié poétique, un espace textuel multiple dont les éléments sont susceptibles d'être appliqués dans le texte poétique concret. Nous appelerons cet espace intertextuel.[2]

Kristeva is mainly concerned with the *fact* that a literary text as a secondary system of signs is inescapably linked to a multitude of other texts, whether by citations or allusions, by transposition of one system of signs into another, or simply by being connected to a specific stock of literary codes and conventions. She is opposed to using the term intertextuality for describing in concrete terms the relations of a text with other so-called source texts ("ce terme a été souvent entendu dans le sens banal de 'critique des sources'").[3] Her broad and therefore somewhat vague conception of intertextuality is at present frequently criticized. Laurent Jenny, for example, asserts that intertextuality does not concern a vague and mysterious field of influences, but that

> l' intertextualité désigne (. . .) le travail de transformation et d'assimilation de plusieurs textes opéré par un texte centreur qui garde le *leadership* du sens.[4]

Jenny suggests, that to speak of intertextuality makes sense only if in a specific text the presence of another text can be located in elements which in some respect are alien to their immediate context:

> nous proposons de parler d'intertextualité seulement lorsqu'on est en mesure de repérer dans un texte des élements structurés anterieurement à lui, au-delà du lexème, cela s'entend, mais quel que soit leur niveau de structuration".[5]

Accepting, as Jenny does, the semantic leadership of the alluding text, Wolf Schmid returns to Bachtin's notion of *dialogical relationships* between words.[6] Contrary to Kristeva, who used Bachtin's ideas to broaden her concept of intertextuality, Schmid returns to Bachtin in order to circumscribe the process of transformation and (semantic) assimilation. According to Schmid, Bachtin's notion of the literary word (text) as an utterance which expresses the position of a specific "author" is most important:

> in order to become dialogical, logical and concrete semantic (predmetno-smyslovye) relationships must be embodied, i.e. they must enter into a different sphere of existence: they must become a word, i.e. an utterance and have an author, i.e. the creator of the given utterance, whose position is expressed.[7]

Bachtin argues that a dialogical relationship between one utterance (word, text) and another manifests itself in what he terms the "double-voiced word" (dvugolosoe slovo). In the double-voiced word two semantic or ideological orientations collide, interact in the (metaphorical) sense of a dialogue. Schmid calls such a dialogical interaction intersemanticity (Intersemantizität). He approaches intertextuality pragmatically and confines his interest to intersemantical relationships between texts incorporated in the wording of a given literary work:

> Wenn wir uns hier mit den Manifestationen der Intertextualität nur insoweit beschäftigen als sie sich als "dialogische Beziehungen" darstellen, zielen wir auf Intertextualität nicht einfach als Relation von strukturierten *Texten*, sondern (. . .) auf Intertextualität als Relation der in den simultan vergegenwärtigte Texten ausgedrückten *Bedeutungen, Sinnpositionen,* und *Ideologien.*[8]

Schmid further maintains that intertextuality is intersemantical only if the presence of a textual source, a "Prätext" Schmid terms it (pre-text hereafter), can be identified in a text as an intentional significatory aspect of the semantic construction of a text. Submitted to these restrictions, intertextuality largely coincides with what is traditionally known as literary allusion. As far as this device is concerned, reference to intentionality on the part of the author seems to be prerequisite. A text cannot allude to a pre-text unless it can be assumed on reasonable grounds that the author of the text has known the specific pre-text.

In his article Schmid discusses four definitions of the literary allusion.[9] The most comprehensive definition is undoubtedly the one designed by Carmela Perry:

> Allusion in literature is a manner of signifying in which some kind of marker (simple or complex, overt or covert) not only signifies unallusively, within the imagined world of the alluding text, but through echo also denotes a source text and specifies some discrete, recoverable property (ies) belonging to the intentions of this source text (. . .), the property (ies) evoked modifies the alluding text, and possibly activates further, larger inter- and intra-textual patterns of properties with consequent further modification of the alluding text.[10]

The present chapter, which will study intertextuality as a montage strategy in Babel's **Red Cavalry**-stories subscribes to Perry's definition and Schmid's lucid elaboration. The restricting definitions of intertextuality provided by these scholars are useful in describing manifestations of intertextuality as forms of montage, i.e. of colliding aspects of "Intersemantizität", of semantic juxtapositions of initially unrelated elements, selected from heterogeneous contexts. Like inner-stories and digressions, intertextual allusions are traditional phenomena in literature which may function according to the "laws" of montage (and indeed often do). In what follows I shall use the term intertextual allusion instead of literary allusion. For the qualifier "literary" puts an unnecessary limitation on the field of research. *Red Cavalry* involves the reader in dialogical patterns not only with other literary texts, but often also with non-literary pre-texts.

It will be clear that the insertion of a pre-text into a text as montage makes sense only if the "strange" properties, the marking elements which enable the reader to establish the pretext have a distinctly conflicting position in their new verbal environment. The inserted marker should create a noticeable effect of discontinuity or contrast. In this respect, the quality of the alluding signal, its material substance, so to speak, is of decisive importance. The chief aim of this study is to describe the attraction-level of the montage, i.e., the conflict status of the marker, and to sketch out the dominant aspects of the hidden dialogical patterns and semantic modifications. The presence of a great variety of pre-texts in *Red Cavalry* has been observed by numerous critics before me. I am happy to be able to start from their excellent work, on which I shall try to elaborate.

2. LITERARY PRE-TEXTS

2.1.

One of the traditional literary modes on which Babel draws in his *Red Cavalry,* is the epic mode of narration. In Babel's hands, the war between Poland and Soviet Russia, or rather the campaign of Budennyj's First Cavalry Army (Konarmija), acquires proportions common to heroic poems of all times. One may even regard *Red Cavalry* in its entirety as a modern epic. It relates to us a series of events which themselves represent a much greater historical event: a radical social change in Western civilization, the end of the old world, the coming of a new era, marked by the first World War and the October Revolution. Babel's awareness of the long-range significance of his epoch is evinced in his vivid evocation of an epic mood. James Falen noted that "Babel's feel for the epic is genuine, and its evocation in his work is extremely effective"[11]. Babel's epic sources are to be found, according to Falen, not only among the ancient classics, but also in the Russian folk-epic—"The Igor Tale" ("Slovo o Polku Igoreve"), and in the nineteenth century epic works by Gogol' (*Taras Bulba*) and Tolstoj (*War and Peace*).

Red Cavalry echoes the epic in several ways. Victor Terras describes the reminiscences of the classic epic (Homer) in the cycle pre-eminently on the diegetic level. He sums up typical epic action motifs (the ride to a strange place where adventure, passion, or even death

is waiting: the ride to a rendezvous with destiny in, e.g., **"The Crossing of the Zbruč"** ("Perechod čerez Zbruč"), **"The Road to Brody"** ("Put' v Brody"), **"Priščepa".**[12]), legendary heroes (the demigods Voroshilov and Budennyj.[13]), heroic martial scenes (Trunov's duel with Fauntleroy; the cavalry charge in **"Česniki"**), which can be read as "Homeric episodes in travesty". As a result of these epic allusions, the events and characters acquire a mythical meaning. Falen reaches a similar conclusion:

> Interpreting contemporary events in terms of models from the past, Babel' describes the Revolution as a "timeless" war, as a part of the unchanging fate of mankind, and its Cossack horsemen—their human traits enlarged to mythic proportions—become Homeric heroes.[14]

According to Falen, Babel's epic vision depends not only on certain diegetic equivalences, on the use of martial themes and a Homeric approach to character, but also involves specific stylistic devices which create an epic mood, devices such as: hyperbolic epithets, apostrophes, and poetic descriptions of the setting.[15]

By using these stylistic devices in a specific manner, Babel not only echoes all past epics, but calls to mind one epic pretext in particular: "The Igor Tale". The presence in the cycle of markers pointing toward this twelfth century Russian folk-epic is clear as day. It has been noted in various studies of Babel's style. Thus, Nilsson points out that the imagery of **"The Crossing of the Zbruč"**, the poetic description of the crossing of the river, reminds readers familiar with Russian literature of "The Igor Tale".[16] Falen also mentions this work as a source of Babel's epic vision but he doesn't go into too much detail.[17] Van Baak pointed out that descriptions of the landscape have functions which are comparable to descriptions of natural phenomena in "The Igor Tale". He mentions, for instance, the "epic escorting of individual heroes in the landscape".[18]

The allusions to "The Igor Tale" are detectable predominantly through equivalences of phraseological material. The alluding signals, the markers, are wrapped in strikingly phrased fragments. It goes without saying, that these moments are alien to their immediate context. As such they can be regarded as points of attraction montage. The reader of *Red Cavalry* is already invited to establish a parallel with "The Igor Tale" in the opening story of the cycle. Through various markers **"The Crossing of the Zbruč"** activates the tale as an intertextual frame of reference to remain operative throughout the cycle.

"The Igor Tale" is referred to in the poetic description of the march toward and the crossing of the river Zbruč. The poetic-ornamental wording of this fragment echoes its hymnographic style. Several images in Babel's story are closely related to it, for instance: "Štandarty zakata vejut nad našimi golovami" (The standards of sunset fly above our heads) relates to "Už vetry (. . .) vejut s morja strelami" (And the winds fly from the sea, like arrows). The effects of expressive descriptions of natural phenomena are roughly the same: qualifications, similes, metaphors provide nature with an active, personified quality.[19] In "The Igor Tale", nature already predicts Igor's lot at the outset of his ride into the unknown, it seems to prevent him from going: "Solnce dorogu emu tmoj zastupilo/ I rano na drugoj den' krovavye zori svet povedajut" (The sun had darkened the road before him/ And early the next morning a bloodshot sunrise announces day-light). Nature reflects the mourning after Igor's defeat: "Ponikaet trava ot žalosti. A drevo pečalju k zemle priklonilos'" (The grass bows in sorrow. Trees bend down to earth in sadness).

Throughout the epic, personification of nature is an important feature of the ornamental style of narration, particularly in the case of Igor's march toward the Donec and the battles with the Kumany. In **"The Crossing of the Zbruč"** ornamental descriptions of nature have a similar role: they reflect not only the army's movement (Volyn' izgibaetsja, uchodit, vpolzaet, putaetsja), but also the dull and slack atmosphere on a hot day in July. The image of the sun rolling along the sky like a chopped-off head foreshadows the coming confrontation with death. The river prepares her deadly traps (zakručivaet penistye uzly svoich porogov). The glittering of the cool majestic moon sheds a cold and indifferent light upon the drowning soldier and his comrades who are struggling to come across. Falen suggests that this type of description may be compared in function to the classical chorus. It gives a kind of indirect comment in response to the depicted events, and expresses the often repressed evaluative perspective of the narrating "I".[20]

The allusion to "The Igor Tale" in **"The Crossing of the Zbruč"** is thus primarily effected through imagery reminiscent of what might be a specimen of Bojan's style in personifying descriptions of spatial elements. The epic passage is an "attraction" moment, at variance with the rest of the story. It breaks off the tone of the opening paragraph and contrasts sharply with the more laconic phrasing of the next paragraph. The equivalence on the level of phraseological material triggers off additional thematic parallels. Take, for instance, the motif of "blindness". Igor fails to recognize the signs of warning expressed by nature, since he is blinded by his eagerness for glory and honor. Unable to form a proper judgement regarding his military capabilities he sets out to fight the enemy by himself instead of fighting them together with other feudal princes. His blindness and conceit leads to a defeat with disastrous consequences. Blindness is also a significant motif in **"The Crossing of the Zbruč"**.[21] Like king Igor, the narrator of *Red*

Cavalry goes on a journey into the unknown, filled with great expectations. He too fails to see the implications of the signs of destruction and death. Only in the second part of the story the observing "I", confronted with the true state of affairs, is forced to abandon his self-delusion.

Another remarkable concurrence in motifs is the symbolic meaning of the crossing of the river. In "The Igor Tale", the Donec does not merely signify the natural boundary between the Russian Soil (Russkaja Zemlja) and the land of the enemy. It is also the borderline between light and darkness, good and evil, heaven and hell, God and the devil.[22] In Babel's story, too, the river has a symbolical meaning of this type. Apart from being a "crossing into Poland", as is more or less suggested, it is a crossing from day to night, from light to darkness, from color to line and sound. But above all it symbolizes the transition from a peaceful atmosphere to war, and on a mental level, from expectations to realities, from blindness to recognition.

Thus in the opening story of *Red Cavalry* a firm frame of reference is established by distinct phraseological and diegetic equivalences with "The Igor Tale". Throughout the cycle, the reader is repeatedly reminded of this epic 'background' through the montage of elements of landscape and nature, particularly the sun, the moon and stars, daybreak and sunset, accompanying martial themes.[23]

Another montage device linked with the epic is the apostrophe. Apostrophes alluding very strongly to the epic genre can be found in **"The Church at Novograd"**. For instance, the digression in which the narrator rhetorically addresses ancient Poland; it breathes a monumental historicism reminiscent of the historic digressions in "The Igor Tale" ("Woe unto you, Res Publica; woe unto you, Prince Radziwill, and unto you Prince Sapieha . . .").[24]

Apart from phraseological and diegetic elements, *Red Cavalry* also has some large-scale compositional idiosyncrasies in common with "The Igor Tale". The aforementioned epic markers are supported in their alluding function by various elements such as an erratic, anachronical sjužet-composition, deliberate oppositions of different styles and a random approach to fact, setting off the present against the past constantly. On account of what I have been saying so far, we may conclude that Babel undoubtedly intended the many references to "The Igor Tale" as a structural element of the semantic universe of his work. The allusions primarily suggest a historical parallel between the events described in *Red Cavalry* and the military campaign of Prince Igor Svjatoslavič in 1185. In view of the fact that Igor's campaign was a failure, and that his defeat had catastrophic consequences for an internally divided Russia, the parallel may well be regarded as a foreboding of doom.

A more important function of the allusion is, however, that it "reflect(s) a vision of the human condition which is characteristic of a heroic world-view, of a heroic society", clashing with brutal aspects of the war.[25] The epic allusions operate within the system of colliding points of view, which, as said, turns the cycle into a polyphonic novel in a modernist tradition. Babel's narrator "imitates" the epic style to create a heroic-epic perspective which stands at variance with other modes of presentation.

2.2.

In the second story of the cycle, **"The Church at Novograd"**, Babel employs some characteristic conventions belonging to the tradition of the *Gothic novel*. Patricia Carden writes:

> Here he (the narrator, M. S.) deals with his attachment to the past, exorcising that attachment by showing it through the distorting lens of the Gothic.[26]

The pre-text to which the story refers cannot be specified. Rather, it consists of a series of texts (novels) which share a number of codes and conventions. The Gothic marker is not restricted to one particular moment in the story, nor does it concern the level of phraseological presentation. The indicator of the literary allusion comprises widely dispersed diegetic elements and narrative-compositional techniques. Therefore, the intertextual correlation with the Gothic pre-text can be established only in retrospect. In such cases the whole text becomes a marker of the source.[27]

"The Church at Novograd" suggests the Gothic tradition in the first place through the presentation of the setting. Carden compares the observing narrator to "that other innocent fascinated by Gothic, Jane Austen's Catherine Morland in *Northanger Abbey*".[28] The church in Novograd and the adjacent presbytery are transformed into a conventional Gothic setting, with hidden subterranean rooms, full of strange elements, creating an atmosphere of terror. The story contains the following examples, some of which have already been mentioned in our discussion of the montage of digressions:

> Rjadom s domom reveli kolokola . . . ; v zmeinom sumrake izvivalas' sutana monacha; ten' monacha kralas' za mnoj neotstupno; dychanie nevidannogo uklada mercalo pod razvalinami doma ksendza, i vskradčivye ego soblazny obessili menja; Vorota kostela raskryty, ja vchožu, i mne navstreču dva čerepa razgorajutsja na kryše slomannogo groba. V ispuge ja brosajus' vniz, v podzemel'e. (. . .) I ja vižu množestvo ognej, beguščich v vysote u samogo kupola.

> The church bells yelled next to the house . . . ; in the snaky twilight a monk's cassock flitted; the monk's shadow followed me about persistently; The breath of an invisible supply glimmered beneath the ruins of the priest's house, and its soothing seduction unmanned

me; The church gates are open, I enter, and to meet me two silver skulls are gleaming on the lid of a broken coffin. Frightened, I dash down into the crypt. (. . .) And I see a multitude of lights darting about, high up in the very dome.

Falen describes these "trappings of a Gothic satire" as follows: "through the story's somewhat sinister symbolism, the Christian temple becomes its obverse, a demonic dungeon-like cellar. The search through the temple's crypt suggests the winding quest through a monster's lair—or through the labyrinthine entrails of the monster itself".[29] It is typical of the Gothic novel that spatial motifs of concealment and horror are psychologically significant.

> One of their (Gothic novels, M. S.) most prominent concerns, though seldom discussed, might grandiosely be called a psychological interest. (. . .) there is a considerable amount of concern for interior mental processes.[30]

The Gothic trappings are a sign of the mental trappings of characters and narrator. Thus the setting in the story is a sign of Pan Romuald's treason, the priest's hidden lusts of the flesh and lustful luxury, of the emotional excitement of the Polish characters (grief, hatred), and the narrator's fascination, fear and moral struggle. Psychological excitement dominates the story on all levels. It not only shows in the spatial presentation, or in the behaviour of the characters (the crazed Robackij, the treacherous Romuald, the bewildered pani Èliza), or in the narrator's emotional digressions, but even in the choice of imagery (Biscuits that smell of crucifixes and that are filled with subtle juice and the rage of the Vatican; and further on: Beneath the black and passionate sky thirsty roses swayed).

One of the reasons why Babel filtered **"The Church at Novograd"** through a Gothic perspective is, according to Carden, to display the narrator's ambiguous point of view, which oscillates between womanish horror and sensual fascination. Mental ambiguity is indeed a characteristic of the Gothic novel: "It emphasizes psychological reaction to evil and leads into a tangle of moral ambiguity for which no meaningful answers can be found".[31] This is a crucial thematic aspect of Babel's story as well. Unable to solve his inner struggle, shifting between moral opposites, the narrator abandons the scene of action (cf. also our discussion on digressions in Chapter Two, section 2).

Another theme which motivates the montage of Gothic elements is Catholicism. Even though there is no concrete "evidence" in the story, it is not too far-fetched to claim that within the Gothic pre-textual field, one text is of particular relevance: *The Monk* by M. G. Lewis. This eighteenth century novel, set in medieval Spain, deals with a Roman Catholic monk Ambrosio, known for his austere way of life and his chastity. However, he falls to the temptations of a woman, and becomes the victim of his sexual desires, which eventually lead him to murder and rape. A similar "blasphemous" evaluation of religion can be found in other Gothic novels:

> The confusion of evil and good which the Gothic novel reflects in its villain-heroes produces a non-Christian or anticlerical feeling. (. . .) To some extent the feeling is simply anti-Catholic.[32]

The intertextual correlation thus enhances an essential thematic aspect of Babel's story. The Catholic double morality, as exemplified by the image of the escaped priest, who is surrounded by signs of sexual weakness and sinfulness, and whose church is involved in worldly affairs, is intensified by the montage of a Gothic frame of reference. This evaluation is countered by the narrator's apparent fascination with the mystical force of the age-long Catholic culture. The echo of Gothic pre-texts is effectively directed towards the expression of this evaluational ambiguity with great aesthetic and emotional force.

2.3.

"The Church at Novograd" alludes to the Gothic tradition through specific themes and narrative-compositional techniques. The marker, as stated, is not confined to one particular element but is an integral part of the overall construction of the story. In this respect it stands apart from most other stories in which montage of literary allusions is restricted to a structurally and thematically isolated text part. Frequently, the marker is an isolated text segment which includes a quite overt authorial hint.

From **"Italian Sunshine"** I now quote the following passage, which refers to Shakespeare's *Romeo and Juliet* staged as an opera:

> Syraja plesen' razvalin cvela, kak mramor opernoj skam'i. I ja ždal potrevozennoj dušoj vychoda Romeo iz-za tuč, otlasnogo Romeo, pojuščego o ljubvi v to vremja kak za kulisami ponuryj èlektrotechnik deržit palec na vyključatele luny.

> The damp mould of the ruins flowered like the marble of opera seats. And I waited, disturbed in spirit, for Romeo to appear from the clouds, a satin-clad Romeo singing of love, while a dismal electrician in the wings keeps a finger on the moon extinguisher.

By means of the montage of this attraction-like passage Babel creates a shift from gruesome reality—the ruined city of Novograd—to the enchanting phantasy of an opera-stage. A transformation which is seemingly motivated by the narrator's drunken exaltation, the result of one of his visits to pani Èliza's presbytery:

> Duša, nalitaja tomitel'nym chelem mečty, ulybalas' nevedomo komu, i voobraženie, slepaja sčastlivaja baba, klubilos' vperedi ijul'skim tumanom.

Filled with tiresome hop, my soul smiled to God-knows whom, and my imagination—a blind and happy old maid, took off into the haze of july.

The transformation of the ruins of Novograd to the stage of Romeo and Juliet is inspired by the effects of a July-moon which sheds its light on the scene. The technician holding his finger on the moon-extinguisher emphasizes the moon motif in relation to the narrator's playful imagination. In Shakespeare's play, July is the time of action. It is the season of extremes, "where a balmy moonlit night is dependent on the heat of the preceding day, its dark, velvet delicacy intensified by contrast with the sun's unmitigated glare. In the charmed darkness of silent summer night it is easy to loose touch with the noisy world of day, so distinct, objective, unveiled".[33] The montage of this Shakespearean phantasy passage primarily effects a double contrast. Harsh every-day reality, the city in ruins, is set off against this Shakespearean moonlit love-scene. At the same time the scene is ridiculed as a stage-trick. Then again, the moonlit night is evoked as a beautiful "imaginistic" vision of the world, signifying the narrator's zest for life ("Blue roads flowed past me like streams of milk spurting from many breasts").[34]

A dominant thematic aspect of **"Italian Sunshine"** is that it compares the minds of two dreamers, who seek refuge from the frustrating misery of their situation: the narrator escapes in his artistic imagination, Sidorov dreams of starting a revolution in Italy.[35] The intertextual reference to *Romeo and Juliet* underlines the correspondence between the narrator and Sidorov. The latter's letter extends the allusion in an ironic manner. Apart from the fact that he wants to go to Italy, it is noteworthy that the name of his bride is *Viktorija*. Some of Sidorov's remarks shed an ironic light on the segment alluding to Shakespeare's drama:

> (. . .) Viktorija, nevesta kotoraja nikogda ne budet ženoj. Vot i santimental'nost', nu ee k rasproetakoj materi . . .

> Vot pogladjat po golovke i promjamljat: 'romantik'. Skažite prosto,—on bolen, zol, p'jan ot toski, on chočet solnca Italii i bananov.

> (. . .) Victoria, fiancée who will never be my wife. Now I am getting sentimental—oh to hell with it . . .

> (. . .) They will only pat you on the head and mumble: 'A romantic.' Say simply: 'He's ill, fed-up, drunk with depression. He wants Italian sunshine and banana's'.

The intertextual correlation furthers the ironic shading of both the narrator and Sidorov. But what is more, it accentuates the contrast and distinction between them. Ljutov's "literary" phantasy is lit by "balmy moonlight", whereas Sidorov longs for the opposite, the Italian sun. It adds to the negative evaluation of Sidorov's "common sense madness", and to the narrator's ironic self-evaluation (the moon-extinguisher; the pink wadding of my imagination).

2.4.

In **"Gedali"** the narrator openly refers to Charles Dickens. Again, this takes place in a singled-out passage in the story, a digression in which the narrator rhetorically adresses Dickens:

> Dikkens, gde byla v tot den' tvoja laskovaja ten'? Ty uvidel by v ètoj lavke drevnostej zoločenye tufli i korabel'nye kanaty, starinnyj kompas i čučela orela, ochotničij vinčester s vygravirovannoj datoj 1810 i slomannuju kastrjulju.

> Dickens, where was your kindly shade that evening? In that little old curiosity shop you would have seen gilt slippers, ship's cables, an ancient compass, a stuffed eagle a Winchester with the date 1810 engraved upon it, a broken saucepan.

This digression follows upon the narrator's sweet memories of childhood, expressed in another digression at the beginning of the story. As noted already in our discussion of digressions in this story, the "ship's cables, an ancient compass" point back to the moment, when he remembered how on Sabbath eves "my child's heart was rocked like a little ship on enchanted waves". A more or less explicit comparison is drawn between old Gedali's shop and the shop of little Nelly's grandfather in Dickens' *The Old Curiosity Shop* (*Lavka Drevnostej*). We recognize the gloomy atmosphere of Dickens' description of the shop, filled with decaying remnants of the past:

> There were suits of mail, standing like ghosts in armour, here and there; fantastic carvings brought from monkish cloisters; rusty weapons of various kinds; distorted figures in china, and wood, and iron, and ivory; tapestry and strange furniture that might have been designed in dreams.

A similar, almost gothic ambience we find in Gedali's shop:

> V ètoj lavke i est' pugovicy, i mertvaja baboč ka (. . .) I on v'etsja v labirinte iz globusov, čerepov i mertvych cvetov . . .

> In the shop are buttons, and dead butterfly, and its small owner goes by the name of Gedali. (. . .) He winds in a labyrinth of globes, skulls and dead flowers . . .

The montage of this literary reference deepens the evaluative tension, which is so essential to **"Gedali"**. On the one hand the association with Dickens within the narrator's mind is apparently generated by a deep sense of affection, connected with tender memories of his childhood. The narrator observes Gedali with undisguised sympathy, comparable to the way Dickens' narrator meets little Nelly, grandfather and grandchild. The former is little and old, like Gedali, and has in his face "marks of deep and anxious thought, which convinced me that he could not be, as I had been at first inclined

to suppose, in a state of dotage or imbecility". Babel clearly linked Gedali to the grandfather in Dickens' novel. They both are figures from the past, and this is symbolized by the contents of their curiosity shops. Their world-views combine wisdom with a childlike naivete, which at first in the case of Nelly's grandfather obtains elements of senility. In the narrator's presentation, Gedali's somewhat childlike outlook is repeatedly emphasized through diminutive forms:

> . . . malen'kij chozjain v dymčatych očkach. (. . .) On potiraet belye ručki, on ščiplet sivuju boroden'ku. (. . .) Èta lavka, kak korobočka ljuboznatel'nogo i važnogo mal'čika, iz kotorogo vyjdet professor botaniki.

> . . . the little proprietor in smoked glasses. (. . .) He rubs his small white hands, plucks at his little grey beard. (. . .) The shop is like the small box of an important and knowledge-loving little boy who will up to be a professor of botany.

Through this emphasis on the childlike smallness of Gedali's appearance, and on the smell of decay and remnants of the past which dominate Gedali's world, the narrator counters the straightforward wisdom and irrefutable logic of the old man's philosophical reasoning with regard to the revolution—his "impossible international". On the other hand, the montage of the Dickens-allusion throws into relief the narrator's nostalgic longing and clashes with his revolutionary bravado.

2.5.

Another interesting literary allusion occurs in the story **"Squadron Commander Trunov"** (**"Èkadronnyj Trunov"**), which is about the heroic death of squadron commander Pavel Trunov. The story begins with Trunov's military funeral, which includes a funeral speech by Pugačev, the commander of Trunov's regiment "about the dead soldiers of the First Cavalry Army, about that proud phalanx which is beating the hammer of history upon the anvil of future ages". The actual story of Trunov's death and of the events leading up to it is told in reversed order, starting from the description of the funeral. This compositional inversion is all the more emphatic because of two inserted fragments which are completely disconnected from the linear action fundament. After giving Trunov's corpse the ritual final kiss the narrator wanders off into "gothic" Sokal. His attention is attracted by "a Galician as lanky and cadaverous as Don Quixote". The association with *Don Quixote* is elaborated in the subsequent description of the Galician:

> Galičanin ètot byl odet v beluju cholščevuju rubachu do pjat. On byl odet kak by dlja pogrebenija ili dlja pričastija i vel na verevke vzlochmačennuju korovenku. Na gigantskoe ego tuloviš če byla posažena podvižnaja krochotnaja, probritaja golovka zmei, ona byla prikryta širokopoloj šljapoj iz derevenskoj solomy i pošatyv-

alas'. Žalkaja korovenku sel za galičaninom na pov-
odu; on vel ee s važnost' ju i viselicej dlinnych svoich
kostej peresekal gorjačij blesk nebes.

This Galician was clothed in a white linen shirt that
reached down to his heels. He was arrayed as though
for his funeral or for Communion service, and he led
by a rope a little tousled cow. Upon his huge body was
set a nimble, tiny, pierced head of a serpent that
waggled beneath a wide brimmed hat of common straw.
The wretched little cow followed the Galician at the
end of its lead. He led it with an air of importance, his
gibbet-like frame cleaving the burning brilliance of the
skies.

The narrator is intrigued by this figure and follows him
into a poor Jewish quarter. One striking detail is piled
upon another: a lane all smoky with thick and nauseating vapors; little charred houses; squalid kitchens; Jewish women like aged Negresses, with excessive bosoms;
a Gipsy blacksmith with greasy hair. Speaking in terms
of actional causality, this passage is in no way related
to the actual story. The motivation behind its implantation seems to be of a psychological/characterological
nature: the narrator shifts from one way of escape to
another: his artistic curiosity, ignited by the strange
Galician. He hopes to find a new story, but is returned
to "reality" by Seliverstov who suddenly accuses Ljutov of having caused Trunov's death.[36] Ljutov then tells
what happened, partly to clear himself from feelings of
guilt and possible blame.

In the course of reading the second part of the story,
which focuses on Trunov's behavior, it gradually becomes clear in what way *Don Quixote* as intertextual
frame bears on the main theme. Trunov is a complex
character in the story. Heavily wounded, he displays sadistic cruelty in killing two prisoners without reason.
On the other hand, he frantically defends revolutionary
justice by preventing a cossack from stealing Polish
uniforms,[37] and he dies like a hero in an epic duel with
four enemy aircraft. All his deeds, however, are shaded
by a sense of mental distortion: he murders cold-
bloodedly, almost kills the aforementioned Cossack,
and his "heroic" death in battle is a deliberate, suicidal
act.

The many signs of death in the description of the
strange Galician Don Quixote fall into place. An ironic
connection exists between Trunov and Don Quixote, the
crazed nobleman who attempts to perform chivalrous
deeds in the face of reality. Trunov, however, unlike the
Cervantes' character, does not win the reader's sympathy. His defence of justice and his heroic death are in
opposition to the brutality of the murders he committed.
He is in a state of desperation, aware of the fact that the
campaign (and possibly the entire Revolution) is on the
brink of complete failure. After the killing of the second prisoner he adresses the narrator (the other protagonist of the story), and orders him to remove the prisoner
from the list. The narrator refuses and adds that Trunov
will have to answer for his deeds.

The allusion to Cervantes' *Don Quixote* activated by
the contrastive description of a Galician peasant, deepens the story's ambiguity. More specifically, it ironically modifies Trunov's contradictory character, his
"epic" heroism, and the narrator's ethical principles
which he holds on to against all odds.

2.6.

"Squadron Commander Trunov" is a pivotal story in
the cycle. It contains clear signs of impending military
defeat. The heavily wounded, demoralized Trunov who
almost single-handedly fights four modern enemy aircraft, symbolically represents the military inferiority of
the Konarmija. This is already indicated at the beginning of the story: Trunov is saluted by "our decrepit old
little canon", "our old little three-incher champed forth
a second time". In his plans for **Red Cavalry** Babel
made the following remarks:

> The Konarmija is retreating. In the face of whom? In
> the face of twenty aeroplanes. (. . .) First meeting with
> Western technology.[38]

The story **"Zamost'e"** recounts the final debacle.
Nearby the town Zamość the Konarmija was trapped
and defeated by the Polish armies. This historical event
is narrated in a very incoherent manner, namely from
the focal point of a totally exhausted, demoralized Ljutov. The story is a shocking montage of disparate
scenes, which are presented in a detached tone, interspersed by striking metaphoric descriptions providing a
sudden insight into the narrator's anxious state of mind.

At some points the imagery of **"Zamost'e"** is reminiscent of contemporary modernist poetry such as Russian
Imaginism, e.g.: "(. . .) and trees like naked corpses set
upright on their feet swayed at the crossroads"; and:
"The sky was cleft by the black crossbar of my horse's
back". Concreteness of both comparé and comparant is
a typical feature of Babel's metaphorical constructions.
It recurs in a great number of his stories. His figures of
analogy are frequently built on a sharp collision between concrete perceptions selected from semantic
fields which are far apart in reality. As a result of their
startling effects upon the reader, Babel's metaphors often stand out as separate units which attract the reader's
full attention. The tendency of the image to function as
an end in itself, combined with its opposing concrete
versus concrete, connects the author with a group of
Russian poets, belonging to the aforementioned movement in literature (Šeršenevič; Mariengof). It was the
creed of these poets that the image is the sole poetic
means to replace logical speech. It should startle, stun,
in order to "rouse the reader from his habitual lethargy
and set his mind working".[39]

There are Imaginistic metaphors in other stories of the cycle. We may think again of "the sun rolling down the sky like a chopped-off head" (**"The Crossing of the Zbruč"**) or of "Night flew toward me on mettlesome horses" (**"Ivans"**). Like the Imaginists Babel often selects his images from everyday life, from the trivial and the gross.[40] The story **"Evening"** (**"Večer"**) provides us with fine examples of this type, for example, when the sun is compared to a lantern and the moon to a splinter:

> Na nebe gasnet kosoglazyj fonar' provincial'nogo solnca. (. . .) I oni zakryli dver' kuchni, ostaviv Galina naedine s lunoj, torčavšej tam, vverchu, kak derzkaja zanosa.

> The squinting lantern of the provincial sun goes out in the sky. (. . .) They had closed the kitchen door, leaving Galin alone with the moon stuck up high like a pert splinter.

T. S. Eliot's *The Lovesong of J. Alfred Prufrock* can be detected in the following constructions: "The raw dawn flowed over us like waves of chloroform. (. . .) Morning oozed over us like chloroform over a hospital table". It is very likely that Babel read *Prufrock* (published in 1917) and used the beginning of Eliot's poem for his story: "When the evening is spread out against the sky / like a patient etherized upon a table". However, there is another interesting literary allusion that I want to discuss extensively. At the very beginning of **"Zamost'e"**, the narrator lies down in a waterlogged hole, ties his horse to his foot and falls asleep. He has a dream which reveals his subconscious self. This dream is the first large episode in the story, and may be considered an extended inner-story. As has already been mentioned in relation to the digression inserted into it[41], it is composed of three sections: 1) a pleasantly erotic experience; 2) a sudden outcry, as a digressive deviation within the inner story; 3) a nightmarish experience of death. The montage of the dream-story first of all creates an effect of contrast. The preceding motifs of pervading wetness, darkness and exhaustion are replaced by a sense of dryness, abundance and tranquility, which is evoked by an almost hyperbolic description of a hay barn on an evening in July, a Chagall-like image of sheaves of wheat flying about in the sky. In his dream the narrator is visited by a woman dressed as if for a ball, in black lace. This scene has an erotic impact, it presents an experience of intimate, physical contact:

> Ona vynula grud' iz černych kružev korsaža i ponesla ee mne s ostorožnost'ju, kak kormilica pišču. Ona priložila svoju grud' k moej. Tmoitel'naja teplota potrjasla osnovu moej duši, i kapli pota, živogo, dvižuš-čegosja pota zakipeli meždu našimi soskami.

> She freed her breast from the black lace of her bodice and raised it to me, carefully, like a wet-nurse. She laid her breast against mine. An aching warmth stirred in the depth of my soul, and drops of sweat—live, stirring sweat—seethed between our nipples.

At this point—after the digressional outcry addressed to the woman, named Margot—a sudden transition takes place in the narrator's mind, whereafter the dream becomes a nightmare as it makes the dreamer undergo his own death. The dreaming "I" cannot escape his fate. The woman who first brought life (food, love) then behaves as if he were a corpse: she falls on her knees and performs a kind of post-mortem ritual which is opposed to the previous wet-nurse ritual. Important for the multilayered function of the dream, seen in relation to the encompassing narrative frame, is the fact that it forms a complex knot of intra- and intertextual references. The intratextual relations are based on a series of contrasts in the dream as well as in the story as a whole. The contrasts are: heat versus cold, and physical and emotional fullness of life versus physical impotence, suffocation, death. As far as the intertextual allusions are concerned: a concrete allusion is marked by the name Margo. This name relates the dream (and indeed the entire story) to the historical novel *La Reine Margot* by Alexandre Dumas (père). In fact, the lyrical digression in the dream might even be a deliberate distortion of a specific scene in Dumas' novel: during Saint Bartholomew's night, a haunted and wounded Hugenot nobleman (la Mole) seeks refuge in the bedroom of queen Marguerite de Valois, the novel's heroine. She embodies an ideal of virtue and beauty; she hides the Hugenot from his persecutors, and proposes to nurse his wounds. In his utter noble-mindedness la Mole is unable to accept this:

> Oh! s'écria la Mole, j'aime mieux mourir que de vous voir, vous, la reine, souiller vos mains d'un sang indigne comme le mien . . . Oh! jamais! jamais!.

The situation of the narrator and, by implication, of the Konarmija with him is thus compared to the fate of la Mole and the Hugenots during Saint Bartholomew's night. The allusion is partly a tacit evaluation of the military situation: the Konarmija is lured into a trap and awaits a large scale massacre. The same goes for the massacre of the Jews in Zamość, which is subsequently sketched by the narrator.

The allusion to *La Reine Margot* enhances the expectation of imminent catastrophe, perhaps of death. However, it involves more than a situational comparison. Van der Eng relates the dream utterance to the courtly love tradition. Indeed, the narrator's behaviour fits the romantic image of the nobleman "willing to undergo the severest ordeals just to be able to see his lady".[42] Within the context of **"Zamost'e"**, one may stretch the interpretation of the allusion even further by activating a second pretext to which Margot refers: Gor'kij's autobiographical novel *V Ljudjach*.[43] In this novel, a fairly plain woman enters the base social environment of the adolescent Aleksej, the hero of the novel. In his phantasy he transforms her into an ideal of virtue and beauty:

She represents for him a dream of regal beauty in the middle of a way of life compounded of his relatives' baseness of soul and the near animal behaviour of the soldiers and washerwomen who work nearby.[44]

He secretly names her "Koroleva Margo" (Queen Margot) after Dumas' heroine and tries to protect her ideal image, fights the 'slanderous' remarks people make about her in a manner which suits a courtly nobleman. One day, however, Aleksej's illusions break into pieces as he finds his Margo in the arms of her lover, a rude soldier: "Ja čuvstvoval sebe poterjavši čto-to i prožil neskol'ko dnej v glubokoj pečali."

Seen within the frame of *La Reine Margot* and *V Ljudjach*, Babel's Margot at first seems to signify faith and hope regarding the aspirations of life. But then the dream allegorically shows how the Zamość-encirclement ruins these aspirations. The "utopian" scene in the hay barn is interrupted by "the earth's calamities", a greater force which renders aspirations illusionary, and brings death. In **"Zamost'e"** the narrator meets with defeat on a military and moral scale. The latter shows itself, throughout the story, in recurrent moments of mental obtusion, estrangement, and the loss of moral control. The narrator pesters a peasant woman for food, for the first time without any sign of remorse.

In sum, the dream is primarily a contrasting unit in the story. It presents a world, abounding in love, safety, food and warmth. This is spatially indicated by the enclosed space of the hay-barn in opposition to the dangerous open space of the field of battle. The intertextual references confined in the dream, and signaled by phraseological and diegetic markers, deepen the contrastive effects of the passage (suggesting love, happiness, beauty) on the one hand. On the other hand, they stress the horror of the situation (St. Bartholomew's night), and involve elements of mental and moral frustration.

3. RELIGIOUS PRE-TEXTS

3.1.

An important pre-text to which the **Red Cavalry** stories regularly refer is the New Testament. As we know from his autobiography, Babel studied the Bible during childhood. This was a result of the ambitions of his father, who wanted his son Isaak to be familiar with the Jewish cultural heritage: "At the insistence of my father, I studied Hebrew, the Bible and the Talmud until I was sixteen", he writes in his short autobiography. The **Red Cavalry** stories allude to the New Testament through a montage of biblical associations: biblical motifs, themes, phraseological idiosyncrasies. The subject has been extensively dealt with by Zsuzsa Hetényi (1981). According to Hetényi, the frequent recurrence of biblical motifs in **Red Cavalry** reflects the author's vision (edinyj vzgljad avtora) not only on the level of poetic language, but also on the scenic level through the presence of churches, popes, frescos, and even on the ideational level of the cycle (v idejnom soderžanii).

Characters' names are sometimes striking by their association with the Old and the New Testament, notwithstanding the abhorrent way of life of those who go by that name. Take for instance the protagonist of the story **"The Life of Pavličenko, Matvej Rodionyč"**, general Pavličenko, whose first name is Matvej, like one of the apostles (before the revolution he was a shepherd). Or the surname of the deacon in the story **"Ivans"**. Patricia Carden paid attention to the fact that "the deacon's name Aggeev comes from the name of the minor prophet of Judea, author of a brief book in the *Bible,* "Haggai" (Russian: Aggej). Moreover, she called to our attention that "Akinfiev's name also has hidden in it a surprising religious association: it hints that his family has belonged to the sect, a branch of Molokans, founded by the Samara merchant Akinfij. Thus, both men's surnames tie them to Russia's religious past".[45]

We refer to our chapter on inner stories for the biblical allusions in the stories **"Pan Apolek"** and **"The Road to Brody"**: Apolek's tale of Christ and Deborah, Afon'ka Bida's parable about a bee and Christ upon the cross, and the ballad he sings about a Cossack who rides to heaven on the day of the beheading (of John the Baptist). Afon'ka Bida, a key character in several stories, is frequently set off against a background of biblical associations. In the story **"Afon'ka Bida"** his head, resting upon the saddle of his dying horse, is compared to a crucifix (golova-kak raspjataja). There is a considerable tension between these biblical allusions and Bida's violent behaviour: in **"The Death of Dolgušov"** (**"Smert' Dolgušova"**) he kills the dying Dolgušov as an act of mercy; his scornful reproof of Ljutov for being unable to do the same almost ends in murdering him. In **"Afon'ka Bida"** we learn of his cruelty from rumors about his violent search for a new horse; in **"In St. Valentine's Church"** (**"U Svjatogo Valenta"**) he partakes in an outrage against a Catholic church in the village Berestecko, a flagrant desecration of Christian relics.

Babel uses biblical allusions to promote the shocking representation of quite a few characters. Without doubt, the Cossack Saska the Christ is the most telling example. His personal history is built on biblical motifs: it is easy to see that "the Christ" is more than just a nickname. His stepfather is a carpenter, like Joseph, he wants to become a shepherd, because "all the saints used to be shepherds". To attain this goal, he no longer defends his mother, but leaves her to the mercy of his syphilitic father.

The projection of numerous Cossack characters on biblical and generally religious motifs relates to the fact that Christianity is the Cossacks' religion. Christianity is an important facet of their socio-psychological universe. This is strikingly evident in words used by D'jakov (**"The Remount Officer"**), confronting the peasants' protest against the confiscation of their horses: "The Father Superior's blessing upon all honest scoundrels" (Čestnym stervam igumen'e blagosloven'e). More striking perhaps is that Babel places several Jewish characters in a Christian perspective as well. Take for instance, Gedali; Hetényi asserts that Gedali in some respects is reminiscent of the apostle Paul:

> Babel presents Gedali as a chosen man: from the very beginning his behavior shows apostolic signs. "He, . . . listens, head bent, to invisible voices wafting down to him". The invisible voice pertains either to God, when heard by Christ and the three apostles (Math. 17:5; Marc. 9:7; Luc. 9:35), or to Jesus, as for instance in the vision which the apostle Paul has on the way to Damascus.
>
> (Acts. 9:5)[46]

In **"The Rebbe"**, Jews, gathered in prayer, are compared to fishermen and apostles. Il'ja the rebbe's son combines Spinoza's powerful brow with the wan face of a nun. The implantation of biblical correspondences in the construction of various characters systematically centers upon effects of contrast. The biblical perspective in which Babel places many of his characters is brought in antithetic opposition to aspects of their behaviour and mental condition. Saška the Christ is a syphilitic who betrays his mother; Afon'ka Bida and Pavličenko are extremely violent characters; Pan Apolek is a heretic. Each of these characters violate the religious values suggested by the biblical frame of reference. Falen asserts that

> by representing incongruous characters as figures of a religious import, Babel' is attempting both to humanize the conception of divinity and at the same time to associate the hopes of the Revolution with religious promises.[47]

This corresponds with Hetényi's interpretation of the biblical allusions with respect to the cossack figures. Since many of these allusions associate characters with apostolic features, we may be led to see the cossacks as a kind of new-fangled apostles, i.e. as bearers of a new myth:

> This method of creating a new myth bears witness of the fact that the author considered the events which took place in the Soviet Union during the nineteen-twenties of great importance for the world.[48]

This conclusion, however, is somewhat incomplete. In my opinion the creation of a new myth is not so much the expression of the author's view. It should rather be seen as a reflection of a general tendency, promoted by state propaganda, to regard the Revolution as an event of mythical proportions. One is more inclined to inter-

pret the contrasting montage of biblical motifs as a touch of irony regarding this tendency. Babel seems to present his "new-fangled apostles" more as debauchers of the old world than as bearers of Utopia.

This is not the case with fanciful and pensive characters, such as Pan Apolek, who do not belong to the stratum of Cossacks. As argued in the chapter about inner stories and digressions, Apolek's heresy, which comes to expression in his biography, in his paintings and blasphemous tale of Christ and Deborah, is an alternative to the traditional teachings of Christianity. Apolek fuses the divine and the earthly into a more humane religion. In this regard he can be compared to the Jewish character Il'ja, who also seems to attempt to reach a synthesis of the Judaistic religious tradition and the ideals of the new order. Il'ja's biblical correspondences partly refer to his heresy, and partly to his ability to combine traditional religious ideologies with the ideology of the new world.[49]

3.2.

The narrator's distancing and aesthetically tuned attitude regarding traditional Christianity, in particular Catholicism, is repeated in his views on traditional Judaism (Hasidism and Jewish Orthodoxy). In the world of **Red Cavalry,** Galicia and Volhynia, Catholicism and Judaism were the main pillars of society. They supported a social configuration consisting of a Catholic community and a Jewish community. Moreover, Christianity and Judaism, more generally, represent the dominant religions in western civilization. These ancient religions largely determined ethical, humanitarian values in the old, pre-World War I societies.

As said in chapter two of our study, the narrator's viewpoint vis á vis the traditional religions is expressed mostly through montage of lyrical digressions. As far as Judaism is concerned attention should be paid again to the stories: **"Gedali"**; **"The Rebbe"**; **"The Rebbe's Son"**. Discussing the digressive deviations, it has already been said that in these stories there are direct references to a considerable number of Judaic religiously philosophical scriptures: twice in **"Gedali"** such references are made through the names of important Jewish philosophers, commentators of the Torah, the Cabala, and the Talmud: Ibn-Ezra (1089-1167); Rashi (1040-1105); Maimonides (1135-1204); in **"The Rebbe"**, Il'ja, the Rebbe's son, is compared to Spinoza, the excommunicated Judaic philosopher; in **"The Rebbe's Son"**, Il'ja carries with him a portrait of Maimonides, and ancient Jewish poems, scribbled on the edges of communist leaflets.[50]

Other, more hidden allusions to Judaic texts are, what Maurice Friedberg calls echoes of the life and works of Rebbe Nahman, the founder of Hasidism. Nahman was a creative writer who expressed his philosophies in short parables, loaded with symbols. Nahman's creed reminds us of the views of Pan Apolek. Nahman, too, was in his time regarded as a heretic by the orthodox Jewry. He did not care about "saints and miracle Rebbes but of princes and shepherds, of anonymous beggars and horsemen, of sages and messengers—and not even Jewish ones at that".[51] Babel alludes to the pre-text of Rebbe Nahman primarily through his choice of names: Gedali is "a name much favored among the Rebbe's followers"[52]; the last name of Rebbe Motalè is Braclavskij. This too is unmistakably an allusion to Rebbe Nahman whose full name was Rebbe Nahman ben Simhah of Braclav.

Rebbe Motale's Hasidic creed reaches its culmination in a conversation with the narrator. As Van der Eng pointed out, a most essential aspect consists in "Widerstand gegen die destruktiven Kräfte der Verzweiflung und (.) Beteiligung am Glücksempfinden, an der Freude Gottes, ungeachtet der Schläge des Schicksals".[53] In this respect Van der Eng quotes the Rebbe's words in reaction to the narrator's information of his putting into verse the adventures of Hersch of Ostropol:

> —Velikij trud,—prošeptal rabbi, i somknul veki,—šakal stonet, kogda on goloden, u každogo glupca chvataet gluposti dlja unynija, i tol'ko mudrec razdiraet smechom zavesy bytija . . .

> —A great task,—murmured the Rebbe, and closed his eyelids,—the jackal whines when he is hungry, every fool has folly enough for despondency, and only the wise man can tear the veil of being with laughter.

The element of "attraction", of a shocking montage effect, of course, resides in the juxtaposition with observations about the ragamuffins seated at the table, the blasphemous aspects etc., as already pointed out in our discussion of digressions.

In **"Squadron Commander Trunov"** (**"Èskadronnyj Trunov"**) the narrator depicts a heated dispute among orthodox and Hasidic Jews about the mystical teachings of the Cabala. The quarrelling Jews mention the Gaon of Wilna, Ilija ben Shlomo (1720-1797), a famous talmudist and persecutor of the Hasidim:

> Evrei sporili o Kabbale i pominali v svoich sporach imja Ilii, vilenskogo gaona, gonitelja chasidov . . .

> —Ilija!—kričali oni, izvivajas', i razevali zarošie rty.

> The Jews were arguing about the Cabala, making mention in their discussions of the name Ilija, Gaon of Vilna and scourge of the Hasidim . . .

> —Ilija!—they screamed, winding and opening wide their hairy jaws.

Il'ja (Ilija, or Elijah), the name of the Gaon and the Rebbe's son, is meant to initiate a referential process in the reader:

The younger Braclavskij's name, Il'ja, a Russian version of the Hebrew Elija or Elijahu, has three major associations. In the Biblical tradition (Kings I and II), Elijah appears as an intransigent prophet, ruthless and fearless in his defence of the faith from unbelievers. In the oral tradition of the Aggadah, Elijah's appearance heralds the advent of the Messiah; it is also in this role that Elijah appears at the Passover ceremony. Finally, in Jewish folklore Elijah is "portrayed as the heavenly emissary sent on earth to combat social injustice. He rewards the poor who are hospitable and punishes the greedy rich".[54]

Babel's choice of names usually has semiotic overtones: the triple intertextual allusion, noted by Friedberg, furthers the emblematic quality of the character. Moreover, it shows the narrator's and perhaps the author's attitude towards Il'ja's world-view. I repeat that Babel intended Il'ja and Pan Apolek as key-figures on the ideational level of ***Red Cavalry.*** Their heresy connects traditional religious philosophies, set in a critical perspective, with a humane standpoint of a socialist type (in Apolek's case this remains implicit). Il'ja and Pan Apolek are placed in antithetic opposition with the primitive Cossacks, but also with the backward Hasidic community as described in **"Berestečko"**. A dissonant note is struck by the student of Rashi's commentaries and the books of Maimonides: Gedali. His comment on the Revolution in terms of good and evil seems to be based on irrefutable logic. A further complication, however, is created by the narrator's unfavorable qualifications of Gedali (ridiculous) and his reasoning (an impossible International).

4. TEXTS OF THE REVOLUTION

The verbal context of the revolutionary rhetoric, signaled by typical forms of phrasing, is another segment of the intertextual field of reference on which ***Konarmija*** is built. Numerous examples of revolutionary rhetoric are dispersed over many stories. In all cases the marking signal, of course, consists of phraseological material. "Words, phrases and syntax typical of the revolutionary period are frequently used in a slightly unsuitable context or in a deformed manner".[55] At various points the text refers to the specific manner in which the official standpoint of the Communist Party was voiced. After the successful Polish invasion of the Ukraine in April 1920, the Communist Party's Central Committee sent out a call for the defence of Russia, a sudden appeal to nationalism

> addressed, not just to the working class to defend the Soviet Republic, but to 'all workers, peasants, and honorable citizens of Rossiya', that vast, vague, mystical empire which the Revolution was supposed to have destroyed. It succeeded in appealing both to the old-fashioned patriots and to the new-fangled revolutionaries. Its language was heavy with talk of ancient rivalries and foreign invasions, with allusions to 1610 and 1812 and 1914.[56]

This curious mixture of Russian nationalism and Soviet internationalism, as Davies calls it, resounds in the phrasing of passages alluding to the epic. The heroic-epic vision in **Red Cavalry,** discussed above, is partly on a par with a revolutionary-propagandistic perspective. "The Igor Tale" is essentially a patriotic work, an appeal to Russia's feudal Princes to join forces.[57] Nationalism pervades the text and finds expression chiefly in the narrator's digressions in which he stresses the threat to Russia, the bravery of the Princes, and the importance of unity. Babel's use of specific hyperbolic epithets, by which he refers to Lenin's speeches, are worth noticing in this respect. "In the revolutionary period much use was made of words which indicated that the Revolution was bringing an enormous change, on an unprecedented world-wide scale".[58] Williams draws attention to epithets such as 'neslychanoe', 'nevidannoe', 'neuv''jadaemoe', 'nebyvaloe', 'nezabyvaemoe', 'neskazannoe', which serve as a kind of recurrent leitmotif, and fuse the epic perspective and the perspective of Communism, with Russian nationalism as a common denominator.

The idiosyncracies of revolutionary rhetoric appear within the speech of characters and sometimes of the narrator. An illustrating example is the character Balmašev, the narrator of the inner stories **"Salt"** (**"Sol'"**) and **"Treason"** (**"Izmena"**). For instance, the statement he makes in **"Salt"** concerning the dubious killing of a peasant woman, already quoted in the previous chapter of our study.

In **"The Life of Pavličenko, Matvej Rodionyč"**, general Pavličenko reads aloud a fake letter from Lenin. He composed the letter himself, imitating official jargon;:

> —Imenem naroda,—čitaju,—i dlja osnovanija buduščej svetloj žizni prikazyvaju Pavličenke, Matveju Rodionyču, lišat' raznych ljudej žizni soglasno ego usmotrenija . . .

> —In the name of the people,—I read,—and for the foundation of a nobler life in the future, I order Pavlicenko, Matvej Rodionyc, to deprive certain persons of life, according to his discretion . . .

"Evening" seems to have revolutionary rhetoric as a central theme. It is a kind of ironic comment on the hollowness of the rhetoric. As shown in our chapter on digressions, the narrator, tired of his life in Konarmija, digests, as it were, the class-struggle in his confused poetic mind. He is reproached by Galin, the political commentator of *Krasnyj Kavalerist,* who shows Ljutov his responsibilities, firing rhetorical slogans at him. The story opens with a digression on the part of the narrator, which directly refers to Galin's speech. It is an ironic comment on the influence of party rhetoric on language: the "brush of iron" from Galin's statement is

comparable to the headlong rails in the first sentences of the narrator's digression quoted on p. 77: ("O regulations of the RCP! You have laid down headlong rails through the sour pastry of Russian tales").

The "curve" in Galin's speech points back to a moment in the story **"My First Goose"** (**"Moj pervyj gus'"**). After winning the Cossacks' sympathy, the narrator reads to them Lenin's speech, held on the second congress of the Komintern: "I read on and rejoiced, spying out exultingly the secret curve of Lenin's straight line". Although the word "curve" was officially used to indicate Lenin's clever adjustments of the Marxist theories to the revolutionary practice, we may non the less detect a touch of irony directed against the "straight line" of revolutionary rhetoric (the headlong rails and the iron brush).

The function of the montage of allusions to texts of the Revolution pre-eminently concerns two aims: it inserts the official policy of the Central Committee as a point of view in the polyphony of voices, and, secondly, it communicates the influence of revolutionary ideals wrapped in rhetoric on the speech and mentality of people. An ironic attitude on the part of narrator and author becomes evident in the unsuitable contexts and deformed manners in which rhetorical slogans are used.

5. CONCLUSION

Ending this chapter, we may repeat that **Red Cavalry** draws on a variety of heterogeneous intertextual frames (pre-texts). In most cases the references to pre-texts are activated, as we have seen, by markers, that is, phraseological, diegetic, or/and compositional features selected from a pre-text and implanted in the alluding text, markers which are differentiated from their verbal environment by distinct effects of contrast. The markers sometimes also form part of otherwise deviating passages (e.g. inner stories; digressions; metaphoric constructions). Through these markers thematic properties of the pre-texts are evoked which bring about a semantic modification of the alluding text. These properties of the source primarily affect the meaning of the story under consideration. This particularly applies to more or less overt literary allusions to concrete literary pre-texts (*Romeo and Juliet; Don Quixote,* etc.). Secondarily, however, the literary allusions also affect the meaning of the cycle as a whole. Dispersed over several stories, the allusions form a systematic representation of an artistic point of view. They frequently lead to an ironic evaluation of events, characters and, at times, of the narrator himself by means of activating parallels with characters and events from literary pre-texts (e.g. **"Italian Sunshine"**).

With the exception of the allusion to "The Igor Tale" in **"The Crossing of the Zbruč"**, the significance of the evoked epic properties mostly pertains to long-term strategies, embracing the whole of the cycle. Allusions to the epic draw events and characters into an heroic, mythological perspective. Effects of irony are usually created through juxtapositions of epic properties with antithetic characterological and action elements (senseless violence; destruction; madness; disillusionment). The same applies to the allusions to religious pre-texts and revolutionary texts: Saška the Christ is parallelled with Christ, but at the same time he is a syphilitic who betrayed his mother; Galin fervently speaks the language of the Revolution, propagating its ideology, while his fervency is apparently linked up with amorous frustration and his words are put in a perspective of hollow rhetoric.

The semantic properties belonging to diverse pre-texts also contract into a chain of corresponding moments dispersed over quite a few stories. Hence the montage functions on two levels of meaning. However, we may establish a third level of meaning where the properties of pre-texts are juxtaposed with each other. The montage of various intertextual frames in the cycle plays in opposition the dominant religious ideologies (Christianity and Judaism) with communism—the "new" ideology, and with an unbound artistic view of the world. These ideational levels in **Red Cavalry** are brought to the fore with increasing acuity. The juxtaposition of opposed cognitive models is above all materialized, i.e. expressed in the words of such characters as Pan Apolek, Il'ja, and Ljutov, the primary narrator. Babel made **Red Cavalry** a battlefield of conflicting worldviews: Judaism, Catholicism (Christianity), Communism, Russian and Polish nationalism, Cossack primitivism and military professionalism are involved in a meaningful dialogue. In addition to inner stories and digressions, the montage of allusions to various intertextual fields (artistic, religious, ideological pre-texts) is essential to the ideational strategy behind the work which presents the world of the Revolution as a crossroad of ideologies, a turmoil of clashing philosophies of life.

Notes

1. Kristeva 1969: 145.

2. Ibid: 255.

3. Ibid 1974: 60.

4. Jenny 1976: 262.

5. Ibid.

6. Cf. Schmid 1983.

7. Bachtin 1972: 152.

8. Schmid 1983: 142

9. Cf.: Górski 1962; Johnson 1976; Ben-Porat 1976; Perry 1978.

10. Perry 1978: 295.

11. Falen 1974: 121.

12. Terras 1966: 142.

13. Ibid.

14. Falen 1974: 191.

15. Cf. also Murphy 1966: 369-370.

16. Nilsson 1977: 67.

17. Cf. Falen 1974: 119.

18. Cf. Van Baak 1979: 44; 1983: 182.

19. Cf. van Baak 1983: 182.

20. Falen 1974: 123.

21. See our analysis of this story in Chapter Five.

22. Cf. Klein 1976.

23. Some examples are presented in: Van Baak 1983: 182-183.

24. See Chapter Two, section two.

25. Terras 1966: 145.

26. Carden 1972: 90.

27. Cf. Schmid 1983: 149.

28. Carden 1972: 90.

29. Falen 1974: 166.

30. Cf. Hume 1969: 283.

31. Hume 1969: 288.

32. Ibid: 287.

33. Gibbons 1980: 60.

34. Cf. Stepanov 1927: 32.

35. See the remarks on the montage of an inner story in "Italian Sunshine" (Chapter Two, section two).

36. Van der Eng speaks in respect of this passage of "intriguing allusions to what might become an inner tale" (1987a: 129).

37. Cf.: Darjalova: 118.

38. Cf. Williams 1984: 293.

39. Nilsson 1970: 40.

40. Ibid: 52.

41. See: Chapter Two, section three.

42. Cf. Van der Eng 1985: 423.

43. Ibid: 424.

44. Borras 1967: 140.

45. Carden 1984: 302.

46. Cf. Hetényj 1981: 235.

47. Falen 1974: 180.

48. Hetényi 1981: 240.

49. Cf. Chapter Two, 92-93.

50. Cf. Chapter Two: 85 ff.

51. Friedberg 1978: 195.

52. Ibid: 194.

53. Cf. Van der Eng 1987b: 338.

54. Friedberg 1978: 197.

55. Williams 1984: 280.

56. Davies 1972: 115.

57. Cf. Klein 1972: 133.

58. Williams 1984: 282.

References

BAAK, J. J. VAN

1979. "The Function of Nature and Space in *Konarmija* by I. E. Babel'", in: Dutch Contributions to the Eighth International Congress of Slavists (Lisse).

1983. The Place of Space in Narration (Amsterdam).

BACHTIN, MICHAIL

1973. *Problems of Dostoevsy's Poetics* (Ann Arbor).

BEN-PORAT, ZIVA

1976. "The Poetics of Literary Allusion", in: *PTL, A Journal for Descriptive Poetics and Theory of Literature,* vol.I/3, 105-128.

BORRAS, F. M.

1967. *Maxim Gorky. The Writer. An Interpretation* (London).

CARDEN, PATRICIA

1972. *The Art of Isaac Babel* (Ithaca/London).

1984. "Babel's *Two Ivans*", in: *Russian Literature,* XV-3, 299-303.

DARJALOVA, L. N.

1968. "Problema istorizma povesti I. Babelja'Konarmija'", in: *Učennye zapiski Kaliningradskogo gosudarstvennogo universiteta,* vyp. 1, 109-122.

DAVIES, NORMAN

1972a. *White Eagle, Red star. The Polish-Soviet War, 1919-1920* (London).

1972b. "Isaac Babel's *Konarmija* Stories, and the Polish-Soviet War", in: *The Modern Language Review,* vol.67, 845-857.

ENG, J. VAN DER

1984a. "The Pointed Conclusion as Story Finale and Cyclic Element in *Red Cavalry*", in: *Language and Literary Theory* (Ann Arbor), 585-594.

1984b. "Äesthetische Dominante und Fiktionalisie—rung. Fiktionalisierung, Wahrheitsanspruch und Intensifierung der Information. Author und Leser".—In: *Text. Symbol. Weltmodell.* (München), 111-130.

1984c. "Babel''s Short Story *Zamost'e*", in: *Signs of Friendship: To Honour A. G. F. van Holk* (Amsterdam), 419-430.

1987a. "Types of Inner Tales in *Red Cavalry*", in: *Text and Context* (Stockholm), 128-138.

1987b. "Komplizierung der Thematik durch dem Mythos. Babel's *Konarmija*", in: *Mythos in der Slawischen Moderne.* Wiener Slawistischer Almanach, Sonderband 20, 327-349.

FALEN, JAMES

1974. Isaak Babel—Russian Master of the Short Story (Knoxville).

FRIEDBERG, MAURICE

1978. "Yiddish Folklore Motifs in Isaak Babel''s *Konarmija*".—In: *American Contributions to the Eighth International Congress of Slavists, Zagreb and Ljubljana,* 2, 192-203 (Columbus, Ohio).

GIBBONS, BRIAN

1980. *Romeo and Juliet* (Introduction), 1-77 (London).

GÓRSKIJ, KONRAD

1964. "Aluzja literacka. Istota zjawiska i jego typologia".—In: *Z historii i teorii literatury.* Seria druga, 7-32 (Warszawa).

HETÉNYI, ZSUZSA

1981. "Biblejskie motive v *Konarmija* Babelja", in: *Studia Slavica Hung.* XXVII, 229-240.

HUME, ROBERT D.

1967. "Gothic versus Romantic: A Revaluation of the Gothic Novel", in: *PMLA,* vol. 84, 282-290.

JENNY, LAURENT

1976. "La Stratégie de la Forme", in: *Poétique. Revue de théorie et d'analyse littéraires,* 27, 257-282.

JOHNSON, ANTHON L.

1976. "Allusion in Poetry", in: *PTL,* vol. 1, 579-587.

KLEIN, JOACHIM

1972. *Zur Struktur des Igorlieds* (München).

1976. "Donec i Stiks", in: *Kul'turnoe Nasledie Drevnej Rusi,* 64-69.

KRISTEVA, JULIA

1969. *Semeiotikè, recherches pour une sémanalyse* (Paris).

1974. *La Révolution du langage poétique* (Seuil).

MURPHY, A. B.

1977. "The Style of Isaac Babel'", in: *The Slavonic Review,* vol. 44, 361-380.

NILSSON, N. Å.

1970. *The Russian Imaginists* (Stockholm).

1977. "Isaak Babel's *Perechod čerez Zbruč*", in: *Scandoslavica,* vol. 23, 63-71.

PERRI, CARMELA

1978. "On Alluding", in: *Poetics,* nr. 7, 289-307.

SCHMID, WOLF

1983. "Sinnpotentiale der diegetischen Allusion. Aleksandr Puskins *Posthalternovelle* und ihre Prätexte".—In: *Dialog der Texte.* Wiener Slawistischer Almanach, Sonderband 11, 141-189.

STEPANOV, N.

1927. "Novella Babelja", in: *I. Babel'. Stat'i i materialy* (Leningrad).

TERRAS, VICTOR

1968. "Line and Color: the Structure of Isaak Babel's Short Stories in *Red Cavalry*", in: *Studies in Short Fiction,* 3, 141-156.

WILLIAMS, GARETH

1984. "The Rhetoric of Revolution in Babel's *Konarmija*", in: *Russian Literature,* XV-3, 279-298.

Zsuzsa Hetényi (essay date March-June 1994)

SOURCE: Hetényi, Zsuzsa. "The Visible Idea: Babel's Modelling Imagery." *Canadian Slavonic Papers* 36, nos. 1-2 (March-June 1994): 55-67.

[*In the following essay, Hetényi traces specific images throughout Babel's work and infers from their use various abstract elements of his ideological outlook.*]

An experienced reader looking at the world tends to perceive his or her ideas as reified and to perceive reality through those ideas. The problem is not that of narration, that is, describing the world from different points of view, but of the notion of "model" in literary studies. Model can be understood as a copy of reality (Plato) or as a system of signs (codes) constructed of the elements of reality, which results in an independent autonomous world ("an analog of the cognised object"). The latter is the basis of Lotman's remarkably powerful semiotic theory of literature, one that should be familiar to anyone involved in textual analysis in the last twenty years.[1]

Let us take one of his axioms as a starting point:

> . . . the artistic model reconstitutes the "parole" of the object. However, in relation to that reality of which we are conscious in the already assimilated artistic model, that model operates as the "langue" which discretely organizes new representations ("paroles").

From this one can arrive at an interpretation of the term "model" that differs, however, from Lotman's. In this view, the writer chooses a number of discrete elements of reality to create his or her new artistic unity. However, this unity will not correspond to external reality, in the same way that a very detailed description is unable to reproduce a visual experience due to the discrete nature of language.

This makes possible another approach to the text, and especially to its imagery. Imagery consists not only of metaphors (usually not longer than a phrase or a sentence), but of longer descriptions as well. There is a balance between intellectual and visual (and sometimes emotional) elements: the image is underlain by an idea. Thus it is through imagery that the idea is transmitted. Babel seems very easily accessible through his imagery, because—as will be demonstrated in reference to his descriptive technique—he deliberately picks those details of the world that are important for constructing an intellectual structure. He views the world from a viewpoint that allows him both to see and to enable the reader to see the organizing principle behind the order, the essential in the incidental. It is a combination of consciousness and intuition; the clue to this structure lies in the writer's philosophy whereby he constructs ideas out of the details derived from visible experience.[2]

An idea, as I understand it, is an intellectual, abstract, and often metaphorical product of the thought process. It is present in images (topoi, metaphorical descriptions) only because of the writer's specific, selective perception or preconceptual attitude. By collating Babel's diary with the stories of his **Red Cavalry** (Конармия) one can discover some important connections that illustrate the way in which Babel creates the image.

In the enchanting description of Gedali's shop, for example, the reader is presented with a long list of objects, yet in the passage in Babel's diary that refers to the real-world version of the shop he considered only two things worth mentioning: "A little philosopher Jew.

An unimaginable shop—Dickens, brooms and golden slippers." / Маленький еврей философ. Невообразимая лавка—Диккенс, метлы л золотые туфли.[3]

Of course, it is possible that the things mentioned in the short story remained only in Babel's memory or that they represent a condensed picture of all the curiosity shops ever seen by Babel. In all probability these things are put together as a result of the preconceptual attitude mentioned above. There is surprising evidence in support of this proposition in the story **"The Rebbe's Son"** (Сын рабби), where Gedali is suddenly shown with "the chicken feathers of his top hat." The cylinder (top hat) and the feathers were mentioned in **"Gedali"** but separately, not even related to each other in the text. However, at the end of *Red Cavalry* one finds this unusual portrait, created by imaginative contamination. A similar discrepancy can be seen in the description of the evening with the rebbe (in **"Rebbe"** [Рабби] and **"The Rebbe's Son"**). Such deliberate discrepancies allow a reader to perceive and analyze these descriptions as consciously constructed images.

The things in Gedali's shop can be divided into two groups representing the two conceptual spheres of mortality and childhood, both of which are mentioned in the first paragraph of the story: "On these evenings my child's heart rocked like a little ship on enchanted waves . . ." / Детское сердце раскачивалось в эти вечера, как кораблик на эаколдованных волнах . . . (II, 29):

4th Paragraph	6th paragraph
antiquities shop лавка древности	buttons пуговицы
gilded slippers эолоченные туфли	dead butterfly мертвая бабочка
ship's cables корабельные канаты	globe глобус
ancient compass старинный компас	skulls черепа
stuffed eagle чучело орла	dead flowers мертвые цветы
1810 Winchester hunting rifle охотничий 'винчестер' из 1810 года	colorful broom made with chicken feathers пестрая метелка из петушиных иерьев
broken pan	dried up flowers

4th Paragraph	6th paragraph
сломанная кастрюля	умершие цветы

These two spheres are connected by two words, standing side by side in the sentence: globe and skull; their mutual globular shapes connote and connect universality and individuality simultaneously. Gedali's outward appearance is delineated according to the same duality: "a little boy who will grow into a professor" / мальчик из которого выгдет профессор (29). His childish features are given in words with diminutive suffixes that are difficult to render in English: "hands" (ручки), "beard" (бороденка), "turret" (башенка), "box" (коробочка) and "water" (водица), among others. On the other hand, his clothing, described as "a floor-length frock coat with three bone buttons" (сюртук до полу с тремя костяными пуговицами), "tinted glasses" (дымчатые очки), and a "black top hat" (черный цилиндр), recalls the appearance of a magician or a sage, living outside time, knowing the secrets of life and death and having all things, but in particular, these beautiful elements of nature—flower, butterfly—transformed for preservation into eternity.[4]

It is worthwhile examining Babel's images in order to discern whether the method of arrangement of the words along certain axes of ideas is significant. Given their nature, the words reflect the ideas as clearly as models do. This feature is a constant element of Babel's approach to the problem of space. In his early, almost journalistic short story, **"The Concert in Katerinenstadt"** (Концерт в Катериненштадте, 1918), the two lexical groups counterbalance the two axes, thus illustrating the fluctuations of history. The old, religious world has been replaced by the new, communist world; the communist club is located opposite the church.[5]

Babel is an author who is extremely sensitive to geometric shapes, to horizontal and vertical dimensions. The abundance of examples illustrating this sensitivity has been analyzed by Joost van Baak in his book, *The Place of Space in Narration*.[6] Quite often the very message of a Babel story is hidden in the spatial figures and relations. In the often quoted passage of the story **"The Church in Novograd"** (Костел в Новограде), it is not the Catholic scenery that is of utmost importance, but the relationship between the Cossacks, appearing at a transcendental height standing under the dome, and the narrator who, at the same time, is deep in the catacombs and, what is more, has lost his way: "I search"; "in fright I hurl myself downwards"; "I see a multitude of lights flickering up high, right under the cupola"; "they lead me out of the cellar"; "skulls . . . no longer frighten me" / "я ищу"—"в испуге я бросаюсь вниз"—"я вижу множество огней, бегущих в высоте, у самого купола"—"они выводят меня из подвала,"—"черепа не пугают меня больше" (9-

10). The Cossacks are glorified in the act of showing the narrator the way out and taking him with them. This is emphasized by the proliferation of comforting first-person-plural pronouns in the next paragraph. It reflects the hope of the narrator that the fatal distance between the Cossacks (height) and himself (depth) can be bridged, and that he can join them.

The situation in which the narrator loses his way is usually metaphorical in Babel's writings. In **"The Death of Dolgushov"** (Смерть Долгушова)—"we bounced back and forth between the walls of fire" / мотал`ись между огневых стен (45)—it foreshadows the conflict at the end of the story, when the position of the narrator is that of a stranger—"not one of us" (не наш). The situation in **"Argamak"** is allegorically unambiguous:

> . . . he carried me away from our lines. I got separated from the squadron and, lacking a sense of direction, wandered for days on end in search of my own; I landed behind enemy lines, spent nights in the ravines, linked up with other companies and was chased away by them.
>
> он выносил меня из рядов, я отбивался от эскадрона и, лишенный чувства ориентировки, блуждал потом по суткам в поисках своей части, попадал в расположение неприятеля, ночевал в оврагах, прибивался к чужим полкам и бывал гоним ими.
>
> (131)

Here again we see the ditch, the depth, as the iconic mark of loneliness and banishment.

Depth in *Red Cavalry* is expressed through several images. The opposition of the castle on the hill and the town in the valley in **"Berestechko"** can be interpreted in several ways. Van Baak interprets it as a contrast between "feudal past and revolutionary present."[7] However, in the description of the town, it is words with negative meanings or associations that predominate together with words connected to the concept of depth and lowness: "below" (внизу), "catacombs" (катакомбы)—twice, and "cellar (подвал)."[8] In all probability, the heart of the matter is the situation of the local Jewry whose life was lowered to the level of almost sub-human existence, and this is the oppressive atmosphere the narrator wants to escape. The world represented by the degenerated countess is going to be destroyed, too, as implied by such epithets and images as "faded ink" / вылинявшие чернила, "nymphs with their eyes poked out" / нимфы с выколотыми глазами (71), the hundred-year old letter written in the language of the now bygone culture of the aristocracy, a family without descendants. The revolution stays poised high above the town, ruling over it.[9]

In the majority of the images, death appears as a super-human (high) and yet, at the same time, an underground (low) realm. In **"The Widow"** (Вдова) we read: "The

bodies of the female orderlies were sticking out every which way *under* the carts while the shy sun was beating *above* the soldiers' sheepskins. The sleepers' boots were tossed about *at random,* their pupils were directed *at the heavens,* and the black *caverns* of their mouths were twisted askew" / Тела санитарок торчали под телегами, несмелая заря билась над солдатскими овчинами. Сапоги спящих были брошены ерозб, зрачки заведены к небу, черные ямы ртов перекошены (108). Here we find an image anticipating the scene in the same story when Sashka holds in her arms the dead Shevelev and says to him "My Jesus Christ" / Иисус Христос мой (108). On the other hand, it repeats the three-dimensional structure of the scene of love (see the discussion below), while also illustrating the unity of the human body with nature, and the helplessness of a sleeping man through the analogy of slumber and death.

Pavlichenko the executioner and his landlord pass through three levels on their way to the landlord's murder. This curious combination of anabasis and katabasis reflects in its three-fold structure certain folklore motifs.[10] This is suggested in values implied by the story's vocabulary levels as well: downstairs, "in the cellar" (погреб) and, along with the motif of treachery, there are examples of base profanity—"boors" (хамы), "son of a bitch" (сукин сын, 58)—while the *skaz*-text depiction of the upstairs scene of the murder includes highly elevated words "hall" (зала), "perambulate" (прохаживаться), "Madam Nadezhda Vasil'evna ran off" / Надежда Васильевна побежали, "[she] saluted me with a sabre" / шашкой мне на караул сделали (58).

Babel's images are similar to models not only because they have these valorising characteristics in their spatial formations, but also because the elements of his imagery can be organized according to certain spheres of concepts. There is a clearly marked tendency in Babel's texts toward abstraction. For instance, he may use an abstract idea as the subject of a sentence with an active verb predicate—as in **"Berestechko"**: "The place reeks in anticipation of the new age, and instead of people there are the faded outlines of border misfortunes walking about it" / Местечко смердит в ожидании новой эры, и вместо людей по нему ходят слинявшие схемы пограничных несчастий (70).

Another characteristic feature appears in the regularly recurring details of his descriptions. Throughout *Red Cavalry,* we encounter the details, chosen from the fullness of reality, to create the models; they are the ones selected to be transformed into ideas. The fifth paragraph of the short story **"The Rebbe"** can serve to demonstrate this:

> White churches gleamed in the distance like fields of buckwheat. An artillery wheel around the corner gave out a groan. Two pregnant Ukrainians came out of a

gate, their jewelry jangling, and sat down on a bench. A timid star lit up in the orange battles of the dusk, and peace, the Sabbath peace, settled onto the crooked roofs of the Zhitomir ghetto.

Белые костелы блеснули вдали, как гречишные поля. Орудийное колесо простонало за углом. Две беременные хохлушки вышли из ворот, зазвенели монистами, и сели на скамью. Робкая звезда зажглась в оранжевых боях заката и покой, субботний покой, сел на кривые крыши житомиоского гетто.

(35)

Though it seems to be a passage of minor importance, nevertheless it contains nearly all the strata of questions that **Red Cavalry** is concerned with: Catholicism, nature, war, physiological femininity and its connection with fertility and rebirth, the heavenly bodies, colour symbolism and questions of Jewish tradition and identity.

As has been shown, in most cases the simple arrangement of the lexical units of Babel's images allows us to approach the model of concepts, the model that brings the reader closer to the non-simple problems of **Red Cavalry.** In the short story **"The Sun of Italy"** (Солнце Италии) Sidorov's character is revealed and explained in a flow of metaphors. The narrator leaves the cozy domestic atmosphere, and the sphere of holiness—"a crown of green fir boughs" / венец из зеленых ветвей ели (26)—and on his way to his quarters he passes a fantastic landscape.[11]

The closing metaphor—"hirsute hand" (волосатая лапа)—generates satanic associations, and there are other examples in the story:

• On the table a *hunchbacked* candle was *smoldering*—the ominous *bonfire* of dreamers. / На столе дымцлась горбамая свеча—зловещий космер мечтателей (26—emphasis, *Zs. H.*).

• . . . dreams leapt around me like kittens. / . . . сны прыгали вокруг меня, как комямя (26).

• Sidorov, the pining murderer . . . dragged me into the corridors of his commonsensical insanity. / Сидоров, тоскующий убийца . . . потащил меня в коридоры здравомыслящего своего безумия (26-27 [cf. maze/labyrinth]).

• Our room was dark, gloomy, everything in it breathed with a nocturnal damp stench, and only the window, filled with the light of the moon, shone like deliverance. / Наша комната была темна, мрачна, все дышало в ней ночной сырой вонью, и только окно, заполненное лунным огнем, сияло, кал избавалене (28).

In the context of the familiar Matthew 6:13—". . . save us from the evil one" / избавь нас от лукавого— the hunch-backed Sidorov, with his dark and deathly, mask-like, face above the yellow fire, is seen to resemble the devil.[12]

There is a generalized metaphor of an oak tree in the story **"The Cemetery in Kozin"** (Кладбище в Козине). Split into two by a thunderbolt, the tree stands over a family tomb. The enumeration of the members of the family, destroyed by historical events, recalls a family tree. The green tombstones might refer to the power of nature, which absorbs everything—both the human body and the culture humankind creates.

One episodic character in the novella **"Ivans"** seems to be a very condensed metaphor.

A bearded peasant in copper glasses and a Tyrolian hat was reading a newspaper off to the side. He caught my gaze and said, "We call ourselves folk, yet we befoul the land worse than jackals. It shames the earth . . ." And, turning away, he went back to reading the newspaper through his big glasses.

Бородатый мужчина в медных очках и тирольской шляпке, читавший в сторонке газету, перехватил мой взгляд и сказал:—Человеки зовемся, а гадим хуже шакалов. Земли стыдно . . . И отвернувшись, он снова стал читать газету через большие очки.

(101)

This character is composed of several sharply differing elements: he has glasses and reads a newspaper as does the narrator in **"My First Goose"** (Мой первый гусь); he has a Tyrolian hat like Apolek's friend, Gottfried; he has a beard, the attribute of the Jews in **Red Cavalry,** and, besides all that, he is a peasant ("мужик"), a detail that absolutely does not fit the other parts of the picture. This episodic figure is an outsider, whose abstract outlook on the world is, when seen from the viewpoint of mankind and the cosmos, markedly distanced.

To decipher the seemingly simple description of the garden at the Novograd church, it is necessary to note first of all the geometric principle: the alley is the horizontal line; thunder at the dome is the vertical line; and the dead legs provide the third dimension, i.e., depth. Second, two groups of words referring to death (D) and femininity (F) must be noted. This polarity is closely related to another description of the same garden, with the same organizing centres in a second story, **"Pan Apolek."**

"THE CHURCH IN NOVOGRAD" (9)	"PAN APOLEK" (23)
(F) outside the window in the garden . . . the lane flows over / за окном в саду . . . переливается аллея	(F) the road pours / льется дорога

(D) night stands outside the window . . . the garden grew stiff / за окном стоит ночь, . . . окоченел сад

(D, F) the black passion of the sky / черная страсть неба

(D) night . . . like a black column / ночь, как черная колонна

(F) thirsting roses were fluttering / жаждущие розы колышутся

(F) shining fruits were suspended / светящиеся плоды повисли . . . the scent of lilies / запах лилий

(D) in the darkness . . . lightning blazes in the cupolas / во тьме молнии пылают в куполах

(D) the dark garden / темный сад

(F) the moon's brilliance streams / лунный блеск струится

(F) under the moon in a shining stream the road flows towards the church / блещущим потоком льется под луной дорога к костелу

Below we will see how words belonging to the sphere of fluidity (pours, overflows, streams, stream, etc.), can be connected with somatic fluid and femininity.

The theme of femininity as a sustaining force runs through *Red Cavalry* in the most literal sense (e.g., in the character of the prostitute Sashka) and in the most abstract sense (in the juxtaposition of rebirth and fertility in nature and in death). The latter seems to be reflected in the closing phrase of the paragraph about the garden in Novograd: the lily overcomes the pine, and their relation may allude to the sexual intercourse of Jesus and Deborah in the legend. The permanent presence of images related to the feminine principle is an essential trait of Babel's world view. It is expressed by metaphors and images of fertility, rebirth, the moon, the night and the evening, and fluidity (although there are variations dependent on the context of individual stories).

Near the beginning of the story **"The Widow"** the stars are joined to the character of Levka: "The stars glow in the darkness like wedding rings, they fall onto Levka, get tangled in his hair, and are extinguished in his shaggy head." / Звезды пылают во тьме, как обручальные кольца, они пылают на Левку, путаются в волосах и гаснут в лохматой его голове (106). The wedding rings elicit an erotic overtone pro-

duced by a landscape corresponding to sexual intercourse: "The feather-grass rustled on the anxious earth, and August stars fell onto the grass." / Ковыль шелестел на потревоженной земле, и в траву падали августовские звезды (108).

It is extremely interesting that the consonants of the name Levka are found in reverse order in the word "kovyl" (feather-grass). The construction of the image carries the same three-dimensional—up, down, horizontal—orientation with the moon and stars, the ditch and the prone bodies of the agonizing Shevelev, and Sashka and Levka making love. In the latter parallel, on the one hand, love and death, and on the other, eating and love, denoted by the same verbs, are drawn together.[13] The simile "a moon like a beggar" correlates with an episodic character from the story **"Sashka Khristos"** who is given a coin that shines like the moon. She says as she beds down with Sashka's father: "You'll be a gentle rain to this old bod. And I'll yield way, way more than you sow . . ." / Дождик на старуху, двести пудов с десятины дам . . . (51). The fluidity and the fertility of nature are closely connected in the sexual context of *Red Cavalry*. The erotic images of water (stream, sea, lake, rain) are well-known motifs of myth and folk genres.[14]

The different hypostases of woman, her role as mother-lover-sister are closely connected from the very outset of Babel's literary work.[15] The most obvious realization of this appears in the story **"The Widow"** and the metamorphosis of its heroine from a prostitute into a Madonna. We find an even more complex correlation of metaphors in "Zamost'e." The metaphors of hole and fluids reek like elements of a Freudian dream: "I . . . lay down in a pit full of water. The soggy earth revealed to me the soothing embraces of the grave." / Я . . . лег в яму, полную воды. Размокшая земля открыла мне успокоительные объятия могилы (110). This dream is about death, but it deals with the sustaining power of nature. Following the methodology outlined above and arranging the words into spheres of concepts, we find that images of fertility and the erotic aspects of fluidity are dominant: "hay" (сено), "threshing" (молотьба), "wheat" (пшеница), "the caress of the hay" (ласка сена); "She pressed her breast against mine. An agonizing warmth shook the foundation of my soul, and drops of sweat, vital, moving sweat, began to boil between our nipples. . . . She . . . stuffed my oral cavity with sweet-smelling hay." / Она приложила свою грудь к моей. Томительная теплота потрясла основы моей души и капли пота, живого, движущегося пота, закипели между нашими сосками. . . . Она забила благовонным сеном омверсмце рта. (110-11). These leading motifs are supplemented by two new elements, namely chloroform, the mark of transition between life and death, and milk, the life-giving fluid.

• The damp dawn *leaked* onto us like waves of chloroform. / Сырой рассвет смекал на нас, как волны хлороформа (111—emphasis here and elsewhere in these examples, *Zs. H.*).

• [Volkov] was writing a letter to his fiancée:

> "My dearest Valia," he wrote, "do you remember me?"
>
> I read the first line, then took some matches out of my pocket and *lit* a pile of *straw* on the floor. . . . The old woman lay down on the *fire* and smothered it with her *breast*. / [Волков] писал письмо к невесте. "Многоуважаемая Валя,—писал он,—помните ли Вы меня?" Я прочитал первую строчку, потом вынул спички из кармана и поджег кучу соломы на полу. Старуха легла на огонь грудью и затушила его.

(112)

• She ran into the vestibule and returned with a pitcher of *milk* and some bread. / Она побежала в сени и вернулась с кувшином молока и хлебом (113).

• The morning *dripped* from us as *chloroform* drips onto an operating table. / Утро сочцлось из нас, как хлороформ сочится на госпитальный стол (113).

Moreover, evening and the night appear as feminine phenomena:

• The July day was merging into night, and the *thickets* (*chashchi*) of the sunset were tossing their heads back above the village. / Июльский день переходил в вечер, чащц заката запрокцдывалцсь над селом (110).

The latter we can place among other parallel metaphors from **Red Cavalry** stories in line with Babel's basic outlook on life:

• Evening wrapped me in the *invigorating moisture* of its twilight bedding, evening pressed its *maternal* hands to my glowing forehead. / Вечер завернул меня в жцвцмельную влагу сумеречных своих простынь, вечер приложил мамерцнскце ладони к пылающему моему лбу (34).

• Night soothed us in our sadness, a light breeze embraced us like a *mother's* skirt, and the *grass* below shone with freshness and *moisture*. / Ночь утешала нас в наших печалях, легкий ветер обвевал нас, как юбка мамерц, и мравы внизу блестели свежестью и влагой (78).

• Evening flew up to the sky like a flock of birds, and darkness placed its *wet* crown upon me. / Вечер взлетел к небу, как стая птиц, и тьма надела на меня мокрый свой венец (124).

They are directly interrelated with the picture of spring given in the story **"Sashka Khristos"**: "The earth was lying in the April dampness. Emeralds gleamed in the hollows. A sour smell was coming off the ground, like off a soldier's woman at daybreak. The first herds were trickling down from the burial mounds, and the colts frolicked in the blue expanses of the horizon." / Земля лежала в апрельской сырости. В черных ямах блистали изумруды. И от земли пахло кисло, как от солдатки на рассвете. Первые стада стекали с курганов, жеребята играли в голубых просторах горизонта (51); or with the famous, often quoted words: "We both looked at the world like at a meadow, a meadow on which women and horses move about." / Мы оба смотрели на мир, как на луг, по которому ходят женщины и кони (65).

All the metaphors of fluidity—life, mother, death—are brought to a common denominator in Gedali's determination of the life-giving elemental force of water as a source of life, as a fluid that sustains the rebirth of nature. As Gedali puts it in **"The Rebbe"**: ". . . All is mortal. Eternal life is granted only to the mother. And when the mother is no longer alive, she leaves behind her a memory that thus far no one has yet undertaken to defile. Memory of a mother nurtures in us compassion, just like the ocean, the boundless ocean nurtures the rivers, and that compassion cleaves the universe . . ." / Все смертно. Вечная жцзнь суждена только мамерц. А когда матери нет в живых, она оставляет по себе воспоминание, которое еще никто не решился осквернить. Память о матери пцмаем в нас сострадание, как океан, безмерный океан пцмаем рецу, рассекающие вселенную . . . (35). This approach to the stream makes a very broad interpretation of the first story, **"Crossing the Zbruch"** (Переход через Збруч) possible. J. Falen thinks of it as an act of transformation and initiation.[16] Inevitably, the meaning of the beginning of a new period of life, the transition into a new life, as well as the transition between life and death (Lethe) and rebirth, must be taken into account when examining the element of femininity, since its atmosphere is strengthened by words like "blossom" (цветут), "virginal" (девственная), "yesterday's blood" (вчерашняя кровь), "the torrents surged between hundreds of horses' legs" / потоки сочатся между сотнями лошадиных ног, "Madonna" (богородица), "lunar serpents" (лунные змеи), and "gleaming caves" (сияющие ямы—6). Additionally, considering the two characters in the second part of the story, the dead body and the pregnant woman, there are three dimensions mentioned here yet again: "upper—river—pit" / поверх—река—яма (height—horizontal dimension—depth).

Conclusions

Babel's poetic imagery reflects a consistent outlook on life and nature. The lexical material of his metaphors in most cases is built into logically interpretable structures and therefore permits an intellectual analysis. This idea, realized in Babel's poetic image, is the concretization of the *idea* in the *eidos,* or, in other words, an intellectual construction is realized in sensuous perception and vice versa, according to each individual's approach to the facts of reality or *Weltanschaung,* whereby we interpret the facts through using our own ideas about reality. The tension accompanying this two-way process resembles the tension generated by the interaction between the two components of a metaphor, in which intellectual and emotional processes, model and intuition, cannot be separated from one another.

Notes

1. Iu. Lotman, *Analiz poèticheskogo teksta,* "Tekst i sistema," (Leningrad, 1972) 119-26. Here and throughout translations from the Russian are by Allan Reid.

2. The concepts of *idea* and *image* originate from the same Greek root ('*idea,*' '*eidos*'). This common origin provided rich material for studies on the meaning of these concepts in Plato and Aristotle. See, for example, P. Brommer, *Eidos et idea: Etude sémantique et chronologique des œuvres de Platon* (Assen, 1940); Cl. Sandoz, *Les noms grecs de la forme* (Bern, 1972); H. Happ, *Hyle: Studien zum aristotelischen Materie-Begriff* (Bern-New York, 1971).

3. I. E. Babel. *Dnevnik 1920 goda.* Pt. 1. The manuscript is held by A. N. Pirozhkova, Babel's widow. Cf. *Sochineniia v dvukh tomakh* (Moscow: Khudozhestvennaia literatura, 1990) vol. I, 362. All subsequent Babel citations are from this edition.

4. For further details see Zs. Hetenyi, "Lavka vechnosti: Gedali Babelia," *Studia slavica Hungarica* 35 (1989).

5. Examples of such replacements include: "the pealing of bells" (звон колоколов)—"The International" (Интернационал); "The Gospels" (Евангелие)—"The House of Soviets" (Дом Советов); "church" (церковь)—"club" (клуб). *Sochineniia* vol. I, 199-201.

6. *The Place of Space in Narration. A semiotic approach to the problem of literary space. With an analysis of the role of space in I. E. Babel's «Konarmija»* (Ph.D. diss.) Studies in Slavic Literature and Poetics (SSLP, 1983), vol. 3 (Rodopi, Amsterdam.)

7. Van Baak, *The Place of Space in Narration,* 58-59.

8. Cf.: See also rot (гниль); stifling (удушливое); rushed (суетливое); squalor (убожество); it never sees the sun (в нём никочда не бывает

солнца); somber (мрачный); reject (отброс); manure (навоз); despondency (уныние); horror (ужас); stench (вонь); faded fecal acidity (протухшая кислота испражнений); stinks (воняет, смердит); rotten (гнилой); faded (слинявший); misfortune (несчастие) 70.

9. Cf. "The cavalrymen slumbered in their *high* saddles" / Бойцы дремали в высокцх седлах (69); "The cloak of the Division Commander Pavlichenko was flying . . . *above* the Staff" / Бурка начдива Павличенки веяла . . . наб штабом, . . . (69); "We rode past the Cossack burial mounds and the *watch-tower* of Bohdan Kmelnitsky" / Мы проехали казачци курганы и вышцку Богдана Хмельницкого (69). Cf. also, how in "Berestechko" the Cossack hides the old Jew's head *under* his armpit before slitting his throat (69).

10. See Zs. Hetenyi, "Eskadronnaia dama, vozvedennaia v Madonnu," *Studia Slavica Hungarica* 31 (1985): 161-69.

11. "A charred city—broken columns and the evil, hook-shaped, little fingers of old women . . . The raw mould of the ruins was blooming . . ." / Обгорелый город—переломленные колонны и врытые в землю крючки злых старушечьих мизинцев . . . Сырая плесень развалин цвела . . . (26); "While returning home I was afraid of meeting Sidorov, my neighbor, who, at night, would put the hirsute hand of his anguish on me" / Возвращаясь домой, я страшился встречи с Сидоровым, моим соседом, опускавшим на меня по ночам волосатую лапу своей тоски (26).

12. "Stooped over . . . his olive-colored, expressionless face"; "And here it is night, filled with a distant and distressing ringing; a block of light in the damp darkness—and in it the deathly face of Sidorov, a lifeless mask hung over the yellow flame of the candle" / Сутулясь, . . . оливковое невыразительное лицо . . . ; . . . И вот ночь, полная далеких и тягостных звонов, квадрат света в сырой тьме—и в нем мертвенное лицо Сидорова, безжизненная маска, нависшая над желтым пламенем свечи. (28).

13. ". . . Levka was chewing meat, crunching and puffing. Once he finished his meat, Levka licked his lips and pulled Sashka into the ditch. . . . Levka was crunching and puffing in the bushes . . ." / . . . Левка жевал мясо, хрустя и задыхаясь. Кончив мясо, Левка облизал губы и потащил Сашку в ложбинку . . . Левка хрустел и задыхался в кустах (107-08).

14. Lüko Gábor, *A magyar lélek formái* (Budapest: Exodus, 1942) 9-61.

15. See the stories "El'ia Isaakovich i Margarita Prokof'evna" (1916) and "Doudou" (1917).

16. J. Falen, *Isaak Babel': Russian Master of the Short Story* (Knoxville: 1974) 137.

Boris Briker (essay date March-June 1994)

SOURCE: Briker, Boris. "The Underworld of Benia Krik and I. Babel's *Odessa Stories.*" *Canadian Slavonic Papers* 36, nos. 1-2 (March-June 1994): 115-34.

[*In the following essay, Briker analyzes Babel's fictional underworld in his* Odessa Tales *within the context of a "larger 'Odessa text,'" or historical and mythological background. He traces the origin of Babel's fictional characters and events to documented notorious individuals, well-known mythologies, and archetypes of Jewish literature prevalent in the city of Odessa.*]

In 1916, a short essay entitled **"Odessa,"** by the then young and unknown writer, I. Babel, appeared in M. Gorky's *Zhurnal zhurnalov.* Using the typical manifesto-like rhetoric of his times, I. Babel predicted in **"Odessa"** that a new literary messiah would come from that sunny port metropolis to break with the literary tradition of grey and foggy Petersburg. While it remains a question whether Babel himself fulfilled the role of such a messiah, he was responsible for helping to shape the popular image of his native city in his *Odessa Stories.* It is also true, however, that an image of Odessa had been formed well before Babel provided the material for his picture of Odessa and its Moldavanka district. This image of the city may be viewed as one "Odessa text."[1] Such a text unites two narrative structures: the structure provided by the history of the city, newspaper reports, urban folklore, and also the structure actualized in literary works.

The very title of one of Babel's *Odessa Stories,* **"How It Was Done in Odessa"** (Как это делалось в Одессе) suggests that the Odessa way of doing things had very distinct features. Indeed, this phrase can be attributed not only to *Odessa Stories,* but to the "Odessa text" in general. While the urban landscape of Petersburg had been associated with the evil and oppressive powers of the Russian Empire, the image of Odessa in the nineteenth century evoked notions of freedom. In the Jewish context, Odessa, though located within the Pale of Settlement, offered a land of opportunity, an "alternative" to America, Argentina, Palestine, or forbidden Petersburg. As one prerevolutionary Odessa writer commented, "If a Jew from the Pale of Settlement does not dream of America or Palestine, know that he will be in Odessa."[2] In addition, Odessa had the reputation of being what historian Robert Weinberg has called the "Russian Eldorado,"[3] a place where easy money could be made. Like Menachem Mendl from Sholom Aleichem's stories, Jewish "Luftenmenschen" set out for Odessa in hopes of realizing their dreams. While these dreams did not necessarily come true, the image of Odessa as a land of opportunity survived throughout the nineteenth century and the beginning of the twentieth century. This helps explain why such literary characters as swindlers, opportunists, and thieves had a better chance of surviving within the context of Odessa's mythopoetic "text" than within that of Petersburg.

The mythologies surrounding the notorious Odessa thieves and bandits constitute an important aspect of the "Odessa text." According to Vladimir Jabotinsky, an Odessa native, journalist, and later a leading Zionist activist, the whole city of Odessa had a reputation among non-Odessa Jews as being a thieving city. He explains: "The word 'thief' in Yiddish (*ganev*) has a much deeper meaning. It characterized a person who would fool you before you fool him—in short, [a person who is] experienced, shrewd, an exaggerator, a speculator . . ."[4] Rumors about Odessa thieves and bandits circulated widely, even extending to faraway lands. In the 1960s, the Australian writer, Judah Waten, who left Odessa in 1914 as a newborn, remembers how his father "boasted that Odessa turned out the most talented thieves in the world, certainly more ingenious, dexterous and brazen then the Warsaw ones."[5]

Babel uses the legendary figures of Odessa thieves and gangsters as the main characters in his *Odessa Stories.* Moreover, Benia Krik's criminal actions constitute the plots of these stories. By "plot," I refer to the Russian usage of *siuzhet,* or, to the more recent term, "story," that is, the "narrated events or characters abstracted by their disposition in the text."[6] In this article I intend to show that the "narrated events" involving Benia Krik and his underworld in Babel's *Odessa Stories* function against the background of a larger "Odessa text." I will also investigate underground folklore featuring underworld "kings" and track some of Babel's Odessa sources. Finally, I will look at Benia Krik and his actions within the historical context of Odessa's experience of Revolution and Civil War, when the real-life Mishka Iaponchik, the prototype for Benia Krik, reached his legendary status.

The *Odessa Stories,* which treat Benia Krik and his gangster activities, include the **"The King"** (Король—1921), **"How It Was Done in Odessa"** (1923), **"The Father"** (Отец—1924), and **"Justice in Quotation Marks"** (Справедливость в скобках—1921).[7] In addition, Babel's later story, **"Froim Grach"** (1934), features "Benia Krik's people" (люди Бени Крика) and is set during the Civil War in 1919. Therefore, I will consider this story as well.

THE PLOT OF THE RAID

While Babel's critics have emphasized his mastery of *skaz* in rendering the Odessa idiom in the **Odessa Stories,** his peculiar treatment of events has usually been taken for granted. Babel's contemporary, K. Paustovskii, records how Babel would polemicize with the critical notion that his stories are held together by style alone. Using formalist terms and clichés, Babel would speculate on the balance of style and plot in his writing:

> "How are my stories held together? With what kind of cement? You'd think that they'd disintegrate at the slightest touch." And then he'd answer his own question by saying that style was the only binding agent; and then he'd laugh at himself. Who could believe that a story could hold up without content, plot or intrigue?[8]

As Babel himself suggested, more unites his stories than style. In fact, a specific, narrative structure underpins many of his stories. In **Odessa Stories,** this structure originates with the gangster raid (налет). The raid may target small shops, factories, or apartments. For Babel's leading bandit, Benia Krik, and his friends, "the raid" signifies the main activity, and it organizes the plots of the stories about Benia Krik. In **"The King,"** for example, the narrator explains the odd familial relationship between the king of gangsters and his wealthy father-in-law, Eikhbaum, by the phrase, "the raid is everything here" / тут все дело в налете (I, 121).[9] The story of Benia Krik's raid on Eikhbaum's farm follows. In **"How It Was Done in Odessa"** Tartakovskii is known by the nickname, "Nine raids" (девять налетов). The tenth raid and its well-known consequences constitute the plot of this story. In **"Justice in Quotation Marks,"** two rival gangsters unexpectedly meet during a single raid. This situation serves as the main conflict of the story. Benia punishes the man responsible for informing both rival parties of the target for an upcoming raid. Although not overtly pertaining to "the raid," the story **"The Father"** ends with an agreement between Benia Krik and Froim Grach to punish the grocer, Kaplun, with a future raid: ". . . and here begins another tale, a tale of the fall of the house of the Kapluns, a tale of slow death, of acts of arson and nocturnal gunfire / . . . и вот тут начинается новая история, история падения дома Каплунов, повесть о его медленной гибели, о поджогах и ночной стрельбе (146).

In Odessa, the practice of "the raid," originated in the political terrorism during the time of the 1905 Revolution. V. Jabotinsky recalls this time, when he writes in his novel that "we all read of the heroic raids against convoys that were transporting gold from the state treasury" (мы все читали о героических налетах на конвои казенного золота).[10] Later, "raids" became the prerogative of criminal gangs and private individuals, and it was called "eks" in street slang (an abbreviation

for "expropriation"). Gangsters involved in these illegal undertakings were labelled naletchiki, or raiders. This type of robbery in Odessa was widespread in the Jewish community. As in Babel's stories, both the instigators and the targets of these crimes were very often Jews. In fact, one journalist compared the raids to the pogroms: "the Jewish masses are pummelled by two scourges—at night by alien scum with clubs, and during the day by our own" (в два кнута хлещут еврейскую массу; ночью дубинками чужая сволочь, днем своя).[11]

During World War I and especially right after the February Revolution in 1917, Odessa newspapers reported rampant raids. Benia Krik's raids most likely originated in the "brazen robberies" of that time. Gangs were composed of former prisoners, who were granted amnesty and released by the Provisional Government. Deserters from the front during World War I often participated in the gangs and provided the gangsters with arms. The state militia recruited young students from gymnasiums and universities to replace the unpopular, though experienced, tsarist police. For example, in the epic poem, *February* (Февраль) by the Odessa poet, E. Bagritskii, the lyrical hero is a university student who serves as the commissar in just such a militia. As commissar, he invades a den of thieves and prostitutes. His interactions with them structures the plot of the poem.

Just as the duel and card game provided a ready-made plot construct for many nineteenth-century Russian literary works, so too did the structure of the raid serve as a ready-made plot for Babel's **Odessa Stories.** Thus, "the raid" serves as the narrative plot even before entering Babel's text. Like other plot constructs, the raid could yield numerous versions. The narrative structure of the raid follows a set of rules, conventions, and an honor code. Using local Odessa newspaper accounts for this period, it is possible reconstruct a master plot of the raid and to trace how Babel refashioned this extratextual material into the raids of his **Odessa Stories.**

A typical raid in Odessa would begin with a letter of extortion received by the owner of a business. In this letter the extortionist would demand that the owner amass a prescribed sum of money and deliver it to a designated place. Such letters invariably contained some of the same clichés found in business letters. But, because of the intent of these letters, the correspondence ultimately produces a pure parody of business correspondence. One letter, addressed to the Odessite, Pinkus, in October, 1917, illustrates the point. It was subsequently published in the daily newspaper *Odesskie novosti,* where it was accompanied by the drawing of a skull and crossbones:

> Dear Comrade Pinkus: On the fourth of August at nine o'clock in the evening, please be so kind as to bring, without fail, 100 rubles to the tram station across from

your house. This modest sum will preserve your life, which is certainly worth more than 100 rubles. Any efforts to evade this payment will lead to major difficulties for you. If you turn to the police, you will be killed immediately. You and your whole family will suffer. We will strike and you will be ruined. Sit on the bench by the tram station and have in one hand an envelope with the money, and in the other a white kerchief. The head of the band of Parisian Apaches will approach, and you will hand the money over to him.

Товарищ Пинкус! Будьте добры и не откажите доставить 4-го августа к 9 часам вечера 100 рублей на станцию трамвая против вашего дома. Эта небольшая сумма сохранит вам жизнь, которая наверное стоит больше 100 рублей. Всякие попытки уклониться от этой подачи принесут вам большие неприятности. Если заявите милиции, будете моментально убиты. Пострадаете вы и ваша семья. Вас разгромят и разорят. Сядьте на скамейке трамвайиой станции и держите в одной руке конверт с деньгами, а в другой белый платок. К вам подойдет атаман шайки парижских апашей и вы ему вручите деньги.[12]

Judging by the relatively modest sum of money demanded in the letter, we may assume that this extortionist was not an experienced gangster. Nevertheless, this bandit certainly knew the formulae for extortion found in the letters of his more experienced brethren: the business-like, detailed description of handing over the money and the accompanied threats. In **"How It Was Done in Odessa"** Babel incorporates into Benia's letter the characteristic features of extortion letters. We should note that the letter reflects this particular pattern more than it does Benia's own speech:

Dear Ruvim Osipovich: Please, by Saturday evening, be so kind as to place under the rain barrel . . . etc., etc. In the case of a refusal, which you have been allowing yourself recently, a major disenchantment in your family life awaits you.

Многоуважаемый Рувим Осипович! Будьте настолько любезны положить к субботе под бочку с дождевой водой . . . и так далее. В случае отказа, как вы это себе в последнее время стали позволять, вас ждет большое разочарование в вашей семейной жизни.

(130)

In **"How It Was Done in Odessa,"** even the narrator who worships Benia Krik seems to mock the letter as a cliché by noting that Benia Krik's letter to Tartakovskii is "a letter very much like all letters written on such an occasion" (130). In the story **"The King"** Babel intensifies the parodic element by imitating Odessa speech patterns in Benia's letter to Eikhbaum. The form of the letter, however, stays intact:

Monsieur Eikhbaum, I am requesting that you place 20,000 rubles beneath the gate at 17 Sofievskaia Street. If you do not do so, such an unheard of happening will befall you that all Odessa will be talking in respect of your person.

Мосье Эйхбаум, « . . . » положите, прошу вас, под ворота на Софиевскую, 17 двадцать тысяч рублей. Если вы это не сделаете, так вас ждет такое, что это неслыханно, и вся Одесса будет от вас говорить.

(121)

We note here that the hero of Il'f and Petrov's *The Golden Calf* (Эолотой теленок), Ostap Bender, an *intellectual* swindler from Chernomorsk-Odessa, also mocks this sort of letter as predictable and this kind of extortion as petty:

A petty con like Panikovskii would write a letter to Koreiko telling him to place 600 rubles under the garbage can out back—otherwise, things would be bad for him, and at the bottom he'd draw in a skull, cross bones and a candle.

(Ch. XII, "The Herculeans")

Мелкая уголовная сошка вроде Паниковского написала бы Корейко письмо «Положите во дворе под мусорный ящик шестьсот рублей, иначе будет плохо»—и внизу пририсовала бы крест, череп и свечу.

(Гл. XII, «Геркулесовцы»)[13]

Failure to respond to letters of extortion represents the first violation of order that ultimately leads to a raid. The second step of the raid follows. The gangsters suddenly appear at the home or business of their victims, pretending to be customers, police officers, soldiers, or else they are garbed in such a way so as to conceal their identity (for example, they might wear robes or masks). Thus, in a 1917 issue of the *Odesskie novosti* newspaper, for example, in the section entitled "Happenings" (Происшествия), we find a typical description of such a scenario:

Around 2:00 a.m. four unknown subjects, wearing masks and armed with revolvers, turned up at a modest dacha near Big Fountain Station No. 1. They broke into the apartment of a certain Mil'rud that was occupied by three men.

"Hands up and don't make a move," shouted one of the bandits. The other bandits stood silently behind their leader, their guns trained on Mil'rud.

. . . Около двух часов ночи четыре неизвестных субьекта в масках, вооруженных револьверами, явились в одну из небольших дач вблизи 1-ой станции Большого фонтана. Они ворвались в квартиру некоего Мильруда, в которой было трое мужчин.

—Ни с места, руки вверх,—крикнул один из вбежавших в комнату грабителей. Остальные грабители, наведя револьверы на Мильруда, молча остановились за спиной своего предводителя.[14]

Even this newspaper report conveys the essentially theatrical nature of the gangsters' entrance. In **"How It**

Was Done in Odessa," Babel also resorts to theatrical gestures in describing how Benia and his friends, who are prepared to raid Tartakovskii's store, make their entrance:

> The next day he and four friends turned up at Tartakovskii's store. Four masked youths with revolvers came barging into the room.
>
> "Hands up," they said and started brandishing their pistols.
>
> На следующий день он явился с четырьмя друзьями в контору Тартаковского. Четыре юноши в масках с револьверами ввалились в комнату.
>
> —Руки вверх!—сказали они и стали махать пистолетами.
>
> (130)

After the letter of extortion and the unannounced visit, "the work" of the raid follows in the sequential order of its constituent events. While threatening the owner or the guards with weapons, the gangsters express their demand. They then get to "work,"—confiscating money or goods. The following real-life report narrates a rather complex procedure of negotiations with guards and clerks before the gangsters get to the safe:

> The bandits demanded that the clerk give them money. The clerk declared that the money was in the safe. The bandits then tried to break open the steel safe, but, when they saw this was more than they could handle, they tried using keys on it. Then they went to the store manager, and took 15,000 rubles before tying him and the guard up.
>
> Грабители потребовали у конторщика выдачи денег. Последний заявил, что деньги в кассе. Тогда грабители попытались взломать железную кассу, но, видя что им это не под силу, решили попробовать ключи от кассы. Затем отправились в квартиру к управляющему конторой и забрали 15 тысяч рублей. Связали конторщика, управляющего и сторожа.[15]

Babel's narrative in **"How It Was Done in Odessa,"** translates this sort of event into dialogue, thus, creating a "scene" in his short story, rather than a narrative summary. Consider the conversation between Benia Krik and the clerk Iosif Muginshtein, when Krik demands that the clerk open the safe:

> "Is Jew-and-a-Half in the factory?"
> "No, the boss's not in the factory" . . .
> "So who's here to be boss then?" . . .
> "I'm here to be boss" . . .
> "Then, may God help you, let's see you open the safe for us! . . .
>
> —Полтора жида в заводе?
> —Их нет в заводе,—. . .
> —Кто будет здесь наконец за хозяина? . . .

> —Я здесь буду за хозяина,—. . .
> —Тогда отчини нам с божьей помощью кассу! . . .
>
> (131)

According to the unwritten master plot, the raid should end with the gangsters getting the money and leaving the scene of the crime. The raids in Babel's stories violate this. In his stories, a violation of the rules and conditions of the raid leads to an unexpected plot twist towards comedy or tragedy, or, in most cases, towards a combination of the two. In **"How It Was Done in Odessa,"** the events of the plot initially correspond to the typical features of the raid. Suddenly, however, it turns into an unplanned and unnecessary death. After the demand for money is made, the clerk Iosif Muginshtein is murdered. In the story, **"The King,"** when the raid is almost over and Eikhbaum and Benia Krik reach an agreement, Benia Krik violates the pattern by falling in love with Eikhbaum's daughter. Consequently, the agreement between Benia and Eikhbaum is broken. In **"Justice in Quotation Marks,"** the violation of the pattern manifests itself as the meeting of two rival gang leaders at the site of a single raid. According to the rules of the raid, "work" should stop if two rival gangsters meet at one raid, while the tipster for the raid should be killed. The plot continues with Benia's revenge against the tipster.

Clearly, the raid and other criminal actions do not dominate all events in the stories featuring Benia Krik. Yet the parodox of the plot of these stories is that Babel sets the criminal raid in the context of the most important events of Jewish family life,—during weddings, funerals, and marriage proposals. By consistently functioning in these archetypal settings, the raid achieves equivalent status as a plot component. In **"The King,"** the raid on Eikhbaum literally concludes with Benia's marriage proposal followed by a prenuptual agreement. In **"The Father,"** the prenuptual agreement precedes the raid on Kaplun. And in **"How It Was Done in Odessa"** the gangsters' raid on Tartakovskii ends with a double funeral procession. The same ritual serves to bury the victim of the raid and his murderer. The leader of the raid and of the funeral procession is the very same Benia Krik. Moreover, in **"The King"** the Jewish wedding of Benia's sister is played out against the background of the raid on the local police station. Benia Krik directs and organizes both the raid and the wedding. His gangsters play two roles, as wedding guests and raider-arsonists. By the end of this story, Babel renders the two events indistinguishable: "When Benia returned home the lanterns were dying out and a glow was lighting up the sky." / Когда Беня вернулся домой, на дворе уже потухали фонарики и на небе занималась заря (126). The extinguishing of the fire at the police station literally coincides with the end of the wedding party at the Krik household.

The family events in which the raid functions in *Odessa Stories* represent the archetypal plots in Jewish literature, as in, for example, the works of Sholom Aleichem. In order to show how the plot of the raid is interwoven with such archetypal plots, it is worth comparing the plot of Babel's story, **"The Father,"** with Sholom Aleichem's short story, "Shprintsa" (1907).[16] In this story Tevye the milkman relates the tragedy of one of his daughters, Shprintsa. Shprintsa falls in love with Aronchik, the dissipated son of a rich widow, who asks her father for her hand. When Aronchik's mother receives the news, Tevye is summoned to the rich widow's dacha. Here Aronchik's uncle demands that Tevye and his daughter leave his nephew in peace, arguing that the daughter of a milkman is no match for a rich heir. The widow, together with her brother and son, suddenly dissappear from the town without a trace. Tevye looks on helplessly as his daughter mourns the loss of her beloved and eventually commits suicide. The comic features of Babel's story notwithstanding, **"The Father,"** follows a very similar plot to Sholom Aleichem's. Froim Grach is also a father whose daughter dreams of getting married. She is interested in Solomonchik Kaplun, the son of a prosperous Odessa grocer. When, however, Froim Grach visits Solomonchik's parents, the marriage proposal is rejected by Mme Kaplun: "I do not want any part of you just as a bride does not want pimples on her face." / Да, я не хочу вас, как невеста не хочет прыщей на голове (140). Like Tevye's daughter, who drowns herself, Bas'ka Grach threatens to end her own life, "or I'll do myself in" / или я сделаю конец моей жизни (139). Up until this point, the story of Froim Grach follows that of Tevye the milkman; both fathers act on behalf of their daughters' wishes and are rejected by the suitors' families. While Sholom Aleichem's Tevye goes on living, accepting his fate with wisdom, pride and humour, the story of Froim Grach takes an unexpected twist. The local smuggler and brothel keeper, Lubka Kazak, comes up with a new match for Bas'ka. Benia Krik and Froim Grach make an agreement that Benia will marry Bas'ka and will punish Kaplun by committing raids on his shop. Benia Krik the gangster plays the role of the long awaited fairy-tale prince. Thus, in **"The Father"** the archetypal tragedy of the Jewish father who cannot find a match for his daughter turns into a gangster's raid and a triumph over the rich. In this way, then, Babel introduces the plots of criminal activity into archetypal events of Jewish literature.

UNDERGROUND FOLKLORE

Babel was not the only writer to incorporate Odessa's local colour into his early stories. As W. Cukerman has shown, between 1919 and 1923, a whole group of young Odessa writers, including Paustovskii, Il'f, Kataev, and Slavin, exploited Odessa material for the setting of their literary works.[17] However, even before the 1920s, stories about Odessa bandits and their raids were already actualized through the medium of urban folklore and local popular culture. Moreover, Odessa underground songs (*blatnye pesni*), which belonged to both the genre of popular entertainment and to urban folklore, cultivated the image of Odessa's thieves and bandits. Thus, Babel and the anonymous authors of the underground songs derived their material from these very same sources, from Odessa's local mythologies, including similar heroes, situations, and mileaux. In order to account for the world which Babel created in his *Odessa Stories,* I will consider the underground songs as literary texts.[18]

Dating back to before the Revolution, the role of the outsider, the man of "the lower depths," served as a common mask for Odessa's local entertainers and comedians. Such figures were often featured in performances at variety theaters, cabarets, and in the summer theaters that flourished in Odessa. The poor and predominantly Jewish outskirts of Odessa, "Moldavanka," which also serves as the locale for Babel's *Odessa Stories,* not only gave a home to its thieves and bandits, but nurtured local popular songs about these figures in its cafes and taverns. The songs of the Odessa underground often combine the traditional, urban, semi-folkloric genres, such as cruel romance (жестокий романс), and prison songs with the specific humour of Yiddish language patterns and jokes of Moldavanka. Like an urban romance, the underground songs often contain a tale or a story. "Moldavanka" became synonymous in these songs with a den of thieves (*malina*), which functions very much contrary to the world at large. During the Civil War, a popular song known in Odessa held that "everyone had gone off for to fight the Civil War, but as for the thieves, they all stayed back in Moldavanka" (Все на войне да на гражданке, А воры все на Молдаванке).

The authors of the texts of these songs used the men of the underground not only as their main heroes, but also as implied narrators. It was said that the authors of the underground songs and the Odessa *naletchiki* could have easily switched roles. Thus, the songs present Odessa and the world at large from the point of view of the bandits and their attitude to crime and justice. Recurrent themes include extortions, encounters with the police, vengeance, and street violence. The heroes featured in these texts lack any pangs of conscience characteristic of the villain in Russian folklore. The narrator of one Odessa song, reminiscent of the real-life Mishka Iaponchik, describes his attitude to life. Though poor, hungry, and wearing patched clothes, he knows that in five minutes he could become rich simply by "signing" a receipt in the bank with his machine gun. The generous nature of his native town Odessa, which, like a mother, cares about her sons whether they are pawns or "kings," nurtures his optimistic outlook. The maternal image of Odessa presented in the song originated with the popular phrase of thieves' jargon, "Odessa-mama."

The thieves and bandits in the songs act according to their own code of behavior and to the laws of their particular world. Thus, murder committed by bandits is often presented as an inevitable act of justice. In the popular song, "Murka" (or, in another version, "Liubka"), the narrator tells how he murdered his fellow bandit, a woman by the name of Liubka, whose connections with the police endangered the thieves. The narrator contends that justice has been served:

> Greetings, my Liubka, greetings, my dear.
> Greetings and farewell!
> You've blown our cover, we're all as good as dead.
> So as a parting shot, I'll have you eat this lead.
>
> Здравствуй, моя Любка, здравствуй, дорогая.
> Здравствуй, дорогая и прощай!
> Ты зашухерила всю нашу малину—
> Так теперь маслины получай.[19]

Despite the grim subject matter of these underground songs, the anonymous authors express a light and humorous attitude towards violence. Moreover, violence is sometimes presented as desirable for the victim. As early as 1917, the young singer and comedian, L. Utesov, performed the role of a newspaper boy in a popular stand-up routine. In one song announcing the most important town news, Utesov described how an old woman was robbed and raped by six bandits. Notwithstanding its disturbing subject matter, the song is nevertheless rather light and cheerful and ends with the old woman's dream of reliving the encounter:

> On Deribasovskaiia at the corner of Richelieu,
> At six in the evening the news came out.
> How some old gal (a fine old babe, all right)
> Six raiders chanced to rape.
> But my, oh my, the old gal's all right.
> And while partaking of her compote
> She dreams, oh my, of taking part
> In yet another raid.
>
> Как на Дерибасовской, угол Ришельевской,
> В шесть часов вечера разнеслася весть.
> У старушки-бабушки, у бабушки-старушки
> Шестеро налетчиков отняли честь.
> Оц-тоц- перевертоц-бабушка здорова.
> Оц-тоц- перевертоц- кушает компот
> Оц-тоц- перевертоц- и мечтает снова
> Оц-тоц- перевертоц-пережить налет.[20]

Such a joyous attitude to violent actions creates the impression that the violence and murders represent not the reality of Odessa streets, but constitute a comic performance. Often violence is described as merry-making. For example, one song, "On Deribasovskaiia they opened a pub" (На Дерибасовской открылася пивная) describes a violent fight between two parties which parodies a then popular Argentinian tango. The story of the violent act is not only accompanied by the melody of tango music, it is referred to as a tango.

> But Kostia the junkman was a fiery fellow:
> He blasted Chubby Churman with a bottle,
> Jammed his fork in a waiter's leg,
> And thus struck up a glorious tango.
>
> Но Костя-шмаровоз был парень пылкий:
> Чурмена жирного он засветил бутылкой,
> Официанту засадил он в ножку вилкой,
> И началося славное танго.

In Babel's **"The King,"** shooting and fighting are part of the merry-making at the wedding:

> At first, the raiders, who were seated in tight rows, felt constrained in the presence of strangers, but after a while they got going. Levka Katsap broke a bottle of vodka over his sweetheart's head, and Monia-the-Artilleryman started firing into the air.
>
> Налетчики, сидевшие сомкнутыми рядами сначала стеснялись посторонних, но потом они разошлись. Левка Кацап разбил на голове своей возлюбленной бутылку водки, Моня Артиллерист выстрелил в воздух.
>
> (I, 123)

Gangsters' slang, together with Yiddish words and expressions, also produces a comic effect. Thus, in the underground songs even the most tragic events are recounted as comic. In the popular song, "From Odessa Prison" (С одесского кичмана), two bandits stop at one of their dens to rest after having just escaped prison. One of them is fatally wounded and realizes that he will not be able to survive. Facing death, he nevertheless expresses his last wishes in comically distorted Russian:

> Comrade Skumbrievich,
> Tell my mum,
> Her son died doin' 'is duty
> Wid 'is rifle in one 'and
> A sabre in t'other,
> And a song in 'is t'roat.
>
> Товарищ Скумбриевич,
> Скажите моей маме,
> Что сын ее погибнул на посте
> С винтовкою в рукою
> И с шашкою в другою
> И с песнею веселой на губе.[21]

The humour of Odessa underground songs also surfaced in poetic form. For example, I. Sel'vinskii bases the plot of one of his poems, "Mot'ka Malkhamoves" (1923), on an anecdote involving a gangster raid in Odessa.[22] In the poem the hero (whose name comes from the Hebrew, meaning angel of death) carries out a raid on a Jewish store, threatening the owners with a bomb. The tragic situation is, in the end, deflated through Mot'ka's joke: the bomb turns out to be a beet. Sel'vinskii's hero shares the title of monarch with Benia Krik, the "King of Moldavanka." Both the hero and the narrator speak a macaronic language which includes Yiddish phrases. Experimenting in his early years with the forms of urban folkloric genres, Sel'vinskii apparently used Odessa underground songs as important sources for his poem.

Like the authors of underground folklore, Babel's narrator treats and reacts to violence lightly, even humorously.[23] In fact, the atmosphere of the festival which surrounds violent events in the underground songs is also evident in Babel's *Odessa Stories*. In Babel's stories, violent events always conclude with triumph and celebration. In the story **"The King"** the raid on Eikhbaum ends happily for both parties: the police raid on Benia Krik's wedding ends with a fire which also constitutes a happy ending, insofar as it represents Krik's triumph over the police. In **"How It Was Done in Odessa,"** there are two murders. However, the tragedy of these two events is diminished by the atmosphere of celebration. The funeral procession that ends the story turns into a carnivalesque coronation of Benia Krik, since immediately following the funeral procession, a cemetery beggar pronounces Benia "king."

The description of the fashions, manners, and luxurious lifestyle of the heroes of Moldavanka also contributes to the carnivalesque atmosphere of *Odessa Stories*. Benia Krik and his gangsters share an appreciation of ostentatious style with the heroes of popular folklore, the kings and knights of Moldavanka. The pseudo aristocratic manners of the gangsters, the exotic colors of their clothing, and the theatrical effects of their appearances in public all constitute what Babel called "Moldavanskii chic." While the author depicts this style in terms of "kitsch" culture, his narrator admires it.

BENIA KRIK, MISHKA IAPONCHIK, AND THE
SOVIET STATE

Babel's critics and the memorists of the time all seem to agree that Mishka Iaponchik (whose real name was Moisei Vinnitskii), the famous Odessa gangster, served as the prototype for Benia Krik. Yet whereas Mishka's notoriety peaked in the years, 1917-1919—the years of Revolution and Civil War in Odessa—Babel's *Odessa Stories* take place before the February Revolution. Mishka Iaponchik himself acknowledged that he had served a ten-year prison sentence before being released in 1917 during an amnesty granted by the Provisional Government.[24] The Soviet writer, Lev Nikulin, noticed this temporal discrepancy between the activity of Babel's Benia Krik and Moisei Vinnitskii: "The Civil-War bandit Mishka Iaponchik was transformed into Benia Krik who dates from the period of reaction that fol-

lowed upon 1905. In any case the combination was unnatural."[25] Although Benia Krik's life does not precisely fit the facts of Mishka Iaponchik's, he nevertheless acquired Mishka's status as an Odessa legend. The title, "king of the streets of Moldavanka," which came to be associated with Benia Krik, originated with Mishka Iaponchik.

The biography of Moisei Vinnitskii, whom some compare to an Odessa version of Al Capone, has yet to be written. I will rely on the memoiristic accounts of his contemporaries to help reconstruct his literary relationship to Mishka Iaponchik. According to one memoirist, Moisei Vinnitskii received the nickname Mishka Iaponchik during the Russo-Japanese War. Vinnitskii served in the War and returned to Odessa with a Japanese wife.[26] While this is not a proven biographical fact, it has served as one of the legends about Mishka Iaponchik. Moreover, the story about Benia's falling in love and marrying Eikhbaum's daughter, the daughter of one of his enemies in the story, **"The King,"** may faintly reflect this tale of Mishka's marriage. L. Utesov, who once witnessed Mishka delivering a speech at a gathering of bandits, gives a more plausible explanation for the nickname: he believed that Mishka was called Iaponchik because of his slanting eyes.[27]

After serving time in a tsarist prison, Mishka Iaponchik became the leader of all the Odessa gangs. During the politically turbulent times of the Civil War, Mishka Iaponchik allied himself with different political groups, such as the Bolsheviks, the anarchists, and anti-pogrom Jewish defense organizations.[28] The most notorious period in Mishka's political career arrived, however, in the spring and summer of 1919, when he collaborated with the Bolshevik regime. At that time the Odessa executive committee assigned Mishka Iaponchik the task of forming a Red regiment out of his bandits to send to the front. Mishka delivered political speeches in the city's theaters to recruit bandits to his regiment, and he became a visible personality.

The establishment of Soviet power in Odessa is also closely connected with Mishka Yaponchik. In his memoirs, the poet, Don-Aminado, recalls the arrival of the Bolsheviks into Odessa in terms of the entrance of Mishka Iaponchik on a white horse. Moreover, to make this image even more striking, Don-Aminado quotes Eduard Bagritskii's poem, "The Ballad of Opanas" (Дума про Опанаса), where he describes the triumphal ride not of Mishka, but of the Red Army Commander, Grigorii Kotovskii:

> The change over in power was extraordinarily simple:
> One side vanished, while another burst into town.
>
> Leading the way on horseback was Mishka Iaponchik,
> the chief of staff.

Bagritskii provided an unforgettable description of this:

With a commander's piercing gaze
He looked the valley over,
While 'neath him his mount did pace
White like confectioner's sugar.

Он долину озирает
Командирским взглядом.
Жеребец под ним играет
Белым рафинадом.[29]

That same year, in 1919, Mishka's collaboration with the Bolsheviks ended, as did his life. When Mishka Iaponchik attempted to desert the front and head back to Odessa, he was killed by a Red commander in charge of a railway station. In the scenario to his film, ***Benia Krik***, Babel depicts how the main hero was lured to one of the stations and killed there.[30] Babel's narrator also refers to Mishka Iaponchik's violent death when he speaks of the "terrible end" of Benia Krik.

Widely circulating historical facts, rumors, and legends contributed to forming the popular perception of Mishka Iaponchik as one of Odessa's rulers. In his novel, *The Green Wagon* (Зеленый фургон), the Odessa writer, A. Kozachinskii, noted that the inhabitants of Odessa included Mishka Iaponchik's name in a rather long list of Odessa's rulers during the Civil War. In his ***Odessa Stories*** Babel projected the image of Mishka Iaponchik as a political ruler onto Benia Krik, the king of Moldavanka in tsarist times.

While popular mythologies perceived the bandits as rulers, the reverse also took place. Opponents of the Bolshevik regime very often equated the Bolsheviks with gangsters. This follows, no doubt, from the fact that the Cheka, the secret police which represented Soviet power, was especially notorious for its cruelty in Odessa. The perception of Chekists as gangsters is reflected in the confusion of the following event. In 1919, rumors circulated that Mishka Iaponchik and the secretary of the Cheka, Comrade Mikhail, were one and the same person. The Chekists published a piece in the local newspaper, stating that their Comrade Mikhail had nothing in common with the bandit, Vinnitskii, and that those who circulated rumors alleging a connection would be persecuted. Clearly, the Cheka wanted to clear one of its comrades from any association with the Jewish bandit. But, for his part, Mishka the bandit also wished to distance himself from any connection with the Cheka in order to preserve his own reputation. Therefore, on the day after the Chekist piece appeared, Mishka Iaponchik used the same newspaper to publish his own letter refuting these rumors. Denying all ties with the Cheka, Mishka emphasized his alliance with the cause of the workers and peasants against the capitalists and the bourgeoisie. Using the political jargon of the time, he set forth his own participation in the partisan movement against the White forces and the Ukrainian National Army. Given the nature of Mishka's

criminal activity at this time, the text of this letter is striking in its earnestness and, ultimately, its irony.[31] Benia Krik's graveside speech in **"How It Was Done in Odessa"** also expresses these political sentiments: "For what did he perish? He perished for the entire working class." / За что погиб он? Он погиб за весь трудящийся класс (135).

The political carnival of Revolution and Civil War in Odessa provide the backdrop for Benia Krik's prerevolutionary adventures in the ***Odessa Stories*** However, in one short story not included in the cycle of ***Odessa Stories***, Babel put political events in the foreground. In fact, in Babel's **"Froim Grach,"** the tragic conflict centers on the clash between the Soviet government and the underworld of Benia Krik. Although Benia Krik himself does not take part in the events of this story, he is mentioned briefly in the opening which focusses on the historical context:

> In 1919 Benia Krik's men attacked the rear of an outfit of White volunteers, hacked up its officers, and made off with a part of its materiel. As a reward for this they demanded of the Odessa Soviet that there be three days of "peaceful uprising . . ."
>
> В девятнадцатом году люди Бени Крика напали на арьергард добровольческих войск, вырезали офицеров и отбили часть обоза. В награду они потребовали у Одесского Совета три дня "мирного восстания" . . .
>
> (II, 254)

The phrase, "peaceful uprising" (мирное восстание) requires some explanation. The Soviet city government set up three days in 1919—May 12-14—for the expropiation of surplus personal belongings, including clothes, boots, food, etc. Though euphemistically called a "peaceful uprising," this event had all the signs of outright robbery. This political operation was cancelled on the second day.[32] When in Babel's **"Froim Grach"** the bandit-followers of Benia Krik demand three days of "peaceful uprising," they also mean the permission to rob freely. Thus, the expression, "peaceful uprising," in the context of Babel's story can be associated both with the action of the Bolshevik Government and thieves' raids. Indeed, the entire plot of the story, **"Froim Grach,"** is based on this semantic ambiguity.

It is clear that the real-life Mishka Iaponchik and his bandits are referred to as "the people of Benia Krik." Moreover, it seems that Mishka Iaponchik may serve as the prototype for one of the characters in the story, Misha Iablochko, since the name, Misha Iablochko, sounds very similar to Mishka Iaponchik. The nickname, Iablochko, probably comes from a popular Civil War song, which circulated in numerous variations:

> Hey, little apple—whe're you headed?
> If it's to the Cheka—you'll be beheaded . . .

Яблочко, куда ты котишься?
В ЧК попадёшь—не воротишься . . .

Babel's story, **"Froim Grach,"** precisely illustrates the popular wisdom conveyed in this song whose text sounds like a warning to Mishka Iablochko.

Indeed, it bears remembering that in **"Froim Grach"** Chekists are hunting for Odessa Gangsters. The year is 1919. Misha Iablochko lures a suspected Cheka informant into taking a leisurely ride along the beach, kills him, and then returns his corpse to his family. Then the same Misha Yablochko, now disguised as an old woman, appears at the yard of the aging bandit Froim Grach and seeks his help in saving his friends from the Cheka. Froim Grach sets out for Cheka headquarters to negotiate with its "chief." However, without due process, Froim Grach is executed by two Red Army soldiers. When the chairman of the Cheka, a newcomer from Moscow, sees that one of the officers is saddened by Froim Grach's death, he explains the motives of the Cheka. Although the Cheka officer accepts these motives, he cannot help but admire Froim Grach and the other gangsters:

> Then having returned to good spirits, he again began to tell the Chekists from Moscow about Froim Grach's life, about how cunning and uncatchable he had been, and about his scornful disregard for his fellow man . . .

> Потом, оживившись, он снова начал рассказывать чекистам, приехавшим из Москвы, о жизни фроима Грача, об изворотливости его, неуловимости, о презрении к ближнему . . .

> (259)

The conflict between the Chekists and the gangsters in this story is realized, then, not only as a political struggle for power, but also as a war between two rival gangs. The Cheka represents one side in this gang warfare. For example, Froim Grach's visit to the Cheka is described in terms of a bandit entering another gang's den:

> "I'm clean, unarmed—nothing in my boots, either, and I didn't leave anyone on guard outside. Let my lads go, chief, just name your price . . ."

> Я пусто,—сказал тогда фроим,—в руках у меня ничего нет, и в чоботах у меня ничего нет, и за воротами на улице я никого не оставил. Отпусти моих ребят, хозяин, скажи твою цену . . .

> (256)

The Chekist's killing of Froim Grach, although lacking the theatrical effect of a criminal act conducted by Misha Iablochko, resembles other murders committed by the bandits. Moreover, the everyday activity of the Cheka consists of a series of killings. In the story such verbs as execute, shoot (расстреливать) function in a context where they connote a trivial procedure: "A month passed before they started to shoot them." . . . "They would shoot them after a brief interrogation . . ." / Прошел месяц, прежде чем их начали расстреливать . . . Их расстреляли после допроса, длившегося недолго . . . (154, 155).

The story ends with the bandits' defeat. However, this is a rather ambivalent ending. It is noteworthy that the Cheka officer appreciates the history of Odessa through the legends about Froim Grach and Benia Krik, "He was really a grand fellow . . . In him you can see the whole of Odessa / Это грандиозный парень . . . Тут вся Одесса пройдет перед вами (256). Thus, for the Cheka officer, an Odessa native, the death of the leader of the gangster world represents the end of Odessa's colorful past. Moreover, the sad feelings of the Odessa Chekist bear some metaliterary implications. If the actions of Froim Grach metonomically substitute for the narrative about him, then the violent death of Babel's Odessa hero may symbolize a forced end to the themes of the **Odessa Stories** in Babel's writing. The text supports this reading, since the past actions of Froim Grach and other bandits are marked by words indicative of narrative. The Chekist Borovoi refers to Froim Grach as "an epic" and "an entire history embodied by that oldster" / это эпопея, . . . целая история с этим стариком (258, 259). He also recalls, "all those amazing stories that have gone off into the past" / все эти удивительные истории, отошедшие в прошлое (259). The acceptance of the cruel order and, at the same time, the lamenting of its consequences constitutes a sentiment to which characters close to Babel such as Liutov from **Red Cavalry** can relate. Thus, in 1934, in the story, **"Froim Grach,"** Babel nostalgically recollects his own rendering of the underworld of Benia Krik in his **Odessa Stories** of the early 1920s. Indeed, the story, **"Froim Grach,"** turned out to be Babel's last story not only about Odessa's criminal world, but about his native Odessa in general.

Notes

1. The semiotic concept of the text of the city has been developed by such scholars as Iu. Lotman and V. Toporov with regard to Petersburg. See, for example, V. Toporov, "Peterburg i peterburgskii tekst russkoi literatury," and Iu. Lotman, "Simvolika Peterburga i problemy semiotiki goroda," in *Semiotika goroda i gorodskoi kul'tury. Peterburg* (Tartu: Uchenye zapiski Tartuskogo Universiteta, 1984).

2. A. Svirskii, "Iz putevogo dnevnika" *Knizhki Voskhoda* No. 7 (1904): 169.

3. R. Weinberg, *The Revolution of 1905 in Odessa: Blood on the Steps* (Bloomington: Indiana University Press, 1993) 1.

4. V. Jabotinsky, "Memoirs of My Typewriter," in *The Golden Tradition,* ed. L. Dawidowich (New York: Schocken Books, 1967) 398.

5. Judah Waten, *From Odessa to Odessa* (Melbourne: Cheshire, 1969) 7.

6. As Shlomith Rimmon-Kennan observes, a story is always a "part of a larger construct, . . . the fictional 'reality' in which the characters of the story are supposed to be living and in which its events are supposed to take place." Shlomith Rimmon-Kennan, *Narrative Fiction: Contemporary Poetics* (London: Routledge, 1990) 6. In our analysis, this large construct is the "Odessa text."

7. "Justice in Quotation Marks" was published in 1921 in the Odessa newspaper, *Na pomoshch'*, and was subtitled "From the Odessa Stories." Later, however, Babel did not include this particular story in his Odessa cycle, in which he grouped "The Father," "The King," "How It Was Done in Odessa," and "Lubka Kazak." Because of its hero Benia Krik and its treatment of the Odessa underworld, I will consider "Justice in Quotation Marks" as part of the 'Odessa cycle,' but I will not consider "Liubka Kazak" within this context. It is noteworthy that the question of what constitutes the 'Odessa cycle' is contentious. For example, Efraim Sicher, treats all nine Odessa-based tales as one cycle—see I. Babel', *Detstvo i drugie rasskazy* (Jerusalem: Biblioteka-Aliia, 1990).

8. K. Paustovskii, "Rasskazy o Babele" in *Vospominaniia o Babele* (Moscow: Knizhnaia palata, 1989) 43.

9. All references to I. Babel's stories are from *Sochineniia v dvukh tomakh* (Moscow: Khudozhestvennaia literatura, 1990). Page numbers are indicated directly in the text. Translations from Russian are by R. L. Busch.

10. V. Zhabotinskii, *Piatero* (Paris: Ars, 1936) 209. On Jabotinsky as a Russian writer and on his novel, *The Five,* see Alice Stone Nakhimovsky, *Russian-Jewish Literature and Identity* (Baltimore: The Johns Hopkins University Press, 1992) 62-69.

11. Zhabotinskii, *Piatero* 209.

12. *Odesskie novosti,* August 19, 1917.

13. This parallel has also been noted by Iu. Shcheglov in his *Romany I. Il'fa i E. Petrova: sputnik chitatelia. «Zolotoi telenok»* (Wien: Wiener Slawistischer Almanach, 1991) 510.

14. *Odesskie novosti,* July 3, 1917.

15. *Odesskie novosti,* August 31, 1917.

16. "Shprintsa" belongs to Sholom Aleichem's cycle of stories, united by the narrator Tevye the milk-man. I have used the Russian edition of his collected works, *Sobranie sochinenii,* vol. 1 (Moscow: GIKhL, 1959) 562-79.

17. W. Cukerman, "The Odessan Myth and Idiom in Some Early Works of Odessa Writers," *Canadian American Slavic Studies* 14.1 (1980): 36-51.

18. Because this type of folklore and popular culture has not been collected and studied by scholars, I have used texts transcribed from tape recordings of local Odessa restaurant performers, such as, Arkadii Severnyi's "Old Odessa" concert. For the approximate dates of these songs, I have had to rely on memoirs of the time. The songs that figure in this section were apparently well known in the years, 1917-1922.

19. K. Paustovskii's fellow passengers sing this song in the train from Kiev to Odessa around 1918. K Paustovskii, *Sobranie sochinenii. Povest' o zhizni,* vol. 4 (Moscow: Khudozhestvennaia literatura, 1982) 673.

20. Utesov recalls this performance forty years later. Although he does not quote this song, he describes it euphemistically: "So, for example, when in fairly frivolous couplets and in accordance with the taste of those days, I sang of the old lady robbed by bandits on Deribasovskaiia Street, the couplets were very vividly perceived and remembered, because towards the end of the war, there were a fair number of robberies in Odessa. L. Utesov, *S pesnei po zhizni* (Moscow: Iskusstvo, 1961) 67.

21. In the late 1920s, thanks to Utesov, who included it in the repertoire of his jazz orchestra in 1928, this underground song became popular throughout the Soviet Union. At that time Utesov was attacked by critics for romanticizing bandits. Even in 1961 he still had to to answer to complaints that he was promoting bandits on stage. Utesov, *S pesnei po zhizni* 147-148. The artist, Iu. Annenkov, quotes the entire text of this song in his novel published in emigration under the pseudonym Temiriazev, *Povest' o pustiakakh* (Berlin: Petropolis) 176-78.

22. Il'ia Sel'vinskii, *Izbrannye proizvedeniia* (Leningrad: Sovetskii pisatel', 1972) 66-69.

23. This attitude in the *Odessa Stories* has been noted by Babel's critics. See Patricia Carden, *The Art of Isaac Babel* (Ithaca: Cornell University Press, 1972) 84-85; Nakhimovsky 97-102.

24. V. Margulies, *Ognennye gody* (Berlin: Manfred, 1923) 180.

25. L. Nikulin, "Isaak Babel'"in *Vospominaniia o Babele* (Moskva: Knizhnaia palata, 1989) 137.

26. Abraham T'homi, *Between Darkness and Dawn* (New York: Bloch Publishing, 1986) 76-77.

27. L. Utesov, "Moia Odessa," *Moskva* 9 (1964): 136-38.

28. The Odessa native, historian S. Borovoi, credits Mishka Iaponchik and his fellow bandits with the important role of preventing anti-Jewish pogroms during the Civil War in Odessa. See Saul Borovoi, *Vospominaniia* (Moscow/Jerusalem, 1993) 75-76.

29. Don-Aminado, *Na tret'em puti* (Moscow: Kniga, 1991) 223-24.

30. Utesov, "Moia Odessa," 138; A. L'vov, *Utolenie pechal'iu* (Vremia i my, 1983) 50-51.

31. Both Mishka Iaponchik's and the Cheka's letters are quoted in their entirety in Margulies 178-82.

32. Margulies 145.

Yuri K. Shcheglov (essay date fall 1994)

SOURCE: Shcheglov, Yuri K. "Some Themes and Archetypes in Babel''s *Red Cavalry*." *Slavic Review* 53, no. 3 (fall 1994): 653-70.

[*In the following essay, Shcheglov identifies the literary archetypes that Babel employs in his story "My First Goose," from* Red Cavalry.]

It is an established fact that the so-called "Southern" (mainly Odessa-based) school of writers enriched Soviet literature of the 1920s with a number of "European" dimensions neglected by the then dominant Russian realist tradition, such as (to name but a few) intertextuality, a focus on language and style, and a sharpened sensitivity to plot and composition. It can be said that in Babel' criticism some of these aspects are just beginning to receive the full measure of attention that they merit. However, the rich fabric of Russian and western cultural subtexts in Babel''s prose and its intricate relationships with various literary and mythological prototypes remain largely unexplored. Among recent studies that begin to fill this gap, the forthcoming monograph in Russian by Yampolsky and Zholkovsky deserves special mention as one of the most comprehensive to date.

The diversity of functions of archetypal and literary motifs utilized by different members of the "Southern" school is readily apparent. While some of them (like Il'f and Petrov) made ample and ostensible use of such elements to parody and debunk traditional "literariness," others (like Valentin Kataev) imbued them with marxist content in endeavors to create Soviet action prose à la Stevenson or Mark Twain; still others (such as Babel' and Olesha) used mythological and literary sources subtly, unobtrusively and highly selectively,

building up subliminal support for their philosophical messages, thematic idiosyncrasies or personal myths. It is this last case that I will demonstrate with regard to one of the most popular stories of Babel's *Konarmiia* (*Red Cavalry*), "My First Goose." First, however, a brief reminder of some relevant elements of Babel's thematic core is in order.

One can argue that the narrator of *Red Cavalry,* Kirill Vasil'evich Liutov, is not endowed with the same unique and "dense" individuality as are the other characters in the book, even those who are minor and episodical. Much of the time he appears as a more or less formal figure, subject to various elements of authorial voice and outlook. In this Liutov resembles those nominal narrators who are not given a voice noticeably distinct from the author's. We tend to be oblivious of their mediatorial presence, let alone of their names and occupations: who remembers such characters of Russian fiction as Anton Lavrent'evich (*The Possessed*) or Colonel I. L. P. ("The Shot")? Only occasionally does Liutov thicken from a purely functional figure into a semblance of a hero in his own right. Then we begin to see that, although he may not possess a character so colorful or sharply etched as most heroes of *Red Cavalry,* he at least has a *problem* that isolates him from the Cossacks at the same time as it affiliates him with another family of heroes—the troubled Soviet intellectuals of the revolutionary era, such as Olesha's Nikolai Kavalerov. As we know, these characters' feelings with respect to the revolution are irreconcilably split between the desire to play an active role in the creation of a new world and the inability to part with the humanitarian and cultural "superstitions" that they have inherited from the past.

In Liutov's case this dilemma is complicated by his ethnic and cultural background. As critics point out, the narrator of *Red Cavalry* "is caught between these groups as he tries to define his position in relation to the humanist tradition of his Jewish heritage and the new values of the Revolution."[1] As Markish aptly has remarked, while Liutov must not be identified with the author, he is one of the author's halves—the Jewish one, "desperately wishing to join the other, revolutionary, Bolshevik one, but without losing the former." According to Markish, Liutov's desire to reconcile tradition and revolution is cerebral and coexists with an estranged and distant view of both. Heritage and novelty are "accepted and rejected simultaneously." The narrator depicts old-style Jewry with the cold preciseness of an aesthete, "often balancing on the brink of active hostility." Nor is he particularly sympathetic towards his bolshevik comrades, who often evoke in him "fear and bewilderment." It is this double allegiance combined with "a position of consistent and uncompromising nonconformism" that ensures a sharp and unbiased view of both sides that constitutes, for Markish, the main strength of *Red Cavalry,* which "was to be Babel''s greatest success, precisely because in no other work did he lean on both of his supports with such confidence and force."[2]

A somewhat different view of Babel''s/Liutov's duality figures in Lionel Trilling's introduction to the English translation of Babel''s works. Even though this critic has failed to discriminate between the author and his hero and rather incautiously quoted Babel''s stories about his allegedly unhappy and humiliated Odessa childhood as a reliable biographical source, the psychological invariants he sees in Babel' are quite relevant. One of Babel''s most persistent motivations, in Trilling's view, was his desire to be "submitted to a test, to be initiated."[3] Detached from the realities of life and painfully conscious of his own fragility and weakness ("spectacles on his nose and autumn in his heart"), Babel''s hero is fascinated by a world imbued with strength, boldness, passion, "sensual freedom," "conscienceless self-assertion," "animal grace," "simplicity," "directness," etc. To partake of this ideal mode of living (whether in Budennyi's Red Cavalry or in the world of old Odessa gangsters), Babel''s hero has to learn violence, to prove to himself and others his ability to commit violent acts, since they are inseparable from the "genuine life" that he craves. However, violence does not come easily to him; the other half of his being is attracted by a wholly different ideal of "realness," whose features—spirituality, compassion, sacrificial humility, "the denial of the pride of the glory of the flesh"—are embodied in such figures as the delicate little sage, Gedali, or the pathetic and helpless Christ in the fresco by Pan Apolek (**"In St. Valentine's Church"**). Concluded Trilling, "The opposition of these two images made his art—but it was not a dialectic that his Russia could permit."[4]

In discussing the ingredients of Babel''s involvement with the revolution, we must not forget *curiosity,* which the writer's biographers and acquaintances unanimously point to as the most salient personal feature of Babel', the "main moving force" of his life.[5] At times Babel''s curiosity is difficult to distinguish from his trademark as seen by Trilling, the "necessity of submitting to [a] test." Falen correctly has pointed out this thirst for experience: "For Babel' the key to both life and art is immersion in experience . . . ***Red Cavalry*** reflects his continuing desire to subject the individualism and self-absorption of the middle-class intellectual to the test of living . . . Almost all of the reminiscences . . . emphasize his insatiable curiosity about life in the raw."[6] Similarly, Carden has merged the two motivations together by explaining Babel''s enlistment in the army as his "curiosity and desire to experience everything from which he had been excluded by the circumstances of his upbringing."[7] However, there need not be a link between the writer's curiosity and his presumed inferiority complex, his need of self-testing, etc. It appears from memoirs about Babel' that he was as interested in

watching and listening as he was in being directly involved in life, and that he appreciated conversations with talkative old women and housekeepers no less avidly than the company of romantic heroes like Betal Kalmykov.[8] Obviously, curiosity was an integral part of that wise joie de vivre which, according to the painter Valentina Khodasevich, made Babel' "an adornment of life for anyone who was lucky enough to know him."[9] The willingness of a curious Babel' to penetrate forbidden and dangerous zones of life is amply illustrated by biographical data—from his early years when the future author of ***Odessa Stories*** took up his quarters at the center of Moldavanka, the district of mob hangouts,[10] to his last years, when he played with fire visiting the "militiamen," as he conspiratorially called the entourage of the chief of the secret police Ezhov, in order, in his words, "to sniff out what is brewing."[11]

It is not irrelevant for this analysis to know to what extent Babel''s curiosity is reflected in his heroes, specifically Liutov. Since Liutov is not defined with any finality and assumes various faculties and features of his creator (such as the knowledge of French in **"Berestechko"**), it would not be unreasonable to credit him with some degree of curiosity as well. And we find it in **"Italian Sunshine"**: the moment that his roommate, the anarchist Sidorov, leaves the room, Liutov hurries to his desk, with trembling hands turns the pages of his books, avidly reads another man's letter . . . It is probably also curiosity that impels Liutov to wander through the curved streets of old Berestechko, peering at the unprepossessing remains of local antiquity and picking up century-old letters, rather than to attend a propaganda meeting organized by his Red Cavalry comrades. Would it not also be natural to assume some of Babel''s curiosity in the intellectual Liutov, if it can be observed even in some of the Cossacks, who explain their violence by a passion for experimentation: "You see, I want to get to know what life really is, what life's like down our way" (**"The Life of Pavlichenko"**)?

Although this article is not the place for a full synopsis of the definitions proposed by Babel' scholars regarding his real-life and literary persona or the main themes of his work, it can be said by way of summing up that Babel''s prose is seen by most critics as highly ambivalent with respect to all values, including the revolution and other manifestations of "raw," elemental life. On the one hand, attraction alternates or mingles with revulsion, the admiration for the revolution's force and genuineness is mixed with horror at its cruelty and dirt. On the other, Liutov's desire to be admitted to the epicenter of this "genuine life" as a spontaneous and equal participant blends with the pathos of an explorer and experimenter, moved by sheer intellectual curiosity and preserving the attitude of a detached viewer even in the midst of turbulent events.

Babel''s **"My First Goose"** displays this ambivalence with exemplary clarity. It is a story of a desire and its fulfillment, enclosed between those two fundamental emotions of the Soviet intellectual of the 1920s, envy and remorse. *Zavist'*, "envy" (towards the new masters of life) and *sovest'*, "conscience" (its pangs) mark the initial and final points of the plot. No less symptomatic is the chain of events connecting them—the hero's mimicry and oppression of kindred human beings in order to get close to those in power, to be invited to their meal. As Carden justly has pointed out, the *bespectacled* old woman whom Liutov pushes in the chest is a creature of the same species as himself, who calls for his sympathy but is rejected because he wants to please the Cossacks.[12] (This old woman has a somewhat different kinship at another level of the story, as I shall try to show later.)

"My First Goose" is a paradigmatic text in more ways than one. Liutov's two encounters—first with the dazzling Savitskii and then with the ruthless and hostile warriors by the fire—illustrate the insoluble duality not only of the hero but of the new reality itself in which there are two inseparable and constantly overlapping facets that can roughly be called "romantic" and "barbaric." This is a dilemma confronted by many heroes of early Soviet fiction who are spontaneously drawn to the revolution yet are dismayed by the discrepancy between the realm of its enthusiastic theorists, poets and visionaries; and that of barbarians, fanatics, dullards or bureaucrats who violently and thoughtlessly translate exciting ideals into disappointing realities. This theme has a wide spectrum of variations in the Soviet fiction dealing with the revolution and its aftermath, socialism; apart from **"My First Goose,"** we recognize it in Olesha's *Envy* in which Kavalerov may secretly desire to join the charismatic Andrei Babichev but is repelled by the narrow-minded brutality of his disciple, Volodia Makarov. This duality of the revolution is famously presented in Sholokhov's *Quiet Flows the Don,* as well as in Pasternak's *Doctor Zhivago,* in the novels of Il'f and Petrov[13] and in other major works of Soviet fiction.

I shall not discuss in detail how this duality of the new world and the ambiguous stance of the *Red Cavalry* narrator translate into the complex imagery and plot of **"My First Goose"** (these more explicit layers of the story's structure have been rather extensively studied). Instead, I shall dwell upon just one or two points which may have some relevance for my immediate topic.

Reading the story in a sound realistic key (that is, temporarily leaving aside its rich literary and archetypal subtext), one cannot fail to notice that the narrator deliberately treats his hosts to a rather coarse, slapstick show. The theatricality of his performance is manifest from the sheer redundancy of the sword that Liutov picks up from the ground to no apparent use, as well as

from the exaggerated belligerence of his gesticulation and speech, rather comic in a little, bespectacled civilian addressing an old woman, yet accepted at face value by his viewers.[14] Liutov's mimicry and calculated simulation as a means of recognition distinguishes him rather sharply from the majority of the intelligentsia heroes of early Soviet fiction, both those who are locked in a love-hate relationship with the revolution and those who just hate it but feign loyalty for survival. Suffice it to compare Liutov with Olesha's Kavalerov, whose behavior in a similar context, whether demanding admission to the Soviet aviation parade or showering venomous philippics upon his nemesis, Andrei Babichev, is always passionate and straightforward. Liutov's vacillation between his readiness to exploit the simplicity of the Red Cavalry heroes, to gain their favors by cunning, on the one hand, and his secret envy for the "flower and iron of their youth," on the other, is a more complex stance. It reminds us not so much of the dismayed intellectuals of a Kavalerov type as of the wise, thoroughly experienced Ostap Bender of the last part of *The Golden Calf,* who, when confronted with the army of enthusiastic builders of the great Turksib railway, is not sure which he desires more, to continue playing his picaresque tricks and manipulating their still rather simple souls for his personal gain, or to lay down his arms and tearfully beg for admission into their happy community.

Another curious detail in the surface plot of **"My First Goose"** is the role played by Lenin's name and text as a form of lingua franca which functions as the final mediator between Liutov and the Cossacks after they have been sufficiently "mollified" by his cavalier treatment of the landlady. In early Soviet mythology the name "Lenin" tends to figure as a password that overcomes distances and class/race barriers (e.g. in Vsevolod Ivanov's *Armored Train 14-69* where the partisans intone the word "Lenin" to get their message across to their American prisoner; in Nikolai Tikhonov's poem, "Sami," etc.). As many other details of the story, this one has an obvious realistic motivation, since Lenin's persona embraced the contrasting halves of the revolution, both theory and practice, and appealed to individuals otherwise divided, educated fellow travelers and brutal bolshevik warriors.[15] At the same time, serving as a kind of magic "sesame," the name preserves a subdued aura of mystique that agrees well with the mythologizing, ritualistic and fairy-tale-like connotations of the story.

Although more could be said about the plot, symbolism and other aspects of **"My First Goose,"** I shall now focus on my main topic, its *archetypal* patterns, that is, literary motifs of ancient, ritualistic and mythological origin which serve as a kind of concealed amplifier enhancing the paradigmatic effect of the story's events. The narrator's ambivalent attitude to the Red Cavalry warriors obviously influenced the selection of these archetypes, which fall into two categories. For that part of the narrator's soul which craves to be tested and accepted into the Cossack brotherhood, the appropriate archetypal counterpart is *Initiation* with its various ritualistic concomitants. The word "initiation" has been used previously in Babel' criticism (by Trilling, Andrew and others), but in a more figurative than terminological sense, that is, without sufficient awareness of those features in **Red Cavalry** which actually reflect the traditional ordeals that adolescents had to undergo to become full-fledged members of their society.

For the other half of his hero's persona, which responds to the revolution with a mixture of intellectual curiosity, estrangement, fear, revulsion and mimicry, Babel' drew not so much on ritualistic sources as on legendary and literary ones; more specifically, on motifs that have to do with *Visiting the Otherworld*. This is a well known topos whose protagonist is an individualist, an outsider who undertakes a journey to forbidden regions to obtain something for himself—an object, a human being, a benefit, a piece of arcane wisdom, etc. To achieve his objective, the hero may have to play the games of the inhabitants of the otherworld, to spy out their secrets, to use stratagems, to cheat and to flee for his life.

Since the initiation rites also imply a journey to the country of the dead, some degree of overlap between the two sets of archetypal motifs is to be expected. However, each of the two groups includes some motifs that are distinctly its own, i.e., either initiatory or demonic par excellence. More importantly, even identical motifs may acquire different overtones depending on which set is activated: with *Initiation* the stress is likely to be on the hero's desire to be assimilated, to submit to ordeals, to fraternize with his new companions and to obey his seniors; while *Visiting the Otherworld* will highlight the dangers and risks of the enterprise, that realm's basic viciousness and hostility to man, and the hero's independence.

To identify initiatory and otherworldly patterns in Babel''s story, I will draw relevant parallels from artistic and literary works rather than from actual myths and rituals, focusing on those texts in which these motifs either appear in their original form or are adapted ("displaced") in more or less recurrent and familiar ways. For *Visiting the Otherworld,* the list of exemplary works, rather predictably headed by Dante's *Divine Comedy* and Gogol''s "The Lost Letter," will include such Russian Romantic stories as Karamzin's "The Isle of Bornholm" and Lermontov's "Taman'." Besides sharing with **"My First Goose"** several collateral details of plot and description, these two narratives resemble Babel''s story in that each features a curious intruder who tries to explore an alien, closed world but who finds it difficult to gain access to it and to establish a common language with its inhabitants. *Initiation* is exemplified by a Spanish picaresque novel and some modern American short stories. Besides these "model" texts, I will also consider several other works of art and fiction and, occasionally, some "raw" anthropological data. Needless to say, this miniature anthology of parallels to **"My First Goose"** is open and can be expanded by additional illustrations from world literature, art and mythology.

After these somewhat prolonged preliminaries, let me recapitulate the motifs in **"My First Goose"** that can be related to one or both archetype clusters:

1) *Sunset.* The sun is setting as the narrator of **"My First Goose"** is led to the lodging of the Cossacks: "The dying sun . . . was giving up its roseate ghost to the skies." In the romantic tradition twilight and the evening landscape constitute a borderline chronotope in which the otherworldly is at its closest to the terrestrial. Whenever a hero ventures into a domain of dark forces, the transition usually takes place in the ambiguous light of the setting sun, at that disturbing and nostalgic hour when the friendly luminary is quickly departing the scene, leaving man alone and helpless in the face of the mysterious forces of the night. The prototype of all such scenes may well be the opening passage of Dante's *Inferno*: "Guardai in alto e vidi le sue spalle / vestite già de' raggi del planeta / che mena dritto altrui per ogni calle" (I.16-18) and "Lo giorno se n'andava, e l'aere bruno / toglieva li animai che sono in terra / da le fatiche loro . . ." (II.1-3). Abundant illustrations are provided by romanticism and the gothic genres. In Gogol''s "Vii" the wanderers arrive at the sinister wayside farm when "the sky was already quite dark, and only a red gleam lingered on the western horizon."[16] In "The Lost Letter" "the sun had set; here and there streaks of red glowed in the sky . . . The farther they went, the darker it grew";[17] in "St. John's Eve" "the sun was gone. There was only a streak of red on one side of the sky. And that, too, was fading. It turned colder";[18] in "A Bewitched Place" "the sun had begun to set."[19] In Radcliffe's *The Mysteries of Udolpho* the macabre castle that the heroine is approaching is "lighted up by the setting sun" and "as she gazed, the light died away on its walls" (II.5). In Lüdwig Tieck's tale "The Blond Ekbert" the traveler meets a mysterious old woman in the dusk and accompanies her to her hut as night falls; a similar evening encounter with an otherworldly stranger occurs in his "Runenberg." A picture of twilight—the last rays of light on the snowy summits, darkness and cold gradually descending on the mountainous landscape—unfolds in Bram Stoker's *Dracula* as the hero nears his destination, the fateful castle, in a coach (chap. 1). The demonic visitor in Bulgakov's *The Master and Margarita* enters Moscow "at the hour of an incredibly hot sunset" when "the windowpanes dazzlingly reflected the fragmented sun that was departing from Mikhail Alexandrovich forever" (chap. 1). Lermontov's "Taman'" slightly deviates from the stereotype in that the narrator

drives up to his new lodging late at night by moonlight. On the whole, however, the constancy of the motif is so obvious that no further examples need be cited.

2) *The frightened guide.* Babel''s narrator is led to the Cossacks' camp by the quartermaster. He warns Liutov of the danger and hints at a possible way of averting it: "Nuisance with specs. Can't do anything to stop it, either. Not a life for the brainy type here. But you go and mess up a lady, and a good lady too, and you'll have the boys patting you on the back." Having introduced the novice to the Cossacks, "the quartermaster, purple in the face, left us without looking back." Narratives with "infernal" overtones often include guides who conduct the heroes to the border of the other world but refuse to accompany them further, sometimes with signs of superstitious fear: "My guide, afraid of he knew not what, implored me to return to the village . . . I looked back, but the boy, my guide, had disappeared" ("The Isle of Bornholm"). "Here our ways must part," says the mysterious companion who has led Christian to the foot of the mountain towards which the latter is attracted by a mysterious force (Tieck, "Runenberg"). An inferno metaphor and the figure of a guide deserting his protégés can be found in *Dead Souls* meandering through the rooms of government offices, Chichikov and Manilov are helped by a civil servant ironically compared to Virgil: "He took them to the president's office, in which . . . sat the president in solitary majesty, like the sun. In this place the new Virgil was so overawed that he did not venture to set his foot in it, but turned back, displaying his back worn as threadbare as a bit of matting and with a hen's feather sticking to it" (chap. 7).

Such moments as the hero's parting with the normal world, abandoning the warmth and security of human company, are quite often highlighted, as are actions that block the hero's way back to safety. Sometimes, as in Babel''s story, the guide literally hands over his charge to his new, ghostly hosts. The vehicle departs from the scene and the newcomer is left alone with his belongings whose bulk, impeding his mobility, ties him to the place. In Stoker's novel the coach driver unloads the passenger's luggage as the carriage sent for him from the castle arrives (cf. "The quartermaster . . . set my little trunk down on the ground"), then hurriedly leaves; the young man "felt a strange chill, and a lonely feeling came over me" (*Dracula,* chap. 1). Pechorin tells his orderly to "unload the trunk and let the cabby go" ("Taman'"). The goat who has brought Ruprecht to the Sabbath "descended low, almost to the earth, and, riding me right up to the crowd, he suddenly tipped me off to the ground . . . and disappeared" (Valerii Briusov, *The Fiery Angel,* chap. 2).

Warnings and advice can come from the guide or other persons whom the traveler meets before embarking on his journey. "We don't go there, and God knows what is going on there," says the boy in "The Isle of Bornholm." "There is one other place, sir, but you wouldn't fancy it. Unwholesome, it is" ("Taman'"). In *Dracula* it is the frightened looks of the peasants and the passengers in the coach that serve as a warning to Harker of the sinister nature of his destination. In Gogol''s "The Lost Letter" the grandfather receives his itinerary to hell from the innkeeper, who, "saying this . . . went off to his corner and would not say another word."[20] Cf. "the quartermaster, purple in the face, left us without looking back."

3) *The inhospitable people by the fire.* In the yard where Liutov is left by the quartermaster "the Cossacks were sitting, shaving one another." Supper is being prepared near by: "Near the hut, on a brick stove, stood a cauldron in which pork was cooking. The steam that rose from it was like the far-off smoke of home in the village." The next time that we see them the Cossacks are "already sitting around their cauldron . . . motionless, stiff as priests." Figures seated around the fire remind us of Goethe's *Faust* where participants of the Walpurgisnacht sit by numerous fires (Mephistopheles to Faust: "Einhundert Feuer brennen in der Reihe . . . Komm nur! von Feuer gehen wir zu Feuer . . .") and of "The Lost Letter": "Only now [Grandad] saw that there were people sitting around a fire . . ." The Cossacks' less than friendly response to Liutov's military salute is close to the gogolian scene in that in neither case do the hosts deign to look at the novice, let alone speak with him:[21]

> So Grandad tossed off a low bow, saying: 'God help you, good people!' No one nodded his head; they all sat in silence and kept dropping something into the fire . . . No one of them glanced at him . . . To this speech, too, there was not a word. But one of the pig-faces thrust a hot brand straight into Grandad's face . . .[22]

Such unanimous, as if by agreement, failure to notice a newcomer may originate either from the hostility and disgust that the dead are known to feel for the living[23] or from the ritualistic notion that the novice is still "unborn" and therefore "invisible" until he is initiated. The latter explanation seems to be more applicable to "The Fourth Day Out from Santa Cruz" by Paul Bowles, a story with no noticeable infernal overtones (see below, 7), while **"My First Goose,"** with its double set of background archetypes, is open to both kinds of associations (see below, 9).

4) *Harassment.* Disregarding Liutov's advances, the Cossacks keep harassing him, throw out his little trunk and tread on his feet. Treating novices in this manner is a familiar fact of army and school life, where the infamous customs of "zuck" and "grandfatherism" (hazing) most probably go back to the ritual harassment and torture that are known from studies on initiation. Typical

of all such scenes are disparaging remarks about the novice's hothouse upbringing, in which the tutors or elders often take the lead: "A new one! From the town! Mommy's son!" or "A little nobleman! Brought up on candies!" (Nikolai Pomialovskii, *Sketches from the Seminary*; Ivan Kushchevskii, *Nikolai Negorev*). Savitskii's taunt "You are one of those kinderbalsams" clearly continues the same tradition. Mocking references to the novice's home and the upbringing he has received there reflect one of the central notions of initiation, a young man's "passing from his mother and the women-folk into the society of the warriors of his tribe."[24] It is therefore no accident that harassment and *derisory references* to the youngster's home are often complemented by another expression of the same archetypal idea, the novice's *longing* for his home. We find this *Heimweh* motif immediately following the mockery in both Russian seminary tales quoted above, as well as in **"My First Goose"**: "The steam that rose from [the pork] was like the far-off smoke of home in the village, and it mingled hunger with desperate loneliness in my head."

5) *Indecent gestures and sounds.* Harassments that the hero has to endure are manifold. In Grimmelshausen's *Simplizissimus* the novice suffers from hunger and is subjected to distasteful practical jokes, when his new companions contrive to make him smell malodorous emissions of their bowels (I.28). This leads us to the gestures of the young Cossack in Babel's story: "He turned his back on me and with remarkable skill emitted a series of shameful noises." The devil's delight in impudent behavior, such as showing his backside, offering it for kisses, etc., is well known.[25] In one of Hieronimus Bosch's paintings a beautiful woman looks at her mirror reflection in the devil's behind. In Briusov's *The Fiery Angel* a newcomer at the Sabbath is required to kiss the devil's backside, "black and emitting a nauseating odor, but yet strangely reminiscent of a human face" (chap. 2). Such acts, in which the hind quarters perform functions normally reserved for the face, are easily explained in terms of "invertedness," another well known characteristic of the underworld.[26] The "backside = face" equation is implied in Nabokov's commentary on Chichikov, whose figure, following Merezhkovskii, he interprets in demonic terms: "Chichikov . . . ecstatically hitting his chubby behind—*his real face*—with the pink heel of his bare foot"[27] (my emphasis). This paradigmatic exchange of roles between face and backside in demonic behavior is evoked in Babel's story by their conspicuous syntagmatic juxtaposition: "A lad with a beautiful Ryazan *face*. . . . turned his *back* on me," etc.

The blond Cossack's pranks recall to us the memorable demon in Dante who "made a trumpet out of his behind" ("ed egli avea del cul fatto trombetta"; *Inferno* XXI.139). This line from Dante serves as an associative link between the behavior of the young Cossack (which, let it be noted in passing, is also described metaphorically, although with a different instrument as vehicle: "To your guns—number double-zero . . . , running fire") and yet another type of activity frequently attributed to demonic creatures: those rather widespread scenes in art and literature where demons use the body (their own, other people's, animals') and its various parts to perform music. Satan's music is body music par excellence. Gogol''s musicians in hell "beat on their cheeks with their fists as if they were tambourines, and whistled with their noses as if they were horns."[28] In Grimmelshausen's novel the devils "trumpeted with their noses till the whole wood resounded therewith"; other musicians at the sabbath play on adders, cats, bitches, horses' skulls, etc. (*Simplizissimus* II.17). A contemporary caricature of Luther presents his body as a bagpipe played by Satan; his nose has the shape of a flute. The Walpurgisnacht musicians mentioned in Goethe's *Faust*—crickets and frogs—presumably use their own bodies as instruments. Some Bosch paintings feature a monster playing its own long nose as a trumpet ("The Hay-cart") and devils blowing into sinners' bodies as if they were wind instruments ("The Garden of Earthly Delights"); one of these sinners has a trumpet sticking from his anus. The elegance of those scenes in which the hind quarters rather than nose, lips or other parts do the job of wind instruments, is in their combination of two otherwise independent demonic features— "music performed on the body" and the previously mentioned "backside-face" inversion.

6) *The hero bespattered with faeces.* The meaning of the young Cossack's motions can be understood in light of yet another series of motifs, also related to the otherworld but this time from a primarily initiatory angle. Some of Liutov's ordeals are prefigured in the picaresque novel "The Story of a Rogue Called Don Pablos" by Francisco de Quevedo, a classic of Spanish baroque. The novel abounds in scenes more or less obviously related to the rites of initiation, including various forms of metaphorical death and rebirth. In chapter 5, as Pablos enrolls in a university, a crowd of fellow students for no visible reason subjects him to a series of cruel jokes. Exclaiming, "This Lazarus must be ready for raising from the dead judging by the way he smells," these new companions surround Pablos and assiduously spit and blow their noses all over him, so that in the end "I was snow-white from head to foot" with saliva and mucus.[29] This procedure is followed by an even more nauseating one: "That crowd of devils let out such a shout that it made me dizzy, and I, to judge from the way they had emptied their stomachs all over me, decided they must use new students as a form of purge to save going to the doctor or druggist." Taking flight, the hero is pursued and kicked by everyone he encounters on his way home. But this is not the end of his calvary: when he returns home the servants, feigning friendly

concern, defecate into his bed at night. Significantly, when these ritualistic tortures are over, peace and harmony sets in between the hero and his tormentors: "We all became friends and from then on all of us in the house lived together like brothers, and neither in class nor on the campus did anyone trouble me again."

Excrement, defecation and urination often figure in initiation rituals and are not uncommon as attributes of the lower world, presumably symbolizing death and decomposition. In some versions of Russian tales Baba Iaga has a "shit leg" (*govnianaia noga*) instead of her proverbial "bone leg." In some initiatory traditions neophites were subjected to loathsome procedures: "they had to drink the urine of their mentor, etc. They were put into a pit filled with excrement and water, bespattered with animals' faeces . . . They had to endure and overcome disgust as well as pain."[30]

7) *"When in Rome, do as the Romans do." Slaughtering birds and animals.* Having endured these trials and fraternized with the students and servants, Pablos decides that he must stick to the same norms of behavior as those around him. In fulfillment of this plan, "I resolved to become a rogue among rogues and to better them if possible . . . First of all I passed a death sentence on all the pigs that wandered into the house, and on all the housekeeper's chickens who strayed from their coop into my room" (chap. 6). We see that both in Quevedo's novel and in Babel''s story the novice's harassment with nauseating body emissions is followed by his hunt after domestic animals and fowl. It is known that in some tribes initiatory tests included killing an enemy, a successful hunt, rapine or cattle stealing, acts "assimilating the members of the warrior band to carnivora." In Sparta an adolescent was sent away to live for a whole year on what he could steal.[31] If the killing of geese, chickens and pigs by Pablos and Liutov can indeed be regarded as a reflection of these ancient customs, Babel''s hero appears to be even closer to the ritualistic prototype than Quevedo's picaro, the goose-killing in the former taking place as part of the test itself, rather than after its successful conclusion, as in the latter.

Several parallels with **"My First Goose"** in "The Fourth Day Out from Santa Cruz" by Paul Bowles are particularly valuable since there are no visible traces of Babel''s direct influence on the American author. The story is placed in the "Initiation" section of Evans and Finestone's anthology of literary archetypes.

> Members of the ship's crew refuse to speak with the new scullery boy Ramon, do not invite him to their meals, give no sign of recognition when he meets them in the port, in short, "behave as if he did not exist." He decides to change this state of affairs at any cost. One day in the open sea he sees a group of sailors at the stern amusing themselves with the plight of a bird fly-

ing after the boat. The exhausted bird desperately wants to land on the deck but is afraid of the people. The sailors make bets on whether the bird will make it or perish. "Ramon's first thought was to tell the men to step back a little from the rail so that the bird might have the courage to land," but then he thinks better of it, considering the ridicule that would have been directed at him for such sentimentality. He runs to the galley, brings the ship's cat and shows him the bird. The animal lies in wait for the bird and leaps at it as it tries to land; the men watch with fascination; seeing the futility of its efforts, the bird stops flying and falls to the sea. The sailors pay their bets; one of them brings from his cabin a bottle of cognac and fills glasses, offering one of them to Ramon: "Have some?"

The killing of a domestic animal takes place in Richard Wright's story "The Man Who Was Almost a Man," which Evans and Finestone also classify as initiatory. The young hero secretly buys a gun and, while trying to shoot, unintentionally kills a horse. When the adults tell him he will have to work two years to compensate the horse's owner, he jumps on a cargo train to flee "away, away to somewhere, somewhere where he could be a man . . ." These parallels support the view that Liutov's actions regarding the goose and the landlady have initiatory overtones and provide a ritualistic motivation for his theatrically exaggerated gestures, in addition to his "realistic" mimicry and desire to impress his none too sophisticated hosts.[32]

8) *The blind old woman with a bird.* Blindness is one of the best known features of Baba Iaga, the guardian of the realm of the dead.[33] More generally, blindness in one or both eyes is a frequent characteristic of various types of otherworld and borderline creatures.[34] One such figure is the blind boy in "Taman'," about whom Pechorin—not without reason, considering the sinister nature of the place—remarks, "I confess I am strongly prejudiced against the blind, one-eyed, deaf, dumb, legless, armless, hunch-backed and so on." On the other hand, the "diffused whites of her purblind eyes" that the woman raises to Liutov evoke both initiation and the realm of the dead since "white [in which some tribes paint neophites, rubbing it, among other parts, over the eyes] is the color of death and invisibility." Other facets of initiation may also apply, such as the neophite demanding and eating Iaga's food in many folktales and rites.[35] As "hostess" of the otherworld (note Babel''s use of the terminological *khoziaika*), Iaga presides over the animal kingdom; wise or prophetic birds quite often accompany demonic female figures in literature and folklore. In Tieck's "The Blond Ekbert" the heroine runs away from such a woman, stealing and eventually killing her bird, which later reappears as the symbol of her guilty conscience (the killing of a bird is generally considered a crime that brings disaster and requires expiation—see *The Ancient Mariner*). The standard features of Iaga's residence in Russian folklore are a hut, a yard, a fence, a gate—all of which are present in Ba-

bel''s story. Another intriguing attribute of the old woman in the latter is spinning ("I . . . went out to the landlady who was spinning on the porch"), a detail rich in mythological connotations, including otherworldly ones: "Yarn and spinning are often associated with the hostess of the lower world."[36]

9) *Ceremony.* "They sat motionless, stiff as heathen priests, and did not look at the goose." This comparison of the Cossacks to priests overtly points to the ritualistic nature of the entire proceeding and has been noticed by commentators.[37] Ceremonial overtones of the Cossacks' behavior are no less obvious in their *not looking* at the goose (or at Liutov), despite the fact that the hero has already accomplished his anti-feat and aroused their sympathetic attention. Why not look? Probably because at this point it is still too *early* to look. Had the Cossacks been overtly watching and discussing Liutov's manipulations with the bird, their conduct would have been little more than just natural and "realistic." However, their actions, as well as Liutov's, have an archetypal facet that imposes a certain amount of ceremony; recognition does not come spontaneously and at once but unfolds in discrete stages following each other in a fixed order. Up to a certain point the warriors "do not see" the novice; after his successful endurance of trials, they will of course begin "to see" him, but not before some final formalities—such as a verbal statement—are performed ("The lad's all right . . . Hey, brother, come down and feed with us . . .").

Having passed the test, the hero reads the newspaper "loudly, like a triumphant man hard of hearing," i.e., he adopts the ceremonious manner of his new comrades, participating with them in the celebration of his transition to a new status. Not only ritualistically solemn, Liutov's metaphorical deafness is yet another hint at his temporary association with the realm of death, whose inhabitants and visitors are prone to sensory deficiencies.[38]

10) *Safe conduct.* In light of the previously mentioned motifs, it is possible to discern an archetypal aspect in Liutov's encounter with divisional commander Savitskii, who has been characterized at the "realistic" level as personifying the attractive, "romantic" facet of the revolution. A hero embarking on a journey to the otherworld can obtain a permission and a safe conduct from some supreme authority to whom those dangerous realms are subordinated. Thus, Dante and his guide often have to explain to the demons and other guardians of the lower world that their peregrination is authorized in the spheres "where they can what they want" ("Vuolsi cosí colà dove si puote / Ciò che si vuole, e piú non dimandare"; *Inferno* III.94-95). As a result of this warning, the devils and monsters, while doing their best to intimidate and hamper the strangers, stop well short of causing them direct physical harm. Something very

similar occurs in **"My First Goose"**: the Cossacks throw out the visitor's trunk as a substitute for the man, but do not actually touch its owner, protected by the quartermaster's announcement that "Comrade Savitskii's orders are that you're to take this chap in your billets, so no nonsense about it." The story's prologue is largely designed to create around Savitskii the aura of a powerful lord presiding over hosts of obedient subjects. This purpose is well served by the grandiose metaphors describing Savitskii's appearance as well as by his thunderous letter to the lesser commander, Ivan Chesnokov.

Besides the two motif clusters outlined above, I would like to point out another possible subtext of Babel''s story that stands in a different relation to it: not an archetypal "amplifier" of its events and images, but a contrasting version, outlining an alternative course of action under identical circumstances.

Maksim Gor'kii's forgotten story "On the Salt" ("Na soli") was published in "The Samara Newspaper" in 1895 and never reprinted until 1968.[39] It is possible, but not necessary, to conjecture that Gor'kii might have shown or told the story to Babel' at an early stage of their acquaintance. Comparing texts with a different treatment of similar themes or plots can make sense regardless of whether their authors were aware of each other's work, engaged in conscious dialogues or polemics, etc., for the stock of recurrent themes, *fabulas,* character types and other ready-made artistic paradigms that "exist" in the anonymous unwritten vocabulary of literature is far greater than it may appear. We should always be ready to allow for the possibility of their unrelated use and even independent generation by various writers.[40]

Gor'kii's hero and first-person narrator comes to look for a job to the salt mines of which he had heard horror stories as a place of back-breaking, unrewarding labor. The assortment of hoboes and jailbirds who work there meet the hero with hostility, shower him with insults and threats, tease him for his spectacles ("Hello, Glass-eyes!"), mockingly deny him access to the common meal ("With us, Maksims are not admitted to the kettle on the first day of work. With us, Maksims eat their own grub on the first day . . . Get the hell out of here!") and subject him to cruel jokes. In his despair the hero addresses them with an angry speech, calling on their conscience and declaring that "I am a human being just like them, that I too want to eat and must work, that I came to them as my equals:—We are all in the same boat,—I said to them,—and must understand each other . . ." In response the workers give him a handful of pennies and ask him to leave, saying he does not belong here. "Nothing will come out of it between you and us . . . Go your way and be thankful you have not been beaten up."

This story apparently does not contain initiatory or otherworldly subtexts, is four times longer than **"My First Goose"** and has limited artistic merit. However, the two narratives have enough common points (including eyeglasses and cauldron) to warrant comparison. The most salient difference between them is their protagonists' contrasting conducts in a basically similar situation. Gor'kii's characters, incorrigible idealists and romantics, respond to the world's evils and injustices with moral exhortations; if these have no effect, they turn to thundering denunciations or extreme, self-destructive acts (cf. the endings of *The Three* or *Foma Gordeev*). The "calculating wisdom of a snake" (Tiutchev: "zmeinoi mudrosti raschet"), to which Liutov has recourse, reflects a new age that has replaced the romantic norms of humanity and common sense with cynicism, violence and absurdity on an unprecedented scale. Open defiance is no longer a viable option, since it is incapable not only of changing the state of affairs but even of producing waves, leaving a trace, setting an example. Any relationships with the new system of power must take into consideration its essential impermeability to moral and rational discourse. Hence the predominance in the twentieth century of more indirect and sly forms of coping, such as mimicry, acting and overzealous conformism, used by many for survival under a repressive world order, and by others for its subtle, ironic debunking.

The latter has its classic examples in such characters as Hašek's Švejk, Erenburg's Julio Jurenito and Il'f and Petrov's Ostap Bender. In Babel''s **"Goose"** we encounter a hybrid case, where the hero is deeply ambivalent vis-à-vis the new order, is painfully conscious of the necessity to lie and dissimulate, yet does so out of motives that are ultimately idealistic and intellectual rather than either purely opportunistic or mocking and subversive. The conciseness and density of **"My First Goose,"** reinforced by its wealth of archetypal connotations, make this story an almost emblematic prototype of many works of later Soviet fiction that address analogous themes.

Notes

1. Carol Luplow, *Isaac Babel's Red Cavalry* (Ann Arbor: Ardis, 1982), 32.

2. S. Markish, "Russko-evreiskaia literatura i Isaak Babel'," in I. Babel', *Detstvo i drugie rasskazy* (Jerusalem: Biblioteka "Aliia," 1979), 332, 343.

3. Lionel Trilling, "Introduction," in Isaac Babel, *The Collected Short Stories* (New York: New American Library, 1975), 20.

4. *Ibid.,* 37.

5. A. N. Pirozhkova and N. N. Iurgeneva, eds., *Vospominaniia o Babele* (Moscow: Knizhnaia palata, 1989), 62, 64, 181, 198, 274, 289, etc.

6. James E. Falen, *Isaac Babel: Russian Master of the Short Story* (Knoxville: University of Tennessee Press, 1974), 126-27.

7. Patricia Carden, *The Art of Isaac Babel* (Ithaca: Cornell University Press, 1972), 11.

8. *Vospominaniia o Babele,* 62.

9. *Ibid.,* 63.

10. *Ibid.,* 15.

11. N. Mandel'shtam, *Vospominaniia* (Paris: YMCA-Press, 1970), I: 341.

12. Carden, 130-31. The analogies between Liutov and the landlady are also noticed by Andrew, who adds important nuances to their interpretation: "The narrator and the old woman are quite clearly linked: they both wear glasses, they are both pushed around . . . By pushing the Old Woman around, the narrator is rejecting what he sees of himself in her, he is deciding that *he* will not be an Eternal Victim." See Joseph Andrew, "Structure and Style in the Short Story: Babel's 'My First Goose'," *Occasional Papers* (Colchester: University of Essex Language Centre, 1974), 14: 18.

13. The relationship between the ideal and real, "earthly" socialism in Il'f and Petrov is discussed in Iu. K. Shcheglov, *Romany I. Il'fa i E. Petrova* (Wien: *Wiener Slawistischer Almanach,* Sonderband 26/1 and 26/2, 1990-91), 11-24.

14. In a similar manner the hero of Babel''s "My First Honorarium" (1928) wins a prostitute's personal sympathy and successfully passes his *sexual* initiation by making her believe a fictional story of his life (note the parallelism of titles).

15. Ironically, it is the same duality of Lenin that enables Liutov to maintain his inner distance: far from merging with his audience in a cathartic co-experience, he leaves it to the Cossacks to enjoy the sheer force and directness of Lenin's speech ("he goes and strikes at it straight off like a hen pecking at a grain") while secretly relishing Lenin's more recondite dialectics ("I read on and rejoiced, spying out exultingly the secret curve of Lenin's straight line"). The issue of "straight line" vs. "curve" in connection with Liutov's duality and with the compromise between him and the Cossacks is convincingly discussed by Andrew ("Structure and Style in the Short Story," 19).

16. Nikolai Gogol', *The Complete Tales,* ed. Leonard J. Kent (Chicago: University of Chicago Press, 1985), I: 136.

17. *Ibid.,* 79.

18. *Ibid.*, 40.

19. *Ibid.*, 199.

20. *Ibid.*, 82.

21. This scene seems to have been a persistent personal symbol in Babel''s life. It reappears with a somewhat different meaning in "Argamak," a story written several years after "My First Goose." "Every night I had the same dream. I am dashing along on Argamak at a fast trot. By the roadside *bonfires are burning,* the Cossacks are cooking their food. I ride past them, and they do not raise their eyes to me. Some salute, others pay no attention: they're not concerned with me. What's the meaning of all this? Their indifference means that there is nothing special about the way I ride. I ride like everybody else, so there's no point in looking at me. I gallop on my way and am happy" (my emphasis). Note the multiple *bonfires* around which the Cossacks are sitting—a more explicit parallel with the Walpurgisnacht scene in *Faust* than the single fire of "My First Goose."

22. Gogol', *The Complete Tales,* 83.

23. V. Ia. Propp, *Istoricheskie korni volshebnoi skazki* (Leningrad: Izd. LGU, 1946), 52-53.

24. Oliver Evans and Harry Finestone, eds., *The World of the Short Story: Archetypes in Action* (New York: Knopf, 1971), 446.

25. In two scenes of Goethe's *Faust* (part 1, sc. 6, with the witch; scene 14, with Faust) Mephistopheles "makes an indecent gesture" ("macht eine unanständige Gebärde"; "mit einer Gebärde"), provoking his partner's admiration in the former case, shock and disgust in the latter. The character of the gesture is not specified.

26. The inversion of human and earthly phenomena typical of the otherworld is discussed and illustrated in S. Iu. Nekliudov, "O krivom oborotne (k issledovaniiu mifologicheskoi semantiki fol'klornogo motiva)," in *Problemy slavianskoi etnografii* (Leningrad: Nauka, 1979); and in Iu. K. Shcheglov, "Dve variatsii na temu smerti i vozrozhdeniia: Chekhov, 'Skripka Rotshil'da' i 'Dama s sobachkoi,'" *Russian Language Journal* (1994, forthcoming).

27. Vladimir Nabokov, *Nikolai Gogol* (New York: New Directions, 1961), 71.

28. Gogol', *The Complete Tales,* 84.

29. White in some initiatory rites is the color of a neophyte who is forcibly painted white from head to toe; white represents blindness and invisibility; see Propp, *Istoricheskie korni volshebnoi skazki,* 60.

30. *Ibid.,* 58, 75.

31. Mircea Eliade, *Rites and Symbols of Initiation* (New York: Harper Torchbooks, 1975), 81, 83, 109.

32. In Wright's story the actual shooting of the horse is preceded by a long episode of buying the gun. The instrument of initiation is thereby "enlarged," the reader's attention is drawn to it, its presentation is "prolonged." Would it not be right to see a similar function in the sword episode of Babel''s story? The narrator picks up the sword without any practical need, just for the sake of pomp (he does not use it to kill the goose). Again, we have explained it "realistically" as showing off but it may also pertain to a ritualistic archetype.

33. Propp, *Istoricheskie korni volshebnoi skazki,* 58-59.

34. See Nekliudov, "O krivom oborotne . . ."

35. Propp, *Istoricheskie korni volshebnoi skazki,* 58-61, 65.

36. V. N. Toporov, "Prizha," *Mify narodov mira* (Moscow: Sovetskaiia entsiklopediia, 1982), 11:344. Andrew has perspicaciously pointed out the symbolic and mythical connotations of the old woman's figure: "The Old Woman is even more emblematic and mask-like than the other characters, and she seems to fulfil a purely symbolic role in the story. It is rather difficult to be precise as to exactly what she symbolizes, but . . . she is central to the narrator's Fate, almost as if she were a supernatural being, meeting the hero at the symbolic cross-roads of his life" ("Structure and Style in the Short Story," 17).

37. *Ibid.,* 12-13.

38. Interestingly, in one of later Chekhov's prose masterpieces, "At Christmas Time" (1899), a pose similar to that of Babel''s Cossacks is associated with blindness: "He stood staring fixedly ahead of him like a blind man" ("on stoial i gliadel nepodvizhno i priamo, kak slepoi"; the sentence is later repeated). It can be said that the "whites of [the old woman's] purblind eyes," the Cossacks sitting "motionless [and] stiff" and Liutov reading "like a triumphant man hard of hearing" form a chain of details that subtly "infect" each other with the seme of blindness through a series of intra- and intertextual similarities and transitions.

39. M. Gor'kii, *Polnoe sobranie sochinenii* (Moscow: Nauka, 1968), I: 189-201, 545-48.

40. Iurii Tynianov used the term "convergence" for this kind of spontaneous growth of identical motifs out of similar thematic functions. He says that

in such cases "the chronological question—'who was the first to say it?'—turns out to be irrelevant." See Iu. N. Tynianov, *Poetika. Istoriia Literatury. Kino* (Moscow: Nauka, 1977), 280.

Igor' Sukhikh (essay date 1999)

SOURCE: Sukhikh, Igor'. "About Stars, Blood, People, and Horses: Babel', *Konarmiia* (*Red Cavalry*), 1923-1925," translated by Vladimir Talmy. *Russian Studies in Literature* 37, no. 1 (winter 2000-2001): 6-26.

[*In the following essay, which was originally published in Russian in 1999, Sukhikh describes* Red Cavalry *as a "fragmentary epic" consisting of "five-minute novellas" and examines this overall structure as well as those of the individual stories, which contribute to it.*]

In the seventh year of the new era (A.D. 1924), Army Commander Budennyi, "having rode into literature on horseback, and criticizing it from the height of his horse" (Gorky), discovered that serving under his command was a slanderer, sadist, and literary degenerate: citizen Babel'.

> Under the fine-sounding, patently speculative title, "Iz knigi *Konarmiia*" [From the book *Red Cavalry*], the hapless author has attempted to depict the life, mores, and traditions of the First Cavalry Army during the hectic period of its heroic struggle on the Polish and other fronts. To describe the heroic struggle of classes never before seen in the history of mankind, one must first understand the essence of that struggle and the nature of classes, that is, one must be a dialectic, a Marxist artist. The author is neither. . . . Citizen Babel' tells us old-wives' tales about the Red Army, he rummages in old-wives' trash and clothes, he recounts with old-wives' horror how a hungry Red Army man takes a loaf of bread and a chicken somewhere; he concocts cock-and-bull stories, slings mud at the best Communist commanders, fantasizes, and simply lies.

Six years later, "rank-and-file Budennyi man" Vsevolod Vishnevskii, when sending to Comrade Gorky his own version—the drama *Pervaia Konnaia* [The First Cavalry Army]—honked the same horn.

> Babel''s misfortune is that he is not a soldier. He was stunned and frightened when he came to us, and this strangely morbid impression of an intellectual is reflected in his *Red Cavalry*. Budennyi could well have been offended and indignant. We former rank-and-file men, too. Babel' gave the wrong thing! He missed a lot. He gave only a tiny bit: a Red Cavalry worn out in battle on the Polish Front. And even then, not in its entirety but *fragments*. Believe a soldier: Our Red Cavalry was not what Babel' has depicted.

The future commander-in-chief of Soviet writers fought with Budennyi for Babel'. The author himself did not fight back; instead, he explained and agreed with him.

"What I saw at Buddenyi's is what I gave. I see that I failed to give any political workers, and, in general, I failed to give a lot about the Red Army; I will, if I can, later." This is what he said in 1925 to Dmitrii Furmanov, the author of *Chapaev* and publisher-editor, using the same lexicon as in the as yet unwritten epistle of Vishnevskii (gave—did not give).

In the early 1930s, at a writers' meeting, he even allied himself with the army commander himself: "I stopped writing because I came to dislike all I had written before. I can't write like before anymore, not one line. It's a pity that S. M. Budennyi didn't think of turning to me at the time to form an alliance against my **Red Cavalry**, because I don't like **Red Cavalry**." The promises to reform and change it, to give "the right thing," remained—perhaps fortunately—unfulfilled.

The book of thirty-four stories (although Babel' had spoken of fifty to Furmanov) was put together in three years and then republished unchanged. In the 1930s, Babel' published two "follow-ups" (**"Argamak,"** dated 1924-30, and **"Potselui"** [**"The kiss"**], 1937), and he even managed to include the former in the next edition. Stylistically, the stories were written "like before." Their subject matter in part duplicates other pieces (**"Argamak—Istoriia odnoi loshadi"** [**"The story of a horse"**] and **"My First Goose"**; and **"The Kiss—Perekhod cherez Zbruch"** [**"Crossing the Zbruch"**] and **"Vdova"** [**"The widow"**]). Those texts could possibly have found their place somewhere in the middle of the collection. Their mechanical placement at the end disrupts the conceived and already developed structure. Today, their place is in an appendix. The *book* gets along nicely without them. These stories merely supplement the "basic text," just as the "Odessa stories" are supplemented by other works on the same topic.

Babel' arrived at the completed, classical **Red Cavalry** in three steps, over three stages of transformation of the raw material of life into a work of art.

The Polish campaign was the penultimate significant episode of the civil war (to be followed by the storming of the Perekop isthmus) and the last desperate attempt to export the Russian revolution to the West. The capture of Kiev by the Poles, the following advance of the First Cavalry Army on Warsaw, the terrible defeat ("'We've lost the campaign,' mutters Volkov, and snores. 'Yes,' I answer." ["Zamost'fe"]), the rollback to the Ukraine, the peace treaty and demarcation of the borders (until 1939)—by the mid-twenties all this had become recent history, still bleeding, but already setting, coated in storybook glaze (hence the protests of Budennyi and "rank-and-file Budennyi men").

The author of the future **Red Cavalry** participated in the Polish campaign (May-November 1920) with documents issued to Kirill Vasil'evich Liutov. The newspaper *Krasnyi kavalerist* [Red Cavalryman] printed reports from its "Sixth Cavalry Division war correspondent" about heroic soldiers, heroic nurses, and heinous enemies.

> Another name, unforgettable for the Sixth Division, must be entered into our heroic, bloody, and sorrowful lists, the name of Konstantin Trunov, commander of the Thirty-fourth Cavalry Regiment, killed August 3, in combat at K. Another grave will be hidden in the shade of the dense Volhynia forests, another noted life, filled with selflessness and devotion to duty, has been sacrificed for the cause of the oppressed, one more proletarian heart has been broken for its hot blood to color the red banners of revolution. The Polish army has gone mad. The mortally wounded pans,[1] meeting their end, are thrashing in mortal agony, piling crime upon stupidity, perishing as they ingloriously enter the grave to their own curses and those of others.

This style of ideological slogans and banalities, flowery metaphors and rhetorical figures of speech would, of course, appeal to the commander of the First Cavalry Army. But then, could an army newspaper print anything else? But in Babel''s stories, such style became an episodic "alien word," an object of detached inspection and refined aesthetic play.

> "Men," then said Pugachev, the regiment's commander, looking at the dead man and standing on the edge of the pit. "Men," he said, trembling and straightening himself out with his arms stiff against his trouser seams, "we are burying Pashka Trunov, the world hero; we are giving Pasha the last honors." And raising to the sky his eyes, inflamed by lack of sleep, Pugachev shouted a speech about the dead soldiers of the First Cavalry regiment and about the proud column that was beating the hammer of history on the anvil of future generations.
>
> **("Eskadronnyi Trunov" ["Squadron Commander Trunov"], 155-56)**

At the same time, Babel' kept a diary, "for himself." It was lost, miraculously retrieved, and published many years after its author's death. It provides a detailed chronicle of the campaign, with candid assessments of friends and foes. The heroic formulas of newspaper articles are emended with scenes of viciousness, plunder, drunken debauchery, and wantonness.

> The Zhitomir pogrom, launched by the Poles and then, of course, the Cossacks. After the appearance of our forward units, the Poles entered the city for three days; Jewish pogrom; cut beards, that's usual; assembled forty-five Jews at the marketplace, then herded them to the slaughterhouse, torture, cut-out tongues, wails all over the square.—Terrible event. Church plundered, ripped raiments, precious, glittering fabrics shredded, on the floor, a nurse dragged away three bundles. . . . Animals, they came to plunder, it's so clear, the old gods are being destroyed.—Must get into the soldier's soul, I do, it's all so awful, animals with principles.— Conversation with artillery battalion commander Mak-

simov, our army is out to earn, not a revolution, an uprising, a free-for-all. It's just a means that the Party condones.

Also preserved are plans and sketches of **Red Cavalry.** While echoing the diary in content, they contain important comments about the form and artistic structure of the future book. "The story swift and fast.—Short chapters filled with content.—One day at a time. Short. Dramatic.—No reflections.—Careful choice of words.— Form of episodes—half a page.—No comparisons or historical parallels.—Simply story.—Style, meter.— Poem in prose." The last definition repeated three times.

Repeating himself, groping, Babel' seeks and ultimately finds an aesthetic formula in which to fit the material of battles and campaigns so common in the 1920s: a poem in prose, a headlong, fast-moving narrative that becomes poetry.

> Babel' fits in well with the Soviet literary landscape of the twenties. Subject-wise, *Red Cavalry* ranks along with the partisan stories and short novels of Vsevolod Ivanov, with Furmanov's *Chapaev,* with Fadeev's *Razgrom* [The Rout], and with a great variety of other works about the civil war. Its naturalism and cruelty, the unruliness of dark, elemental forces let loose by the revolution are no more noteworthy and no more shocking than that same Vsevolod Ivanov's, or Artem Veselyi's. His florid style is no more florid or vivid than the magic verbal fabric of Andrei Platonov or the fearless experiments of the *Serapion Brothers,* or the inimitable color of *Tikhii Don* [And quiet flows the Don].
>
> (Sh. Markish)

This is true and at the same time not true at all. While coinciding with many of his contemporaries subject-wise, Babel' veers away from them aesthetically, and first of all genre-wise.

Chapaev, The Rout, Rossiia, krov'iu umytaia [Russia, washed in blood], *And Quiet Flows the Don,* and Platonov's main books (*Chevengur* and *Kotlovan* [The pit]) were different transformations of the novel. Apparent in Ivanov's partisan short novels and a great number of other works on the civil war was a naturalist, essayist foundation. Such "military physiologies" also on the whole inherited the psychological detail, ramification, and unhurried pace of larger forms and were, genre-wise, amorphous. It is quite impossible to apply to them criteria of brevity, thorough word choice, or rhythm. The closest *aesthetic* ally of the author of **Red Cavalry** was a writer who started out a little earlier and differed widely in subject matter. "To the thunder of cannons and the clanging of sabers, Zoshchenko begat Babel'," was how a limerick of the twenties recorded that link. The fate of both is linked with the short-story genre of Russian prose.

In 1937, in a talk with young writers, Babel', while stating that, from his point of view, Lev Tolstoy was the leading Russian writer, went on to explain, almost physiologically, why he could not follow Tolstoy's method.

> The thing is that Lev Nikolaevich Tolstoy had the temperament to describe all twenty-four hours of the day, moreover, remembering all that had happened to him, while I, apparently, have only enough temperament to describe the most interesting five minutes I had experienced. Hence the appearance of this novella genre.

Babel' realized only too well that "this genre" was somewhat alien to the Russian soil.

> I think it would be useful to talk about the story technique, because this genre is not well regarded in our country. It must be said that this genre never flourished especially here, and the French were well ahead of us. Actually, our real novella writer is Chekhov. With Gorky, most of his stories are abbreviated novels. Tolstoy's, too, were abbreviated novels, except for "Posle bala" [After the ball]. This is a real story. In general, here people do not write stories very well; they are more inclined to novels.

Naturally, he finds the working definition of the novella not "here" but "there."

> I read the definition of the novella in a letter from Goethe to Eckermann: a small story of the genre in which I feel more comfortable than in others. His definition of the novella is very simple: it is a story about an unusual event. Maybe that's not correct, I don't know. Goethe thought so.

With his involvement with the new, searing subject matter ("Why do I have this unending anguish? Because I am far from home, because we are destroying, moving like a whirlwind, like lava, hated by all, life is torn asunder, I am present at a never-ending wake"), Babel' became the creator of a new type of story combining the poetics of everyday "novelty" with modernist expressiveness and eccentricity.

Red Cavalry is a book of "unusual events," of five-minute novellas. In this context, as a genre, Babel' is closer not to Fadeev and Platonov but to Zoshchenko, the author of *Rasskazy Sinebriukhova* [Stories of Sinebriukhov], with his idea of the indescribability of the new reality by old creative means.

Babel' takes great pains to arrange neatly this small, fragmentary genre, diversifying it and making it rich in opportunities and perspectives.

The book contains novellas in the precise sense of the word: jokes, anecdotes, unusual events with a required *pointe,* a totally unexpected ending that leaves the reader shocked.

In a strange house, the totally unsuspecting narrator sleeps alongside a dead body (**"Crossing the Zbruch"**). An infant tenderly nursed all night by another cavalry-man turns out to be a sack of salt—and Balmashov "gives it" to the scheming woman black-marketeer (**"Sol'"** [**"Salt"**]). A deacon-deserter who shams deafness, after three days of torture at the hands of his guard actually becomes deaf (**"Ivany"** [**"Two Ivans"**]).

In other cases, there is no unusual event in the story. People are simply traveling somewhere, conversing, writing letters, singing . . . But here, too, the plot is constructed according to the laws of the novella rather than of the abbreviated novel. The novella's eventful *pointe* is replaced by a *mot,* a word ("Has *a word* been found?"), a striking aphorism, which flares up at the end and relieves the intensity and expectation mounting throughout the novella.

"And we heard the great noiselessness of a cavalry attack" ("Kombrig dva" [Combrig 2]). "O, death, O, covetous one, O, greedy thief, why have you not spared us, just for once?" (**"Kladbishche v Kozine"** [**"The Kozino cemetery"**]). "[B]ut we will see each other in the Kingdom of Heaven, to put it bluntly, though there is a rumor going around that the old fellow up in heaven has not got a Kingdom but a real whorehouse, and since there's enough clap here on earth, so, perhaps, we will not see each other" (**"Prodolzhenie istorii odnoi loshadi"** [**"The story of a horse, continued"**]).

"With Babel', just one little word, or some magic formula, becomes the gravitational center of an episode," notes E. Kogan, a researcher of the *Red Cavalry* drafts. "In some cases, such a verbal clot appears a priori, before the situation. It drifts from episode to episode, and the author has to try out different plot settings before it merges with a precious find."

In *Red Cavalry,* the traditional novella-situation and novella-anecdote come along with the novella-formula and novella-aphorism. Naturally, there are cases when a word bolsters and reaffirms a novella's point.

Here is how the hero concludes his story of gruesome revenge against his merry *barin* [landlord], Nikitinski, in the novella **"Zhizneopisanie Pavlichenki, Matveia Rodionycha"** [**"The life and adventures of Matvei Pavlichenko"**]:

> "With shooting—I'll put it that way—with shooting you only get rid of a chap. Shooting's letting him off and too damn easy for yourself. With shooting you'll never get at the soul, to where it is in a fellow and how it goes and shows itself. But I don't spare myself, and I've more than once trampled an enemy for more than an hour. You see, I want to get to know what life really is and how it is inside me."

(90)

In **"Smert' Dolgusheva"** [**"Death of Dolgushev"**], after shooting Dolgushev Afon'ka Bida growls: "You people in specs take about as much pity on our brothers as a cat on a mouse."

Another method Babel' uses to achieve creative diversity is through different narrators.

The greater part of the book (twenty-three of the thirty-four novellas) is written in the style of a personal narrative as told by the principal character—the "autopsychological hero"—a witness of, and participant in, the events. In only four cases he is named Liutov. In the other novellas he is just "I," with occasionally varying biographical details. The later **"Argamak"** is done in the same manner.

In seven novellas Babel' displays a classical narrative style. We have the word of the hero, a picturesque, paradoxical character created not just through action but by purely linguistic means. This is Vas'ka Kurdiukov's letter in **"Pis'mo"** [**"A letter"**] about how they "finished off" two enemies—father and son (variations of *Taras Bulba*); another letter from the gloomy and enigmatic Sokolov with a request to send him to make revolution in Italy (**"Solntse Italii"** [**"Italian sunshine"**]; another letter and an explanatory note to a magistrate from Nikita Balmashov (**"Salt," "Izmena"** [**"Treason"**]); an exchange of messages between Savitskii and Khlebnikov (**"The Story of a Horse," "The Story of a Horse, Continued"**); and Pavlichenko's story-confession (**"The Life and Adventures of Matvei Pavlichenko"**).

"The Kiss," written later and appended to the book, is essentially an alien idiom. Although Liutov is commonly considered to be the hero, actually the narrator differs significantly from "people in specs" (he is a squadron commander, he "unsaddled two Polish officers in battle," and flaunts his brutality) and should be regarded as an objective hero with an intellectual rather than common-folk vocabulary.

In the novella **"Prishchepa,"** the narrator refers to the hero's story but recounts it himself, presenting the central character's thoughts, but not his speech.

Finally, three novellas (**"Nachal'nik konzapasa"** [**"The remount officer"**], **"The Kozino Cemetery,"** and **"The Widow"**) hve no narrator or storyteller. They are presented objectively, in the third person. But here, too, the pure anecdote about the clever D'iakov (the most carefree and "problem-free" novella of the book) differs markedly from the poem in prose, a lyrical sigh at a Jewish cemetery (the shortest and "non-plot" novella).

Babel' rallies the hidden possibilities of the small genre, testing its strength, diversity, and depth.

Although Babel' published his first writings God knows where (in the Odessa newspaper *Izvestiia*, the magazine *Shkval, Pravda, Prozhektor, Lef, Krasnaia nov'*), he always had in mind, as R. Bush demonstrates, an inte-grated image: The first newspaper and magazine publications, at the level of novella compatibility, compositionally reflect the structure of the final version of ***Red Cavalry.***

The book of poetry, with its specific structure, became an accepted form already in the nineteenth century (Baratynskii's *Sumerki* [Dusk] and Fet's *Vechernie ogni* [Evening lights]) and really took hold in the Silver Age (Annenskii, Blok, Akhmatova, Pasternak, and many others).

One of the first to start building books of stories was, I think, Chekhov (*Khmurie liudi* [Gloomy people], *V sumerkakh* [At dusk], and *Detvora* [Children]). But then, were there not also [Pushkin's] *Povesti Belkina* [Tales by Belkin] and the experiments of the romanticists (V. Odoevsky's *Russkie nochi* [Russian nights])?!

Red Cavalry, as a book of novels, becomes a metagenre, an analogue and rival of the novel (another example of this kind is Zoshchenko's *Sentimental'nye povesti* [Sentimental stories]).

Sergei Eisenstein, the director of *Bronenosets "Potemkin"* [Battleship Potemkin], who had already worked with Babel' on the script of ***Benia Krik,*** fully realized the novelty of Babel''s structure. In an article written in 1926, he stated:

> The understanding of the cinema is now entering a *"second literary period,"* a phase of drawing closer to the symbolism of language. Of speech. Of speech, which gives symbolic (meaning not literal) and "imagery" to a very concrete material connotation through *contextual juxtaposition,* that is, *montage.* In some cases—in unexpected or unusual juxtaposition—it acts as a "poetic image." "Bullets whine and scream. Their complaint builds up intolerably. Bullets strike the earth and fumble in it, quivering with impatience."
>
> (Babel')

The example from **"Death of Dolgushev"** is not serendipitous; it is basic. Two years later, Eisenstein would say that Babel' "will forever remain an irreplaceable supplementary 'reader' for the new *cinematic imagery.*"

The structure of ***Red Cavalry*** can thus be organically described in the language of another art form: as a montage of frame bits within the novella and a montage of novella episodes in the whole of the book. Here, many of the opening frames ("The Comdiv 6 communicated today that Novograd-Volynsk was taken at dawn" [8]; "The Sixth Division was mustered together in the wood outside the village of Chesniki, awaiting the signal to attack" [191]) and formulae-aphorisms ("We'll die for a sour pickle and the world revolution"—"A horse is a friend . . . A horse is a father" [193]) can be interpreted as captions of this colorful silent film.

In any artistic arrangement the most significant, demarcated parts are the beginning and end. **Red Cavalry** starts with **"Crossing the Zbruch."** This page-and-a-half text presents almost all the topics and motifs that provide the structural basis of the book.

"**'Crossing the Zbruch'** doesn't have this crossing" (F. Levin). To be fair, we should note that the novella does have a crossing, but with just one colorful, graphic frame, half a paragraph:

> The blackened Zbruch roars, twisting itself into foamy knots at the falls. The bridges are destroyed, and we wade across the river on which rests a majestic moon. The horses are in to their cruppers and the torrent gurgles past hundreds of horses' legs. Somebody sinks, calling out loudly against the Mother of God. The river is dotted with square black patches—the carts—and is full of confused sounds, of whistling and singing that rise above the bright hollows and the serpentine trails of the moon.
>
> (8-9)

With respect to the *pointe* of each novella, its title is indeed "misleading," camouflaging. It is a notch for the memory, a point on the map, a formal place marker (compare **"Kostel v Novograde"** [**"The Novograd Church"**], **"Put' v Brody"** [**"The road to Brody"**], **"The Kozino Cemetery," "Berestechko," "Zamost'e,"** and **"Chesniki"**). But from the perspective of the book, the title introduces an important timeframe: the roads along which shouting, cursing, singing people are traveling somewhere on horseback.

A luxurious noon is followed by evening, then night. The sun, moon, and stars become anchor details of landscape descriptions, no longer detailed, as in the first novella, but concisely packaged into one or two sentences, or even just into a comparison or epithet.

The road leads to a house, moreover, a strange one—a place to spend the night, a chance shelter (compare the image of the family home in M. Bulgakov's *Belaia gvardiia* [White Guard]).

It is a Jewish home, and the fate of the Jewish world and the philosophy behind it becomes a constant theme of the book (**"Ghedali," "Rabbi,"** and **"Syn rabbi"** [**"The rabbi's son"**].

In passing, an instantaneous punch in the very first paragraph-frame provides a historical parallel: "Our noisy rearguard convoy is spread out over the road from Brest to Warsaw built by Nicholas I over the bones of peasants" (8).

From here begins the motif of death persistently pursued throughout the entire novella: the orange sun rolls down the sky like a decapitated head; the evening coolness drips with the smell of yesterday's blood and of killed horses; silence overpowers all; Comdiv 6 is pursuing the Combrig on a heavy stallion, firing at him twice between the eyes.

Death flows like water through nature and through history, seeping even into dreams, thus preparing for the shocking finale, the novella's full stop: "She . . . removes the blanket from the sleeping man. Lying on his back is an old man, dead. His glottis has been torn out and his face split in two; his beard is clotted with blue blood resembling a piece of lead" (10).

The words of the pregnant daughter concluding the novella (another connective joint: a coming birth with a past death) project not grief or sorrow but an almost preternatural pride.

> "The Poles killed him," says the Jewess, shaking the mattress, "and he begged them: 'Kill me in the back yard so that my daughter doesn't see how I die.' But they did as it was most convenient to them. He died in this room and thought of me. And now I'd like to know," cried the woman with sudden terrible violence, "I'd like to know where you'd find in the whole world another father like my father!"
>
> (10)

Beyond the unemotional words of a military report lies a world of overwhelming beauty and Shakespearean passions.

The first killers in the book are Poles, the nominal enemy. But then everything intermixes, diffuses, and turns into one bloody mess. **Red Cavalry** has not got a single natural death (save for an old man in the later story **"The Kiss,"** who does die suddenly, albeit without outside help). On the other hand, plenty of people are shot, cut down, and mutilated. The thirty-four novellas offer twelve firsthand accounts of deaths, with many other mass slaughters mentioned in passing. "Prishchepa went from neighbor to neighbor, leaving behind him the trail of his blood-stained footprints. He set fire to villages and shot Polish headmen for hiding" (94).

In "Stikhi o neizvestnom soldate" [Verses about an unknown soldier], O. Mandel'shtam would later write about "millions killed for nothing . . . massive, wholesale deaths in the sky." The action in Babel''s book takes place under this sky.

A father *rezhet* [slashes] his Red-Armyman son, while another son *konchaet* [finishes off] his dad (**"A Letter"**). Pavlichenko *topchet* [tramples] the former landlord (**"Life and Adventures of Matvei Pavlichenko"**). Konkin *kroshit* [wipes out] Poles, then, together with a fellow soldier, *snimaet vintami* two men [put them out of action with rifles], while Spir'ka *vedet* [conducts] another man to Dukhonin's headquarters to check his documents, and, finally, the narrator *oblegchaet* [relieves] a proud old Pole (*Konkin*). Nikita Balmashov, with the help of his trusted rifle, also *konchaet* [gives it] to a deceitful black-marketeer woman (**"Salt"**). Trunov *vsunul sabliu v glotku* of a prisoner [thrusts his sword into the prisoner's neck], Pashka *raznes cherep* of a lad [sends his skull flying], then enemy airplanes *rasstreliali* [shoot], first Andriushka, then Trunov, with their machine guns (**"Squadron Commander Trunov"**). Galin with the white spot in his eye, a contributor to the newspaper *Krasnyi kavalerist,* savors the violent deaths of emperors.

> "Last time," says Galin, narrow-shouldered, pale and blind, "last time, Irina, we considered the shooting of Nicholas the Bloody by the Ekaterinburg proletariat. Now we will go on to another tyrant who died the death of a dog. Peter III was strangled by Orlov, his wife's lover, and Paul was torn to pieces by his courtiers and his own son. Nicholas the Rod poisoned himself; his son fell on March 1, and his grandson died of drunkenness. You need to know all that, Irina."
>
> (**"Vecher"** [**Evening**], 132)

What a diversity of synonyms! And not one of them that denotes a simple, natural death.

In the world of **Red Cavalry** it is difficult to escape and survive not only for people. "I grieve over the bees. The fighting armies have treated them most brutally. There are no bees left in Volhynia now" (**"The Road to Brody"**). "All torn and singed and dragging his feet, he led a cow out of the stall, put his revolver in its mouth, and fired" (**"Prishchepa,"** 94).

Most pages of the book are painted in the brightest color—red. That is why the sun here looks like a decapitated head, the blazing sunset reminds one of approaching death, the autumn trees oscillate at the crossroads like naked corpses.

Blood and death are equalizers for friend and foe, for right and wrong. "Pashka is dead, and there is no one to judge him on earth, and I would be the last to judge him" (**"Squadron Commander Trunov,"** 159).

"What is our Cossack?" Babel' writes in his diary. "Many things: looting, daring, professionalism, revolutionary zeal, brutal cruelty. We are the vanguard, but of what?"

The novella frames in **Red Cavalry** are arranged by contrast and juxtaposition, with no comforting connectors or soothing reflections.

One character strips prisoners and corpses; another plunders a church; the third tortures an unfortunate deacon, his unrecognized double; the fourth dies heroically in an encounter with airplanes; the fifth sees treason even in a hospital, among the doctors treating him; the sixth suddenly becomes an able brigade commander with the "imperious indifference of a Tartar khan"; the seventh dreams of killing the king of Italy to spark a revolutionary fire; the eighth, a Red Cavalry Christ, travels quietly and peacefully with the rear-guard convoy playing an accordion; the ninth issues inane orders to flog his own infantry, the common soldiery; the tenth prefers his favorite horse over the [Communist] Party . . .

On rereading Babel' in the late 1950s, film director G. Kozintsev (another director!) was carried away by "the burning instant of life observed" in his books, noting that the writer had discovered an entire "continent": "the soldier of the civil war."

The inhabitants of Babel''s continent are people on horses, moral centaurs. They are united by an intensity of external manifestations, unbridled feelings, passion—for horses, the Party, women, the revolution. Participants in the just ended civil war, they are hyperbolized, enlarged, and presented in remote epic perspective. Like Gogol's Zaporozhye Cossacks, or perhaps "Achaean menfolk" embarking on a campaign to Warsaw in search of Helen—the world revolution.

It was Gorky who compared Babel''s Cossacks with the Zaporozhye Cossacks: "Babel' illuminated the fighting men . . . from within and, in my view, better and more truthfully than Gogol did the Zaporozhye Cossacks." E. Pomianowski, the Polish literary scholar and Babel' translator, did not agree and elaborated:

> No, he did not illuminate them. He simply transferred them to another level, to the level of a *skaz* [tale], the epic form of which ennobles the heroes by its very method of narration. Even the beginning of the *Iliad* would have been but the story of a row between two unwashed *atamans* [chieftains] in a hand-to-hand fight over a wench, had it not been for the seriousness and brilliance that Homer, with his hexameter, forces us to see in this brawl.

An objective, epic view explains much in the poetics of **Red Cavalry**: the unflappability, the superficial impartiality with which tragic events are recounted, specifically, death. The most famous example, which shocked so many, is from **"Berestechko"**:

> Right under my window some Cossacks were shooting an old, silver-bearded Jew for spying. The old man was uttering piercing screams and struggling to get away. Then Kudria, of the machine-gun section, took hold of his head and tucked it under his arm. The Jew stopped screaming and set his legs apart. Kudria drew out his dagger with his right hand and carefully, without splashing himself, cut the old man's throat. Then he knocked on the closed casement.
>
> "Anyone who cares may come and fetch him," he said, "You're free to do so."
>
> The Cossacks disappeared behind a corner.

(120)

Naturalism in descriptions and in object details—an extreme, indicative frame in the novella "Two Ivans": "Loading my saddle on my back, I went along the overturned edge of a field and stopped at a turning to satisfy a natural need. Having relieved myself, I buttoned up and felt drops on my hand. I lit a little lantern, turned around and saw, lying on the ground, the corpse of a Pole spattered with my urine." In the first editions there was another detail, later removed by either the author or the censor: "It dripped from his mouth, trickled between his teeth, and pooled in his empty eye sockets" (171).

Love in **Red Cavalry** is not romantic meetings under the moon (they occur only in the later novella **"The Kiss"**), not decadently convoluted, capricious feelings but open, blunt passion, unbridled erotics. Sashka, the "lady of all the squadrons," copulates with another man almost before the eyes of her dying former partner. Several hours later, that same man strikes her in the face for being in no hurry to send the dead man's mother "the orphan's share" (**"The Widow"**). The washerwoman Irina goes to sleep with the heavy-jowled cook Vasilii right in front of Galin, who loves her and "educates" her (the one who lectured about assassinated emperors) (**"Evening"**).

As it moves back into epic perspective, the last war becomes history. But at the same time history becomes another of its victims, crushed in the millstones of the belligerent sides. One feels pity and compassion not only for people but also for the shattered legend.

According to Babel', "the burning history of the outskirts" is molded by the proximity of several tribes. "The Jews here threaded the gain of the Russian muzhik[2] to the Polish pan, and the Czech colonist to the Lodz factory" (121). Lying peacefully in the cemetery in Kozin are four generations spanning 300 years. And today, people still go to the synagogue; they argue about Hassidism and celebrate the Sabbath. However, now all this is taking place against a different background.

> In Berestechko itself, the old order had been given an airing: but it was still firmly rooted here. . . .
>
> Berestechko reeks unredeemably even now, and a violent smell of rotten herrings emanates from all its inhabitants. The little town reeks on, awaiting a new era; but instead of human beings there go about mere shadows of frontier misfortunes.
>
> (122)

In **"Zamost'e,"** the narrator suddenly awakes out of a terrible dream in which eros and thanatos are irresistibly intertwined and intermixed, like milk and blood, only to find himself in another horror.

> In the stillness I could hear the far-off breath of groaning. The smoke of secret murder strayed around us.

> "Somebody is being killed." I said. "Who is it?"
>
> "The Poles are getting the wind up," the muzhik answered. "The Poles are killing the Jews."
>
> . . . The muzhik made me light a cigarette from his. "The Jews are to blame for everything on our side and on yours. There'll be mighty few of them left after the war. How many Jews are there in the whole world?"
>
> "Ten million," I answered, putting the bridle on my horse.
>
> "There'll only be 200,000 left," cried the muzhik.
>
> (178, 180)

From this Jewish milieu and culture come two noteworthy heretics. One, an old shopkeeper, like a character out of a Dickensian novel, dreams about a sweet revolution and an improbable International. "And I want an International of good people; I would like every soul to be taken into account and given first-category rations. There, soul, please eat and enjoy life's pleasures" (**"Ghedali,"** 32).

The other, a young man with the face of Spinoza, a rabbi's son and a Bolshevik, dies at some forgotten railway station near Rovno—the death of the last of the princes, the end of that Hassidic culture.

In **Red Cavalry,** the Polish element is as multidimensional and multifaceted. The church is an ever present landmark: "White churches gleamed in the distance, like buckwheat fields. . . . It was almost midday when I had finished and was free at last. I went up to the window and saw the Berestechk temple—white and mighty. It was gleaming in the warm sunlight like a china tower" (148). The Poles (like the Cossacks) "cut up the Jews." But the Poles also include slaughtered prisoners, and meaninglessly proud shliakhta,[3] and the old bell-ringer fearlessly defending his temple.

The Polish tribe, too, has its heretic. Pan Apolek, a strange wandering painter, is one of the few in the **Red Cavalry** world who creates rather than destroys. He works to order but does not sell himself. Like the painters of the Renaissance, he joins the mundane with the celestial; he transfers down-to-earth life to icons, transforming sinners into saints. He cherishes his own apocrypha—of Christ pitying the unfortunate Deborah, who had borne his son, whom "the priests concealed."

In the argument about Apolek's art, despite its jocular style, some sentiments extremely important to Babel' slip out.

> "He has made saints of you in your lifetime," cried the Vicar of Dubno and Novokonstantinov in answer to the crowd's defense of Apolek. "He has surrounded you with the unspeakable attributes of holiness—you—

thrice fallen into the sin of disobedience, distillers of brandy in secret, merciless usurers, makers of false weights and merchants of your own daughters' innocence."

"Your holiness," then said limping Vitol'd, a buyer-up of stolen goods and the keeper of the cemetery, "who will tell the ignorant people about the things in which the all-merciful Lord God sees truth? And isn't there more truth in the pictures of Pan Apolek who satisfies our pride than in your words so full of blame and aristocratic wrath?"

(55)

The question of the "buyer-up of stolen goods" is rhetorical. It is apparent where the truth lies in this dialogue about painting and morality. Apolek seems to be the only apostle in the bloody flow of life racing somewhere. It is not for nothing that, along with the "naïve and colorful" portrait icons, the narrator gives him (this time in the novella **"U sviatogo Valenta"** [**"In St. Valentine's Church"**]) a painting with a spark of genius.

At that instant the velvet curtain beside the altar swayed, shook and slipped to one side. A niche was revealed in the blue depth of which, against a background of cloud-furried sky, ran a bearded figure in a Polish great coat of orange—barefooted, with torn and bleeding mouth. A hoarse cry pierced our ears then. I saw that the man in the orange coat was being followed by hatred and overtaken by his pursuers. He put out a hand to ward off the coming blow, and blood flowed from that hand in a purple stream. . . . The figure in the niche was none other than that of Jesus Christ—the most extraordinary image of God I have ever seen in my life.

(152-53)

Apolek's icon is the Savior seeking liberation from a world where nothing can be changed. The wandering painter's art is not Catholic (although the icon hangs in a church), just as Ghedali's International is not Judaism. It is simply Christianity, the gospel of the street—of Socrates, of Skovoroda, of an as yet unknown preacher from Judea.

A disciple of Apolek is what the narrator would be—and is.

The wise and beautiful life of Pan Apolek went to my head like an old wine. In Novograd-Volynsk, among the ruins of a town swiftly brought to confusion, fate threw before my feet a New Testament that had lain concealed from the world. Hallowed with ingenuousness, I made a vow then to follow Pan Apolek's example. And the sweetness of meditated rancor, the bitter scorn I felt for the dogs and swine of mankind, the fire of silent and intoxicating revenge—all this I sacrificed to my new vow.

(48)

The narrator's "I" bonds the fragmentary epos of **Red Cavalry.** It is, of course, not biographical, although Babel''s **Red Cavalry** pseudonym is mentioned in the novellas several times.

Babel''s status—a staff official of "commander" rank, with his own orderly, sufficiently independent of the rank and file, and with a modicum of influence—has nothing in common with the status of the "bespectacled," wretched Kirill Liutov, a stranger to the Cossack crowd seeking to ingratiate himself with them.

(V. Kovskii)

But neither is there some concocted biography or prescribed image of Babel''s central figure. The narrator *is there,* but he is legendary, elusive, faceless, like Homer or Boian,[4] whose strings "twanged the glory" of eleventh-century centaurs. Instead of a biography, the narrator has a system of signatory details and reactions, which are, moreover, shifting and contradictory. He may be a Russian or a Jew, a newspaperman or a rear convoy officer with an orderly, a bungler and dreamer, or a quite able and tenacious cavalryman.

These images, masks, and transformations are united, it seems, by one key metonymic detail.

I handed him a paper whereby I was to be attached to the staff of the division.

"Put it down in the Order of the Day," said the Comdiv, "put him down for every satisfaction save that of the front. Can you read and write?"

"Yes, I can read and write," I replied, envying the flower and iron of that youthfulness. "I graduated in law from St. Petersburg University."

"Oh, you are one of the *Kinderbalsams,*"[5] he laughed. "Specs on your nose. What a nasty little object! They've sent you along without any enquiries; and this is a hot place for specs."

(**"My First Goose,"** 35)

Opposite the moon, on the bank of a sleeping pond, I was sitting—spectacled, with boils on my neck and bandages on my legs.

(**"Evening"**)

Red Cavalry is a book about a *Kinderbalsam* in specs in a redskin land. He is a person from the outside, an observer, and a witness attempting, as the poet said, "to flow like a drop with the masses," but organically incapable of this. The world dream blinding the eyes of other cavalrymen and blending with pogroms, pillage, a flippant attitude toward the lives of others and one's own death is not, it seems, alien to him. He keeps trying to appear as one of them, to get rid of his "moral specs." But the most he can do is wring the neck of a goose or frighten old women with a gun. He cannot shoot a dying man at the latter's own request and goes into "the unforgettable attack near Chesniki" with an unloaded weapon: "The Poles go for me, and I don't go for them."

It is as though the narrator has stumbled into the Red Cavalry from out of the nineteenth century. He is related to Tolstoy's Pierre (also bespectacled) or Garshin's heroes who went to war "to suffer with the people," to present their chests to bullets but not punch holes in others.

But this paradoxical situation—side-by-side, but not together—helps the hero to understand both Sashka's meekness and Akinfiev's frenzy, thoughts of the Hassids, and the gospel of Apolek.

Babel''s hero is split in more important ways than Russian-Jew or correspondent-staff worker. He is also a centaur: a participant in the Red Cavalry campaign and at the same time an epic viewer and painter of it. To an artist, it is good to be a viewer from the outside.

There is no air in the book's novella tales. The science of hate blinds the characters. In their eyes the world is transformed into a black-white empty space that just has to be overcome. "Then we began to pursue General Denikin, and killed thousands of them and drove them into the Black Sea" (**"A Letter,"** 14). "We were wiping out the *shliakhta* up beyond Belaia Tserkov'. We were wiping them out and making a clean job of it so that even the trees went and bent" (**"Konkin,"** 113).

Italy to Sidorov, who is dreaming to kill its king, is sunshine and bananas. The narrator of that same novella, **"Italian Sunshine,"** sees the real Italian landscape in the devastated town on the Zbruch River.

> The signed town—columns broken and dug into the earth, the malevolent, crooked, little fingers of old women—seemed to me raised up aloft into the air, as snug and chimerical as dream-visions. The crude brightness of the moon flowed over it with inexhaustible force. The damp mould of the ruins flowered like the marble of opera seats. And I waited with an uneasy mind for Romeo to appear from the clouds—a Romeo in satin and singing of love—while a dismal electrician in the wings keeps a finger on the switch of the moon.
>
> (23)

The true romanticist is not the boring ideological killer Sidorov, but the narrator, who is thus able to visualize the scene after the battle.

The opera comparison in **"Italian Sunshine"** is not accidental. In his story **"Probuzhdenie"** [**"Awakening"**] Babel recalls a rebuke of his Odessa acquaintance and critic of his first stories: "Your landscapes look like descriptions of stage settings." Nevertheless, the luxurious, colorful, blazing, decorative qualities of Babel''s landscapes are retained in *Red Cavalry.* Babel''s epic characters are natural precisely on such a stage, which, incidentally, they themselves do not notice. The art of seeing the world belongs to the narrator.

In his early essay, **"Odessa"** (1916), Babel asks rhetorically: "If one thinks about it, will one not find that there never has been a truly joyous, shining description of sunlight in Russian literature?" "The literary Messiah, whom people have been awaiting for so long and so fruitlessly," he goes on to predict, "will come from there: from sunlit steppes surrounded by sea."

And then he appears a decade later, to see the sun, at a most unsuitable time of civil discord and bloody campaigns.

> Yesterday was the first day of slaughter at Brody. Having lost our way on the blue earth we had no knowledge of it, not I nor my friend Afon'ka Bida. . . . The rye was tall, the sun resplendent, and the soul, all undeserving of those blazing, winged skies, longed for drawn-out tortures."
>
> (**"The Road to Brody"**)

> Andriushka . . . unbuttoned the old man's trousers, shook him slightly, and began to pull them off the dying man. . . . The sun came out of the clouds at that moment and impetuously surrounded Andriushka's horse, its lively pace and the devil-may-care swing of its docked tail.
>
> (**"Squadron Commander Trunov"**)

Babel''s sunsets and nights, moons, stars, and simply the details of his surrounding world are just as original, vividly picturesque, as though lit up with theater lights, and sharp as a sudden gunshot.

> Night flew toward me on mettlesome horses. The whole universe responded with vociferations from the transport wagons, and on the earth, girdled about with shrill sounds, the roads disappeared. Stars crept forth out of the fresh womb of night, and deserted villages blazed on the horizon.
>
> (**"Two Ivans"**)

Iurii Olesha, author of *Zavist'* [Envy], whom Babel in a later interview called a fellow Odessite and a writer of "the Odessa, southern Russian school," "in his old age . . . opened a metaphor shop." Babel' would have been a must in this imaginary shop, featured in the most prominent places. The goods in *Red Cavalry* number in the hundreds. Metaphors (more strictly speaking tropes: comparisons, hyperboles, etc.) flash in every point of the text and not just illuminate the plot space but acquire independent value of their own.

The world of people crushed by suffering and blinded by hate is colorless. God's world, even mutilated by war, is amazing and stunning. Far from despoiling it, blood, urine, and tears accentuate its poetry and beauty.

The most famous aphorism from Viktor Shklovskii's "critical romance" about Babel' (1924), on the whole a very penetrating piece, has been: "The meaning of Babel''s method is that he speaks in one and the same voice of stars and gonorrhea." This is one-sided and inaccurate. What is remarkable in *Red Cavalry,* among other things, is the range of intonations, the architectonic structure of the book. The matter-of-fact tone of speech about horrible things, which had taken aback contemporaries (some saw it as deliberate aestheticism) melds with the style of a military report or protocol, of a comic story, of lofty rhetoric and the exalted lyricism of the "poem in prose."

The fragmentary epic of **Red Cavalry** stands at an intersection of stylistic experiments of the twenties: from the verbal blizzards of Pil'niak to the bare simplicity of Dobychin, from the everyday life tales of Zoshchenko to the philosophical incorrectness of Platonov.

The book begins and ends with a road. **"Crossing the Zbruch"** presents almost all significant motifs. The three concluding novellas are the finale: They close the story lines and develop the summary formulae-aphorisms.

"Posle boia" ["After the battle"] is based on a dispute with Akinfiev, who just cannot understand "them as get muddled in the fight and don't put no cartridges in the pistols." The final formula stresses—retroactively—the principal quality of the bespectacled Kinderbalsam: his paradoxical pacifism and irrational "Molokanism."[6]

> The village was swimming and swelling, and muddy clay was oozing from its dismal wounds. The first star glimmered above me and fell into the clouds. The rain lashed the willows and spent itself. Evening flew into the sky like a flock of birds, and darkness crowned me with its watery wreath. I felt all my strength ebbing away, and bent beneath the funereal garland, continued on my way, imploring fate to grant me the simplest of proficiencies—the ability to kill my fellow men.

In **"Pesnia"** ["The song"], Sashka Koniaev, alias Sashka the Christ, sings a Kuban' song reminiscent of either an old romance or a new Yesenin. The simple tune transforms people: The narrator stops threatening the old landlady with a revolver and tries to go to sleep with good thoughts, the old woman herself reflects that she is a woman dreaming of her bit of serendipitous happiness. "Those songs are indispensable to us. No one can see an end to the war, and Sashka the Christ, our squadron's singer, is not yet ripe for death" (207).

In **"Syn rabbi"** ["The rabbi's son"], the narrator, for the first time in the **Red Cavalry** world, discovers his double. In **"My First Goose,"** the narrator mentions the manuscripts and tattered old clothes that had fallen out of his trunk. In the last novella there is a similar situation, but here the narrator is collecting "the scattered belongings of the Red Army soldier Bratslavsky" that had fallen out of the dying man's case.

> His things were strewn about pell-mell—mandates of the propagandist and memorandum books of the Jewish poet; the portraits of Lenin and Maimonides lay side by side: the knotted iron of Lenin's skull beside the dull silk of the portraits of Maimonides. A lock of woman's hair lay in a book, the Resolutions of the Party's Sixth Congress, and the margins of communist leaflets were crowded with crooked lines of Hebrew verse. They fell upon me in a mean, depressing rain—pages of the Song of Songs and those revolver cartridges.
>
> (212)

The rabbi's son manages to do what the narrator was never able to do: to meld Russian and Jewish, literature and revolution, a lock of woman's hair and party resolutions. Perhaps that is why he dies?!

> He died before we reached Rovno. He—that last of the princes—died amid his poetry, phylacteries, and coarse linen leggings. We buried him at some forgotten station or other. And I, who can scarcely contain the tempests of my imagination within this primeval body of mine, was there beside my brother when he breathed his last.
>
> (212)

Brother—the final word of the novella, the cycle, the book. Some try to ascribe it religious meaning, seeing the narrator's "kinship" to Jewishness or his "affinity" to the Hassidic wise men. But the thing is that, within the structure of the book built according to the laws of "the closeness and unity of the poetic line," this episode and this definition also rhyme with each other.

In **"Two Ivans,"** a novella about unrecognized Russian doubles, the pacifist deacon and his torturer Ankifiev, the earlier quoted naturalistic scene with the body of the dead Pole covered with urine is followed by a connotational blow, another of Babel''s formulas. "With the Commander-in Chief Pilsudsky's proclamation, I wiped away the smelly liquid from the skull of my unknown brother, and went on, bent beneath the weight of the saddle" (171).

The narrator's brother is not only the rabbi's son, Red Army man Bratslavsky, but also the unknown dead enemy (no one has yet suspected the narrator of being of Polish descent). Similarly, he lists as friends the meek Sashka the Christ, the raving lover of horses, Savitsky, the reckless Afon'ka Bida.

It was not Babel' who said: And all ye are brethren (Matthew 23:8). But he essentially talks about the same thing. The narrator's exuberant imagination seeks to found an "International of Good Men" in the world of **Red Cavalry.** The trouble is that good people, as Bulgakov's Ieshua says, do not know of their goodness or brotherhood.

> "Pan comrade, the International is eaten with—"
>
> "It's eaten with gunpowder," I answered the old man, "and flavored with the best blood."
>
> (32)

And one more good man who, not suspecting how he would be ridiculed many years later, wrote a review (or signed someone else's).

> Citizen Babel' was unable to see the great upheavals of class struggle, it was alien and objectionable to him, but he does, however, see, with the passion of a sick sadist, the quivering breasts of a Cossack woman conjured up in his imagination, her bare thighs, and so on. He sees the world "as a meadow crossed by naked women, stallions, and mares." Indeed, with such an imagination, one can only write slander about the Red Cavalry.

Budennyi may have been a good military leader, but he was a bad, biased, and ill-tempered reader.

> We were both of us rocked by the same passions. Both of us looked upon the world as a meadow in May—a meadow crossed by women and horses.
>
> **("The Story of a Horse")**

The dispute with Budennyi did not erupt because the renowned cavalryman knew nothing about poetry (although, indeed, he did not). What was worse is that he wanted to write a different myth into history, a different picture of the actions, roles, and objectives of his troops and their political commissar. The system, consolidated by the iron hand of that commissar, gave the powers that be a monopoly on creating myths, on describing events, past and current. Only talented appointees had the right of such description. Babel''s talent was of a different, unearthly origin. That is why he perished.

They say that history is written by the winners. No, alas, no.

(E. Pomianovskii)

Notes

"Konarmiia" is a contraction of "Konnaia armiia," that is, "Cavalry Army." *Red Cavalry* is the title of the English translation of the book by Nadia Helstein, published (and copyrighted) in 1929 by Alfred A. Knopf. The translations of all quotes from *Konarmiia* in this article, as well as the titles of the respective novellas, have been taken from this translation. I have, however, ventured to correct several apparent mistranslations, as well as to adapt name transliterations to the current accepted Library of Congress standard. Page references to this edition will follow each citation in parentheses.—Trans.

1. The term *Pan*, in Polish, means "gentleman," "owner," or "landlord" and is used as a common address for "Mister." In Russian, depending on the context, *Pan* may be used simply as an address to or among Poles or, in a somewhat derogatory sense, as denoting Poles in general.

2. *Muzhik*, a Russian peasant, may also refer colloquially to any man.

3. *Shliakhta* is the term for Polish small-landed gentry; in Russian, it is also a derogatory reference to Poles in general.

4. Boian is the legendary bard of Russian legends and *bylinas*.

5. *Kinderbalsam* is derogatory slang for students.

6. Molokanism refers to the Molokan Christian religious sect that originated in Russia.

Edyta M. Bojanowska (essay date July 2000)

SOURCE: Bojanowska, Edyta M. "*E Pluribus Unum*: Isaac Babel's *Red Cavalry* as a Story Cycle." *Russian Review* 59, no. 3 (July 2000): 371-89.

[*In the following essay, Bojanowska maintains that* Red Cavalry *is best understood as a story cycle. Bojanowska illuminates the "basic patterns of cohesion" that provide a sense of unity to the collection and applies Mikhail Bakhtin's conception of the story-cycle form to Babel's genre-defying work.*]

Red Cavalry's form has perplexed critics since its first publication in 1926. The work has been described as an epic, a lyric poem, a baroque novel, a novel of stories, a loose collection of stories unified by a theme, and a series of anecdotes.[1] While each of these approaches illuminates a certain aspect of the work, a full appreciation of *Red Cavalry*'s masterful design and its wealth and complexity of meanings requires an approach that will take the work for what it appears to be: a cycle of short stories, that is, a series of short narratives composed and arranged by the author to form a coherent whole. Despite acknowledgements of *Red Cavalry*'s unified structure, the question of what exactly holds the cycle together has so far received only perfunctory treatment.[2] In this article I will attempt a more comprehensive—though by no means exhaustive—analysis of *Red Cavalry*'s basic patterns of cohesion. I also will demonstrate a close interdependence of formal structure and thematic developments in the work. In conclusion I will consider some implications of Mikhail Bakhtin's narrative theory for the genre of the story cycle and will discuss the cycle's differences from the novel form. *Red Cavalry* baffles its readers for what they take to be its unresolved tensions, stark juxtapositions, and ambiguities in the narrative voice. The work's open-endedness fully justifies this reaction. Yet an approach to *Red Cavalry* as a whole, as a work of a particular genre that generates meanings in ways peculiar to itself, is likely to dispel some of this bafflement.

Isaac Babel himself treated his work as a unified whole. He referred to the stories as "chapters of *Red Cavalry*" and resented having to publish some of them separately:

"I published for money a few foul (*pakostnykh*) fragments in the local *Izvestiia,* foul—simply because they are fragments."³ Each separately published story was marked as a fragment of **Red Cavalry.** Babel's concern with the cycle's structure is documented by a letter to his censor and editor, Furmanov, concerning changes in the titles and ordering of the stories.⁴ Babel was a meticulous and painstaking craftsman known to revise a story even twenty-two times according to Paustovsky's well-known anecdote about "Liubka the Cossack." Babel's correspondence with publishers and editors is overrun with pleas for additional advance payments and for extensions of deadlines—to make time for yet another revision. At least ten such extensions preceded **Red Cavalry**'s publication.⁵ Such assiduity in crafting the stories and arranging them in a volume suggests that the stories' ordering was carefully considered. All these facts point to the need of interpreting **Red Cavalry** holistically.

My approach to **Red Cavalry** is informed by Forrest Ingram's pioneering study of the story cycle genre.⁶ He defines a story cycle as "a book of short stories so linked to each other by their author that the reader's successive experience on various levels of the pattern of the whole significantly modifies his experience of each of its component parts." Ingram applies the term "pattern" in a broad sense, to include both the regular and irregular recurrence of an element. He discusses static patterns (such as framing devices or titles), yet asserts that the dynamic ones—such as the recurrence and development of characters, motifs, and symbols—are far more important in binding the stories into a whole. Ingram likens the dynamic pattern to the motion of a wheel whose rim represents recurrent elements that "rotate around a thematic center." Thus, "the thematic core of a cycle expands and deepens as the elements of the cycle repeat themselves in varied contexts."⁷ Such recurrence relativizes the element itself and influences the "thematic core" as well. Later contexts add dimensions to the original usage of an element, yet in retrospect the original usage is itself affected by this expanded context. Ingram's sensitivity to a story cycle's unique dynamism, to its unceasing back-and-forth movement between *pars* and *toto* makes his insights most useful for the methodology of dealing with story cycles. In my discussion of **Red Cavalry** I will identify some of its dynamic patterns and thematic cores and will explore the dynamic between motifs reappearing in various contexts. Since space does not allow me to recapitulate the reader's "successive experience" (from Ingram's definition) of the cycle story-by-story, I will limit myself to discussing the implications of a particular ordering of stories only for a few sequences.

On the macro-level, the cycle is unified by the theme of the Russo-Polish War of 1920, and by its narrator, Liutov. However, Liutov's status is not clearly defined and his narrative life does not follow a logical path of events. There is no consistent pattern to his incarnations as a propaganda officer and as a soldier on active service.⁸ In fact, sometimes this issue remains ambiguous (as in **"The Death of Dolgushov"** or **"Berestechko"**). In some stories he is an observer, in others a participant. He relates the stories he has heard, and also plays the role of an omniscient narrator (for example, in **"The Widow"**). Liutov's functions as a character and a narrator are inconsistent. It is his role as a unifying perceiving consciousness of the world he describes that adds cohesion to the cycle. Robert Maguire perceptively highlights the crucial aspects of this consciousness:

> He is a Bolshevik whose loyalties are eroded at every turn by scruple, sentimentalism, and a deep sense of a past both dead and vital. He is an intellectual who is incapable of defining welling problems of conscience, morality, and ethics forced on him by experience. Liutov, then, stands outside everything. . . . [He] longs to find an allegiance that will put together all these conflicting and incomplete identities; yet circumstances compel him to make constant acts of allegiance that he knows fall short of perfection.⁹

Maguire's characterization captures well the conflict and the flux of Liutov's consciousness. Thus the kind of cohesion that this consciousness will impart to the cycle cannot be static; various stories will plot its different (often conflicting) aspects.

While the war theme and the persona of Liutov undoubtedly contribute to the work's unity, its remarkable cohesiveness owes the most to the recurrence and development of subthemes, motifs, and characters—Ingram's "dynamic patterns." I argue that the cycle is composed of three structural-thematic blocks. The first ten stories describe life behind the front line and set up most of the work's themes, motifs, and symbols. These are reworked in the main block of twenty-three stories that center around the front-line experience. The final block of one to three stories, depending on the edition, reconnects with the opening stories, thus foregrounding further the work's cyclical structure.¹⁰ I will trace **Red Cavalry**'s dynamic patterns within and throughout these three blocks.

The opening story, **"Crossing the Zbrucz,"** contains the essence of the whole cycle.¹¹ Most fundamentally, it indicates the various viewpoints that the narrator will adopt throughout **Red Cavalry.** The opening paragraph introduces the impersonal perspective of a laconic and objective observer, removed from the reality he describes by the intellectual awareness of larger historical conditions that have shaped it. This is inherent, for example, in the reference to Nicholas I who built the road to Warsaw "on the bones of peasants" (p. 140). The second paragraph introduces a collective perspective, as the narrator portrays a division of Cossacks, of whom he is one, crossing the river. This fragment also foreshadows the tension between Liutov's simultaneous belonging to and separateness from the community of Cossacks: though he is part of the group, the visceral captivation with the beauty of the landscape appears clearly his own. The third section brings to the fore an aspect of Liutov's identity. He now is a Russian Cossack—billeted in a house of Polish shtetl Jews (the reader does not yet know that Liutov himself is Jewish). He reacts to the house's filthiness with contempt and indignation. He watches the Jews "skip[] about . . . *monkey-fashion,* like *Japs* in a circus act" (p. 42, emphasis added). These epithets underscore his perception of the Jews' "otherness": they appear to him non-human and non-Russian. The story's ending, however, shows Liutov revising his dismissive attitude. In a gesture of humane empathy he withholds his own commentary and instead gives full voice to the pregnant Jewish woman whose father, as Liutov learns, had been massacred by the Poles. Her anguished cry closes the story: "I should wish to know where in the whole world you could find another father like my father" (p. 43). The story opens with a matter-of-fact, declarative communiqué and unexpectedly concludes on a poignant personal question to which no answer is—nor can be—given. In an ideological sense, this movement from an assertion to an often perplexed and unanswerable question is characteristic of the work as a whole. A narrowing focus, shifting from a detached, impersonal vision, through a collective experience to an individual one, reappears throughout *Red Cavalry,* as does the motif of stepping outside oneself to experience "the other." "Crossing the Zbrucz" also introduces many themes that will run through the cycle, for example, the abuse of civilians and the moral deterioration of the Cossack army (Liutov's dream), as well as the motif of regeneration amid chaos and death (the proximity of pregnancy and death), which will become prominent in the cycle's concluding stories. The motif of crossing, of trespassing, indicated in the story's title, will also recur in the cycle, as the narrator enters new realms of experience, and as he slowly descends into the hell of war atrocities.

The pivotal story in the first block is **"Pan Apolek."** Liutov's meeting with the eponymous village painter is a turning point in his life. Nowhere else in the book does he so openly comment on the effects of his experience: "I then made a vow to follow Pan Apolek's example. And the sweetness of meditated rancor, the bitter scorn I felt for the curs and swine of mankind, the fire of silent and intoxicating revenge—all this I sacrificed to my new vow" (p. 55). Pan Apolek has portrayed as saints the same people whom the narrator approached earlier with hostility and scorn. Some belonged to the Jewish villagers who initially appalled Liutov in "Crossing" (incidentally, both stories are set in Novograd). The lame convert Yanek is portrayed as St. Paul and the

loose woman Elka as Mary Magdalene. Polish Catholics, Pan Romuald and Pani Eliza, described by Liutov in **"The Church at Novograd"** with jaundiced Bolshevik clichés, appear on Apolek's paintings as John the Baptist and the Virgin Mary. The pledge to follow Pan Apolek's example implies undiscriminating empathy with other human beings, whether a pathologically vicious Cossack, a filthy and grotesque shtetl Jew, or a treacherous Pole. As Patricia Carden remarks, Pan Apolek's example also implies that "true humanity demands not only the acceptance of man in those attributes that elevate him, but also in those . . . that we despise."[12] She is right to stress the importance of compassion that Liutov sees in Apolek's humanism. "[A presage of mystery touched me]" (*Predvestie tainy kosnulos'menia*)—these words of Liutov mark his stepping onto the path of reevaluating his previous moral and artistic beliefs, the path on which Pan Apolek serves as a beacon.[13] Liutov's "new vow" is manifest in *Red Cavalry*'s affinity with Apolek's murals, both being, as Iribarne remarks, "brilliant tableau[x] of unsaintly figures."[14]

In the first block's last four stories Liutov attempts to sort out his allegiances. The world of the Jews, with their culture, tradition, and humanistic ideals appears to him noble and precious, but stifling. The Cossacks, with their commitment to the revolution that will create a new and better world, with their vitality and heroism, captivate Liutov, but their cult of violence, and cold-blooded, often mindless cruelty, repel him. The ordering of the stories reflects Liutov's wavering. **"Gedali"** and **"The Rebbe,"** which stand for the Jewish tradition, alternate with **"My First Goose"** and **"The Road to Brody,"** which represent the Cossack values, the ones Liutov resolves to uphold, though he remains an outsider in both worlds.

"Gedali" and **"The Rebbe"** pose a question that will resurface in later stories: Could the downtrodden of this world, exploited and decimated by antirevolutionaries and revolutionaries alike, improve their lot by joining the revolution? Gedali expresses his confusion and doubt: "The Revolution is the good deed of good men. But good men do not kill. So it is bad people that are making the Revolution. But the Poles are bad people too. Then [who will tell Gedali] which is Revolution and which is Counter-Revolution?" (p. 71). This valid reservation is problematized by **"The Rebbe,"** which questions whether a continued allegiance to tradition remains a viable option for the Jews. The story portrays Hasidism as barren and bankrupt, implying that it keeps the chosen nation in the "Zhitomir ghetto" (p. 78). The Rebbe's "unruly" (p. 79) son, Il'ia Bratslavskii, *will* join the Revolution.[15]

"The Road to Brody," which closes the first block, shows Liutov, another Jewish revolutionary, on his way to the front line. The story also laconically suggests

Liutov's initiation into battlefield slaughter: "The chronicle of our workday offenses oppressed me without respite, like an ailing heart" (p. 81). The story's final paragraph concludes simultaneously the story itself and the whole introductory block, offering different meanings on each of these planes. Within the context of the story, the passage suggests Liutov's relief at having escaped death in an ambush that the Poles set up near Brody: "O Brody. . . . I could already sense the deathly chill of orbits suffused with tears grown cold. And here I am being borne away at a jolting gallop, far from the dented stones of your synagogues" (p. 82). However, as a conclusion to the whole block, most notably in the context of **"Gedali"** and **"The Rebbe,"** these sentences indicate that Liutov is leaving behind all that has so far been associated with the synagogue and Jewishness, that is, the passivity of a victim, on the one hand, and humanism, peace, and culture, on the other.[16] The passage conspicuously stands out in the story, which triggers an impulse to read it in these two perspectives. So far the story has been describing in detail concrete events and conversations, following, "nose to the ground," so to speak, concerns as to who did what when. The exclamation "O Brody" brings this flow to a sudden halt. The unanticipated pathos of the passage and the sudden distance it creates take the reader by surprise and encourage him to follow the narrator by taking a step back and pausing for reflection. Not only is the story over; the first "act" of *Red Cavalry* is over. It is time for an intermission. In addition to the thematic distinction between the first ten stories and the ones that follow, this passage provides further support for marking the block boundary here and not elsewhere. Moreover, the liminality is also geographical, since Brody was an important check point between Russia and the Polish provinces of the Habsburg Empire.

Interestingly, **"The Road to Brody"** exhibits a deliberate lack of focus. Three-fourths of the story is devoted to Afon'ka Bida's bucolic stories. Then comes the paragraph about the Brody ambush (Is it, then, the story "proper," considering the title?). The conclusion takes on yet another dimension, as I have just shown. Quite a few other stories are similar composites of more than one story line (for example, **"Zamość," "Cześniki"**). This technique underscores the fluidity of narrative boundaries in the cycle and encourages a reading that will transcend them.

In the main block of stories Liutov fulfills his promise to follow Pan Apolek's example of universal humanism and through his art ennoble seemingly less suitable subjects. The character of Prishchepa appears as one of Liutov's unsaintly Apolek-like vignettes: "a young Cossack from Kuban—a tireless [bully, kicked out] from the Communist Party, a future rag-and-bone man, a carefree syphilitic, and a happy-go-lucky fraud" (p. 108). The story of Pavlichenko, victimized by his mas-

ter until the revolution provided him with an opportunity to lynch him (which he does slowly and sadistically), bears the title *"zhizneopisanie,"* ironically suggestive of the genre of saints' lives. Liutov now withholds his opinion about Pavlichenko, but portrays him in a more positive light when he reappears in **"Cześniki"** as a disciplined soldier and a prudent commander, unaffected by the rampant anarchy in the Soviet army. Although both stories are independent, self-contained units, the readers might conceivably be tempted to revise *ex post facto* their reading of **"Pavlichenko"** [**"The Life of Pavlichenko Mativej Radionych"**] after seeing the hero's redemptive qualities in the **"Cześniki"** episode. Perhaps the lynching, though morally wrong, had an expurgating, regenerative influence upon him? Could the Revolution have tempered Pavlichenko's bloodthirstiness or harnessed it for positive ends? Or perhaps the reader will choose not to reconcile the two behaviors: are they two separate sides of Pavlichenko's personality?

To ask a more fundamental question: to what extent does Babel resolve the moral dilemmas he poses? We follow Liutov into new fields of experience, see old acquaintances—like Pavlichenko—in new situations, and are invited to see the world through their eyes. By making us experience a character's perspective and by showing his various aspects, Babel makes us question and test our most basic moral beliefs. Perhaps the most disturbing aspect of *Red Cavalry* is Babel's insistence on constructing seemingly plausible situations or states of mind in which killing *might appear* justified. Rather than leading us to condone evil and violence, Babel aims at exposing the immense complexity of any moral action and, consequently, of any moral judgment. Instead of resolving a moral dilemma, he often chooses to dramatize it. The possibilities of balancing stories and of shifting narrative viewpoint inherent in the story cycle genre aid him well in this task.

Yet not all is left unresolved. **"In St. Valentine's Church"** shows how the epiphany occasioned by Pan Apolek's art makes Liutov revise his contemptuous and hostile attitude toward "the other," here: Polish Catholics. Poles were added to this structural category in the initial block, in **"The Church at Novograd,"** which also initiated the motif of a sacrilegious plundering of a church. The change in Liutov's attitude is already apparent in the contrasting descriptions of the two churches. The Novograd church is a treacherous place: "Bone buttons sprang beneath our fingers, icons split down the middle and opened out, revealing subterranean passages and mildewed caverns" (p. 46). The church of St. Valentine, on the other hand, emerges as an almost immaterial oasis of tranquility: "It was full of sunshine, full of dancing sunbeams, airy pillars, a kind of cool gaiety" (p. 140). The framing of the story between the portrayals of the violence of war in the preceding **"Afon'ka Bida"** and the following **"Squadron Commander Trunov"** enhances this effect. Similarly, Babel creates "lyric relief" by inserting a brief poetic interlude, **"The Cemetery at Kozin,"** between the stories about Pavlichenko and Prishchepa, both laden with violence.[17]

Another "control" for Liutov's change in attitude in **"In St. Valentine's Church"** is his portrayal of Kurdiukov. He was introduced in the initial block in **"A Letter"** as an example of a morally anesthetized revolutionary, with Liutov ultimately withholding his opinion. In contrast, **"In St. Valentine's Church"** does signal Liutov's criticism of Kurdiukov's part in desecrating the church, which consists in simulating intercourse with an army nurse. Liutov describes him with scorn: "Kurdiukov the half-wit straddled her as if on horseback, shook as though in the saddle, and pretended to be satisfying his lust" (p. 140). In portraying other *Red Cavalry* characters, such as Pavlichenko or Afon'ka Bida, Liutov also alternates what I will call mediated and unmediated descriptions. I will use these terms as shorthand labels—I do not wish to claim that an objective, unmediated narrative in absolute terms is possible.[18] I merely wish to indicate the two poles of the spectrum, a relative contrast between an opinion expressed (with varying degrees of articulation or openness) and an opinion withheld (which does not preclude its existence).[19]

Pan Apolek, Liutov's role model, reappears metonymically in the masterpieces of St. Valentine's Church that bear the indelible mark of his "heretical and intoxicating brush" (p. 141). The central epiphany in the story occurs when a falling curtain reveals Pan Apolek's statue of Jesus Christ, so lifelike that everyone at first takes him to be alive.[20] From Liutov's perspective, Apolek's Jesus combines "sameness" (he is a Jew, like Liutov) with "otherness"—he wears a Polish coat (Poles are the enemy) and is pursued by his oppressors, as the Poles are pursued by their enemies, the Russians. Liutov's revelation is triggered by a sudden awareness of a basic bond that connects him with all humanity, one that transcends the differences of ethnicity, nationality, and religion.

This is borne out by yet another alignment of motifs. The description of the bell-ringer's wife, who implores Liutov to stop the desecration of St Valentine's Church, evokes the portrayal of the harrowed old woman in **"My First Goose"** who, broken by the weight of wartime violence, threatens to hang herself when Liutov kills her goose. The pupils of the bell-ringer's wife "were infused with the white moisture of blindness, and were brimming with tears" (p. 139). The woman in **"Goose"** "raised . . . the diffused whites of her purblind eyes" (p. 75). The predicament of both women signals the ill treatment of the civilian population in the territories conquered by the Cossacks. Yet the purblind

eyes also suggests the women's affinity with the severely short-sighted and bespectacled Liutov. Thus the image symbolically links the victim with the oppressor. Babel's use of the purblind eyes motif exemplifies the way a cycle creates symbols. As Ingram explains, the repetition of an element in various contexts "amplifies and deepens [its] significance to such an extent that it becomes a symbol."[21] Babel's symbolic use of the half-blind eyes suggests an interpretation that Liutov as a moral being and artist remains connected indiscriminately to other human beings, that no single faction, nation, army, or ethnicity can claim his exclusive allegiance.

The main block of stories also develops the initial block's other thematic embryos. The idea of an ideal, humane revolution contained in Gedali's notion of an International of good people returns in **"The Story of a Horse"** and **"The Story of a Horse, Continued."** The former story portrays Khlebnikov, an idealistic Bolshevik who renounces his party membership when the party fails to redress his just claim and return his horse to him. Khlebnikov's idealistic view of the Revolution echoes Gedali's: "The Communist Party . . . was founded, as I understand it, for joy and sound justice without limit, and it ought to consider the small fry also" (p. 112). However, a disparity between this ideal and his individual experience makes Khlebnikov disillusioned with the revolution. In **"The Story of a Horse, Continued,"** in turn, Khlebnikov renounces his cynicism and acknowledges the need to overcome the individual and espouse the collective. In a letter to Savitskii, who now holds possession of the horse, he expresses joy that his horse advances the revolutionary cause by serving a war hero. Savitskii's cynical reply provides yet another ironic inversion of Khlebnikov's idealism. He jocosely lists the dead brothers-in-arms and off-handedly mentions that Khlebnikov's horse is also dead. The conclusion of Savitskii's letter stands in stark contrast to the earnestness and simple-hearted kindness of Khlebnikov: "We shall meet again, to put it bluntly, in the Kingdom of Heaven, though there is a rumor going around that the old fellow up in Heaven has not got a kingdom at all, but a regular whorehouse, and clap there's plenty of on earth as it is, and so it is quite on the cards that we shall not see one another again" (p. 162).

Another issue that **"Gedali"** raised earlier, the question of the Revolution's promise for the oppressed masses it now liberates, resurfaces in **"Beresteczko"** and **"Afon'ka Bida,"** this time with clearly pessimistic overtones. Beresteczko and its miserable inhabitants await a new era with hope: "The town reeks on, awaiting a new era, and instead of human beings there go about mere faded schemata of frontier misfortunes" (p. 120). The Soviet promises sound enticing: rule belongs to you, no more masters. Yet the Soviets' ability to live up to these promises is undermined in the story through references to Bohdan Khmelnitsky and Napoleon, who failed to deliver on their alluring promises, and by the historical context of Khmelnitsky's infamous pogroms that in the seventeenth century decimated the Jewish population in this area.[22] On a smaller scale, Babel's Cossacks repeat this inglorious historical topos by murdering an elderly Jew suspected of spying, which further undermines their credibility. The infantry unit in **"Afon'ka Bida"** is drafted from the same milieu as the Beresteczko inhabitants (the most destitute Galician peasants and Jews). The Cossacks' scandalous treatment of these poorly armed soldiers in bast sandals shows that Russian Communists are no better than Polish masters: the Cossack horsemen round them up like cattle and whip them. Afon'ka Bida gladly partakes in this lashing spree, and amuses himself by shouting commands to these soldiers as to a dog: "Look out . . . [n]ow go and catch fleas!" (p. 133).

By the time the reader encounters **"Afon'ka Bida,"** the abuse of civilians by the warring armies already constitutes an expanded "thematic core," to use Ingram's term. What follows is some elements that have been "rotating" around this core in the initial block of stories:

1) In "Crossing" Poles raid the Jewish woman's house and murder her father.

2) In "The Remount Officer" red cavalrymen confiscate draft horses; the peasants consider this a plunder that deprives them of means to farm the land.

3) "My First Goose" describes Liutov's killing of a goose that belongs to a despairing old woman, a gruesome and grotesque initiation rite through which Liutov hopes to gain acceptance among Cossacks.

Toward the end of the main block, **"Zamość"** and **"The Song"** will add new motifs to this theme of abuse.

Liutov's portrayal of Afon'ka Bida in a number of stories gives the reader a good cross-section of a Cossack soul. In **"The Road to Brody"** Afon'ka shows his humane, benevolent face: he sings Cossack ballads and tells a touching story about a bee. Liutov calls Afon'ka his friend. **"The Death of Dolgushov"** reveals Afon'ka's capacity for compassion—he weeps over leaving behind wounded comrades who will inevitably fall prey to the Poles. The story also shows that Afon'ka possesses something that Liutov will always lack: an ability to perform a mercy killing on a fatally wounded comrade who begs for a bullet. Afon'ka berates Liutov for what he sees as Liutov's weakness and lack of compassion, and threatens to kill him. Liutov's admiration of Afon'ka—now with an admixture of horror—is replaced by repulsion in the story **"Afon'ka Bida."** Afon'ka displays more sympathy for his horse (like

Kurdiukov in **"A Letter"**) than for the infantry soldiers, whom he whips "for fun." His unorthodox ways of finding a new horse, which include going single-handedly behind the enemy lines, though courageous, display the full extent of his anarchic nature. (He is nicknamed after the anarchist commander, Makhno, under whom Sidorov, the anarchist in **"Italian Sunshine,"** served.) Liutov becomes entirely disillusioned with Afon'ka when the latter defiles the shrine of St. Valentine (**"Afon'ka Bida"**), and in a drunken stupor performs a cacophonous "concerto" on the church organ (**"In St. Valentine's Church"**).

An important theme running through ***Red Cavalry*** is the role of propaganda in forming the New Man that the Revolution was to create. The story **"Salt"** shows how the propagandist (mis)conception of collective revolutionary goals serves simply as an excuse for completely arbitrary, amoral acts. The story's hero, Balmashev, takes pity on a woman with a small baby who begs to be taken aboard the train, but when he discovers that she has fooled him by pretending that a bag of salt is her child, he throws her off the moving train and shoots her. He addresses her with a harangue full of Communist slogans: "You, abominable woman, you're more counterrevolutionary than the White General who goes about on a horse that cost a thousand. . . . He can be seen from everywhere, that general can . . . but you . . . can't be seen no more than a flea can, and you go biting away for all you're worth" (p. 126). The entranced line of this rhetoric leads Balmashev to assert that the woman is a traitor and a dangerous threat to the Revolution. He considers it a revolutionary duty to kill her: "I . . . washed away that stain from the face of the workers' land and the republic" (p. 126). Balmashev's initial act of kindness predisposes us toward him and makes us try to accept his rationale for killing the woman. Yet the incongruity between the facts and Balmashev's rhetoricized version of them remains puzzling. The story in its entirety consists of a letter to an editor (Liutov?), but unlike **"A Letter,"** **"Salt"** lacks a narrative frame—it stands on its own and the narrator in no way guides the reader in evaluating Balmashev's act.

The next story, **"Evening,"** adds a new dimension to the Balmashev question. The story also portrays a character who views the world through the prism of propagandist clichés, but now the portrayal is rather comical. The efforts of the love-stricken Galin to win the heart of a washerwoman by raising her revolutionary consciousness appear futile and ridiculous. The story's conclusion shifts to a more somber tone, as it becomes clear that Galin's immersion in propagandist newspeak has deprived him completely of the ability to communicate emotions. After catching a glimpse of the washerwoman snuggling in bed with someone else, Galin turns to Liutov with the following words: "The Cavalry Army

. . . is the social focus effected by the Central Committee of our Party. The revolutionary curve has thrown into the first rank the free Cossacks still soaked in many prejudices, but the Central Committee's maneuvering will rub them down with a brush of iron" (p. 130). This is hardly what one would expect from a scorned lover. The juxtaposition of **"Salt"** and **"Evening"** in the text is significant. The (tragi)comical treatment of propaganda in **"Evening"** may retroactively influence our interpretation of its detached, unmediated presentation in **"Salt."** But, one may ask, can we really read **"Salt"** through the prism of **"Evening"**? After all, they are connected neither by plot nor character.

Even if the answer to this question is negative, **"Evening"** does seem to indicate the direction in which the propaganda theme will develop. Indeed, Balmashev himself reappears in **"Treason,"** now as a quixotic figure, more comical than even Galin in **"Evening."** Babel's use of *skaz* in **"Treason"** to render Balmashev's inflated revolutionary zeal and propagandist indoctrination resembles Zoshchenko's use of this technique. Balmashev and his friend come to a hospital for treatment, but steadfastly refuse to surrender their weapons and clothes for sterilization, accusing the staff of betrayal: "What contagion could there be in a sharp Kuban saber except for the enemies of our Revolution?" (p. 174) The party affiliation of the person in charge of the storeroom is a vital issue in their dilemma. After the hospital staff finally drugs them and puts them in hospital clothes, they start a riot. The story ends, like **"Salt,"** with a tirade against ubiquitous treason, but now Balmashev's fulminations clearly cannot be taken seriously.

As I have mentioned, the balancing of the unmediated and mediated stories forms a pattern in *Red Cavalry.* The unmediated portrayals of Kurdiukov, Pavlichenko, and Balmashev in **"A Letter,"** **"Pavlichenko,"** and **"Salt,"** respectively, are in each instance balanced by the mediated ones in **"In St. Valentine's Church,"** **"Cześniki,"** and **"Treason."** The unmediated portrayals are based on the characters' own speech, which allows Liutov to withhold his opinion, while the mediated ones appear mostly as Liutov's narratives, Liutov's opinion being embedded in the tone, structure, and symbolism of the stories. (**"Treason,"** kept in a letter form, is an exception, though a degree of evaluation is suggested by its addressee, an investigator, and by the comic absurdity of Balmashev's self-portrayal.) The unmediated stories are among the most enigmatic ones in the cycle. The lack of narratorial comment in these stories proves all the more unsettling since they portray human behavior in the absence of law and moral rules. Pavlichenko's improvisation of a fictitious party order that allows him to kill his former master makes a mockery of a moral sanction: "I . . . takes out my book of orders and opens it at a blank page and reads, though I can't read

to save my life. 'In the name of the nation . . . and for the foundation of a nobler life in the future, I order Pavlichenko, Matthew son of Rodion, to deprive certain people of life, according to his discretion.' 'There,' I says, 'that's Lenin's letter to you'" (p. 105). Stories about Kurdiukov and Balmashev also portray morally arbitrary actions justified by idiosyncratic conceptions of the advancement of the revolutionary cause. Babel balances the mediated and unmediated stories to capture Liutov's quest for a resolution of the dilemmas arising at his first contact with these characters, dilemmas that the reader certainly shares. The reader may either see the mediated versions as relevant to their interpretion of the unmediated counterparts, or may consider them separately, as reflections of particular stages of Liutov's cognitive journey through the world of war. The genre of a story cycle allows for both possibilities. However, the presence of the same characters in the parallel stories, and often in the context of the same problem (for example, morality vs. the revolution), requires that the issue of the relation between these stories be addressed in one's reading.

There is a definite sense of direction in Babel's development of the propaganda theme. Balmashev is an avid reader of the *Red Trooper,* the propagandist rag for which Liutov writes articles. The same paper equips Balmashev with the specious rationale for his refusal to be disarmed in the hospital: "the *Red Trooper* says about our international position that it's real terrible, and that the horizon is full of clouds" (pp. 174-75). That propaganda makes one blind is suggested on the literal level in the description of Galin's walleye and twitching eyelid. The story **"Squadron Commander Trunov"** compares interestingly with Babel's actual article about Trunov, **"More of Such Trunovs,"** which he published in the *Red Trooper* under the name of Liutov. The article is a propagandist funeral panegyric of Trunov: "Yet another illustrious life . . . was given for the cause of the downtrodden; yet another proletarian heart was broken in order to paint the banners of the Revolution with its hot blood."[23] Babel's fictional portrayal of Trunov, on the other hand, is problematized: although he dies a heroic death, he has earlier butchered prisoners of war and tried to force Liutov to falsify their number in an official report.

Liutov himself at the beginning of the campaign views reality through the eyes of a propaganda officer. In **"The Church at Novograd"** he commits a more refined version of the Balmashevian discourse: "Here is Poland, here is the proud distress of the *Res Publica*! And I, a violent intruder, spread out a lousy mattress in a church abandoned by its priest, and placed beneath my head folios in which were printed hosannas to the Most Excellent and Illustrious Head of State, Joseph Pilsudski" (p. 45). Yet Liutov liberates himself from the propaganda's seductively cocksure and thunderous voice in the stories that follow, for example, in **"In St. Valentine's Church,"** which balances **"The Church at Novograd."**[24] In fact, in the course of his war experience he comes to despise *any* form of propaganda, whether Soviet or Polish, and goes as far as to claim brotherhood with his enemy. This is how Liutov relates his unintentional defilement of a Polish soldier's corpse: "I felt splashes of something on my hand. I lit my little lantern . . . and saw lying on the ground the corpse of a Pole I had splattered with my urine. . . . With Commander-in-Chief Pilsudski's proclamation I wiped the skull of my unknown brother" (**"Two Ivans,"** pp. 155-56). This gesture symbolizes Liutov's ultimate rejection of propaganda as a reliable cognitive and moral guidepost.

The theme of propaganda has also a metaliterary significance: it is a type of discourse whose objectives and methods are antithetical to those of a story cycle like *Red Cavalry.* Propaganda aims at persuading its audience; it selects and links "stories" and events in such a way as to project a monistic vision of reality. A story cycle like *Red Cavalry,* in contrast, presents a multiplicity of truths and casts events and characters in a wide range of moral perspectives. Rather than attempting to persuade, it invites interpretive pluralism. Thus, built into the cycle is a competing model of a narrative, one that gradually becomes undermined and discredited. It is therefore arguable that on the metaliterary level, the theme of propaganda provides the cycle with an opportunity to accentuate the prerogative of its own poetics.

The main block's final group of stories portrays a growing deterioration of the army that is losing the campaign. (This theme has been initiated by Liutov's dream in the opening **"Crossing the Zbrucz."**) In **"Zamość"** Liutov reaches the nadir of his war experience. He spends the night in a ditch full of water, with his horse tied to his leg: "The sodden ground offered me a soothing embrace of the [grave]" (p. 168). His dream about a woman named Margot stands in juxtaposition to Sidorov's plea to his fellow conspirator, Victoria, in **"Italian Sunshine."** Yet the escape that Liutov finds in Margot is not the prospect of a "heroic" deed (an assassination of an autocrat), but his own death. Like the opening story, **"Zamość"** also mentions a pogrom perpetrated by the Poles and Liutov's camouflaged Jewish identity (his conversation with an anti-Semitic peasant who takes Liutov for a non-Jew).[25] The next day, when his housekeeper refuses to feed him, he threatens to burn down her house. In contrast to **"My First Goose,"** in which Liutov's act of terror was motivated by a desire to insinuate himself into the Cossacks' good graces, he now commits a parallel act out of sheer desperation to obtain the necessary sustenance. The story ends on a somber note: "'We've lost the campaign,' muttered Volkov. . . . 'Yes,' I answered'" (p. 172).

By depicting commanders who are about to disobey orders, **"Cześniki"** presages the breakdown of army morals that will reach its apogee in **"After the Battle."** The latter story relates the events of the Cześniki battle in which the Poles won a spectacular victory, as five thousand Cossacks fled in disarray after a brief skirmish. The Russian army has deteriorated to the point that the Cossacks turn against one another. Liutov, trying to collect his men for another attack, approaches Gulimov, who refuses to follow the order unless Liutov moves to the attack first. In the ensuing conflict Gulimov threatens to kill Liutov, and Liutov buries his nails in Gulimov's face.[26] Later, Akinfiev, who accuses Liutov of not having put cartridges in his rifle during the Cześniki battle, does the same to Liutov's face.

Although these last stories represent the absolute lowest circle of the hell of war, they also offer glimmers of hope, of life, of a regenerative force—though the work's ending cannot be deemed uplifting on account of these images. Liutov's prayer to fate in **"After the Battle"** for the ability to kill a fellow man may be viewed as a sign of the degeneration of his earlier humanistic ideals, but it may also be seen in positive terms: despite all he has experienced, Liutov is still unable to kill. The motif of life at the juncture with death, most often though not exclusively symbolized in sexual intercourse, becomes a prominent motif toward the end of *Red Cavalry.* As I have mentioned earlier, it appears already in the cycle's first story, this brilliant miniature of all of *Red Cavalry,* in the image of a pregnant Jewish woman mourning her dead father. In **"The Widow,"** the nurse Sashka abandons her dying lover and makes love to his helper in the nearby bushes. In **"Treason,"** the hospital—an institution that saves human lives—is situated in Kozin, the location of a cemetery in an earlier story. The Russian word *shashki* appears in **"Treason"** in two different meanings and contexts: as the bellicose Kustov's "sword," and as the "checkers" which the recovering patients make from bread, the symbolic food of life. The story **"Cześniki,"** whose title would suggest that it will focus on the battle, is half devoted to Sashka getting her mare covered by the commander's stallion. The case of Sandy the Christ is more ambiguous. In **"The Song"** he offers to make love to the elderly woman psychologically destroyed by war, by which he recapitulates the gesture of Christ in Pan Apolek's story, who in the same way took pity on Deborah, abandoned by her bridegroom. On the other hand, an earlier story (**"Sandy the Christ"**) has shown Sandy become infected with a sexually transmitted disease, which compromises his gesture of love to the old woman in **"The Song."** This profoundly ambivalent image closes the main block of *Red Cavalry* stories.

The concluding stories do not resolve *Red Cavalry*'s conflicts or provide an overarching meaning to the whole book, as some critics have suggested.[27] On the contrary, countless ambiguities and irresolutions are built into every seeming conclusion. What all three endings share, however, is a tendency of returning to the beginning of *Red Cavalry,* thus endowing the book with a cyclical structure.

"The Rebbe's Son" may be seen as a positive ending: the revolution wins over a prominent representative of a group which in earlier stories harbored skepticism toward communism—the Jews. This person is Il'ia, the last prince of a Jewish dynasty. An overview of Il'ia's belongings may also imply a possibility of reconciling personal and cultural values with collective, revolutionary ones. This optimistic resolution, however, is undermined by Il'ia's demeaning death and burial at a forgotten station. In addition, the possibility of Il'ia's messianic role (is Il'ia—Elijah the new Prophet?) is undermined by images of "emaciation and impotence."[28] Liutov's fraternal identification with Il'ia provides another twist: it may imply that what Il'ia stands for will live in Liutov. Yet Liutov earlier has called a dead Polish soldier his brother as well. Does Liutov's identification with Il'ia and the Pole suggest simply his recognition of the basic bond between human beings? The story invites various interpretations. **"The Rebbe's Son"** contributes to the cyclical structure of *Red Cavalry* by evoking a recollection of Zhitomir, which is chronologically Liutov's first recorded experience of the campaign (while in Novograd he reminisces about his earlier stay in Zhitomir). By relating further events of Il'ia's life, the story looks back to **"The Rebbe"** from the first block of *Red Cavalry.* The thrice-repeated "do you remember" accentuates this pattern of reconnection.

"Argamak," though slightly more optimistic, is similarly ambiguous. The story may suggest that Liutov has found his place among the Cossacks, but the terms of the Cossacks' acceptance ironically undermine this conclusion: stopping to stare at him and his horse does not connote friendship. Liutov remains an outsider and a grotesque misfit. Horsemanship alone does not secure the status of a true Cossack; further training in killing geese without pangs of remorse—not to mention killing people—would be needed. *Red Cavalry* never shows Liutov learning that. Like **"The Rebbe's Son," "Argamak"** refers the reader to the beginning of the cycle. "The Cavalry Army has gained possession of Novograd-Volynsk" (p. 196), announces Liutov, which takes the reader back to the opening sentence of the book: "The Commander of the VI Division reported: Novograd-Volynsk was taken at dawn today" (p. 41).

"The Kiss" represents the most optimistic version of a *Red Cavalry* ending. Joost van Baak is right to attribute the surprisingly positive overtones of **"Argamak"** and **"The Kiss"** to the fact that they were written much later than *Red Cavalry* proper, "under the ideological pressure of the thirties."[29] **"The Kiss"** reworks the theme

and plot of Chekhov's eponymous story. Yet while Chekhov's hero never again meets the mysterious woman who kissed him and comes to see his life as purposeless and incomprehensible, Babel's hero finds the woman, makes love to her, and discovers purpose in revolutionary struggle. The story's conclusion affirms the revolutionary path as the only natural one. Liutov's Cossack companion finds it by animal-like instinct: "We . . . found ourselves in a ploughed field [without a path]. Surovtsev straightened up in the saddle, looked right and left, gave a whistle, sniffed for the right direction and breathed it in with the air; then he leaned forward and shot off at a gallop" (p. 373). Nonetheless, the story has its ironic pitfalls. The woman's father remains skeptical about Liutov and Surovtsev's triumphant vision of "the right direction": "In order not to cloud his happiness, he tried [not to notice] our bloodthirsty bravado, the loudmouthed simplicity that in those days we brought to the solution of all world problems" (p. 368). Liutov's promise of a better life for the woman may be impossible to keep: the story **"Zamość"** has already related the Russian defeat. The context of **"Beresteczko,"** which alludes to Bohdan Khmelnitsky and Napoleon, whose armies rolled through these territories leaving behind a path of destruction, magnifies this doubt. (Both stories also use the motif of a liaison between a local woman and a foreign soldier, which encourages an interpretive connection.) Again, the story provides closure to the cycle by reporting the Russians' crossing of the Polish border, which recapitulates the "crossing" from the opening story and takes the reader again to the beginning of the war and of *Red Cavalry.*

In its cyclical structure, recurrent themes and motifs, and in the pattern of Liutov's reexamination of his values and beliefs as he enters new fields of experience, *Red Cavalry* emerges as a coherent, closely knit whole. I would therefore agree with the proponents of treating *Red Cavalry* as a novel insofar as the need for a holistic approach is concerned. In a letter of 1929, Babel himself admitted to gravitating toward the novelistic form in his early years: "Before I always tried to write (*razmakhivalsia na*) novels, and what would come out instead were stories, shorter than a sparrow's tail."[30]

Jan van der Eng offers the most convincingly articulated "novel approach" to *Red Cavalry.* He views the work as a modernist novel among whose features he lists a shifting ironic viewpoint, secondary narrators, truncated transitions between narrative sections, and non-indicated flashbacks.[31] Yet considering the proliferation of story cycles in the nineteenth and twentieth centuries, these features may arguably suggest the opposite direction of influence. The novel itself may be undergoing a "contamination" by the story cycle poetics—a process parallel to the novelization of the epic (a previously dominant genre) so insightfully described by Bakhtin. More important, van der Eng's insistence on fitting the work into a novelistic mold causes him to smooth out and tie up more than seems warranted. The "clear developmental line" that he sees in the events, characters, and especially the narrator seems to me much less clear, at times even zigzaggy or circular (in ways that the qualification "modernist" no longer accounts for it).[32] Van der Eng's focus on the narrator's development, conditioned precisely by a novelistic expectation, also appears somewhat forced. *Red Cavalry* is only in part about Liutov. By choosing the story-cycle form Babel could be attempting to "dethrone" the main protagonist (here also narrator), to deemphasize his *Bildung* relative to that of his novelistic counterpart. Even the *kind* of narrator that Liutov is underscores this tendency. His centrifugal consciousness prompts him to suspend his ego in encountering the various "others"; his initial impulse is always the experience of the object itself rather than the discovery of the object's relation to him. Finally, any novel approach, including van der Eng's, inevitably tends to consider the story cycle a poor version of the novel: rather than be judged on its own, the cycle is shown to barely meet the novel's standards. Therefore, instead of justifying *Red Cavalry*'s deficiencies as a novel, I consider it more productive to investigate what the work gains by *not* being one. While arguing a holistic approach to *Red Cavalry* I have thus far stressed the connections and linkages in the work, a comparison with the novel form now requires a comment upon the relative separateness and autonomy of stories and voices within a story cycle.

Forrest Ingram's study of the story cycle genre again offers valuable insights for this comparison. He notes that story cycles accentuate "the rhythmic pattern of the telling" and deemphasize the time relationships among stories.[33] This certainly occurs in *Red Cavalry.* For example, Liutov's transformation into a soldier in active service (though not consistently maintained) happens imperceptibly in the work; its timing and circumstances are unimportant. Only one of the concluding stories reports this event. Many stories stand out, as it were, from the main time framework, the 1920 Polish campaign (for example, **"Sandy the Christ"** or **"Prishchepa"**), or are completely "timeless" and static (**"The Cemetery at Kozin"** or most of **"Discourse on the *Tachanka*"**). While it is true that prehistories of characters (as in **"Prishchepa"**) or lyrical passages (as **"Kozin"**) also appear in novels, stories collected in a cycle are equipolent parts of the whole, and not departures from the main story line due to each story's autonomous, self-contained status. Ingram's rhythmically patterned telling characterizes sequences of individual stories (such as the ones describing the deterioration of the Cossack army) and of the major blocks; for example, the main block's development of the initial one's thematic embryos. The abandonment of the causal-temporal relationships in a cycle for the sake of the rhythmic patterns of thematic development allows for a greater ideological focus and flexibility while the work's unity and cohesion is simultaneously preserved.

Another vital contrast with the novel is the cycle's emancipation of peripheral characters. Ingram notes that the action of the cycle is always centered in the action of a given story.[34] Hence, in a cycle, a story of a secondary character is not a digression from the main plot, as it would tend to be in a novel. For as long as the character occupies the spotlight, he or she is the center of interest. In *Red Cavalry* such "peripheral" characters as Afon'ka Bida or Pavlichenko assume an even greater prominence by reappearing in a number of stories that modify and complement their portrayal in the stories where they are central.

It is arguable, if we take *Red Cavalry* as a model, that the genre of a story cycle is better suited for representing the flux of contemporaneity and for achieving the open-ended dialogue of heteroglossia than Bakhtin's venerated novel.[35] Bakhtin's definition of the novel hinges on the interillumination of various social languages through dialogue. *Red Cavalry* matches this definition. The languages of Russian Cossacks, Poles, Catholics, rabbis, shtetl Jews, Communists, anti-Communists, anarchists, and village artists, among others, dialogically illuminate and refract one another. Contrary to Bakhtin's assertion, however, the novel is not unique in combining the "subordinated, yet still *relatively* autonomous [compositional-stylistic] unities . . . into the higher unity of the work as a whole."[36] It is true of cycles as well. Moreover, the autonomy of each story and character in a cycle weakens the links of subordination of various stylistic unities and discourses into the "higher unity." Therefore, it seems more natural for the story cycle than for the novel to convey inconclusive, open-ended contemporaneity.

Bakhtin also praises the polyphonic novel for representing the man who "ceased to coincide with himself," and for capturing "the dynamics of inconsistency and tension between various factors of his image."[37] Here again the Babelian cycle surpasses the Bakhtinian novel. As *Red Cavalry* demonstrates, in a story where a character occupies the central position, he or she receives a fully dramatized, independent voice. The portrayals of that character from different viewpoints in a number of other stories show his or her other selves and voices. The autonomous status of each story makes the genre perfectly suited for leaving the tensions between these voices unresolved, and for allowing these different selves to remain unmerged into a coherent, unified identity. Who is Afon'ka Bida? A Cossack raconteur with poetic leanings? A compassionate comrade? An awesome yet terrible mercy-killer? A cruel degenerate? An anarchist? A drunken wretch? The answer is that he is a hybrid of all the above, he "does not coincide with himself." The variety of vantage points and of stories in which these different selves and voices are plotted makes the "inconsistency" and the "tension" all the more palpable.

The role of plot in the two genres also offers revealing differences. Bakhtin revels in the novelistic word that is "half-ours and half-someone else's," that serves as the battleground of various ideological values and points of view. *Red Cavalry* abounds in such internally conflicted words. The struggle within Liutov between authoritarian discourse, such as political dogma, and other people's internally persuasive discourse, to use Bakhtin's term, serves as a good example. Bakhtin asserts that these discourses remain "incomplete and unresolved," though he himself sees plot—and the undeniable degree of resolution and closure that it offers—as a constraint on his notion of the novel's openness.[38] He conveniently underestimates the power of plot in evaluating discourse. If openness is the ideal, the generic features of the story cycle give it an advantage over the novel. First, in each story the narrator appears as if anew; his voices, views, and attitudes may fluctuate between stories. As a result the reader never relies on his word as authoritative. Liutov's internally persuasive discourse never liberates itself from another's discourse, even in the concluding stories. Second, the novel may have a plot and subplots, or at best a few parallel plots. *Red Cavalry* has thirty-six plots. While connected by the narrator and certain themes, they are nonetheless autonomous. Even when a character appears in a few stories, each time the plot is new. All these factors undermine the power of plot in *Red Cavalry* to resolve anything. In short, I believe that Babel's story cycle fulfills the potential of Bakhtin's model of a narrative more fully than the novel. The Bakhtinian analysis of several story cycles could quite likely yield interesting results.

Although this article has focused on *Red Cavalry*'s sources of cohesion, my concluding discussion of the cycle's internal *separateness,* necessitated by the comparison with the novel, has added a crucial counterpoise without which the picture of the genre would be incomplete. Separateness and cohesion are simultaneously at work in the cycle, and their continuous interplay is crucial for the genre's idiosyncratic dynamic. A feature of the story cycle which relies in turn on the *connectedness* of its parts is its special blend of irony (I am concerned here with the irony that operates between, not within, individual stories). An ironic reading of this kind requires an assumption that the characters and motifs reappearing in various stories are meant to be read in the context of one another. This has been my approach to *Red Cavalry* in this article, and it has been motivated by the insufficient attention given to it by the existing scholarship. Yet the cycle's constant pull between independence and interdependence makes ironic correspondence a potential that is constantly questioned: these are, after all, separate stories. Assuming they *are*

interrelated, establishing specific ironic juxtapositions presents further difficulties, due to the proliferation of plots and contexts in a cycle. According to one of D. C. Muecke's definitions, irony consists in placing an element, without comment, in an invalidating or corrective context.[39] While the mediated and unmediated portrayals of various characters in *Red Cavalry* offer ample incongruities and incompatibilities (an indispensable ingredient of irony), do the mediated stories invalidate or correct the unmediated ones? No unequivocal answer to this question is possible. This latent irony, this irony "with a question mark," represents the story cycle's unique generic feature and contributes to *Red Cavalry*'s ideological dynamism and uncompromising open-endedness.

Notes

1. Respectively, Marc Slonim, *Portrety sovetskikh pisatelei* (Paris, 1933), 145; A. Arkhipov, "Uroki," *Neva* 6 (1958): 187; Louis Iribarne, "Babel's 'Red Cavalry' as a Baroque Novel," *Contemporary Literature* 14, no. 1 (1973): 58-77; Jan van der Eng, "*Red Cavalry*: A Novel of Stories," *Russian Literature* 33 (1993): 249-64; Stanley E. Hyman, "The Identities of Isaak Babel," *The Hudson Review* 8 (1956): 622-23; and Edward J. Brown, *Russian Literature since the Revolution* (Cambridge, MA, 1982), 89.

2. See, for example, Carol Luplow, *Isaak Babel's "Red Cavalry"* (Ann Arbor, 1982); Efraim Sicher, *Style and Structure in the Prose of Isaak Babel* (Columbus, OH, 1986); and Agnes Gereben, "The Syntactics of Cycles of Short Stories," *Essays in Poetics* (April 1986): 44-75.

3. Letter to I. V. Evdokimov, 16 April 1926, and letter to I. L. Livshits, 17 April 1923, both in Isaak Babel', *Sochineniia,* 2 vols. (Moscow, 1990), 1:243, 238. All further quotes from Babel's letters will be taken from this edition. All translations of Russian texts other than Babel's stories are mine.

4. Letter to Furmanov, 4 February 1926, ibid., 244.

5. Dmitrii Furmanov, *Sobranie sochinenii* (Moscow, 1961), 4:340.

6. Forrest L. Ingram, *Representative Short Story Cycles of the Twentieth Century: Study in a Literary Genre* (The Hague, 1971). The subsequent studies do not make radical departures from or add substantial elaborations to Ingram's model of the genre. See Susan G. Mann, *The Short Story Cycle: A Genre Companion and Reference Guide* (Westport, CT, 1989); and J. Gerald Kennedy, ed., *Modern American Short Story Sequences: Composite Fictions and Fictive Communities* (New York, 1995), both of which fine-tune Ingram's notions and provide insightful case studies (Mann's

book also sketches the genre's history). In the Anglo-American criticism Ingram's study has inspired a plethora of projects similar to mine.

7. Ingram, *Representative Short Story Cycles,* 19, 20, 21.

8. For example, he is the former in "The Rebbe," "Evening," and "The Rebbe's Son"; the latter in "Afon'ka Bida," "Two Ivans," and "After the Battle."

9. Robert A. Maguire, *Red Virgin Soil* (Ithaca, 1987), 328.

10. The original 1926 edition ends with "The Rebbe's Son." In 1932, Babel adds "Argamak." The inclusion of "The Kiss" in the posthumous editions is based on Babel's wife's indication that the author intended to do so.

11. *Isaac Babel: The Collected Stories,* trans. Walter Morison (New York, 1974). My emendations are marked by square brackets. In-text parenthetical references to stories in the cycle are to the Russian text published in Babel', *Sochineniia,* vol. 2. David McDuff's most recent translation, *Collected Stories* (New York, 1994), is noteworthy for its use of the uncensored Russian text published in Israel in 1979. Morison's translation, however, surpasses McDuff's stylistically, especially in its rendition of *skaz* (for example, in "Treason" or "Pavlichenko"). Following McDuff's example, however, I will use Polish spelling for Polish place names rather than follow Morison in transcribing them from Russian. The most important changes are: Beresteczko (compare with Morison's "Berestechko"), Cześniki ("Chesniki"), Zamość ("Zamoste"), Zbrucz ("Zbruch"). I will also use a more direct translation of "Perekhod cherez Zbrucz"—"Crossing the Zbrucz" (Morison's "Crossing into Poland"), and of "Rabbi" and "Syn rabbi" (Babel uses the Hebrew word, not the Russian "*ravvin*") as "The Rebbe" and "The Rebbe's Son" (Morison's "The Rabbi" and "The Rabbi's Son"). I will also use the Library of Congress system for transliterating Russian names, such as "Liutov" or "Il'ia" (compare with Morison's "Lyutov" and "Ilya").

12. Patricia Carden, *The Art of Isaac Babel* (Ithaca, 1972), 135.

13. Babel', *Sochineniia* 2:18. There may be other parallels between Liutov and Pan Apolek. Apolek's identity is not clear but he may be Jewish. He is described as having a thin neck—a frequent attribute of Babel's Jewish characters (for example, the Jewish woman's sons in the first story). He claims to have been christened, but he may be lying in order to gain employment from Catholics.

His stories and murals reveal little care about Christian dogma. Apolek and Liutov (and Babel) may thus be seen as artists working in fundamentally hostile communities: the former among Polish Catholics, the latter among Russian Cossacks. In working *for* them, they need to balance their own artistic vision with the employer's tastes and views. Perhaps in this respect Apolek also provides a model for Liutov. For an extra fee Pan Apolek will paint the customer's enemy as Judas in a monstrous Last Supper scene, just as Liutov will write propagandist articles for a Communist rag. Both, however, can also create great art.

14. Iribarne, "Babel's 'Red Cavalry,'" 65.

15. See also Efraim Sicher's brilliant investigation of the issue of Jewishness in Babel in *Jews in Russian Literature after the October Revolution* (New York, 1996).

16. The motif of renouncing Jewishness and espousing the Revolution has already appeared in "The Rebbe," when Liutov leaves the rebbe's house and rushes back to the propaganda train to finish an article for *Red Trooper.* It will reappear in "The Rebbe's Son."

17. For a compelling reading of the story see Joost van Baak, "Isaac Babel's 'Cemetery at Kozin,'" *Canadian Slavonic Papers* 36, no. 1-2 (1994): 69-87. Van Baak makes a compelling argument for the story being an important "nodal point in the semantics and composition of *Red Cavalry*" (ibid., 69).

18. See Wayne Booth's exposé of the "objective fallacy" of authors and readers, *The Rhetoric of Fiction,* 2d ed. (Chicago, 1983).

19. Indeed, the spectrum approach to the study of narrative viewpoint has been gaining acceptance over the rigid binary approach. See, for example, Susan Lanser, *The Narrative Act: Point of View in Prose Fiction* (Princeton, 1981).

20. Babel quite likely took the trick from Maupassant's 1885 novel *Bel-Ami,* in which the narrator describes a work of art (a painting of Christ walking on water) as if the event it depicts were actually taking place ([New York, 1975], 357, 400-401).

21. Ingram, *Representative Short Story Cycles,* 201.

22. Sicher, *Jews in Russian Literature,* 98.

23. Babel', *Sochineniia* 1:202.

24. For a contrasting interpretation of the propaganda theme see Gareth Williams, "The Rhetoric of Revolution in Babel's *Konarmija*," *Russian Lit-*

erature 15 (1984): 279-98. Williams's article, though rich in fascinating minutiae, remains unconvincing. In order to argue Babel's acceptance of propaganda and revolution, Williams disregards problematic passages, glosses over irony whenever it suits his purpose, and imputes to Liutov mental leaps that lack any textual evidence.

25. In this curious dream, Liutov's death merges with a sexual climax and is followed by an eery Christian-pagan funeral ritual. Margot prays to Jesus and then places five-kopek coins on Liutov's eyelids and stuffs his mouth with hay. Upon awakening, Liutov becomes imagistically transformed into a figure of a cross formed by the "black crossbar of [his] horse's back" and by his leg that was "sticking in the air, caught fast in the tight noose of the bridle." The blood trickling down his face, "torn by the weeds of the steppe," further likens Liutov to a Christ figure (p. 169). An image of Jesus, so frequently encountered in the Jewish art of the period (most notably in Chagall; see, for example, Sicher, *Jews in Russian Literature,* 40-71) signals the martyrdom of the Jewish people and in this story connects Liutov with the Jews being massacred in the Zamość pogrom whose groans he hears through the tumult of battle.

26. Gulimov also sends a bullet by Liutov's ear. This act acquires symbolic significance when read in the context of "Two Ivans," in which Akinfiev repeatedly fires his pistol near the ear of Aggeev, who evades active service by pretending to be deaf. Thus, a shot fired by someone's ear, like the purblind eyes or the thin neck motifs, becomes a symbol: it labels a person as a deserter.

27. See, for example, Allan Reid, "Isaak Babel's *Konarmiia*: Meanings and Endings," *Canadian Slavonic Papers* 33, no. 2 (1991).

28. Sicher, *Jews in Russian Literature,* 104.

29. Joost van Baak, "Story and Cycle: Babel's 'Potseluj' and Konarmija," *Russian Literature* 15 (1984): 326.

30. Babel', *Sochineniia* 1:296.

31. Van der Eng, "*Red Cavalry*: A Novel of Stories."

32. Ibid., 261.

33. Ingram, *Representative Short Story Cycles,* 23.

34. Ibid., 22.

35. Mikhail Bakhtin, *The Dialogic Imagination: Four Essays,* trans. Caryl Emerson and Michael Holquist (Austin, 1981), 35.

36. Ibid., 262 (emphasis added).

37. Ibid., 35.

38. Ibid., 345, 349.

39. D. C. Muecke, *The Compass of Irony* (London, 1969), 23.

Rachel Rubin (essay date 2000)

SOURCE: Rubin, Rachel. "Imagine You Are a Tiger: A New Folk Hero in Isaac Babel's *Odessa Tales*." In *Jewish Gangsters of Modern Literature,* pp. 15-49. Urbana: University of Illinois Press, 2000.

[*In the following essay, Rubin outlines the ways in which Babel's gangster-protagonists transmute the banality of Odessa ghetto life into something remarkable and memorable. She also demonstrates that a large portion of Babel's writing stems from his love for his home, and that his admiration of Odessa's vitality manifests itself in the form of powerful, engaging, and lawless characters.*]

> And Benya Krik had his way, for he was passionate, and passion rules the universe.
>
> —Isaac Babel, **"The King"**

Isaac Babel's colorful Odessan gangsters loom larger and wilder than life, and the responses of his readers at home and abroad have tended to reflect this. "Babel's Odessa is a fairyland," writes Andrey Sinyavsky, "where local images and national traits are surrounded by a halo of legend." James Falen agrees: "Everything about the gangsters is exaggerated and fantastic." Frank O'Connor quips, "if I were dependent for my idea of reality on the Odessa gangsters of Babel I should be in a bad plight indeed."[1] These glorious bandits tower above the cramped Jewish ghetto, liberated from its deprivations by the brilliance of their iniquity.

If the resplendence of their deeds exceeds the credible, the aplomb of these gangsters is not out of proportion with the impact of these stories upon the literary world. Babel wrote seven short stories—totaling around sixty pages—about Benya Krik (Benny the yell), passionate "gangster and king of gangsters."[2] These few pages—though frequently overshadowed critically by Babel's longer and better-known story cycle *Red Cavalry*—were groundbreaking for a host of diverse writers, including those to be treated in this study. The effect of their publication upon the literary world, recalled Konstantin Paustovsky, author of several affectionate memoirs of Babel, was like being hit in the face with a stream from a siphon.[3] The story of the literary gangster must start here, in the Jewish ghettos of prerevolutionary, cosmopolitan Odessa.

With *Odessa Tales,* Babel inaugurated the Jewish gangster theme into "high" literature, although stylized Jewish criminals had certainly inhabited popular and folk forms in Russia and the United States.[4] By taking the folk character of the social bandit and investing his experience with complex motivations, political immediacy, and modern ambivalence while allowing him to remain glorious, Babel created a character with unusual allure for Jewish intellectuals in the New World of America as well as in the new Soviet Union. In order to trace the important figure of the Jewish gangster in modern American prose, one must first look to Babel's rogue heroes.

Babel's elevated portraits nourished a fascination on the part of European and American writers with modern underworld figures. Most important, his treatment of Jewish gangsters as ideal studies in social, artistic, linguistic, and political modernity remains influential for writers on both continents. The reminiscences of Robert Pinsky, in addition to hinting at the remarkable geographic and temporal range of the stories' impact, disclose exactly what so many Jewish writers found compelling about Benya Krik. Pinsky connects indulgent memories of his own grandfather, a New Jersey gangster, with a readerly appreciation of Babel's gangsters, noting that "one of the many things that interest me . . . is the process of mythologizing and glamorizing." Of shady gangster toughness—a blow in the face of Jewish tradition—Pinsky contends, "the point . . . is not assimilation but something like assurance."[5]

For Pinsky, Babel's creations signal a healthy bravado, spelling an "attractive counterforce" to the typical Jewish underdog. But most interesting is the self-consciousness in Pinsky's blueprint; his emphasis on the *process* of mythologizing points to a *rhetorical invention*—the image of the gangster—who will serve the needs of a marginalized Jewish writer. The connection between writer and gangster proposed by this study starts with Babel's Odessa tales. These stories are the first to pair the two as artistic foils, turning the gangster from a literary device into a metaliterary device: if the writer were more like the gangster, the stories suggest, he or she could respond effectively to anti-Semitism, craft a hardy Jewish identity, and be at home in the polyvocal modern city (not only its Jewish ghetto), whether Odessa or New York.

This relationship between artist and killer was emphasized by the New York intellectual Lionel Trilling, who in 1955 wrote a short introduction to a major English translation of Babel's short stories. Trilling's introduction would become a cornerstone of Babel's American reception and an important meditation upon the place of the Jewish intellectual in America. Trilling, whose admiration for the stories cannot always cloak a certain squeamishness, writes what amounts to a summary of Babel's first American reception (even invoking his own experience reading Babel's stories twenty-five years earlier). Trilling recalls how to those American

writers and artists whose attentive eyes were fixed on the "Russian experiment" came the complicated Isaac Babel, who always "speaks of art with the language of force."[6] In Babel, Trilling sees a Jewish artist torn between peace, which is associated with the memory of Babel's father groveling before a Cossack soldier, and war, which is associated with the gangster Benya Krik, who creates his own future.

Whatever expectations about Soviet art may have circulated, Babel's violent stories closed a chapter in shtetl-centered portrayals of Jewish life, while establishing new categories for other writers to contend with. Drawing heavily from the seminal Yiddish writers Sholem Aleichem and Mendele Moykher-Sforim, known for their humorous chronicling of Russian Jewish life at the turn of the century, Babel attaches elements of satire and dissonance: he thereby not only produces the shock of his own Odessa tales, but also insists upon a look below the charming surface of the earlier texts. *Man without a World,* a fake "lost" Yiddish film by the American filmmaker Eleanor Antin, captures this well in an aside: an explanatory "scholarly" note scrolls across the screen at the beginning to explain that the film's backers had rejected Babel as a possible screenwriter because they desired a shtetl film, pure and simple, without any of the lurid or bizarre complications for which Babel was well known.

Babel's grim adaptation of Yiddish idiom to Russian and the modern experience shaped another generation of Yiddish writers across the ocean in America. For instance, Jacob Glatshteyn's poem "Sheeny Mike" (1929), which tells of the rise and fall of a dead Jewish gangster in a New York neighborhood, is noticeably indebted to **Odessa Tales.**[7] The escapades of Babel's gangsters seem to inspire not only the subjective introspection of Glatshteyn, but also the sardonic humor of Ornitz, the offhanded cruelty of Fuchs, and the heightened pathos of Gold. The most striking aspect of this band of criminals is how truly they resist old categories. This fluidity perhaps more than anything else indicates the true stamp of Babel's imagination.

Like his unruly gangsters, Babel has continued to evade critical templates. During his life and posthumously, during his peak of productivity and during the years when he was practicing what he termed the difficult genre of "silence," Babel has worn too many provocative and seemingly contradictory hats to allow anyone to be completely at ease with him. He has been hailed and reviled as the first real Soviet writer; as the first integrated Russian Jewish writer; as the literary ancestor of the score of younger Russian writers who began under his impress; as a martyr to Stalinism; as a devoted Bolshevik and even Chekist (the Soviet Secret Police, later called the KGB); as an uncompromising chronicler of the horrors committed by *both* armies in the Civil

War; as a celebrator of Jewish folkways and collective identity; as a self-hating Jew who rejects and ridicules the world of his parents and commits the mind-boggling trespass of admiring that ancient enemy of the Jews, the Cossacks.[8]

Babel's reception at home and abroad has reflected an ambivalence corresponding to the complexity of the author's own position. Like many of his contemporaries, Babel was arrested during the Stalinist purges (in 1939, which was relatively late) and ultimately executed; predictably, the content of his writings emerged as a component of his indictment. He was officially rehabilitated by the Soviets in 1954 during the process of de-Stalinization and cleared of all charges, but a specter continued to haunt his reputation in the Soviet Union. Those of Babel's works that were republished in the Soviet Union following the clearing of his name were issued in tiny printings and in sharply edited form; suppressed diaries, correspondence, and the like continue to surface in archives in the former Soviet Union. Even able critics from outside the Soviet Union are frequently more comfortable explicating Babel's accomplishments as existing *in spite of* his politics, rather than considering methodically how Babel's political philosophy contributed to the formation of his inimitable aesthetic. Although superlatives are commonly linked to his name, a full critical biography of Babel remains to be written.

Babel himself has contributed to this elusiveness: his autobiographical stories are typically misleading. Even his often-anthologized two-page scrap of an autobiography ("Avtobiografiya") contains several misleading or inaccurate descriptions. One thing Babel is straightforward about is his trickiness. The boy-narrator of **"In the Basement"** tells the reader directly, "I was an untruthful child," effectively warning the reader not to confuse artistic truth with fact.[9] Likewise, the narrator of **"Moi pervyi gonovar"** (**"My first fee"**) cites lying as his first professional venture as a writer: he entertains a prostitute with a fabricated life story and elicits her sympathy; she returns his money.[10]

It is precisely from these lacunae of indeterminacy, however, that some of the most relevant truths about Babel emerge. Isaac Emmanuelovich Babel was born in Odessa in 1894 into a secular, lower-middle-class Jewish family. Although his autobiographical writings indicate that he spent his entire childhood in this Black Sea port city, his biographers assert that shortly after his birth, the Babel family moved to nearby Nikolayev, where Babel's sister was born; they did not return to Odessa until 1905. This immediate discrepancy, unremarkable enough for any writing tossed into the vexed category of autobiographical fiction, is consequential in two ways: it indicates Babel's obstate tendency toward the enigmatic; and more specifically, it manifests his relentless privileging of the port city of Odessa.

TALES OF ODESSA

Even the most cursory biographical or critical sketch of Babel must also be a portrait of his beloved Odessa. The Odessa of Babel's day was the most cosmopolitan city in Imperial Russia. Odessa was an important port town founded shortly after Peter the Great established his capital of St. Petersburg; its population (until the devastation of World War II) consisted of a substantial mix not only of Russians but also Ukrainians, Jews, Greeks, Moldavians, Poles, Germans, Turks, Karaites, Bulgarians, Armenians, French, and Italians.[11] By the time Babel was born, Odessa had become the largest Jewish settlement outside of Poland, the population of Jews having grown from 246 in 1795 to 152,634 in 1904.[12] Odessa boasts a mild climate (especially compared to the frigid Russian winters pictured by Dostoevsky and Pasternak), bathing beaches, and a variety of available delicacies such as fresh fruits and vegetables. This appeal, coupled with the attraction of its ethnic diversity, has always given the city a remarkable drawing power and reputation as charmingly "exotic" among tourists, artists, and writers. Patricia Herlihy writes that by the 1880s Odessa's image as "an El Dorado for Jews and gentiles alike had flashed throughout the Pale."[13] Maurice Friedberg, in his study of Odessa during the last twenty-odd years (the title of which, *How Things Were Done in Odessa,* is borrowed from Babel), maintains that in recent times "Odessa appears to have retained more color, more spunk, more irreverence than most Soviet cities."[14]

Babel's warmth toward his hometown is a constant force in his writing. Besides providing the milieu for the adventures of Benya and his gang, Odessa is the setting of some deeply moving childhood stories (**"Pervaya lyubov'"** [**"First love"**], **"Awakening,"** **"Story of My Dovecote,"** and others) and numerous less famous works. Additionally, Babel wrote several discursive pieces dealing with Odessa, and in his personal correspondence frequently refers to its appeal and color, especially in terms of language.[15] His wife, Antonina Nikolaevna Pirozhkova, recalled that in Odessa Babel would coach her to listen for typically Odessan phrases.[16] Although the formalist theorist Victor Shklovskii is credited with later identifying a discrete Odessan literary tradition, Babel remarked on more than one occasion that Odessa was uniquely capable of producing the kind of writer that the changing world was awaiting.[17]

In his essay on the emergence of modernism, Raymond Williams cites the "miscellaneity of the metropolis" as a key factor in the production of formally experimental literary works. Williams connects aesthetic innovation with the collision of different native languages or traditions and the shedding of provincialism that occurs in the complex metropolis: the sophisticated social environment produces a heightened self-consciousness, and as a result language is "more evident as a medium—a medium that could be shaped and reshaped—than as a social custom."[18] (The Jewish American short-story writer Grace Paley more simply and graphically described a "lucky composting" that began for Babel in Odessa.[19]) Babel frankly declares the diverse and changing cultural milieu in Odessa to be the source of his own inspiration, especially his attention to language. In an early essay on Odessa, he explicitly connects regionalism with linguistics, ethnicity, history, literary power, and law:

> Odessa ochen' skvernii gorod. Eto vsem izvestno. . . . Mne zhe kazhetsya, chto mozhno mnogo skazat' xoroshego ob etom znachitel'nom i ocharovatel'nyeshem gorode v Rossiiskoy Imperii. Polovinu naseleniya ego sostavlyayut evrei. . . . Bednykh evreev iz Odessy ochen' pugayut gubernatory i tsirkulyary. No sbit' ikh s pozitsii nelegko, ochen' uzh starodavnyaya pozitsiya. Ikh i ne sob'yut i mnogomy ot nikh nauchitsya.

> Odessa is an awful place. Everybody knows how they murder the Russian language there. All the same, I think there's a lot to be said for this great city, which has more charm than any other in the Russian Empire. Half the population consists of Jews. . . . Poor Jews in Odessa are very confused by provincial governors and official forms, but it's not easy to get them to abandon positions they took up a very long time ago. You can't get them to do that, but you can learn a lot from them.[20]

This early jibe marks a connection between language and difference that is an important reason for creating fictional gangsters. In the opening lines of the essay Babel concretizes this connection textually, giving two pithy examples of the "nasty" (*skvernii*) way Odessans speak. The first example underscores the notion of difference: instead of saying "a big difference," Odessans say "two big differences" ("vmesto 'bolshaya raznitsa' tam govoryat 'dve bolshie raznitsi'").[21] The second example invokes place or regionalism: Odessans, Babel claims, mispronounce the phrase "here and there."

Babel responds directly to critics of Odessan speech, such as the novelist Yevgeny Zamyatin, who was innovative and unconventional in his own prose but oddly resistant to what he considered to be "contamination" of the Russian language. Zamyatin writes:

> In the Western provinces, the Russian language has been corrupted by Byelo-russian and Polish influences; in the provinces of southern Russia, by admixtures of Polish, Ukrainian and Yiddish. The use of southern and western provincialisms in dialogue is, of course, entirely legitimate. But it would be a gross error to introduce them into the text, into the author's comments or descriptions of landscape. This fault is especially pronounced in the works of southern writers, since the worst adulteration of the language has occurred in the south and particularly in Odessa.[22]

The threat of language contamination seems to be a common way of articulating and deflecting anxiety about other blendings—in particular, miscegenation. (I discuss this deflection at length in chapter 3, on Mike Gold.) In this light, the highest tribute paid in the stories to Benya Krik—that he could spend the night with a Russian woman and she would be satisfied—perhaps vocalizes a fear on the part of anti-Semites as well as an internalization of this fear as desire on the part of the Jewish narrator.

Babel, on the other hand, makes the case for language blending as the way to achieve literary excellence.[23] To do this, he mimics in his essay the "charm" of this integrated city in the language he uses. He interjects frequently in French (the language in which, at fifteen, he wrote his first stories)—Odessa possessed important trade connections with France—but translates the Yiddish word *luftmensch* into Russian, rendering it literally as *chelovek vozdukha,* or "person of the air"; in short, he uses a Yiddish idiom to coin a new Russian phrase.[24] Not only is *luftmensch* a Yiddish idiomatic expression referring to someone insufficiently grounded in daily reality, but the figure of the luftmensch is a standard of Jewish folk and "high" literature that is invoked by a myriad of Jewish writers, including Babel.[25]

Whether Babel's notion of an Odessan "literary messiah" is an overstatement may be open to debate.[26] But the halls of the Odessa Literary Museum show inarguably that the city has produced some of the most important Russian writers, as well as Yiddish and Hebrew ones: Babel himself, of course, and also Konstantin Paustovsky, Yurii Olesha, Valentin Kataev, the team Ilf and Petrov, the poet Eduard Bagritsky, and Mendele Moykher-Sforim, the undisputed founder of both modern Hebrew and modern Yiddish literature; the list could also include important work done in or about Odessa by Anton Chekhov, Alexander Kuprin, Ivan Bunin, and Sholem Aleichem.

The work of these writers, taken together with historical accounts, indicates that Odessa also excelled at the production of criminals. As critics have noted, "high" writers of Babel's generation seemed to be obsessed with criminal or near-criminal types, and Odessa supplied ready material: according to Konstantin Paustovsky, there were two thousand professional criminals in the Jewish Moldavanka district of the city, which was "one of the shabbier quarters [of Odessa]. . . . It was dirty, poor, noisy, overcrowded, and dangerous."[27] Leon Trotsky called Odessa "perhaps the most police-ridden city in police-ridden Russia."[28] Paustovsky opens his volume of memoirs of Odessa with a chapter headed "Forerunners of Ostap Bender"; by describing the city's criminal population in terms of a literary character, Ilf and Petrov's rogue hero from *The Twelve Chairs* and *Little Golden Calf,* he makes an imaginative link between gangsters and writers. Paustovsky goes on to testify to the fascination these characters had for his group of young writers, which included Babel:

> What has made me think of him [Ilya Ilf] and his hero, the fearless racketeer Ostap Bender, is that even in those grim days racketeering flourished in Odessa. Even the most spineless caught the infection. They, too, came to believe in the ancient law of the junk-market: "If you want to eat, know how to sell the sleeves of a waistcoat."
>
> In time, the rackets infiltrated even our literary and journalistic milieu.[29]

Despite the grip that the actual gangsters had upon the public imagination of Odessa, it is no accident that the linguistically fastidious Babel, known for the obsessive attention he paid to the choosing of each word in his stories, named his cycle of stories after Odessa rather than after the gangsters. Babel's text mirrors the heterogeneity and turbulence of the city: a host of different vernacular voices present themselves, frequently without narrative mediation; clichés and banalities are passed off as high drama; literary conventions ranging from the folkloric to the epic are invoked and then abruptly undercut. For instance, an astute reader might recognize "Laugh, Clown" as the aria from Leoncavallo's *Pagliacci,* but will be startled to hear it belted out by the horn of a gangster's bright red car. Of course, the Russian formalist critics had already coined the term *ostranenie,* or defamiliarization, to describe this quest for the frisson of novelty.

Babel relies upon *ostranenie* to make topical points about the status of Jews, and the Jewish writer, in Russia. At the same time that Babel was beginning *Odessa Tales,* the Jewish writer and critic Lev Lunts groped toward a definition of the Russian Jewish identity, writing in a letter to Maxim Gorky, "I'm a Jew, staunch, loyal, and glad to be one. And I'm a *Russian* writer. But I'm also a Russian Jew, and Russia is my homeland, which I love more than any other country. How does one reconcile these?"[30] Babel uses the textual instability he models upon the commotion of Odessa to recreate in the reader a sense of anxiety and paradox that mirrors the position of the Jews in Imperial Russia.

Most important, however, Babel's stories create a climate of estrangement, in which familiar situations are frequently not what they seem to be or what they used to be. Estrangement is necessary to his portrayal of a society on the cusp of shattering technological and political changes.[31] This overarching sense of estrangement situates Babel's poignant self-consciousness as a product of a way of life that is about to end—one that Babel himself, when he joined the revolution, was actively working to end. A number of other modernist writers in "great power" countries were at this time ac-

knowledging their own untraditional use of language as a rebellion against themselves as products of their imperial nations. For instance, in his account of the "lost generation" of the 1920s, Malcolm Cowley recalls his circle of intellectuals as thinking that "life . . . is joyless and colorless, universally standardized, tawdry, uncreative, given over to the worship of wealth and machinery." Confronting this problem, Cowley writes, "the intellectuals had explored many paths; they had found no way to escape; one after another they had opened doors that led only into the cupboards and linen closets of the mind." The closest thing to an answer for young writers in the twenties, according to Cowley, was a belief in "form, simplification, strangeness."[32] This account of the modernist impulse, with its sense of pathos and impotency in the artists' intellectual hatred of themselves as well as their culture, speaks to Babel's own sense of distance and alienation, even as he joined forces with the Bolsheviks.[33]

This keenly felt alienation might be Babel's greatest literary obsession. The works in his *Childhood* stories focus on a Jewish disunion from the natural world.[34] His *Red Cavalry* tales thrust a lone Jewish intellectual into the company of uneducated Cossacks. The stories in *Odessa Tales* address the sense of alienation by setting up a highly visible system of insider/outsider paradigms that are constantly in flux. By using gangsters, as James Falen has aptly remarked, Babel managed to create characters who are "*in* but not *of* the ghetto."[35] Because of their "profession," the gangsters represent an assault on traditional Jewish values and folkways as surely as the Bolshevik Revolution does in *Red Cavalry.*

At the same time, however, the gangsters are useful to the Odessa community. They are able to move among worlds in a way that others cannot, thereby bridging many realms: legal with illegal, Jewish with non-Jewish, ghetto with mainstream. The ambiance of the wedding Benya Krik hosts for his sister Deborah attests to the gangster's role as sui generis diplomat:

> Nezdeshnee vino razogrevalo zheludki, sladko perelamybalo nogi, durmanilo mozgi i vyzyvalo otryzhku, zvuchnuyu, kak prizyv boevoi truby. Chyorny i kok s "Plutarkha", pribyvshego tret'ego dnya iz Port-Saida, vynyos sa tamozhennuyu chertu pusatiye butylki yamayskogo roma, maslyanistuyu maderu, sigary s plantatsii Pirponta Morgana i apel'siny iz okrestnostei Ierusalima.

> (**"Ko"** [**"Korol'"**], 243)[36]

> Wines not from these parts warmed stomachs, made legs faint sweetly, bemused brains, evoked belches that rang out sonorous as trumpets summoning to battle. The Negro cook from the Plutarch, that had put in three days before from Port Said, bore unseen through the customs fat-bellied jars of Jamaica rum, oily Madeira, cigars from the plantations of Pierpont Morgan, and oranges from the environs of Jerusalem.

> (**"K"** [**"The King"**], 207-8)

This ritual meal is truly a feast of the gods, attended by Jews as well as their friends. Konstantin Paustovsky recalls Babel remarking:

> "You remember Blok—'I see the enchanted shore, the enchanted distance.' [From "The Unknown Lady" (Neznakomka).] He got there all right, but I won't. I see that shore unbearably far off. I'm too sober. But I thank my lucky stars that at least I long for it. I work till I drop, I do all I can because I want to be at the feast of the gods and I'm afraid they'll throw me out."

> He took off his glasses, and wiped his eyes on the sleeve of his patched jacket.

> "I didn't choose to be born a Jew," he said suddenly. "I think I can understand everything. Only not the reason for that black villainy they call anti-Semitism."[37]

Taken together, these two passages show the gangsters as having a unique ability to overcome "that black villainy."

The special capacity of urban transgressors to unite is crucial to the story **"Froim Grach,"** which details the death under socialism of Ephraim Rook, the old-style gang leader who gives Benya his underworld start. An officer of the Soviet intelligence agency says of Grach, "He's a fantastic fellow . . . you will see the whole of Odessa in this man" (**"FG"** [**"Froim Grach"** (English)], 13). Grach is described as "huge as a house" (**"FG,"** 13), an image establishing him as connecting many discrete rooms that could have very different inhabitants. His ability to encompass so much is facilitated by his outlaw position as someone heedless of convention. The tale of the modern city is the tale of the glorious gangster.

BENYA'S YELL

What does a criminal do to rules of language? Babel's king of gangsters, Benya Krik, occupies the same transgressive space linguistically that he does legally, speaking an unforgettable admixture of Russian, Yiddish, Odessan jargon, and thieves' argot. In other words, he commits crimes in speech; Benya Krik might have been who Babel was thinking of in his essay **"Odessa,"** when he made the facetious observation that Odessa is a terrible place because of the way people speak there. Babel was eventually condemned by Stalinist critics for this very crime: violating the Russian language through an assault on its "purity" evinced largely by his use of vernaculars.[38]

Indeed, scholarship about Babel has tended to appropriate with admiration this notion of assault from Babel's Soviet detractors; James Falen, for instance, comments that Babel "murders in art," while V. I. Pritchett asserts that he "was a man who hit one in the belly."[39] In such descriptions, Babel becomes the Jewish gangster, as grand in his way as Benya Krik.

The "assault" represented by Benya Krik's vernacular Russian is what makes him an important gangster in the world of the stories, and also to the writers in Europe and America who came under Babel's influence. Acts of physical violence or terror occur in each of the Odessa tales. But Benya is a gangster of language more than anything else. His acceptance by the gang, recounted in **"How It Was Done In Odessa,"** is couched in terms of extraordinary speech acts. When, with forceful and colloquial eloquence, he demands that Ephraim Rook take him into his band of thieves, Ephraim responds appreciatively to Benya's words *as such,* remarking that "Benya says little, but what he says is tasty. He says little, and one would like him to say more" (**"H"** [**"How It Was Done in Odessa"**], 213). In **"Justice in Parentheses"** the narrator closely echoes Ephraim Rook's assessment of Benya's speech, saying, "The king speaks and he speaks politely. This frightens people so badly that they never ask him to repeat" (**"JP"** [**"Justice in Parentheses"**], 256).

These descriptions seem to indicate how the laconic Babel, whose revisions of his stories apparently consisted largely of obsessively cutting any words that could be considered extraneous, would have measured his own literary success. In his reminiscences of Babel, Paustovsky has him frequently performing excruciating revisions: "Babel would go up to it [his manuscript] and stroke it gingerly like a half-tamed beast. He often got up at night and reread three or four pages by the light of a wick-lamp, hemmed in by thick dictionaries standing on their sides. Every time he found a few more unnecessary words and triumphantly crossed them out. 'Language is clear and powerful,' he used to say, 'not when there is nothing more you can add to a sentence, but when there is nothing more you can cut out.'"[40]

By gifting Benya with the realization of Babel's own creative ideals, Babel equates initiation into gangsterhood with the highest achievement as a writer. The gangsters are inventive and daring; moreover, they have found a way to be semantically forceful. Benya's gangster nickname, *krik,* means yell. On more than one occasion, Babel drew connections between the ability to shout and the ability to write well. Paustovsky remembers Babel saying: "Writing! I've got asthma and I can't even shout properly, but a writer can't mumble—he has to shout at the top of his voice. You can bet Mayakovsky didn't mumble; and then there was Lermontov, slamming his verse into our faces."[41] Benya Krik, a masterful Jew whose very name is "shout," must then represent an exemplary Jewish writer.[42]

Indeed, Benya Krik makes ample "professional" use of his literary abilities. During his first raid as a member of Ephraim Rook's gang—before he has earned the nickname "King"—Benya passes the time while the money is being placed into a suitcase by telling stories—stories *about Jewish life*:

Nervnyi Solomon skladyval v chemodan den'gi, bumagi, chasy i monogrammy; pokoinik Iosif stoyal pered nim s podnyatymi rykami, i v eto vremya Benya rasskazyval istorii iz zhizni evreiskogo naroda.

("**Kak**" ["**Kak eto delalos' v Odesse**"], 250)

The nervous Solomon was packing cash, securities, watches, and monograms in a suitcase; the late Joseph stood before him with his hands in the air, and at that moment Benya was telling anecdotes about the life of the Jewish people.

("**H**," 217; translation altered)

Engaged in a crime, the gangster becomes chronicler for the Jews. In fact, here it is precisely Benya's actions as a Jewish criminal that have provided the occasion (not to mention the audience) for him to act as Jewish "writer."

Throughout this story, Babel's equation of Jewish speech with Jewish gangsterism is explicit. During the raid, the clerk Joseph is killed, and Benya—who feels responsible although he was not the one who fired the shot—arranges a lavish funeral. The elder Arye-Leyb recounts how Benya—who, he takes pains to point out, was not yet called the King—came to the front of the gathering:

—Chto khotite vy delat', molodoi chelovek?—podbezhal k nemu Kofman iz pogrebal'nogo bratstva.

—Ya khochu skazat' rech',—otvetil Benya Krik.

I on skazal rech'.

("**Kak**," 254)

"What have you in mind, young man?" cried Kaufman of the Burial Brotherhood, running over to him.

"I have it in mind to make a funeral oration," answered Benya Krik.

And a funeral oration he made.

("**H**," 221)

Benya's oration is compelling through its evocativeness rather than anything resembling logic. He arrives in his red car, which trails smoke and flame and plays an aria from *Pagliacci*. Stretching forth his arms toward the people and standing upon a mound of earth, he speaks in seeming non sequitur that nonetheless captures the bleakness of ghetto life—a bleakness that Benya has overcome partly through his verbal flamboyance.

"Gospoda i damy. . . . Vy prishli otdat' poslednii dolg chestnomu truzheniku, kotoryi pogib za mednyi grosh. . . . Chto videl nash dorogoi Iosif v svoei zhizni? On videl paru pustyakov. Chem zanimalsya on? On pereschityval chuzhie den'gi. Za chto pogib on? On pogib za ves' trudyashchiisya klass. Est' lyudi, uzhe obrechennyie smerti. I est' lyudi, eshchyo ne nachavshie zhit'."

("**Kak**," 254)

"Ladies and gentlemen and dames. . . . You have come to pay your last respects to a worthy laborer who perished for the sake of a copper penny. . . . What did our dear Joseph get out of life? Nothing worth mentioning. How did he spend his time? Counting other people's cash. What did he perish for? He perished for the whole of the working class. There are people already condemned to death, and there are people who have not yet begun to live."

("**H**," 221)

When Benya has departed in his improbable automobile, it is his oration, rather than an act of physical prowess, that earns him the name "King." After Joseph's murder, Benya Krik and Joseph's former employer, Tartakovsky, clash dramatically over how much of a pension Tartakovsky will award to the dead man's mother—but, as Falen observes, "the battle here . . . is a thing of words."[43]

The high social stakes of Benya Krik's battles can be best understood through an intertextual reading of "**Sunset**" with an event from Babel's childhood that he fictionalized in two stories, "**The Story of My Dovecote**" (1925) and "**Pervaya lyubov'**" ("**First love**"; 1925). Each story revolves around a generational conflict; to resolve it, the young generation is called upon to create its own meaningful cultural arguments. Ultimately, the gangsters emerge as the only Jews with the resources to rectify the traumas of Babel's Jewish childhood.

In "**The Story of My Dovecote**," an adult narrator recalls his experience as a boy in the 1905 pogrom in Odessa. The Odessa pogrom was part of a large wave of pogroms that year, affecting more than 650 Jewish communities (including Odessa) during the course of a single week. At least three hundred of Odessa's 160,000 Jewish residents were killed; thousands more were wounded, and forty thousand were financially ruined. It was not unusual for Russian soldiers to participate in these attacks.[44]

The narrator of "**The Story of My Dovecote**" relates that all his life he had longed to own a dovecote. It is not until the age of nine that his wish is realized: after frenzied studying, the boy is admitted to secondary school (despite suffocating quotas on Jews and discriminatory examinations) and his father rewards him with the wherewithal to buy wood to build a hutch and three pairs of pigeons to stock it with. But while the boy is still in the marketplace, a pogrom breaks out, and a mob forms to kill the boy's grandfather. Grandfather Shoyl is brutally murdered, and although the boy and his parents are hidden by gentile neighbors and go unharmed, a cripple who had been beloved by children smashes the boy's pigeons against his face. This moment is the horrifying dramatic climax of the story:

Ya lezhal na zemle, i vnutrennosti rasdavlennoi ptitsy stekali s moego viska. Oni tekli vdol' shchek, izvivayas', bryzgaya i osleplyaya menya. Golubinaya nezh-

naya kishka polzla po moemu lbu, i ya zakryval poslednii nezaleplennyi glaz, chtoby ne videt' mira,
rasstilavshegosya peredo mnoi. Mir etot byl mal i
uzhasen.

("**Is**" ["**Istoria moei golubyatin**"], 46)

I lay on the ground, and the guts of the crushed bird
trickled down from my temple. They flowed down my
cheek, winding this way and that, splashing, blinding
me. The tender pigeon-guts slid down over my forehead, and I closed my solitary unstopped-up eye so as
not to see the world that spread out before me. This
world was tiny, and it was awful.

("**SD**" ["**The Story of My Dovecote**"], 262)

"**Pervaya lyubov'**" takes place later the same day; the
boy is taken to the gentile neighbors where his parents
are hiding. The emotional crux comes when the boy,
still splattered with feathers and blood, witnesses his father groveling before a Cossack on horseback during
the pogrom. The sympathetic female neighbor, about
whom the boy has previously had disturbing erotic visions, washes the blood and feathers off his face and
kisses him on the lips.

This bloody smashing of the pigeons remained an affecting memory-image for Babel into adulthood; Paustovsky recalls him weeping, "I came safely through a
Jewish pogrom as a child, only they tore my pigeon's
head off. Why?"[45] The opening lines of "**Sunset**" invite
an intertextual reading with the pogrom narrative. Mendel Krik's younger son, Levka, has fallen in love with a
girl named Taybel, and Taybel, as the story's narrator
reminds us repeatedly, is Yiddish for dove (pigeon).
When Levka tells his abusive father of his infatuation,
Mendel verbally destroys her:

—Ty polozhil glaz na pomoinitsu,—skazal papasha
Krik,—a mat' ee bandersha.

("**Z**" ["**Zakat**"], 280)

"You have taken a fancy to a slut," said Papa Krik,
"and her mother keeps a whorehouse."

("**S**" ["**Sunset**"], 141)

For this symbolic pigeon-crushing and for other acts of
cruelty, Mendel has been nicknamed by the town "Mendel Pogrom."

Unlike Babel's weak intellectual father, who grovels
before the Cossack officer, or the boy, who is unable to
save his pigeons or even understand their destruction,
Benya Krik responds with decisive action. He galva-
nizes his brother and sister to kill their father. The three
siblings (with Benya standing "on the left by the dovecote" [S, 147]) severely beat Mendel, the pogrom.

The parallel is suggestive in two ways. In the first place,
Jews like Benya—violent, illicit, potent—appear to be
the ones who can react usefully to the anti-Semitism

that Babel told Paustovsky he cannot comprehend. In
the second place is the casting of the father in the role
of the pogrom: to save themselves from victimization,
Jews must reject the filiopiety and pacifism that is associated with them, and murder the world of their fathers.
It is tragic, but ultimately necessary.

"**Sunset**" does not end with the beating of Mendel. The
story goes on for some pages to evoke pity for, or even
partially to redeem, the old man. It is fitting that Levka,
the brother whose dove is crushed, should be the one
overcome with grief for his defeated father:

—Benchik,—skazal on,—my muchaem starika. . . .
Sleza menya tochit, Benchik.

("**Z**," 290)

"Benchik," he said, "we are tormenting the old
man. . . . It makes me cry, Benchik."

("**S**," 153)

It may be necessary to dispose of one's Jewish parents
to avoid becoming the helpless boy who comes home
covered in bloody feathers, but the psychic cost is great.

The significance for the Soviet artist of this outlaw
shedding of generational and cultural baggage is conveyed in a minute but compelling image in "**Sunset**."
The night following the beating of Mendel, an unseen
phonograph starts to play Jewish songs. These songs—
written, no doubt, in a minor key—drift through a tawdry and malevolent night in which a keen ambivalence
regarding the death of lyricism is projected onto the
very landscape:

Zvezdy rassypalis' pered oknom, kak soldaty, kogda
oni opravlyayutsya, zelenye zvezdy po sinemu polyu.

("**Z**," 287)

Stars—green stars on a dark-blue background—were
scattered in front of the window like soldiers relieving
themselves.

("**S**," 150)

Almost immediately, the music, a lovely but atavistic
cultural production of Mendel's generation, ceases. It is
a grand Babel success that the whole trajectory is accomplished in one sentence: "A phonograph started
playing Jewish songs, but then it stopped" ("**S**," 150).

* * *

The Odessa tales not only establish gangsters as consequential cultural actors, the stories directly—and favorably—compare their creative abilities to the skill of
writers. A professional writer, who acts as an educated
framing narrator for the folk narration of the elder
(*starik*) Arye-Leyb, is introduced into the text of "**How**

It Was Done in Odessa." This young writer discovers that he could learn much about his own craft by observing the successes of Benya Krik.

The literate narrator begins the story with a series of questions about Benya's ascent. But it is the silver-tongued Arye-Leyb who understands and relates what really transpired. Arye-Leyb is an elderly Jew who earns his living praying for the dead (consequently he is often to be found in the cemetery, the cemetery wall being his usual vantage point). As James Falen observes, Arye-Leyb is associated with the biblical Aaron, whose stature derives from his speaking abilities; he accompanies his stuttering brother Moses ("little lisping Mose" in the stories) before the Pharaoh to negotiate freedom from slavery for the Jewish people. A profound separation exists between Arye-Leyb and the writer-narrator of **"How It Was Done in Odessa,"** in terms of their speech habits and their ability to understand the workings of Moldavanka. Although the writer-narrator establishes a relationship with Arye-Leyb (if nothing else they are both observers and tellers), he speaks standard Russian where Arye-Leyb's Russian is noticeably Yiddish-inflected. (For instance, Arye-Leyb uses the article *ob* exclusively—akin to using "an" exclusively in English—but the unnamed narrator does not.) His standard speech marks him as an outsider, and he seems unaware or uncomprehending of events that shook the whole town.

The literate narrator is tormented by an impotence that seems to result from his overintellectualism. His effeteness is counterpoised to the character of the vibrant gangsters. The writer-narrator, it is made clear, will never be called "the King" as Benya Krik is called, for he has "spectacles on his nose and autumn in his heart":

> Chto sdelali by vy na meste Beni Krika? Vy nichego by ne sdelali. A on sdelal. *Poetomu on Korol', a vy derzhite figu v karmane.*
>
> ("**Kak,**" 127; emphasis added)

> What would you have done in Benya Krik's place? You would have done nothing. But *he* did something. *That's why he's the King, while you make a fig in your pocket.*
>
> ("**H,**" 212; emphasis added; translation altered)

Since Benya, who "did something," has earned the nickname "King" by distinguishing himself verbally (at Joseph's funeral and in his "business" negotiations), the implied comparison is linguistic. Dispensing with the sort of writer who "does nothing"—whether he partially or fully represents Babel's own sense of self—represents a break from the literary past and acknowledges the exhaustion of lyricism as a viable literary mode. The masturbatory, furtive image of the milquetoast writer "making a fig in his pocket" adds to the picture

of the inadequate artist as possessed of a frustrated masculinity. Arye-Leyb's formula that the writer can do nothing because he has "spectacles on his nose and autumn in his heart" would resonate deeply among American readers. For example, in Daniel Fuchs's bitter novel *Summer in Williamsburg*—which also ponders whether gangsters are the ones truly able to accomplish great deeds—a young aspiring writer, whose character presents a mockery of frustrated Jewish masculinity, paraphrases the words to read, "I have pimples on my face and tears in my eyes." Likewise, Philip Roth, a writer as concerned as anyone with the intersections among ethnicity, masculinity, and creativity, picks up on Babel's "definition" of a Jewish writer in his novel *The Ghost Writer* (an irreverent, obtrusively Jewish romp through modernist literary history), adding to it "and blood in the penis."[46]

This contrast between the intellectual's sterility and the gangster's power prompted Stephen Marcus to complain in the *Partisan Review* that "Babel respected Jews only when they answered the violence done to them with violence. . . . These stories of Odessa seem to me unpalatable."[47] It is worth pointing out that within Marcus's reproach resides an acknowledgment that Babel had created in the gangster a Jew who was not a victim.

TAKING THE "MAMA" OUT OF MAMA-LOSHEN

With Benya's yell as a possible model, the Odessa tales grope toward a powerful new definition of the Jewish writer that is both potent and activist. Babel posits this ideal in a visibly masculinist rhetoric:

> Tak vot—zabud'te na vremya, chto na nosu u vas ochki, a v dushe osen'. Perestan'te skandalit' za vashim pis'mennym stolom i zaikat'sya na lyudyakh. Predstav'te sebe na mgnoven'e, chto vy skandalite na ploshchadyakh i zaikaetes' na bumage. Vy tigr, vy lev, vy koshka. Vy mozhete perenochevat' s russkoi zhenshchinoi, i russkaya zhenshchina ostanetsya vami dovol'na.
>
> ("**Kak,**" 246)

> Forget for a while that you have spectacles on your nose and autumn in your heart. Cease playing the rowdy at your desk and stammering while others are about. Imagine for a moment that you play the rowdy in public places and stammer on paper. You are a tiger, you are a lion, you are a cat. You can spend the night with a Russian woman, and satisfy her.
>
> ("**H,**" 212)

Here a bold solution is offered to the writer's torment of impotence: by envisioning himself as a gangster—even for a moment—the Jewish writer can redeem his own masculinity. This would turn out to be one of Babel's literary legacies, one that a number of Russian and American writers would find deeply compelling. In a number of ways, they would explore how this vision of the writer as gangster translates into creative literature.

Battling literary impotence was a driving force behind many modernist artistic techniques, according to Sandra M. Gilbert and Susan Gubar in their seminal work, *No Man's Land: The Place of the Woman Writer in the Twentieth Century.* Gilbert and Gubar offer a fascinating analysis of the sexualized linguistics of modernist and postmodernist writing. Their compelling discussion of male modernist fantasies regarding "what they *as men* could do with that common language" is extremely suggestive in terms of Babel's various literary toughs—especially the Jewish gangsters.[48] Ultimately, Benya Krik and his company appear to be engaged in the same enterprise as moderist writers like James Joyce: the "parabolic wresting of patriarchal power from the mother tongue."[49]

Babel's grotesque portraits of actual maternal bodies (such as the awesome Lyubka Cossack, with her enormous, milkless breasts) have been noted by critics; it is more fruitful for my purposes to consider his use of motherhood as a theoretical construct implying generational continuity and what Nancy Chodorow calls sociofamilial "relatedness"—a line that Babel seems eager to interrupt. It is through the mother that Jews inherit their Jewishness and babies acquire language. Walter J. Ong points out: "Our first tongue . . . is called our 'mother tongue' in English and in many other languages, and perhaps in all languages is designated by direct or indirect reference to mother. There are no father tongues—a truth that calls for deeper reflection than it commonly commands."[50] The concept of motherhood (and its intimate connection to language) provides the key to the writerly reason for Babel's creation of Jewish gangsters: a de-domesticization of the mother tongue.

Historically the Yiddish language has been dogged by its association with the mother (it is known to Jews as the *mama-loshen,* a cozy form of mother tongue) and the banalities of everyday life; as a vehicle for Jewish culture, it was degraded at the expense of the holy tongue, Hebrew. Prayer books for women were the only ones in Yiddish. The "grandfather" of modern Yiddish literature (first named so by his admirer Sholem Aleichem), the Odessan Mendele Moykher-Sforim (Mendele the book peddler), saw it as his job to transcend the trite history of Yiddish: "In my time, the Yiddish languuage was an empty vessel, containing naught but gibes, nonsense, and fiddle-faddle, the jabber of fools who had nothing to say. *Women and vulgar folk* read it."[51] Identification of the Yiddish language as female was characteristic before Mendele "forge[ed] it into a modern Yiddish literary instrument."[52] Sholem Aleichem's contemporary critics hailed him for raising Yiddish literature above the level of a "kitchen language" and for nursing the mother tongue to adulthood. Sholem Aleichem drafted a pamphlet, "Shomar's Mishpot" (Shomar's trial), condemning Yiddish writers of romances and serial novels, which were associated with women readers.

Benya Krik's task is to take the Yiddish language further away from the passive Jewish mothers. In this light the slaughter of milk cows in **"How It Was Done in Odessa"** is of great significance: it indicates Benya Krik's need to murder domesticity in order to establish his control over the vernacular. While Benya and his gangsters kill the passive cows, conventional womanhood becomes the greatest threat:

> Vo vremya naleta, v tu groznuyu noch', kogda mychali podkalyvaemye korovy i telki skol'zili v materinskoi krovi, kogda fakely plyasali, kak chernye devy, i baby-molochnitsy sharakhalis' i vizzhali pod dulami druzhelyubnykh brauningov,—v tu groznuyu noch' vo dvor vybezhala v vyreznoi rubashke doch' starika Eikhbauma—Tsilya. I pobeda Korolya stala ego porazheniem.
>
> ("Ko," 241-42)

> During the raid, on that dreadful night when cows bellowed as they were slaughtered and calves spilled and slithered in the blood of their dams, when the torch-flames danced like dark-visaged maidens and the farm-women lunged back in horror from the muzzles of amiable Brownings—on that dreadful night there ran out into the yard, wearing naught save her V-neck shift, Tsilya the daughter of old man Eichbaum. And the victory of the King was turned to defeat.
>
> ("K," 206)

Not only are the cows dying pathetically, but their calves are slipping around in their mothers' blood, a painful inversion of the Jewish law that accounts for the "milk" and "flesh" categories: an animal should not be cooked in its own mother's milk. Jewish law also specifies how an animal must be slaughtered (which in addition to the kind of animal is what qualifies meat as kosher). Benya, therefore, kills Mosaic law.[53]

Benya Krik's masculine victory over Jewish domesticity is demonstrated by the passage's overtly gendered symbology. Benya and his men appear in Eichbaum's yard at night holding aloft poles and brandishing phallic guns, knives, and fists. They terrify not only the dying cows but also the dairymaids (*baby-molochnitsy*) and farm women (*rabotnitsy*). And when Tsilya runs across the yard and turns Benya's thoughts to love of women and marriage, it constitutes a "defeat." Love of a woman as the road to defeat would become a convention of Jewish and non-Jewish gangster stories (and hard-boiled detective fiction).

Babel facetiously gestures toward the Jewish marriage impulse as interfering with creativity and adventurousness in an early introduction to a neverpublished collection of stories by young Odessan writers:

Tut vse delo v tom, chto v Odesse kazhdyi yunosha—
poka on ne zhenilsya—khochet byt' yungnoi na okean-
skom sudne. I odna u nas beda,—v Odesse my zhenim-
sya s neobyknovennym uporstvom.

The whole point of this book is that in Odessa every
youth—until he marries—wants to be a cabin-boy on
an ocean-liner. We have only one problem: in Odessa
we are unusually insistent upon marrying.[54]

Like other Odessans, Benya Krik is certainly unusually
insistent upon marrying; in the four Odessa tales he is
shown marrying two different women. In order that
marriage not spell the defeat of the King, Benya Krik
must prevent the female voice from retaining control of
the mother tongue. In **"Justice in Parentheses,"** he has
to silence his pregnant wife to conduct business with
the narrator:

Takoe u menya bylo mnenie. I zhena korolya s nim
soglasilas'.

—Detka—skazal ei togda Benya,—ya khochu, chtoby
ty poshla otdokhnut' na kushetke.

("Sp" [**"Spravidlivost' v skobkakh"**], 257)

Such was my opinion. And the King's wife agreed with
it.

"Child," Benya said to her then, "I want you should go
and rest on the couch."

("JP," 255)

Somewhat chillingly, the wife's pregnancy serves to
connect her viscerally with the cows murdered in the
presence of their calves in **"The King."** The gangster's
success depended upon killing the cows; the writer can
approximate this success by muting the woman.

Viktor Shklovskii measures Babel's artistic success on
the terms set up by Babel himself. Shklovskii, perhaps
responsible for the most astute characterization of Babel's style—"[his] principal device is to speak in the
same tone of voice of the stars above and of gonorrhea"—feels sure that Babel could spend the night with
a Russian woman and satisfy her, because a Russian
woman loves a good story.[55] In other words, Shklovskii
feels that Babel has taken his own advice and envisioned himself as a gangster while he is writing, the result being that he has overcome the aspects of Jewishness debilitating to an author's manhood.

While this equation of penis and pen is an old one, Babel's reinvestment of the *mama-loshen* with a masculine, immediate tone associates him with leading modernists worldwide who were experimenting with a
multiplicity of voices and a corresponding multiplicity
of language forms. Babel scholars have tended to trace
the origins of his vernacular technique to Russian ornamentalist writers such as Andrei Remizov (1877-1957)

and Nikolai Leskov (1831-95). But as Gilbert and
Gubar's work indicates, Babel's attempt to reinvent
Yiddish needs to be placed into a context of formal and
thematic radicalism that characterized literature (and the
other arts) during the period surrounding World War I.

This radicalism demonstrated the breakdown of the
dominance and absolute assurance of nineteenth-century
Western European bourgeois aesthetics (foreseeing an
end, or at least a realignment, of the total political and
economic domination of the great powers of the nineteenth and early twentieth centuries). Some modernist
writers, notably T. S. Eliot, lamented this passing of
cultural certainty, but many "ethnic" writers saw instead
a widening of artistic possibility, an opportunity for
them to find what William Boelhower calls a possible
ethnic cultural space.[56] For these writers, there was room
for celebration of the liberality of the movement, in
which multiple languages could interact on something
like equal ground. For instance, the American poet William Carlos Williams, in *Spring and All* (1923), explores forms of American English, advertisement language, official and quasi official language, parodies of
literary language, and much vernacular speech, including some African American language as poetic material.
Williams's use of the vernacular underscores the poems' thematic digs at the stiffness of the standard literary language from which the speakers deviate.

Babel makes a kindred case for the newly achieved literary potential of the vernacular in his story "Guy de
Maupassant," in which a Jewish woman makes a pallid
translation of de Maupassant's work into Russian because the Russian she uses is too pure, "the way Jews
used to write Russian." The implication is that now—as
the male narrator realizes—there are more possibilities.
Revising her translation, he understands that in good
literature, "all kinds of weapons may come into play"
(**"GM"** [**"Guy de Maupassant"**], 331). The idea of
style as a weapon—implied here is Jewish style in particular—invokes once again the act of powerful Jewish
writing as assault. The American writer Raymond
Rosenthal recognized that Babel "was not simply a Jew
writing in the language of Turgenev and Dosto-
evski, . . . he was a genius who spoke with a new inflection."[57] In the Odessa tales, the modern frisson of
Yiddish is both amplified and embodied in the forceful-
ness of its speakers, who are violent criminals.

Ultimately, in these stories, the "othered" language appears more "authentic" than the standard; Babel's move
away from the domesticity of the vernacular is also a
move away from the condescension to the vernacular
on the part of the standard. His reinvention of Yiddish
in gangsters' mouths marks a rejection of nineteenth-
century romantic uses of "dialect"—characterized, for
instance, by Ivan Turgenev's representations of Russian
serfs or Harriet Beecher Stowe's representations of African American slaves. This move once again associates

Babel's language experimentation with the work of leading modernist writers outside of Russia. James Joyce in *Ulysses* lampoons the nineteenth-century sentimental condescension of the official literary language for the vernacular:

> —Do you understand what he says? Stephen asked her.
>
> —Is it French you are talking, sir? the old woman said to Haines. Haines spoke to her again a longer speech, confidently.
>
> —Irish, Buck Mulligan said. Is there Gaelic on you?
>
> —I thought it was Irish, she said, by the sound of it. Are you from the west, sir?
>
> —I am an Englishman, Haines answered.
>
> —He's English, Buck Mulligan said, and he thinks we ought to speak Irish in Ireland.[58]

Benya Krik's Yiddish is not textually patronized; on the contrary, the under-pinning of Yiddish in Benya's words is the source of Babel's literary "assault" in the Odessa tales.

We receive Benya's words in Russian, but they destabilize that language, inflected as they are with Yiddish idiom, hyperbole, and sardonic tone:

> Vyshla gromadnaya oshibka, tetya Pesya. No razve so storony Boga ne bylo oshibkoi poselit' evreev v Rossii, chtoby oni muchilis', kak v ady? I chem bylo by plokho, esli by evrei zhili v Shveitsarii, gde ikh okruzhali by pervoklassnye ozera, goristy vozdukh i sploshnye frantsuzy? Oshibayutsya vse, dazhe Bog. Slushaite menya ushami, teotya Pesya. Vy imeete pyat' tysyach na ruki i pyat'desyat rublei v mesyats do vashei smerti,—zhivete sto dvadtsat' let.
>
> ("Kak," 252-53)

> A terrible mistake has been made, Aunt Pesya. But wasn't it a mistake on the part of God to settle Jews in Russia, for them to be tormented worse than in Hell? How would it hurt if the Jews lived in Switzerland, where they would be surrounded by first-class lakes, mountain air, and nothing but Frenchies? All make mistakes, God not excepted. Listen to me with all your ears, Auntie Pesya. You'll have five thousand down and fifty rubles a month till you croak—you should live a hundred twenty years.
>
> ("H," 219; translation altered)[59]

Benya's outburst is strongly evocative of the Tevye stories by Sholem Aleichem (the first of which appeared in 1894). The embattled Tevye endlessly and intimately wrangles aloud with God over the state of his world. In one memorable harangue in the story "Today's Children," Tevye bemoans the fact that he must work endlessly serving the rich in order to earn his paltry living. What he wants to know—given that there is no shame in working for a living—is "where does it say in the Bible that Tevye has to work his bottom off and be up at the crack of dawn every day when even God is still snoozing away in bed?"[60]

Babel's literary involvement with Sholem Aleichem is extensive. He did his own translations of Sholem Aleichem into Russian because he felt that previous renderings were poor, and he translated some works that had not been previously translated. Babel also wrote a screenplay based on Sholem Aleichem's novel *The Adventures of Menachem-Mendl*. According to Babel's wife, he said that he worked on Sholem Aleichem "to feed his soul."[61]

The complicated relationship of Babel's Odessa tales to works by Sholem Aleichem, particularly the Tevye stories, is worth some attention. Babel's invocation of the quintessential Yiddish writer indicates a self-awareness on Babel's part of the relationship of his Jewishness to his own cultural work and a resultant desire to place himself in a literary ancestral line that included Jewish writers as well as Russian ones like Turgenev, to whom Babel also pays homage.[62] The presence within Babel's Russian text of Sholem Aleichem's Yiddish text manifests a subversive approach to the Russian language itself, one that carries Babel's well-documented use of vernacular above the level of stylization and demonstrates the historical and ideological depth of Babel's polyphonous aesthetic.

Babel's famous obsession with temperament, particularly Jewish temperament, owes much to Sholem Aleichem's Tevye. Tevye is a milkman; his job is delivering milk, cheese, and butter to the wealthy people who summer nearby. But the word Sholem Aleichem uses to describe Tevye (*milkhiker*) does not literally mean milkman. In fact, the word is a coinage on Sholem Aleichem's part, created not from the Yiddish word for milk (*milkh*) but from the word *milkhik*, which refers to a dietary category: according to kosher law, milk and flesh cannot be combined, so a meal consists of foods from either the *milkhik* group or the *fleyshik*.

Sholem Aleichem uses these kosher dietary categories to establish two temperamental types. Tevye the milkman is frequently contrasted with more worldly, aggressive, and financially successful butchers. He is concerned about giving his eldest daughter in marriage to the successful butcher Lazer-Wolf not only because he is old enough to be her father, but because he is a butcher: "'A diamond,' I say, raising my voice, 'and twenty-four carats too! You'd better take good care of her and not act like the butcher you are.'" Tevye not only hesitates to engage his daughter to Lazer-Wolf, he refuses to sell him his cow, lamenting, "It's just a sin to hand over a poor innocent beast to be slaughtered. Why, it says in our holy Bible. . . ."[63]

Despite the fact that Tevye's innocence and benevolence cannot triumph, Sholem Aleichem treats him lovingly. Although Tevye's rebellious daughters are generally vindicated in their strivings to direct the course of their own lives, often against the wishes of their father, it is the gentle Tevye who commands the reader's sympathy precisely because of his utter lack of bitterness. The metaphor of milk and milkiness was one that Sholem Aleichem would return to on several occasions during his lengthy career, taking pains to place himself squarely in Tevye's camp.

Babel, on the other hand, is appalled by the tendency of Jews to possess the "milky" temperament. The problem of milkiness is a repeated theme of *Red Cavalry*: for example, a Cossack comrade scolds Lyutov for riding into battle without any cartridges in his revolver, telling him, "you're a Molokan [a member of a pacifist sect that took its name from the Russian word for milk], one of them milk-drinkers. . . . I've got a law written down about Molokans that says they ought to be wiped out. They worship God."[64] There is also the story of Matvei Pavlichenko, a dreamy herdsman whose problem, as he voices it in the story's opening lines, is that he smells dreadfully of milk: "As for my heart—you know what it's like, Natasya; there isn't nothing in it, it's just milky, I dare say. It's terrible how I smell of milk." Matvei ultimately solves his problem of milkiness by trampling his master to death "for an hour or maybe more." He goes on to become a Red General.[65] Unlike Sholem Aleichem, Babel privileges the fleshy, active world. The vibrancy of his gangsters is elevated at the expense of bookish introspection.

Babel, as he establishes his typology, returns again and again to images of milk or milkiness. The female presence among the gangsters, Lyubka Cossack, who runs a brothel and smuggler's hangout, is a potent and awesome figure. She reigns wholly over her inn. Her nickname reflects the vitality and force that drew Babel toward the Cossacks in *Red Cavalry*. Lyubka is also a mother—not only a mother, but the mother of a child with a king's name: David. This powerful and untamed figure is unable to produce milk for the baby:

> Mal'chik potyanulsya k nei, iskusal chudovishchnyi ee sosok, no ne dobyl moloka.

> **("LK" ["Lyubka Kozak"]**, 149)

> The child strained toward her, bit at her monstrous nipple, but achieved no milk.

> **("L" ["Lyubka the Cossack"]**, 239)

While Tevye the milk(ish)man cannot bear to think of slaughtering a milk cow, Benya the gangster, in the pivotal scene discussed earlier, arranges a mass slaughter of milk cows. Benya writes a series of letters to Zender Eichbaum, who owns sixty milk cows, demanding that he leave twenty thousand rubles in the entrance to an Odessa building or else "something unusual will happen to you" (205). When the letters go unanswered, Benya acts:

> Benya otbil zamki u saraya i stal vyvodit' korov po odnoi. Ikh zhdal paren' s nozhom. On oprokodyval korovu s odnogo udara i pogruzhdal nozh v korov'e serdtse.

> **("Ko,"** 241)

> Benya beat the locks from the door of the cowshed and began to lead the cows out one by one. Each was received by a lad with a knife. He would overturn the cow with one blow of the fist and plunge his knife into her heart.

> **("K,"** 206)

The scene is a gruesome one, with the pathetically lowing animals falling in gore at the feet of Benya Krik, king of gangsters and killer of cows.

The resolution of Benya's challenge to Eichbaum represents a final inversion of the Tevye stories. Benya's raid ends when Eichbaum's daughter Tsilya runs across the yard in her shift, and Benya falls in love with her. No longer concerned with the twenty thousand rubles, he wants to marry Tsilya. Marriage of the daughters is the organizing principle of the Tevye stories (which have even been translated under the name *Tevye's Daughters*). Tevye has seven daughters, and his biggest concern is finding them appropriate husbands; his fall is measured by the growing *in*appropriateness of each successive union. By having the violent Benya Krik force his way into a wedding with the milkman's daughter, Babel turns him into another traditionally inappropriate husband and Eichbaum into a less lovable—but also defeated—Tevye. (The name Tsilya sounds quite a bit like Tseitl, the name of Tevye's eldest daughter.) Thus, Benya Krik comes to represent the end of Tevye's world.

But Babel the revolutionary must welcome the end of Tevye's world, and even find a kind of harsh and tragic beauty in the inevitability of its demise. *Odessa Tales* often revisits the theme of "today's children" who find it necessary to annihilate the ways of their parents. As often as not, it is the kind of passivity represented by Tevye that they are rejecting. Benya's father Mendel, a drayman, is associated also with Tevye, who always appears in a cart behind his horse. In Babel's later story **"Sunset,"** Benya and his siblings overthrow their father in a violent and righteous acting out of the dilemma of "today's children." If the Tevye stories represent a version of Turgenev's *Fathers and Children* from the point of view of the father,[66] the forward-looking Benya Krik stories, seizing upon this same filial conflict, display an underlying tension of Babel's oeuvre: the sometimes tragic need for young generations to destroy and devour the past:

> [Benya] razognal lyudei palkoi, on ottesnil ikh k vorotam, no Levka, mladshii brat, vzyal ego za vorotnik i stal tryasti, kak grushu.

—Benchik,—skazal on,—my muchaem starika. . . .
Sleza menya tochit, Benchik. . . .

—Sleza tebya tochit, otvetil Benchik, i, sobrav vo rtu
slyunu, on plyunul Levke eyu v litso.—O nizkii brat,—
prosheptal on,—podlyi brat, razbyazhi mne ruki, a ne
putaisya u menya pod nogami.

("Z," 290)

[Benya] scattered the crowd with a stick and drove
them back to the gate, but Levka, his younger brother,
took hold of him by the collar and began to shake him
like a pear tree:

"Benchik," he said, "we are tormenting the old
man. . . . It makes me cry, Benchik. . . ."

"It makes you cry, does it," Benchik replied, and collecting all the spittle in his mouth, he spat in Levka's
face. "Oh, lowdown brother," he whispered, "vile
brother, free my hands and don't get in my way."

("S," 153)

The question that remains for Babel is what role Yiddish will play after it has been divested of the traditional Jewish "milkiness."

* * *

Babel's revisions of Sholem Aleichem's seminal Yiddish texts are part of his continual exploration of the
role Yiddish language, literature, and culture might play
in the radically reorganized world of the Soviet Union.
(Babel's Jewish American counterparts would be moved
to consider this same question in an American context.)
To understand how Babel envisions Yiddish functioning
in the Soviet context, it is helpful to take a broader look
at his systematic use of vernacular forms, a technique
called *skaz* (from the Russian root "say"), to represent
collectivity and Marxist materialism. Definitions of *skaz*
by formalist critics in the 1920s tended to posit a classical (or Hegelian) dialectic, wherein the literary or standard language acts as a thesis, the *skaz* voice forms an
antithesis, and whatever artistic resolution occurs is the
synthesis.[67] This system demands a rather rigid presupposition of one official and one unofficial language
within a *skaz* work.

Babel, however, takes more from the Marxian dialectic,
which is not as straightforward. Although Marx's model
is primarily bipolar, in that he indicates two major contending forces (the bourgeoisie and the proletarian
classes), he also allows for the existence of other
classes, such as peasants or petite bourgeoise, that do
not fit neatly into a two-part paradigm.

This notion of the collision of a number of forces sheds
light on Babel's use of *skaz*, which emphasizes a plurality of Russian voices rather than the duality suggested by Bakhtin's description of *skaz* as "double-
voiced." Babel seeks to convey the different speech

patterns of Cossacks, peasants, Jews, Ukrainians, and
street criminals. It is important to expand the definition
of *skaz* beyond the traditional two-part official/unofficial
schema, because the various language forms Babel uses
may have entirely different subtextual meanings.

Yiddish becomes emblematic of the Marxian model of
social evolution, for it is by nature a language of fusion. Its very composition—with elements of vocabulary, grammar, pronunciation, and syntax cobbled together from German, Hebrew, Russian, Polish, and later,
English—reveals the history of Jews' interactions with
other cultures. According to Benjamin Harshav, the
irony implicit in this layering is "the meaning of Yiddish": "The vocabulary of Yiddish is rather poor in
comparison with English or Russian, but each word has
an aura of connotations derived from its multidirectional and codified relations not just within a semantic
paradigm, as in other languages, but to parallel words
in other source languages, to an active stock of proverbs and idioms, and to typical situational clusters. . . .
Since each word may belong to several heterogeneous
or contradictory knots, ironies are always at hand."[68]
The presence of Yiddish in the stories, with its "contradictory knots" of influence, helps to position Jews as
particularly able to represent "all of Odessa" (as the
gangster Froim Grach did for the Cheka officer).

The transgressor/bridger role of the gangsters, owing to
their particular location as Yiddish speakers and criminals, is evident in Benya's eloquent demand that Efraim
Rook accept him into the gang:

Grach sprosil ego:

—Kto ty, otkuda ty idesh' i chem ty dyshish?

—Poprobui menya, Froim,—otvetil Benya,—i perestanem razmazyvat' beluyu kashu po chistomu stolu.

—Perestanem razmazyvat' kashu,—otvetil Grach,—Ya
tebya poprobuyu.

I naletchiki sobrali sovyet, shtoby podumat' o Benye
Krike.

("Kak," 247)

Rook asked him:

"Who are you, where do you come from, and what do
you use for breath?"

"Give me a try, Ephraim," replied Benya, "and let us
stop smearing kasha over a clean table."

"Let us stop smearing kasha," assented Rook. "I'll give
you a try."

And the gangsters went into conference to consider the
matter of Benya Krik.

("H," 213; translation altered)

"Kasha" as Benya uses the word dovetails with a Russian idiomatic expression for convoluted talk or making
trouble.[69] But the word "kasha" also occurs in Yiddish

to represent a thorny or perplexing question—and not as one of the 20 percent of Yiddish words that entered Yiddish from Slavic languages. The "kasha" in Yiddish is an Aramaic word that comes from descriptions of rabbis arguing "difficulties" of Talmud scholarship.

Babel's emphasis on the signifying nature of Yiddish suggests that Jews possess the tricky combination of ethnic culture and internationalism that Lenin called for, and therefore should naturally be successful at creating a new working-class culture. Lenin asserts in his "Critical Remarks on the National Question" (1913) that "our slogan is: the international culture of democracy and of the world working class movement," but also maintains that "it is true . . . that international culture is not non-national."[70] The Yiddish of the Odessa tales encompasses both of these mandates: it interacts with Russian, enacting an ipso facto internationalism, and yet it remains powerfully and identifiably Jewish.

But Babel still needs gangsters to act as his integration-ists: he was, as I have noted, keenly aware that Jewish participation in the cultural fund will be resisted. The elderly Arye-Leyb, who recounts the rise of Benya in **"How It Was Done in Odessa,"** expresses this sense of exclusion from the Russian cultural fund by darkly inverting a familiar convention of fairy tales. Russian fairy tales frequently end with a "validating" formula, such as, "How do I know? Why, I was there, and I ate and drank and danced until dawn." Arye-Leyb borrows this formula, but instead points out that he was *not* present, that he was excluded—a sly move he uses more than once.

Arye-Leyb's subversive use of storytelling convention is an example of how Babel deliberately thwarts his reader's literary expectations; to borrow Jonathan Culler's terminology, Babel's tales demand of their reader a high level of literary competence, but having established what seems like a familiar pattern (in this case the fairy tales), Babel frequently yanks out the rug of convention. For instance, in **"The King,"** Arye-Leyb describes how the gangsters shot into the air because "if you don't fire into the air, you may kill someone" (**"K"**, 206). Although James Falen overdignifies this joke as indicative of the gangsters' underlying "bourgeois respect for caution and tradition," he does recognize the deflating effect of this one-liner on the gangsters' supposed daring.[71] Actually, what Arye-Leyb does is pass off as humane or prudent an old joke—or rather one of a whole category of jokes—about Jewish "schlemiels" attempting either to avoid or to survive conscription into the tsar's army. Ruth R. Wisse repeats several variants on this theme in her book *The Schlemiel as Modern Hero*: "On the battlefield he cries: 'Stop shooting! Someone might, God forbid, lose an eye!'"; "A Jew . . . was suddenly arrested by the challenge of a border guard: 'Halt, or I'll shoot!' The Jew blinked into the beam of the searchlight and said: 'What's the matter with you? Are you crazy? Can't you see that this is a human being?'"; and so forth.[72]

The myriad jokes on this subject (Babel's included) were a way for Russian Jews to confront a problem that was both serious and severe. According to regulations set up by Nicholas I, a specified number of Jews over the age of eighteen were to be drafted into military service for a period of twenty-five years (children of twelve could be taken for several years of training before the twenty-five-year term). Since parents whose sons were forced into the army could assume they would never see them again, extreme measures were taken to prevent this from happening: young men fled into the woods, swapped names and identities with the dead, and submitted to mutilation such as blinding to render them undesirable for conscription. The association of the seemingly invincible gangsters with the desperation and pathos of ordinary Jews reminds the reader of the cultural vulnerability from which such extraordinary Jews as Benya Krik had sprung.

The cultural vulnerability of the Jews in Moldavanka is mirrored in the author's relationship to the standard literary language. Babel's community language was Yiddish; his earliest language of scholarship was Hebrew; and standard Russian was something he associated with formalized institutions of learning, an association burdened with duress and discrimination: "I was only nine, and I was *scared stiff* of the exams. In both subjects, *Russian language* and arithmetic, I couldn't afford to get less than top marks. At our secondary school the *numerus clausus* was stiff: a mere five percent."[73] Rather than being entirely native either to the world of the folk or to the world of standard usage—a dichotomy frequently used to describe the motivation behind *skaz*— Babel is alien to both: his Jewish background divides him from the literary language, and his revolutionary politics and relatively cosmopolitan education distance him from the "folk." Therefore, the most useful way of looking at language choice in Babel is not in terms of "official" versus "unofficial" speech. Leiderman's fluid categories of "translated" and "translating" verbiage are more appropriate.[74] These categories are neither as fixed nor as valanced as "official" and "unofficial"; instead, the counterpoised languages define each other's status according to which form controls a given situation. Leiderman's system allows not only for the presence of multiple voices, but also for the language forms to occupy *either or both categories in different contexts,* which is crucial for Babel. In the Odessa tales, Yiddish and other vernaculars are sometimes translated and sometimes translating, demonstrating shifting balances of linguistic power, and frequently an intentional subversion of literary hierarchies that leaves the standard, educated form on the bottom. For instance, when the narrator of **"Sunset"** explains that "Taybel is Yiddish for dove," the educated Russian reader is placed in the position of not having been able to understand without the assistance of someone who speaks Yiddish. This sense of upheaval accounts for the unusually bifurcated tone of the story **"Froim Grach,"** in which the lens through which events are understood switches midstory from the consciousness of the gangsters to the consciousness of a troubled, sincere agent of the secret police who is grappling with questions about what the Soviet collective requires.

The intensely personal nature of Babel's chronicling of a struggle for collectivity is perhaps the most poignant aspect of his work. Writing during the thick of the civil war that consolidated the power of the Soviet government, Babel had to wrestle with the position of art within that new society. Multiple *skaz* voices help him to be an artist of the collective, to get away from the intimate "I" of earlier literature, and to avoid the limitations of what came to be called *meshchanstvo,* or petty, cowardly individualism. The vernacular voices make their own conclusions, judgments, and observations, operating as a kind of class-conscious Greek chorus in their independent commentary:

> . . . Papasha Krik lezhal borodoyu kverkhu.
>
> —Kayuk,—skazal Froim Grach i otvernulsya.
>
> —Kryshka,—skazal Khaim Drong, no kuznechnyi master Ivan Pyatirubel' pomakhal ykazatel'nym pal'tsem pered samym ego nosom.
>
> —Troe na odnogo,—skazal Pyatirubel',—pozor dlya vsei Moldavy, no eshche ne vecher. Ne videl ya togo khloptsa, kotoryi konchit starogo Krika. . . .
>
> —Uzhe vecher,—prerval ego Ar'e-Leib, nevedomo otkuda vzyavshiisya,—uzhe vecher, Ivan Pyatirubel'. Ne govori "net", russkii chelovek, kogda zhizn' shumit tebe "da."
>
> ("**Z,**" 285-86)

> . . . Old man Krik was lying with his beard in the air.
>
> "Curtains," said Froim Grach and turned away.
>
> "It's all over," said Chaim Drong, but Pyatirubel the blacksmith wagged his forefinger under Chaim Drong's nose:
>
> "Three against one," said Pyatirubel. "What a disgrace for the Moldavanka. But it's not night yet. . . ."
>
> "It is night," interrupted Arye-Leyb, who had suddenly appeared from nowhere. "It is night, Ivan Pyatirubel. Trust a Russian to say no when life is crying out yes."
>
> ("**S,**" 148)

The materialist quality of *skaz* provides the stories with a semblance of plurality.

A product of Babel's renunciation of the intimate is the objectification of language as a thing-in-itself, possessing cultural or moral meaning of its own. This objectifi-

cation is foregrounded in **"Justice In Parentheses."** The primacy of language itself, and its multiplicity of function (as medium, character, artifact, setting, and so forth), are established immediately, in the story's opening lines:

> Pervoe delo ya imel s Benei Krikom, vtoroe—s Lyubkoi Shneiveis. Mozhete vy ponyat' takie slova? Vo vkus etikh slov mozhete vy voiti?
>
> ("**Sp,**" 256)

> The first deal I had was with Benya Krik, the second, with Lyubka Shneyveys ["Snow-white"]. Can you understand the meaning of such words? Are you able to penetrate the flavor of such words?
>
> ("**JP,**" 254; translation altered)

In this story as well as each of the others, Benya's utterances (especially his two letters, "reproduced" without mediation in **"The King"** and **"How It Was Done in Odessa"**) seem suspended on the page in a way that is extraordinary in dialogue. Benya's unforgettable language becomes not only a means to express an experience but also a self-conscious part of that experience, and therefore a concrete artistic artifact:

> —Idite k svoemu semeistvu, Tsudechkis,—obrashchaetsya ko mne korol',—v subbotu vecherkom, po vcei veroyatnosti, ya zaidu v "Spravedlivost'." Voz'mite s soboi moi slova, Tsudechkis, i nachinaite idti.
>
> ("**Sp,**" 257-58)

> "Go back to your family, Tsudechkis," the king says to me. "On Saturday evening, in all probability, I'll pay a visit to Justice. Take my words with you, Tsudechkis, and go."
>
> ("**JP,**" 256)

Here Benya's words are gifts that Tsudechkis can carry with him; shortly thereafter, Tsudechkis compares Benya's words to a boulder.

"Justice in Parentheses" is littered with instances of words as things, starting with the naming of the collective the gangsters plan to rob as "Justice." The word "justice" is ironically concretized in the existence of the collective, but it is once again underscored as language by the story's title, which, by placing it "in parentheses," forces the reader to picture it on the page.

This concretizing of language ultimately calls attention to every speech act as *art*. The chatty, persistent narrator of **"Justice in Parentheses"** refers to his tale not as "*istoriya*" but as "*rasskaz,*" which usually refers to a written form, even as he reinforces the folksy orality of the tale, warning his reader, "It's better not to carry this story into the side-streets" (256). Along the same lines, language becomes a major national product in the conclusion of **"Lyubka Cossack:"**

I na sleduyushchii den' Tsudechkis prishel za funtom neobranderolennogo tabaku iz shtata Virginiya. On poluchil ego i eshche chetvertku chayu v pridachu. A cherez nedelyu, kogda ya prishel k Evselyu pokupat' golubei, ya uvidel novogo upravlyayushchego na Lyubkinom dvore. On byl krokhotny, kak ravvin nash Ben Zkhar'ya. Tsudechkis byl novym upravlyayushchim.

On probyl v svoei dolzhnosti pyatnadtsat' let, i za eto vremya ya uznal o nem mnozhestvo istorii. I, esli sumeyu, ya rasskazhu ikh vse po poryadku, potomu chto eto ochen' interesnye istorii.

("**LK,**" 269)

And the next day Tsudechkis looked in for his pound of unbonded tobacco from the State of Virginia. He received it, and a quarter pound of tea into the bargain. And a week later, when I called on Yevzel to purchase some pigeons, I saw the new manager in Lyubka's yard. He was tiny, like our Rabbi Ben-Zkharya. The new manager was Tsudechkis. He stayed in the job some fifteen years, and during this time I heard many a tale about him. And if I am able I will tell them all one after the other, for they are very entertaining tales.

("**L,**" 242)

The tea, the tobacco, the pigeons, and the gossip about Tsudechkis are linked as fine products: goods are imported and stories exported in a reasonable exchange.

* * *

The last of Babel's gangster stories, **"Froim Grach,"** could be described as a conclusion to the Odessa tales: if the previous stories celebrate the gangsters' linguistic victories, this one shows their final silence. The story relates how the venerable old gang leader Froim Grach, huge, one-eyed, and scarred, goes alone and unarmed to the Cheka building to speak in defense of his "boys," who are being wiped out by the new Soviet regime. A Cheka interrogator, Sasha Borovoi, receives him and leaves briefly to gather all the interrogators and commissars in town so that they might listen to this "legend" who "was the real boss of Odessa's 40,000 thieves" (FG, 14). But when Borovoi returns, he finds Froim Grach's body sprawled under a tarpaulin. The head of the Cheka, who understands that Borovoi is upset, presses his hand compassionately but asks him:

—Otvet' mne kak chekist,—skazal on posle molchaniya,—otvet' mne kak revolyutsioner—zachem nuzhen etot chelovek v budushchem obshchestve?

—Ne znayu,—Borovoi ne dvigalsya i smotrel pryamo pered soboi,—navernoe, ne nuzhen.

("**F**" ["**Froim Grach**"], 259)

"Tell me as a Chekist," he said after a pause, "tell me as a revolutionary: what good was this man for the society of the future?"

"I don't know." Borovoi sat motionless and stared in front of him, "I suppose he wasn't."

("**FG,**" 15)

As a member of the Soviet collective, Borovoi is well aware that an aging thug like Froim Grach has little to offer a socialist society. As an individual, however, he regrets the stilling of the gangster's vibrant voice. Borovoi himself begins to tell the Chekists from Moscow all about the life of Froim Grach, but even as he describes "his cunning and elusiveness, and . . . his contempt for his fellow man," he knows he is marking a loss: the end to "all these extraordinary stories that are now a thing of the past" (**"FG,"** 15).

The Jewish Gangster in the Land of the Soviets

While Babel used his Odessa gang to muse upon what Jews could offer to the revolution and what they would have to sacrifice to it, a handful of Russian Jewish writers followed by taking the figure of the Jewish gangster firmly into the Soviet period. Among the most interesting of these is Venyamin Kaverin's novella *Konets khazy* (End of the gang; 1924). Kaverin's Jewish gangster, Shmerl Turetskii Baraban, represents, according to Hongor Oulanoff, "a 'modernized' version of Benya Krik, the superb and generous 'King.'"[75] Babel and Kaverin delineate the same social transformation—the emergence of the Soviet state—and the figure of the Jewish gangster is a crucial transitional figure for both writers. But they are looking at modernization from opposite sides of the cavern, so that Benya, with his pseudorevolutionary graveyard oration and his run-in with the Cheka, barely glimpses the changes that have already come to pass in *Konets khazy.*

Baraban and his gang—Volodya the Student, Sashka Barin, Five-Spot, and Frolov—are indubitably products of their modern, postrevolutionary city. While Benya burns down the local police station and extorts money from a cattle owner who eventually becomes his father-in-law, Baraban and his company calculate how to use advanced technology to break into the GosBank (State Bank, in Sovietese).

Kaverin's gangsters belong in the ranks of the savvy criminals and quasi criminals who populate the literature of the New Economic Plan (NEP), manipulating with varying degrees of shadiness and violence the NEP's relative looseness. Responding to the economic chaos precipitated by the civil war, a chaos described in the opening of *Konets khazy,* the government introduced the plan in 1921, establishing a permissive policy toward small business and manufacturing, and even speculation. As Maurice Friedberg would have it, Jews in large numbers welcomed the chance to reestablish themselves in traditionally "Jewish" professions, and subsequently turned up in a host of anti-Semitic literary portraits as black-marketeers, moneylenders, profiteers, and crooked businessmen.[76] Questionable morality in legal business under the NEP is briefly thematized in *Konets khazy,* too; Sashka Barin and a couple of henchmen organize a raid on the profits of "one NEPer on Mil'onni Street" with even less compunction than usual and with no small amount of implied reader sympathy.[77] They also rob a Jewish jeweler who cries out in cowardly fashion that the money does not belong to him.

Although one cannot but think of Benya Krik when reading Kaverin, the flamboyant Shmerl Turetskii Baraban most resembles a less charming Ostap Bender, the opinionated, self-aggrandizing con man/protagonist of Ilya Ilf and Yevgeny Petrov's humorous novel *Dvenadtsat' stul'ev* (The twelve chairs; 1928), who is probably a Jew.[78] Bender is extremely—perhaps tellingly—coy about his background; the only piece of information he offers about his past is a repeated, enigmatic claim that his father is a Turkish citizen. This claim may even be an oblique reference to Kaverin's gangster, who goes by the trade name of Turkish Drum. At any rate, Baraban is striving for the level of competence and savoir faire that the "smooth operator" Bender claims as his Soviet birthright. Bender's feeling of ease and belonging in the new Soviet society represent the realization of Baraban's dreams. When Baraban and Sashka Barin have entered the sleeping Pineta's apartment, the sarcastic Pineta demands to know who they are. Baraban answers with a grandiose air that is to become characteristic:

> —To est' ya khochu skazat', chto u menya na golove est' shishka, iz-za kotoroi ya po nasledstvennosti stradayu ostrym lyubopytstvom. Naprimer, seichas mne ochen' khochetsya uznat', kto zhe vy, chyort vas vos'mi, takie?
>
> Sashka Barin skosil na nego glaza i zakuril novuyu papirosu.
>
> —My nalyotchiki,—ob'yasnil on dovol'no ravnodushno.
>
> —My organizatory,—popravil Baraban,—vy nichego ne poteryaete ot znakomstvo s nami.[79]

> "That is, I want to say, that on my head I have a bump, on account of which I suffer by heredity from acute curiosity. For instance, now I very much wonder who, the devil take you, are you?"
>
> Sashka Barin squinted at him and lit up a new cigarette.
>
> "We're criminals," he explained fairly indifferently.
>
> "We're organizers," corrected Baraban. "You have nothing to lose from acquaintanceship with us."

By calling himself an "organizer," Baraban establishes himself as a willing participant in his modernized surroundings, even though his claim is degraded. He has a passion for following parliamentary procedure during criminal huddles and for planning heists "according to the newest system."[80] He even falls in love with a stenographer, the exemplar of the modern working girl. Ostap Bender, created a few years later, has the opportunity to act upon Baraban's comic claim; among other endeavors, he encounters a convention of confidence men and women that parodies Soviet trade unions and congresses and recalls Baraban's eagerness to be a "modern" gangster. Babel didn't get a chance to tell this part of the story, although it seemed that he intended to; before his arrest he had told his wife that he was working on a novella about a Jewish gangster in the age of Sovietism: "I'm writing a novella in which the main character is a former Odessa gangster like Benia Krik. . . . I want to show how this sort of man adapts to Soviet reality. Kolya Topuz works on a collective farm during the time of collectivization, and then he goes to work in a Donbass coal mine. But since he has the mentality of a gangster, he's constantly breaking out of the limits of normal life which leads to numerous funny situations."[81] Although the social context may have changed, Babel continues to picture the gangster as someone larger than life, free from limitations that hobble others, and able to entertain and instruct as a result.

THE END OF THE GANG

Sympathy between writers and gangsters notwithstanding, Babel most likely did not intend to script his own end at the hands of Soviet intelligence in **"Froim Grach."** Nonetheless, when he was executed at the age of forty-six, his own "extraordinary stories" abruptly became a thing of the past. Reportedly, at his arrest on May 16, 1939, Babel was led off complaining that he had not been permitted to finish.[82] Like the gangster Froim Grach, Babel had more stories to tell.

It is impossible to comment at this point in history upon the tragedy and waste of Babel's murder without sounding banal, especially in light of his undisputed dedication to the ideal of a communist society; but there is something almost fitting in the official mystery that has surrounded his death, the details of which were largely unknown until recently and are still emerging. It is as though Babel's death returns his readers to the indeterminacy with which I began: the enigma he sought to fashion out of his own life. The charges against him were fantastic and purple, but eventually he "confessed" under torture to numerous crimes against the Soviet government, including having provided André Malraux with secrets of Soviet aviation.[83] On January 26, 1940, Babel's appeals—in which he vehemently rescinded the testimony he had given under torture and urgently requested a lawyer—were answered with a death warrant. The next day he was shot. With the writer's death, his character Froim Grach's final message, which he had come to deliver in defense of his gang, became painfully profound: "Boss . . . who do you think you're killing? You're killing the best. You'll be left with nothing but riff-raff, boss" (**"FG,"** 15).

Notes

1. Andrey Sinyavsky, "Isaac Babel," 92; Falen, *Isaac Babel,* 79; O'Connor, *Lonely Voice,* 190.

2. Four of these stories constitute the cycle anthologized as *Odessa Tales*: "The King" (1921), "How It Was Done in Odessa" (1923), "The Father" (1924), and "Lyubka Cossack" (1924). Three additional stories chronicle Benya Krik and his gang: "Sunset" (1928), "Froim Grach" (1933), and "Justice in Parentheses" (1921; throughout the text, I have Americanized McDuff's translation of Babel's title from "Justice in Brackets").

   Soviet publishing history is complicated; frequently, three dates are relevant: the date a work was written, the date of its first publication (which may well have been abroad), and the date of its first Soviet edition. Babel apparently wrote the stories of the Odessa cycle between 1921 and 1923; the dates given above represent their first publication in Soviet literary journals. "Justice in Parentheses" was published in 1921 with the subhead "From the Odessa Tales," but it was not included by Babel when he put the four others together as a cycle in the early 1920s. "Sunset" was written four years later but seems not to have been published until 1964; the 1990 Soviet (Khudozhestvennaya literatura) edition notes that the last page is missing. "Froim Grach" was first published in New York in 1963. In May 1933, Babel wrote some relatives that three new stories, including "Froim Grach," were being considered by the editors of a literary anthology to be called *God XXVI* (Year 26). The stories were returned with a note from the writer A. Fadeev saying that they were being rejected for Babel's own sake, since they were "unsuccessful."

   In addition to these seven stories, Babel wrote a film scenario called *Benya Krik* (1926) and a dramatic version of "Sunset," *Zakat* (Sunset; 1928).

3. Harold Bloom, *Isaac Babel,* 113.

4. Jeffrey Brooks's fascinating study of Russian kopeck novels at the turn of the century, *When Russia Learned to Read,* notes that popular chapbooks frequently featured Jewish villains and often chronicled the feats of well-known Jewish gangsters such as Misha Yaponchik ("Mike the Jap").

5. Pinsky, *Poetry and the World,* 144-45.

6. Trilling, introduction, 31.

7. Glatshteyn belonged to the Yiddish modernist literary movement called introspectionism (*in zikh*). He and his colleagues, although they were almost without exception multilingual, chose to write in Yiddish as a muscular cultural assertion; their goal, as they saw it, was to adapt Yiddish to the experience of the Jew in modern America.

8. For a fuller exposition of what Gregory Freidin calls "the whole complex of ideas, texts, and events that have come to be associated with Babel's name," see Freidin, "Isaac Babel," 1889.

9. Babel, "In the Basement," 293. This ploy recalls Fyodor Dostoevsky's *Notes from Underground* (Zapiski iz podpol'ya), in which the narrator immediately warns the reader that he has "lied out of spite" (91).

10. This chain of events in "Moi Pervyi Gonovar" (My first fee) also associates storytelling with prostitution as a profession—an association that later arose for Babel under circumstances outside of his artistic control in 1924, when Commander of the First Cavalry Army Semyon Budennyi accused him of libeling the First Cavalry. Budennyi called Babel a whore in a newspaper article titled "Babizm Babelya iz *Krasnoy novi*" (The sluttishness of Babel from *Red Virgin Soil*). *Red Virgin Soil*—one of the most important and prestigious literary journals of the Soviet 1920s—was the original publisher of Babel's stories from both *Red Cavalry* and *Odessa Tales*; the title of Budennyi's article in Russian contains a pun linking Babel's name and the Russian word *baba,* a rude sobriquet for a woman.

11. See Friedberg, *How Things Were Done in Odessa.*

12. Baron, *The Russian Jew,* 67.

13. Herlihy, *Odessa,* 253.

14. Friedberg, *How Things Were Done in Odessa,* 1.

15. For instance, Babel frequently prefaces turns-of-phrase with the clarification "As they say in Odessa . . ." (see his letters in *Sochineniya v dvukh tomakh,* vol. 1).

16. Pirozhkova, *At His Side,* 85.

17. See Shklovskii, "Yugo-zapad" (Southwest).

18. Raymond Williams, *Politics of Modernism,* 45, 46.

19. Paley, foreword, viii. Paley also acknowledges that her own chosen form, the short short story, "probably couldn't have happened without Babel's work" (ibid., xix).

20. Babel, "Odessa," 26.

21. Babel, "Odessa," 62 (my translation from the Russian version; this passage is omitted in Hayward's English translation).

22. Zamyatin, "On Language," 180.

23. For a clear example of Babel's opinion of the value of "pure" Russian, see his short story "Guy de Maupassant" (1920-22). The narrator describes an attempt by a Russian Jew to translate de Maupassant from French into Russian, an attempt that is unsuccessful because it is too correct and carefully devoid of Jewish inflection: "Raisa Bendersky took pains to write correctly and precisely, and all that resulted was something loose and lifeless, the way Jews wrote Russian in the old days" (331).

24. In an interesting circular move, Max Hayward, in his translation of this essay into English, turns *chelovek vozdukha* back into *luftmensch* (Babel, *You Must Know Everything,* 28).

25. Examples of the literary *luftmensch* include Hershele in Babel's "Shabbos Nakhamu," Benjamin in Mendele Moykher-Sforim's *Travels of Benjamin III,* Munves in Daniel Fuchs's *Homage to Blenholt,* and Menachem-Mendl in Sholem Aleichem's *Adventures of Menachem-Mendl.* Israel Zangwill wrote a humorous short story entitled "The Luftmensch."

26. Babel, "Odessa," 30.

27. Quoted in Herlihy, *Odessa,* 128, 28.

28. Quoted ibid., 281.

29. Paustovsky, *Years of Hope,* 11. The jazz-band leader Leonid Utesov also writes about Odessa's gangsters (including Misha Yaponchik) in his reminiscence "Moya Odessa" (My Odessa; 1964).

30. Lunts to Gorky, 1922, quoted in Erlich, *Modernism and Revolution,* 118.

31. Babel's diaries (and some of his essays for publication) deal extensively with social reorganization in the early Soviet period; see, for instance, Babel, *1920 Diary*; and "Evacuees," "Premature Babies," "Palace of Motherhood," and "Blind Men," in Babel, *You Must Know Everything.*

32. Cowley, *Exile's Return: A Narrative of Ideas,* 77, 100. In a subchapter entitled "Historical Parallel," Cowley adds that Russian and American writers had in common a vision that "going to Europe" could mean aesthetic salvation. Babel did in fact make three long trips to France, and he wrote often of his admiration for the French short-story writer Guy de Maupassant (including the story named after the writer that deals with a search for artistic truth).

33. It is important not to apply Cowley's theory of modernism too broadly here; although Russia before the revolution was a huge empire often included on lists of the great powers, in practice it was an economic colony of the major capitalist nations. Moreover, as I discuss in detail later, Babel's position as a pure product of his country's dominant culture is dubious. Nonetheless, something of this impulse of self-denial is present in his work.

34. The need for Jews to become closer to the natural world was a major focus of the enlightenment (*haskalah*) movement among European Jews in the late eighteenth and nineteenth centuries. The founder of modern Yiddish literature, Mendele Moykher-Sforim (who was involved with the enlightenment movement for many years), frequently thematized the Jewish tendency to be cut off from nature in his novels; in order that Jews might have access to natural science, he published Hebrew translations of popular biology texts.

35. Falen, *Isaac Babel,* 62.

36. Stories by Babel that were my primary sources are cited in the text of this chapter with the abbreviations listed below. Russian-language quotations from these works are transliterated from Babel, *Detsvo i drugie rasskazy*; although supposedly accurate Soviet and post-Soviet Russian complete issues of Babel's work are now available, I find this émigré edition to be the most reliable and free of errors or changes, especially in terms of vernacular Russian forms. The English translations of these primary works are taken from Babel, *The Collected Stories of Isaac Babel* (trans. Walter Morison), with three exceptions: "Froim Grach" excerpts are from Babel, *Isaac Babel: The Lonely Years* (trans. Max Hayward); "Justice in Parentheses" excerpts are from Babel, "Justice in Brackets," in *Isaac Babel: Collected Stories* (trans. David McDuff); and "Sunset" excerpts are from Babel, *You Must Know Everything* (trans. Max Hayward). In several instances I made minor adjustments to these quoted translations, as I have noted in the citations.

F: "Froim Grach" (Russian)

FG: "Froim Grach" (English)

GM: "Guy de Maupassant"

H: "How It Was Done in Odessa"

Is: "Istoriya moei golubyatin"

JP: "Justice in Parentheses"

K: "The King"

Kak: "Kak eto delalos' v Odesse"

Ko: "Korol'"

O: "Odessa"

L: "Lyubka the Cossack"

LK: "Lyubka Kozak"

S: "Sunset"

SD: "The Story of My Dovecote"

Sp: "Spravidlivost' v skobkakh"

Z: "Zakat"

37. Paustovsky, *Years of Hope,* 141.

38. See Sicher, *Style and Structure,* 77.

39. Falen, *Isaac Babel,* 91; Pritchett, "Isaac Babel," 16.

40. Paustovsky, *Years of Hope,* 125.

41. Paustovsky, "Few Words," 279.

42. A satire by Ping-Pong entitled "Nashi Pozhelaniya k 10-Letiyu Oktyabrya" (Our wish for the tenth anniversary of the October revolution; 1927) focuses on Babel's long period without publication and makes a wry joke about the significance of Benya's name: "Just put out something, if only a yell, as long as it isn't Benya the Yell" (Izdai khot' chto-nibud', khot' krik, / No chtob on ne byl Benei Krikom). The extremely thorough bibliography in Efraim Sicher's *Style and Structure in the Work of Isaak Babel'* called my attention to this piece.

43. Falen, *Isaac Babel,* 106.

44. Figures are taken from Baron, *The Russian Jew,* 56-58.

45. Paustovsky, *Years of Hope,* 141.

46. Fuchs, *Summer in Williamsburg,* in *Three Novels,* 155; Philip Roth, *Ghost Writer,* in *Zuckerman Bound,* 30. Taking a further page out of Babel's book, Roth refers in an interview to the craft of writing as "a kind of gangsterism" (Brian D. Johnson, "Intimate Affairs," 256).

47. Marcus, "Stories," 407.

48. Gilbert and Gubar, *No Man's Land,* 253. Mendele Moykher-Sforim makes this writerly oedipal fantasy explicit in his "Notes for My Biography," where he describes his artistry as a sacred calling: the elevation of the mother tongue. Mendele describes his success at that calling this way: "I fell in love with Yiddish and bound myself to that language forever. I found for her the perfumes and fragrances that she needed, and she became a charming lady who bore me many sons" (42). Following this remarkable assertion is a list of his Yiddish works.

49. Gilbert and Gubar, *No Man's Land,* 260.

50. Ong, *Fighting for Life,* 36.

51. Mendele Moykher-Sforim, "Notes for My Biography," 41 (emphasis added).

52. Howe and Greenberg, *Treasury,* 73.

53. A similiar ritual slaughter accounts for one of the most famous moments of *Red Cavalry*: in "My First Goose," Lyutov kills his landlady's goose in a manner forbidden by Jewish law; shortly thereafter he sits down to a meal of pork with the Cossacks.

54. Babel, "V Odesse kazhdiy yunosha . . ." (In Odessa every youth . . .), 358 (my translation). Although the anthology Babel's one-page essay was intended to introduce never appeared, the essay itself was subsequently published in the Soviet Union in 1962 (*Literaturnaya gazeta,* January 1).

55. Shklovskii, "Isaac Babel," 12-14.

56. For a discussion of this concept of ethnic trilogies, see Boelhower, "Ethnic Trilogies."

57. Rosenthal, "Fate," 126.

58. Joyce, *Ulysses,* 12.

59. According to the Bible, Moses lived 120 years; wishing Aunt Pesya a life this long is not merely evidence of Benya's extravagance but in fact reflects a convention of conversational Yiddish.

60. Sholem Aleichem, *Tevye the Dairyman,* 47.

61. Pirozhkova, *At His Side,* 107.

62. In the following passages, Babel borrows from Sholem Aleichem, but makes his images violent:

> . . . the bride looked at the groom with one eye, licking her chops like a cat who had swiped some sour cream.
>
> (Sholem Aleichem, *From the Fair,* 9)

> With both hands she was urging her fainthearted husband toward the door of their nuptial chamber, glaring at him carnivorously. Like a cat she was, that holding a mouse in her jaws tests it gently with her teeth.
>
> (Babel, "The King," 211)

63. Sholem Aleichem, *Tevye the Dairyman,* 40, 36.

64. Babel, "After the Battle," 186.

65. Babel, "Life and Adventures of Matthew Pavlichenko," 101, 106.

66. Ruth Wisse suggested this comparison to me.

67. See Eikhenbaum, "Illyuziya skaza" (The illusion of skaz; 1918), and "Kak sdelana 'Shinel' Gogolya" (How Gogol's *Overcoat* was made;

1919); Vinogradov, "The Problem of Skaz in Stylistics" (1925); and Bakhtin, *Problems of Dostoevsky's Poetics.*

68. Harshav, *Meaning of Yiddish,* 39.

69. Efraim Sicher points this out in his extremely useful book *Style and Structure in the Work of Isaak Babel'*, 77.

70. Lenin, "Critical Remarks," 92.

71. Falen, *Isaac Babel,* 82.

72. Wisse, *Schlemiel,* 23, 3. Evidence of how widespread this particular subject of humor was can be found in the fact that the formulation Babel uses about shooting into the air is repeated verbatim by Woody Allen in the duel scene in his comedy of Russian Jewish life *Love and Death* (1975).

73. Babel, "Story of My Dovecote," 251 (emphasis added).

74. Leiderman, "I ya khochu," 11.

75. Oulanoff, *Serapion Brothers,* 134 (transliteration made consistent).

76. Friedberg, "Jewish Themes," 196. Some examples of satiric literature of this period portraying Jews under the NEP are Mikhail Kozakov's *Povest' o karlike Makse* (Tale about Max the dwarf; 1926); Yulii Berzin's *Ford* (1928); and Matvei Roizman's *Minus shest'* (Minus six; 1931). Other works about criminality under the NEP (but not necessarily Jewish criminality) are Valentin Kataev's novel *Raztrachiki* (The embezzlers; 1928); Leonid Leonov's *Vor* (Thief; 1927); and Ilya Ilf and Yevgeny Petrov's *Dvenadtsat' stul'ev* (The twelve chairs; 1928) and its sequel, *Zolotoi telyonok* (Little golden calf; 1931).

77. My translation of Kaverin, *Konets khazy* (End of the gang), 268. No English version of this work has been published; subsequent translations are also my own.

78. Some critics refer outright to Bender as a Jew or a half-Jew, and some skirt the issue; in fact, there is no hard evidence in the novel to prove it. One of the authors—Ilf, whose real name was Faizelburg—was Jewish. The name Ostap could be a corruption of the Jewish name Osip, and Bender is believable as a Jewish name, but it could also be German. The fact that the Jewish American comic filmmaker Mel Brooks made a movie version of *The Twelve Chairs* probably indicates that Brooks, at least, had some sense of Jewishness in the novel.

79. Kaverin, *Konets khazy,* 241.

80. Ibid., 286.

81. Pirozhkova, *At His Side,* 107.

82. Ibid., 113.

83. Freidin, "Isaac Babel," p. 1911.

References Cited

In cases where I relied on the Russian version of a work but quoted an English translation in the text, the two versions are included here as a single entry. Unless otherwise indicated, page numbers cited throughout this book refer to the reprint editions listed below.

Babel, I. E. [Isaac Emmanuelovich Babel]. "After the Battle." In *The Collected Stories of Isaac Babel.* Trans. and Ed. Walter Morison. 182-87. New York: New American Library, 1955. "Poslye boya." 1920. Reprinted in *Detstvo i drugie rasskazy.* 221-25. Jerusalem: Aliya, 1979.

————. "Avtobiografiya." 1932. Reprinted in *Detstvo i drugie rasskazy.* 7-8. Jerusalem: Aliya, 1979.

————. "Awakening." In *The Collected Stories of Isaac Babel.* Trans. and Ed. Walter Morison. 304-14. New York: New American Library, 1955. "Probuzhdenie." 1930. Reprinted in *Detstvo i drugie rasskazy.* 68-75. Jerusalem: Aliya, 1979.

————. *Benya Krik: A Film-Novel.* Trans. Ivor Montagu and S. S. Nolvandov. Westport, Conn.: Hyperion Press, 1973. *Benya Krik: Kinopovest'.* 1926. Reprinted in *Sochineniya v dvukh tomakh* 2:406-46. Moscow: Khudozhestvennaya literatura, 1990.

————. *The Collected Stories of Isaac Babel.* Trans. and Ed. Walter Morison. New York: New American Library, 1955.

————. *Detstvo i drugie rasskazy* (Childhood and other stories). Jerusalem: Aliya, 1979.

————. "The Father." In *The Collected Stories of Isaac Babel.* Trans. and Ed. Walter Morison. 223-33. New York: New American Library, 1955. "Otets." 1924. Reprinted in *Detstvo i drugie rasskazy.* 270-79. Jerusalem: Aliya, 1979.

————. "Froim Grach." Trans. Max Hayward. In *Isaac Babel: The Lonely Years, 1925-1939.* Trans. Andrew R. MacAndrew and Max Hayward. Ed. Nathalie Babel. 10-15. New York: Farrar, Straus, 1964. "Froim Grach." 1933?/1963. Reprinted in *Detstvo i drugie rasskazy.* 292-97. Jerusalem: Aliya, 1979.

————. "Guy de Maupassant." In *The Collected Stories of Isaac Babel.* Trans. and Ed. Walter Morison. 328-37. New York: New American Library, 1955. "Gyui de Mopassan." 1920-22. Reprinted in *Detstvo i drugie rasskazy.* 81-89. Jerusalem: Aliya, 1979.

————. "How It Was Done in Odessa." In *The Collected Stories of Isaac Babel.* Trans. and Ed. Walter

Morison. 211-22. New York: New American Library, 1955. "Kak eto delalos' v Odesse." 1923. Reprinted in *Detstvo i drugie rasskazy.* 246-55. Jerusalem: Aliya, 1979.

———. "In the Basement." In *The Collected Stories of Isaac Babel.* Trans. and Ed. Walter Morison. 293-304. New York: New American Library, 1955. "V podvale." 1929. Reprinted in *Detstvo i drugie rasskazy.* 58-67. Jerusalem: Aliya, 1979.

———. *Isaac Babel: Collected Stories.* Trans. and Ed. David McDuff. New York: Penguin Books, 1994.

———. *Isaac Babel: The Lonely Years, 1925-1939.* Trans. Andrew R. MacAndrew and Max Hayward. Ed. Nathalie Babel. New York: Farrar, Straus, 1964.

———. "Justice in Brackets." In *Isaac Babel: Collected Stories.* Trans. and Ed. David McDuff. 254-59. New York: Penguin Books, 1994. "Spravidlivost' v skobkakh." 1921. Reprinted in *Detstvo i drugie rasskazy.* 256-62. Jerusalem: Aliya, 1979.

———. "The King." In *The Collected Stories of Isaac Babel.* Trans. and Ed. Walter Morison. 203-11. New York: New American Library, 1955. "Korol'." 1921. Reprinted in *Detstvo i drugie rasskazy.* 239-45. Jerusalem: Aliya, 1979.

———. "The Life and Adventures of Matthew Pavlichenko." In *The Collected Stories of Isaac Babel.* Trans. and Ed. Walter Morison. 100-106. New York: New American Library, 1955. "Zhizneopisanie Pavlichenki, Matveya Rodionycha." 1924. Reprinted in *Detstvo i drugie rasskazy.* 152-57. Jerusalem: Aliya, 1979.

———. "Lyubka Cossack." In *The Collected Stories of Isaac Babel.* Trans. and Ed. Walter Morison. 234-44. New York: New American Library, 1955. "Lyubka Kazak." 1924. Reprinted in *Detstvo i drugie rasskazy.* 263-69. Jerusalem: Aliya, 1979.

———. "Moi pervyi gonovar" (My first fee). 1922-23/ 1963. Reprinted in *Sochineniya v dvukh tomakh* 2:245-53. Moscow: Khudozhestvennaya literatura, 1990.

———. "My First Goose." In *The Collected Stories of Isaac Babel.* Trans. and Ed. Walter Morison. 72-76. New York: New American Library, 1955. "Moi pervyi gus'." 1924. Reprinted in *Detstvo i drugie rasskazy.* 129-32. Jerusalem: Aliya, 1979.

———. *1920 Diary.* Trans. H. T. Willetts. Ed. Carol J. Avins. New Haven, Conn.: Yale University Press, 1995.

———. "Odessa." In *You Must Know Everything: Stories, 1915-1937.* Trans. Max Hayward. Ed. Nathalie Babel. 26-30. New York: Farrar, Straus, and Giroux, 1966.

———. [Bab-El, pseud.]. "Odessa." 1916. Reprinted in *Sochineniya v dvukh tomakh* 1:62-65. Moscow: Khudozhestvennaya literatura, 1990.

———. "Pervaya lyubov'" (First love). 1925. Reprinted in *Detstvo i drugie rasskazy.* 49-57. Jerusalem: Aliya, 1979.

———. "Shabbos Nakhamu." 1918. Reprinted in *Detstvo i drugie rasskazy.* 19-25. Jerusalem: Aliya, 1979.

———. *Sochineniya v dvukh tomakh* (Works in two volumes). Moscow: Khudozhestvennaya literatura, 1990.

———. "The Story of My Dovecote." In *The Collected Stories of Isaac Babel.* Trans. and Ed. Walter Morison. 251-64. New York: New American Library, 1955. "Istoriya moei golubyatin." 1925. Reprinted in *Detstvo i drugie rasskazy.* 36-48. Jerusalem: Aliya, 1979.

———. "Sunset." In *You Must Know Everything: Stories, 1915-1937.* Trans. Max Hayward. Ed. Nathalie Babel. 135-54. New York: Farrar, Straus, and Giroux, 1966. "Zakat." 1924-25/1964. Reprinted in *Detstvo i drugie rasskazy.* 280-91. Jerusalem: Aliya, 1979.

———. "V Odesse kazhdiy yunosha . . ." (In Odessa every youth . . .). 1923. In *Sochineniya v dvukh tomakh* 2:358. Moscow: Khudozhestvennaya literatura, 1990.

———. *You Must Know Everything: Stories, 1915-1937.* 1966. Trans. Max Hayward. Ed. Nathalie Babel. Reprint, New York: Farrar, Straus, and Giroux, 1969.

———. *Zakat* (Sunset). 1928. Reprint, Letchworth, England: Prideaux Press, 1977.

Baker, Carlos. *Ernest Hemingway: A Life Story.* New York: Charles Scribner's Sons, 1969.

Baker, Houston. "Caliban's Triple Play." In *"Race" Writing and Difference.* Ed. Henry Louis Gates Jr. 381-95. Chicago: University of Chicago Press, 1986.

Bakhtin, M. M. *Problems of Dostoevsky's Poetics.* Trans. and Ed. Caryl Emerson. Minneapolis: University of Minnesota Press, 1984.

Baron, Salo W. *The Russian Jew under Tsars and Soviets.* 2d ed. New York: Macmillan, 1976.

Berzin, Yulii. *Ford.* Petrograd: n.p., 1928.

Bloom, Harold, ed. *Isaac Babel.* New York: Chelsea House, 1987.

Boelhower, William. "Ethnic Trilogies: A Genealogical and Generational Poetics." In *The Invention of Ethnicity.* Ed. Werner Sollors. 158-75. New York: Oxford University Press, 1988.

Brooks, Jeffrey. *When Russia Learned to Read: Literacy and Popular Literature, 1861-1917.* Princeton, N.J.: Princeton University Press, 1985.

Budennyi, S[emyon]. "Babizm Babelya iz *Krasnoy novi*" (The sluttishness of Babel from *Red Virgin Soil*). *Oktyabr'* 3 (1924): 196-97.

Cowley, Malcolm. *Exile's Return: A Literary Odyssey of the 1920s.* New York: Viking, 1951.

———. *Exile's Return: A Narrative of Ideas.* New York: W. W. Norton, 1934.

Dostoevsky, Fyodor. *Notes from Underground* (Zapiski iz podpol'ya). Trans. Mirra Ginsburg. New York: Bantam, 1974.

Eikhenbaum, B. M. "Illyuziya skaza" (The illusion of skaz). 1918. In *Skvoz' literatura: Sbornik statei.* 152-56. Leningrad: Academia, 1924.

———. "Kak sdelano 'Shinel' Gogolya" (How Gogol's *Overcoat* was made). 1919. In *Skvoz' literatura: Sbornik statei.* 171-75. Leningrad: Academia, 1924.

Eliot, T. S. "Notes toward the Definition of Culture." 1948. Reprinted in *Christianity and Culture.* 79-187. New York: Harcourt Brace Jovanovich, 1988.

Erlich, Victor. *Modernism and Revolution: Russian Literature in Transition.* Cambridge, Mass.: Harvard University Press, 1994.

Falen, James. *Isaac Babel: Russian Master of the Short Story.* Knoxville: University of Tennessee Press, 1974.

Freidin, Gregory. "Isaac Babel." In *European Writers of the Twentieth Century.* Ed. George Stade. 11:1885-1915. New York: Charles Scribner's Sons, 1993.

Friedberg, Maurice. *How Things Were Done in Odessa: Cultural and Intellectual Pursuits in a Soviet City.* Boulder, Colo.: Westview Press, 1991.

———. "Jewish Themes in Soviet Russian Literature." In *The Jews in the Soviet Union since 1917.* Ed. Lionel Kochan. 188-207. New York: Oxford University Press, 1978.

Fuchs, Daniel. *Three Novels by Daniel Fuchs: "Summer in Williamsburg," "Homage to Blenholt," "Low Company."* New York: Basic Books, 1961.

Gilbert, Sandra M., and Susan Gubar. *No Man's Land: The Place of the Woman Writer in the Twentieth Century.* Vol. 1, *The War of the Words.* New Haven, Conn.: Yale University Press, 1988.

Glatshteyn, Jacob. "Sheeny Mike" (Shini Mayk). 1929. In *American Yiddish Poetry: A Bilingual Anthology.* Trans. and Ed. Benjamin Harshav and Barbara Harshav et al. 241-46. Berkeley: University of California Press, 1986.

Harshav, Benjamin. *The Meaning of Yiddish.* Berkeley: University of California Press, 1990.

Herlihy, Patricia. *Odessa: A History, 1794-1914.* Cambridge, Mass.: Harvard University Press, 1986.

Howe, Irving, and Eliezer Greenberg, eds. *A Treasury of Yiddish Stories.* New York: Schocken Books, 1953.

Ilf, Ilya, and Yevgeny Petrov. *Dvenadtsat' stul'ev; Zolotoi telyonok* (The twelve chairs [1928]; Little golden calf [1931]). Moscow: Khudozhestvennaya literatura, 1990.

Johnson, Brian D. "Intimate Affairs." In *Conversations with Philip Roth.* Ed. George J. Searles. 254-58. Jackson: University Press of Mississippi, 1992.

Joyce, James. *Ulysses: The Corrected Text.* 1922. Reprint, New York: Vintage Books, 1986.

Kataev, Valentin. *Raztrachiki* (The embezzlers). 1928. Reprint, Moscow: Federatsya, 1933.

Kaverin, Venyamin. *Konets khazy* (End of the gang). 1924. Reprint, Moscow: Khudozhestvennaya literatura, 1980.

Kozakov, Mikhail. "Povest' o karlike Makse" (Tale about Max the dwarf). 1926. Reprinted in *Chelovek padayushchii nits* (Man falling prostrate). 99-160. Leningrad: Priboi, 1930.

Leiderman, N. "I ya khochu internatsionala dobrykh lyudei . . ." (And I want an international of good people . . .). *Literaturnye obozrenie* 10 (1991): 11.

Lenin, V. I. "Critical Remarks on the National Question." 1913. Reprinted in *Lenin on Literature and Art.* 88-95. Moscow: Progress Publishers, 1967.

Leonov, Leonid. *Vor* (Thief). 1927. Reprint, Moscow: Khudozhestvennaya literatura, 1979.

Love and Death. Dir. Woody Allen. Rollins and Joffe, 1975.

Man without a World. Dir. Eleanor Antin. 1991.

Marcus, Stephen. "The Stories of Isaac Babel." *Partisan Review* 23, no. 3 (1955): 400-411.

Mayakovsky, Vladimir. *"The Bedbug" and Selected Poetry.* Trans. Max Hayward and George Reavey. Ed. Patricia Blake. Bloomington: Indiana University Press, 1973.

Mendele Moykher-Sforim. "Notes for My Biography." 1889. Trans. Gerald Stillman. In *Selected Works of Mendele Moykher-Sforim.* Ed. Marvin S. Zuckerman, Gerald Stillman, and Marion Herbst. 31-46. Malibu, Calif.: Joseph Simon-Pangloss Press, 1991.

———. *Selected Works of Mendele Moykher-Sforim.* Ed. Marvin S. Zuckerman, Gerald Stillman, and Marion Herbst. Malibu, Calif.: Joseph Simon-Pangloss Press, 1991.

———. *The Travels of Benjamin III.* In *Selected Works of Mendele Moykher-Sforim.* Ed. Marvin S. Zuckerman, Gerald Stillman, and Marion Herbst. 353-74. Malibu, Calif.: Joseph Simon-Pangloss Press, 1991.

O'Connor, Frank. *The Lonely Voice: A Study of the Short Story.* 1962. Reprint, New York: Harper Colophon, 1985.

Ong, Walter J. *Fighting for Life: Contest, Sexuality, and Consciousness.* Ithaca, N.Y.: Cornell University Press, 1981.

Oulanoff, Hongor. *Serapion Brothers.* Paris: Mouton and Co., 1966.

Paley, Grace. Foreword to A. N. Pirozhkova, *At His Side: The Last Years of Isaac Babel.* Trans. Ann Frydman and Robert L. Busch. South Royalton, Vt.: Steerforth Press, 1996.

Paustovsky, Konstantin. "A Few Words about Isaac Babel." In *You Must Know Everything: Stories, 1915-1937,* by Isaac Babel, 275-83. New York: Farrar, Straus, and Giroux, 1966.

————. *Years of Hope.* Trans. Manya Harari and Andrew Thomson. London: Harvill Press, 1968.

Ping-Pong [pseud.]. "Nashi pozhelaniya k 10-letiyu oktyabrya" (Our wishes for the tenth anniversary of the October Revolution). *Na literaturnom postu* 20 (1927): 128.

Pinsky, Robert. *Poetry and the World.* New York: Ecco Press, 1988.

Pirozhkova, A. N. *At His Side: The Last Years of Isaac ́Babel.* Trans. Ann Frydman and Robert L. Busch. South Royalton, Vt.: Steerforth Press, 1996.

Pritchett, V. S. "Isaac Babel: Five Minutes of Life." In *Lasting Impressions: Selected Essays.* 16-19. London: Chatto and Windus, 1990.

Roizman, Matvei. *Minus shest'* (Minus six). Berlin: Kniga i Stena, 1931.

Rosenthal, Raymond. "The Fate of Isaac Babel, a Child of the Russian Emancipation." *Commentary* 3, no. 2 (1947): 126-31.

Roth, Philip. *Zuckerman Bound: A Trilogy and Epilogue. "The Ghost Writer," "Zuckerman Unbound," "The Anatomy Lesson," "Epilogue: A Prague Orgy."* New York: Fawcett Crest, 1985.

Shklovskii, Victor. "Isaac Babel: A Critical Romance." In *Isaac Babel.* Ed. Harold Bloom. 9-14. New York: Chelsea House, 1987.

————. "Yugo-zapad" (Southwest). *Literaturnaya gazeta,* 5 January 1933, 3.

Sholem Aleichem. *The Adventures of Menachem-Mendl.* Trans. Tamara Kahana. New York: Putnam, 1969.

————. *From the Fair: The Autobiography of Sholom Aleichem.* Trans. and Ed. Curt Leviant. New York: Viking, 1985.

————. *Shomar's mishpot, oder der sud prisyazshnikh oyf alle romanen fun Shemer.* 1888. Reprint, New York: Clearwater/YIVO, 1980.

————. *"Tevye the Dairyman" and "The Railroad Stories."* Trans. Hillel Halkin. New York: Schocken Books, 1987.

————. *Tevye's Daughters.* Trans. Frances Butwin. New York: Crown, 1949.

Sholokhov, Mikhail. *Tikhii Don* (And quiet flows the don). 1928-40. Reprint, Moscow: Khudozhestvennaya literatura, 1985.

Sicher, Efraim. *Style and Structure in the Work of Isaak Babel'.* Columbus, Ohio: Slavica Publishers, 1985.

Sinyavsky, Andrey. "Isaac Babel." In *Isaac Babel.* Ed. Harold Bloom. 87-95. New York: Chelsea House, 1987.

Trilling, Lionel. Introduction to *The Collected Stories of Isaac Babel.* Trans. and Ed. Walter Morison. New York: New American Library, 1955.

Utesov, Leonid. "Moya Odessa" (My Odessa). *Literaturnaya Rossiya.* 21 August 1964, 6-17.

Vinogradov, Viktor. "The Problem of Skaz in Stylistics." *Russian Literature Triquarterly* 12 (Spring 1975): 237-52.

Wald, Alan. *Writing from the Left: New Essays on Radical Culture and Politics.* New York: Verso, 1994.

Walsh, George. *Public Enemies: The Mayor, the Mob, and the Crime That Was.* New York: W. W. Norton, 1980.

Warshow, Robert. "The Gangster as Tragic Hero." 1948. Reprinted in *The Immediate Experience.* New York: Atheneum, 1970.

Weidman, Jerome. *I Can Get It for You Wholesale.* 1937. Reprint, London: Bodley Head, 1984.

Weinryb, Bernard. "Anti-Semitism in Soviet Russia." In *The Jews in Soviet Russia since 1917.* Ed. Lionel Kochan. 288-320. New York: Oxford University Press, 1972.

West, Nathanael. *A Cool Million.* 1934. Reprinted in *The Collected Works of Nathanael West.* 277-380. New York: Penguin Books, 1981.

————. *The Day of the Locust.* 1939. Reprinted in *"Miss Lonelyhearts" and "The Day of the Locust."* New York: New Directions, 1962.

What Happened to Mary? Writ. Horace G. Plympton. Edison, 1912.

Williams, Raymond. *The Politics of Modernism: Against the New Conformists.* New York: Verso, 1989.

Williams, William Carlos. *Spring and All.* 1923. Reprinted in *The Collected Poems of William Carlos Williams.* Ed. A. Walton Litz and Christopher MacGowan, vol. 1 (1909-39). 175-236. New York: New Directions, 1986.

Wisse, Ruth R. *The Schlemiel as Modern Hero.* Chicago: University of Chicago Press, 1971.

Zamyatin, Yevgeny. "On Language." 1919-20. Reprinted in *A Soviet Heretic: Essays by Yevgeny Zamyatin.* Trans. and Ed. Mirra Ginsburg. 175-89. Chicago: University of Chicago Press, 1970.

Zangwill, Israel. "The Luftmensch." In *Ghetto Comedies.* New York: Macmillan, 1907.

———. *The Melting-Pot.* 1909. Reprint, New York: Macmillan, 1932.

FURTHER READING

Biography

Sicher, Efraim. "The Trials of Isaak: A Brief Life." *Canadian Slavonic Papers* 36, nos. 1-2 (March-June 1994): 7-42.

> Offers a brief biography of Babel, setting the writing and publication of his major works in the context of his life. Sicher stresses the development of Babel's themes and the various degrees of reception and rejection his work received, first in revolutionary, and then in Stalinist Russia.

Criticism

Baak, Joost van. "Isaak Babel's 'Cemetery at Kozin.'" *Canadian Slavonic Papers* 36, nos. 1-2 (March-June 1994): 69-87.

> Argues that Babel's "Cemetery at Kozin" functions as a kind of thematic and structural centerpoint to *Red Cavalry,* offering a stationary moment of reflection in which the narrator assesses and mourns for what has been lost, rather than a recounting of events.

Bar-Yosef, Hamutal. "On Isaac Babel's 'The Story of My Dovecot.'" *Prooftexts: A Journal of Jewish Literary History* 6, no. 3 (September 1986): 264-71.

> Focuses on Babel's "The Story of My Dovecot," calling it an autobiographical tale and a work in which the author's attitude toward the Jewish condition developed from ambivalence to sympathy.

Bloom, Harold, ed. *Isaac Babel,* New York: Chelsea House Publishers, 1987, 277 p.

> A collection of twenty essays on Babel and his work written by a number of noted critics and scholars of Russian literature and presented in chronological sequence. The essays include those by Viktor Shklovsky, Lionel Trilling, Ilya Ehrenburg, James Falen, and Efraim Sicher, among others.

Danow, David K. "A Poetics of Inversion: The Non-Dialogic Aspect in Isaac Babel''s *Red Cavalry.*" *The Modern Language Review* 86, no. 4 (October 1991): 939-53.

> Argues that much of the visceral power of *Red Cavalry* derives from Babel's extremely sparse use of dialogue and his correlating tendency to juxtapose ghastly events with lyrical outbursts, rather than with mediating or reactive conversation.

———. "The Paradox of *Red Cavalry.*" *Canadian Slavonic Papers* 36, nos. 1-2 (March-June 1994): 43-54.

> Interprets *Red Cavalry* as a study in paradox, both that of an overlaid present and past, and that of co-existing human tendencies toward inflicting suffering, on the one hand, and creating art and beauty, on the other.

Eng, Jan van der. "*Red Cavalry*: A Novel of Stories." *Russian, Croatian and Serbian, Czech and Slovak, Polish Literature* 33, nos. 2-3 (1 April 1993): 249-64.

> Analyzes the structure of Babel's *Red Cavalry,* focusing on those elements that allow its stories to function as self-contained entities while simultaneously fitting into the overarching framework of a novel.

Erlich, Victor. "Art and Reality: A Note on Isaak Babel's Metaliterary Narratives." *Canadian Slavonic Papers* 36, nos. 1-2 (March-June 1994): 107-14.

> Traces the relationship between art and reality as developed in Babel's work, not only as it relates to his narrative devices, but also as a central theme to which he returns constantly throughout his career.

Hetényi, Zsuzsa. "'Up' and 'Down,' Madonna and Prostitute: The Role of Ambivalence in *Red Cavalry* by Isaac Babel." *Acta Litteraria: Academiae Scientiarum Hungaricae* 32, nos. 3-4 (1990): 309-26.

> Considers Babel's *Red Cavalry* a new mythology that nevertheless draws its primary symbols from biblical narrative and Christian iconography, simply inverting, modernizing, or altering their meaning, so as to convey paradox and ambivalence.

Kellman, Steven G. "The Birth of a Batterer: Isaac Babel's 'My First Goose.'" *Bucknell Review* 44, no. 1 (2000): 102-07.

> Critiques Babel's "My First Goose" in terms of patriarchal rites of passage, including martial brutality, oppression of women, and cruelty toward animals.

Luck, C. D. *The Field of Honour: An Analysis of Isaak Babel's Cycle* On the Field of Honour *(Na pole chesti), with Reference to Gaston Vidal's* Figures et anecdotes de la Grande Guerre. Birmingham, England: Department of Russian Language & Literature, University of Birmingham, 1987, 84 p.

> Maintains that the source for three war stories Babel wrote before he created *Red Cavalry,* entitled "On the Field of Honour," "The Deserter," and "The Family of Old Man Maresko," have as their source two war stories written by a French captain, Gaston Vidal, in 1918.

Nesbet, Anne. "Babel's Face." *Russian, Croatian and Serbian, Czech and Slovak, Polish Literature* 42, no. 1 (1 July 1997): 65-83.

> Approaches Babel's work to uncover a self-portrait of the author, while addressing issues of identity and image throughout his stories. Nesbet concludes that this pursuit for narrative identity resolves only into more paradox and mystery, rather than a definitive "face" or image of the author.

Reid, Allan. "Isaak Babel's *Konarmiia:* Meanings and Endings." *Canadian Slavonic Papers* 33, no. 2 (June 1991): 139-50.

> Attempts to correct previous interpretations of Babel's *Red Cavalry* by examining the work's conclusion. Reid argues that Babel's story-cycle achieves neither "linear development" nor resolution but rather repeats its theme throughout, thereby linking the ending with the beginning.

Rougle, Charles, ed. *Red Cavalry,* Evanston, Ill.: Northwestern University Press, 1996, 176 p.

> Collects three previously published essays on Babel's *Red Cavalry* by Carol Luplow, Milton Ehre, and Victor Terras. Rougle also offers a brief biography of Babel and an examination of *Red Cavalry* in the context of the Polish-Soviet War of 1920.

Safran, Gabriella. "Isaak Babel's El'ia Isaakovich as a New Jewish Type." *Slavic Review* 61, no. 2 (summer 2002): 253-72.

> Postulates that in the figure of El'ia Isaakovich, from the short story "El'ia Isaakovich and Margarita Prokof'evna," Babel became the first writer to successfully portray a strong Russian-Jewish character, a literary type that is neither a victim nor an exploiter of other Russians, but a personification of positive change.

Sicher, Efraim. "The Jewishness of Babel." In *Jews in Russian Literature after the October Revolution: Writers and Artists between Hope and Apostasy,* pp. 71-111. Cambridge: Cambridge University Press, 1995.

> Charts the development of Babel's national and ethnic identities, demonstrating that he did not fit in with either the tradition of Russian-Jewish writers nor with the Bolshevik and Soviet authors of post-revolutionary Russia.

————. "Babel's 'Shy Star': Reference, Inter-reference and Interference." *New Zealand Slavonic Journal* 36 (2002): 259-75.

> Considers Babel's work in the context of his cultural and ethnic situation, stressing the tension between his Jewish heredity and his status as an acclaimed Russian author.

Stine, Peter. "Isaac Babel and Violence." *Modern Fiction Studies* 30, no. 2 (summer 1984): 237-55.

> Traces the theme of violence in Babel's work, which he considers a symptom of the author's irresistible urge to tell the truth about the nature of human passion and suffering.

Additional coverage of Babel's life and career is contained in the following sources published by Thomson Gale: *Contemporary Authors,* **Vols. 104, 155;** *Contemporary Authors New Revision Series,* **Vol. 113;** *Dictionary of Literary Biography,* **Vol. 272;** *Encyclopedia of World Literature in the 20th Century,* **Ed. 3;** *European Writers,* **Vol. 11;** *Literature Resource Center; Major 20th-Century Writers,* **Ed. 2;** *Major 21st-Century Writers; Reference Guide to Short Fiction,* **Ed. 2;** *Reference Guide to World Literature,* **Eds. 2, 3;** *Short Stories for Students,* **Vol. 10;** *Short Story Criticism,* **Vols. 16, 78;** *Twayne's World Authors;* **and** *Twentieth-Century Literary Criticism,* **Vols. 2, 13.**

The Ambassadors

Henry James

The following entry presents criticism on James's novel *The Ambassadors* (1903). For discussion of James's complete career, see *TCLC*, Volumes 2, 11, 24, and 47; for discussion of the novel *The Portrait of a Lady* (1881), see *TCLC*, Volume 40; for for discussion of the novel *Daisy Miller* (1879), see *TCLC*, Volume 64.

INTRODUCTION

The Ambassadors is widely acknowledged as one of James's greatest literary achievements. Ranked with the other two "master works" of his so-called late period, *The Wings of the Dove* (1902) and *The Golden Bowl* (1904), *The Ambassadors* is regarded by many critics as the most formally precise and artistically integrated of all James's novels. Through its deftly orchestrated narration and its psychological explorations of character, the novel confronts fundamental questions of morality, perception, personal integrity, and the myth of the American abroad—the encounter of the New World with the Old. *The Ambassadors* has also been lauded as the work in which James refined many of the literary techniques and concerns that shaped the direction of the modern novel in the twentieth century, and which influenced such later writers as James Joyce and Virginia Woolf. These include his method of "scenic progression" and point-of-view narration, the art of "indirect suggestion," and the relationship between subjective experience and external reality. Although not all critics today would agree with the author's own assessment of *The Ambassadors* as "quite the best" of all his writings, they generally concur that it is one of the two or three masterpieces that established James as the first great novelist of the modern period and one of the most imposing figures in twentieth-century literature.

PLOT AND MAJOR CHARACTERS

Lambert Strether, a middle-aged man of sensibility and imagination from Woollett, Massachusetts, has arrived in England at the request of Mrs. Newsome, a wealthy widow who is his employer and fiancée. Strether's mission is to act as Mrs. Newsome's "ambassador" and rescue her son, Chad, from a presumed entanglement with an unknown Frenchwoman, which has kept him from returning to America. Mrs. Newsome has hopes that upon his return Chad will work in the family business and marry Mamie Pocock, sister of Chad's brother-in-law. Strether's romantic and financial future with Mrs. Newsome depends on his successful return from this mission. While in England Strether joins an old friend, Mr. Waymarsh, and forms a new friendship with Maria Gostrey before continuing on to London, and eventually Paris, to confront Chad. Both Waymarsh and Gostrey assist and advise Strether on his travels.

When Strether meets Chad and his mistress, the Countess Madame de Vionnet, he is enchanted by their appearance and genteel manners and his focus gradually shifts away from his duties to Mrs. Newsome. Strether is confronted with the fact that he is middle aged and that many opportunities have already passed him by. Nostalgia and longing overtake him as he enjoys the company of Chad and his young friends. The seductive possibilities of Paris coupled with Strether's own sense of loss prompt his well-known speech to Little Bilham, which James credits as the origin of the novel: "Live all you can; it's a mistake not to." In a reversal of all the New England values and expectations he held at the start of his mission, Strether decides to help the Countess and convince Mrs. Newsome that Paris has had positive effects on Chad. Waymarsh advises him to either abandon his mission or continue with his original plan, but Strether refuses this advice and attempts to construct a compromise. At one point, Chad even becomes willing to return to Woollett, but ironically it is Strether who now convinces him to remain in Paris.

At this point in the narrative, Strether's failure and doomed fate become inevitable. The novel's hourglass structure emerges as the hero's original intentions and observations reverse. He is replaced by another "ambassador" when Mrs. Newsome sends her daughter, Sarah Pocock, to carry out her orders and bring Chad home. Unlike Strether, Sarah does not delight in Chad's surroundings or friends, and she soon exposes the superficiality of Chad's "improvement" in Paris when she convinces him to return home. Chad recognizes that his attachment to the Countess has no future because she is already married. For him, it is advantageous, both financially and personally, to return to the family business and a willing bride. Strether's enchantment with Paris and the genteel society he has experienced begins to diminish as Chad's intentions become apparent. When Strether refuses to give his blessing on Chad's decision to leave, he also rejects any possibility for reconciliation and forgiveness upon his own return to Woollett. Strether makes this decision to preserve his own integrity and because he does not want to be responsible for what he foresees as Chad's boring and unsatisfying life in Woollett.

In the final section of the novel, Strether discusses the outcome of events with Maria Gostrey. Mrs. Newsome's will has been carried out and Strether's relationship with her is most certainly over. Strether acknowledges that he will go "home to infamy." Secretly in love with Strether, Gostrey invites him to stay in Paris with her, but he declines. He is convinced that his involvement in the events must remain selfless and free of strategy. Strether must return to Woollett and accept the damage he has done to himself. To allow himself to be saved by Gostrey would be to forfeit the sacrifice he has made and to diminish the "vision" he has achieved as a result of his ordeal.

MAJOR THEMES

One of the most-discussed themes in *The Ambassadors*—indeed, what many critics consider the central theme—is the myth of the American abroad and the

juxtaposition of opposing cultures and conflicting sensibilities symbolized in the novel by Woollett and Paris, and the respective characters from both worlds. But although James structures his novel around the polarities of Woollett and Paris, the depictions of each is hardly unambiguous, as a number of recent commentators have noted. Both societies demonstrate positive and negative qualities. While Woollett is ultimately depicted by James as the more inhibiting of the two cultures, with its over-reliance on commerce, productivity, social status, and moral inflexibility, Paris is not merely "a jewel brilliant and hard," but shows that the capacity to enjoy life carries the risk of cynicism, relativism, and lack of moral purpose. James treats both American innocence and European culture with more than a touch of comic irony. Many critics argue that, despite its symmetry and balanced structure, *The Ambassadors* does not offer a clear conflict between two cultures but instead explores the limitations of one culture—the American—from a distant setting and in light of another.

Another important theme in *The Ambassadors* frequently debated by critics is that of consciousness and self-awareness, especially as reflected in the character of Strether. Indeed, the drama and interest of the novel center on the perceptions, judgments, and consciousness of James's hero, and the key question of what, in the end, he comes to *see* and understand as a result of his experiences. On one level, the matter of consciousness is closely linked to James's technique of "scenic progression" and his expert control of his narration through the impressions of his main character (whom James referred to as his "Poor Sensitive Gentleman"). Through Strether's evolving perspective—his first impressions of his mission; his altered opinions as he succumbs to the beauty of Paris and the charms of his young companions; his nostalgia for youth; and his ultimate "vision" of life—James dramatizes the limitations of subjectivity and the failings of perception itself to bridge the gap between personal experience and external reality. At a deeper level, the theme of consciousness is enacted in Strether's movement towards his own epiphany and sense of self-knowledge, culminating in his crucial speech to Little Bilham in Gloriani's garden: "Live all you can."

Related to the theme of consciousness or vision is that of youth and age. As many critics have noted, age plays an important role in Strether's experiences and his interpretation of events. His sense of personal loss and his overly romantic attachment to youth cause him to misinterpret facts, misjudge people, and attempt to achieve vicariously through others what he failed to experience during his own youth. On one level, the theme is enacted in the ironic reversal of Strether's and Chad's roles during the course of the novel. Whereas Strether opens the novel as the "mature" man with a mission to rescue Mrs. Newsome's youthful and irresponsible son, it is he who is overcome by the charms of youth and urges Chad to stay in Paris. On the other hand, Chad appears to mature, agreeing to return home and accept his appointed position in the family business. But, as numerous critics have asserted, such a reading oversimplifies both Strether's character and James's intent. Despite his self-deprecation, Strether is a noble soul who truly seeks to understand life, to confront moral issues honestly, and to see "things as they were." While he fails at one mission, he heroically succeeds at another, more personal, one. By the end of *The Ambassadors,* Strether has gained an awareness of himself and his situation, of morality and beauty, that places him above most other of James's protagonists.

Finally, strategy is an important theme running through *The Ambassadors.* Central to the novel is the ambassadors' mission: to convince Chad to return home. Strether's failed attempt and subsequently Sarah's success are largely as a result of strategy. Upon Strether's arrival in Paris, his plans for persuading Chad are quickly reversed as he himself is persuaded by the genteel society of Paris. Sarah is unyielding to the pleasures and charms of Paris. She never wavers from the mission nor her initial predisposition and eventually convinces Chad to come home with her. Paradoxically, Mrs. Newsome is both powerful and vulnerable. She insists upon her will being carried out, yet she is unable to act herself. Her only strategy is a passive one, to send "ambassadors" until her will is accomplished. Also significant is Strether's rejection of strategy at the end of the novel. He refuses to save himself because he wants his actions to remain pure.

CRITICAL RECEPTION

As previously noted, James considered *The Ambassadors* "quite the best, 'all round,' of all my productions." But many early critics reacted ambivalently to the novel. Whereas some found evidence of James's immense technical skill in the novel, others faulted it for its perceived obscurity, verbosity, and lack of meaningful action—what H. G. Wells referred to, in his description of James, as a "leviathan retrieving pebbles." After James's death and in the global upheaval following the First World War, *The Ambassadors* and most of James's work fell into near obscurity. His subtle, artistic, and romantic portraits of the social and psychological dilemmas of upper-class characters appeared particularly inconsequential and out of step with the times. But *The Ambassadors* and the James canon experienced a critical revival in the 1940s and 1950s. Although critics disagreed over the ultimate success of the novel and the exact nature of Strether's experience in Paris, most praised James's subtleties of characterization and found a depth of philosophical and psychological meaning in the work that had been ignored by previous critics.

Continuing a trend that dates back to the earliest interpretations of the novel, a number of recent critics have examined the nature of Strether's epiphany and the "process of vision" in James's narrative. Collin Meissner, for example, has regarded Strether as James's embodiment of the guiding principle of "permutation" in the novel. Phyllis van Slyck has speculated that the "emphasis on Strether's passivity and vulnerability has made it more difficult to observe the consistency and power of Strether's gaze and the philosophical consequences of his discoveries." And Kevin Kohan has questioned the popular assumption that Strether's experience in *The Ambassadors* is one of liberation, stating that James demonstrates that both the "epistemological perspectives" of Mrs. Newsome's Woollett and Madame de Vionnet's Paris are "essentially oppressive because both are oriented toward a kind of absolute, either positive or negative." Others have reexamined James's female characters and their role in the novel. Marianne DeKoven has argued that the story's modernist form and ideas are conflated in the figure of Madame de Vionnet, whom she called the "representational lynchpin" of the novel. And Richard A. Hocks has asserted that "it is time to acknowledge the extent to which Mrs. Newsome—insensitive, unimaginative, the antithesis of Jamesian fine consciousness and the routinely dismissed representative of everything that Strether must escape—is right." A number of recent critics have also focused on the role of commerce, capitalism, and consumption in *The Ambassadors,* especially in terms of the apparent dichotomy between Woollett and Paris. The amount and variety of interpretations of *The Ambassadors* attest to the novel's continuing interest for contemporary critics and scholars. Indeed, only *The Portrait of a Lady* (1881) and *The Turn of the Screw* (1898) from the James canon have generated more criticism. The importance of *The Ambassadors* in the history of English literature has perhaps been best summarized by Dorothea Krook: "If the English and American novel of the twentieth century is stuffed to the seams with 'psychological reasons,' the model and inspiration may well be *The Ambassadors,* and Henry James the first great novelist of the Age of Psychology."

PRINCIPAL WORKS

A Passionate Pilgrim, and Other Tales (short stories) 1875
Roderick Hudson (novel) 1876
The American (novel) 1877
The Europeans (novel) 1878
French Poets and Novelists (criticism) 1878
Watch and Ward (novel) 1878
Daisy Miller: A Study (novel) 1879

Hawthorne (criticism) 1879

The Madonna of the Future and Other Tales (short stories) 1879

Confidence (novel) 1880

The Portrait of a Lady (novel) 1881

Washington Square (novel) 1881

*Daisy Miller: A Comedy in Three Acts (play) 1883

The Siege of London. Madame de Mauves (novellas) 1883

The Art of Fiction (criticism) 1884

A Little Tour in France (travel essays) 1884

The Bostonians (novel) 1886

The Princess Casamassima (novel) 1886

The Aspern Papers. Louisa Pallant. The Modern Warning (novellas) 1888

Partial Portraits (criticism) 1888

A London Life (short stories) 1889

The Tragic Muse (novel) 1890

The American (play) 1891

The Real Thing, and Other Tales (short stories) 1893

Theatricals. Two Comedies: Tenants. Disengaged (plays) 1894

Theatricals, Second Series: The Album. The Reprobate (plays) 1894

Guy Domville (play) 1895

Embarrassments (short stories) 1896

The Other House (novel) 1896

The Spoils of Poynton (novel) 1897

What Maisie Knew (novel) 1897

The Two Magics: The Turn of the Screw; Covering End (novellas) 1898

The Awkward Age (novel) 1899

The Sacred Fount (novel) 1901

The Wings of the Dove (novel) 1902

The Ambassadors (novel) 1903

The Golden Bowl (novel) 1904

English Hours (travel essays) 1905

The American Scene (travel essays) 1907

The Novels and Tales of Henry James. 26 vols. (novels, novellas, and short stories) 1907-18

The High Bid (play) 1908

Views and Reviews (criticism) 1908

Italian Hours (travel essays) 1909

The Outcry (novel) 1911

A Small Boy and Others (autobiography) 1913

Notes of a Son and Brother (autobiography) 1914

Notes on Novelists, with Some Other Notes (criticism) 1914

The Ivory Tower (unfinished novel) 1917

The Middle Years (unfinished autobiography) 1917

The Sense of the Past (unfinished novel) 1917

Within the Rim and Other Essays, 1914-15 (essays) 1918

The Letters of Henry James. 2 vols. [edited by Percy Lubbock] (letters) 1920

Notes and Reviews (criticism) 1921

The Art of the Novel: Critical Prefaces (criticism) 1934

The Notebooks of Henry James [edited by F. O. Matthiessen] (notebooks) 1947

The Complete Plays of Henry James [edited by Leon Edel] (plays) 1949

The Complete Tales of Henry James. 12 vols. [edited by Edel] (novellas and short stories) 1962-64

*This play is an adaptation of the novel *Daisy Miller.*

CRITICISM

Jan van Rosevelt (essay date fall 1994)

SOURCE: Rosevelt, Jan van. "Dining with *The Ambassadors.*" *Henry James Review* 15, no. 3 (fall 1994): 301-08.

[*In the following essay, Rosevelt investigates the significance of food and consumption in* The Ambassadors. *Rosevelt asserts that James uses the prevalent controlling metaphor of food in his novel "to represent several levels of signification at once in his depiction of the formation of individual consciousness and identity."*]

Henry James's fiction is, as Robert L. Gale notes, rich in figures of speech, with an "imagistic density [of] four images per one thousand words" ([*The Caught Image: Figurative Language in the Fiction of Henry James*] 8). One of the few categories of imagery in James that Gale has not really addressed in his otherwise comprehensive work on figurative language in the fiction of James, *The Caught Image,* is that of eating or food. Neither is indexed by Gale, though he mentions in passing that one type of figure that a "more exhaustive examination . . . might turn up" could be that of food (197). An examination of *The Ambassadors* does not need to be very exhaustive to discover images of food or references to eating or drinking—by my (rough) count these occur over one hundred times in the novel.

But it is not just the frequency of these appearances that gives them significance. If one looks at food in *The Ambassadors* with the aid of established psychological, sociological and anthropological concepts, patterns of meaning emerge. Food is important by itself; it is a "perceptible phenomenon, unique in the number of senses affected and in the intensity of affect" (Jones ["Perspectives in the Study of Eating Behavior"] 262). Food is the means by which the individual reproduces herself, Mervyn Nicholson points out, as sex is the means of species-reproduction; thus the individual performs an "act of self creation daily" by eating (["Food and Power: Homer, Carroll, Atwood and Others"] 37).

Audrey Richards puts it bluntly: "Nutrition as a biological process" she says, "is more fundamental than sex . . . the individual man can exist without sexual gratification, but he must inevitably die without food" (qtd. in Goody [*Cooking, Cuisine and Class*] 15). It is impossible to separate eating and life for a "truly individual identity"; indeed, Judeo-Christian tradition identifies the origin of "self-consciousness and history" with "an act of eating: Adam and Eve's theft of forbidden fruit" (Nicholson 37). The act of eating is not only associated with knowledge, but also with the acquisition of knowledge, with shared insight, with the growth of individual consciousness.

With the eating of the forbidden fruit came not only knowledge, of course, but also mortality as well. If eating is identified with life and creation, it also clearly involves a process of destruction. The existence of the eater requires that there be an eaten, and these relational roles are not always stable.

The Ambassadors, which centers on the middle-aged Lambert Strether's trip to Paris in order to bring back his fellow American, the young Chad Newsome, is about life and knowledge, about the growth of consciousness. Strether becomes intrigued with the idea of the propagation of the individual's self-hood, fascinated by what he sees as the maturation of young Newsome. Oscar Cargill says that "the story of *The Ambassadors* is . . . of the growth of a man, belatedly, from innocence to maturity" ([*The Novels of Henry James*] 313). The Adam figure is Strether, rather than Chad, whose innocence has already been lost when the novel begins.

If the novel is about the absorption of life, it is appropriate that the work is replete with metaphoric or depicted acts of eating or tasting. Many of the references to dining or drinking are dead metaphors or parts of tropes, as is the mention of Maria Gostrey's "appetite for news," or Jim Pocock's "healthy appetite" for sightseeing. Certainly "some congruous fruit of absolution," "the cup of his impressions," or "he had settled his hash" do not refer to actual comestibles, but James's repeated recourse to such figures keeps that level of meaning alive (*AM* [*The Ambassadors*] 240, 211, 172, 59, 315).[1] Many other references to eating or drinking are made in passing and seem to have little import outside of serving purely as atmosphere, being something that the characters do in the course of the novel. Clearly, however, as Nicholson says, "in life, eating is a routine necessity, but in literature eating is always a symbolic act" (38).

Henry James was noted for his fondness of food and company. In reading Leon Edel's biography of James, one is struck by the aptness of Edel's description of him as "dining out strenuously" ([*Henry James: A Life*] 540). Edwin Sill Fussell says that "nostalgia is certainly

the word for *The Ambassadors,*" that it carries out the Jamesian "notion of revisiting, the motif of nostalgic return" ([*The French Side of Henry James*] 177, 179) that is to be found throughout James's work, and Daniel Mark Fogel sees the novel as one of James's "positive enactments of the Romantic dialectic of spiral return" ([*Henry James and the Structure of the Romantic Imagination*] 175). For James, France and especially Paris were associated with food. During his 1872 stay Edel tells us "the waiters in the restaurants were his chief society" (135). Towards the end of his lengthy 1875-76 sojourn, James writes his mother that there are no longer any professional or social reasons for his continuing on and, wistfully, that "it is rather ignoble to stay in Paris simply for the restaurants" (Edel 320). His memoirs of his earliest years, in *A Small Boy and Others,* are replete with remembered food, and he remarks at "the warm rich exhalations of subterranean cookery with which I find my recall of Paris from those years so disproportionately and so quite other than stomachically charged" (*SB* [*A Small Boy and Others*] 393). James's evocation of food in *The Ambassadors* may flow in part from his attempt at recalling the France of his earlier years. Like Proust, perhaps James found the trail to recollection through the powerful associations of the taste and smell of remembered food.

If Henry James's return to England in 1869 commenced with "as he put it, a 'banquet of initiation'" (Edel 94), much the same might be said of Lambert Strether's fictive arrival in Europe. In the famous opening sequence of the novel, the certainty of Strether's dining with his friend Waymarsh is described as "the fruit of a sharp sense," and his "consciousness of personal freedom" at being in Europe is "a deep taste of change" (*AM* 17). His initial landing at Liverpool is a "qualified draught of Europe," but "a potion at least undiluted" by the presence of his fellow American, Waymarsh (*AM* 18).

When Maria Gostrey strikes up an acquaintance with Strether at the hotel in Chester, there are several moments of awkwardness. When Miss Gostrey introduces the possibility of mutual friends, which would impart a gloss of propriety on their speaking without formal introduction, Strether is unable to make anything of this gambit, and "they were left together as over the mere laid table of conversation. Her qualification of the mentioned connexion had rather removed than placed a dish, and there seemed nothing else to serve" (*AM* 19).

Conversation is a ritual, like dining; later, Waymarsh's suggestion that Strether "be kind" to Sarah Pocock by cooperating in convincing her brother Chad to return to America becomes a "present," the suggestion being offered "as on a little silver breakfast tray" (*AM* 270). Words become something to be consumed, knowledge is taken in, and as Strether remarks "one does fill out some with all one takes in, and I've taken in, I dare say, more than I've natural room for" (*AM* 31). Here Strether seems to be referring to food, but this passage is echoed later by Chad when he says "of course Mother's making things out with you about me has been natural. . . . Still, you must have filled out." This and Strether's reply that "it was 'filling out' enough to miss you as we did" seem to alter the meaning, to fill it with significance, to repeat the metaphor of information as food (*AM* 99).[2] Eating is in itself a form of communication, a way of establishing a relationship among people. In *Totem and Taboo,* Freud claims that from the earliest times "eating and drinking with a man was a symbol and a confirmation of fellowship and mutual social obligations," that it provided a "binding force" (*Works* [*The Standard Edition of the Complete Psychological Works of Sigmund Freud*] XIII, 134). More recently, anthropologists have theorized that the very origin of human society is linked to the development of food-sharing behavior among early protohumans. Glynn Isaac says that food-sharing behavior among humanity's earliest ancestors had evolutionary consequences. Food is linked to communication, and "language serves in modern human societies not only for the exchange of information but also as an instrument for social adjustment and even for the exchange of misinformation. . . . Food-sharing and the kinds of behavior associated with it probably played an important role in the development of reciprocal social obligations" (Isaac ["The food sharing behavior of proto-human hominids"] 106).

Throughout the novel, moments of shared eating are occasions for the exchange of information or misinformation. The Latin roots of the word "companion," of course, signify its derivation from the idea of sharing bread. The "crunch of the thick crusted bread" (*AM* 71) delights Strether as he tells his friend Waymarsh about meeting Little Bilham at Chad's. When Strether and Chad later meet over coffee, Chad is "buttering his roll" and Strether "munched toast" as Chad proposes that Strether visit Madame de Vionnet (*AM* 142). Near the conclusion of the novel, as Strether pays his last visit to Madame de Vionnet, he looks about him carefully, gathering the details of his impressions to him. He reflects that "No, he might never see them again—this was only too probably the last time; and he should certainly see nothing in the least like them. He should soon be going to where such things were not, and it would be a small mercy for memory, for fancy, to have, in that stress, a loaf on the shelf" (*AM* 317).

Memories become food, a source of nourishment, here bread, the biblical staff of life. Earlier, at Gloriani's garden party, bread is seen as less essential. There, Strether had reflected disparagingly on Chad's "profusely dispensing *panem et circenses*" (*AM* 118). This phrase ironically prefigures Waymarsh and Mrs. Pocock's later activities in Paris, which seem to Strether to consist of Waymarsh "putting before [Mrs. Pocock] a hundred francs' worth of food and drink, which they'll scarcely touch . . . and the circus afterwards" (*AM* 243).

Significantly, though dining "nose to nose," Waymarsh and Sarah Pocock are said to "scarcely touch" their food (*AM* 242). Their relationship is apparently nonsexual. C. G. Jung proposes a close connection between the "hunger libido" and the "sexual libido" in humans, as evidenced by "numerous and innate correlations between the functions of nutrition and sexuality" ([*Psychology of the Unconscious.*] 161). Dining is an obvious metaphor for sexual relations throughout the book, as in the heightened scene when Strether and Maria Gostrey first dine "at his hotel face to face over a small table on which the lighted candles had rose-coloured shades; and the rose-coloured shades and the small table and the soft fragrance of the lady—had anything to his mere sense been so soft—were so many touches" (*AM* 42).

When Strether later lunches with Marie de Vionnet, he has in effect taken up Chad's side against Mrs. Newsome. Although he still refuses to admit to himself the nature of Chad and Marie's involvement, he is working to advance their affair, and Strether helps "her to the dish that had been freshly put before them" as he helps her to satisfy her appetite for Chad. On another level, it is knowledge that is referred to. Strether tells Mme. de Vionnet, as he serves her, that he has written Chad's mother, and "I've told her all about you," which evokes the immediate response of "Thanks—not so much. 'All about' me" (*AM* 179). What is at question here is how much Strether knows to tell. There is the playing out of the game of competing ideas of what is going on, the controlling of information and rationing of communication. Oscar Cargill calls this scene, with its descriptive passage of "their intensely white table-linen, their *omelette aux tomates,* their bottle of straw coloured Chablis," an example of "impressionistic picturing" (*AM* 176). He endorses the view that this is "pure enrichment . . . calculated to demonstrate Strether's capacity to taste and enjoy" (Cargill 327). But the workings of the scene are more complex than this, depicting what Strether calls "the smash in which a regular runaway properly ends," the occasion where "his surrender [was] made good" (*AM* 177). In one of the many descriptive linkages of the novel, Madame de Vionnet is described as "a woman who, between courses, could be graceful with her elbows on the table. It was a posture unknown to Mrs. Newsome" (*AM* 178). Unknown to Mrs. Newsome, perhaps, but Chad Newsome is earlier described with his elbows on the table. Chad has left behind the manners of Massachusetts and is linked with those of Paris.

The vivid impressions of the dejeuner scene with Mme. de Vionnet are contrasted by the meal Strether has in the "small slippery *salle-à-manger*" at his hotel after he has learned from Waymarsh that Mrs. Pocock is about to relay her mother's ultimatum, and "he perceived the whole thing to be really at last upon him" (*AM* 267). Here Strether has a "brief consumption of coffee and a roll," in the room "so associated with rich rumination," with "various lonely and absentminded meals" (*AM* 267). Here Strether has chewed upon the limited information given him, or that he has allowed himself to see, puzzling over the maneuvers of the Woollett contingent, which he has cut himself off from, and as yet an alien to the expatriate community. His life is likened to a cappucino, "the whole enigma, whipping up in its fine full-flavoured forth the very principle, for good or for ill, of his own, of Strether's destiny" (*AM* 267).

Near the conclusion of the novel, Strether goes to confront Chad, and to urge his continuation in the liaison with Mme. de Vionnet. He imagines, as he pauses for breath on the stairs, feeling the weight of his years, that Chad has had "a supper of light cold clever French things, which one could see the remains of there in the circle of the lamp" (*AM* 333). Chad denies that he has any notion of leaving Marie, saying that "I'm not a bit tired of her." It seems to Strether that Chad is speaking "of being 'tired' of her almost as he might have spoken of being tired of roast mutton for dinner" (*AM* 337). Chad, we might suspect, has had his fill of "clever French things." James's use of "mutton" is also interesting, given that word's long use in British slang to refer to "food for lust; loose women, prostitutes" (*OED* [*Oxford English Dictionary*]), particularly in the phrase "mutton dressed as lamb," meaning a middle-aged or older woman dressed as though she were young, as Mme. de Vionnet is described as appearing.

If Madame de Vionnet is by implication presented in terms of food, as something to be consumed, this is not the only time in the novel that individuals are so viewed. Strether speaks jokingly of the possibility of Waymarsh "serving me up," or analyzing him (*AM* 40). In comparison to the budding Jeanne de Vionnet, he thinks of himself as "the most withered of the winter apples" (*AM* 248). Chad asks him, "Don't you count it as anything that you're dished—if you are dished? Are you, my dear man, dished?" (*AM* 285). Later Chad asks, "Haven't I been drinking you in?" (*AM* 340). The new Chad is described in terms of food: "that he was smooth was as marked as the taste of a sauce" (*AM* 97). When Waymarsh remarks that Little Bilham cannot be a good American, Miss Gostrey asks, "What is it . . . to be one?" and continues, "It's such an order, really, that before we cook you the dish we must at least have your receipt" (*AM* 87). Little Bilham himself, in response to Miss Barrace's mock-accusation that he had "come over [to Europe] to convert the savages" and had let them convert him instead, replies "they haven't gone through

that form. They've simply—the cannibals!—eaten me; converted me if you like, but converted me into food. I'm but the bleached bones of a Christian" (*AM* 125).

Strether is described as Chad's "mother's missionary" (*AM* 135), and in all the old jokes, it is clear how missionaries usually fare with cannibals. Strether's first name obviously alludes to the eponymous hero of Honoré de Balzac's novel *Louis Lambert* (1842), but it also suggests "Lamb-ert": innocence, sacrifice—food. James shows Strether thinking to himself at one point, perhaps punningly, that "it was clearly better to suffer as a sheep than as a lamb. One might as well perish by the sword as by famine" (*AM* 177), this last an echo of the earlier Old Testament reflection "He might perish by the sword as by famine" (*AM* 78). Jack Goody describes the sacrifice as "the offering that feeds both the living and the dead (as well as the divine)" (11). Strether is caught between the demands of the American past and his European present, with the unseen but much felt presence of Mrs. Newsome corresponding, possibly, to the Old Testament deity. More to the point, for the American innocent abroad, in James, there is a real danger of being consumed by the older European culture, swallowed Saturn-like, perhaps. Strether protests to Mrs. Pocock that "Chad's been affected so beautifully. The proof of the pudding's in the eating" (*AM* 279). In Paris, all of life is somehow to be consumed; while walking in the garden of the Tuileries, it seems to Strether that "the air had a taste as of something mixed with art, something that presented nature as a white-capped master-chef" (*AM* 59).

But this danger of devourment comes not only from the Old World. If, in the garden party in Book Fifth, Gloriani is described as part of the "covertly tigerish" "great world," there is also something fierce about Woollett, which menaces its strayed Lambert Strether (*AM* 133). Jim Pocock says of his wife and his mother-in-law that "they don't lash about and shake the cage . . . and it's at feeding time that they're quietest. But they always get there." Strether echoes "they always get there!" with a nervous laugh, because, as James tells us, "It was as if a queer truth in his companion's metaphor had rolled over him with a rush. She *had* been quiet at feeding time; she had fed, and Sarah had fed with her, out of the big bowl of all his recent free communication, his vividness and pleasantness, his ingenuity and even his eloquence" (*AM* 216).

Perhaps there is a reflection here of James's own feelings, as he sent his writing off to be serialized in New York. Words are something to be consumed, to be eaten or tasted, as the "lemon-coloured volumes" of French fiction, "as fresh as fruit on the tree" that appear throughout the novel are a "kind of low-priced consommation" (*AM* 63, 67). Literature is seen as a form of discourse where the production of the author is to be consumed and digested by the reader.[3] Strether looks at the Paris bookstall and finds it "delicate and appetising," with an "impression" like "one of the pleasant cafes" nearby (*AM* 67). In this passage, as John Rignall notes, "the metaphorical substitution of cafe for bookstall blurs the distinction between intellectual and physical appetites" and "conveys the sensuous appeal of the book as commodity" ([*Realist Fiction and the Strolling Spectator*] 117).

In the end, of course, words, like Chad's attempt to charm his sister, have "buttered no parsnips" (*AM* 255). When Strether chances upon Chad and Marie de Vionnet at their assignation by the river, and must admit to the carnal nature of their liaison, the three awkwardly share a meal of a *côtelette de veau à l'oseille* (*AM* 305). Strether reflects that "there had been simply a *lie* in the charming affair. . . . It was with the lie that they had eaten and drunk and talked and laughed" (*AM* 311). It is not only his naiveté that bothers him, but also "his sense of what, over and above the central fact itself, he had to swallow"; that is, "It was the quantity of the make-believe involved and so vividly exemplified that most disagreed with his spiritual stomach" (*AM* 313). This passage echoes another in an early short story by James, **"Poor Richard,"** when Richard Laudle realizes his gaucheness and "gulped down the sickening fact of his comparative, nay, absolute ignorance of the great world represented by his rivals" (**"PR"** [**"Poor Richard"**] 209).

James himself, in his Preface to *The Ambassadors,* indicates that "the essence of *The Ambassadors*" is contained in Lambert Strether's speech to Little Bilham in Book Fifth, with its concluding imperative, "Live!" (*AM* 1, 132). The central fact of life, as Freud took it from Schiller, is that "hunger and love are what moves the world." In Freud's *Civilization and Its Discontents,* hunger represents "the instincts which aim at preserving the individual" while the "chief function" of love is "the preservation of the species" (*Works* XXI, 117). For James, these concepts remain central, though perhaps more complex; there are many levels of hunger and consumption in *The Ambassadors,* as there are many kinds of love and knowledge. With his usual economy, or foreshortening, James has used the motif of food and eating to represent several levels of signification at once in his depiction of the formation of individual consciousness and identity.

There are several other linking and controlling metaphors and images in the novel: water, painting, and the theater are some of the more obvious. I would argue that one of the most pervasive and versatile is that of food and its consumption. Ultimately, as Fussell points out in his reading of *The Ambassadors,* "one of our last visions of Paris, and one of our best, is of the remnants of Chad's late supper . . . of 'light cold clever French

things' . . . and we notice that the food, just before or just after our closing the back cover of the book, has already begun to turn into something else . . . soon it will be no more, that represented food, and that represented Strether" (214).

Notes

1. Metaphors of food and drinking appear throughout James' work, as does food imagery. There is the "delicious companionship of thought" (*SY* 62), the drunken and loquacious picnic in "A Landscape-Painter," where the trio "talked with our mouths full" (*LP* 129), the "fruit of his imagination" (*AB* 326) in "The Author of Beltraffio," and "the sweet taste of Albany" (*SB* 7), among many others. Often, like the central image of *The Golden Bowl,* a "drinking-vessel larger than a common cup" (*GB* 116), the food/drinking aspect becomes subsumed in other metaphoric levels of meaning.

2. James uses this metaphor in other works. The early story "A Passionate Pilgrim" (particularly rich in food imagery) has the narrator overhearing fellow Americans in an English coffee-room and "a large portion of their conversation made its way over the top of our dividing partition and mingled its savor with that of my simple repast" (*PP* 230).

3. James strikingly recurs to this metaphor in a letter to Edmund Gosse of 26 October 1911, when he writes of having the latter's book on Denmark, "Which I *taste* very much. But I am still tasting it—in a large spoonful a day, & have but waited to write you till I licked the ladle, if not the platter, clean" (*SL* 258). Similarly, in *A Small Boy and Others,* James writes of his early fascination with Edgar Allan Poe that "he lay upon our tables and resounded in our mouths, while we commenced to satiety, even for our boyish appetites, over the thrill of his choicest pages" (*SB* 64).

Key to Works by Henry James

AM: *The Ambassadors.* Ed. S. P. Rosenbaum. New York: Norton, 1964.

PR: "Poor Richard." *The Complete Tales of Henry James.* Ed. Leon Edel. Vol. 1. Philadelphia and New York: Lippincott, 1962.

SB: *A Small Boy and Others.* London: Macmillan, 1913.

Other Works Cited

Cargill, Oscar. *The Novels of Henry James.* New York: Macmillan, 1961.

Edel, Leon. *Henry James: A Life.* New York: Harper, 1985.

Freud, Sigmund. *The Standard Edition of the Complete Psychological Works of Sigmund Freud.* 24 vols. Trans. and ed. James Strachey. London: Hogarth, 1973.

Fogel, Daniel Mark. *Henry James and the Structure of the Romantic Imagination.* Baton Rouge: Louisiana State U P, 1981.

Fussell, Edwin Paul. *The French Side of Henry James.* New York: Columbia U P, 1990.

Gale, Robert L. *The Caught Image: Figurative Language in the Fiction of Henry James.* Chapel Hill: U of North Carolina P, 1964.

Goody, Jack. *Cooking, Cuisine and Class.* Cambridge: Cambridge U P, 1982.

Isaac, Glynn. "The food sharing behavior of proto-human hominids." *Scientific-American* 238 (April 1978): 90-108.

Jones, Michael Owen. "Perspectives in the Study of Eating Behavior." *Folklore Studies in the Twentieth Century.* Ed. Venetia J. Newall. Woodbridge, UK: D. S. Brewer, 1980. 260-65.

Jung, C. G. *Psychology of the Unconscious.* Trans. Beatrice M. Hinkle. New York: Moffat, 1916.

Nicholson, Mervyn. "Food and Power: Homer, Carroll, Atwood and Others." *Mosaic* 20 (1987): 37-55.

Oxford English Dictionary. 2nd ed. 1989.

Rignall, John. *Realist Fiction and the Strolling Spectator.* London and New York: Routledge, 1992.

Claire Oberon Garcia (essay date spring 1995)

SOURCE: Garcia, Claire Oberon. "The Shopper and the Shopper's Friend: Lambert Strether and Maria Gostrey's Consumer Consciousness." *Henry James Review* 16, no. 2 (spring 1995): 153-71.

[*In the following essay, Garcia disagrees with the standard reading of* The Ambassadors *as a novel that depicts a conflict of oppositions—such as that between civilized Europe and commercialized America, between "aesthetic" and "economic" cultures—arguing instead that "the commercial and aesthetic ways of determining value" in* The Ambassadors *are "interrelated, shaped by the power and effects of consumer culture, the result of late nineteenth-century Western capitalism."*]

Toward the close of the nineteenth century, Matthew Arnold described culture as emphasizing "becoming something, rather than having something" ([*Selected Prose*] 208). Henry James's *The Ambassadors* has usually been read as a description of the conflict between the values of what James called "the world of grab" and the world of culture. When I began my study of James's 1903 novel, I set out to explore the relationship between the language of money and the language of art. I was struck, however, by James's pervasive use of economic imagery in a novel that purportedly describes "a process of vision" (*AM* [*The Ambassadors*] xxx). Although the novel has traditionally been read as one of James's "international novels," which describe the confrontation between European and American mores and values, my examination of James's use of commercial metaphors and financial imagery reveals there is no tidy dichotomy between the money-grubbing values of industrial Woollett and the civilized, ideal values of European culture. Unlike *The Golden Bowl,* in which economic imagery is associated with Verver and the Prince, and Maggie's language and imagery is stubbornly subversive of commercial rhetoric, *The Ambassadors* is characterized by economic language and imagery on all levels of the narrative. Despite the often disconcerting preponderance of money imagery in the text, it has received little critical attention to date, perhaps because *The Ambassadors,* as one of James's most subtle and superbly wrought novels, is so congenial to formalist criticism. But I believe this novel is more historically engaged than it appears. James wrote *The Ambassadors* when Western economies and culture were undergoing a period of transition. At the turn of the century, the American and European economies were being transformed from production to consumption economies. The American Gilded Age, with its economic boom and national fascination with great and sudden wealth, was waning. Advances in communication and distribution channels were creating a new mass market, and advertising was developing into a profession with affinities to the arts and sciences. Through its pervasive economic imagery, *The Ambassadors* provides an arena for the voices of competing value systems and exemplifies the effects of a nascent commodity culture on the human imagination and on human relationships. *The Ambassadors* goes beyond contrasting the values of a materialistic, capitalist culture with those of an older, more civilized society. Rather than claiming that a particular value system is superior to its "opposite" (European rather than American, aesthetic rather than economic, imaginative rather than social, etc.), the novel demonstrates that the economic, political, and historical forces that shape human consciousness operate in all aspects of human life and that, at the turn of the century, American evaluative judgments are all shaped by the influence of an emerging commodity culture. In the aftermath of the economic boom of the Gilded Age, the language of money provides a way of talking about fundamental issues of value: "For just as money is a universal equivalent into which all other commodities must be translated to establish their value, so also James uses economic language as the dominant code to fix the value of characters and ideas in his writing"

(McCormack [*The Rule of Money*] 1). The depiction of the relationship between Maria Gostrey and Lambert Strether, especially in the opening book, establishes the dominance of economic value as a trope for the rest of the novel.

I do not want to suggest that economic value structures are more fundamental than any other, but I do believe that at the time *The Ambassadors* was written the question of the value of money had a particular power over the American imagination. In William Dean Howells's novel *The Rise of Silas Lapham* (1885), which was written during the height of the Gilded Age, a character observes, "there's no doubt but that money is to the fore now. It is the romance, the poetry, of our age. It's the thing that chiefly strikes the imagination" (60). At the turn of the century, the idea of wealth, the dynamics of capitalism, and the values of the emerging consumer culture all played a role in structuring individual consciousnesses and imaginations. Thus, codes of meaning related to business dominated both the American consciousness and the rhetoric of the age. Again, this is not to assert that economic value systems are more fundamental than the other value systems operating in James's late work (in other words, that his novels can be "explained" in terms of economics), but rather that the business dynamics are, in a sense, prior.

T. J. Jackson Lears sees the hunger to experience "real life" as symptomatic of the educated bourgeoisie's response to new pressures at the turn of the century. Disoriented by the loss of the religious and social structures that gave meaning to human life, the American bourgeoisie was plagued by a feeling that Lears characterizes as "weightlessness": "Indeed, a feeling that one can call weightlessness reinforced the spreading sense of unreality among the educated bourgeoisie. As liberal Protestantism became assimilated into the secular creed of progress, as Satan became an Evil Principle and hell a metaphor, the preferred personal style shifted from shrill earnestness to formulized benevolence. Religious beliefs have historically played a key role in defining an individual's sense of reality. Without distinct frameworks of meaning, reality itself becomes problematic; the individual slides into normlessness, or anomie" (["From Salvation to Self-Realization"] 9). As an antidote to this feeling of "weightlessness," the educated middle-class American developed an intense desire for "real life." According to Lears, "this quest for 'real life' was the characteristic psychic project of the age" (10). The protagonists of James's three completed late novels exemplify this desire, which Lears sees as one of the hallmarks of the rising consumer culture: "This reverence for 'life' as a value in itself was a new development in American cultural history. Never before had so many people felt that reality was throbbing with vitality, pulsating with unspeakable excitement, and always just out of reach. And, most important . . . the feeling

of unreality helps to generate longings for bodily vigor, emotional intensity, and a revitalized sense of selfhood" (10). This "revitalized sense of selfhood" is exactly what Lambert Strether is seeking when he steps off the boat at the beginning of *The Ambassadors.* Through trying to recapture a sense of the "life" that he believes he has missed, Strether discovers a "way of seeing" that becomes, by the end of the novel, his identity and his ethos.[1] Strether is often read as a man who is both oppositional to and outside of "the world of grab." But Strether's vision is profoundly influenced, if not created by, the values of "the world of grab," or what more recent thinkers have dubbed "consumer culture."

It is deceptively comfortable to accept the apparently bifurcated terms of *The Ambassadors.* If one does, one reads it as a story about two competing systems of value: in Arnoldian terms, Philistinism versus civilization. On one side is Woollett: the vulgar Pococks, the narrow-minded Mrs. Newsome, and the common object that has generated millions for succeeding generations of Newsomes and will generate millions more if the object can be advertised effectively enough. On the other side is Europe: the glittering and elusive city of Paris, the "wonderful" and equally elusive Madame de Vionnet, and the qualities of Strether's developing consciousness. But the fact that economic concerns and imagery invade and color the aesthetic issues raised in the text subverts the idea of two independent value systems or discourses.

Barbara Herrnstein Smith describes what she calls the "double discourse of value" in contemporary Western thought:

> On the one hand there is the discourse of economic theory: money, commerce, technology, industry, production and consumption, workers and consumers; on the other hand, there is the discourse of aesthetic axiology: culture, art, genius, creation and appreciation, artists and connoisseurs. In the first discourse, events are explained in terms of calculations, preferences, costs, benefits, profits, prices, and utility. In the second, events are explained—or rather (and this distinction/opposition is as crucial as any of the others), "justified"—in terms of inspiration, discrimination, taste (good taste, bad taste, no taste), the test of time, intrinsic value, and transcendent value. The decisive moves in the generation and maintenance of this double discourse of value are commonly made under the quasi-logical cover of *We must distinguish between*: for example, we must distinguish between mere price and intrinsic value, between mere consumers and discriminating critics, between true artistic creativity and mere technological skill, and so forth. The question posed here and throughout this study is, *must* we and, indeed, can we?
>
> ([*Contingencies of Value*] 127)

Fundamental to my reading of *The Ambassadors* is the dismantling of the binary oppositions that critics have seen operating in the novel and that have prevented them from seeing the work as a response to very specific economic and cultural pressures of the Western world at the turn of the century. Critics have insisted on "distinguishing between" the economic and aesthetic discourses in *The Ambassadors,* but a close examination of the text will make it difficult to "distinguish between" the two. Rather than being antithetical, the commercial and the aesthetic ways of determining value at the turn of the century are interrelated, shaped by the power and effects of consumer culture, the result of late nineteenth-century Western capitalism. This is not to reduce all aspects of human life and feeling to economics, but to suggest that the processes of consciousness, knowledge, and evaluation are conditioned by historical and cultural forces that function in all realms of human discourse. There is no stance "outside" culture from which to critique it. The interesting question is how the issues are articulated, the tensions mediated, and an ethical vision forged in the complex and provocative text of *The Ambassadors.*

Despite the apparent tensions in the text between financial success and moral integrity, "the world of grab" and civilization, economics and aesthetics, the real problem confronting Strether is not which of the elements in each of these oppositions is superior (for he finally turns away from them all), but the difficulties of establishing an idea of "good," a ground for ethical behavior, in a culture that perceives even people and relationships as commodities that can be bargained for, bought, and sold. It is significant that Chad Newsome, whom Strether is commissioned to rescue from the immorality of Paris and to encourage to return in order to see the family business through a period of immense profit, rejects his European life and exchanges it not only for the prospect of even greater wealth than his family already possesses, but also for the brave new frontier of advertising, the dynamo of consumer culture.

The commercial and the aesthetic ways of determining value at the turn of the century are not independent of each other. The economic, political, and historical forces that shape human attitudes are at work in all realms of human activity. Evaluative judgments, whether within the realm of finance, interpersonal relationships, or aesthetics are all influenced by cultural factors formerly assumed to be "outside" the particular discourse. The economic dynamics of late-nineteenth-century American capitalism influence the major characters in *The Ambassadors* and their ideas about what gives human life value—what, in moral terms, constitutes "a good life." Despite James's apparent belief in the incompatibility of financial success and moral integrity, of "the world of grab" and authentic civilization, and of economics and aesthetics, in this novel value is construed not in opposition to but in accordance with the dynamics of industrial capitalism and the values of consumer culture.

In the opening chapters of the book, the narrator uses a startling amount of commercial language. The result is to establish money and its social effects as a powerful context and subtext for the development of Strether's vision. Strether's moral education—which, for James, is the same thing as an aesthetic one—takes place not in opposition to the power of money, but in ambivalent conversation with it. If one looks at *The Ambassadors* as a cultural document that expresses, on various levels, the values and tensions of the world in which it was produced, one can see it not so much as an unequivocal affirmation of a single value system, but as an arena where several value systems struggle with each other.

BUSINESS AND GOODNESS

Lambert Strether's mission to Europe on his fiancée's behalf is a business trip. Although Mrs. Newsome has two compelling reasons to desire her son Chadwick's return to the United States—to get him into the family business and to get him married—it is the business interest that predominates. Strether's mission has the air of an attempt at moral salvation—Woollett (i.e. Mrs. Newsome, whose rigorous vision is the epitome of Woollett's values) imagines the woman involved with Chad as very "bad"—but the concern seems to be more about the effect of this liaison on the family business than on the state of Chad's soul. Chad's paramour is not "bad" because she threatens Chad's sexual purity, for even Woollett has "accommodate[d] itself to the spirit of the age and the increasing mildness of manners" and accepts the fact that young men, especially if they go to Paris, are going to acquire sexual experience (*AM* 51). The unknown woman is most threatening as a force that prevents Chad from fulfilling his function as a man in capitalist society: obeying his father's will and increasing the prosperity of the business.

From the opening paragraph, the narrator and Strether constantly refer to Strether's mission as "the business."[2] It is not surprising that Strether's dominant metaphor for his rescue mission should be business-related. According to James, a preoccupation with commerce is a fundamental characteristic of the culture and consciousness of New England.[3] In his **"Project of Novel,"** a prospectus for *The Ambassadors* that James submitted to Harper and Brothers in 1900, he describes Strether as "an American, of the present hour and sufficiently typical New England origin" who "has always been occupied, and preoccupied, in one way and another, but has always, in all relations and connections, been ridden by his 'New England conscience,'" which James sees as structured by the dynamics and effects of commercial relations (*CN* [*The Complete Notebooks of Henry James*] 543, 544).

As he disembarks from the steamer, Strether reflects that his "business" would be "a trifle bungled" if his friend Waymarsh's face was the first thing he encountered in Europe, before the "note" of the experience could be established (*AM* 1). Here "business" refers to Strether's attempts to be receptive to the "note" of Europe. Like a detective, Strether wants to reconstruct the chain of events that led up to "the crime"—Chad's defection from Woollett. The use of the word "business" in the opening scene of the novel is particularly interesting because it describes what is essentially a process of consciousness with a commercial term. Strether repeatedly states, to himself and to others, that in order to fulfill his mission he must "see things for what they are," a phrase that Matthew Arnold used to describe scientific passion (205).

Strether's stance as a scientific, pragmatic detective begins to slip even as he justifies his decision to delay contacting his friend Waymarsh in order to allow himself a few hours of what he conceives to be a "freedom" to experience the first "draughts" of Europeanness. Waymarsh, the "voice of Milrose"—a town that represents even more than Woollett does the traditional American values—would compromise the objectivity of Strether's initial impressions (*AM* 19). Yet the metaphor the narrator chooses to describe Strether's feeling of freedom is an appropriately "Woollettian" one: "he was like a man, who, unexpectedly finding in his pocket more money than usual, handles it a while and idly and pleasantly chinks it before addressing himself to the business of spending" (*AM* 2). James uses a similar metaphor later in the novel when Strether wanders the streets of Paris, savoring the city's "sharp spell": "Strether hadn't for years so rich a consciousness of time—a bag of gold into which he constantly dipped for a handful" (*AM* 78).

Even after Strether has surrendered to Europe to the extent that he can promise Madame de Vionnet that he will "save her," his structures of expression and perception are still rooted in economically conscious rhetoric (*AM* 180). Newly open to different ways of evaluating people, relationships, and experience, he still can reflect that "it was only for the moment, but good moments—if he could call them good—still had their value for a man who by this time struck himself as living almost disgracefully from hand to mouth" (*AM* 205). His letters to Woollett have grown less frequent as the situation grows more "complicated," but he refers to his task as "the other great commerce [which] he had to carry on" (*AM* 205-206). The symbolic gesture of his surrender to Paris is, typically, a purchase: Victor Hugo's vision of the past in "convenient terms." Strether's grand gesture towards "living all one can" consists in his ownership of the books that, "giving the rein for once in a way to the joy of life, he had purchased in seventy bound volumes, a miracle of cheapness, parted with, he was assured by the shopman, at the price of the red-and-gold alone" (*AM* 208). Sitting in the nave of Notre Dame, basking in the atmosphere of historic reverence

and the triumph of his bargain, he finds that "what his thought had finally bumped against was the question of where, among packed accumulations, so multiform a wedge would be able to enter. Were seventy volumes in red-and-gold to be perhaps what he could most substantially have to show at Woollett as the fruit of his mission?" (*AM* 208). Again, we have the Woollettian preoccupation with investment and yield: that one must have something to "show for" one's efforts. Even though the Hugo volumes represent to Strether a world of values distinct from those of Woollett, this incident underscores the ambiguous status of values that ostensibly lie outside the realm of economic value. The volumes are at once a dramatic symbol of Strether's psychic surrender to Paris and "only" books: as objects, they are insufficient emblems of his transformation and commodities that can be bought or sold, cheap or dear. Jennifer Wicke describes Strether's feelings toward these books and the "lemon-colored" volumes (*AM* 107) that he remembers from his youth as an attempt to "decommodify" books; his "reverence for these authorless, titleless books bespeaks his nostalgia for books he can imagine are produced in another way, decommodified, as it were. . . . Books outside the market system are his little totems of reassurance" (Wicke [*Advertising Fictions*] 107-108). Yet he can only attempt to appropriate this world by the gesture of purchasing them, and getting them cheaply at that.

An American Agent

Lambert Strether finds a natural ally in the character James called the "*ficelle*" of the novel, Maria Gostrey. An American with Milrose and Woollett connections who lives in Europe, she serves as a transitional figure between America and Europe. That James himself characterizes Maria Gostrey as a "light *ficelle*" and not a "true agent" in the novel (*PL* [*The Portrait of a Lady*] 53) should not lead the reader to underestimate her importance not only as a confidante to Strether, the "true agent" of the novel, but also as a powerful figure of significance in her own right. As Ruth Bernard Yeazell points out, "Miss Gostrey may help both Strether and the reader to see the truth, but that truth is inseparable from her personal manipulation of it" ([*Language and Knowledge in the Late Novels of Henry James*] 71). The thread that Gostrey uses to guide both the reader and Strether to "the truths" of the novel, the light that she is able to shed on apparently dark and inscrutable objects of interpretation, comes from her ability to observe and to traffic in competing value systems. As a *ficelle,* the character of Maria Gostrey provides a field for the interaction of these value systems. When he learns that someone has lent Gostrey an expensive box at the Théâtre Français, "The sense of how she was always paying for something in advance was equalled on Strether's part only by the sense of how she was always being paid; all of which made for his consciousness, in the larger air, of a lively, bustling traffic, the exchange of such values as were not for him to handle" (*AM* 90).

It is Maria Gostrey who bluntly presents the troubling questions of value in the story. From the beginning of the novel, much of the conversation between Gostrey and Strether centers around money and its effects; the language of these themes permeates the opening books of the text even when the topic of discussion is not explicitly financial.

Gostrey introduces herself to Strether as a "general guide to Europe," a "companion at large" who can steer the naive American tourist through the labyrinth of the Old World. She declares that "there is nothing [she doesn't] know": "I know all the shops and the prices—but I know worse things still" (*AM* 12). In the prospectus for **The Ambassadors,** James had emphasized her role as a professional shopper: "She calls herself the universal American agent . . . She sees people through. She shops with them in Paris. She shops with them in London, where she has a tailor of her 'very own.'" She takes to Strether because she realizes at once that he is "better than the most bloated and benighted of the California billionairesses she has ever seen through the great round of Paris purchases" (*CN* 546). This characterization of her knowledge and skills as primarily consumerist reveals the interests of her "clients," who may purport to come to Europe in order to see museums, to imbibe the air of old civilizations, and to educate themselves, but who end up attempting to acquire culture and history through purchasing it. James's description also reveals the place of consumer information on Gostrey's scale of values: to possess an intimate and unerring knowledge of shops and prices is somehow awful, yet it defines her identity.

Gostrey makes it clear, however, that her clients cannot *purchase* her services; her services themselves are not a commodity. She is not a professional companion such as existed at that time for the sole purpose of introducing nouveaux riches Americans to European society. When Strether asks her how she is "rewarded" for her services (juxtaposing the idea of "love" to money, alluding to the colloquial phrase—always negative—that one would not do something "for love or for money"—in other words, without being paid), Gostrey replies that she is not rewarded. She is free from the necessity of being paid for her work because she is an unmarried woman with a small but independent income. James describes her as "inordinately modern, the fruit of actual, international conditions" both social and economic (*CN* 546). What else could a modern American woman with a sufficient discretionary income *do* at that time but shop? Shopping is paradigmatic female behavior in a consumer culture:

> As the proportion and volume of goods sold in stores rather than produced in the home increased, it was women, rather than men, who tended to have the job of purchasing them. . . . middle- and upper-class ladies were occupied with the beautification of both their homes and their own persons. The superfluous, frivolous associations of some of the new commodities, and the establishment of convenient stores that were both enticing and respectable, made shopping itself a new feminine leisure activity.
>
> (Bowlby [*Just Looking*] 19)

In James's prospectus for the novel, he states that most of Gostrey's madly shopping clients are female: "She comes over with girls. She goes back with girls. She meets girls at Liverpool, at Genoa, at Bremen" (*CN* 546).

There are many similarities between Maria Gostrey's and Lambert Strether's situations in the economic system in which they move. They are both feminized by consumer culture: Strether is a failure in a society in which a man's identity is defined by his ability to make money, and capitalist society has feminized Maria Gostrey by offering her an identity as a spender. She is both bargain shopper and shopper's friend. Both Strether and Gostrey describe themselves as "outside" the business of making money, but each in his or her own way epitomizes the vision and values of consumer culture. The allegiance between Maria Gostrey and Lambert Strether is not based solely on the subtle affinities between their rather ambiguous social and economic positions. Strether recognizes that Gostrey, like himself, is "out of it," and Gostrey declares that "our realities are what has brought us together. We're beaten brothers in arms" (*AM* 31). When Gostrey tells Strether that he is superior to his successful friend Waymarsh, Strether protests, proclaiming himself "a failure" because he has "never made anything" (*AM* 30). Gostrey responds by asserting that her own superiority is due to the "futility" of her efforts to succeed. If Gostrey represents the American female consumer par excellence, who not only purchases but also encourages others to purchase, Strether can be seen as a man who has been emasculated by capitalist culture.

Strether's son died at the age of ten, so he is without issue; in terms of patrimony, he is without father and without son. The capitalistic value system in which he has what Waymarsh refers to as a "fierce" interest has deprived him of manhood. As Strether says to his friend, if he does not marry Mrs. Newsome he "miss[es] everything—[he's] nowhere" (*AM* 77). Strether points out to Gostrey that she, despite her alienation from the American ideal of success, is "expensive"—she has "cost" him something already by urging him to reject his conception of himself as a failure (*AM* 31). What she has cost him is his own acceptance of the value system that negates him.

Both Gostrey and Strether serve wealthy Americans—Strether directly, as Mrs. Newsome's ambassador to her son, and indirectly, as the editor of the review that advocates a social reform that does not threaten the material well-being of the prosperous New Englanders who support it. At the time of his mission to Europe, Strether's only "presentable" identity—to use his own words—has been "reduced" to being the name on the cover of the review, which Mrs. Newsome "magnificently pays for and which [he], not at all magnificently, edit[s]" (*AM* 44): "He was Lambert Strether because his name was on the cover, whereas it should have been, for anything like glory, that he was on the cover because he was Lambert Strether" (*AM* 59). Strether, of course, has a compelling personal financial interest in the successful completion of his mission. Chad's return to the Newsome business will enable the fulfillment of his father's will, which is to allow the business to "boom" (*AM* 77). Chad, as the only son, is apparently the only person who can accomplish this under the terms of the father's last document. Strether tells his friend Waymarsh that it is "indispensable . . . that Chad should be got back" because, as Waymarsh bluntly says for him, "If you have your own man in it . . . you'll marry—you personally—more money. She's already rich, as I understand you, but she'll be richer still if the business can be made to boom on certain lines that you've laid down" (*AM* 77). Strether responds that it was not he who laid them down, but the all-wise Mr. Newsome, who is described in the prospectus as "hard, sharp, and the reverse of overscrupulous" (*CN* 547). Strether, even as his wife's new husband, will not be able to head the family business; if a man's identity in Strether's world is commensurate with his ability to generate money, Strether is a failure as a man.

Likewise, Maria Gostrey's past and its role in determining her present identity is vague. Strether and the reader know that she moves in the right circles, but we do not know how or why she has access to these circles. Although we know that she went to school with Marie de Vionnet, we know little else of her history. What is significant here is not that the background information on Strether and Gostrey is vague, but that the details the reader *is* given define their economic and social identities. Strether alludes to "the wreck of hopes and ambitions, the refuse heap of disappointments and failures" of his past, and also to "the fact that he had failed . . . in everything, in each relation and in half a dozen trades, as he liked luxuriously to put it" (*AM* 45, 58). As a New Englander who once entertained commercial aspirations, he evaluates his present life in an accountant's terms: "Oh, if he *should* do the sum no slate would hold the figures!" (*AM* 58). His life, in short, does not "add up" to very much; he has had a range of experiences that "count for" nothing because none of these experiences have resulted in monetary success.

The collection of "lemon-coloured volumes," now soiled and still unread, becomes instead a symbol of his failure, "a symbol of his long grind and his want of odd moments, his want moreover of money, of opportunity, of positive dignity" (*AM* 61). Strether envies his friend Waymarsh in two respects: his friend's ability to maintain his dignity despite being deserted by his wife and the fact that he "had made a large income," "for the figure of the income he [Strether] had arrived at had never been high enough to look any one in the face" (*AM* 19). The suggestion here is that, in the social milieu Strether aspired to, a man's value is identified with his income.

As Maria Gostrey and Lambert Strether get to know each other, much of their conversation naturally involves establishing facts about Strether's economic and social position. Gostrey is one of the few characters in the novel who can talk frankly about money. Despite her gentility and "outsider" status, she has the soul of a "commercial person."[4] Gostrey refers to her social life and activities as "the shop," and even though Strether is not one of her clients, their conversations are called "commerce": "[This perfection of tact] . . . had kept him out of the shop, as she called her huge general acquaintance, made their commerce as quiet, as much a thing of the home alone—the opposite of the shop—as if she never had another customer" (*AM* 240). In the **"Project of Novel,"** James in several places associates Gostrey metaphorically with the world of commerce and retail; for example, when Strether speculates on the possible awkwardness of what he may discover about Chad's relationship with the Frenchwoman and her daughter, the few lines of Gostrey's response and James's narrative are resonant with shopping imagery:

> "Oh," says Miss Gostrey, "don't be too sure, in advance, of the shade of your awkwardness. There are many kinds; of every colour and every price. But perhaps!"
>
> Chad meanwhile introduces Strether to other friends; Miss Gostrey, on her side, produces a type or two out of her own store; and the business of our hero's enjoying himself . . . goes apace.
>
> (*CN* 556)

Although the relationship between Strether and Gostrey is compared to "the home"—which is domestic, intimate, and individual—as opposed to "the shop," James's use of the word "commerce" to describe their interaction compromises the opposition. The use of the word "customer" slyly suggests that their relationship is not quite as different from Gostrey's relationship with her "general acquaintance" as they would both like to believe. Gostrey provides her "brother-in-arms" with the same services she would provide any other client. She promises to "see him through" Europe if he will "give [himself] up" to her (*AM* 13); she calls her relationship with him a "job" and there is an unwritten contract between them with specific "terms of understanding" (*AM* 13, 23). Like a skillful advertiser, she is a creator of a need that she will professionally fulfill: "She was surely not to break away at the very moment she had created a want" (*AM* 23). The late nineteenth century in the United States provided the ground for the commercial revolution of mass marketing; for the first time in history, products were not only manufactured and distributed to fill pre-existing needs, but also needs were created and cultivated so that products could be sold to fulfill them. In her undercover, ironic way, Gostrey is allied with Chad and his ilk.

Gostrey makes clear that her work in Europe actually supports the bourgeois American way of life: "I'm—with all my other functions—an agent for repatriation. I want to re-people our stricken country. What will become of it else? I want to discourage others" (*AM* 24). She ironically sees herself as a secret worker for the project of keeping the American bourgeois culture strong and untained by its contact with Europe.[5]

When Strether first visits Gostrey in Paris, he is struck by how crowded her apartment is with *things*:

> Her compact and crowded little chambers, almost dusky, as they at first struck him, with accumulations, represented a supreme general adjustment to opportunities and conditions. Wherever he looked he saw an old ivory or an old brocade, and he scarce knew where to sit for fear of a misappliance. The life of the occupant struck him of a sudden as more charged with possession than Chad's or than Miss Barrace's; wide as his glimpse had lately become of the empire of "things," what was before him still enlarged it; the lust of the eyes and the pride of life had indeed thus their temple . . . objects all that caught, through the muslin, with their high rarity, the light of the low windows. Nothing was clear about them save that they were precious.

> (*AM* 83)

Maria Gostrey recognizes and pays homage to the power and appeal of things; her relentless appetite for bargains—she acquires the rare and the beautiful for less than they are worth—is testimony to that recognition. Her apartment is a "shrine," a "temple" to "precious" objects, suggesting that she endows them with an almost religious importance.

Later, when Strether first visits Marie de Vionnet's apartment, he contrasts the living quarters of the two "Marys." Gostrey's apartment, like Chad's, is the product of serious shopping; Gostrey's possessions are "vulgarly numerous." Madame de Vionnet's possessions, on the other hand, are the result of "transmission" rather than "acquisition."[6] Looking at the accumulation of rare and beautiful things in the aristocratic house, Strether is aware of how many things might have been given up rather than acquired for financial reasons; he cannot imagine the family selling "good" objects in order to acquire "'better' ones," as the aspiring middle-class American family does routinely (*AM* 172).

In his critique of contemporary American society in *The American Scene* (1907), James describes a new, bifurcated society. The society is divided into the economic and social realms, and the turf is disbursed according to gender. The American man, preoccupied by business and by the accumulation of money, can "never hope to be anything *but* a businessman" and so leaves the most important "two thirds of apparent life"—the social—to the women (*AS* [*The American Scene*] 345, 346). In the upper classes, the male laborers liberate the females of the family so that the females may busy themselves with the more interesting and significant aspects of life.

The reader can recognize, in Strether's admiration of Madame de Vionnet's relationship to objects, the same removal of the idea of "woman" from the ugly but absolutely essential realm of money-getting. Yet this sort of female is the product of the male's acquisitive efforts. Madame de Vionnet, as an old-world aristocratic woman in a setting of wealth and privilege, is romanticized by Strether as far removed from "the world of grab." She is so foreign, so "Other" to his American imagination that her wealth has been quietly "transmitted" rather than busily hunted down. One could look at the two Marys of the novel—Maria Gostrey and Madame de Vionnet—as representing competing values. Marie de Vionnet is associated with the illusions of aesthetic discourse, whereas Maria Gostrey, the pander of culture and commodities to wealthy Americans, is associated with economic discourse. Yet, as the plot reveals, Madame de Vionnet is no more removed from the world of grab than she is from the world of sexual desire.

SHOPPING: DESIRE AND FREEDOM

It is perfectly appropriate that Maria Gostrey should take Waymarsh and Strether on a walk through the commercial district of Chester. We are told in few words that she and Strether had viewed the historical landmarks the previous day, and perhaps Waymarsh is already familiar with them. At any rate, Gostrey introduces the men to a city of products available for purchase and consumption, a playground for the leisure class. The three stroll around the famous arcade of shops. Strether indulges in "the full sweetness of the taste of leisure," excusing his enthusiasm before the shop windows to his friend in terms of a "plea of a previous grind" (*AM* 27).

The walk awakens desire in Strether—the desire to purchase. The shop windows "fairly make him want things that he shouldn't know what to do with. It was by the oddest, the least admissible of laws demoralizing him now; and the way it boldly took was to make him want more wants" (*AM* 27). While Waymarsh, characteristically, "most sensibly yielded to the appeal of the more useful trades . . . of ironmongers and saddlers," Strether becomes "shameless" with "dealers in stamped letter-paper and smart neckties," and Gostrey has to restrain her new friend's compulsion to buy by permitting him only the purchase of a pair of gloves and by promising to take him to the Burlington Arcade, where he can get more for his money (*AM* 27). Waymarsh has been silently disapproving throughout the walk, though Strether is unable to tell whether he disapproves of the foreignness of the city, of the assault on ideas of New England thrift, or of Maria Gostrey's role as the "woman of fashion" initiating Strether into a "wicked" society. Even Waymarsh, however, apparently succumbs finally to the allure of the shop windows, impulsively dashing into a jeweller's shop and proceeding to spend a large though unspecified amount of money on an unspecified object or objects.

While waiting for Waymarsh to emerge from the glittering abyss, Gostrey and Strether discuss the relationship between money, freedom, and power. Strether sees Waymarsh's lunge into the jeweller's shop as a strike "for freedom," an assertion of his own power against what he perceives to be the corrupt and wicked power of Europe as personified by Maria Gostrey, and, by association, the bedazzled Strether (*AM* 29).

It would seem at first glance that James is juxtaposing two concepts of freedom here: the freedom derived from having the power of money—the power to purchase—and the freedom in which Maria Gostrey deals and which Strether is, in his own words, "trying" (*AM* 30). Ruth Bernard Yeazell sees Strether as suggesting that Gostrey's freedom is one of "remorseless analysis":

> "Remorseless analysis," Strether implies, means freedom—freedom presumably from the remorse with which Woollett, Massachusetts, is so obsessed, but freedom in a larger sense as well. For to talk like this is to question the meaning of the very words one uses, and to question meaning is finally to question value itself . . . by asking Strether if Waymarsh's success is to be measured in cash, Maria indirectly calls attention to the possibility of other meanings and other values. And by putting her question so bluntly, she suggests that making money is really but a crude definition of success—a definition which she subsequently confirms when proclaiming her delight that Strether is by such a definition a failure.

> (Yeazell 70)

The characterization of Maria Gostrey as someone who opens up, both directly and indirectly, the possibility of other value structures is absolutely correct, I believe, but the dichotomy between the two kinds of freedom is not clear and unambiguous in the text itself. The context of the conversation and the language of the dialogue create questions and ironies that do not allow the reader to accept a simple juxtaposition of the finer free-

dom of observation, conversation, and verbal analysis and the crude freedom of being able to buy whatever one wants (or, to use Arnold's broader term, freedom as the ability to "do what one wants").

First, as I have endeavored to show, both Gostrey and Strether are deeply compromised by the economically based system of values of the American Philistine class. In fact, Maria Gostrey sees herself as working to support this system of values in her own subtle way. If she has not become a success in Waymarsh's terms, it is not for want of trying. She and Strether are outsiders to the world of American success but not because of faults they have seen and could not accept in that system of values. Strether and Gostrey did not choose to reject the Philistine definition of success; they are both "beaten" by the system in which they have striven and failed. If they have insights into the weaknesses and cruelties of the system, it is because they have known them through desire and experience, not through ideological criticism.

Second, Waymarsh, before his bolt into the jewelry shop, has played the austere, thrifty New Englander to the frivolous Strether, who for once has the opportunity to delight in the play between materialistic desire and enticing objects; Strether can act, for an afternoon at least, as a member of the leisure class. The "remorseless analysis" that characterizes Strether and Maria's conversation is turned toward "passers, figures, faces, personal types" and objects, such as gloves and neckties, in shop windows. Their conversation transforms what they see into commodities. Strether and Gostrey see people—other subjects—as objects, as "types," just as later, at the theater, the people on both sides of the footlights seem to Strether to be "types." Types are categorized according to their style, their appearances, and the observers' habitual expectations. To see a human being as a "type" is to reify him or her. Waymarsh interprets Strether's and Gostrey's remarks as "exemplif[ying] in their degree the disposition to talk as 'society' talked" (*AM* 28). "Society" is a term that refers to the upper classes and their assumed economic privilege.

Strether and Gostrey's conversation not only reduces the people who pass before them to the same ontological status as the neckties and gloves in the shop windows, but also highlights, to Waymarsh and to the reader, the notion that consciousness itself has become reified. Just before Waymarsh dashes to the jeweller's, Strether reflects, "He thinks us sophisticated, he thinks us worldly, he thinks us wicked, he thinks us all sorts of queer things" (*AM* 29). What James juxtaposes here is not crude materialism with higher issues of taste and discrimination, or even simply the expressive power of language with the acquisitive power of money. Strether and Gostrey are "worldly," delighting in the variety of people and objects offering themselves to their acquisitive instinct. As observer/shoppers, they "rummaged and purchased . . . sifting, selecting, comparing" as Chad and Gostrey do when decorating their apartments (*AM* 172). Strether and Gostrey are more than merely window-shopping in a literal sense; their observations of objects and passersby demonstrate what Jean-Christophe Agnew terms "acquisitive cognition"—"the characteristic perspective of consumer culture" (67). In commodity culture, "cultural orientation becomes one with cultural appropriation. We read clothes, possessions, interiors, and exteriors as representing more or less successful accommodations to the world of goods, and in so doing we rehearse in our minds the appropriation of that social world via the commodity. We consume by proxy. We window-shop" (Agnew ["The Consuming Vision of Henry James"] 73). Gostrey's and Strether's "worldliness," which sets off such a reaction of repulsion in Waymarsh, is rooted in the entrenchment of their vision and values in consumer culture. Waymarsh is drawn to make his "extraordinary purchase" out of what Strether calls his "sacred rage," which has its roots not in the materialistic values of the Gilded Age but in the "real tradition" of American Puritanism with its willful unworldliness and faith in the judgment of conscience. Waymarsh is reacting to the detachment of his companions' "remorseless analysis," their preoccupation with the signs of style and value in both people and objects for sale (which are undifferentiated in their contemplative gazes). Waymarsh's "sacred rage" represents a kind of American purity and is, ironically, a gesture *against* materialism:

> Of all Strether's acquaintances Waymarsh proves to be "most in the real tradition" of American culture and pleads for the "purest veracity." Uncompromising in his judgements and unimpressed by subtleties, he is still not as narrow in his vision as the Woollett clan. . . . He always acts from consistent motives. The "sacred rage" repeatedly attributed to him by Strether and his witty friends is no mere patriotic bluster but the genuine impatience of the New World with the Old, with its inefficiency and imperfections. Waymarsh rebels against the sophisticated influence which Maria Gostrey is having on Strether during their cultural pilgrimage in Chester by striking out on his own to buy something expensive at a jeweller's. . . . It is a demonstration of independence, the independence that American money can buy.
>
> (Bellringer [*The Ambassadors*] 104)

There is something high and fine and superior about Waymarsh's militancy that even Madame de Vionnet's circle of aesthetic friends recognizes; Miss Barrace declares, upon first meeting him, that he would be a "*succés fou*" in artistic circles—a completely different kind of success from the American economic success to which Gostrey and Strether refer (*AM* 80). He is the noble distillation of a type, and as such his judgment of European society does carry some moral force. Waymarsh's impulsive purchase is disinterested; it is an affirmation of freedom, nothing more or less:

"I hope he hasn't paid," she said, "with his last [penny]; though I'm convinced he has been splendid, and has been so for you."

"Ah no—not that!"

"Then for me?"

"Quite as little.". . . .

"Then for himself?"

"For nobody. For nothing. For freedom."

(*AM* 31)

There is, indeed, something pure and "sublime" about Waymarsh's spending money in this way (*AM* 31). His extravagance in the jewelry shop, like his later attempts to buy Miss Barrace things that cost "hundreds and hundreds," is, Strether realizes, "an opposition" (*AM* 190, 191). In James's prospectus for *The Ambassadors,* the character who is to become Waymarsh in the final text is "Waymark"—implying that he is one who "marks the way": the rigid, moralistic, pragmatic New England way. Waymark, in the prospectus, is "an overworked lawyer in an American business community": "Waymark (never having, previous to this, been out of his lifelong setting at all), fails to react, fails of elasticity, of 'amusement,' throws back on suspicion, depreciation, resentment, really; the sense of exteriority, the cultivation of dissent, the surrender to unbridgeable difference" (*CN* 544, 545).

Later, in Gloriani's garden, when Strether again compares himself unfavorably to Waymarsh's "success," it is once more in terms of his friend's American authenticity rather than mere financial power. Miss Barrace has just declared Waymarsh in Europe "wonderful," like the Indian chief who is impassive before the "power" of the president—"the Great Father." Strether, already dazzled and beguiled by what he perceives as the "Europeanness of Europe" distilled in Gloriani's garden, reflects sadly "how little he himself was wrapt in his blanket, how little, in marble halls, all too oblivious of the Great Father, he resembled a really majestic aboriginal" (*AM* 145). Waymarsh has the ability to see the world with a penetrating and straightforward gaze; unlike Strether, he does not need the help of glasses to be able to see: "he fixed, with his admirable eyes, his auditor or his observer; he wore no glasses and had a way, partly formidable, yet also partly encouraging . . . of looking very hard at those who approached him" (*AM* 17).

In this text, the values epitomized by American and European cultures are not simply presented as contrary to each other. James performs an ambiguous inversion of the relationships between the ideal and the material, the idea of Europeanness and the idea of Americanness. Ironically, Waymarsh's extravagance serves to depreciate and transcend the power of money, while Gostrey and Strether's "civilized" attitudes and talk are valorized only in the commodified world of burgeoning capitalism. Waymarsh's bolt can be seen both as a challenge to and an appropriation of the power of commodities and the style-conscious consumer culture in which Gostrey and Strether are entangled.

The speaker of the injunction to "Live—live all you can," which provided James with the "germ" of ***The Ambassadors,*** was William Dean Howells. In "The Art of the Adsmith" (1907), Howells foresaw the dominance of advertising as a cultural institution and its effect on consciousness. He envisioned the advertising man as the "supreme artist of the twentieth century. He may assemble in his grasp, and employ at will, all the arts and sciences" (*Literature* [*Literature and Life*] 271). Howells even predicted the ascendance of advertising over the commodities it sells: "Evidently it can't keep on increasing at the present rate. If it does, there will be no room in the world for things; it will be filled up with the advertisements for things" (270). Howells's fictitious narrator goes on to wonder if the supreme adsmith could even, with the help of technology and an artist's skill, bypass words altogether and penetrate a consumer's consciousness directly. His interlocutor asks despairingly, "But what is to become of a race when it is penetrated at every pore with a sense of the world's demand and supply?" (271). The narrator speculates that, engorged with advertising, a sort of "immunity" to advertising may develop in society (it is either that immune reaction or madness). In the narrator's idea of civilization, no commodities would be produced, "much less foisted upon the community by adsmiths" (272).

Strether, who at the conclusion of ***The Ambassadors*** emphatically possesses "nothing," inadvertently demonstrates what happens when a consciousness is "penetrated at every pore with a sense of the world's demand and supply." Unable to accept the values of either Paris or Woollett, choosing to reject "having something"—gaining any tangible or intangible benefit from his experience—Strether finds nonetheless that he cannot even "be something."

Notes

1. "Live all you can; it's a mistake not to. It doesn't so much matter what you do in particular, so long as you have your life. If you haven't had that, what *have* you had? . . . I see it now. I haven't done so enough before—and now I'm too old; too old at any rate for what I see" (*AM* 153).

2. "His idea was to begin business immediately, and it did much for him the rest of his day that the beginning of business awaited him" (*AM* 53); "But his own actual business half an hour later was with a third floor on the Boulevard Malesherbes" (*AM* 67); "What has that to do with it? The only

thing I've any business to like is to feel that I'm moving [Chad]" (*AM* 125); "he wants me so furiously to meet them, know them and like them, that I shall oblige him by kindly not bringing our business to a crisis till he has had a chance to see them again himself" (*AM* 128); "conscious as he was, and as with more reason, of the determination to be in respect to the rest of his business perfectly plain and go perfectly straight" (*AM* 148); "[Maria Gostrey's] answer in an instant rang clear. 'Because I wish to keep out of the business [Strether's project]'" (*AM* 159). Even the depiction of the "process of vision" that drives the novel is described by Strether as "the business": "He had determined Chad to wait, he had determined him to see; he was therefore not to quarrel with the time given up to the business" (*AM* 318). Madame de Vionnet, in her final conversation with Strether, juxtaposes the two words most associated with her and the values of her world with the word "business," which here refers to her relationship with Strether. Strether, who has idealized both Madame de Vionnet and her relationship with Chad, feels that he cannot continue to be friends with her after he discovers that she is, indeed, Chad's mistress; upon hearing his plea for her to "be easy"—a state that is associated with Chad—she replies, "And not trouble you any more, no doubt—not thrust on you even the wonder and the beauty of what I've done; only let you regard our business as over, and well over" (*AM* 407).

3. In his autobiography, *Notes of a Son and Brother,* James wrote that commercial exchange defined the social order and the human relationships within it; the New England culture of his boyhood was, as Alan Bellringer relates, "a social order (so far as it *was* an order) that found its main ideal in a 'strict attention to business,' that is to buying and selling over a counter or a desk, and in such an intensity of traffic as made, on the part of all involved, for close localisation" (Bellringer 9). The small-scale retail commerce of James's boyhood was replaced, in the economic expansion that swept the United States after the Civil War, with large-scale industrialization. Whereas before the Civil War American industry was based on hand labor, now products were turned out by the thousands by machines. The cities of New England, stoked by the influx of millions of European immigrants, became major manufacturing centers.

4. This reference to Christopher Newman appears numerous times throughout *The American.*

5. James's emphasis in this conversation on the word "spent" is telling:

> "That's my little system; and, if you want to know," said Maria Gostrey, "it's my real secret,

my innermost mission and use. I only seem, you see, to beguile and approve; but I've thought it all out and I'm working all the while underground. I can't perhaps give you quite the formula, but I think that I practically succeed. I send you back spent. So you stay back. Passed through my hands—"

"We don't turn up again?" The further she went the further he always saw himself able to follow. "I don't want your formula—I feel quite enough, as I hinted yesterday, of your abysses. Spent!" he echoed. "If that's how you're arranging so subtly to send me I thank you for the warning."

For a minute, amid the pleasantness—poetry in tariffed items, but all the more, for guests already convicted, a challenge to consumption— they smiled at each other in confirmed fellowship.

(*AM* 25)

James plays with two meanings of the word "spent" here: he means at once the depletion of energy and the utter exhaustion of resources as well as the disbursement of money. With the avidly acquisitive Americans, hungry for "culture" and its objects, these two meanings collapse into one another. When Gostrey and Strether smile at each other in that moment of immediate sympathy and understanding, they do so with an ironic awareness of the context of Gostrey's portrayal of American Philistine culture and her role in perpetuating it: the very pleasant, calculatedly English garden created, like the hotel, for the consumption of foreign guests who are seeking to purchase experience.

6. "His attention took [the books] into account. They were among the matters that marked Madame de Vionnet's apartment as something quite different from Miss Gostrey's little museum of bargains and from Chad's lovely home; he recognized it as founded much more on old accumulations that had possibly from time to time shrunken than on any contemporary method of acquisition or form of curiosity. Chad and Miss Gostrey had rummaged and purchased and picked up and exchanged, sifting, selecting, comparing; whereas the mistress of the scene before him, beautifully passive under the spell of transmission—transmission from her father's line, he quite made up his mind—had only received, accepted, and been quiet" (*AM* 172).

Key to Works by Henry James

AM: *The Ambassadors*. Oxford: Oxford U P, 1985.

AS: *The American Scene*. Bloomington: Indiana U P, 1985.

CN: *The Complete Notebooks of Henry James*. Ed. Leon Edel and Lyall H. Powers. Oxford: Oxford U P, 1987.

PL: *The Portrait of a Lady*. Harmondsworth: Penguin, 1984.

Other Works Cited

Agnew, Jean-Christophe. "The Consuming Vision of Henry James." *The Culture of Consumption: Critical Essays in American History, 1880-1980*. Ed. Richard W. Fox and T. J. Jackson Lears. New York: Pantheon, 1983. 65-100.

Arnold, Matthew. *Selected Prose*. Ed. P. J. Keating. London: Penguin, 1970.

Bellringer, Alan W. *The Ambassadors*. London: George Allen and Unwin, 1984.

Bowlby, Rachel. *Just Looking: Consumer Culture in Dreiser, Gissing, and Zola*. New York: Methuen, 1985.

Howells, William Dean. "The Art of the Adsmith." *Literature and Life*. New York: Kennikat P, 1968. 265-72.

———. *The Rise of Silas Lapham*. New York: Norton, 1982.

Lears, T. J. Jackson. "From Salvation to Self-Realization: Advertising and the Therapeutic Roots of the Consumer Culture (1880-1930)." *The Culture of Consumption: Critical Essays in American History, 1880-1980*. Ed. Richard W. Fox and T. J. Jackson Lears. New York: Pantheon, 1983. 3-38.

McCormack, Peggy. *The Rule of Money: Gender, Class and Exchange Economics in the Fiction of Henry James*. Ann Arbor: UMI Research P, 1990.

Smith, Barbara Herrnstein. *Contingencies of Value: Alternative Perspectives for Critical Theory*. Cambridge: Harvard U P, 1988.

Wicke, Jennifer. *Advertising Fictions: Literature, Advertisement, and Social Reading*. New York: Columbia U P, 1988.

Yeazell, Ruth Bernard. *Language and Knowledge in the Late Novels of Henry James*. Chicago: U of Chicago P, 1976.

Marianne DeKoven (essay date spring 1997)

SOURCE: DeKoven, Marianne. "Walking on Water: The Metropolitan Feminine in *The Ambassadors*." *The Henry James Review* 18, no. 2 (spring 1997): 107-26.

[*In the following essay, DeKoven argues that in* The Ambassadors *James conflates a number of different ideas, including "modernist form and epistemology," "maternal and actively sexual" femininity, and "cosmopolitan modernity." DeKoven asserts that this confla-*

tion "crystallizes defining characteristics of modernist narrative," and that its "representational lynchpin is James's complex treatment of Madame de Vionnet."]

"Women were thus endlessly absorbent, and to deal with them was to walk on water . . . it took women, it took women; if to deal with them was to walk on water what wonder that the water rose? And it had never surely risen higher than round this woman" (***AM*** [***The Ambassadors***] 322).[1] "This woman" is Madame de Vionnet. The flooding water she figures, and that figures her, seems at this crucial moment in the text threatening to drown both her and Strether so imminently that he must represent his miraculous, impossible task in "deal-[ing] with" (controlling) her as "to walk on water." The flood however is on the point not of drowning anyone but rather of becoming Madame de Vionnet's tears.[2] It strikes Strether after "taking a long look at her" that "'You're afraid for your life!,'" a revelation that produces this response: "A spasm came into her face, the tears she had already been unable to hide overflowed at first in silence, and then, as the sound suddenly comes from a child, quickened to gasps, to sobs" (322).

This conversion of the dire but miracle-inducing female flood to childish, pitiable female tears corresponds in the text to Strether's decision at last to take (on his own terms and in his own time of course) Waymarsh's advice—"Look here, Strether. Quit this" (74)—quit Paris and the complex nexus of possibilities it represents in the novel. Strether's exist from Paris, his putative return to Woollett, literally marks the boundary of the world of the novel. James cannot sustain the modernist forms and knowledges that the novel discovers, locates in, and makes figurally coterminous with Paris: the radical epistemological and stylistic complexity and indeterminacy of his Major Phase style. At the heart of this novel's modernism is the labyrinthine, shifting, self-reversing quest, undertaken by a privileged narrative center of consciousness (Strether), for a continually deferred knowledge—Paris, in this novel, has precisely the unstable, multifaceted self-contradictoriness of the modernist narrative form James uses to represent it. When Strether leaves Paris at the end of the novel, James renounces that modernist narrative form, returning, as if in substitution for the translation back to Woollett he finds it redundant or impossible to narrate, to determinate, self-consistent premodernist modes of knowledge and representation at once less dangerous and less promising.

At the center of Paris, literally for this novel, is Madame de Vionnet in her house.[3] I will argue here that ***The Ambassadors*** enacts a multiple conflation of modernist form and epistemology (the Major Phase style) with radical history (the Revolution and the ongoing struggle for democracy), with a femininity both maternal and actively sexual (Madame de Vionnet), and with

cosmopolitan modernity (Paris). This conflation, which does not appear in such clear, powerful form anywhere else I know of, crystallizes defining characteristics of modernist narrative. Its representational linchpin is James's complex treatment of Madame de Vionnet. This treatment is most accessible through analysis of water imagery, as is so often the case with representations of the feminine in early modernist narrative.[4] The novel journeys inward to Madame de Vionnet in her house, then, unable to bear what it finds, withdraws.[5]

I

> He recognised at last that he had really been trying all along to suppose nothing.
>
> (*AM* 313)

Strether is an "ambassador" only in the most ironic sense: he is a failed ambassador, an ambassador-manqué.[6] I will argue here that he is in fact the opposite of an ambassador. He is not the authorized signifier of a legitimate, phallogocentric national signified, an absence-made-presence, but rather a *flâneur,* that self-propelled, unauthorized vector of illegitimate metropolitan anonymity. Further, he is a Parisian *flâneur* of an unusually plotted, narrativistic kind. His motion is not random or nonlinear. He is a voyager rather than a wanderer, whose seemingly desultory movement is in fact relentlessly directed. He is not, like his fellow voyager into modernist form and consciousness Marlow, penetrating into the heart of darkness at the other end of the world from (and constituting the enabling condition for) the modernist metropolis, but is steadily penetrating into the heart of that metropolis itself, the heart of light: Paris, the "lighted city" (281), the *Ville Lumière.*

As ***Ambassadors*** criticism has generally known, whatever there is of value and danger in the world of the novel, whatever is not-Woollett, is Paris. The accounts or descriptions of what constitutes that value and danger are almost as multiplicitous as the meanings of the novel itself. As Leavis notoriously complained in *The Great Tradition,* evidently finding the question unanswerable rather than merely rhetorical, "What, we ask, is this, symbolized by Paris?"; critics have been answering ever since,[7] and I will be no exception, offering here one more answer. I will argue that Paris is metropolitan modernism as the potential for egalitarian revolution embodied in the sexuate maternal feminine, embodied in turn in the character Marie de Vionnet.[8]

A discussion of what I mean by "metropolitan modernism" will follow shortly. With "sexuate maternal feminine," I reinvoke the figure at the center of my argument in *Rich and Strange* and at the heart of much French feminist theory, particularly that of Luce Irigaray and Julia Kristeva. Most relevant to the study of modernism is the notion that this erotic maternality, repressed, disenfranchised, allied with and relegated to the unconscious both of the individual psyche and of Western culture, erupts into representation along with the unconscious at the Freudian turn of the century. The emergence of this gendered unconscious into representation—not the feminine in general but specifically the erotic maternal—takes place visibly, demonstrably, in the destabilizations of language and form that characterize modernism and the avant-garde, because these destabilizations disrupt the orderly, naming, sense-making function of language privileged by the dominance of logos in patriarchy.

Luce Irigaray, in *Speculum of the Other Woman,* uses Plato's parable of the cave to propose that dominant modes of representation in patriarchy were founded on the denigration and suppression of the womb, as figured by the cave. Plato's cave is at the heart of James's imagistic structures in **The Ambassadors.** The life-originating and primary image-making carnal power of the womb-cave, in Plato's myth of the foundation of Western representation, is repressed in favor of, and therefore made the always-returning unconscious of, logos, the sun, the abstract paternal power of the regime of truth. Using figuration she finds in Plotinus, Irigaray shows how the liquidity of the maternal origin (water is the preeminent feminine element in Western mythology) is frozen, recontained, deprived of threat and power, redefined as a matte, iced surface that exists only to reflect the light of the paternal sun (168-179; the significance of this phase of Irigaray's work will become clear in subsequent analysis of James's representation of Madame de Vionnet).

In *Rich and Strange,* I use Irigaray's work to analyze modernism's formal dislocations, particularly its indeterminacy and self-contradictoriness (the qualities that make it "rich and strange"), as markers of the eruption into representation at the turn of the century of the empowered maternal feminine. This erotic maternal figure in turn (literally) embodies, in modernist figuration, the radical egalitarian political movements, primarily feminism and socialism, that Perry Anderson designates the "revolutionary horizon" of the period: the continually lurking possibility, at once terrifying and alluring to the modernists, of total political and cultural change. The pervasive, feminine-gendered water imagery in early modernist narrative is a prime site of the representation of ambivalence toward the eruption of the sexuate maternal feminine, as symbolic of and conflated with feminism and socialism. My argument here focuses on the ways in which **The Ambassadors** extends this conflation to include the modern metropolis. I abbreviate this extended conflation as "the metropolitan feminine." James's characteristic modernist ambivalence toward the metropolitan feminine determines both the novel's fascination with, and its ultimate repudiation of, the symbolic nexus of Paris.

In this reading of the novel, the key scene of discovery or revelation is not the sequence in book 11, chapters 3 and 4, where James finally allows Strether to read the purloined letter stating in black and white that Chad's relations with Madame de Vionnet have been actively sexual all along. I see that sequence rather as a recontainment: a narrativization of the impossibility for James of representing directly, in Paris, using modernist forms, Madame de Vionnet's active sexuality.

This scene of putative revelation but actual recontainment—the sex scene, such as it is for James—takes place not only outside Paris, but entirely within the premodernist past: the "oblong gilt frame" (302) of "a certain small Lambinet that had charmed him, long years before, at a Boston dealer" (301). As S. P. Rosenbaum's useful and concise note in the *Norton Critical Edition* explains, while James in **A Small Boy and Others** describes Lambinet as "'summ[ing] up for the American collector and in the New York and Boston markets the idea of the modern in the masterly,'" in fact "it has been pointed out [by John L. Sweeney in his introduction to **The Painter's Eye**] . . . that the village scene which reminds Strether of Lambinet is described as if it were an Impressionist painting" (301, n.4). That is evidently the case: Strether remembers the Lambinet as a "special-green vision . . . the poplars, the willows, the rushes, the river, the sunny silvery sky, the shady woody horizon" (301). The rustic scene as it unfolds around him within "the oblong gilt frame" is described in nearly identical, even more painterly language: "the sky was silver and turquoise and varnish; the village on the left was white and the church on the right was grey" (302); "whiteness, crookedness and blueness set in coppery green" (306). I would add that "the idea of the modern in the masterly" at the time James was "a small boy" *was* Impressionism. Further, James locates Strether's encounter with the Lambinet in premodernist Boston, destination of the Fitchburg train, capital of provincial, Puritan New England ("long years before . . . in the maroon-coloured, sky-lighted inner shrine of Tremont Street" against the "background of the Fitchburg Depot" [301]), an explicit contrast to metropolitan Parisian modernism.[9]

The "oblong gilt frame" of the premodernist social, cultural, and artistic past continues to enclose the scene wherever Strether moves through it: "the oblong gilt frame disposed its enclosing lines" (302); "he . . . lost himself anew in Lambinet" (303); "[h]e really continued in the picture . . . all the rest of this rambling day . . . and had meanwhile not once overstepped the oblong gilt frame" (305); "for this had been all day at bottom the spell of the picture" (306). When Chad and Marie appear in their damning boat on the river of impunity, "expert, familiar, frequent . . . [knowing] how to do it." "It was suddenly as if these figures, or something like them, had been wanted in the picture, had been wanted more or less all day" (307). Within the confining frame of the premodernist past, "the old text"[10] of Puritanical, Victorian melodrama, the liberating metropolitan modernity of Marie's maternal sexuality is recontained and discredited as something banal and altogether familiar: her sin, her guilty secret. Suddenly, in a full repudiation of the modernist indeterminacy at which this novel has painfully and gloriously arrived, constructed around the undecidability of Chad's relations with Marie, those relations are revealed as decidable and decided, guaranteeing a conventional plot after all: Chad and Marie are simply illicit lovers. *The Ambassadors* has been harboring and concealing a very explicit, simple, unitary knowledge; Mrs. Newsome and Sarah Pocock, and therefore Woollett, were right all along. When Strether decides at last to cast his lot with Madame de Vionnet despite her "sin," and to make it "all right" (to "pay") by renouncing for himself all she gives him, he orchestrates a highly melodramatic scene with Chad in which Strether "appeal[s] to him by all [he] hold[s] sacred," telling him, in the tritest language of melodrama, language glaringly at odds with the complex subtleties and ironies of James's Major Phase style, that he would be a "brute" and "a criminal of the deepest dye" if he left Marie (336).

Strether's relations with Maria Gostrey are also recontained at the end of the novel, equally dramatically revised to conform to the old premodernist text. In the beginning of the novel, Strether followed Maria Gostrey through the Rows of Chester and into the heart of the feminine modernist Parisian metropolis; at the end *he* takes *her,* passively acquiescent and silent, on a shopping expedition. The consumer culture that enabled her mobility is turned against her at the end to reinstitute her conventional feminine positioning.

The culmination of Strether's Parisian journey is not that bucolic day trip *out* of Paris, to an extra-urban past of culture and art. The culmination is rather the sequence succeeding it, book 12, chapters 1 and 2, in which Strether re-enters Paris, going straight this time to its center, Madame de Vionnet in her house, in possession of the knowledge that will allow him at last to see, because he has determined to renounce it, what is really there: "the vibration of the vast strange life of the town . . . the fierce, the sinister, the acute" (315). That turn-of-the-century Paris was both the quintessence and the prime locale of urban modernity, of modernism as a movement enabled by and located within that modernity, requires no demonstration. Benjamin's "Paris, Capital of the Nineteenth Century" is really about Paris as the capital of modernity, as his quote from Michelet's *Avenir! Avenir!* makes clear: "*Chaque epôque rève la suivante*" (148). Even without that quote, it is evident that Benjamin's subject throughout this essay is, as he repeatedly says, Paris as modernity.

Benjamin's arguments concerning the interrelations of metropolitan modernism and commodity culture provide the necessary context for understanding James's irreducible ambivalence toward Chad Newsome and to his relations with Madame de Vionnet. Chad is at once civilized ("improved") and immoralized ("degraded") by Madame de Vionnet, and therefore, in this novel's and modernism's equation, by consumerist modernist metropolitan Paris. Because advertising is modernist form's powerful legacy to consumerism, Chad's success at consumerism juxtaposed with his interest in advertising locates him at precisely the point where the imbrication of artistic modernism with consumer capitalism is clearest.[11] As far as my argument in this essay is concerned, I would emphasize Benjamin's assumption that Paris is in effect the historical body, within capitalism, of emergent modernism.

Raymond Williams makes this argument explicitly in his essay "Metropolitan Perceptions and the Emergence of Modernism": "It is now clear that there are decisive links between the practices and ideas of the avant-garde movements of the twentieth century and the specific conditions and relationships of the twentieth-century metropolis" (Williams uses "avant-garde" interchangeably with "Modernism" and "modern art").[12] Williams argues that metropolitan modernism emerged within late nineteenth-and early twentieth-century "capital cities, and especially within the major metropolises," because "there was at once a complexity and a sophistication of social relations, supplemented in the most important cases—Paris, above all—by exceptional liberties of expression" (44); "a new kind of open, complex and mobile society" (45). Modernist works, Williams argues, are therefore constituted by, and at the same time represent, "the vitality, the variety, the liberating diversity and mobility of the city" (43). Further, "[t]his complex and open milieu contrasted very sharply with the persistence of traditional social, cultural and intellectual forms in the provinces and in the less developed countries" (44-45): Paris contrasted with Woollett, precisely the founding binary of *The Ambassadors.*[13] Though Williams does not mention *The Ambassadors,* he could well have had the guests in Gloriani's garden in mind when he wrote of "the miscellaneity of the metropolis—which in the course of capitalist and imperialist development had characteristically attracted a very mixed population, from a variety of social and cultural origins—and its concentration of wealth and thus opportunities of patronage" (45).

These metropolitan dislocations were the primary cause of the detachment of the artistic medium, particularly language, from its cultural embeddedness as social convention, accompanied by its conversion into a thing in itself, its own most important referent. This abstraction and self-referentiality constituted the precondition and defining characteristic of modernist formal practice. In the modern metropolis, Williams argues, "the only community available" to the modernist artists was "a community of the medium; of their own practices" (45):

> within the very openness and complexity of the metropolis, there was no formed and settled society to which the new kinds of work could be related. The relationships were to the open and complex and dynamic social process itself, and the only accessible form of this practice was an emphasis on the medium: the medium as that which, in an unprecedented way, defined art.
>
> (46)

The Ambassadors both exemplifies and directly represents Williams's argument, with the materiality, the opaque self-refeentiality of its language and the multiplicity and indeterminacy of its knowledges both enabled by an figured by Paris, whose exciting "openness and complexity" attach to Madame de Vionnet and her house.

With Madame de Vionnet, James radically revised the *flâneur* tradition that epitomizes Benjaminian consumerist-modernist Paris. As Rachel Bowlby argues in "Walking, Women and Writing," the masculine figure of the *flâneur* is inextricably connected to the feminine figure of the "passante," the prime but disappearing object of the *flâneur*'s wandering gaze.[14] She is fugitive because he is on the move: "Her passing is really his, as he zooms by just catching sight of her" (12). Bowlby finds that for Baudelaire, in his *Fleurs du Mal* poem "A une passante," this feminine figure, who appears clothed in mourning, is erotic, maternal, and also split:

> Death-dealer and life-giver, a mother. A twofold mother . . . nourishing eye and evil eye, '*la douceur qui fascine et le plaisir qui tue*'. Anonymous: any woman, '*une femme*'. And also the one and only, the unique woman. . . . Two women seen in one. She is '*noble*', '*majestueuse*', a queen or goddess . . . unavailable, inaccessible, she is not to be approached. At the same time the woman of the street, the street-walker. A fast ('*fugitive*') lady. The whore, undomesticated, whose home is the *maison de passe*, the street inside.
>
> (9-10)

James takes the projected, reified figure of masculine fantasy, the "passante," and, without altering the defining characteristics that Bowlby makes clear, retaining especially this figure's contradictory combination of sexual inaccessibility and sexual availability, gives her subjective agency in the narrative. He gives her a voice, a character, and a home that reimagines the "street inside." Just as the character of Strether undoes conventional gender positions,[15] the character of Madame de Vionnet undoes the modes of representation historically aligned with those gender positions, replacing them with the modernism of the metropolitan feminine.

Before I return to the text of James's novel, I want to locate Madame de Vionnet in one more social-historical context: the altered relationship of women to the city at the turn of the century, as analyzed recently by Judith Walkowitz in her work on late Victorian London.[16] Walkowitz shows us women moving out into the city in new ways in the 1880s. No longer "matter out of place," or automatically sexual prey (though heterosexual significations remained in complex play on these urban streets),[17] women charity workers, social workers, and proto-sociologists were able to transform for their purposes the urban space opened by consumerism's enfranchisement of women as legitimate public shoppers, claiming both mobility and agency in the East End.[18] While Madame de Vionnet is in no way directly associated with these women, and at least ostensibly occupies a social space antithetical to theirs (aristocratic and artistic/bohemian Parisian "high society"), she moves as freely through modernist Paris as they do through East End London. Like them, she is unescorted, mapping her own trajectory in pursuit of her own purposes, enabled but not determined by the public spaces of consumer culture. At two pivotal points in the novel, in Notre Dame and in Sarah Pocock's hotel room, we find her arrived before Strether, having traveled to her destination alone. James does not go as far as actually representing her in transit—again, we see her already arrived, and her solitary urban journeying is only implied. These solitary arrivals give her nonetheless an aura of independence and autonomy in notable contrast to the characteristic positioning of women in bourgeois domestic fiction, where they are generally either visited at home or escorted out.[19] Even Maria Gostrey, except in our first, premonitory (of her double Marie) encounter with her in the Chester hotel lobby, appears either at home, at a social gathering, or out in company with Strether. Mamie Pocock, Marie's "opposite number" in many senses of that term, epitomizes this characteristic bourgeois fictional enclosure of women: Strether images her administering tea in a Woollett drawing room, and we encounter her trapped on the balcony of her Paris hotel room, unable to go out for want of a suitable male escort.[20]

Women's urban mobility exists in the context of consumer culture, for James as for the turn-of-the-century historical moment of his novel. This connection is clear in the use I have already noted of Maria Gostrey, Madame de Vionnet's avatar and less threatening double, as doyenne of Strether's introductory shopping trip through the Rows of Chester, avatars themselves of Paris's Benjaminian arcades.[21] Strether's opening shopping trip chaperoned by Maria Gostrey signals the text's preoccupation with the reconstruction of gender in urban modernity; the reversal of that chaperone relation at the end—the reinstatement of conventional patriarchal gender relations—signals James's retreat from that reconstruction.

II

the elements were different enough from any of her old elements, and positively rich and strange

(WD [The Wings of the Dove] 149)[22]

Strether's wilful and necessary misreading of Madame de Vionnet's relationship to Chad, his strenuous, liberating effort to "suppose nothing," corresponds to his misreading, or incomplete, partial, distorted reading, of the historical provenance of Madame de Vionnet's house. Just as James requires Strether to define Madame de Vionnet to himself as nonsexual in order to be able to experience the possibilities her sexuality, embodied in Paris, opens up, Strether must also define her historical and social position to himself as exclusively aristocratic, patrilinear, untouched by either the commodity culture of modernist Paris or the democratic upheavals that enabled and defined it.

On his first visit to Madame de Vionnet's house, in book 6, chapter 1, Strether establishes a series of contrasts to the domestic interiors of the consumerists Chad Newsome and Maria Gostrey in order to locate in the difference of Madame de Vionnet's residence "the ancient Paris that he was always looking for" (*AM* 145). This "ancient Paris" is exaggeratedly aristocratic and palpably secluded from Parisian modernity. The court from which the visitor gains entrance to the house is in the "high homely style of an elder day," and speaks to Strether of the aristocratic "habit of privacy, the peace of intervals, the dignity of distances and approaches" (145). Once inside, Strether notices, not perfectly selected objects, as he does in the homes of Chad Newsome and Maria Gostrey, but rather the "ancient Paris that he was always looking for" visible in noble architectural elements: in "the immemorial polish of the wide waxed staircase and in the fine *boiseries,* the medallions, mouldings, mirrors, great clear spaces" (145). This emphasis on lasting architecture and on long perspective within empty space as metaphor not only of freedom from bourgeois consumerism but also of the distance between classes, makes the aristocratic provenance of the house seem independent of the activities of its contemporary occupant, with aristocratic tradition and family superseding the bourgeois democratic individual.

Such objects as there are also refer not to Marie de Vionnet herself but to her "ancient" lineage: "He seemed at the very outset to see her in the midst of possessions not vulgarly numerous, but hereditary cherished charming" (145). These "hereditary cherished charming" possessions, in opposition to the "vulgarly numerous possessions" of democracy's consumer, mark

> Madame de Vionnet's apartment as something quite different from Miss Gostrey's little museum of bargains and from Chad's lovely home; he recognised it

as founded much more on old accumulations . . . than on any contemporary method of acquisition. . . . Chad and Miss Gostrey had rummaged and purchased and picked up and exchanged, sifting, selecting, comparing; whereas the mistress of the scene before him, beautifully passive under the spell of transmission—transmission from her father's line, he quite made up his mind—had only received, accepted and been quiet.

(145-46)

At stake here are entire historical-social-cultural nexes, with strongly marked class and gender alignments. On the one hand is the preconsumerist past of aristocratic, paternalistic hegemony assigned to Madame de Vionnet, and on the other, a potentially gender-egalitarian consumerist bourgeois modernity, to which Chad and Maria have equal access. Consumerism involves the activity of individual agents (they "rummaged and purchased and picked up and exchanged, sifting, selecting, comparing"), while Madame de Vionnet can only passively receive and accept the "transmission from her father's line," "be[ing] quiet" like the silent, silenced woman of traditional misogyny.

Strether bolsters this positioning of Madame de Vionnet by linking her to the Empire, which he describes explicitly as "the post-revolutionary period" (145). The word "revolutionary" marks the return of the repressed, absented democratic revolution with which James's novel, but not Strether until its climactic moments, actually associates Madame de Vionnet. That one of the figures she reminds Strether of in this scene is Madame de Staël also powerfully undercuts her "quiet" receiving and accepting of the transmission from her father's line. This association with Madame de Staël also signals what will become apparent in book 12, chapter 1: that the trappings of traditional feminine passivity and of an aristocracy secluded from urban modernity are exaggerated, distorted figures marking precisely, in their exaggeration and distortion, the repression that this modernist novel, articulated through Strether's own consciousness, temporarily undoes. As such, they function to protect Strether from his own potential knowledge that Marie de Vionnet's active sexuality is the same thing as the democratic, modernist Paris that has set him free, liberated him from the old text of Woollett, presided over by Mrs. Newsome, this novel's ultimate Irigarayan frozen mother: the "particularly large iceberg in a cool blue northern sea" (298).

Perhaps the most extreme moment of this deployment of aristocracy as class marker of the text's suppression of Madame de Vionnet's revolutionary maternal sexuality comes in book 9, chapter 1, when she informs Strether that "'We're marrying [her daughter] Jeanne'" (237). In narrating Strether's response to this arranged aristocratic marriage, James uses language that stunningly predicts Irigaray's, indicating the embodiment in

Madame de Vionnet-as-aristocrat of Irigaray's repressed maternal origin, the womb-cave of Plato's myth as frozen by patriarchy:

> they stood there together so easily in these *cold chambers of the past.* . . . The sense he had so often had, since the first hour of his disembarkment, of being further and further "*in,*" treated him again at this moment to another twinge . . . feeling as if he had even himself been concerned in something *deep and dim.* . . . It was—through something *ancient and cold* in it— what he would have called the *real thing.*
>
> (237-38, italics added to emphasize the Irigarayan language)[23]

James has set the stage in ample detail for Marie's liberation from this frozen class pedestal.

At the beginning of book 12, before bringing Strether to Madame de Vionnet's house one last eye-opened time, James takes him to the *Postes et Télégraphes,* the "big one on the Boulevard" (314), to reply to her *petit bleu* inviting him to visit her that night. He writes his reply "on the Boulevard, also in the form of a *petit bleu.*" This scene establishes, as the context of Strether's final encounter with Marie, the Parisian public space of urban modernity. Further, James's free indirect narration of Strether's view of the *Postes et Télégraphes* also establishes the Revolution of 1789 as the historical context of Strether's final encounter with Marie. Strether feels "in the air of" the *Postes et Télégraphes*

> the vibration of the vast strange life of the town, the influence of the types, the performers concocting their messages; the little prompt Paris women, arranging, pretexting goodness knew what, driving the dreadful needle-pointed public pen at the dreadful sand-strewn public table; implements that symbolised for Strether's too interpretative innocence something more acute in manners, more sinister in morals, more fierce in the national life. After he had put in his paper he had ranged himself . . . on the side of the fierce, the sinister, the acute. He was carrying on a correspondence, across the great city, quite in the key of the *Postes et Télégraphes* in general. . . .
>
> (315)

This passage barely requires explication. The "types" and the "prompt Paris women" wielding their "dreadful needle-pointed public pen at the dreadful sand-strewn public table" brilliantly condense allusions both to urban modernity and to the Revolution, in its fearful, guillotining manifestation as the Terror. As E. J. Hobsbawm argues, in the aftermath of the Revolutionary Centennial of 1889 and in the context of Perry Anderson's notion of the turn of the century as "revolutionary horizon," the Revolution meant democracy.[24] At the *Postes et Télégraphes,* classes and races are mixed together, as to a lesser extent (constrained by the class boundaries of modernism itself) they were in Gloriani's garden, as a concatenation of "types." Women are writing (and their writing is experienced as the most frightening aggression), moving freely through public urban space, motivated by their own desires. Concurrently, James invokes networks of modern urban communication and at the same time the guillotine of Mme Defarge with her "dreadful needle-pointed public" knitting. James's irreducible ambivalence toward metropolitan feminine modernity, which Strether is at last free to express, could not be more clear. The Boulevard and the *Postes et Télégraphes* are at once the exciting locus of the "vast vibration" of the "great city," language that Williams echoes ("the vitality, the variety, the liberating diversity and mobility of the city" ["Metropolitan" ["Metropolitan Perceptions and the Emergence of Modernism"] 43]), and also the terrifying ("dreadful public") locus of "the fierce, the sinister, the acute."

Without a paragraph break, Strether goes on to think of his relationship with Madame de Vionnet as "mix[ing]" him up in the "typical tale of Paris" produced by the *Postes et Télégraphes.* The "most significant" aspect of this "typical tale . . . in respect to himself" is Strether's "preference for seeing his correspondent in her own best conditions. . . . He liked the place she lived in" (315). By making Madame de Vionnet's home the best setting for the "typical tale of Paris," James has Strether connect that house to democratic, gender- and class-egalitarian urban modernity; heretofore he defined it by its separation from that milieu, its seclusion within an aristocratic, anti-democratic, patriarchal "ancient" ness (*ancien régime*). Again, what makes the difference, what enables this revision of Madame de Vionnet's social-historical positioning, is Strether's knowledge of her active sexuality. The novel has positioned Madame de Vionnet's house at the center of Paris for Strether all along—it is clearly the destination to which his modernist voyage is carrying him (the equivalent of the Inner Station for Marlow in *Heart of Darkness*), as he moves from Chester to London to Paris, and then through successive layers of the Parisian onion: the great public gardens, Maria Gostrey's house, Chad's house, Gloriani's garden, to, at the center of the novel, the first visit to Madame de Vionnet.

James prefaces Strether's final visit to Madame de Vionnet's house with a singularly, self-consciously explicit water image. Strether wishes

> that somebody was paying something somewhere and somehow, that they were at least not all floating together on the silver stream of impunity. Just instead of that to go and see her late in the evening, as if, for all the world—well, as if he were as much in the swim as anybody else. . . .
>
> (315)

The "silver stream of impunity" recalls the putative "revelation" scene of book 11, and like that scene it invokes the association of water with Madame de Vionnet's sexuality, recontained now within the "stern" morality of Woollett as "impunity" or not "paying." In "sternness alone now wouldn't be sinister," the reflection that precedes the "silver stream" passage, James reiterates the connection of Madame de Vionnet to the "sinister" life of metropolitan Parisian femininity, opposing it not to the aristocratic past but to Woollett.

As evening approaches, the day turns "to heat and eventual thunder" and Strether reflects that "there had been times when he believed himself touching bottom. This was a deeper depth than any . . . by evening his irresponsibility, his impunity, his luxury, had become . . . immense" (316). Engulfed in dangerous and, finally, climactically erotic water imagery—no icebergs or "ancient and cold chambers of the past" here—Strether arrives at Madame de Vionnet's house. While he makes Strether wait for Marie to appear, James allows him to give us a full, explicit, powerful page resituating that house historically. Perhaps as an "effect of the thunder in the air," Strether hears, as he sits in this crucial house, "as if excited and exciting, the vague voice of Paris" (317) itself. This is the "voice" produced by the "vibration," now connected to thunder, of the "vast strange life of the town." "Strange" as in "rich and strange"; "vast" as in Plotinian figuration of the chaotic matter of the mother's body; "vibration," "voice" and "thunder" as in the pre-Oedipal echo Plato hears in his womb-cave, the repressed/returning, unsilenceable presymbolic voice of the maternal origin.[25]

After admitting that the aristocratic seclusion of Madame de Vionnet's Faubourg St. Germain is penetrated by the "vague voice of Paris," the Jamesian narrator makes an even more remarkable admission:

> Strether had all along been subject to sudden gusts of fancy in connexion with such matters as these [the "vague voice of Paris"]—odd starts of the historic sense, suppositions and divinations with no warrant but their intensity. Thus and so, on the eve of the great recorded dates, the days and nights of revolution, the sounds had come in, the omens, the beginnings broken out. They were the smell of revolution, the smell of the public temper—or perhaps simply the smell of blood.
>
> (317)[26]

The sound of the mother's voice becomes the smell of her body, bloody from menstruation and childbirth as from the revolution with which her body is figurally associated.[27] Madame de Vionnet, freed from the passive silence of aristocratic patrilinear seclusion, her house penetrated by this "excited and exciting" noise, now becomes not Madame de Staël but "Madame Roland on the scaffold" (317). That personification is a perfect figure of modernism's irresolvable ambivalence toward revolution, invoking at once, appropriately in the figure of a nonvirginal woman dressed in white (Madame de

Vionnet is dressed "in the simplest, coolest white," and Madame Roland dressed in white for her execution), the terror of the Terror ("the scaffold") and also the greatness of Revolutionary ideals (Madame Roland was, as the Norton note helpfully informs us, "a famous intellectual and moderate French revolutionary executed in 1793 during the Reign of Terror . . . her last words were 'O Liberty! What crimes are committed in your name'" [317 n.5]).

James goes on, on the next page, to refer to Madame de Vionnet as "something old, old, old, the oldest thing he [Strether] had ever personally touched" (318), linking her again to the maternal origin that is suppressed and repressed in patriarchal culture.[28] He then uses imagery to describe her that recalls his famous characterization of Paris as "all surface one moment . . . all depth the next" (64), an image used there to describe a "jewel brilliant and hard," but equally applicable to water and clearly referring to water here. Strether sees her as "a mild, *deep* person, whereas he had had on the occasion to which their interview was a direct reference a person committed to movement and *surface* and abounding in them" (318, italics added). Madame de Vionnet *is* modernist Paris: the "metropolitan feminine." Again, James makes clear in this sequence the conflation, at the heart of this novel and of modernism, of formal indeterminacy (undecidability of surface and depth), of the sexuate maternal feminine figured as water, of democratic revolution, and of metropolitan modernity.

The partial, distorted reading of Madame de Vionnet's (house's) historical provenance that dominates the novel is not overtly corrected until book 12, but cracks in this misreading appear at various points in the novel, through which both the empowered maternal and also the ethnic fluidity of urban modernity signal fleetingly but distinctly to the reader. Marie (Mary) de Vionnet's embodiment at once as Paris and as the sexuate mother, precisely the embodiment that changes Strether but that he must refuse to acknowledge, is suggested in her identification in book 7, chapter 1 with Notre Dame de Paris.[29] The other Mary, Maria Gostrey, as less threatening double and also avatar of Marie de Vionnet, embodies the same figuration. The two Marys were childhood friends; Maria quite literally leads Strether to Marie and then "covers for" her. Once Marie emerges, Maria fades, her light, at first much stronger than any Strether had seen heretofore, eclipsed. Maria Gostrey's apartment is also an avatar of Marie's house, but it is not, at least at first, less threatening: because Maria herself is so much more manageable, James can use her apartment to represent some of the referents that cannot yet emerge in relation to Marie.

James's description of Maria's apartment, on Strether's first visit there in book 3, chapter 2, is for him remarkably direct. In it, he makes very clear his linkage of consumerist metropolitan modernity with the maternal origin, the womb-cave of Plato's parable. The two features of Maria's apartment that James both emphasizes and links are its "accumulations" (80) of bought objects and its resemblance to a cave:

> wide as his glimpse had lately become of the empire of "things," what was before him still enlarged it; the lust of the eyes and the pride of life had indeed thus their temple. It was the innermost nook of the shrine—as brown as a pirate's cave. In the brownness were glints of gold; patches of purple were in the gloom; objects all that caught, through the muslin, with their high rarity, the light of the low windows. Nothing was clear about them but that they were precious, . . . The circle in which they [Strether and Maria] stood together was warm with life. . . .
>
> (80)

I quote this passage at length because I want to make clear the aura of the "rich and strange" that permeates this description of Maria's brown womb-tomb, her numinous cave-shrine of the empire of things, warm with erotic maternal life.

A different sort of preview of the final unveiling in book 12 comes in the preface to the dialogue between Strether and Little Bilham in Gloriani's garden, in book 5, chapter 1, that James cites as the precis of his central theme. Appropriately, this sequence also introduces Madame de Vionnet to Strether and to the reader. James's description of Gloriani's house and garden explicitly foreshadows our first view of Madame de Vionnet's house:

> a small pavilion, clear-faced and sequestered, an effect of polished parquet, of fine white panel and spare sallow gilt, of decoration delicate and rare, in the heart of the Faubourg Saint-Germain and on the edge of a cluster of gardens attached to old noble houses. Far back from streets and unsuspected by crowds, reached by a long passage and a quiet court, . . . grave *hôtels* stood off for privacy, spoke of survival, transmission, association, a strong indifferent persistent order. . . . Strether had presently the sense of a great convent. . . .
>
> (119)

The content and even some of the language in this passage are repeated almost verbatim in the first description of Madame de Vionnet's house. But here, the paean to aristocratic tradition and noble seclusion from "crowds" is interspersed with a different element entirely, a different note, as James might say: metropolitan modernist Paris itself, precisely what the narrator insists Gloriani and his *monde* escape.

Immediately preceding the above description of Gloriani's house and garden as aristocratic haven comes a description of his guests—"the people before him [Strether], in whose liberty to be as they were he was aware

that he positively rejoiced. His fellow guests were multiplying, and these things, their liberty, their intensity, their variety . . . were in fusion in the admirable medium of the scene" (119). "These things" may be "in fusion" in James's "scene," but they are in opposition to his description of the setting.[30] In fact, James uses to describe the guests almost the same language that Williams uses in his description of metropolitan modernity: Williams invokes "the new kind of open, complex and mobile society" ("Metropolitan Perceptions" 45), the "complexity and . . . sophistication of social relations, supplemented in the most important cases—Paris, above all—by exceptional liberties of expression" (44); "the vitality, the variety, the liberating diversity and mobility of the city" (43). Further, the "quiet court" set "far back from the street and unsuspected by crowds" has the effect of giving Strether, "more than anything yet, the note of the range of the immeasurable town" (*AM* 119).

This "range" includes, as Williams emphasizes, a modernist diversity of ethnic and national origin, a diversity that James emphasizes in Little Bilham's account of Gloriani's entourage and that Strether evidently finds intriguing. What to Strether are "types tremendously alien, alien to Woollett" (121) are to Little Bilham "all sorts and sizes. . . . There are always artists . . . ambassadors, cabinet ministers, bankers, generals . . . even Jews" (122). When Strether asks whether there are "'any Poles'" among the "'*femmes du monde*,'" Bilham replies "'I think I make out a "Portuguee." But I've seen Turks'" (122). Madame de Vionnet's English seems to Strether "like a precaution against her passing for a Pole. There were precautions, he seemed indeed to see, only when there were really dangers" (127-28). Maria describes Marie in her schoolgirl incarnation as "polyglot as a little Jewess (which she wasn't, oh no!)" (138). And in our final encounter with Marie, after her flood has turned to tears, she even incorporates into Jamesian feminine metropolitan modernity a representation of the working class, appearing to Strether "as vulgarly troubled, in very truth, as a maidservant crying for her young man" (323).[31] For James, as for Williams, the freedom, diversity, mobility and immeasurable range of metropolitan modernity are in dialectic most importantly with the provincialism James calls Woollett.[32]

III

> There it stands, accordingly, full in the tideway; driven in, with hard taps, like some strong stake for the noose of a cable, the swirl of the current roundabout it.
>
> (preface to *AM* 2)

James's repudiation and recontainment of Marie de Vionnet's empowered maternal flood as tears, in the scene that opened this essay, signals and represents his closing repudiation and recontainment of modernist Paris. "Walking on water" is at once a feat of miraculous communion and also an act of evasion and control. As the perfectly, irreducibly ambiguous figure "walking on water" indicates, Marie de Vionnet both gives Strether everything and becomes everything he must renounce. Both his enlightenment and his renunciation take place "on her back": in walking on water he walks on her.

The Alvin Langdon Coburn photograph that James used as the frontispiece for the first volume of *The Ambassadors* in the New York Edition, the photograph on the front of the Norton Critical Edition, entitled by James *By Notre Dame,* provides a powerful visual emblem to reinforce the verbal figure of "walking on water" (fig. 1).³³ It is a photograph of a bridge over the Seine, with characteristic Parisian houses ethereal in the bright light along the top of the composition, one and a half arches of the bridge darkly, stolidly dominating the center, and the lower third to half of the composition the Seine itself, comprised mostly of the dark shadows cast by the undersides of the arches. The overall effect is of enormous, dark, watery holes, the flowing, maternal underbelly of Paris, spanned by the man-made structure that at once embraces and transcends it, with the very top of the photo suggesting that transcendence. James's title *By Notre Dame* reinforces its connection to the sexuate maternal feminine and therefore to Marie de Vionnet as what I have argued is the metropolitan feminine.³⁴

"The Future of the Novel," written in 1899 and therefore almost contemporaneous with *The Ambassadors,* provides a useful conclusory paradigm for this essay. James begins on a censorious, retrograde note, using the flood metaphor to figure the democratic reading masses in very negative terms:

> The flood [of fiction] at present swells and swells, threatening the whole field of letters, as would often seem, with submersion. It . . . directly marches with the rapid increase of the multitude able to possess itself in one way and another of the *book.* . . . There is an immense public, if public be the name, inarticulate, but abysmally absorbent. . . . The diffusion of the rudiments, the multiplication of common schools, has had more and more the effect of making readers of women and of the very young . . . the ladies and children—by whom I mean, in other words, the reader irreflective and uncritical.

(AC [The Art of Criticism] 242-45)

With "abysmally absorbent" we return to the "walking on water" passage that marks the conversion of Marie de Vionnet from flood to tears. This is the James whose Strether must renounce Paris/Marie, the modernist as misogynist, anti-democratic elitist, a by now wearyingly familiar figure.

As James thinks about the "elasticity" of fiction, however, the way "it moves in a luxurious independence of rules and restrictions" *(AC* 246), the necessity of "ex-

periments" for its continued vitality (247), and "the immense variety of life" fiction must represent, that "will stretch away to right and to left" (247), his tone and political stance shift markedly from the right to the left. The essay ends on a note diametrically opposite to that of its opening:

> It would be curious—really a great comedy—if the renewal [of fiction] were to spring just from the satiety of the very readers for whom the sacrifices [to propriety] have hitherto been supposed to be made [i.e., to "the ladies"]. It bears on this that as nothing is more salient in English life today, to fresh eyes, than the revolution taking place in the position and outlook of women—and taking place much more deeply in the quiet than even the noise on the surface demonstrates—so we may very well yet see the female elbow itself, kept in increasing activity by the play of the pen, smash with final resonance the window all this time most superstitiously closed.

(AC 250)

This passage gives us surface and depth, as in water, Paris and Marie de Vionnet; the female elbow simultaneously pushing the pen and smashing the window, like the excited and exciting, strange, fierce, sinister, acute, dreadful needle-pointed public pen of the Parisian women in the *Postes et Télégraphes.* **"The Future of the Novel"** encompasses precisely the same irreducible ambiguity that governs *The Ambassadors,* produced by the irresolvable ambivalence of early modernism toward the egalitarian politics of the metropolitan feminine. In **"The Future of the Novel,"** as in *The Ambassadors,* we go down to the water but we come up dry.

Notes

1. Strether also represents to Little Bilham the great thing he (Strether) has missed in life, in the pivotal scene in Gloriani's garden, book 5, chapter 2, by means of flood imagery: "'Better early than late!' This note indeed the next thing overflowed for Strether into a quiet stream of demonstration that as soon as he had let himself go he felt as the real relief. It had consciously gathered to a head, but the reservoir had filled sooner than he knew, and his companion's touch was to make the waters spread" (131).

2. Isabel Archer's momentary immersion in the flood of erotic possibility at the end of *PL* [The Portrait of a Lady], as she considers embracing Goodwood, is recontained as her tears in a remarkably similar sequence—see *Rich and Strange,* 12-14.

3. This assertion has not always appeared self-evident. In the high new critical phase of James criticism represented by the 1964 first edition of the Norton Critical Edition of *The Ambassadors,* Rosenbaum indicates that James's revisions of the novel for serial publication, omitting some scenes

between Strether and Chad, created the impression, erroneous according to Rosenbaum, "that Strether's relationship with Mme. de Vionnet is more basic to the novel than his relationship with Chad" ("Editions and Revisions" 357). Without the father-son relationship at its center, the novel loses significance for Rosenbaum. The son displaces the sexuate mother in masculinist New Criticism, but in James's novel, the conflation of Paris with Madame de Vionnet is evident throughout. Chad himself notifies Strether and the reader of this conflation in book 4, chapter 1, when in response to Strether's interrogation about his involvement with a woman, he says "'Don't you know how I like Paris itself?'" (100).

4. For an extended analysis of water imagery as site of the eruption of an empowered sexuate maternal femininity in modernism, see *Rich and Strange.* For previous work on water imagery in *AM,* linking Strether's close association with images of floating to his centerlessness and to his ambiguous gender identity, see Wise and Abbott, respectively.

5. This reading of the novel's ending, hardly original with me, is nonetheless at odds with James's statement in "Project of Novel" that Strether "has come so far through his total little experience that he has come out on the other side . . . so quite other that, in comparison, marrying Miss Gostrey would be almost of the old order. Yes, he goes back other—and to other things" (*PN* ["Project of Novel by Henry James."] 403). However, within the ellipsis in the above quote is a contradictory remark: "He must go back as he came—or rather, really, so quite other. . . ." In light of this contradiction and of the fact that "Project" was written before the novel and therefore quite possibly was revised by it, and also by way of "trusting the tale," I persist in the tradition of seeing Strether as renouncing Paris at the end: "Not, out of the whole affair, to have got anything for myself" (*AM* 344).

6. See Rivkin for a deconstructive analysis of the trope of the ambassador in this novel.

7. See for example "The Meaning of Paris in *The Ambassadors*: A Disagreement" (*AM* 438-42).

8. I employ the awkward term "sexuate," often used in translations of French feminist theorists, because the connotations of "sexual" would be somewhat misleading. "Sexuate" is intended to convey a pervasive condition, a defining characteristic, rather than an activity or one attribute of many.

9. "Reduced to about two hundred fifty examples from the foreign section, the collection [from the 1913 Armory Show] then moved on to Boston, where it was shown at Copley Hall. . . . Boston was never really aroused. The show was neither a financial nor a publicity success. Other cities clamored for it . . . but the instigators . . . decided, in the words of Walt Kuhn, to 'chop it off in Boston'" (Brown 166-67).

10. In *Rich and Strange,* I use "old text" to designate the constellation of narrative forms and the social possibilities they represented that preceded the emergence of modernism at the turn of the century.

11. For a different reading of Chad's interest in advertising, aligning him with Woollett's capitalist barbarism over against Madame de Vionnet's European high culture, see Greenslade.

12. For example: "It is not only the continuity, it is also the diversity of these themes, composing as they do so much of the repertory of modern art, which should now be emphasized. Although Modernism can be clearly identified as a distinctive movement . . . it is also strongly characterized by its internal diversity of methods and emphases: a restless and often directly competitive sequence of innovations and experiments, always more immediately recognized by what they are breaking from than by what, in any simple way, they are breaking towards" (43). Using the terms "modern art" and "Modernism" here, Williams clearly also encompasses the avant-garde.

13. For a different but not entirely incompatible theoretical framework in terms of which to understand this founding binary, see the discussion of American literature as a "post-colonial" formation defining itself against the cultural institutions of "the metropolitan centre" in Ashcroft (2). This framework highlights the ambiguity of James's self-positioning in relation to Parisian metropolitan modernity as "the vast bright Babylon" (64), and Woollett as locus classicus of provincialism.

14. Bowlby discusses the *flâneur* in works by Huart, Baudelaire, and Proust.

15. On Strether's feminized masculinity, see for example, Abbott and Silverman.

16. For an account of London as urban modernity in the feminist modernism of Virginia Woolf, see Squier.

17. Walkowitz discusses this ambiguity in "Going Public." Walkowitz cites the "representational codes of the era [the 1870s-80s] that continued to polarize womanhood into two categories, of the fallen and the virtuous. But we might also say that these opposing categories were always ambiguous, and that they demanded a regulatory force of observers to police the boundaries" (8).

18. See Walkowitz, *City of Dreadful Delight,* "Shopping Ladies," 46-50, in chapter 2: "Contested Terrain: New Social Actors," 41-80.

19. Breaches of this feminine positioning in nineteenth-century fiction by women occur as marked demonstrations of a protagonist's unusual independence. Two instances that come most immediately to mind are Elizabeth Bennet's solitary, muddy excursion on foot through the fields to visit Jane at Bingham's house and Jane Eyre's lonely sojourn after running away from Thornfield. In both cases, of course, this exceptional independence is recontained by its morally sanctioned purpose.

20. See Posnock for a fascinating discussion of the role of balconies in *AM.*

21. James also has Maria Gostrey refer to the Burlington Arcade as a synecdoche for London, Strether's training camp for Paris, in this scene. Benjamin of course aligns the emergence of modernist Paris with the emergence of consumer capitalism.

22. I am indebted to Marcia Ian for calling my attention to this passage.

23. I am aware that this reading reverses the standard alignment of Europe with reactionary aristocracy and America with egalitarian democracy. The patterns of this complex text are multiple and over-determined.

24. "Nevertheless [despite fears of regicide], the major controversial issue raised by the centennial was not monarchy but democracy. . . . France had finally chosen to be a republic and a democracy in the 1870s. Its rulers had deliberately chosen to define themselves as the heirs of the Revolution . . . Jacobinism was the touchy part of the Revolution and, in 1889, Jacobinism meant democracy" (Hobsbawm 70-71).

25. The echo from within the womb-cave in Plato's parable of the cave constitutes a crucial element of Irigaray's analysis of the repressed/returning maternal origin in patriarchal representation, in *Speculum of the Other Woman,* "Plato's Hystera," 263-65.

26. See also Posnock on this material.

27. I discuss this chain of associations in *Rich and Strange.* See also Paulson and Theweleit for comparable discussions of these figural associations.

28. This is the central argument of Irigaray's *Speculum.*

29. Mary as the prime figure in Western culture of the simultaneous representation and repression (desexualization) of the sexuate maternal feminine has been crucial to both Irigaray and Kristeva. See for example Irigaray, *Je, Tu, Nous,* and Kristeva, "Stabat Mater."

30. This contradiction in fact follows the form of Williams's definition of "residual, dominant and emergent" cultural formations, where the residual aristocratic formation co-exists alongside the still-emergent modes of democracy. See Williams, *Marxism and Literature.* For a complementary discussion of the layering or sedimentation of urban space, where older spatial-social-political forms and more recent developments interpenetrate, see Lefebvre.

31. James used a similar figure for the protagonist of *TS* [The Turn of the Screw] in order to emphasize her inferior class position. See *Rich and Strange* 38-63.

32. As James says in the preface, Paris represents "more things than had been dreamt of in the philosophy of Woollett" (8).

33. For a discussion of James's use of these photographs, see "Editions and Revisions" (*AM* 365-66).

34. James indicates suggestively, in his preface to *The Golden Bowl,* that these photographic images should be "optical symbols or echoes, expressions of no particular thing in the text, but only of the type or idea of this or that thing" (*AC* 380).

Works by Henry James

AC: *The Art of Criticism.* Ed. William Veeder and Susan M. Griffin. Chicago: U of Chicago P, 1986.

AM: *The Ambassadors.* 1903. Introd. S. P. Rosenbaum. New York: Norton, 1964.

PL: *The Portrait of a Lady.* 1881. New York: Signet, 1963.

PN: "Project of Novel by Henry James." *The Ambassadors.* New York: Norton, 1964. 375-404.

TS: *The Turn of the Screw.* 1898. *The Turn of the Screw and Other Stories.* Harmondsworth: Penguin, 1969. 7-121.

WD: *The Wings of the Dove.* 1902. Harmondsworth: Penguin, 1965.

Other Works Cited

Abbott, Reginald. "The Incredible Floating Man: Henry James's Lambert Strether." *Henry James Review* 11 (1990): 176-88.

Anderson, Perry. "Modernity and Revolution." *New Left Review* 144 (March-April 1984): 96-113.

Ashcroft, Bill, Gareth Griffiths, and Helen Tiffin, eds. *The Empire Writes Back.* London: Routledge, 1989.

Benjamin, Walter. "Paris, Capital of the Nineteenth Century." *Reflections.* Ed. Peter Demetz. New York: Schocken, 1978. 146-62.

Bowlby, Rachel. "Walking, Women and Writing." *Still Crazy After All These Years.* London: Routledge, 1992. 1-33.

Brown, Milton W. "The Armory Show and Its Aftermath." *1915: The Cultural Moment.* Ed. Adele Heller and Lois Rudnick. New Brunswick: Rutgers UP, 1991. 164-84.

DeKoven, Marianne. *Rich and Strange: Gender, History, Modernism.* Princeton: Princeton UP, 1991.

Greenslade, William. "The Power of Advertising: Chad Newsome and the Meaning of Paris in *The Ambassadors.*" *ELH* 49 (1982): 99-122.

Hobsbawm, E. J. *Echoes of the Marseillaise.* New Brunswick: Rutgers UP, 1990.

Irigaray, Luce. *Speculum of the Other Woman.* Trans. Gillian C. Gill. Ithaca: Cornell UP, 1985.

———. *Je, Tu, Nous: Toward a Culture of Difference.* Trans. Alison Martin. New York: Routledge, 1993.

Kristeva, Julia. "Stabat Mater." *The Kristeva Reader.* Ed. Toril Moi. New York: Columbia UP, 1986. 160-86.

Lefebvre, Henri. *The Production of Space.* Trans. Donald Nicholson-Smith. Oxford: Blackwell, 1991.

Paulson, Ronald. *Representations of Revolution (1789-1820).* New Haven: Yale UP, 1983.

Posnock, Ross. "Going to Smash: Violence in *The Ambassadors.*" *The Trials of Curiosity: Henry James, William James and the Challenge of Modernity.* New York: Oxford UP, 1991. 221-49.

Rivkin, Julie. "The Logic of Delegation in *The Ambassadors.*" *PMLA* 101 (1986): 819-31.

Silverman, Kaja. "Too Early/Too Late: Male Subjectivity and the Primal Scene." *Male Subjectivity at the Margins.* London: Routledge, 1992. 157-81.

Squier, Susan. *Virginia Woolf and London: The Sexual Politics of the City.* Chapel Hill: U of North Carolina P, 1985.

Theweleit, Klaus. *Women, Floods, Bodies, History.* Vol. 1 of *Male Fantasies.* Minneapolis: U of Minnesota P, 1987.

Walkowitz, Judith. *City of Dreadful Delight.* Chicago: U of Chicago P, 1992.

———. "Going Public: Shopping, Streetwalking, and Sexual Harassment in Victorian London's West End." Unpublished essay, 1993.

Williams, Raymond. *Marxism and Literature.* Oxford: Oxford UP, 1977.

———. "Metropolitan Perceptions and the Emergence of Modernism." *The Politics of Modernism.* London: Verso, 1989. 37-48.

Wise, James N. "The Floating World of Lambert Strether." *Arlington Quarterly* 2 (1969): 80-110.

Collin Meissner (essay date spring 1997)

SOURCE: Meissner, Collin. "Lambert Strether and Negativity of Experience." *Studies in the Novel* 29, no. 1 (spring 1997): 40-60.

[*In the following essay, Meissner focuses on the process of "permutation," as reflected in the character of Strether, as a guiding principle in* The Ambassadors. *James intentionally develops the concept, the critic argues, to construct "a more clear picture of the whole process of understanding as it functions in James's hermeneutics."*]

> "And then the justice,
> In fair round belly with good capon lined,
> With eyes severe and beard of formal cut,
> Full of wise saws and modern instances,
> And so he plays his part."

[1]

The conclusion of James's outline for **The Ambassadors** raises a difficult question for students of James's fiction. The outline calls for a final conversation between Maria Gostrey and Lambert Strether in which Strether is given "a clear vision of his opportunity" with Maria.[2] In the final text James remains faithful to this last attempt at connection between the pair. The interesting question comes in James's reason for Strether's refusal of Maria's offer of marriage. James explains how Strether "*can't* accept," how he "won't," or "doesn't," that it's "too late," for such an intimate partnership at this stage of his life. These are reasons we can understand given our insight into Strether at the conclusion of all that has happened. But James goes on to explain how Strether "has come so far through his total experience that he has come out on the other side—on the other side, even, of a union with Miss Gostrey" (p. 390). The question here is what does it mean to pass so through an experience that you come out on the other side, that you emerge into a world completely altered? Into what world, that is, does Strether emerge? To reason through James's suggestion is to confront the whole notion of experience and understanding not only in **The Ambassadors,** but in all of James's projects up to this late novel.

The difficulty of making sense of **The Ambassadors**'s end, particularly Strether's refusal to ground himself in Maria Gostrey, is doubly compounded, first by the permutations of Strether's subjectivity throughout the course of his Parisian experience, and second, by the ambiguity of the novel's closing comment—"'Then there we are!'"[3] Readers have long wondered where "we are" points to, for Strether and Maria Gostrey as much as for themselves. To ask this question, one James purposely plants at the novel's close, is to ask about the basic structure of understanding as it functions in James's hermeneutics.[4] In a persuasive and insightful deconstructive reading of *The Ambassadors,* Julie Rivkin, employing what Derrida refers to as "'the logic of supplementarity,'" argues rather forcefully that what I refer to as the permutations of Strether's subjectivity are "supplementations," a manifestation of the "logic of delegation" which governs the entire novel's narrative structure; in Rivkin's words, a "principle" of "displacement . . . compensating for sacrifices by creating a chain of ambassadors" beginning with James, moving through the Preface, embodied in the text, and made manifest in the "plurality dictated by the text's own logic of delegation—not *The Ambassador* but, rather, *The Ambassadors.*"[5] The outcome of Rivkin's analysis is to show that what Strether discovers "as he replaces one truth about experience with another is that there is no stopping point in this logic of revision" (["The Logic of Delegation in *The Ambassadors*"] p. 828). But in focusing on supplementarity, Rivkin deconstructs all notions of self in the novel and leaves Strether without *any* ground on which to come to understand the personal and public impact of his Parisian experience in so far as it assists in the development of his conception of self as permeable.[6] And one wonders here whether an argument that focuses on a deconstruction of the self in *The Ambassadors* retraces the ground Strether has already deconstructed over the course of his Parisian experience? After all, isn't the goal for James and Strether not to get rid of or to "supplement" the self, but to make that self porous? To this extent *The Ambassadors* can be read as a text that tries to relocate rather than get rid of the self, and this includes a relocation outside deconstruction.

Furthermore, Rivkin's reading of the novel not only intensifies the ambiguity of Strether's final "'Then there we are!'" because just as it leaves Strether stuck, looking for yet another possible supplementary authority, it also leaves the reader out of the interpretive equation, in that all too typical role of passive spectator only too willing to watch but not be engaged in (Strether's) interpretive adventure. And while Rivkin rightly accords the concept of revision a crucial place in James's aesthetics, particularly revision of self, her deconstructive "supplementarity" is based more on a principle of replacement than revision, on resignation and passive observation than active participation. To this extent Rivkin sees Strether as continually displacing himself, continually living vicariously through the experiences of others as opposed to coming to understand and revise himself

through the collective body of his personal and observed experiences. The difference here between Rivkin's "supplementarity" and what I call Strether's "permutations" is crucial because it suggests, in Rivkin's argument, that all Strether can ever come to understand of himself comes through "an infinite chain, ineluctably multiplying the supplementary mediations" that stand between Strether and himself (Derrida, qtd. in Rivkin, p. 819). "Permutations," on the other hand, suggest Strether is consistently and actively revising and expanding *his* conception of self and is more in keeping with James's own remarks about understanding from his Preface to *The American* where he says "The real represents to my perception the things we cannot possibly *not* know, sooner or later, in one way or another."[7] If we substitute "self" for "real" in James's formulation, a substitution James's fiction encourages, then reading Strether's developing sense of self and his conception of what has happened and is happening both in Paris and in Woollett as a series of permutations allows us perhaps a more clear picture of the whole process of understanding as it functions in James's hermeneutics.

In dramatizing how Strether works through the competing versions of his subjectivity—his potential-filled youth, his cowed present self, his possible future—to arrive at his eventual rebirth, James reveals several pitfalls associated with all hermeneutic projects, the most misleading, perhaps, being the unconscious interpretive projection upon a yet to be encountered reality. The most obvious and well-documented example in *The Ambassadors* is Mrs. Newsome's projected and imposed interpretation of Madame de Vionnet. But Lambert Strether too is guilty of a creative projection that leads him to misread his situation as much as Mrs. Newsome does hers. More specifically, Strether is guilty of a double projection, the second of which builds upon the exploded image of the first. Strether is guilty first of projecting an image of Chad Newsome as a vulgar youth who has fallen into the clutches of a base and venal woman. When this turns out not to be the case, Strether immediately overcompensates by making Chad an idealized image of his own youthful and morally circumspect self. Both interpretive projections, as we shall see, debilitate Strether's capacity for understanding, and, in doing so, underscore James's artistic concerns with what he saw as the limitations of imposing any ready-made form of mediation upon what is strange.

That James objected strongly to the easy reliance on conventions of understanding has been the focus of a number of studies which deal with James from the perspective of various phenomenologies. The most fully developed phenomenological reading of James comes in Paul Armstrong's *Phenomenology of Henry James* (1983), which examines Jamesian consciousness and morality by way of phenomenologists such as Husserl,

Heidegger, Merleau-Ponty, and Ingarden among others. In addition to Armstrong's extensive analysis, Michael Wutz's "The Word and the Self in The Ambassadors" (1991) makes a strong case for reading "Strether's vision . . . as a phenomenological perception of the world, as an intending consciousness engaged in the act of apprehension."[8] Wutz offers a powerful analysis of Strether's developing understanding that language is not "the simple medium of truth but an artful instrument to make himself and others believe what is not true" (p. 97). As Wutz argues, in coming to realize that the "world is what it is only through the imprint of the word" Strether is brought to a point of awareness in which he is finally able first to "question his quasi-Puritan literality, with its simple equation of sign and thing," and then to throw over Mrs. Newsome's proscriptive restrictions and embrace the freedom his Parisian experience finally makes available to his changed consciousness (p. 97). Both Armstrong and Wutz employ phenomenological readings to substantiate the "deeply ethical impulse" that informs James's work (Wutz, p. 100). As Armstrong shows, where James "argues that the morality and truth of a novel depend at bottom on how the artist knows the world, so phenomenology finds that morality and truth in general can claim no other foundation than lived experience."[9] In pointing out how "ethics depends on experience" in James, Armstrong shows how James challenges the "conventional certainties about knowledge and human activities" and exposes Woollett-like conventions as "socially codified ways of interpreting the world and relating to others" (p. 5). James's fiction directly challenges individuals like Mrs. Newsome, *The American*'s Madame de Bellegarde, or *The Turn of the Screw*'s Mrs. Costello who profess objective standards of ethical behavior while actually hiding behind "culturally contingent customs that organize experience along particular lines and that owe their existence to the agreement of the community to practice them" (Armstrong [*The Phenomenology of Henry James*], p. 5).

It is just this question of codified ways of knowing and culturally contingent ways of being and understanding James puts under scrutiny in *The Ambassadors.* And while the phenomenologists Armstrong marshals in his study shed various types of light on the cultural and ethical contingencies one finds in James, the problem of how one begins to interpret, how one comes to understand what it is to understand not just oneself, but a text, another person, or a culture in James, is worth a few more words. Since Armstrong's study follows a more purely phenomenological path he omits Hans-Georg Gadamer's hermeneutical branch of phenomenology. And while Gadamer comes out of the phenomenological tradition, namely that of Schleiermacher, Dilthey, Husserl, Heidegger, and Wittgenstein, Gadamer sees understanding as less an act of transcendental consciousness, as does Husserl, and more as an event in which we come to understand not so much the text or person or thing before us, but how we stand in relation to it and to our immediate historical situation. As Gerald Bruns has argued, Gadamer sees "the task of hermeneutics" as an effort "to clarify situations of this sort."[10] For Gadamer, understanding presupposes belonging to a tradition and is always of a subject matter. Gadamer continually forces us to ask what light a text throws on what matters to us. In addition, understanding always entails application; it cannot be the solitary act of a disengaged ego because understanding a text entails understanding the claim it has upon you. According to Gadamer's hermeneutics, one is always exposed to the text one seeks to understand and understanding itself always takes the form of action. In the context of *The Ambassadors,* one thinks here of Strether's final understanding of the relationship between Chad and Madame de Vionnet. The applicability of Gadamer's hermeneutics, his analysis of hermeneutical situations and how one comes to understand them is thus directly relevant to the hermeneutic struggle Strether experiences in *The Ambassadors.* For while Husserl's phenomenology can help explain the larger social texts which determine meaning in Woollett and, to some extent in Paris, Gadamer's hermeneutics is much more able to capture the subtleties behind the epistemological crises that not only Strether, but the reader too experiences through the course of *The Ambassadors.* And by clarifying how we come to understand the subtleties of James's text, Gadamer enables us to better appreciate the vital and actively engaged quality of Jamesian aesthetics.

Gadamer's analysis of how foreconceptions and projections operate in understanding is helpful in coming to understand the hermeneutic trap Strether lays for himself. In examining Heidegger's description of how understanding inevitably takes place in a hermeneutic circle, Gadamer refers to Heidegger's insistence that "what we call 'Throwness' belongs together with that which is projected."[11] To summarize briefly, this means that our being "thrown," in Heidegger's sense of the word, means accepting and understanding the limits of the "ground" we've been "thrown" upon.[12] The "ground" includes all the conditions of our existence, all that has gone into the construction of our consciousness and character, all that we know of ourselves, and all that operates below the level of what can be directly known. In short, Heidegger's "throwness" means being always already situated in regard to external phenomena. Strether's "throwness" involves the whole nature of relations with Woollett, his status as Mrs. Newsome's factotum, and his awareness of his youthful desires. Both Heidegger and Gadamer show how one's "throwness" or, in Gadamer's language, one's foreconceptions and prejudices can have a contaminating effect on interpretation. As Gadamer explains, "All correct interpretation must be on guard against arbitrary fancies and the limitations imposed by imperceptible habits of thought . . .

which originate in [the interpreter] himself" (*TM* [*Truth and Method*], p. 236). Gadamer's point here is important in relation to Strether and to the reader of James's texts. For Gadamer, "A person," let's say Strether or a reader of *The Ambassadors*, "who is trying to understand a text," let's say Chad, or Madame de Vionnet, or *The Ambassadors*, "is always performing an act of projection." The reader always projects forward, extending meaning "as soon as some initial meaning emerges," which allows him to revise his earlier expectation (*TM,* p. 236). This, of course, is what it is to be open to the possibilities of the text.

If I can stick with Gadamer a few moments longer his assistance in our understanding of Strether and *The Ambassadors* will become evident. Throughout his analysis of understanding Gadamer repeatedly warns that the possibility of true understanding can occur only when the interpreting subject is aware of "the tyranny of hidden prejudices" which invariably prevent the text (or other person) from "assert[ing] its own truth against one's own fore-meanings" (*TM,* pp. 239, 238). The only requirement, Gadamer explains, is our remaining "open to the meaning of the other person or of the text" (*TM,* p. 238). This, to be sure, runs exactly contrary to Woollett's understanding of interpretation. James depicts Mrs. Newsome as an advocate of the narrowly realistic tradition he believed limiting to fiction because it is the product of a covert ideology that purports to present a real picture of life while secretly confining that life within a closed system. For James, as for Gadamer, the failure of hermeneutics occurs when the interpreting subject refuses to acknowledge the requirements of revision so as to modify understanding in light of newly-acquired knowledge. An individual—Mrs. Newsome as Realist author—who remains essentially sealed off from life seeks to extend control over the world by confining what James understood to be an ever-evolving and fluid reality within a method of perception based on a strict management of reality.[13]

It's interesting to note how often commentators identify Mrs. Newsome with philosophical positions, especially those positions that claim to possess a surefire method for understanding and behavior. Ross Posnock, for instance, has cited Mrs. Newsome's "implacable rationality" as an indication of her "Cartesian method."[14] As a New Englander of her time Mrs. Newsome strikes one as an example of the Puritan internalization of the Law both Henry James—Sr. and Jr.—held with a good deal of impatience and skepticism. Henry James Jr.'s complaint about Puritan rigor such as Mrs. Newsome's was centered on his conception that individuals such as the Woollett doyenne draw their absolutes and certitudes from within and carry out their own self-serving positions through a self-ratifying spiritual authority. Both descriptions—Mrs. Newsome as the embodiment of a strict interpretive methodology or Puritan zeal—are par-

ticularly apt, for Mrs. Newsome leaves nothing to chance, refuses to accept the possibility that the individual has anything less than absolute control over her own moral agency.[15]

Indeed, without exception, each of Mrs. Newsome's acts—from wanting to bring Chad home, to choosing an Ambassador who will act her agent in Paris, to redeploying an alternate in Sarah Pocock, to severing relations with Strether—is an attempt to extend control over her world. James's characterization of Mrs. Newsome as "all cold thought," as an agent who operates via an understanding that simply "doesn't admit surprises," sets her in direct opposition to James's understanding of art and life (22:220). To be sure, Mrs. Newsome's closure is indicative of what Gadamer would say is a refusal to acknowledge the claim upon one that experience makes. To be able to "work the whole thing out in advance" suggests Mrs. Newsome deals with knowledge as though it were a quantifiable thing with which she's filled to the brim (22:222). And this is exactly how Mrs. Newsome approaches the world, not just as though reality were a finite quantity one could contain, but that mastery depends upon containment, depends, that is, on eliminating life itself. Strether's final realized picture of Mrs. Newsome is thus galvanic. Despite his multiple and fluid descriptions of Chad, of Madame de Vionnet, of Paris, he is unable to penetrate Mrs. Newsome's interpretive fortifications: "I haven't touched her. She won't *be* touched. I see it now as I've never done; and she hangs together with a perfection of her own . . . that does suggest a kind of wrong in *any* change in her composition" (22:222). For Mrs. Newsome, one has a certain number of experiences that matter and then understanding of "the world" comes into sharp focus. Life, like the ideology of realism James found such a masquerade, is itself a process of strict control, of stasis.

A final word from Gadamer brings the point home, especially if we think of someone like Sarah Pocock's interpretation of Madame de Vionnet, and, as I will show, Strether's interpretation of Chad.

> If a person is trying to understand something, he will not be able to rely from the start on his own chance previous ideas, missing as logically and stubbornly as possible the actual meaning of the text until the latter becomes so persistently audible that it breaks through the imagined understanding of it. Rather, a person trying to understand a text is prepared for it to tell him something.
>
> (*TM,* p. 238)

Sarah, of course has been commissioned by Mrs. Newsome to find Chad and Madame de Vionnet exactly as Woollett had originally projected—a wayward son caught in the web of a base and venal woman. Woollett, to paraphrase Gadamer, is not prepared to be told anything else. And that's exactly the response Strether meets with when he pleads Madame de Vionnet's case with Sarah Pocock. When Strether says, "She has struck me from the first as wonderful. I've been thinking too moreover that, after all, she would probably have represented even for yourself something new and rather good." Sarah's response is as quick as it is predictable. Woollett doesn't need anything new: "a 'revelation'—to *me*: I've come to such a woman for a revelation?" (22:202). Ironically, Sarah's refusal to be open to the possibility of newness here reminds us of Strether's reference to Mrs. Newsome's "perfection" of "composition"; in both cases what James underscores is the essential closedness of these interpretive subjects (22:222). In James's larger hermeneutic explorations, Sarah's and Mrs. Newsome's closed-mindedness is analogous to the narrowly-realist and often lifeless fiction he felt constrained art within coercive or forced limits. As his fiction repeatedly shows, James waged a constant struggle against subjectivities such as Sarah's and her mother's for the sake of his readers and his belief in art's living qualities. In James's critique, petty orthodoxies would impose a static form upon what he saw as a fluid and ever-modulating reality. The Sarah Pococks, Mrs. Newsomes, and Gilbert Osmonds of the world gain their power over others by taking away any medium in which understanding can take place. What James shows in *The Ambassadors* and throughout his career is how works of art and ways of interpreting that mirror Sarah's and Mrs. Newsome's conceptual horizon are actually a denial of life, and should be seen as a denial of interpretation, since such rigid formulations undermine what James saw as the protean and destabilizing power of mimesis.

Each of these interpretive projections, then, is an example, in varying degrees, of the hermeneutic circle. James uses this process to show how interpretation is always already influenced by one's expectations. He suggests throughout his novels that one's expectations invariably lead to a moment of destabilizing bewilderment in which what was anticipated turns out to be altogether other, and that all attempts to fix reality, to make it conform to a pre-established picture, lead one to accept the counterfeit for the real thing, or the shadow for the substance. To this extent, James's hermeneutics anticipates Gadamer's own understanding of the hermeneutic circle. Gadamer thinks of the hermeneutic circle not so much as an interpretive procedure, but as a way of describing the rationality of everyday life, where understanding as a mode of being requires openness and flexibility precisely because the singularity and unpredictability of experience necessitates that our judgements be in a process of constant revision. James too, as we have seen, understood that flexibility and openness are part of this quotidian rationality. James's attention to *how* his characters understand as much as *what* they understand adds another dimension to his texts in

that the reading subject is invariably drawn into the text and led to examine along with the perceiving character the whole process of understanding. While the character projects hypotheses in an attempt to grasp the whole of reality, the reader is carried along and invariably led to participate through either questioning the character's hypotheses or by projecting his or her own. This dynamic of living forward and understanding backward characterizes all of James's late style and lends itself particularly well to analysis from a phenomenological perspective. Edward Casey makes a point about the "specifically phenomenological method" that lends insight to the nature of James's narrative method I'm describing. Phenomenology, Casey explains, "places special stress on firsthand or direct description thereby minimizing recourse to . . . highly mediated constructions . . . What is sought in the implementation of such a method is an accurate description of a given phenomenon *as it presents itself to one's own experience,* not an explanation of its genesis through reference to antecedent causal factors." Thus, what the reader discovers as **The Ambassadors** unfolds and Strether's understanding of things is increasingly called into question is the degree to which he or she is authorially involved in constructing expectations of Chad, of Madame de Vionnet, of Strether, and of James, expectations based on what has been presented, and what we assume or project to be the case. In this way James's late narrative refinements foreground the extent to which what we already believe or what we want to be the case shapes our understanding of what is.[16]

Reading James's narrative experiment through Gadamer's understanding of foreconceptions and prejudice allows us to get to the bottom of James's own hermeneutics. By explaining the degree to which understanding always involves an interpretive crisis and demands an ongoing conceptual reconstruction, Gadamer offers a way of reading that succeeds in elevating the typical James text, such as **The Ambassadors,** to a fully live and active work of art. As such, the Jamesian text's fundamental openness can be finally expressed. Such a text, James realized, demands a reader's participation, but rewards that effort by allowing the reading subject to carry over into the world the aesthetic experience not as an escapist abstraction, but as a meaningful event that has an immediate and direct application to reality as measured in the reader's expanded and active understanding. In Gadamer's formulation this means allowing the text to open itself before the reader and "begin to speak." Only then, explains Gadamer, as though commenting on a text like **The Ambassadors,** can understanding begin, for to "understand a text is to come to understand oneself in a kind of dialogue."[17] Thus, James's narrative strategy in texts like **The Ambassadors** is to diminish authorial power so as to liberate the reader's mind. The benefits of such a liberation extend beyond the boundaries of literature itself. Rather than accepting passively the author's version of things, the reader finds James's texts a place where active minds meet and change. To understand Jamesian hermeneutics along these lines is to see how James's aesthetics work towards giving art an active voice that demands an enlightened engagement from its audience. Sadly, it is perhaps because of this demanded and threatening requirement that so many readers find James so easy to avoid or so easy to misunderstand.

James accentuates the tension between imposition, adaptation, and revision in his hermeneutics by having Strether's interpretive categories come under pressure the moment he disembarks in Europe. This interpretive crisis becomes critical for Strether when Woollett's absolutist interpretation of Chad is shattered by the appearance of what to Strether is someone altogether other than the anticipated Chad Newsome. When the metamorphosed Chad thwarts Strether's ability to know by imposition, Strether experiences a hermeneutical crisis, and responds by falling back on yet another preconception. As his critical skills, his ability to respond perceptively to the situation, abandon him, Strether fills his gap in understanding with an already produced image. The rapidity with which Strether moves from a mild contempt for Chad to aesthetic enchantment with him catches the reader by surprise. The shift in Strether's perception is partially "represented by the fact that Chad had been made over" (21:150). However, it's not just that Chad has been made over by others; Strether himself completes the make over when he ascribes to Chad his own moral uprightness. James makes the reader aware of this transference when he has Strether answer the question "whom should I enjoy being like" with the following sudden recognition: "It was the click of a spring-he saw the truth . . . 'Oh, Chad!'—it was that rare youth he should have enjoyed being 'like'" (21:220). The result of Strether's transference is crucial for it is what disables him from taking the true measure of Chad and Madame de Vionnet and forces not just Strether, but the reader into yet another hermeneutic circle. That is, when Strether overwrites Chad's identity with the fantasized image of his own youthful self he effectually removes the original Chad Newsome from his interpretive horizon and takes away any ground on which understanding can take place for the reader as much as for Strether.

The consequences of this transference are far-reaching for everyone involved in *The Ambassadors,* reader included. Once Strether grants to Chad his own moral character, he can't help but see the relationship as "virtuous." Strether becomes like a character in a play who actually believes the roles all the other players are inhabiting to be their real identities. And since his is the center of consciousness through which all experiences are mediated, everyone and everything involved is artificially ennobled. And this is exactly what happens. Af-

ter all, Strether's elevated belief in the people involved doesn't just condition his understanding of them, it also influences their understanding of themselves, a point brought into sharp focus when Marie de Vionnet breaks down into uncontrollable sobs during her final conversation with Strether (22:285-86). For despite their additional qualities, Chad is a womanizer, Madame de Vionnet an adulteress, and Little Bilham a liar. Maria Gostrey calls Strether's attention to his power over reality when she remarks that "you dressed up even the virtue" of it all (22:300). How readers make their way through the elements of fancy and reality in Strether's experience is directly proportional to their ability to understand Strether better than he does himself. That readers become unavoidably caught up in and then suspicious of Strether's ability to understand what's going on testifies to the novel's success at inducing an epistemological crisis in its reading audience. James's intended provocation of such a crisis in *The Ambassadors* elevates the text to the status of a practical hermeneutics and makes readily apparent literature's direct application to reality. In other words, the reader's reaction to Strether's self-coerced understanding is an empirical demonstration of how the James text first refuses to be constrained within a typical reading experience, and second, how that text goes so far as to interrupt and then revise the reader's own interpretive process.

How Strether winds up the only one involved in *The Ambassadors* unable to see the truth about Chad's and Madame de Vionnet's relationship is an interesting study in how easily one can fall victim to what Gadamer calls the tyranny of hidden prejudices. When Strether looks closely at Chad he is own over by the (at least superficial) change. By showing the way Strether constructs reasons for his new conviction, James is able to highlight the degree to which all understanding is necessarily composed and therefore suspect. Strether reasons from Chad's improved appearance that the woman involved must be good, since "the product of her genius" appears so impressive (21:236). Once Strether arrives at his assumption that the affair is virtuous, every experience is filtered through a distorting medium that serves more to corroborate than illuminate his preconceptions. Part of the novel's irony is that the more apparent the affair's adulterous nature becomes for the reader, the more Strether seems determined to believe in its platonic quality. When pressed by Little Bilham, Strether admits to attributing "a very high ideal of conduct" to Chad (21:285). Strether's misperception of Chad dramatizes again the mistake of closing the hermeneutic circle prematurely with a fixed interpretation. The deeper Strether falls into his projected image of Chad, the more impressive Chad appears, and the more impressive Chad becomes for Strether, the more Strether finds him the envied realization of his own youthful desires. Strether makes explicit the transference of his identity in admitting to Maria Gostrey that the couple is his "surrender," his "tribute, to youth," and that they offer him a chance to make "up late for what I didn't have early." As Strether asserts, the "point is they're mine. Yes, they're my youth; since somehow at the right time nothing else ever was" (p. 207). Strether's remark, of course, extends itself beyond the text with the reader's ineluctable query: "what are they to us, and why?"

Once Strether abandons what we could call a hermeneutics of suspicion[18] and allows a mentally produced image to stand between him and a more complete understanding of his experiences, he becomes susceptible to the very modulations of perception James saw as simultaneously wondrous and hazardous. What James dramatizes through Strether's attempt to struggle his way toward understanding is how easy the situation of reality can change with a subtle shift in the perceiver's perspective. Once again James's house of fiction metaphor is an apt explanation of what goes on in life. Since Strether sees Chad as the embodiment of his own youth and Madame de Vionnet as the magnificent artist whose hand has wrought the change in Chad, every action that involves these characters is conditioned within Strether's interpretive paradigm. In demonstrating this mediating process James shows that what things are, what they mean, and how we understand them is often as much a product of the subjective package we carry with us as of any innate or unmediated quality in the thing itself. Strether's interpretation of his encounter with Madame de Vionnet in Notre Dame shows this hermeneutic persuasion at work. As far as Strether is concerned Marie de Vionnet's presence in the church proves the extraordinary nature of her relationship with Chad.

> This attitude fitted admirably into the stand he had taken about her connexion with Chad on the last occasion of his seeing them together. It helped him to stick fast at the point he had then reached; it was there he had resolved that he *would* stick, and at no moment since had it seemed as easy to do so. Unassailably innocent was a relation that could make one of the parties to it so carry herself. If it wasn't innocent why did she haunt the churches?—into which, given the woman he could believe he had made out, she would never have come to flaunt an insolence of guilt. She haunted them for continued help, for strength, for peace-sublime support which, if one were able to look at it so, she found from day to day.
>
> (22:10)

The interrogative dynamic reveals the depth of James's analysis of the circular character of understanding here. Strether makes a question-begging assumption about the nature of the relationship, then posits that Marie de Vionnet's presence in Notre Dame proves the relationship's virtuousness, and finally concludes from his premises that she wouldn't be in the church to begin with were the relationship different from what he thinks.[19]

Though Strether's interpretive wanderings dramatize what both James and Gadamer agree are the pitfalls associated with the attempt to hypothesize about or project meaning upon reality, so too do they make manifest the need to be ever and always open to the possibility of contradiction, perplexity, and the refusal of reality to be confined within an interpretive paradigm. Accordingly, as much as Strether's own mind dupes him with regard to Chad and Madame de Vionnet, so too does it allow him to escape the blind and unforgiving rigor of Woollett's restrictive vision. Throughout his Parisian experience Strether surrenders his imagination, lets it open to the possibilities of Paris. Indeed, Strether's giving his imagination free reign and his misreading of Chad and Marie de Vionnet are complementary, for from the moment he sees Chad as the manifestation of his youth, his free-floating imagination takes care of the rest and enables him, ultimately, to get a much better understanding of the affair than does Sarah Pocock who merely identifies it as a cheap adultery and condemns it accordingly. Martha Nussbaum has characterized this shift in Strether's consciousness as a readiness to surrender, to be passive, to revel in the particularity of life: "a willingness to surrender invulnerability, to take up a posture of agency that is porous and susceptible of influence, is of the highest importance in getting an accurate perception of particular things in the world."[20] Strether's unhesitating acceptance of "particularity," Nussbaum goes on to say, "involves a willingness to be incomplete, to be surprised by the new" (["Perceptive Equilibrium"] p. 71). In this way, Strether's experience of reality, that is to say of other people, and of course of himself, matches the structured dialectic of bewilderment and enlightenment, where one is the condition of the other's possibility. This is how James understood our experience of reality. It might not be too paradoxical to say that the failure of understanding becomes the medium of understanding, but Jamesian hermeneutics comes down to something *like* that. James makes this point repeatedly through the course of his career. For instance, in the Preface to the *Princess Casamassima* James claims it "seems probable that if we were never bewildered there would never be a story to tell about us."[21] Strether's own celebration of life's bewildering multiplicity echoes James's:

> "It isn't playing the game to turn on the uncanny. All one's energy goes to facing it, to tracking it. One wants, confound it, don't you see?" he confessed with a queer face—"one wants to enjoy anything so rare. Call it then life"—he puzzled it out—"call it poor dear old life simply that springs the surprise. Nothing alters the fact that the surprise is paralysing, or at any rate engrossing—all, practically, hang it, that one sees, that one *can* see."
>
> (21:167-68)

Strether's celebration of the uncanny, of course, flies in the face of Woollett's paradigm of interpretive confinement and is precisely what Gadamer means by the hermeneutical experience. For Gadamer such an experience brings about a release from constraints and makes possible a condition of openness. That Strether recognizes "the fact that the surprise is paralysing" but also responsible for his new-found ability to see, parallels exactly Gadamer's sense that the hermeneutical experience involves a break-down of one's conceptual framework and leaves one suddenly naked with respect to the world. But one shouldn't interpret Strether's condition at this stage of his development as James's advocacy of a simple open-mindedness. For James a simplistic *laissez-faire* disengagement is every bit as much a form of mediation as is the rigidity of Sarah Pocock's conceptual apparatus. The former is forever in danger of being overrun and disabled by the latter, a point James makes forcefully when he has Strether's sense of things challenged by Sarah Pocock's narrowly referential realism. Sarah's refusal to see Chad and Madame de Vionnet as Strether does so astonishes the latter that he is led not only to question his ability to understand but to ask about the nature of reality itself. However, there's more at stake in the stand-off between Strether and Sarah than competing modes of vision. James makes a larger point about experience and interpretation in general. Rather than merely privilege the beginnings of Strether's openness, James goes so far as to suggest that openness is the most nearly natural state and that prejudice is a learned behavior that must be unlearned if understanding is to occur at all. James dramatizes this idea through Sarah's experiences in Paris, particularly the development of her "virtuous affair" with Waymarsh. To be sure, Sarah's relationship with Waymarsh is important because through it James suggests the line between virtue and adultery is not so easily drawn, that there are degrees of each. The stand-off between these ambassadors is made more difficult for the reader because both share in the truth, so far as the reader is able to determine. In having the reader want to modify Sarah's judgement and see Chad and Madame de Vionnet as more than adulterers James is able to show how interpretive categories are always insufficient when applied to particular circumstances.

Through the course of **The Ambassadors** everything builds to a final moment of bewilderment: the famous country scene in which Strether feels himself moving about within a Lambinet painting. Nowhere in the novel is Strether more responsible for transfiguring his impressions to suit his mental landscape or more oblivious to the solipsism James exploited in developing his center of consciousness technique, and nowhere in James's fiction (other than, perhaps Isabel Archer's searching night vigil) does James so effectively highlight the epistemological crisis yoked to the hermeneutical experience. The moment of bewilderment occurs when something from outside Strether's framed vision intrudes and transcends his ability, momentarily, to absorb and make

sense of the event. Only when Chad and Marie de Vionnet drift into Strether's picture does Strether realize the full extent of his mistake about the larger reality of their affair (22:256). The sudden explosion of Strether's frame of reference matches exactly James's understanding of reality as an unfixable, ever-expanding horizon, what William James referred to as a "multiverse."[22]

To answer why Strether doesn't recoil at the sudden realization of the affair's adulterous component is to get at the role attunement (what Rivkin calls the "logic of revision") plays in Jamesian hermeneutics (p. 829). To be sure, the recoil is expected by all, including the reader. James makes these concerns apparent through Maria Gostrey's observations of Strether at the time of his disabusement: the "difference for him might not inconceivably be an arrest of his independence and a change in his attitude—in other words, a revulsion in favor of the principles of Woollett. She had really prefigured the possibility of a shock that would send him swinging back to Mrs. Newsome" (22:296). That Strether doesn't retreat to "the principles of Woollett," despite the high personal cost of his break with Mrs. Newsome, explains how far he has moved the other way, towards a celebration of the uncanny. To accept the uncanny is to accept bewilderment as a condition for understanding, to accept reality as a continually enlarging horizon. And in coming to accept and possibly even welcome the possibility of bewilderment as a condition of understanding, Strether learns, as Rivkin has argued, that "experience, the truth of life" which he believed was stable, is more correctly to be understood as "something detached from any fixed ground" and not only "revisable" but even "multiple" (p. 828). This revision of consciousness seems to be James's larger point in **The Ambassadors**. We recall James's remark in his preliminary notes for the novel that the "idea of the tale" centered on "the revolution that takes place in the poor man."[23] Thus, Strether's capacity to respond to the situation, his being able first to assimilate it and then revise his understanding in a way that acknowledges his respect for Madame de Vionnet and his commitment to her relationship with Chad as a good thing shows how much Strether has learned to be open to the probability of bewilderment. The sudden revelation that "the couple thus fixing his attention were intimate" tests Strether's ability to think about adultery in a way inaccessible to his Woollett self (22:278). That he succeeds demonstrates James's idea that understanding and interpretation, if they are to occur at all, demand action.

Strether's epiphany comes not in his realization of the simple truth of the couple's intimacy, nor in his refusal to revert to Woollett's principles, but from his determination of "absolutely preventing" Chad "from so much as thinking of" abandoning Marie de Vionnet (22:311). The reader should not underestimate the remarkable reversal Strether undergoes during the course of his Parisian experience. How Strether responds to Chad and Madame de Vionnet is as much a surprise to himself as to all observing him. Sent on an embassy to force Chad's return to "the general safety of being anchored by [Mrs. Newsome's] strong chain," Strether winds up doing his best to break the chain at the very moment he finds all of Woollett's expectations of baseness verified (21:71). In counseling Chad to remain, Strether deploys the severe moralist's language of Woollett for what can only be seen as the anti-Woollett position and pleads for fidelity within adultery:

> "let me accordingly appeal to you by all you hold sacred . . . You'd not only be, as I say, a brute; . . . you'd be a criminal of the deepest dye . . . You owe her everything—very much more than she can ever owe you. You've in other words duties to her, of the most positive sort; and I don't see what other duties—as the others are presented to you—can be held to go before them."
>
> (22:311-13)

The determination of his insight is crucial for Strether because it's what allows him to begin the active dissociation of his past from his present reality. Rather than live by projection, Strether begins his engagement with life by learning to live through his experiences individually and coming to understand those experiences on their own ground. The degree of Strether's successful transformation can be measured in three phases. First, in his recognition of and subsequent refusal to fall in step with Mrs. Newsome's systematic, fixed hermeneutic. Second, in his rigorous and selfless defense of Madame de Vionnet, especially when he could either remain silent or acquiesce to Sarah Pocock's condemnation of her (22:203-04). And, third, by his final refusal to pass judgement on Madame de Vionnet and Chad, even when he becomes aware of how he has been manipulated into complicity with the pair: "that his intervention had absolutely aided and intensified their intimacy, and that in fine he must accept the consequence of that" (22:278).

But it isn't enough for James to show that Strether has learned to think differently. Understanding in James's hermeneutics always takes the form of action. Strether's revaluation of what it means to be faithful, to be obligated, indeed, to be ethical can be explained by Gadamer's analysis of experience. The experienced person, Gadamer tells us, is not someone who "knows everything and knows better than anyone else," like Mrs. Newsome, but is someone who is

> radically undogmatic; who, because of the many experiences he has had and the knowledge he has drawn from them is particularly well equipped to have new experiences and to learn from them. The dialectic of experience has its own fulfillment not in definitive knowledge, but in that openness to experience that is encouraged by experience itself.
>
> (*TM*, p. 319)

This experienced person is what, for example, Isabel Archer or Lambert Strether come to be. And by experienced I do not mean the more simple notion of worldliness (where experience is the opposite of innocence). Nor do I mean the sense captured by some of James's Europeans who, though worldly, are impervious to experience. These characters are fazed by nothing, nothing reaches them. What I see as more central to James's experiment in *The Ambassadors* (hence my recourse to Gadamer) is the emphasis on how the product of experience is not knowledge but openness. The condition of openness Gadamer talks about is like Aristotle's notion of *phronesis,* where experience leads to a kind of practical wisdom. An experienced person in this sense is responsive, capable of acting in the sense of carrying through in a situation. An experienced person in Gadamer's thinking is someone who is practiced in coping with human situations, living through them, making sense of them, doing what is called for. Strether's actions at the end of *The Ambassadors,* his refusal to align himself with the Pococks or to bend under Mrs. Newsome's pressure reveal his final openness and ability to cope with and make sense of everyone, including himself. Thus, for James (like Gadamer), experience brings an ability to see what a situation calls for, an ability to respond. It is to this extent that *The Ambassadors* can be seen as a *vade mecum* for James's hermeneutics.

James demonstrates how completely Strether meets the requirements of the experienced person in his final conversation with Marie de Vionnet. Fully expecting condemnation, Marie de Vionnet acknowledges how she must appear "[s]elfish and vulgar" to Strether (22:281). However, rather than criticize her, Strether demonstrates his sensitivity to her role in the affair and his understanding not only that the particular often outweighs the "universal," but that ethical values themselves must be fluid if they are to have currency in life. In examining this aspect of Strether's developing understanding of contingency Armstrong argues convincingly that *The Ambassadors* "suggests that the choice of an interpretive attitude is itself an ethical decision" and that as "an international drama, *The Ambassadors* explores how conventions institutionalize ways of being with others. It suggests that there are as many possible forms of personal relations as there are cultural codes" (*Challenge* [*The Challenge of Bewilderment*], pp. 100, 102). Thus, far from categorizing Madame de Vionnet as an adulteress, as Woollett's restrictive paradigm demands, Strether finds her situation much more complex and alive, larger than the simple facts Sarah Pocock throws in his face (22:203-04). Strether completes his ethical and interpretive revolution by offering Madame de Vionnet praise and support: "You've been making, as I've so fully let you know I've felt, . . . the most precious present I've ever seen made" and "[t]here's something I believe I can still do" (22:283, 288).

However, Strether's proposal of aid raises an important question about the conclusion of **The Ambassadors.** James goes to great lengths to reveal the degree of change. But experience, in order to be properly called experience is always disruptive, always takes away something we heretofore had accepted as understood. For instance, Chad's and Madame de Vionnet's intimacy presents Strether with a new and better understanding of their affair, a revelation which then brings about a reassessment of his entire interpretive system. The sea change experience brings is explained as the negativity of experience in Gadamer's hermeneutics. For Gadamer "'experience' in the real sense is always negative."

> If we have an experience of an object, this means that we have not seen the thing correctly hitherto and now know it better. Thus the negativity of experience has a curiously productive meaning.
>
> (*TM*, p. 317)

The immediate comparison, of course, is Strether's experience of the affair. But several others give an indication of how deep Strether's experiences reach and complete they become. He once again revaluates Chad, bringing him back to earth as "none the less only Chad" (22:284), and he finds himself able more fully to understand Mrs. Newsome as impermeable, like "some particularly large iceberg in a cool blue northern sea" (22:223). Strether's metaphor is important as it not only calls attention to the hardness of Mrs. Newsome's understanding, but also how much of her had remained hidden beneath her quiet surface.[24] Maria Gostrey focuses our attention on Strether's more complete understanding of Mrs. Newsome's power when she compares her to a block whose size is difficult to determine: "Little by little it looms up. It has been looming for you more and more till at last you see it all" (22:223). Gostrey's depiction captures exactly James's belief that since the interpreting subject is inside reality, any attempt to grasp the whole of it is thwarted by the limits of the interpreter's perspective. Mrs. Newsome so completely made up what Strether had understood as his reality, his life in Woollett, that only a shift in perspective, a view from the other side of the Atlantic, gave him sufficient distance to see the whole of her influence. Strether's last word on his understanding of the Woollett doyenne is, as he explains to Maria Gostrey, that "'She's the same. She's more than ever the same. But I do what I didn't before—I *see* her'" (22:323).

That experience, its productive negativity as Gadamer describes the process, has consequences in James's hermeneutics becomes apparent at the conclusion of James's novels. Throughout James's work characters move through experiences that ultimately leave them, as in the case of Isabel Archer, "consistently wise" but simultaneously disconnected from the world they had inhabited (**The Portrait** [*The Portrait of a Lady*], 3:145). Christopher Newman ends his European experience ricochetting back and forth between Paris and New York, unable to settle down in either. **The American** closes with Newman left between worlds. Similarly, **The Portrait** ends with Isabel Archer supposedly on a train somewhere between the escape Caspar Goodwood offered and the restraint Osmond demands. The reader never sees her arrive. Hyacinth Robinson, we recall, finds his place in suicide. The point here is that James takes his characters through a series of experiences that refine their consciousness so that they finally approach mirroring his own, but he ends their development there, as though to be responsive in the Jamesian sense means being dissociated from a fixed, localized world and aware that subjective identity is an ongoing project of negotiation between self and others, and between what is inside and what is outside. The parallel between the characters and James is clear, for James too belonged to no particular country or no particular world. Indeed, James celebrated his expatriatism as an example of his cultivated alien and nonidentity posture, as yet another way of breaking down boundaries. In his words: "I aspire to write in such a way that it would be impossible . . . to say whether I am at a given moment an American writing about England or an Englishman writing about America . . . and so far from being ashamed of such an ambiguity I should be exceedingly proud of it, for it would be highly civilized."[25] In **The Ambassadors** Marie de Vionnet calls Strether's attention both to the consequences of his experiences and how they have left him disconnected from his former world. As he leaves her for the last time, supposedly before his return to Woollett, Madame de Vionnet forces Strether to recognize the impossibility of returning to the Woollett he left behind: "'Where *is* your 'home' moreover now—what has become of it? I've made a change in your life, I know I have; I've upset everything in your mind as well; in your sense of—what shall I call it?—all the decencies and possibilities'" (22:282). The question is so important for James's strategy in **The Ambassadors** that twice in the novel's last scene he has Maria Gostrey ask Strether "'To what do you go home?'" (22:325).

The answer to this question has involved readers of James from the moment of **The Ambassadors'** publication. It is perhaps enough to say that Strether goes home to nothing, or that the first step in the direction of Woollett brings about the completion of his life, so far as James was interested in it. Strether, for his part, agrees that the return to Woollett will "amount to the wind-up of his career" (22:294). "Career" here is unmistakably to be read as "life," a connection James establishes by having Strether imagine what the future holds now that he is fully aware of social relations in Paris and his complicity in their development.

He had been great already, as he knew, at postpone-ments; but he had only to get afresh into the rhythm of one to feel its fine attraction. It amused him to say to himself that he might for all the world have been going to die—die resignedly; the scene filled him with so deep a death-bed hush, so melancholy a charm. That meant postponement of everything else—which made so for the quiet lapse of life; and the postponement in especial of the reckoning to come—unless indeed the reckoning to come were to be one and the same thing with extinction.

(22:293)

Extinction is one of the consequences of experience in James's hermeneutics. Extinction in the sense of being unable to inhabit the world one had heretofore known, unable to be the person one had heretofore been. Stre-ther, as James mentions in **The Ambassadors'** **"Project,"** has "come so far through his total little ex-perience that he has come out on the other side." The "other side" here, seems to be the other side of fiction. For one thing that happens at the end of almost all of James's major novels, to characters like Strether, and Isabel Archer, and Maggie Verver, and, interestingly, Christopher Newman, is the characters are no longer containable within any plot or story. This is perhaps why Strether backs away from Maria Gostrey's offer. Resolution of his life is still premature, old as he is. He is no longer a character in a novel. Viewed from this perspective *The Ambassadors'* famous final "'Then there we are!'" can be read as a coda for all of James's work (22:327). "'Then there we are!'" is James's in-junction to readers to carry the dialogue they have been having with the text out into the world at large. "'Then there we are!'" is simultaneously the beginning and the end of a spell, for as the reader puts down the book and adjusts his or her enhanced gaze upon the world it is al-most as though James reaches out and draws back a curtain to reveal a world that has been sufficiently al-tered as a result of the reading experience. For James, art could be no less. For James this was what "the high and helpful . . . civic use of the imagination" amounted to.[26] It is perhaps enough to say that beyond that James didn't care to go.

Notes

1. William Shakespeare, *As You Like It* (2.7.153-57), *The Riverside Shakespeare,* ed. G. Blakemore Evans, et. al. (Boston: Houghton Mifflin, 1974), pp. 369-400.

2. Henry James "Project of Novel," in *The Ambassa-dors,* ed. Leon Edel (Boston: Houghton Mifflin, 1960), pp. 373-91.

3. Henry James, *The Novels and Tales of Henry James,* 26 vols. (New York: Charles Scribner's Sons, 1909), 22:326. Subsequent references will be from this edition and are cited parenthetically by volume and page number in the text.

4. Paul Armstrong addresses this issue and suggests Strether's "last words defy the expectation of clo-sure" since they "both assert and deny the deter-minacy of reality," *The Challenge of Bewilder-ment* (Ithaca: Cornell Univ. Press, 1987), pp. 95-96.

5. Julie Rivkin, "The Logic of Delegation in *The Ambassadors,*" *PMLA* [Proceedings of the Mod-ern Language Association of America] 101 (1986): 822-31, 819-20.

6. Ross Posnock argues that James continually sought to "revise the bounded self of 'bourgeois circumspection'" so as to develop a "permeable self" which he considered "an experimental ven-ture to enlarge the self's range of modalities," *The Trial of Curiosity: Henry James, William James, and the Challenge of Modernity* (New York: Ox-ford Univ. Press, 1991), p. 168. Posnock's remarks about James's notion of a "permeable self," like mine about the roles of revision and permutation, see in *The Ambassadors* a logic of interpretation which offers a counter statement to Rivkin's "del-egation" and "'supplementarity.'" And while I find myself in agreement with much that Rivkin says of Strether's experience, I end up with a com-pletely different sense of Strether's self and a con-ception of James's hermeneutics which Rivkin's "logic" would qualify considerably.

7. Henry James, "Preface" to *The American* in *Henry James: Literary Criticism,* ed. Leon Edel (New York: New American Library, 1984), 2:1053-1069, 1062-63.

8. Michael Wutz, "The Word and the Self in *The Ambassadors,*" *Style* 25 (1991): 89-103, 89.

9. Paul Armstrong, *The Phenomenology of Henry James* (Chapel Hill: Univ. of North Carolina Press, 1983), p. 5.

10. Gerald Bruns, *Hermeneutics Ancient and Modern* (New Haven: Yale Univ. Press, 1992), p. 9. I am indebted to Gerald Bruns for his assistance in helping me trace Gadamer's phenomenological origins here.

11. Hans-Georg Gadamer, *Truth and Method,* trans. Garret Barden and John Cumming (Crossroads: New York, 1985), p. 232. Cited hereafter as *TM.*

12. See Martin Heidegger, *Being and Time,* trans. John Macquarrie and Edward Robinson (1927; rpt. New York: Harper and Row, 1962), pp. 344-46. I'm in-debted here to Paul Armstrong's discussion of Heidegger's concepts of "thrownness" and "ground." See Armstrong's *The Phenomenology of Henry James* (Chapel Hill: Univ. of North Caro-lina Press, 1983), p. 19.

13. How fully Mrs. Newsome follows a line of strict referentialism, cementing words and referents together in order to impose, as opposed to work towards, understanding has led Julie Rivkin to see the Woollett doyenne as "almost a parody of the absent author" who is determined, through her proscriptive interpretive schema and ambassadorial delegates, to validate and thus universalize her "new England conception of identity as a stable reality" (pp. 824, 29).

14. See Posnock, *The Trial of Curiosity*, p. 225.

15. Posnock sees Mrs. Newsome's rigidity as an implacable attempt to fend off the possibility of difference. In his words, she's "a veritable fortress against difference, surprise, or alteration" (p. 225).

16. Edward Casey, *Imagining: A Phenomenological Study* (Bloomington: Univ. of Indiana Press, 1976), pp. 8-9 (emphasis added). Paul Armstrong sums up the dialectic between the reader's understanding of Strether's experiences and Strether's own in his *Challenge of Bewilderment* (Ithaca: Cornell Univ. Press, 1987). "The reader's challenge," Armstrong explains, "is not only to know Strether's world better than he does by taking fuller, more considered advantage of available clues. James also asks us to understand *how* Strether understands more acutely than he himself can—to develop a more sophisticated self-consciousness about the process of interpretation which his groping quest for knowledge dramatizes than even this extraordinarily reflective character can, given his many pressing involvements" (p. 77).

17. Hans-Georg Gadamer, *Philosophical Hermeneutics,* trans. David E. Linge (Berkeley: Univ. California Press, 1976), p. 57.

18. Paul Ricoeur, *Hermeneutics and the Human Sciences,* ed. and trans. John B. Thompson (Cambridge: Cambridge Univ. Press, 1981), pp. 32-40.

19. In following Strether's and James's logic here I am aligning myself with what Edwin Fussell has referred to as the "Protestant prejudice," which leads Strether to misunderstand Marie de Vionnet's "presence in church," along the following lines: since she is a Catholic "she must be innocent because sinners don't go near churches, they take right hold of themselves and amend their lives," *The Catholic Side of Henry James* (Cambridge: Cambridge Univ. Press, 1993), p. 152.

20. Martha Nussbaum, "Perceptive Equilibrium: Literary Theory and Ethical Theory," in *The Future of Literary Theory,* ed. Ralph Cohen (New York: Routledge, 1989): 58-85, 71.

21. Henry James, "Preface" to *The Princess Casamassima* in *Henry James: Literary Criticism,* vol. 2., ed. Leon Edel (New York: New American Library, 1984), pp. 1086-1102, 1090.

22. William's comment is worth considering for its similarity to Henry's project in *The Ambassadors.* "Visible nature," according to William, "is all plasticity and indifference,—a moral multiverse, as one might call it, not a moral universe," *The Will to Believe and Other Essays in Popular Philosophy* (1897; reprint, New York: Dover, 1956), pp. 43-44.

23. Henry James, *The Notebooks of Henry James,* eds. F. O. Matthiessen and Kenneth B. Murdock (New York: Oxford Univ. Press, 1947), p. 227.

24. Jim Pocock alerts Strether to the deceptive quality of the Newsome women when he first meets Strether in Paris. When Strether notes his surprise to Jim that Sarah didn't show claws, Jim informs Strether that "you don't know her well enough . . . to have noticed that she never gives herself away, any more than her mother ever does . . . They wear their fur smooth side out—the warm side in . . . They don't lash about and shake the cage . . . and it's at feeding-time that they're quietest" (22:86-87).

25. *Henry James Letters,* ed. Leon Edel, 4 vols. (Cambridge: Harvard Univ. Press, 1974-84), 1:142.

26. Henry James, "Preface" to "The Lesson of the Master" in *Henry James: Literary Criticism,* 2:1230.

Phyllis Van Slyck (essay date fall 1997)

SOURCE: Van Slyck, Phyllis. "Knowledge and Representation in *The Ambassadors*: Strether's Discriminating Gaze." *Criticism* 39, no. 4 (fall 1997): 557-79.

[*In the following essay, Van Slyck proposes "a radically new reading of Strether's subjectivity in* The Ambassadors,*" asserting that the character's awareness at the novel's end is not merely one of "renunciation," but the gradual discovery "that the freedom he seeks is not to be found in the illusion of power"—characterized by tropes of masculinity—"but rather in its opposite, in the vulnerable acceptance of fragmentation."*]

The things we see somehow manifest something that transcends both the features disclosed by vision and the consciousness of the one who sees. What there is then are not things first identical with themselves, which would then offer themselves to the seer, nor is there a seer who is first empty and who, afterward, would open himself to them—but something to which we could not be closer than by palpating it with our look, things we could not dream of seeing "all naked" because the gaze itself envelops them, clothes them with its own flesh.

—Maurice Merleau-Ponty[1]

1

In the late James, there is a consistent emphasis on the function, the meaning and the validity of the gaze. As major characters discover that their idealized images of others, even of themselves, are flawed, their fundamental belief in human wholeness, coherence and integrity is challenged. That crucial moment when a character discovers the limitations, the frailty of his vision, is epitomized in the climactic scene of *The Ambassadors* when Strether encounters Chad Newsome and Madame de Vionnet in the French countryside. Maud Ellman argues that in this encounter, Strether discovers, not only his own blindness, but the lack in all vision; that is, he sees not only the illicit relationship between Chad and Madame de Vionnet, but, more importantly, his own failure of vision, his own mortality: ". . . he realizes that his vision all along has masked a lack."[2] If, as Ellman suggests, Strether's awareness parallels that of the viewer who discovers the anamorphic blot, the death's head in Holbein's famous painting, "The Ambassadors,"[3] then Strether experiences important insights into his own subjectivity, insights which suggest a level of understanding not generally attributed to him.[4]

I would like to propose a radically new reading of Strether's subjectivity in *The Ambassadors,* one which challenges critical readings to date and suggests that Strether's journey reflects a tacit but very definite confrontation with the fundamental illusion of the core self. The surface hesitation and uncertainty figured in his language, his gestures, his actions, his reflections, consistently point to an inner struggle in which Strether questions the definition of his identity imposed upon him by his society, in particular by Mrs. Newsome, and begins to explore, on his own terms, the significance of his personal history and the meaning of his subjectivity. As Strether separates from Mrs. newsome, he engages in an act of mourning for his youth which he defines initially as a failure to have acted, to have seized his desire. However, as he follows the trajectory of his desire, initially through an identification with the "masculine" self-representation of Chad Newsome,[5] Strether comes to see the limitations of conventional notions of masculinity. What Strether gradually discovers is that the freedom he seeks is not to be found in the illusion of power characterized by masculine control and repression but rather in its opposite, in the vulnerable acceptance of fragmentation. Thus the whole evolution of Strether's project and his position at the end of the novel documents, much more than a process of renunciation on the part of a bewildered and indecisive

gentleman as he discovers Mrs. Newsome's callous rigidity and Madame de Vionnet's subtle deception. It delineates Strether's painful discovery and gradual acceptance of own incompletion. Strether may be seen, therefore, not as a modern but as a postmodern hero: his seeming passivity, his indecisiveness, his "femininity" challenge conventional masculinity which privileges phallic potency in order to sustain the illusion of wholeness, coherence, and power.[6]

Such a reading of Strether's character grants him a degree of agency, discriminating purpose, and courage which has been obscured by readings which emphasize his passivity and detachment.[7] *The Ambassadors*' highly sensitive hero is most often seen as a representative of his author's subjectivity, reflecting James's preference for a perceptive but detached and protected way of being in the world. Sally Sears notes that "Strether . . . joins the long list of characters in James . . . who achieve their strongest emotional satisfactions by observing the lives of others";[8] Kaja Silverman observes that "The prototypical Jamesian character is the one who, like Lambert Strether, gets nothing for him or herself 'out of the whole affair'—the one who is, moreover, precisely marked by vulnerability,"[9] and Carren Kaston argues that Strether "assume[s] the burden of emotions that do not derive from . . . or serve [his] own interests . . . the result is a kind of absence from both self and world."[10] A number of readings have linked Strether's passivity to the idea that he is essentially "feminine,"[11] and psychoanalytic criticism has contributed to the notion that Strether is a victim of unconscious forces, discerning unresolved oedipal issues in his relationship with Mrs. Newsome, unacknowledged homoerotic feelings in his relationship with Chad Newsome and repressed sexual desire in his relationship with Madame de Vionnet.[12]

This emphasis on Strether's passivity and vulnerability has made it more difficult to observe the consistency and power of Strether's gaze and the philosophical consequences of his discoveries. Strether *is* James's quintessential hero not because he is passive or detached but because he redefines action as a powerful kind of reflective vision[13] which calls into question the very nature and purpose of conventional masculine behavior. His apparent detachment, even his "femininity," is, in fact, a highly vulnerable and self-critical kind of analysis, through which Strether gradually repositions himself. Understanding the particular nature and power of Strether's vision and action requires a repositioning of ourselves as readers. The belief that Strether's subjectivity is less than fully mature, that his detached "feminine" stance is a substitute for a more courageous, "masculine," kind of action and involvement with others,[14] privileges traditional gender codes and fails to account for the profound changes in Strether which the novel explores.

THE AMBASSADORS

A Novel

by

HENRY JAMES

AUTHOR OF "THE AWKWARD AGE" "DAISY MILLER"
"AN INTERNATIONAL EPISODE" ETC.

NEW YORK AND LONDON
HARPER & BROTHERS PUBLISHERS

In the course of his journey Strether attempts to compose a coherent reality through a series of representations; however, these portraits of other characters are consistently undermined, their contents subtly challenged. His representations of Chad, Mrs. Newsome, Maria Gostrey, and Madame de Vionnet all contain a mysterious element which is the key to both the shattering and the ultimate enlargement of Strether's vision. Just as the anamorphic object, the naked skull in the foreground of Holbein's painting, catches the observer in its trap,[15] in each of his representations Strether uncovers a mystery, a "stain,"[16] a blot, something which shatters the coherent image he tries to construct. In composing and examining his portraits of others, Strether apprehends a gaze which looks back at him, forcing him to assess the failure of his own vision and his own coherence. In Lacanian terms, we may say that Strether's representations compel him to "see [himself] seeing [himself]" and this "reflecting reflection . . . reduce[s] the subject . . . to a power of annihilation."[17] In this moment, Strether confronts not only the limitations of perception but the illusion that the self, any self, is whole, coherent, powerful or, even, fully knowable. That is, Strether may be said to experience what Lacan describes as a "decentring from the consciousness of self,"[18] and his consciousness ultimately reflects what postmodernists refer to, after Foucault, as an awareness of "the shattered self."[19]

Several critical readings of James's novels explore the idea that his characters engage in creative constructions of self and other, and some of these readings suggest that such activities raise questions about the nature of subjectivity. Most argue, however, that James's fiction dramatizes the difficulties and moral dangers of such creative seeing, implicitly defending an essentialist notion of self. Leo Bersani maintains that for James's characters, "fictional invention . . . constitutes the self,"[20] and he argues that the later novels "dramatize the difficulties of living by improvisation."[21] Don Anderson maintains that *The Ambassadors* comments extensively on the nature of aesthetic form, and that one aspect of the self-reflexive character of the novel is the emphasis placed on Strether's "framing, shaping and structuring" of his experience; however, he believes that James's point is to demonstrate the dangers, for moral insight, of those activities.[22] Susan Griffin claims that "Jamesian seeing [is] an active interested struggle both to create and to preserve the self,"[23] Julie Rivkin notes that, initially, Strether "still thinks of penetrating facades, touching at the bottom and arriving at the 'truth,'"[24] and Priscilla Walton maintains that Strether "desires coherence [but] does not yet realize that it is unattainable."[25] Except for Walton's and Rivkin's, these readings do not explore the challenge to essentialism implicit in Strether's approach to knowledge, and none interprets Strether's insights as offering a challenge to the belief in a core or essential self.[26] Strether's representations raise fundamental questions about how one can know another subject; however, the moral and epistemological dangers of this enterprise lie not in the uncontrollability of perception but in believing that such control is necessary or desirable. In fact, one of the most explicit themes of *The Ambassadors* concerns the dangers of believing in such control, as Strether's growing knowledge of Mrs. Newsome's limitations suggests. *The Ambassadors* traces a revolution in Strether's consciousness as he gradually rejects the false objectivity which governs Mrs. Newsome's perspective and learns to accept a more fragile perspective, associated with Madame de Vionnet, through whom he learns to live with ambiguity.

From the outset, Strether reveals a complex and contradictory, but far from passive, set of intentions. In order to clarify Strether's subtle agency, let us consider what he actually does. He goes on a quest for Mrs. Newsome to retrieve her son; the reward for successful completion of this task will be marriage to Mrs. Newsome. However, instead of moving to complete the task, as requested, Strether, from the moment he arrives in Europe, begins to question the purpose and validity of his mission. Once he encounters Chad and then meets Madame de Vionnet, he becomes extremely active, but not in the conventional masculine sense. Subjecting everything he sees to an acute visual and emotional examination, Strether creates a series of images, a comprehensive visual text, through which he begins to question his relationship with Mrs. Newsome. In allowing himself to be emotionally seduced by Paris and Madame de Vionnet, Strether is fully aware that he is violating the terms of his contract with Mrs. Newsome, and although his ambiguous position causes him much confusion and concern, he persists in his course. Strether then proceeds to reverse Mrs. Newsome's test: just as she has sent him over to fulfill her expectations, through deliberate inaction (he refuses to return home and insists that Chad remain with him), he forces Mrs. Newsome (or, rather, her emissaries) to come to Paris. What Strether wants to find out is whether or not Mrs. Newsome (embodied in her daughter, Sarah Pocock) is spiritually capable of seeing what he has seen, of appreciating Madame de Vionnet. Both Mrs. Newsome and Sarah fail his test just as he has failed theirs. His imposition of this test brings about the end of his relationship with his fiancée, and if he experiences some ambivalence, it is certainly not strong enough for him to swallow his pride and make amends with her. Finally, Strether also faces the "truth" of the relationship between Chad and Madame de Vionnet: he grapples with his own self-blinding desire to see Madame de Vionnet as "pure," and accepts her imperfection and vulnerability without sacrificing his beautiful portrait of her. Thus, Strether is not necessarily as naive or passive as some critics have suggested; his reflective, voyeuristic way of understanding the world is, in fact, extremely active, but it is an approach which reflects a questioning and gradual rejection of masculine resolve and action in favor of a more complex (possibly feminine) understanding of agency and knowledge. Strether's increasing ability to see, imaginatively, creatively, aesthetically, is precisely his most important skill. Far from blinding him, it enables him to glimpse the complexity, the ambiguity and, ultimately, the mystery of others.

When Waymarsh asks Strether, "Then what did you come over for?" and he replies, "Well, I suppose exactly to see for myself—without their aid" (133), James's hero articulates a subtly rebellious intention to separate his own perceptions from those of Mrs. Newsome, suggesting a private purpose clearly at odds with his ostensible mission.[27] In fact, it is his deep sense of loss, of having missed out on something important in life, much more than his mission, which most insistently and poignantly shapes his response to Europe: "There were sequences he had missed and great gaps in the procession: he might have been watching it all recede in a golden cloud of dust" (118). Although he believes that he has somehow failed to assert himself and therefore failed to "live," Strether's quest for experience is undertaken, not through an assertion of "masculine" resolve (though he is aware that this is what his mission and Mrs. Newsome demand) but rather through a consistent rejection of the conventional masculine position. As early as his initial encounter with Maria Gostrey, it is clear that Strether is unable to make even the pretence of adopting a masculine stance. Each effort Maria makes to define and accept Strether in conventionally masculine terms is rejected: when she tells him she likes his name (63), he tells her she won't have heard of it (65); when she observes that he looks as if he is doing something wrong, he admits he is afraid of her. This fundamental vulnerability, which has been seen as a kind of self-emasculation,[28] may instead suggest a tacit questioning of the masculine position Mrs. Newsome has imposed on her emissary. The reunion with Waymarsh which follows his encounter with Maria confirms such a reading, for Strether wishes only to put distance between himself and his friend's repressive and conventionally masculine point of view. Like Mrs. Newsome, Waymarsh asserts complete authority and imposes a single coherent interpretation, a set of judgments about Europe and its inhabitants with little reference to external facts. Waymarsh's gruff and judgmental resistance to "the ordeal of Europe" (71), his rigid moralism, mirrors Strether's own future: utter compliance with a predetermined code which will deny him the possibility of experiencing life on his own terms.

Observing his companions, Waymarsh, Maria Gostrey, Chad Newsome, Madame de Vionnet and then the Pococks who come to replace him, Strether composes portraits of each of them, only to glimpse something behind the surface image which challenges their coherence. Like the viewer standing before Holbein's painting who sees the naked skull only when his angle of vision shifts, Strether, once he has arrived in Europe, begins to see the rigid preconceptions of his New England counterparts; and, through this "double consciousness," he is partially able to suspend the values which have been imposed on him and to explore alternative ways of seeing which do not privilege masculine control and which do not necessarily lead to a single, coherent, representation of another. In thus identifying the lack in all vision, Strether's visual representations of others point to something Lacan refers to as "an encounter with the real."[29] That is, Strether's images allow him to glimpse, for a brief moment, that unnameable reality which lies outside the symbolic order ("the sphere of culture and language"[30]) and which therefore defines the inadequacy of perception and the limitations of knowledge. And, since each portrait also reflects Strether's own lack, as he projects his own desire for completion onto his subject, it marks a stage in the process of mourning Strether undergoes as he gradually relinquishes his belief in the illusory ideal of masculine power and coherence and redefines himself as a vulnerable desiring subject.

2

"I began to be young, or at least to get the benefit of it, the moment I met you at Chester, and that's what has been taking place ever since."

—*The Ambassadors,* 305

In this matter of the visible, everything is a trap . . .

—Lacan[31]

In Book Second of *The Ambassadors,* when Maria Gostrey comes to dine with Strether at his hotel, she immediately becomes an image of his lost desire: "Miss Gostrey had dined with him . . . face to face over a small table on which the lighted candles had rose-coloured shades; and the rose-coloured shades and the small table and the soft fragrance of the lady . . . were so many touches in he scarce knew what positive high picture" (89). As Strether gazes at the "broad red velvet band" which encircles Maria's neck, the moment is infused with uncertainty, for his masculine identity is decentered: "What . . . had a man, conscious of a man's work in the masculine world to do with red velvet bands?" (90). This image of desire is thus a trap: the red velvet band is the "stain" in the picture, generating in Strether "fresh backward, fresh forward, fresh lateral flights" (90) and challenging the masculine control of Mrs. Newsome and the power of her contrasting and distinctly asexual "ruche" which reminds him of Queen Elizabeth.

Strether recognizes that, in tempting him to enjoy her seductive femininity, Maria challenges him to defy Woollett's definition of appropriate masculine behavior.

But Strether sees something more. In contrasting Mrs. Newsome's repressiveness to Maria's seductiveness, Strether resents the way Mrs. Newsome has denied him an important kind of pleasure: "With Mrs. Newsome, there had been no little confronted dinner, no pink lights, no whiff of vague sweetness . . . one of the results of which was that at present, mildly rueful, but with a sharpish accent, he actually asked himself *why* there hadn't" (90-91). It is, in fact, Woollett's refusal to enjoy life that accounts in part for Strether's own failure. As he gazes at Maria, he suddenly sees himself being seen by her and, reflected in her gaze, is his own nothingness. He recalls "the period of conscious detachment occupying the centre of his life," "the grey middle desert . . ." after the death of his wife and child (91). Strether's poignant reflection initiates the first stage in his act of mourning, for he recognizes the fundamental truth that he himself is not *in* the picture, that he has lived, essentially, on the sidelines, allowing others to dictate the rules. As he turns his gaze inward, Strether discerns that his failure is only partially a result of his literal inaction; it is also based on his unacknowledged acceptance of Woollett's repressive codes.

As the rigid representation of reality as "truth" inscribed by Woollett is juxtaposed to the more complex, ambiguous reality suggested by Paris, the latter offers Strether the space of fantasy and therefore a way in which he can explore alternatives to Woollett's values. From his private dinner with Maria, Strether is transported to the theater where he feels "as if the play itself penetrated him" (92). Noting that "The figures and faces in the stalls were interchangeable with those on the stage" (92), Strether allows himself to enter the world of representation. It is as if he senses that he can take the risk he failed to take in his youth by allowing himself to be duped, by giving up control of his gaze, what Lacan refers to as the laying down of one's gaze.[32] When Chad Newsome silently enters this theater in the midst of the performance, he, too, becomes part of the *tableau vivant*. Instantly, for Strether, Chad is much more than Chad: his "massive young manhood" (166) takes on mythic proportions, and he becomes an "irreducible young pagan" embodying the enviable power and potency of youth. Chad's apparent maturity and confidence challenges Strether, making him feel "like a schoolboy" (155). But Chad's palpable masculine presence, "perhaps enviable," is also "ominous" (166). This encounter with Chad, like the subsequent encounter with the famous artist, Gloriani, forces Strether to confront his ambivalence about his own masculinity. When the sculptor challenges Strether with his gaze, Strether feels exposed, tested, put on trial. Gloriani's powerful gaze, like Chad's "pagan" masculinity, seems literally to penetrate Strether's psyche: it is "a long straight shaft sunk by a personal acuteness that life has seasoned to steel" (200). Yet, gradually, the phallic potency of Chad and Gloriani is called into question: Chad has

an air of "designedly showing himself"; his "palpable presence" is, in effect, a "presentation"; his "sense of power" is "oddly perverted" (169-70), and Gloriani soon betrays "a charming hollow civility on which Strether wouldn't have trusted his own full weight a moment" (250). If Strether is initially seduced, even rendered "feminine," the object of the masculine gaze, as the phallic imagery surrounding Gloriani and Chad suggests, it is also a moment in which Strether glimpses the inherent lack in this phallic stance.[33]

Strether's focus slowly shifts from Chad's sexuality to the fact that Chad is no longer Chad but, seemingly, a different person, a product of the fantasy space of Paris both he and Strether have entered. Chad's transformation fascinates Strether, for, until this moment, he has viewed identity as something given, and this belief has been a source of his hopelessness. The idea of a new, radically different identity begins to undermine Strether's preconceptions—about Chad and about himself. Initially, Strether falls back on an essentialist metaphor to describe Chad's transformation: once "shapeless," Chad has been put into a "firm mould" and "turned successfully out" (167). However, Strether's image raises paradoxical, even contradictory questions about the nature of identity. At what point does the "mould" impose itself? Can one be shattered and then "remoulded"? Does the "mould" alter the surface only or the entire person? If Chad's "mould" can be broken, why can't Strether's?

A closer connection between Chad's altered surface and Strether's own identity is established shortly after their initial encounter when Strether analyzes his own personal history using the same "mould" image in the scene James fondly refers to as the "germ" of his novel. "The affair of life—couldn't, no doubt, have been different for me," he tells Little Bilham, "for it's at the best a tin mould . . . into which, a helpless jelly, one's consciousness, is poured—so that one 'takes' the form . . . and is more or less compactly held by it . . ." (215). On the surface, his insistence on this image suggests that, for Strether, it has always been too late, and the tone of lament that emerges as he contemplates his loss seems to confirm a kind of hopelessness: "There were some things that had to come in time if they were to come at all. If they didn't come in time they were lost forever. It was the general sense of them that had overwhelmed him with its long slow rush" (214). However, through a recognition of his emotions, through a reliving of his loss, Strether reaches a new and vulnerable place. Towards the end of this scene, Strether asks Little Bilham, "But what am I to myself?" (216). In this moment, we may say that Strether's identity is "split"; that is, he recognizes a separation between the one who speaks ("myself") and that which is represented by the speech act ("I").[34] He has begun to recognize that there is always a gap between the "self" (however it is defined) and the various ways that "self" is represented, that the "self" both is and is not its various representations, however they are "moulded." It is clear that Strether's discovery of the "new" Chad has helped him to see that the original "mould" may be broken. Indirectly, Chad has liberated Strether to examine his own identity in a way which holds out the possibility of hope.

As Strether seeks to understand his own personal lack, Chad and Madame de Vionnet become conscious projections of his own desire: "The point is that they're mine. Yes, they're my youth; since somehow at the right time nothing else ever was" (306). Through Chad, Strether enters into a relationship with Madame de Vionnet, and, in her, Strether creates a fantasy object, a substitute for his lack, through whom he vicariously experiences the love he missed in his youth. When Strether meets Madame de Vionnet, he recognizes that he is being tempted, tested, drawn in, invited to relinquish his own controlling gaze. However, what initially distinguishes Madame de Vionnet from Mrs. Newsome is not her sexuality or her capacity to create mystery; it is her ability to reach Strether in a very personal way, to make emotional contact with him. This is something she does silently and, seemingly, without effort. When Strether has his first private meeting with Madame de Vionnet, he finds her "seated, near the fire . . . with her hands clasped in her lap and no movement, in all her person, but the fine prompt play of her deep young face" (238). In terms of Woollett's repressive codes, once again, Strether feels that he is losing touch with reality, and he notes the powerful effect of Madame de Vionnet's personal style: "she had only after all to smile at him ever so gently in order to make him ask himself if he weren't already going crooked" (211).

As Lacan suggests, the artist "invites the person to whom this picture is presented to lay down his gaze there as one lays down one's weapons."[35] Madame de Vionnet is a true artist, and she represents herself in such a way that Strether is emotionally disarmed: "Then it was that he saw how she had decidedly come all the way; and there accompanied it an extraordinary sense of her raising from somewhere below him her beautiful suppliant eyes" (238). Her vulnerability is defined in a portrait in which she is the outsider, rather than Strether: "He might have been perched at his doorstep and she standing in the road. . . . It had been sad of a sudden, with a sadness that was like a cold breath in his face" (238-39). Her isolation is, in this moment, a mirror image of his own, for, like Strether, she seeks to rectify the past, to have the love, intimacy that was denied her in her youth. Although Strether does not know that her personal history and present desire bear a similarity to his own, his gaze has been trapped because he has glimpsed something behind the image which reminds him of himself, a vulnerable incompletion. As Strether's fragmentation finds its reflection in Madame

de Vionnet, she becomes "an all powerful signifier that will make up for the lost object";[36] in this way Strether begins to mourn and come to terms with his own incompletion.

In contrast to the controlling and rigid masculine image of Mrs. Newsome, Madame de Vionnet's power is defined in a complex and elusive image of ambiguity and mystery. Strether is struck by her infinite variety and multiplicity, by her capacity to reshape ordinary experience into something mythical: "Above all she suggested to him the reflection that the *femme du monde*—in these finest developments of the type—was like Cleopatra in the play, indeed various and multifold. She had aspects, characters, days, nights. . . . She was an obscure person, a muffled person one day, and a showy person, an uncovered person the next" (256). However, a "stain" in the portrait makes it impossible for Strether to shape a coherent image. As with Maria's red velvet band and Chad's pagan masculinity, Madame de Vionnet's sexuality (figured in Strether's recognition that she is not only a "goddess still partly engaged in a morning cloud" but also a "sea-nymph waist-high in the summer surge" [256]) is a surface clue, pointing to something deeper, something which renders Strether's gaze inadequate. In the midst of attempting to "render" her, Strether abandons his effort to compose a coherent image: ". . . thanks to one of the short-cuts of genius, she had taken all his categories by surprise" (257). Within a deliberately composed frame, Strether's portrait is all chaos; however, it is a chaos which he embraces because it identifies precisely what is lacking in his relationship with Mrs. Newsome. As Priscilla Walton suggests, Madame de Vionnet "actually personifies the open text"; she "helps Strether to evolve away from a single referential reading toward polyvocal interpretation."[37] Madame de Vionnet's ambiguity evokes in Strether a sense of mystery and delight; however, the part of her which persistently eludes definition also points to the unformed and unnameable "real" which lies behind all symbolic structures. The presence of this mystery undermines the essentialist position that one's own or another's subjectivity can be fully defined.

Strether's commitment to Madame de Vionnet reaches its climax, not when he achieves clarity, for this is impossible, but in the instant when her ambiguity is most irreducible. When he enters the cathedral of Notre Dame one afternoon seeking "a refuge from the obsession of his problem" (271)—that of the choice between Mrs. Newsome and Madame de Vionnet—Strether seems, almost literally, to step outside himself and to see himself in the act of disengaging from Woollett, from the world that insists that he take a clear position and act decisively, that he condemn those who do not fit Woollett's mold. He sees himself as "a plain tired man" seeking refuge from "the hard outer light" (271). Within the cathedral, Strether discerns a mysterious woman whose mood, he senses, matches his own. However, he imagines this woman to be more profoundly at peace than he can ever be: "she had placed herself, as he never did, within the focus of the shrine, and she had lost herself, he could easily see, as he would only have liked to do . . ." (273). Once again, however, something in the picture, subtly undermines the peaceful image Strether has created.

Even before Strether knows that this is Madame de Vionnet, an implicit contradiction challenges the coherence of his portrait: if she seems, on the one hand, "one of the familiar, the intimate, the fortunate," she is neither "prostrate" nor "bowed," but only "strangely fixed" (273). He asks himself, "But what had such a woman come for if she hadn't come to pray?" (273). Shortly after discovering that the mysterious woman is in fact Madame de Vionnet, Strether makes a commitment to believe in her. That is, paradoxically, at the moment he recognizes that his image of Madame de Vionnet is his own construction ("she reminded our friend . . . of some fine firm concentrated heroine of an old story" [273]), he decides that the relationship between Chad and Madame de Vionnet must be pure: "Unassailably innocent was a relation that could make one of the parties to it so carry herself" (276). A shift has occured in Strether's consciousness, from a commitment to "reality" as objectively knowable to a commitment based on personal and subjective choice: it is, in a sense, a contract made between the perceiver and his subject.

Although Strether recognizes that his commitment to Madame de Vionnet will destroy his relationship with Mrs. Newsome, he experiences in this alliance a moment of personal liberation: ". . . he made, under Madame de Vionnet's protection . . . his first personal point" (339). Or, as he tells Sarah, somewhat perversely, "'What has really happened has been that, all the while, I've done what I came out for'" (339). In his refusal to return home at Mrs. Newsome's command or to act decisively in bringing Chad around, Strether forces Woollett to come to Paris, and Woollett's test of his values becomes Strether's test of theirs."[38] When the representatives of Woollett confront the representatives of Paris, Strether can truly assess the distance he has traveled. In the emotional contrasts between Sarah Pocock and Madame de Vionnet, Strether is able to see clearly the source of his complaint against Mrs. Newsome. The two adversaries meet, at Sarah's hotel, in a climactic *tableau vivant,* which Strether observes from the sidelines. The two pairs of gazes, Sarah's and Madame de Vionnet's, challenge each other. As Strether watches Mrs. Newsome's emissary deal with Madame de Vionnet, he sees "something fairly hectic in Sarah's face" (335). Madame de Vionnet, in contrast, strikes him as "prepared infinitely to conciliate." Her eyes are "exquisitely expressive" where Sarah's gaze reveals only "a dry glitter that recalled to him a fine Woollett winter

morning" (339). Sarah speaks "a little piercingly" whereas Madame de Vionnet "breathe[s]" her words "to the air" (340). Repeatedly, the rigid harshness of Sarah is contrasted to the skillful feminine gentleness of Madame de Vionnet. Strether's complaint about Sarah is that she cannot appreciate alterity or ambiguity; in fact, she is morally opposed to it, for it threatens her own coherence and control. What he is waiting for her to see is precisely what is impossible for Sarah or her mother to understand, that one must risk ambiguity and concede control, that the inability to do so is not based on moral rectitude but a cowardly adherence to a single controlling self, and a harsh rejection of the vulnerability and incompletion which Strether has come to share with Madame de Vionnet.

Shortly after this confrontation between Woollett and Paris, Sarah effectively disposes of Strether, letting him know how deeply his admiration for Madame de Vionnet has hurt Mrs. Newsome. In the wake of this rejection, Strether looks squarely at the original sense of loss (the failure of vision and resolve in his life) which has haunted him, and his mourning enters a new phase. As if he has reached the end of his journey, Strether finds himself alone once again in Chad's rooms, where his quest for his own "masculinity" began. In a private moment of reflection which so often marks a dramatic climax for a Jamesian character, Strether brings the empty unformed past into the present, feels it, for the first time, as a palpable thing:

> He felt, strangely, as sad as if he had come for some wrong, and yet as excited as if he had come for some freedom. But the freedom was what was most in the place and the hour; it was the freedom that most brought him round again to the youth of his own that he had long ago missed. He could have explained little enough to-day either why he had missed it or why, after years and years, he should care that he had; the main truth of the actual appeal of everything was none the less that everything represented the substance of his loss, put it within reach, within touch, made it, to a degree it had never been, an affair of the senses. That was what it became for him at this singular time, the youth he had long ago missed, a queer concrete presence, full of mystery, yet full of reality.

> (426)

This is Strether's fullest moment of personal recognition, a poignant awareness of his loss. However, Strether is not simply mourning his failure to *be* the masculine subject Chad represents. Given his astute and reflective scrutiny of his youthful alter ego's perfect yet hollow masculinity ("a smile that pleased exactly in the right degree" [427]) and his powerful recognition that Mrs. Newsome's coherence is also flawed, Strether's apprehension of his own lost youth, his failed masculinity, is really a metaphor for a more universal lack, one which embraces Chad, Mrs. Newsome and even Madame de Vionnet, that of human frailty and incompleteness, and, ultimately, mortality. He has been "brought round again to the youth of his own that he had long ago missed"; in his experience of this loss, Strether completes his act of mourning. We may say then that Strether is now aware of his fragile subject position, of the fact that no one is master of his representations, of himself or of anyone else. The individual is always, literally, outside the picture, that is, outside the world he represents to himself through images. As Lacan observes, "The picture, certainly, is in my eye. But I am not in the picture. That which is light looks at me, and by means of that light in the depths of my eye, something is painted . . . but something that is an impression . . . which is in no way mastered by me."[39] "Individuality is both one's 'true' self and someone else's fiction, thus inherently alien or other."[40] If Strether experiences "the substance of his loss," he also discovers his "freedom": in this moment, he begins to accept his shattered self.

Strether is now able to analyze Sarah Pocock with a new kind of integrity and strength, and a clarity of vision he has not had before. In a conversation with Maria Gostrey, he creates a harsh portrait that explains his rejection of Mrs. Newsome and the values of Woollett. "That's just her difficulty," Strether tells Maria, speaking of Sarah, but, in actuality, invoking Mrs. Newsome, "that she doesn't admit surprises . . . that she's all, as I've called it, fine cold thought. She had, to her own mind, worked the whole thing out in advance, and worked it out for me as well as for herself . . . there's no room left; no margin, as it were, for any alteration" (447). In Sarah's rigidity, Strether sees Mrs. Newsome's controlling masculine essentialism as something which inscribes an emotional and intellectual prison; he sees that, for him, too, there will be no room, no margin for "alteration."[41] When Maria suggests the possibility of modification ("You've got to make over, altogether, the woman herself?"), Strether's reply is almost brutal: "What it comes to . . . is that you've got morally and intellectually to get rid of her" (447). In effect, this is Strether's real (and little noted) moment of active renunciation and growth. In his rejection of Mrs. Newsome, Strether renounces his belief in a single, coherent image of his own life; he no longer wishes to have "the whole thing [worked] out in advance" (447).

Strether continues to assess Mrs. Newsome's rigidity, ("his eyes might have been fixing some particularly large iceberg in a cool blue northern sea . . ." [448]) in a blatant phallic image which stands in stark contrast to Madame de Vionnet's fluid and mysterious subjectivity. The warmth and grace, the sexuality and imagination which characterize Madame de Vionnet are profoundly absent. Strether's comparative portraits of Mrs. Newsome and Madame de Vionnet, his clear rejection of the former and his embrace of the latter, articulate his plea for the possibility of imagination and mystery, with the

recognition that real control, coherence or wholeness is illusory and the effort to sustain that illusion is soul destroying. Mrs. Newsome cannot see beyond her own constructs; she cannot return Strether's gaze. Her absence is emblematic of her blindness, and her blindness is emblematic of her inability to connect, to love. In contrast, Madame de Vionnet, in the end, can do nothing but see; she returns Strether's gaze and reveals herself as a vulnerable subject. It is this same vulnerability which defines Strether's own progress. Through his own willingness to "lay down his gaze," Strether comes to acknowledge the mystery of the other. Not ceding his desire for mystery is also what brings about an understanding of the frailty of the constructed self, the illusion that lies behind all vision and psychological acts of representation.

3

"What more than a vain appearance does the wisest of us know?"

—Little Bilham, *The Ambassadors*, 204

The world is merely the fantasy through which thought sustains itself.

—Lacan[42]

There remains, for Strether, a final confrontation which will enable him to come to terms with his own image-making and his own mortality. Strether's climactic picture, his "Lambinet," in which the values of Boston (where he first saw the Lambinet) and of the French countryside come into open conflict, forces Strether to confront directly the most threatening aspect of the world he has sought to understand through his representations. As the small boat which holds Chad and Madame de Vionnet comes into view, the lady with the parasol turns, and Strether glimpses her face. In the moments leading up to this scene, Strether has recognized that he has been at the height of his composing ("There had been all day at bottom the spell of the picture . . . essentially more than anything else a scene and a stage . . ." [456]). What collapses then is not the "reality"— whatever that may be—but Strether's own image-making process. The frame of Strether's picture breaks open: its contents become chaotic: the boat, so tranquil a moment before "went a little wild" (462); the pink parasol, so perfectly reflecting the controlled center of interest Strether believes he wishes to maintain, exposes for a brief moment and then eclipses Madame de Vionnet. The sublime facade of Strether's ideal love-object is destroyed, exposing not only Madame de Vionnet's deception, but also her frailty, her mortality.

The scene which follows this dramatic tableau explores not only the collapse of Strether's illusion, but the inevitable replacement of that illusion, underscoring the fact that "the real," that which lies behind all image-making, can only be glimpsed briefly before it is lost to the necessary language of representation. In the awkward dinner which Strether, Chad and Madame de Vionnet are forced to share, subsequent to their chance meeting, each of them continues to play the role which has been previously agreed upon. It is now Chad's and Madame de Vionnet's "fiction and fable" which are "inevitably in the air"; it is they who have "something to put a face upon" (465). Their elaborate posturing underscores the necessity of the mask—the arbitrary shape which must be given to identity.[43] The gazes they exchange are opaque; they deny what each actually sees. Yet it is as if the naked skull is present at the table, for Strether now sees another image behind the mask: Madame de Vionnet's performance falters "as if she had asked herself . . . what after all was the use" (466). Strether knows, for the first time, that Chad and Madame de Vionnet have lied to him; they know, for the first time, that he sees their masks. But the masks Strether now sees are the mould he has been struggling to understand from the beginning: they are the shape each individual assumes, the necessary but wholly inadequate language which reflects both the lie and the truth of subjectivity. The real "lie" is the illusion that any real distinction is possible between "true" and "false" representations of the self because that distinction is based on the illusory belief in an essential and knowable core self. The deconstruction of Strether's "Lambinet," the breaking open of the frame of his most important picture, brings about not only a dramatic reversal, but the shattering of his belief in a coherent subjectivity—for Madame de Vionnet—and, ultimately, for himself.[44]

In Strether's private meditation following his return to Paris, he struggles to reconcile the contradictory images of this relationship: "He kept making of it that there had been simply a *lie* in the charming affair" (466); yet he also sees "the deep, deep truth of the intimacy revealed" (468). In the end he recognizes that the "lie" and the "truth" must both be accepted. In his last meeting with Madame de Vionnet, Strether embraces her contradictions in a complex portrait in which her mythic elements have been subdued but not lost: "She was older for him to-night, visibly less exempt from the touch of time . . . he could see her there as vulgarly troubled, in very truth, as a maidservant crying for her young man" (483). The vulnerability Madame de Vionnet evinced during their first private encounter is present again and her trouble has been named; however, for Strether, she has lost neither her mystery nor her beauty: "she was as much as ever the finest and subtlest creature, the happiest apparition, it had been given him, in all his years, to meet . . ." (483).

Why, then, does Strether "abandon" Madame de Vionnet, and how does his position at the end of the novel reflect an acceptance of the shattered, fragmented nature of all subjectivity? Critics have focused on Stre-

ther's consistency as the ambassador who claims to seek nothing for himself, yet the renunciation he professes is not consistent with his emotional stance or his actions throughout the novel.[45] On the contrary, his real mission has been a personal one: that is, despite his disclaimers, he has struggled consistently to discover and to *have* something for himself, at last. As James puts it, ". . . his fingers close, before he has done, round the stem of the fullblown flower . . ." (Preface, 33). Once Strether has separated from Mrs. Newsome, from the phallic mother, he recognizes that he can "toddle alone" (303). And Madame de Vionnet has been Strether's sublime or ideal love object, through whom he has finally confronted his desire. But she is also the fantasy object through whom he has successfully learned to mourn his lost self. Like Hamlet, in learning to mourn, Strether is able to reconstitute his own identity.[46]

In his final portrait of Madame de Vionnet, Strether redefines knowledge—not as rigid certainty—but as trust, based on the exchange of images we create and choose to believe in. If, initially, Strether's decision to see one thing, is, simultaneously, a decision not to see something else, ultimately, in his portrait of Madame de Vionnet, he embraces her contradictions. Perhaps, then, what is most important is precisely what Strether's journey allows him to keep: a kind of truth which is based on this subjective trust: ". . . once more and yet once more, he could trust her. That is he could trust her to make deception right. As she presented things the ugliness—goodness knew why—went out of them" (477). In this moment, Strether understands that all knowledge is a cultural construction and an act of faith.

Madame de Vionnet has shaped Strether's "encounter with the real"[47] his glimpse behind the screen of language, of representation. Moreover, Strether's clear rejection of the controlling stance of Mrs. Newsome is a rejection of an essentialism which privileges a false coherence. As he tells Maria, "I do what I didn't before—I *see* her" (510). Strether's acceptance of the complex identity of Madame de Vionnet has resulted in a profound decentering of Strether's own subjectivity. This decentering, however, is not a failure, a weakness, but a strength, because his belief in the symbolic order (the "vanitas" of Holbein's ambassadors) has been challenged. The question James raises in the preface to the novel ("Is there time for reparation?") has been answered in the affirmative. Strether's dynamic, shifting and ambiguous images have enabled him to redefine his mission and to acquire the courage necessary to confront and accept his own shattered self.

Notes

1. Maurice Merleau-Ponty, *The Visible and the Invisible,* ed. Claude Lefort, trans. Alphonso Lingis (Evanston, IL: Northwestern University Press, 1968), 131.

2. Maud Ellman, "'The Intimate Difference': Power and Representation in *The Ambassadors*," in *Henry James: Fiction as History*, ed. Ian F. A. Bell (London: Vision, 1984), 110.

3. In *Henry James and the Lust of the Eyes* (Baton Rouge and London: Louisiana State University Press, 1993), Tintner identifies this painting as a possible source for both the title and the major themes of James's novel. She notes that James did not title his novel until 1900, after the correct identification of Holbein's subjects (the French ambassadors, Jean de Dinteville and Georges de Selve), and she strengthens the association between Holbein's painting and James's novel in her analysis of the *carpe diem* and *memento mori* themes which are represented in both works: iconographically in Holbein's painting through the anamorphic object (the naked skull) in the foreground and thematically in James's novel (92).

4. Ellman is drawing on Lacan's analysis of Holbein's painting: ". . . the singular object floating in the foreground, which is there . . . in order to catch . . . in its trap, the observer . . . reflects our own nothingness, in the figure of the death's head" (*Four Fundamental Concepts*, ed. Jacques-Alain Millar, trans. Alan Sheridan [New York and London: W. W. Norton, 1977]), 92.

5. "'Oh Chad!'—it was that rare youth he should have enjoyed being 'like,'" (*The Ambassadors* [London: Penguin, 1986], 217). All further citations from James's novel are from this edition and will be noted parenthetically in the text.

6. See Priscilla Walton who argues that *The Ambassadors* "frustrates Realist Masculine searches for singular meaning" (*The Disruption of the Feminine in Henry James* [Toronto: University of Toronto Press, 1992], 103).

7. Susan Griffin notes that two misconceptions can be traced to the beginnings of James criticism: "that observation and experience are opposed in James, and that the Jamesian protagonist is a 'passive observer,' a cerebral, almost bodiless being, completely detached from the world of experience" (*The Historical Eye: The Texture of the Visual in Late James* [Boston: Northeastern University Press, 1991], 396). She cites as the earliest example, Percy Lubbock's 1920 essay, "The Mind of the Artist."

8. Sally Sears, *The Negative Imagination: Form and Perspective in the Novels of Henry James* (Ithaca: Cornell University Press, 1968), 120.

9. Kaja Silverman, *Male Subjectivity at the Margins* (New York and London: Routledge, 1992), 159.

10. Carren Kaston, *Imagination and Desire in the Novels of Henry James* (New Brunswick: Rutgers University Press, 1984), 3.

11. Leslie Fiedler calls Strether "the most maidenly of all James's men" (*Love and Desire in the American Novel* [New York: Stein and Day, 1966], 293); Matthiessen claims that "neither Strether nor his creator escapes a certain soft fussiness" (39), and William R. McNaughton argues that "Strether is not only humiliated but emasculated," (*Henry James: The Later Novels* [Boston: Twayne, 1987], 69). Reginald Abbott offers a psychoanalytic reading of a "floating" Strether immersed in the waters of feminine consciousness," ("The Incredible Floating Man: Henry James's Lambert Strether," *The Henry James Review* 11 [1990]: 178) extending James N. Wise's earlier reading of Strether as "a man floating between two mental reactions without a center of self-knowledge or self-reliance on which to build a foundation for decision," ("The Floating World of Lambert Strether," *Arlington Quarterly* 2 [1969]: 84).

12. Abbott claims that Strether is repeatedly placed in "a feminine context," that from the outset, "gender reversal" characterizes his relations with women. "What Strether finds in Europe . . . is not sexual activity or fulfillment but sexual . . . use at the hands of women. . . . Strether is not a kept man, but his maleness is of use to Mrs. Newsome and Madame de Vionnet . . . as a way to preserve their power" (180). Silverman (158) and Elizabeth Dalton discern evidence of a Freudian "primal scene" in Strether's discovery of the relationship between Chad and Madame de Vionnet ("Recognition and Renunciation in *The Ambassadors*," *Partisan Review* 59 [1992]: 462). For a reading of the homoerotic connection between Chad and Strether, see Georges-Michael Sarotte, *Like a Brother, Like a Lover: Male Homosexuality in the American Novel from Herman Melville to James Baldwin* (New York: Anchor, 1978), 203-11.

13. For readings which emphasize the importance of vision in *The Ambassadors*, see J. A. Ward who maintains that for Strether, "vision is action, it represents a full participation in experience" ("*The Ambassadors*: Strether's Vision of Evil," *Nineteenth Century Fiction* 14 [1959]: 45). Daniel Mark Fogel notes that James's essential premise is "the intrinsic value of the process of vision" (*Henry James and the Structure of the Romantic Imagination* [Baton Rouge: Louisiana State University Press, 1981] 47), and Susan Griffin argues that in James, "visual perception is not detached intellection. . . . Seeing is an active means of adapting to the world" ("The Selfish Eye: Stre-

ther's Principles of Psychology," *American Literature* 56 [1984]: 396).

14. Richard Chase argues that "the general lack of masculine reciprocation, especially in Strether himself, accounts in part for . . . the softness at the center of life . . . in James's novel" (*Twelve Original Essays on Great American Novels,* ed. Charles Shapiro [Detroit: Wayne State University Press, 1958], 136).

15. Lacan, *Concepts,* 92.

16. Lacan defines the "stain" as "that which governs the gaze most secretly and that which always escapes from the grasp of that form of vision that is satisfied with itself in imagining itself as consciousness" (*Concepts,* 74). Madame de Vionnet's ambiguity enables Strether to glimpse this split between what can be known/seen and what consistently escapes his representations.

17. Ibid., 81.

18. Lacan, "The Function and Field of Speech and Language in Psychoanalysis," *Ecrits: A Selection,* trans. Alan Sheridan (New York: Norton, 1977), 80.

19. Foucault attributes this notion to Bataille who "makes us aware of the shattering of the philosophical subject" ("A Preface to Transgression," in *Language, Counter-Memory, Practice: Selected Essays and Interviews,* trans. Donald F. Bouchard and Sherry Simon [Ithaca: Cornell University Press, 1977], 43). Foucault elaborates: "The breakdown of philosophical subjectivity and its dispersion in a language that dispossesses it while multiplying it within the space created by its absence is probably one of the fundamental structures of contemporary thought" (42).

20. Leo Bersani, *A Future for Astyanax: Character and Desire in Literature* (Boston: Little Brown, 1976), 132.

21. Bersani takes the idea of creative composing to an almost anarchic conclusion: "What James asks us to do in his later fiction is to detach the notions of reality and probability from all such external references—which is to say that he would encourage us to believe that our range of experience can be as great as our range of compositional resource" (132). Strether's compositions can be rescued from such relativism/anarchy by looking at the way Strether gradually defines an incomplete subjectivity as a valid basis for personal knowledge.

22. Don Anderson, "Can Strether Step into the Same River Twice? *The Ambassadors* as Meta-Novel," *Sydney Studies in English* 10 (1984-85): 70.

23. Griffin, 18.

24. Julie Rivkin, *False Positions: The Representational Logic of Henry James Fiction* (Stanford: Stanford University Press, 1996), 75; originally published as "The Logic of Delegation in *The Ambassadors,*" *PMLA* 101 (1986): 819-31.

25. Walton, 109.

26. Walton suggests that "Madame de Vionnet actually personifies the open text, which she then helps Strether to interpret plurally. Strether evolves through each woman's tutelage to the point where he, too, ultimately, embraces multiplicity" (105); Rivkin argues that in the course of the novel, "the model of a single explanatory reality behind all appearance is challenged . . ." (76).

27. Several critical readings regard Strether as initially committed to his mission. Sears, for example, describes him as "fully primed with the Woollett concept" (109), undergoing change only after he encounters Chad and Madame de Vionnet. But Strether's mission is psychologically compromised before he meets anyone: in his desire that Waymarsh's countenance not be "the first 'note' of Europe," for example, since Waymarsh is clearly a stand-in for Mrs. Newsome.

28. See Abbott and Wise.

29. Lacan, *Concepts,* 53: ". . . the real emerges as that which is outside language and inassimilable to symbolization" (Dylan Evans, *An Introductory Dictionary of Lacanian Psychoanalysis* [London and New York: Routledge, 1996], 159). According to Lacan "The real . . . stands 'behind' the reality constituted in and by our use of language and only hints at its operative presence in the variety of failures or ruptures or inconsistencies that mark this symbolic reality . . ." ("Television," trans. Denis Hollier, Rosalind Krauss, and Annette Michelson, *October* 40 ([1987]: 10).

30. Ellie Ragland-Sullivan, *Jacques Lacan and the Philosophy of Psychoanalysis* (Urbana and Chicago: University of Illinois Press, 1987), 131.

31. Lacan, *Concepts,* 93.

32. Ibid., 101.

33. Jonathan Lee explains Lacan's analysis of the phallus thus: "The phallus . . . serves to signify that fullness of being, that complete identity, the lack of which is the fact of our ineluctable want of being" (*Jacques Lacan* [Amherst: University of Massachusetts Press, 1990], 67).

34. Lee glosses Lacan's tripartite structure of the human subject: "The Lacanian subject is the uneasy coexistence of three distinct moments. There is, first of all, the real 'presence that is speaking to

you,' the speaking body, the subject of the actual act of enunciation. Secondly, there is the symbolic subject indicated by the *je* of the speaking body's discourse, the subject of the statement actually uttered. The third moment of the subject, distinct from both the speaking body and the *je,* is the imaginary *moi* constructed early in childhood to give the subject an identity that it really lacks" (82). Evans explains the concept of the split subject thus: ". . . the subject can never be anything but divided, split, alienated from himself . . . the split denotes the impossibility of the ideal of a fully present self-consciousness; the subject will never know himself completely . . ." (192).

35. Lacan, *Concepts,* 101.

36. Lee, 118.

37. Walton, 105, 110.

38. F. W. Dupee makes this point in *Henry James* (New York: Sloane, 1951), 241.

39. Lacan, *Concepts,* 96.

40. Ragland-Sullivan, 106.

41. According to Rivkin, Mrs. Newsome is "the absent authority who stands behind all the novel's ambassadors, she sends her delegates off with the express understanding that they alter nothing of that for which they stand in . . . her fixity of purpose makes it impossible for her to imagine any shift or deviation" (67-68).

42. Lacan, "Television," 10.

43. As Lacan notes, "How can one deny that nothing of the world appears to me except in my representations?" (*Concepts,* 81.)

44. Ellman comments extensively on this scene in relation to Lacan: "'There is something whose absence can always be observed in a picture,' hints Lacan. What bursts through the picture frame at last, like the return of the repressed, are the unbidden figures of sexuality" (109). Like Silverman and Elizabeth Dalton ("Recognition and Renunciation in *The Ambassadors, Partisan Review* 59 [1992]: 462), Ellman discerns the site of a primal scene; however, Ellman links this insight to Lacan's more complex notion of the subject's annihilation.

45. See Holland and Matthiessen.

46. See Lacan's discussion of *Hamlet* in "Desire and the Interpretation of Desire in Hamlet" in *Literature and Psychoanalysis,* ed. Shoshana Felman (Baltimore and London: Johns Hopkins University Press, 1977).

47. Lacan, *Concepts,* 53.

Richard A. Hocks (essay date 1997)

SOURCE: Hocks, Richard A. "Multiple Germs, Metaphorical Systems, and Moral Fluctuation in *The Ambassadors.*" In *Enacting History in Henry James: Narrative, Power, and Ethics,* edited by Gert Buelens, pp. 40-60. Cambridge: Cambridge University Press, 1997.

[*In the following essay, Hocks examines an actual incident—in which William Dean Howells declared to a young companion named Jonathan Sturges: "Live. Live all you can: it's a mistake not to"—which James credits as the inspiration for his novel* The Ambassadors. *Hocks looks at James's multiple versions of this "germ speech," their tonal differences, and their effect on an interpretation of the novel. In addition, Hocks studies Strether, the main character of the novel, and his "predicament" of moral ambiguity.*]

A remarkable feature of Henry James's great novel, **The Ambassadors,** is that its genesis and composition bespeak his unprecedented 'ease' and sense of assurance regarding its artistic merit, yet the novel's central 'register' of consciousness, Lambert Strether, the figure who carries all the weight of James's easeful composition and comprises the medium for James's artistic unity, is a character in opposition to those very elements suggested by his creation: burdened with regrets and ambiguity, 'groping' for interpretation, bewildered by his experiences, Strether morally fluctuates in his need 'to be right'. An analogous contradiction is that Strether's ambassadorial power, delegated by Mrs. Newsome, is systematically frittered away so that other ambassadors arrive to replace him, whereas James himself rejoices at his successful delegation of artistic consciousness to Strether, a favourite among his fictional 'deputies'. To see whether this general feature of **The Ambassadors** evokes any sense of difficulty or is merely an erroneous confusion between subject-matter and craftsmanship, it may help to re-enact the essential history of the book's composition and gradually inquire into Strether's predicament.

I. Multiple Germs

One of the better-known cases in American literature of a single generative incident which gave rise to a major novel is the famous 'germ' of **The Ambassadors,** when William Dean Howells stood in a Parisian garden owned by James McNeill Whistler sometime in 1894 and declared to his young thirty-year-old *confrère,* Jonathan Sturges, 'Live. Live all you can: it's a mistake not to.' Rarely has a single genetic source so successfully initiated and eventually pervaded a hefty novel, playing itself out in multiple directions and culminating in what James later called 'frankly, quite the best, "all round", of all my productions' (*LC*-11 [*Literary Criticism*], 1306).[1] Besides its being James's last novel published serially, *The Ambassadors* is also the only James novel with a surviving prose Scenario, sent to Harper's in 1900 and entitled **"Project of Novel"**, a document the novelist himself in a letter to H. G. Wells two years later wrongly believed was destroyed.[2]

It may surprise even readers familiar with this book and some of its vast scholarship to realize that there are probably more than half a dozen extant versions of the 'germ', some before the novel, one within it, and some after it. To be sure, the actual number of versions depends, as such things generally do, on how you count. The *very* first version of the 'germ' speech is, of course, not preserved, because it was related to James by Sturges. But whatever Howells actually said to Sturges in McNeill Whistler's garden was less than what James said in his first entry in his *Notebooks* 18 months later, 31 October 1895: "'Oh, you are young, you are young—be glad of it: be glad of it and *live*. Live all you can: it's a mistake not to. It doesn't so much matter what you do—but live. This place makes it all come over me. I see it now. I haven't done so—and now I'm old. It's too late. It has gone past me—I've lost it. You have time. You are young. Live!'" (*CN [The Complete Notebooks of Henry James]*, 141). James immediately adds, 'I amplify and improve a little—but that was the tone. It touches me—I can see him—I can hear him.' Henry James, I dare say, not only 'hears' Howells, he already begins to reinvent Howells's outburst on the spot; he responds with more than Wordsworthian 'wise passiveness' to the impulse transmitted by Sturges's account the previous evening. By the end of his productive 'self-talk', James has come a surprisingly long way into his 'Howellsian' character and situation, all in the space of roughly 1,400 words; the man is a widower, coming out to retrieve the son of a widow to whom he is engaged to be married; he is fifty-five; he undergoes a total 'volte-face' of his mission; he feels the 'dumb passion of desire' even though 'it's too late, too late *now,* for HIM to live'; he is 'literary almost . . . The Editor of a Magazine . . . not at all of a newspaper.' James even thinks in terms of the tale's burgeoning genre, of his 'deepen[ing] the irony, the tragedy' (*CN,* 141-2).

James initially conceives the ambience of his character's situation to be one of sorrow, of tragedy, and irony. Later he will add more consciously the element of comedy to the novel. To this day, however, all readers and critics alike of *The Ambassadors* have to deal with its beautifully mixed tonal mode. Like *Don Quixote,* which elicits its 'hard' and 'soft' readings, each of which may go in and out of fashion, *The Ambassadors* can modulate from a sort of Freudian 'Mourning and Melancholia' text to a sharp comedy of manners tethered to curiosity, bewilderment, miscalculation, and misinterpretation—somewhat like Molière. James preserves this mixed mode right to the very last lines of the novel itself,

when we read that Maria Gostrey 'sighed it at last, all comically, all tragically, away' (*AB [The Ambassadors]*, II, 327; bk. 12, ch. 5). Her 'sigh', we might well say, started all the way back with his, the man in the garden's, in the earliest versions of the germ. Et in Arcadia Ego.

The third germ comes from James's remarkable **"Project of Novel"**, the 20,000-word Scenario sent in the autumn of 1900 to Harper & Brothers after his agent, James B. Pinker, had first seen it. Partly because of its length and amplitude, James's 'Project of Novel' is an extraordinary piece of writing, at times resembling one of his own nouvelles, at other moments reminding the reader, almost with a jolt, that this 'text' is actually an extended statement to his publisher, yet one which also resembles the procreative self-talk found in the *Notebooks.* Indeed, Martha Banta's observation ten years ago about James's notebooks generally, that they reveal his 'access to the writer's workplace' and the 'principle of rank organicism let loose upon the world', is exemplified to a high degree in the **"Project of Novel"**.[3] Our responding to it as a creative work is salutary, I think, if only to turn our minds away momentarily from the sort of issue we usually attend to, such as Waymarsh's name being 'Waymark' or Little Bilham's being 'Burbage', or such matters as Strether's young son having died in a swimming accident, or that the 'vulgar article of domestic use' produced by Mr Newsome in Hartford or Worcester (not yet Woollett) is 'to be duly specified'—which of course it never was (*CN,* 547). These issues, I say, are momentarily put aside if we attend instead just to the way James conceives and moulds his main character, allows Strether's consciousness to unfold, then punctuates the Scenario with clusters of dialogue between Strether and Gostrey, Strether and Chad, Strether and Marie, simulating in advance and in miniature the picture/scene modulation which is a hallmark of *The Ambassadors* itself. If one has ever spent much time studying James's tales, his **"Project of Novel"**, I would argue, really 'wants to' act like a tale and either cannot quite do it, or else all but does it, depending on your emphasis. James divides the Scenario into a formal prologue followed by three numbered untitled sections of symmetrical length, each corresponding to successive stages in Strether's experience and burdensome discoveries. Such structuring and numbering, together with its spider-like descent into the web of Strether's mind, is what makes the Scenario reminiscent of a Jamesian tale. The one major ingredient missing, however, is his rich imagery, the highly metaphorical language of James in 1900, the same year, for example, that he penned **"The Great Good Place"**, with its abstract language in tandem with highly charged metaphors and conceits. This lack of such imagery—there is hardly any in the Scenario—is mainly what prevents me from suggesting that **"Project of Novel"** is to *The Ambassadors* what the Rembrandt sketch, let us say, is to the major oil canvas. What makes one think of the analogy, however, is the obvious parallel of a major artist doing in effect something like a preliminary sketch.

In this Scenario we actually get two statements of the germ, thus constituting versions three and four in my count. The first and richer of the two comprises the entire prologue, which suggests that, structurally speaking, the prologue stands in relation to the three numbered untitled sections that follow pretty much as does the Scenario itself to the composed novel. In any case, James now formally identifies the episode as 'my starting-point' and 'the germ of my subject'. The incident now is far more delineated than in 1895. First of all, he carefully evokes the Sunday afternoon garden party and meticulously explains the geography and architecture of the 'old houses of the Faubourg St.-Germain', identifying the residence and garden both of McNeill Whistler (here called simply 'a friend of mine') and also a very similar house 'contiguous' with it in which James himself had spent considerable time. This careful preliminary description soon gives rise to a cascade of personal associations and memories analogous to the nostalgic mood and ambience out of which the 'anecdote' of the older 'distinguished and mature' man's lament to the younger man bursts forth. James reads into the Howells figure the pith and precision of his character's emotion, calling it at one point a sense of seductive European charm that—for an American—'was practically as new, as up-to-that-time-unrevealed (as one may say) as it was picturesque and agreeable' (*CN,* 541-2). Gradually he approaches the speech by writing:

> Well, this is what the whole thing, as with a slow rush the sense of it came over him, made him say: 'Oh, *you're* young, you're blessedly young—be glad of it; be glad of it and *live.* Live all you can: it's a mistake not to. It doesn't so much matter what you do—but live. This place and these impressions . . . that I've been receiving and that have had their abundant message, make it all come over me. I see it now. I haven't done so enough before—and now I'm old; I'm, at any rate, too old for what I see. Oh, I *do* see, at least—I see a lot. It's too late. It has gone past me. I've lost it. It couldn't, no doubt, have been different for me—for one's life takes a form and holds one: one lives as one can. But the point is that *you* have time. That's the great thing. You're, as I say, damn you, so luckily, so happily, so hatefully young . . . Don't, at any rate, make *my* mistake. Live!'
>
> (*CN,* 542-3)[4]

James immediately comments, 'I amplify and improve a little, but that was the essence and the tone.' These words, of course, are the identical ones he spoke to himself five years earlier, prompted by Sturges' anecdote. Clearly, each time he 'amplifies and improves a little' his inch turns into a more extended ell and he

guesses still more of the unseen from the seen. In any case, he summarizes the germ-episode and concludes his prologue by referring to the foregoing as the 'dropped seed' from which 'the real magic of the *right* things' was 'to spring' (*CN,* 543). This seems to be a Jamesian template for genesis, composition, and nascent interpretation all together.

There is also a briefer second version of the germ in the Scenario—my number four (or your number three if you wish to designate the actual Sturges conversation with Howells the 'ur-text'). It occurs in Scenario section II, its placement co-ordinating with its mid-point stage in the plot. James refers to the 'very special note . . . alluded to in my few preliminary pages'—i.e. earlier in the prologue (*CN,* 556). He alludes again, too, to '"do"[ing] the occasion and the picture', 'evok[ing] the place and influences', and he also speaks of Strether as our 'fermenting friend', and of the moment charged with 'wonderful intensity . . . a real date' (*CN,* 557).

A number of intriguing issues engage the James critic when he or she puts down this Scenario and thinks about the novel. None of them is really independent of the originating germ because of its extraordinary interconnection with all that occurs in the book it brought forth. Yet one can, surely, distinguish between certain ideas that are more or less emphasized in the Scenario and the novel respectively. For example, James makes a great point of saying he must, and will, 'do' Mrs. Newsome in the novel, though she never directly appears; and all readers agree that is just what he did. On the other hand, he does a superb job of summarizing and specifying all the advantages that Strether stands to lose if he sides with Chad and Marie away from Mrs. Newsome and Sarah Pocock, whereas in the novel itself the particularity of that sacrifice has to be mostly inferred by the reader, except for one episode on Chad's balcony, in which the young man, apparently testing the waters for any cupidity in Strether (and finding none), alludes suggestively to all that Strether will have to renounce. Chad is suggestive, yes, but not comprehensive nor with James's own solidity of specification found in the Scenario. The key here was James's committed point of view: that is, Strether's character as 'deputy' throughout the story virtually disallows such specific massing together of his own advantages-in-jeopardy, because Strether has no more fundamental drive for worldly goods than has, say, Merton Densher in *The Wings of the Dove.*

Another important feature for one who comes to the Scenario with both the novel and the 1895 notebook entry in mind is that James is marrying a comedy of manners to the book's melancholia. That is, he continues to speak of Strether as 'rueful', and the proposed work as '[t]he whole comedy, or tragedy, the drama, whatever we call it' (*CN,* 564). The plot-directed reversals begin to cascade, the second wave of ambassadors arrives, 'Waymark' finally gets his second wind with Sarah, Jim Pocock is ready to live all *he* can—these and many other similar elements achieve that Quixote-like suspension referred to earlier, as the comic personality of the book competes with its originating meditative theme of 'too late', found back in James's February 1895 Notebook. Such competing moods, however, do not change James's hope, at the end of the Scenario, that this work would possess the structure and, one assumes, the beauty of 'a rounded medallion, in a series of a dozen hung, with its effect of high relief, on a wall' (*CN,* 575-6). Considering his eventual judgment of the work and its effective twelve-book structure, one must assume James believed he had indeed crafted some such medallion-like series—despite, for instance, the continuing scholarly dispute about the alleged reversal of chapters 28 and 29 in the first American and New York Editions, a debate most recently joined by Jerome McGann. Since the dispute inevitably involves the question of temporal sequence, perhaps its lesson is to remind us that, in late James, much of the 'main' action occurs retrospectively, is recollected in the mind at a sometimes unspecified 'future' moment. Right or wrong, McGann's hypothesis makes us appreciate the non-linear element within James's late narrative method.[5]

II. METAPHORICAL SYSTEMS

The fifth version of the germ is, of course, the fully realized episode in the second chapter of Book Fifth of *The Ambassadors.* When a reader examines this powerful moment in the novel itself on the heels of studying the October 1895 notebook entry and then the prologue to the 1900 Scenario, he or she perforce is struck by the evolving progression of all three versions. First, the preliminary ambience of the occasion stressed by James in the Scenario is now extended and distributed over the first chapter of Book Fifth and half-way into the second; Strether is given ample time to imbibe the seductive charm of the visual scene in Gloriani's garden, of letting the 'rather grey interior' of his mind 'drink in for once the sun of a clime not marked in his old geography' (*AB,* I, 196-7; bk. 5, ch. 1). James follows this with the impact of Strether's introduction to Madame de Vionnet, who impresses him as has no one since his arrival from America except, quite arguably, the transformed Chad himself, who immediately whisks her away after Strether receives the full measure of her charming presence, leaving him alone once more with Little Bilham and thus ready to deliver the germ speech.

The speech in *The Ambassadors,* far more than in the Scenario, has the character of a full soliloquy, except that Little Bilham's presence, of course, disqualifies it technically as soliloquy. James, as the poet says, loads his rift with ore, principally by interlacing the rhetorical stages of the speech with figurative language presum-

ably welling out from Strether because of the emotion and intensity of the moment.

> It's not too late for *you,* on any side, and you don't strike me as in danger of missing the train; besides which people can be in general pretty well trusted, of course—with the clock of their freedom ticking as loud as it seems to do here—to keep an eye on the fleeting hour. All the same don't forget that you're young—blessedly young; be glad of it on the contrary and live up to it. Live all you can; it's a mistake not to. It doesn't so much matter what you do in particular, so long as you have your life. If you haven't had that what *have* you had? . . . I see it now. I haven't done so enough before—and now I'm old; too old at any rate for what I see. Oh I *do* see, at least; and more than you'd believe or I can express. It's too late. And it's as if the train had fairly waited at the station for me without my having had the gumption to know it was there. Now I hear its faint receding whistle miles and miles down the line. What one loses one loses; make no mistake about that. The affair—I mean the affair of life—couldn't, no doubt, have been different for me; for it's at the best a tin mould, either fluted and embossed, with ornamental excrescences, or else smooth and dreadfully plain, into which, a helpless jelly, one's consciousness is poured—so that one 'takes' the form, as the great cook says, and is more or less compactly held by it: one lives in fine as one can. Still, one has the illusion of freedom; therefore don't be, like me, without the memory of that illusion . . . Do what you like so long as you don't make *my* mistake. For it was a mistake. Live!
>
> (*AB,* I, 217-18; bk. 5, ch. 2)[6]

Apart from the pacing of this speech (James says, 'with full pauses and straight dashes, Strether had so delivered himself' (*AB,* I, 218; bk. 5, ch. 2)) and the iterative use of the word 'mistake' somewhat like incremental repetition in poetry, it is the striking insertion of the metaphors which seem to bind this moment to the novel as a whole, thus collaborating James's view that the germ stretches out from one end of the book to the other. For example, the train that Strether laments to have missed, even though it awaited him past departure time, so to speak, is finally 'caught' by him later in Book Eleventh ('selected almost at random', says the text (*AB,* II, 245; bk. 11, ch. 3)) when he rides it to the French countryside and eventually chances upon Chad and Madame de Vionnet in an attitude inferring their sexual intimacy, thereby collapsing his own elevated interpretation of what Little Bilham has called their 'virtuous attachment'. In other words, the train metaphor points directly across the canvas of the novel to its great recognition/meditation scene, which, reminiscent of Isabel Archer's all-night vigil in *The Portrait of a Lady,* might likewise be described with James's language from the later Preface to *The Portrait* as, 'obviously the best thing in the book, but . . . only a supreme illustration of the general plan' (*LC*-II, 1084). Next, the metaphor of the 'great cook' and his 'tin mould' for ornamental jellied dishes, although its immediate function is surely to represent the limitations of free agency, is another image that extends across the entire book in both directions, establishing connection with Strether's series of meals that act as benchmarks of his European apprenticeship. First there is his recollection of dining out back home with Mrs. Newsome during the excitement of his very different evening dinner in Book Second at his London hotel with Maria Gostrey, whose dress is '"cut down", as he believed the term to be, in respect to shoulders and bosom, in a manner quite other than Mrs. Newsome's' (*AB,* I, 50; bk. 2, ch. 1). Then there is the soft sensual meal later on the left bank with Madame de Vionnet in Book Seventh after he runs into her by accident at Notre Dame Cathedral, a meal that marks still greater initiation away from the Puritan tone of his evenings out with Mrs. Newsome and also, to Strether's own surprise, distancing him even from his London outing with Maria Gostrey. Still later, there is the meal set for him by the hostess at the Cheval Blanc in the rustic village Strether wanders into in Book Eleventh. He is 'hungry', has worked up an 'appetite', and is told by the hostess that 'she had in fact just laid the cloth for two persons who, unlike Monsieur, had arrived by the river—in a boat of their own'. Strether is even offered 'a "bitter" before his repast' (*AB,* II, 254; bk. 11, ch. 3). It culminates in the awkward meal he shares with Chad and Marie de Vionnet after he accidentally espies them, 'too prodigious, a chance in a million', in the boat together, after which all three must sit down to eat (*AB,* II, 257; bk. 11, ch. 4). His 'bitter' thus becomes his 'repast', so to speak, and the three eventually continue the charade, though thinly, by riding back to the city on the train. No wonder Strether later that evening in meditation thinks of Chad and Marie's make-believe as 'disagree-[ing] with his spiritual stomach' (*AB,* II, 265; bk. 11, ch. 4).

The tin-mould metaphor functions also, however, as the principal signifier of consciousness and freedom, or more properly, as both the limitations and felt experiences of human freedom. James chooses the germ speech itself as the repository within the novel to embed the book's central philosophical question, whether or not we act as free agents. Strether is, of course, a character, not the author, and yet a certain number of readers tend to read this book as in part a kind of spiritual autobiography. Even if one does not identify Strether all that closely with James, one does sense that at least these particular statements about the nature of consciousness and freedom are, for James, unusually authorial. But, then again, when Strether goes on to say, 'don't be, like me, without the memory of that illusion', we feel we *are* back with the character, with the 'mature and distinguished man' who originated, distantly, in Howells. The concept of there being varying degrees of fixed sensibility and consciousness, from plain to ornamental, in tandem with the concept of freedom as illu-

sion, is an intricately mediating philosophical stance between the traditional competing arguments of freedom and determinism; and it answers remarkably to the nuanced position taken by Henry James's brother William James in his philosophical doctrines.[7] What should be stressed in this regard is that Henry James's philosophical 'indeterminism', to appropriate William James's term, is given credence not only by the sheer variety of consciousnesses and the positive side of freedom as an actual, functioning illusion, but also by the emphatically 'chance' encounters that transpire in the novel, such as Strether's encounter with Marie at Notre Dame or with the couple in the boat at Cheval Blanc at the end of a train 'selected almost at random'. With its metaphorical systems, *The Ambassadors* seems composed like a web in which, when you 'touch' in one place, the entire design vibrates.

What James has done with the germ speech in the novel, then, is to take the all-too-human moment and weave his philosophical, thematic, and psychological values onto it through a poetics of metaphor and motif, a process suggesting those linked 'medallions' he hoped for in his Scenario to Harper's. Even the metaphor of the clock, whose loud ticking Strether associates with freedom, is implicitly a complex image consistent with these ideas above: for while the clock is rhetorically associated with the free European life, as opposed to New England constriction, the self-same image is psychologically associated with the speaker's feeling that for him it is 'too late', which is precisely why the clock ticks so loud. The sense that Strether cannot ultimately transcend his own temperament—which is also the sense in which 'the illusion of freedom' sounds its negative side—is captured at the end of the novel in Book Twelfth, when Strether humorously compares himself and his adventure to one of the figures on the clock in Berne, Switzerland, who came out on one side, 'jigged along their little course in the public eye, and went in on the other side' (*AB,* II, 322; bk. 12, ch. 5). Like the actual train rides compared to the metaphorical trains, the Berne clock diminishes the expectations of free autonomy proposed by the ticking metaphorical clock. Despite his sense of new personal freedom after he disembarks from America, despite his fermenting declaration to live, despite his cultivating European appetite, Strether cannot transcend his own temperament, even though his, fortunately, is one greatly embossed and not at all dreadfully plain. No wonder Emerson in his great bittersweet essay 'Experience' denominated 'temperament' as one of the 'lords of life' that will not brook transcendence.

The sixth and seventh versions of the germ reside briefly in two letters to Howells, written exactly a year apart in 1900 and 1901. He speaks of the work as 'lovely— human, dramatic, international, exquisitely "pure", exquisitely everything; only absolutely condemned, from the germ up, to be workable in not less than 100,000 words' (*HJL* [*Henry James Letters*], IV, 160). 'From the germ up' insinuates the same sense of ease and frictionless composition found again and again with *The Ambassadors.* The second letter to Howells comes after James has completed the novel and sent it off to Harper's. This statement—my number seven—is also the one in which he finally declares to Howells that he himself was the germ-source.

James now expounds in his own way a curious paradox about his creative process: that Howells is at once deeply disconnected from the novel while, in another sense, and only after the fact, very much connected with it. '[M]y point', he says, 'is that it had long before—it had in the very act of striking me as a germ—got away from *you* or from anything like you! had become impersonal and independent. Nevertheless', James continues, 'your initials figure in my little note; and if you hadn't said the five words to Jonathan [Sturges] he wouldn't have had them (most sympathetically and interestingly) to relate, and I shouldn't have had them to work in my imagination. The moral is that you are responsible for the whole business' (*HJL,* IV, 199). Both sides of this alchemic equation are rather compelling. That is, Howells had turned into the 'distinguished and mature' literary man almost immediately in James's gestation process. At the same time, James's half-humorous insistence that Howells is 'responsible' for it all reaffirms the deep and mysterious sense of life's interconnectedness. Philosophically speaking, it is William James's definition of unity as residing in conjunction, contiguity, and ambulation through every intervening part of experience rather than transcendence; dramatically, it is one with Strether's lament and defense to Sarah Pocock's accusations that '[e]verything has come as a sort of indistinguishable part of everything else' (*AB,* II, 200-1; bk. 10, ch. 3); genetically, it is the recognition that the initials 'W. D. H.' in his 1895 notebook entry signal an initiating germ whose metamorphosis extended all the way through to the completion of the novel.[8]

The eighth and final version of the germ is found in James's New York Preface to *The Ambassadors,* written in 1909. This last version is, in one sense, the most exuberant commentary, primarily because James, in rereading the novel, was struck afresh by the sheer extent to which the initiating germ permeates the book from one end to the other. In no other Preface does he speak like this: '[n]othing is more easy than to state the subject of **"The Ambassadors"**', or '[n]othing can exceed the closeness with which the whole fits again into its germ', or '[n]ever can a composition of this sort have sprung straighter from a dropped grain of suggestion', or 'never can that grain, developed, overgrown and smothered, have yet lurked more in the mass as an independent particle' (*LC*-II, 1304-5). And so he takes us

yet again to Strether's 'irrepressible outburst' to Little Bilham in Gloriani's garden on Sunday afternoon, this time rendering the germ speech from bits and combinations of language found in the 1895 Notebook, the prologue to the Scenario, and from the novel itself, although much reduced and hence considerably diminished in size from the novel's extended 'soliloquy'. James reiterates the point that he can remember 'no occasion on which, so confronted [with a germ], I had found it of a livelier interest to take stock, in this fashion, of suggested wealth'. For this reason he concludes that '[f]ortunately thus I am able to estimate this as, frankly, quite the best, "all round", of all my productions' (*LC*-II, 1305-6). The word '[f]ortunately' is the key word here, in part because the germ itself was such a fortunate one, but, more importantly, because James sensed that, given such a quintessentially ideal 'seed', had the book composed from it *not* been successful, that fact might have invalidated his conception of his own creative process. The note of compositional ease suffuses this entire Preface: at one point he compares the writing process to 'the monotony of fine weather', at another point he says that the steps and stages of his 'fable' placed themselves with such promptness that he himself huffed and puffed 'from a good way behind, to catch up with them, breathless and a little flurried, as [I] best could' (*LC*-II, 1306, 1311).

This Preface, of course, addresses a number of other items, mostly technical ones, which have long since been the province of James scholarship and criticism. The most familiar include the necessity to restrict the point of view to Strether as a third-person 'register' (together with the comparative drawbacks of first-person narration); the more complicated function of a *ficelle* figure like Maria Gostrey transcending her role; the successful 'alternations' of picture and scene; the successful presence, throughout, of the 'grace of intensity'. And yet, beyond these technical considerations, James obviously feels the deep presence of his hero, whose germ speech is now called 'melancholy eloquence', whose opportunity allows James to 'bite into' the 'promise of a hero so mature', and whose fundamental character allows him the 'immeasurable' chance to '"do" a man of imagination' (*LC*-II, 1306-7). Upon rereading the novel, James sees that the power of this germ's habitat in the depths of Strether's psyche is what enables the novel both successfully to have '"led up" to' the melancholy outburst in the garden and, just as important, to have followed through with '[Strether's] very gropings' to the end (*LC*-II, 1309, 1313). One of James's most perspicacious remarks in this respect is that Strether's irrepressible outburst to Bilham is likewise 'the voice of the false position' (*LC*-II, 1309). Such an assessment may open up the novel for a critique of Strether by a certain kind of critic so predisposed, yet it equally permits an empathetic approach to him by a very differently minded critic, since a 'false position', for the latter, is still the human one; and besides, it resides more or less half-way through Strether's adventure and does not necessarily mean to characterize the ending—where the first critic, so to speak, already awaits and says it does. These opposing critical positions, each responding to Strether's declination of Maria Gostrey's proffered love and his decision to leave for home, have solid enough Jamesian justification: the first has the continuity of Strether's deepest unyielding 'temperament', the Emersonian lord of life; the second has James's commitment to a dynamic central character, one who can have a *Bildungsroman* experience in middle age, and who lives in a William Jamesian world where things are never static but always 'in the making'.

III. Moral Fluctuation

'She keeps *him* up—she keeps the whole thing up . . . She has simply given [Chad] an immense moral lift, and what that can explain is prodigious' (*AB,* I, 283-4; bk. 6, ch. 3). So speaks Lambert Strether to Little Bilham in the flush of his new allegiance to Chad and Marie de Vionnet. But here also is Strether later in the novel after the Cheval Blanc episode: '[Marie] had but made Chad what he was—so why could she think she had made him infinite? She had made him better, she had made him best, she had made him anything one would; but it came to our friend with supreme queerness that he was none the less only Chad' (*AB,* II, 284; bk. 12, ch. 2).

These passages are in no wise special to the novel, but they do typify the continual fluctuation of Strether's moral assessment, not only of the younger couple, but also of his entire experience of Paris, Europe, and the ambassadorial mission. Strether's ongoing dialectic of faith and suspicion does not arise because his moral rigour is lax or even intermittent—quite the opposite—but because James situates him deep within an interpretive field of reality-as-flux, so that his own consciousness must enter into and complete whatever he seeks to know. When he attributes to Chad's 'moral lift' the capacity for 'prodigious explanations', he gives away the secret to, and reveals the problem of, James's own narrative invention: that ethics are never separable from the ceaseless process of knowing; and that process, within William James's pluralistic universe, is both never ending and less what one might observe than how one understands. When James sends Strether to Chad's apartment for the very last time on Madame de Vionnet's behalf, and he has to climb up four flights 'without a lift', the reason is only superficially that 'the lift, at that hour, [had] ceased to work' (*AB,* II, 306, 305; bk. 12, ch. 4); the deeper narrative reason is that Strether no longer believes in the Chad of the 'moral lift'. Even the physical world of the novel reshapes and re-presents itself in answer to the interpretive world through James's metaphorical system; the same prin-

ciple is at work as Strether now sees from the Boulevard below the 'more solid shape' of Chad on the balcony in sharp contrast to the early substitute-shape of Little Bilham the first time he arrived at that address (*AB,* II, 305; bk. 12, ch. 4). Chad's 'solidity' answers to Strether's now less luminous interpretation of him; his 'shape', moreover, replaces that of the 'amiable' Bilham, author of the heretofore soothing phrase, 'virtuous attachment'.

Paul Armstrong affirms rightly that, by 'focusing on Strether's "groping" efforts to understand, James transforms the composing powers of consciousness into the central action of his narrative'.[9] This feature opens up the novel and makes it a 'hymn' to William James's 'ambulatory rather than saltatory relations, in which the "intervening parts of experience"—i.e. Strether's "process of vision"—supersede every other consideration'.[10] And yet, this very feature means that explanations, however 'prodigious', do not bequeath assurance or agreement from others. When Strether first encounters the 'transformed' Chad, for instance, his 'burden of conscience' compels him to 'communicat[e] quickly with Woollett'; however, 'his heart always sank when the clouds of explanation gathered'. For '[w]hether or no he had a grand idea of the lucid, he held that nothing ever was in fact—for any one else—explained. One went through the vain motions, but it was mostly a waste of life' (*AB,* I, 141; bk. 3, ch. 2). This judgment certainly proves true with Mrs. Newsome, whose reaction to Strether's copious 'explanations' in his letters is an abrupt silence followed by her decision to launch a second ambassadorial delegation headed by her daughter Sarah.

But the problem of explanations for others, Strether learns, can prove no more severe than it does for oneself. When he lunches on the quay with Marie de Vionnet after their chance encounter at Notre Dame, he recollects that his dinner with Maria Gostrey in London 'had struck him as requiring so many explanations. He had at that time gathered them in, the explanations—he had stored them up; but it was at present as if he had either soared above or sunk below them—he couldn't tell which; he could somehow think of none that didn't seem to leave the appearance of collapse and cynicism easier for him than lucidity' (*AB,* II, 13; bk. 7, ch. 1). The supreme irony, therefore, is that, in a novel where reality-in-the-making dictates how one understands rather than what one sees, the status of explanations—whether for another or even for oneself—is dubious.

And yet, were we to 'step back' momentarily to the realm of simple perception, so-called, the situation would be more of the same than one might think. Susan Griffin demonstrates convincingly that Strether's visual perception throughout *The Ambassadors* illustrates the functionalist psychology associated with William James:

hence 'the active, interested, attentive nature of functional perception means that in the act of seeing, Strether shapes his world and his past'.[11] Griffin agrees that his 'self-interested activity' of perception is never solipsistic but is limited by certain 'outside determinations of his environment';[12] so that Strether's 'interaction between arranged environment and attentive eye' bespeaks the functionalist system enunciated in William's *Principles* rather than the associationist schools he opposed.[13] What all this suggests is that, much as William's earlier psychology adumbrates his later pragmatistic philosophy, so Strether's interested and attentive selectivity at the very nexus of perception adumbrates what Armstrong eloquently defines as his 'bridge over the darkness [through] the ceaseless meaning-making of consciousness' at the higher levels of reality and interpretation.[14] In short, not only does James's distinctive narratology emphasize understanding over observation, as noted earlier, but observation itself in late James, by virtue of its functionalist mode, repeats—or does it initiate?—the shaping agency distinctive to Jamesian consciousness. So if all 'explanations' are eventually problematic, they come by it honestly having emerged from the level of 'simple' perception.

James's narrative epistemology, as I have just defined it, results in Strether's inevitable moral fluctuation. If only he were monistic, if only prescriptive and a priori like Sarah and her mother, he could escape the dialectic of faith and suspicion. But he would not then be the medium of consciousness in the late James. As it is, he illustrates instead William James's insistence that pragmatism, unlike rationalism, disallows 'moral holidays', because one can never rest on the laurels of the transcendent absolute if one inhabits a universe both plural and in constant flux, where ideas, even the most profound and useful ones, are 'transitional'. In *The Ambassadors,* 'virtuous attachment' is just such an idea; it undergoes as many modifications of meaning in the hands of James and his protagonist as does Walter Besant's dictum that one should write from experience at the hands of James the critic, in **"The Art of Fiction"**. Just as Strether generally 'reconstructs' Chad after meeting him anew in Paris, then 'reconstructs' him after critical episodes culminating in Cheval Blanc, so too does he fluctuate from Chad as pagan to gentleman, as smooth to brute, as knowing how to live to, potentially, 'a criminal of the deepest dye' should he desert Marie (*AB*, II, 311; bk. 12, ch. 4).

Such profound interdependence of ethical imperatives and interpretive attitudes is epitomized by the great boat scene at Cheval Blanc. Armstrong insightfully proposes that

> even when Strether confronts reality, James is more interested in how his hero understands than in what he sees. Strether learns the truth about Chad and Madame de Vionnet not by facing unmediated facts but by following out the implications of various clues. Never given direct evidence of their intimacy, Strether must ponder a series of small, subtle signs requiring skilful reading.[15]

This formulation of Strether's discovery evokes Michael Polanyi's theory of 'tacit' and 'focal' knowledge expounded in works like *Knowing and Being* and *Personal Knowledge,* and it does so not only because of the linear descent of *Gestalt* thought from William James, but also because Henry James, like both William and Polanyi, seems bent on capturing the human processes of construal along the lines of a humanistic science.[16] A comparable formulation of the same episode is this: 'Strether actively and radically meets the discovery; he enters into a reciprocal relation with it, grafting meaning while receiving in kind; he empties every possible insight about himself, his previous assumptions, the thoughts of the two lovers in having to deal with *him,* and even the imagined responses of those back at Paris, into it.'[17] In stressing the active shaping of Strether's consciousness in the face of life's fluidity, both formulations suggest why Strether's 'gropings' make him vulnerable to deception: he is a believer, and, within his dialectic, suspicion, though inevitable, is never sought, whereas faith is always welcomed. Strether's moral stance in this regard seems that of William James's in **"The Will to Believe"**, especially his theme that '[d]upery for dupery, what proof is there that dupery through hope is so much worse than dupery through fear?'[18]

And yet, Strether's moral fluctuation, though seasoned with good humour in William's spirit up through the final breakfast scene with Maria Gostrey, also resonates with that undertone of melancholia James first detected in the germ and continued to convey in all his subsequent versions of it, as when denominating Strether 'rueful' or addressing the novel's mixed tragedy/irony mode, as discussed earlier. The problem for 'poor Strether', as he is so often called, is, in his own words to Maria, that he truly needs '[t]o be right' (*AB,* II, 326; bk. 12, ch. 5) in the face of all the bewilderment and fluctuation he has experienced. Yet how does one do that in a world that can only begin with 'Strether's first question', and only end with 'Then there we are!'—in other words, an indeterminate world going everywhere horizontally but nowhere vertically? As usual, Armstrong provides the best answer one can find: 'The most we can hope for, James seems to suggest, is a sense of integrity—a sense that our lives have composed themselves into a whole that we can accept as our own . . . By espousing the value of integrity, James asserts that we can live a moral life; but *The Ambassadors* also shows that integrity, as an ethical goal, is infinitely variable and open to interpretation'.[19] The norm Strether invokes is ultimately existential, grounded on the structure of experience and belief in 'the illusion of freedom' with both its positive and negative poles, and answering to William's iterative claim of pragmatistic thought as both 'tender and tough-minded'. But in late James these norms are intrinsic rather than extrinsic values, derived neither from society nor a priori imperatives. While problematizing the issue of representation in a way that stamps his modernity, James, like Strether, must somehow steer a middle course between reality and interpretation, thereby evoking William's 'mediating philosophy', on one side, and the hermeneutical circularity of phenomenology he anticipates, on the other. The phenomenological James is one with William's concept of the never-ending confluence of experience-as-apparent, wherein one must not distinguish where one cannot experientially divide. On this account, Strether is most 'phenomenological' in his anxiety-based defense to Sarah's attack in the same speech that begins, 'Everything has come as a sort of indistinguishable part of everything else.'[20]

For Strether, there has been something exhilarating in the ambiguity of a woman who 'had taken all his categories by surprise' (*AB,* I, 271; bk. 6, ch. 3) and who spoke 'now as if her art were all an innocence, and then again as if her innocence were all an art' (*AB,* I, 116; bk. 9, ch. 1). But even pragmatistic novelty can turn rueful as when Strether later ponders 'the general spectacle of his art and his innocence, almost an added link and certainly a common priceless ground for them to meet upon' (*AB,* II, 278; bk. 12, ch. 1). Regarding this irony, a reader may swing back and forth between its grimness and its good humour. But, either way, William James, in '**The Moral Philosopher and the Moral Life**', rings true for Strether when he insists: 'Neither moral relations nor the moral law can swing *in vacuo.* Their only habitat can be a mind which feels them; and no world composed of merely physical facts can be a world to which ethical propositions apply.'[21] Nevertheless, Joyce Rowe represents a certain type of reader when she claims that, like Huck or Ishmael, Strether 'ends a spiritual orphan' whose 'finale forces us to reconsider once again the cost of American moral idealism'.[22] If this position goes too far and ignores the book's comedic side, it does do justice—more than justice—to the 'rueful' melancholia intrinsic in James's germ. Once again, William James seems to address the issue when he writes that 'there is always a *pinch* between the ideal and the actual which can only be got through by leaving part of the ideal behind . . . Every end of desire that presents itself appears exclusive of some other end of desire . . . Some part of the ideal must be butchered and [the moral philosopher] needs to know which part.'[23]

Although 'to butcher' sounds much too coarse for Strether (who is called by Waymarsh a 'fine-tooth comb' not fit 'to groom a horse' (*AB,* I, 109; bk. 3, ch. 1)), he

does, ultimately, cut away parts of his ideal. He severs himself from Mrs. Newsome, like the Hegelian slave who comes to a new consciousness of her as under the gaze and censure of the master. He severs himself from Marie de Vionnet, even though he also tries valiantly to persuade Chad not to desert her. And he severs himself from Maria Gostrey, whose companionship he has cherished and who offers him her love. As a quondam ambassador, he has known power for a time and then squandered it, as I suggested at the beginning of this chapter. In regard to such power, he resembles his predecessor, Fleda Vetch, in *The Spoils of Poynton,* and his successor, Merton Densher, in *The Wings of the Dove,* both of whom renounce their possibilities for control on behalf of a more compelling need for personal integrity—a comparable need, if you will, 'to be right'. In this respect he is unlike Maggie Verver in *The Golden Bowl,* who combines the shaping burden of consciousness with the gradual acquisition of power other than the composing 'powers' of consciousness *per se,* although such momentous power makes it impossible, finally, for Maggie to feel very sanguine about, and thus certain of, her being right. Perhaps one overlooked clue to Strether's lack of ultimate power acquisition is that his character is a reconceived, rewritten draft of Christopher Newman in *The American*: for, whereas Newman sought in a woman 'the best article in the market' (*AM,* [*The American*] 49) but still came up empty, Strether insists '[n]ot, out of the whole affair, to have got anything for myself' (*AB,* II, 326; bk. 12, ch. 5); and, whereas Newman spoke of wash tubs and leather as his business ventures, Strether never names the Woollett 'article'. Perhaps still another connection, albeit a less direct one, is to *The Turn of the Screw,* wherein a person in possession of delegated power misuses it and thereby loses Jamesian integrity in her obsession 'to be right'.

Nevertheless, neither these nor other analogues can account for Strether. His predicament, like his ethic, remains intrinsic to him, and also to the remarkable germ that brought him forth. His power *does* remain that of consciousness, and there is no reason to disbelieve him when he tells Maria of his returning home that 'I shall see what I can make of it' (*AB,* II, 325; bk. 12, ch. 5). At the same time—indeed, perhaps for the same reason—a reader senses that at least some part of Strether refuses Maria Gostrey because, unlike Marie de Vionnet, she never *has* taken all his categories by surprise—the very surprise that can trigger 'melancholy eloquence'.

Notes

1. This assessment is, of course, from James's Preface to the New York Edition. For a possible 'subconscious' connection between Strether's 'Live' speech and James's early character of Louis

Leverett in 'A Bundle of Letters' (1879), see Oscar Cargill, *The Novels of Henry James* (New York: Macmillan, 1961), 304.

2. Cf. J. Donald Crowley and Richard A. Hocks, eds., *The Wings of the Dove: Norton Critical Edition* (New York: Norton, 1978), 454-5.

3. Martha Banta, '"There's Surely a Story In It": James's Notebooks and the Working Artist', *Henry James Review*, 9 (1988), 155-7.

4. James's reiteration of the 'too late' theme in all major versions of the germ speech is likewise anticipated in an earlier notebook entry, 5 February 1895, which begins, 'What is there in the idea of *Too late*' (*CN*, 112).

5. The dispute about the chapters, that is, has taken an entirely new 'reversal' by McGann's essay, in which he argues that it was the first English Edition—which James did *not* use for his Scribner's revision—that has the chapters in the wrong order; whereas the first American Edition—which James did revise from—had the chapter sequence right all along (the original magazine text in *The North American Review* had omitted chapter 28 altogether). Hence, for McGann, all the editions we used to believe had it 'wrong' have been right, and the ones we now think have 'corrected' it have it wrong! (Jerome McGann, 'Revision, Rewriting, Rereading; or An Error [Not] in *The Ambassadors*', *American Literature*, 64 (1992), 95-110.) See S. P. Rosenbaum, ed., *The Ambassadors: Norton Critical Edition*, 2nd edn. (New York: Norton, 1994), 360-1, for a cogent refutation of this view.

6. It is noteworthy that this central speech was not substantially revised from either the first American or first English editions, aside from the removal of a few commas in keeping with James's general style in the New York Edition (cf. Henry James, *The Ambassadors* (New York: Harper, 1903), 149-50); furthermore, it is just possible that the metaphorical train's receding 'whistle' may be James's punning 'signature' for the originating germ-location at the home of James McNeill Whistler.

7. For a fuller interpretation along these lines see Richard A. Hocks, *Henry James and Pragmatistic Thought: A Study in the Relationship between the Philosophy of William James and the Literary Art of Henry James* (Chapel Hill: University of North Carolina Press, 1974), 152-87, as well as section III of this chapter.

8. A year later, in 1902, one still finds this 'germ-like' sentiment in James's letter to Edith Wharton, wherein he expresses his 'desire earnestly, tenderly, intelligently to admonish you while you are young, free, expert, exposed (to illumination) . . . admonish you, I say, in favour of the *American Subject*. There it is round you. Don't pass it by— the immediate, the real, the ours, the yours, the novelist's that it waits for. Take hold of it and keep hold, and let it pull you where it will' (*HJL*, IV, 235-6).

9. Paul B. Armstrong, *The Challenge of Bewilderment: Understanding and Representation in James, Conrad, and Ford* (Ithaca: Cornell University Press, 1987), 63.

10. Hocks, *Henry James and Pragmatistic Thought*, 158.

11. Susan M. Griffin, *The Historical Eye: The Texture of the Visual in Late James* (Boston: Northeastern University Press, 1991), 33.

12. Hocks, *Henry James and Pragmatistic Thought*, 177.

13. Griffin, *Historical Eye*, 51.

14. Armstrong, *Challenge of Bewilderment*, 105.

15. Ibid., 92.

16. Michael Polanyi, *Knowing and Being* (University of Chicago Press, 1969); *Personal Knowledge: Towards a Post-Critical Philosophy* (University of Chicago Press, 1958).

17. Hocks, *Henry James and Pragmatistic Thought*, 63.

18. William James, *Essays on Faith and Morals* (Cleveland: World, 1962), 58.

19. Armstrong, *Challenge of Bewilderment*, 102.

20. By far the best discussion of James and post-William Jamesian phenomenology remains Paul B. Armstrong, *The Phenomenology of Henry James* (Chapel Hill: University of North Carolina Press, 1983); Merle A. Williams, *Henry James and the Philosophical Novel: Being and Seeing* (Cambridge University Press, 1993), however, combines Merleau-Ponty, Husserl, and Derrida in her approach to James.

21. William James, *Essays*, 190.

22. Joyce A. Rowe, *Equivocal Endings in American Literature* (New York: Cambridge University Press, 1988), 98.

23. William James, *Essays*, 202-3.

Abbreviations

AB: *The Ambassadors*, New York Edition, 24 vols. (New York: Scribner's, 1907-9), vols. XXI, XXII.

AM: *The American,* New York Edition, 24 vols. (New York: Scribner's, 1907-9), vol. II.

CN: *The Complete Notebooks of Henry James,* ed. Leon Edel and Lyall H. Powers (New York: Oxford University Press, 1987).

HJL: *Henry James Letters,* ed. Leon Edel, 4 vols. (Cambridge, Mass.: Belknap-Harvard University Press, 1974-84).

LC-II: *Literary Criticism: French Writers, Other European Writers, the Prefaces to the New York Edition,* ed. Leon Edel with the assistance of Mark Wilson (New York: Library of America, 1984).

Kevin Kohan (essay date December 1999)

SOURCE: Kohan, Kevin. "Rereading the Book in Henry James's *The Ambassadors*." *Nineteenth-Century Literature* 54, no. 3 (December 1999): 373-400.

[*In the following essay, Kohan examines, through a study of specific "texts" within the novel, the popular assumption that Strether's experience in* The Ambassadors *is one of liberation. Kohan asserts that the novel concludes with "an ambivalent middle way," in which James demonstrates that both the "epistemological perspectives" of Mrs. Newsome's Woollett and Madame de Vionnet's Paris are "essentially oppressive because both are oriented toward a kind of absolute, either positive or negative."*]

Post-structuralist critics commonly read Henry James's *The Ambassadors* (1903) from the Parisian point of view, approving Madame de Vionnet's skeptical "vast, bright Babylon"[1] and rejecting Mrs. Newsome's dull, Woollettian rationalism.[2] Julie Rivkin, for example, after a lengthy discussion of Jacques Derrida and the logic of the supplement, concludes that

> what Mme de Vionnet comes to reveal is that behind representation there is no firm ground. The supplements that make up representation, delegation, and ambassadorship are potentially infinite. Indeed, she confirms what Strether had already begun to learn from Maria Gostrey—that property (as the self of proper names, the wealth of family, the propriety of behavior, and the presence that stands behind representation) is itself an effect, a product of the interplay of likenesses and likelihoods, the intersubstitution of representations. In Mme de Vionnet's world, there are no final authorities of the sort Mrs. Newsome claims to be; there are only ambassadors.[3]

Similarly, Maud Ellmann asserts that the novel "reveals that representation means the death of origins. In the realm of power the monarch [Mrs. Newsome, a figure of the 'origin'] is unseated by the very instruments of tyranny."[4] Ellmann assumes that the Woollettian perspective has been overthrown for the more elusive, though dangerous, power-representation nexus operating in Paris, Mrs. Newsome's tyranny undone by its own (suppressed) textuality. Likewise, Mary Cross argues that "*The Ambassadors* is a story of signifiers, a narrative of the process of denomination by which words categorise the world. The names for things, especially for his experiences, give Strether . . . great trouble. . . . It is his triumph, eventually, 'to find the names,' only to discover that they do not settle anything; the signifiers are in motion and the process of denomination keeps coming undone."[5] And in another vein, Richard Salmon concludes his discussion with this assertion:

> As a character in a book that is also prospectively subject to commodity display, Strether is simultaneously "inside" and "outside" the scene of his own representation.[6] . . . The artifice of Strether's representation, which would underlie the mimetic surface of a "realistic" narrative, is itself open to textual display.[7]

The difficulty with all of these readings, however, is that to conclude that the Parisian aspect of Strether's education is dominant, indeed represents a final "triumph," one must ignore the subtle equation that James establishes between the a priori rationalism of Woollett's Mrs. Newsome and the semiotically sensuous skepticism of Paris's Madame de Vionnet. Both epistemological perspectives, the novel suggests, are essentially oppressive because both are oriented toward a kind of absolute, either positive or negative. It is certainly the case that Newsome's impersonal rationalism assumes a decidedly omniscient cast, her lofty intentions expecting to narrate Strether's Paris mission without digression or lacunae. In Paris, however, de Vionnet is the ostensible author of another kind of text, one that would release its characters from the burden of knowing and into a world of desire—her Paris is religiously secure in its anti-realist assumptions. Strether's negotiations between the Scylla of rationalist control and the Charybdis of textual play conclude not with the victory of one over the other, but with the realization of an ambivalent middle way, shorn of "final authorities" yet not resigned to be lost in a world undone.[8]

But if the two kinds of texts are correlatives, then to recognize the failing of Parisian textuality is to recuperate something of Newsome's "tyrannical" book. Post-structuralist critics not only misread Strether's education in Paris as a kind of liberation, but they also try to suppress James's intransigent commitment to realism. *The Ambassadors,* I suggest, makes the now unfashionable literary argument that certain assumptions of a realist epistemology cannot be overwritten by a representational economy ruled by desire. This is the James of clear distinctions, stable discriminations, and hard facts—asserted here more forcefully, perhaps, than anywhere else in his fiction because the assertion is made right in the teeth of textualist indeterminacy. To put this another way, it is time to acknowledge the extent to which Mrs. Newsome—insensitive, unimaginative, the antithesis of Jamesian fine consciousness and the routinely dismissed representative of everything that Strether must escape—is *right*.

The grounds for questioning Mrs. Newsome's authority are strong; indeed, they are made to seem overpowering. Her attempted narration of Strether's experience in Paris and of Chad's corruption there is so utterly saturated with clear intent that it sustains itself, even flourishes, when not constrained by any medium of expression: when she does *not* write, her presence is all the more imposing:

> It struck him [Strether] really that he had never so lived with her as during this period of her silence; the silence was a sacred hush, a finer clearer medium, in which her idiosyncrasies showed. He walked about with her, sat with her, drove with her and dined face-to-face with her . . . and if he had never seen her so soundless he had never, on the other hand, felt her so highly, so almost austerely, herself: pure and by the vulgar estimate "cold," but deep devoted delicate sensitive noble.

(II, 47)

Her text is essentially invisible, beyond the corruption of simple mediation, and her authorship insists on a sustained "sameness" even in its "idiosyncrasies." The "sacred hush" that permits this essential Newsome to make itself present for Strether calls forth a kind of prayer: Mrs. Newsome is "deep devoted delicate sensitive noble," the accumulated adjectives and alliteration of the "d" producing an uncanny effect. The elimination of commas denies separation of the words, blurring them all into an over-arching, inarticulate hymn, the rhythm of the triple "d"s subsiding into the slide of the "s" and the roll of the "o." We notice less what is said by each of these terms than the intention of praise animating them. Mrs. Newsome's intentionality allows itself to be incarnated through Strether, but he is similarly expected to erase himself in the transcendent speech of his author. Strether resists, and Sarah, who effects a more perfect translation of Newsome's intention—she carries over the woman herself, "the whole moral and intellectual being or block" (II, 239), so that Strether can feel, after lengthy conversations with Sarah, that it was "as if he were dealing directly with Mrs. Newsome" (II, 112)—brings a missive from the other side (a holy tablet, almost, being the first letter or telegram actually quoted in the novel despite the flurry of correspondence sent in both directions across the ocean): "Judge best to take another month, but with full appreciation of all re-enforcements" (II, 45). That first word "Judge"—both verb and noun (the "I" of the telegram disappears into its action)—announces her voice

to the novel in its singular insistence that knowing, acting, and being are essentially both one thing and the "best."

But the absolute rigor of Mrs. Newsome's vision of Chad that she attempts to pass to Strether is, in fact, questioned from the first words of the novel ("Strether's first question . . ." [I, 3]), and the success of her perspective in adequately defining the terms of the relationship between her son and Paris (and "bad" women) is almost immediately dismissed by the narrative voice. The subtle trap here, however (and it is one into which post-structuralist critics typically fall), is that the certainty of Newsome's conception, which presumes to account for a limited set of evidence (lack of written correspondence from Chad and his lengthy stay in Paris when wealth, position, and family await him back home) with a definite conclusion, is itself subjected to a most summary dismissal—the kind of rejection that signifies in James inadequate consideration, a lack of imagination. Strether immediately strays from what he considers more sober courses of action by falling in with Mrs. Gostrey, an event and a relation that he assures her will cost him his past "in one great lump" (I, 45)—the feeling of separation, disjunction, and dislocation is extreme—a complete break with the past that is here immediately announced and later becomes the broken ground of Strether's action when he tells Chad to remain in Paris. Much later in the novel—in Book Eleventh, just before the final revelation—Strether offers this assessment of the nature and quality of Mrs. Newsome's assignment and the character she puts forth through it:

> "That's just her difficulty—that she does n't admit surprises. It's a fact that, I think, describes and represents her; and it falls in with what I tell you—that she's all, as I've called it, fine cold thought. She had, to her own mind, worked the whole thing out in advance, and worked it out for me as well as for herself. Whenever she has done that, you see, there's no room left; no margin, as it were, for any alteration. She's filled as full, packed as tight, as she'll hold, and if you wish to get anything more or different either out or in—."

(II, 239)

Gostrey completes this thought by noting that any alteration would require a complete "make over" of the woman herself, to which Strether offers the definitive assertion, "What it comes to . . . is that you've got morally and intellectually to get rid of her" (II, 239). The disruption that the opening pages of the novel begin to trace is Strether's retreat from the intense figure of Newsome's compact conception, his sense that he could not be "booked, by her vision" (II, 241) in the face of European impressions. But the extreme nature of both Newsome's interpretation and the reaction against it that Strether here asserts (one must "get rid of her") signals a curious parallel between the rejected version and the newly accepted one in Paris.

The reversion to Parisian values occurs most decisively in Book Third with Chad's unexpected late arrival at the theater: he enters the box occupied by Strether, Gostrey, and Waymarsh and has a profoundly unsettling effect on Newsome's wayward agent. James underscores the dramatic character of Chad's sudden appearance by aligning it with the rise of the curtain and the fall of the theater crowd's hush, signaling the beginning of a performance both below on the stage and above in Strether's theater box. At both locations a moment of revelation, an unveiling, is about to occur, the unfolding of a moment of aesthetic effect.[9] Chad's presence, protected and made awful by the "decorous silence" of the crowd attentive to the other stage, occupies the absolute center of Strether's own consciousness and exerts a powerful authority by virtue of the enforced absence of conversation. If Mrs. Newsome is herself absent from the novel except through her "book," which sustains itself through vanishing delegates, then Chad "himself," to Strether, has been entirely erased, and in his place stands an alien figure who seems to concentrate the art of performance within his very person. The figure assaults Strether's sensibility by presenting an absolute incongruity that defies cognitive access and utterly destroys the pretensions of the Newsome prediction in a shattering epiphany of alterity:

> He was in presence of a fact that occupied his whole mind, that occupied for the half-hour his senses themselves all together. . . . The phenomenon that had suddenly sat down there with him was a phenomenon of change so complete that his imagination, which had worked so beforehand, felt itself, in the connexion, *without margin* or allowance. . . .
>
> He asked himself if, by any chance, before he should have in some way to commit himself, he might feel his mind settled to the new vision, might habituate it, so to speak, to the remarkable truth. But oh it was too remarkable, the truth; for what could be more remarkable than this sharp rupture of an identity? You could deal with a man as himself—you could n't deal with him as somebody else.

(I, 136-37; emphasis added)

Chad's physical appearance deepens the sense of disorientation. His black hair now streaked with gray and his face betraying no sign of Woollett's influence, Chad seems not only to have subverted his origin but also to have triumphed over the irreversibility of time itself: "It would have been hard for a young man's face and air to disconnect themselves more completely than Chad's at this juncture from any discerned, from any imaginable aspect of a New England female parent" (I, 140).[10] Even at the level of physical authorship Chad has introduced a "rupture" that defies continuity and intelligibility.

But Chad's appearance creates its radically disjunctive effect precisely because an equally extreme vision had set the stage of Strether's expectations. Undoubtedly,

Mrs. Newsome's closed-world sterility encourages immediate flight, an immersion into a world apparently its opposite—one dominated by fiction, ruled by desire, and sharp with the sense of possibility. Chad stands before Strether in the theater box as a testament to everything that Mrs. Newsome is not. But before this performance of performance (Chad's staging of the superiority of the stage, the aesthetic life), Strether sees the Newsome "book" performed on that other stage, played there as a drama in which "there was a bad woman in a yellow frock who made a pleasant weak good-looking young man in perpetual evening dress do the most dreadful things"; and Strether finds himself drifting into "a certain kindness . . . for its victim" (I, 53-54). The implication of the stage doubling of the prewritten Woollett version of Chad's affairs is that the certainty provided by Newsome is in its "fine cold thought" already the companion of an imagination suited for the melodramatic theater; such a thought is not the opposite of the lurid imagination but its correlative. Strether's immersion in Parisian "aesthetic life" presents itself as a radical break from Woollett but is in a crucial respect a *continuation* of it, although in a different register. Indeed, Newsome's book and Chad's revelatory appearance are both said to leave Strether "without margin." Chad's explosive appearance thus replays the Newsome book as visual stage rather than documented truth, but it depends on a strictly parallel though inverted principle: what is presented here cannot be doubted. Mrs. Newsome claims to know Chad's situation; Chad himself insinuates that Strether knows *nothing*. Woollettian certainty gives way to dogmatic skepticism.

Despite carrying Newsome's brief with him to Paris, Strether has also arrived equipped with one capacity entirely suited to appreciate Chad's dramatic performance: an ability to live or think outside the confines of his immediate context. During his first conversation with Gostrey at the station Strether tells her that he wants "out of the terror." He explains: "I'm always considering something else; something else, I mean, than the thing of the moment. The obsession of the other thing is the terror. I'm considering at present for instance something else than *you*" (I, 19). If Newsome's certainty makes her (and her perfect representatives, one of whom Strether proves himself not to be) blind to radical variations beyond the book of her expectations, then Strether recognizes that whatever element of Newsome's perspective he carries with him implies a deflection of attention from present objects of intentionality—the overarching, transcendental intention dominates to the point of erasure of the actually present. Certainty, that is, obscures the qualifications evident in the present. Strether's "terror," his obsession with the "other thing"—what he will find, what Chad will turn out to be—is also an incessant looking ahead, waiting for confirmation of what has already been decided. This is not Newsome's own understanding of her vision, but Strether, weak transporter of that view, extracts from it its functional character, which accords perfectly with what Chad needs to achieve his effect. Strether's terror will no longer be of his own alienation from the present but rather of his sudden confrontation with and absorption in the present—or rather, the "present," the moment, only as the "other thing" itself, the Other made manifest. Chad's alterity is terrifying and attractive at the same time because at this stage it seems to overturn Strether's alienation and deliver him over to a present that is more than simply the thing itself: Chad is shockingly there (Strether's attention diverts not in the smallest degree; during the performance he considers nothing else) and, at the same time, so completely not there by virtue of his difference. The perpetually "different" of Strether's "something else" that threw his consciousness forward to the next thing or away to abstraction and expectation becomes, through and in Chad, lodged in the present itself as perpetual self-difference. Chad, then, is not the representative for Strether of absolute experience (as Rivkin suggests);[11] rather, Chad's shattering presence/absence breaks experience itself. The secret compatibility of Newsome's certainty and Chad's performed skepticism lies in their shared exploitation of obsession: the former denies the present in its yearning for the a priori, the latter clutches desperately at the present in order to sever rational connections (the tendrils of its enemy) and insinuate dissonance into the heart of experience. The Other and the One are companions.

Newsome's book posits, in effect, an absolute continuity from Woollett to Paris: both a continuity of authorship (mother as son's unquestionable source of identity and of moral, social, and financial security) and a continuity of temporal connection in causation (Chad must be as he was, or an intervening cause has usurped the mother's role, an interruption that must be of comparable force to a mother's authorship). Chad's text purports just the reverse—not continuity but break, radical change, temporal disruption. His gray-streaked hair indicates his dislocation from Woollettian time and his occupation in a world where time, rather than marking its own autonomy, represents the quality of experience. In such a world Strether's authority is undermined since it relied in part on his own mature age. Before presenting his arguments to Chad, Strether realizes that the effect of Chad's dramatic self-presentation—connoting social grace, tact, and experience—serves to reverse their relative age relation: "If he was himself moreover to be treated as young he wouldn't at all events be so treated before he should have struck out at least once. His arms might be pinioned afterwards, but it would have been left on record that he was fifty" (I, 143). With time undermined by Chad's self-staging, Strether feels himself converted into a passive observer of the performance, watching it "like a schoolboy wishing not to miss a minute of the show" (I, 139).

And in a world of the timeless show, "one simply couldn't know" (I, 150). After Strether refuses to answer Mrs. Gostrey's question about the objects produced in Woollett by the Newsome industry, the narrator intrudes with this comment:

> But it may even now frankly be mentioned that he in the sequel never *was* to tell her. He actually never did so, and it moreover oddly occurred that by the law, within her, of the incalculable, her desire for the information dropped and her attitude to the question converted itself into a positive cultivation of ignorance. In ignorance she could humour her fancy, and that proved a useful freedom. She could treat the little nameless object as indeed unnameable—she could make their abstention enormously definite.
>
> (I, 61)

Gostrey's "cultivation of ignorance" and her conversion of the unnamed to the unnameable permits an imaginative "freedom" precisely by forcing, even in this trite (but indicative) case, epistemological questions to the side: it is not known, and so cannot be known—on this assumption, "fancy" has its widest play. Strether adopts this attitude with reservations—he continues to speculate about Chad's "type"—but in the face of Chad's transformation, explanations are not only deemed inadequate but also are regarded as either irrelevant or as mere constructions for the sake of personal convenience, just as time itself is reduced to little more than an accoutrement of style. Chad and de Vionnet, it is implied, play upon a sensibility inclined, like Gostrey's, to convert the unspecified into the absolute absence of grounds. On this assumption a "virtuous attachment" is a safe designation of the secret connection because, not being revealed by the name, it becomes something that simply cannot be known. Strether is thus not being educated, as Mary Cross argues, "to find the names"; on the contrary, he is being encouraged to think that any name will do, because naming is impossible. The text of desire functions in the absence of the proper name.

The epistemological abyss signaled by Chad's appearance leads Strether in two directions, each sustained by the assumed irrelevance of Newsome's perspective and its claim to "know" Chad and Paris (Sarah later remarks that she "knows Paris," a comment that provokes derision, if not from Strether then at least from the reader utterly seduced by the aesthetic education vicariously achieved through him). With de Vionnet outside the Notre Dame church, Strether, in the pleasure of her company and in his satisfaction at escaping his affairs with Chad, reflects that in London things "had struck him as requiring so many explanations . . . but it was at present as if he had either soared above or sunk below them—he couldn't tell which; he could somehow think of none that didn't seem to leave the appearance of collapse and cynicism easier for him than lucidity" (II, 13). The destruction of Woollettian certainty provokes either delusions of grandeur or fantasies of tremendous impotence, both issuing from the avoidance of explanations that could reconfirm at all the connection Chad has with the Newsome world. Strether's extreme self-constructions in the desire text (soaring or sinking) suggest that, while he may have switched his allegiance from Woollett to Paris, he is still bracketed within traditional rationalist and skeptical thought. Ricoeur criticizes these philosphies as being confined "within the problematic defined by the search for a certainty that would be an absolute guarantee against doubt," or the negation of that guarantee. They result in either the "exalted subject" of the Cartesian tradition, according to which the subject is the source of certainty, the god prior to God (able to "save" us from the evil genius of doubt); or in the "humiliated subject" of the equally hyperbolic Nietzschean tradition, according to which the self is a mere "grammatical habit," an effect rather than a cause of "signification" (Ricoeur, pp. 16, 15). It is interesting, however, that James's novel suggests that the humiliated subject of skepticism can also become the exalted subject since, with the burden of certainty utterly destroyed so that even fallible knowledge is renounced, the mere "grammatical" subject may just as well be a god (everything) as a cipher (nothing)—the absolute criterion flattens everything into equivalence, including the opposition between rationalism and skepticism.

Gloriani's garden party, at which Strether unleashes his "live all you can" speech, is crucial in this regard, for here James defines the essence of Strether's aesthetic education as a submission to glittering appearance and the play of surface.[12] The party puts on display the "vast bright Babylon" of Paris, where "differences [were not] comfortably marked"—a city that could take "one's authority away" (I, 89). At Gloriani's party an "assault of images" produces an almost religious seduction of the senses, the "young priests" dazzling and mysterious in a world that "had the sense of names in the air, of ghosts at the windows, of signs and tokens, a whole range of expression . . . too thick for prompt discrimination" (I, 196). With discrimination and explanation undermined by the richness of potential reference, the only basis for interpretation is a quasi-empirical submission to sensation, as rationalism is undermined by the flux and breadth of shifting surface. Gloriani himself, master-artist (or at least poseur-aesthete), wears a "medal-like Italian face, in which every line was an artist's own, in which time told only as tone and consecration" (I, 197), his body so conforming to the principle of surface—itself lit, as it were, by the "special flare, unequalled, supreme, of the æsthetic torch"—that time itself, the marker of both progress and decay, the foundation from which we recognize empirical distinctions, is no more than a shade of his color or a tone of his note, subservient to aesthetic effect.

Little Bilham tells Strether, in short, almost (for James) fragmentary sentences, that Gloriani "has some secret. It's extraordinary. And you don't find it out. He's the same to every one. He does n't ask questions" (I, 199)—Gloriani's divine-like mystery depends both on the creation of a known secret (knowing that the secret exists, but not what the form contains) and his own avoidance of inquiry. And Bilham continues the game by also blocking further inquiry from Strether as to the true cause of Chad's transformation by saying, "I can only tell you that [a virtuous attachment is] what they pass for. But is n't that enough? What more than a vain appearance does the wisest of us know? I commend you . . . the vain appearance" (I, 202-3). Strether later observes that "you've all of you here so much visual sense that you've somehow all 'run' to it. There are moments when it strikes one that you have n't any other" (I, 206). And indeed, James suggests that not having any other is tantamount to eliminating *being* altogether—being (or presence) is erased by the omnipotence of representation and seeming. The irony in Bilham's recommendation is self-protecting; it does not qualify the statement so much as it preemptively wards off serious criticism, and Strether's capture in the coils of these self-reflexive games makes him wonder whether inquiry itself is appropriate, a false note: "Was it after all a joke that he should be serious about anything? He envied Miss Barrace at any rate her power of not being. She seemed, with little cries and protests and quick recognitions, movements like the darts of some fine high-feathered free-pecking bird, to stand before life as before some full shop-window" (I, 204). Of course the meaning of the second sentence here is that Strether envies Barrace's power of not being serious, but the syntax creates the flickering image of Barrace simply not being, of her power to not be. And the impression is reinforced by the opening two words of the next sentence (its subject—with its verb so long delayed that the subject is isolated, suspended—attaches, in effect, to the conclusion of the previous sentence, which itself depended for completion on an absent phrase ["serious about anything"]). Thus the reader, reading over the sentence-appearance, ignoring for the moment the rule of the period, finds this meaning: Barrace had the power not to be; she seemed.

The (dis)embodied aesthetic skepticism that seduces Strether is thus based on the rejection of the possibility of gaining a conceptual grasp of underlying principles (or causal foundations) and on an acceptance of the force of display as the primary source of meaning ("stand[ing] before life as before some full shop-window"). The meaning that this visual experience yields, though, is not meaning at all from the rationalist perspective, which would require firm distinctions and careful discriminations; this is "meaning" as the flow of interconnected, endlessly shifting appearances, the movement of "signs in the air," and the realization that, as Strether says, "everything [comes] as a sort of indistinguishable part of everything else" (II, 200-201).

The capacity to act under the jurisdiction, as it were, of Newsome's book is thus destroyed, and Strether either lapses into or ascends toward a state of perpetual delay (this is the double result of the aesthetic skepticism). His predisposition to postpone drawing conclusions and to avoid making hasty decisions is seriously exacerbated by the final abandonment of his previously held, definite plan. The sense of urgency that he felt after the first shock of Chad's theater appearance, an urgency prompted by the anticipation of the loss of future opportunity to "strike out," is replaced by a desire for luxurious postponement and the fanciful exploration of possibility. At the Notre Dame church, his mind full of romance and Victor Hugo, Strether fantasizes a sweeping dramatic context around the image of a lone woman whom he observes sitting forward in the shade of a chapel. The heroine of his desire turns out to be Madame de Vionnet, but the fantasy is triggered by the "supreme stillness" and "prolonged immobility" of her nameless shadow, kneeling in prayer in the "sacred shade" of the grand church (II, 6,7), where judgment is forbidden: "Justice was outside, in the hard light, and injustice too; but one was as absent as the other from the air of the long aisles and the brightness of the many altars" (II, 5). These centers of dark inaction, these aisles filled with "figures of mystery and anxiety" (II, 5) who crave a transcendent illumination beyond the mundane world (the light of the priest's stage against the shade of the audience's domain, where, if both justice and injustice have no hold, then action and consequence are made irrelevant), attract and encourage Strether's imaginative play but push further away the reality of the present and the possibility of effective initiative.

Strether soon argues for stasis—Chad should remain in Paris—and writes letters back to Newsome that are devoid of meaning and barely qualify as genuine acts of consciousness:

> he was of course always writing; it was a practice that continued, oddly enough, to relieve him, to make him come nearer than anything else to the consciousness of doing something: so that he often wondered if he hadn't really, under his recent stress, acquired some hollow trick, one of the specious arts of make-believe. Wouldn't the pages he still so freely dispatched by the American post have been worthy of a showy journalist, some master of the great new science of beating the sense out of words?
>
> (II, 45-46)

The "new" science defies "sense" and relies on flash and show; the "new" Chad destroys *New*some's sense brought over from Woollett; and the Old World cultivates the sacred appearance that permits no crass "knowing." De Vionnet's triumph is to make the origin *old* (the already familiar), to un-originate it, so that what is left is mere relief in "always writing."

But Strether soon finds himself charged with other duties—primarily to de Vionnet—that are even more imposing in their form than those issued to him by Mrs. Newsome, since they are cast in terms consonant with what Sarah implicitly denounces as "religious" Paris. He promises de Vionnet that he will report favorably to Mrs. Newsome of Chad's associations, thus committing himself to "save" de Vionnet from disrepute and from Chad's possible abandonment. The word *save* is "exorbitant" (I, 255), as Strether recognizes, and implies an onerous responsibility—a promise to fulfill a contractual obligation analogous to Newsome's own demand that Strether act as her ambassador to Chad, but pitched to the key of de Vionnet's Catholicism. After meeting her at the Notre Dame church, Strether reconfirms his promise and realizes that the connection thus ratified places him in the service of one whose seriousness outweighs Newsome's own (II, 22). The obligation is a "golden nail" of commitment, binding him deeply and irrevocably—however gilded, dazzling, and rich the instrument of affixation. It is important, though, that the agency thus conferred on him with such seriousness counters the Woollett contract in its granting of autonomy to the agent. After Strether demurs that the whole thing is "not [his] affair" (II, 22), de Vionnet insists that since he has taken it up, he is still intensely implicated in shaping Chad's and her own destiny. Strether submits and affirms her characterization of his role:

> "You can't in honour not see me through," she wound up, "because you can't in honour not see *him*."
>
> . . . He took it all in, he saw it all together. "No," he mused, "I can't in honour not see him."
>
> Her face affected him as with an exquisite light. "You *will* then?"
>
> "I will."
>
> (II, 22)

To *see* is here translated as to *will*. Chad's theater performance has made clear that seeing is a rather paradoxical matter and can no longer be a metaphor of knowing; it is rather a recognition of aporia that forbids acting according to precedent. Newsome, however, relied on loyalty and duty, providing for Strether a clear plan of action, which Sarah eventually fulfills with greater success. But of course Sarah does so by submerging her identity into that of Mrs. Newsome, becoming little more than a perfect substitute, a transparent medium for her principal's intent. The paradigmatically "logocentric" Sarah-Mrs. Newsome relationship, with Newsome's book of certainty deploying a marker that ideally vanishes at the deliverance of the author's inviolate intent, is mirrored by Strether's relationship with de Vionnet, for his acceptance of the duty that she gives him implies the opposite extreme, based on undecideable difference, of self-assertion rather than self-abnegation: "I will."

Since in Paris, however, the possibility of intelligibly directed action is for Strether almost eliminated, his "I will" is radically dissociated from the "I know" of meaningful decision and implies instead the acceptance of responsibility without precedent or history—a radically aporetic ethical decisionism. Strether's will wanders "in a maze of mystic closed allusions" (I, 279), tempted to focus exclusively on the patterns of relationships and the symmetry and implications of their construction—all without endeavoring to discover the inner spring that has launched the entire Parisian drama: the secret of the relationship between Chad and de Vionnet. Trying to recover his past sense of initiative, Strether encourages Little Bilham to marry Mamie. He remarks:

> "I want . . . to have been at least to that extent constructive—even expiatory. I've been sacrificing so to strange gods that I feel I want to put on record, somehow, my fidelity—fundamentally unchanged after all—to our own. I feel as if my hands were embrued with the blood of monstrous alien altars—of another faith altogether."

> (II, 167-68)

But the strange gods of Paris provoke in Strether his own version of the "sacred rage," more pronounced than Waymarsh's, to appear somehow "different. . . . But better" (I, 46, 45). Rather than leading him to perform a decisive action, his will and rage transform him into a kind of demigod able to save de Vionnet despite his "pinioned" arms on the corporeal level (I, 143). He tells Gostrey, "I'm extremely wonderful just now. I dare say in fact I'm quite fantastic, and I should n't be at all surprised if I were mad" (II, 40); and later, "I think of everything" (II, 113). Strether's confidence wanes, of course, since his intellectual superiority is a negative one—against Sarah, his knowing is that he does not know—but the assumption of transcendence, tied to material incapacity, is finally thrust upon him as "the hero of the drama" (II, 179), the one upon whom all the consequences will fall. He will suffer for the others: "Yes, he should go to the scaffold yet for he would n't know quite whom. He almost, for that matter, felt on the scaffold now and really quite enjoying it" (II, 186). The sacrifice (the word resonates throughout the novel) of his interests (primarily financial, with the removal of Newsome's patronage) is explicitly connected with Strether's emerging centrality—achieved not through a "logocentric" domination of affairs but through his rigorous lack of specific knowledge and his negative realization that he knows either everything (II, 113) or nothing (II, 233). Strether's power is dependent on his practical immobility and his certain skepticism. At the end of the process, which provokes a desire to "want more wants" (I, 40), is a Strether narrated by a text from which the word *judge* has been eliminated.

* * *

Time, though, reasserts its linear aspect, and with it returns the muted efficacy of linear causality, the uneradicable but qualified foundation that underwrites the Newsome book. Strether's "school-boy" youthfulness before Chad's Book Third performance cannot sustain itself for long, and the play at age reversal and manipulation—the game of simulated youth—begins to lose its appeal. Gostrey has told him that he is "youth," and he has replied:

> "Of course I'm youth—youth for the trip to Europe. I began to be young, or at least to get the benefit of it, the moment I met you at Chester, and that's what has been taking place ever since. . . . Chad gives me the sense of it, for all his grey hairs, which merely make it solid in him and safe and serene; and *she* does the same, for all her being older than he, for all her marriageable daughter, her separated husband, her agitated history."

> (II, 50-51)

But with the erosion of Chad's sudden theatrical effect, subjective time created through the staging of personality gives way to autonomous time that marks both the accumulation of experience and "the menace of decay" (II, 185). The gradual resurrection of linear temporality signals the emergence of the necessary separation between present empirical experience on the one hand and memory, imagination, and representation on the other, which had so confusedly merged with one another for Strether in Paris. At the height of his fantastic, "mad" state of mind, "it was the way of nine tenths of his current impressions to act as recalls of things imagined" (II, 6). But the show given to him (by Chad, de Vionnet, and the others), and the dramas that he writes himself (dead letters to Newsome, romantic fantasies about de Vionnet), lose some of their power to enchant when viewed not from the spectator's position, nor from the author's, but from the critic's. Chad's miraculous transformation into an accomplished older gentleman of Paris is played again for Strether's scrutiny by de Vionnet and the hopelessly vulgar sensualist Jim Pocock. De Vionnet, resolved to do "everything" for Chad's cause, seduces Jim's approval by making herself "about twenty years old . . . as young as a little girl" (II, 182). After the "virtuous attachment" acquires a more determined reference, however, Strether "could think of nothing but the passion, mature, abysmal, pitiful, [de Vionnet] represented, and the possibilities she betrayed. She was older for him to-night, visibly less exempt from the touch of time; . . . and yet he could see her there as vulgarly troubled, in very truth, as a maidservant crying for her young man" (II, 286). De Vionnet's display of feigned youth for Jim is not only a technique of deception but also a kind of self-betrayal, a debilitating acquiescence to the constructions of fantasy. Once the "show" is uncovered the Parisian desire-text begins to lose its power, for there is after all something grounding those "names in the air."

And that grounding is recognized only from a distance, a critical distance that resists the conflation of experience and critical reflection. Just before discovering Chad and de Vionnet in the country together, Strether reflects on his own lost youth and the opportunity that Paris has given him to recapture it:

> He could have explained little enough to-day either why he had missed it or why, after years and years, he should care that he had; the main truth of the actual appeal of everything was none the less that everything represented the substance of his loss, put it within reach, within touch, made it, to a degree it had never been, an affair of the senses. That was what it became for him at this singular time, the youth he had long ago missed—a queer concrete presence, full of mystery, yet full of reality, which he could handle, taste, smell, the deep breathing of which he could positively hear. It was in the outside air as well as within.

> (II, 211)

Strether here moves from considering the representation of his loss, which brings it "within reach"—a locution signifying the approximation of the represented experience to the reality, which yet remains ultimately inaccessible—to a most emphatic assertion of actual possession of that lost reality: the loss becomes a concrete presence that *is* within reach, which indeed he can directly "handle, taste, smell." The slide from representation to bodily experience—the phantasmagoric, miracle world of Paris seen as providing "an affair of the senses"—superimposes imaginative reconstructions over physical time until the distinction is utterly broken: this "queer concrete presence" is the total absorption of physical time into the time of desire, memory, and imagination. De Vionnet is understood to be a creature caught in time rather than its master (the deep traditionality of her home and property that initially helps to create her impression on Strether later reinforces the sense of her desperation). And Strether, as he climbs the stairs for his last meeting with Chad, begins to feel old and to know that, according to the primitive law of succession, he will feel even "older . . . the next day" (II, 306). Thus the way is prepared for the distinction between representation and physical time to reassert itself.[13] And with its revival, Newsome's book returns to place in question Chad and de Vionnet's Parisian desire-text.

The revelation of Book Eleventh, central to any critical discussion of the novel, when compared to the revolutionary epiphanies preceding it, is more properly thought of as an anti-revelation, a dynamic shift that gives the lie to the pretensions of transcendence implicit in both the extreme rationalism of Woollett and the radical skepticism of Paris. But with the Parisian sensibility uppermost in Strether's consciousness, the shift is most drastically away from the intensely "fictional" and ungrounded Parisian epistemology. Post-

structuralist critics emphasize that James's account of the scene and its immediate aftermath is awash with metaphors of self-reflexivity, but they miss the larger critical context within which these metaphors operate.[14] Strether transforms a leisurely day in the French countryside into a virtual absorption within a long-remembered Lambinet painting, and the sense that fiction, imagination, memory, and desire are inextricably linked with—even determinative of—his experience is incessantly underscored. The possibility of distinction seems hopeless:

> For this had been all day at bottom the spell of the picture—that it was essentially more than anything else a scene and a stage, that the very air of the play was in the rustle of the willows and the tone of the sky. The play and the characters had, without his knowing it till now, peopled all his space for him, and it seemed somehow quite happy that they should offer themselves, in the conditions so supplied, with a kind of inevitability. . . . Not a single one of his observations but somehow fell into a place in it; not a breath of the cooler evening that was n't somehow a syllable of the text. The text was simply, when condensed, that in *these* places such things were, and that if it was in them one elected to move about one had to make one's account with what one lighted on.

> (II, 253-54)

Strether's fantasy of luxurious satisfaction, framed by the Lambinet painting, depends on the notion that this "scene" and "stage" harmoniously connect the worlds of nature and of his own desire; that the "flow" of sensation, though never yielding knowledge, is harmonious in its singularity. Indeed, the feeling is part of Strether's sense that time "slipped along so smoothly, mild but now slow, and melting, liquefying, into his happy illusion of idleness" (II, 251). But the "sharper arrest" (II, 255) provided by the appearance of Chad and de Vionnet in a boat on the barely rippling water represents the intrusion of definite discrimination into the field of smooth, liquid indeterminacy.[15] The incredible coincidence that Strether should meet them in this compromising circumstance is attributed to the fact that "fiction and fable *were,* inevitably, in the air, and not as a simple term of comparison, but as a result of things said" (II, 262). "Surface and sound" (II, 259) help them to negotiate the extremely awkward social occasion, but the significant difference realized by Strether is that, though within the realm of "things said" fiction could not be compared to "reality," the disjunction between what is said and what has presented itself has become crucial.

Unlike the other revelations, which were designed and controlled by the actors involved in order to achieve a certain effect, the incongruous appearance of the boat has an intelligibility that cannot be controlled by any of its spectators. De Vionnet slips into a French so studded with "idiomatic turns" that Strether cannot follow her, and she conducts a "comedy" of indirection to help them smooth over the sense that the encounter is "quite horrible" and that a scene of violence has just been averted (II, 260, 265, 258). But the fiction cannot re-name the "miracle of the encounter" (II, 258) and bring it within the desire-text, for that text, here so densely concentrated, has pushed the very notion of desire to its limit in order to reveal its inevitable source: the two lovers, seen on a flat, paperlike surface, mark a stable contiguity that cannot be subverted by representational construction: they are irrevocably bound together until such real time has elapsed that their boat can reach shore. James emphasizes that Strether sees the boat move "with the slow current": "They came slowly, floating down, evidently directed to the landing-place near their spectator" (II, 256). After the mutual recognition, sensations become "sharp," discriminations and decisions are made rapidly, in an "instant" or a matter of "seconds" (II, 257), while the boat makes its way to the shore. Whatever fiction is planned during these moments, and however time is "cut" by markers of intention, the slow drift *makes* the time for Strether to draw his conclusions about the two figures locked into the autonomous temporal current. The two, writers of but also written by the desire-text, are "lovers" metaphorically and, as their capture within physical time intimates, literally as well. And what is summoned is not silent fascination or childish passivity but a tremendous "amount of explanation" (II, 259).[16]

This resurgence of the need for explanation resurrects Newsome's rationalistic conception of Chad's state of mind and affairs in Paris: she understood that the only force capable of superseding her own physical authorship of her son would be an authorship operative at an equally fundamental, physical level. And it is de Vionnet, the older woman, creator of Chad and the "mother" of his transformation in Paris, who proves to fulfill this function and provide a reference for Newsome's prediction. In this light, Newsome's book is vindicated, for the sense of fiction dominating after the "revelation" is no longer controlled by desire as method, frame, and style of perception; instead the fictionalizing is orchestrated as a response to the ineluctable fact of de Vionnet's authorship, that fundamental connection whose meaning is traceable back to Woollett. The spring of this play is known and defines its quality: at the heart of the show is "the deep, deep truth of the intimacy revealed" (II, 266). And this is the sense to be drawn from James's incessant underscoring of the fictionality of Strether's experience in the countryside. The intimacy had not been named, but it *is* nameable; its truth is not exterior to the capacities of representation, requiring a (Levinasian) radical break or epiphany, nor is its truth simply "constructed" by Strether's aesthetic method of conceptualization. The desire-text turns in on itself so that desire—the physical desire that connects Chad and de Vionnet—becomes the subject of the book

that catches the meaning of its evasions "in the eye of nature" (II, 258). Thus de Vionnet becomes the victim of her own text: the author idolatrously worshiping her own construction is defeated by unlimited desire:

> With this sharpest perception yet [that de Vionnet fears Chad's desertion], it was like a chill in the air to him, it was almost appalling, that a creature so fine could be, by mysterious forces, a creature so exploited. For at the end of all things they *were* mysterious: she had but made Chad what he was—so why could she think she had made him infinite? . . . The work, however admirable, was nevertheless of the strict human order, and in short it was marvellous that the companion of mere earthly joys, of comforts, aberrations (however one classed them) within the common experience, should be so transcendently prized . . . the real coercion was to see a man ineffably adored.
>
> (II, 284-85)

James here asserts common experience over the private infinite, the work or the text of the "strict human order" over any text that calls for an ineffable adoration, and earthly joys over transcendent desire. With Newsome's book back in play but heavily qualified, Strether recognizes that however constraining the Woollett view was, "the real coercion" emerges from the text built by desire alone, a text in which one "move[s] among miracles" (II, 301).

After Strether realizes the true nature of the relationship between Chad and de Vionnet, he also understands that his cognitive failure was sustained by a childish fear of assuming the authority that his age and experience confer.[17] The elaborate "make-believe" manipulations of Chad and de Vionnet may have bottomed out in a crisis of "revelation," laying bare the lies that so disagree with Strether's "spiritual stomach" (II, 265), but his own role has also been crucial: he has presumed that nothing could be known about the object of his inquiry. The "school-boy" Strether, sitting before Chad's play at the theater box, must give way to the adult who knows that "it was all very well for him to feel the pity of its being so much like lying; he almost blushed, in the dark, for the way he had dressed the possibility in vagueness, as a little girl might have dressed her doll" (II, 266). Indeed, "he had really been *trying* all along to suppose nothing" (II, 266; emphasis added)—the desire-text, for all its grace, freedom, and charm, requires an unacknowledged effort to ward off the collapse of doubt. As Gostrey observes to Strether after he has been shocked back into his actual age, "things must have a basis," a foundation commensurate with what is built upon it: to "dress . . . up . . . the virtue" so that it is disconnected from an "intimate" and physical ground is to be either "grandly cynical . . . [or] grandly vague" (II, 300).

Strether does not "swing . . . back" (II, 296) to the principles of Woollett—certainty and moral inflexibility guided by a maturity beyond experience—but neither does he accede to the religious aestheticism exemplified by Chad's dramatic self-definition or intimated in the task of "saving" de Vionnet. His rejection of the extremes of both texts, and his understanding that both nevertheless convey a partial truth—Woollettian referential verticality (Chad *is* having an affair; lies *have* been told) and Parisian laterality (the quality and texture of experience cannot be reduced to utility)—is a reconciliation that James recognized as highly precarious. Chad combines the two texts in an entirely different way, drawing on the coercive elements of each: a combination of transcendent desire with hard practicality, a kind of instrumental reason according to which "knowing" means nothing more than "knowing how to get what one wants."[18]

But what Chad wants is subject to infinite change. His enthusiasm for advertising, which he declares "an art like another, and infinite like all the arts" (II, 316), turns the highly aestheticized Parisian epistemology to the tasks of commerce, the principal lure of Woollett's claim that Chad should "return." He will indeed return with more potent skills, uniquely suited to exploit the modern world of the image-market, an arena of beastliness (II, 313) where the primary goal is to manipulate desire. Chad's synthesis ironizes desire to such an extent that the last surviving criterion of value is the avoidance of boredom: he will leave de Vionnet when he is "tired of her" (II, 312). Strether's only course in this new world of miracles—but the miracles are thoroughly secularized—is to attempt a "curse" and "to appeal to [Chad] by all [he] hold[s] sacred" (II, 311), to satirize Chad's tepid irony by pushing Chad's synthesis against its own transcendental implications. The curse draws on the absolutist cast of both the Woollett book and the Paris play by purporting to establish a direct link between worldly affairs and the absolute narrator: if Chad fails in his responsibility to de Vionnet, then he invites a narration of damnation.

Strether's own apparent rejection of Gostrey's proposal at the end of the novel must be understood in this light. Critics usually discuss the ending as another of those Jamesian renunciations of personal ties (particularly carnal ones), as Strether (enacting James's own anxieties) turns away from the dangers of real sexual and emotional entanglement. But the novel's last line—"Then there we are!" (II, 327)—is less Strether's definitive rejection than his decision point, James's complex staging of possibility: "then" (implying sequence and causality) "there" (grounding in place, but also a place not simply "here") "we" (stressing commonality, the shared condition unbreakable by absolute difference) "are" (culminating in copresence where the temporal, the spatial, and the ethical intersect). Strether may leave but he hasn't yet, and what he says communicates merely a condition of possibility. A real decision is enabled in a scene infused with a sense of the past and of the commitments of the present. These final words are thus the critical counterpart to Chad's radical self-staging, which was designed to subvert commonality, overthrow personal history, and dis-enable judgment. Strether does not renounce Gostrey; rather, James simply releases Strether from narration, leaving his character where the other narrators would not. Newsome and de Vionnet attempted to write with or against the transcendent, and even Strether deployed a satirical narration of Chad's fate. But James affirms the true synthesis of texts, of desire and knowledge, by lifting his hand in the name of finitude.

Notes

1. Henry James, *The Ambassadors,* 2 vols., vols. 21-22 of *The Novels and Tales of Henry James: New York Edition* (New York: Charles Scribner's Sons, 1909), I, 89. Further references are to this edition and appear in the text.

2. James criticism, from the first, has considered the "international theme" by, in part, comparing American and European cultural values (mention frequently being made of James's comment that America lacks a tradition, or at least the institutions of a formal tradition) and translating America and Europe into their metaphorical significances. European "experience," "decadence," or "sophistication" and American "innocence," "naiveté," or "energy" are the often-invoked rough heuristic identifications made to characterize the two worldviews that come into conflict in James's novels. While the history of James criticism betrays no decided preference for one side of this binary over the other, Derridean or post-structuralist critics inevitably champion Paris for its representational skepticism.

3. Julie Rivkin, "The Logic of Delegation in *The Ambassadors,*" *PMLA* [*Proceedings of the Modern Language Association of America*], 101 (1986), 829-30.

4. "'The Intimate Difference': Power and Representation in *The Ambassadors,*" in *Henry James: Fiction as History,* ed. Ian F. A. Bell (London: Vision Press, 1984), p. 111.

5. Mary Cross, *Henry James: The Contingencies of Style* (London: MacMillan, 1993), p. 100.

6. Salmon is, of course, calling on the familiar Derridean inside/outside paradox, but Strether's "undecideable" position both within and without his representations of himself is not really all that surprising unless one expected self-representations to be either totally accurate and comprehensive or utterly false and illusory.

7. Richard Salmon, "The Secret of the Spectacle: Epistemology and Commodity Display in *The Ambassadors,*" *Henry James Review,* 14 (1993), 52.

8. Against Derrida's abyssal logic of the supplement, I would counter Paul Ricoeur's more worldly fallibilism, which insists on the important connection between knowledge and action and is particularly apropos *The Ambassadors*: "We should not . . . forget that the passage from inadequate ideas, which we form about ourselves and about things, to adequate ideas signifies for us the possibility of being truly *active*. In this sense, the power to act can be said to be increased by the retreat of passivity tied to inadequate ideas. . . . This conquest of activity under the aegis of adequate ideas makes the work [Spinoza's text] as a whole an *ethics*. Thus there is a close connection between the internal dynamism worthy of the name of life and the power of the intelligence, which governs the passage from inadequate to adequate ideas. In this sense, we are powerful when we understand adequately our, as it were, horizontal and external dependence with respect to all things, and our vertical and immanent dependence with respect to the primordial power that Spinoza continues to name 'God'" (Paul Ricoeur, *Oneself as Another,* trans. Kathleen Blamey [Chicago: Univ. of Chicago Press, 1992], p. 316).

9. Nicola Bradbury notes that "when the [first meeting between Chad and Strether] finally takes place, it is in contrast with the kinetic tension of the preparatory movement, with its series of other, less important, interviews, that this, with its curiously static quality, stands out" (*Henry James: The Later Novels* [Oxford: Clarendon Press, 1979], p. 49). Indeed, the static quality of the scene signals an intensification of the present moment as well as its explosion as radical difference; time, for Strether, pivots on this moment and seems to reverse itself.

10. The language employed here may for the present-day reader recall the work of Emmanuel Levinas, who attempts to open a kind of thinking outside representation's appropriation of the Other as an aspect of the Same. For Levinas this escape is available in a radical experience of alterity, an epiphany of the face that signifies an absolute exteriority (see Emmanuel Levinas, "The Face Speaks," in his *Totality and Infinity: An Essay on Exteriority,* trans. A. Lingis [Pittsburgh: Duquesne Univ. Press, 1969], p. 67). Representation, on this account, is idealistic and solipsistic, a mode of access to the not-self that ultimately imprisons one, as Ricoeur characterizes the Levinasian view, in the "stubbornly closed, locked up, separate ego" (Ricoeur, p. 337). In James's text, however, where Chad's appearance is indeed rendered as an epiphany of disruption, an extreme ethics of radical alienation is challenged as being as corrosive as its appropriating counterpart.

11. See *False Positions: The Representational Logics of Henry James's Fiction* (Stanford: Stanford Univ. Press, 1996), p. 76.

12. While this speech is indeed central to the novel's concerns, it should not be taken as unproblematically affirmative, a simple declaration of James's overriding theme. In the narrative context, the plea that one should live all one can is interwoven with a notion of life that is entirely ephemeral.

13. I would like to note here John B. Brough's comment: "With regard to time's structure, . . . one might put the following suggestions before the deconstructionist: There may be plural times and concepts of time, but they will share certain fundamental features; these times may not fit the pattern of a single, unified, linear time, but they do presume the conception of such a time in certain respects; finally, the possibility that all particular times may implicitly have a place in a single all-embracing time should not be foreclosed by an a priori conception of what is metaphysical and what is not" ("Husserl and the Deconstruction of Time," *Review of Metaphysics,* 46 [1993], 535). Indeed, as M. C. Dillon has argued, a metaphysical understanding of time is more properly attributed to Derrida, who relies on "the Eleatic conception of time and its relation to being. Only if being is equated with immutability/eternity and becoming is relegated to mere appearance on the grounds of the nonbeing of that which changes, only then does the founding aporia of real eternal now versus unreal passing now generate itself. The deconstruction of presence rests on the assumption that there is a formal necessity that time in our epoch be conceived in this Eleatic way" (M. C. Dillon, "The Metaphysics of Presence: Critique of a Critique," in *Working through Derrida,* ed. Gary B. Madison [Evanston, Ill.: Northwestern Univ. Press, 1993], p. 201). Derrida is able to introduce representation into the heart of Husserlian presence, for example, only by making this assumption; the result is the subversion of the distinction between real and constructed time.

14. John Landau sees *The Ambassadors* as a novel that "reveal[s] aberrations in the representation or mediation of things, which themselves become indeterminate and, perhaps, ultimately inaccessible. *The Ambassadors* . . . engages the radical impossibility of apprehending experience directly" ("*A Thing Divided": Representation in the Late Novels of Henry James* [Cranbury, N.J.: Fairleigh Dickinson Univ. Press, 1996], p. 56). Landau's reading stresses the Parisian disruption of the Woollettian representational economy, but it ignores Strether's sudden realization that Paris obscured what, in a limited way, Woollett knew

about Chad's transformation. Landau quotes at length the passages leading up to the crucial reversal, but he has nothing to say about Strether's revulsion at having avoided explanation or his realization that things must indeed have a foundation. Instead, Landau concludes his look at the Lambinet scene this way: "Here all the terms and modes through which experience is mediated merge and meld. It is as though this interpenetration and the overwhelming evidence of the mediated aspect of experience is the very condition which from the outset was in the nature of Strether's embassy. Pictures, play, nature, art, texts, all combine to contribute to Strether's sense of well-being, his general confidence. The representative from Woollett has finally recognized that the distinctions he had come to Paris to make must disappear in the network of interpenetrations in which he has perforce to function. . . . The multiplicity of codes in the symbolic order is *the thing* he became aware of, and it is thus impossible to represent parts of it without implicating the whole" (p. 76). Yes, but soon after this grand ironic set-up Strether loses his confidence and feels that he has been a fool. The Woollettian distinctions are curiously resurrected right in the heart of the Lambinet, where all of this fictionality suddenly bottoms out.

15. Paul G. Beidler wisely avoids reading *The Ambassadors* from an excessively Parisian point of view, arguing instead that "the Lambinet chapters . . . portray Strether's greatest triumph of the novel, for it is here that Strether finally breaks free of the destructive Paris aesthetic" (*Frames in James: "The Tragic Muse," "The Turn of the Screw," "What Masie Knew," and "The Ambassadors"* [Victoria, B.C.: English Literary Studies, Univ. of Victoria, 1993], p. 80). Beidler denounces the Paris aesthetic on the grounds that its main premise is inaction: "Action is vulgar under the Paris aesthetic, and beauty is found in one's potential, not one's endeavors" (p. 88). I think that this view is accurate, yet Beidler down-plays the damning similarities evident between that aesthetic and the underlying assumptions of the Derridean analysis that he undertakes. He reads the post-Lambinet Strether as finding a synthesis of Woollett and Paris, but by reading this binary strictly in terms of ethics and aesthetics, respectively, he allows the Parisian *epistemology* to have unchallenged supremacy. He thus concludes: "Strether has left the oblong gilt frame behind now and has re-entered the drama of Paris as an active participant, an entity now to be reckoned with. The difference is that Strether now knows, as the others do, that he is acting in a drama, a fiction in which everyone has, like Chad and Madame de Vionnet, 'something to put a face upon'" (p. 91).

16. Richard D. Hathaway argues that "we must do as Strether did: we must float with, not fight, the flow; we must relax into the tensions of opposites. We must accept a multiplicity that cannot always be resolved into a simplicity. We have to go with the ghosts" ("Ghosts at the Window: Shadow and Corona in *The Ambassadors*," *Henry James Review,* 18 [1997], 84). And de Vionnet, of course, is one of these ghosts with whom we should relax, since "the medium in which she floats is soft as a ghostly sigh, as soft and tantalizing as phosphorescence" (p. 81). Mrs. Newsome, however, must be rejected because "Woollett-mindedness cannot abide ghosts" (p. 84). Yet floating serenely on the soft waters may be no protection against a sharp arrest that transforms floating into the slow time of critical reflection, the kind that permits the partial recover of Mrs. Newsome's book. De Vionnet, caught in this time, is no longer so ghostly. Hathaway also deploys the usual post-structuralist tactic of calling on an absolute standard to undermine knowledge claims when he remarks: "We may think we now know the truth about Marie and Chad, but we don't; we know only the image, the surface appearance. We have never seen into their minds, their history, their hearts, as lovers of each other" (p. 91). But of course there is always more to know. Only if knowing is made to mean total, divine apprehension does the acquisition of any particular fact, however crucial, not count as knowing. The point is that Strether did not know Chad and de Vionnet *were* lovers, and it is only with that fact that Strether can begin to wonder about any of the other questions that Hathaway mentions.

17. In his description of the novel that he sent to Harper and Brothers in 1900, James comments that "all the value of [Strether's] total episode, and all the enjoyment of it, has precisely been that 'knowing' was the effect of it," and that only in the face of this knowing does Strether have "a beautiful chance . . . not to shirk" (Henry James, "Project of Novel," in *The Complete Notebooks of Henry James,* ed. Leon Edel and Lyall H. Powers [New York: Oxford Univ. Press, 1987], p. 571).

18. This is a paraphrase of a description in *The Wings of the Dove* (1902) of Kate Croy, another figure who combines the artist's touch with ruthless practicality (see Henry James, *The Wings of the Dove,* 2 vols., vols. 19-20 of the *New York Edition* [New York: Charles Scribner's Sons, 1909], II, 226).

Siobhan Peiffer (essay date spring 2002)

SOURCE: Peiffer, Siobhan. "Commerce and Freedom in *The Ambassadors.*" *Henry James Review* 23, no. 2 (spring 2002): 95-104.

[*In the following essay, Peiffer discusses questions of economic exchange and independence as they relate to personal freedom and choices made by characters in* The Ambassadors.]

When H. G. Wells criticized Henry James in *Boon,* he described an author who created "no people with defined political opinions, no people with religious opinions, none with clear partisanships or with lusts or whims [. . .] no poor people dominated by the imperatives of Saturday night and Monday morning [. . .]" ([*Boon, The Mind of the Race, The Wild Asses of the Devil, and The Last Trump*] 96). In James's famous response, he attacked the assumption that well-crafted literature is irrelevant to everyday existence. "I regard it as relevant in a degree that leaves everything else behind," he writes. "It is art that *makes* life, makes interest, makes importance, for our consideration and application of these things, and I know of no substitute whatever for the force and beauty of its process" (*HJL* [*The Letters of Henry James*] 490). "Opinions" and "Monday morning[s]" are enriched by the force and beauty of James's fiction, and an awareness, in turn, of his writing's sociological context helps to explain better many of his characters' moral decisions. Yet while the critical "paradigm shift from literary to cultural criticism," as Ross Posnock has termed it, has lavished attention on many James works (["Henry James and the Limits of Historicism"] 273), critical attention to *The Ambassadors* has yet to plumb the metaphors of commerce within the novel and allusions to commerce in other novels in relation to the book's historical context.[1] Such examination would help to explain more fully Lambert Strether's ethical development.

It is the "rightness" of Lambert Strether's final choice in the novel that must be understood. In the final scene of *The Ambassadors,* Strether decides to return to a life without job, wife, or financial support, and calls his decision "right"—the right ending to his story and the right choice morally. Yet a choice so pure as to be entirely "right" may be impossible in realist fiction. In her analysis of justice and late-nineteenth-century American novels, Wai Chee Dimock writes that novels' endings, by never seeming entirely "right," become through this "sense of mismatch" an "eloquent dissent from that canon of rational adequation" forwarded by legal or philosophical rhetoric ([*Residues of Justice*] 10). Stories prove "commensurability," in Dimock's phrasing (9), to be a lie—the commensurability of the justice's scales or, perhaps more fundamentally, of the perfect economic exchange. Commerce supports the ideal of a

quantified worth for every identifiable particular, yet does so only by making this worth dependent, ever-changing, and malleable, a product of circumstance rather than a fundamental, or even a universal, descriptor. In *The Ambassadors* Strether learns the power of commerce to govern exchanges between people, as well as purchases of things, and confronts the "mismatch" that results. The relation of Strether's moral development to Basil Ransom's in *The Bostonians* builds an idea of freedom and economics specific to James's American past.

Dimock's use of American nineteenth-century realist novels to study questions of commensurability is not an arbitrary choice. It is a canon whose historical context—dominated by the slaveholding Confederacy and its aftermath and by the rise of industrial factory-based capitalism—naturally makes the question of economic and judicial equality particularly cogent. And as Brook Thomas has argued, the rights of citizenship were indistinguishable, during Reconstruction, from the rights to buy and sell. "The first right listed in the 1866 Civil Rights Act was the right to make and enforce contracts, thus guaranteeing freedmen's ability to contract their labor to gain property," he writes, and "the 14th Amendment was designed in part to leave no doubt that the 1866 Act was constitutional" ([*American Literary Realism and the Failed Promise of Contract*] 38).

To remember this "identification of freedom with a system of contractual labor" is to dismiss many analyses of late-nineteenth-century Supreme Court decisions, such as *Plessy v. Ferguson,* supporting segregation, and *Lochner v. New York,* supporting exploitation of workers. Both used the Fourteenth Amendment as justification, which prompts critics like Kenneth Warren to see both as part of "a retreat that moved the body of Northern public opinion to an acceptance of policies and decisions mandating the social, political, and economic subordination of the nation's freedmen" (*Black and White* [*Black and White Strangers*] 38). But as Thomas rightly notes, there was no "retreat": "the Court did not move away from the morally responsible social intent of the 14th Amendment toward an immoral, or at best amoral, economic interpretation for the simple reason that the amendment was economic and moral from the start" (40). To reformers, of course, a change of legal definition was easier than a radical alteration of economic patterns. Perhaps for this reason, the reforming energy of Northern abolitionists was, toward the end of the century, re-channeled into female suffrage, an area where simple legal enfranchisement could again seem like a victory. Yet for that triumph to be a true freedom, or for abolition to be, would require an economic enfranchisement that remained as impossible for women at the century's end as it was for African Americans. Warren is correct when he urges a reading of James's work "against the backdrop" of slavery and segregation

(*Black and White* 38), for it haunts the economics so important to his fiction: In James's subtle exploration of freedom and purchase, slavery is effectively eradicated only through participation in the commerce that drives so many of his metaphors.[2] But in *The Ambassadors* and *The Bostonians* James shows that the American ethos of personal liberty—the freedom to choose—depended often on an economics of possessing others or, more insidiously, enslaving the self.

Claire Oberon Garcia rightly notes that though "Strether is often read as a man [. . .] outside of 'the world of grab,'" his "vision is profoundly influenced, if not created by" its commercial values (["The Shopper and the Shopper's Friend"] 155). She sees this as an inevitable outcome of the novel's historical moment in late-nineteenth-century capitalism, a time when "codes of meaning related to business dominated both the American consciousness and the rhetoric of the age" (154). In *The Ambassadors,* however, James looks farther and tests economic "codes of meaning" by driving them toward logical extremes: slavery or prostitution. Early in his Parisian sojourn Strether is brought up short by Chad's question, "Do you think one's kept only by women?" (101). The challenge makes Strether wince not only because it voices the hitherto-only-suspected status of Chad's connections in Paris, but also because it so closely approaches a criticism of Strether's own position. Strether is kept by a woman; he is a failure because he is not economically independent, because he is a purchased commodity maintained by Mrs. Newsome and later "handed over" or "given away" (127). Strether's debt is so large that Mrs. Newsome can direct his movements, sending him to Paris, for instance. She is both his business superior and his future wife, and the possibility for coercion in the two relationships seems remarkably alike—a fact of which Strether seems painfully conscious. While slavery and prostitution usually assume a male purchaser, both Strether and Chad must confront the possibility that female economic power, and female sexuality, can also take control of men.

This reversal (and its ramifications for Strether and other men) has a powerful Jamesian echo: Basil Ransom, in *The Bostonians,* also considers what it might be like to be "kept by a woman." After Ransom's move north, the narrator describes his run-down environment to summarize that "we need, in strictness, concern ourselves with it no further than to gather the implication that the young Mississippian [. . .] had not made his profession very lucrative" (191). In Ransom's New York, as in Strether's and Mrs. Newsome's Woollett, success means economic independence. Basil has therefore failed. Even poverty, however, cannot prevent him from quitting his job as tutor to Mrs. Luna's son. The reason is simple: "it was disagreeable to him to have pecuniary relations with a lady who had not the art of

concealing from him that she liked to place him under obligations" (197). Mrs. Luna wants these "obligations" to include marriage, and, like Mrs. Newsome, she knows that economic debt is a sure way to lead toward a more permanent tie. The only reason that Ransom momentarily considers such a relationship is to publish his views in a journal that is to be supported by Mrs. Luna, much as Strether's Review is supported by Mrs. Newsome. But Ransom is more wary than Strether: even for his journalistic career, Ransom will not go into a permanent debt—a slavery—to Mrs. Luna. To him it would be a perversion. Since women, he believes, are "essentially inferior to men" (197), they should naturally depend on rather than support men economically. In Ransom's opinion, women are owed nothing more than the "tax" of chivalry, a small debt discharged out of vast stores of male power (198). Even the prototypical virtue of the Southern male here becomes an economic quantity. To Ransom, a man not "earning his fee" and granting women small percentages relinquishes a large part of his masculinity. To be economically controlled by a woman is to be even more definitively emasculated (197). Ransom "would have despised himself if he had been capable of confessing to a woman that he couldn't make a living. Such questions were none of their business [. . .]" (205). The neat play on "business" concludes Ransom's use of economics in his philosophy of white male superiority. Business is the domain of men, and women must keep well out of it; men control women as they control economic exchange.

Basil's anxiety here comes from his need to be owning rather than owned, and *The Bostonians* shows that such need stems from a nostalgia for the self-defining power to buy and sell slaves. In conversation with Mrs. Birdseye, Basil jokes that the South was "a good cause" and "meant this allusion to the great Secession and, by comparison, to the attitude of the resisting male (laudable even as that may be) to be decently jocular" (221). The comparison of two equally laudable (to Basil's mind) efforts of resistance depends not on a jocular connection but on their similarly economic impetus. James's allusion to Ransom's past makes this clear: near the start of the story, he writes that Basil "had more than once reflected that a moderate capital was an aid to achievement. He had seen in his younger years one of the biggest failures that history commemorates, an immense national *fiasco,* and it had implanted in his mind a deep aversion to the ineffectual" (17). The direction and sequence of Basil's thoughts here are no accident: to Basil, the Civil War *fiasco* is a failure of capital; its principal lesson is the need for economic, not political or social, viability.

Olive "loses" Verena to Basil in part because she capitulates to his equation of capital and power. She uses Basil's slave-holding past as a particularly damning criticism—she calls him "a man who, no doubt, desired to treat women with the lash and manacles, as he and his people had formerly treated the wretched coloured race"—but desires just as badly as he to possess Verena with similar totality.[3] Verena must be hers: Olive doesn't "wish to think of the girl's belonging to anybody but herself" (111) and looks for "a chance to take a more complete possession of the girl" (132). She eventually *buys* Verena from her father "for a very considerable amount" (168). The fact that Olive, a Northern abolitionist and suffragette, purchases a woman to work for the cause of women's liberty, shows how far she is from fighting true oppression. (In a fitting detail, Mrs. Tarrant, the daughter of a famous abolitionist, uses Olive's check to hire a female domestic: "servile, mercenary labour" [175].) Female liberation could have meant a transcendence of old male-female relations of purchaser-and-commodity, but Olive's actions guarantee that this will not be the case. She is willing even to contemplate Verena's marriage to the rich Henry Burrage, not from thoughts of the girl's feelings, self-expression, or relative liberty, but because partnership would mean "a large command of money" (317).

Such grasping for money accedes to the conflation of male-female power relations with economic power relations, and this, in practical terms at the time of *The Bostonians,* dooms women to the subordinate position occupied by African Americans during slavery. In *The Portrait of a Lady,* written five years before *The Bostonians,* Mrs. Touchett calls "poor American ladies" "the slaves of slaves." It is Henrietta who responds, Henrietta, the novel's principle example of female liberation, who earns her own way through writing journalism. She tells Mrs. Touchett that American women are "the companions of freemen." But this guarantees nothing, as Mrs. Touchett cynically notes: "They are the companions of their servants—the Irish chambermaid and the Negro waiter. They share their work" (89).[4] Olive will not admit this, of course. When she asks Basil about the status of his own female relatives in Mississippi, Ransom tells her that their only happiness was "not to think about it too much, and to make the best of their circumstances." Olive interprets this as subjugation by male authority—"You mean that you have traced a certain line for them, and that that's all you know about it!" she tells Basil (258-59)—but it is rather subjugation by Reconstruction poverty. Without any purchasing power, dependent on their male kin, Basil's female relatives must do the work once performed by slaves. Olive herself, an independent woman with her own wealth, may seem a model for the liberated female, but she does not recognize that she perpetuates a commercial system enslaving most of her sex.

As Thomas notes, the real freedom of the Fourteenth Amendment was the freedom of the former slave to contract his own labor and thus to earn the power of individual economic control (38). James recognized that

liberty must begin with economic liberty, and impugns not only Olive and Basil but a larger category of hypocritical late-nineteenth-century "reformers" who wish to support the cause of equality without altering their own economic superiority. In an essay on Emerson, James quotes approvingly the elder Bostonian's question: "Does he not do more to abolish slavery who works all day steadily in his own garden, than he who goes to the abolition meeting and makes a speech? He who does his own work frees a slave" (*SC* [*Selected Literary Criticism*] 83). James's essay also remembers "the great meeting in the Boston Music Hall, on the first day of 1863, to celebrate the signing by Mr. Lincoln of the proclamation freeing the Southern slaves," when Emerson read from his "Boston Hymn." James excerpts the climactic verse: "Pay ransom to the owner / And fill the bag to the brim. / Who is the owner? The slave is owner / And ever was. Pay *him!*"[5] Emerson realizes that "independence" must mean the capacity for credit, and, thus, that America must recognize its immense debt to those who worked as slaves.[6] James, who wrote his appreciative essay a year after he published *The Bostonians,*[7] would have included the "ransom" to women. But James's Ransom will never pay Emerson's "ransom." Nor will Olive.

More perceptive than either Basil or Olive, Strether tries to ransom himself as he frees others. Like *The Bostonians, The Ambassadors* shows that independence is based on the exercise of economic liberty. Strether and Maria Gostrey "realize" early in the book that when Waymarsh dashes for a jeweler's shop, where "he may buy everything," he "has struck for freedom" (39). That freedom is an especially American concern is confirmed by Jeanne's innocent remark: "Oh but I'm almost American too. That's what mamma has wanted me to be—I mean *like* that; for she has wanted me to have lots of freedom" (154). Waymarsh tries almost comically to short-circuit the process in one blunt and efficient mass purchase, but Strether, with less "capital" of money or experience, is already indebted to Mrs. Newsome; he cannot exercise independence in one rush but must instead purchase or borrow resources of experience and perception from Maria. His own ransoming becomes more complicated than any in *The Bostonians,* for in *The Ambassadors* debts—and worth of all sorts—have become much more uncertain.

The Bostonians sees payment and ownership as an all-or-nothing affair: the model is slavery, Olive or Basil must possess Verena entirely, and all debts are infinite. Olive, for instance, "considered men in general as so much in the debt of the opposite sex that any individual woman had an unlimited credit with them; she could not possibly overdraw the general feminine account" (141). In *The Ambassadors,* economic value has acquired a fineness of gradation. The shift reflects a triumphant new economy based on paper money and interested credit rather than capital assets like land and slaves. In American economic history, nineteenth-century commercial expansion was coupled with a fervent national debate about the status of currency. Paper money advocates fought against "gold bugs" who argued that the entirely manufactured value of printed bills would undermine a system more properly grounded on the "inherent" worth of gold. Though the debate was, as Ian Bell notes, "the clear paradox of one form of abstraction competing with another on the contradictory grounds of its supposedly 'natural' materiality" (["Money, History and Writing in Henry James"] 23), the concern for a bill's ability to be counterfeited, revalued, re-signified and re-inscribed was an aesthetic as well as a financial fear. Criticism of paper money used the example of art and writing to show that paper inscriptions were too changeable and too insignificant to act as a standard of worth (Shell [*Money, Language and Thought*] 5-23). The possibility of currency fluctuation revealed a deeper truth—the relative, transient nature of all value-fixing systems—that could rock aesthetics as well as commerce.

Though paper money had won the argument by the time of *The Bostonians*—Basil Ransom must send "greenbacks" home to his female relatives in Mississippi (194)—Basil clearly pines for the embodied wealth of slaves, the South's economic standard, which had provided him with position and power.[8] For Lambert Strether, debates about the changeable value of inscriptions on paper jeopardize self-worth in more than one way. He bases his identity on the writing on the cover of his Review, a relationship he finds precisely backwards: "He was Lambert Strether because he was on the cover, whereas it should have been, for anything like glory, that he was on the cover because he was Lambert Strether" (61). His identity is all appearance, for the Review is all cover: when Maria asks, "What kind of Review is it?" he replies, "Well, it's green"—an answer which not only confirms the journal's superficiality but links that superficiality to the fickle worth of paper greenbacks (50). Strether is an editor, whose job it is to make the green cover worth more, which will increase the worth of the Review, which will increase the worth of his own name, which exists in Woollett only because of the green cover. He can contract his labor and assert his individuality only by making that individuality one more product of fluctuating value. (In his autobiography, "Notes of a Son and Brother," James cherished the defining memory of "the very greenbacks [. . .] into which I had changed the cheque of my first earned wage." This wage, also, came from a literary review [*AU* [*Autobiography*] 476].)

The Ambassadors shows people to be valued like currency—then makes currency of variable value. Chad may return to a job in advertising, "at this time of day the secret of the trade" according to Strether, an art of

manipulating demand and exploiting the full range of possible perception (339). But it is not just advertising: all writing assigns worth, and James's novel often conflates two senses of "account," financial record and written narrative. Strether is compulsively writing "accounts" home to Mrs. Newsome to pay off the vast "account" he owes her, and it is the interruption of Mrs. Newsome's letters to him that makes him believe she has ceased to support him financially (195). As the unnamed product of the Woollett manufacture seems to wait for Chad's advertising to grant it a name and a price, even Chad himself can find his identity and self-importance only through economics: since his new job meant "money, to very large amounts," as Strether explains to Maria at the start of the novel, "if he'll pull himself together and come home, [. . .] he'll find his account in it" (47). Accounts (letters, stories, debts) must shuttle constantly among James's characters, because in the economic construction of identity, one is always dependent on the valuation of others. When the Pococks arrive in Paris, for example, Strether wants from them "an account more full and free of Mrs. Newsome's state of mind than any he felt he could now expect," for this account will "prove to himself that he was not afraid to look his behaviour in the face"; he is "impatient to know the cost" and "ready to pay in instalments" (198). Experiences and people have their prices, but all prices are set by demand; Strether can know his own only when he knows what others think. "The finely conscious Jamesian hero is a spectator at a slave market," writes Alfred Habegger. "But even though he is supposed to be a good observer, he doesn't understand that it is a slave market until he learns that he himself has been bought and sold" (254).

Strether cannot leave this market, but unlike Olive and Basil, he is aware of it and begins to use its forces to better purpose. Only by asserting debts owed to him can he begin to pay off his own and buy himself back; only by limiting the freedom of others can he begin to free himself. He prevents his and Chad's reentry into Woollett's economics by calling Chad to account. Chad wants to return, and Strether tells him "you're absolutely free to do as you choose" but in the next moment reminds him, "what you owe me." Chad asks, "How can I pay?" and Strether replies, "By not deserting me. By standing by me" (189). Chad is "freed" from Woollett's commercial demands only by another debt. Strether uses the same tactic to keep Chad with Madame Vionnet. "You owe her everything," he tells the younger man (338) and advises Chad to leave her only if he has "got all that can be got," knowing that "there will always be something to be got" (337). Like Basil Ransom, Strether began his tale wincing at the prospect of being "kept" by a woman; he assumed that virtue and economic dependence were incompatible. Now, figuring a relationship as a business exchange guarantees that Chad will do the right thing. The codependencies of commerce keep both parties aware of mutual debt and make an absolutely "free" action as unnecessary as it is impossible. Quite early on, the perceptive Miss Gostrey articulates what Strether himself has barely learned of Madame Vionnet and her "virtuous" attachment to Chad. "Your idea is that it can be virtuous—in any sense worthy of the name—only if she's *not* free?" (117). Strether's idea proves true—and, as always in James, the subordinate aside is as important as the principal clause. "In any sense worthy of the *name*," Maria specifies, for while a name may be an arbitrary verbalization of worth (like an advertisement or a novel), virtuous action depends on an awareness of accounts, a consciousness of debts and credits.⁹

Through explorations of commerce, *The Ambassadors* realizes what *The Bostonians* could not: complete freedom is as undesirable as complete enslavement. Characters must recognize what they owe through what they are owed; they must recognize their liberties through their conscriptions. Keeping each condition partial and dependent prevents morality from becoming a slave market, where every transaction erases the entire self as it erases all possibility of future economic agency. What liberation there is may be partial, but its very incompleteness makes it possible. In *Playing in the Dark,* Toni Morrison has analyzed how every knowledge of independence depends on its opposite; in many American novels, she writes, "freedom has no meaning [. . .] without the specter of enslavement [. . .] the signed, marked, informing, and mutating presence of a black slave" (56). Throughout the book, she shows slavery to be the defining other of self-fashioned individualism in American protagonists during and beyond the nineteenth century. In *The Bostonians* and *The Ambassadors,* James shows slavery as the limit and death of economic activity as it was the limit and death of freedom.¹⁰ It is the dream of commensurability, to use Dimock's word, that James troubles through the ethical education of his characters. In them, the specter of enslavement has become a necessary internal awareness of the free purchasing subject.

This leaves Strether, at the close of *The Ambassadors,* with a heightened sense of what he found in the second paragraph: "that his relation to his actual errand might prove none of the simplest. He was burdened, poor Strether—it had better be confessed at the outset—with the oddity of a double consciousness" (18).¹¹ F. O. Matthiessen writes that Strether "symbolizes the illusion of free will" ([*Henry James*] 26). It is in Strether's own recognition of the illusion that he is able to grant others, and himself, a fuller measure of freedom. Basil Ransom had to possess Verena to avoid Mrs. Luna's possession and to seem an independent, economically successful man; Strether can abandon his indebted position with Mrs. Newsome without taking the "exquisite service" of Maria. He thus resolves instead "not, out of

the whole affair, to have got anything for myself," nothing but the "wonderful impressions" that comprise his new sensibility (345). The ending of *The Ambassadors* absorbs the lessons of *The Bostonians* to become James's fullest representation of free and equal relations between two Americans, and between a man and a woman.

Notes

1. Several older studies give limited attention to commercial images in *The Ambassadors*. Dietrichson argues that the "evil nature of late-nineteenth-century New England commercialism—represented by Woollett and Mrs. Newsome with her family and also by Mr. Waymarsh, a lawyer friend of the protagonist, Lambert Strether—is revealed, especially through the contrast made with the social and aesthetic beauty of the Parisian world" (86-87). None of the ambassadors from Woollett are so obviously "evil" and none of the Parisians so obviously "good" as to make this statement true. Dietrichson also believes that Strether and Chad "stand for contrasting attitudes to money: Strether, a responsible, unselfish one which subordinates pecuniary wants and wishes to moral obligations, Chad a selfish, grasping one which makes him disregard these obligations for the sake of pecuniary advantage and social status" (147). This is also overly reductive: Chad would not treat Madame Vionnet as he does were he interested only in pecuniary advantage and social status, and Strether would not be in Paris were it not for certain pecuniary wants and obligations. Mull's approach is more nuanced, and his textual analysis detailed: he analyzes how the money in James's writing "becomes a nexus of meanings, significant in the totality of its relations, rather than a thing determinately meaningful in itself" (5). His book has few specific things to say about *The Ambassadors,* however. In a more recent essay, Garcia addresses some of the failures of these earlier views, beginning with the important assertion that "there is no tidy dichotomy between the money-grubbing values of industrial Woollett and the civilized, ideal values of European culture" (152).

2. Economics is one of James's most pervasive tropes. See Dietrichson (68) and Mull (12).

3. Many critics have identified a similar conservatism in Olive and Basil. Fetterley, for instance, writes that "Olive believes ultimately neither in herself nor in women nor in their cause or movement. Her similarity to Ransom is not simply that they are both possessive, jealous, and conservative, but that they both see as inevitable the patriarchal system" (137).

4. Person shows how James links racial and gendered hierarchies, arguing that "*The Bostonians*

transposes gender and race through a complex process of subject positioning" (293).

5. For the complete poem, see "Boston Hymn" (Emerson 211-14).

6. Current arguments for slave reparations foresee possible cases based on both breach of contract and damages. Both tacks put the economic power to make contracts at the center of a truly free citizenship. See "Making the Case for Racial Reparations."

7. Emerson's notion of the economics of slavery was clearly important to *The Bostonians,* and one of the early inspirations for *The Bostonians* was a reference to "numberless projects of social reform" in a letter from Emerson to Carlyle that James read in 1883 (Edel 311).

8. The fact that slaves were the true currency of the South is demonstrated by Confederate paper money, which was imprinted with the images of slaves "usually contented and sometimes smiling"; Firestone writes that "southern banks enshrined slavery in their monetary system to remind those who came in contact with their bills that the institution was the region's economic bedrock."

9. "The process, that of the expression, the literal squeezing-out, of value is another affair [. . .]," James wrote, describing his composition process, in the preface to *The American.* "It's all a sedentary part—involves as much ciphering, of sorts, as would merit the highest salary paid to a chief accountant" (*AN* [*The Art of the Novel*] 312).

10. I do not want to suggest that James's direct representations of race always transcend Morrison's analysis. In *The American Scene* James also uses the African American as a way to define himself, the documenting observer (Blair [*Henry James and the Writing of Race and Nation*] 207). See also Warren ("Still Reading" ["Still Reading Henry James?"] 282-84).

11. Though W. E. B. DuBois's use of "double consciousness" appeared in 1897, Warren argues against an allusion: "DuBois and James adapted the term from a host of other sources" (*Black and White* 12). A profitable comparison, however, need not assume direct influence. James did admire *The Souls of Black Folk* (*AS* [*The American Scene*] 418).

Works by Henry James

The Ambassadors. Ed. S. P. Rosenbaum. New York: Norton, 1964.

AS—The American Scene. London: Chapman, 1907.

AN—The Art of the Novel. London: Scribner's, 1934.

AU—Autobiography. Ed. Frederick W. Dupee. London: Allen, 1956.

The Bostonians. New York: Random, 1956.

HJL—The Letters of Henry James. Ed. Percy Lubbock. Vol. 2. London: Scribner's, 1920.

The Portrait of a Lady. New York: Norton, 1975.

SC—Selected Literary Criticism. Ed. Morris Shapira. London: Heinemann, 1963.

Other Works Cited

Bell, Ian F. A. "Money, History and Writing in Henry James: Assaying *Washington Square.*" *Henry James: Fiction as History.* Ed. Ian F. A. Bell. London: Vision, 1984. 11-48.

Blair, Sara. *Henry James and the Writing of Race and Nation.* Cambridge: Cambridge UP, 1996.

Dietrichson, Jan W. *The Image of Money in the American Novel of the Gilded Age.* New York: Humanities, 1969.

Dimock, Wai Chee. *Residues of Justice: Literature, Law, Philosophy.* Berkeley: U of California P, 1996.

Edel, Leon. *Henry James: A Life.* New York: Harper, 1985.

Emerson, Ralph Waldo. *Poems of Emerson.* London: Oxford UP, 1914.

Fetterley, Judith. *The Resisting Reader: A Feminist Approach to American Fiction.* Bloomington: Indiana UP, 1978.

Firestone, David. "When Slaves and Currency Were One: Interpreting the Images of Toil That the Confederacy Used on Its Money." *New York Times* 6 Mar. 2001: E1.

Garcia, Claire Oberon. "The Shopper and the Shopper's Friend: Lambert Strether and Maria Gostrey's Consumer Consciousness." *Henry James Review* 16 (1995): 153-71.

Habegger, Alfred. *Gender, Fantasy and Realism in American Literature.* New York: Columbia UP, 1982.

"Making the Case for Racial Reparations." *Harper's* Nov. 2000: 37-51.

Matthiessen, F. O. *Henry James: The Major Phase.* Oxford: Oxford UP, 1946.

Morrison, Toni. *Playing in the Dark: Whiteness and the Literary Imagination.* Cambridge: Harvard UP, 1992.

Mull, Donald L. *Henry James's "Sublime Economy": Money as Symbolic Center in the Fiction.* Middletown: Wesleyan UP, 1973.

Person, Leland S. "In the Closet with Frederick Douglass: Reconstructing Masculinity in *The Bostonians.*" *Henry James Review* 16 (1995): 292-98.

Posnock, Ross. "Henry James and the Limits of Historicism." *Henry James Review* 16 (1995): 273-77.

Shell, Marc. *Money, Language and Thought: Literary and Philosophical Economies from the Medieval to the Modern Era.* Berkeley: U of California P, 1982.

Thomas, Brook. *American Literary Realism and the Failed Promise of Contract.* Berkeley: U of California P, 1997.

Warren, Kenneth W. *Black and White Strangers: Race and American Literary Realism.* Chicago: U of Chicago P, 1993.

———. "Still Reading Henry James?" *Henry James Review* 16 (1995): 282-85.

Wells, H. G. *Boon, The Mind of the Race, The Wild Asses of the Devil, and The Last Trump.* London: T. Fisher Unwin, 1915.

FURTHER READING

Criticism

Guilds, John Caldwell. "Pragmatic Humanism in *The Ambassadors* and *Absalom, Absalom!*: A Philosophical Link between James and Faulkner." In *Value and Vision in American Literature: Literary Essays in Honor of Ray Lewis White,* edited by Joseph Candido, pp. 151-67. Athens: Ohio University Press, 1999.

> Finds similarities between James's *The Ambassadors* and William Faulkner's *Absalom, Absalom!,* particularly in regard to their "convictions about the role of man" in "an affirmative philosophy at odds with naturalism."

Hathaway, Richard D. "Ghosts at the Windows: Shadow and Corona in *The Ambassadors.*" *Henry James Review* 18, no. 1 (winter 1997): 81-96.

> Examines polarities in *The Ambassadors,* including contrasting images of light and dark, and the ways in which these oppositional forces create multiplicity of meaning rather than contradiction in the novel.

Hoover, David L. "Altered Texts, Altered Worlds, Altered Styles." *Language and Literature* 13, no. 2 (May 2004): 99-118.

> Explains and provides examples of the process of "text alteration," modifying the opening paragraph of *The Ambassadors* in several different modes to illuminate the importance of authorial style and its connection to interpretation.

Krook, Dorothea. *Henry James's* The Ambassadors: *A Critical Study,* New York: AMS Press, 1996, 132 p.

> Book-length study designed for the nonspecialist as an introduction to *The Ambassadors,* focusing primarily on the central role of "consciousness" as James defined it in his novel.

Menton, Allen W. "Typical Tales of Paris: The Function of Reading in *The Ambassadors.*" *Henry James Review* 15, no. 3 (fall 1994): 286-300.

> Traces the influence of nineteenth-century literature about Paris on James's characterization of Lambert Strether.

Parsons, Deborah L. "The Note/Notion of Europe: Henry James and the Gendered Landscape of Heritage Tourism." *Symbiosis* 2, no. 2 (October 1998): 225-40.

> Discusses ideas of travel and tourism as they relate to Strether's and Gostrey's experiences of Europe in *The Ambassadors.*

Roraback, Erik S. "Money, Temporality and Bio-Power in *The Ambassadors.*" *Litteraria Pragensia* 9, no. 18 (1999): 1-25.

> Analysis of *The Ambassadors* centered on the concept of "essence," especially as reflected in Martin Heidegger's "historical idea of Being," in order to shed new light on the traditional reading of the novel "as the story of a latecomer to the realization of life as an art-form."

Scherzinger, Karen. "'Lurking Ghosts': Metaphor, *The Ambassadors,* and Henry James's Population of the American Scene." *Henry James Review* 24, no. 2 (spring 2003): 168-79.

> Focuses on James's return to America, particularly New York, and his sense of alienation chronicled in *The American Scene.* Scherzinger connects the use of metaphor in this work to that in *The Ambassadors.*

Smith, George. "Manet, James, and Postmodern Narrative." *Henry James Review* 17, no. 1 (winter 1996): 30-9.

> Discusses postmodern tendencies in the works of "modernists" Claude Manet and Henry James. Smith scrutinizes the "interartistic aesthetic" present in Manet's painting *Olympia* and James's novel *The Ambassadors.*

Westervelt, Linda A. "'A Modest Retreat': *The Ambassadors,* by Henry James." In *Beyond Innocence, or the Altersroman in Modern Fiction,* pp. 30-49. Columbia: University of Missouri Press, 1997.

> Reviews the process of ultimate awareness or insight that takes place in several of James's middle-aged characters featured in a number of works written between 1892 and 1908. With respect to *The*

Ambassadors, Westervelt concludes that Strether undergoes a reflection process that "does not merely lead to remorse, but offers an insight that he regards as an advantage."

Additional coverage of James's life and career is contained in the following sources published by Thomson Gale: *American Writers*; *American Writers: The Classics,* Vol. 1; *American Writers Retrospective Supplement,* Vol. 1; *Beacham's Encyclopedia of Popular Fiction: Biography & Resources,* Vol. 2; *British Writers,* Vol. 6; *Concise Dictionary of American Literary Biography, 1865-1917*; *Contemporary Authors,* Vols. 104, 132; *Dictionary of Literary Biography,* Vols. 12, 71, 74, 189; *Dictionary of Literary Biography Documentary Series,* Vol. 13; *DISCovering Authors*; *DISCovering Authors: British Edition*; *DISCovering Authors: Canadian Edition DISCovering Authors Modules: Most-studied Authors* and *Novelists*; *DISCovering Authors 3.0*; *Encyclopedia of World Literature in the 20th Century,* Ed. 3; *Exploring Short Stories*; *Literature and Its Times,* Vol. 2; *Literature Resource Center*; *Major 20th-Century Writers,* Eds. 1, 2; *Major 21st-Century Writers*; *Novels for Students,* Vols. 12, 16, 19; *Reference Guide to American Literature,* Ed. 4; *Reference Guide to English Literature,* Ed. 2; *Reference Guide to Short Fiction,* Ed. 2; *St. James Guide to Horror, Ghost & Gothic Writers*; *Short Stories for Students,* Vol. 9; *Short Story Criticism,* Vols. 8, 32, 47; *Supernatural Fiction Writers,* Vol. 1; *Twayne's United States Authors*; *Twentieth-Century Literary Criticism,* Vols. 2, 11, 24, 40, 47, 64; and *World Literature Criticism.*

Iris Murdoch
1919-1999

(Full name Jean Iris Murdoch) Irish-born English novelist, philosopher, poet, short fiction writer, essayist, and playwright.

The following entry presents an overview of Mrudoch's life and works. For additional information on her career, see *CLC*, Volumes 1, 2, 3, 4, 6, 8, 11, 15, 22, 31 and 51.

INTRODUCTION

Iris Murdoch's contribution to twentieth-century literature is formidable. During a writing career that spanned more than forty years, the Anglo-Irish writer produced twenty-six novels, five books of philosophy, five plays, one libretto, two volumes of poetry, and two collections of essays on philosophy and literature, as well as criticism, verse, and short fiction. Her philosophical expertise—particularly regarding Platonist and existentialist theory, morality, and ethics—informs both her fiction and nonfiction writings. As a novelist, Murdoch has been compared to the great writers of the nineteenth century, particularly Fyodor Dostoevsky, George Eliot, and Charles Dickens, because of her intricate plots, rich imagination, preoccupation with ethics and moral philosophy, and her emphasis on the complex interrelationships of her characters. Murdoch wrote primarily in the realist mode, rejecting stream-of-consciousness writing and other experimental styles of the modernist era. She is admired for her storytelling, her blending of abstract philosophical ideals with concrete narrative, her careful and abundant use of detail, and her powerful imagination. In her novels, where the supernatural and ordinary coexist, Murdoch infused everyday life with mythic and symbolic significance. Her novels are concerned with the intricacies of human living and the exploration of the themes of morality, religion, power, truth, and love.

BIOGRAPHICAL INFORMATION

Murdoch was born July 15, 1919, in Dublin, Ireland, the only child of Irene Alice Richardson Murdoch and Wills John Hughes Murdoch. When she was only one year old, her father's civil service career required that the family move to London, but they continued to visit Ireland during vacations. Murdoch's early education began at the Froebel Institute in London, where she stud-

ied until she was twelve. In 1931 Murdoch received a scholarship to attend Badminton Boarding School in Bristol. She began writing articles there, many of which were published in the school newspaper. She continued her education at the Somerville College, Oxford, where she studied classics, philosophy, and history. In 1939 Murdoch began publishing in Oxford's student-run literary magazines, the *Cherwell* and *Oxford Forward*. As an undergraduate she became interested in Marxism and joined the British Communist Party, but remained a member for only one year. In 1942 she graduated from Oxford with a degree in classic literature, language, history, and philosophy.

During World War II Murdoch joined the civil service and worked in the Treasury in London. Her wartime experiences led her to accept a position with the United Nations Relief and Rehabilitation Administration (UNRRA) to help those displaced by the war. While employed by the United Nations, Murdoch traveled to Belgium where she met the French existentialist Jean-Paul Sartre and the novelist and poet Raymond Queneau, whose writings influenced the early development of her philosophical ideas. Because of her short involvement with the British Communist Party, the United States denied Murdoch a visa in 1946, and she was forced to decline a graduate scholarship from Vassar College. Instead, Murdoch spent a year at Newnham College, Cambridge, before returning to Oxford in 1948 as a philosophy lecturer and fellow of St. Anne's College.

In 1953 Murdoch published *Sartre, Romantic Rationalist,* a critical examination of Sartre's use of the novel form as a vehicle for his philosophical ideas, a path Murdoch would follow in her own writing career. Murdoch purportedly wrote and destroyed five novels she deemed unfit for publication before her debut novel, *Under the Net,* was published in 1954. Two years later she married John Bayley, a novelist and professor of English literature at Oxford. She retired from Oxford in 1963 and lectured part-time at the Royal College of Art in London until 1967, when she finally gave up teaching to pursue writing on a full-time basis. Her diverse and prolific writing career is marked by several awards and honors. She received the James Tait Black Memorial Prize in fiction in 1974 for *The Black Prince* (1973), the Whitbread Literary Award in 1974 for *The Sacred and Profane Love Machine* (1974), and the Booker Prize in 1978 for *The Sea, the Sea* (1978). In 1987 Murdoch was made a Dame Commander of the Order of the British Empire by the British government. In 1998 *Under the Net* appeared on the Modern Library's list of "100 Best Novels of the Twentieth Century." Murdoch's writing career ended only after she was diagnosed with Alzheimer's disease. Her final novel, *Jackson's Dilemma,* was published in 1995. On February 8, 1999, Iris Murdoch died in Oxford, England.

MAJOR WORKS

Although Murdoch was a prolific writer, publishing on average a novel every eighteen months of her career, critics have discerned a small number of recurring themes and philosophical issues in her work. These include the Platonic conceptions of truth and goodness, the importance of morality and religion in human life, the role of art and love in shaping moral behavior, the nature of human freedom and the power of individuals to control the lives of others, the relationship of appearance and reality, and what critic Lorna Sage referred to as Murdoch's "aesthetic of imperfection."

Complicating interpretations of Murdoch's fiction is the fact that she worked both as a philosopher and a novelist. Indeed, critics often view her novels as fictional explorations of the moral and aesthetic concepts established in her various philosophical essays and books. In

this regard, her first novel, *Under the Net,* is interpreted in light of her early existentialist writings, specifically her critical study of Jean-Paul Sartre, whereas the novels of her so-called mature phase—such as *The Time of the Angels* (1966), *The Nice and the Good* (1968), *The Black Prince,* and *The Sacred and Profane Love Machine*—are deeply concerned with problems of good and evil, truth and reality, and the power of love to redeem or destroy—concepts proposed in her 1969 essay "On 'God' and 'Good'" and more fully examined in her book of Platonic philosophy *The Sovereignty of Good over Other Concepts,* published in 1967.

Of the novels of Murdoch's "early phase"—those written before *The Time of the Angels*—critics consider *Under the Net, The Bell* (1958), *A Severed Head* (1961), and *The Unicorn* (1963) to be her most accomplished works. In general, these novels deal with the philosophical concepts of truth and love, with the responsibilities and bond of marriage, and with the realization of the "otherness" of people. Of the group, *Under the Net* is the most philosophical and contains the seeds of many of Murdoch's later novels. The narrative focuses on Jake Donoghue, the first of many failed-artist narrators in Murdoch's fiction, who attempts to establish a pattern for his life in order to insulate himself from the impact of "contingencies," or random events that are not part of his design for living. In the course of the novel, Jake comes to accept contingency as a necessary part of life while acknowledging the influence of others, thus freeing him to love. But *Under the Net* is also a novel about language, specifically the inability of language to convey truth and its power to conceal rather than expose reality. The central image of the "net" in the novel reflects the net of language in which humans are trapped and unable to escape into the "silence" of understanding.

Commentators generally concur that Murdoch's mature or major phase begins in the mid-1960s, with the publication of *The Time of the Angels* or, in some cases, with *The Nice and the Good.* The works of this period, especially those published after *An Accidental Man* (1971), break out of the more overt formal constraints of the earlier novels: generally, they are longer and their settings more expansive; they dispense with the use of chapter divisions as a formal structural device; and their philosophical viewpoints are more complex. They also examine more explicitly the moral and aesthetic themes tentatively explored in Murdoch's earlier novels. These include the philosophy of art, the nature of good and evil, the sacred and profane aspects of love, and the problem of a morality of "the Good" in a world where faith in God and religion has been replaced by the power of the individual. The concept of the "enchanter" figure—the hero who seeks to undermine the simpler characters by testing the quality of their goodness—also appears in a number of these later novels, such as Carel

Fisher in *The Time of the Angels,* Julius King in *A Fairly Honourable Defeat* (1970), and Bradley Pearson in *The Black Prince.*

Many critics consider *The Black Prince* and *The Sea, the Sea* to be the master works of Murdoch's mature period. The former is an intricately structured novel that includes a book within a book, four postscripts written by characters other than the narrator, and an "Editor's Foreword" written by "P. Loxias," the narrator's alter-ego and Murdoch's personification of Apollo, the god of art and eros. Bradley Pearson, the protagonist and narrator, is a retired civil servant writing what he hopes will be his great novel. But the plot turns as Pearson is accidentally and innocently drawn into the scene of a murder, for which he is arrested and convicted. While in prison he contemplates his life and completes his literary masterpiece on art and love, a process that is possible only because of what he has suffered. The loss of self in the pursuit of art, depicted in Pearson's story, is a theme to which Murdoch returned in many of her novels. In the case of *The Black Prince,* the very destruction of ego leads to greater truth through the art that is created. Some critics have noted parallels between the novel and Shakespeare's plays *The Tempest* and *Hamlet.* The postscripts contradict the narrator's rendering of events and encourage alternate readings of the novel. In its use of such self-conscious narrative techniques, *The Black Prince* is considered one of Murdoch's most postmodern works of fiction.

The Sea, the Sea is also somewhat metafictional and unusual in its structuring. Like *The Black Prince,* it features a book within a book, the "inner story" consisting of the autobiography of the narrator, Charles Arrowby, who is writing his life story in an attempt to purge himself of egoism. Through the process of revisiting his past, Arrowby meets an old lover with whom he tries to rekindle a relationship. His obsession with this woman persists despite the fact that she has married and changed significantly since their youth. Arrowby's obsession and false sense of reality indicate that his attempt at redemption through art is a failed one. In addition to the themes of illusion and morality, Murdoch's novel examines such issues as manipulation, humility, consequence, and the interconnectedness of all things. Once again, in reading this novel, critics have drawn parallels between Murdoch and Shakespeare. Specifically, Arrowby's attempt to set aside manipulation and selfishness mirror Prospero's retirement from magic in *The Tempest.*

There is a critical consensus that Murdoch's major phase ends with the publication of *The Good Apprentice* in 1985. After this she wrote four more novels and two books of philosophy, including her most detailed study of morality and Platonic ideals, *Metaphysics as a Guide to Morals,* in 1992. The late novels explore familiar themes, such as the redemptive and destructive power of love, the relation of religion and morality, the concept of the Good, the failed artist, and the idea of the "enchanter" or demon-figure who achieves control over the lives of others. Of the late novels, critics generally consider *The Book and the Brotherhood* (1987) and *The Message to the Planet* (1989) to contain the richest characterization and imaginative treatment of the moral and aesthetic issues that dominated Murdoch's life. *Metaphysics as a Guide to Morals* is based on a series of meditations, from a wide variety of perspectives, on the question of the role of metaphysics in ethics. Noted Murdoch scholar Maria Antonaccio has argued that the work is Murdoch's greatest achievement in philosophy because its structure mirrors the tension between the ordering frameworks of metaphysical thought, on the one hand, and the contingency and messiness of the actual human condition, on the other. Other critics, such as Barbara Stevens Heusel, have maintained that *Metaphysics as a Guide to Morals* presents the most comprehensive view of Murdoch's moral universe and that the work is essential reading to a fuller understanding of Murdoch's fiction.

CRITICAL RECEPTION

Murdoch's critical reputation has grown steadily since the publication of *Under the Net* in 1954, though her works have also encountered a number of detractors. One difficulty with assessing Murdoch is that she defies classification: she is not a modernist or postmodernist, though with respect to the latter designation many critics have discovered postmodern techniques and themes in her work. Unlike many of her female contemporaries, she is not a feminist writer, attested to by the fact that most of her protagonists and narrators are men and her female characters, despite their education and intelligence, are noticeably absent from the public world of her novels. And, despite her affinity with the sprawling, realistic novels of the nineteenth century, she is not a traditionalist. Complicating the issue is Murdoch's dual position as both novelist and philosopher. In fact, a central issue in Murdoch criticism, present from the very beginning, is the question of her "location" as a writer of fiction: is she a philosophical novelist, a realistic novelist, or a postmodern novelist? Despite ongoing disagreement on this central question, commentators generally agree that, in her best works, Murdoch is a powerful thinker, an excellent storyteller, a figure approaching Shakespeare in her depiction of character, and a daring writer who built compelling stories on her philosophical ideals. Detractors have faulted Murdoch for her failure to integrate the elements of myth and realism in some of her novels, for the repetitive nature of her themes, and for what Lorna Sage, writing in 1977, called her "aesthetic of imperfection"—the paradoxical, ambiguous, ambivalent, and inconclusive nature of her novels. Following Sage, critics began to see this unsettling quality of Murdoch's fiction, which became more apparent as her career progressed, as an intentional theme, one based on the central idea that human experience, truth, and reality cannot be abstracted or contained by language and consolidating thoughts.

Contemporary criticism, for the most part, has continued the work begun by previous critics. Recent essays have revisited Murdoch's recurring themes of love, power, and freedom, and her frequent reference to previous narratives, myths, and plays. Critics have continued to analyze Murdoch's interaction with Shakespeare's works, particularly in *The Black Prince*. Others have focused their comments on the portrayal of sexuality or gender roles in Murdoch's work. Much critical attention is still devoted to the connection between philosophy and art as it appears in her novels and her philosophical writings. Heusel has summarized their interdependence in Murdoch's novels: "Art and philosophy use imagery in different ways to describe the world; for Murdoch, philosophy is a rational activity, while fiction draws on unconscious as well as rational activity. Neither discourse can capture all of life's mystery. Her novels contribute images of minds thinking—reflecting inner as well as outer experience; her philosophy contributes metaphysical pictures or systems that may be used as guides to the Good. Her distinguishing philosophy from literature does not, however, signify that she walls one off from the other. She is continually empowered by each discourse, and in turn each empowers the other." Despite various new areas of interest in the work of Iris Murdoch, what remains most constant is an abiding respect for the author, and an appreciation of her tremendous accomplishments.

PRINCIPAL WORKS

Sartre, Romantic Rationalist (philosophy) 1953
Under the Net (novel) 1954
The Flight from the Enchanter (novel) 1956
The Sandcastle (novel) 1957
The Bell (novel) 1958
A Severed Head (novel) 1961
An Unofficial Rose (novel) 1962
*A Severed Head [with J. B. Priestley] (play) 1963
The Unicorn (novel) 1963
The Italian Girl (novel) 1964
The Red and the Green (novel) 1965
The Time of the Angels (novel) 1966
†The Italian Girl [with James Saunders] (play) 1967
The Sovereignty of Good over Other Concepts (philosophy) 1967
The Nice and the Good (novel) 1968

Bruno's Dream (novel) 1969
A Fairly Honourable Defeat (novel) 1970
The Servants and the Snow (play) 1970
An Accidental Man (novel) 1971
The Black Prince (novel) 1973
The Sacred and Profane Love Machine (novel) 1974
A Word Child (novel) 1975
Henry and Cato (novel) 1976
The Fire and the Sun: Why Plato Banished the Artists (philosophy) 1977
The Sea, the Sea (novel) 1978
A Year of Birds: Poems (poetry) 1978
Nuns and Soldiers (novel) 1980
The Three Arrows (play) 1980
The Philosopher's Pupil (novel) 1983
The Good Apprentice (novel) 1985
Acastos: Two Platonic Dialogues (philosophy) 1986
The Book and the Brotherhood (novel) 1987
‡The Black Prince (play) 1989
The Message to the Planet (novel) 1989
Metaphysics as a Guide to Morals (philosophy) 1992
The Green Knight (novel) 1993
Jackson's Dilemma (novel) 1995
Existentialists and Mystics: Writings on Philosophy and Literature (essays) 1998
Something Special: A Story (novella) 1999

*This play is an adaptation of the novel *A Severed Head*.

†This play is an adaptation of the novel *The Italian Girl*.

‡This play is an adaptation of the novel *The Black Prince*.

CRITICISM

Douglas Brooks-Davies (essay date 1989)

SOURCE: Brooks-Davies, Douglas. "Iris Murdoch's *The Black Prince*: Overthrowing the Tyrant and Inscribing the Feminine." In *Fielding, Dickens, Gosse, Iris Murdoch and Oedipal* Hamlet, pp. 151-79. London: Macmillan, 1989.

[*In the following essay, Brooks-Davies considers the thematic importance and organizational influence of Shakespeare's* Hamlet *in Murdoch's novel* The Black Prince.]

> I will arise and go to my father, and will say unto him, Father, I have sinned against heaven, and before thee, and am no more worthy to be called thy son.
>
> Luke 15:18-19

Iris Murdoch's novel ***The Good Apprentice*** (1985) opens with these verses from the parable of the prodigal son as Edward Baltram, guilt-ridden over the death of his friend Mark, begins his quest for his natural father, Jesse Baltram. The same verses are used in ***Henry and Cato*** (1976) at the point where Cato has renounced the priesthood, has been apparently abandoned by Beautiful Joe, the youth whom he loves, and has heard of the death of his friend Father Milsom:

> And he thought: I will arise and go to my father, and will say unto him, Father, I have sinned against heaven and before thee, and am no more worthy to be called thy son.[1]

Edward Baltram reaches Jesse, 'that enormous dark figure concealed behind the curtain of the future',[2] after attending a seance at which he is urged 'Come to your father' (p. 62). He meets him at his strange fantasy of a house, Seegard; but Jesse subsequently drowns and is discovered by Edward in the river that runs past Seegard at a spot where there is 'a cluster of willows which seemed to stir his memory' (p. 434). The father, known by Edward throughout his life only by his absence, has now finally departed. Or has he? ***The Good Apprentice,*** in a way characteristic of Murdoch's novels, invites the reader to make equations that imply theological and philosophical riddles. Jesse, brought home from the river by the tree men, is somehow the Biblical Jesse, celebrated for his sons, the root of Isaiah 11 from whom the branch and flower Jesus will grow; so that he is at once dead and not dead, though the status of his existence is left teasingly open. In the last part, 'Life after Death', Edward relegates him to the province of memory by beginning to read Proust at the end, while the Bloomsbury graffiti writers have inscribed *Jesse Lives* and *Jesse Baltram is King* 'on a wall near the British Museum' (p. 519). ***The Good Apprentice*** could be a ghost story; it is clearly concerned with the Freudian area of the uncanny. Equally clearly, with its ghostly king of a father, its haunted son, its drowning by a memory-stirring cluster of willows, it is one of Murdoch's *Hamlet* fictions, even though it does not name the play.

The naming of Hamlet is, this late in Murdoch's writing career, scarcely necessary, for ***The Good Apprentice*** is recognisably the climax to a group of *Hamlet* fictions that began with ***The Black Prince*** (1973) and includes ***Henry and Cato, The Sea, The Sea*** (1978) and ***Nuns and Soldiers*** (1980). Of these last three ***Henry and Cato*** is closest to ***The Good Apprentice,*** beginning as it does with Henry, Cato's symbolic twin, about to take possession of his ancestral lands, his father dead and his elder brother just having been killed in a car crash. Henry's story, however, unlike Edward's, contains teasing acknowledgements of *Hamlet.* His mother, Gerda (Gertrude), loved his elder brother more than she loved

him, so that in many ways ***Henry and Cato*** is about Henry's revenge on Gerda, raising questions about his psychological complicity in the death of his father and elder brother, as when he feels 'panic, terror, a kind of nebulous horror as if he were a man destined by dark forces to commit a murder for which he had no will and of which he had no understanding' (p. 59). His image of himself fractured by maternal deprivation and indifference, he identifies with the victims of torture and imprisonment that people the Max Beckmann paintings that haunt the novel[3] and, also, with Hamlet:

> He had an instinctive identification with heroes beginning with H. Homer. Hannibal. Hobbes. Hume. Hamlet. Hitler. What a crew. Only his own name seemed empty, a sort of un-name, another cause for resentment, unredeemed by kings.

(pp. 70-1)

A son's quest for, and supplication before, his father is a fundamental theme in Murdoch's later fiction but, as in ***Henry and Cato,*** the prodigal son motif is almost invariably shadowed by its Oedipal negative—supplication, in other words, seems to be a penance for entertaining patricidal desires, and the impetus for the paternal quest seems to lie firmly in the patterns of patricide and atonement noticed by Freud in *Moses and Monotheism* and *Totem and Taboo.*

Hamlet is one of many threads in Henry's story, as it is in Charles Arrowby's in ***The Sea, The Sea*** or in ***Nuns and Soldiers,*** with its pub called 'The Prince of Denmark' situated near Fitzroy Square.[4] In all of these novels, in fact, *Hamlet* is present yet somehow residual, as if they are texts haunted by a ghost that has been relieved of its burden and is making a rather awkward appearance as a super-annuated guest celebrity. This is even true of ***Nuns and Soldiers,*** which appears to be retelling *Hamlet* from Gertrude's point of view (the central woman is again named Gertrude and within a year of her husband's death she has made an o'er hasty second marriage to a young man half her age) but rapidly turns its (albeit related) centres of interest elsewhere: to the question of vocation and the nature of God, the function and value of art, the question of national identity, and so on.

Hamlet's tameness as an allusive force in these novels can be attributed directly to its centrality in ***The Black Prince,*** where Murdoch encountered the play head on and almost (but not quite) laid its ghost once and for all as she created in Bradley Pearson, the novel's autobiographical narrator, a writer so involved with *Hamlet* that it takes him some four hundred pages to disclose the extent of his obsession. A main clue to his monomania is the elaborate tutorial on the play given by Bradley to Julian, the daughter of his rival novelist friend Arnold Baffin, which fulfils for ***The Black Prince*** the function fulfilled by the performance of *Hamlet* in *Tom Jones* and *Great Expectations,* inviting the reader to relate inset text to frame text and elevating *Hamlet* as a mirror of dazzling reflective power.

The essence of the tutorial is Bradley's Oedipal understanding of *Hamlet,* which at once raises questions about the status of the male narrator in relation to the author herself. Murdoch habitually identifies with men and writes from the male viewpoint, but a main argument of this chapter will be that **The Black Prince** is a mimetic text, self-consciously about the tension between male narrator and female author as it is focused by Shakespeare's most Oedipal and (arguably) most misogynistic play.[5] As Bradley erects a Platonic theory of art on the foundations of Ernest Jones's Oedipal *Hamlet* and, of necessity, repudiates the notion of woman as creator and thinker, we hear Murdoch's female self insistently query his interpretation of women and his assumptions about the nature, role, and gender of the artist. Bradley enables Murdoch to enter a paradigmatic male mind and survey the extent to which this phenomenon rejects and dishonours the feminine, while the Oedipal *Hamlet* permits her to overhear the mystery of male encountering male in the form of father and son arguing over woman as both maternal and sexual love object.

In **The Black Prince,** then, Murdoch takes the Oedipus complex as a sadly true working definition—even explanation—of the relationship between the sexes, of Christianity and of Platonist theories of art.[6] In exploring the terrifying depths of Oedipal male myopia it demonstrates a feminist alternative as Julian survives Bradley's obsession to become a poet. In the end, rather like that other radical mid-seventies re-vision of *Hamlet,* Fay Weldon's *Remember Me* (1976), where Madeleine's ghost displaces that of patriarchal Old Hamlet with his cry of 'remember me', **The Black Prince** is a story of woman's revenge on the male for his oppression and suppression of the feminine.

By a neat coincidence **The Black Prince** was published in the same year as Harold Bloom's Oedipally anxious *Anxiety of Influence.* To his astonishing theoretical fiction of 'strong poets, major figures with the persistence to wrestle with their strong percursors, even to the death'[7] Murdoch's theoretical fiction responds by revealing how puny a concept of strength is that is predicated upon the humiliation and misprision of woman.

APOLLO, MARSYAS, AND HAMLET

HAMLET:

What have you, my good friends, deserved at the hands of Fortune that she sends you to prison hither?

GUILDENSTERN:

Prison, my lord?

HAMLET:

Denmark's a prison

ROSENCRANTZ:

Then is the world one.

HAMLET:

A goodly one, in which there are many confines, wards, and dungeons, Denmark being one o' th'worst.

(*Hamlet,* II.ii)

It is helpful to begin with a plot summary. Bradley is a divorced, fifty-eight year old former tax man who has taken early retirement in order to follow his writing career. As the novel opens he is packed and ready to leave his London flat for a rented seaside house called Patara. There he hopes he will find the solitude and silence he needs to enable him to overcome his writer's block:

For the first time in my life I wanted silence.

Of course, as might be pointed out with barbed humour, I had always in a sense been a devotee of silence. Arnold Baffin once said something like this to me, laughing, and hurt me. Three short books in forty years of sustained literary effort is not exactly garrulity. And indeed if I understand anything that is precious, I did understand how important it was to keep one's mouth shut until the right moment even if this meant a totally voiceless life.[8]

Arnold, Bradley's former *protégé,* is in Bradley's view as prodigal and intemperate with words as Bradley is thrifty and chaste.

The narrative begins with the aftermath of a row between Arnold and his wife during which he hits her with the poker and, simultaneously, the irruption into Bradley's life of two figures from his remote past, his divorced, remarried, and subsequently widowed wife Christian, and her brother Francis Marloe. Bradley tries to comfort Rachel and, eventually and momentarily, becomes her awkward and impotent lover while repudiating overtures from Christian and being forced to care for his sister Priscilla, who deposits herself in his flat in a state of nervous breakdown after being left by her husband Roger for a much younger woman. To complicate this characteristically Murdochian plot further, the Baffins' daughter Julian has appeared and requested from Bradley tutorials on *Hamlet* which she is preparing for an examination. The possibility of going to Patara having receded under the pressures of all this contingency, Bradley agrees. While giving her a long tutorial Bradley falls in love with her. Despite parental resistance and imprisonment, Julian escapes to Bradley and drives with him to Patara. Their seaside idyll is interrupted by Arnold, who reveals Bradley's age to Julian and tells her of Priscilla's suicide. The narrative ends with Rachel telephoning Bradley (as Arnold had telephoned him at the beginning) asking for help. She has hit Arnold with the poker and he is dead. Bradley is accused of the murder, tried, and found guilty.

The narrative is framed by two forewords, the editor's and Bradley's, and six postscripts, by Bradley, Christian, Francis, Rachel and Julian, and the editor. Bradley's postscript, the first and longest, tells of his trial and, again, of his love for Julian and his view of the nature of artistic inspiration; those by the *dramatis personae* (to use the novel's own phrase) apportion varying degrees of blame to Bradley. The editor's reveals that Bradley has died in prison of cancer and defends Bradley's story as art: 'Art tells the only truth that ultimately matters. It is the light by which human things can be mended' (p. 416).

At the centre of **The Black Prince,** then, is Bradley's narrative; at its extremities are the contributions of the editor, a certain P. Loxias. Loxias's foreword tells us that he got to know Bradley in prison; that they 'found in each other the blessings of friendship'; that Bradley sensed in him 'his *alter ego*'; and that he, Loxias, is 'in more than one way responsible for the work that follows' (p. 9). *Loxias* is, as many have recognised, an epithet for Phoebus Apollo, god of the sun and of poetry.[9] Does his presence before Bradley in prison suggest that Bradley, at his physical nadir, achieves, like Milton's Samson, his moment of glory, the spiritual possession by the divine that he has been seeking all along? This is a possibility that is reinforced by the appearance of the cave and the sun image ('This morning I had felt like a cave-dweller emerging into the sun. [Julian] was the truth of my life' (p. 285)) that invites a comparison with this passage from **The Sovereignty of Good**:

> Our attachments tend to be selfish and strong, and the transformation of our loves from selfishness to unselfishness is sometimes hard even to conceive of. . . . One might say that true morality is a sort of unesoteric mysticism, having its source in an austere and unconsoled love of the Good. When Plato wants to explain Good he uses the image of the sun. The moral pilgrim emerges from the cave and begins to see the real world in the light of the sun, and last of all is able to look at the sun itself.[10]

The ideal relationship between the Good and art is explained by Murdoch in **The Fire and the Sun,** her other major Platonic philosophical work: 'the relation of art to truth and goodness must be the fundamental concern of any serious criticism of it'; 'good art thought of as symbolic force rather than statement, provides a stirring image of a pure transcendent value, a steady visible enduring higher good'.[11]

But to see Bradley as an *illuminatus* into the mysteries of Apollo would, in the end, be naive, as most of **The Black Prince**'s critics agree; for the point is that he

knows what he is aiming at, does experience illumination of a sort, but is in the end brought up short by his moral blindness. What critics disagree on is where Bradley's failure and blindness lie. The answer to this problem is, though, clearly presented in the *Hamlet* tutorial where Bradley assumes the truth of the Freud-Jones Oedipal reading of the play in order that he may then proceed to his explanation of it as a confession about the nature of creation by Shakespeare the artist. Bradley's procedure neatly demonstrates the dependence of his male-oriented theory of artistic inspiration on the Oedipus complex, and Murdoch achieves through it the more general exposure—demolition, even—of the woman-repudiating aspect of the Plato who is, in so many other ways, fundamental to her thinking. For the most that the feminine can ever be to Bradley, as to all mainstream Platonists, is a stepping stone to the male god. Here is the revealing crux of the *Hamlet* tutorial which is placed, literally and symbolically, *en abysme,* in the middle of the novel:[12]

> 'Did Shakespeare hate his father? Of course. Was he in love with his mother? Of course. But that is only the beginning of what he is telling us about himself . . . He has performed a supreme creative feat, a work endlessly reflecting upon itself, not discursively but in its very substance, a Chinese box of words as high as the tower of Babel. . . . *Hamlet* is words and so is Hamlet. He is as witty as Jesus Christ, but whereas Christ speaks Hamlet is speech. He is the tormented empty sinful consciousness of man seared by the bright light of art, the god's flayed victim dancing the dance of creation. . . . How veiled that deity, how dangerous to approach, how almost impossible with impunity to address, Shakespeare knew better than any man. *Hamlet* is a wild act of audacity, a self-purging, a complete self-castigation in the presence of god . . .'.
>
> (pp. 199-200)

This is apparently inspired, and after uttering it Bradley reports himself 'exhausted, almost dazed, damp with sweat from head to foot as if I were outlined with warm quicksilver', thus perceiving himself momentarily as Mercury, messenger of the gods, patron of language and music, symbol of both substance and goal of the alchemists' work, guide of and communer with the souls of the dead.[13] Yet, gifted by his nascent love for Julian with such Hermetic eloquence and perception, what does Bradley see after all but an Oedipal Shakespeare performing a masochistic and exhibitionistic ritual of self-abasement before a sadistic god who is the 'great . . . and . . . terrible godhead' of his prison confession (p. 390) and in effect nothing more than a projection of the feared terrible father, product of Oedipal fantasy? Bradley's Shakespeare is, of course, Bradley himself, whose name partly anagrammatises into Bard Spear. (As B. P. he is also Hamlet, the Bard's son, one of the Black Princes of the novel's title.)

The myth that underlies Bradley's vision in the tutorial and beyond it is a favourite with Murdoch, that of

Apollo and Marsyas. Male orthodoxy as exemplified by the Neoplatonists construed Apollo's flaying of Marsyas the flautist as, to quote Axel in *A Fairly Honourable Defeat* (1970), an image of 'the inevitable agony of the human soul in its desire to achieve God'. For them the violation of the body revealed the beauty of the soul. To Dante, the myth offered validation of his artistic self.[14]

Bradley's use of the myth is in this tradition, but his Oedipal preface brilliantly deconstructs the Neoplatonist orthodoxy to suggest the myth's historical origin in one of the ancient battles between patriarchy and matriarchy. The Apollo who emerges now is the destroyer and woman hater, equivalent of the Hamlet who, identifying Gertrude with Ophelia (p. 195), vilifies and destroys them. This reading recalls that Marsyas was playing the flute, Pallas's instrument, when he challenged Apollo to the contest which he lost: recalls, in other words, that Apollo's lyre vanquished the voice of the goddess of wisdom and that the victory was greeted with almost universal grief: 'the country people, the sylvan deities, fauns . . . the nymphs, all wept'.[15] Bradley reveals a view of the flayed victim and the god that is absolutely homoerotic and attributable, as Francis Marloe insists, to his Oedipal relationship with his parents. Francis may be bumptious, self-advertising and intolerable, but his perception of Bradley is truer than many critics have been prepared to allow. Bradley's suspicion of his Freudianism ('My mother filled me with exasperation and shame but I loved her. (Be quiet Francis Marloe.)' (p. 15)) is itself suspect.

The deconstructive process continues after the tutorial:

> I opened the window and a breath of slightly cooler air entered the room, polluted and dusty, yet also somehow bearing the half-obliterated ghosts of flowers from distant parks. A massed-up buzz of various noise filled the room, cars, voices, the endless hum of London's being. I opened the front of my shirt all the way down to the waist and scratched in my curly mat of grey hair.
>
> (p. 201)

A couple of pages earlier Bradley has described his chest hair as 'copious but grizzled. (Or, if you prefer, a sable silvered)' (p. 197), thereby identifying himself as Old Hamlet (I.ii.240-2). This, together with the Mercury-quicksilver description that he applies to himself just before he opens the window in the above quotation, suggests that, as he now faces Julian, he has summoned up and combined several of the souls of the mythological and fictional dead. Bradley confronting Julian recalls Apollo confronting Marsyas but transformed now into a tableau in which Bradley is Old Hamlet and simultaneously his own dead father confronting himself-as-son in the shape of Julian as Hamlet. The feminine is totally excluded as Bradley contin-

ues: 'So you played Hamlet. Describe your costume', and the issues raised by this multiple image are resolved, or at least clarified, by the phrase that Bradley now quotes at Julian: 'She was dreamy, combing her layers of greeny-golden hair with long fingers, seeing herself as Hamlet, sword in hand. "Here thou incestuous murderous damned Dane—"' (p. 202). For if quotations and allusions are to mean anything in this riddle of a novel, this one says that Bradley's ecstatic tutorial vision has merely stimulated, brought right into the foreground, the preoccupation with Oedipal incest from which he began. His words are, of course, Hamlet's last, death-dealing, words to Claudius as he gives him the poison. Following Ernest Jones's lead (as Bradley himself does) in applying principles of doubling and inversion to the text, we must infer that what we have here, at the centre of this particular Chinese box, is Bradley as his own (Old Hamlet) of a father accusing his Julian-Claudius-Hamlet of a self of incest guilt.[16]

The fact that Julian is a girl and therefore, in the pantheon of Bradley's subconscious, 'really' Ophelia, as Bradley has already acknowledged (p. 196), merely reinforces the Oedipal inference. Oedipally father and son are identified; so that Bradley as Old Hamlet accusing himself in the form of Julian-Hamlet by using words directed by Hamlet at the dying Claudius is also Bradley as lover of his mother confronting her as Ophelia. As Bradley remarks to Julian's baffled commonsense after she has said that she cannot 'see why [Hamlet] should think Ophelia is Gertrude, they're not a bit alike': 'The unconscious mind delights in identifying people with each other. It has only a few characters to play with' (p. 195).

Bradley opens the window onto his claustrophobic hothouse of a tutorial about the agonies of the male creator exultant before the father god, and what enters is 'cooler air . . . bearing the half-obliterated ghosts of flowers from distant parks'. The language is beautifully, hauntingly, metaphorical: parks are female spaces 'down among the women';[17] and the air, suffused with the dust of death (as in the church near Patara later) bears the ghostly memory of the Ophelia flower maiden infinitely multiplied to embrace all mothers, muses, and *animae* that the Apollonian artist has erased through the exercise of his rampant and excluding male ego.

If Apollo silenced the feminine when he vanquished Pallas's reed flute, he also humiliated and denied her at Patara. Bradley's seaside retreat borrows its name from the Lycian town which was celebrated for its temple of Apollo,[18] and the point of the name is not to compound riddles, though it might on the face of it seem as though it is, but rather to clarify in yet another way the relationship between Bradley's Apollo-based theory of art and the sexual humiliation and denial of the feminine.

It is at Patara that Bradley rapes Julian, an act born out of his knowledge of his sister, Priscilla's, suicide and his decision to do nothing about it for the moment, not even tell Julian: "'Oh Bradley, please, don't be so rough, please, Bradley, you're hurting me." Later on she was crying. There had been no doubt about this love-making. I lay exhausted and let her cry' (p. 328).

By any criterion this has been the 'love-making' of an egotistical sadist and fantasist. Startled by Julian's meta-morphosis into Hamlet he has grabbed at her and pushed her into the bedroom and onto the bed. Afterwards, she has been monosyllabic and numb, aware of the omi-nous presence of demons, those Murdochian symbols of malignant fantasy: "'Let's draw the curtains. I feel bad spirits are looking in at us'" (p. 330). When they start to talk, Julian confesses to feeling 'quite impersonal', Bradley to having 'come through [his] ordeal'. In terms of the Platonist ideology to which Bradley subscribes, he has been possessed by 'the god, the black Eros' (p. 331), has enjoyed a *raptus* that has taken him signifi-cantly nearer the 'greater and more terrible godhead', Apollo (p. 390), and has communicated his power to Julian. But if we see him as one of Iris Murdoch's courtly lovers, like Montague Small in **The Sacred and Profane Love Machine** (1974) and, above all, like Charles Arrowby in **The Sea, The Sea,** then his posses-sion ceases to be the gift of a god which he has passed on to another and becomes instead merely the willed projection of what Murdoch has called 'fantasy-myth',[19] the freedom-denying reduction of another to the myopia of one's own perceptions.

As we know, the symptom of Bradley's myopia is his preoccupation with Hamlet and Ophelia. And so, just as the *Hamlet* tutorial's ecstasy had collapsed into the rev-elation of Bradley's Oedipal obsession, the Patara ec-stasy is undermined, too. He has violated Hamlet in or-der to produce Ophelia:

> She was [now] wearing the blue dress with the white willow-spray pattern which she had been wearing when she fled. . . . There had been a lot of tears but none now. She looked so much, and beautifully, older, not the child I had known at all, but some wonderful holy woman, a prophetess, a temple prostitute.
>
> (pp. 330-1)

The willow is Ophelia's emblem, sign that Bradley, like Hamlet, has drowned the girl in the flow of his outra-geous egotism. When he proceeds to equate holy woman with *hetaira,* as if there could be no difference between holiness and prostitution, the relevance of the Patara al-lusion becomes clear, for at the centre of the cult of the Pataran Apollo was a prostitute.

Our authority here is Herodotus, whose comment is embedded, significantly, in his description of the shrine of Baal (Zeus Belus) in Babylon:

> But no image has been set up in the shrine, nor does any human creature lie therein for the night, except one native woman, chosen from all women by the god, as say the Chaldaeans, who are priests of this god.

> These same Chaldaeans say (but I do not believe them) that god himself is wont to visit the shrine and rest upon the couch, even as in Thebes of Egypt, as the Egyptians say (for there too a woman sleeps in the temple of Theban Zeus, and neither the Egyptian nor the Babylonian woman, it is said, has intercourse with men), and as it is likewise with the prophetess of the god at Patara in Lycia, whenever she be appointed; for there is not always a place of divination there; but when she is appointed she is shut up in the temple dur-ing the night.[20]

The more one's mind plays on this passage, the more shabby Bradley becomes. He is a sham Apollo who has brought his own concubine to his Pataran temple, and the god he admires so much is after all no better than a Soho punter, dangerously akin to Baal, the most-named and ill-reputed pagan god of the Old Testament. Israel goes whoring after him and his para-deities (Judges 8:33), serves him (II Kings 17:16), and her prophets prophesy by him (Jeremiah 2:8). To follow him is to abandon the path of goodness and of truth. Herodotus's linking of Apollo Patareus with Baal is crucial to this novel which names Julian after one of the great medi-eval visionaries of the mystery of divine love (p. 55) and calls Bradley's divorced wife Christian, though she is partly Jewish ("'Our mother was a Christian convert'", Francis tells Bradley, who had courted, mar-ried, lived with, and divorced Christian without ever discovering the Jewish connection (p. 148). The link suggests that Bradley's Apollo is a false god whose need for a temple harlot testifies less to his godhead, his power to bestow the divine *raptus,* than it does to his subjection to the goads and tugs of the flesh and the fantasies of his own depraved mind; it suggests that he needs this specially selected woman for much the same reasons that Hamlet needs to vilify and sexually humili-ate Ophelia.

Herodotus indicates that Apollo was not present at Pat-ara all the time. He was there, as Servius informs us in his brief but crucial note on *Aeneid,* IV.143, for the six winter months of the year, spending the six summer months at Delos. The line that prompts Servius's note describes Aeneas as 'like Apollo when in winter he leaves Lycia and the river Xanthus and visits maternal Delos' when he appears in order to go hunting with Dido.[21] Once the hunt has started, a severe rainstorm leads the two to shelter in a cave and make love: 'on that day were sown the seeds of [Dido's] suffering and death'. Rumour reports 'how they were now spending all the long winter together in comfort and self-indulgence, caught in the trap of shameful passion'. Later, Jove's messenger, Mercury, will tell Aeneas to abandon Dido so that he may fulfil his 'great destiny', the founding of his Latian kingdom. Patriarchy and the heroic code mass all their might against what the outraged Iarbas calls *a mere woman, a vagrant* (*femina . . . errans*; l.211), and Dido, cursing Aeneas's faithlessness, kills herself.

Servius's explanation of the simile at line 143 makes Aeneas into Apollo Pataraeus hibernating with his temple prostitute until the call to his greater duty forces him to leave her. And clues in Murdoch's text nudge us into connecting *Aeneid,* IV with Bradley's Patara. For one thing, Patara is recorded on the name plate in 'Italian lettering' (p. 311); for another, a piece of driftwood picked up by Julian has had etched on it by the sea 'a sort of delicate sketch of an old face, a sketch such as some Italian artist, Leonardo perhaps, might make in a rather abstract way in his notebook' (p. 313). *Italian* in both instances invites the speculation that we are pondering fragments of Roman history, that as Bradley makes his way with Julian to Patara he is treading a path into an archaic past in which he will assume the role not just of Apollo but of Aeneas-Apollo, and that Julian will be forced into the role of Dido-like *hetaira.*

Then, fifty pages later, after his trial and sentence for Arnold's murder, Bradley meets his double, P. Loxias, Apollo Loxias, Apollo the oblique, Apollo the crooked one, reputedly so named from his riddling and ambiguous oracles.[22] As Loxias, matching narrative mode to name, tells us in his foreword, 'What follows is ambiguous and sometimes tortuously told. Man's searchings and his strugglings are ambiguous and vowed to hidden ways' (p. 9). But in the end they are perhaps not quite so hidden. For if Apollo Pataraeus permits Bradley to fulfil his Hamlet fantasy and use Julian as a whore, then Apollo Loxias reveals the reason why he needed to do so in the first place: 'I own no lord but Loxias; him I serve', declares Tiresias to Oedipus in Sophocles's *Oedipus Tyrannus.* The blind seer, who knows what the god knows, names him at this point in the play as the arch-riddler and master of the Oedipal secret. The name will be used later by Jocasta when Oedipus begins to suspect that he may have killed his father, and, later still, Oedipus will name him: 'Loxias once foretold that I should mate with mine own mother, and shed with my own hands my own father's blood'.[23] The mystery encoded in the epithet Loxias is thus the Oedipal mystery, and in finding his way to Loxias at the end of his life Bradley confronts this fact in its stark and horrifying simplicity.

Ophelia's Sisters

HAMLET:

> Now get you to my lady's chamber and tell her, let her paint an inch thick, to this favour she must come.
>
> (*Hamlet*, V.i)

Despite his difficulty in deciding how to open his narrative, Bradley knows that it ought to begin with an image of hurt womanhood, either 'with Rachel's tears, or Priscilla's. There is much shedding of tears in this story' (p. 21). He knows, too, that the origins of this image lie in his parents' papershop and his relationship with his dead parents and with Priscilla (pp. 14-15). In the event, however, he decides to begin with Francis Marloe, who stands on his front doorstep 'with copious greyish longish frizzy hair' emanating 'something significantly ill-omened' and riddlingly mutters "'She's back. . . . He's dead. She's back'" (pp. 23-4). Old Hamlet returns from the dead to tell of murder; Francis irrupts, ghostlike, into Bradley's life to tell of the apparent return from the dead of Christian, the divorced wife whom Bradley has erased from his memory: 'I . . . was able to feel that she had died' (p. 25). Christian returns as a *revenant* ('Francis had certainly raised ghosts himself of a particularly nasty kind' (p. 52)), but before we see her Bradley focuses his narrative attentions on Rachel. Arnold has 'killed' her as Bradley 'killed' Christian and invites Bradley round to view the result. As Bradley describes her we discover a middle-aged Ophelia who is a double for Christian and also for Bradley's dead mother:

> There was a darkening reddish bruise under one eye and the eye was narrowed, though this was hard to see because the eyelids of both eyes were so grossly red and swollen with weeping. Her upper lip was also swollen on one side. There were traces of blood on her neck and on her dress. Her hair was tangled and looked darker as if wet. . . .
>
> (p. 34)

It is as if Bradley is a sadistic voyeur at the aftermath of some orgiastic primal scene, already relishing his attack on Julian at Patara. The assault itself has been perpetrated by Arnold, of course. But the act of describing and recreating it makes it Bradley's, and in any case the two are paired like Henry and Cato, Cain and Abel, Claudius and Old Hamlet. Arnold's killing of Rachel because 'she was yelling like a fury and saying awful things about my work' (p. 37) parallels Bradley's infinitely earlier banishing of Christian because 'I say her as a death-bringer. Some women are like that' (p. 25). To both, woman is threat and destroyer, and both, in this opening scene at least, express the need to turn the totem woman into Ophelia: Arnold by battering her with a poker and then pouring a jug of water over her; Bradley by reliving the scene in such minute detail.

This Ophelia-vision of Rachel will soon empower Bradley to become her (rather ineffectual) lover. In the meantime Murdoch gives Bradley a moment of perception that locates his Ophelia syndrome in the fundamental human and animal need for a scapegoat:

> She sighed very deeply and flopped her hand back on to the bed, lying now with both hands symmetrically by her side, palms upward, like a limp disentombed

Christ-figure, still bearing the marks of ill-treatment. Tufts of cut hair adhered to the dried blood on the bosom of her blue dress.

(p. 39)

This is, symbolically at least, 'the blue dress with the white willow-spray pattern' which Julian wears for her escape to Patara and puts on after her rape (p. 330); but here it drapes an Ophelia perceived as the ultimate masochist's victim, Christ. As Beautiful Joe will say of the crucified Christ in *Henry and Cato,* 'If a gang done that, they'd get ten years even if the bugger survived' (p. 69). This particular bugger in the form of Rachel survives to have her revenge by killing one of the gang (Arnold) and giving the other (Bradley) his ten years. Furthermore, Rachel as Christ gives her name to Christian, another of the survivors at the end of this novel which teases us, particularly at the beginning of Part 3, with the question of evolutionary success and failure. These, then, are the basic elements from which Murdoch creates in *The Black Prince* her feminist attack on the Oedipus complex as it parades itself under the mask of male sentimentality over the 'Hamlet vocation'.[24]

Bradley's description of Rachel's bedroom, too, is paradigmatic. The room is shared by Rachel and Arnold, though we would never suspect this from his hard-eyed Juvenalian (and Hamlet-like) concentration on cosmetics and the frailties of the female body:[25]

> A dressing-table can be a terrible thing. . . . The plate glass 'table' surface was dusty and covered with cosmetic tubes and bottles and balls of hair. The chest of drawers had all its drawers gaping, spewing pink underwear and shoulder straps. The bed was chaotic, violent, the green artificial silk coverlet swooping down on one side and the sheets and blankets creased up into a messy mass, like an old face. . . . The whole room breathed the flat horror of genuine mortality, dull and spiritless and final.

(p. 38)

This is Rachel's deepest private self mercilessly exposed, yet there is hurt here as well as Bradley catalogues these images of female vulnerability and the grave of a bed; for the sheets and blankets, creased 'like an old face', anticipate sobbing, desperate, and ugly Priscilla who is herself a transfigured hieroglyph of their dead mother, whose death bed Bradley is recreating here ('My mother lived to see my first book published. She was proud of me' (p. 15); 'Priscilla's woebegone tearful face was crumpled and old. Had she every really resembled my mother?' (p. 85)).[26] And it is out of this vision of the Rachel-mother and Bradley's speculation as he walks back to his 'cosy womb' of a flat (p. 22) that she might still be 'lying like a disfigured corpse staring at the ceiling' (p. 53) that Julian enters the narrative. The moment is brilliantly achieved, for 'she' is at first a 'he' as Bradley's dreamlike perception insists that this strangely posturing figure can exist only as an adjunct of his obsessed self intoning a funeral liturgy over the dead Ophelias who inhabit the burial chambers of his mind:

> He was standing upon the kerb and strewing flowers upon the roadway, as if casting them into a river. . . . [He] appeared to be chanting some form of repetitive litany. I now saw that what he was strewing was not so much flowers as white petals. Where had I seen just such petals lately? The fragments of white paint which the violence of Arnold's chisel had dislodged from the bedroom door. . . . I had paused and had been watching him for some time and was about to set off again towards the station when, with one of those switches of *gestalt* which can be so unnerving, I realized that the light had deceived me and that this . . . was a girl whom I knew. It was Julian Baffin, Arnold and Rachel's teenage daughter and only child. (So named, I need hardly explain, after Julian of Norwich.)

(pp. 54-5)

Julian, then, emerges out of Bradley's fixation on Rachel as corpse and simultaneously out of his image of himself as Rachel's attacker: s/he is strewing the petals of white paint he (as Arnold) had created by chiselling at the door in his attempt to view the woman he had battered and 'drowned' with the jug of water. (The white paint-petals probably derive, in Bradley's fevered mind, from white violets and thus complicate the issue further by meshing with Ophelia's 'violets [which] withered all when my father died' (IV.v.182-3) and punning homophonically on *violets* and *violence*.) This moving icon is also wonderfully proleptic in her refusal to remain bound within Bradley's Hamlet-engineered prison, however: she opposes his sick fantasy with the totemic power of her name and as her Julian self scatters, as Ophelia never quite managed to, the remembrances of an unwelcome lover to the winds.

If Julian is at once within and beyond Bradley's fantasies then Priscilla is completely inside them, constantly threatening and finally achieving suicide, another middle-aged Ophelia who now presents herself at Bradley's front door, pushes her way into the bedroom, and lies there, 'pitiful and ugly. . . . Her swollen face, the scene in the dim light, reminded me of Rachel' (p. 74). Bradley has literally become the hero of his own novel, that 'nebulous work' he has described slightly earlier as 'now a *nouvelle,* now a vast novel, wherein a hero not unlike myself pursued, amid ghostly incidents, a series of reflections about life and art' (p. 62). The 'ghostly incidents' continue as Bradley leaves his flat with its enshrined Priscilla to visit Christian in the time capsule of their old flat, the lease of which she has retained. In fact, the journey from Priscilla to Christian is no journey at all, for his unconscious with its limited number of characters to play with (p. 195) perceives them as aspects of one figure. Inevitably, therefore, Priscilla moves in with Christian, and Bradley discovers in them the twinned obverse and converse of a maternal Ophelia, dead yet alive, ugly yet with a haunting mermaid-like beauty, Priscilla dressed in a black *negligée* and looking ancient juxtaposed against Christian dressed in green, combing at her reddish-brown hair with her fingers (p. 110).

Bradley replays the scene later when Julian returns to Priscilla the Chinese bronze of a lady riding on a water buffalo that Bradley has given her but which really belongs to Priscilla:

> [Julian] pushed the water buffalo lady along the coverlet, as if she was amusing a child. . . .
>
> Julian had retreated to the bottom of the bed. . . . [She] looked as if she were begging Priscilla's pardon for being young and good-looking and innocent and unspoilt and having a future, while Priscilla was old and ugly and sinful and wrecked and had none.
>
> (pp. 134-5)

The bronze itself merely reiterates Bradley's obsession. The buffalo keeps its rider out of the water but gets so damaged during the course of the novel that we get the feeling that she, like Ophelia, is in danger of death by water. She ghosts Priscilla, so that both become witnesses to the sterile negative imposed on women's history by the Oedipal male. For Bradley's corpselike sister, apparently the victim of self-loathing after being rejected by her husband Roger in favour of his young mistress, Marigold, is really bearing the burden of Bradley's separation anxiety, that moment, constantly replayed in his mind, when he first discovered that *fort* need never necessarily be followed by *da*.

The point emerges with appalling clarity when Bradley goes down to Bristol to confront Roger, misses his train home and rings his flat to speak to Priscilla but gets no reply:

> Ships are compartmental and hollow, ships are like women. The steel vibrated and sang, sang of the predatory women, Christian, Marigold, my mother: the destroyers. I saw the masts and sails of great clippers against a dark sky. Later I sat in Temple Meads station and howled inside myself, suffering the torments of the wicked under those pitiless vaults. Why had no one answered the telephone?
>
> (pp. 109-10)

The phone wires, like the string on the balloon he chases after a few pages later (pp. 123-4), are his umbilical link with the maternal feminine, the fact of whose perpetual absence his mind recreates obsessively by flinging up corpse after corpse as if it were a superhuman gravedigger. And so: 'Priscilla, do try to relax, you're as rigid as a corpse' (p. 133); and (when Bradley and Rachel are holding hands on the verandah, sitting awkwardly in deck chairs): 'So two corpses might ineptly

greet each other on resurrection day' (p. 118); and '[Rachel] led me by the hand, and in a moment we were in the bedroom where I had seen Rachel lying like a dead woman with the sheet over her face' (p. 155).

Indeed, Bradley's unconscious mind flickers from Priscilla to Rachel and back again so rapidly that it is not all that clear which of them he is seeing in bed at any given time. It is, therefore, no surprise that after Priscilla's funeral Rachel should appear at the door of Bradley's flat, as Priscilla had first appeared there, bearing a message from the deepest recess of his memory:

> Seeing Rachel there in the flat was like a bad trip in a time machine. There was a memory-odour like a smell of decay. I felt distressed, physically repelled, frightened. Her wide round pale face was terribly familiar, but with the ambiguous veiled familiarity of a dream. It was as if my mother had visited me in her cerements.
>
> (p. 354)

In his first discussion of *Hamlet* with Julian, Bradley had asserted that 'the ghost was a real ghost' (p. 160), but it is not until this appearance of Rachel that we know how he can be so certain. He is, simply, possessed by the ghost of his mother, a terrifying fictional counterpart to the Edmund Gosse of *Father and Son.* His life is one long attempt to repair the damage of severance and umbilical dismemberment by acts of remembrance which betray him by refusing to remember anything except corpses.

Death and, more importantly, the fear of death inform Bradley's view of women. Unlike the Neoplatonist, for whom death is the welcome and necessary prelude to union with the divine, and unlike Freud's ideal old man who embraces the goddess of death as the final mother of his life,[27] Bradley repudiates death while living it constantly. It is out of his repudiation and fear that his tutorial on *Hamlet* springs, with its attempt to transcend the stuff of Oedipal conflict ('Did Shakespeare hate his father? Of course. Was he in love with his mother? Of course.' (p. 199)) that is baffled by the pressing presence of 'the half obliterated ghosts of flowers from distant parks'. And it is his horror of maternal absence and death that defines his feelings for Julian, turning his hexaemeron of love—that 'new world' which he creates at the beginning of Part 2—into yet another fantasy of destruction. Despite his present from the shoe shop, Bradley can only leave Julian as, in the sagely choric words of Francis, he left Priscilla, 'fruitless and bootless. Fruitless and bootless' (p. 133).

Arrival at the Past

HAMLET:

> What man dost thou dig it for?

GRAVEDIGGER:

> For no man, sir.

HAMLET:

> For what woman, then?

GRAVEDIGGER:

> For none neither.

HAMLET:

> Who is to be buried in't?

GRAVEDIGGER:

> One that was a woman, sir; but rest her soul, she's dead.

(Hamlet, V.i)

If Bradley's vision of his 'mother . . . in her cerements' sounds rather gothic, even reminiscent of Frankenstein's dream of his mother in her shroud, then that is predictable too; for **The Black Prince** is, like *Frankenstein,* a text written by a woman to disclose, through the image of a male creator, the mystery of woman as artist.[28]

In Victor Frankenstein's dream his kiss kills, turning Elizabeth into 'the corpse of my dead mother' at the moment his grotesque giant of a baby leaps into life. Bradley, similarly, has the doubtful gift of being able to link birth and the charnel, most obviously when, on the third day of his new world of love, he becomes tormented by the memory of kissing Julian: 'I felt her flesh upon my lips. Phantoms were bred from this touch. I felt like a grotesque condemned excluded monster' (p. 246). This makes him the creature rather than the creator, a reversal that has to be understood as a consequence of his earlier speculation about the moment when he actually fell in love with Julian: 'I had known this child since her birth. I had seen her in her cradle. I had held her in my arms when she was twenty inches long' (p. 205).

Through this moment of memory which signals the birth of love Bradley literally re-creates Julian. But what Murdoch is concerned with charting is not so much the degree of his unselfing here, his loss of his obsessional centre, as the continuing reflexiveness of his experiences, his refusal, even when irradiated by love, to take his eyes off Julian's copy of *Hamlet,* his inability to escape from the self-created demon of Priscilla: 'Priscilla got up and walked stiffly towards the bed. She got into it. It was like a corpse climbing into its coffin. She pulled up the bedclothes' (p. 224). Priscilla is the Rachel of the beginning and his dead mother. The *volte face* which registers Bradley's change from creator, as he recalls baby Julian, to excluded creature, as he feels her flesh upon his lips, is, then, explained by the intervening image of Priscilla. This woman who constantly proclaims that she is going mad and that she will kill herself is Bradley's archetypal Ophelia and his absent mother. When he turns the eye

of love on Julian he, like Frankenstein, can do nothing but replicate images of death which present and re-present his exclusion from the maternal presence. In Bradley's memory his kiss has transformed the flesh of his Julian baby into that of his dead mother which means that he, in turn, becomes the baby, repudiated and rejected. The quotation continues: 'How could it be that I had actually kissed her cheek without enveloping her, without becoming her? How could I at that moment have refrained from kneeling at her feet and howling?'

Bradley's death-dealing myopia dominates his view of Julian for the rest of the novel:[29] When she is kept by her parents from seeing him he imagines her 'locked . . . in her room. I pictured her lying there and crying, a tumbled figure of despair with her shoes off and her hair all tangled. (The vision filled me with pain, but it was rather beautiful too.)' (pp. 289-90): a clear enough example, if we still needed one, of the way his aesthetic perceptions are dictated by his Oedipal needs as the imprisoned Julian becomes 'beautiful' in direct proportion to her approximation to her battered shoeless mother of the beginning and the desperate and equally shoeless Priscilla.[30] When he actually sees her at St Cuthbert's, Philbeach Gardens, he reiterates the identification, recognizing what she will look like at fifty and comparing her with the Rachel of the beginning (p. 294) in a setting which symbolically juxtaposes the Ophelia vision against the strengths of the archetypal feminine:

> Pale green angelica-coloured light entering through Victorian stained glass failed to dissipate the magnificent and soothing gloom of the place. Framing an elaborate reredos apparently made of milk chocolate, a huge melancholy rood screen which looked as if it had been rescued from a fire at the last moment announced that *Verbum caro factum est et habitavit in nobis.* Behind a sturdy iron railing at the west end a murky dove-pinnacled shrine protected the font, or perhaps the cave of some doom-obsessed sibyl or one of the more terrible forms of Aphrodite. Powers older than Christ seemed to have entered and made the place their own. High above us a black-clad figure paced along a gallery and disappeared.

(p. 294)

If Rachel's appearance at the flat after Priscilla's funeral is a trip in a time machine for Bradley, presenting him with a Miss Havisham-like image of his dead mother, then in this scene at St Cuthbert's it is Murdoch as narrator who discloses further and more dizzyingly archaic vistas into the realm not just of the mother but of the Mother. For it reveals the primal powers of the Goddess herself, the ancient one whose representative Julian is simply by virtue of being a woman: the powers, in other words, that Apollo perceived in the richly reedy register of Marsyas's pipe and that Bradley is perpetually having to suppress, for they speak of female freedom and creativity, the death of male hegemony.

In this superb *tour de force* Murdoch presents the Goddess both as she was and as she is, filtered through the distorting lens of male perception and appropriation, at once Ophelia and Aphrodite. The font, now the preserve of the male Christian Trinity, expands to suggest that it contains the water from which Aphrodite was born, and its dove of the Holy Spirit reverts momentarily to its ancient meanings as Aphrodite's bird and, simultaneously, because of the naming of 'some doom-obsessed sibyl', sybilline dove of Dodona.[31] The 'black-clad figure', similarly, is at once a priest, dedicated by his vocation to suppressing and denying the powers of the Goddess and exalting in their place the creative powers of a male deity ('The Word was made flesh': John 1:14), and primordial Eros, born, according to the ancients, in close conjunction with Mother Earth.[32]

Meanwhile the whole scene is suffused with aqueous light from the stained glass which catches and defines Julian as she sits beside Bradley 'with her weary lucid face and her blue dress with white willow leaves on it' (p. 295). She has escaped from her parental prison into this more insidious one, created by Bradley in collusion with the powers of Western Christendom with their preference for women in the form of dead martyrs.

It is, then, with a Saint Ophelia wrested from the shrine of the archaic goddess of love that Bradley proceeds to Patara, home of the woman-denying god. Before he does so, however, he returns to his flat and is subject to one more visionary moment in which the powers of the feminine are evoked, too late to be seized by Bradley, perhaps, but nonetheless insistently and urgently there, registering their refusal to be suppressed and silenced. Entering the flat he hears 'a curious noise such as some bird might make, a sort of descending "woo-oo"' (p. 298). It is Priscilla, voluntarily discharged from her electric shock treatment (that last resort of medical males confronted with mad Ophelias), uttering her womb cry that encodes her sense of loss at having had no babies (compare p. 149) and her sense of unity nevertheless with the creative feminine. The cry also makes her a dove of Aphrodite and a Dodonian dove, archaic and strong, a female voice that overrides the voice of the male god, a memory trace from way beyond the strait-jacket of Bradley's reductive unconscious mind. When Bradley peeps in to view the source of the sound she is, of course, just Priscilla again, reeking of formaldehyde and thus a preserved corpse of an Ophelia who announces, at the threshold to Part 3, that the journey Bradley is finally to make is a retreat into a historical past that images his psychological regression. It stops short at Patara, home of Apollo the woman-destroyer, because Bradley's Apollo fixation renders him incapable of breaking through to the shrine of the Goddess in whichever of her 'terrible' manifestations.

Patara signifies the possession and humiliation of woman in the name of the god. It is an ancient temple exposed, as through the opening up of a vast fissure in the earth's crust, to Bradley's view, and as he travels towards it with Julian he begins to talk in terms of geological time, posing momentarily in his backward flight as a mid-nineteenth-century evolutionist:

> 'There isn't any future. We shall go on and on driving this car forever. That's all there is.'
>
> 'You mustn't speak like that, it's false. Look, I've brought brown bread and toothpaste and a dustpan.'
>
> 'Yes. That's a miracle. But it's like fossils which religious men used to think God put there when He created the world in 4000 BC so that we could develop an illusion of the past.'
>
> 'I don't understand.'
>
> 'We have an illusion of the future.'
>
> 'That's wicked talk and a betrayal of love'.
>
> (p. 307)

Julian holds up her pathetically ordinary and tangible domestic purchases as an act of faith in her and Bradley's love for each other, as an assertion of her belief in the powers of Aphrodite. Bradley counters by identifying her as a Philip Gosse vainly adhering to a divine law that is denied by the evidence. But Bradley's progressive evolutionary stance is itself regressive. In refusing Julian's offer of absolute love (p. 309) he doubts the redemptive power of Aphrodite, forcing Julian back into the Ophelia mould just as, in St Cuthbert's, he had viewed her as Ophelia in denial of the ancient feminine powers that were resonating there in response to her. Now, to prove her love, she jumps out of the moving car in a gesture of symbolic suicide. And what Bradley discovers when he runs back to her is an image that would have delighted Rossetti, Millais, and all those other connoisseurs of Hamlet's bedraggled beloved:

> The creamy moon had become smaller and paler and more metallic. Darkness began to thicken about us in the dense air as we held each other in silence.
>
> 'Bradley, I'm getting cold, I've lost my sandals.'
>
> I let go and swivelled my body round and began kissing her cold wet feet as they lay dinting a cushion of damp spongy moss. Her feet tasted of dew and earth and the little green frond-flowers of the moss, which smelt of celery. I clasped her pale wet feet in my arm and groaned with bliss and longing.
>
> (p. 310)

By refusing Julian's offer of love Bradley ensures the perpetuation of the Ophelia icon, and the archetypal planet of the feminine registers her protest by becoming 'smaller and paler and more metallic'. When they reach Patara Bradley's necrophilia reaches even more astonishingly Iachimo-like proportions:[33]

I went into the bedroom. Julian, in a mauve and white flowered petticoat with a white fringe was lying on the bed deeply asleep. . . . She lay on her back with her throat exposed as if to the knife. Her shoulders, pale in colour, were as creamy as the moon at dusk. . . .

(p. 311)

Maybe this overgoes even Iachimo: maybe this is Hamlet lusting after Ophelia when she has just been dragged dead from the river.

* * *

Just for a moment, though, and by an accident (to use one of Murdoch's favourite words) the gods are kind. Bradley and Julian sleep side by side in total unawareness of each other and waken to a piscatory idyll of Elizabethan intensity which offers Bradley yet another chance of redemption from the Oedipal bind. It is a visionary transmutation of *Hamlet's* graveyard scene in which earth's buried bones and decomposed corpses become, as in a Shakespearean romance or the third book of Spenser's *Faerie Queene*,[34] the sea's washed treasures: a sheep's skull, stones and shells, and a piece of driftwood. All are beautiful, speaking of a world that is totally opposite to the underworld of ghosts and demons in which Bradley habitually walks. Here, outside Patara itself, Ophelia can be erased after all. The sheep's skull parodies the skulls of *Hamlet's* Act v and ponders Hamlet's 'is not parchment made of sheepskins' (v.i.112) by presenting the substantial reality that underlies parchment's impermanence, a reality born of transformation through the power of the sea that echoes the magic performed in *The Tempest's* 'Full fathom five'.[35] The stones and shells, less obviously worked on by the sea, are simply its gifts, beautiful in themselves. But the driftwood has been fashioned even more so than the skull into a supreme art work for its cracks and wrinkles have all been:

> Smoothed and joined by the sea water until it looked like a sort of delicate sketch of an old face, a sketch such as some Italian artist, Leonardo perhaps, might make in a rather abstract way in his notebook. I took the sheep's skull. . . . It had been smoothed and caressed and polished until it seemed more like a work of art, some exquisite fabrication in ivory, rather than one of nature's remnants.

(p. 313)

These art works are pure, born from the sea like dreams from the unconscious mind, fully formed and healing.[36] The external signals which have pointed to a journey into the past—the geological debate; Patara's name; the fact that it is written in 'bold Italian lettering'—are now confirmed as having heralded for Bradley a potentially benevolent night journey. He has gone to sleep with drowned Ophelia; he has awakened after that 'precious, precious night' to the sea's solution to that image: the

fact of metamorphosis. The sea's message is that the art work is the product of process, a process that is in part analogous to that of dream work. Julian places the wood in the centre of the chimney-piece where we might expect to find a clock. It is an emblem of Bradley's escape from the time capsule which he shares with the corpses of his parents, the Priscilla corpse, wet and shoeless Rachel, and Ophelian Julian. In the wood's 'delicate sketch of an old face' lies the answer to Bradley's earlier obsessive comments on Priscilla's and Rachel's aged faces. Bradley knows, as he picnics by the sea with Julian, that he has entered a magically redemptive space:

> It was just perfect communion and rest and the kind of joy which comes when the beloved and one's own soul become so mingled with the external world that there is a *place* made for once upon the planet where stones and tufts of grass and transparent water and the quiet sound of the wind can really *be*. It was perhaps the other side of the diptych from last night's moment of seeing Julian in the twilight lying motionless beside the road. But it was not really connected, as moments of pure joy are not really connected with anything. And human life which has such moments has surely put a trembling finger upon nature's most transcendent aim.

(p. 314)

It *is*, of course, connected, as dead Catherine beyond the window is connected to living Heathcliff, and as Alice's daily life is connected to looking-glass land. If Bradley could retain the joy and make the connection he would be well on his way towards the Good. But he cannot, and the image of his failure is a church which he and Julian visit in the evening of that same day:

> After tea we drove over to the big church and walked about inside its bony emptiness. . . . There was no stained glass, only huge perpendicular windows through which the cool sun shone on to the pale rather powdery stone of the floor, casting a little shadow into worn *requiescats* many centuries old. The church in the flat land was like a great ruined ship or ark, or perhaps like the skeleton of some enormous animal, under whose gaunt ribs one moved with care and pity. We trod in silence with soft feet, padding and prowling, separated from one another and yet connected, pausing and gazing at each other across slanting shafts of powdery air, leaning back against the pillars or against the thick wall where the cold damp stone was like the touch of death or truth.

(pp. 315-16)

The connection which Bradley describes here is false, the contaminated product of his anxiety-ridden self, for it is perceived through the powdery dust that speaks of death and separation. Where St Cuthbert's had revealed a possibility of redemption rooted in the ancient cults of matriarchy, this church exposes Bradley's deathly regressiveness in all its bleakness. It is a ship and therefore, to him at least, like the ship at Bristol (p. 109), image of the womb and of the mother as traitor who has to be destroyed for her treachery. And so Bradley relishes the powdery stone with its reminders of death and then imagines the church into a re-membered dinosaur skeleton, ultimate reminder, despite the human ingenuity expended on its articulation, of death and extinction, and exact opposite of the sheep's skull and the transfigured piece of wood.

Bradley's wish to kill, to punish every woman because of his mother's betrayal of him with his father and her abandonment of him through dying, now reaches Priscilla, who kills herself, thus finally completing her enactment of Ophelia's history and fulfilling Bradley's fantasy of humiliation and domination: 'I wanted to take Priscilla in my arms and make her live again . . . I was stricken with guilt and horror at my unforgivable failure to keep my dear sister alive' (pp. 324-5). He decides, of course, not to tell Julian about the suicide until he has made love 'properly' to her which means, simply, that he now performs the necrophiliac act he has promised earlier. With Priscilla, image of his mother (p. 82), dead on his own terms, Bradley revives her in Julian, rapes her, then turns her afterwards into Pataran temple prostitute.

The sea, earlier on the vehicle of the unconscious mind with its storehouse of treasures, now turns hostile, releasing malevolent demons, one of which will take the form of Arnold Baffin, who will come that night and batter away at the front door like the sheriff at the 'Boar's Head', Eastcheap, when he comes to call another old man from his fantasies to a cold world based in the realities of decay and mutability (*I Henry IV*, II.iv). Arnold ends the saturnalia by telling Julian the Oedipal truth of Bradley's love for her. It is, of course, as Murdoch's dazzling narrative complexities insist, only one aspect of the truth, but it convinces Bradley, who falls asleep with Julian still at Patara, dreams of Priscilla, and wakens to a 'ghastly' room and house from which Julian is obviously absent. She has fled 'in her blue willow pattern dress', an Ophelia created by Bradley to help him re-enact once more that perpetual drama of maternal deprivation by which he lives.

Bradley goes to Priscilla's cremation and then to his flat, where he is tortured by Julian's absence. It is then that Rachel comes, bringing the 'memory-odour like a smell of decay': 'it was as if my mother had visited me in her cerements' (p. 354). Bradley insists on seeing his mother but the 'real' Rachel is intent on bringing him 'back to reality' (p. 357), though she does it in terms guaranteed to aggravate his obsession:

> 'You are the sort of person who goes around in a dream smashing things, No wonder you can't write. You aren't really here at all. Julian looked at you and made you real for a moment. I made you real for a moment be-

cause I was sorry for you. Now that's all over and all that's left of you is a sort of crazy spiteful vampire, a vindictive ghost.'

> (p. 363)

For what happens next (after Bradley has, with Francis's help, ripped up Arnold's complete works and flung 'the white cascading sheaves of print' so that they rise around him like Ophelia's river (p. 364)) is that Bradley tells Francis how much he loved his mother and recalls the names of other women he claims to have loved: 'Annie. Catherine. Louise. It's odd how names remain, like skeletons with the flesh fallen away. They designate something that happened. They give an illusion of memory. But the people are gone as if they were dead. Perhaps they are dead. Dead as Priscilla . . .' (p. 367). Rachel has, in effect, uttered a curse that turns Bradley's mind sufficiently to make him actually suffer, for a moment at least, the fate of Ophelia; for he speaks at the end of this section in the words of Ophelia herself maddened by a parent's death: '"But oh if she would come back in the morning! What was it you said? A concentration camp. I'll meditate on that. Good night. Thank you, thank you. Good night"' (p. 368). The 'she' whose return he hopes for is Julian. But by now Julian is merely a sign for Bradley's mother, 'dead and gone' and laid 'i'th'cold ground' (*Hamlet*, IV.v.29-30, 70).

Rachel's psychological revenge for having been an Ophelia for so long rapidly becomes physical revenge when she summons Bradley by phone: 'I hardly recognized her. Or rather, I recognized her as a portentous *revenant*, the weeping distraught figure of the beginning of the story' (p. 375). She has killed Arnold, Bradley is accused of the murder, and Rachel does nothing to exculpate him. Ophelia—the Ophelia engendered by Bradley at the opening of his narrative—has returned like Weldon's Madeleine[37] and had her revenge, relegating her only begetter to a prison cell in which, as in his flat, he looks out onto an 'old brick wall' (p. 391; p. 22) and muses on his mad water maiden:

> What we [Bradley and Loxias] have seen together is a beauty and a glory beyond words, the world transfigured, found. It was this, which in the bliss of quietness I now enjoy, which I glimpsed prefigured in madness in the watercolour-blue eyes of Julian Baffin. She images it for me still in my dreams.

> (p. 391)

* * *

The point of ending with a trial is, as in Fryniwyd Tennyson Jesse's *A Pin to See the Peepshow* (1934) or Beryl Bainbridge's *Watson's Apology* (1981), to remind us how impossible the uttering of truth is and therefore how fragile the verdict born of that impossibility. And beyond the trial in ***The Black Prince*** lie further reminders of the hermeneutic nightmare spawned by the fall of the tower of Babel in the form of the postscripts. What this structural detail conveys unequivocally, though, is that the females have survived; or, at least, those outside Bradley's family circle have. The voice that was silenced when Apollo claimed victory over Marsyas is now liberated in the survivors Christian, Rachel, and the poet Julian. They speak partially, egotistically, embarrassingly, but they are alive and, in Julian's case at least, acutely perceptive; for it is she who finds her way through the hiccupping syntax of her postscript to a statement, in defiance of Apollo Loxias, about the feminine nature of language: 'the highest art is poetry because words are spirit at its most refined: its ultimate matrix' (p. 410).

Matrix shimmers here, registering *pregnancy* and *womb* among its meanings.[38] Julians 'words are spirit . . . : its ultimate matrix' answers Bradley's 'Hamlet is words and so is Hamlet' (p. 199) by proposing the possibility of a completely feminine discourse, the liberation of language from the neo-Freudians' phallogocentric Babel and its relocation in *ruah,* feminine spirit.[39]

This is the root meaning of **The Black Prince,** a text in which Murdoch writes as a man and yet from which 'something about the female predicament' emerges. Actually it is rather more than 'something'. It is a text which releases its fictional narrator into his own novel of ghostly pursuit (a fiction 'wherein a hero not unlike myself pursued, amid ghostly incidents, a series of reflections about life and art' (p. 62)) and makes him the scapegoat for several thousand years of Oedipal patriarchy. The assertiveness of Loxias's voice at the end is an irrelevant mythological fossil except insofar as it confirms Rachel's identification of Apollo as 'a notorious rapist and murderer, a well-known musical virtuoso, whose murder, by a peculiarly horrible method, of a successful fellow-musician made the headlines some considerable time ago' (p. 407) and narrates the survival of 'the little bronze of the buffalo lady' (p. 415). The males in this novel speak for the death-instinct; the female voice, fractured and shell-shocked though it is at the end, speaks for life, prophesying that spirit as matrix will dispel the ghostly presence of the fathers and their anxiety-ridden sons. This most brilliantly and elaborately sustained *Hamlet* fiction, in other words, turns its source text on its head, dismissing its accrued male mythology of kings, usurpers, sibling rivals, tormented fathers and avenging sons and offering in its place a countertext of feminine revenge that, playing with the Freudian oppositions *thanatos* and *eros,* implicitly subverts any text produced under the anxiety of influence, and especially those devoted to perpetrating *Hamlet's* patriarchal fictions.

Notes

1. *Henry and Cato* (London: Chatto and Windus, 1976), p. 195.

2. *The Good Apprentice* (London: Chatto and Windus, 1985), p. 197.

3. Henry claims to be writing a book about Beckmann, the German Expressionist painter who died in 1950. His paintings are referred to several times (most notably on p. 96), but more importantly the novel's dominant images—of fire, candle light, imprisonment, and violence—are consciously (if not solely) Beckmannesque.

4. Charles worships Shakespeare, has acted the part of Hamlet (*The Sea, The Sea* (London: Chatto and Windus, 1978, p. 38), glimpses a Tibetan Buddhist significance to it when he responds to his cousin James's description of *bardo* with '"For in that sleep of death what dreams may come" . . .' (p. 384; *Hamlet,* III.i.66), and at the end of the novel notes cryptically: 'Took Miss Kaufman to *Hamlet* and enjoyed it' (p. 501). Elizabeth Dipple, *Iris Murdoch: Work for the Spirit* (London: Methuen, 1982), ch. 10 pursues some of the *Hamlet* clues in *Nuns and Soldiers,* which appeared too late for Richard Todd's *Iris Murdoch: The Shakespearean Interest* (London: Vision Press, 1979), which is perceptive on the earlier fiction.

5. In 1978 she agreed that she 'perhaps identif[ies] with men more than with women, because the ordinary human condition still seems to belong more to a man that to a woman . . . if one writes "as a woman", something about the female predicament may be supposed to emerge. And I'm not very much interested in the female predicament': J. I. Biles, 'An Interview with Iris Murdoch', *Studies in the Literary Imagination,* XI (1978), 115-25; p. 119. The idea of 'mimesis'—assumption of the male personality in order to discover its limitations, structure, etc., with the intention of recovering 'a possible operation of the feminine in language'—is taken from Luce Irigaray, *This Sex Which Is Not One,* tr. Catherine Porter (Ithaca: Cornell U.P. 1985), p. 76, who has also been invoked by Deborah Johnson, *Iris Murdoch* (Brighton: Harvester, 1987), p. 35, in her feminist approach to *The Black Prince.* What astonishes me as a man is the brilliance of Murdoch's mimetic intuitions. It is worth noting, though, that despite her intention (as I see it, anyway) to recover language for the feminine, the narrative structure that Murdoch's fictions perpetuate remain essentially patriarchal in their Oedipal teleology. For other comments on the emergent feminine in her fiction, see Steven Cohan, 'From Subtext to Dream Text: The Brutal Egoism of Iris Murdoch's Male Narrators', *Women and Literature,* II (1982), 222-42.

6. For Murdoch's Platonism, see W. K. Rose, 'An Interview with Iris Murdoch', *Shenandoah,* XIX

(1968), 3-22, and her Platonist essays *The Sovereignty of Good* (London: Routledge and Kegan Paul, 1970) and *The Fire and the Sun: Why Plato Banished the Artists* (Oxford: Clarendon Press, 1977). Her narrative concern with the Oedipus complex is discussed by, e.g., Cohan *art.cit.* (n. 5) pp. 228-31, and P. J. Conradi, *Iris Murdoch: The Saint and the Artist* (London and Basingstoke: Macmillan, 1986), p. 77.

7. *The Anxiety of Influence,* p. 5.

8. *The Black Prince* (Harmondsworth: Penguin, 1975), pp. 17-18. Subsequent quotations are identified by page references within the text.

9. E.g. Jane Sturrock, 'Good and the Gods of *The Black Prince*', *Mosaic: A Journal for the Comparative Study of Literature and Ideas,* X (1977), 133-41, page 136-7: J. F. Stewart, 'Art and Love in Murdoch's *The Black Prince*', *Research Studies,* XLVI (1978), 69-78, pp. 75-6: Elizabeth Dipple, *op. cit.* (n. 4 above), p. 112: Conradi, *op. cit.* (n. 6 above), p. 187 and n.

10. *The Sovereignty of Good* (n. 6 above), pp. 91-2.

11. *The Fire and the Sun* (n. 6 above), pp. 72,76.

12. It is at the centre as 'The Mousetrap' is at the centre of *Hamlet,* and fulfils a similar function of interior duplication and amplification: e.g., Jean Ricardou, *Le nouveau roman* (Paris, 1973), pp. 47-75.

13. On Mercury as quicksilver, and his other meanings, see C. G. Jung, *Alchemical Studies,* tr. R. F. C. Hull, Bollingen Series, XX (Princeton, N.J.: Princeton U.P. 1967), sect. IV. Jung's significance in the novel, probably as an opponent of Freud, is guaranteed by Arnold's 'shadowy' discipleship (p. 187); and Bradley's vows of silence, as novelist and as lover (e.g. pp. 213, 252), are in part Hermetic: see Edgar Wind, *Pagan Mysteries in the Renaissance,* rev. edn (Harmondsworth: Penguin 1967), pp. 12 n. 196 and plate 23 on Hermetic silence as communion with the One. The tradionally hermaphroditic nature of alchemical Hermes points to a Jungian answer to the Oedipus complex within the novel: it is expelled through recognition and assimilation by the male of his feminine *anima*. For the definition of the *anima,* see Jung, *Psychological Types, or the Psychology of Individuation,* tr. H. Godwin Baynes, (London: Kegan Paul, Trench, Trubner, 1923), pp. 588-99, esp. pp. 594-5 and 597-8. The latter states: 'With men the soul, *i.e.* the anima, is usually figured by the unconscious in the person of a woman', and suggests how a failure to project the soul-image can result in homosexuality or narcissism. See also Jung's *Man and His Symbols* (London: Aldus Books and W. H. Allen, 1964), pp. 177-88.

14. *A Fairly Honourable Defeat* (Harmondsworth: Penguin, 1973), p. 41. Wind's discussion of the myth in *Pagan Mysteries,* ch. XI, as a battle between 'the relative powers of Dionysian darkness and Apollonian clarity' is characteristically astute (*ed.cit.,* n. 13 above, p. 173). On the same page he quotes Dante's prayer to Apollo: 'infuse me with your spirit as you did Marsyas when you tore him from the cover of his limbs'. This view of the myth informs Dipple's reading of the novel (*Work for the Spirit,* pp. 108-32) and, to a large extent, Conradi's (*Saint and Artist,* pp. 187-9).

15. Ovid, *Metamophoses* VI.392-4, tr. F. J. Miller, Loeb edn (London and New York: Heinemann and Putnam's, 1929), p. 315. The political implications of the story—as a battle between the forces of Apollo and the mother goddess—are taken for granted in, e.g., William Smith, *Dictionary of Greek and Roman Biography and Mythology,* 3 vols (London 1862-64), II.962-3, *s.v.* Marsyas. Note that Plato banishes the flute in *Republic,* 399 D-E, thereby explicitly exalting Apollo over Marsyas.

16. For the dizzying principles of doubling, see Ernest Jones, *Hamlet and Oedipus* (London: Gollancz, 1949), ch. 7, and, for a slightly different approach, Frank Kermode, *Forms of Attention* (Chicago and London: Univ. of Chicago Press, 1985), ch. 2.

17. Fay Weldon, *Down Among the Women* (London: Heinemann, 1971), ch. 1 and Jocelyn's epilogue.

18. As Sturrock and Stewart (see n. 9 above) both noticed without, however, going back to sources.

19. Murdoch, 'Against Dryness', *Encounter,* XVI (1961): repr. in Harold Bloom, ed., *Iris Murdoch* (New York, New Haven, Philadelphia: Chelsea House Publishers, 1986), pp. 9-16; p. 15.

20. Herodotus, Book I, paras 181-2, tr. A. D. Godley, Loeb edn (London and New York: Heinemann and Putnam's, 1931), I.227. Henry in his state of moral myopia in *Henry and Cato* is excited by the idea of Stephanie Whitehouse's past as a prostitute and at one point imagines her as a *hetaira* (p. 165). For Apollo as woman-hater see J. E. Harrison, *Prolegomena to the Study of Greek Religion* (Cleveland and New York: World Publishing Company, 1966), pp. 394-5.

21. *Aeneid,* IV.143-4. Servius's note reads: 'nam constat Apollinem sex mensibus hiemalibus apud Pataram, Lyciae civitatem, dare responsa: unde Patareus Apollo dicitur: et sex mensibus aestivis apud Delum . . .': *Servii Grammatici qui feruntur in Vergilii Carmina Commentarii,* ed. G. Thilo and H. Hagen, 3 vols (Leipzig, 1878-87), I.489.

22. Liddell and Scott, *Greek-English Lexicon, s.v.*: 'from Apollo's "crooked", i.e. ambiguous, oracles'.

23. *Oedipus Tyrannus,* l.410 (Tiresias); l.853 (Jocasta); ll.994-6 (Oedipus). Quoted from Loeb *Sophocles* tr. F. Storr, I (London and New York: Heinemann and Macmillan, 1912). The play abounds in epithets and names of Apollo; Loxias is used in these instances and one other neutral instance (by the Chorus, l.1101). Dipple, *Work for the Spirit,* p. 112, misses the Oedipal connection by locating the name in Aeschylus's *Agamemnon,* though Conradi, p. 284, n. 6, suspects the Sophoclean truth.

24. A useful phrase that I have borrowed from Martin Greenberg's *The Hamlet Vocation of Coleridge and Wordsworth* (Iowa City: Univ. of Iowa Press, 1986).

25. See the attack on cosmetics in Juvenal's *Sixth Satire,* ll.457-73 and, for some at least of its influential subsequent history, F. A. Nussbaum, *The Brink of All We Hate: English Satires on Women, 1660-1750* (Lexington: Kentucky U.P., 1984).

26. Bradley identifies Priscilla with their mother on page 82: 'I felt for my misguided mother pain and shame which did not diminish but qualified my love. I was mortally afraid of anyone seeing her as absurd or pathetic, a defeated snob. And later still, after her death, I transferred many of those feelings to Priscilla.'

27. For the Platonist view in Murdoch, see Lynette Hunter, *Rhetorical Stance in Modern Literature: Allegories of Love and Death* (London and Basingstoke: Macmillan 1984), pp. 106-20; for Freud, see *The Theme of the Three Caskets, SE,* XII.301, *cit.* ch. 2, n. 35 above.

28. The classic account of this reading of *Frankenstein* remains that of Gilbert and Gubar, *The Madwoman in the Attic* (New Haven and London: Yale U.P., 1979), ch. 7.

29. The Apollo on whom Bradley models himself is thus not just Apollo the woman-hater (above, n. 20) but Apollo the death-giver, whose name derives from Greek *apollumi,* to destroy: William Smith, *Dictionary* (n. 15 above), I.230. Luce Irigaray's reversal of the Platonic cave myth to show (among other things) how Plato's sun blinds man to the feminine also foregrounds Apollo the destroyer: see ref. in n. 31 below.

30. It is worth noting here that Richard Todd has rightly identified Bradley as a foot fetishist: 'The Plausibility of *The Black Prince*', *Dutch Quarterly,* VIII (1978), 82-93.

31. The doves of Aphrodite are a commonplace; for the doves of Dodona as the oracular voices of the wise women see, e.g., Pausanias, *Description of Greece* VII.xxi.2. Murdoch is revisiting here the Jungian archetype of the feminine cave: Johnson, *Iris Murdoch* (above n. 5), ch. 4, discusses its appearance in her fiction and directs attention to the relevance of Luce Irigaray's feminist deconstruction of the Platonic cave-sun metaphor in *Speculum, de l'autre femme* (tr. G. G. Gill (Ithaca: Cornell U.P., 1985)).

32. Hesiod, *Theogony,* l. 120. This is the same Eros that we find in Plato's *Symposium,* 178B.

33. Shakespeare's *Cymbeline,* II.ii. The further analogy, with Tarquin's rape of Lucretia, is made by Iachimo himself at the beginning of the scene.

34. *Faerie Queene,* III.iv.18, 23 and, especially, *Pericles* and *The Winter's Tale.*

35. The song resounds hauntingly through *The Sea, The Sea* (e.g. p. 364); Morgan sings (or quotes) it to Peter in *A Fairly Honourable Defeat* as an example of something human that is 'good, . . . intact and precious and absolutely beautiful' (Penguin edn (1973), pp. 188-9); to cite only two instances of its relevance to Murdoch's fiction.

36. Murdoch said in a 1978 interview that 'Ideas in art must suffer a sea-change': Bryan Magee, *Men of Ideas: Some Creators of Contemporary Philosophy* (London: BBC, 1978), p. 277; and the idea of the transmuting power of the sea, as well as the sea as source, is omnipresent in her thinking. Thus, James tells Charles riddlingly, in *The Sea, The Sea,* that 'Plato was descended from Poseidon on his father's side' (p. 176). Interestingly, dreams are a narrative obsession in the novel that followed *The Black Prince, The Sacred and Profane Love Machine* (1974).

37. See p. 154 above.

38. Apollo is specifically enemy of the womb, signified by his dragon-opponent Delphyne: see Carl Kerényi, *The Gods of the Greeks,* tr. Norman Cameron (London: Thames and Hudson, 1951), p. 51: *cit.* Mary Daly, *Gyn/Ecology* (London: The Women's Press, 1987), p. 62 and n.

39. On this see, for example, D. J. Gelpi, SJ, *The Divine Mother: A Trinitarian Theology of the Holy Spirit* (Lanham, New York, London: University Press of America, 1984). The 'Jew' pun in Julian's name (which contrasts with Jewish-born Christian's) emphasises the Jewish tradition of feminine spirit here.

David J. Gordon (essay date 1995)

SOURCE: Gordon, David J. "The Good Apprentice: 1954-1966." In *Iris Murdoch's Fables of Unselfing,* pp. 116-37. Columbia: University of Missouri Press, 1995.

[*In the following essay, Gordon examines Murdoch's early novels, focusing on the novelist's development and, especially, on thematic concerns.*]

The ten novels that Iris Murdoch published between *Under the Net* (1954) and *The Time of the Angels* (1966) were widely read and reviewed. Especially to those who read also such essays as "The Sublime and the Beautiful Revisited" and "Against Dryness," which eloquently related the art of the novel to moral philosophy, she seemed an important new writer as well as a very readable one. In light of the more ambitious work of the seventies and eighties, the work of this period does looks slighter than it once did, but a few of the early novels still hold up well—especially *The Bell*—and each of them makes new moves both conceptually and formally. In this chapter I want to chart the development of the novelist during these years with particular emphasis on the rapid advance of her thematic material and on the challenge she faced to find forms that would enable this material to realize its expressive potential.

Commentary on the early novels has tended to take its cue from Murdoch's own distinction between "closed" and "open" forms, that is, between those in which pattern is tight and those in which it is more relaxed—*The Flight from the Enchanter* and *A Severed Head,* versus *The Sandcastle* and *The Bell.* Murdoch implied (speaking to Hobson) that the open novels more nearly approximated an artistic ideal, whereas she felt fonder of the closed novels because they expressed more of herself. The open novels (relatively open, that is, because all of Murdoch's novels are quite patterned) allowed for more depth of characterization, but the closed ones were marked by more intensification of a favorite theme, a theme illustrated (she explained to Rose) by Mischa Fox (*FE* [*The Flight from the Enchanter*]) and Honor Klein (*SH* [*A Severed Head*]) as "power characters . . . deified by their surrounding followers." Both kinds grow out of *Under the Net,* but the rapid advance of her ideas broke the mold of that first novel, in which the enchanter and the saint were combined in one figure. It was the enchanter who received development first, because, as Linda Kuehl justly remarked about the early novels, Murdoch was "more fascinated by enchantment than by the struggle against illusion." But she was certainly concerned as well with notions of freedom and virtue and with intimations of saintliness, which develop from *Under the Net* to *The Sandcastle* and *The Bell.* Indeed, since her ideas of both good and evil developed so rapidly, it became difficult to find a form to contain them, a form that worked both as novel and as fable.[1]

The period from 1961 to 1966 in Murdoch's career is usually thought to be her weakest, but *An Unofficial Rose* broke new ground in its extended presentation of

a figure of good, and *The Unicorn* and *The Time of the Angels,* whatever their weaknesses, greatly clarified the ideas of evil, with which the novelist would continue to be concerned. The other two novels of this period, *The Italian Girl* and *The Red and the Green,* are less ambitious efforts in the same directions, but the first refined the use of an illusioned narrator, and the second gave voice to the romantic writer hidden inside the ironist and the anti-romantic novelist, a voice that later flowered in such major achievements as *The Black Prince* and *The Good Apprentice.*

It is odd forty years later to remember that *Under the Net* was grouped after publication in 1954 with the postwar school of "angry young men," who welcomed the vulgar upstart and scoffed at the snobbish establishment. It is true that its protagonist, Jake Donaghue, has no regular job, pays no rent, spends his time getting into scrapes, and, in spite of his frenzied efforts to sort things out, generally enjoys his footloose freedom. But Jake is in fact an aspiring writer, even if by his own proud report he has "been turned out of more places than any other member of the English intelligentsia" (*UN* [*Under the Net*] 139). And his creator's concerns are not really social and political but philosophical and literary, having to do with the difficulty of seeing the situations of other people truly and of finding language fine enough to capture another person's elusive particularity.

Byatt commented that what Murdoch did have in common with Kingsley Amis and John Wain in this first novel "was an interest in rapid comedy, and the long English tradition of the farcical episodic novel." The sprightly, picaresque tone and bohemian social milieu turned out not to be the right vehicles for her themes, and indeed its tone and milieu were admittedly borrowed from Beckett's *Murphy* and from *Pierrot mon ami* by Raymond Queneau, to whom it is dedicated. Murdoch herself spoke dismissively of *Under the Net* later on—in 1970 to Hayman and in 1986 at a symposium (*Amst* 109)—and in retrospect it may be regarded as an uncharacteristic performance. Byatt in an essay of 1976 (with a 1986 postscript) considered it her "most satisfying" novel perhaps because it looks more avant-garde than its successors and we are reluctant to think of a retreat from an avant-garde position as an artistic advance. But Murdoch herself understood its structural weakness very well, pointing out to Conradi how little the Jake-Hugo conflict engages the other characters, especially the women. As a result of this disjunction, some elaborate episodes (Jake's stealing the trained dog, pursuing the elusive image of a woman in Paris on Bastille Day, and trying to find Hugo on the huge movie set in "contingent" South London) are bustling without being either amusing or suggestive.[2]

But the narrator, however self-deceived, knows that the central interest of his story lies in his friendship with

Hugo, which begins drolly when they are sequestered together during a cold-cure experiment and results in the only real give and take in the novel, the only real testing of views and attitudes. In these scenes, there is at issue a conflict that has genuine importance for Murdoch and hence for her readers.

Hugo's expressive diffidence combines Sartre's respect for situational particularity and distrust of stories because they are "lies," Weil's association of virtue and powerlessness (though wealth and power come to him, Hugo will renounce them and become a humble watchmaker in Nottingham), and Wittgenstein's skepticism about philosophical language as an instrument for capturing the truth of experience (for such language is "a coarse net through which experience slips" ["TL" ["Thinking and language"] 28], "a final network which we cannot creep under" [MGM [Metaphysics as a Guide to Morals] 234]). Hugo has so pure a respect for the concrete and unique that he distrusts all theory, but Jake finds theory necessary to the writer's task of understanding.

Jake writes up his talk with his new friend in the form of a Platonic dialogue called The Silencer, an excerpt of which is given to the reader. In it the Jake persona (Tamarus) makes the strong enough point that civilized, rational animals are inevitably "theory-making animals" because life "to be lived has to be understood." But the Hugo persona (Annandine) asks if a theory can help you when you are in doubt about what to do. "What I speak of," he says, "is the real decision as we experience it; and here the movement away from theory and generality is the movement toward truth. All theorizing is flight. We must be ruled by the situation itself, and this is unutterably particular. Indeed it is something to which we can never get close enough, however hard we may try, as it were, to crawl under the net" (UN 80-81). This is impressive but extreme. As Tamarus says, it would "cut all speech, except the very simplest . . . making life unendurable" (81).

Annandine responds with words that evoke Murdoch's own visionary aspiration but also, in their very absoluteness, imply the compromise that must be made. "Why should life be made endurable? I know that nothing consoles and nothing justifies except a story—but that doesn't stop all stories from being lies. Only the greatest men can speak and still be truthful. Any artist knows this obscurely; he knows that a theory is death, and that all expression is weighted with theory. Only the strongest can rise against that weight. For most of us, for almost all of us, truth can be attained, if at all, only in silence. It is in silence that the human spirit touches the divine" (81). Annandine outlines here the program for a saint or a supreme artist, but Tamarus knows that art must use language and story. Silence can only be intimated through speech—a theme of Beck-

ett's, too—though Murdoch herself did not explore the bearing of this insight on literary form. When Hugo late in the novel comments on The Silencer, he tells Jake he cannot remember any of that. It sounds remote to him. He is half-wedded to silence already.

Until near the end, Hugo is perceived by us as more a figure of mystery and power than a saint. This may seem confusing in light of Annandine's (and finally also Hugo's) absolute embrace of contingency, but the confusion is illuminating. The absolutely necessary man (the compelling enchanter) may lead us toward the Good as much as the absolutely contingent one, and Hugo is the one at least as much as the other. Zohreh Sullivan comments, "Hugo is an unknowing innocent center rather than a deliberate manipulator of others' fantasies."[3] True, he is in this respect unlike Mischa Fox in Murdoch's next novel, The Flight from the Enchanter, but he is like Mischa in being charismatic, "a person of the utmost fascination."

Disassociating the magician (or artist) and saint after Under the Net, Murdoch in a sense spends the next forty years trying to associate them again. At the end of her first novel, she steers her artist-to-be clear of these future complications by having him make Hugo-like renunciations and learn a Hugo-like respect for contingency. Jake will give up lucrative translating and do his own work, sacrifice a payoff so that he can keep the aging dog that saved his life one night on the cold Embankment, and try to curb his need to impose meaning on experience, letting "things take shape deeply within me" (UN 327).

The Flight from the Enchanter introduces a theme its author recognized as central to her vision, "the way in which people make other people play the role for them of gods and demons."[4] A circle of people in London, centering on Rosa Keepe, who once turned down Mischa Fox's offer of marriage, are spellbound by Mischa the enchanter, and their complicity with his power over them makes them unable to break free into the undramatic and ego-deflating light of truth. One is reminded of Plato's image of chained figures who mistake the reflected firelit images for reality, but there are two notable additions, both suggesting the influence of Weil. One is the idea of a demonic source for the enchantment. The other is the implication that the ability to see the truth—an ability only present in one character, who is placed to the side of the main action—requires a spiritually arduous unselfing.

In Under the Net, the illusion that binds the protagonist is dispelled by the (benign) enchanter himself, and both Jake and Hugo discover their true work after renunciation. But Murdoch's second novel is, throughout, a tale of entrapment, as Byatt implies in noting its pervasive imagery of traps and hunts. It gives us a more sinister picture of the human condition, in spite of a fairy-tale atmosphere that prevents us from taking much interest in the individual characters. (Howard German helps account for this atmosphere by finding allusions to such works as *Through the Looking-Glass* and *Hansel and Gretel,* although Conradi hints at the novel's intended depth when he aptly describes its central moment at Mischa's party as a "*skandal* scene" reminiscent of Dostoevsky and anticipating a technique used repeatedly in her own *A Fairly Honourable Defeat.*)[5] In the final chapter, Rosa, still under Mischa's spell, asks the one character free of his influence to marry her, but Peter Saward turns her away, saying, "Some god or demon makes you say it, but you do not really want it" (*FE* 287).

Sustaining this central idea results in a tight novelistic structure, but the price paid for such patterning is that almost every scene seems contrived, and hardly any action is credible. Coincidences multiply; doors open at inopportune moments; living arrangements seem dictated by novelistic convenience rather than by probability. The melodramatic quality of the novel is epitomized in young Annette, who is on two occasions shown with breasts bared by an accidentally torn dress and twice attempts to commit suicide. Our interest in *The Flight from the Enchanter* now consists mainly in observing how the relatively inexperienced author tries to embody a fast-developing cluster of ideas. Most notably, she tests the idea that a certain kind of evil, spreading from the spiritual air of Central Europe, has a seductively coercive quality capable of arousing the imaginations of persons in civilized, postwar London.

Mischa Fox's background suggests a German provenance without a specific link to Nazism. The glance of his one brown eye and one blue eye somehow paralyzes those who would seek definite knowledge about him. He is said to be "capable of enormous cruelty" (*FE* 31), but this remains rather vague. We learn that he is "a bit of a press lord and general mischief-maker" (118), and we see him trying to buy out by blackmail a marginal journal that Rosa and her brother have inherited from their suffragist mother and the mother's now elderly friends, feminists of an earlier age. Mischa is also shown to be capable of emotional blackmail, especially with Nina the refugee dressmaker and with Annette, who is also a kind of refugee in that her family lives on the Continent and she has quit school.[6] He pays Nina's rent and expects her to be available when he visits, but his purpose remains mysterious, and the result is that she has no private life and feels like someone whose only hope is in flight—a vain hope in this case because she is driven to suicide when she believes too quickly that all refugees are about to be deported. Annette also, after Mischa's seductively sadistic speech about women, feels like a puppet in his hands, but proves young enough, despite her humiliations, to survive. Even Rosa,

who has some measure of autonomy, feels "lost in a forest" when she looks at him and desires to be "at his mercy" (240-41). The several incidents of overt violence in the book, throwing and breaking things, are committed by her and Annette, Mischa's *victims,* just as the confused narrator, not the enchantress, is responsible for the blows struck in *A Severed Head.*

Some insight into the enchanter's motives is provided later in the novel when Mischa reveals to Peter that as a child he had felt a compassion for the suffering of animals so keen that it drove him to acts of cruelty against them. Peter reflects, "How strangely close in this man lay the springs of cruelty and pity" (*FE* 208). This picture of Mischa seems to grow out of Weil's idea that we exert what power we have, and those who have suffered pass suffering on. It's an important idea for Murdoch, who is less interested in cruelty as such than in the relation between suffering and selfishness, who indeed would track the basis of aggressive acts to hurt vanity.

Since she wants Mischa to operate by fascination rather than force and yet be plausible as a center of power, she needs to augment the coercive aspect of his role through accomplices. In this novel the chief accomplice is Calvin Blick, called "the dark half of Mischa's mind" (*FE* 280). He is the first of many Murdochian antagonists who become moral instructors as well. Blick tells Annette, "The notion that one can liberate another soul from captivity is an illusion of the very young" (221). And to Rosa he offers the novel's darkest wisdom, a curious mixture of Plato, Weil, and (the pessimistic) Freud: "You never will know the truth, and you will read the signs in accordance with your deepest wishes. That is what we human beings always have to do. Reality is a cipher with many solutions, all of them right ones" (278).

I will pass over the demonic Lusiewicz brothers, who complicate Rosa's life; the morally mediocre civil servant John Rainborough, who mainly helps his creator make plot connections and provide background information to the reader; and the nonagenarian Mrs. Wingfield, a friend of Rosa's mother and a mildly amusing comic creation of a Dickensian stamp, because they suggest little that is original in Murdoch's art or thought, but I should say a word about Peter Saward, who extends the concept of the near-saint, which Murdoch would go on to develop with considerable originality. He is said to be a friend of Mischa's though free from his influence, the only person around who, as Mischa himself recognizes, is not maddened by the enchanter. Peter is a scholar obsessed with a hieroglyphic text that can't be deciphered until a bilingual text comes along. When one finally does, he knows that he has been on a wrong track from the beginning, and accepts his failure. Thus his spiritual independence is seen to have come from his ability to be "good for nothing," in sharp contrast to Mischa's victims, who in their egoism are hungry for spiritual significance. Our picture of this pointless virtue is augmented when we learn of his (arrested) tuberculosis and of his vain courtship of Rosa. To Rainborough, illness seems to have made "Saward not weaker but more powerful," giving him "a personality without frontiers" (*FE* 28, 31). He is, in short, a suggestive sketch for Murdoch's later and fuller attempts—in Ann Peronnet, Tallis Browne, and others—to demonstrate that good is more interesting than evil. As the dying Guy Openshaw will say in *Nuns and Soldiers,* "Only in our virtues are we original, because virtue is difficult, and we have to try, to invent, to work through our nature against our nature" (74).

I have commented earlier on most of what is original in *The Sandcastle* and *The Bell*—in the one, the critique of freedom and Bledyard's questioning of art; in the other, the working out of alternative moral ordeals (worldly and priestly) and alternative views of the good life. In the context of this chapter, I will develop a bit more fully another quality in these two books, the way they open up the inner life of certain characters (Mor and his adolescent children; Michael and Dora). I choose two moments from *The Sandcastle* that linger in the mind as illustrative of this new and welcome sensitivity, and I will comment briefly on the inwardness of *The Bell* in a somewhat different way.

Early in *The Sandcastle,* when Mor does not yet know that he is falling in love with Rain, he is teaching a Latin class and, worried about running out of time, asks a bright student to translate, although Mor is not sure that the passage, from Propertius, is suitable for boys and does not like the bright student's influence on his rebellious son:

> 'While the light remains,' said Carde, speaking slowly in his high deliberate voice, 'only do not forsake the joy of life. If you shall have given all your kisses, you will give too few. And as leaves fall from withered wreaths which you may see spread upon the cups and floating there, so for us, who now as lovers hope for so much, perhaps tomorrow's day will close the doom.'

> 'Yes,' said Mor, 'yes. Very nice, Carde. Thank you. Now you can all go. Rigden, wait a moment, would you?'

(*S* [*The Sandcastle*] 40)

We sense beneath the propriety of his words (especially in that second "yes") how moved Mor is by this beautiful translation and, in his summons to dull Rigden, how constrained are his feelings. Murdoch has given us a glimpse of the man's heart with complete delicacy. The second incident concerns Mor's adolescent son and daughter, whose rebelliousness and mysticism, respectively, do not hide from us their fear of their normally

dependable father's dangerous new interest. After picking wildflowers one day, they suddenly decide to go on a "sporting raid" of Rain's room, where they are awed to discover a love letter from their father, and when Rain suddenly enters, they are bewildered and impulsively offer her the flowers, a tribute to her fascination that is perfect because quite unintended.

As for *The Bell,* I am tempted to cite some fine passages that illustrate her developing skill in representing the thinking of fictional characters, but I will instead join in a critical chorus. Byatt admired *The Bell* as Murdoch's "most successful attempt at realism" among the early novels. Dipple admired its "generous, ruminative mode." For John J. Burke Jr., it is "the real turning point in [her] career as a novelist." And Murdoch herself felt, as she told Simon Blow, that she had first found her style in *The Bell,*[7] adding a decade later, "I think *The Bell* is the best of my earlier novels" (*Amst* [*Encounters with Iris Murdoch*] 109). The gain in maturity and ease, not really surpassed until *The Nice and the Good* (1968), derives in part from the setting, a lay religious community in the Gloucestershire countryside, which allows the characters to talk about and reflect on the moral life quite naturally.

A Severed Head not only deploys its internal narrator more skillfully than did *Under the Net* but also begins to break new ground in connecting erotic adventure to power by way of the myth of Apollo and Marsyas. Honor Klein is an anthropologist of German Jewish background who has studied traditional Japanese rituals, and she tells Martin Lynch-Gibbon, who is seeking a "colossal and powerful love such as I had never known before": "Being Christian you connect spirit with love. These people [the Japanese] connect it with control, with power" (*SH* 54, 96). Murdoch informed her agent Norah Smallwood that she chose "Honor Klein" because she "wanted a strong name."[8] Honor is both the German Jew as potent source of dark wisdom and a figure out of D. H. Lawrence: "'You cannot cheat the dark gods, Mr Lynch-Gibbon,' she said softly" (64). We hear also about her "dark love," "her dark assassin's head," "her eyes upon me like a cold sun" (138, 170, 177). She and her brother are, for Martin, "an infernal pair," who have invited him to travel far away, to "Los Angeles, to San Francisco, to Tokyo" (171). In what is evidently meant to be the novel's most shocking scene, Martin opens an unlocked door and discovers them in bed together. Byatt comments: "The way in which Martin Lynch-Gibbon acquires the strength of magical influence to stand up to Honor Klein is by observing her in bed with her brother, and thus becoming involved in the violation of the incest taboo." Murdoch adds to her picture of this demon-lover the image of a Samurai sword, once drawn by Honor slowly across her thigh, and later used to sever a thrown napkin as a mock-decapitation. Honor describes her own fascination for Martin as that of "a severed head" (182), reminding us of the connection made earlier by Martin's sculptor-brother (whose busts, separated from bodies, made Martin uneasy) between the head of Medusa, severed by Perseus, and Freud's speculation that "the head can represent the female genitals, feared not desired" (44). Interviewed by Ruth Heyd, Murdoch spoke of Honor as a conqueror of self-deception and a favorite character, but she is clearly more interested in Honor's power to create enchantment than to dispel illusion.[9]

A Severed Head is a sophisticated but very self-conscious fiction, in which, as Dipple rightly says, the characters themselves, instead of being revealed, "adorn their activities with the products of their education." Byatt's description is kinder but not so different: "comedy shading into French bedroom farce combined with Jungian psycho-analytic method and cool philosophic wit."[10] But it does manage to hint at the spiritual dimension of power through its allusions to the Marsyan myth, which Murdoch will richly develop.

An Unofficial Rose is the first of five novels published from 1962 to 1966—including *The Unicorn, The Italian Girl, The Red and the Green,* and *The Time of the Angels*—that mark a transition between Murdoch's early and mature periods, a time when her moral vision, if not formal inventiveness, develops very rapidly. Especially in the three most ambitious novels of this group—*An Unofficial Rose, The Unicorn,* and *The Time of the Angels*—we can perceive a new conceptual energy straining against the limits of the narrative form, which in turn seems to rely as if for security on nineteenth-century precedents. *An Unofficial Rose* is dependent on the form and style of Jamesian high comedy, *The Unicorn* and *The Time of the Angels* on the conventions of the Gothic novel. "Good" and "evil" are not yet well integrated, but perhaps each had to be explored separately and even carried to excess, which would help to explain the seeming perverseness of Ann's virtue in one novel and the unabashed Gothic excesses in the other two. I would not disagree with Dorothy Winsor that the Gothicism of *The Unicorn* and *The Time of the Angels* may have seemed a dead end to Murdoch, but they also seem to have taught her something about the moral problematics of suffering and sadism.[11]

The most readable and attractive of the group is *An Unofficial Rose,* perhaps because of the congeniality of the Jamesian influence. The manner in which its clever female schemers (Mildred, Emma, Miranda) practice upon its well-meaning but less clever males (Hugh, Felix, Penn) is clearly reminiscent of Jamesian comedy, and in fact there are a number of sentences that might actually have been written by James, suggesting that Murdoch may be deliberately teasing her own indebtedness. Of course the Jamesian influence has not gone un-

noticed. Byatt called *An Unofficial Rose* Murdoch's "most Jamesian book" and, later, perceptively related Ann to James's Maggie Verver by way of John Bayley's analysis of Maggie in his critical study, *The Characters of Love* (1960), specifically referring to his idea that Maggie "finds in the refuge of convention and deliberate 'ignorance' salvation both for herself and for the others."[12] Ann Peronnet's husband, Randall, maddened by her lack of "form, structure, will, something to encounter, something to make me *be*" (*UR* [*An Unofficial Rose*] 32), has abandoned her and their rose-nursery in Kent to take up with Lindsay Rimmer in London. His father, Hugh, has become absurdly obsessed, after his wife's death, with the idea of reviving an adulterous affair of long ago with Emma Sands, a writer who employs Lindsay as companion-secretary. Randall cannot successfully lay claim to Lindsay except by persuading his father to sell a valuable Tintoretto inherited from his wife. Hugh is shocked at first by the proposal, but, guided by Mildred, an old flame and his neighbor, he persuades himself that Randall faces the same situation he once faced with Emma and should be given the opportunity he did not take, to live all he can. Meanwhile Mildred seeks to win Hugh for herself and also to match Ann with her younger brother Felix, an officer and a gentleman, who has long loved her. When Randall's new situation becomes known, Felix declares his love, and much of our interest in the latter half of the novel is tied up with the question of why, in spite of her reciprocal love for Felix, Ann cannot see her way to accepting him. I have commented earlier on Ann's goodness itself, but I want to focus here on the aesthetic problem it presented for Murdoch.

Ann does not respond, as people do, in terms of resentment and calculation. She cannot see herself other than married to Randall, for her loyalty is the product of an involuntary inner necessity rather than of a desire for love and happiness, and so she awaits the unlikely return of her unworthy husband. (The possibility of this return and thus of Ann's obligation to wait is a point driven home sharply by her demonic daughter, the ironically named Miranda, who has herself been secretly in love with Felix and is now dedicated to preventing her mother from getting him, even though he will then marry a girl in India and be lost to her as well.) Ann's refusal, therefore, is scarcely perceived by us as a renunciation.

The novel's evocation of Henry James, in fact, leads us to miss in Ann, compared to Milly Theale or Maggie Verver, the presence of a purifying power. Ann seems, Dipple observed, "too pallid to carry her central role." In her creator's opinion, reported by Bellamy, she may be simply "not interesting enough."[13] Among the more persuasive reasons offered by her critics for this relative weakness are the constrictive patterning of the plot, the inherent difficulty of embodying a concept of imageless good, and the weakness of Randall as an oppositional figure. The strong oppositional figure is really Miranda with her dangerously magical dolls and dagger, whose presence in the house is to Ann "menacing, a source of strange rays" (*UR* 276), but Miranda remains a mostly covert presence during the action, brought forward finally to help resolve the plot.

When Henry James shifts the center of consciousness to Milly or Maggie, a surge of new energy comes into play. But in *An Unofficial Rose,* after the first quarter, which is presented from Hugh's fair-minded perspective, the point of view moves about opportunistically among the other characters including Ann, and when we do see the situation from her point of view, we do not see very clearly. Murdoch tries to invest her with an authentically negative force: "There must be no drama here, no foothold for the imagination" (114); "It was scarcely a matter of 'motives.' She had had no motives. Her whole life had compelled her" (274). Ann herself admits that others see her as the spirit that denies. Of course she is no Mephistopheles, just the opposite, but unless we can imagine some sort of moral victory in the sacrifice of her Felix, her happiness, the sacrifice seems perverse.

But as my discussion of Ann in chapter 2 should imply, I point in this chapter to a limitation, not a fundamental failure, for the characterization, particularly in the dialogue involving Douglas Swann, adds a new conceptual subtlety to the representation of good that will contribute to the remarkable success of Tallis Browne.

Murdoch's "moral psychology" was fairly well worked out by the early 1960s, but *An Unofficial Rose* must have also made clear to her how difficult it is to have a character who occupies a novel's center space embody Good. Later, the saintly figure is put more to the side (Theo Gray, Brendan Craddock, Stuart Cuno) or, in the single, remarkable case of Tallis Browne, is allegorized. But before Murdoch was ready for these characters, the nature of what she meant by evil had to be further developed, and she explored the subject by way of critiquing spiritual—especially Christian—suffering.

The unicorn, a symbol of Christ, is identified in *The Unicorn* with Hannah Crean-Smith, whose mental suffering is exploited by a few and is seductive to a circle of others through whose eyes we see her. Murdoch believed that *The Unicorn* was a more thoughtful book than *The Flight from the Enchanter, A Severed Head,* or *The Italian Girl,* a meditation about "the ambiguity of the spiritual world itself, about the curious connexions there are between spirituality and sex."[14] One sees what she means—and the novel is indeed rich in ideas— but whether it is an effective narrative is doubtful.

The first chapters could have been drawn almost unchanged from the nineteenth-century Gothicist, Sheridan Le Fanu. An educated and sensible Englishwoman named Marian Taylor, whom the reader trusts, accepts a job as governess in a remote castle in "an appalling landscape" (*U* [*The Unicorn*] 7) that is recognizably Irish but never quite specified. The interior of Gaze castle is imaged by oil lamps, murky corridors, heavy furniture, and, against a background of mystery, social rituals that reflect a high bourgeois level of comfort and culture. Marian's duty is to be companion and reader for a beautiful, strange lady who seems to be an unchained prisoner in her own home. We hear talk of fearful events that occurred seven years earlier: of Hannah's adulterous connection with a young man from the only other family in the vicinity, of her cliff-top struggle with her jealous husband, who fell, was maimed but survived, and who from his distant residence in New York seems to have directed his old friend Gerald Scottow, a suavely forceful man, to serve as his wife's jailer, which he does by using "guilt" as the principal means of enforcement. Now that seven years are almost up, it is superstitiously believed that the term of captivity is about to end.

From this opening we might expect only a naive fable to emerge, hardly the sort of "ethically controlled fantasy" that Robert Scholes had in mind. But the Gothic trappings are evoked only intermittently thereafter as Murdoch pursues her major concern, which is *not* a psychological study of Hannah's guilt but the idealization of Hannah's sorrowful beauty among persons who are drawn to feel for her a love that enhances their own image of self.[15] These persons include chiefly Marian, Effingham Cooper (who is visiting the Lejours, having once been the tutee of Max Lejour and the fiancé of his daughter Alice), and a countryman named Denis Nolan, a sort of pagan Christ who tries to assume and purge Hannah's guilt but ultimately fails because of his hatred for her husband.

We tire of the suspense, since the central action is a condition of impasse, the result of a reluctance on the part of those who "love" Hannah either to rescue her or simply to leave Gaze. Marian and Effingham at one point attempt a rescue but it aborts, and they feel sucked in all the more. Toward the end of what feels like too long a book, Murdoch does provide resolving action, but it comes so swiftly and neatly as to seem merely incredible. Hannah kills Gerald and drowns herself; Denis, trying to save her and not knowing she is already dead, kills the returning husband; and the former love, Pip Lejour, kills himself while cleaning his gun. Finally we learn that Hannah had left her money not to any of her worshippers but to Max Lejour, who refused to pay court.

The two most interesting moments of the story occur, first, when there is a false but believed report that Hannah is simply about to leave with Gerald and the returned husband and, second, when the spell is broken by her death. With a comical suddenness that is surprising yet apt, the others thereupon resume their pursuit of *other* erotic goals; it is as if these normal pursuits (which are just as self-regarding as their worship of Hannah but far more ordinary) had been simply put "on hold." So Marian turns amorously to Denis, and so Effingham, as he boards the train for England, thinks amorously of Marian. Their release from captivity to Hannah is shown to be merely a return to a more usual kind of captivity.

We see the story mainly through the eyes of Marian and Effingham. Marian's point of view works better because her difficulties of understanding are practical ones, whereas Effingham is one of Murdoch's "really fat and monumental egoist[s]" (*U* 268). He diddles his correspondent Elizabeth, engages Alice's affections to escape Elizabeth, and after a moving farewell to the Lejours, "he anticipated that he would weep in the taxi all the way to the [airport]. But on that journey he was in fact chiefly engaged in wondering whether he had not been too forward in kissing Carrie [the maid] at the moment of departure" (267). Murdoch jeers at him so often that he seems a curious vehicle even for the momentary spiritual insight she attributes to him in the face of possible death. It is Max Lejour, however, who is the novel's true wise man, and it is he who critiques most subtly spiritual suffering. The example of Hannah might suggest that Murdoch is merely critical of such suffering, thinking it a kind of moral masochism. Yet Max reads to Effingham a passage in Aeschylus that tells us "we must learn by suffering. As sad care, with memories of pain, comes dropping upon the heart in sleep, so even against our will does wisdom come upon us" (80). An important distinction is made here between two kinds of suffering. One is romantic, self-indulgent, and, like false freedom, a function of will. The other comes against our will and tests us: it is the pain of unselfing. *The Unicorn* shows how easily we can be deceived by the appearance of selfishness. Hannah, after all, is not a sleeping princess held against her will; she is a woman capable of violence who has allowed her guilt to be manipulated by those she hates and her suffering to be romanticized by those she thinks she loves.

The Italian Girl is one of three novels—along with *A Severed Head* and *The Black Prince*—that Murdoch chose to recast in dramatic form. (She also wrote two original plays, of minor interest, *The Three Arrows* and *The Servants & The Snow*.) One can see why. Its brevity, single plot, and pivotal turnabout make it suitable for such adaptation. But novelistically its "pilgrimage from appearance to reality" is too quick and schematic to engage much emotion, and it is studded with facile surprises and melodramatic improbabilities. Murdoch told Rose that it was a story about "coming home to mother and settling down with mother," by which she apparently meant that Edmund's attachment to his now dead mother is transferred to the motherly Maria, but Edmund's interest in his mother is not really dramatized, nor does the sketched-in romance with Maria accumulate any incestuous resonance. Even less realized are the changes the other characters undergo: we do not feel that Otto has been "broken and made simple by a knowledge of mortality" (*IG* [*The Italian Girl*] 153), that Isabel is no longer a "machine" but someone who can "see" (163), or that the mischievous David (the only character with a bit of life) must return to Russia because "one cannot escape from the suffering of the world" (152). Since the novel is not highly regarded by critics and since I have earlier discussed its use of the internal narrator, I will leave it at that.

The Red and the Green (1964) is also slightly regarded, for different, more complicated reasons that throw some light on the primary aesthetic challenge Murdoch faced. It is the only one of her novels with a historical setting—Dublin during Easter week, 1916—and is thick with details about actual events, persons, and places. Moreover, it dramatizes the kinds of questions that the abortive rebellion historically generated and that are familiar to most of us through Yeats's poem "Easter 1916." Was the Rising foolish (given the promise of Home Rule) or brave? Is Ireland a backwater where nothing happens or indeed a land that nurtures heroes? But the most important anomaly of this novel is that its structure is not essentially ironic. It is a romance, thereby also departing in spirit from Yeats's poem, phrases of which are woven into it. The front cover in the Penguin edition advertises "a story of terrible beauty and glorious death." Yeats's oxymoronic phrase "terrible beauty" is given some play (enough to allow us to read the story of its major character, Pat Dumay, as a fable of unselfing), but the stress falls on the romantic second phrase, "glorious death." The novel is a retrospective tribute to the bravery of youth in a time of crisis.

The story revolves around two cousins, Andrew and Pat, the one Protestant Anglo-Irish, the other Irish Catholic, who find themselves on opposite sides at the time of the Rising. In an epilogue dated 1938, Frances, who had been engaged to Andrew but secretly in love with Pat, speaks from "the workaday middle of her life," telling her anti-romantic husband and too romantic son (each a foil figure) of those distant days and what happened to those she knew, with particular emphasis on Pat's death at the end of the Rebellion and Andrew's the next year in France: "'They were inconceivably brave men,' said Frances suddenly gripping the table. . . . She did not really think all that much about the old days; and yet now for a moment it seemed to her that these thoughts were always with her, and that she had lived out, in those months, in those weeks, the true and entire history of her heart, and that the rest was a survival" (*RG* [*The Red and the Green*] 279).[16]

Although the story Murdoch makes for us in ***The Red and the Green*** is exciting, thanks in part to the suspense provided by the ticking of the clock toward the foreknown conclusion, it is scarcely more than melodrama, with almost none of the symbolic resonances we value in her work. Its most interesting picture is that of Pat, a soldier whose consummate intensity is like that of an artist. It may seem strange that a soldier could be a figure of religious significance for Murdoch, but "if [Pat] could have believed himself a poet, a creator of any kind, capable of lifting out of the muck and mess of life some self-contained perfect object, this would have seemed to him a goal worthy of his powers. But he knew, bitterly, that this salvation was not given to him" (82). So he is *like* an artist, lover, or saint in scorning the morally mediocre, in feeling that he belongs "not to himself but to some design of history" (77). The novel's other interesting figure, satirically conceived, is Frances's Uncle Barney, "by vocation a failed priest" (99), who thinks about Good and about his inability to achieve it because he cannot renounce drink, the "other" woman, and most of all, his self-indulgent memoir, in which he records well-written resentments against his long-suffering wife. He is roused to action by the Rising but literally shoots himself in the foot, though an expert marksman, and so misses out on the climactic action. Even these characters, however, are more explained and analyzed than truly presented, and so there is relatively little interaction between "story" and "idea," the integration of which is always the clue to the aesthetic success of any single novel.

Like ***The Unicorn, The Time of the Angels*** enlists Gothic trappings in a serious intellectual purpose, to explore the nature of evil, but whereas Hannah Crean-Smith's Christian suffering is used as a magnet to elicit the egoism of others, Carel Fisher is himself an Antichrist who acts vengefully out of his belief in the Grand Inquisitor's sad wisdom that goodness is too hard for human beings. The novel ought to be more impressive than it is, for, along with Dostoevsky, it brings into play such weighty material as Nietzsche's and Heidegger's proto-existentialist death-of-God theologies. But the novel is too self-conscious in its use of this material. Carel *reads* Heidegger rather than exemplifying his ideas, and even this is only indicated once, and comically, when his innocent maid (and mistress), Pattie O'Driscoll, out of curiosity reads an open page (partly quoted for us) and is bewildered to the point of terror.[17]

Louis Martz considered ***The Time of the Angels*** Murdoch's "only truly philosophic novel," and Murdoch herself (Rose reported) acknowledged that, in it, "philosophy comes into the very center of the plot." But its use of philosophy, as Byatt put it, is "mannered." Dipple takes the book more seriously by stressing a complex

trinitarian allegory that is not really dramatized, based on what happened between Carel and his two brothers before the story began.[18]

Carel's blasphemies are accompanied by his sexual enslavement of dark Pattie and fair Elizabeth, the sugarplum fairy and swan princess of Tchaikovsky, whose music suffuses his prisonlike home. His daughter, Muriel, hoping to be a writer, is so intimidated by him that she cannot pronounce his name. But all this seems more lurid than frightening. Perhaps it is too late in the day to frighten us with the idea that God is dead and therefore all is permitted. Or perhaps we don't feel an underlying despair in Carel's satanism. Or perhaps the story itself as it unfolds, though effectively oppressive in the atmosphere it creates around the deserted rectory in the East End, is too predictably shocking.

We are more than prepared for the story's major surprise: Elizabeth, Carel's presumptive niece, is also his forced mistress. And the further surprise, that she is his daughter, loses its shock value because the background explanation is cobbled together on the spot. When we learn, early on, that Muriel keeps a supply of sleeping tablets in case of despair, we know they will be used somehow and perhaps by Carel, since the resolving action of a novel so dominated by his presence is likely to be his death. The only twist is that, in dying, he leaves his daughter a legacy of damnation, and ruins Pattie's chance of marriage with the saintly porter, Eugene Peshkov. The destinies of Pattie and Eugene are fairly predictable too, given the stress on *her* deep innocence and *his* long victimization in Eastern Europe and at the hands of his scapegrace son: *she* will take up a new life helping refugees in Africa; *he* will revert to his old conviction that "after all the world was just a camp" (***TA*** [***The Time of the Angels***] 233).

An air of luridness pervades theme as well as plot. Carel is said to have laughed in church, and he wants to announce from the pulpit that there is no God. He will be "the priest of no God" (***TA*** 170), reminding an American reader of Flannery O'Connor's Hazel Motes, who, however, is a semi-literate and half-comic figure. Murdoch has Carel declare that no one has yet really believed that God is dead: "Perhaps Nietzsche did for a little. Only his egoism of an artist soon obscured the truth" (171). "Suppose," Carel declares to his brother, Marcus, who refuses to believe what he hears, "only evil were real. . . . The death of God has set the angels free. And they are terrible" (172-73). With this image of "demonized angels," softened by Muriel's former teacher, who is trying to understand him, to "irresponsible psychological forces" (194), Carel seeks to shock his brother and Murdoch to shock her readers, who may or may not feel the desired effect. For me the shock is too deliberate, but certainly Carel is a more interesting Murdochian satanist or scourge than Nick Fawley or Gerald Scottow, an important warm-up for Julius King.

The modicum of resistance to Carel's ideas generates some interest. Several persons are suspicious enough to make repeated inquiries with the intention of perhaps intervening: Norah Shadox-Brown, a retired headmistress; Marcus himself; and Anthea Barlow, a psychiatric social worker from the pastorate. Liberals all, they prove inadequate to the task of comprehending a radical evil. A more interesting form of resistance derives from a triangulated argument involving Carel, Marcus, and the Bishop. Marcus, who is writing a book about the idea of the Good, is alarmed by the Bishop, who, despite his bland interest in the pleasures of the tea table, states a belief in a severe Kierkegaardian Christianity that makes Marcus cry out, "You've taken away all the guarantees" (*TA* 95), setting him up to be terrified later by hearing his brother say that "goodness is impossible for us human beings" (174). The Bishop's argument about the pointlessness of Good is undermined by his complacency, but it functions dramatically to alarm Marcus and to make Carel's ideas sound more acceptable. Marcus seems to be endorsing a Murdochian position, wanting to salvage from Christianity the idea of the Good. But he is too soft for this ambition, as Eugene is too soft for saintliness. Marcus degrades the Good (whereas Carel inverts it), but, unlike Rupert Foster in *A Fairly Honourable Defeat,* he is permitted to recognize that what he wanted to say cannot be expressed as theory and thus permitted to accept a lower level of achievement. Murdoch gives one of her Platonists a measure of sympathy after he admits his basic mediocrity.

Interesting in some ways, *The Time of the Angels* is on balance too stilted, too much a series of tableaux. Yet a number of its ideas and strategies are refined in the novels ahead. And it rounds off impressively twelve crowded years of apprenticeship.

Notes

1. Hobson, "Lunch with Iris Murdoch," 28; Rose, "Interview," 14; Kuehl, "Iris Murdoch: The Novel as Magician / The Magician as Artist," 357.

2. Byatt, "Iris Murdoch," 215; Ronald Hayman, "Out of the Tutorial," 13; Byatt, "Iris Murdoch," 228; Conradi, *Saint and Artist,* 44.

3. Sullivan, "The Demonic: *The Flight from the Enchanter,*" 72-73.

4. Rose, "Interview," 14.

5. Byatt, "Iris Murdoch," 221; German, "Allusions in the Early Novels of Iris Murdoch," 365; Conradi, "Iris Murdoch and Dostoevsky," 45.

6. A manuscript of the novel at the University of Iowa shows that Murdoch's original idea was to make *all* the major characters refugees (Conradi, *Saint and Artist,* 52). In 1983 she remarked, "I've only recently realised that I'm a kind of exile, a displaced person. I identify with exiles" (Haffenden, "Haffenden Talks to Iris Murdoch," 33). And in 1991 she linked this personal interest with her own school experience and her work in the UNRRA camps for displaced persons after the war (Meyers, "Interview," 106).

7. A. S. Byatt, "Shakespearean Plot in the Novels of Iris Murdoch," 90; Dipple, *Work for the Spirit,* 147; John J. Burke Jr., "Canonizing Iris Murdoch," 494; Blow, "Interview," 24.

8. Murdoch to Smallwood, February 21, 1961, in Murdoch Collection.

9. A. S. Byatt, "*A Severed Head* and *The Unicorn,*" 118; Heyd, "Interview," 143.

10. Dipple, *Work for the Spirit,* 148-49; Byatt, "Shakespearean Plot," 90.

11. Winsor, "Solipsistic Sexuality in Murdoch's Gothic Novels," 130.

12. Byatt, "Iris Murdoch," 224. It is relevant to note that Murdoch married Bayley in 1957, a few years before his study was published. Among her other early novels, the ones that show most stylistic indebtedness to James are *A Severed Head* and *The Unicorn,* written just before and just after *An Unofficial Rose,* suggesting a certain period (1959-1962) when this influence peaked. But Conradi reminds us that "James continued to haunt Murdoch at least until *Nuns and Soldiers,* which partly reworks the plot of *The Wings of the Dove*" (*Saint and Artist,* 59).

13. Dipple, *Work for the Spirit,* 150; Bellamy, "Interview," 136.

14. Rose, "Interview," 17.

15. I disagree, then, with Byatt's description of *The Unicorn* as "a case history in purely Freudian terms" (*Degrees of Freedom,* 133). Nor is guilt the real theme of any later novel, even *A Word Child* or *The Philosopher's Pupil.*

16. A connection between the circumstances depicted in Murdoch's novels and those known to us of her personal life does not often suggest itself, but *The Red and the Green,* though hardly a confessional work, does seem to be a special tribute to her Irish background; one remembers in particular that her adored father, who later became an eminent civil servant in Whitehall, was a cavalry officer during the Great War. Donna Gerstenberger shrewdly remarks that the author's feelings seem to be distant from her story *until* the end, when the weight of final judgment suddenly and arbitrarily falls on Frances, whereupon all distance

and irony are dropped, and the final effect is "a tribute to Ireland" (Gerstenberger, "*The Red and the Green,*" 70). Two comments that Murdoch herself made bear out this impression of personal involvement: "That was a very special case, the novel about Ireland, because it was something I knew about and felt about very deeply . . . the thing was very close to me emotionally" (*Amst* 108); "I think my father was a really good man; I didn't realize how remarkable this was until later on. He was a great inspiration to me and certainly the greatest influence on my life" (Meyers, "Interview," 103).

17. It is interesting to note that, when asked by Hugo Brunner in 1968 to write a parody of Heidegger, Murdoch declined, saying that she hadn't time, then added, "Anyway Heidegger is his own best parody" (see Murdoch Collection [1968]).

18. Martz, "The London Novels," 52; Rose, "Interview," 10; Byatt, "Shakespearean Plot," 90; Dipple, *Work for the Spirit,* 72-74.

Abbreviations

BOOKS BY IRIS MURDOCH

FICTION

Note: Years indicate first publication. Citations are from the Penguin editions.

FE: The Flight from the Enchanter (1956)

IG: The Italian Girl (1964)

RG: The Red and the Green (1965)

S: The Sandcastle (1957)

SH: A Severed Head (1961)

TA: The Time of the Angels (1966)

U: The Unicorn (1963)

UN: Under the Net (1954)

UR: An Unofficial Rose (1962)

NONFICTION

MGM: Metaphysics as a Guide to Morals. London: Chatto and Windus, 1992.

ESSAYS AND REVIEWS BY IRIS MURDOCH

Amst: Murdoch's responses in *Encounters with Iris Murdoch.* 1986. Ed. Richard Todd. Amsterdam: Free University Press, 1988.

tl: "Thinking and Language." *Proceedings of the Aristotelian Society* 25 (1951): 25-34

Barbara Stevens Heusel (essay date 1995)

SOURCE: Heusel, Barbara Stevens. "*Metaphysics as a Guide to Morals* and Iris Murdoch's Ongoing Dialogues with Other Philosophers." In *Patterned Aimlessness: Iris Murdoch's Novels of the 1970s and 1980s,* pp. 1-22. Athens: University of Georgia Press, 1995.

[*In the following essay, Heusel considers* Metaphysics as a Guide to Morals, *asserting that an understanding of Murdoch's moral concerns expressed in this work "and her stance in relation to other philosophers enlightens any reading of her novels."*]

Iris Murdoch's desire to think about the lives of human beings and their relationship to morality has drawn her simultaneously to writing philosophy and fiction. Her novels "are *not connected* with philosophy," she insists (Letter to the author, April 24, 1993).[1] Art and philosophy use imagery in different ways to describe the world;[2] for Murdoch, philosophy is a rational activity, while fiction draws on unconscious as well as rational activity. Neither discourse can capture all of life's mystery. Her novels contribute images of minds thinking—reflecting inner as well as outer experience; her philosophy contributes metaphysical pictures or systems that may be used as guides to the Good. Her distinguishing philosophy from literature does not, however, signify that she walls one off from the other. She is continually empowered by each discourse, and in turn each empowers the other. An understanding of Murdoch's moral concerns and her stance in relation to other philosophers enlightens any reading of her novels.

Murdoch seems to think her job as a philosopher is not only to create her own philosophy but also to scrutinize others' philosophies: examining how they work, applying to them the questions that have been asked for centuries, and coming up with her own analysis of what a given philosophy contributes to the larger system of ideas. Calling herself a "Wittgensteinian neo-Platonist" (Chevalier, *Rencontres* 90), she is a thinker who has the special knack of seeing within an idea a whole spectrum of positions and of holding all the positions in her mind as she weighs their strengths and weaknesses. This is the way she proceeds in *Metaphysics as a Guide to Morals* (1992), her major philosophical text. Here she studies conceptual change: looking at the old Western truths in light of new ideas about truth, juxtaposing Cartesian concepts and those of quantum physics, or Platonic idealism and structuralism—the broad term she uses to include not only Saussurean systems but also the poststructuralism and deconstruction that have swept Western academia.[3] According to Murdoch, Jacques Derrida, who has said that "Heidegger is the last metaphysician," is himself a metaphysician and his structuralism (deconstruction) "look[s] like another metaphysic" (*MGM* [*Metaphysics as a Guide to Morals*] 197). She argues that structuralist theory in general and Derridean practice in particular, "by its removal of the 'old' idea of truth and truth-seeking as moral value," inhibits philosophical study of conceptual change: "If all meaning is deferred our ordinary distinctions, for instance between what is clearly true and what is dubious and what is false, are removed and we begin to lose confidence . . . in what is made to seem the simple, old-fashioned, ordinary concept of truth" (*MGM* 194).[4] Like any metaphysician, Derrida is incapable of opting for *not* creating systems, Murdoch points out, and is therefore also incapable of ending metaphysics.

Murdoch's vision is large and comprehensive; she wants to save not absolute truth, not Platonic forms (they are only indicators), but the relationship between what is outside the body and what is inside the mind, no matter how arbitrary that relationship is. She has the ability to tolerate more incongruities than the philosophers who find that her work is unorthodox. Murdoch has always preferred moral philosophy to analytic or linguistic philosophy. Since her days at Oxford and Cambridge, she has been leery of jumping onto any philosophical bandwagon. Immersed during her school days at Oxford in the atmosphere of the analytical philosophy of Bertrand Russell, A. J. Ayer, Gilbert Ryle, and Ludwig Wittgenstein, she preferred the moral philosophy of G. E. Moore and Plato. The closest she has come to joining the dominant or popular philosophical crowd was during her twenties when she discovered existentialism. But her first published work, *Sartre, Romantic Rationalist* (1953), demonstrates her clear-sighted criticism of existentialism (see chapter 4). Since 1977 she has been publicly contemplating Derrida's deconstruction, which she flatly labels "plausible amoralist determinism" (*MGM* 198). Yet Murdoch is able to empathize with Derrida and others who are comfortable with forms of determinism: "it satisfies a deep human wish: to *give up*, to get rid of freedom, responsibility, remorse, all sorts of personal individual unease, and surrender to fate and the relief of 'it could not be otherwise'" (*MGM* 190). She finds that structuralism, including deconstruction, threatens empirical views of truth and value.[5]

While the determinist may be inhibiting the study of philosophical change, however, the moral collapse in contemporary society is an immediate and more concrete problem. Murdoch has argued moral philosophy with a dogged attentiveness much of her life, and she insists that the ideal of a transcendent good, which Derrida obfuscates, is "essential to both morality and religion" (*MGM* 511). She envisions humans struggling to apprehend a perfection that they can only vaguely understand. *Metaphysics as a Guide to Morals* is her reiteration that Plato's proof of the necessity of Good is "a background to moral philosophy, . . . a bridge between morals and religion, and . . . [is] relevant to our new disturbed understanding of religious truth." She insists,

furthermore, that the world needs a theology that "can continue without God" and without the supernatural (*MGM* 511) and a metaphysics that can, as the title of her book reminds readers, point to morals.

Murdoch defines traditional metaphysics as "a search for hidden *a priori* determining forms, constituting an ultimate reality" (*MGM* 6), in other words, a transcendent or deduced system that strives "to reach the basis of things and show us what . . . *must* be there" (*MGM* 259). She therefore shares with the structuralists a yearning for structures. "Philosophers are artists," she writes, "and metaphysical ideas are aesthetic; they are intended to clarify and connect, and they certainly satisfy deep emotional needs" (*MGM* 37). The metaphysical process connects "different considerations and pictures so that they give each other mutual support" (*MGM* 511). With each change of worldview comes a change of images. Younger generations of metaphysicians consider issues from a new worldview and determine to break the old pictures, their goal being to demythologize the illusions or errors made by earlier metaphysicians. Some philosophical moves, like the early Wittgenstein's separation of fact and value, demythologize and yet manage to remove errors without destroying mystery or the cultural horizon. Murdoch has persistently employed the "terms of ordinary language and its 'naive' truth values" (*MGM* 199) to argue that mystery is as important as duty and reason. She summarizes the process, going so far as to say that "demythologisation is not a single road, nor need it imply or *mean* a disappearance of myths and icons, or some profound 'rectification' of ordinary language. The modern scene includes (I hope) an enlargement of our concept of religion through our greater tolerance and knowledge of other religions" (*MGM* 454). Rituals, by sparking the imagination, provide sources of energy. Some metaphysicians, however, attempt to obliterate the cultural horizon or, overwhelmed by their hubris, imagine that they do. Such egoism takes them too far. In fact, the major development one notices in Murdoch's philosophical stance since *Sovereignty of Good* (1967) is her struggle with this new brand of demythologizing that denies the overarching cultural background of truth.

This chapter explores Murdoch's many-layered vision by showing the way she has employed four decades of dialogue with her fellow philosophers to hammer out a practicable moral philosophy that celebrates the Good. In *Metaphysics as a Guide to Morals,* Murdoch stands like a rock of classical Greek moderation amid the waves of contemporary theoretical interpretation. She warns of the difficulty of finding a balance between "faithfulness to the text" and "inventiveness."[6] In regard to literary theory, Murdoch seems to want to find a mean between the formalist who argues that a complete understanding of the text is possible and the deconstructionist who argues that there is no one answer because meaning is always deferred and finding meaning is an ongoing process. For her, theorizing can often become an end and may unfortunately become "another way of losing the original" (*MGM* 510). With this problem always in the foreground, her larger philosophical argument has as its central issues the relation of value and fact, of consciousness and thought, and of art and philosophy to morality. Her philosophy dramatizes a broad range of voices who speak to these issues.

Being also a storyteller, Murdoch makes it easy for the reader to watch the unfolding of her philosophical process and to take part in her digressions and qualifications. For her, the history of philosophy reveals a series of metaphysical systems hypothesized by a series of philosophers, many demythologizing the immediately preceding system. Being herself more an iconoclastic pilgrim than a demythologizer, she portrays in **Metaphysics as a Guide to Morals** a sequence of dramas, in each of which one philosopher demythologizes another. Although she does not depict the sequence in explicitly Freudian terms, the pattern is familiar: each generation must overthrow the preceding one,[7] substituting its own construct D for the construct C, which in its day superseded construct B, and so on. Such a drama recalls Harold Bloom's "anxiety of influence," each genius arguing that he had found the center of things, Heidegger's "*Dasein*" replacing Schopenhauer's "will" replacing Kant's "thing-in-itself" replacing Locke's Substance. Murdoch can only be an outsider in these scenes, having no father per se to overthrow. She did, however, identify with Elizabeth Anscombe and Phillippa Foot, who served as valuable role models.[8] To put the sequence of male philosophers in perspective, Murdoch ingeniously adopts what she elsewhere calls "a mythological or dramatic mode of presentation"; in "Broken Totality," an unpublished chapter of **Sartre, Romantic Rationalist,** she uses the expression to describe seeing the world made up of dramatic personalities and scenes (133).[9] When Murdoch stages such philosophical conflicts, readers' excitement is more visceral if they recognize this strategy. Adopting a Renaissance perception of life as a drama and human beings as dramatis personae, Murdoch peoples her texts with major characters (Plato, Wittgenstein, Kant, and Sartre) and minor ones (Anselm, Descartes, Schopenhauer, and Derrida). Weaving her own philosophy out of particular concepts promulgated by the major characters, she demonstrates her logical agreements and disagreements with all of them. While she never posits a continuum reaching from good to evil, it is clear that she would place Plato at the former extreme and Nietzsche and Derrida at the latter.

A major new emphasis in Murdoch's ongoing discussion of epistemology is "the idea of a self-contained unity or limited whole . . . [as] a fundamental instinctive concept." She argues in the opening sentences of the first chapter of **Metaphysics as a Guide to Morals,**

"We see parts of things, we intuit whole things. We seem to know a great deal on the basis of very little." Furthermore, her jumping in in medias res focuses on the drama of human perception, the point where inner and outer experience meet, assuming her reader's knowledge of the mechanics of perception and cognition. In simply saying "We see parts," she assumes the reader is an observer who knows how the human eye works together with the brain to grasp a whole picture when only parts can be seen. Her immediate challenging of contemporary discussions of "the self" raises the stakes: "Oblivious of philosophical problems and paucity of evidence we grasp ourselves as unities, continuous bodies and continuous minds" (*MGM* 1). In this discussion of self-contained unity, she makes gestures toward arguments concerning the Lacanian "self" and the Derridean *aporia,*[10] apparently assuming that the reader knows that infants enter the Mirror Stage between six and eight months of age and begin to learn that they are discrete entities. Of course, she does not say that humans have unity or that time and space have continuity, but often her references to the ontological givens of Western culture are unclear, perhaps ambivalent. For example, she heartily disagrees with Martin Buber's reading of Plato: "Philosophy is grounded on the presupposition that one sees the absolute in universals" (quoted in *MGM* 461). For Murdoch, Buber's statement is an example of a common misunderstanding of Plato's doctrine: "all is patently not one, our human world is not determined by a hidden unity or universal harmony, we are strained and stretched out (like the *Anima Mundi* in the *Timaeus*), we live with intuitions of what we also realise are very distant. . . . Plato spoke only of (perhaps) glimpsing the Form of the Good" (*MGM* 462).[11] Even Socrates did not achieve it. Even so, Murdoch's saying that human beings "assume the continuity of 'time and space'" implies that society will consider abnormal anyone who never absorbs these concepts. To achieve the fast-paced opening of **Metaphysics as a Guide to Morals,** she sacrifices the specificity that might result from defining as broad a term as *instinctive.* She forces her reader to question whether such expressions as *instinctive* and *common sense* have precise meanings, inside or outside philosophical discourse.[12]

Murdoch had good reason to organize the first two chapters of **Metaphysics as a Guide to Morals** in a way that calls attention to the diminished valuation of morality by modern and postmodern culture. Opening with value, as she sees it manifested in Plato's philosophy and in art, creates the opportunity to dramatize a crucial problem: Kant's and the early Wittgenstein's separation of fact and value. Their segregating "value in order to keep it pure and untainted" resulted in "a marginalisation of 'the ethical'" (*MGM* 25). Marginalizing value calls into question the cherished unities such as the self and the art object and concepts such as history and truth: as Nietzsche, Heidegger, and Derrida have suggested, the Greek horizon of our culture is, in Nietzsche's phrase, being "sponged away" (**MGM** 2).

In the struggle over the demise of value, Murdoch occupies a position of moderation.[13] She is not blind to the jumbled, rudderless condition of the contemporary world, one manifestation of which is the global reemergence of fundamentalism, and another the ubiquitous exploitation of powerless and poor people. Nor does she find Derrida's picture of humans drowning in language to be an empirical reality, let alone a beneficial insight. She describes as elitist his suggestion that only authors and philosophers have any control over the ocean of language in which all people are submerged. Her position on language is more complex. Agreeing with Saussure's descriptive theory of language because it includes the qualitative "*as if* it were a vast ocean of linkages and possibilities over which we cannot see very far" (**MGM** 274), Murdoch disagrees with any metaphysician's need to freeze a living organism like language.

Decades ago Murdoch jettisoned the ideas of Descartes and the concept of a personal deity. She insists that "God does not and cannot exist. But what led us to conceive of him does exist and is *constantly* experienced and pictured" (**MGM** 508). She will not, however, dismiss as valueless the intuitive unities people create for themselves. One might think she would see these as illusions. Cynics who are rendering innocuous the traditional icons, rituals, and ceremonies of the Greek, Judeo-Christian heritage ignore the evidence that human beings are moral and that this condition is inherent. Murdoch acknowledges the same moral failure in society as the cynic who "might say of our age that it is the end of the era of 'the virtuous individual,'" but she also recognizes "the remarkable continued return to an idea of goodness as unique and absolute" (**MGM** 427). For Murdoch, philosophers are certainly free to think extreme positions in the abstract—doing so is part of the philosophical give-and-take—but it is an abuse of power when philosophers impose such abstract positions on people who have to live with them at a concrete level. For philosophers like Nietzsche to prophesy, or decree, that God is dead is thus to act amorally. His prophecy creates an escapist fiction—"moral-less, value-less societies of the future"—making more difficult the ordinary lives of ordinary people (**MGM** 473).[14] Saint Paul's dictum, Be careful that your sin does not make some other person fall, seems appropriate here. Grounding her argument in a simple reality, Murdoch raises the issue of whether the ordinary parent teaches the ordinary child the Nietzschean notion that God is dead or that goodness is dead. She questions whether parents can find values in the husks of the old rituals to nurture their children's latent goodness. Moreover, she reminds the reader that most children ultimately learn to judge whether a smile is "mocking" or "tender" and learn moral concepts through vocabulary like "generous," "gentle," "reckless," "envious," "honest" (**MGM** 385). She emphasizes Wittgenstein's statement in *Culture and Value* that certain experiences of upbringing could lead a person to believe in God (**MGM** 415).[15] Wittgenstein also argues that the duty of teachers of young children is to train them in the "world picture" of the culture to give them a foundation for learning.

In *Metaphysics as a Guide to Morals,* as in Murdoch's earlier philosophical writings, Plato is central to the discussion of the pictorial nature of the philosophical process and of language. As she has always contended, morality depends on cognition and language, the imagery of vision: "Our world, source of our deep imagery and thought-modes, is a visual world. . . . We know when we are being satisfied with superficial, illusory, lying pictures which distort and conceal reality" (**MGM** 462). Here Murdoch distinguishes between deep "dominant metaphors in metaphysics," which humans easily recognize, and other pictures that easily fool them. Activities such as "'change of aspect' and 'seeing as' are ubiquitous [human] activities" (**MGM** 279), according to Murdoch and Wittgenstein. There is, however, a negative aspect to these image-making and image-apprehending potentialities of the mind, which exacerbate the already prevalent fantasizing and make humans victims of illusion. Plato theorizes many levels of illusion, particularly *eikasia,* "the lowest condition in the Cave" (**MGM** 317).[16] Murdoch finds that Platonism, the ground for Western cultural ideas, continues to be a vital guide; she continues to consider the metaphysics of vision (knowledge, attention) as less egoistic than the metaphysics of movement (will), as I will discuss later in regard to Kant and Wittgenstein. Because Christianity absorbed Platonism, both metaphysics are part of secularized Christian culture. For her, paradoxically, although humans have an instinctive idea of self-contained unity (**MGM** 1), no hidden unity determines the world (**MGM** 462). She writes in a letter: "There is no clear set up unity. (We set up our only unities.)" (Letter to the author, April 24, 1993).

A poet as well as a philosopher, Plato generated apt images long since buried in the collective unconscious or simply in the cultural ideology. His parable of the spiritual quest from appearance to reality employs the images of the cave and of the sun, the Form of Good which is the supreme unifying power. Murdoch employs not only in her philosophy but also in her novels the images surrounding the pilgrimage and Plato's Forms—"models, archetypes: universals, general concepts as distinct from particular entities, and, in their ethical role, moral ideals active in our lives, radiant icons, images of virtue" (**MGM** 10). The pilgrimage is inspired by "the disturbing magnetism of *truth,* involving *ipso facto* a purification of energy and desire in the light of a vision of what is *good*" (*MGM* 14). Such a position of "moral spiritual *desire*" obviates the issues of determinism and discontinuity (*MGM* 24). The advantages of the Platonist myth are its simplicity and its lack of dependence on the continuation of religious belief, but, she asserts, "religion can exist without this western concept of a personal God" (*MGM* 432). She considers Platonism a valid alternative to a religion dominated by suffering and masochism. Meeting the other through love and perceiving the other without fantasy create a change of consciousness.

By emphasizing otherness and inner speech, Plato's texts offer a rationale for sowing the seed of love. Although Murdoch expressly places Plato first in *Metaphysics as a Guide to Morals* in order to focus on conceptions of unity, especially art, she does foreground love and inner change by explaining the transformation of "base egoistic energy and vision (low Eros) into high spiritual energy and vision (high Eros)" (*MGM* 24). To demonstrate the part the other plays in the process, Murdoch quotes in *The Fire and the Sun* (1977) a dialogue from *Sophist*. Her use of this quotation argues that the other sets up not a binary system but a larger spectrum: "not-being does seem to be rather interwoven with being (240c), and the stranger explains that not-being is not the opposite of being, but that part of being which is different or other (257-58). When we deny that something is X, we are not denying that it *is* but asserting that it is other" (*FS* [*The Fire and the Sun*] 29). The discourse of love requires disciplining oneself to do "the work of attention" in discovering and seeing the other, and not just one other but many. The metaphor of vision can help explain how one goes about altering the consciousness by changing vocabulary and eventually composing a new self. "Goodness," Murdoch writes, "is connected with the attempt to see the unself, to see and to respond to the real world in the light of a virtuous consciousness" (*SG* [*The Sovereignty of Good*] 93). Plato says, according to Murdoch, "truth and knowledge live, and plausibility and falsehood too" in inner speech (*FS* 30). Incorporating Plato's concept of energy to explain moral change, a notion Freud takes from Plato, helps Murdoch to dramatize a "slow shift of attachments wherein *looking* (concentrating, attending, attentive discipline) is a source of divine (purified) energy" (*MGM* 25). Gathering all the value in the Idea of the Good, Plato sees it working in humans as love or Eros (*MGM* 50).

The philosophers with whom Murdoch identifies best are those who possess a religious sensibility, including the major characters important to her philosophical drama: Plato, Kant, and Wittgenstein, philosophers who combine conceptions from Plato and empiricism.[17] In a letter to me, she responded to a question about the perceived distance between Platonism and empiricism: "I

see no problem about Plato and 'empiricism.' . . . Plato's Ideas are not distant abstractions but concern the perception of what is real (as contrasted with our usual conditions of casual egoistic illusion)" (Letter to the author, January 12, 1983). Just as humans can perceive objects and sounds, they can perceive evidence of good in the world. For Plato, knowledge comes from sense experience as long as it is informed by the knowledge of the Idea or participates in the Idea. Believing knowledge comes from sense experience, Plato and Murdoch, like Kant and Wittgenstein, share a belief in transcendence (e.g., Wittgenstein writes of metaphysics as "seen against the background of the eternal" [*MGM* 422]). Wittgenstein makes these distinctions clear to metaphysicians in his first published work. "*Tractatus* Wittgenstein," as Murdoch calls the early Wittgenstein, "like Kant, has two 'subjects,' one which is locked on to the world of fact, and one which is totally independent of the world" (*MGM* 27).[18] Wittgenstein carries further the task of separating these two; Murdoch worries that this "division of language itself between fact and value not only isolates and diminishes value, it may damage the concept of truth" (*MGM* 455). She faults early Wittgenstein and Kant for their well-meaning but problematic separating of fact from value. By doing so they unwittingly participated in laying the groundwork for the contemporary condition of Western philosophy. Her criticism doubtless explains her preference throughout *Metaphysics as a Guide to Morals* for the "*Tractatus* Wittgenstein." She appears to funnel much of her reading of *Philosophical Investigations* through her Oxbridge-G. E. Moore-Elizabeth Anscombe view of Wittgenstein.

Murdoch would have certainly preferred a more Platonic path for Kant and Wittgenstein. Nevertheless, she expresses great respect for both men and is quite positive about her agreements with them. She does not appear to have changed her mind significantly over the years about either's contributions to philosophy. In *Metaphysics as a Guide to Morals* she devotes more energy and space to Wittgenstein's ideas than to Kant's, perhaps because Wittgenstein stops just short of where she treads. She does not keep silent, as Wittgenstein, in a letter to Friedrich Waismann, said he wanted to do: "to put an end to all the claptrap about *ethics*—whether intuitive knowledge exists, whether values exist, whether the good is definable" (quoted in *MGM* 29). *Metaphysics as a Guide to Morals* discusses Wittgenstein's refusal in the *Tractatus* to analyze "what is higher in order to keep it (its own kind of magic) safe, to emphasise its separateness, its inevitably *mystical* character, its silence, its absolute lack of connection with science, that is with the empirical world" (422). Such refusal Murdoch finds frustrating.

Ultimately Wittgenstein's investigation made him uncertain about using any language to talk about religious sensibility and ethical vision. He begins to analyze the tension between fact and value in "A Lecture on Ethics" (1929), a text not found in the index of *Metaphysics as a Guide to Morals.* For him, the act of discussing ethics is nonsensical: "our words will only express facts," considering that "the essence of the Good has nothing to do with facts and therefore cannot be explained by any proposition" ("Lecture" 7, 15). He humbly admits sharing a characteristic with humans in general: needing to challenge one's own factual, scientific language in order to attempt to communicate absolute judgments, trying "to go beyond the world and that is to say beyond the significant language":

> My whole tendency and I believe the tendency of all men who ever tried to write or talk Ethics or Religion was to run against the boundaries of language. This running against the walls of our cage is perfectly, absolutely hopeless. Ethics as far as it springs from the desire to say something about the ultimate meaning of life, the absolute good, the absolute value, can be no science. What it says does not add to our knowledge in any sense. But it is a document of a tendency in the human mind which I personally cannot help respecting deeply and I would not for my life ridicule it.
>
> ("Lecture" 11-12)

Later, in the *Tractatus,* he explains his view about the sense of life: "the sense of the world must lie outside the world. . . . [I]n it no value exists" (6.41).[19] In *Metaphysics as a Guide to Morals,* Murdoch compares Kant's "phenomenal world . . . devoid of value, self-contained and absolute" with the factual world of the *Tractatus* (222).

She further argues that Wittgenstein, unable to talk about transcendental reality, left it out of the *Tractatus.* Not being able to find a perspective from which to view ethics, he points to a value somewhere else, already there outside his world: "Ethics is transcendental" (6.421). Murdoch describes Wittgenstein's decision about examining ethics in this way: "We *enact* morality, it looks after itself"; Wittgenstein's solution is "to say nothing except what can be said, i.e. propositions of natural science—i.e. something that has nothing to do with philosophy" (*MGM* 30). Since he cannot change the way the world is, his relation to it must be that of an "attitude of mind" (*MGM* 54). Murdoch says he conveys in *Tractatus* "a strong impression of his own moral style"; she agrees with him that humans "rightly accept many things as mysteries" (*MGM* 282). She does not, however, agree that "'talk about' moral decisions, whether 'rational,' or 'philosophical,' or 'ordinary,' . . . [is] itself suspect and likely to be other than it seems" (*MGM* 315). She insists that, as a moral philosopher, she has no choice but to raise the issue of value and to talk about inner thought.

Murdoch cites two letters to demonstrate that Wittgenstein's often reiterated refusal to talk about morality and ethics and his cordoning off of whatever is tran-

scendental argue that, for him, the transcendental exists. Speaking of the *Tractatus* in a letter to Ludwig Ficker, Wittgenstein says, "The book's point is an ethical one. . . . I believe that where many others today are just gassing I have managed in my book to put everything firmly in place by being silent about it" (quoted in *MGM* 28-29). Wittgenstein's irony is also evident in a letter to Waismann: "Anything we might say is *a priori* bound to be mere nonsense. Nevertheless we run up against the limits of language. . . . This running up against the limits of language is *ethics*" (quoted in *MGM* 29). For Wittgenstein, what is beyond is ethics. Murdoch also points out that at least three of Wittgenstein's texts reveal his religious sensibility. *Culture and Value* discusses "religion and even God," arguing that "suffering 'deepens' our lives and drives us toward some sense of an absolute" (*MGM* 415-16). *Notebooks* 1914-1916 focuses on ethics, and the last section of the *Tractatus* proposes a "religious view" (*MGM* 415). Wittgenstein, like Kant, wanted to save a "safe space for (some form of) religious faith" (*MGM* 50). Murdoch also wants to save a space.

Because of Wittgenstein's ethical vision, Murdoch finds more in him to proclaim than to contest. Wittgenstein allows for the mysterious, and therefore allows for intuition, even if he will not talk about either. His celebration of mystery demonstrates his respect for the other, the alien. In accepting that humans have experiences of thought that are "initially beyond and hidden," Murdoch wants Wittgenstein to agree that "at the borderlines of thought and language we can often 'see' what we cannot say" (*MGM* 283). He, however, will only say this much: There are "cases where someone has the sense of what he wants to say much more clearly in his mind than he can express in words" (*CV* [*Culture and Value*] 79). He says even less about language's relationship to inner thought in *Philosophical Investigations.* Both philosophers nevertheless situate their thinking at the borders where reason and imagination, the obvious and the mysterious, meet. Even though Murdoch cannot have Wittgenstein as an ally in the argument about the way experience is recorded, she is empowered by his oeuvre: his method of questioning concepts and his logical arguments have influenced not only her rationale for ethical action but also her empirical worldview, her definition of language, and her attitude toward the thought process. In the same 1983 letter to me that I quoted above, she acknowledges the breadth of his effect on her thinking: "I have been affected (I hope) by his slow and meticulous methods of working. Also, I agree with many of the fundamental ideas and methods in *Philosophical Investigations,* and with the solutions therein of various problems about meaning and thought, old Cartesian problems and those posed by British empiricism" (Letter to the author, January 12, 1983).[20] Wittgenstein's willingness to question the very foundations of philosophy fascinates Murdoch and seems to have contributed to her ability to open her own imagination to the chaos of contingency. A surprising number of his conceptions—especially his "illusion-free perspective on reality,"[21] which reveals his debt to Plato's parable of the cave (259)—meet her need for a cultural ideal grounded in her Greek, Judeo-Christian heritage.

Murdoch has incorporated many of his concepts into her own philosophy and has freed herself from traditional restraints in the same way he had done. The difference between Murdoch's explicit moral philosophy and the early Wittgenstein's ineffable moral sensibility is a difference in style—the Austrian genius brooding over his perceptions and the British social critic attempting to stem a tide. In her 1971 collection of philosophical essays, *The Sovereignty of Good,* Murdoch takes an empirical stance similar to Wittgenstein's:

> I assume that human beings are naturally selfish and that human life has no external point or telos. . . . I can see no evidence to suggest that human life is not something self-contained. There are probably many patterns and purposes within life, but there is no general and as it were externally guaranteed pattern or purpose of the kind for which philosophers and theologians used to search. We are what we seem to be, transient mortal creatures subject to necessity and chance.
>
> (*SG* 78)

Here Murdoch agrees with Wittgenstein that life is self-contained and that no general pattern, such as Derridean language theory, determines the world.

But even with this view, Murdoch's reaction to life is an ethic of love, a philosophy of unselfing, ascesis. For her, an "active moral agent" focuses "a just and loving gaze . . . upon [an] individual reality" (*SG* 34). Using the discourse of love requires disciplining oneself to do "the work of attention";[22] if one thinks in loving words, one can move toward becoming moral, the imperative to love preparing the mind to create a groundwork of values that allow the will to rest. Murdoch's finding such a precedent for a moral response to this condition "of contingent states of affairs" is analogous to Wittgenstein's return to the same traditional background in *Philosophical Investigations* (published posthumously in 1953). Having accepted the empirical view of the universe but dissatisfied with the empiricist's picture of humans and their potential, both philosophers opt for the Greek, Judeo-Christian view of humans as creatures with religious sensibility. In their respective philosophies they do discover an answer to the dilemma of whether to be moral in an immoral world. Each proposes that if humans would search for "an illusion-free perspective on reality" and accept contingency, they could put their energy into attending to and being awed by the complexity and mystery of life.[23] Such sensibility can lay the groundwork for good. While jettisoning the

traditional linguistic concepts of the *Tractatus,* Wittgenstein retains his underlying moral sensibility in *Philosophical Investigations.* Ethics, he insists, must grow out of a humble realization that human beings cannot find the conceptual models to describe the whole of reality, or "the truth." That sensibility clearly forces Wittgenstein to see the world as a miracle, not a battleground for egoistic self-assertion.

Emphasizing her ethic of love, Murdoch, like Wittgenstein, refuses to accept the ethic of principle that has obsessed Kant and his successors. One problem Murdoch finds with the Kantian moral imperative—"survey all the facts, then use your reason" (*MGM* 26)—is that moral discrimination is almost always inherent in the defining, selecting, and evaluating of facts. Murdoch seems incredulous that anyone would think there are "sets of neutral facts": "In deciding what the initial data are we are working with *values.* Value goes right down to the bottom of the cognitive situation" (*MGM* 384). For Murdoch, "To be conscious is to be a value-bearer or value-donor" (*MGM* 256). Whereas Kant based his morality on reason, not imagination, Murdoch's morality requires imagination.

The greater problem with the Kantian view is that it conceives of a moral sensibility that depends on technique and centers on ego: "'How shall I act?' seems to most of us the paradigmatic ethical question," writes James C. Edwards, "and it seems only to admit answers formulated in terms of general and substantial first principles; 'Act only on that maxim which you can at the same time will to become universal law' or 'Act always so as to produce the greatest good for the greatest number'" (*Ethics Without Philosophy* 238). Based on this perception, the moral life demands knowledge of what the greatest good is. Since morality is then necessarily a riddle and a long, arduous struggle, one must search for right principles of action. Such principles are hidden and must be discovered, tested, and decided on; and, of course, such determinations depend heavily on pseudoscientific analysis. The will is in charge of this problem of technique, which deals with people in a conspicuously paternalistic fashion—as objects that need to be treated morally.

Insisting that her readers keep in mind Wittgenstein's unorthodox use of the concept *will,* Murdoch demonstrates that what the early Wittgenstein called the will was actually "not a particular thrust or emotive drive among others, but a total change of being in relation to everything" (*MGM* 53-54). Murdoch feels it necessary to make the following distinction: for Wittgenstein, "change of being, *metanoia,* is not brought about by straining and 'will-power,' but by a long deep process of unselfing" (*MGM* 54). It is a change of "attitude of mind." This metaphysical idea of will employed by Schopenhauer, early Nietzsche, and young Wittgenstein is "a liberating force capable of removing the illusions and miseries of mundane egoism" (*MGM* 54). Using Simone Weil's phrase, Murdoch contends that this unorthodox use of the concept *will* is better "set aside" as "a recipe for moral improvement." Even though Wittgenstein does not suggest how one follows the path to good, Murdoch calls him a "brave young man," one who reflects in *Notebooks 1914-1916* "a strong impression of his own moral style" (54): "The life of knowledge is the life that is happy in spite of the misery of the world [because it] can renounce the amenities of the world" (81).

In contrast to the Kantian view, Murdoch and Wittgenstein conceive of a moral sensibility that centers on miracle and mystery, activating love rather than egoism. Schopenhauer and Wittgenstein see Kant's concept of duty "as a narrow mandatory account of the moral life" (*MGM* 448); for Kant, "truthfulness is an unconditional duty" (*MGM* 383). Instead, Schopenhauer and Wittgenstein opt for moral sensibility as opposed to "'duty' . . . a mere arbitrary listing of divinely commanded particular tasks" (*MGM* 295). It is "inadequate," Murdoch writes, "to define morality solely in terms of duty, and without reference to quality of consciousness" (*MGM* 383). Moral attraction to Christ or to the Form of the Good is innate; Kant disapproves of such an intuitive attraction (*MGM* 24). For Murdoch, constant attention to changing one's consciousness is primary: the growth being "a slow shift of attachments wherein *looking* (concentrating, attending, attentive discipline) is a source of divine (purified) energy" (*MGM* 25). This kind of sensibility distrusts the Kantian principle, which can lead one to idolize duty and make duty the center of the moral life, the ostensible reason for Jesus' confronting the Pharisees.

Love, as Murdoch defines it—getting beyond the self—is an occasion for an immediate, instinctual response. Murdoch in her fiction rather than her philosophy, and Wittgenstein in his philosophical writings, show transactions they see in the world but refuse to interpret; a tempting analogy involves the early Jews who were too awed by their God to name him. Moral autonomy, rarely achieved and never permanent, seems to come, according to Murdoch, from successfully learning to discover good and to pay attention in all its permutations. Murdoch says in **"The Idea of Perfection"** that "the argument for looking outward at Christ and not inward at Reason is that self is such a dazzling object that if one looks there one may see nothing else. . . . Where virtue is concerned we often apprehend more than we clearly understand and *grow by looking*" (31). Although Wittgenstein does not employ the word *love,* he does insist on the same selfless "attention to the individual realities" that Murdoch demands.

Murdoch and Wittgenstein each find that the state of a person's mind determines his or her religious sensibility. For example, in **Sovereignty of Good,** in reference to reveries, Murdoch writes that religion "regards states of mind as the genetic background of action: pureness of heart, meekness of spirit. . . . Our states of consciousness differ in quality, our fantasies and reveries are not trivial and unimportant, they are profoundly connected with our energies and our ability to choose and act. And if quality of consciousness matters, then anything which alters consciousness in the direction of unselfishness, objectivity and realism is to be connected with virtue" (*SG* 83-84). Astonishment at the existence of the world dominates Wittgenstein's state of mind, as is evident in the *Tractatus*: "It is not *how* things are in the world that is mystical, but *that* it exists" (proposition 6.44); and in "A Lecture on Ethics" (1929): "Now in this situation I am, if I want to fix my mind on what I mean by absolute or ethical value. And there, in my case it always happens that the idea of one particular experience presents itself to me which therefore is, in a sense, my experience *par excellence.* . . . I believe the best way of describing it is to say that when I have it *I wonder at the existence of the world*" (8). The earlier *Notebooks 1914-1916* reveal his discovery that the sense of life is wondrous: "Ethics does not treat of the world. Ethics must be a condition of the world" (77). Murdoch empathizes with Wittgenstein's argument in the *Tractatus* for attending to "the world in a detached manner from the outside, as if it were a work of art" (*MGM* 31). Her understanding of his position in *Philosophical Investigations* is not as clear. She calls prophetic Wittgenstein's now famous proposition 6.44, while at the same time disagreeing with his view that there is no place for an idea of moral facts, or a moral vocabulary. What argues most eloquently for the moral sensibility of both Murdoch and Wittgenstein is the humility each manifests in the presence of life's awesome mystery. Murdoch and Wittgenstein both see that the blatantly obvious symptom of the diseased human understanding is bewitchment, extremism, or following "a total creed" (**"SBR"** [**"The Sublime and the Beautiful Revisited"**] 255).[24] Neither espouses the kind of "total creed" that Kant or Sartre did; Wittgenstein's thinking was open to many voices, as Murdoch's continues to be.

Kant has long served as the whetstone to her growth as a philosopher. For decades she has been grounding her arguments in his. In 1953, in the draft of an unpublished chapter of **Sartre, Romantic Rationalist,** Murdoch voiced a traditional position: Kant "set the scene upon which the dramas of philosophy are still enacted" by instituting two crucial notions: the transcendental solution—the world's structure "is determined for us by elements which are held in common between subject and object"—and the idea that "the mind is *free* to impose law upon itself in accordance with the absolute demands of reason" (125-26). In 1992 she said that Kant, whose thoughts about God began the modern age, is among "the greatest systematic 'demythologisers' of Christianity" (*MGM* 444) and that he opened space for agnosticism, encouraging the eventual movement toward seeing God as duty or as superscientist (*MGM* 440). She uses Kant in her argument to support her reliance on the traditional givens, such as "intuitive certainty" (*MGM* 439), crediting him with recognizing reason as a universal faculty that helps each person judge right and wrong: "What is absolute and unconditional is what each man clearly and distinctly knows in his own soul" (*MGM* 439). The categorical imperative is Kant's ontological proof. Moral good is an absolute that one can discover empirically: "As for God, must we just say that it is *as if* he were there, there is a *space* left for faith?" (*MGM* 439). As I discuss later, Murdoch endorses this "as if" strategy.

Murdoch's eclecticism makes room for Kant's contention that each person has knowledge of good and for her own reaction to the effect Kant's extremism has had on modernism, especially literary modernism. Kant has, in her opinion, influenced the state of mind or quality of consciousness manifested during the first half of the twentieth century. For many years, criticism of Murdoch's novels has been stuck on a distinction Murdoch made in a 1959 essay about the dichotomy between two branches of liberalism: scientific liberalism (e.g., linguistic empiricism) and existentialism. For her, neither branch pays enough attention to the complexity of human beings, their interaction, and their inner life. Her many disagreements with Kant, which she explains in this essay, **"The Sublime and the Beautiful Revisited,"** grow out of his "equation that virtue is freedom is reason. Virtue [for him] is not a knowledge of anything," Murdoch reasons; "it is rather an ability to impose rational order" (**"SBR"** 248). Kant's total creed includes the ultimately romantic view of the personality, which leads to both the "strength and the . . . weakness of the Liberal theory of personality." Murdoch uses the term *liberal* in the "traditional historical sense" as "the philosophy of John Stuart Mill is a Liberal philosophy" (**"SBR"** 248). Calling both existentialism and linguistic empiricism neo-Kantian, she argues that they have these motives and doctrines in common: they "are against traditional metaphysics, attack substantial theories of the mind, have a touch of puritanism, construe virtue in terms of will rather than knowledge, emphasize choice, [and] are markedly Liberal in their political bias" (**"SBR"** 253). Throughout her career, Murdoch has wished to "purge" the liberal theory of its romanticism: its emphasis on the moment of choice for the solitary moral agent (**"SBR"** 248).[25] For Murdoch, Kant's romanticism and his moral imperative come from the same condition: desiring to "turn away from the chaos of empirical inwardness to the clarity of overt actions" (**"SBR"** 254). For her, such a turning away is an escapist illusion. Her desire is to capture the "thingy-

ness," the particular and the eccentric in human personality, not to accede to the monistic will. She celebrates these qualities in Sartre's texts even while criticizing his romanticism.[26]

The alteration of consciousness and its moral quality have been central to Murdoch's philosophy and her novels. For her, a decline in literature is tied to a decline in morality. The issue she raises in *Metaphysics as a Guide to Morals* is a continuation of her intention in **"The Sublime and the Beautiful Revisited,"** in which she addresses "changes in the portrayal of characters in novels as symptoms of some more general change of consciousness" (**"SBR"** 247). Such a change involves paradigm shifts in Western discourses: physics, history, philosophy of science, and linguistics. Murdoch's philosophical outlook here tilts her argument toward the "anti-religious," "non-moral" thrust of the late structuralist metaphysics (*MGM* 200). The worldviews of linguistic empiricism ("the tradition of Moore and Wittgenstein") and existentialism ("the work of Sartre") correspond to bourgeois convention and neurotic rebellion, respectively. Rather than describing these poles as ends of a continuum, Murdoch finds them to be the two alternatives from which novelists choose in fleshing out these two prevalent worldviews. Her diagnosis is that ills inherent in the philosophies are also inherent in the modern decline of literature (**"SBR"** 253). Her examination of Sartre and his philosophy shows that she diverges from his concepts at the point where his characters become less rounded than characters have traditionally been in the texts of such authors as Tolstoy and George Eliot. Sartre, himself a complex and rounded human being, produces "Totalitarian Man," a romantic character who whines and then surrenders to neurosis or to "*Angst,* which is *Achtung* minus confidence in universal reason" (**"SBR"** 254). For her, the opposite extreme provides no better representation of real people: "Ordinary Language Man," in life or in novels, surrenders to convention, his choices being subject to the rules of society. These two opposing philosophies are enemies of understanding, and the devaluing of humanity that they promulgate suggests to Murdoch that exploration of human beings is no longer valuable. Because the philosophical and literary establishment has what Wittgenstein would have described as diseased human understanding, literature has found it difficult to create robust characters—real personalities with real consciousnesses.

Moreover, Murdoch accuses modern writers of being unwilling to record chaos and contingency and of desiring "significance completely contained in itself," not writing of "what is feared": "history, real beings, and real change" (**"SBR"** 260). The modern novel is either "a tight metaphysical object" that is self-contained or the other extreme, "a loose journalistic epic" (**"SBR"** 264). Yearning to escape such a binary trap, Murdoch wants to treat the two opposites as ends of a continuum between which she and other novelists can construct fiction based in contingency. Her emphasis in her moral philosophy and in her novels on human consciousness strongly suggests that she finds unhealthy the contemporary dearth of Lears and Hamlets. Life is made of muddle, and good art records the contingencies. What modern novelists fail to recognize, she says, is that "virtue is not essentially or immediately concerned with choosing between actions or rules or reason, nor with stripping the personality for a leap [but] with apprehending that other people exist" (**"SBR"** 269-70). This argument's very clarity—that human consciousness is a moral value to be recorded—has proved a trap for some critics.

Throughout her philosophical writings, Murdoch has seemed annoyed with philosophers who, because they cannot figure out how mental processes work, give up and assume that there is nothing to analyze or discuss publicly. She explores in ***Metaphysics as a Guide to Morals*** the broad differences among philosophers, who at one extreme assume the idea of the "contents of consciousness" as if consciousness were a container, while those at the opposite extreme, like phenomenalists Russell and Ayer, "have postulated 'sense data' which may or may not be said to be strictly introspectible" (***MGM*** 219-20), what Murdoch calls a behaviorist stance. Somewhere toward the middle of the spectrum, Hume and Berkeley assume "atomic mental contents, impressions, ideas" (***MGM*** 219). Kant would not accept that scientific knowledge came from Hume's association of ideas or that conceptions of time and space "presupposed these conceptions" (***MGM*** 221). Kant argued that the "understood, experienced world was a product of conjoined forms of organisation (*a priori* and empirical concepts)" (***MGM*** 221-22).

Murdoch is being traditional in grounding her argument in Kant's analysis of the rational mind as moral. Putting cognition at the center of his philosophy, Kant demonstrates the mind organizing experiences. In the draft of the unpublished chapter of ***Sartre, Romantic Rationalist,*** Murdoch alludes to Kant's texts to ask whether science represents mental events in legitimate or valid ways. According to Murdoch, Kant sees the mind not only "as constituting a real objective world for itself, but as seeking at the same time to comprehend this world as a complete rational intelligible system. (The mind is like a static grid through which reality pours; it is also like a dynamic movement toward a more complete and intelligible ordering of everything that is.)" (125). Decades after referring, in that unpublished chapter, to the mind as "a static grid" and in ***Under the Net*** to Wittgenstein's "fine square network," a symbol of theorizing without getting under the net to reality, Murdoch refers to language as a network: "Language is transcendental, a final network which we cannot creep

under" (***MGM*** 234). Murdoch keeps circling back in her philosophical essays to the need for philosophical research on "inner mental happenings" (**"NP"** [**"Nostalgia for the Particular"**] 243). She bewails the modern philosophers' (especially linguistic analysts') disregard of such a need, insisting that Ayer and Ryle cannot enlighten the definition of *thinking* by simply dividing and subdividing mental phenomena. What is more important to her than pseudoscientific analysis is the fact that an artist such as Rainer Maria Rilke can deal in words that reveal the "rich and pregnant" particulars (***MGM*** 258). Calling for concerted attention, Murdoch reiterates the need to go beyond logic and grapple with "the cloudy and shifting domain of the concepts which men live by" (***MGM*** 122).

Recalling that the concept of the individual has presupposed the idea of consciousness since Homer, Murdoch pursues her study of the mind's "'moment-to-moment flow and the procedure . . . of the inner monologue or inner life'" (***MGM*** 259). Questioning how much increased awareness has exacerbated the contemporary predicament, she contemplates the ways thought runs through the mind: thoughts flow by and are mostly lost to memory. To illustrate her explanation of William James's term *stream of consciousness,* she cites Molly Bloom, a character in Joyce's *Ulysses* (***MGM*** 258). Her motive here is to ask whether "every moment [is] morally significant," suggesting that all "our 'presents' are very various in quality" (***MGM*** 257). Teachers of writing know that students can record their own streams of consciousness while overhearing them flow, an example of an empirical commonsense proof for Plato's point that "truth and knowledge live, and plausibility and falsehood too," in inner speech (***FS*** 30). Every writer will no doubt fail, however, to keep up with the ubiquitous movement that Hegel calls the *ragbag.* Murdoch has been attempting to pin down this issue of "the moving substance of our mind" at least since she brought up the question in regard to Moore in her 1952 essay, **"Nostalgia for the Particular."**

Four decades later, when ontological uncertainty is a powerful threat to humankind, Murdoch continues to call for examination of "self-existence [that] continues unknown in the dark": "This concerns what it is to be human, the enigma at the centre" (***MGM*** 258). Perhaps for her, the human is a limited whole, the transcendental part being the center of darkness or the unconscious—the centered self being merely an outworn cultural illusion. Murdoch suggests that the study of the enigma of the self could end in doubt, in "relativism, cynicism, doubts about morals, doubts about *order*" (***MGM*** 258). She sees herself as a philosopher who is willing to look into the deep dark of the cave, the void,[27] and still control her human anxiety, an attitude similar to Rilke's when he describes Cézanne as looking objectively at reality with the focused "attention of a dog"

(*MGM* 246). Just as Rilke suggests that it is good to *say* art instead of judging it, Murdoch finds it desirable to *say* all of reality without judging it. In the regression of certainty and absolute reference points, the battles that she records in her philosophical writing—because they are about the human condition—continue to be played out in her novels.

Notes

1. Letter to the author. Murdoch continues: "My books are just about the jumble of the mysterious world as we know it."

2. Murdoch says art and philosophy uncover the same reality: "The artist makes us see what is, in a sense manifestly and edifyingly open to discussion, *there* (real), but unseen before, and the metaphysician does this too" (*MGM* 433).

3. Murdoch does not distinguish in the usual way among structuralism, deconstruction, modernism, and postmodernism. She chooses to use the "old original term [structuralism] as it is informative and less ephemeral" (*MGM* 5).

4. Murdoch says that Derrida employs "the old idea of total coherence . . . to inspire a way of life which excludes the value of individually establishable truths" (*MGM* 197).

5. Paul de Man said in 1986 that "the real debate of literary theory is not with its polemical opponents but rather with its own methodological assumptions and possibilities . . . ; resistance to the introduction of linguistic terminology in aesthetic and historical discourse about literature is only one particular version of a question that cannot be reduced to a specific historical situation and called modern, post-modern, post-classical or romantic" (*Resistance to Theory* 12).

6. Murdoch says she is "aware of the danger of inventing [her] own Plato" (*MGM* 510-11).

7. For Murdoch, art and language point to a reality, or value, beyond themselves. For example, impressionism, as well as cubism and abstract painting, she insists, have demonstrated that the artist is "not a demythologising 'ironist' . . . [but] authoritatively asserts the presence of the *transcendent object.*" She values "the familiar concepts of individual object, individual person, individual meaning, those old and cherished 'limited wholes'" (*MGM* 5).

8. Ved Mehta categorizes Murdoch in the late 1940s as a part of Oxford's squadron of feminine philosophers along with Anscombe and Foot: "they and Richard Hare make up the constabulary of moral philosophy at the university" (*Fly and the Fly-Bottle* 53). The three women were "united," however, "in their objection to Hare's view that the human being was the monarch of the universe, that he constructed his values from scratch" (*Fly and the Fly-Bottle* 56). Murdoch began to lecture at Oxford as a Fellow of St. Anne's College, and she served until 1963 as university tutor in philosophy (Tominaga and Schneidermeyer, *Murdoch and Sparks* xi).

9. Also marked "Chapter IX," this portion (125-36) survives in the *Sartre* manuscript housed at the University of Iowa Libraries.

10. Jacques Lacan writes that there is no sense of a separate self until a third party breaks up the symbiotic relationship of the child to its mother. He thinks the Other is the locus of the constitution of the subject. The deconstructive act uncovers in a text the *aporia,* or gaps, that reveal the author's blind spots. Paul de Man writes that deconstruction is unearthing "hidden articulations and fragmentations within assumedly monadic totalities" (quoted in Lentricchia and McLaughlin, *Critical Terms* 215).

11. Preferring "the language of encounter or dialogue, not contemplation," Buber charges Plato with "opticis[ing] thought" (quoted in *MGM* 463).

12. For proof that good exists, Murdoch recommends the use of common sense and intuition rather than the arguments of philosophers, which are most often circular arguments for what is already known. She suggests that individuals look empirically at their own conscious activity: "the idea of perfection haunts all our activity, and we are well aware of how we try to blot it out." Showing great respect for the nonphilosophical person, Murdoch believes that "the ordinary fellow 'just knows,' for one is speaking of something which is in a sense obvious, the unique nature of morality" (*MGM* 428).

13. Murdoch even attributes moderation to Wittgenstein, who says that philosophy "leaves everything as it is" (quoted in *MGM* 2).

14. Murdoch's use of the word *ordinary* does not imply a hierarchy of value on which philosophers or thinkers inhabit higher rungs than other people. Human beings are ordinary when they are not occupying a particular role. For example, Murdoch says that a male represents ordinary humans and that ordinary human beings continually compare and contrast "language with the *extra-linguistic* world" (*MGM* 195).

15. Murdoch's method in *Metaphysics as a Guide to Morals* is similar to Wittgenstein's in *Philosophical Investigations*: "traveling over a field of

thought criss-cross in every direction" (*PI* [*Philosophical Investigations*] ix). For instance, Murdoch returns to a subject, and sometimes to a specific example, at various places in her text. In chapter 3 she cites Wittgenstein's *Culture and Value* to make a point about transcendence (*MGM* 75); ten chapters later, she cites the same page of the same text (*MGM* 415) to make a similar point.

16. Murdoch foregrounds the similar optical view of theologian Martin Buber that "the Greeks established the hegemony of sight over the other senses"; the optical world became the world (*MGM* 461), and the optical character became part of philosophy. Her only complaint about Buber's stance is his blindness to Plato's irony, an aporia that she also finds in Cornford. She quotes Buber, for example, as saying that "the character of the contemplation of particular objects . . . [is that] the object of this visual thought is the universal as existence or as a reality higher than existence.

17. Edwards says that Wittgenstein discusses the conception of *showing* twenty-three times in the *Tractatus* (*Ethics Without Philosophy* 14-15).

18. When Wittgenstein wrote the *Tractatus*, he was blinded by the assumption of Western philosophy that human beings can have views or pictures of reality. He also presaged his later theory by contending that "ethical matters lie outside the realm of thought . . . and must be *shown* rather than *said*" (Edwards, *Ethics Without Philosophy* 73).

19. "The world is nothing," according to Edwards's paraphrase of Wittgenstein, "but a collection of contingent states of affairs, altering concatenations of eternally existent simple objects; these contingent configurations are utterly independent of one another; belief in the causal nexus is superstition. In this atomistic world there is no sense of life to be found; there is only what happens. Neither is the sense of life to be found in thought, for thought is always thought about the world" (*Ethics Without Philosophy* 204).

20. As Murdoch commented to Mehta, "Most English philosophers . . . share certain assumptions of Wittgenstein and Austin" (*Fly and the Fly-Bottle* 57).

21. Edwards describes Wittgenstein's perspective in this way.

22. Murdoch borrows the word *attention* from Simone Weil (*SG* 34).

23. Edwards focuses exclusively on Wittgenstein rather than placing him in the same context in which Murdoch's *Metaphysics as a Guide to Morals* discusses him. Furthermore, Edwards goes further than Murdoch: he infers from the entire body of Wittgenstein's work, and from Wittgenstein's vision of the sound human understanding revealed in *Philosophical Investigations*, the centrality of Wittgenstein's ethical vision and religious sensibility to his oeuvre.

24. Wittgenstein argues that traditional Western scientific philosophy leads to a diseased, narcissistic human understanding when it is dominated by logic alone (Edwards, *Ethics Without Philosophy* 224-29). In *Remarks on the Foundations of Mathematics*, Wittgenstein says, "The philosopher is the man who must cure himself of many sicknesses of the understanding before he can arrive at the notion of a sound human understanding" (157).

25. Murdoch's clear examination of nineteenth- and twentieth-century philosophy in the draft of her unpublished chapter of *Sartre* (n. 9, above) helps explain her movement away from both existentialism and scientific realism.

26. Criticism of Murdoch's novels often refers to her examination of "totalitarian man" and "ordinary language man."

27. The dark condition Murdoch calls the void can be the result of suffering, guilt, desperation, bereavement, emptiness, loss of personality, or loss of energy (*MGM* 500).

Abbreviations

IRIS MURDOCH'S PHILOSOPHY:

FS: *The Fire and the Sun*

MGM: *Metaphysics as a Guide to Morals*

"NP": "Nostalgia for the Particular"

"SBR": "The Sublime and the Beautiful Revisited"

SG: *The Sovereignty of Good*

LUDWIG WITTGENSTEIN'S TEXTS:

PI: *Philosophical Investigations*

CV: *Culture and Value*

Hilda D. Spear (essay date 1995)

SOURCE: Spear, Hilda D. "*The Green Knight*." In *Iris Murdoch*, pp. 107-20. London: Macmillan, 1995.

[*In the following essay, Spear offers a critique of Murdoch's fantasy* The Green Knight, *claiming that the novel "melds together aspects of Christian myth with those of Arthurian legend."*]

Between the publication of *The Message to the Planet* and *The Green Knight* (1993) Murdoch published the most extensive of all her philosophical works, *Metaphysics as a Guide to Morals* (1992). For the reader of her novels it is not compulsory reading but it is a fascinating expansion of, and reflection on, many of the themes she has dealt with in fiction, particularly in the later books. We can see, too, how the novels themselves reflect her philosophical ideas:

> We fear plurality, diffusion, senseless accident, chaos, we want to transform what we cannot dominate or understand into something reassuring and familiar, into ordinary being, into history, art, religion, science
>
> (***MGM*** [*Metaphysics as a Guide to Morals*] pp. 1f.)

or, we might add, into novels which are able to reinstate the old mythologies whilst simultaneously exploring the contemporary problems of morality which we have been faced with ever since Nietzsche declared the death of God.

The struggle in the novels to set out some sort of 'guide to Goodness', which has become more acute as time has progressed, is here argued more singlemindedly; the adversaries in Murdoch's search for truth are not here, as in the novels, wayward characters tossed about by the contingency of being, in a world where order is constantly at odds with chance, but fellow-philosophers who have pursued or are pursuing their own solutions to the problem of morality. What is especially valuable to the reader of her novels is that certain philosophical concepts, as Murdoch understands them and as she employs them in her fiction, are discussed minutely and are considered from various points of view. Of particular interest to the reader of her novels is the dialectic concerning the connections between language and truth which runs throughout the book. At the end of such discussions we are left in no doubt as to Murdoch's own philosophic stance, though she is never dogmatic. She reaffirms her admiration for Platonic philosophy; she questions the validity of the structuralist argument; she offers a detailed investigation of Derrida's ideas and—even if ever so kindly—finally dismisses them with a cogent examination of value:

> The fundamental value which is lost, obscured, made not to be, by structuralist theory, is truth, language as truthful, where 'truthful' means faithful to, engaging intelligently and responsibly with, a reality which is beyond us. . . . 'Truth' is learnt, found, in specialised areas of art where the writer (for instance) struggles to make his deep intuitions of the world into artful truthful judgment. This is the truth, terrible, delightful, funny, whose strong lively presence we recognise in great writers and whose absence we feel in the weak, empty, self-regarding fantasy of bad writers.
>
> (***MGM,*** pp. 214f.)

Metaphysics as a Guide to Morals is by far the longest of her philosophical books, which, unlike her novels, have been, until this point, short and concerned with certain limited aspects of philosophical thought. Like her first published book, ***Sartre: Romantic Rationalist,*** however, it is intricately bound up with the discussion of the way that language works and can be usefully seen as an aid to the understanding of what she as novelist expects to achieve in her novels: it examines the question of Good without God which has been a matter of concern in so many of the novels as well as in the earlier philosophical work; it considers the place of religion in the modern world; it looks at the concepts of good and evil, of truth, of duty, to pick out just a few of the themes relevant to the novels; and it devotes a chapter to the ontological proof of God's existence, which we observed in Chapter 6 above has become increasingly a topic in the more recent novels. It almost inevitably seems to lead us to the novel which follows it, ***The Green Knight.***

This latest novel melds together aspects of the Christian myth with those of Arthurian legend. It is a heavily symbolic novel which tantalises and exercises the mind with snatches of quotations, will-o'-the-wisp recalls, and well-known references, the relevance of which is often simultaneously obvious and more subtly obscure, offering the reader an immediate link with observed reality, yet leaving the imagination space in which to expand.

The novel begins in Kensington Gardens on a chilly, wet October day, when two middle-aged women, old friends since their schooldays, are walking, exercising Bellamy's dog, Anax, himself one of the principal characters in the book. Through the conversation of Louise Anderson and Joan Blacket we are introduced to most of the other characters as well as to what at first appears to be the focal centre of the plot—the death of an assumed mugger at the hands of Lucas Graffe, a scholarly academic historian, friend of both the Anderson and Blacket families and, as Joan says, an 'eccentric'. The first words of the novel, however, should alert us to the current of 'fairy' or magic which is to underlie the plot: "'Once upon a time there were . . .'". They are the words that begin a thousand fairy stories and, with intentions at least partially similar to Murdoch's, Joyce's *A Portrait of the Artist as a Young Man* begins with the same words, as Stephen Daedalus's father tells him a bedtime story.

Joan and Louise are immediately placed at opposite poles in the black and white of fairy story, Joan the 'bad girl', Louise the 'good girl', Joan's life one of 'lawlessness' and 'disorder', Louise 'docile' and bringing into their joint lives the 'soothing possibility of order' (***GK*** [***The Green Knight***], p. 1). Joan and Louise are by no means at the moral centre of the story but to some extent the two women are reflected in the Graffe brothers who are, for despite the reputation of reserve he has fostered in the minds of his acquaintances, Lucas resembles no one so much as Julius King in *A Fairly Honourable Defeat,* whilst his younger brother Clement is the anxious worrier about moral rectitude whose desire for truthfulness is constantly put at risk by Lucas.

The fairy-tale element of the novel is reinforced through Louise's three daughters, but especially through Moy, the youngest of the 'three little girls' in Joan Blacket's fairy story. For Moy, everything around her is imbued with life, can think and can feel, and she experiences somewhat whimsical mystic happenings when the stones which she has collected with such loving care move about in her room; apparently even Anax observes this phenomenon. A rather heavier symbolism rests on Moy, however, when her anthropomorphism leads to her encounter with the swan in the Thames, an incident recalling the classical story of Leda and Zeus and suggesting her as the chosen of the gods; later, at the end of the novel, the 'silkies' call her back to join them in the sea but the sea-myth is thwarted by Anax, who helps his master, the spiritually-inclined Bellamy to save her.

The Green Knight has many of the attributes of a thriller, though it is certainly not a 'whodunnit' for we know from the outset who commits the murder. What we do not know is the identity of the victim or even for sure whether he was indeed murdered, for, like the legendary Green Knight, he appears to rise phoenix-like from his own ashes. When Louise first observes Peter Mir, despite the darkness, she notices his green umbrella. We soon become aware that green is Peter's colour; he wears a 'dark green tweed jacket' (*GK,* p. 103), a 'chic green tie' (*GK,* p. 122), a 'sort of green' suit (*GK,* p. 194) and he claims to be a member of the Green Party (*GK,* p. 194). It is Aleph who first suggests that he is the Green Knight. Certainly, like the Green Knight, he was struck down by a blow to the head and he undergoes resurrection (thought not immediate resurrection) to challenge Lucas on moral grounds. There are many similarities with the story of *Sir Gawain and the Green Knight* but there are also many differences, and after Peter's second death Clement ponders on the original mediaeval story and concludes that 'it's all mixed up' (*GK,* p. 432); but by this time Clement has seen clearly 'what is fundamental . . . Peter saved my life and gave his life for me' (*GK,* p. 430); the evangelical Christian ring to these words makes us realise that if Peter Mir is the Green Knight from pagan romance, he is also a Christ-figure.

Like Christ, he is a Jew and his physical characteristics are Jewish; like Christ, he is unmarried; more significantly, however, it is constantly emphasised that he died to save Clement: even Lucas acknowledges that 'one man can die for another' (*GK,* p. 91). He suffers physical pain before his death; he is resurrected and he seems to offer the possibility of redemption. It would not be merely simplistic but wrong to suggest that Peter, when he regains his memory after reliving his death experience, changes from the pagan Green Knight to the Christian hero, for the Green Knight himself was chivalrously moral, offering a challenge and a test to the knights of King Arthur's court; furthermore, Peter claims to have recovered his understanding of the Buddhist, not of the Christian, faith for, like James in *The Sea, The Sea,* he had become a Buddhist, though the blow on his head had made him forget this. We may perhaps see, however, this second experience as akin to the Pentecostal fire, which brings about a change from the Old Testament Dispensation of justice—an eye for an eye—to the New Testament Dispensation of mercy and love. The two myths continue to run parallel to each other; Peter offers the Green Knight's token punishment to Lucas but his [Peter's] second death is that of Christ; as a representative of Christ, Peter has died, first to save Clement and secondly to break all spells and set everyone free (see *GK,* p. 448). At his 'Last Supper'—the party at his house—which follows his resurrection into the fulness of life and precedes his second death, twelve invited guests arrive and he talks to each of them in turn; when Tessa arrives, she is both the thirteenth—the bringer of ill-luck—and the betraying Judas. Once more it is all mixed up! What is not mixed up, however, is the fact that the novel is again struggling with the problems of morality, of Good and Evil, of the place of God and religion in a godless world.

The moral theme is explored in various ways. Bellamy James is the main seeker after God, his whole life 'a religious quest' (*GK,* p. 23), which his conversion to Roman Catholicism has not resolved. Like Cato in *Henry and Cato* he considers entering the priesthood but does not do so; rather, like Catherine Fawley in *The Bell* he decides to give up the world and enter a monastery in an enclosed order, to cut himself off from social life and dedicate himself to Truth. Much of the serious religious discussion in the novel is to be found in the exchange of letters between Bellamy and his mentor, Father Damien, whose philosophy seems in many ways to accord with that of Murdoch herself.

Even without Father Damien to tell us, however, we are aware that Bellamy has romanticised the religious life, that the monastery is to be for him an escape from reality and that, moreover, he is playing a Christian role to disguise from himself the very fact that he has not convinced himself of Christ's existence, first in the flesh and then in the spirit: 'if we have a mystical Christ can that be the real Christ? Is a mystical Christ "good enough"? Could there be Christ if *that* man never existed at all?' (*GK,* p. 41). Here he is rehearsing one of Murdoch's own worries:

Perhaps (I believe) Christianity can continue without a personal God or a risen Christ, without beliefs in supernatural places and happenings, such as heaven and life after death, but retaining the mystical figure of Christ occupying a place analogous to that of Buddha: a Christ who can console and save, but who is to be found as a living force within each human soul and not in some supernatural elsewhere.

(*MGM,* p. 419)

This is the very position that Bellamy adopts after Father Damien tells him that he has lost his faith and just before what he, Bellamy, is to interpret as the vision on the road to Damascus when he sees Peter burning in the Pentecostal fire. It is not an orthodox Christian belief but is based on the dictum of the thirteenth-century Christian mystic, Meister Eckhart, which Father Damien refers to in several of his letters to Bellamy: 'do not seek for God outside your own soul' (*GK,* p. 266). Bellamy returns to this concept later in his conversation about religion with Peter Mir and it is one that is discussed minutely again and again in *Metaphysics as a Guide to Morals*; it is able to fit in with the modern rejection of God but at the same time to retain a faith in a 'Good-based' morality; it is this contemporaneity of thought which makes Murdoch revere Eckhart as 'a thinker for today' (*MGM,* p. 354).

Though Bellamy has lost his vision of a personal God he has not lost his desire to have an 'avatar' or a 'mediator' whom he can venerate; he is a man for whom religion is a necessity and he believes that he has received a sign; Peter is to be his path to goodness, yet, when Peter is taken away to Dr Fonsett's clinic, it is Emil who solves the realistic problems of Bellamy's life: 'You will stay with me . . . You must get your dog back' (*GK,* pp. 372f). We have been strangely affected by the plight of Anax for, despite the love bestowed on him by Moy, his loyalty to the master who has deserted him is absolute; early in the novel, through Moy's anthropomorphic interpretation of Anax's mind, the dog too enters the realm of religious thought in almost the very words spoken by Mary Magdalene when she found Jesus's empty sepulchre (see *GK,* p. 21 and St John, 20, 2 and 13). His reconciliation with his master when he is reclaimed helps Bellamy to find his purpose in life:

'I've got so much to do, I'll find that job [Father Damien] spoke of, and yes he was right about happiness, don't be miserable thinking you can't be perfect. . . .'

(*GK,* p. 471)

Quite a different sort of goodness is apparent in Moy. A vegetarian by conviction because of her concern for all living things, she is the youngest of the three Anderson girls and she celebrates her sixteenth birthday during the course of the novel. She is seen as a strange child,

even by her friends and relations, for she appears to live in a slightly different world from them, a world in which everything, animate and inanimate, is endowed with its own life. Under such circumstances ordinary life becomes almost untenable and she is in a constant agony of apprehension about the feelings of such natural objects as rocks and stones. Her 'goodness', however, is Milton's 'fugitive and cloistered virtue', a kind of naïve innocence which has not had to cope with temptation:

Aleph said, 'Innocence can't go on and on.'

[Moy] 'Yes it can, if you just *don't do things.*'

Sefton said, 'Being human, we are already sinners, we aren't innocent, no one is because of the Fall, because of Original Sin.'

'The Fall is ahead,' said Moy, 'and I am afraid of it. How can evil and badness begin in a life, how can it *happen*?'

(*GK,* p. 18)

By the end of the novel the Fall is still ahead for Moy but we know it is approaching; she has lost her mystic powers which had earlier made the stones in her room move, her fey powers have faded and she is suffering the agonies of unrequited love. Yet Moy, we believe, unlike Charles in *The Sea, The Sea,* comes out on the other side of innocence into goodness.

By far the most significant discussion of Good and Evil in the novel, however, centres on Peter Mir's death and resurrection. How does he become involved in the original act of aggression, the intention of Lucas to kill his brother Clement? The first version of the story, that put about by Lucas and Clement, and that which everyone believes at the time, is told to us by the narrator; the true version emerges later. Murdoch sets the details of the scene with care: it is past midnight on a summer evening; Lucas gets Clement completely drunk before taking him in the car to a remote place amongst trees and construction rubble with the pretence of showing him something but with the intention of striking him on the head with a baseball bat and killing him. As the murder weapon begins to descend Clement senses it and tries to spring away, observing as he does so 'the figure beside Lucas of another man' (*GK,* p. 85). The theatricality of the scene is only equalled by its religious implications: the mysterious third figure manifests himself at the crucial moment and saves Clement's life at the apparent expense of his own; when Lucas returns from his self-imposed exile he explains, 'one man can die for another' and Clement asks, 'So he died for me?' (*GK,* p. 91); a little later, as they continue to talk, Lucas comments 'An angel might have stayed my hand' (*GK,* p. 92). Immediately after this conversation we are introduced to the figure of Peter Mir—revived, resurrected, or perhaps an avenging angel from the beginning: 'An angel', Peter explains to Bellamy, 'is a messenger of the divine, a messenger is an instrument, sometimes an unconscious one' (*GK,* p. 299); though he was at the time applying the words to Lucas, we are able to conceive of Peter himself as some sort of mystic messenger, an instrument of justice.

In *A Fairly Honourable Defeat* the demonic figure of Julius King is responsible for Rupert Foster's death but is able to shrug it off, appearing to feel no guilt and no responsibility for his actions. Before the return of Peter Mir it looks as though this will be exactly the stance of Lucas Graffe; he has invented a story to tell to the world, he has involved Clement in his machinations and he appears to feel no remorse. When Peter appears, however, he demands justice, thought it is soon apparent that it is not legal but moral justice that he is seeking. He rehearses what justice must demand, 'the idea of retribution is everywhere fundamental to justice', so that Lucas's 'just punishment would seem to be . . . a blow upon the head delivered with equal force' (*GK,* p. 126), in other words the Old Testament justice of 'an eye for an eye'; more germane to Peter's sense of justice, however, is his desire that Lucas should acknowledge his sin and confess the truth to his friends, the implication behind this demand being that truth is greater than mere justice. Lucas's sin is not only against Peter but also against Clement; furthermore, he has trapped Clement into compounding the sin, for Clement, who is normally decent and truthful, essentially good, has become embroiled in his brother's evil.

On several occasions Bellamy describes Lucas as 'anti-Christ' but he nevertheless loves him. We have seen in earlier novels, particularly in *The Time of the Angels,* how the evil can attract and inspire love and Lucas is certainly loved by a number of the characters in this story. We feel, nevertheless, that the love accorded to Lucas is not sufficient to bring about his salvation; thus the resolution of the plot seems difficult to understand, for Peter, resurrected a second time, recognises that his feelings of hatred and vengeance are more harmful to himself than to Lucas, metes out symbolic justice and makes peace. Lucas, on the other hand, appears to take the reconciliation cynically; even the symbolic retribution of the small slit between his ribs is inflicted not to bring Lucas to a sense of moral right but in order to complete Peter's healing. We might observe that the two stories—that of Gawain and that of Christian redemption are again brought together here; the symbolic retributive wound is a significant aspect of justice in the Gawain legend whilst the wound given to Lucas is, like that of Christ in the Crucifixion, in the side, a connection made for us by Lucas himself when he equates Clement with doubting Thomas. When Clement asks whether the event was about forgiveness, Lucas concurs with the suggestion and ends up with the outrageously smug act of forgiving Clement for 'all the suffering you

caused me when we were children' (*GK,* p. 322). It would appear that he, like Julius King, has learned nothing and his piece of the story ends with him taking Aleph from her family and, again like Julius, leaving the country.

The last short section of the novel is entitled "They Reach the Sea". For Murdoch the sea is both attractive and awe-inspiring; here it signifies the end of all the journeys, all the quests and we can perhaps see the regenerate characters as 'finding god in their own souls'. Sefton and Harvey are ecstatically happy together in Florence. By the sea, the last acts of the play are played out: Moy emerges from her dark night of the soul and from a near-death experience into a revitalised anticipation of the future; Bellamy, in saving Moy, finds his life transformed; only over the lives of Louise and Clement a question-mark hangs. Through musing about Peter, Louise expresses the sorrows of Christianity:

> 'how can we ever be happy now? Peter didn't die *for* anything, he died accidentally, senselessly - he appeared out of a mystery which I have never understood, and now he has vanished leaving all *this* behind. . . .'
>
> (*GK,* p. 454)

Clement, on the other hand, strives to see the point of it all and finally expresses the joys of Christianity: 'And so . . . we betray him, we explain him away, we do not want to think about him or puzzle about him or try to make out what he was in himself . . .' But then follows the triumphant acceptance of belief, 'Peter saved my life, he gave his own life for mine' (*GK,* p. 456). It is a concept that he repeats frequently to himself; he does not see Peter as an instant saviour of them all but he finds him as a god in his own soul.

The Green Knight is highly theatrical, though the technical ingenuities which peppered the earlier novels are largely absent, the most obvious being simply the butcher's knife hidden in Peter Mir's presentation umbrella. Like the narrator of *The Sea, The Sea,* Clement is an actor, though a very much less successful one, and one who has allowed his private life to take precedence over his public role. Actors have frequently trod the boards, and plays and theatre played significant parts, in Murdoch's novels. The reunion between Clement and Louise which takes place in the 'bijou' theatre south of the river should remind us that their first meeting had taken place in an empty theatre when Teddy Anderson had brought her along to meet Clement; it may also recall for us the reunion (albeit temporary in their case) between Jake and Anna in the little Mime Theatre in Hammersmith Mall in *Under the Net.*

As we have observed, however, what has been most striking throughout the novels, has been the way in which Murdoch uses 'spectacle' to enhance her plots.

This partly explains her tacit refusal to abandon the premodernist tradition of descriptive detail; we are required to see characters, places, actions as she has envisaged them. We are also frequently put in the remarkable position of viewing incidents as well as experiencing them. In *The Green Knight* there are numerous dramatic incidents, from Harvey's accident on the bridge early in the novel to Bellamy's rescue of Moy from the sea almost at the end. Harvey's two exploits on the Italian bridge are presented to the reader in quite different ways; in the first account we walk the bridge with Harvey himself, part of the action, feeling both his fear and his elation; we see the second walk at the end of the novel through Sefton's eyes and, as spectators, experience vicariously her dread, observing her and observing Harvey only through her fear.

The event which is treated most theatrically, however, is the reenactment of the murder scene. From the first Peter has seen it as 'a sort of rite of purification—a sort of mystery play' (*GK,* p. 250) and, following this, Clement has decided to make it into some sort of histrionic performance. He is convinced of the necessity of this after, returning to the original scene, he sees in his mind's eye, in slow motion and in all its horror, what happened in the original incident and envisages what might have happened. The scene he views is his own near-death and what he clearly at that moment believes was the actual death of Peter Mir. He fears that the reenactment of the scene might bring about a repetition of the violence and perhaps another death for Peter; he thus decides that he must be the director of the play that is to be acted out in order to prevent a recurrence of the original incident. Yet the action is taken out of his hands as we view Peter, bathed in burning light before he falls to the ground like Saul on the road to Damascus; unlike Saul, he is not struck blind but, as in the biblical story, those around him are speechless, unsure of what has happened and they have to take him home. Like Saul, however, Peter has undergone a conversion, the avenging spirit of the Old Testament has left him; he remembers God, as he explains to Bellamy, though it is his Buddhist beliefs he recalls and the Buddha in the soul.

The problem with this novel is that the reader's retrospections and expectations are constantly changing and the theatricality of many of the events does not dispel our unease: if Peter had, indeed recovered from Lucas's blow, is it possible that Lucas would not have been informed? Moreover, we are told quite unequivocally that 'the "assailant" had died without regaining consciousness' (*GK,* p. 88); in this case Lucas would surely have been tried for manslaughter, if not for murder. We are then left with the belief that Peter Mir is a mystical figure, the 'third' who walked beside the two brothers and saved Clement's life and who then became an avenging angel. The difficulty with this interpretation is the conversion of the avenging angel into an angel of mercy, his seizing by Dr Fonsett and his later reported death. Why do Bellamy and the others not go to the Nursing Home to see Dr Fonsett and ask to attend the funeral? To argue in such a way suggests, I believe, a failure of imagination. The answers to such questions lie in the supernatural and fairy-tale element of the story. Life and death are mysteries; we cannot account for them; the various myths, legends and fairy tales embedded in *The Green Knight* are, as Clement reflects, 'somehow jumbled up and all the wrong way round' (*GK,* p. 431). The not-completely-Green Knight, the inchoate Christ-figure, the fey Moy with her Rapunzel pigtail, the evil magician Lucas, the failed Holy Man Bellamy are pieces of separate jigsaw puzzles which have all been thrown together; they may never come together as a rational whole but they recreate pictures in our minds, fed by our varying stores of knowledge and imagination.

The Green Knight with its mysticism, its interest in religion, its philosophical viewpoints is a far cry from the first novel *Under The Net.* Both novels, however, appear at first to illustrate Murdoch's belief in contingency. We have seen in Chapter 2 above how Jake's trust in 'a sufficient reason' for everything (*UTN* [*Under the Net*], p. 24) was undermined by events. Here, in the most recent novel, we are aware once more of the way in which chance seems to rule our lives. The encounter which was intended to lead to the death of Clement was interrupted by the chance appearance of Peter, as he explains:

> 'How was it that you and I met on that dark summer night? You of course were there with intent, I as the most accidental of strollers. A minute either way and we would never have met.'
>
> (*GK,* p. 314)

Thus Lucas's carefully laid plans are frustrated. In the second encounter Clement plans everything in detail once again, and once again the plans are frustrated. Yet, in this later novel there is a strong suggestion that the events as they happened were not left to chance, that it was a mystical but predestined intervention that saved Clement's life, that it was a single incident in a titanic contest between two magicians, the Good and the Evil, between, perhaps, God and Satan. If so, Evil is certainly not vanquished for Lucas lives to accept jauntily his token punishment and to move on to his next evil deed, the abduction of Aleph and the destruction of trust between members of the Anderson family. Like Julius King, like Milton's Satan, like those tied to the Buddhist Wheel, he moves on to another sphere of activity.

The interest in theatre is, as we have seen in all the novels, a continuing one, but in the course of time it seems to me that it has become less spontaneous and more of a structural device. Actors and actresses, theatres and plays dominate the novels almost as often as do writers and books, confirming Murdoch's strong interest in the theatre, particularly in the works of Shakespeare. The looking-in on little theatrical scenes which is so much a part of the actual writing of the earlier novels (see particularly the discussion of *The Bell,* pp. 29f above) has gradually given way to more deliberate dramatic structuring. There are several occasions in *The Green Knight* when most of the characters are brought together in one place, a device of increasing interest to Murdoch because of its dramatic potential. The first of these, a gathering of the Andersons and Blackets and their friends, is staged in order to introduce them to Peter Mir; it is at this introductory meeting that Peter Mir invents his role of psychoanalyst, a role in which both the reader and the other characters in the drama believe until the final grand dinner party in Peter's house. The next such gathering is the masked party to celebrate Moy's sixteenth birthday; because it is a masked party, all the participants assign themselves roles. Peter assumes that of a bull and Moy that of the wise owl who leads the bull into the celebrations; the mythological connections with Zeus who changed into a bull in order to seduce the maiden Europa and with Minerva the wise (whose symbol is an owl), who was born out of Zeus's head are both there and not there; like the mediaeval legend, they are 'all mixed up', thus avoiding a glib symbolic interpretation and simultaneously awakening our imaginations. We might also remember that the owl is a symbol of desolation in the Bible,[1] and of the three girls Moy (certainly at this point in the story) is the saddest and loneliest. The third gathering, which encompasses the *dénouement,* is the party at Peter's house which has been discussed briefly above.

Furthermore, not only have actors such as Charles Arrowby or Clement Graffe become major characters in the novels but also discussion of the role of 'acting', the conscious or subconscious substitution of—or perhaps interplay between—imagination and reality have become dominant. Clement, the actor, sees the whole plot of *The Green Knight* in terms of some sort of play 'the slow enactment of an awful pantomime' (*GK,* p. 329). The book is divided into five sections like the five acts of a play; Clement identifies the various 'Acts' as the three 'events': the original assault on Peter, its replay, and 'Act Three'—the infliction of symbolic justice (see *GK,* p. 329), belonging respectively to sections 1-3 of the novel. On the other hand, he thinks that Peter's party is to be Act Four, but the fact that it occurs in section 3 suggests that the real Act Four recounts the death of Peter Mir and the various engagements that take place in section 4, whilst in section 5, the final Act or the Resolution, they reach the sea (*GK,* p. 451). Thus, we can see the whole novel as consciously using the framework of a Shakespearean drama.

The ethical and philosophic content of the novels has also changed and grown over the years. *Under the Net* posited a comparatively straightforward moral problem, which was not much complicated by the introduction of a religious dimension in *The Bell.* Later novels, however, enter into philosophic discussion about the nature of Good and Evil, about the existence or non-existence of God, about the relation of morality to religion and about mystic beliefs such as Buddhism, Judaism or, indeed, Christianity itself. Most people shift their religious and political perspectives as they grow older, responding to their own explorations and investigations. Murdoch is no exception and perhaps more than most people she has pursued trains of thought that have led her through many philosophic and moral mazes. Her present position as 'Christian fellow-traveller' (see above, p. 11) would seem to represent the religious stance she takes in *The Green Knight,* where Christian morality prevails without God; at the same time, she has not shut the door on the imaginative possibilities of mystic and supernatural belief.

The most striking change in the course of the novels is, I think, that of atmosphere and tone, yet it is difficult to pin down. All the novels have their light moments and some, such as *A Severed Head,* may be seen as almost pure comedy, but, particularly in the later novels, there is a kind of moral seriousness which is not apparent even in novels such as *The Bell* or *The Unicorn.* The plots of the novels are just as gripping, exciting and unpredictable but the reader, whilst still reading for the story is being forced to consider philosophical and moral concepts. Rather than being given answers, we are offered questions which stimulate our minds and send us back to reread the novels, long as they are, again and again.

Note

1. See, for instance, Psalm 102.6, 'I am like a pelican of the wilderness: I am like an owl of the desert.'

Bran J. Nicol (essay date spring 1996)

SOURCE: Nicol, Bran J. "Anticipating Retrospection: The First-Person Retrospective Novel and Iris Murdoch's *The Sea, the Sea.*" *Journal of Narrative Technique* 26, no. 2 (spring 1996): 187-208.

[*In the following essay, Nicol discusses the ways in which the first-person retrospective novel differs from the memoir or confessional novel, and using Murdoch's* The Sea, the Sea *as an example, discusses how a unique relationship between the narrator and reader is created.*]

This paper concerns the first-person retrospective novel, one in which a narrator tells a story about his or her own past. My reasons for using this term rather than more common ones like 'the confessional novel,' 'the memoir novel' or 'the personal novel,' are linked to my appreciation of its qualities. Unlike multiple first-person narratives (*Wuthering Heights* or Conrad's Marlow tales, for instance) the first-person retrospective novel has only one narrator; unlike first-person present-tense fiction (like the diary novel or the journal novel) this narrator is looking back on the past after a period of time has elapsed. These distinguishing features—the retrospective dimension, the narrator's autonomy—combine, I think, to give the first-person retrospective novel a peculiar rhetorical power. In what follows I want to explain this assertion, first by proposing that the form of the first-person retrospective novel invites us to read it in a particular way, and second by undertaking a reading of Iris Murdoch's **The Sea, the Sea** in light of my conclusions.

READING THE FIRST-PERSON
RETROSPECTIVE NOVEL

It seems right to begin the discussion of retrospective narrative by looking back. Käte Hamburger's influential 1957 work *The Logic of Literature* argues that the first-person novel is uniquely equipped to convey the impression of reality. This, she suggests, is not because of the style in which it is written nor its subject matter, but is a feature of the very form itself. The language that characterises the first-person novel (for example, the narrator's avoidance of verbs of inner action in the description of another character) makes it inhabit the realm of the *feigned,* that which masquerades as something it is not, rather than the *fictive,* which does not attempt to hide its artificiality. Unlike the third-person novel it "posits itself as non-fiction, i.e., as a historical document," to the extent that in some novels "it cannot be determined with certainty whether we are dealing with a genuine autobiography or with a novel" (Hamburger 312, 314-15). Hamburger's isolation of first-person narrative from the rest of fiction has been criticized because it is based too much on 'logic' rather than actual textual practice (see Bronzwaer), and her proto-structuralist approach to narrative theory has been supplanted by the more scientific method of the narratologists. Yet, in my view, her conviction about the mimetic effect of the first-person novel remains essentially accurate—especially in the case of the first-person retrospective novel.

This becomes clear if we consider the structure of this kind of fiction. In his modification of previous formalist-structuralist definitions of the basic parts of a narrative, Genette describes fictional narrative as essentially a tripartite structure comprising *story, text* and *narration.*[1] This third category refers to the production of the text, and is the one we are mainly concerned with here, for it is, in the words of Peter Brooks, "the level at which narratives sometimes dramatize the means and agency (real and fictive) of their telling" (Brooks [*Reading for the Plot*] 328n18). Genette stresses that text is the only part which is *real*; story and narration remain abstract elements of the textual equation. In other words, the account into which the raw material of the story has been shaped actually exists before the reader: it is a real object (the book itself) which the reader holds in his or her hands. Only by using this object can s/he begin to piece together the stuff of the story and imagine the process of narration. While this relationship between the three categories of course prevails in the first-person retrospective novel in the same way it does in all narrative, I think they also interact in another way. The structure of first-person retrospective narrative is such that Genette's second and third categories of narrative (text and narration) are also part of the first. The story element includes an event which is not always explicitly featured within, but which we know must occur, namely the narrator's composition—and narration—of the novel. In other words, the reader deduces that the chronological sequence of events which makes up the story (A, B, C, D . . . etc.) must always end with Event Z: Narrator Tells Story.[2] We might describe this final stage as possessing an almost uncanny quality; not unlike a ghost wandering through the text, it is present yet absent, something vital to the plot yet not exactly part of it.

This formal outline suggests that a distinct (Russian) formalist logic prevails in the first-person retrospective novel: the motivation of its story is its telling. More importantly, it also explains (in a different way from Hamburger's theory) the sense of authenticity I spoke of above. The illusion is created and maintained that the book we are reading is not a work of fiction created by the author whose name is on the cover, but a fictionalized version of the past constructed by the narrator. In *Studies in the Narrative Technique of the First-Person Novel,* Bertil Romberg—one of several critics I shall be dealing with whose work builds on Hamburger's concept of the feigned reality statement—insists that the impression of verisimilitude is principally the result of the "epic situation" (Romberg [*Studies in the Narrative Technique of the First-Person Novel*] 34). Just as "all epics can ultimately be related to a situation where a narrator presents a story orally to a listening public" (33) so, Romberg believes, the reality effect of a first-person novel is enhanced (or collapsed) by the author's incorporation of the epic situation into the novel—the narrator may reveal that he or she is speaking or writing the account or may appear among the characters. Where the epic situation is not a part of the third-person novel because it is *outside* the fiction, in the first-person novel it belongs to it. But while Romberg is right to argue that the epic situation brings a sense of authenticity to the narrator's discourse, I would take issue with his view that it requires to be *incorporated* by the author or else the novel's reality effect is threatened. It is easy to imagine a real autobiography where the author provides no insight into his situation at the time of writing, but does not collapse its sense of authenticity. The very nature of the retrospective first-person narrative means that the epic situation is always *implied*: it is the supplementary part of the text I spoke of above, 'element Z' of the 'story.'

There is historical support for the view of the first-person novel as a feigned reality statement if we think of the tradition, as old as the novel itself, where a fictitious author or editor presents a narrative as genuine (e.g., *Robinson Crusoe),* or of the determination of nineteenth-century critics to regard all first-person narrative as autobiography (e.g., *Jane Eyre).*[3] The work of critics like Hamburger and Romberg can explain how even nowadays—in more enlightened times—the first-person retrospective novel tends toward realism. The autodiegetic narrator maintains a degree of autonomy not matched in other forms. While the reader is constantly aware that this surrogate author is a fictional creation, s/he also possesses an independence quite unlike even the most realistically drawn character in a third-person text, because every word of the narrative originates only from him or her. This figure is individualized by no other narrator (except where there is another in the same text, like the shadowy editors of Nabokov's *Pale Fire* or Iris Murdoch's **The Black Prince),** and there are no direct interruptions in his or her text by a heterodiegetic narrator who represents the views of the implied author. Our mental construction of this persona is not limited to what he 'writes' on the page; rather, we must tap into the silences around his words for a sense of this fictional author existing in a world surrounding his text and actually constructing his narrative, just as we do with a real author. This illusion of autonomy has the effect of placing the author more emphatically 'under erasure,' in post-structuralist terms, than is the case in other texts. In an important sense, the presence of the 'real' author is negated, for like Laius, he has begotten a being who is unquestionably his but who also has a life of his own and has usurped him.

To equate the narrator of a text with its author is of course contentious from a narratological point of view. While Genette is happy to speak of the "author-narrator" on occasion, he does not wish the comparison to be taken too far, and cautions those critics who

> identify the narrating instance with the instance of 'writing,' the narrator with the author . . . a confusion that is perhaps legitimate in the case of a historical nar-

rative or a real autobiography, but not when we are dealing with a narrative of fiction, where the role of narrator is itself fictive, even if assumed directly by the author.

(Genette [*Narrative Discourse*] 213)

Within the context of poetics, the branch of criticism concerned with identifying and describing objectively each individual part that goes together to form the whole narrative, Genette is of course right. The real writing of the novel, we know, can only be done in the real world, a place where the narrator does not exist, no matter how strong is the sense of reality transmitted by the first-person novel. The narrator performs the *narrative function,* that is, s/he is used by the real author to convey the story to the reader. My point, though, is that a great many first-person retrospective narratives invite the reader to *imagine* that the narrator is also the novelist, and to take this knowledge into account when interpreting the text. The conventions of reading dictate that the reader must, up to a point, suspend disbelief and accept the fictional world as 'real.' The author-narrator, and his implied function beyond the time of the story, is part of this world. This is not to deny that many novels give the impression of being oral rather than written monologues (e.g., Camus's *La Chute,* Kazuo Ishiguro's *The Remains of the Day).* Yet even in these novels the sense of reality remains powerful, for the narrator still seems in sole control over his material. My point here is not that the narrator *replaces* the novelist in first-person retrospective fiction, but that—whether he seems to be speaking or writing—he occupies a position analogous to that of the real author.

Structuralist critics do, in any case, recognize that the narrator's role as fictive author means that s/he is not confined to the world of the novel. Todorov, for example, advises that "the person who 'recounts' the book" has "a unique position" and cannot be treated in the same way as other fictional characters in a novel (Todorov [*Introduction to Poetics*] 40), while in Genette's system this person occupies two different narrative levels; s/he is not just autodiegetic but extradiegetic: "author-narrators . . . are at the same level as their public—that is, you and me" (Genette 229). Susan Lanser's useful categorization of the various levels at which the world of the story is brought to the reader expands on this point. The "public" narrator, as distinct from the "private" narrator, who can speak only in the world of the novel, functions as "creator and authority" in this world and is unique among narrators in that s/he addresses someone 'outside' the text (Lanser [*The Narrative Act*] 137-38). It is worth noting that transgressing the textual boundary in this way carries a significant implication for the effect of the novel: although it serves ultimately to strengthen the reality effect, paradoxically it also works against it. The narrator exists as a person composing a novel in both a fictional world and the 'real' world. His or her book is simultaneously an arte-fact in both worlds, and serves as a bridge between the two. The interaction of such worlds is a characteristic metafictional device and is bound to result in a subtle raising of ontological questions. To ask: 'which level of reality does the narrator belong to?' corresponds to the question 'which level of reality do we belong to?'. If the narrator inhabits both our world and his or her own, do we inhabit a fictional world too? **The Sea, the Sea,** which we shall return to below, would have us think so, addressing the reader as if s/he is familiar, from cover-age in the 'real' media, with its narrator's status as a well-known public figure.[4]

All of this would be of descriptive value only, were it not for the fact that the hero's 'writing' of the narrative has a crucial bearing on the content of some novels, and must be taken into account as we interpret them. Although Genette and Todorov, as we have seen, show some concern with the status of the first-person author-narrator, their task remains that of classifying the differ-ent types of narrator in fiction, and does not extend to the semantic ramifications of the narrator's apparent re-sponsibility for the material in the text. This is also largely the case with other major narrative theorists. While we can see a discussion like Booth's on unreli-able narration, for example, as taking some account of these implications, we require a fuller analysis of the way the formal character of the first-person retrospec-tive novel, as we have discussed it, contributes to its content. Steven Kellman's work on what he calls the self-begetting novel (although it does not draw explic-itly on narrative theory) goes some way to providing this, as it is concerned with how the status of the author-narrator has much to do with the meaning of the novel. The self-begetting novel is distinguished by a circular movement in both structure and theme: it "projects the illusion of art creating itself. . . . it is an account, usu-ally first person, of the development of a character to the point at which he is able to take up his pen and compose the novel we have just been reading" (Kellman, "Self-Begetting" [*The Self-Begetting Novel*] 1245). The self-begetting novel is thus a self-reflexive commentary on itself, "a happy fusion of form and content" (1246), its central concern the story of its own composition. It thereby projects the illusion of narratorial autonomy that I have described: its protagonist is not only the subject of the story but also the producer of the whole novel in which he features, making the real author ap-pear redundant.

One of Kellman's example texts is Iris Murdoch's **Un-der the Net,** and a look at how the form of this novel invites us to interpret it serves, by way of a conclusion to this first section, to clarify the position I have argued so far. Kellman demonstrates that this text bears many of the self-begetting novel's trademarks, including the physical begetting *motif* itself (to liken the process of composing a novel to giving birth), a cast of artists, much metafictional reflection on art, and intertextual connections with what he suggests is the guiding force behind the sub-genre, the French literary tradition. Its hero, Jake Donahue, is a typical solitary self-begetting hero, looking for a direction in life that his novel will ultimately provide. Kellman shows how Jake's *éduca-tion sentimentale*—his movement from wanting "every-thing in my life to have sufficient reason" (24) at the beginning of the book to an appreciation of the contin-gent world at the end—coincides with the realization of his dormant desire to write a novel.

Of course, not all first-person retrospective novels con-form as neatly as **Under the Net** to Kellman's require-ments for the self-begetting novel. The great majority of hero-narrators throughout literary history do not *con-sciously* decide to write a fiction and by doing so beget a self, and their novels seldom feature the array of typi-cal themes and imagery Kellman identifies. Moreover, as Kellman reminds us, certain third-person works like Gide's *Les Faux-Monnayeurs* and Joyce's *Ulysses* fea-ture a central character who attempts to author himself into existence by writing a novel. He does suggest, however, that these novels are "somewhat peripheral to the self-begetting tradition" (Kellman, "Self-Begetting" 1248-49) because they also contain an extradiegetic narrator, and this seems to me to point to a significant fact: the self-begetting novel is most effective when it is a first-person retrospective novel.[5] Surely, that is, the self-begetting novel achieves maximum effect when it is a feigned reality statement? By the same token, the first-person retrospective novel is, in a sense, a self-begetting novel: it is as self-sufficient as legitimate ex-amples of Kellman's sub-genre because its narrator seems responsible for creating the novel we read.

Kellman's reading of **Under the Net** indicates why it is important to take into account the role of the author-narrator when interpreting first-person retrospective nar-rative. The point is emphasized when we set his reading against another, one by Deborah Johnson in her recent feminist study of Iris Murdoch, in which the novel is treated as first-person narrative but, in my view, under-estimated as a feigned reality statement. Johnson bases her reading on Irigaray's principle that "the 'feminine' is that which is repressed or elided in discourse," and concludes that as female author beneath the male narra-torial persona, Iris Murdoch can deconstruct the mi-sogyny of the external narrative by attacking from within. This works, Johnson says, by a process by which the postures Jake continually strikes in his narrative are revealed to be inadequate; the person Jake sees himself as is continually shown to be at odds with the reader's impression of him. As an example, Johnson quotes a passage from the scene where Jake is reacquainted with his former girlfriend Anna in the props room of a mime theatre:

I took her wrist, and for an instant saw her eyes wide with alarm, very close to mine, and then in a moment I had thrown her, very carefully, onto a pile of velvet costumes in the corner of the room. My knee sank into the velvet beside her, and straightaway a mass of scarves, laces, tin trumpets, woolly dogs, fancy hats and other objects came cascading down on top of us until we were half-buried.

(Johnson [*Iris Murdoch*] 21; Murdoch 39)

The irony that flavours this scene is of a straightforward (and characteristically for Murdoch, visual) kind, which works by inviting the reader to imagine how the action described would actually look. Jake's impression of himself as a gallant romantic 'Hollywood' hero of the 1950s is comically subverted by the cascade of theatrical objects on top of him.

Johnson's feminist reading of Murdoch is largely persuasive, despite the author's determinedly non-feminist stance.[6] Less convincing, however, is her conviction that the deconstructive voice in the narrative belongs to Iris Murdoch. To regard Murdoch's first-person narration as solely a device that exposes the illusory nature of the male position is to miss the full significance of the 'silent,' subversive element of the *narrator's* discourse. To put this another way, although Johnson's reading does not pretend to be a comprehensive narrative theory, it does depend upon a conception of the first-person form which holds that the author's creative domination over his or her material is evidenced, for example, by ironic discrepancies between what the narrator means to say, and what the author has determined this should reveal. The narrative theorist Lorna Martens has offered a more systematic exposition of this theory. She describes the semantic structure of the first-person novel, as it first seems to the reader, as a "narrative triangle" (derived from Jakobson's communicative triangle, sender-receiver-message), the points of which represent what she calls the "fictive narrator," the "fictive reader" (the implied reader) and the "narrated world" (the subject matter of the story). This three-way relationship results in an illusion of autonomy that makes it difficult to determine whether the first-person text is fictional or non-fictional. Yet she also contends that there *is* a distinction between fictional and genuine narratives.

If we read carefully and suspiciously, we may be able to denaturalize the narrator's discourse and find points in the text that support, belie, or simply enrich a reading based on voluntary acceptance of the fiction that the narrator alone is speaking.

(Martens [*The Diary Novel*] 35)

The authority of the narrator over all the material, Martens concludes, is therefore undermined by the existence of a second narrative triangle that envelops the first, the points of which are "author," "reader" and "novel."

But Martens's theory, though it is ultimately a faithful reflection of what occurs in first-person narrative, does not take full enough account of the narratorial autonomy that is an integral part of the concept of 'feigned reality' she elsewhere invokes. How, in practice, do we distinguish between the real and fictional author? We may know that the second triangle exists, but we cannot determine when we are actually in contact with it. Without recourse to extra-textual material, it is impossible to attribute with any certainty *any* intrusion whatsoever into the original narrative triangle (narrator/narrated world/reader) *to the author*. It must be remembered that in a novel where the hero and the narrator are the same person, the narrative works on two main temporal levels. There is the time of the present, in which the narration takes place, and the time of the past, in which the events told of actually happen. (In Genette's terms, these time-spheres correspond to the "extradiegetic" and "diegetic" levels of narration.) This dual form means the narrator's character is in effect split into two different manifestations of the same self, one who narrates and one who experiences (or focalizes).[7] (We might usefully say that these two selves correspond respectively to the 'text' and 'story' elements of the novel's form.) The distance between these two *personae* varies, in Franz Stanzel's words, "from identification to complete estrangement" (Stanzel [*A Theory of Narrative*] 213), according to whether the narrator is wiser after the events he recounts. Dorrit Cohn characterizes this distinction systematically, using the terms "dissonance" and "consonance" for each pole in the scale of identification (Cohn [*Transparent Minds*] 143-72).

Jake Donahue, as Kellman demonstrates, is clearly a dissonant narrator. This means that to concentrate solely on the *author's* deconstructive position in the discourse, as Johnson does in her reading of **Under the Net,** is to overlook that of the *narrator,* the surrogate author. Iris Murdoch does discreetly 'attack from within' in the novel, but by ensuring that the wiser voice of the narrator's remembering self underpins the deluded experiencing self. The implied author is thus equivalent to Jake Donahue's second self. In other words, it is just as much the narrator himself, in his creative role, who deconstructs the section of narrative that relates to his pre-enlightened persona. He has undergone a transformation as a result of the experience he describes, and this has caused him to distance himself from the person he was at the time of the story. To return to the episode in the prop room quoted by Johnson, it is completely plausible that the comic irony which operates there derives from Jake's *own* desire to expose the counterfeitness of his experiencing self, to question his tendency to relegate those around him to props in his personal drama. It is even plausible that Jake is aware of his early misogynism. In Irigaray's terms, the enlightened narrator is equivalent to the 'feminine' part of the discourse.

WRITING THE FIRST-PERSON RETROSPECTIVE
NOVEL: THE SEA, THE SEA

Peter Brooks suggests that "we would do best to speak of the *anticipation of retrospection* as our chief tool in making sense of narrative" (Brooks [*Reading for the Plot*] 22-23). This insight, as I hope the discussion of **Under the Net** has already indicated, applies in a distinctive way to the first-person retrospective novel. It is a form that requires us to follow the logic of the feigned reality statement: the reader must look forward to the point at which the narrator looks back. **Under the Net,** however, is a *bona fide* self-begetting novel, and thus lends itself easily to the kind of interpretation I have advocated. I want therefore to undertake a reading of another Iris Murdoch novel, **The Sea, the Sea,** the form of which is altogether more complex.

Murdoch says in her book on Plato that "the subject of every good play and novel" is "the pilgrimage from appearance to reality" (**The Fire and the Sun** 14). **The Sea, the Sea,** most critics agree, is about this pilgrimage. Famous theatre director Charles Arrowby retires to a lonely house by the sea—his "cave" (4)—to write his memoirs. There he will be able to reject the theatrical world of power and magic and "learn to be good," in other words, learn to distinguish between illusion and reality. Yet the inside of a cave, as Plato's famous metaphor illustrates, is where illusion resides, and Charles has another ordeal to face before he can finally reach the end of his pilgrimage. A chance meeting with the woman he loved and lost in his youth plunges his mind into chaos and he sets out to force her back to him. To pass fully from the state of *eikasia* to enlightenment he must therefore recognize that he has relinquished power in one form merely to grasp it in another. Previous interpretations of **The Sea, the Sea** have argued this case thoroughly, though opinions vary as to whether its hero's pilgrimage is successful.[8] To read the novel as a first-person retrospective novel, keeping in the forefront of our minds the fact that Charles Arrowby figures as its author, not only enables us to resolve the question of his enlightenment, but also results in a new reading of the text, not incompatible with others, but which does involve a notable shift of emphasis. I propose that the novel tells of a Proustian quest for truth, to which Charles's narrative project is central; the lessons he learns from this quest allow him finally to reject solipsism. His dual preoccupation with the distant past and with the form of his work contribute to the novel's neat synthesis of form and content. **The Sea, the Sea** is a retrospective novel and a novel about retrospection.

The book is divided into three sections, **"Prehistory," "History"** and **"Postscript: Life Goes On,"** which document respectively the periods before, during and after his involvement with Hartley. For the present purpose, however, it is useful to divide the novel into a slightly different tripartite structure. The first part, which takes up the first hundred pages and is narrated from Charles's house (called Shruff End) at the beginning of one summer, is written in a diary form that mixes present tense description of his environment with wistful recollections of his far past. Here he is deeply interested in the process of writing, avidly re-reading and commenting upon his work and repeatedly updating the reader on his epic situation. (The present tense gives his self-analysis an added immediacy, as if the reader is looking over his shoulder as he writes.) He is just as concerned with the form of his work and how it suits his purpose, referring to it variously as a diary, a memoir, a chronicle and a "novelistic memoir." We are launched into the second part of the novel (a few pages after the beginning of 'History') as the main story unexpectedly takes off. This section contains the bulk of the novel and is narrated in the past tense, from London (mainly) and Shruff End. It consists chiefly of action and the occasional reminiscence of the far past and, unlike the first part, is seldom interrupted by the narrator's reflections. Although in this section Charles provides several glimpses into his epic situation, these are mostly statements of narrative intention ("I will now describe what happened next" [207]) which reveal nothing more about his present circumstances. The final short section (the Postscript) is set in August of the same year (the whole convoluted narrative takes place, we can deduce, during one summer) and reverts to diary form. The epic situation is again referred to as we realize that Charles is writing from his cousin James's flat in London, and indeed has been for much of the previous section.

The structure of **The Sea, the Sea** differs from **Under the Net** and other examples of 'pure' first-person retrospective form because a substantial part of the novel is in the present tense. Yet, in essence, it remains formally retrospective, for the book as a whole is built upon the familiar narrative trajectory of first-person retrospective fiction we spoke of above, where a story is begun at a particular time in the past and gradually brought up to the present, revealing the situation of the narrator at the time of writing. The existence of the first section does not threaten this view of the novel's form but suggests simply that the author has chosen to tell the early part of his story by including a journal kept at the time. Nevertheless, while I regard **The Sea, the Sea** as essentially a retrospective fiction, its structural difference from the other novels has an important implication for my reading of the text. Because the book opens in the present tense, we know that Charles began writing *before* the events which come to form the plot have occurred. This means that the narrator's motive for writing the book is not born with these events, as it is in **Under the Net,** but has been formed before.

In the first section Charles is clear about the function he intends his book to perform. Recently, he confesses, he has felt the "need to write something that is both personal and reflective." He has "very little sense of identity" and this, he implies, must be put right; it is "time to *think* about myself at last" (3). His book is central to this process:

> This is for permanence, something which cannot help hoping to endure. Yes, already I personify the object, the little book, the *libellus*, this creature to which I am giving life and which seems at once to have a will of its own. It wants to live, it wants to survive.
>
> (2)

Yet despite his admission that he wants to examine his character through autobiography, he is not forthcoming about what exactly this task involves. Amidst the wealth of allusions to literary works (e.g., *The Tempest*, Valéry's 'Le Cimetière Marin') comparison with one in particular stands out, which I think explains in more depth why he writes. At Caen in 1978, just after completing the book, Murdoch suggested an affinity between her work and "the tradition of Proust." Proust's great novel, the archetypal self-begetting novel, is an important intertext in **The Sea, the Sea.** As well as subtle allusions to this work (for instance, James mentions Proust, and there is a gay man called Gilbert[e]) Murdoch's novel is also a study of obsessive, jealous love which explores the theme of illusion and reality. John Bayley's comment that for Proust, "A can never love B but only his idea of B, and *vice versa,* with confusing and depressing results," could apply equally to **The Sea, the Sea** (Bayley [*The Characters of Love*] 161). Both narrators aim to write about what is personal in order to illuminate what is universal, or as Charles puts it, to "reflect about the world through reflecting about my own adventures in it" (3).

This is not the place for a full comparison of the two novels. Most relevant to my reading of **The Sea, the Sea** is simply the fact that, like Marcel, Charles believes in reminiscence as the source of truth. Like his precursor Charles sifts through the experiences of what he calls his "far past"—memories of his friends and acquaintances in the theatre, his parents and his Aunt Estelle and cousin James—to find the one period where he thinks truth is located, the time he spent long ago with his childhood sweetheart Hartley. Describing his mind, characteristically, as a cave, Charles explains it is illuminated by the memory of Hartley, "the great light towards which I have been half consciously wending my way." He alludes to the Platonic origin of the metaphor, wondering if this light is "a great 'mouth' opening to the daylight, or . . . a hole through which fires emerge from the centre of the earth" (77). The process of writing about this memory is central to discovering if this light is really, as he imagines, "the light that reveals the truth" (79).

He is impressed by the strange power of writing, which enables shadowy areas of the past to be brought to light.

"Since I wrote [about Hartley]," he says, "so many more pictures of her, stored up in the dense darkness of my mind, have become available" (87). He is equally struck by the *form* of his narrative. When meditating on form—as he often does—it is noticeable how often he refers to the specific act of joining together past and present. In the early stages he considers structuring the narrative in order to "bring the story gradually up to date and as it were float my present upon my past" (3). Later, when he decides that his narrative will allow him to "inhabit the far past or depict the scarcely formulated present," he comments revealingly that

> The past and the present are after all so close, so almost one, as if time were an artificial teasing out of a material which longs to join, to interpenetrate, and to become heavy and very small like some of those heavenly bodies scientists tell us of.
>
> (153)

There are many other instances where a less explicit reference to past and present is made. The significance of this, I think, is that the quasi-autobiographical form itself links the narrator's past with his present by incorporating the experiencing and the narrating selves. The form of his novel thus promises to join together Charles's past and present. While the activity of writing makes the past more visible to the present, narrative form goes one step further and makes them one.

Those who have written about **The Sea, the Sea** have recognized its concern with the nature of artistic form. Several suggest that Murdoch is characteristically showing how reality will always defeat any attempt to impose form onto it. Elizabeth Dipple, for example, says that certain episodes at the beginning of the novel which interrupt Charles's reflections in prose—the disturbing vision of a sea monster, his vain attempts to attach a rope to the rocks to help him climb out of the sea after a swim, his concern at having been sent no letters—represent the unwelcome intrusion of the real contingent world into his stylized life-in-art. It is true that Murdoch is here commenting on the consolatory nature of artistic form. Like a great many of her characters, Charles displays an uneasiness about the contingent world. He is struck by the "*senselessness*" of the rocks outside his house and takes up the "obsessive task of collecting stones" (242) and ordering them on his lawn. But this only partly explains why the novel foregrounds the question of *narrative* form to such a degree. Dipple's view that the intrusion of contingency makes it "impossible" for Charles "to order a carefully exclusive diary" is unconvincing. It is never his intention to maintain "a smooth elegance of form" (Dipple [*Work for the Spirit*] 277). His uncertainty about what to call his narrative (diary, memoir, etc.) does not stem from frustration about forces he cannot control affecting it, but because he is happy to modify its form to cater for new requirements in the telling of his story. He is always content to see his work as an amalgamation of forms in which he can "rumble along" (2) as he pleases. Charles is of course uneasy about contingency, but there is another function that the form of his work must fulfill, more immediately important than presentation: the interpenetration of his past and present selves.

Once we recognise that Charles sets out to write his journal specifically to recapture the past, we can read the events that make up the plot of his novel in another way. The reflective first section of his journal is not, as it first seems, rudely hijacked by the events of the present, but is something that has been intended to serve as a *prelude* to these events. This section, "Prehistory," ends with Charles claiming to be haunted by the past (a fact suggested all along by his former lover Rosina occupying his house and pretending to be a ghost) and wondering, "Can a woman's ghost, after so many years, open the doors of the heart?" (89). Soon after this, as if conjured up by his possessed prose itself, the real Hartley appears in his life. The intensity with which he immediately hurls himself into pursuit of her is the result of more than simply the rekindling of dormant love. It is the inevitable reaction of a man obsessed by his past who now comes face to face with it. He is not attracted to Hartley physically or cerebrally, he wants her because she is an embodiment of a lost world of innocence. He describes their childhood love as innocent, kept secret from their friends, involving only caresses not sex, "a passion and . . . a love of purity that can never come again and which I am sure rarely exists in the world at all" (80). In her presence he feels "so helplessly, vulnerably close to my childhood" (327). Given his fascination with the period of his youth, it is not altogether surprising that he is patently unable to recognise that the Hartley he has carried around in his imagination is quite unlike the dull, elderly, comfortably married woman she is now.

Charles's deep desire to revisit the past means that his attempt to capture Hartley is a way of doing literally what he first intended to accomplish metaphorically by writing his novel. She represents his past; by reclaiming her, he can possess it. Her significance in this sense is suggested when Charles, having failed to prise her away from her husband, imprisons her (in an episode reminiscent of Proust) in a locked room in Shruff End. Furthermore, meeting her again causes him to ponder the close proximity of past and present with renewed vigour. Looking over old photographs of Hartley as a child, he tries "to trace the similarities, to build connections between the young face and the old, the old face and the new" (156). She makes him "whole as I have never been since she left me" (186).

From her 'prison' Hartley remarks on Charles's "curiosity, like a tourist, you're visiting me, visiting my life and feeling superior" (300). He is indeed a kind of tour-

ist, but her words suggest a more apt comparison: in Murdoch's work curiosity and superiority are often seen as qualities of the novelist (for example: Arnold in *The Black Prince* and Monty in *The Sacred and Profane Love Machine*). And Charles is a novelist; although his narrative never entirely loses its pretensions to factual truth, he comes to realize that he is writing a novel. When we take into account the completed novel as a whole—written of course by Murdoch, but masquerading as Charles's—we can see that in a sense his metaphorical capture of Hartley is a success. He imagines telling her one day about the other great love of his life, Clement, and reflects, "How important it seems to continue one's life by explaining oneself to people, by justifying oneself, by memorializing one's loves" (244). Hartley herself is "memorialized," captured within his novel. Because he is successful in this aim, it follows that his attempt at wrapping up the diverse elements of the world is not wholly in vain either. Peter Conradi has pointed out that the sea is the ultimate example of formlessness (Conradi [*Iris Murdoch*] 249). But in a way Charles does manage to build form around it: the sea is metaphorically contained in his novel, as its title indicates. In applying form onto reality he is altogether more successful than has previously been acknowledged. Dipple is right to point out that the book's "meandering refusal of closure" (Dipple 85) comically highlights the problems of ending a work of fiction. There is, nevertheless, a circular unity about the book; Charles begins by writing a meditative diary in a strange house and ends that way too. Although its form is undoubtedly ragged, he does manage to create a self-contained art object with the quality of "permanence" he envisages. Dipple suggests that what Charles is trying to do in his narrative can be explained by Murdoch's argument that "one of the deep motives for literature is that one is defeating the formlessness of the world" (Dipple 276). While this motive more often than not leads her characters to create bad art, we must remember that Murdoch sees a positive value in this too, provided form does not console at the expense of truth. Like every artist Charles does succeed, in a small way, in "defeating the formlessness of the world."

Up to a point, then, Charles does manage to secure his past within the pages of his novel. But does this mean his mission is a success? So far we have discerned two aims behind his preoccupation with his far past: a desire to comprehend the *truth* of the past, and a corresponding wish to unite his past and present selves. His renewed involvement with Hartley has done nothing to suggest that his first aim is likely to be fulfilled, for he is just as unable to penetrate the "terrible mystery" of why she left him as he was at the start of the novel. As far as his second aim is concerned, Charles gradually comes to realize that the connective power of narrative form is illusory. Writing his novel teaches him the lesson that he is always already separated from even his most recent past. The very activity of narration implies a detachment from experience. (All narrative, Genette says, is retrospective.) This is especially noticeable in the **"Prehistory"** section of Charles's narrative, which employs the form of narration common to journal or epistolary novels, which Genette calls "interpolated" (because it occurs "between the moments of the action"): "Here the narrator is at one and the same time still the hero and already someone else: the events of the day are already in the past, and the 'point of view' may have been modified since then" (Genette 217-18).[9] In the early passages of his diary, Deborah Johnson remarks "Charles is divided from his luminous present by the very act of writing about it" (Johnson 47).[10] Describing an experience lets him see how it could be bettered:

Oh blessed northern sea, a real sea with clean merciful tides,
not like the stinking soupy Mediterranean!
They say there are seals here, but I have seen none yet.

(2)

On a wider level, telling the story of his recent exploits forces him to examine his actions more objectively simply by virtue of describing them. In other words, his narrating self is already becoming divorced from his experiencing self.

In the long second part of the novel, narrated in the past tense, Charles's narrating self first appears consonant with his experiencing self. That is, he gives the impression that he still endorses his recent actions and emotions. As Charles's mind becomes full of questions when reflecting upon an occurrence (a way of thinking that resembles the Dostoevskyan hero) he usually finds a way of discrediting the interpretation which the reader can see is the most likely:

Or was it naïve to expect confidences from a woman I had not seen for more than forty years? I had kept her being alive in me, but to her I might simply be a shadow, an almost forgotten schoolboy. I could not believe this. Was she perhaps on the contrary still so much in love with me that she dare not trust herself to see me?

(139)

He clings repeatedly on to the fact that the "evidence was not conclusive and could be read in other ways" (158). Gradually, however, his narrating and experiencing selves become more dissonant, and his tone reveals a subtle but unmistakable questioning of some of his previous actions or opinions: "I had lost control of my life and of the lives with which I was meddling. I felt dread and a terrible fatalism. . . . I had wakened some sleeping demon, set going some deadly machine; and what would be would be" (310). The confession of

"meddling" is almost hidden amidst his deterministic reasoning, but lends the passage the distinct tone of remorse. In another example, he seems half-aware that he has been deluded about his relationship with Hartley: "I felt for her a desire which was marvellously indistinguishable from pure love" (279). As in **Under the Net,** the hero's narrating and experiencing selves have become separated. Finally enlightened, Charles reaches the point where he can say,

I had deluded myself throughout by the idea of reviving a secret love which did not exist at all. . . . I accused Hartley of being a 'fantasist' . . . but what a 'fantasist' I have been myself. I was the dreamer, I the magician. How much, I see as I look back, I read into it all, reading my own dream text and not looking at the reality.

(499)

This recognition is the conclusion of his pilgrimage from appearance to reality, which we could describe as a movement from narratorial consonance to dissonance. Central to his enlightenment is the realization that he cannot fully inhabit his past self, despite the power of narrative form. James has already hinted at this, asking his cousin:

What is the truth anyway, that truth? As we know ourselves we are fake objects, fakes, bundles of illusions. Can you determine exactly what you felt or thought or did? We have to pretend in law courts that such things can be done, but that is just a matter of convenience.

(175)

Only much later, after James's death, does Charles begin to realize the significance of what James says, that retrospective writing can bring only a limited degree of self-knowledge:

Time, like the sea, unties all knots. Judgements on people are never final, they emerge from summings up which at once suggest the need of a reconsideration. Human arrangements are nothing but loose ends and hazy reckoning, whatever art may otherwise pretend in order to console us.

(477)

To confirm this point it is worth considering the section titles, which—if we follow the logic of the feigned reality statement—Charles must have added after completing the novel, and which reveal in a concise way the truth he discovers. The most immediate past, the story about re-encountering Hartley, is consigned to "History." Life must go on, despite and because of what has happened in the past. Charles ends the novel aware of the journey he has undertaken, looking into the future not the past: "Upon the demon-ridden pilgrimage of human life, what next I wonder?" (502).

Notes

1. He outlines these categories in *Narrative Discourse,* the English publication of part of *Figures III,* originally published in 1972. I am using the

English translations of Genette's original terms—*histoire, récit* and *narration*—used by Rimmon-Kenan in *Narrative Fiction.*

2. Seymour Chatman notes that the story contains both the "content or chain of events" and what he calls "existents (characters, items of setting)" (*Story and Discourse* 19).

3. See, for example, Lennard J. Davis, *Factual Fictions*; Ian Watt, *The Rise of the Novel* and, for an interesting discussion of the nineteenth-century view of first-person narrative, especially how it links to aspects of gender, Susan S. Lanser, *The Narrative Act.*

4. See Brian McHale, *Postmodernist Fiction.* Such formal self-consciousness might explain why, although it is present throughout literary history, the first-person novel is perhaps the representative fictional form of a postmodern age obsessed with subjectivity. See also Bradbury and Fletcher, "The Introverted Novel."

5. Kellman's proviso that the self-begetting novel is "*usually* first person" (my italics) is explained by the fact that a novel like Butor's *La Modification,* which he discusses in his book, is famously written in the second person. This device functions in fact in the same way as the first person, for it is clear that the narrative originates from one man, the hero.

6. Murdoch commented at a conference at Caen that although she is aware of woman's self-consciousness in society, she wishes "to write about things on the whole where it doesn't matter whether you're male or female."

7. Leo Spitzer is credited with first employing the terms "experiencing self" and "narrating self" for this distinction. Leo Spitzer, *Stilstudien II,* 1923. Other terms have been coined. For example, Hans Robert Jauss uses "the remembering I" and "the remembered I" in a 1955 study of Proust's great novel. However, like Romberg, I prefer Spitzer's terms, because they suggest the centrality of actual experience to the first-person narrator.

8. Richard Todd, for example, thinks Charles has changed, Conradi is not convinced that any of Murdoch's narrators achieve lasting enlightenment, and Deborah Johnson believes Charles "settles eventually on a partial truth, on an incomplete illumination" (Johnson 91).

9. Genette's discussion of this kind of narration contains other insights which are relevant to *The Sea, the Sea.* He regards it as the most complex type of narration "since the story and the narrating can become entangled in such a way that the latter has

an effect on the former," a development, as we have seen, which occurs in Murdoch's novel. In *The Sea, the Sea,* as Genette also says, "the journal form loosens up to result in a sort of monologue after the event" (Genette 217).

10. Johnson's theory of the deconstructive subtext, discussed above, is more convincing applied to present tense narrative.

Works Cited

Bayley, John. *The Characters of Love.* London: Constable, 1960.

Bronzwaer, W. J. M. *Tense in the Novel: An Investigation of Some Potentialities of Linguistic Criticism.* Groningen: Wolters-Noordhoff Publishing, 1970.

Brooks, Peter. *Reading for the Plot: Design and Intention in Narrative.* Cambridge, Mass.: Harvard University Press, 1992.

Chatman, Seymour. *Story and Discourse: Narrative Structure in Fiction and Film.* Ithaca, New York: Cornell University Press, 1978.

Chevalier, Jean-Louis, ed. "Rencontres avec Iris Murdoch." Centre de Recherches de Littérature et Linguistique des Pays de Langue Anglaise, Université de Caen, France, 1979.

Cohn, Dorrit. *Transparent Minds: Narrative Modes for Presenting Consciousness in Fiction.* Princeton, New Jersey: Princeton University Press, 1978.

Conradi, Peter J. *Iris Murdoch: The Saint and the Artist.* 2nd ed. Basingstoke: Macmillan Press, 1989.

Davis, Lennard J. *Factual Fictions: The Origins of the English Novel.* New York: Columbi University Press, 1983.

Dipple, Elizabeth. *Work for the Spirit.* London: Methuen, 1984.

Fletcher, John and Bradbury, Malcolm. "The Introverted Novel." *Modernism 1890-1930* ed. Malcolm Bradbury and James McFarlane. Harmondsworth: Penguin, 1976. 394 415.

Genette, Gérard. *Narrative Discourse.* Trans. Jane E. Lewin. Oxford: Basil Blackwell, 1980.

Glowinski, Michal. "On the First-Person Novel." *New Literary History* 9 (1977-78): 103-14.

Hamburger, Käte. *The Logic of Literature.* Trans. Marilyn J. Rose, 2nd revised ed. London: Indiana University Press, 1973.

Johnson, Deborah. *Iris Murdoch.* Brighton: Harvester Press, 1987.

Kellman, Steven G. "The Fiction of Self-Begetting." *Modern Language Notes* 91 (December 1976): 1243-56.

_____. "Raising the Net: Iris Murdoch and the Tradition of the Self-Begetting Novel." *English Studies* 57 (February 1976): 43-50.

_____. *The Self-Begetting Novel.* London: Macmillan, 1980.

Lanser, Susan S. *The Narrative Act: Point of View in Prose Fiction.* Princeton, New Jersey: Princeton University Press, 1981.

McHale, Brian. *Postmodernist Fiction.* London: Methuen, 1987.

Martens, Lorna. *The Diary Novel.* Cambridge: Cambridge University Press, 1985.

Rimmon-Kenan, Shlomith. *Narrative Fiction: Contemporary Poetics.* London: Routledge, 1983.

Romberg, Bertil. *Studies in the Narrative Technique of the First-Person Novel.* Lund: Almqvist and Wiksell, 1962.

Stanzel, Franz. *A Theory of Narrative.* Trans. Charlotte Goedsche, 2nd ed. Cambridge: Cambridge University Press, 1984.

Todd, Richard. *Iris Murdoch.* London: Methuen, 1984.

Todorov, Tzvetan. *Introduction to Poetics.* Trans. Richard Howard. Brighton: Harvester Press, 1981.

Watt, Ian. *The Rise of the Novel.* Berkeley: University of California Press, 1957.

Elizabeth Dipple (essay date 1996)

SOURCE: Dipple, Elizabeth. "*The Green Knight* and Other Vagaries of the Spirit; or, Tricks and Images for the Human Soul; or, the Uses of Imaginative Literature." In *Iris Murdoch and the Search for Human Goodness,* edited by Maria Antonaccio and William Schweiker, pp. 138-68. Chicago: University of Chicago Press, 1996.

[*In the following essay, Dipple stresses the referential nature of Murdoch's fiction and the fact that her works defy any definitive reading. After offering commentary on key scenes in* The Book and the Brotherhood *and* The Message to the Planet, *Dipple offers a critique of Murdoch's imagery, metaphors, and allusions in* The Green Knight.]

I

I must first address the question of the crazed title of this paper, especially in the light of its apparently overblown alternatives and repetitions. Simply put, it has to do with both the nature of literary studies at this time and the techniques Iris Murdoch uses to maximize the primary functions of literature as a useful genre. In her practice of the tough art of novel writing, she persistently displays a subtle sense of fictional construction at a very sophisticated level, while at the same time she uses novels to address deep human issues. These are connected to the quality of moral action both in the realm of the quotidian world, where most of her characters fail in myriad small and large ways, and in the religious sphere, where she describes the soul's persistent yearning for a perfection that, as her most spiritually advanced characters repeatedly say, only a saint could achieve. Murdoch is at once well aware of the limitations of all too many contemporary novels, and of the ways in which imaginative literature can wrongfully feed the human desire for spectacular displays of magical supernaturalism.

Let me first put Murdoch's work into the context of contemporary literary studies. The critical climate in which literature could flourish has changed qualitatively over the last several years in a way that renders the central concerns of this conference on the work of Iris Murdoch of limited interest to the majority of professional literary critical practitioners, for whom the text itself is secondary to sets of theory generated before the advent of fictional intervention. I look at this decline of interest in the ethical, aesthetic, spiritual, and personal on the part of my colleagues in literature departments warily and often sadly. The prevailing atmosphere among most professional literary critics gives real urgency to the practice of an alternative criticism that stretches the moral and aesthetic imagination dwelling within the human subject, and calls for the practice of a continuous patience while the dominant materialist movements wear themselves out, as they inevitably must. Fortunately for the fate of the study of literature, various kinds of beneficial criticism do exist—in the Bakhtinian studies of Caryl Emerson and Saul Morson, for example, in the ethos of Martha Nussbaum's philosophical literary criticism, in the rigorous, formal, aesthetically oriented work of some practicing poets like Robert Pinsky and Mary Kinzie or fictionists like J. M. Coetzee, and in the efforts of an increasingly large number of workers in the literary vineyards who wish to infuse reading with an apprehension of the path through experience, to a knowledge of the radical insufficiency of material existence, and hence to the divine. I am not myself comfortable with much of the work of the latter group, however, in that the pressure of traditional religions can lead too often to a simplistic misuse of literary texts as a corollary of settled belief. This practice can easily become a dogged essentializing of broad elements that are present in the text but are easily distorted by the heavy hand of dogmatic conviction or religious fantasy. Because of the nature of Murdoch's fiction, with its religious suggestiveness, this issue must early be cleared away as irrelevant to a just and accurate reading of her texts.

In her novels, Murdoch, through specific characters and extended thematics, again and again warns against the dangers of fantasy and illusion in the face of the apparently supernatural, especially because of the human tendency to find miracles and quasi-divine comforts everywhere. In her recent book, ***Metaphysics as a Guide to Morals,***[1] she urges the uses of a discriminating and disciplined imagination. Through the following quotation I focus attention on only a small portion of her extended discussion in order to stress the potential power of religious infusion in the literary and its severe limitations as fantasy or dogma:

> High imagination is passionately creative. . . . The spiritual life is a long disciplined destruction of false images and false goods until (in some sense which we cannot understand) the imagining mind achieves an end of images and shadows (*ex umbris et imaginibus in veritatem*), the final *demythologisation* of the religious passion. . . . I want to see the contrast [between fantasy and imagination] . . . positively in terms of two active faculties, one somewhat mechanically generating narrowly banal false pictures (the ego as all-powerful), and the other freely and creatively exploring the world, moving toward the expression and elucidation (and in art celebration) of what is true and deep. . . . 'Truth' is something we recognize in good art when we are led to a juster, clearer, more detailed, more refined understanding. Good art 'explains' truth itself, by *manifesting* deep conceptual connections. Truth is clarification, justice, compassion.

> (*Metaphysics* [*Metaphysics as a Guide to Morals*], 319-21)

A serious reader of literature, as opposed to an ideologue, recognizes that the function of the imagination in any of its definitions is opposed to a wholesale acceptance of the strong concept of cultural or social constructivism—the idea that human beings are more or less passively shaped by the dominant discourses and ideologies of their culture. This constructivist theory, however, is now in firm control in many fields of academic inquiry and is seldom questioned. Central concepts of constructivism itself are not primarily negative, of course, and indeed can offer help in such fields as the anthropology of literature—a movement that cries out for new thought instead of the kind of ideological borrowing that is now too often going on. A philosopher of science, Arthur Fine, rescues the field. He points out that our ideas are indeed socially formed, arranged and rearranged in subtle ways as two or more (indeed, multiple) minds work through local conversations, reading, discussions of other topics, or human discourse of any sort, toward shifts and changes in our individual apprehension of the world. This continuous, ongoing process keeps us within the world, using our local experience and solving problems within that experience.

In terms of Fine's principle of the Natural Ontological Attitude—NOA (pronounced Noah)—this sort of subtle constructivism does not trap us in a socially determined mode, but rather allows us to open the doors to ethical and aesthetic considerations, as well as to a renewed critique of social and scientific constructivism. One important thing that Fine's NOA work teaches a literary critic is that the rigidity of theory or the tight, Marxist/Feminist political-cultural nexus of current ideology lacks the fluidity of mind and strong attention necessary for real analysis or a sensitive listening to the work at hand. As Fine puts his case in another context: "NOA . . . is an open, particularist and nonessentialist attitude to science. It promotes a no-theory attitude [of letting the ontological chips fall where they may] toward truth, and thus avoids the metaphysics of [scientific] realism or metaphysical constructivism."[2]

For Murdoch, as for a thinker as unlike her as Fine, all human problems are indeed local in very specific ways. Given her carefully enforced novelistic repetitions, the reader of Murdoch's fiction is always aware of the need to work slowly through the dense and often contingent material that crowds each novel. Although central ideas—such as her complex concept of the good, the muddle of contingency in the experienced universe, or the fallacy of comforting unitive thought—may be passed on from novel to novel, their context is always skewed, renewed and reworked by the freshly conceived structure in which they appear.

As Murdoch's novelistic production advances through time, there is a consistent increase in compositional strength and a progressive refinement in her metaphoric reach. About a dozen years ago I wrote a book on Murdoch's fiction, feeling at that time that *The Black Prince* (1973) was her best novel. I argued moreover that the earlier novels, although of great interest, lack the density of the later work. Another way of putting this was to use Henry James's vocabulary, as Murdoch herself has done, thus opening the door for most of her critics endlessly to reiterate her opinion as I do here: She moved steadily from her tendency toward tightly controlled plots and form to the "big baggy monsters." She became more like James, more like the nineteenth-century novelists and particularly the Russians. In reading individual Murdoch novels, one feels that occasionally Tolstoy and almost always Dostoevsky is tapping on one's shoulder. And behind the whole oeuvre is the encompassing, disruptive spirit of Shakespeare.

This particular intertextual insight does not get the reader very far, however. It can lead too easily to generalized readings of the novels, to a misprision of the particular which Murdoch has labored intensively to create. Imaginative literature dies under the hammer blows of a priori theories: If one considers the task of author and reader as somehow shared within certain areas of cognition, then each participates in the tension of constructivism, of the making of the text within usable mental boundaries. This shared responsibility is not frivolous, nor is it a property of simplistic first readings.

After the publication of her twenty-fourth novel, *The Message to the Planet* (1989), I became convinced that it and the previous work, *The Book and the Brotherhood* (1987), could productively be seen as paired novels and that each indicated a stride forward from her already impressive record in the most recent previous books. Not only was she consistently and relentlessly driving her standard of fiction forward from the early novels to the high achievements of the 1970s and early 1980s, but she was also working more freely and successfully within strong structural and metaphorical areas that set these novels both qualitatively and narratologically apart from those that preceded them. Having decided this, but feeling nevertheless that this attitude might be a temporary disaffection based on current enthusiasms, I went back and carefully reread *The Good Apprentice* (1986), which is individuated and surprising in its own right. It was not until the publication in Britain of *The Green Knight* in the summer of 1993, however, that my overly tidy pattern of response was bent if not entirely broken. Murdoch's sudden entry into the Arthurian world as one of her intertexts led to a myth-ridden area which both she and her novelistic characters, standing in for her authorial viewpoint, had always forsworn, passionately preferring the open, particularized sphere of Shakespeare's plays. For Murdoch's fiction, the implied magic, the fantasy-ridden mythology, and the potential trumpery of that romance tradition had previously appeared to be too distractive for such a serious writer. Indeed, they have too often tempted modern writers and readers easily with an illusionary/visionary world like that of Charles Williams or like John Cowper Powys's *A Glastonbury Romance,* a Modernist quasi-Arthurian saga that one of the characters is languidly reading through much of Murdoch's *The Green Knight.* I therefore began this novel armed with suspicion. However, I rapidly came to the conclusion that it is one of her most compelling books and one that develops ideas suggested in her earlier work but which are here taken into new dimensions.

The strength of the novels seems to me to grow progressively through a ceaseless rethinking of thematics within the new framework of each book. In other words, although many of Murdoch's critics, particularly the journalistic ones, have claimed to be unable to distinguish one novel from the other and to feel that once you are in the phenomenology of Murdoch's world you know all the rules, the opposite is more often true. Her novels constantly surprise because repetitive patterns lull the inattentive and generalizing reader into a kind of mental softness, from which one is suddenly awakened by an often infuriating series of reversals that, on

first reading, meet strong reader resistance. When the Russian Formalist Victor Shklovsky came up with the term *ostrannenie,* "defamiliarization," Mikhail Bakhtin attributed it to that quality of Tolstoy's writing that makes the reader reperceive the world as somehow adequately, mimetically represented in the fiction, but also made strange and "other." This insight can be taken a small step further in Murdoch's case: As novel readers, we both recognize and rethink the two structures involved—our perception of the experienced world represented by fiction and, held in tension against this, the structure of the fictional representation that we thought we could master.

Fiction has an important task, that of disarming and alienating its readers from their sense of security in the world they perceive in habitual ways. Within Murdoch's particular agenda, the slippery presentation of narrators, of characters, of action reversing logical expectation, robs the reader of interpretative certainty. I find again and again in teaching Murdoch's novels to students, who too often and willingly attach themselves to brutally singular meanings, that I must answer their queries by saying that I simply do not know why such-and-so happens, or why a certain character says a particular something. I can, however, present a series of possibilities (although even in presenting that series I feel that a better reader might come up with a better list). Because the novels are so crowded with myriad details, all significant from one point of view or another, any reading feels small and eccentric in the face of the crowded, resonant text. The multiple interpretations called out by Murdoch's work defy the single reading, or the smug sureness of the theoretician.

Although Murdoch does not in any general or straightforward way reflect the thought patterns of the postmodernist novelists who have appropriated several of the ideas of the American "pragmatist" C. S. Peirce, her novels can be seen as participating in a version of realism the reading of which demands a *mise-en-abyme* structure. In terms of the multiplicity of adequate readings of her fiction, then, it is helpful to look at Peirce's stripteasing explanation of the problem of representation within a context that chimes with the ambitions of any one of Murdoch's recent novels: "The meaning of a representation can be nothing but a representation. In fact, it is nothing but the representation itself conceived as stripped of irrelevant clothing. But this clothing never can be completely stripped off; it is only changed for something more diaphanous. So there is an infinite regression here. Finally, the interpretant is nothing but another representation to which the torch of truth is handed along; and as representation, it has its interpretant again. Lo, another infinite series."[3]

In a very real sense, Murdoch's mimetic representation of a flimsy world of infinite interpretational regress is hermeneutically analogous to her apprehension of the spiritual questing of the religious soul. As a case in point, one can refer to **Henry and Cato** (1976), where the Catholic priest Brendan Craddock tries to call Cato back to the rigors of the church: "The point is, one will never get to the end of it, never get to the bottom of it, never, never, never. And that never, never, never is what you must take for your hope and your shield and your most glorious promise" (p. 339). In an increasingly secular world, one central use of literature as practiced by Iris Murdoch is to detach us from the illusion of determinate meaning, in both fiction and the spiritual life.

II

The toughness, the flex and play of Murdoch's dense fiction can be approached through her Ovidian instincts, a possibility I put forward in order to focus on the particular achievements of her most recent novels. The hellenistic idea of the "continuing song" of literature, put forth and practiced by Callimachus (third century B.C.), is part of the complex intertwining of Ovid's *Metamorphoses* (A.D. 7-8), a long narrative poem in fifteen books thematically linked by ideas of transmutation. Here the structuralist intuition of the endlessly relational aspect of literary knowledge (and for Murdoch one would have to add art historical and religious knowledge as well) is useful. Jonathan Bate, who in his excellent recent book *Shakespeare and Ovid* gives the best radical critique of Ovid that I have read, is aware that Ovid is par excellence a poet of Derridean *différance*—of differentiation and endless deferral.[4]

Murdoch, who has studied and heavily criticized the excesses and traps of the various structuralisms in **Metaphysics as a Guide to Morals,** however, is also a fastidious reader of Shakespeare, whose plots, characters, and themes she incorporates obliquely and iconoclastically into her own fiction. Shakespeare's grasp of the contingent, the tragic, and the performed life alters her understanding of Ovid, whom I suspect sets her route. In major respects, Murdoch's art lives in a milieu of oblique commentary on Shakespeare's techniques as well as on those she has learned from her enormous interest in the Venetian Ovidian painters of the cinquecento, particularly Titian. Again and again she evokes those mythological paintings, derived from Ovid and transmuted into the spiritual allegories of the Italian Renaissance, particularly the image of Titian's *Flaying of Marsyas*, of *Actaeon and Diana*, and *Perseus and Andromeda*, to mention only the major ekphrases of the Ovidian Venetian connection. The lens of Titian's representations turns continuously into transmuted visions—Diana hunting actively in the foreground while Actaeon is roughly torn by the hounds in the misted background, Marsyas overturned in body as well as mind by a torturing, flaying Apollo. The transmutation of the myth is everything to Ovid, and his freedom before the idea of metamorphosis is seized on by Murdoch's own sense of literary, intertextual inversion.

It would, however, be a serious disservice to Murdoch's fiction to say that she is wholly or even largely dependent on an Ovidian frame of reference. What I imply when I say that her style is Ovidian has to do much more with methodology, with a sense of succession in novel after novel, as a long continuing song unfolds discretely and freshly with each new presentation. Living as her fiction does very much within the real world of the late twentieth century, Murdoch's method of imagistic and metaphoric presentation goes widely beyond the strictures of classical mythology. The purpose of the central part of my study is to illustrate how her imagery, metaphors, and allusions work, as one senses that within every one of her fictions books endlessly talk to books within the minds of the narrator, the characters, and the readers, who share in the process of constructing a world in which the images and stories of the past beget story after story in the present. This endlessly generative process ties every reader to a large referential frame from western literary and art historical culture, from Judeo-Christian texts, Buddhism, Hinduism—in short, the whole panoply of cultural armor that a privileged, educated audience wears and wishes to embellish.

Herein, I might add almost parenthetically, lies a problem that Murdoch's fiction neither engages in nor attempts to apologize for. The social doctrines now endemic in cultural criticism bounded by narrowly doctrinaire Marxism, the strictures of multiculturalism, and radicalized feminism make most culturally elitist art of any sort (the buzzword is "museum art") blameworthy. The blame is doubled when the issues also involve ethical or spiritual examinations beyond the materialist expositions of politicized issues like race, class, and gender. Murdoch uses these issues when they are useful to the larger designs of her fiction or of her ethical thought, but she sturdily refuses to reduce the learned world that our hard-won education presents us with. (For which Allah be praised.) Even a critic like Nicholas Spice, whose occasional reviews of Murdoch's novels in *The London Review of Books* are among the most insightful work to be done in short measure on the books under review, felt obliged—no doubt under the pressure of the materialist concentration of thought in current Britain—to chastise her mildly for presenting the moral action of **The Green Knight** against a background with no socioeconomic or historical depth. It is essentially outside the boundaries of this paper to defend Murdoch on this front, or to concentrate attention on her no doubt elitist but strong conviction that education, through a broad reconception of its function and content, is necessary for us as a society to retain any kind of access to virtue. I will simply say that in **The Green Knight,** Sefton, one of the three sisters who are almost enchanted princesses, lives in a glorious haze of passionate book learning (her field is history) which feeds and enriches her imagination. Sefton is, to my mind, a mythical representation not only of the wisdom that her real name, Sophia, allegorically points to, but also of the high progressive feeling of liberation and clarification that a genuine, disciplined search for manifold, not merely politicized, knowledge can give us.

III

In carrying out even a brief analysis of Murdoch's recent fiction, it seems clear, at least to me, that two points are imperative: (1) It is essential not to clog the investigation with theory. An overtheorized approach stops the fluidity and multidirectional aspect of the novels at the same time as it calls attention to itself rather than to the more challenging job of trying to gather some of the salient aspects of these broadly beckoning artifacts. (2) A fruitful reading should be aware of but significantly separated from heavy reliance on Murdoch's recent philosophical work, *Metaphysics as a Guide to Morals.* This generically different product has been broadly touted as the primary guide to the fiction, as it is to her interpretations of the moral and spiritual life. The close intertwining of literature, art, ethics, and religion present in that volume is of extraordinary interest, but if misused it can also be seen as a sort of unfriendly takeover of the experience of reading, of thinking about fictional writing, of being in the old Lutheran sense one's own priest. Reading the novels side by side with this capacious inquiry is too much like relying on the pretheorized aspects of *The Golden Bough* in all Modernist anthropological studies. I believe that Murdoch wants readers to have a go on their own, helped but untrammeled by her own powerful interpretative, authorial hand. I am not simply raising spectres of the Barthesian idea of the absence, which he called "death" of the author; but it is clear to me that the novels must also make their own way within the responsiveness of the individual reader.

I will begin by examining specific but brief scenes in *The Book and the Brotherhood* and outlining the broad contours of *The Message to the Planet,* as a preparation for engaging in a study of some central metaphors in Murdoch's next novel, *The Green Knight.* A few small episodes from *The Message to the Planet* illuminate something important about Murdoch's mastery over technique. At one crazed point in his obsessive, Kafkaesque experience, Alfred Ludens, whose surname evokes the image of *homo ludens* and is ultimately connected to the idea of play and interpretation, comes upon a shed full of muddled up, injured bicycles. Their presence on the estate is carefully heralded by a posted sign. Ludens, marred to a satiric degree by his reliance on book culture and its accompanying semiotic confusions, instantly begins to interpret what seems to be the locutionary force of this sign: "Free Bicycles. Ludens contemplated the notice which was prominently set up inside the gates on the side of the gravel drive. Free bi-

cycles? Unwanted bicycles offered gratis? Bicycles released to wander like free-range hens? Or a protest: unjust to bicycles, bicycles lib?" (p. 67). The exact genesis and status of these bicycles are never given, but Ludens, in this essentially charming scene, comically stands in for the reader faced with a text and a feeling of compulsion toward its interpretation. Like every other image in this densely written book, however, the bicycles are part of a larger pattern that passes incrementally through the plot. First, there is the description of Ludens's potential fiancée, Irina, on her bicycle going for a ride with him and then her final appearance with her preferred lover where they are also on bikes. Second, we are told that the current area of Ludens's historical scholarship is a study of Leonardo who, inter alia, was the inventor or conceiver of the bicycle. Finally, compellingly, the novel takes us into a dream sequence that strikes at the heart of the novel:

> He dreamt that he was in a large empty room, lit from above by grey daylight, rather like one of the studios of the art college, only larger. He was alone, standing in the middle of the room, frightened, expecting some person or some happening. A door opened at the far end and Leonardo came in. Leonardo was tall, young, with long pale flowing hair and brilliant luminous eyes. He was dressed in a long white smock or shirt which might have been a painter's overall, but which Ludens realised was the garb of a priest. He felt at that moment a wave of delicious and terrible emotion. . . . [Leonardo] said to Ludens in a peremptory tone, 'You must go on your bicycle and take this message to Milan.' He handed the piece of paper to Ludens. Ludens said, 'B-b-but, sir, I haven't got a b-b-b-bicycle.' Leonardo, pointing to the paper, said, 'There's your bicycle!' Ludens looked down and saw the drawing of the bicycle which he had shown to Irina. He cried, 'But, sir, this is not a bicycle, this is a drawing of a bicycle.' Leonardo said, 'You can ride it if you try hard enough.' As he turned to go Ludens called after him, 'What about the message?' The reply was, 'That is the message.'

(pp. 281-82)

In keeping with the narrator's slippery feeling for aporia or connotative dead-endedness, this dream is left without comment and the text abruptly turns to the more frivolous preoccupations of the novel's characters. The resonance of Ludens's quasi-nightmare is both comical and profound, but it is clear that Murdoch as implied authorial voice intends readers to do their own work. The novel's commitment to exploring the nuances and snares of the spiritual life infuses even an apparently secular dream, for Leonardo appears as a priest (of meaning and interpretation perhaps). Ludens's stammer, which occurs only when he is neurotically upset, is in evidence and indicates that even his subconscious responds through his physical disability. The art historical reference to the Surrealist movement in painting is particularly important, in that it reminds the reader that, within Murdoch's subtle revisions of realism, art—and by extension her novels as well—is significantly sur-real, anti-real, in touch with the irrational and contin-gent. Ludens's objection that a drawing of a bicycle can't be ridden to Milan like a real bicycle evokes the most famous painting of the genre, Magritte's *pictorial* representation of a pipe labelled *Ceci n'est pas une pipe,* which reminds the viewer that the various forms of mimesis are not equivalent to the *Ding an sich* of the phenomenal world. A painting of a pipe is not a pipe. A picture of a bicycle is a representation whose empirical function is automatically symbolic.

Most crucially for this novel, the idea of message is fore-fronted in the dream and throughout the fiction, for Ludens is convinced that Marcus Vallar, with what Ludens perceives as his nearly supernatural power, can write out and *publish* a salvational message to the vio-lent, damaged, post-holocaust planet. At the point of re-union with Ludens after a long, mysterious absence, Marcus had indicated that he did indeed have a mes-sage, or perhaps *was* in himself a message. In the light of such illusionary power, he had dubbed Ludens his messenger, vaguely and rather incoherently following the pattern of John the Baptist's role during Jesus' preparation for his ministry. As the novel demonstrates, the vehicle of human desire for a sublime coherence is not a practical reality but an artifact, a picture, some-thing made from individual human genius and yearning, something that doesn't exist in the phenomenal world but that we can somehow learn to ride intelligently when we know its and our limitations and capacities. The message of the novel is that there is *no* message to the planet beyond the rubble out of and through which we ride as well as we can, hoping not to be intruded upon by fantasy and the unreality of ecstatic solutions, keeping on the road to a symbolic Milan.

The length of my discussion of one image, touching on the profundity of these two scenes' most obvious con-notations will, I hope, serve to indicate how endless the task of literary criticism is when one thinks about this complex, image-spinning novel. It might be possible to shorten the task, but not without failing in the critic's only genuine contract—that between the work of art and our power to interpret its function in human lives, as cognition darts through the conscious and uncon-scious minds, aided by the constant pressure and ten-sion put upon us by the narration itself. There is a sig-nificant duality in any reader's reception of a work of art: on the one hand, the reader/viewer undergoes a sense of "extasis," of standing outside the boundaries of our lived quotidian life; on the other hand, the work of art causes us to reflect steadily on our own broken, dis-jointed, experienced world. This intermingling of two realms constitutes the primary nature of our reception of art, and in this sense it is unlike our apprehension of any other human experience. It also means that each reader/critic has a specific and difficult responsibility to

develop and ponder the to-and-fro movement of the work's inter-suggestive detail. Readers interpret not only the broad outline of the characters and action, but also the local line-by-line, word-by-word detail. As I said previously, leaning on Fine's theory of NOA, all problems are local, all tasks immediate, all attention to-tal.

Of her three most recent novels, ***The Book and the Brotherhood*** can perhaps most simply and directly be used as a methodological paradigm for key elements in Murdoch's work. Applying such an argument to this atypical novel requires a reasoned explanation. I will begin by going back to ***Nuns and Soldiers*** (1980), where Anne Cavidge, a nun who has left the convent after 15 years to rejoin the secular world, picks up on novel-reading, a frivolous pastime that she had for-sworn during her period of religious vocation: "She in-spected them with amazement. There was so much het-erogeneous *stuff* in a novel. She had been interested in pictures once. . . . One day she walked along the river as far as the Tate Gallery and looked at the Bonnards. They affected her rather as the novels did, marvellous, but too much. . . . Anne had been reading *Little Dor-rit,* it was amazing, it was so crammed and chaotic, and yet so touching, a kind of miracle, a strangely naked display of feeling, and full of profound ideas, yet one felt it was all true!" (pp. 53-54). ***The Book and the Brotherhood*** is like conventional novels of the sort de-scribed by Anne Cavidge's reaction in its being crammed with heterogeneous stuff, and brimming with complex episodes that can at first look chaotic. In addi-tion to this sense of repleteness or plenitude, it also in-cludes ironic parodies of the traditional novel—comedic closure in marriage, for example, and the overly fortu-itous tying up of the futures and destinies of all of the characters. There is an ostensibly omniscient narrator, a strong antagonist and a doubtful protagonist, and a care-ful alignment of characters over a broad range of points of view. Its putative slogan is enunciated by Jenkin Riderhood, who is perhaps the novel's most admirable character: "The brotherhood of western intellectuals versus the book of history." This tidy way of dealing with ***The Book and the Brotherhood,*** however, doesn't correspond to the puzzling experience of reading the book, although Charles Newman, reviewing it in *The New York Times Review of Books,* exuberantly reacted to it as an amazing, crowded, multiply complex novel that was everything an extended fiction should and can be, in addition to being brilliantly political without mentioning or being bogged down by the specific de-tails of politics.

Why, then, does the experience of reading this novel with care work so strongly against such straightforward exuberance and generalization? I have always found it impossible to imagine Murdoch's actual process of writ-ing. I know, of course, about the fountain pen, the time conscientiously set aside, the extraordinary fecundity of her plot-spinning imagination, her careful planning and subsequent conviction of authorial control over and knowledge of what she is doing. But I cannot conjecture where and how and through what constructive thought processes her manifold affects are produced. Habitual novel readers always begin their analysis with the narrator, and certainly the apparently omniscient narrators of the novels are difficult to pin down. In *The Book and the Brotherhood,* one can perceive the choices being made about which minds to enter and in what order. In offering an analytic presentation of individual characters, the narrator is capacious, generous, amusing, and often heartbreakingly direct. There is, nevertheless, a strong sense of constriction and limitation: This narrator strains against limitations and must be described in Bakhtinian terms as a third-person restricted narrator. The voice is one of restrained skepticism and careful silences. The shifting uncertainty of the narration obliquely demonstrates the difficulty inherent in the formation of meaning—a difficulty that the characters also have in committing themselves to action. The novel has been constructed so that the characters and reader alike experience the unfathomable and even infuriating difficulty of locating meaning in a text. Frequently, long conversations occur without adequate identification of the speaker, so that the reader sometimes has to count back to see who is saying what, an old habit of Murdoch who, like Henry James, has a spirited interest in the dramatic functions of all fictions.

Most significantly, this restricted narrator cannot enter directly into the minds of the novel's two most dubious (perhaps wicked) characters, Violet Hernshaw and the massively negative but occluded David Crimond. Added to these peculiarities is the sense of absence: The narrator is present for reportage but for nothing else. There is a notable absence of judgment, or didactic function, or self-revelation—and, above all, of location. The reader is stymied by the absence of a sense of where this narrator might stand: From where does one view the scene? What is the perspective? Clearly this narrator is friendly but alien from us and is not connected to the characters. Perhaps this is what Thomas Nagel called the view from nowhere? One driving force behind the construction of a narrator is that one must get the technical job done: hence, in this novel, the arrangements of action and the parody of closure. In an earlier novel, *The Philosopher's Pupil* (1983), the narrator actually became part of the action—a gamesome trick much used in one way or another by contemporary novelists like Martin Amis or John Fowles. But in *The Philosopher's Pupil,* the game is unusually and elaborately witty and parodic: The narrator N creates N's town or Ennistone, in which he tries to manipulate intractable characters, thereby demonstrating the impossibility of

interpreting the sequence of action he puts into play. As in *The Book and the Brotherhood,* he forces closure and then smugly, cleverly reflects on his job:

> The end of any tale is arbitrarily determined. As I now end this one, somebody may say: but how on earth do you know all these things about all these people? Well, where does one person end and another person begin? It is my role in life to listen to stories. I also had the assistance of a certain lady.

> THE END

> (p. 576)

Where does a character begin? Where does a narrator? Where a novelist?

Unsettling as the narrator's mystery is in *The Book and the Brotherhood,* the presentation of character and event is equally slippery—or perhaps the trickiness of the narrator fundamentally alters the potential securities of the novel. Certainly there is an interestingly evocative structure based on plausible triads: first, there are the flower women, Rose, Lily and Violet, who like Milton's flower lady, Eve, are unable to concentrate on very much beyond their own passional nature. The more absorbing triad of men compellingly falls into the symbolic Hindu pattern suggested at the beginning of the book when Crimond's intense, grim, concentrated Highland dancing reminds Jenkin of Shiva. The association of the women with flowers indicates something deeply old-fashioned if not entirely Miltonic and hence genuinely satiric: Lily, and, particularly, Rose define themselves only in terms of the men, living and dead, on whom their dull lives are built. Violet's dangerously neurotic self-pity and destructive mothering of Tamar, the only novelistically well-developed example of the younger generation, also appear to spring from the fact that she cannot have a life or the will to live without the accompaniment of a man or his money. Because no adequate man appears on the scene until Gideon takes over the situation late in the book, Tamar must take on the male role, bury her academic hopes, quit Oxford, and support the catastrophic Violet. Jean Cambus too defines her life in terms of men, and escapes the trilogy only because she is a pawn between the two major male antagonists, Crimond and Gerard Hernshaw, while her husband Duncan, like Jean, holds a fully human—active, but nonsymbolic—role in the novel. If Crimond is Shiva the destroyer god, then Gerard, with his languid allegiance to the classics of western culture, can be read as Vishnu the preserver. Holding the balance is the third figure in the trinity—Brahma the creator, who in the development of Hinduism diminished as Vishnu and Shiva shared power over the universe. Jenkin Riderhood ambiguously plays the role of a doomed Brahma.

This schematized, structural reading is ingenious, and may be one of the tricks built almost casually into the formal aspect of the novel. It certainly in no way corresponds to the reader's discontent. Putting aside Crimond momentarily, as well as the renewed Tamar who is set to become an ominous power figure at the end, we are left with characters who are limp, helpless, almost effete. The central characters are in their fifties and are mostly idle. Only Jenkin really works for a living, while Crimond toils on, unabashedly financed by the brotherhood who are now his enemies, for an unconscionable number of years on his great book. The arrogant, younger character, Gulliver Ashe, is too conceited to submit to a menial job; everybody else either retires early or sits helplessly around, contemplating a long gone golden youth when Sinclair—Rose's brother and Gerard's lover—was still alive. His accidental death seems to have frozen their developmental capacities decades ago, and although we can perhaps follow their lives with sympathy, their claustrophobic stalling diminishes them.

Indeed, there is something decidedly surreal about these characters, as though they are frozen pictures emerging from the subconscious. Plausible to an uncanny degree, they also feel like tricks of the spirit, or like the uncommitted moral flotsam and jetsam that makes them an easy target for the evil impersonated by Crimond. Their separation from the opaqueness of a continuously sought after, almost inconceivable good is palpable and is part of the overriding feeling of absence in this novel. Their paralysis appears to come from something profound, a failure to commit themselves to the present, and to a sense of energized meaning that might force them into purposeful action. Sinclair, dead, unwillingly governs them, and even the belligerent spirit of the old professor, Levquist, at the Tolstoyan opening of the novel, is unable to goad their central representative, Gerard, into useful activity. They live in a state of nostalgic reminiscence of their younger lives and of the culture they learned in university. Levquist makes it clear that Gerard has frittered away his life and that it is too late now to write the book on Plotinus. With no capacity for self-evaluation, Gerard assumes his superiority to Jenkin Riderhood in front of their old teacher, only to be caught up short by Levquist's acerbic tongue: "A pity he's let his Greek slip so. He knows several modern languages. As for 'getting anywhere', ridiculous phrase, he's teaching isn't he? Riderhood doesn't need to get anywhere, he walks the path, he exists where he is. Whereas you . . . were always dissolving yourself into righteous discontent, thrilled in your bowels by the idea of some high thing elsewhere. So it has gone on" (p. 24). It is starkly and depressingly true that Gerard is stalled by his languid desire for mountaintops and philosophical spiritual summits. He lives falsely and egotistically within a mind-dependent image of himself on some spiritual and moral high ground. At the same time he, like so many other characters in the book, is

unable to commit himself to the quotidian world, to seeing and acting in order to create, if not meaning, at least the necessity of commitment within his present milieu.

Setting himself up against the destructive power of Crimond, Gerard waxes briefly but wanes rapidly. At the end of the novel, when he declares that he will study and work toward a definitive, crushing book that will serve as an antidote to the impressive tome Crimond has finally finished, one cannot believe him. The only acceptable interpretation I can see is that Gerard's plans fit into the parodic design of the novel's closure. In this respect, his ambition is equivalent to Jean and Duncan Cambus's second reclamation of their marriage, as they head, both keeping their lies and secrets to themselves, into a life of idle, unproductive "happiness" in France. In other words, Gerard moves from forefront to background, and the reader is left with the sense that he is at best an uncertain antagonist to Crimond. Murdoch devises the structure so that readers are left to work out their own interpretation of the ending to the novel, and indeed that final resolution is subjective or mind-dependent to an extraordinary degree.

It is important to note too that as the reader becomes committed to *The Book and the Brotherhood,* there is an accompanying commitment to certain ideas of anti-realism which can be profitable within the mimetic practice of fiction. The sense that these characters live in a crowded, locatable phenomenal world where people act and stories happen is undercut by their surreal aspect. This frozen unreality battles against the narrator's sympathy for them and entrance into their hearts and minds. If the narrator were more reliable, more perspectively situated, this novel would be more in line with conventional realism. In other words, the taut anti-realist and anti-foundational functioning of the novel, so crucial to its place in experimental modes, would evaporate. Murdoch's task is notably large and exacting, because, within the performative direction of this fiction, she opens up technical paths that occlude traditional realism and strike out toward a world where the mind does its own choosing.

The Book and the Brotherhood can thus be read as a sour commentary on the difficulties human beings confront when they try to work through the formation of meaning to the point of commitment and action.

Embedded in the fiction, however, is another important struggle that alters the contours of the novel and reduces the interpretation I have been at pains to adumbrate. This struggle centers on Jenkin Riderhood, the only character at home in the world and all its smallest particularities. Humble and unpretentious, he is neither bound to the past nor dismissive of the two would-be antagonists, Crimond and Gerard. When Levquist says that he walks the path, that he just is what he is, we rapidly indentify him as one of Murdoch's characters of the good. He is the only character among the brotherhood who tries for genuine perspective and wishes to locate himself within meaning and significance: He says, "Well, where is my battle? I'd like to be somewhere out at the edge of things. But where is the edge?" (p. 16), and later Gerard mentally acknowledges his power: "Gerard had always recognised his friend as being, in some radical even metaphysical sense, more solid than himself, more dense, more real, more contingently existent, more full of being. . . . It was also paradoxical (or was it not?) that Jenkin seemed to lack any strong sense of individuality and was generally unable to 'give much of an account of himself'. Whereas Gerard, who was so much more intellectually collected and coherent, felt sparse, extended, abstract by contrast" (pp. 122-23).

Jenkin says that he just wants to know what is happening on the planet, but he keeps the book he is reading on liberation theology a secret from Gerard, almost as though he were shielding his frailer friend from reality. His sudden death shocks even the immovable Crimond, whose activities and interferences are the principal agents of that death, to tears. Jenkin's extinction leads to a series of narcissistic internal narratives, in which central characters among the book's inhabitants egotistically warp the tale in order to make themselves its guilty center. The characters' unreliability, their need to interpret through the lens of their own being, is an illustration *in parva* of the generative fecundity of experimentation within this novel.

Jenkin is a hint in the fiction of a better world of acting, doing, living within workable meaning. He has no narcissistic image of himself at the center of things and is satisfied with the fringe. When Gerard "proposes" to him, Jenkin breaks into a *fou rire,* while at the same time he is sensitive to what it is in Gerard that would lead to such a proposal. In like vein, and unlike Gerard, Rose, and Gull, he alone declines to deride and belittle Crimond's Marxist project; instead, he cuts through to the heart of the matter: "Look, David, it won't do. . . . There's a large lie in it somewhere" (p. 341). Brief, trenchant, without bitterness or jealousy, Jenkin's statement has the ring of truth—and oddly enough the reader believes this very brief critique, although the contents and central argument of Crimond's great book are never revealed to us. In other words, we sense truth, because we see someone acting on it. At the heart of the novel, then, the real antagonists are Crimond and Jenkin, potential evil versus potential good. Jenkin lives in the novel to extend a temporary, limited, but just estimation of the plight of others, rather than as an agent of antagonism. His violent removal from the plot leaves Crimond withdrawn and in some perhaps minor way defeated.

On the other hand, Crimond as character forms a significant link between this secular novel and the intensely complex, doubly plotted next novel, *The Message to the Planet.* As part of an entirely secular novel, Crimond can be perceived as a magical source of power, whose primary attribute is a misuse of others. He exudes a conviction that the very concept of the soul in a bourgeois, Marxist-leaning, self-absorbed world is pointless: "What's the use of a soul, that gilded idol of selfishness! I've sold it and I'm going to *do something* with the power I've got in exchange. . . . You all idolise your souls, that is yourselves" (p. 340). Mysterious and fascinating, Crimond is grim within the many realms of his destructive power. But he also wishes to create, like Shiva, whose metaphor is simultaneous destruction and creation. With Gerard/Vishnu weakened, and without the balancing power of Brahma, he represents the materialist, technologically driven, intellectually rarefied anti-soul of a terrifying new world order.

IV

Crimond's spiritual/mystical counterpart in *The Message to the Planet* is Marcus Vallar, a tormented man whose dubious powers begin with the Christlike restoration of the almost dead Patrick to life. Patrick is a poet, who lyrically eulogizes his savior, and becomes, as another character puts it, a "resurrection bore." (I lack the space to balance the morally horrific secular plot, seen through the consciousness of Franca, against the hermeneutical one, interpreted by Ludens; I will concentrate briefly only on the latter.) Ludens jealously attaches himself to Marcus, assured that he can become the effective agent of Marcus's great book which, in Ludens's obsessed view, will send a necessary and absolute message to the planet. It is oddly interesting that Ludens, a secular, Kafkaesque Jew, should adore (even idolize) Marcus—but technically he is necessary to highlight the ambiguous problem of meaning within the novel. Again, that meaning is entirely mind-dependent, because Ludens, playing with his interpretations, creates an idea of Marcus that the action and diverse thought patterns of the novel are calculated to deny. Ludens's view of events is manically book-oriented, and never during Marcus's lifetime does Ludens give up on the idea that the written word is utterly central. He buys pens and notebooks for Marcus, he cajoles him, he tries himself to take notes on the contradictory and shifting intellectual fumblings that Marcus gropes through. Hopelessly dismayed by Marcus's sudden access to mystical power, not only over New Age travelers but over virtually everyone else, Ludens is particularly unnerved by the startling authority Marcus, during his "showings," has over the skeptical and truth-telling Gildas.

Marcus is a remarkable human and novelistic phenomenon, a creation at once readable as an evil, power-seeking charlatan and equally interpretable as a positive phenomenon, particularly in his brooding over the unspeakable pain of the Holocaust and during his powerful manifestations of himself to the crowds on the porch of his cottage at the private mental hospital where, according to his cynical daughter Irina, he richly deserves to be. Ludens's fiction-making, mind-dependent antirealism misinterprets Marcus at every turn, a factor which helps to hide him in plain view. At the same time, Marcus seems to be an exemplification of Murdoch's view of the ontological proof: His spirituality and divine message are created by the perceiver out of some magnetic energy that he possesses. Thus, little Fanny looks at him entranced and enchanted, Gildas kneels, and even Ludens, who finally reluctantly stands at some distance before him, looks and finds his own interpretation—not of the holy, but of the horrors of the spiritual world: "With a slight effort, [he] managed to focus his attention on the face. . . . It was as if Marcus's head, leaving his body and very much enlarged, had advanced towards him, hanging in space at a point half-way from the yew wall and the Stone. The face that he saw was contorted with grief . . . and the most dreadful fear" (p. 428). Consumed with anguish over the Holocaust, seeing himself as does Rozanov in *The Philosopher's Pupil* as beyond good and evil (and hence evil, as Gildas emphatically states), Marcus is also a wounded monster, a new Minotaur, a human reflection of mythic horror. Ludens has heard Marcus describe himself, and no doubt this information feeds Ludens's image of him: "It was as if some evil being came to me and overthrew everything and accused me of everything and made me see myself as something terrible, something loathsome, a monster" (p. 378). The brilliant but unreadable psychiatrist, Marzillian, sees him as someone headed inexorably for death, but even he cannot unravel his mystery or decode the mysterious language he records from Marcus's bedroom shortly before his death. Marcus finally represents something wholly other, mysterious, beyond psychiatry, a spiritual being whose local habitation and name are insufficient to the humbler tasks of reality. He is an image or a series of images and metaphors, but as Gildas says in another context: "One must beware of images, they console and are made to be destroyed" (p. 416). In the stringency of Murdoch's novels, this statement indicates why Marcus must take leave of life and of the novel.

V

While Marcus Vallar is a compellingly mysterious image larger than the human subject's capacity to understand, the Green Knight of the next novel is even more so. This is not merely because he is necessarily the more interesting character, but because he derives his very existence from the heart of literature, not only through his intertextual rubbing against the fourteenth-century poem, *Sir Gawain and the Green Knight,* writ-

ten in the West Midland dialect, but because he is so self-consciously a construction outside the arena of rational discourse. In a sense one can argue that Crimond, Marcus Vallar, and Peter Mir (the Green Knight) are all out of the range of our perception, except through the surfaces of their actions and words. Each of them is veiled from us by the narrator and as such kept beyond our interpretative range.

The only other novel that departs from Murdoch's normative but unusual rendition of realism so boldly is *A Fairly Honourable Defeat* (1970), where she worked out an atypical allegory of the eternal combat between Christ and Satan, good and evil, for the human soul. The Trinity is bizarrely represented as a moribund family, where only Tallis, the Christ figure, will be able to endure in a world where the great angels have been set free to abuse their moral intelligence. Julius King, the Satan figure, bears some relation to Lucas Graffe of *The Green Knight,* but nothing in the analogy really holds up to serious analysis. Murdoch's vocabulary when talking about her work is infectious, and ever since her first novel, *Under the Net* (1954), critics have written endlessly about her opposing the artist with the saint. The creation of metaphoric (or allegorical) characters in *The Green Knight,* however, is quite separate from and qualitatively different than any novel that precedes it. Although it is clear that the Green Knight (Peter Mir) and Lucas Graffe are in opposition as two powerful magicians, one possibly good and the other evil, the focus of the novel is on Peter Mir.

Rivaled only by Dickens in her name-play, Murdoch here outdoes herself, calling attention by having Peter Mir translate his surname from Russian as meaning both "world" and "peace." No one needs to be told that Peter is the rock on which the Christian church was founded. This latter identification leads us into an allusive tangle, because Moy, of whom more later, lives amid collected rocks and stones, which she endows with spirit, moving them through her adolescent psychokinetic power. The name game does not end there, of course, and can drive one into a veritable tizzy of association. After Peter Mir, however, the naming of the three teen-aged Anderson sisters by their now dead father as Alethea, Sophia, and Moira—Truth, Wisdom, Destiny—is most significant. In depicting these three, Murdoch takes on her biggest challenge in the book—to give them both allegorical and "real" existence. The three have long since taken matters into their own hands, labeling themselves Aleph, Sefton, and Moy, but the problem persists and is, indeed, elaborately expanded: Aleph as the first letter of the Hebrew alphabet is fraught with symbolism, Sefton evokes connotations, among others, of awe and high regard, and Moy, i just *moi,* "myself." The novel begins by placing them outside of the experiential world through Joan's mocking quotation of the dormouse's tale from *Alice in Wonder-*

land: "Once upon a time there were three little girls. . . . And they lived at the bottom of a well." They exist as a trilogy of fairy princesses, of ripe young women about to be plucked by life. A great deal of energy goes into an account of this plucking, or their emergence from the well or Romance tradition.

By the end of the book, they have all been transposed from the magical world of "milk"—the protective aura of the house in Hammersmith, which they inhabit as their castle of allegory. All of them, even sixteen-year-old Moy, have entered another realm, as the time of change and metamorphosis, heralded by the appearance of Peter Mir, the great shapeshifter and catalyst, and instituted by his magical symbolic being. Peter Mir's very presence scatters metaphors through the novel in a trail as lush and connotative as any tangle of weeds.

For those readers who do not know *Sir Gawain and the Green Knight,* Clement gives a vague run-through of the plot late in the novel. This poem, which is one of the glories of late medieval times, has deep resonance within this fiction, not least because Peter Mir self-consciously fashions himself as a contemporary parody of the mighty giant who disturbs the Christmas celebrations at Arthur's court by insisting on a game of death. Peter hides out in a pub called The Castle, an ironic reference to Bercilak's castle. He carries a green umbrella which is also a knife. He always wears something green, as though to present himself not as a person but as a self-contrived image. A green girdle, linked with Bercilak's lady in the poem, is picked up by Moy as she leads the Minotaur-Mir to her birthday party. As he is taken away by the demonic psychiatrist, Fonsett, ultimately to die, Peter leaves behind his last green garment, a cravat, which is taken up and carried off by Sefton.

There are, however, other important connotations in the medieval poem that I would like to call attention to. It is, above all, a poem about courage and fear, justice and mercy. Courage and justice should, in a virtuous sphere, win; in a world where the knights are not magical but human, Gawain fails not in chastity but in fear, accepting the lady's green girdle on the third day at Bercilak's court, because he is assured by the lady temptress that it will save him from the beheading he has accepted as part of the Green Knight's challenge. He expects justice, but hopes—even cheats—for mercy. The Green Knight who is also Bercilak gives him both, only nicking him on the third stroke of the axe, because he succumbed in fear to the temptation of the lady's girdle. In Murdoch's novel, Lucas receives only a small cut between the ribs (causing Clement/Mercy to faint). Lucas is no Gawain, although he is much admired as an historian and revered by most of the characters. He never acknowledges guilt, shame, or awareness of the moral intensity of the situation. It is, however, marvel-

ous to watch Peter Mir's performance of mercy after he has followed an almost Shylock-like path of revenge. His insistence on reenacting in the park the original scene which "killed" him leads to a flashing light and a total metamorphosis, during which he discovers what he had lost through his death and recovery: God, and an attendant mercy that transforms his murderous, justice-ridden intention. This metamorphosis within Peter Mir leads to a steady rippling of metamorphoses throughout the characters of the novel, as one era ends and another begins.

Another important point stemming from the original Gawain poem has to do with two important details left out by Clement in his rough summary of the story. The gigantic Green Knight with his green horse carries a sprig of holly in his hand. His real castle is a burial mound. He is at a remove from the potential source material for the poem, in that he is a sort of nature god, lord of the living in nature and the dead. Elderly Welsh folk still talk about childhoods where Christmas had no Dylan Thomas sentimentality but involved taking birds and holly through the woods to propitiate the malign spirits of nature. In Murdoch's novel, Peter's magnetic power seems to be connected with nature: The technicians of modern medicine are at a loss over the wound of the Philoctetes figure, Harvey, but Peter Mir lays on his hands and the foot instantly responds. Moy, the rock-, spider-, animal-loving animist, as a character recognizes and "knows" Peter as he does her. On his death and the completion of everyone else's metamorphoses, she enters the sea in a pagan baptism among the seals where, like the Green Knight, she fearlessly sees death. This new Moy feels that she, like Peter Mir, must leave the world as she's known it, perhaps to go to India where the spiritual life might be more available.

The manuscript containing the original Gawain poem (Mus. Brit. Cotton Nero A, x) precedes that poem with the long didactic poem *Cleannesse,* which has always been seen as ideologically tied to *Gawain.* The connotation of cleanness as virtue in all its connotations is present in the doubly plotted tale of the Gawain poet, and the temptation to its opposite, uncleanness, is evoked in both plots as well—in its challenge to the moral purity of the Arthurian court and in the denotation of uncleanness as unchaste or defiled. The sexual underlay of Murdoch's novel is strong, with Lucas's smoldering sexuality hinted at through connections with Joan, his secret proposal to Louise long ago, and his rapacious theft of Aleph. The same is true, but somehow not as salacious, in the case of Peter Mir, who is suspected of being after Aleph, calling her the Princess Alethea and giving her, not the lovely stone necklaces that he gives to her sisters, but a diamond V-shaped collar—V for Veritas or the Virtue in his own family insignia, *Virtuti Paret Robur.* Murdoch's novels always crackle with erotic energy, about which not enough has been written or said, and in this one there is a passionate sense of hidden Eros.

Peter Mir's primary identification for most readers is, no doubt, his Christlike identification through his death and resurrection. Dogged realists will continue to fault Murdoch for this "death," which is, like Desdemona's, medically lax. Slammed on the head with a weighted baseball bat (for Americans, this sounds odd, but I assume it is a short leaded rounders bat, not the three-foot-plus thing swung by American players in their national sport), Peter Mir apparently dies but is revived magically and secretly by a team of Aesculapian doctors of whom Fonsett is the demonic representative. By superhuman strength, Peter maintains an aura of normal humanity during a brief period before he is reclaimed by the doctors and relapses to the world of the dead. Like the Old Testament God, he is justice itself until metamorphosed into the mercy of Christ. I myself do not put much stress on this interpretation, finding it not as interesting as his related identifications, especially those associated with his role as scapegoat and his possible apocalyptic function.

For a partial reading of his performance as scapegoat, I turn briefly to the work of René Girard, in his book of that title.[5] Girard's theory of mimetic desire, in which one person's love object is claimed or mimetically desired by another, is played out by Lucas Graffe's interpretation of his brother Clement's love for their mother. Lucas's resulting hatred leads to a determination to kill his brother, Cain-like, for that mother's preferring Clement over him. As Girard sees it, mimetic violence, when it arises, can only be stopped by claiming an innocent victim and putting him to death as an embodiment of the obstacle to all desires. Thus, there is constant potentiality for mimetic violence between twinned antagonists. Within this rigid scheme, Peter Mir can be seen as the innocent victim—as was Christ, as was the Minotaur, in whom Murdoch is also deeply interested in this novel and in *The Message to the Planet*. I mentioned earlier in this paper that theory fails as a response to the fluidity of Murdoch's fiction, and I therefore want to cut against the grain of Girard's idea by referring to the idea of the apocalyptic which is also strong in *The Green Knight.*

Peter Mir, during his premetamorphic manifestation as Justice, quotes an image that, as Lucas points out, is used both in Isaiah and Revelation: "The heavens shall be rolled together—as a scroll—" (p. 253). In the Apocalypse, this occurs after the opening of the sixth seal and indicates the end of life in the universe. The two brothers engage in a fascinating conversation about Peter's possible existence in an after-death state—in a *bardo* (like Charles Arrowby in *The Sea, The Sea*), or the Christian limbo, or Hades, or, as Lucas puts it, "the brain may continue to operate in some twilight way,

ticking on like a machine" (p. 254). In apocalyptic thinking, men appear from the skies or from nowhere, rather than being violently killed and hence excluded from society. An apocalyptic arrival can be seen in the person of Peter Mir (or the Green Knight in the medieval poem) as an abrupt and unstoppable inclusion of a concealed person or spirit whose authority is imposed on the world. Peter Mir demands that he be allowed into the tight coterie of the novel's characters, having no friends or connections of his own except for the jaunty Australian publican at The Castle. His entrance leads to a metaphoric millennium conceived through the idea of metamorphosis. At the end of the book, all is changed, and the apocalyptic being exits of his own free will. As he says to Bellamy, "Now I can go straight on *through* it all" (p. 354).

Peter Mir exists at the extreme boundaries of real life and the spiritual world, through both of which we wander as we read, following now this lead, now that, now this myth, now that. As a liminal figure, he participates in both worlds but cannot be clearly located. His places fade, and we are left remembering his transfiguration, his magnetism, his total commitment to enacting a metaphorically constructed emblem, trying to make his way in the experiential world. As a thinker, Iris Murdoch is committed to agency and action within the material world, whereas Peter Mir is pledged to hearkening in this limbo to a different spiritual sphere. His temporary "life" within a literary work is insubstantial and the contradictory literary self he presents throughout the novel is not important to his ultimate function. He does *not* fit in the assemblage of characters; apparently, he does not want to—his will is other-oriented, and what he perceives in people is their moral, spiritual, or allegorical being. Of course he loves truth, and so Alethea; he recognizes wisdom and book-learning and admires Sefton; he *knows* who Moy is. In order to "go through it all" as an apocalyptic figure, he goes from death to resurrection and life in the world and back to death. He has begun the new era, and like Christ, the original apocalyptic figure in western culture, he departs, leaving it behind.

Who is the Moy he knows and who knows him? Who is this late adolescent girl who lives her life in an experienced present and ponders a difficult future? She is what Peter Mir was in a sense, but whereas he is made of images, she, perhaps, is the only anti-metaphorical anti-mythical character in the book. She sees the details, the suffering, she is at home in the natural world and full of imaginative creativity, of yearning love for all beings. She is also a creature of loss, of suffering, of a world that she chooses not to mess up with book learning. Her loss of the beloved dog Anax breaks her heart even more than the fact that she can never have

Harvey, her heart's desire. Like a sprite, she embodies human spiritual yearning, committed to the world to which the reader is condemned.

The final character I want to look at briefly is Bellamy James, who is oddly emblematic of the strength as well as the folly of humankind. I think he stands for the vagaries of the human spirit—and in his weaknesses and inchoate love he, like the feckless Frances in **The Black Prince,** stands in for us. Comically afflicted by fantasies about angels, and especially the warrior archangel Michael, he is absurdly greedy for romanticized religious experience. He wants visions, the dark night of the soul, and all the tempting images of religious consolation. Finally, and above all, he wants to serve Peter Mir, who unwillingly becomes his Christ. Drolly chided by his priest for his vaguely gnostic fancies, he nevertheless is a bel-ami (as Percival called himself in Chrétien's romance), someone who crosses all boundaries and is loved or tolerated by everyone in the book. Emil seizes him and the wonderful Anax at the end of the novel and returns him to life in the world, although he remains full of spiritual longings. He loves both the evil Lucas and the metamorphic Peter Mir and is a figure of two worlds—the metaphoric and the real. His stumbling presence ties the novel more firmly to the "real" than anything else in the book. His double participation represents the human valence of Murdoch's artistic endeavor. The reader, like Bellamy, tends to want a world energized by spirit and has to settle for considerably less. The English painter and mystic, Cecil Collins, expresses what Bellamy wants through art and the spiritual life: "Art is a point of interpenetration between worlds, as a marriage of the known with the unknown, for it is the unknown that freshens our life. In Art we can converse with that abundant life whose energy glows through the sad terrestrial curtain of time."[6]

Iris Murdoch's novels, on the other hand, strive to exist at the crossroads adumbrated by Peter Mir and Marcus Vallar and even the brittle, mysterious Crimond. Whereas her earlier novels tended to set up a dichotomy between saint and artist, she now works toward another configuration, in which a single complex character carries an enormous weight of metaphoric power beyond the boundaries of the possible. It is this sense of stretch that makes the most recent novels so ambitious from both a spiritual and literary point of view. It also makes them tough, experimental, tenuous, unabsorbable. Murdoch, who has never read the work of Mikhail Bakhtin, operates fully within his definition of the "unfinalizability" of the literary work—that sense that the last word about our lives cannot be written nor the final analysis achieved.

Notes

1. Iris Murdoch, *Metaphysics as a Guide to Morals* (New York: Allen Lane/Penguin Press, 1993); hereafter referred to as *Metaphysics*.

2. Arthur Fine. "Science Made Up: Constructivist Sociology of Scientific Knowledge," in *The Disunity of Science: Boundaries, Contexts, and Power,* eds. P. Galison and D. Stump (Stanford: Stanford University Press, 1995).

3. C. S. Peirce. *Collected Papers,* vol. 1, ed. Charles Hartshorne and Paul Weiss (Cambridge: Harvard University Press, 1960), sec. 339.

4. Jonathan Bate, *Shakespeare and Ovid* (Oxford: Clarendon Press, 1993).

5. René Girard, *The Scapegoat,* trans. Yvonne Freccero (Baltimore: Johns Hopkins University Press, 1982).

6. Cecil Collins. *A Retrospective Exhibition* (London: Tate Gallery, 1989), 37.

Zahra A. Hussein Ali (essay date 1997)

SOURCE: Ali, Zahra A. Hussein. "A Spectrum of Image-Making: Master Metaphors and Cognitive Acts in Murdoch's *Bruno's Dream.*" *Orbis Litterarum* 52, no. 4 (1997): 259-79.

[*In the following essay, Ali investigates the role of metaphor in* Bruno's Dream, *which Murdoch used not merely to illuminate character or theme, but to demarcate "the characters' progressions along their individual spiritual journeys."*]

One of the fascinating aspects of **Bruno's Dream** is the way Iris Murdoch employs metaphors to invigorate the text with tension.[1] In this novel, metaphor-making is not merely a device to further aesthetize descriptions of objects, nor is it a handy index which reveals the psychological make-up of the characters, nor yet is it an instrument to elucidate vague realities; it is paradoxically, and yet intrinsically, an act of weaving problematics and conflict into the perception of various important realities: the reality of self-identity, the reality of other or non-self, and the reality of Good, the Murdochian equivalent of God.[2] It is thus unjust to make judgments similar to the one Richard Todd has made in his introductory book on Iris Murdoch; Todd wrote:

> "An area of potential though self-imposed disadvantage may lie in the very use of the flashback mode, which presents Bruno's arachnological and philatelic interests as thin, concessive tokens not integrally characterizing him in the way that Ducane's [a character in Murdoch's *The Nice and the Good*] interests in Roman Law may be said actually to illuminate the latter's personality."[3]

This paper intends, therefore, to analyse metaphor-making (Bruno's "arachnological interests" being at the heart of this human activity), as an inadequate act of cognition, and to explain the necessity of effacing all metaphors; it is my argument that this act of effacement is the proper gauge to demarcate the extent of the progression of the spiritual journeys all the major characters seem to undertake. Because metaphors abound in the text, I will be highly selective; this study will exclude synchronically limited and extemporally forged metaphors, and will concern itself with master metaphors: metaphors that are consciously constructed as willful acts of cognition, *i.e.*, purposive readings of self and the ontological world; let me add that the focus of this paper necessarily entails excluding some characters who, though major, do not possess master metaphors.

In her theoretical speculations on Platonic discourse Murdoch points out that the imagination is not morally neutral; metaphors, as the articulation of the imagination par excellence, are very serious matters because they shape our moral visions and our self-identity. They can illuminate but they can also be a bane and a blindness to the spiritual eye within. In *Metaphysics as a Guide to Morals* she writes:

> "Moral improvement . . . involves a progressive destruction of false images. Image-making or image-apprehending is always an imperfect activity, some images are higher than others, that is nearer to reality. Images should not be resting places, but pointers toward higher truths. The implication is that the highest activities of the mind, as in mathematics and mysticism, are imageless."[4]

Image-making then, is ineluctably discordant with truth-seeking, yet we think in images; it is our dominant mode of cognition, and often, we are tempted to substitute image for reality.

Bruno's Dream is pivoted on two central presences: the solid actuality of death and the monolithic image of the spiders. Janie Greensleave, Bruno's wife, Gwen, his daughter, Maureen, his mistress, Parvati, his Indian daughter-in-law, are all dead, and Bruno himself hardly leaves his deathbed as he obsessively ponders his approaching mortality. As for the spiders, Bruno peers over voluminous entomological books; in his room we encounter dead and live spiders, and many of his dreams enfigure them.

From an aesthetic and formal perspective, characterization in the text is controlled by a taxonomy of metaphors: the spiders signify conceptualized, closed readings of reality or cognition (characters as ordinary, average human beings), while death signifies perceptual (or visionary) open readings (mystics.) From a philosophical and a thematic perspective, death and spiders generate symmetrical patterns of juxtaposition; Bruno and Lisa weave metaphors at the opposite end of a spectrum: Bruno perceives self and God in total concretion—he is a spider; God is a spider. Lisa, however,

signifies God in total silence, in imagelessness; Bruno's discourse is that of the completely sayable, whereas Lisa continuously pays tribute to the unsayable. Indeed, Bruno's metaphor-making and Lisa's refusal of it are allegories of fundamentally opposed modes of being: materialism and asceticism. The patterns of juxtaposition are symmetrical but not radically so; Murdoch's artistry blurs and opaques any rigidity in form or pattern: at the novel's end, Bruno pilgrimages toward asceticism, while Lisa succumbs to materialism and Danby Odell's sexual appeal.

Bruno's Dream opens with a depiction of the lowest stage or quality of Bruno's consciousness. In his smelly, sordid, dark room the entomologist is afflicted by remorse; he has estranged himself from Miles, his only son, by making racial remarks about not wanting "coffee-coloured grandchildren" (p. 12), and he has ignored Janie's deathbed calls and entreaties and has refused to go upstairs to hear her last words. He has been afraid of Janie's curses because of his infidelity. More poignantly, however, Bruno is afflicted with the fear of the annihilation of his consciousness:

> "Three weeks ago he had overheard Adelaide saying to Nigel, 'He won't be coming downstairs anymore'. He had felt a sense of injustice and a thrill of fright. How could he concede that 'any more?'"

> (p. 5)

Death is nothing but the dissolution of the only certain and meaningful entity that anchors his being, that is, his ego:

> "He feared something that was present with him, the whimpering frailty of his being which so dreaded extinction."

> (pp. 300-301)

Bruno must invent ways of survival: "He must, with a part of his mind, look always away from *that* [death or suffering], and not let the structure of his personality be destroyed by what it could not bear" (p. 301).

Bruno was and still is a materialist and a hedonist; as a materialist he effects will power in the face of death:

> "He must live three years anyway, he had to do that so as to cheat the income tax, to live three years was a statutory requirement. When I ought to be thinking about death I am thinking about death duties, thought Bruno. That was not really altruism. It was more like a pathetic inability, even now, to divest himself of property."

> (p. 6)

As a hedonist, he feels no guilt in having had "set house" and "played at domesticity" with seductive Maureen, a "nymph of the cinema age." And when Bruno recalls sharp, erotic images of her—Maureen—"dressed only in a blue necklace, dancing the Charleston" (p. 13) he still feels a "warm rush to the centre of that dry schematic frame" (p. 14).

But despite his wrongdoings, Bruno conceptualizes his self, to borrow a phrase from Murdoch, as a "moral centre or substance;" by deliberately moulding the conception of his past to accord with this premeditated self-image, Bruno projects himself as the victim of his family's cruelty, and not as their victimizer, even in any partial or slight sense. He protests against Janie's anger and her withholding of forgiveness: "Janie behaved so badly to me" (p. 15), and although his infidelity is obvious, he remains tragic, even more tragic than epic heroes: "Agamemnon was killed on his first night home from Troy. But Agamemnon was guilty, guilty" (p. 15). As for his estrangement from Miles, he places the blame squarely on his son:

> "It was so unfair to have been made to carry the moral burden of his careless talk, to carry it for years until it became a monstrous unwilled part of himself. He had not wanted Miles to marry an Indian girl. But how soon he would have forgotten his theories when confronted with a real girl."
>
> (p. 11)

Bruno's bedridden world is fluid and pictorial; it consists of remembering dead female faces and of browsing through the pages of voluminous spider books. To control the fear of the fragmentation of his consciousness, Bruno must seek the image of a unified self; he therefore yearns for stable forms and master metaphors. As an entomologist, Bruno seeks this image in science; he comes to believe that his metaphysical certainties must fit into the paradigm of science itself. As with scientific discourse regarding natural laws, Bruno attempts to enfigure as much as possible in the smallest number of metaphors. Under the banality of his human condition he reduces his self-identity to that of the pathetic, ageing immortality of Tithonus, but more concretely he is a spider:

> "He no longer looked into the mirror though he could feel sometimes like a mask the ghost of his much younger face. . . . He knew that he had become a monster, animal-headed, bull-headed, a captive Minotaur. He had a face now like one of his spiders, *Xysticus* perhaps, or *Oxyptila,* that have faces like toads. Below the huge emergent head the narrow body stretched away. . . . He lived in a tube now, like *Atypus,* he had become a tube. *Soma Sema.*"
>
> (p. 7)

Bruno draws the metaphoric grid tightly not only around the concept of self, but also around the concept of God. Like self, God is objectified and rationalized according to the logic of deduction which intrinsically tends to reductivism. In one scene Bruno wakes up from a nightmare and, for comfort, converses with Nigel, his live-in male nurse, about his metaphoric process of conceptualizing God:

> "When I was very young . . . I thought of God as a great blank thing, rather like the sky, in fact perhaps He *was* the sky, all friendliness and protectiveness and fondness for little children. . . . Later it was different, it was when I first started to look at spiders. Do you know, Nigel, that there is a spider called *Amaurobius* which lives in a burrow and has its young in the late summer, and then it dies when the frosts begin, and the young spiders live through the cold by eating their mother's dead body. One can't believe that's an accident. I don't know that I imagined God as having thought it all out, but somehow He was connected with the pattern, He was the pattern, He *was* those spiders which I watched in the light of my electric torch on summer nights."
>
> (p. 99)

This passage signifies cognitive and moral degeneration; from intuitive, almost imageless, phenomenological awareness of God in childhood, Bruno's mind descends into a false, imagistic, formal configuration; in childhood God is ontologically external, in adulthood God is internalized as something private and personal. This second stage of metaphor-making is not only a "semantic impertinence", to use Paul Ricœur's words, or a linguistic sayable trap, but also a catalyst of moral sensibility; here metaphor does not point beyond or deeper, it reifies itself as the embodiment of ultimate truth, of all that is necessary and transcendental. Bruno's figuration is both an epistemological impasse and an *aporia.*

It would not be going too far to say that Bruno's master metaphor functions upon his consciousness as magic and fetishism, for Bruno imbues the spiders with the allure of the ancient; he tells Adelaide that "spiders existed a hundred million years before flies existed" (p. 26), and, of course, before Man did too. Bruno confers upon them the glamour of nobility: "O spiders, spiders, spiders, those aristocrats of the creepy-crawly world, he had never ceased to love them" (p. 9); he associates them with the fascination of rituals, those "memories of summer nights when he was sixteen, seeing in the light of his electric torch the delicate egg-laying ritual of the big handsome *Dolomedes* spider;" and as their devotee he ascribes to them sacred claims upon his attention as if they were theological texts: "I ought to have been a recluse, lived in the country like an eighteenth-century clergyman with my books of theology and my spiders" (p. 9). Having failed to write extensively on spiders, and neglecting his correspondence with Vladimir Pook, the eminent Russian entomologist, Bruno feels that he has "failed" and "betrayed" the spiders; by contrast, he does not feel that he has failed his son or betrayed his wife.

Bruno's metaphor-making is a yearning for control over the contingent world, for it involves casting reality in simple dualistic forms; the pivot of this dualism is that of the male versus the female, or rather that of the centrality of the male and the marginality of the female. The intensity and the sustaining of female reality depends on the intensity of the male consciousness, and death's fragmentation of male consciousness, *i. e.,* his own, annihilates the female category altogether. Bruno muses:

> "It was odd to think that Janie and Gwen and his mother and for all he knew Maureen now existed more intensely, more really, here in his mind than they existed anywhere else in the world. They are a part of my life-dream, he thought, they are immersed in my consciousness like specimens in formalin. The women all eternally young while I age like Tithonus. Soon they will have that much less reality."

(p. 10)

Another aspect of this dualism is the male's embodiment of amorality, and the female embodiment of morality: "He had never bothered with religion, he had left that to the women, and his vision of goodness was connected not with God but with his mother" (p. 10); and in his conversation with Nigel, Bruno recounts that in adulthood God "receded altogether, He became something that the women did, a sort of female activity" (p. 100). Needless to say, Bruno gives this dualism a deterministic nature simply to serve as an easy justification for his moral laxity.

Dangerously, however, the dualistic vision engenders cynicism and nihilism in Bruno's mind; life or consciousness is only illusion and fantasy: "There is just the dream, its texture, its essence, and in our last things we subsist only in the dream of another, a shade within a shade, fading, fading, fading" (p. 10). Moral regeneration is impossible: "As one grows older . . . one becomes less moral, there is less time, one bothers less, one gets careless" (p. 10); and it is pointless: "Was there any point in starting to think about it all now, in setting up the idea of being good now, of repenting or something?" (p. 10). Bruno would like to pray, but "What is prayer if there is nobody there?" (p. 10).

Perhaps the best literary device that epitomizes the dangerous workings of metaphor-making as inadequate cognition and as a trap of solipsism is the *mise-en-abyme.* Broadly speaking this device relates to narrative structuring and achieving textual self-referentiality; literally, the term means "to be thrown into the abyss," and it connotes the "recurring internal duplication of images of an artistic whole, such that an infinite series of images disappearing into invisibility is produced—similar to what one witnesses if one looks at one's reflection between two facing mirrors."[5] One, however, can approach *mise-en-abyme* as a device for depicting the quality of consciousness, that is as a technique of characterization. Bruno's consciousness and his sense of self-identity travel between two facing mirror-images:

his actual hideous face much disfigured by cancer and the primordial spiders in his much-thumbed books; Bruno, who does not consciously look into mirrors anymore, is nevertheless peering into one constantly, and his consciousness regresses infinitely into spiritual lethargy, despair, and the vertigo of solipsism:

> "But there was no God. I am at the centre of the great orb of my life . . . until some blind hand snaps the thread. I have lived for nearly ninety years and I know nothing. I have watched the terrible rituals of nature and I have lived inside the simple instincts of my own being and now at the end I am empty of wisdom. Where is the difference between me and these little humble creatures? The spider spins its web, it can no other. I spin out my consciousness, this compulsive chatter, this idle rambling voice that will so soon be mute."

(pp. 303-304)

Let me point out in passing that I find Frank Kermode's reading of the presence of the spiders in the novel as nothing but a "brief manual of arachnology . . . deftly divided and served to us in whispers" very uncritical.[6]

Indeed, Lucien Dällenbach's remark in his excellent book, *The Mirror in the Text,* that *mise-en-abyme* signifies a "vicious circle" "depth and vertigo" and has the associations of "paradox and *aporia,*" is helpful in understanding the moral dangers of mirror-images in Murdoch's text.[7] For, Arachne-like, Bruno perceives self as solitary, fallen, and smitten with some transcendental curse. Bruno, of course, is committing idolatry, "taking the shadow for the real" as Murdoch would put it. Definitely, Bruno's room, always dark, the curtains often tightly pulled down, and his habit of figuring out the time of the day, usually after great uncertainty, by the shadows the leaking rays of the sun make on the walls, is emblematic of the Platonic myth of the cave. To exit from the cave of illusion, images should be approached, to use Murdoch's phrasing, as "ladders to be thrown away after use;" true mysticism is the effacement of imagery; in western mysticism, she once pointed out, "beyond the last image we fall into the abyss of God."[8]

Lisa Watkins, at the opposite end of the spectrum of image-making, seems, at the outset of the novel, to be in the abyss of God; she is an ex-nun of the Poor Clares Order, an ex-communist, and is now a teacher in one of the poorest sections of London. After Miles's disastrous first meeting with his father, Lisa, like a Good Samaritan, initiates an embassy of reconciliation. Not that Lisa is beyond and above the human muddle; she has passionately, yet silently, fallen in love with Miles on his wedding day to her sister Diana. Nevertheless, and in contrast to all the other characters, Lisa possesses deep respect for the old social structures, particularly marriage and family, and an ability to see the particular without tainting it with egotistic fantasy. These qualities she persistently endeavours to hold even after Miles's discovery of her secret passion, and even after his confession of mutual love. By rejecting, or by "killing" Miles's love, she intends to keep her higher love pure and "uncontaminated". Lisa's moralistic utterances are curt, imageless and austere; to the beseeching Miles she says, "You're married to Diana, she's given you her life. It's not just a calculation" (p. 225). To subvert Miles's hedonistic intentions of working out a plan for the love triangle—keeping two separate lodgings for the sisters, one as wife, the other as mistress—Lisa resorts to the wilful act of leaving England for India to volunteer for the Save the Children Fund.

Obviously, Lisa is the mouthpiece of Platonic Murdochian views, but what she particularly embodies in light of the focus of this paper is the anti-Wittgensteinian, anti-structuralist, and, one may add, very Greek and Cartesian, concept of "substantial self," that is, "self as unified active consciousness, living between appearance and reality." In other words, Lisa's characterization represents Murdoch's idea of self as a "moral centre" which stubbornly refuses to be "dislodged by psychoanalytical psychologists and 'literary' deconstruction," philosophical trends which Murdoch often discusses under the labels of "behaviourism" and "linguistic determinism."[9]

In light of the above analysis, Lisa's final surrender to Danby's love, her new "smart clothes" and her rides in a "speedy sport car," are not moral regressions as much as they are a realistic fitting into this normative concept of self; in other words, they are gestures of familiarization. Self-abnegating Lisa is afraid of committing the trangression of "nullification of the inner" by separating value or duty toward Diana and respect for marriage (what is outer) from her deep ardent passion for Miles (what is inner). Only by gauging the inner by the outer, private desires by the sense of duty to attend to external reality, does Lisa cogitate a clear, truthful, imageless understanding of her domestic dilemma, and is, therefore, able to eschew purely aesthetizing her love for her brother-in-law.[10] The acceptance of Danby's love, which is slightly more than just mundane and sexual, is a wilful flight from the temptations of the purely aesthetic. Lisa does not, as Peter Conradi contends, become a "beautiful *hetaera*" who simply "returns to the cave."[11]

Nigel's illusory mysticism may generate equivocality about Lisa's position within the spectrum of metaphor-making. I find Donna Gerstenberger's view of Nigel as an earnest "practitioner of Hindu mysticism and a source of a good deal of the book's wisdom" inaccurate.[12] Furthermore, William Hall's analysis of Nigel as the blissful "man of realisation" and as the true mystic who "alone at night progresses through the stages passed through by Buddah . . . the night before his enlightenment" is cursory.[13] That ***Bruno's Dream*** embodies two juxtaposing poles; that "at one pole of the novel

stands . . . Nigel, eastern consciousness—quietest, self-abnegating: at the other Bruno—western ego consciousness (that is significantly dying)" is indeed ungrounded.[14] Highly discriminating, though not going far enough, is Elizabeth Dipple's assessment of Nigel as a "failure" yet "useful to the fiction," as "unhinged in some radical way," a character only parodying sacred rituals, pretending that he is an "all-seeing God."[15] To clarify and secure Lisa's stance as the bearer of the highest quality of consciousness in the novel, I will digress briefly and explain why any approximation of Nigel's position to Lisa's is fallacious, and how his metaphor-making is actually similar to Bruno's cognitive impasse.

Like Bruno, Nigel has a master metaphor of self-identity—he is God, a strange coadunation of the Christian and Hindu deities; London is "his night city, it is a place of pilgrimage" (p. 85). When Nigel "strides among the Londoners, prayers rise up about him hissing faintly, like steam" (p. 86); his divine nature makes him a "looker-on at inward scenes"(p. 86). Like the Ganges, the Thames is a "sacred river" which "rolls on at his feet black and full, a river of tears bearing away the corpses of men" (p. 86). When blissful, Nigel's smile is the "tender forgiving infinitely sad smile of almighty God" (p. 88).

However, this general master metaphor of self as God takes on at times a highly particular colouring; Nigel mythologizes himself as the avatar of Shiva, the extremely enigmatic Indian God, who is both destroyer and reproducer. Behaviouristic imitation of Shiva's actions abounds.[16] One of the attributes of Shiva is that he is the Lord of dancing; Nigel, through his reeling dance, achieves a Nirvanic mystical vision of one "Concentric Universe" of a "holy city" turning within the "ring of equatorial emerald," and within the "lacticogalactic wheel" (p. 27). In this vision, Nigel sees the stages of the creation of the cosmos: black "void," then inception of consciousness, self, and time, then finally the essence of existence, namely, the two warring "terrible angels" of love and death struggling with each other but eventually "oneing in magnetic joy" (p. 28). Nevertheless, and despite its poetic and aesthetic charm, Nigel's Nirvanic vision is delusory and depraved; when the dance ends, he hears Bruno's call for help, apparently after waking up from a nightmare, but Nigel who "hears the calling and the weeping" with "magnified precision," ignores Bruno and blissfully "lies prostrate upon the floor of the world" (p. 29). His room is his world, and the old man's call is far away in another world" (p. 29). Nigel's indifference signifies moral failure which occurs because the inner does not intermesh with the outer.

Besides ritualistic imitations (dance as fount for visions) Nigel indulges in behaviouristic and verbal parodying. For instance, paradox is the source of Shiva's power and enchantment; it is believed that Shiva engages in both enstatic trance and in ecstatic dance; when he is covered with ashes, he is illuminated with radiant external light, but within he remains dark. On his night journey barefooted Nigel, whose feet are "muddied" and whose hands are "red with rust" (p. 85), perceives truthful images of the human condition; ironically, however, his mystical journey is nothing but acts of eavesdropping and voyeurism, stark violations of others' privacy that obliterate any ethical context for the journey and its induced visions. With mud on his feet, rust on his hands, Nigel is deep in the abyss of solipsism.

But Nigel's meddling with paradox has yet another aspect; to enchant his hearers, Nigel empowers his discourse with contradictions. In earnest, Bruno asks, "What is God made of?" Nigel replies, "Why not spiders? The spiders were a good idea" (p. 101); however, later in the conversation Nigel asserts that "It wouldn't matter if He was all sex" (p. 101). Nigel confesses to Bruno that he loves God because God makes him "suffer," although it "does not matter whether we are saved" (p. 101). Bruno is beguiled, and tells him "You understand almost everything."

But perhaps the power of Nigel's discourse is mostly demonstrated during his only encounter with Diana. Diana, who feels depressed by the discovery of the mutual passion between Lisa and Miles, ponders suicide and steals Bruno's tablets. Nigel, who knows her intentions, corners her in the living room, terrorizes her, and makes her sit still by pinioning her arms. He dictates his precept about the proper attitude she must adopt toward Lisa's and Miles's love affair, what he calls the "task," of making "a new heaven and a new earth:" "Relax. Let them walk on you. Love them and let them walk on you" (p. 237). In paradoxical terms, he tells how he comes to know about others' private lives:

> "I am God . . . or it can be that I am the false god, or one of the million million false gods there are. It matters very little. The false god is the true God."
>
> (p. 237)

Besides Nirvanic dance, and the excessive employment of paradox, Nigel parodies Shiva in yet a third way. The Indian God is the archetype of the erotic ascetic. Nigel seems free from materialistic impulses; he is, for example, absolutely apathetic about Bruno's precious stamp collection; nevertheless, his world is highly eroticized. When in Nirvana, he perceives God as a "jet black orgasm" (p 102), and in his reeling dance he perceives "Om Phallos" as the initial stage of the creation of the cosmos (p. 28). Moreover, his bizarre dealings with Danby and Will, his twin brother—he follows the drunk Danby through his hilarious night journey to see Lisa, and he ties down the violent Will with an elaborate rope trap to reveal to him Adelaide's unchastity, and later stages a duel between these two men—spring

from his suppressed homosexual love for both men. Nigel's eroticism augments his moral failure, his pretension of being free from desire adds to his insincerities, and his erotic drives mock his religiosity.

One may be tempted to argue that Nigel is the archetype of the wise and holy fool, the holy adept who, although possessor of the deepest insights, behaves like a madman. To be sure, outwardly Nigel resembles this archetype; he is a sort of outcast and seems not to fit into the social hierarchy of London, and his discourse is hostile to our normative values of pride and egoism. On close examination, however, and contrary to the credibility of the archetype, Nigel flaunts his wisdom in a dogmatism which he himself violates: "up any religion a man may climb" (p. 237); Nigel is not beyond or above the common, normative, human motivations; he is a seeker of power, a ruthless magician, and a builder of torture machines. After Danby pairs off with Lisa and Will marries Adelaide, Nigel writes Danby a confessional letter in which he speculates about the meaning of the Thames-side duel he had arranged, the event he elatedly describes as his "Russian roulette of the soul":

> "To have you both before me pointing loaded pistols at each other was the acting out of a fantasy. And how absolutely, when it came to it, you were both of you clay in my hands. How easy it proved to make you do exactly what I wanted."
>
> (p. 286)

Nigel cannot be the fool because his machines have much cunning, and he is not wise because his moral sense is hollow. He does not engage in any acts of purification, whether through self-discipline or renunciation; only at the end of the novel when he loses both male lovers does he decide to go to India as volunteer for the Save the Children Fund in an attempt at self-abnegation.

The point I am making is that Nigel's metaphoric conceptualizations ingeminate Bruno's metaphoring as an expression of false concretism. Bruno's image-making impresses itself on Nigel's consciousness, and it augments Nigel's epistemological impasse. In the scene where Bruno drafts his spiritual regression he recounts how in country churches God seemed to him no longer "an official who made rules" or a "bureaucrat" who made "checks and counterchecks" but as "something rather lost and pathetic, a little crazed perhaps, and small" (p. 100). This particular image weaves itself into Nigel's consciousness and into his mode of metaphor-making; toward the end of the novel he tells Diana he looked like God because "Maybe this is how God appears now in the world, a little unregarded crazy person whom everyone pushes aside and knocks down and steps upon" (p. 237).

Significantly, Nigel's master metaphor traps his consciousness in dualistic forms and naive binarism; when he pinions Will's wrists and ankles in his torture "machine" he philosophizes about the inevitability of the chastisement: "You are the other half of myself, a weird brutish alien half, doubtless a lesser half, but connected to me by an ectoplasmic necessity" (p. 210); because of this metaphysical logic of necessity Will needs Nigel as "the brute needs the angel, as the tender back needs the whip and as the suppliant neck the axe" (p. 211). While Bruno's dualistic conceptions are shallow and sexist, Nigel's are sadistic and perverse.

Nevertheless, it would be simplistic to view Nigel through his demonic dark intentions only; to his credit he subverts Diana's mythologized self-image of the smitten, romantic, suicidal maiden tormented by the cruelty of her lover; the subversion of this image becomes the preparatory step to her understanding of pure, unpossessive love. The discourse of **Bruno's Dream** bathes all the characters in comedic light, and Nigel is no exception. The cunning builder of torture machines is easily knocked down by the drunk Danby and hits a lamp-post; he stages a duel between his two lovers, a sort of thrilling sexual game, only to panic at its possible outcome; and despite his philosophical utterances, some very Murdochian in tone—for instance "A human being hardly ever thinks about other people" (p. 286)—he makes shallow statements, "groans" to indicate understanding during a conversation, ridiculously chews the "lank end of a lock of dark hair" (p. 100), and often looks like a "slice of a human being" (p. 100).

Now that the danger of Nigel's master metaphor has been elucidated, it is appropriate to revert to Lisa's attitude to metaphor-making. The gist of her misgivings is plain: to weave metaphor and reality so as to make their fibres indistinguishable gives rise to ethical perplexity and spiritual blunders; to perceive the women as spider "specimens in formalin" is to make Maureen retain an erotic presence only, and it is to reduce or allegorize Janie as an unforgiving puritanical animus. Only when Janie is not a specimen in formalin does Bruno assume with great certainty the tender reconciliatory intentions behind her death-bed calling.

Aesthetically—that is from the perspective of characterization in the text—and in an oblique way, Lisa's continuous labour of dismantling and effacing Bruno's imagery has the aura of a sacred activity, for her role of reinscribing the inadequacy of positivistic and totalizing metaphors, or any similar forms of misleading concretism, echoes the Second Commandment's credo: "Thou shalt not make unto thee any graven image" Or, to be more specific, Lisa's task is to rearrange the mental patterns of Bruno's consciousness by a kind of intellectual and linguistic shock treatment, that is by systematically nullifying and replacing his metaphors with simple, direct imageless language which points to the world outside. During one of her visits to Bruno, he ponders, "I'd like to know what I'm *like*;" Lisa replies, "perhaps

there isn't any such thing;" Bruno ignores this remark and declares his wish to get the past "into focus" to define what he "really feels about it all" (p. 175). Lisa, who designates the present as the only space for genuine moral visions, points out, "One doesn't necessarily feel anything clear at all about the past. One is such a jumbled thing oneself" (p. 175). However, not comprehending her meaning, Bruno forges another self-image: he must have been a "demon" to Janie. Patiently, Lisa points out that "Human beings are not demons. They are much too muddy" (p. 176). Lisa's utterances not only exhibit a hostility to metaphors, but they also show a preoccupation with shared, social linguistic frames that are moral and imageless.

So while Bruno's utterances accentuate the similarities between image (always a subjective mental construct) and reality (a certain action, event, or object), thus eclipsing all differential dimensions, Lisa's utterances express difference and disparity; to Bruno image and reality are one, to Lisa images are always inadequate and asymptotic: metaphors can approximate the perception of an experience, but they cannot capture or arrest that experience. Philosophically, Lisa's stance warns us about what metaphors must not do: reconcile us to the contingency of the world. Since the imagination has "synthetic power", to use Murdoch's Kantian phrasing, image-making, intrinsically and ineluctably, involves a desire to seek hegemony and integration; it reconciles self and the world in order for self to dominate, mould, and contain the world. However, while she tries to restore difference and dissimilarity between language and reality, Lisa simultaneously tries to establish rapprochement between language and silence.

Lisa's asymptotic reading of images and her awareness of the deficiency of all metaphor-making associates her with the idea of death and silence, but let me point out how the text posits these two terms: death is the redemptive moral and wilful act of unselfing, and silence is perception in imagelessness; both death and silence are forms of asceticism, of abstention from limiting reality to subjective structures. In an oblique way, death and silence function in the text as non-material forms of the Kantian sublime. It is in this de-mythologizing sense that love, as Lisa holds from the outset of the novel and Diana comes to believe later, is both death and silence. Silence is a formal constituent of moral language and death is the exemplary metaphor for our moral attitude. The purpose of death and silence is to keep egotism under check, to open up inner space where the other nonself can exist, and to reinstall the social contract much threatened by modernity. In short, silence and death are the antidote to the tempting marginalization of the world.

The category of silence often poses an epistemological crisis, because it constantly points out the breach between the way self subjectively structures meanings and the way the world, or the ontological category, decimates these meanings. There is always a sense of the illegitimacy of one's reading, of one's own metaphor-making, and a sense of frustration that positivistic, consoling metaphors or paradigms cannot, after all, explain away the contingent world. Miles's crisis is exemplary; having written his lengthy poem about Parvati's tragic death immediately after it happened, he cannot write any longer; he has exhausted his vocabulary and his images; it is only after Lisa leaves him and, therefore, forces him to attend to reality silently, disinterestedly, does his literary talent rejuvenate itself with a new language and a new vision. Wisdom is getting the joke that all our metaphors are futile, that silence is emancipating.

Lisa's metaphors are sparse, and when her consciousness accidentally and infrequently forges them, they do not linger either in her memory, or in the reader's: however, one synchronically active metaphor is an exception. Walking in the Brompton Cemetery with Diana, and having just finished meeting Bruno, Lisa remembers her father's death which she had witnessed alone. Although Lisa had held his hand and had expressed her love, he had not understood and had not wanted to know the nature of love and death. Like Bruno at the outset of the novel he was perceiving death as nothing but annihilation of self, and his fright was like a horrible "physical struggle." Diana, who did not witness her father's death, tries to elicit from Lisa a metaphor that can capture his awful fright, but Lisa has no metaphor: "I think one almost absolutely forgets the *quality* of scenes like that" (p. 137); all metaphors fail because "It's like no other fear, it's so *deep*. It almost becomes something impersonal" (p. 138). Nevertheless, Lisa can convey "the dimensions of what love would have to be;" it is like "a huge vault suddenly opening out overhead" (p. 138).

This metaphor arrests us, for it sets in order a moral vision, sharp and apocalyptic in its dimensions of self, death, and the world: the vault of self opening out, love and death (self-abnegation) leading to emancipation, and the world, vast and separate, clearly being seen. The idealistic metaphor summons up traditional images from our collective unconscious: resurrection, rebirth, new horizons or space, and a new language which obliterates naive binarism and, instead, installs reciprocation because it embeds death in life.

Unlike Bruno's and Nigel's egoistic and positivistic master metaphors, Lisa's is speculative and is constructed from the perspective of the dead person buried in the vault. Her metaphor echoes Murdoch's speculations on what pictures (she often cites Christ on the cross as an example) ought to do: lead to "moral illuminations" play a "protective or guiding role," function as "moral refuges" and as "perpetual starting points."[17]

Lisa's metaphor diachronically travels in the text; from a formal point of view it parallels the resurgence of Bruno's metaphor of God as a "pathetic" and "crazed" person in Nigel's consciousness, and it contests the impressions of Nigel's master metaphor on Diana's higher consciousness.

The genesis of Diana's higher consciousness takes place in the last chapter, after Lisa initiates her own new, busy, eroticized life with Danby; Diana is thus forced to take up the task of caring for Bruno. Bruno, who has lately suffered a fall in the basement while trying to save his stamp collection from the flooding water of the Thames, is now totally bedridden as well as mentally confused and incoherent. At first, Diana tends him as a "kind of consoling inevitability," as "something compulsory" a "duty" (p. 309), she hopes the new task will help her cope with Miles's recent aloofness due to an outpour of new literary activities, and will also help her re-establish a "natural relationship" with Danby, who early on in the novel flirted boldly with her. The habit of tending Bruno, however, turns into a "blank unanxious hopeless love," "the most pointless of all loves" (p. 309).

From the perspective of this paper, what is interesting about Diana's new consciousness is the way it embodies a sharp and climactic presentation of the conflict between the two approaches to metaphor-making in relation to reality - the identicalness of metaphor and reality (Niger), or their asymptoticality, their infinite apartness (Lisa). But let me give the lengthy but necessary quotation first:

> "She tried to think about herself but there seemed to be nothing there. Things can't matter very much, she thought, because one isn't anything. Yet one loves people, this matters . . . Her resentment against Miles, against Lisa, against Danby had utterly gone away. They will flourish and you will watch them kindly as if you were watching children. Who had said that to her? . . . Relax. Let them walk on you. Love them. Let love like a huge vault open out overhead . . . She lived the reality of death and felt herself made nothing by it and denuded of desire."

> (p. 310-11)

One sees the resurgence of Lisa's single asymptotic metaphor of love as an open vault and the disappearance of Nigel's master metaphor of self as God; however, and despite the antithetical relationship of the two modes of metaphor-making, one sees resolution and synthesis; Nigel's Christ-like, moralistic sayings, now purged of their idiosyncratic nature—Diana cannot even remember that Nigel said them—intermesh with both Lisa's metaphor of the vault and with Diana's new Platonic thoughts. The mark of Diana's spiritual progression is not only the successful sifting of our normative values and the underscoring of love as the absolutely central one, but it is also her joyous and animating failure to forge any positivistic image of self; self as nothing is the true, mystical imageless perception of self-identity.

I have devoted much space to Lisa's role; however, the undoing of images is not the task of only Murdochian mystics; the text includes two other subversive agents: the flooding Thames and the spiders themselves when shown and not seen—that is when they appear as entities separate from Bruno's consciousness, and are described from the external viewpoint of omniscient narration.

With their non-human, solitary and solid existence in the midst of the spiritual perplexity and epistemological muddle of the characters, the spiders' presence adds a comedic dimension to the text. The polysyllabic, unfamiliar, and difficult entomological names—*Micromatta vivescens, Ciniflo farox, Drassodes lapidosus,* render them the embodiment of the maddeningly and irritatingly particular. Indeed, the spiders' presence provides a kind of constructive humorousness because their role is to save the novel's moral vision from Bruno's totalizing master metaphor by turning God into an alien and separate reality which demands our attention. Another related aspect of the spiders' role is to provoke the wholesome, though metaphysically painful, awareness that the grid of our metaphors, and generally of all our forms of cognition, cannot encompass reality. Simultaneously then, the spiders point to the thereness of the world and to the evanescence of Bruno's master metaphor; as a result, they simultaneously invite pleasure in the vast ontological world and vexation at the narrowness of all images.

Significantly, the spiders are everywhere: in the gardens, in Bruno's room, on the window casements, in the lavatory; they uncontrollably occupy space in the text as though to mock the limited inner space of those who cogitate by means of metaphors. If Bruno caricatures God by means of the reductive image of the spiders, the spiders mock and subvert the shallow, gender-based binarism governing his consciousness because they then appear as substantial, genderless, and highly particular.

But besides their comedic role when shown by the omniscient narrator, the spiders, when actually seen by Bruno, eventually get associated with a recurrent Murdochian philosophical concern: the necessary defeat of what Murdoch calls "theories of coherence". I can detect two occasions where this concern is imparted. In the first instance the spiders are associated with the idea of the sublime: In an unusual dream Bruno saw that:

> "God had hung up above him [Bruno] in the form of a beautiful *Erisus niger,* swinging very very slightly upon a fine almost invisible golden thread. God had let down

another thread toward Bruno and the thread swung to and fro just above Bruno's head and Bruno kept seizing it and it kept breaking. The light fragile touch of the thread was accompanied by an agonizing and yet delightful physical sensation."

(p. 301)

In Kant's philosophy the sublime is a moment of intense moral awakening generated by the realization that vast and infinite phenomena (or objects) do not conform to our rational faculty; the failure of our finite rational faculty and its fabricated images to assimilate these infinite phenomena paradoxically fills us with tension and delight. The concept of the sublime, let me add, entails the asymptoticality of metaphors.

Bruno's realization of the sublime (the impossibility of seizing the entire thread) is momentary, for suddenly in this dream "the *Erisus niger* seemed to be growing larger and larger and turning into the face of Bruno's father" and this face "filled up the whole sky" (p. 301); nevertheless, I would argue that the metamorphosis of God-spider into the familiar face of a father (God as father), an image which connotates origin, human ties, and external authority, is a progressive step towards the perception of Good, because it is a less solipsistic image, has a root in our collective unconscious, and engenders in Bruno a yearning for God.

In the second instance, Bruno sees a fly caught in a spider's web; Diana catches the spider, puts it in a cup, and both Bruno and she are delighted to see that the big *Araneus diadematus* has a "big white cross on her back" (p. 303). Bruno remarks that "In the Middle Ages they said she was holy because of the cross" (p. 303). The image of the cross, an image which points beyond the muddled human world, and which is a "moral refuge" and a "ladder" for moral improvement, and the allusion to the Medieval, the major period of theological speculations, mysticism, and sainthood, diametrically contrasts with Bruno's sordid world of stultifying and reifying metaphors. The cross in the Middle Ages created an overarching sense of reality which bound together all aspects of human life. By contrast, Bruno's master metaphor intensifies his loneliness, his alienation, and his sense of a fragmented, private modern world. Because the spiders are the antidote to theories of coherence, or of totalization, they generate self-doubt and they therefore create a positive awareness of the possibility of regeneration.

In contrast to the intermittent presence of the real spiders, the threat of the flooding Thames looms apocalyptically and persistently throughout the text; the river provides the comedic perspective which could, at any moment, displace the substantiality of the master metaphors. As a comedic force, therefore, the river is iconoclastic, for it smashes and washes away both the mythologized spiders in Bruno's house, and the black wooden box of the precious stamp collection, the very symbol of his materialism. The flood itself is a rebuttal of the profaned sacred (God as a spider) and the sham valuable (stamp collection). The boisterous sound of the waters in Bruno's basement is the boisterous sound of comedy which mocks the vulnerability of all sayable metaphors, and which qualifies all hermeneutics and readings of reality. Like Bruno's struggle with the flooding waters in his basement, morality is a cognitive struggle against the enchantment of images.

The crux of Bruno's final cognitive struggle and its resultant cognitive triumph is how to retrieve a true grammar of morality by which feelings or values, such as love and Good, can be articulated in ordinary, imageless language. But to achieve this grammar Bruno must first scrutinize his inner self and begin to critique its contents and its quality:

> "He had loved only a few people and loved them so badly, so selfishly. He had made a muddle of everything. Was it only in the presence of death that one could see so clearly what love ought to be like? If only the knowledge which he had now, this absolute nothing-else-matters, could somehow go backwards and purify the little selfish loves and straighten out the muddles."
>
> (p. 305)

Furthermore, since his imagination is reduced to its last resources, he must look for value in new places; he must adopt a new point of reference: the transcendental logic of love and death:

> "Had Janie known this at the end? For the first time Bruno saw it with absolute certainty. Janie must have known. It would be impossible in this presence [of death] not to know. She had not wanted to curse him, she had wanted to forgive him."
>
> (p. 305)

The triumph of Bruno is his redefinition of self and reality. Self, or inner consciousness, is a moral centre and the "bearer of value," lively, free from "deterministic pressures," exuberantly engaged in free moral choices; and despite its propensity to fantasize, it can exhibit momentary acts of pure cognition.[18] As for reality, it is contingent and prismatic, separate and alien, constantly demanding our attention, our images of it always asymptotic. But moral progress, though antithetical to reality, must gauge self against reality, it is to see the particularity of all objects in the outside world.

In conclusion, **Bruno's Dream** is one of Iris Murdoch's best achievements, because it reveals how Platonism can still be a valid antidote to some of our cognitive problems generated by modernity.

Murdoch's highest triumph, however, is the way she subtly interweaves her Platonism with the glaringly ordinary and quotidian.

Notes

1. The edition used in this study is Iris Murdoch, *Bruno's Dream* (New York: The Viking Press 1969).

2. Murdoch explains that "the proper and serious use of the term 'Good' refers us to a perfection which is perhaps never exemplified in the world we know . . . and which carries with it the ideas of hierarchy and transcendence. . . . The self, the place where we live, is a place of illusion. Goodness is connected with the attempt to see the unself)." See Iris Murdoch, *The Sovereignty of Good* (London: Ark Paperbacks, 1986), p. 93.

3. Richard Todd, *Iris Murdoch* (London: Methuen, 1984) p. 68.

4. Iris Murdoch, *Metaphysics as a Guide to Morals* (New York: Allen Lane-Penguin Press, 1992) p. 317.

5. Jeremy Hawthorn, *A Glossary of Contemporary Literary Theory* (London: Edward Arnold, 1992) p. 149.

6. See Frank Kermode, "Bruno's Dream" in: *Modern Critical Views: Iris Murdoch.* Harold Bloom (Ed). (New York: Chelsea House Publishers, 1985), p. 21.

7. Lucien Dällenbach, *The Mirror in the Text,* translated by Jeremy Whiteley and Emma Hughes (Chicago: The University of Chicago Press, 1989) p. 24.

8. Murdoch, *Metaphysics*, p. 318.

9. *Ibid,* p. 162.

10. See Iris Murdoch's essay "Wittgenstein and the Inner Life" in: *Metaphysics,* pp. 269-92.

11. Peter Conradi, *Iris Murdoch: The Saint and the Artist* (London: Macmillan Press, 1986) p. 101.

12. Donna Gerstenberger, *Iris Murdoch* (London: Associated University Presses, 1975) p. 47.

13. William Hall, "Bruno's Dream: Technique and Meaning in the Novels of Iris Murdoch" in: *Modern Fiction Studies,* 15.3 (1969) p. 437.

14. *Ibid* p. 439.

15. Elizabeth Dipple, *Iris Murdoch: Work for the Spirit* (Chicago: The University of Chicago Press, 1982) p. 179.

16. In this section I am indebted to the excellent book of Lee Siegel, *Laughing Matters: Comic Traditions in India* (Chicago: The University of Chicago Press, 1987).

17. Murdoch, *Metaphysics*, p. 17.

18. *Ibid.*, p. 149.

Roberta S. White (essay date 2000)

SOURCE: White, Roberta S. "Iris Murdoch: Mapping the Country of Desire." In *British Women Writing Fiction*, edited by Abby H. P. Werlock, pp. 23-41. Tuscaloosa: University of Alabama Press, 2000.

[*In the following essay, White studies the central importance of love in Murdoch's fiction, stating that "love obsesses her characters and drives her plots." According to White, "love and the good" is one of the supreme concepts which Murdoch "attempts to illuminate in both her philosophical writings and her novels."*]

> [Murdoch] uses love the way some Arab tribes in North Africa used mud to build whole cities. Sometimes she uses it as various agricultural people use fire to clear the land.
>
> Anatole Broyard[1]

Love is the stuff of Iris Murdoch's twenty-four novels, out of which she erects her fictional structures. Love is also a narrative strategy she uses to burn off her own talkiness and tendency to abstraction, blasting away her characters' assumptions about themselves and making way for new growth. Murdoch seldom describes the workaday world; her settings, London and the English countryside, are heightened and energized by desire. In all its varieties, perverse and possessive to ennobling, love obsesses her characters and drives her plots; love is also one of the supreme, problematic concepts—love and the good—which she attempts to illuminate in both her philosophical writings and her novels.

Murdoch evidently conceives of her fiction as new space to be opened up and explored. In her first novel, ***Under the Net*** (1954), Jake observes that a novel is like a natural landscape: "Starting a novel is opening a door on a misty landscape: you can see very little but you can smell the earth and feel the wind blowing" (177-78). Fiction provides space for the discovery of experience and the testing of ideas. In the grand tradition of the nineteenth-century novel, Murdoch creates serious-minded characters, ample settings, and big old-fashioned plots with many twists. Her modernity manifests itself in the rootlessness of her characters, their uncertainty of identity, the dark comedy of their erotic life, and their sometimes desperate search for values in a world from which God is conspicuously absent.

Despite the length of her novels, Murdoch has no interest in producing histories or sagas. One therefore need not observe chronology in exploring her anatomy of love. Her novels resemble a series of experiments performed to reveal moral, psychological, and spiritual aspects of human behavior. Frequently she puts in motion an instance of obsessive love or desire and then scrutinizes, in a sympathetic but rather clinical way, the psychological and moral states induced in the lover, who is usually male and rather weak. The results often prove comic, but only because Murdoch judges humans by the highest standards of behavior; her novels are suffused with human sympathy as well as high intelligence. Moreover, according to Murdoch's Platonic philosophy, sexual love, for all its inherent comedy, is also a powerful energy capable of assuming higher forms. In her book on Plato and art, ***The Fire and the Sun*** (1977), she claims that "Plato's Eros is a principle which connects the commonest human desire to the highest morality and to the pattern of divine creativity in the universe" (33). The event of falling in love, she writes, "is for many people the most extraordinary and most revealing experience of their lives, whereby the centre of significance is suddenly ripped out of the self, and the dreamy ego is shocked into awareness of an entirely separate reality" (36). On yet another level, the literary artist, like Plato's Demiurge, creates worlds out of a love that resembles the lower forms of love, with all the usual attendant dangers of egotism and delusion.

Instances of obsessive love in Murdoch's novels range across a wide spectrum. At one extreme, revelation of hidden perversity, such as the sibling incest in ***A Severed Head*** (1961) or the father-daughter incest in ***The Time of the Angels*** (1966), impels melodramatic plots in which unsuspecting persons are abruptly exposed to the breaking of taboos. A revelation of Dionysian forces rends the screen of civilized behavior, and the onlooker's world turns upside down. This is not to label these novels themselves Dionysian; they do not provide steamy reading. On the contrary, Murdoch emphasizes not the gratification of desire, but the aching experience of desire and the dislocations it causes in the psyche. Despite her various experiments with gothic horror—additional examples include ***The Unicorn*** (1963) and ***The Italian Girl*** (1964)—Murdoch's fictional mode remains Apollonian and comic. In no more than four or five of her twenty-four novels does death, betrayal, or unfathomable evil overwhelm the potential for comedy, and even in these novels the dailiness of life frequently asserts itself in comic fashion.

At the other extreme looms a higher, selfless, transcendent Eros, more often pointed to as an ideal or felt in moments of epiphany than actually practiced; as Jake learns from his pursuit of Anna in ***Under the Net,*** such ideal love would mark the end of desire and even of longing to know the other person. It would amount to full acceptance of the otherness of the other, "and this too is one of the guises of love" (268). Ideally, as Murdoch writes in ***The Fire in the Sun,*** "Carnal love teaches that what we want is always 'beyond,' and it gives us an energy which can be transformed into creative virtue" (34). But the path to creative virtue is rarely taken, and usually Murdoch deals with more common themes—love triangles, adultery, unreciprocated desire—though often with a bizarre twist, such as sixty-year-old Charles Arrowby's obsession with Hartley in *The Sea, the Sea* (1978). Long ago Hartley was his youthful sweetheart, "the jewel of the world" to him; she continues to obsess Charles to such an extent that he kidnaps her and holds her as a prisoner of love even though she is now a confused and rather decrepit old woman.

In Murdoch's novels love proves so capricious, unpredictable, irrational, and contrary to the conscious wishes and intents of the ego and practical needs of the self as to seem like an external force. As Hugh Balfounder insists in *Under the Net,* "anyone can love anyone, or prefer anyone to anyone" (255). A memorable instance of this arbitrariness occurs in *The Book and the Brotherhood* (1987). Gerard Hernshaw experienced the most intense love of his life at age eleven, a passion whose object was a small parrot named Grey with clever yellow eyes and scarlet wing tips. Although he symbolically equates his lifelong grief for the absence of Grey with his sorrow for his dead lover Sinclair and for "all the agony and helpless suffering of created things" (590), it is nonetheless Grey whom Gerard so poignantly and rather ludicrously mourns, the particular other being, beautiful and replete.

Desire portrayed as a force contrary to the will of the ego invites Freudian interpretation. But in *The Sacred and Profane Love Machine* (1974) Blaise Gavender, a psychotherapist, finds that his understanding of Freudian mechanisms neither helps nor inhibits the treatment of his patients any more than it offers him the least guidance in his own wayward love life, which entangles him in the usual messes. One might just as well call upon any old notions or superstitions to explain the inexplicable phenomenon of love's arbitrariness. In *The Black Prince* (1973), one of her finest novels, Murdoch amusingly draws upon the psychology of love in Shakespeare's time, when, for example, Robert Burton diagnosed love as a melancholic disease of the liver that drives lovers "headlong like so many brute beasts." Despite all the counsels of reason, "they will do it," Burton writes in his *Anatomy of Melancholy* "they will do it, and become at last void of sense; degenerate into dogs, hogs, asses."[2]

In *The Black Prince,* Bradley Pearson narrates, from prison, the story of his ill-fated love for Julian Baffin, a young woman nearly forty years his junior. Julian's mother, Rachel, herself in pursuit of Bradley, warns him, "it's nearly midsummer and you are, perhaps, reaching the age when men make asses of themselves"

(239). Even before the publication of *The Black Prince,* critic Robert Hoskins noted that several of Murdoch's novels resemble midsummer night's dreams, comic novels of love gone awry in summery settings.[3] Here Bradley, a writer and serious intellectual, ironically plays the role of Bottom. Bradley's life is already complicated by three other women—Rachel, his suicidal sister Priscilla, and his ex-wife Christian—when he feels helplessly drawn to Julian in a fetishistic way: her legs, feet, body smells, and hair overwhelm and madden him. From the moment he falls for her in the middle of their *Hamlet* tutorial, his stomach feels hollow, his knees dissolve, his teeth chatter, and his face takes on a waxen smile (172). This aging lover comically experiences transcendence, anxiety, longing, jealousy ("like a red-hot knitting needle thrust into the liver"), desire, humiliation, and so on (209). Murdoch details every phase of love's foolishness. Bradley confesses his love to Julian only after listening to the opening of *Der Rosenkavalier,* and then vomiting in Covent Garden out of sheer lovesickness. When he loses Julian and goes to prison for a crime that Rachel commits, the bludgeoning of Julian's father, Bradley narrates his story in a posthumous novel within the novel, *The Black Prince,* subtitled "A Celebration of Love," edited by P. Loxias (Apollo in disguise).

In *The Black Prince* we thus have the curious situation, often repeated in Murdoch's novels, of a woman novelist anatomizing and memorializing the erotic features of a woman character through the transfixing gaze of an adoring male. (A useful study could be made of the importance of *hair* in her novels as an erotic and aesthetic display of the vital, enticing "otherness" of the adored person.) This intertwining of genders, reminiscent of Shakespeare's playfulness with gender-shifting characters like Rosalind and Olivia (male actors playing women who play men), produces startlingly actual and vivid views of women—they seem wholly present. Murdoch supports the feminist movement, but she rarely brings feminist issues into her fiction; rather, she sets out to break down what she sees as arbitrary and limiting definitions of gender and of love. Delicate males and boyish women with androgynous names abound in her work; not just homosexuals and bisexuals, but virtually everyone is capable of same-sex love, often hovering somewhere between friendship and Eros. Like Virginia Woolf before her, Murdoch sets out to define and hence legitimize varieties of human attraction previously undefined and therefore unacknowledged.

Ambivalence about gender abounds in *The Black Prince.* When Bradley first sees Julian strewing bits of love letters in the street, he thinks she is a boy in dark trousers and jacket. He becomes aroused by her when she is wearing his socks, and he cannot make love until she dons her Hamlet costume, breeches, tunic, and chain. The comedy of the gender-bending and the lovesickness is at once dark, funny, and tragic because the first-person narration traps us inside Bradley's confession and his pain.

A self-conscious narrator, Bradley also theorizes about his own dilemma and its relation to his writing. Like Stephen Dedalus in *Ulysses,* Bradley presents a theory of *Hamlet* at the center of **The Black Prince,** that is, in the tutorial scene with Julian. *Hamlet* is postmodern in its intricate self-reflexiveness. Bradley describes it as "a work endlessly reflecting upon itself . . . in its very substance, a Chinese box of words . . . a meditation upon the bottomless trickery of consciousness and the redemptive role of words in the lives of those without identity, that is human beings" (166). Yet paradoxically *Hamlet* also reveals Shakespeare's deepest beliefs: "He is speaking as few artists can speak, in the first person and yet at the pinnacle of artifice" (166). Here Murdoch gives us a clue to her own work: **The Black Prince** is an intricate fiction within a fiction, and yet we may assume that, as Shakespeare revealed himself most when most disguised, so Murdoch speaks most candidly when artfully hidden in the guise of Bradley Pearson (BP, Black Prince, B. Person). Bradley comments: "Almost any tale of our doings is comic. We are bottomlessly comic to each other. Even the most adored and beloved person is comic to his lover. The novel is a comic form, and makes jokes in its sleep [as Bradley has just made a pun on Bottom]. . . . Yet it is also the case that life is horrible, without metaphysical sense, wrecked by chance, pain and the close prospect of death. Out of this is born irony, our dangerous and necessary tool" (58). Irony is dangerous because it kills sentiment, and a necessary tool because it converts life's horrors into something bearable, a dark joke, a rhetorical gesture, or a work of literary art that distances us one step away from the pain, allowing us to contemplate it. More recently, in her philosophical lectures entitled *Metaphysics as a Guide to Morals* (1992), Murdoch argues that "Novels are, however sad or catastrophic, essentially comic" (97). The novel is an "open" form that embraces more of life's ordinariness than other genres do: "Characters in novels partake of the funniness and absurdity and contingent incompleteness and lack of dignity of people in ordinary life" (97).

The comedy of ordinary life often arises in Murdoch's novels when, like Bottom, people delude themselves with dreams of romance. As Joyce Carol Oates notes in a review, "Murdoch's philosophical position is austere, classical, rigorously unromantic, and pessimistic. Not that the pessimism precludes comedy: on the contrary, it is probably the basis of the comic spirit."[4] In *An Unofficial Rose* (1962) the traditional plot device of the love triangle, an unstable situation always conducive to irony, is repeated in three generations of would-be lovers, representing a continuity of foolishness that seems as ingrained as original sin. As the novel opens, Hugh

Peronette, a retired civil servant aged sixty-seven, realizes at his wife's funeral that "he had not really known what was in her heart" (20). Ignorance of the hearts of others repeats itself, realistically, in virtually every relationship in this novel and throughout Murdoch's work, leading to possibilities of both illusion and disenchantment. In this most Jamesian of Murdoch's novels, Hugh feels an unpleasant touch of complicity in his desire to help his son Randall leave his dutiful wife Ann and daughter Miranda to run off with the big blonde Lindsay Rimmer. Randall, once a talented horticulturist now given to drink and self-indulgence, feels, probably rightly, that Ann's unselfishness is ruinous to him; she lacks "form," lives too much for others, and seems amorphous. His father, Hugh, who failed to make his own leap to "freedom" in an affair with Emma Sands many years ago, sells his treasured Tintoretto to finance Randall's high-style elopement with Lindsay, thus freeing Emma, so Hugh hopes, from her own involvement with Lindsay, her secretary and "gaiety girl." In the third generation, Hugh's grandson Penn imagines himself the courtly lover of his cousin Miranda, a demonic pubescent girl-woman who plays with dolls but cherishes a secret crush on her mother's admirer Felix Meecham.

Randall's love for Lindsay, like his father's love for Emma and his nephew's love for Miranda, is delusory and romantic in the extreme: "Randall's love for Lindsay has come violently and suddenly, the entire transformation of the world in a second, a wild cry after a long silence, the plunge of a still stream into a deep ravine" (65). Randall understands neither Emma's lesbian interest in Lindsay nor her control of Lindsay through the purse strings, and not until after the elopement does he learn what is in Lindsay's heart, mainly self-interest and vulgar avarice. Having taken the plunge, he will soon tire of her and move on to other aimless affairs. And Hugh, no better off for having abetted Randall, loses Emma, who finds herself another "gaiety girl," Jocelyn.

Randall's rose nursery at Grayhallock, which once provided meaningful work for him, no longer holds meaning, and the pervasive motif of the rose symbolizes disenchantment rather than love. *An Unofficial Rose* is Murdoch's anti-romance of the rose, a work of comic irony in which three types of characters disastrously interact. The manipulators, who, like Emma Sands and young Miranda, resemble the Medusa-women in several of Murdoch's novels, keep their hearts to themselves, act in their own self-interest, and sometimes manage to attain their desires. The selfish fools, or erotic dreamers, Hugh, Randall, and Penn, obsessed and deluded with love, always act in their own self-interest yet ironically fail to attain their desires. Unselfish fools, like Ann, act against their own self-interest, convinced they serve a higher good. When soldier Felix offers to Ann his love and a more felicitous life, she bungles her own chance for happiness by concealing her feelings from him, imagining herself attached forever to the worthless Randall and letting herself be manipulated by her daughter Miranda. An interesting variation on the unselfish fool is Hugh's old friend Mildred, an amiable, elderly woman married to a suspected pederast, who wants Hugh for herself but acts against her own interest by encouraging him to sell the Tintoretto, thus freeing Ann for marriage to Felix, Mildred's brother. Mildred's unselfishness pays off in the end because, although her matchmaking fails, she gets Hugh to herself on a slow boat to India.

The notion of a romantic setting, of spaces made sacred for love, also receives comic treatment in *An Unofficial Rose*. Randall's foolish flight to Rome with Lindsay creates a virtual map of erotic excess: "Randall made of Rome a sort of map of love, a series of lovepilgrimages where places were identified by embraces and ecstasy. . . . He took Lindsay to the Appian Way and made love to her behind the Tomb of Caecilia Metella. He took her to the Palatine and made love to her in the Temple of Cybele. . . . He took her to the Catacombs. He took her to the English Cemetery and would have made love to her on Keats's grave, only some American ladies arrived" (308-9).

The idea of a map of love is not a joke, however, in *Nuns and Soldiers* (1981). Sacred places in the warm south, in this case natural features of the French countryside, have the power to redeem, to transform, and to make a space for love. Whereas *An Unofficial Rose* comically exposes the folly of romance, *Nuns and Soldiers* tests the possibility of authentic love. More deeply concerned with the moral life, *Nuns and Soldiers* is comic in the traditional sense with its happy ending in which love triumphs over, in this case, class distinctions, disapproving relatives, and clashing values.

Again a death sets the plot in motion. Guy Openshaw, the cohesive intellectual and moral force in both his marriage and his extended family ("*les cousins et les tantes*"), dies prematurely after urging his wife, Gertrude, to seek happiness with another man such as his upright friend the Count. Gertrude's grief turns to love, some would say hastily—the *Hamlet* theme appears all on the surface here—when at her summer home in France she falls in love with Tim Reede, an indifferent painter and amiable hedonist whose irresponsibility and moral laxity most vividly contrast him to Guy. (Guy was the sort of stern agnostic who longed for an afterlife only so that he might be judged.) In her relationship with Tim, Gertrude has all the advantages: maturity, money, upper-bourgeois status, and a firmer moral sense. The crucial question is whether Tim can rise to the occasion of their love. In fact, both Gertrude and Tim have doubts as to whether their love might be a

midsummer delusion. Tim wails, "We're under a spell. But when we go away it will fade. You'll see I'm just a dull fellow with ass's ears. Gertrude, you are deluded, you can't love me, I'm not educated, I'm not clever, I can't paint, I'm going bald" (188). Such irony and doubt are in themselves saving graces. And the "sacred" places in the French countryside which Tim encounters and sketches, a daunting old rock face and a pure crystal pool, are ritual markers of his emotional growth, preparing him for the new, serious love of Gertrude. But when they marry, Tim conceals from Gertrude his longtime affair with the hapless artist Daisy Barrett. When Gertrude learns the truth, Tim, having little faith in himself and their love, returns to Daisy. Tim and Gertrude are reunited at last, in France, after Tim undergoes a literal test by water and symbolic rebirth in which he is nearly drowned in a rushing underground canal and spewed into the sunlight again. These adventures are an objective correlative for the journey to truth and openness essential to their marriage. The transformative factor, purging love of its delusional folly for Gertrude and Tim, is the presence of the genuine Eros, which makes itself felt in their first moments of dancing, wine, and lovemaking: "There was no doubt about the *fact* of her being in love with Tim and Tim being in love with her. This was the real, the indubitable and authoritative Eros: that unmistakable seismic shock, that total concentration of everything into one necessary being, mysterious, uncanny, unique, one of the strangest phenomena in the world" (194).

The magic of Eros is counterbalanced by the secondary characters and their loveless fates. Anne Cavidge and the Count, a lapsed nun and a soldier "in the army of the moral law" (42), ultimately lose out in the love triangles of Tim-Gertrude-Count and Anne-Count-Gertrude. Anne keeps her love for the Count secret, selflessly urging his suit with Gertrude, and finally immigrates to America, "the spy of a non-existent God" (62). And the Count permits himself to be co-opted when Gertrude offers him a "love-treaty" allowing him to remain a special member of her inner circle and live on the scraps of love she dispenses to him in the name of friendship. For the sake of avoiding romantic fantasy in *Nuns and Soldiers,* Murdoch surrounds her warm, rather Lawrentian love story (true Eros) with these cool, Jamesian ironies, and the reader feels the chill.

Murdoch, like Virginia Woolf, frequently views sexual identity as ambiguous and heterosexual orientation as provisional. Moreover, she follows both Woolf and Rosamond Lehmann in treating homosexuality sympathetically and naturally within the context of her mainstream fiction. Homosexual, bisexual, and lesbian characters abound in her novels, in and out of their closets, some of them noble and lonely, some treacherous, some silly, about like everyone else. In *A Fairly Honorable Defeat* (1970), Julius King (emperor-ruler?), a serious mischief-maker, performs a cruel experiment on Murdoch's behalf: he sets out to destroy both a stable, well-established marriage and a similar monogamous homosexual relationship. Julius calls his trick "a midsummer enchantment, with two asses!" (255). In a scarcely believable plot twist, Julius turns out to have been both a scientist working on biological weapons and, before that, a survivor of Belsen—and yet it makes thematic sense that one who has suffered and perpetrated two of the most unthinkable horrors of the twentieth century should play the role the cynic who idly wishes to prove love illusory. The experiment yields mixed results, a fairly honorable defeat. The heterosexual marriage ends in disaster: using falsely planted letters, Julius manipulates Rupert Foster and his unstable sister-in-law Morgan into a romantic affair, after which Rupert and his wife break up and Rupert drowns in the backyard pool under ambiguous circumstances. But the homosexual couple, Simon Foster and Axel Nilsson, manage to survive the suspicions Julius disseminates between them when Julius manufactures evidence of an affair between Simon and himself. Actually, Axel never doubts Simon's faithfulness, but he feels deeply hurt by the lies that Simon tells in order to cover up the *appearance* of his guilt. In the end, Axel and Simon are united by their honesty and the presence of the true Eros; like Gertrude and Tim in **Nuns and Soldiers,** they will remain in their challenging marriage. As his name implies, Axel is the more stable of the two men; the relationship revolves around him. Detesting the loose promiscuity of the underground gay scene, Axel has moderate opinions on love halfway between those of the cynic Julius and the optimist Rupert, who drowns believing in love as an absolute. Axel tells Simon that "Almost all human love is bloody selfish. If one has anything to hang onto at all one clings to it relentlessly. . . . To take refuge in love is an instinct and not a disreputable one" (424). Whereas Axel brings to the marriage intellectual power and unvarnished truth, simpler Simon is closer in his nature to the spirit of Eros. At the end we see Simon and Axel together in an authentic midsummer dream, on holiday in France, drinking wine in a sunny garden among the vine leaves, anticipating happiness.

Homosexuality is also crucial to the moral and spiritual problems presented in **The Bell** (1958). The novel's two most dynamic characters, the conscious seekers of self-understanding, are Dora Greenfield, who faces choices between values of flesh and spirit, and Michael Meade, a homosexual lay preacher, who has difficulty reconciling his erotic needs with the higher callings of the spirit. Murdoch's rural setting establishes a clear demarcation between the naturally pagan surroundings of woods and lakes, where erotic trysts occur, and the ascetic life of the Anglican Benedictine nuns, cloistered until death in their abbey. Just outside the abbey walls lies Imber Court, which Michael has established as a lay community for people who can live neither in the world nor out of it. Dora, unhappily married to a rather rigid, judgmental art historian, is in her spontaneity and careless ways allied—as her name implies—with the pagan green world, and she detests "the spiritual ruling class" of Imber Court. She gains a new sense of autonomy by participating in the mischievous adventure of retrieving an ancient monastic bell from the lake, a bell whose symbolic associations are related more to aesthetic and sexual knowledge than to the spirit. In a moment of revelation, the Botticellis, Pieros, and Gainsboroughs in the National Gallery also strengthen Dora's inner being; she is not so much dumb Dora as an inarticulate woman who experiences wordlessly the calm, the conferred dignity, and the consolation of great art, "and her heart was filled with love for the pictures" (191). By the end of the novel Dora feels ready to leave behind both her dry husband and her loosely hedonistic summer lover and move forward to begin a new life in Bath.

Whereas Dora appears to arrive at an aesthetic synthesis of spirit and flesh through art, Michael seems more deeply torn and more deeply made to suffer by society because of his hidden homosexuality and his attraction to young men. Being gay kept Michael from the priesthood. Some years earlier, Michael, then a schoolmaster, fell passionately in love with a student, Nick Fawley, and although the idyll amounted to nothing more than holding hands and bestowing light caresses, Nick cruelly betrayed Michael to the headmaster, implying that more serious behavior had occurred. History repeats itself. Nick is present at Imber Court, and so is Toby Gashe, a charming, callow boy who looks like Donatello's *David*. When Michael kisses Toby in the woods after drinking too much cider in the village, satanic Nick betrays Michael a second time by inducing Toby to "confess" the story to Michael's colleague James Tayper Pace, a hard-nosed moralist and homophobe. Thus, Michael's sexual preferences are revealed and the community of Imber Court dissolved. Despite its melancholy ending, **The Bell** is often comic, its implications positive. The emergence of a stronger Dora and a wiser Michael at the end actually endorses the values they embody: her healthy paganism and his deeply thoughtful spiritual questing. Whereas James Tayper Pace preaches a Calvinistic Christianity that insists upon the preeminence of moral legalism, Michael Meade, as his name suggests, preaches a mediate path of realistic striving toward perfection starting with an affirmation of one's identities and abilities, a pilgrimage that Murdoch clearly endorses.

The pattern of an inner journey or pilgrimage occurs with increasing frequency in Murdoch's novels, always carrying the possibility of a movement toward enlightenment. Joyce Carol Oates proposes, "the work that is central to an understanding of Murdoch's oeuvre is Plato's allegory of the cave: I suggest that all of Murdoch's novels are commentaries on it" (31). While one might argue that nearly any serious work of fiction aims at extricating ourselves from the cave, Murdoch's novels explicitly allude to Plato's allegorical setting. In *Metaphysics as a Guide to Morals* she insists, "We must transform base egoistic energy and vision (low Eros) into high spiritual energy and vision (high Eros)" (24). "Eros" she defines as "the continuous operation of spiritual *energy,* desire, intellect, love . . . the force of magnetism and attraction which joins us to the world. . . . It gives sense to the idea of loving good, something absolute and unique" (496). This notion of love as a transformable magnetic energy binding us to the world, and possibly to the good, helps to explain some crucial dramatic moments in her novels.

For example, Charles Arrowby in *The Sea, the Sea* misinterprets Plato's myth and inverts the meaning of the cave when he imagines his love for the illusive long-lost Hartley to be the genuine article, mistaking his desire for reality: "O my darling, how clearly I can see you now. Surely this is perception, not imagination. The light in the cavern is daylight, not fire" (79). Clearly, Bottom's dream is also the dream of the prisoner in Plato's cave. By the end of the novel, after several disastrous encounters with Hartley and her family, Charles somewhat more willingly acknowledges Hartley's existence as another human being, apart from his desires, and though scarcely enlightened, he is better prepared to confront whatever comes next in his "demon-ridden pilgrimage" (502).

A literal cave serves as the means to enlightenment in *The Nice and the Good* (1968) when John Ducane, a good man who fancies himself capable of judging others, undergoes a series of moral crises while investigating the suicide of a colleague. The climax occurs when John becomes trapped in a rapidly flooding sea cave at high tide while attempting to rescue Pierce, son of the widow Mary Clothier, and Pierce's dog Mingo. In the icy cold Ducane manages to guide Pierce and the dog up through a narrow rock chimney and finally out into the light and safety. Such physical ordeals constitute a means of moral testing in Murdoch's novels, just as the features of Plato's cave constitute metaphors for states of the soul's enlightenment. First Ducane learns to acknowledge his own pitiful, self-preoccupied mortality: stranded in a flooding shaft, he sees himself as "a little rat, a busy little scurrying rat" (263). Then, vowing to kill the rat in himself, he thinks "If I ever get out of here I will be no man's judge" (263). And finally he reaches an understanding that "To love and to reconcile and to forgive, only this matters. All power is sin and all law frailty. Love is the only justice" (263). Mary, fearing her son drowned, carries this understanding one step further; she feels "a love so impersonal and so cold it can scarcely be recognized, a love devoid of beauty"

(265), a love that she can feel for the dead, like Gabriel Conroy in Joyce's story "The Dead."

A momentary glimpse of this same selfless love is granted to Effingham Cooper in *The Unicorn.* Facing imminent death, mired in a liquid hole of mud in a bog that literally sucks him down into the earth, Effingham sees that, given the extinction of the self, "What was left was everything else, all that was not himself, that object which he had never before seen and upon which he now gazed with the passion of a lover" (167). Effingham sees "with a clarity which was one with the increasing light, that with the death of the self the world becomes quite automatically the object of a perfect love" (176). Although Effingham survives, he fails to bring his vision of love of the world down to the realm of lower Eros, for he is an ineffectual bureaucrat enmeshed in the irresistible mechanism of a gothic horror plot.

Even without Murdoch's writings on Plato, a quasi-Platonic pattern reveals itself in the fiction, a pattern variously influenced by the mysticism of Eastern religions, the psychological insights of existentialism, and the moral teachings of Christianity. Advancing beyond illusions about the self and others and beyond the demands of the self, the soul (mind) on its way to enlightenment must experience the death of the ego, learn to love others in all their incomprehensible otherness, and learn to love the world without the self, thus perhaps attaining a glimpse of *the* good. Successful pilgrimages like this are rare, and they do not make very good fiction anyway. Murdoch wisely chooses to weave her fiction from the failures and compromises of ordinary life, its comedy and grim ironies, but the underlying presence, not so much of a value system as of a systematic pursuit of value, makes itself urgently felt in her work.

The nightmare experience of a life utterly lacking in love is beautifully portrayed in *A Word Child* (1975), arguably Murdoch's finest novel. The narrator, Hilary Burde, presents himself to the reader as a man made irredeemably brutal, harsh, and unlovable by the burden of remorse and self-loathing he carries as a result of having caused the death of Anne Jopling, wife of his friend Gunnar, when the two men were young Oxford dons. Rising out of the most abject origins through serious linguistic study, Hilary managed to ruin his academic career by falling in love with Anne and then causing the motor accident in which she died even as she was trying to break off her affair with Hilary. He regards himself as a murderer, his life blackened forever. In this winter's tale of rain, fog, mist, and snow, Hilary's extreme pessimism creates a dark cosmos around him; rendered in the light of Hilary's brutally precise language, his London emits a stark, almost splendid, misery. Barely existing in a deadening government job, Hilary rigidly parcels out his weeks into "days" when he dines with various people, including his hapless mistress Thomasina and his half-sister Crystal, a very plain and simple soul and the object of his only (tense and possessive) affection. His particular hellish cave is the Inner Circle of the Underground, where he likes to ride round and round until the station bars open.

In *A Word Child* Murdoch employs a favorite device, the twice-told plot, enacted first as tragedy and second as tragicomedy. Hilary's past redounds upon him when Gunnar's second wife, Lady Kitty, "courts" Hilary through her maid, a mysterious Indian girl called Biscuit, in order to enlist Hilary's help in exorcising Gunnar's own obsession with the past and the ghost of Anne. Hilary eventually reconciles with Gunnar until he learns of Hilary's infatuation with Kitty. A scuffle on a jetty leads to Kitty's death in the freezing Thames and Hilary's near-death ordeal in the rushing water.

Murdoch powerfully engages the reader in *A Word Child* not only by her direct, forceful style and suspenseful plot, but also through the particular tone of Hilary's narration and the relation it establishes with the reader. We are invited to engage deeply in Hilary's story, but not allowed to love him: the excessiveness of his remorse and the brutality of his candor leave room for neither pity nor love. Hilary cannot live within the circle of humanity until he finally comprehends that his remorse need not be infinite, since it is not logical. Having "raged at the accidental," Hilary has nonetheless insisted "upon being the author of everything," a victim of the gods himself playing God (382). In the denouement, which occurs in T. S. Eliot's church, Hilary learns to weep and "to conjugate the verb of love" (380). His painful and reluctant journey out of his cave is dramatized within the reader, through one's slow, unwilling process of identification with this dark, recalcitrant character.

Murdoch's recent novels continue to hold out the possibility of metaphysical discovery. As their titles imply, *The Philosopher's Pupil* (1983), *The Good Apprentice* (1985), *The Book and the Brotherhood* (1987), and *The Message to the Planet* (1989), all long, ambitious novels, demonstrate Murdoch's increasing preoccupation with searching out truth, apprenticing oneself to it, and inscribing and imparting it. Even more prominently than in her earlier work, magical places in these novels—the underground hot springs of Ennistone in *The Philosopher's Pupil,* the mysterious towered house Seegard in *The Good Apprentice,* or the garden at Ballmain with the mysterious Axel Stone in *The Message to the Planet*—exert a force field, transforming the characters who enter them in a way that parallels love's transformations of the ego. From her early experiments with the gothic, Murdoch learned to use atmospheric settings as pervading presences that could manifest enchantments or inflictions of the soul, like Hannah Crean-

Smith's castle Gaze in *The Unicorn.* In these later novels, the "sacred" spaces seem to promise revelations from a place beyond the self to searchers like Edward in *The Good Apprentice* or Alfred Ludens in *The Message to the Planet.* Frustratingly, and realistically, however, Murdoch always stops short of revelation, bringing us back to the realm of lower Eros.

In *The Message to the Planet,* for example, Ludens, whose gloomy nature belies his name, loves and loses the young Irini, daughter of his friend Marcus Vallar (valor?). But the one Ludens really loves is Marcus, a mysterious charismatic figure and modern-day prophet without a religion who, having advanced, like Dr. Faustus, through various forms of learning—mathematics, art, philosophy—finally turns to forms of mysticism. Marcus commits suicide after preaching to a multitude of New Age believers who have followed him to Ballmain, a rural mental institution, and who end up stoning him. Christian, Jewish, and pagan themes and symbols so deeply infuse this novel that much seems at stake—at least to his disciple Ludens—in Marcus's quest for truth, some universal understanding, perhaps. The disappointment to both Ludens and the reader occurs as Marcus's papers are burned, the meaning of his final act is indecipherable, and the planet must go on without receiving the message. *The Message to the Planet* is a fine novel, a satisfying "read," but it nonetheless leaves the reader profoundly unsatisfied about the religious and metaphysical questions it raises. This dissatisfaction is obviously deliberate, a lesson. Murdoch raises frustrating questions about the existence of God and the nature of reality. One has no choice but to reexamine and to doubt the faith one has placed, as a reader, in both Marcus and Iris Murdoch's novel, a self-examination that continues after the novel is put aside.

Another messianic figure makes an appearance in London and later dies in a mental hospital in *The Green Knight* (1993), but in this case Peter Mir, a Russian Jewish Buddhist whose name means "world" and "peace," manages to carry out a series of morally significant actions before his mysterious demise. Physically intervening in a Cain-and-Abel struggle between two brothers, Lucas and Clement, Peter accidentally receives the blow to the head meant for Clement and then serves as the bearer of both justice and mercy for Lucas by administering a symbolic nick to Lucas's flesh, as the Green Knight did to Gawain. Successive chapter titles—"Justice," "Mercy," and "Eros"—suggest an upward moral progression, as do the several allusions to Dante's *Purgatorio* and the work of the Pearl Poet. With its bright imagery of medievalism and pervasive references to art and magic, *The Green Knight* is more festive in tone than Murdoch's several previous novels. She hints at a splendid dream of universal love, never to be synthesized or realized, but perceived only in scattered form among the great religious traditions and the stories and arts of East and West.

"Art, especially literature," Murdoch writes in **The Fire and the Sun,** "is a great hall of reflection where we can all meet and where anything under the sun can be examined and considered" (86). The house of fiction, with its many mansions, represents for Murdoch a place where teaching and learning about human nature can naturally occur; she opens up fictional spaces for that reflective purpose. The novelty and pleasure of her novels—the suspense, adventure, and wild twists of plot—keep the enterprise from ever seeming academic. Murdoch has a fine power of story-telling, and she fabricates her narratives out of love as she defines it: the energy that binds mortal fools to one another and to their world.

Notes

1. Anatole Broyard, "In the Emergency Ward of the Mind," *New York Times Book Review* 4 Feb. 1990: 3.

2. Robert Burton, *The Anatomy of Melancholy* (6th ed., 1651; New York: Farrar and Rinehart, 1927), 737.

3. Robert Hoskins, "Iris Murdoch's Midsummer Nightmare," *Twentieth Century Literature* 18.3 (July 1972): 191-98.

4. Joyce Carol Oates, "The Novelists: Iris Murdoch," rev. of *The Sea, the Sea,* by Iris Murdoch, *New Republic* 18 Nov. 1978: 28. Further page references are given in the text.

Katherine Weese (essay date fall 2001)

SOURCE: Weese, Katherine. "Feminist Uses of the Fantastic in Iris Murdoch's *The Sea, the Sea.*" *Modern Fiction Studies* 47, no. 3 (fall 2001): 630-56.

[*In the following essay, Weese contends that in her novel* The Sea, the Sea *Murdoch employs the fantastic mode to disrupt dominant and traditional novelistic conventions, and to compel both her characters and her readers to reconsider the scope and nature of reality as defined by "patriarchal institutions."*]

While many critics employ the term "fantastic" to describe aspects of Iris Murdoch's novels, none has systematically explored her work in conjunction with theories of the fantastic. Similarly, because Murdoch is often considered a writer who happens to be a woman rather than a woman writer, little exists in the way of feminist criticism of her work. Yet by examining Murdoch's Booker Prize-winning novel, **The Sea, the Sea,** at the intersection of feminist narrative theories and theories of the fantastic, we can place Murdoch's work within a body of contemporary women writers' fiction that employs some degree of postmodern experiment in narrative form, but that nonetheless retains strong ties to a realist tradition.[1]

Murdoch's **The Sea, the Sea** fits Tzvetan Todorov's category of the fantastic as articulated in *The Fantastic: A Structural Approach to a Literary Genre.* Todorov defines the fantastic as an unresolved moment of hesitation during which the reader or characters cannot decide whether seemingly supernatural events depicted in fiction are meant to be taken as real in a world with its own sets of laws, where supernatural events seem normal and undisturbing (marvelous fictions); or whether naturalistic explanations account for these events, which take place in our historical world and are bound by the laws we know (uncanny fictions). While Todorov has come under attack for his very narrow definition of the fantastic text, nonetheless several of his insights—and the ways in which critics following on his heels have developed those insights—bear on Murdoch's novel, especially in light of Todorov's explorations of the connection between the fantastic and the real. Toward the end of *The Fantastic,* Todorov asks, "Why does the literature of the fantastic no longer exist?" (166). The answer that he proposes stems from his conviction that while "the category of the real [. . .] has furnished a basis for our definition of the fantastic" (167), "today we can no longer believe in an immutable, external reality, nor in a literature which is merely a transcription of this reality" (168). Todorov concludes that in the twentieth century, the classic fantastic tale is replaced by the "generalized fantastic," which "no longer has anything to do with the real" (173-74). Iris Murdoch herself writes that "[w]e can no longer take language for granted as a medium of communication. Its transparency has gone. We are like people who for a long time looked out of a window without noticing the glass—and then one day began to notice this too" (**Sartre [Sartre, Romantic Rationalist]** 64). But Murdoch's fiction, along with that of many other contemporary women writers, allows critics to draw a very different set of conclusions than does Todorov about the continued existence of fantastic literature and about the relationship of that literature to what we call the "real." **The Sea, the Sea** is a novel in which instances of the unreal highlight the author's social and historical concerns, particularly the construction of gender roles. Murdoch and other contemporary women writers use fantastic devices that seem to straddle the boundary that Todorov proposes between the marvelous and the uncanny. Murdoch employs seemingly impossible events, at least one of which—James's miraculous rescue of his cousin Charles—is *not* resolved into the uncanny, but she sets this event squarely within our historical world. Murdoch, in her contemporary revision of the Gothic novel, employs the fantastic to disrupt conventional narrative practice and to force both her characters and the reader to "scrutinize the categories of the patriarchal real" (Cranny-Francis [*Feminist Fiction*] 77).

Many theorists of the fantastic have followed Todorov in his conclusion that literature of the fantastic no longer exists except as what he terms the "generalized fantastic." For example, Gerhard Hoffman extends Todorov's ideas about the generalized fantastic, and Christine Brooke-Rose speaks of a "displaced" fantastic to describe postmodern versions of the fantastic.[2] The novels on which these critics of the fantastic focus—mostly metafictions written by male authors of the 1960s and 1970s—need not employ supernatural devices of any kind; rather, the generalized fantastic is the self-referential world these fictions create, where character, self, history, reality, and truth are all simply textual constructions and hence "unreal." But as numerous feminist critics have explored, embracing the "generalized fantastic" poses a problem for women authors, given that women have historically been denied self-representation. Murdoch and her contemporaries of course acknowledge that one cannot simply return to a view of language as a transparent conveyor of an incontestable truth. Gayle Greene, for example, finds that contemporary women's fiction "bridges [the] gap between naive realism and esoteric experimentalism, enlisting realism while also employing self-conscious devices that interrogate the assumptions of realism" ([*Changing the Story*] 22). As she and numerous other feminist narrative theorists point out, while women's contemporary fictions differ from many male metafictionists' works insofar as their narrative experiments may seem less radical in form, nonetheless these experiments may actually be more radical in their social and political implications.[3] In an interview that took place ten years prior to *The Sea, the Sea*'s publication, Murdoch disdained contemporary experimental writing: "I would like to be thought of as a realistic writer [. . .]. I want to talk about ordinary life and what things are like and people are like [. . .]. Whether one could use experiment in the interest of this is something I have wondered about" (**"Iris Murdoch"** 73). *The Sea, the Sea* takes up precisely this project as Murdoch not only explores the lives of real people but uses experiment—including narrative self-consciousness and fantastic devices—to interrogate commonplace assumptions about the nature of gender. As Gary Goshgarian puts it, "Murdoch is directly concerned with [. . .] the artificial mystiques and myths of womanhood that deny women recognition as free, independent, and contingent human beings" (["Feminist Values in the Novels of Iris Murdoch"] 519).

Though feminist theorists do not necessarily deal with literature of the fantastic in their discussions of contemporary women writers (indeed, frequently they have either explicitly devalued the fantastic—an already marginal fictional mode—or have paid scant attention to its increasingly widespread use in women's contemporary fiction),[4] nonetheless their insights bear importantly on this body of literature since contemporary women authors' treatment of the fantastic falls in line with their treatment of narrative experiment. That is, while many authors carried the critique of representation to an extreme in metafictions that fall into that category of the generalized fantastic, most contemporary women authors rejected the idea of the generalized fantastic, instead employing fantastic devices that recuperated the relationship between the fantastic and the real that Todorov considers central to the classic fantastic tale. Contrary to the claims of many critics of the fantastic, then, the fantastic has not become synonymous with the most extreme kinds of narrative experimentation but does continue to exist in a middle ground between experimentation and realism, a middle ground occupied by authors such as Margaret Atwood, Barbara Kingsolver, Toni Morrison, and also by Iris Murdoch in *The Sea, the Sea*.

At the same time that she was working on this novel, Murdoch also published *The Fire and The Sun: Why Plato Banished the Artists* (1977), in which she writes that Plato's "criticism of art extends and illuminates the conception of the shadow-bound consciousness" (5). For Plato,

> form in art is for illusion. [. . .] Enjoyment of art deludes even the decent man by giving him a false self-knowledge based on a healthy egoism: the fire in the cave, which is mistaken for the sun, and where one may comfortably linger, imagining oneself to be enlightened. [. . .] The artist deceives the saving Eros by producing magical objects which feed the fantasy life of the ego and its desire for omnipotence.[5]
>
> (66-67)

Though Murdoch sees art in more positive terms than does Plato, she agrees that "magic in its unregenerate form as the fantastic doctoring of the real for consumption by the private ego is the bane of art" (79). Rather, life should be "a pilgrimage from appearance to reality" (2). *The Sea, the Sea* conjures up Plato's allegory of the cave: the main character Charles speaks frequently of "the world of shadows" (57) and of being chained. He writes early on, "I remember James saying something about people who end their lives in caves. Well, this, here, is my cave" (4). Once Charles begins to tell his tale, the reader will envision him as a prisoner—handcuffed, able to see only the images and shadows of reality thrown in relief on the cavern wall of his mind, fully believing that he sees the real thing in the shadows, ghosts, or phantoms he perceives. It is through his journey out of the cave, as it were, toward a definition of femininity not bound by the conventions of the classic Gothic plot, that Murdoch employs the fantastic to dismantle the patriarchal real.

"[W]hatever bondage we may be held in by [dark powers], however they may confine and cripple us, is a function of the moment in which we live[. . . . T]he Gothic reveals that monsters of fantasy come, not from deep within our minds, but from the forms of identity and selfhood shaped by our conventional reality" (Day [*In the Circles of Fear and Desire*] 192). So writes Patrick William Day, who reminds us that the Gothic genre is not a universal one, but one that reveals "the historicity of the imagination" (192).[6] In the hands of Iris Murdoch, the Gothic self-consciously explores the connection between the romance plot and the social construction of both masculinity and femininity. Published in 1978, *The Sea, the Sea* situates itself at the moment of the women's movement (at one point the narrator Charles Arrowby refers to "Women's Lib" [316]), but unlike many contemporary Gothic novels that focus upon the heroine's development, Murdoch's work focuses upon the change in consciousness of her central male character, the prototypical Gothic antagonist.[7] Central to this change are the fantastic devices that Murdoch employs throughout the novel, devices that, while serving as part of the novel's Gothic machinery, simultaneously subvert the conventions of the genre, in particular its narrative of patriarchal domination, its story of rescue and control.

Throughout *The Sea, the Sea,* the narrator's self-conscious ruminations on narrative form provide fertile ground for exploring the connections between the novel's narrative strategies and its representation of gender roles. *The Sea, the Sea* opens with a section called **"Prehistory"** that both introduces the supernatural elements of the novel and establishes narrator Charles Arrowby's preoccupation with aesthetic form. Charles, a London director and actor, records in a diary his decision to leave the city and to move to his current location, an eerie old house called Shruff End. In this setting, perched precariously on a bluff overlooking the sea, he plans to write something of his life—exactly what, he isn't sure, but he is confident that he will eventually "find [his] literary form" (3). He goes to Shruff End to withdraw from the world he has known, promising that he will become a hermit and, like Shakespeare's Prospero, repent a life of egoism and "abjure magic" (2-3). Charles is unable to escape his past, however; it revisits him in various forms as figures from the past disrupt his solitude by the sea. Two former actors with whom he has worked, Gilbert and Peregrine, intrude upon him at Shruff End, as do two actresses and former lovers, Lizzie and Rosina. James, a cousin that Charles has not seen in some years, also makes surprise visits. Finally, one day Charles believes he also sees his former love Hartley, a figure from the past preceding Charles's London theater days. Convinced that in Hartley he can find a way to recapture the innocence of his youth, he becomes obsessed with her, and with the idea of rescuing her from the husband whom he considers to be abu-

sive. His writings about and treatment of Hartley reveal that far from abjuring magic and egoism, Charles is still deeply embroiled in both, a fact that becomes clear from his preoccupation with literary form.

Throughout the first section of the novel, Charles exhibits an extraordinary self-consciousness about his writing, calling it a diary, a chronicle, and a memoir; his writings in this section, up until the point when he begins to obsess about Hartley, are loose and rambling observations. But when he turns to consider Hartley, he muses, "if one had time to write the whole of one's life like this bit by bit as a novel how rewarding this would be" (99). Thick into his new subject matter, he finally admits, "So I am writing my life, after all, as a novel. Why not? It was a matter of finding a form, and somehow history, my history, has found the form for me" (153). Though Charles quickly supplants history in general with his personal history, Murdoch, who titles the long middle section of her novel "History," suggests not only a collusion between narrativized historical accounts and traditional novelistic form, but also a collusion between the personal and the political, particularly where the social construction of femininity is concerned.[8] The story Charles tells is the larger story of society's patriarchy, its subordination of women to male authority, and its circumscription of female identity to the domestic realm.[9] Charles's novel is conventional both in its story line and in its linear structure: Hartley is his "alpha and omega" (77); life with her would "connect [Charles's] end with [his] beginning in a way that was destined and proper" (371). In thus constructing his story according to the principles of teleology, Charles adopts precisely the narrative form that feminist critics have identified as masculinist, while Murdoch's self-consciousness about history, individual and societal, undermines the novel that Charles writes and critiques the ideology on which it is based.

Charles's role as a director in the London theater provides a revealing commentary on the link between his formal self-consciousness and his treatment of women. Charles writes, for example, that "actors regard audiences as enemies, to be deceived, drugged, incarcerated, stupefied" (33), and that "drama must create a factitious spell-binding present moment and imprison the spectator in it" (36). The images of incarceration and assault that he uses to describe the theater characterize as well Charles's dealings with Hartley. In classic Gothic fashion, he locks her in a secret room in his house, imprisoning her literally just as he imprisons her metaphorically in his story, his house of fiction. Thus his conception of art as a means of power and magic surfaces in his "novelization" of Hartley, in the aggression of his narrative form itself. Until the end of the novel when he abandons his "history," nothing enables him to see that his relationship with Hartley is based less on love than on power, or that his narrativizing impulse, his attempt to force Hartley to become the heroine of a traditional love story, is an act not of tenderness but of aggression. As Steven Cohan points out, "the narrator's egocentric attempt to impose form onto experience through his fantasy of love actually manifests a predatory attack on woman" (["From Subtext to Dreamtext"] 236).

Charles's compulsion to narrativize his history with Hartley is critiqued through the fantastic devices of Murdoch's novel. In his work on the fantastic, Todorov examines the special affiliation between narrative and the fantastic, concluding that the fantastic mode is particularly appropriate to the narrative model, since supernatural episodes disturb the stable situation at the beginning of a narrative and require resolution in order for equilibrium to be re-established ([*The Fantastic*] 162-65). Todorov does not theorize that the fantastic creates new narrative forms, merely that it is especially suited to established, general narrative patterns. But by coupling these claims with feminist theories of narrative, we can see how the fantastic would be especially suited to disrupting not just stable plot situations but also traditional narrative patterns. Central to feminist narrative theory is the idea that narrative forms are ideological, or as Margaret Homans puts it, "narrative structure is cognate with social structures" (["Feminist Fictions and Feminist Theories of Narrative"] 5). *The Sea, the Sea* is profoundly and self-consciously concerned with the ideological implications of plots, with the ways that narrative has shaped cultural constructions of gender, and with the ways that alternative discourses and narrative techniques can disrupt dominant constructions of femininity, literary and historical (such disruptions accomplished in large part through the novel's fantastic devices). The instances of the fantastic in *The Sea, the Sea* raise questions for Charles regarding the reality status of his story and offer a counter-narrative that returns Charles from his social withdrawal at Shruff End to the world of messy, contingent reality.[10] The fantastic elements that disrupt the continuity of his narrative—especially the gruesome sea monster—cannot easily be fitted into his reductive world where everything constitutes part of the artistic pattern he imposes on events. In this capacity, the ghosts and monsters that haunt his mansion are by-products of his world view that haunt him and reveal the error of his ways, eventually forcing him to acknowledge a different kind of reality. That is, the fantastic elements of the novel that cause Charles to hesitate, in Todorov's terms, over what is real and what is not, eventually cause him to question the "reality" of his novelistic version of the Hartley romance, to question his use of genre—in particular the Gothic romance plot—to construct gender.

Theories of the female Gothic illuminate Murdoch's project in *The Sea, the Sea*. Karen Stein points out that in the traditional Gothic, "males are portrayed as heroes struggling to define themselves and working for personal power and success in all aspects of human endeavor while females, according to Joanna Russ, have only one role, 'the protagonist of a Love Story'" (Stein ["Monsters and Madwomen"] 125-26). This model certainly accounts for the way in which Charles views both himself and Hartley. Furthermore, according to Stein's work on the female Gothic,

> in the Gothic mirror, the [female] self is reflected in the extreme poses of rebel, outcast, obsessive seeker of forbidden knowledge, monster. Monsters are particularly prominent in the work of women writers, because for women the roles of rebel, outcast, seeker of truth, are monstrous in themselves. For a man to rebel, to leave a comfortable home and to search for truth are noble acts. [. . .] For women, however, such assertions of questing self-hood have been deemed bizarre and crazy; consequently the Gothic mode—and in particular the concept of self as monster—is associated with narratives of female experience.
>
> (123)

But Murdoch subverts the conventions of the female Gothic: it is not the female self that becomes monstrous, but the male self who casts woman as nothing other than the protagonist of a love story. Indeed, when Charles describes the monster, he is "vague about its exact distance away" from him (21): Murdoch offers the monstrous as a metaphor for Arrowby's own patriarchal project.

While jealousy is the most straightforward of the demon's significations,[11] all of the scenes in which Charles describes the monster or the monstrous qualities he sees in others also reveal Charles's fear of female sexuality. The monster's mouth recurs as a key terrifying image. When he first describes the monster, he writes, "*I saw a monster rising from the waves.* [. . .] I could also see the head with remarkable clarity, a kind of crested snake's head, green-eyed, the mouth opening to show teeth and a pink interior" (19). And when Rosina first appears at Shruff End, before Charles realizes she has been "haunting" him, he notes that "her mouth, enlarged by lipstick, was huge and moist. [. . .] I suddenly then, as I was staring at her, saw a vision: it was as if her face vanished, became a *hole,* and through the hole I saw the snake-like head and teeth and pink opening mouth of my sea monster" (104-05). He recalls his Aunt Estelle's singing from his childhood and comments, "it is probably in some way because of Aunt Estelle that the human voice singing has almost always upset me with a deep almost frightening emotion. There is something strange and awful about the distorted open mouths of singers, especially women, the wet white teeth, the moist red interior" (60). He notes later that "singing is of course a form of aggression. The wet open mouths and glistening teeth of the singers are ardent to devour the victim-hearer. Singers crave hearers as animals crave their prey" (312). In addition to recalling quite explicitly the description of the sea monster, Charles's comments about singing also endow the women in the novel with sirenlike qualities, suggesting the danger of their sexual allure.[12] In the conventional Gothic novel, feminine sexuality is often portrayed as something monstrous and unacceptable; in *The Sea, the Sea,* female sexuality, in any form other than traditional submission, terrifies Charles.[13] Charles, then, divides women into binary opposites, virgin and whore, in keeping with the "male disgust with woman's sexuality, the male hatred and fear of woman's awful procreative power and her 'otherness,' which lies at the root of the female gothic" (Stein 124). He distinguishes Hartley from the other women in his life because he considers her asexual, wanting always to describe their relationship in terms of its purity, to exclude Hartley from monstrous female sexuality. Writing of their relationship in the past, he claims, "[W]e were chaste, and respected each other absolutely and worshiped each other chastely" (80). Fantasizing about their future, he speculates, "Hartley and I would live alone, secretly, [. . .] in a little house by the sea [. . .] and the old innocent world would quietly reassemble itself around us" (371). Yet when Hartley rejects him, she, too, becomes monstrous as Charles exhibits a fear of her inner self and projects the sea serpent's qualities onto her: "she began to fight me, silently, violently, and with a surprising strength, kicking my ankles, writhing her body about. [. . .] I caught a glimpse of her open mouth and of her glistening frothy teeth" (232). In the same scene, Charles "sh[ies] away in horror from the *interior* of [Ben and Hartley's house] and of that marriage" (238-39; emphasis added), because in that marriage, Hartley is a sexual being, fallen and impure. Only very late in the novel does Charles begin to accept Hartley's sexuality: "[I]t occurred to me for the first time to wonder, had Ben and Hartley come together through *sexual attraction?*" (436).

While Charles is repeatedly drawn to other women's surfaces, finding their "insides" repulsive,[14] he claims that he wants desperately to "have access to [. . . Hartley's] interior being" (295), which he assumes to be purer, more submissive than the other women's interior selves. Murdoch constructs an elaborate metaphor around Charles's assumptions about Hartley's sexuality and his attempts to penetrate to Hartley's interior: the mysterious "inner room" at Shruff End, which he describes as "the chief peculiarity of the house, and one for which I can produce no rational explanation" (14).[15] Charles writes at one point that Hartley is "a pale partly disembodied being, her face hanging always just above my field of vision like an elusive moon" (170). This description is woven in with a string of related images throughout the novel. Charles envisions early in the narrative "a face looking at me through the glass of the inner room." (69). He considers three possible explana-

tions: first, he saw his own face reflected in the room's window; second, someone very tall or standing on something did peer out at him; or third, he saw "the moon reflected in the inner glass" (69). At first he settles on the third explanation (his preference being to privilege surface, not to wish to acknowledge depth, to admit of something in the inner room), but after he learns Rosina has been haunting his house, he favors the second.

Charles's drive is, of course, to recuperate Hartley—to strip her of her "truth" by making her conform to his world view, by making her tellable or representable. Thus he tries desperately to narrativize the events that take place in the inner room and to contain the threat or excess that Hartley herself might be seen to represent. While he may ultimately be unsuccessful in this endeavor, nonetheless his attempts and Hartley's passive responses to them allow a second reading of the function of her character in the novel, as a critique of the stereotypical Gothic heroine. Thus, when Charles has disturbing dreams about Hartley's death, the mysterious face in the inner room takes on for him a new significance, the language of the novel linking Charles's description of the mysterious face explicitly with Hartley's elusive "moon" face. At one point he dreams that Hartley is carried away by a "black prince" (a playful allusion to Murdoch's earlier novel of that title, whose narrator resembles Charles) and that "her head hung back over his shoulder as if her neck was broken" (147); next he dreams that he "found a new secret room at Shruff End, and a woman lying dead in it" (199). After he "captures" Hartley and actually locks her in the inner room to keep her from returning to Ben, he dreams that he sees Hartley there and that she is very tall, or that she is standing on something, but then he realizes "that she was suspended from the lamp bracket. She had hanged herself" (309). When he wakes from the dream, he reluctantly goes to look through the window into the inner room:

> I stood, holding my candle, and looking at the long inner window which was now like a glossy black mirror; and it occurred to me that I was shunning the drawing room not out of propriety but because of the appalling possibility that I might see Hartley actually looking out. And then I suddenly remembered the face which I had seen looking at me through the dark glass; and I thought, that face was *too high up.* It could not have been the face of someone standing on the floor. It was just at the level at which Hartley's face would have been if she had really hanged herself.
>
> (309-10)

In his mind, Hartley is a model of "true" femininity according to traditional Gothic representations of womanhood, while the reader will interpret the inner room motif and its accompanying imagery as suggestive of Charles's inability really to see into women's interiors or inner beings, and of his continuing tendency to see only surfaces or socially constructed ideals of femininity, since the Hartley he envisions in the inner room is the stereotypical masochistic Gothic heroine.

Michelle Massé's *In the Name of Love* provides a way to read masochism not as a personal weakness but as both a symptom of social trauma and, in psychoanalytic terms, as an attempt to bring to the surface a recognition of oppression.[16] Through Freud's account of the repetition compulsion, Massé accounts for the Gothic pattern of a woman moving from her domineering father's house to a husband's house that is supposed to grant her freedom but in actuality turns out to be simply a version of the same. In *The Sea, the Sea,* Hartley's repetition compulsion manifests itself not in the move from a father's house to a husband's, but in the shuttling back and forth she does (or is forced to do) between a husband and a suitor who are doubles of each other.[17] Massé "reconsider[s] the erased, retrospectively trivialized heroine's text and the trauma and repetition that give it shape," arguing that "repetition in the Gothic functions as it does for certain other traumas: the reactivation of trauma is an attempt to recognize, not relish, the incredible and unspeakable that nonetheless happened. [. . .] The originating trauma that prompts such repetition is the prohibition of female autonomy in the Gothic, in the families that people it, and in the society that reads it" (11-12). Rather than locate the source of Gothic heroines' suffering in those heroines' "faults," Massé suggests "looking instead at the encapsulating social systems that engender repeated trauma" ([*In the Name of Love*] 19) and that give rise to what she identifies as the genre's most "ominous" implication: "the refusal of the heroine's existence as subject" (11, n. 2).

Murdoch explores in her "love" triangle the destructive underside of gender roles assigned not only to the female Gothic protagonist but also those assigned to the male Gothic antagonist. Her use of the surface/depth trope comments not only upon Hartley but also upon Charles and ultimately challenges social constructions of masculinity. He himself is all "surface," his identity—of which he says he has "very little sense" (3)—stemming from popular portrayals of the male Gothic hero in which he becomes trapped. Charles evinces a perverse fascination with the antique mirror at Shruff End, to which he is "especially attached" (15), and which gives him the illusion that he has become someone he can at last represent to the reader. He describes the mirror in some detail:

> I have now been polishing the big oval mirror in the front hall (which I think I mentioned before). This fine thing (date eighteen ninety?) is perhaps the best 'piece' in the house. The glass is beveled and somewhat spotted but remarkably luminous and silvery, so that the mirror seems like a source of light. [. . .] Since I have

> just spent a while gazing at myself in this mirror it is perhaps time to attempt to describe my appearance."

> (31-32)

The mirror provides him with some "light" into his self, by providing the illusion of a coherent whole, like the ego formation the mirror provides according to Lacan's theory of the mirror phase. Murdoch suggests, however, that the self Charles sees there is not only narcissistic but illusory, an image, like his other visions of "reality."[18] Though he locks Hartley up, Charles himself behaves like a caged animal: "I ran about like a frenzied animal in a cage which batters itself painfully against the bars, executing the same pitiful leaps and turns again and again" (199). As Lindsey Tucker points out, Charles is both "the enchanter and the enchanted" (["Released From Bonds"] 382): he is locked in his own devices, as much the prisoner of his delusions of power as anyone around him, trapped by Gothic conventions and social constructions of masculinity.

If we extend Massé's observations to pertain to the male antagonist, as Murdoch's novel invites us to do, we can apply her theories of Gothic repetition to illuminate Charles's situation. His initial efforts to remake himself merely replicate the same old formulas, a tendency most evident in Charles's insistence that he has gone to Shruff End to retire from the theater, to "abjure that magic, drown my book," to make the "surrender of power, the final change of magic into spirit" (39), while in truth he replicates his theatrical powers by subjugating Hartley and writing another book of magic, a fantastic doctoring of the real. Toward the end of the novel, Charles becomes aware of his own repetition compulsion: "[I]t is strange to think that when I went to the sea I imagined that I was giving up the world. But one surrenders power in one form, and grasps it in another" (500). Hartley, caught in her own repetitive horror, partially allows Charles finally to recognize his own perpetuation of the Gothic plot, to acknowledge his participation in patriarchy and the denial of female subjectivity, and at last—and with great difficulty—to abandon his "history," with all its implications of the link between his personal history and the sociohistorical reality of male domination and female submission.

This recognition on Charles's part depends ultimately on his interactions with his cousin James. While Charles has constructed a story of male domination, a story of rescue and control, it is ultimately he who winds up being rescued by James. In a twist on the conventional Gothic plot, Murdoch offers an alternative model of masculinity, introducing through the character of James another instance of the fantastic, which, like the other fantastic devices she employs, disrupts Charles's version of his "history." James's miraculous rescue of

Charles, which is never fully explained, in effect challenges and changes the reality of male domination and prompts Charles to reconsider his patriarchal version of the "real."

James, a practicing Tibetan Buddhist, believes that "every tiny action has its consequences" (384). Like Charles, James participates in magic and powerful tricks of his own. James, however, fully recognizes the danger of power, whereas Charles is seduced by it. The difference in the cousins' use of magic is that James "understands [his tricks'] meaning and their consequences" (Tucker 387) and is willing to take responsibility for them. For example, he recounts to Charles the story of how, when he was in Tibet, he tried to practice a certain trick, "raising one's bodily warmth by mental concentration" (446), because he thought that he could generate enough heat to keep both himself and his companion warm enough to survive a cold night in a mountain pass. But, James laments, "there wasn't enough heat for two. Milarepa died in the night [. . .]. He trusted me. . . . It was my vanity that killed him" (447). James exercises his powers again, with more success, in the final "fantastic" instance of the novel. Peregrine, in a fit of jealousy, pushes Charles into a dangerous part of the sea called Minn's Cauldron, where the waters are so rough and the rocks so steep that it is impossible for him to climb out. And yet, miraculously, he is saved. Weak, feverish, and with no memory of who pushed him or how he survived, Charles at first believes that the sea monster was in the ocean pool with him and has saved him by lifting him out. But after Charles has recovered from the fever that follows his near-death experience, he suddenly recalls that he wrote down something about the event and hid it in his room. The piece of paper he finds reveals that James saved him from drowning "by coming down like some animal [into the cauldron. . . .] He was not climbing down with footholds and handholds like a man, he was creeping down on the smooth surface like some sort of beast. [. . .] Then James, as he crept right down into the churning whirlpool, detached himself from the rock like a caterpillar. There was an effect as of something sticky and adhesive deliberately unsticking itself" (468-69). Charles, who has earlier noted James's peculiarly deformed "feet like hands" (330), concludes that this memory of James's transformation must be accurate, even if the sea monster itself was not real. James's metamorphosis helps trigger Charles's own more mundane transformation from a romantic, solipsistic individual to a more socially responsible one.[19]

"What finally does lay Gothic horror to rest," writes Michelle Massé, "is the refusal of masculinist authority as the only reality to which one can turn and return" (39). Massé also observes that "in the interpersonal realm of the Gothic, both the beaten *and* the beater must change" (265). Though traces of Charles's old self

and his delusions remain throughout the postscript, he adopts many of James's wise attitudes toward his obsession with Hartley, at last admitting that she was "a phantom Helen" (492), and that he has "relax[ed] [his] hold upon Hartley, or rather her image, her double, the Hartley of [his] mind," recognizing his "acts and thoughts as those of madman" (491). The concluding postscript demonstrates, in its random form as well as in its themes, how the contingency of history disrupts the surface of Charles's novelistic endeavor. Charles comes to recognize what Peregrine tells him: "You've made it into a story, and stories are false" (335). As he approaches the end of his book, he abandons the part called "History" and begins the postscript with a comment on the nature of closure:

> That is no doubt how the story ought to end, with the seals and the stars, explanation, resignation, reconciliation, everything picked up into some radiant bland ambiguous higher significance, in calm of mind, all passion spent. However life, unlike art, has an irritating way of bumping and limping on, undoing conversions, casting doubt on solutions, and generally illustrating the impossibility of living happily or virtuously ever after; so I thought I might continue the tale a little longer in the form once again of a diary, though I suppose that, if this is a book, it will have to end, arbitrarily enough no doubt, in quite a short while.
>
> (477)

Charles's syntax itself here illustrates his point: his numerous clauses bump and limp on much like the postscript itself, which exhibits what Elizabeth Dipple calls a "deliberate and extended refusal to end" ([*Iris Murdoch*] 276). Indeed, as she points out, Charles "rejects the novelistic shape of an ending which his morning visitation by four seals had given him and which earlier he would have seized on as artistically apropos, and accepts the formless, anti-artistic, shapeless reality of life instead" (298). Charles rejects the clarity and intensity of artistic closure: he writes instead that "if this diary is 'waiting' for some final clarificatory statement which I am to make about Hartley it may have to wait forever" (490).

James might be said to represent a feminine principle in the novel, or the feminine side of the masculine self, one whose qualities oppose those of the Gothic male. But while James provides welcome relief to Charles's unrelenting and violent egotism, James's character is not wholly unproblematic.[20] In fact, James, who tells Charles that "we must practice dying" (445), offers a "solution" to the problem of violence that proves limited and ineffective. His discourse on this matter resembles certain ideas presented in Derridean thinking, namely the idea of pure difference, which Murdoch finally rejects just as she rejects Charles's attempt to construct a reality based on a naive view of language's ability to make things present. For James, because "the good are unimaginable" (445), dying would seem to be the only way to be truly good, the path James finally chooses in the end. The letter that Charles receives about James's death near the novel's end reveals that "Mr. Arrowby died in happiness achieving all. I have written for cause of death on the certificate 'heart failure,' but it was not so. There are some who can freely choose their moment of death and without violence to the body can by simple will power die. It was so with him" (473). Though James believes that his act, the surrender of power through death, constitutes the only available act of goodness, this withdrawal might be read simply as another version of Charles's withdrawal to Shruff End.

James has explained to Charles that most souls, after death, enter a "sort of limbo" called "bardo," where one meets one's "attendant demons." At the moment of death, one has the chance to avoid bardo and "to become free. At the moment of death you are given a vision of all reality which comes to you in a flash. To most of us this would be [. . .] something terrifying and dazzling and incomprehensible. But if you can comprehend and grasp it then you are free" of "attachments, cravings, desires, what chains us to an unreal world" (385). Though James is often viewed as the voice of wisdom in the novel, here the obtuse Charles's objections to his philosophy actually prove insightful. Charles objects that he "always thought that goodness was to do with loving people, and isn't that an attachment?" He then states that "all this giving up of attachments doesn't sound to me like salvation and freedom, it sounds like death" (445). Of course Charles's means of creating an attachment with Hartley is, as we have seen, violent and destructive, but the novel suggests that the impulse he has toward loving people is not in itself something to be viewed negatively, merely that it must shift from a relationship of dominator and dominated to a relationship of social equality. Instead of embracing James as Charles's wholly "good" double, Murdoch proposes a merger of the cousins' characters; she suggests that one needs to affect the world positively, not negatively, as James believes, but she suggests that one must affect it positively in a different manner than Charles has attempted to do at Shruff End. In this regard, Murdoch's vision resembles that of John McGowan, who distinguishes between "negative" and "positive" versions of freedom, describing the former as the freedom the individual can achieve only apart from any involvement in the social context which he or she opposes, and the latter as the freedom "possible within the terms of membership in a society" ([*Postmodernism and Its Critics*] 15). Instead of withdrawing from the world or giving up all attachments, even love, Charles continues to live very much in the world, but with a recognition that he must put an end to the historical reality of male domination by facing the fact that his concept of femininity is not a true one.

In the last image of the novel, Murdoch suggests the possibilities that the world holds for Charles. We have seen how Charles has a problematic relation to interiors, which Murdoch treats in two different ways: on the one hand, he is trapped in a cave, chained to the world of shadows and images, without access to the world of reality outside the cave; on the other hand, he fears women's "inner beings" and projects monstrous qualities onto women that actually reflect his own interior qualities. Both sets of images demonstrate Charles's inability to face what is real. As Charles ends his "History," however, when he is lying out on the rocks, he sees "into the vast soft interior of the universe which was slowly and gently turning itself inside out. I went to sleep, and in my sleep I seemed to hear the sound of singing" (475). This scene shows Charles's progress out of the entrapping house at Shruff End, as the world turns itself "inside out." The sound of singing here contrasts with the terror Charles has previously associated with women's singing; in conjunction with his peaceful vision of the world turning inside out, the image further suggests that the novel's Gothic horrors have been laid to rest. Indeed, Charles's last entry in the book furthers shows that Charles has resolved the interior/exterior conflict. He tells us that the demon casket in James's flat, of which he has been so protective, "fell off its bracket. The lid has come off and whatever was inside it has certainly got out. Upon the demon-ridden pilgrimage of human life, what next, I wonder?" (502). This incident has a distinctly comic, rather than horrific, tone and seems to open the way for many possibilities to follow, suggesting not only that Charles himself has escaped entrapment but also that he will no longer attempt to trap others in secret inner rooms. In his demon-ridden pilgrimage, he has put to rest his monstrous masculinity, his patriarchal world view.

The negativity that James represents in the novel is mirrored finally in the treatment of Hartley's character as well. In spite of Charles's attempts to contain Hartley by narrativizing her and by locking her in the inner room, both Hartley and the inner room become almost like excesses which cannot be wholly contained by his love story. Charles, as James points out, has turned Hartley from a real person into a ghost: "Some kind of fruitless preoccupations with the past can create such simulacra [. . .]. She is real, but what reality she has is elsewhere" (352-53). Hartley ultimately defies representation, her reality remaining elsewhere. Upon first beginning to remember her, Charles terms their story "untellable" (78); upon looking for her likeness in the museum, Charles comments, "She was a vast absence" (170), and in his final impression of her, she appears to him, as she will to the reader, as someone whose face is "strangely blank" (493). Her very blankness itself might be construed in Kristevan terms as a disruptive force. Kristeva notes, for example, how the principal of the feminine in the text constitutes a "truth" that has no self and that is found "in the gaps of identity," existing in "negativity" as a force that disrupts the symbolic (["About Chinese Women"] 150-53), in this case the patriarchal order of discourse that Charles represents. Hartley's "truth," defined by negativity, opposes the patriarchal "truth" that Charles wants to impose upon her in his socially constructed definition of femininity. As Rosemary Jackson suggests of literature of the fantastic, "it exists [. . .] as a muted presence, a silenced imaginary other. [. . .] By attempting to transform the relations between the imaginary and the symbolic, fantasy hollows out the 'real,' revealing its absence, its 'great Other,' its unspoken and unseen" ([*Fantasy*] 180).

Yet Murdoch presents as well a positive female alternative to Hartley's ghostliness, to her ultimate absence from the text: she depicts the transformation of Rosina from one who plays at being poltergeist, haunting Charles in his mansion, to one who gives up that role and enters the real world by taking political action. Once Hartley has disappeared from the text, much of Charles's final commentary concerns the fate of Rosina, who "had the fierce charm of the rather nasty girl in the fairy-tale who fails to get the prince, but is more interesting than the girl who does, and has better lines too" (73). Rosina and Peregrine reconcile when they have killed off the demon of jealousy that stood between them. Rosina, once "black, a black witch" (345), gives up that "nasty" role; dressed all in white she announces that she and Perry are "going to bring theatre to the people" in Ireland (435). Perry has earlier denounced Ireland quite vehemently as a hopeless cause. Interestingly, in this conversation between Charles and Perry, Murdoch links the subject of women with the subject of Ireland, proposing a connection between patriarchal and colonial domination.[21] In order to undertake this project with Perry, Rosina has also given up the part of Calypso that she's always wanted to play. Charles notes, "that had the hard touch of reality all right" (436), suggesting that Rosina's decision to give up playing Calypso, who keeps Odysseus on her island in isolation, constitutes her own move back into the real world. Charles learns later that "Peregrine is doing well with his theatre in Londonerry and is becoming quite famous as a propagandist for peace in Ireland. Rosina is equally enthusiastic and is rumoured to have become politically conscious and power-mad" (482). This socially symbolic power is quite distinct not only from Charles's version of power but also from the power Rosina used to haunt Charles at Shruff End and to prevent him from being with Lizzie. Rosina, who serves as an alternative to James by choosing activism over withdrawal, fights domination on behalf of others. Through the character of Hartley, the dominated, Murdoch both critiques the patriarchal society that perpetuates Gothic plots and subtly suggests ways in which Hartley's ghostliness or negativity subverts Charles's project; through the character of Rosina, Murdoch creates a woman who in a

positive fashion resists domination and awakens from the Gothic nightmare in which she has been trapped.

Notes

1. On both the difficulty of placing Murdoch within the contemporary canon and on the relationship between realism and experimentalism in postwar fiction, see Nicol, chapter 1.

2. Hoffman argues that the fantastic should include the "active play, creativity, the imaginative construct" that characterizes fictions by Barth, Barthelme, Coover, and Pynchon. According to Hoffman, in works by these and other contemporary authors, Todorov's concept of the fantastic (hesitation) is replaced by "a radical negation of the recognizability or explainability and even the need to recognize or explain" (320). There results a "non-meaning which the human being, accustomed to and constituted by meaning-building practices, must conceive as 'irreal,' as fantastic" (320). Brooke-Rose writes that "if the only feature that distinguishes the pure fantastic from the uncanny and the marvellous is ambiguity, which in turn is shared with some non-fantastic fiction, we must either emphasize (as Todorov does) that this ambiguity concerns only the supernatural [. . .], or treat other such non-'fantastic' texts as a displaced form of the fantastic, which is what I shall be doing in this book" (65).

3. See Hite 2; Frye 37-38; and Greene 19-22. Greene claims that while Murdoch is a contemporary woman writer who employs metafictional elements in her novels, she does not do so within the context of feminism (25). *The Sea, the Sea,* however, as well as Murdoch's earlier and similar novel, *The Black Prince,* provide perfect examples of novels that employ metafiction in the service of feminist ideals.

4. While there exists a large body of critical literature on women's fantasy and science fiction, there is little criticism of the fantastic itself in contemporary women's literature. In the 1990s, while there has been renewed attention to the supernatural as it appears in the works of multi-ethnic writers (see, for example, Winsbro), the widespread appearance of the fantastic in white women authors' works has not been fully considered. For an exception, see Hite, which provides an insightful analysis of the fantastic dimension of Margaret Atwood's *Lady Oracle.*

5. Compare Murdoch's comments in "Against Dryness," in which she suggests that form falsifies by imposing wholeness on the individual and the world, resulting in fantasy. In contrast, "reality is not a given whole. [. . .] Our sense of form,

which is an aspect of our desire for consolation, can be a danger to our sense of reality" (30-31). Reality, according to Murdoch, is something that transcends the individual (26) and that is difficult to know. Similarly, in "The Sublime and The Beautiful Revisited," she comments:

> There is a temptation for any novelist, and one to which if I am right modern novelists yield too readily, to imagine that the problem of a novel is solved and the difficulties overcome as soon as form in the sense of a satisfactory myth has been evolved. [. . .] There is then the much more difficult battle to prevent that form from becoming rigid, by the free expansion against it of the individual characters. [. . .] A novel must be a house fit for free characters to live in; and to combine form with a respect for reality with all its odd contingent ways is the highest art of prose.
>
> (271)

In fact, the reader might identify Arrowby as the type of novelist Murdoch speaks against: he is one who ignores the contingent messy reality of everyday life and who creates characters that are not free, namely Hartley. In the "novel" he produces, Hartley's "freedom" (in Murdoch's terminology, "free" is synonymous with "real"—a free character behaves like a real person in the real, contingent world) is severely restricted because Charles, who casts Hartley into a conventional social role, resembles modern authors who "deny freedom to the fictional individual either by making him merely part of his creator's mind, or by treating him as a conventional social unit" ("The Sublime" 266).

6. See also the portion of Massé's argument that addresses the Gothic's relation to social and historical reality and refutes claims that the Gothic is merely "escape literature" (18-20).

7. See, for example, Stein's argument that recent women authors "are creating new heroines who grow into personhood through their quest for experience and knowledge [. . . .] T]hese new writers are changing the Female Gothic symbols of victimhood and persecution into new sources of strength" (136-37). Likewise, Massé identifies two contemporary Gothic novels, *Linden Hills* and *Lady Oracle,* that resist what she identifies as the masochistic strain in earlier Gothic fictions. According to Massé, many, but not all, contemporary women authors writing in the Gothic mode create fictions in which women are freed from patriarchal authority and do establish identities of their own.

8. In considering the structure of Murdoch's novel and her narrative strategies, one should compare the implications of her form to what Hayden White postulates. White argues that the

value attached to narrativity in the representation of real events arises out of a desire to have real events display the coherence, integrity, fullness, and closure of an image of life that is and can only be imaginary. [. . .] Does the world really present itself to perception in the form of well-made stories, with central subjects, proper beginnings, middles, and ends, and a coherence that permits us to see "the end" in every beginning? Or does it present itself more in the forms that the annals and chronicle suggest [. . .]?

(24)

Earlier in the same essay, White points out that "the chronicle [. . .] often seems to wish to tell a story, aspires to narrativity, but typically fails to achieve it. More specifically, the chronicle usually is marked by a failure to achieve narrative closure. It does not so much conclude as simply terminate" (5). These ways of writing history correspond remarkably to Murdoch's project in *The Sea, the Sea,* where Charles's "History" section is narrativized history, marked by all the wishful thinking White identifies as inherent in this mode, while the "prehistory" and postscript more closely resemble the chronicle.

9. Massé writes that in the traditional Gothic, "history, both individual and societal, is the nightmare from which the [female] protagonist cannot awaken and whose inexorable logic must be followed" (12). She further points out that "heroines of the Gothic [. . .] have the same expectations as those around them for what is normal. Their societal contract tenders their passivity and disavowal of public power in exchange for the love that will let them reign in the interpersonal and domestic sphere" (18).

10. Compare here Murdoch's statement in "The Sublime and the Beautiful Revisited," where she comments on what she sees as the romantic, solipsistic character of recent fiction, where "what is feared is history, real beings, and real change, whatever is contingent, messy, boundless, infinitely particular, and endlessly still to be explained; what is desired is the timeless non-discursive whole which has its significance completely contained within itself" (260).

11. Not only Charles but all characters who act possessively out of jealousy become demons to the other characters in some form. Charles links Rosina, jealous of his relationship to Lizzie, with the monster on at least two separate occasions. Ben, we learn from Hartley, is jealous of Charles and for years has suspected his wife of a secret affair with him. Hartley says, "Ben's ideas about you have been like—like demons in our lives" (229). Finally, Perry, too, who is jealous of Charles's affair with Rosina, comments that when one is

wounded in love, "one's soul becomes numb with the endless blows—and of course one becomes a sort of fiend one-self, that goes without saying, one becomes ingenious in evil" (161). Compare also Murdoch's statement in an interview: "The notion of the intrusion of demons—well, I feel this is something that happens in life. Not necessarily that people really are demons but that they play the role of demons for other people" ("Iris Murdoch" 68).

12. For quite some time Charles excludes Lizzie, another former lover, from his association of women with the monstrous. Lizzie remains in his mind completely submissive, the ideal Gothic heroine. She finds Charles's power and possessiveness attractive; she tells him at one point, for example, that she wants him "to be the lord and the king as [he's] always been" (189); Charles in turn refers to her as an obedient "dog reading his master's tiniest movements" (359). Yet when Charles finds out that she and his cousin James have known each other prior to his introducing them, he immediately assumes they have a sexual relationship and considers Lizzie "spoiled," associating her, too, with the terrifying singers (409).

13. The siren connotation is especially appropriate in *The Sea, the Sea* since the sirens lured men to their deaths by drawing them near to the dangerous coast, where they would be dashed against the rocks and drowned. Ben and Hartley's son, Titus, dies in precisely this manner, when he is unable to climb safely out after swimming and drowns from a blow on the head. But in this context, too, Murdoch undermines Charles's revulsion at female sexuality, for Titus is not the victim of sirenlike singers but of Charles's own egotism. In his eagerness to appear strong and youthful to Titus, he neglects to warn the boy that climbing out of the sea can be treacherous. He realizes later, "My vanity destroyed him" (459).

14. Charles describes Rosina, for example, as the "most stylish, the most gorgeously artificial" (73); he sees all the women from his past in portraits in the London museum he visits: "Lizzie by Terboch, Jeanne by Nicolaes Maes, Rita by Dominichino, Rosina by Reubens, a perfectly delightful study by Greuze of Clement" (170). While he has not seen Hartley's portrait among the women in his past pictured in the museum, such is the case only because he has not yet painted it. Charles thinks of Hartley as a work of art he can create: "Hartley lay like a seed in my heart and grew again, purified as of old. It was only now clear to me how very much I had *made* that image, and yet I could not feel that was anything like a fiction. It was more like a special sort of truth [. . .]. I had

smoothed Hartley's brow and unclouded her lovely eyes as the years went by, and the ambiguous tormenting image had become a gentle source of light" (428). The novel's attention to the exterior/interior opposition, its fascination with both surfaces (portraits, mirrors, windows that act as mirrors) and interiors (inner rooms and open mouths), also plays an important role in Murdoch's critique of patriarchal domination, especially of those versions of the Gothic that refuse to grant women any identity other than shallow and supplicating victim of male aggression. Charles's fear of interiors is commensurate with his obsession with his own narrative form: in his attempt to write a perfect, coherent, seamless novel about himself and Hartley, he must ignore depth, the contingency of history, and the events that surround him, and quite aggressively attempt to force them into the pattern he creates in his mind.

15. Claire Kahane analyzes how Gothic mansions reflect the female body and discusses women characters' ambivalence toward the maternal body; in *The Sea, the Sea*, the association of the inner room with Hartley and her sexuality comments more explicitly on Charles's response to the female body than on Hartley's own, just as Murdoch reverses the trope of monstrosity to reflect upon the male character rather than the female.

16. As Stein also points out, "[T]he women who have been most acceptable to patriarchal culture are those who have been powerless; passive rather than active, self-sacrificing rather than self-assertive, meek rather than bold. [. . .] Through centuries of conditioning women have internalized this male-created division and, consequently, much of their behavior can be understood as reaction to this reductionism" (124).

17. While Charles believes that he is offering Hartley "freedom," his own discourse is full of dramatic ironies that suggest the collapse of boundaries between Charles and Ben:

> A dose of Ben, after having been with me, after having had the seeds of liberty sown in her mind, might very well wake her up to the possibility, then the compelling desirability, of escape. A dose of Ben would make her concentrate at last. It would be better thus, because she would make her own clear decision, not simply acquiesce in mine. If she could feel a little less frightened, a little less trapped, then she would decide to come. [. . .] I ought never to have locked her up, I saw that now. [. . .] I had given her the role of prisoner and victim, and this in itself had numbed her powers of reflection.

(357)

18. When Rosina breaks the mirror as part of her haunting, Charles is "very sorry" (55) and intends to keep the undamaged frame, but at the end, when he leaves Shruff End and takes up residence in James's London flat, he notes that he "resisted the temptation to keep the *art nouveau* oval mirror which Rosina broke" (479), suggesting his progress beyond conforming to cultural expectations reflected in the surface of the mirror.

19. In this particular fantastic instance, Murdoch's novel works against the commonplace claim that the fantastic has become meaningless in postmodern literature. Thus while Jackson, for example, argues that in twentieth-century literature, transformation happens "without the will or desire of the subject," that "metamorphosis in the modern fantastic [. . .] is no longer redemptive and [. . .] perverse images of mutilation/horror/monstrosity have taken precedence over utopian dreams of the superhuman or magical transformation of the subject" (81), we see in Murdoch's novel that the fantastic maintains its redemptive function: James wills his metamorphosis into the strange creature capable of rescuing Charles, using his powers for good, turning the monstrous into the miraculous.

20. Critics have tended to view James either too negatively or too positively. Dipple sees him as someone sinister and dangerous, as much to be condemned as Charles for his use of magic (293-96); she takes too literally his own self-assessment. Tucker, on the other hand, believes James to be a source of pure good, a saint, yet she fails to examine critically some of his problematic statements and attitudes. Murdoch's novel, I think, suggests something between these two extreme views about the nature of James's magic.

21. Another way that Murdoch highlights the colonial theme is by drawing heavily upon *The Tempest,* a drama that raises issues of both colonial and patriarchal domination. See Tucker's comparison of the various characters in *The Sea, the Sea* to characters in Shakespeare's work.

Works Cited

Brooke-Rose, Christine. *A Rhetoric of the Unreal: Studies of Narrative and Structure, Especially of the Fantastic.* Cambridge: Cambridge UP, 1981.

Cohan, Steven. "From Subtext to Dreamtext: The Brutal Egoism of Iris Murdoch's Male Narrators." *Women and Literature* 2 (1982): 222-42.

Cranny-Francis, Anne. *Feminist Fiction: Feminist Uses of Generic Fiction.* New York: St. Martin's, 1990.

Day, William Patrick. *In the Circles of Fear and Desire: A Study of Gothic Fantasy.* Chicago: U of Chicago P, 1985.

Dipple, Elizabeth. *Iris Murdoch: Work for the Spirit.* London: Methuen, 1982.

Frye, Joanne S. *Living Stories, Telling Lives: Women and the Novel in Contemporary Experience.* Ann Arbor: U of Michigan P, 1986.

Goshgarian, Gary. "Feminist Values in the Novels of Iris Murdoch." *Revue des Langues Vivantes* 40 (1974): 519-27.

Greene, Gayle. *Changing the Story: Feminist Fiction and the Tradition.* Bloomington: U of Indiana P, 1991.

Hite, Molly. *The Other Side of the Story: Structures and Strategies of Contemporary Feminist Narrative.* Ithaca: Cornell UP, 1989.

Hoffman, Gerhard. "The Fantastic in Fiction: Its 'Reality' Status, Its Historical Development, and Its Transformation in Postmodern Narration." *Year-book of Research in English and American Literature* 1 (1982): 267-364.

Homans, Margaret. "Feminist Fictions and Feminist Theories of Narrative." *Narrative* 2.1 (1994): 3-16.

Jackson, Rosemary. *Fantasy: The Literature of Subversion.* London: Methuen, 1981.

Kahane, Claire. "The Gothic Mirror." *The (M)other Tongue: Essays in Feminist Psychoanalytic Interpretation.* Ed. Shirley Nelson Garner, Claire Kahane, and Madelon Strengnether. Ithaca: Cornell UP, 1985.

Kristeva, Julia. "About Chinese Women." *The Kristeva Reader.* Ed. Toril Moi. New York: Columbia UP, 1986. 153-55.

Massé, Michelle A. *In the Name of Love: Women, Masochism, and the Gothic.* Ithaca: Cornell UP, 1992.

McGowan, John. *Postmodernism and Its Critics.* Ithaca: Cornell UP, 1991.

Murdoch, Iris. "Against Dryness." 1961. *The Novel Today: Contemporary Writers on Modern Fiction.* Ed. Malcolm Bradbury. Glasgow: Fontana, 1976. 23-31.

———. *The Fire and The Sun: Why Plato Banished the Artists.* Oxford: Oxford UP, 1977.

———. "Iris Murdoch, Informally." Interview with William K. Rose. *London Magazine.* June 1968: 59-73.

———. *Sartre, Romantic Rationalist.* 1953. New Haven: Yale UP, 1967.

———. *The Sea, the Sea.* New York: Viking, 1978.

———. "The Sublime and the Beautiful Revisited." *Yale Review* 49.2 (1960): 247-71.

Nicol, Bran. *Iris Murdoch: The Retrospective Fiction.* New York: St. Martin's, 1999.

Stein, Karen F. "Monsters and Madwomen: Changing Female Gothic." *The Female Gothic.* Ed. Juliann E. Fleenor. Montreal: Eden, 1983. 123-37.

Todorov, Tzvetan. *The Fantastic: A Structural Approach to A Literary Genre.* Trans. Richard Howard. Ithaca: Cornell UP, 1975.

Tucker, Lindsey. "Released From Bonds: Iris Murdoch's Two Prosperos in *The Sea, the Sea.*" *Contemporary Literature* 27.3 (1986): 378-95.

White, Hayden. "The Value of Narrativity in the Representation of Reality." *The Content of Form: Narrative Discourse and Historical Representation.* Baltimore: Johns Hopkins UP, 1987. 1-25.

Winsbro, Bonnie. *Supernatural Forces: Belief, Difference, and Power in Contemporary Works by Ethnic Women.* Amherst: U of Massachusetts P, 1993.

W. S. Hampl (essay date fall 2001)

SOURCE: Hampl, W. S. "Desires Deferred: Homosexual and Queer Representations in the Novels of Iris Murdoch." *Modern Fiction Studies* 47, no. 3 (fall 2001): 657-73.

[*In the following essay, Hampl discusses the presence in Murdoch's fiction of a non-threatening version of homosexuality, one in which supposedly gay characters are liable to experience heterosexual relationships but never have sex with other homosexuals.*]

In the moving memoir *Elegy for Iris,* John Bayley, the widower of Iris Murdoch, writes that Murdoch "had an odd streak of romanticism about gay men and was apt sometimes to be naïve in her assessment of who was what" (188). This comment and Bayley's claim that Murdoch could brilliantly describe the physical details of characters without having "any instinctive sense of how those characters function in themselves, on the humbler level" (66) are actually quite enlightening to readers who attempt to analyze Murdoch's homosexual characters and the manner in which her texts intricately queer positionalities and sexualities.

Although Murdoch's texts are filled with homosexual characters, Murdoch's readers quickly realize that her fictional versions of homosexuality are light years removed from any versions of homosexuality in the real world; in other words, Murdoch's fiction is much stranger (and not necessarily more comforting) than truth. This disparity in Murdoch's work—her literary treatment of homosexuality versus a real-world version of homosexuality—proves to be increasingly problematic, not to mention bizarre. Even when she writes a fine novel, *The Green Knight* (1993), that indicates

queer possibilities for re-configurations of the family unit (or the "desire-ability" of queer relationships), the reader realizes that Murdoch's optimism surprisingly arrives after an extensive and observable history of unrealistic (even nonsensical) treatments of homosexuality.

Murdoch's most intriguing and successful configuration of a queer family unit appears in her Shakespearean *The Green Knight,* which demonstrates that conventional notions of desire and sexuality break down. A brief summary of some of the subplots of the novel follows: the text describes the dissolution of a long-term homosexual relationship between Clive and Emil. Murdoch writes against the grain of stereotypical homosexual hysteria: Emil, after Clive leaves him for another man whom Clive "loves more," does not fall apart. Having been happy with Clive, he decides to now enjoy life by himself. His later advances toward Bellamy, who considers becoming a priest, are politely refused, and still Emil is content. Later, Bellamy decides to live together with Emil, without sex, and be happy; Bellamy even imagines a future for them, living together in India, "adopting" the young woman Moy. Such a family unit may best (only?) be identified as queer, and indeed, queer family units are, as a result of the destruction of traditional sexual categories, the point toward which Murdoch's writings commonly strive.[1]

Before approaching the queer politics of *The Green Knight,* I would like to examine the homosexual politics of some of her earlier novels, which reveal male characters who are insecure in their sexualities and the sexualities of others, male characters who desire other male characters (who do not reciprocate but do not mind being desired), and male characters whose homosexual dreams or futures never come to pass. Readers could find such tropes in a plethora of Murdoch's texts, but the present analysis will limit itself to two texts per homosexual trope (with additional examples in the endnotes). Queer politics are built upon the foundation laid by homosexual politics, and a knowledge of Murdoch's treatment of homosexuality is integral to an understanding of her works.

In this connection, Murdoch's texts reveal themselves to be strangely and strikingly at odds with one important aspect of Foucaultian theory. In his interview "Friendship as a Way of Life," Michel Foucault says: "I think that's what makes homosexuality 'disturbing': the homosexual mode of life, much more than the sexual act itself [. . .] To imagine a sexual act that doesn't conform to law or nature is not what disturbs people. But that individuals are beginning to love one another—there's the problem" (["Friendship as a Way of Life"] 136-37). According to Foucault, most of those people who are uneasy about homosexuality are troubled by the notion that two men or two women might love each other; Foucault posits that love makes people uncomfortable, not sex.

However, in Murdoch's novels, the opposite occurs: Murdoch repeatedly has male characters who love or fall in love with each other,[2] but she never writes that these same characters ever have sex. This lack is blatant when one considers not only how often Murdoch's heterosexual characters eagerly jump into bed with each other, but also the gleeful detail with which the texts often describe such heterosexual couplings. Obviously, Murdoch's deferment of homosexual desire complicates homosexuality, for by taking the sex out of *homosexual,* Murdoch's texts leave only the prefix, meaning *same,* and the texts therefore provide pals, not partners.[3]

Besides de-sexing homosexuality, Murdoch's texts in addition demonstrate that homosexuality is a fluid category of identification, that being homosexual is not a rigid or lasting category of (self-) identification. In other words, with Murdoch, we get gay today (maybe), but maybe not tomorrow. Although few would dispute that sexualities are malleable categories, Murdoch's understanding or literal conceptualization of homosexuality is so very fluid that Murdoch's readers, bearing in mind that her homosexual characters do not engage in homosexual acts, might well ponder what Murdoch means (or even suggests) when she writes of homosexuality.

It follows, then, that Murdoch's texts include an ersatz version of homosexuality. This psuedo-homosexuality in Murdoch's novels is still present in contemporary society, recalling a humorous anecdote in David M. Halperin's *Saint Foucault.* Writing about problems with the word "queer" and noting that the term "provides a means of de-gaying gayness," Halperin notes the ultimate results of what happens when sexual categories melt down. He relates that one of his friends "reports about a certain New England women's college, [where] all the women who are sleeping with men identify themselves as lesbians and all the women who are sleeping with women identify themselves as bisexuals. Hence the stunning headline of a recent lesbian 'zine: LESBIANS WHO SLEEP WITH WOMEN!" ([*Saint Foucault*] 65-66). Halperin's short aside serves to show that people (including authors) are free to (and invariably do) deconstruct, reinvent, rename, (re-) appropriate sexual norms and labels, but when people do this type of work and take (with the best of intentions, no doubt) this work to the extreme, the labels no longer make sense.

In other words, most people in society (excluding, apparently, certain members of society affiliated with a particular New England women's college) have a certain understanding of *lesbian* and *gay* and would not be surprised by the notion that lesbians sleep with women or that gay men sleep with gay men. (To reiterate, Foucault's position is that people are relatively untroubled by such homosexual couplings; Murdoch's novels fail to include such homosexual couplings). Only when the traditional meanings of such labels disintegrate does the fact that some people sexually prefer others of their own gender become headline news.

As previously mentioned, Halperin's story is strikingly similar to some of the bizarre sexual identifications in several of Murdoch's novels. Two of Murdoch's novels in particular, ***The Philosopher's Pupil*** (1983) and ***A Fairly Honourable Defeat*** (1970), are case studies of characters who are unsure or insecure of/in their sexualities and sexual relationships. For instance, in one dizzying plot twist in ***The Philosopher's Pupil,*** Emma, who is male, eventually identifies as homosexual, despite (not because of) the fact that he has a sexual experience with Pearl, who later identifies as lesbian. In fact, Pearl's following statement occurs shortly after the characters engage in some less-than-thrilling heterosexual (?) intercourse: "I think I can only love my own sex. Like you [Emma]. Not that anything has ever come of it" (485). The sexual politics of the novel are eerily disturbing: Pearl, never acting on her sexual desires toward other women, is celibate until Emma. Thus, in ***The Philosopher's Pupil,*** although gay men may love gay men and gay women may love gay women, Murdoch's narrative throws sexual orientation to the winds: a homosexual man has sex with a homosexual woman, and gayness is thereby de-gayed.

Such incidents expand in importance when considering Murdoch's earlier novel ***A Fairly Honourable Defeat,*** which contains a homosexual couple, the reticent Axel and the flamboyant Simon. The characters are quite different from each other: Stephen Adams writes that Rupert is "a paragon of civilised manhood" and Simon "throws himself wholly into prettification, flower-arranging and interior design" ([*The Homosexual as Hero in Contemporary Fiction*] 176-77). Although Peter J. Conradi claims that Murdoch's depiction of the couple as "happy" is "a small triumph" ([*"A Fairly Honourable Defeat"*] 87), the reader should judiciously consider the power dynamics within Axel and Simon's relationship, especially when Axel muses whether he might have "blighted Simon's life," whether the once happily-promiscuous Simon might not really be heterosexual after all:

> Axel also went off into long speeches about the unfairness of an older person imposing love upon a younger person. He speculated about whether he had not blighted Simon's life. He wondered whether Simon might not really be heterosexual after all. He pictured Simon happily married to some charming long-legged twenty-two-year-old girl. He provided Simon with several splendid children. He gave a favourable estimate of Simon's possibilities as a father.
>
> (157-58)

One may perhaps describe the above as a homosexual character's engaging in a heterosexual fantasy, for even if Axel has his own doubts of his partner Simon's homosexuality, the reader certainly does not. Critics have duly noted that Murdoch's love-plots often "work as a series of unveilings, of the discovery of erotic substitutions" (Johnson ["Iris Murdoch's Questing Heroes"] 56), and indeed, Murdoch herself has a character in *A Fairly Honourable Defeat* who claims, "There is no relationship [. . .] which cannot quite easily be broken and there is none the breaking of which is a matter of any genuine seriousness. Human beings are essentially finders of substitutes" (233). These substitutions, however, are generally understood as substitutions between heterosexuals.

A Fairly Honourable Defeat clearly demonstrates that Axel's day-dreaming is not about any value-free erotic substitutions, but rather about the frequent cruelty and self-absorption of this particular character. Yet the text presents Murdoch's nonsensical homosexuality as actually quite plausible. Through Axel, Murdoch's text sanctions the possibility that Simon is having an affair with a heterosexual female, his sister-in-law Morgan. Early on, the text reveals that Axel jealously dislikes Morgan: "Simon was far too diffident to imagine that Axel disliked Morgan because Simon loved her. Yet that in fact was the origin of the dislike" (33). This jealous animosity festers throughout the novel, and Axel, having already distressed himself and Simon over Simon's theoretical heterosexuality, eventually asks Simon: "You didn't have any sort of love passage with either Morgan or Julius?" (392). Despite years in a monogamous homosexual relationship with Simon, Axel questions whether his partner is having an affair with either a heterosexual woman or else a heterosexual man.

Complicating Axel's unfounded suspicion that his long-term partner is in fact "really" heterosexual, Murdoch's text allows the possibility that Simon is either "vulgarly flirting" or even having an affair with Julius. The powerful effect of this possibility is not to be underestimated, for Julius is able to blackmail Simon by threatening to "reveal" to Axel that Simon has strayed from monogamy and has been making passes. The threat works because Simon strongly suspects that Axel will believe Julius's claim, and as seen above, Axel specifically questions Simon about his relationship with Julius.

Thus, **The Philosopher's Pupil** and **A Fairly Honourable Defeat** demonstrate that although *homosexual* may be what-one-is, *homosexual* is not all-that-one-is.[4] Sexuality becomes increasingly problematic: gay men both engage in sex with lesbians and also wonder whether their own partners are heterosexual. Understandably, not a few people have trouble accepting or even acknowledging "playing fast and loose" with sexual orientation in this way. For instance, in *One Hundred Years of Homosexuality,* Halperin writes: Now *both* the notion that an act of heterosexual aggression in itself makes the aggressor suspect of homosexual tendencies *and* the mirror-opposite notion that a person with marked homosexual tendencies is bound to hanker after heterosexual contacts are nonsensical to us, associating as we do sexual object-choice with a determinate kind of "sexuality," a fixed sexual nature" (33). Halperin's use of *nonsensical* in the above passage parallels the reactions of many readers to Murdoch's portrayals of sexual desires: by and large in Western society, most heterosexual men do not chase other men (regardless of the sexuality that these chased men claim), and most homosexual men do not yearn for sexual fulfillment with women. However, the sexual identities of Murdoch's characters suggest that a character's "being" homosexual does not preclude him or her from having or actively seeking sexual relationships with both heterosexual men and women. Such a version of homosexuality is, to use Halperin's word, nonsensical: it is a very small minority indeed of real-life homosexuals who would ever practice their sexuality in the way Murdoch's literary creations do.

Such fluid (albeit non- or anti-realistic) representations of sexual desire(s) help explain the lack of homophobia in Murdoch's texts, for *homosexual* ultimately becomes an arbitrary label of little descriptive value. To be sure, Murdoch's texts are filled with characters who wonder whether some other character may be gay or queer, but this gossip is fairly benign, for Murdoch's texts don't really *believe* in homosexuality. That is to say, if Murdoch's fictions contain solely homosexual characters liable to engage in heterosexual relationships or else homosexual characters who never engage in sex with other homosexual characters, then homosexuality, for all intents and purposes, fails to exist.

Murdoch's characters could also be described as omnisexual. In fact, omni-sexuality is suggested by Eve Sedgwick's claim that "many people have their richest mental/emotional involvement with sexual acts that they don't do, or even don't *want* to do" ([*Epistemology of the Closet*] 25). Her novels are filled with instances of heterosexual male characters who do not react in disgust when they learn of other male characters who sexually desire them. In Murdoch's (omni-) sexually-charged narratives, any character, regardless of gender, may be fair game, but due to sexless homosexual relationships, characters have nothing to fear.

Two texts in which male characters do not mind at all that they are desired by other male characters are **The Book and the Brotherhood** and **A Word Child**. In the first of these texts, Gerard tells his longtime friend Jenkin that they should be together:

> Look, Jenkin, this is serious, it's the most serious thing in the world, in my world. I want to get to know you

better, much better, I want to come closer to you, I want us to share a house, I want us to live together, to travel together, to *be* together, I want to be able to see you all the time, to be with you—I want you to *come home*—you've never had a home—I want you to come home to *me*. I'm not saying this is possible, I'm telling you what I want, and very very much want—and if you consider what I say and understand it you'll see why it is I don't want you to go away.

(360-61)

Surprised by this powerful, poignant admission of love and desire, Jenkin jocosely queries whether this "proposal of marriage" includes sex as well, to which Gerard replies, "Why not, but that's not the point. It doesn't matter" (361).

But *it,* meaning sex, does in fact matter, both in Murdoch's texts and in real life. Several critics have noted that Murdoch frequently incorporated her experience of life into her novels (Spear I), and because she knew many happy homosexual couples, her textual rendering of homosexual couples is often considered to be sympathetic (Bove ["New Directions"] 189). Yet, a representation of a (homo-) sexual relationship in which sex doesn't matter is hardly sympathetic; on the contrary, such a representation serves to erase (homo-) sexuality.

"Homosexual" desire "appears" in a second text, *A Word Child* (1975), when the reader learns that the homosexual character Clifford has carefully (and *naturally,* in Murdoch's texts) appraised the heterosexual character Hilary as a possible partner. Even though Hilary identifies as heterosexual, he does make the following comment: "It was not that I was in any way homosexual, though I sometimes attracted men" (35). Hilary knows that he has, true to form, attracted Clifford and that Clifford has examined him and found him an unacceptable choice:

That [Clifford] had hoped to find a partner in me, had with the most exquisite tact and discretion tried me for this role, now seemed to belong to the remote past, a kind of legend of a time which may not even have existed in reality, but which pervaded and determined the present, coloured it certainly. Nothing was said of course, and I received no confidences about Clifford's life.

(74)

Despite being put under such scrutiny, Hilary remains close friends with Clifford. Hilary disclaims any type of homophobia: "I harboured no prejudice of this sort [against homosexuality]. If I shuddered at all it was at what was sexual rather than at what was homosexual" (74). *A Word Child,* then, contains a supposed homosexual (because Clifford offers no personal confidences, the reader has no knowledge of any of his only-presumable homosexual activities) who chases a heterosexual who does not mind being chased.

Clifford comes to a rather sudden end in *A Word Child,* committing suicide toward the text's conclusion. Though Clifford's relationship with Hilary had been strictly platonic with no suggestion of any possible future consummation,[5] the text, by ridding itself of the homosexual character, definitively disallows any chance of such a consummation. Murdoch's texts commonly employ such a plot device: they introduce two male characters who display some degree of homosexual interest toward each other (though sometimes the interest is one-sided), only to violently remove (that is, "kill off") one of the characters.[6]

Earlier I quoted Sedgwick to suggest that some people voyeuristically enjoy or experience sex. These people don't necessarily have to be engaged in a sexual act (and indeed, some people may mentally engage in a sexual act that they would never consider physically participating in) to gain pleasure from it. However, what Sedgwick is taking as a given is that these people have the choice, ability, or, to be Foucaultian, the *power* to mentally engage in this type of voyeurism; Murdoch's characters do not. Although, as stated earlier, sex does in fact matter, my purpose is not to argue the benefits, degree of pleasure, or politics of voyeuristically experiencing a sexual act as opposed to actually/physically experiencing a sexual act. Instead, my aim is to note that Murdoch's "homosexual" characters often perish, quite suddenly, before their respective texts allow these characters to act upon their desires.[7] Thus, homosexual acts in Murdoch's texts are always deferred, considered to be something that might—definitely not *would*—have been.

Two examples of death's deferring of possible homosexual relationships occur in *The Book and the Brotherhood* and *The Good Apprentice* (1985). In the first of these texts, as already mentioned, Gerard propositions Jenkin, and although Jenkin is certainly not repulsed by the offer, he is not able to arrive at a definite conclusion about what he will do:

Jenkin had never had a homosexual relation or dreamt of considering his close friendship with Gerard in that light—nor did he now allow himself to wonder what exactly it was which now existed and previously had not. What he felt was a sudden increase of being. Gerard had *called* to him, and the echoing call stirred things in deep places. Come live with me and be my love. Perhaps, after all, this changed everything?

(370-71)

Perhaps Gerard's sudden offering of love does change everything for Jenkin, but the reader will never know, for Murdoch's text does not afford Jenkin a future; instead, he is accidentally shot before he can either accept or refuse Gerard's offer (468).

A second example of a homosexual dream deferred appears in *The Good Apprentice,* in which Edward, the son of a bisexual father, Jesse, surreptitiously gives his friend Mark some drugs, and Mark shortly thereafter perishes in an accident. Grieving very much for Mark's untimely death, Edward wails: "Oh my dear, oh my darling, my poor lost one, my poor dead one, come to me, forgive me, I'm sorry, oh my love, my love, I'm so sorry, help me, help me, help me" (11). Later, Mark's sister, Brownie, asks Edward whether he and Mark had had a homosexual relationship. Edward replies that they had not and then realizes that such a relationship "was something which might have happened in that long future which he had, together with Mark, destroyed" (309). Although Edward tells Brownie that just as he had not sexually desired Mark, neither had Mark sexually desired him (Edward), even as Edward speaks these words, he thinks, "Can I be certain? [. . .] God, how this hurt, this unexpected opening up of things that might have been, further torture chambers and caverns of pain" (310). Due to Mark's untimely death, both the reader and Edward realize that any possible homosexual relationship between him and Mark is permanently deferred.

Having considered Murdoch's literary presentations and complications of homosexuality, we can now consider *The Green Knight* and analyze how this later text both aligns itself with and contradicts Murdoch's previous novels. As previously mentioned, this particular novel courageously offers a new understanding of the configurations of a queer family. Before examining the particulars of this queer family, I would first like to provide some explication of my use of *queer.*

As David Halperin notes, whereas gay identity is usually rooted in homosexual object-choice, queer identity is not:

> Queer identity need not be grounded in any positive truth or in any stable reality [. . .] "queer" does not name some natural kind or refer to some determinate object; it acquires its meaning from its oppositional relation to the norm. Queer is by definition *whatever* is at odds with the normal, the legitimate, the dominant. *There is nothing in particular to which it necessarily refers.* It is an identity without an essence.
>
> (*Saint* 62)

In other words, *queer* is never meant to be a synonym for *gay,* or, as Michael Warner succinctly notes, "'queer' gets a critical edge by defining itself against the normal rather than the heterosexual" ([Introduction to *Fear of a Queer Planet*] xxvi). The definition of *queer* is pretty much dependent upon the person(s) using the word, but what is important to remember is that queer is somehow at odds with mainstream—as opposed to specifically heterosexual—society.

Thus, *queer* is like a two-edged sword: its benefit and its downfall is that the word can be applied to whatever is at odds with the normal, and people are bound to dis-

agree over whether the term is used "correctly." Because of the flexibility of the term, some commentators have trouble with its being used at all, under any circumstances.[8] Halperin notes the purpose of *queer* is to "define (homo)sexual identity oppositionally and relationally but not necessarily substantively, not as a positivity but as a positionality, not as a thing but as a resistance to the norm" (*Saint* 66). My queer reading of *The Green Knight* is intended to point out how Murdoch uses her traditional tropes related to homosexuality and then takes them further into different, affirming, queer directions.

The text contains Murdoch's usual trope of characters insecure of their sexualities; the reader of *The Green Knight* discovers Bellamy, a homosexual male literary figure "who [does] prefer his own sex, but seem[s] to find no difficulty in remaining chaste" (24). Here we have business as usual: a homosexual character who (knows that he) desires other males but never acts upon his homosexual desires. Alarmingly, *The Green Knight* suggests that Bellamy is almost virginal. The text informs the reader that Bellamy was previously involved in a relationship with a certain Magnus Blake; however, the relationship was entirely chaste. After the breakup of this relationship, Bellamy later has a nervous breakdown (44-45). Years later, Bellamy, when feeling sorry for himself, thinks, "I have no wife and no children, I have put away my dog and he has forgotten me. Magnus Blake has forgotten me and I have forgotten him" (368). Magnus Blake seems to be Bellamy's first and only passionate love, and a chaste love at that. The closest Bellamy comes to sexual activity is when he wishes that the handsome young man, Harvey, were also a homosexual: "Bellamy also wished that Harvey was gay, but had put away this wish together with many other world wishes" (76). Ironically, though, Bellamy is the character who counsels Harvey about sex: "it will all come to you, some god will explain it to you, it will all be clarified, it will all be *easy*" (76). So instead of sexual fulfillment, the text suggests chastity and asceticism that is mysteriously powerful enough to be able to impart wisdom to a younger generation.

And Bellamy is not the only gay male character who is chaste. Midway through the novel, the text introduces Emil, who has recently parted ways with his partner, Clive:

> There is another partner waiting for me, a teacher whom I knew long ago—his name is solitude [. . .]. I shall come back here to an empty flat and close the door, and I shall lean back against the door, as I recall I used to when I was young, and breathe deeply and feel the *deep* relief and liberation of coming home to solitude, coming home to *myself.*
>
> (311)

Throughout the text, true to Murdoch's established form, never does Emil mention his sex life with Clive.

Emil never mentions missing his sexual experiences with Clive, and the reader only assumes that their relationship was sexual because homosexual relationships typically involve sex.

However, Murdoch complicates her already complicated writing on chastity by having one chaste homosexual character sexually pursue the other. Such an occurrence—to suggest that a homosexual man has a libido—is a rare moment in her fiction. This acknowledgment of sexual desire surfaces in a conversation between Emil and Bellamy, when Emil asks the following:

> Really, it seems that there are two questions. Do you want to be chaste? Do you want to live alone? It seems that you want to be chaste, all right. But that need not prevent you from living with another person. All right, you have not wanted to before, perhaps because you could not find a worthy person. Here I present myself. As we know, you have already, if I may use the traditional phrase, rejected my advances. All right, all right. That matter will not be pursued. The point is that you have been living here successfully [with Emil] for a while, we are old friends, we know each other well, we are on the way to knowing each other very well. Why not simply stay here? I need you, I think you have discovered that you need me [. . .]. Here you can be happy [. . .] you know we love each other.
>
> (426)

In the above passage, the reader discovers that sex really does matter, even if mattering just a little bit, and even if the reader discovers that sex only occurred in the past. Emil has "made advances" toward Bellamy.

Though one should not underestimate the fact that Bellamy rejects Emil's advances, one must also admit that the making of these advances brings Murdoch's text into a more realistic realm (especially for a writer so closely associated with literary realism) of homosexual representation. What this means is that in the real world, people make choices about their sexual partners, and sometimes people refuse other people's offers. By demonstrating a refusal of a sexual proposition (and by writing this refusal as "no big deal"), Murdoch endows her characters with real-life adult sexual behaviors. The behavior is also queer given that few people would choose to remain on extremely amiable terms with a person who has rejected a sexual offer.

That being said, it should then come as no surprise that Harvey and Bellamy work into Murdoch's trope of men who are (nonsensically) desired by other men. Although Harvey does not acknowledge that Bellamy may wish circumstances to be different between them, Harvey does not really mind if other characters associate him with Bellamy. When Harvey finally does "discover" sex, he tells his friend and future wife, Sefton; however, he thinks that she thinks that he has discovered sex

with Bellamy: "You're thinking perhaps that Bellamy was the person—I had that experience with—it wasn't him, it was Tessa" (390). Harvey clears the air, but he is not vehement in his protest. Of course, readers of Murdoch would not expect an admission of sex between men, for her characters never reveal that such acts occur. (Recall that Bellamy refuses Emil's advances). The dialogue that does in fact occur fits into Murdoch's pre-established textual conventions.

Murdoch's third trope, that of a possible homosexual future that is deferred by death, is altered in ***The Green Knight.*** Although Bellamy and Emil temporarily live together, Bellamy leaves, unsure of what (or whom) he wants. In this particular text, the threat of death occurs, but not to either of the homosexual characters; instead, the character threatened is the young female character, Moy, who risks drowning and ultimately plays a large part in both Emil's and Bellamy's lives.

Writers such as Stephen Adams have noted how Murdoch often employs water imagery to signify redemption. Murdoch's use of water imagery signals that Bellamy's rescue attempt is also a kind of rebirth.[9] After hearing his dog, Ajax, barking, Bellamy notices a form in the sea and runs out to rescue the person:

> He threw off his encumbering overcoat and crossed the sand and entered the sea, stepping awkwardly, clumsily, concentrating on continuing to stand up. Water came pouring into his boots, he was walking upon sand, stopping at every step as he advanced, meeting the repeated violent blows of the breaking waves, hearing himself calling, crying out into the tearing wind, his mouth filling with sea water [. . .] the sea took him and he saw above him the inner hollow of the tall wave breaking over him and he saw its dome of translucent green light as he fell backwards under it, choking with water, experiencing death. The next moment he found he was still alive, scrabbling in the ferocious undertow.
>
> (468)

Bellamy is baptized or reborn upon successfully maneuvering out of the sea with the person he rescues. When he gets back to land, he realizes some of the physical changes occurring in his environment: "the tide is going out, and the weather has changed too. The wind had dropped and there was more brightness in the sky, and he thought, that was the light which I saw when I was under the dome of the wave" (469).

Just as the elements have changed, so has Bellamy. He has "seen the light": "Yes it is true, I love Emil, and Emil loves me [. . .] we shall live together and stay together" (465). Bellamy's admission is not only an acknowledgment that Emil, who has previously claimed to love the now-dripping character, indeed loves Bellamy but is also an epiphany wherein Bellamy realizes that he actually returns Emil's love. Although the sex is still absent, the love is not.

However, the text concludes with the queer suggestion that Emil and Bellamy will both recommence their relationship and also include Moy in it: "I'll look after Moy, and Emil will help her to get into an art school, perhaps we could adopt her, or sort of" (472). Such a family configuration is in alignment with Halperin's suggestion of what might constitute a queer family: "'Queer,' then, demarcates not a positivity but a positionality vis-à-vis the normative. [. . . I]t could include some married couples without children, for example, or even (who knows?) some married couples *with* children—with, perhaps, *very naughty* children" (*Saint* 62)

Again, though Bellamy's planning of the relationship between him and Emil does not specifically include sex, the text reveals that such a relationship is finally a possibility. Neither Emil nor Bellamy perishes at the conclusion of the novel. Finally, one of Murdoch's texts allows for the possibility not just of a homosexual relationship, but of a queer family: two fathers and a daughter. How "naughty" Moy might be is subject to dispute, but when one remembers that the text reveals that she has telekinetic powers and suggests that she will leave her mother and sisters, her "real" or biological family, for this other type of familial arrangement, *queer* seems the best word to describe this new arrangement.

John Bayley writes that "[Murdoch] wanted, through the novels, to reach all possible readers, in different ways and by different means" ([*Elegy for Iris*] 26). Although Murdoch may have wanted to include homosexuals among her circle of possible readers, her portrayal of homosexual characters is at times alarming, inaccurate, and/or nonsensical. Murdoch's texts cater to heterosexually-prurient and homosexually-prudish audiences. Especially troublesome is her death-trope, by which (possibly) homosexual characters never get the chance to act upon their sexual desires. However, *The Green Knight,* though maintaining some of Murdoch's more problematic tropes related to homosexuality, manages, if not to break completely from these tropes, then to alter them to such a degree that the possibility for queer relationships is provided: neither Bellamy nor Emil fall out a window (*The Good Apprentice*) or are shot (*The Book and the Brotherhood*) so as to avoid a possible sexual experience. Murdoch finally allows for the existence of queer desire-ability and a queer reconfiguration of the family.

Notes

1. See, for instance, the conclusion of Murdoch's *A Fairly Honourable Defeat,* where upon Rupert's death, his widow, Hilda, leaves Britain to start a new life in America with her son, Peter, and her sister, Morgan. Even though Peter has previously propositioned his aunt, Morgan has refused his advances. It follows that the queer family unit in America will be celibate.

2. See, for instance, Murdoch's *A Fairly Honourable Defeat,* in which Axel openly remarks, "You don't have to amuse me, Simon. I love you" (33).

3. See, for instance, Murdoch's *A Fairly Honourable Defeat,* in which Simon continually refers to Axel not as a partner or a lover, but instead as "friend." Though Axel later forms the opinion that their relationship is "in the crudest possible sense, nothing but sex after all" (158), this conjecture, given Axel's discomfort with being touched and given also the novel's silence on gay sex acts, emerges as surprising, to say the least.

4. See, for instance, Murdoch's *A Word Child,* in which Christopher, who has previously had a homosexual relationship with Clifford, "turns straight" and marries a female character, Biscuit (386).

5. Just the same, note that Hilary more strongly mourns Clifford's death than Hilary does that of his heterosexual love-interest, Kitty (380).

6. Let me provide three examples. In Murdoch's *Henry and Cato* (1976), Cato kills the young man for whom he yearns, Beautiful Joe. In *The Message to the Planet* (1990), Ludens desires and more or less stalks Marcus, only to have Marcus eventually commit suicide. Finally, in *The Nice and the Good* (1968), the reader discovers that Theo has had an affair in India with a young novice; nothing comes of this affair, however, because the young man soon drowns.

7. I would note, however, that Sedgwick does not trap herself within this same problem. She does not write that thinking about sex is even more important than, or just as important as, engaging in sex to all people all of the time. To those who would argue what Sedgwick, then, does not, I would query how they would justify such a claim in combination with Murdoch's ideas about redemption through suffering and her participation in the literary tradition of realism.

8. See, for instance, Siegel.

9. Compare, for instance, Murdoch's *The Bell* (1958), when Dora jumps into the sea.

Works Cited

Adams, Stephen. *The Homosexual as Hero in Contemporary Fiction.* London: Clarke, 1980.

Bayley, John. *Elegy for Iris.* New York: St. Martin's, 1999.

Bove, Cheryl. "New Directions: Iris Murdoch's Latest Women." Tucker 188-98.

Conradi, Peter J. "A Fairly Honourable Defeat." Tucker 85-105.

Foucault, Michel. "Friendship as a Way of Life." *Ethics: Subjectivity and Truth.* Ed. Paul Rabinow. New York: New, 1994. 135-40.

Halperin, David M. *One Hundred Years of Homosexuality: And Other Essays on Greek Love.* New York: Routledge, 1990.

———. *Saint Foucault: Toward a Gay Hagiography.* New York: Oxford UP, 1995.

Johnson, Deborah. "[Iris Murdoch's] Questing Heroes." Tucker 48-60.

Murdoch, Iris. *The Bell.* New York: Viking, 1958.

———. *The Book and the Brotherhood.* New York: Penguin, 1987.

———. *A Fairly Honourable Defeat.* 1970. New York: Penguin, 1972.

———. *The Good Apprentice.* London: Chatto, 1985.

———. *The Green Knight.* 1993. New York: Penguin, 1995.

———. *Henry and Cato.* 1976. New York: Viking, 1977.

———. *The Message to the Planet.* New York: Viking, 1990.

———. *The Nice and the Good.* New York: Penguin, 1968.

———. *The Philosopher's Pupil.* New York: Viking, 1983.

———. *A Word Child.* New York: Penguin, 1975.

Sedgwick, Eve Kosofsky. *Epistemology of the Closet.* Berkeley: U of California P, 1990.

Siegel, Lee. "The Gay Science: Queer Theory, Literature, and the Sexualization of Everything." *The New Republic.* 9 Nov. 1998: 30+.

Spear, Hilda D. *Iris Murdoch.* New York: St. Martin's, 1995.

Tucker, Lindsey, ed. *Critical Essays on Iris Murdoch.* New York: Hall, 1992.

Warner, Michael. Introduction. *Fear of a Queer Planet: Queer Politics and Social Theory.* Minneapolis: U of Minneapolis P, 1993. vii-xxxi.

Richard Todd (essay date fall 2001)

SOURCE: Todd, Richard. "Realism Disavowed? Discourses of Memory and High Incarnations in *Jackson's Dilemma.*" *Modern Fiction Studies* 47, no. 3 (fall 2001): 674-95.

[*In the following essay, Todd critiques Murdoch's last novel,* Jackson's Dilemma, *arguing that attempts to assess the work based on its signs of the author's incipient battle with Alzheimer's disease are misleading. Todd maintains that rather than interpret the novel's brevity and its markedly different treatment of reality compared to her earlier works, critics should consider whether, in this book, Murdoch was attempting a deliberate disavowal of realism and embarking on a new phase in her career, one that was cut short by her death in 1999.*]

Reading Iris Murdoch's **Jackson's Dilemma** (1995) offers a not wholly dissimilar experience to that offered by reading Virginia Woolf's *Between the Acts* (1941), in the sense that both are the final works of their authors. As such, and in view of the biographical knowledge we have, both novels raise questions as to the mental state of their authors during the period of composition. In what follows I shall argue that the answers to such questions are not straightforward and that in each case both writer and work suffer diminishment when careless assumption replaces thoughtful attention.

There are, of course, significant differences between the two cases. Virginia Woolf (1882-1941) took her own life shortly after completing (but before revising) her last work. The gradual mental and physical decline of Iris Murdoch (1919-99) as a result of Alzheimer's disease led to her death from pneumonia four years after the publication of her final novel. Woolf's last novel was published posthumously under the supervision of Leonard Woolf, who left it unrevised in detail: it has therefore never been read—indeed, cannot be read—without the knowledge of the tragedy it has always retrospectively been seen as fostering. Murdoch's last novel, in contrast, appeared while its author was still alive, and the questions it has come to raise have to do with how far Alzheimer's had encroached upon her astonishing powers of memory during its composition. The reviews **Jackson's Dilemma** received show that it certainly caused some puzzlement, and in some cases disappointment, among its first readers. Most strikingly it is different from its immediate predecessors in being very much shorter than them. Indeed, it is the shortest Murdoch novel since **The Italian Girl** (1964). Not until more than a year after the appearance of **Jackson's Dilemma,** however, did the news of its author's cerebral degeneration became public. The problem was first described in 1996 in the international press as "writer's block." By 1997 it was acknowledged to be Alzheimer's, with the most knowledgeable and, indeed, intimate account, John Bayley's *Iris: A Memoir* (American title: *Elegy for Iris*) not appearing in Britain until 1998 and the United States until 1999. Bayley's memoir appears to date the perceived onset of the illness to 1994.

The effect of *Between the Acts* never having been read publicly without knowledge of its *Nachleben* has meant that discussions of it are bound to be predicated, far more than is the case with any of Woolf's other novels, on seeking textual traces of insanity. Yet, as Hermione

Lee argues, the first and longer of Woolf's two suicide notes to her husband "is not the letter of an irrational or mad person, but of a person in despair, with no sense of a future, and suffering from a terrible fear of the possibility of a breakdown with no prospect of recovery. The writing of the letter, and the act it presaged, though an act *in extremis,* was rational, deliberate and courageous" ([*Virginia Woolf*] 757).

This suggests that the textual traces we should seek are not so much those of insanity but of a much more diffuse kind that encompasses extremes of courage and despair. Certainly *Between the Acts* does span an extraordinary range. At one end of the spectrum, we have the daringness of the play on names (such as that of the vamp Mrs. Manresa) coupled with the inner insistence of Mrs. Swithin that it is wrong to play on people's names (28) (unbeknownst to her, Mrs. Swithin herself has a nickname, "Old Flimsy" [23]), or such things as the unflattering self-portrait of Miss La Trobe. At the other end, we have the grotesque episode of the snake choking in the act of trying to swallow a toad ("It was birth the wrong way round—a monstrous inversion" [72]), or the equally claustrophobic indecisive and repetitive motif, "Will it be wet, will it be fine?" Also consider this remarkable passage, in its own way also frighteningly claustrophobic: "The room was empty. Empty, empty, empty; silent, silent, silent. The room was a shell, singing of what was before time was; a vase stood in the heart of the house, alabaster, smooth, cold, holding the still, distilled essence of emptiness, silence" (30). These extremes can be seen as representing—at one end of the scale—an intelligence so fine that it has virtually uncoupled itself from any relation to the quotidian realities on which the novel's narrative matrix seems to insist (such as the opening discussion of the village cesspool, or the persistently characteristic dialogue), and—at the other—a self-reflexive irresolution or even impasse that might well foreshadow the kind of despair of which Lee writes so perceptively. Yet both ends of the spectrum offer us quintessential Woolf.

The case of *Jackson's Dilemma,* as already indicated, is rather different. A few of the novel's first readers (most likely close personal acquaintances) may well, it is true, have formed a perception that something was "wrong," and perhaps seriously so. Yet what they and others, including most reviewers, were primarily faced with was the issue of the novel's brevity, rather than the idea that the novel represented a distillation of Murdoch's craft (as *Between the Acts* does that of Woolf, at least on the basis of the brief account above). Only later will readers begin (however strong their resistance) to search Murdoch's last novel for evidence that the author's memory might already have been failing. In this way, the brevity of the novel cannot but be brought into the discussion in terms that suggest that by 1993 or 1994 (the date of composition of *Jackson's Dilemma*)

Murdoch was already finding it difficult to carry the plot and detail of a six hundred page novel in her mind.[1] Yet it seems proper to challenge this view, for to hold to it blindly or unthinkingly is to pre-empt or hijack a more discerning argument that can be distilled from some of the more intelligent responses. This argument maintains that despite certain manifest flaws *Jackson's Dilemma* is nevertheless quintessential Murdoch. In making this claim I shall be asking to what extent this novel's apparent disavowal of realism is deliberate and whether, when read in such terms, it does not suggest that had Murdoch lived longer, she would in retrospect be seen to have been entering yet another phase in her work.

Many interviews and profiles attest to the fact that the final long-hand version of each Murdoch novel was written out in two drafts—a process that took place only after the entire novel had been constructed entirely from memory following a preliminary draft. The final version involved (at most) minor revision but no significant act of composition. Such a method of creation naturally would make Murdoch reliant on her memory to an extent that may well be almost unique. Although annotations and synopses were made, apparently no notebooks survive, nor is there, to my knowledge, any surviving working draft material, although notes and scraps must once have existed.[2] Such manuscripts as do exist (many of them now housed at the University of Texas at Austin) are thus the completed final drafts, from which the typescript used to prepare the page proofs issued by Chatto & Windus was prepared. Murdoch's refusal to be copy-edited, unwaveringly respected by her longtime editor at Chatto, Norah Smallwood, became a staple topic of reviewers from the 1980s onwards. When Carmen Callil became her editor after Smallwood's death and made cuts to one of the novels, the material (as Peter Conradi pointed out in his *Guardian* obituary) was restored at Murdoch's insistence.

It is true that many, although not all, reviews of *Jackson's Dilemma* were dismissive. Somewhat surprisingly, the book was not even noticed in *The London Review of Books*. The 1999 obituary section of the *Encyclopaedia Britannica* summed up her final work crisply and dismissively: "The troubling formlessness of her last novel, *Jackson's Dilemma* (1995), was a sad harbinger of [Murdoch's] encroaching Alzheimer's disease." Yet, surely, whatever else this novel might stand accused of, it is not formlessness: the rapid, skilful, even peremptory, assemblage of the characters was noted by several readers and the characteristically Shakespearean-comic manner in which a marriage dance is rescued out of apparent chaos, completed, and a solitary figure left as some kind of comment on the pattern, was felicitously described by Kate Kellaway in *The Observer*: "[the] great beauty of *Jackson's Di-*

lemma is that it is not, as it would first appear to be, a flight from the enchanter but a headlong rush towards enchantment. Murdoch quotes from Hölderlin: 'But where danger is, rescue is ready too'" (16). Those reviews that were on the whole cool were more likely to exemplify the nuance expressed by Brad Leithauser in *The New York Times*: "The story is a psychologically rich tale of romances thwarted and revived. The writing is a mess" (["The Good Servant"] 6). Yet criticisms of Murdoch's writing style are not new. They were perhaps most authoritatively and forcefully expressed by Christopher Ricks, who reviewed **The Red and the Green** in 1965 and **Nuns and Soldiers** in 1980, taking Murdoch's style primarily to task for its overuse of "a sort of" or "a kind of."[3] For Ricks these quirks were not merely irritating but attested to an inability (not, admittedly, always or invariably present) to write with the exactitude demanded by the thought being expressed. Indeed, one of the major problems in assessing Murdoch's work critically has increasingly been the extent to which her own thoughts and those of her characters are to be disentangled from each other. By the end of the 1970s many critics and reviewers agreed that during much of the 1960s Murdoch's writing had lost its initial panache and bite, becoming careless and formulaic and ushering in a phase famously characterized by William F. Hall as "the doldrums" (["*Bruno's Dream*"] 443). And, indeed, once Murdoch's views on being copy-edited became generally known, reviewers started to express the belief that were this proscription to be lifted, the novels would gain in concision and effectiveness. The full implications of such a view are never sufficiently developed by those who promote it—although, of course, everyone's writing, can gain from the input of another reader.[4] One striking shortcoming of criticisms of Murdoch's style lies in a failure on the part of her detractors to distinguish between the form of narration (is the narrator omniscient or focalized?) and the remarkably consistent voice. This does raise a number of problems. It must be admitted (and would probably be generally conceded) that outside the range of voice of the group or clique her characters form, there are lapses, but are these genuine lapses arising from an imperfect ear, or a casual attitude to discourse outside a narrow class boundary? It is difficult to say. Thus, while the discourse of Norman Monckley, the father of the little girl Austin Gibson Grey has run over and killed in a road accident while drunk, and Norman's blackmailing attempts to get Austin to help him publish his appalling novel in **An Accidental Man** (1971) are genuinely grotesque and indeed funny, other excursions into proletarian discourse will strike many readers as embarrassingly off-key. One thinks of the language used by the group of thugs beating up a black customer in a Chinese restaurant in **A Fairly Honourable Defeat,** an act resolved by Tallis Browne's physical intervention; or this **Jackson's Dilemma** extract, set at the church where Edward and Marian were to have been married: "[. . .] as they approached, there were some friendly and courteous faces, and Benet quickly led his party through. Only a few stared with amusement, most lowered their eyes, some bowed their heads, and there were a few incoherent murmurs of sympathy. One youth (on holiday) who said loudly. 'Too bad, chum, she's bolted!' was hushed up by others" (34). Such discourse raises the question, to be returned to, of when exactly the action in this novel is supposed to be set—it is hard to imagine this particular kind of British demotic as belonging to any period within the past four or five decades.

The consensus on Murdoch's style, then—on the writing expressed both in the narrative voice, whether this be first- or third-person, as well as in the dialogue—is fairly general and can be seen as an aspect of the subject-matter, even of "Murdochland" itself. That said, it cannot be denied that there are some strange inconsistencies in **Jackson's Dilemma.** Are they a playful tripping-up of the reader that is consistent with the steady disavowal of accurate realism that critics such as Lorna Sage (and myself) claim characterizes Murdoch's late work? Or are they "genuine" lapses, such as might, whether deliberately or not, be brought about by a trick of memory? Reviewing **Henry and Cato** in 1977, Sage came up with the luminous idea of an "aesthetic of imperfection" (["The Pursuit of Imperfection"] 68), and this concept underlies the next part of this essay.

There are at least three inconsistencies on page 108 of **Jackson's Dilemma,** and they may serve to exemplify the extent of the problem. They concern the sisters Marian and Rosalind Berran. Firstly, we have already been told that Rosalind, who is the younger, is also the more scholarly and career-minded of the two, and that once both left school, Marian forgot her French and Italian. On page 108 Rosalind, in addition to keeping these languages up, is said to be learning Russian, whereas earlier (page 92) we were told that her third language is German. On the other hand, it might be argued that the earlier passage is being told by the omniscient narrator, whereas the focalizer on page 108 is Marian. The mis-remembering *might,* therefore, be Marian's. Secondly, the passage on page 108 describes Marian's cruise to Australia (where she stays instead of going on to New Zealand and meets Cantor Ravnevik). En route she stops off at "Ceylon." Sri Lanka has not been "Ceylon" since 1972, yet in its context here (as well as in view of Cantor's and, indeed, Marian's impetuousness) this voyage seems to occur no more than two or three (or is it, in terms of a chronology the novel elsewhere suggests, five to seven?) years before the events in the novel's "now." In this "now" (in addition to a "youth" who can shout words such as "chum" and "bolted"), there is some lively discussion of women priests. The Church of England voted to ordain women priests in 1992, and the first ordinations took place in 1994, so this theme at least is clearly topical to the period of composition of *Jackson's Dilemma.* There is also, in this novel, the observable presence of beggars in London's streets (a feature of the 1980s Thatcherite landscape) and pound coins (also introduced in the 1980s). All this raises a larger question (already touched on) of when the novel is supposed to be set, and whether and to what extent anachronisms in Murdoch's work are deliberate (a question we may also ask concerning the third inconsistency). Thirdly, then, it is while Marian is on this sea-voyage, presumably somewhere in the southern Pacific, that Uncle Tim dies; on page 108 Marian receives a telegram with the news, and telegraphs condolences from Australia. Yet a previous description of Uncle Tim's obsequies and cremation clearly states that "Marian and Rosalind were both with their mother in Canada" (90). Again, it is hard to say whether this passage is Marian's own memory at odds with that of the narrator and how we are to take the anachronisms themselves: telegrams bearing this kind of news seem to belong to an earlier era. This point needs making with all the more vigor in light of the return of Marian with Cantor Ravnevik to Australia: in terms of a realistic chronology this must be nearer five or, at the most, seven years after her cruise, assuming Marian was eighteen then and twenty-five now. We are told that Rosalind is now twenty-three, but this detail still does not resolve the problem, already indicated, of how much time has actually elapsed since Marian's visit to Australia and the "now" of the novel's present.

Such disparities and apparent anachronisms could and have been ascribed to carelessness. Yet they have been so increasingly present in the later novels of Iris Murdoch that we are surely entitled, even compelled, to ask along with Sage, whether something more complex is not at issue—whether a dispersal with or dissipation of any need for consistency in a presentation of the contingent or circumstantial stuff of life, what Sage terms "[a mocking] of the critical demand for totalities, [making] fiction seem a living process" (68), is taking place. Whatever *is* taking place, it seems quite different from what Sage sees as the inferior opposite of an aesthetic of imperfection: Murdoch's "voice" as heard in this passage is not "formulaic" in the same sense as the perhaps justifiably labeled "formulaic" writing of the 1960s (which featured telling without showing, the crude use of symbolism, and the authorial intrusion that seems to leave certain scenes ending in tableaux). Nor is it to be confused with the famously intriguing misquotation of the first sentence of Proust's *Du Côté de chez Swann* at the end of *The Good Apprentice* (1985), which may either be a dim reflection of Murdoch's own quotidian habits, or represent some quite other kind of misremembering altogether. What we find instead in the novels to which *Jackson's Dilemma* forms a conclusion is a numinous mysteriousness about these disparities and

anachronisms amounting to a finely-wrought sense of playful fantasy, almost perhaps a jokiness, that casts its inimitable light on Murdoch's conception of what, in *The Fire and the Sun,* she termed "[s]trong agile realism" (84). Reviewing this last novel, Lorna Sage wrote of the patterning that there "is always a kind of joke about the permutations of sexual and social relations which are to surprise everybody into a glimpse of contingency, and this [novel] is no exception except that this time the surface of social illusion is dealt with very sketchily and impatiently" ("Amongst Entities" 25). A strong agile realism of this kind can surely permit its own disavowal—indeed, that is its essence.

The comparison with Woolf made at the start of this essay was not arbitrary. It was intended to press the idea that in addition to what has been suggested above, both writers had a wholly distinctive *voice,* and that this voice remained audible to the end of their writing careers. I have tried in the case of Murdoch briefly to characterize that voice, especially but not exclusively insofar as it finds expression in *Jackson's Dilemma.* It must be conceded that the characteristic Murdoch "voice," a voice inseparable from the physical and intellectual vistas of "Murdochland," seems to have developed fully and recognizably during and, above all, after the "doldrums" period, sounding most clearly and distinctively in the novels of the 1970s and the 1980s. Indeed, it may be possible to account in some measure for the doldrums themselves in terms of a search for a style. This is, after all, a writer who said famously in her 1953 study of Sartre that "he has the style of the age" ([*Sartre*] 7). The major shortcoming of her fiction of the 1960s was always seen to exist not so much at the level of macrocosmic plotting but at that of a formulaic use of language to describe certain scenarios, particularly (as suggested above) the tableau-esque note on which individual chapters ended. (In this context it is worth observing that Murdoch dispensed largely with chapters in much of the fiction from the mid 1970s until the end of her career, returning to five very long chapters in *The Green Knight* and to the shorter and more conventional chapterization of her earlier work in *Jackson's Dilemma* itself.)

In maintaining this, I find I am endorsing the view I put forward in 1984 that Murdoch's career to date "[had] fallen into a number of phases and stages leading her from the influence of post-war existentialist fiction to a position now peculiarly her own" ([*Iris Murdoch*] 14-15). I now argue, further, that this process continued until the end of her career. It therefore seems worth reminding ourselves of an earlier, crisper style, a style influenced by Murdoch's reading of French existentialist fiction, prior to the doldrums, in the fiction of the 1950s.

There is a fascinating passage illustrating this early style that has to do centrally and absolutely with the recuperation of a memory in the very first published novel, *Under the Net* (1954). This passage is quoted with approbation by Geoffrey Leech in his 1969 stylistics textbook, *A Linguistic Guide to English Poetry.* Leech is impressed by the way Murdoch manages to turn a cliché—"trying to track down something in the back of your mind" ([*A Linguistic Guide to English Poetry*] 27-28)—into this: "While I was thinking these thoughts a little stream was running softly somewhere in my mind, a little stream of reminiscence. What was it? Something was asking to be remembered. I held the book gently in my hands, and followed without haste the course of my reverie, waiting for the memory to declare itself" (*Under* 81-82). For Leech, this passage "gives a precise, vivid account of the experience [it describes] by apt choice of vocabulary (*reminiscence, reverie*), and by a syntax that imitates the thought process being recalled: 'What was it? Something was asking to be remembered'" (27).

The formulaic, inward-looking, seemingly unintentionally self-parodic style into which Murdoch's writing had degenerated in the 1960s, and the recovery towards a newly recognizable quintessence in the 1970s, have been documented by many commentators.[5] There is less consensus about the very long novels of the 1980s, with some commentators feeling that Murdoch had once again lost her touch. Others pointed with great effectiveness to a novel such as *The Good Apprentice* (1985) to show how the solipsistic discourse pertaining to the long central section describing the world of Seegard, with its absurd but unforgettable rituals, a kind of closed community presided over by Mother May, cannot but be a form of self-conscious parody, reminiscent of *The Bell* (1958). The kind of writing characteristic of the 1980s onwards has moved so manifestly far away from quotidian realism that it appears to parody itself in a now serious and outward-looking manner. Yet, it is worth remembering that forty years ago Murdoch wrote: "Most modern English [*sic*] novels indeed are not *written.* One feels they could slip into some other medium without much loss. It takes a foreigner like Nabokov or an Irishman like Beckett to animate prose language into an imaginative stuff in its own right" (**"Against Dryness"** 29).

It is defensible in this context to extend the concepts of "style" and "discourse" quite explicitly to encompass such matters as the portrayal of children and adolescents. Here one might think of the attributes of their world such as clothing and (in Murdoch's case) the absence of those technological paraphernalia that have, as the 1980s and 1990s progressed, become steadily apparent in the "real" world. Such attributes and absences have increasingly taken Murdoch's young people away from what might thus be considered normative. We might contrast the young people in the last novels with the level of acutely observed actuality characterizing the world of Dora Greenfield (her dresses, her jazz

records) in *The Bell.* Yet, to assume that Murdoch is *not capable* of imagining children and adolescents does not logically follow. Certainly, it might be argued that for her, children and adolescents are fey or even demonic, often though not always lonely (she spoke repeatedly of imaginary siblings and a harmless obsession with twins), and possessed of a degree of sexual awareness that in our own censorious age may be felt to be beyond what is acceptable. Yet, on the other hand, she did, on occasion, create genuinely loveable and normal children, such as the Biranne twins, Edward and Henrietta, in *The Nice and the Good* (1968).

In this sense Edward Baltram's half-sisters Ilona and Bettina, the Anderson daughters in *The Green Knight,* and Bran Dunarven in *Jackson's Dilemma* are allotropes of each other: all occupy fantasy worlds (as indeed we all do), and all are capable of springing surprises on us as well as the world they occupy. Thus the "something terrible and unexpected [that] happen[s]" at the beginning of *Jackson's Dilemma* (5)—the stone thrown through Edward Lannion's window at Hatting—is revealed at the end to have been launched by his biological son, Bran, who wryly comments: "Somebody had to start something" (193). Despite his crucial role in galvanizing the book's action, Bran remains very much on the sidelines, portrayed through the eyes of others. In this way his role oddly counterpoints that of Jackson himself. There is a disproportionate amount of observation of others by the majority of this novel's characters and little inward focalization. Do these characters see themselves as Benet sees himself towards the end of *Jackson's Dilemma*: "He thought, I am nobody now. He was the beginning of nobody" (215)? Yet Jackson, Benet, and Bran are far more intriguing to the reader than are most of those characters who are constantly observing, gossiping, or prattling about them. The one exception might be Owen Silbury, whose sado-pornographic paintings and squalor-ridden "entities" are never explained to us (yet why should they be?), and who is really the only character who attempts to "see" Jackson on Jackson's own terms. This kind of "seeing" should be kept distinct from what appears to be an epiphany toward the very end of the novel, where Mildred finally gets her chance to approach Jackson at the Penndean wedding party of Edward and Anna.

> Mildred found herself turning towards Jackson. She trembled, she shuddered, she thought he is different, he is more, even more, handsome, his dark eyes are larger, so calm and glowing, his lips are gentle, his expression is loving, he is secure because Benet has forgiven him, no, no, *he* has forgiven *Benet*! But it isn't that, he has changed, like in suffering, like a seachange, that is in Shakespeare isn't it, his skin is different, darker and more glowing, when he went away it was for another incarnation, he belongs with people who go on and on living, perhaps it is Tibet or somewhere else, how old is he, a hundred years, a thousand years, they come like guardian angels, they *are* guardian angels, now he

is talking to me in a strange language, yet I understand, I reach out my hand and touch his hand, and his hand is burning. I am speaking to him and he is speaking to me, he has the stigmata, he was beaten like Christ was beaten, he is damaged, like the Fisher King in disguise, he is afraid of being caught up with by those who know his shame, and how he was found in a cardboard box in the rushes beside the river.

(232)

Here I suggest Jackson is created in Mildred's image, ending up as the victim of her thoughts about him, rather than being accorded the distance and respect for his otherness that Owen gives him. Other characters, too, seem unable to recall what Jackson has said to them. I shall return briefly to this point at the end. I have raised it here to suggest that if what I have argued is true, or even only approximately so, then we may at least be able to claim that Murdoch comes closer in this novel than perhaps anywhere else to realizing the "peripheral" character; to managing the astonishing achievement, in a deliberately short novel, of pulling it apart; and to surrounding that achievement with a mysteriousness for which all too few readers were prepared to give her credit.

It is frequently noted that the worlds of Murdoch novels comprise little "courts." In the present context of her style and discourse, one aspect of *Jackson's Dilemma* may have irritated some readers, yet it, too, seems to point to a new phase relating to the essence of belonging to the court. There is an abundance of italics in the prose, along with an abundance of words or phrases enclosed within inverted commas. This aspect of Murdoch's writing is not as intensely present in her earlier works as it is here. The italics invariably occur as a means of expressing not just strong emotion, but of recording its uniqueness, perhaps even attempting to commit it to memory in an action that will ensure that it is imprinted on the individual consciousness of a member of the court forever. Rosalind, observing (without being seen) the events on the blighted marriage-day, as those guests who have not been reached in time are being received by Benet and the Rector, thinks: "Oh how *weird* it was, and *terrible,* what an *extraordinary* scene as if some great ceremony were being performed. [. . . T]hey will never forget it, / shall never forget it. And—they will never forgive it" (37). This peculiarity of italicization within focalized thought is not infrequently connected to the recuperative act of memory in this novel. The inverted commas are equally interesting, for they seem to point to a group discourse that becomes particularly evident in the opening chapters of the novel as the characters are briskly and deftly introduced. The introduction of Edward and Benet is conventionally omniscient. If they are seen through eyes other than the narrator's, then it is through their own. This is particularly true of Benet, whose introduction merits a rather longer quotation (and contrasts with his later thoughts on being "nobody"):

Leaving at last the silence of the library, Benet moved towards the drawing room, pausing in the hall to survey himself in the long mirror. [. . .] Ever since childhood Benet had wondered what he looked like. This wonder was connected with 'Who am I?' or '*What* am I?' Benet had discovered quite early in life that Uncle Tim shared this lack of identity. They sometimes discussed it. Does everyone feel like this, Benet had wondered. Tim had said that no, not everyone did, adding that it was a gift, an intimation of a deep truth: 'I am nothing.' This was, it seemed, one of those states, achieved usually by many years of intense meditation, which may be offered by the gods 'free of charge' to certain individuals. Benet laughed at this joke. Later he took the matter more seriously, wondering whether this 'gift' were not more likely to precede a quiet descent into insanity. Later still he decided that, after all, 'I am nothing,' far from indicating a selfless mystical condition, was a vague state of self-satisfaction experienced at some time by almost anyone. Yet more profoundly he wondered whether Tim, thought by so many of his friends and acquaintances to be 'rather dotty,' were not really a receiver of presents from the gods.

(11)

As we have seen, "I am nothing" approximates a thought to which Benet will return at the end of the novel. But this early passage can almost be seen as a distillation of the uses of inverted commas in the novel, and it culminates in the one I see as the most characteristic. The inverted commas may enclose existential questions ("Who am I?"), a mantra ("I am nothing"), a joke ("free of charge"), a judgment ("gift") and finally an assertion reached in his absence—now in this case literally, since Tim is dead—by the group ("rather dotty"). Mildred Smalden speaks "in what some called an 'aristocratic voice'; others said 'like a headmistress.'" When she stays in Hatting she "had 'her own room'" (16). Again, these uses of the inverted comma all serve to fix characteristics, prejudices, habits in the communal memory. Similarly, Tuan (against all the evidence as it might appear to a reader) "was deemed not to be gay," and Owen Silbury "was tall, becoming stout, but remained handsome, even 'dashing,'" saved from a descent into alcoholism "(it was said) by the saintly attentions of Mildred" (18). Yet again, in various ways, these discursive characteristics fix the characters in relationships to each other and in doing so serve a mnemonic purpose.

In her review of *Jackson's Dilemma,* Molly McQuade reveals another feature of the communal discourse that it seems appropriate to include here. Writing of the novel's dialogue, she points out that "[p]eople are always checking up on each other, often over the phone, their words staccato, brisk, mundane. [. . .] Buttoned-up or banal as they may sound, these conversations are efforts to retrieve vital information, to secure a more hopeful state of mind, to console or compensate for tragic blunders—to survive" ([Rev. of *Jackson's Dilemma,* by Iris Murdoch.] 36) This seems extremely astute, but still I wish to qualify it by placing more emphasis on the mnemonic compulsiveness of this kind of dialogue, the almost desperate attempt to "fix" evanescent experience. (Yet, what can be more evanescent than dialogue, especially over the phone?) The "survival" of which McQuade speaks would therefore become existential in the way that had both troubled Benet and left Uncle Tim apparently unmoved. What is it to be nothing or nobody? If human nature and identity is constructed out of our memory, then the desire to want to cling on to it seems the most natural instinct.

The preceding discussion has, then, suggested three ways in which the group discourse found in *Jackson's Dilemma,* while quintessentially Murdochian, has been intensified to a degree not seen in any of her preceding work. Without going down the fruitless path of trying to connect any description of the novel's discourse with the novelist's encroaching loss of memory, it should still be possible to argue that matters of existential identity were becoming particularly important to Murdoch during this novel's gestation. It is clear that small lapses (if that is what they are) such as the disparities between Marian's experience of her voyage to Australia and what "really" happens during this time apart could be said to represent a subconscious rehearsal of mnemonic technique. That style could not and should not, of course, be held to "foreshadow" Alzheimer's in any meaningful way.[6]

Rather than attempt to reverse laboriously into this cul-de-sac, I want in conclusion to return to the issue of existential reality, the lack of which Benet fears. Just as we cannot read *Between the Acts* without knowing what followed, we cannot read *Jackson's Dilemma* without taking into account John Bayley's anecdote of what appears to be the onset of the disease. It would seem that the novel had already largely been written, or even completed, and Murdoch's remarks to Bayley, as cited in *Elegy for Iris,* do not seem to me those of someone gestating a character, but rather of someone looking back on that character and seeing the construct of which he is a part gradually fading away: "'It's this man Jackson,' she said to me one day with a sort of worried detachment. 'I can't make out who he is, or what he's doing.' I was interested, because she hardly ever spoke of the characters in a novel she was writing. [Iris] looked serious, even solemn and puzzled. 'I don't think he's been born yet'" (213). I would like to suggest that Benet and Jackson were conceived of in a characteristically Murdochian way. Their relationship to each other is of a kind that, with minor variations, persisted intermittently throughout her career. For example, we see it in Mischa Fox and Calvin Blick in *The Flight from the Enchanter* (1956): here Calvin is Mischa's "other half" in the sense that he is the malevolent carrier-out of much of Mischa's power-play. We encounter another version of this "other-half" relationship in *A Fairly Honourable Defeat* (1970), when Julius King, another enchanter figure, recognizes in the virtuous Tallis Browne

his own alter ego. Murdoch was intrigued by the strategy in J. M. Barrie's *Peter Pan* (1904), in which the actor playing the children's father, Mr. Darling, doubles as Captain Hook.[7] Behind all this may lie the Platonic idea that each creature is constantly in search of its other half. The *kind* of role fulfilled by Calvin-Mischa or Julius-Tallis is different in each case, but each of these characters Murdoch would later in her career come to describe explicitly as "high incarnations," whether good or evil. In each of these cases, both "halves" of the composite are "incarnate." Before proceeding to examine the relation between Benet and Jackson, we may rapidly remind ourselves of the archetypes found in the novels.

While the "artist-saint" dichotomy—about which many of her commentators, notably Peter Conradi, have written—was present from the very beginning of Murdoch's career, it gradually became transformed under the influence of what Conradi and others have called her "Christian Buddhism." Thus, **Under the Net** itself presents what is by the standards of the later work a fairly straightforward conception in which the garrulous artist Jake Donaghue is in effect (as a hack translator and reviewer *manqué*) a fake, and his ascetic friend Hugo Belfounder is, or at least is perceived by Jake to be, a much more serious figure eliciting fear and respect. Yet of the two men, it is Jake who can disseminate the words, whereas Hugo's discourse tends toward silence: he is, as Murdoch was later to put it in an interview with Michael Bellamy, a type of "the truthful, formless figure" (**"An Interview"** 135). This dichotomy recurs in later work, perhaps most compellingly in **The Black Prince** (1973), a novel in which the artist becomes enmeshed with the myth of Apollo and Marsyas. In her second novel, **The Flight from the Enchanter,** Murdoch's readers were introduced to another type. Malcolm Bradbury appears to have been among the first to apply the term "psychopomp" to Mischa Fox and his various and later allotropes. Such an enchanter or power figure is always accorded a degree of deference by the characters that surround him (the character is invariably male). By the end of the novel, this deference is frequently seen to have rested on self-inflicted misprisions as to each character's place in patterns that attain great complexity in the later novels. Unlike Mischa Fox, Julius King in **A Fairly Honourable Defeat** (1970) may be thought of as one of Murdoch's more successful baroque examples: these are invariably of middle-European, often Jewish, ancestry and seem to owe much to Murdoch's fascination with Elias Canetti. John Ducane in **The Nice and the Good** is a more "realistic" kind of power figure (there is also a fascination with a Scottish Calvinist background, as with David Crimond in **The Book and the Brotherhood** [1987]); Ducane's perception of his own shortcomings is perhaps the most acute in any of the novels. All this will be familiar ground to Murdoch's readers. What fewer have noticed is that in the later novels, perhaps notably from **The**

Sea, the Sea 1978) onwards, the figure of the psycho-pomp tends to become closely identified with one of the characters making up the artist-saint dichotomy. Thus, it is possible to see the narrator Charles Arrow-by's cousin James as playing "saint" to Charles's "art-ist"; yet, in this novel what seems new about James is that he possesses that inscrutability that causes the sur-rounding characters to defer to him. This combination serves to unveil a further Murdoch type: the Dosto-evskian holy fool. The entire constellation, personated by James, also testifies to Murdoch's distinctive con-ception of Buddhism. For James is one, perhaps the most fully realized, of her "high incarnations" (although a general interest in Eastern thought can be traced at least back to *Bruno's Dream* [1969] and probably much further, to *An Unofficial Rose* [1962]). A character such as James is to be seen as "recurrent": it seems that he (again, these characters are all male) has been languish-ing in the Tibetan "Bardo" for a while before returning to earth in whatever form. We may see an avatar of this kind of figure in (say) Tallis Browne (*A Fairly Ho-nourable Defeat*), and it is worth noting that the utter squalor in which Tallis lives, although not unique in the canon, reappears intriguingly in Owen Silbury and the "entities" that clutter up his house. Reviewing *Jack-son's Dilemma*, Lorna Sage perceptively pointed out that of all Benet's friends it is Owen who is most per-sistent in trying to "lure Jackson away, [. . .] 'borrowing' him to sort out fuses, gardens, dinners, lives" ("Amongst Entities" 25).

In *Jackson's Dilemma*, we may see Mildred as she sees herself. Her holiness may be mocked, by Owen in particular, and in characteristically indulgent fashion, by the author herself. Still, she wishes to be one of those who "[n]ot just busily, efficiently [. . .] feed the poor, but [. . .] do so in humility, out of love, out of deep spiritual belief, as *servants*" (206). In doing so they, and she, would become nothing—and she discov-ers that such a vocation is not for her, not least because of her involvement with the Anglican priest Lucas Beg-brook. And in one sense Mildred gets Jackson *right*: he grants her a vision; though in another sense she is wrong: he is a construction of her own mind. In this re-spect, as Sage saw, it is probably Owen who is the most hard-headed about Jackson.

The abjection expressed by Mildred in her wish to be-come Jackson's servant is not new, for servants are re-current figures in the whole of Murdoch's fiction. On the very first page of *Under the Net* we encounter Finn (Peter O'Finney), who is described by the narrator Jake Donaghue as

> [not] exactly my servant. He seems often more like my manager. Sometimes I support him, and sometimes he supports me; it depends. It's somehow clear that we aren't equals. [. . .] But people do get the impression that he is my servant, and I often have this impression too, though it would be hard to say exactly what fea-

tures of the situation suggest it. Sometimes I think it is just that Finn is a humble and self-effacing person and so automatically takes second place.

(7)

Yet, it is hard to think of another relationship elsewhere in the oeuvre that is more comparable to that of Jack-son (who has no other name) and Benet. It is true that the manservant Fivey, in *The Nice and the Good* (1968) has a certain amount in common with Finn, yet Fivey differs from Finn in possessing multiple identities, ex-pressed as regional Celtic nationalities, according to whose service he is in. But seen from the viewpoint of the end of an entire career, Jackson is accorded various characteristics that neither Finn, as conceived in *Under the Net,* nor even Fivey can possess:

> [Marian] said to him, sipping the coffee, "How old are you?"
>
> This startled Jackson. He wondered which of his ages he should most tactfully offer. He said, "Forty-three."

(48)

Until the appearance of this novel, one might have said that as Murdoch's high incarnations are identified and explored in the last novels, the picture they present is fairly stable. They are invariably male, as we have seen. They are usually also single, in many ways domesti-cally incompetent, and at times they exhibit behavior almost farcically at odds with the powers they are re-puted to possess. In this sense, the most extreme ex-ample is Jesse Baltram in *The Good Apprentice* (1986), who is in fact sequestered for much of the novel and is barely coherent when he does emerge. As a father fig-ure to Edward Baltram, he is utterly incapable of any-thing approaching adequacy.

This, at least, would have seemed to have been the pic-ture hitherto. It is true that Julius cleans up the un-speakable squalor in Tallis's kitchen, but the kitchen is Tallis's, and a figure such as Jesse is more typical. It seems clear that we are being invited to see Jackson as some kind of incarnation (like his avatars he has no fixed identity, as the passage about his "ages" demonstrates). Jackson, in contrast to many of these avatars, can do everything, and in effect what we find in this novel is, it seems to me, something new: Benet (who has no sense of identity) dithers about whether or not to employ Jackson, reluctantly employing then sack-ing and then again re-employing him. Jackson carries out tasks not just for Benet but for many other charac-ters in the novel. The recurrent fatigue both characters suffer, the suggestions of role reversal—all these sug-gest that at one level the dilemma facing Jackson is whether to remain a high incarnation. If he is what he is, he seems to find many aspects of mortality, those as-pects having to do with human interaction, unbearably difficult. (In this sense he reminds us of Julius King, who as we learn from the end of *A Fairly Honourable*

Defeat is always much better, healthier, when not surrounded by people.) The characteristic reversal we discover at the end of *Jackson's Dilemma* is also—in terms of the preceding novels—unexpected, in that it is an action of a boy, Bran, that has set the novel's plot moving. And yet, after all, it is not unexpected: Jackson by his very nature would not initiate a plot, although he does enter Benet's life, as he enters the lives of others.

Jackson's Dilemma, then, is a disturbing novel in the sense that its *Nachleben* invites readings that seem inappropriately to confuse the cerebral condition of its writer with the deliberate aesthetic of imperfection her work offers. Among its considerable achievements we should place near or, indeed, at the very top of the list the capacity to create more in the way of a novel with peripheral characters than she had ever done before. In so doing, she went as far as she had ever done in fulfilling her avowed aim of pulling the texture of her fictions apart. Yet one would expect, mainly on the basis of views expressed in interviews, that were this aim to have been reached, the novel might have been even longer than its predecessors.[8] Instead, with her last novel, Murdoch managed to return to the scale (and to some extent the world) of her earliest work. In this sense *Jackson's Dilemma* can actually be seen as in many respects representing the summation of her achievement. No British novelist of her generation thought more profoundly about realism: her conception of strong agile realism allowed her to plot and narrate with astonishing suppleness and pliability. This essay has attempted to examine how these facets operate in the area of the discourse of memory. It has paid particular attention to how what Murdoch would have agreed should be termed "unselfing" can lead, at least in some of her high incarnations and the ways in which they operate in the everyday world, to virtue.

Notes

This essay is dedicated to the memory of Malcolm Bradbury (1932-2000). whose knowledge of modern English-language fiction was unrivalled, and who stimulated my interest in Iris Murdoch at a crucial point in my career by commissioning a study on her work for Methuen's Contemporary Writers series.

1. At some stage quite early on in Murdoch's career, the choice was made (presumably by her London publisher Chatto & Windus) to select October, traditionally the British book market's best month, for releasing the newest Murdoch novel. For a long while, until the takeovers of the 1980s and 1990s, she was their highest-profile quality fiction lead. Even if she had completed a given novel by (say) the previous November, there would be a year's wait between completion and publication. (This is not, or is no longer, customary practice in London's publishing world.) Thus, composition might well have occurred two or even three years before publication. It is worth bearing in mind—as it is corroborated in Bayley (211-14)—that Murdoch was wrestling with *Jackson's Dilemma* as early as 1994 and very likely as early as 1993, the year of publication of her penultimate novel, *The Green Knight.* Murdoch withdrew this novel for consideration for the 1994 Booker Prize because John Bayley was that year's Chair.

2. During a visit to Amsterdam in October 1986, Iris Murdoch described to me how, when moving from Steeple Aston, Oxfordshire, to North Oxford, she and John Bayley had destroyed an immense amount of paper-work by tearing it up into little pieces before burning it, on her account so that not even the refuse collectors would be able to make use of it. While this paperwork may have included correspondence, it seems more likely that it would largely have consisted of draft work that had accumulated over the preceding three decades, in a household of clutter described vividly in the Bayley memoirs.

3. Among novelists critical of Murdoch's style are John Updike, whose views are close to those of Ricks, and Angela Carter, who accused Murdoch's writing of blandness. Some of these attitudes, it must be accepted, are not wholly without justification, but they apply to particular phases of Murdoch's career rather than to the entire oeuvre.

4. John Bayley documents his sole writerly intervention in a Murdoch novel, involving the first chapter of an early draft of *The Bell* (1958) (41-44).

5. Such commentators include A. S. Byatt, Elizabeth Dipple, Richard Todd, and Peter Conradi, although they are not all in complete agreement.

6. It is worth noting that the Bayley memoir describes how Murdoch's own mother (who was only 19 when Murdoch was born) was hospitalized with dementia when in her late 70s, and suggests that from that time Murdoch may have known that on hereditary grounds she was at a higher-than-average risk of suffering the same fate.

7. This rather special kind of sinister, nightmarish double-casting has its counterpart in the operatic repertoire. Murdoch, in whose work opera plays an occasional role, may well have been aware of the double-casting of the children's mother and the witch in Engelbert Humperdinck's *Hansel and Gretel* (1893) or, most terrible of all, Dr. Schön and Jack the Ripper in Alban Berg's *Lulu* (1929-35).

8. Murdoch has touched on this theme in interviews with, among others, Christopher Bigsby, John Haffenden, and Richard Todd.

Works Cited

Bayley, John. *Elegy for Iris.* New York: St Martin's, 1999.

Bradbury, Malcolm, ed. *The Novel Today: Contemporary Writers on Modern Fiction.* London: Fontana, 1977.

Byatt, A. S. *Degrees of Freedom: The Early Novels of Iris Murdoch.* London: Vintage, 1994. Rpt. of *Degrees of Freedom: The Novels of Iris Murdoch.* London: Chatto, 1965.

Carter, Angela. "The Nun's Story." Rev. of *Nuns and Soldiers,* by Iris Murdoch. *The Guardian* 4 Sept. 1980: 14.

Conradi, Peter. "Dame Iris Murdoch." Obituary. *The Guardian.* 9 Feb. 1999: 18.

Dipple, Elizabeth. *Work for the Spirit.* London: Methuen, 1982.

Haffenden, John. *Novelists in Interview.* London: Methuen, 1985: 191-209.

Hall, William F. "*Bruno's Dream*: Technique and Meaning in the Novels of Iris Murdoch." *Modern Fiction Studies* 15 (1969): 429-443.

Kellaway, Kate. "Towards Enchantment." *The Observer Review.* 1 Oct. 1995: 16.

Lee, Hermione. *Virginia Woolf.* 1996. London: Vintage, 1997.

Leithauser, Brad. "The Good Servant." Rev. of *Jackson's Dilemma,* by Irish Murdoch. *The New York Times Book Review.* 7 Jan. 1996: 6.

Leech, Geoffrey N. *A Linguistic Guide to English Poetry.* London: Longman, 1969.

McQuade, Molly. Rev. of *Jackson's Dilemma,* by Iris Murdoch. *Boston Review.* 21.1 (1996): 36-37.

"Murdoch, Dame Iris." Year in Review 2000: Obituary. *Encyclopaedia Britannica.* 2000. <http://www.britannica.com/eb/article?eu=367581&hook=673508#673508.hook>.

Murdoch, Iris. "Against Dryness." Bradbury 23-31.

———. *A Fairly Honourable Defeat.* 1970. Harmondworth: Penguin, 1972.

———. *The Fire and the Sun: Why Plato Banished the Artists.* 1977. Oxford: Oxford UP, 1978.

———. "An Interview with Irish Murdoch." Interview with Michael Bellamy. *Wisconsin Studies in Contemporary Literature.* 18 (1977): 129-40.

———. Interview with Christopher Bigsby. *The Radical Imagination and the Liberal Tradition: Interviews with English and American Novelists.* Eds. Heidi Ziegler and Christopher Bigsby. London: Junction, 1982. 209-30.

———. *Jackson's Dilemma.* London: Chatto, 1995.

———. *Sartre: Romantic Rationalist.* 1953. London: Fontana, 1967.

———. *Under the Net.* 1954: Harmondsworth: Penguin, 1960.

Ricks, Christopher. "A Sort of Mystery Novel." Rev. of *The Red and the Green,* by Iris Murdoch. *New Statesman.* 22 Oct. 1965: 604-605.

———. "The Daisychain of Passion." Rev. of *Nuns and Soldiers,* by Iris Murdoch. *The Sunday Times.* 7 Sept. 1980: 43.

Sage, Lorna, "Amongst Entities." Rev. of *Jackson's Dilemma,* by Iris Murdoch. *Times Literary Supplement.* 29 Sept. 1995: 25.

———. "The Pursuit of Imperfection." Rev. of *Henry and Cato,* by Iris Murdoch. *Critical Quarterly.* 19.2 (1977): 61-8.

Todd, Richard. Plenary Discussion. *Encounters with Irish Murdoch.* Ed. Richard Todd. Amsterdam: Free UP, 1988. 96-110.

———. *Iris Murdoch.* New York: Methuen, 1984.

Updike, John. Rev. of *The Philosopher's Pupil,* by Iris Murdoch. *New Yorker* 15 Nov. 1983: 197.

Woolf, Virginia. *Between the Acts.* 1941. Harmondsworth: Penguin, 1953.

Jack Stewart (essay date winter 2002)

SOURCE: Stewart, Jack. "Metafiction, Metadrama, and the God-Game in Murdoch's *The Unicorn.*" *JNT: Journal of Narrative Theory* 32, no. 1 (winter 2002): 77-96.

[*In the following essay, Stewart defines the type of metafiction at work in* The Unicorn, *positing that the novel is, "to some degree, an allegory of reading." Stewart shows how the metafiction in* The Unicorn *opens for critical inspection the "mythicizing impulses in author and characters that constitute the act of narration."*]

Iris Murdoch is not usually thought of as an experimental novelist, although Robert Scholes, Patricia Waugh, and other critics have commented on her use of metafiction. But in *The Unicorn* (1963), she highlights the literary/psychological tendency to mythmaking in her own fiction through a stylized use of Gothic narrative and settings.[1] Murdoch's metafiction, which mainly exposes the fiction-making illusions of her characters, is heuristic rather than formalistic in the postmodern sense. Waugh, who observes that "metafiction explores the concept of fictionality through an opposition between the construction and the breaking of illusion," places Murdoch's novels "at one end of the spectrum," where "fictionality [is] a theme to be explored," but "formal self-consciousness is limited" ([*Metafiction*] 16, 18-19). She asks: "Why do metafictional novelists so frequently concern themselves with the problem of human freedom?" (119) Why, one might add, does Murdoch treat the problem of freedom metafictionally in *The Unicorn*? The answer has to do with the way she deconstructs the Gothic fantasy of the text and her characters' illusions.[2] As Peter Brooks says of *Heart of Darkness*, "[the] reader's own incapacity to sum up—the frustration produced by the text—is consubstantial with his dialogic implication in the text" ([*Reading for the Plot*] 260-61).

Mark Currie defines metafiction as "a kind of writing which places itself on the border between fiction and criticism" and emphasizes "the strong reciprocal influence between discourses which seem increasingly inseparable" ([*Metafiction*] 2, 3). In "[the] postmodern context," he notes, "the boundaries between art and life, language and metalanguage, and fiction and criticism are under philosophical attack" (17-18). Inger Christensen similarly observes that metafiction "focuses on the difference between art and reality and displays its consciousness of this distance" ([*The Meaning of Metafiction*] 22). Murdoch's novelistic discourse constructs a spellbinding mythos, while at the same time disclosing the reality of human relations that lies behind appearance. As a novelist, she is suspicious of the power of mythmaking; but *mythos* is connected with *telos* and "the reading of narrative . . . is animated by [what Barthes calls] the 'passion for (of) meaning'" (Brooks 177).

In *The Unicorn,* where discourse is ultimately demythologizing, Murdoch dramatizes the construction and collapse of fantasies and illusions. If "the goal of literary work . . . is to make the reader no longer a consumer, but a producer of the text" (Barthes [*S/Z*] 4), Murdoch as philosophical fabulist encourages the reader to participate in her character's illusions, but also to deal critically with issues of freedom and reality. For Scholes, Marian and Effingham "suggest two kinds of readers and two ways of encountering a book like *The Unicorn,* which is itself a 'fantasy of the spiritual life': the reader who, like Marian, becomes engaged in the events and touches good and evil through imaginative experience; and the reader who, like Effingham, remains aloof 'through egoism, through being in some sense too small'" ([*Fabulation and Metafiction*] 74). *The Unicorn* is, to some degree, an allegory of reading. Metafiction opens a gap between *mythos* and philosophical commentary that invites understanding: it examines the story, as fictional pattern, from the inside, laying bare mythicizing impulses in author and characters that constitute the act of narration.[3] Murdoch pre-

sents a cast of characters trapped in a state of Gothic enchantment or illusion, a state that the implied reader enters and absorbs, before learning to stand back and criticize it.

In **"The Sublime and the Beautiful Revisited,"** Murdoch notes that "the individuals portrayed in the [great] novels are free, independent of their author, and not merely puppets"; she comments on "how almost impossibly difficult it is to create a free and lifelike character" and on the "difficult battle to prevent [the] form from becoming rigid, by the free expansion against it of the individual characters" (257, 267, 271). She wants to construct "a house fit for free characters to live in" (271), yet the focal character in *The Unicorn* is imprisoned at Gaze Castle under a seven-year spell. The mirror motif and images of seeing are implicitly metafictional, for (to cite Genette on Proust) "the work is ultimately . . . only an optical instrument the author offers the reader to help him read within himself" (261). The characters attempt to "read" each other, gazing at facial expressions as if they were inscriptions in a secret code. The process of understanding is subverted, when one self projects illusions onto another in a search for identity.

J. Hillis Miller cites a parallel situation in Meredith's novels, in which "[e]ach [character] lives by speculation, by its reflection of the lives of others in itself, or by seeing itself reflected in the mirrors of others" ([*Ariadne's Thread*] 104). He takes it as axiomatic that "I always read my own face in the mirror of other people. We can never encounter another person face-to-face in that person's otherness or enter into a direct relation with that otherness . . ." (199). This axiom relates to Murdoch's sense of "the opacity of persons" (**"Against Dryness"** 20). Hannah particularly presents a blank or dazzling surface that mirrors the fantasies of those who gaze at her. She conforms, in Miller's terms, to "[a] model of interpersonal relations [that] sees selves as nothing but a locus traversed by fleeting signs"—which, for Murdoch, constitutes inauthenticity. "Such selves seek to ground themselves in others by drawing others to themselves, but each such self succeeds only in experiencing its solitude and nonentity" (Miller 219-20). In Hannah's transactions with Effingham, it is unclear who is more active and who more passive, who the analyst and who the analysand. As in Freud's narrative of the Wolf Man, "the self is bound in illusory relations" (Brooks 279).

Murdoch's novelistic discourse merges with, then undermines, the mythic superstructure. The "fiction/criticism boundary" (Currie 4) is crossed as characters in *The Unicorn* read each other, invent stories about each other, and act out imaginary roles in scripts derived from literature or legend. Christensen notes that in Sterne's *Tristram Shandy,* "[the] reader is not considered merely a passive receiver of the narrative, but shares in the making of the work. To the extent that he is drawn inside the work . . . his role changes from the more passive one of *reader* to that of *narratee,* sharing at times in the compositional task" (28). If Murdoch is too much in command of her *mythos* and too much concerned with philosophical understanding to share the task of composition with her reader, she does tutor that reader metafictionally—as Max tutors Effingham on the relevance of Plato's ideas to Hannah's predicament. To respond fully to the novel's tightly interwoven thematic nexuses of illusion-falsehood-power-destruction, on the one hand, and seeing-reality-love-freedom, on the other, the implied reader must follow philosophical clues implanted by the author or given directly by one character to another. Success depends on "[the] narrative *competence* of the reader . . . which enables him both to decipher more and more quickly the narrative code in general or the code appropriate to a particular genre or a particular work, and also to identify the 'seeds' when they appear" (Genette [*Narrative Discourse*] 77).[4] For instance, Marian, the main focalizer, "[finds] herself still, sometimes disconcertingly, unable to 'work out' the relations of the individuals to each other" (*Unicorn* 30). Metafictionally, her difficulty relates both to the author's struggle with the plot and to the reader's effort to understand it. According to Waugh, "*Metafiction* is a term given to fictional writing which self-consciously and systematically draws attention to its status as an aretefact in order to pose questions about the relation between fiction and reality" (2). Waugh notes that "[m]etafictional texts thus reveal the ontological status of all literary fiction: its quasi-referentiality, its indeterminacy, its existence as words and world" (101). This skeptical slant is consistent with Murdoch's insistence on the "opacity of persons," which rules out omniscient narration or first-take reading. Interpretation and moral insight have priority over fantasy in Murdoch's novels, but do not preclude it, any more than Umberto Eco's semiotics limits his fantastic invention in *The Name of the Rose*. In convincing narratives, illusion is dialectically linked with reality. In *The Unicorn,* the focus is on the second-degree fictionality of the characters' interpretations of their own and others' roles. Murdoch gravitates to that metafictional dimension in order to underscore the difference between such fictions of the self and ontological reality. In *The Unicorn,* the ego's compulsion to spin tales or fabricate fictions about itself and others gives rise to "narrative[s] within the narrative," or metanarratives as Genette calls them (228, n. 41). Effie's and Marian's speculations about Hannah are played off against each other at the *metadiegetic* level of the discourse.[5] Just as "[e]very proper history presupposes a metahistory" (White [*Tropics of Discourse*] 71), every proper (i.e., self-reflexive) fiction embraces a metafiction. Hannah, aware of Effie's Courtly Love scenario, talks about being the hero in his story, which, at

the metadiegetic level, she is. As she is also the focus of Murdoch's novel, her awareness of her fictionalized image enables the reader to critique Effie's fantasy and parallels her own iconic status in the text.

Reading Murdoch is a learning process, and Max, Effie's tutor in philosophy, and Marian, his pupil/teacher, function hermeneutically.[6] These characters try to read the darkly Gothic situation through myth, legend, or fantasy and make up roles for themselves and others through which they try to assimilate, or see through, an opaque "reality."[7] Just as Wilkie Collins, in *The Moonstone,* "uses multiple narrators to maintain interest and to create a nearly epistemological form of suspense, a deep uncertainty of perspective" (Brooks 169), Murdoch uses a pair of focalizing characters in *The Unicorn.* Marian, who embodies the reader's curiosity, ironically misreads her role:

> "Why have I come?" said Marian. Her own place in the story occurred to her for the first time. The ghastly tale had become a reality all about her, it was still going on. And it was a tale in which nothing happened at random.
>
> (64-65)

Murdoch's transposing of the last two sentences into free indirect discourse shows how ready Marian's mind is to "narrativize" or reconstruct events in terms of a "pattern." Her realization is self-reflexive in two ways, highlighting the character's distorted apprehension of her situation and the fictionality of the plot.[8] In "[a] prophetic flash of understanding," Marian thinks: "That was what she was for; she was for Gerald Scottow: his adversary, his opposite angel. By wrestling with Scottow she would make her way into the story" (65). Murdoch's use of free indirect discourse expresses Marian's illusions about herself: her self-confidence is derived from inexperience and lack of self-knowledge. It is a measure of her misreading of the plot that she thinks she can breeze in and counteract the seven-year spell with a cheerful burst of reality. Denis and Max, in their different ways, also misjudge Hannah's case, the one because of his own goodness and the other because of his fixation on the *idea* of goodness, both assuming that her suffering is spiritual expiation and that she should be allowed to complete it.[9]

Waugh notes that "explicit intertextual reminders are common in metafictional novels" (113), Scholes that "[i]magination feeds on previous imagination" (214). In *The Unicorn,* an aura of romanticism, melancholy, and enchantment is reinforced by allusions to Mme. de Lafayette's *La Princesse de Cleves* and Paul Valery's "La Cimitiere Marin," which Marian is reading with Hannah. Given Hannah's cipher-like quality, the allusion to purgative suffering in *La Princesse de Cleves* is, at best, a tantalizing but misleading clue to an unfulfilled potentiality. Hannah reads, with her tutor Marian, about a spiritual path that she fails to follow, but whose trace has been inscribed in the text. Effie's captivation with "Courtly Love" suggests sublimation and role-playing through a grammar of indirect discourse: "He was to be in love with Hannah, he was to be Hannah's servant . . ." (73). He passively accepts a role assigned by literary convention, rather than trying to reshape actuality. Hannah's very remoteness and unattainability attract him and leave him free to fantasize. His reading of her rationalizes romance, self-pleasing mysticism, and inertia and he exploits her existence for egotistical purposes. His romantic dream is inscribed upon a "dreary trance-like solipsism," like Dora's in *The Bell* (192), and his attempts to become Hannah's lover are perfunctory—in the mirror she holds up he simply watches himself perform the role of Courtly Lover. The truth, that something in him feebly wants to confront, constantly eludes him, so that his attraction to Hannah becomes a parody of metaphysical or spiritual questing. His psychoanalytically astute secretary Elizabeth's comments on Courtly Love—its decadence, unreality, and romanticism—supply a reality check on his motives.

Effie's Freudian interpretation of his own character as unconsciously determined by the Oedipal pattern, is a speech act parodically (and metafictionally) intended to exonerate him of all freedom and responsibility (232-33). It is not "the 'simple' Freudian sub-structure of the myth" that Byatt ([*Degrees of Freedom*] 152) takes it to be, so much as an instance of "double-voiced discourse" (Bakhtin [*The Dialogic Imagination*] 324-26), containing a technically correct but largely irrelevant diagnosis, which the subject manipulates to avoid confronting his own existential freedom and responsibility. His second-hand self-analysis reveals his retrospective and introspective tendencies to narrativize reality, rather than act in the present. Given the shifting contexts of speech in the novel, Elizabeth's Freudian analysis (uncontaminated by the ego's excuses) is more reliable.

Metafiction suits the generic premise of Gothic legend, in which a fantasy mechanism or fate selects fixed roles, with which characters align themselves. Hannah, in self-conscious complicity, knows more about Effie's illusions than he does himself: "You suffer, yes," she says. "But I'm a story for you. We remain on romantic terms" (91). Effie will do anything to avoid confronting reality, which is why his experience of Being in the bog (160-68) is so salutary yet so short-lived. He makes sure that his relationship with Hannah remains on the level of illusion, with their roles pre-cast by literary tradition. Accepting a "pattern" requires playing a role in a preconceived script, rather than generating one's own story. Legendary patterns, like those of the Unicorn (null and void) and Sleeping Beauty (displaced), replace reality, so that scripting and interpreting—slotting oneself into a role and reading the drama from a se-

lected perspective—become more significant than acting freely. Miller's deconstruction of "Figures" (256) applies to Hannah, who is also a "mask" or "rhetorical figure"—a blank space "disfigured" by the legend of the Unicorn. Effie cannot awaken the "Sleeping Beauty," because he himself prefers dream to reality.

Gerald's lecture to Marian about destiny, pattern, and authority (150-51) maintains a constant duality—are the characters free to choose their own acts or are they forced to act out a prearranged scenario? There is tension between "the primary fabula" or plot and "the embedded fabula" or legend. Mieke Bal (who expounds these terms), notes that "[the] embedded story can explain the primary story, or it may resemble the primary story" ([*Narratology*] 52-53). Alternatively, their relation may be ironic, highlighting illusions as in Murdoch's novel, where the Sleeping Beauty legend, with its seven-year spell, relates ironically to the main plot and the characters' belief in the legend's predictive power. Murdoch wants to examine the power of myth while dramatizing it, but cannot do so without manipulating her characters for the sake of the plot[10]—which demonstrates the magnetic power of *mythos*, at both primary and embedded levels.

Gerald's question, "Do you think there really *is*, for Hannah, an inside and an outside any more?" (150), blurs boundaries between self-structuring illusion and external reality. He gives "pattern" "absolute authority" over individual lives, although no grounds can be found for it other than fear and fantasy. The legend of the seven-year spell offers him a politically expedient reading of events, which he can manipulate for the sake of power, and he overawes Hannah's subjects with a mystique that plays on their illusions. A critical analysis of Gerald's language shows that he is asking Marian to sacrifice her freedom and accept the destruction of her identity for a "higher" purpose—a tactic that relates him to O'Brien in Orwell's *1984*. Gerald dominates Marian through an illocutionary act in which rhetoric subsumes semantics. "Pattern," like any metaphysical system, offers transcendence and consolation amid personal conflict, facilitating escape from reality at the price of relinquishing freedom.[11]

Gerald's relation to Marian is homologous with an omniscient author's relation to characters who must conform to plot. Self-abasement before the mechanics of the situation demands paralysis of the will, ennobled by an illusion of redemptive suffering and of cooperation with a higher cause. But existential reality springs from freely chosen action, rather than submission to external authority or system, be it legendary or Hegelian. By giving up her autonomy in order to become an icon in other people's imaginations, Hannah binds them to her in imprisoning illusions. This disguised form of power ("enchantment") subverts the freedom to be oneself that makes love possible.

Metafiction is a hermeneutic strategy. "In reality every reader is, while he is reading, the reader of his own self," claims Proust (qtd. in Genette 261), while Eco points out that "the surrogate reader is as common in fiction as the figure of the detective or any similar dramatised interpreter" (qtd. in Currie 4). The implied reader sees through Gerald's brainwashing of Marian, by recognizing how the power motive distorts his argument. As Enchanter, Gerald rationalizes a mythic structure in order to rob his victim of intellectual freedom. The novel does more than carry one along under a Gothic spell; it deconstructs its own myth[12] by presenting a *dialectic* of fantasy and reality that actively involves the reader. Rather than simply inviting the reader to share the character's illusions and then disillusioning him by conjuring tricks, as Fowles does in *The Magus,* Murdoch unmasks the process that generates illusions. She expects the reader to see the motives behind Gerald's speech. His sinister statement that "'freedom' has no meaning" ought to alert the reader to an agenda of enslavement. The speech approaches double-voiced discourse, because it is infiltrated by an ongoing authorial dialectics: Murdoch herself believes neither in absolute freedom nor in determinism, but in "degrees of freedom" (**"Against Dryness"** 19) that are the result of conscious choices.

For Byatt, "the problems of freedom or lack of it are . . . most starkly seen" in *The Unicorn*; comparing the novel with *A Severed Head,* she concludes: "All is not permitted, but neither are we not free at all" (146, 178). Byatt's double negative underlines the difficulty of defining freedom in positive terms and recalls Murdoch's strictures on overplaying the concept. In the novel, Max Lejour says: "Freedom may be a value in politics, but it's not a value in morals" (97). His reason is that "[w]hat we can see determines what we choose" (100).[13] His didactic dialogue with Effie on the Unicorn image, the Greek concept of *Ate,* the *Phaedrus,* and recognition of Good and Evil is meant to instruct the reader in philosophical themes. Yet seeing the Good falls short of acting selflessly to produce it and Max, engrossed in Platonic philosophy, overvalues contemplation at the expense of action. The metafictional equivalent of his perspective would be reading and interpreting the novel without attempting to grasp the distinction between fantasy and ontological reality.

Inclusion of a philosophical tutor and his pupil in the novel is clearly heuristic. In the concentrated metadiscourse in Max's study, the shift from plot-mythos to plot-interpretation is abrupt: if the half-drunk Effie fails to grasp the lesson, the implied reader is expected to do better. Such scenes might tend to become "allegories of reading," but Murdoch is using novelistic rather than unmediated philosophical discourse, and the density of imagined characters and contextualization of their speech acts creates a vital hermeneutics, far removed

from allegory. The fact that a philosopher, speaking as authorial surrogate in a Platonic tutorial intended to edify the reader, has criticized the existential concept of freedom does not mean that Gerald's indictment of freedom, in the scene where he subjugates Marian, is similarly endorsed by the author. The contextual implications of the two speech acts are completely different: as Chatman says, "'[u]tterance meaning' is word-sequence meaning plus a context, the locution plus its illocutionary force" ([*Coming to Terms*] 79). Max is conducting an open search for understanding with "negative capability"—all *too* negative, because he fails to act (the irony of a literary/philosophical mind)—while Gerald is exercising will-to-power in a "politicized" speech act, backed up by physical and emotional pressure, and is clearly capable of violent action. "The best lack all conviction, while the worst / Are full of passionate intensity" (Yeats, "The Second Coming"): Max, who might help Hannah, only thinks about her; Gerald imprisons and finally possesses her.

Waugh observes that "[some metafictional novels] involve characters who manipulate others explicitly as though they were playwrights or theatrical directors . . ." (117). Gerald assumes such a directorial, quasi-authorial power towards Marian and the rest of the cast at Gaze. He imposes his own far from disinterested view on Marian's rescue attempt, denying Hannah the capacity of distinguishing between "inside" and "outside," subjective and objective, and so denying her the possibility of free choice. Asserting Hannah's mystical function in a plot structure that has absolute authority and that "Maid Marian" cannot conceive of, he robs the latter of her independence by plausible arguments, backed up by an attractive and intimidating presence. Like the charismatic Mischa Fox in *The Flight from the Enchanter,* Gerald applies erotic as well as intellectual force to confuse Marian and subvert her freedom. His tactic is to invert the normal scale of values, substituting irrational but internally coherent myth for vagaries of individual impulse and action. He reads Marian's mind in order to divide and conquer it, reimposing the spell she wanted to break and bringing her more fully within the enchanted circle of Gaze. In her encounter with Gerald, Marian experiences a complex defeat, in which her innermost self is disclosed, entered, possessed, and subverted. Gerald's act of psychic rape reduces her to the status of a trembling child, robbed of her ability to think or act freely. Rather than being herself and making her own decisions, she must accept a supporting role in a drama whose outcome she cannot affect. Consequently, her blurred and teary gaze fixes once more on Hannah as an object of fantasy, rather than as a potentially free and unreified subject.

Metafictional texts problematize the relation between fiction and reality, as Murdoch does for epistemological and moral, rather than formal, ends. Effie's momentary experience of Alice's reality, despite his infatuation with Hannah, is rendered in metafictional dialogue: "[She's] the real side of the story, the real person, the real object of love. It's as if I'd been, all the time, looking into a mirror, and only been vaguely conscious of the real world at my side" (208). Given the fantasy of the *princesse lointaine* that holds him in thrall, "happiness," for Effie, would be "the achievement at last of a real action" (208), namely loving Alice. But this is impossible because, at the diegetic level he remains a character in a fiction and at the metadiegetic level he deliberately substitutes fantasy (self-pleasing images produced by the ego) for reality (the existence of others and the world outside the ego). "[A]ll our failures are ultimately failures of love," says the Abbess in Murdoch's **The Bell** (237), and Alice Lejour's failed love for Effie—which stems from his lack of attention to her reality—is an ironic mirror image of his illusory love for Hannah:

> As soon as you began to love her [Alice says], that made my love for you into something else. I became a sort of *spectator.* I had *a role* of being the generous rejected one. And since your love was hopeless too there was *a structure and a story* on which I could rest. And so I stopped just loving you and I was consoled.
>
> (266; emphasis added)

Truth is a function of relationships and Effie's opting for a fantasy Other immediately displaces Alice's genuine feelings, allowing her to play a role. Murdoch foregrounds metaphors of theatricality and fictionality to contrast with a reality that is further distanced by retrospective and introspective narration. Alice's reflections are scripted in past tense without quotation marks, her first-person story embedded within another's autoreferential narrative. This device implies automatism or a low degree of freedom.

Conversely, Marian is initiated into reality by her love for Denis, which produces a kind of "alienation effect," liberating her from the psychodrama that obsessively works its way out among the protagonists.

> With the return to Gaze she felt again her connexion with the house and with the drama it had contained. But she felt towards it rather as one who is leaving a theatre after some tragic play, worn, torn, yet rejoiced and set free with a new appetite for the difficult world. . . . Denis was real to her, mysterious, awkward, unfamiliar, infinitely to be learnt, but real.
>
> (204)

Metafictionally, the house is a microcosmic image of the novel's *mythos,* focalized by Marian, whose feelings are cathartic yet premature, for the "tragic play" has not yet reached its climax. She has come to Gaze to discuss poetry and fiction with Hannah and her assumptions are frequently based on literature, underlining the metafictionality of the text. Amused by Effie's "renunciation" of her, Marian mistakes the genre of drama they are performing, contradicting her previous assumption that it is tragic: "It was like a comedy by Shakespeare. All the ends of the story were being bound up in a good way" (209). So the text comments metafictionally on the tendency of fiction to fabricate an "All's Well that Ends Well" illusion of closure, as well as the tendency of actual people to interpret experience through "story lines."

Rimmon-Kenan observes that "[genre] conventions establish a kind of contact between the text and the reader, so that some expectations are rendered plausible, others ruled out, and elements which would seem strange in another context are made intelligible . . ." ([*Narrative Fiction*] 125). Genre affects outcome and interpretation of genre programs expectations. Murdoch's text presents itself alternately as Gothic melodrama, fairytale, comedy, and tragedy. The irony is that Marian has misread the genre, just as the reader has been misled by a series of plausible metanarratives. Murdoch's Gothic drama turns out to be tragic, rather than comic, while the comic frame-text and philosophical subtext bracket the central fabula and deconstruct fantasy. Violet Evercreech reduces the childish outsiders who aspired to be heroic actors to mere spectators. As the drama continues to unfold without their being able to "wrestle" their way into it, she mocks Marian's and Effie's inertia: "You both feel you are sitting out the end of some rather tedious film, don't you, where you already know what's going to happen?" (209). Violet's words are metafictional and proleptic: Marian and Effie haven't a clue as to the horrors that will occur when pent-up emotional forces locked up in the plot-mythos are finally unleashed. Tragic events are about to occur as *Ate* works its way out; the principal characters have invested a demonic energy in the story that surpasses their will to control. Violet's grim warning, "While you are playing ring-a-roses others are working the machine" (210), suggests that the plot is being manipulated from within. Even as Violet's remarks "contribute to an implied metanarrative commentary . . . by emphasizing the fictionality of the fabula" (to cite Bal 98), the dramatized spectators' sense of fixed fate and powerlessness is itself seen to be a fabrication or excuse.

After Hannah has been broken by Scottow, she seems about to start weaving another "more majestic, more terrible spell" to keep reality at bay. Instead, she confesses: "Do you know what part I have been playing? That of God. And do you know what I have been really? Nothing, a legend. A hand stretched out from the real world went through me as through paper" (218). Acting in "[a] dream" that parallels her textual role, Hannah has played the God-game, submitted to the very temptation that might seduce an author into omniscient control. For subliminally it is the author who plays God with her characters, although Murdoch wants (impossibly) to release them into their freedom, breaking the spell of Gaze Castle at the end of the novel, as Prospero breaks his wand at the end of *The Tempest*. To this end, the author communicates with the reader through a metafictional shadow-play, speaking ventriloquistically through Hannah about her own fiction and the way it pits illusion against reality: "I have lived on my audience, on my worshippers. I have lived by their thoughts, by your thoughts—just as you have lived by what you thought were mine. And we have deceived each other" (218-19). In this double-voiced discourse, Hannah's sudden shift from third person to second person and from "audience" to individual interlocutor reflects the narrator's address to the reader.

Anti-hero and audience mirror each other, for both are guilty of preferring fantasy to reality and self-projected, self-reflecting shadow-play to Being. By her very passivity, which falsely suggests an inner spiritual activity, Hannah—usurping the authorial role in an embedded God-game—disseminates fantasized, legendary narratives in her lovers, worshippers, jailers, observers, and "surrogate readers." Speaking "as if delivering some sober, much-debated judgement" (219), this irresponsible fabricator of illusory stories tells Marian:

> I needed my audience, I lived in your gaze, like a false God. But it is the punishment of a false God to become unreal. . . . You have made me unreal by thinking about me so much. You made me into an object of contemplation. Just like this landscape. I have made it unreal by endlessly looking at it instead of entering it.
>
> (219)

Here fiction criticizes its own fictionality, which depends upon the capacity to generate illusions. Existentially, Hannah, as author of a false, "unreal," self-image, has turned for-itself into in-itself and subjective reality into "an object of contemplation" (219). The legendary allusion is to the Lady of Shalott, spellbound by reflections of a world she is weaving into images of art and unable to enter the real landscape outside. The ironic parallel is with Max Lejour, who seeks the truth but endlessly gazes at Gaze, contemplating Hannah, without attempting to rescue her from her enclosed world. Her derealization of the landscape by gazing at it is ironically homologous with his suspension of her reality by speculating about her at a distance, instead of entering into relations with her.

Ghostlike or schizophrenic, Hannah alienates herself from reality and becomes a hollow sham falsely animated by other people's projections. Her refusal to function as a free, authentic self undersores the metafictionality of her confession. Her palindromic name[14] suggests that she is a cipher, without moral or psychological core, a blank mirror empty of metaphysical signifi-

cance. "You all attributed your feelings to me," she complains. "But I had no feelings, I was empty. I lived by your belief in my suffering. But I had no real suffering. The suffering is only beginning—now" (219). Peter Conradi speculates that "the absent centre perhaps points to Murdoch's own negative theology or secular mysticism in which the Good can be described only in terms of what it is not, and any attempt to incarnate or define it must finally be vain" ([*Iris Murdoch*] 123). The centripetal pressure on Hannah's role, at any rate, finally implodes it, along with her self-sustained enigma, vindicating Violet's existential judgment that she is no legendary Unicorn, but a violent and guilty creature who has failed to achieve self-understanding.

The diegetic substructure of the story is psychological rather than mythic, showing the baleful power of *Ate*. Hannah seems on the point of awakening to reality just as the curtain is about to come down. But she has not done the work of suffering and self-recognition that would purge her and so is bound to re-enact her violent impulses at the end of the seven-year cycle. Refusing to act is itself a kind of action, as Pip Lejour and Max find out to their cost; Hannah refuses to act until acted upon by Gerald and then her revenge and suicide are a vivid enactment of Ate. Even Effie realizes, in retrospect, that "Max had been right perhaps when he said that they had all turned towards [Hannah] to discover a significance in their own sufferings, to load their own evil on to her to be burnt up" (268). Hannah is complicit with this role of ritual scapegoat, although it does not match her inner reality. The effect of compulsive repetition in the plot is enhanced by intertextual allusion to Henry James's Gothic masterpiece—"Yet it was merely the turn of the screw, the turn to the next spiral" (228). Textuality is reified by reference to the metaphoric axis of substitution: "He has *become* him," Denis says. "Gerald is Peter now. He has Peter's place, he is possessed by Peter, he even looks like Peter . . ." (229). Here the plot approximates a theatrical mechanism in which characters are interchangeable pawns in the author's hands—as in Murdoch's novel *A Severed Head* (1961), which she later turned into a play.

But the teleological pattern of the main plot is gradually revealed. As Miller writes, "[n]arrative event follows narrative event in a purely metonymic line, but the series tends to organize itself or be organized into a causal chain. . . . The end of the story is the retrospective revelation of the law of the whole" (18).[15] Thanks to Murdoch's use of spatialized frames demarking a zone of relative reality from one of illusion—the Gothic spell has power within the "domaine" of Gaze; ordinary reality lies outside—the spectator-survivors (powerless to influence events) are left to interpret the plot as surrogate readers.[16] Hannah's suicide calls forth a politics of competing narratives. Rejected by the central drama because he cannot bring reality into it or sustain a vision of Being that goes beyond the ego, Effie's hollow triumph is to survive and abscond with "the story" of his enchantment. Disqualified from action, he preserves the memory of his illusions.

> [Effie] needed time to decide upon his own view of the story, to regroup his emotions, to sketch out his own salvation. . . . He did not want Max to contain him in any picture of the destiny of Hannah. The story, after all, was his, he had suffered enough for it.
>
> (237)

Effie, living ambiguously in the two worlds of diegetic and metadiegetic discourse, tries to elude the philosopher's more powerful narrative that would subsume and reinterpret his own. His alienation is apparent in the way he instinctively transposes reality into "story." Shoving responsibility aside, he "feel[s] that perhaps it was all inevitable and we were all something in Hannah's dream. . . . He thought of her now as a doomed figure, a Lilith, a pale death-dealing enchantress: anything but a human being" (266, 268)—in short, he blatantly romanticizes.[17]

As well as substituting mythic masks for Hannah's opaque reality, Effie brushes aside the issue of moral authenticity, leaving to Max "[that] vision . . . of the good forced into being as the object of desire, as if one should compel God to be" (268). Whereas Max focuses too much on moral vision and not enough on the suffering human subject's needs, acting too late to avert disaster, Effie, losing his belief in the God-game, settles for fictionality and the mundane routine of his own ego: "It had been a fantasy of the spiritual life, a story, a tragedy. Only the spiritual life has no story and is not tragic" (268). His double-voiced self-contradiction underlines the split between fantasy and reality and marks the character's inauthenticity: "He himself would hurry back to his familiar ordinary world. . . . He would try to forget what he had briefly seen" (268-69). Metafictionally, his role parallels that of a reader who refuses moral engagement with the text and, having dwelled in its imaginative space, dismisses it as reified fantasy, denying the insights it offers.

In **The Unicorn,** Murdoch constructs a labyrinth of Gothic melodrama, only to deconstruct it metafictionally. Her textually self-conscious use of legend and genre sets up false expectations in the reader, who has to correct them by reading against the grain. Murdoch's art subsumes the seductive pleasures of fantasy in the serious aims of philosophy, converting the reader's libidinal energy, with its delight in fantasy, into a "passion for meaning" or understanding. As the implied reader loses his or her way in the labyrinth of plot, the pleasures of insight begin to compensate for the frustrations of fantasy. Without formally disrupting the novel's imaginative premises, metafictional clues activate the

reader's awareness, so that imaginative and emotional energy is reinvested in existential and ontological thinking. While characters misread their situations and remain opaque to each other, their shortfalls in understanding make them partly transparent to the reader, who learns to re-read their readings of self and other in the relativizing light of ego psychology. The characters' illusions produce "internal" fictions that hide their reality, but rather than simply exploiting such illusions for the sake of a spellbinding story, the novelist impels the reader to see through them. In deconstructing ego-authored fantasies, she challenges the reader to think critically not only about the characters' complicity with illusion or capacity for seeking the truth, but about the self and its potential relations with others and with Being. The narrator's seriously playful dialogic and metafictional tactics engage the reader's critical imagination in an interpretive act that becomes increasingly sensitive to nuances of self-deception or self-knowledge. Murdoch's metafictional experiments function heuristically to stimulate curiosity, exploiting possibilities inherent in closed and open fictional forms and empowering a hermeneutics ultimately directed towards understanding the self and enlarging the reader's view of reality.

Notes

1. According to David J. Gordon, "[the] first chapters could have been drawn almost unchanged from the nineteenth-century Gothicist, Sheridan Le Fanu" (129).

2. As Linda Kuehl puts it, Murdoch's "metaphysical fantasy . . . employs stock fairytale, mythic, and Gothic devices and transforms them into literary correlatives of the author's philosophical vision" (347). Scholes observes of *The Unicorn* that "the conventions provide a frame of reference for the reader, helping him orient himself, but they also provide material for ironic or parodic scrutiny by the author, who manipulates [them] . . ." (59).

3. As Seymour Chatman observes, "a narrative text . . . contains within itself, explicitly or implicitly, information about how to read it" (83). Chatman adds that "the implied author is the reader's source of instruction about how to account for the selection and ordering of [the text's] components" (84).

4. Roland Barthes defines the *hermeneutic code* as "all the units whose function it is to articulate in various ways a question, its response, and the variety of chance events which can either formulate the question or delay its answer; or even, constitute an enigma and lead to its solution" (17). For Shlomith Rimmon-Kenan, "[the] hermeneutic aspect of reading consists in detecting an enigma (a gap), searching for clues, framing hypotheses, trying to choose among them and (more often than not) constructing one finalized hypothesis" (128).

5. *Diegesis* "designates the universe of the first narrative," *metadiegesis* that of second-level narrative-within-the-narrative (Genette 228, n. 41; see also 231-34).

6. As Elizabeth Dipple notes, an extreme hermeneutics such as Eco's regards "all novels as 'machine[s] for generating interpretations'" (Currie, ed. 224).

7. Paul Coates finds "a dialectic of realism and fantasy, representation and solipsism, at the heart of all writing" (1).

8. As Scholes observes, "Marian see[s] herself as entering a 'tale' which has materialized around her; a tale in which nothing happens at random. . . . [Yet she] is a character in a tale by Iris Murdoch, who is certainly the God of this little fictional universe—a very careful God, who will let nothing happen at random" (65-66). The text comments metafictionally on the God-game that every author is compelled, to some extent, to play.

9. Murdoch's concept of the central character, originally based on Simone Weil's mystical theology, changed during the writing (see Heyd 142), reducing Hannah from a paradigm of suffering to a source of illusion and ultimately a structural device.

10. According to Kuehl, "Murdoch is unable to give her characters a free and independent existence because they are cast in predetermined roles and are invested with intellectual concepts and associations . . ." (355).

11. Murdoch, in *The Sovereignty of Good,* observes: "Art presents the most comprehensible examples of the almost irresistible human tendency to seek consolation in fantasy and also of the effort to resist this and the vision of reality which comes with success" (64).

12. Miller explores "the way the novel [as a genre] deconstructs itself in the process of constructing its web of storytelling" (23).

13. According to Scholes, "Iris Murdoch is teaching us how to read allegorically in *The Unicorn* . . . almost imperceptibly moving from conventional mysteries of motivation . . . to the ideational mysteries of philosophy" (60). This move is plainly perceptible in Max's tutorial.

14. According to Scholes, Hannah's first name (which reads the same forward or backward) suggests "a duplicity or ambiguity in the significance of her life," counteracting the more serious suggestion of her surname, Crean-Smith, which contains the anagram, "Christ-name" (68-69).

15. Brooks similarly maintains that "the energy that belongs to the textual hero's career and to the reader's expectation . . . maintains the plot in its movement . . . toward recognition and the retrospective illumination which will allow us to grasp the text as total metaphor . . ." (108).

16. Waugh (111) compares the way that Fowles in *The Magus* and Murdoch in *The Unicorn* shift from realistic frames to Gothic settings, while Scholes observes that "Marian and Effingham come from the 'real' world into Gaze, just as we readers come into a work of fiction" (63).

17. Kuehl refers to Murdoch's "technique of molding characters into legendary figures" (354), implying her indulgence in romantic or Gothic imagination before the plot deconstructs it.

Works Cited

Bakhtin, M. M. *The Dialogic Imagination: Four Essays.* Ed. Michael Holquist. Trans. Caryl Emerson and Michael Holquist. Austin: U of Texas P, 1981.

Bal, Mieke. *Narratology: Introduction to the Theory of Narrative.* 2nd ed. Trans. Christine Van Boheemen. Toronto: U of Toronto P, 1997.

Barthes, Roland. *S/Z.* Trans. Richard Miller. New York: Hill, 1974.

Brooks, Peter. *Reading for the Plot: Design and Intention in Narrative.* Cambridge, MA: Harvard UP, 1992.

Byatt, A. S. *Degrees of Freedom: The Novels of Iris Murdoch.* London: Chatto, 1965.

Chatman, Seymour. *Coming to Terms: The Rhetoric of Narrative in Fiction and Film.* Ithaca: Cornell UP, 1990.

Christensen, Inger. *The Meaning of Metafiction: A Critical Study of Selected Novels by Sterne, Nabokov, Barth and Beckett.* Bergen: Universitetsforlaget, 1981.

Coates, Paul. *The Realist Fantasy: Fiction and Reality Since "Clarissa".* London: Macmillan, 1983.

Conradi, Peter J. *Iris Murdoch: The Saint and the Artist.* London: Macmillan, 1986.

Currie, Mark, ed. *Metafiction.* New York: Longman, 1995.

Dipple, Elizabeth. "A Novel which is a Machine for Generating Interpretations." Currie 221-45.

Eco, Umberto. *The Name of the Rose.* New York: Warner-Harcourt, 1984.

Fowles, John. *The Magus: A Revised Version.* New York: Laurel-Dell, 1978.

Genette, Gerard. *Narrative Discourse: An Essay in Method.* Trans. Jane E. Lewin. Ithaca, NY: Cornell UP, 1980.

Gordon, David J. *Iris Murdoch's Fables of Unselfing.* Columbia: U of Missouri P, 1995.

Heyd, Ruth. "An Interview with Iris Murdoch." *University of Windsor Review* 1 (1965): 138-43.

Kuehl, Linda. "Iris Murdoch: The Novelist as Magician/ The Magician as Artist." *Modern Fiction Studies* 15 (1969): 347-60.

Miller, J. Hillis. *Ariadne's Thread: Story Lines.* New Haven: Yale UP, 1992.

Murdoch, Iris. *The Bell.* London: Chatto, 1958.

_____. *The Flight from the Enchanter.* London: Chatto, 1956.

_____. *The Sovereignty of Good.* London: Routledge, 1970.

_____. *A Severed Head.* 1961. New York: Compass-Viking, 1963.

_____. "The Sublime and the Beautiful Revisited." *Yale Review* 49 (1960): 247-71.

_____. *The Unicorn.* 1963. Harmondsworth, Middlesex: Penguin, 1966.

Rimmon-Kenan, Shlomith. *Narrative Fiction: Contemporary Poetics.* 1983. London: Routledge, 1989.

Scholes, Robert. *Fabulation and Metafiction.* Urbana: U of Illinois P, 1979.

Waugh, Patricia. *Metafiction: The Theory and Practice of Self-Conscious Fiction.* London: Methuen, 1984.

White, Hayden. *Tropics of Discourse: Essays in Cultural Criticism.* Baltimore: Johns Hopkins UP, 1978.

Margaret Moan Rowe (essay date spring 2004)

SOURCE: Rowe, Margaret Moan. "Iris Murdoch and the Case of 'Too Many Men.'" *Studies in the Novel* 36, no. 1 (spring 2004): 79-94.

[*In the following essay, Rowe critiques a number of Murdoch's novels to demonstrate the claim that women of "public stature" and intellectual force are noticeably absent from her fiction. According to Rowe, "in Murdoch's world, intellectual women are very much relegated to the private, domestic sphere, while the world of professions, the public world, is male dominated."*]

In *The Flight from the Enchanter* (1956), Rosa Keep makes several efforts to save the *Artemis,* a women's periodical founded by her dead mother and Mrs. Camilla Wingfield. One such effort involves visiting Mrs. Wingfield, an eighty-three year old suffragette, in an attempt to convince her to save the periodical she helped establish. That visit, one of Murdoch's great comic scenes, has Rosa telling how the *Artemis,* now edited by her younger brother Hunter, is in danger of being taken over by Mischa Fox, described as "'press lord and general mischief-maker.'" Rosa's account is interrupted by Mrs. Wingfield who exclaims: "'There are too many men in this story'" (114). When reading Murdoch's novels, many a reader or critic, especially a female reader or critic, has been tempted to repeat Mrs. Wingfield's comment about male omnipresence.

Yet, despite Mrs. Wingfield's criticism, women characters come in for a fair share of prominence in *Flight.* Ironically enough, that novel is as close as Murdoch comes in her fiction to giving a prominent role to what its characters refer to as "female emancipation" (169). Written before the publication in 1954 of her first novel, *Under the Net, Flight* can be read as Murdoch's ur-novel, introducing so many of the themes that figure in novels that follow.[1] Within the thirty chapters of *Flight,* Murdoch weaves a myriad of interests (e.g., the attraction to power relationships, particularly the Magus-disciple axis, the connection between sexuality and love, the interest in marginalized communities, the lure of intellectual quests, the relationship between good and evil). Most of those interests figure prominently in the twenty-four novels that follow-not so "female emancipation." Elizabeth Dipple judges the *Artemis* subplot in *Flight* "as close as Murdoch ever gets to an extended feminist statement" ([*Iris Murdoch*] 140). And she is correct.[2]

From Jake Donaghue in *Under the Net* to Martin Lynch-Gibbon in *A Severed Head* (1961) to Hilary Burde in *A Word Child* (1975), male narrators are everywhere in Murdoch's fictional world, particularly in the novels written before 1980. And when not actually narrating their stories, male characters and their psychological, ethical, and social dilemmas occupy center stage. Murdoch favors male rivalry as a narrative complication and often stages it as conflict between brothers or cousins as in *A Severed Head, The Time of the Angels* (1966), *An Accidental Man* (1971), *Henry and Cato* (1976), *The Sea, The Sea* (1978), *The Good Apprentice* (1985), and *The Green Knight* (1993). Another form of male rivalry that she explores is the master-disciple relationship; the love-hate it engenders in works such as *The Flight from the Enchanter, The Bell* (1958), *A Fairly Honourable Defeat* (1970), *The Black Prince* (1973), *The Philosopher's Pupil* (1983), *The Book and the Brotherhood* (1987), and *The Message to the Planet* (1989) is as intense as any blood feud.

The preeminence of male rivalry in Murdoch's work is not surprising from a writer who told Michael Bellamy in 1977:

> I identify with men more than women, I think. I don't think it's a great leap; there's not much difference really. One's just a human being. I think I'm more inter-

ested in men than women. I'm not interested in women's problems as such, though I'm a great supporter of women's liberation-particularly education for women-but in aid of getting women to join the human race, not in aid of making any kind of feminine contribution to the world. I think there's a kind of human contribution, but I don't think there's a feminine contribution.

(["An Interview with Iris Murdoch"] 133)

I quote at length from her response to Bellamy because Murdoch's position *vis à vis* "women's liberation" is a complex one.

Murdoch asserts that men and women are the same, or at least "'there's not much difference really.'" Then she goes on to suggest there is a great difference: somehow men are already there. Their presence defines the human race. Women have to join the human race and a principal route to that connection is education. Certainly Murdoch's own educational pedigree—student at Oxford and Cambridge, Fellow at Oxford where she taught philosophy—supports her view of education. That same intellectual pedigree seems to have given Murdoch a sense of security caught in a 1976 interview with Sheila Hale, wherein Murdoch insists:

> But although, I, too, am prejudiced on behalf of the downtrodden group to which I belong, the subject bores me in a way. Women who think of themselves as something separate are joining a kind of inferiority movement, like women's clubs. I realise I am lucky. I have never felt picked out in an intellectual sense because I am a woman, these distinctions are not made in Oxford.

(["Women Writers Now"] 180)

Education gave Iris Murdoch entre into the intellectual life of her times; her work in both philosophy and literature assured her a prominent place in that life. It is no accident that Murdoch's final philosophical work, **Existentialists and Mystics** (1997), has a foreword by George Steiner, an intellectual mandarin among mandarins. Steiner points to Murdoch's prominence as a philosopher: "In at least three fields, the study of Platonic and Kantian ethics, the introduction to British students and readers of French existentialism and its Kierkegaardian roots, and in the inquiry into the nature of art and beauty, Iris Murdoch has made contributions which, alone, would ensure something of her international stature" (x). Then there are her considerable literary contributions to add in. Both the philosophy and the fiction add up to a significant "human contribution." Murdoch's stature as an intellectual is undisputed. There is a public record of that stature in the existence of her texts, critical reviews, comments by George Steiner and others. Through education and distinguished work, Iris Murdoch is not only able "to join the human race" but also to win a prominent place in it.

What intrigues me is the marked absence of the woman as *public* intellectual in Murdoch's fiction, especially in the light of her own status as such. I underscore "pub-

lic" to suggest intellectual activity subject to notice beyond a circle of friends and social acquaintances, activity often registered in the world of work. This kind of achievement, however, is not reflected in her fiction, where there are no female characters able to approach anything remotely like public stature. In Murdoch's world, intellectual women are very much relegated to the private, domestic sphere, while the world of the professions, the public world, is male dominated. But then so is the world of education, the very means by which Murdoch sees women joining the human race.

I

Even as recently as 1995 in **Jackson's Dilemma,** Murdoch's last novel, intellectual interests remain largely a male preserve. Uncle Tim, Thomas Abelson (called Tuan) and Benet Barnell are very much at home in the world of ideas, particularly with philosophical, theological, and literary issues. Not so the female population in **Jackson's Dilemma.** Marian and Rosalind Berran are the marriageable young women in the novel; of the two, only Rosalind is given anything like intellectual ambition: "her ambition was to study art history and if possible also be a painter" (91). By the novel's end, Rosalind is married and discovers that her husband is wealthy: "Now she could paint *and* try the Courtauld" (224). Try is an interesting verb. Contrast the sweet amateurism of Rosalind's aspirations with the weighty amateurism of Benet Barnell, university man and retired civil servant: "There on the desk was his book about Heidegger, open at the page where he had left it such a little while ago. Benet perused the page which he had written" (68).[3] Higher education, whether at universities or art institutes, while available to women in Murdoch's world, is still very much a masculine domain—even in 1995.

Not much changed in the thirty-eight years that separate **Jackson's Dilemma** and **The Sandcastle** (1957), Murdoch's "academic" novel. Education, particularly university education, is a male right (at least for middle- and upper-class men). The novel, set in a boy's school, centers around the career and marriage of William Mor, a history teacher. (Teachers in Murdoch's world are also most often male.) The bulk of the narrative is given over to Mor's affair with Rain Carter, a painter and the daughter of Sydney Carter, a more celebrated painter. The affair is dull going for the reader; of much greater interest is Mor's relationship with his wife, Nan, and his children, Felicity and Donald.

Mor is disappointed in his wife's narrow life; he had tried to educate her: "He had always known that she was intelligent. He had imagined that she would turn out to be talented. The house was littered with the discarded paraphernalia of subjects in which he had hoped to interest her [. . .]" (13). Because of that failure and for class reasons as well, Mor stresses education for his children, and despite straitened circumstances sends his daughter to boarding-school and forces his son to prepare for a college entrance examination in chemistry. Nan, on the other hand, wants to have their daughter leave school and start on a typing course so that Felicity might have "'a good career [. . .] [as] secretary to some interesting man.'" Mor rejects his wife's practicality: "'I don't want her to be secretary to some interesting man,' said Mor, 'I want her to be an interesting woman and have someone else be her secretary'" (12).

What never becomes clear in what Nan sees as Mor's "'sentimental feminism'" (13) is just what makes an interesting woman. And the narrative is not intent on that clarification; it is Donald's rebellion and his missing the much-awaited Cambridge entrance exam that gets Mor's attention and acts as a rival, albeit a pale one, to his passion for Rain Carter. The novel ends with Felicity telling her father that she would like to stay in school and Mor speculating that "'later on perhaps you'll go to a university'" (285). Felicity is—perhaps—a candidate for "'a university'" by default.

Few of Murdoch's female characters in the nineteen novels published prior to 1980 even go to university. And those few who have access to university and earned degrees do not garner the intellectual cachet enjoyed by male characters with university affiliation. Take the case of Morgan Browne in *A Fairly Honourable Defeat.* Morgan, a linguist, returns to England after her affair in America with Julius King, a celebrated biologist, ends. Here, I want to stress the absence of an adjective attached to linguist and the presence of an adjective attached to biologist. Morgan often seems to be playing a part; Julius King fully inhabits his academic identity. Seeking a refuge, Morgan flees to the household of her sister Hilda and her brother-in-law Rupert Foster. Julius King ends up in the same locale because he, Rupert and Axel Nilsson, Rupert's colleague in the Civil Service, are university friends. Rupert, self-described as "'a Sunday metaphysician,'" has for eight years been writing a book about "'real virtue'" (27), an enterprise that provides the idea field in *A Fairly Honourable Defeat.* The question of whether or not real virtue exists forms the matter of reflection and conversation for the network of male intellectuals in the novel: Rupert, Julius, Axel, and Tallis Browne, historian, and Morgan's estranged husband. Morgan's conduct fuels part of the discussion, but she is not herself a discussant nor a member of the intellectual network.

In fact, the only character who describes Morgan as an intellectual is her sister Hilda Foster, and that term comes into play to serve Hilda's self-description when she contrasts herself as "'not one of your trained minds'" (25). Axel Nilsson makes an interesting comment on the difference between Hilda and Morgan when he notes: "'Morgan means well but she's fundamentally a very silly person. Hilda is far more genuinely a rational being, though like so many women she preferred marriage to the development of her mind. Morgan's a lightweight'" (33). Presumably, Morgan the lightweight did initially prefer to develop her mind (or at least attend university), but that development leads to little. She, herself, describes her manuscripts as "'The stuff on theoretical linguistics which I was working on when I went to that extremely consequential conference in South Carolina'" (55-56).

Her work is "stuff." The conference is "extremely consequential," but not for professional reasons. According to Hilda, "'She met Julius on the second day. She went for a fortnight and stayed two years'" (15). All that time, Morgan focuses on Julius who has time to work on his science. Her initial preference leads to the same choice Hilda makes: all for love. But Hilda has the social support of marriage; in her liaison with Julius, Morgan does not.

Axel's judgement that "Morgan's a lightweight" reverberates throughout the novel. Her work is "stuff" to her and the matter of comic confusion for Rupert and Hilda:

> [. . .] that book she was writing on glossy what was it?
>
> Glossematics.
>
> What a word! How clever of Morgan even to know what it means!
>
> (14)

For Julius King, the academic super star, Morgan's intellectual work is the object of contempt. For Julius, linguistics is not intellectually respectable; he tells her that "'The trouble with your subject is that it isn't one'" (257). He views Morgan as having "'the intellectual equipment of a sixth-form mistress or a literary critic'" (259). Even Tallis, Morgan's long-suffering husband and the keeper of her manuscripts, sees her as "'hopelessly theory-ridden'" (213). Morgan's university training and the development of her mind lead to a very nebulous destiny. After being used by Julius in a terrible ethical experiment that ends the Fosters' marriage and precipitates Rupert's suicide, Morgan and her sister leave England for America, and Morgan takes "a university job on the West Coast" (443).

Before turning away from *A Fairly Honourable Defeat,* I want to return to Hilda Foster and her self-definition early in the novel. In response to Hilda's claiming not to be "'one of your trained minds,'" Rupert Foster replies: "'Well you could have been, only I snatched you up so early. You don't regret it do you darling, not having been to a university? You know it isn't important.'" To which the canny Hilda responds:

"'Yet it's important that Tallis got a second. You mention it about once a month'" (25). "Having been to a university" and won the glittering prizes is decidedly important in making intellectual claims in Murdoch's fictional world.

II

By 1980 and the publication of the magnificent *Nuns and Soldiers,* the glittering prizes of university life are within reach of women characters—or at least seem to be. More than any other novel before or after it, *Nuns and Soldiers* presents strong and fascinating women. Its action revolves around two university friends, Gertrude Openshaw (nee McCluskie) and Anne Cavidge: "They had been prize students together, clever Anne Cavidge, clever Gertrude McCluskie. They were two strong women who might have been rivals for the world. They had divided it between them" (51). Separated for fifteen years, the Cambridge friends are reunited when Anne, newly exited from a Roman Catholic Convent, shows up at Gertrude's flat in the last's days of the latter's husband's dying of cancer. In one way, they have divided a world—if not the world; Gertrude and Anne are the Martha and Mary of the narrative in Luke 11: 38-42:

> Now as they went on their way, he entered a village; and a woman named Martha received him into her house. And she had a sister called Mary, who sat at the Lord's feet and listened to his teaching. But Martha was distracted with much serving; and she went to him and said, "Lord, do you not care that my sister has left me to serve alone? Tell her then to help me." But the Lord answered her, "Martha, Martha, you are anxious and troubled about many things; one thing is needful. Mary has chosen the good portion, which shall not be taken away from her."

Before her marriage to Guy Openshaw, patriarch of an extended grouping of family and friends, Gertrude had been a teacher, but losing a child "and feeling that Guy needed her presence at home, [. . .] she gave up her work" (17). She also planned to write a novel "[. . .] but was soon dissuaded by Guy, and of course she came to agree. Did the world need yet another mediocre novel? For a while she employed herself as Guy's research assistant." Gertrude accepts the narrative judgment that the abandoned novel would be "mediocre." Guy's "book about justice, punishment and the criminal law" (23) progresses until his death. Gertrude's world of houses and domestic obligations is not so far from Hilda Foster's all for love in *A Fairly Honourable Defeat.* Gertrude, too, plays handmaiden to her husband although more self-knowingly than Hilda Foster: "Guy's 'formative influence' in their married love was discreetly admitted by Gertrude, while at the same time she announced herself as a woman not easily dominated" (17).

Anne Cavidge's conventual life seems nothing but a dominated life—at least to Gertrude. Hostile to religion, Gertrude's immediate response to Anne's arrival is to see her friend as someone from the Dark Ages:

> What did you do in *there,* I mean in the way of intellectual pursuits, or was it all prayer and fasting?
>
> I taught some theology and Thomist philosophy, but it was so specialised and sort of simplified—I couldn't sell it outside. It wasn't a very intellectual order.
>
> So you said at the start, and amazed me! You sacrificed your intellect to those charlatans!
>
> I could teach Latin, French, Greek maybe—
>
> You wasted all those years—You must start thinking again.
>
> (49)

Gertrude's patronizing conclusion is wonderfully ironic in light of Murdoch's depiction of Anne Cavidge's years as a nun. Anne, after all, is the Mary figure in this novel. Thinking and reflection have been her way of life, her "good portion."

At the outset, "Clever Anne Cavidge, in her desperate flight from the world, had shrewdly decided to make the sacrifice of the intellect as early and as irrevocably as possible" (56). But that proves vain and impossible for her. The intellect channeled toward holiness leads her out of the convent and back into the world:

> her ideas were changing, the shape of her cosmos was changing, making what was far near, and what was near far. But what these so-natural changes did, and out of their fullness and their sweetness, bring to her at last for her pain, was a profound urgent notion, felt increasingly as a *duty,* that she must now move away to *some other place.*
>
> (59-60)

That other place is temporarily with Gertrude as witness to her struggle with widowhood and her triumph in a new marriage. Tempted by her love of Peter, a bogus Polish Count, Anne flirts with becoming part of the world of homes and established relationships. But the Count, still in love with the remarried Gertrude, prefers "to stay forever as [Gertrude's] courtier, within the light of her countenance" (460).

By the end of *Nuns and Soldiers,* Gertrude and Anne once again divide the world, at least geographically. But for all the dramatic change of its focusing on women characters, the conclusion of *Nuns and Soldiers* confines women to the world of a separate sphere. Leaving Ebury Street for Hammersmith with her new and younger husband Tim, Gertrude becomes the matriarch of a new Openshaw circle. Ever self-satisfied, she tries to keep Anne within her orbit: "'you're *our* nun. We need you—'" (470) she cries as Anne tells her of her plans to join a group of Poor Clares in America.

Deborah Johnson correctly reads this text as one that goes on "to explore, with increasing depth and flexibility, the inter-relationships among the female characters" ([*Iris Murdoch*] 70). But this is a singular departure in Murdoch's presentation of women characters. It does not seriously alter what I have described as Murdoch's male-gendered public world. Intellectual as she is, Anne Cavidge has no public role as an intellectual. Johnson and other female critics want to see *Nuns and Soldiers* as a more radical—even feminist—turn in Murdoch's response to "female emancipation" than the novel actually is. Olga Kenyon, for example, wants to argue that in *Nuns and Soldiers* "Murdoch begins unconsciously to share a feminist revaluation of women" ([*Women Novelists Today*] 40). The assertion is easier to make than to prove.

Certainly by 1980 and the publication of *Nuns and Soldiers,* Murdoch had abandoned a seeming obsession with first-person, and equally obsessed, male narrators in favor of an omniscient narration that privileges the views of a number of characters. As Cheryl Bove maintains: "One important result of this decentering strategy is that it allows for more narration through the consciousness of her women characters" ([*New Directions*] 193). Barbara Stevens Heusel makes an even more elaborate claim when she says of novels written in the eighties and after: "A review of Murdoch's novels shows that marginal women characters have become less marginalized in the later novels and that the male thinkers have become marginalized" ([*Patterned Aimlessness*] 140). Heusel then goes on to offer readings of but two novels, *Nuns and Soldiers* and *The Message to the Planet,* to support her generalization.

Neither the narrative bill of rights for female consciousness that Bove advances nor the "less marginalized" position that Heusel describes, however, explains why Murdoch's female characters continue to inhabit a separate sphere. In the novels that follow *Nuns and Soldiers,* all for love is still the mantra for Murdoch's female characters. *The Philosopher's Pupil* is a good case in point. This sprawling book of nearly six hundred pages opens with George McCaffrey trying to drown his wife Stella. Two reasons are offered for this serious breach in domestic decorum. According to the narrator, "George had one of his rages" (1); according to Stella, he is "'crazy with fear because Rozanov is coming'" (5). John Robert Rozanov, a renowned philosopher/historian, is the native son, returning home to establish a domicile in Ennistone for his granddaughter Hattie. Rozanov had also been a teacher of both George and Stella and has become an obsession of George's: "Some pupil-teacher relationships last a lifetime. George maintained his side of the relationship, though it is doubtful whether Rozanov animated his" (78).

Of more importance to my argument, however, is that Stella, too, is "the philosopher's pupil." Rozanov had early recognized Stella's talent for philosophy, a talent that the deluded George does not have. But Stella the student had suppressed her gift to support George; N, the narrator of the novel, notes: "'And you gave up philosophy, in case George realized you could do it and he couldn't!'" (370). After marriage, she makes even more elaborate intellectual sacrifices. An outsider in the closely knit community of Ennistone, Stella Henriques, "daughter of an English diplomat of Sephardic Jewish extraction [. . .] was said to be 'academic' and 'awfully clever,' though she gave up her studies on marriage" (31). In a dialogue between Stella and N, she reveals that her marriage itself had become her study. "'My holy place is George,'" she tells N (365); later she admits to N: "'I am George'" (369). Stella's absorption in George keeps her from everything else. Even N, sympathetic to Stella whom he saves after George attempts to drown her, sees the limitations of Stella's all for love. By the end of the novel, George and Stella are reconciled after George has a brainstorm on the Commons and asks to be returned to Stella. N offers a wry summation of the "happy ending":

> I lately expressed the hope to Stella that now that life has become (it seems) more predictable she should stop regarding George as a full-time occupation, and consider harnessing her excellent mind to some coherent and developing intellectual study. She says that no doubt she will, but 'not yet', that perhaps she will 'write something'. I am afraid that at present she is more concerned about George's mind than about her own.
>
> (565)

George is obsessed with Rozanov, the thinker; Stella is obsessed with George, the philosopher's lesser pupil.

Obsession with male characters is the order of the day for central female characters in *The Book and the Brotherhood* as well. Rose Curtland and Jean Cambon (nee Kowitz) are school friends. Neither woman is the writer of the book in the novel's heavily gendered title; both are connected to the brotherhood only through familial or romantic associations. Each woman has academic credentials. An Oxford graduate, "Jean was a clever academic who should, Rose felt, have 'done something' instead of just being a wife" (12). Rose

> had studied English literature and French at Edinburgh. She had done a variety of things, never achieving anything which could be called a career, taught French at a girls' school, worked for an Animals' Rights organisation, been a 'women's journalist', tried to write novels, returned to part-time journalism and ecology. She did unpaid social work and occasionally went to (Anglican) church. She had a small annuity from a family trust which she felt she might have been better off without; she might have tried harder.
>
> (11)

Neither woman tries hard in the public sphere; both, however, have major occupations as handmaidens to male intellectuals.

The novel opens at the Commem Ball at Oxford, an event that draws the brotherhood of Gerard Hernshaw, a retired Civil Servant, Jenkin Riderhood, a teacher, and Duncan Cambon, a Civil Servant. Rose Curtland is attached to the brotherhood because she is the sister of Sinclair Curtland, a deceased member of the group and Gerard's lover. Rose has spent most of her adult life loving Gerard. The past links the group and part of that past was the decision to underwrite David Crimond's "long quasi-philosophical book" (98). No book has been completed as the novel opens, but Crimond, who had "remained on the extreme left while the others now held more moderate opinions" (99), appears at the Commem Ball. As a result of that appearance, Jean Cambon leaves her husband Duncan and elopes with Crimond for a second time. She tells Duncan: "'You and I connect through our weaknesses. Crimond and I connect through our strength'" (73).

The Jean/Crimond relationship is intense and produces a violent end in which Duncan shoots Jenkin while aiming at Crimond. What it also produces is the same old separate spheres even though Crimond sees himself and Jean as above the ordinary: "'We are both from elsewhere, we are visitors here, aliens'" (311), he tells her. Crimond's view of women is anything but alien. When Jean charges him with thinking women inferior, Crimond responds: "'All men think that [. . .] And most women too. Why deny it, women are different, their brains are different, they're weaker [. . .].'" He quickly exempts Jean from the downtrodden group by naming her "'an errant spirit'" (310-11).

Crimond begins the relationship by talking a kind of intellectual equality: "He lectured her on how she must find some employment, chided her for not using her talents." Crimond first urges Jean to "do a degree, take a course, study a language." But his apparent openness to her intellectual development and her choosing gives way to standard patriarchal domination. She asks to help him with his work; he says no. Finally, "She suggested a short course in computer science, but Crimond did not like computers. He was also very firmly against her trying to learn any philosophy. Another difficulty was that he did not really want her to be away from the house" (166). So much for the new order. Jean settles for the age-old female occupation: "She was *living* upon love [. . .] She had never experienced *presence* so vividly before, the total connection with another being, the interpenetration of bodies and souls, the intuitive absolute of mutual self-giving, the love of two gods" (167).

"The intuitive absolute of mutual self-giving" is but one of the lies Jean Cambon tells herself about her relationship with Crimond. Blinded by her own selfishness,

Jean remarks to her friend Rose: "'you've never been deified by love, you're a quiet girl, you're a puritan really, in the depths of your heart you feel that sex is wrong'" (306). Neither is "deified" by love, but Rose has a firmer grip on the actuality of her relationship with Gerard. As early as the Commem Ball, Rose recognizes: "I've wasted my life on this man, I've waited though I've known I'm waiting for nothing, he has accepted so much and given so little in return." Those thoughts are barely registered, however, before another view surfaces: "how ungrateful I am, he has given me his precious love, he loves me and needs me isn't that enough? Even if he does think of me as a sort of ideal sister" (9).

Murdoch's characterization of the watchful and waiting Rose is one of the triumphs of *The Book and the Brotherhood.* Cheryl Bove sees Rose as "another representation of the female as victim" (193). I have a problem with the too simple term "victim" that Bove uses—this in spite of her move to read later Murdoch novels as more feminist friendly. In *Iris Murdoch: A Life,* Peter Conradi writes persuasively of Murdoch's "consistent refusal to depict women only as victims" (393). Even though her women characters occupy a separate sphere, particularly in reference to intellectual and professional possibilities, there is no lack of psychological complexity in those characters. With or without work in the world, Rose Curtland is a complex character faced with choices. Something of her complexity is caught in the scene after Crimond, having rejected Jean, proposes to Rose. As with her thoughts about Gerard, Rose's thoughts about Crimond's offer are filled with subtleties:

> How can I make sense, how can something like this happen so quickly? But it has happened—and it's impossible, it's deadly, it must simply be stopped and killed. I must drown these thoughts. The least weakness could make a catastrophe, a desolation. No one must know. How could I live if Gerard knew? If anything were to happen—it could only go wrong—and that would break me, it would break some integrity, some dignity, some pride, something by which I live. I can't risk my life here. But, oh, what pain, a secret pain that will be with me forever. I must be faithful to my real world, to my dear tired old world. There is no new world.
>
> (415)

Rose Curtland is one of the many savvy female witnesses to male egoism in Murdoch's fiction. The novel ends with Gerard planning to write a book in response to Crimond's published book. Rose is to be his research assistant, as major an intellectual role as is open to women in *The Book and the Brotherhood.*

The intellectual possibilities for women seem more promising—at least for awhile—in *The Green Knight.* For once, the master-disciple relationship, so dear to

Murdoch and so often gendered as male as I indicated earlier, involves a woman disciple, Sophia (called Sefton) Anderson. Sefton is one of three sisters whose progress forms one of the narrative strands in the novel. The master in *The Green Knight* is Lucas Graffe, mysterious historian. Graffe's hatred of his brother Clement precipitates an attempted fratricide that leads to injuring Peter Mir and then involving that stranger with the circle of friends and relatives around the Graffes and Andersons. My interest, however, is with the narrative strand woven around the Anderson sisters, particularly Sefton, the intellectual: "She was said to be too bookish, obsessed with learning and passing exams, only interested in serious conversation" (13).

At eighteen, Sefton has completed her exams and is awaiting her results. "Destined for the university" (8), she is presented as reticent, controlled, and a bit androgynous: "She did not care for clothes but wore shabby, often second-hand, corduroy jackets and trousers, and cheap men's shirts" (13). Sefton identifies with Hannibal and Odysseus; she is also devoted to Lucas Graffe and their tutorials:

> Lucas was not only a good and exacting teacher, he was a great scholar. She had been told, as a child, that Lucas was awfully learned and clever, but this had meant little. Now, coming to him from the agreeable domain of her thoroughly worthy schoolteachers of history and of the classical languages, she felt like an ambling walker confronted by a cliff. The standards which she perceived, though still hazy to her, were terrible ones.
>
> (272)

The intellectual-erotic spell is broken by Lucas (secretly involved with Sefton's sister Aleph) who ends the master-disciple relationship, commanding Sefton to "'Remember that this [being an historian] is a lifelong dedication, you are entering upon it as into a religious house, something to which you must give your whole life, you must grow into being a scholar.'" Lucas closes with the admonition: "'Do not marry [. . .] Solitude is essential if real thinking is to take place'" (274).

Sefton's solitary and scholarly vocation is short-lived as she falls in love with Harvey Blackett, also eighteen and planning to study modern languages in London. Her first response to falling in love is negative: "I am *losing* myself, I am in a state of *warfare,* of confusions and compromises and base dissension and deceit. I must not become this other person, this cowardly, overthrown defeated person" (392). But true to all for love, Sefton does become "this other person" reflected in her dress: "Sefton was wearing a dark green dress of very fine corduroy pulled in at her waist by a red belt. Her abundant reddish brown hair, grown a little longer, was combed back from her brow, her green hazel eyes shone, her firm lips were parted, her pale face, blush-

ing, glowed" (444). The novel ends with talk of a future marriage between Sefton and Harvey with nary a mention of her scholarly ambitions.

III

Interestingly, for a writer whose fiction is so overwhelmingly linked to male protagonists with professional identities, Murdoch offers few depictions of characters in a work place. The activities in the factory and at the Special European Labour Immigration Board in *Flight from the Enchanter* are Murdoch's most extensive forays into that arena. Ironically enough, the scenes at SELIB present a picture of female power in a public space. Murdoch describes the grade of Organizing Officer as having "been invaded by an army of young women who, appointed initially as typists, had rapidly set about bettering themselves, and having once got a foothold in this new territory advanced with formidable speed" (85). That connection between women, work, and power remains an anomaly in Murdoch's fiction. In *Bruno's Dream* (1969), the Greensleave printing works inspire Danby Odell's joy: "He loved the works, the clattering noise, the papery dust, the tribal independence of the printers, he loved the basic stuff of the trade, the clean-cut virginal paper, the virile elemental lead" (22). Still, that joy is soon enough supplanted by his passion for Diana and the domestic trappings around her. The world of Whitehall in *The Nice and the Good* and in *A Word Child* is sketchily developed. Hilary Burde offers a virtual non-description of his work environment in *A Word Child* when he notes: "I worked in Whitehall, in a government department, it boots not which. I worked in the section called 'establishments' which deals with the administration of the office itself" (6). Burde does spend some time recording territorial skirmishes with co-workers, skirmishes with a quaintly domestic tinge:

> The Room had been rearranged. My desk had been moved out of the bay window and put facing the wall on the near side where Reggie Farbottom's desk used to be. Edith Witcher's desk had moved onto the carpet and into the bay in place of mine, and Reggie's desk was now just behind hers, also on the carpet and facing out of the window.
>
> (69)

As Burde admits "Very little of my story actually takes place in the office" (28)—a truth for most of Murdoch's male protagonists.

In *A Severed Head,* Martin Lynch-Gibbon declares that "it was on my palate alone that the firm of Lynch-Gibbon depended" (60), but he is perfectly content to absent himself from the office and leave the work of the wine merchant to secretaries. Blaise Gavender of *The Sacred and Profane Love Machine* (1974) "knew he was some sort of charlatan" (20) in his practice of psychotherapy and spends his time fantasizing about giving up his work. Bradley Pearson's saga begins after he retires from the world of work in *The Black Prince.* Leaving the Civil Service and claiming his uncle's inheritance, Benet returns to his avocation, philosophy, in *Jackson's Dilemma.* Economic means make semi- or full retirement an engaging possibility for many of Murdoch's male characters; thus, the drawing room rather than the board room dominates her settings.

Lorna Sage reads Murdoch as "feminizing the whole human condition. The individual is pictured enmeshed in 'relations' surrounded by fixtures and fittings [. . .]" ([*Women in the House of Fiction*] 74). I would not go that far, but would argue that Murdoch's creation of a feminized landscape is her most radical gesture toward the emancipation of what she called in the Hale interview: "the downtrodden group to which I belong." Sage goes on to describe Murdoch's world as one in which "men are pulled by the text's gravitational field into a domestic orbit" (80). That is true, but it is a domestic orbit soon colonized by male egoism. The result is often catastrophic as the overweening egoism of so many of the male characters that might have been disciplined by the rituals and constraints of the work place, tempered by the presence of male "equals," wrecks havoc in the home place.

In *The Sea, The Sea,* the novel for which Murdoch won the Booker Prize in 1978, Charles Arrowby, a successful director, retires to the seacoast where he finds his first love whose life he disrupts with his egomaniacal pursuit. In a rare moment of narrative truth-telling, Arrowby declares: "'I'm beginning to feel like a terrorist'" (307). He is not alone in Murdoch's world. Father Carel Fisher in *The Time of the Angels* (1966) is the domestic tyrant at his most repellent. In the incestuous and closed world of his rectory, Fisher acts with demonic certainty and declares: "'With or without the illusion of God, goodness is impossible to us. We have been made too low in the order of things'" (165). Fisher's psychological and physical oppression of his daughters is Murdoch's most chilling depiction of evil, but Fisher's drive to dominate, while the most extreme, is not the only example of domestic tyranny in Murdoch's middle-class world. At its heart, that world is often a site of domestic terror and women are most often the object of that terrorism.

Blaise Gavender and Emily, his second wife, construct a funeral pyre in *The Sacred and Profane Love Machine,* and the narrator describes them as people working "silently, surreptitiously, feverishly, like people trying to conceal a crime." They seek to obliterate any sign of Harriet, Gavender's first wife, from the house over which she presided. The outline of Hood House is brightened by funeral flame:

A perpetual bonfire burnt in the garden on to which the spouses, usually avoiding each other in this chore, quietly piled Harriet's more dispensable belongings, the poor rubble of Harriet's finished life: the contents of her desk, her childhood mementoes, the water-colours of Wales, her books of recipes, her news-paper cuttings about her father's regiment, picture postcards from her father and brother, drawerfuls of cosmetics and combs and ribbons and old belts, even underwear. The strange funeral pyre gradually consumed them all.

(339)

Obliteration also appeals to the ever-violent George McCaffrey in *The Philosopher's Pupil,* and he enacts his domestic rage against the netsuke prized by his wife Stella:

George burst in with his hammer, eagerly anticipating the work of destruction. But the window-sill was bare. He looked about the room, opened the drawers: gone. The little gaggle of ivory men and animals had disappeared. Stella must have come, foreseeing his rage, and taken them away. She treasured them as tokens of her father's love. George felt a pang of jealous misery and frustration.

(138)

I would term Murdoch a laureate of unhappy families,[4] creating as she does a middle-class landscape of tragicomic proportions. Responding to a question from Jean-Louis Chevalier about the Gothic terrors in her work, Murdoch disavowed that exotic language and asserted that "'It is ordinary life that I'm talking about which after all is full of horrors'" (85). Material security does not necessarily translate into emotional and psychological security in Murdoch's complicated world, many of whose "'horrors'" are associated with the misuse of power, one of the "ailments of Romanticism" that she discusses in **"Against Dryness"** (1961). In that essay, she declares:

We are not isolated free choosers, monarchs of all we survey, but benighted creatures sunk in a reality whose nature we are constantly and overwhelmingly tempted to deform by fantasy. Our current picture of freedom encourages a dream-like facility; whereas what we require is a renewed sense of the difficulty and complexity of the moral life and the opacity of persons.

(20)

Murdoch's male protagonists often deform reality. Kingsley Widmer aptly notes that "Murdoch's novels do, and often do-in, philosophical claims, but almost obsessively they do, and do-in, self-deluded and self-destructive intellectual males" (["The Wages of Intellectuality . . . and the Fictional Wagers of Iris Murdoch"] 16). I would go a step further and underscore Murdoch's focus on self-deluded and other-destructive males in her fictional world. These are characters who act as though their homes were their castles, characters who see themselves as monarchs of all they survey. The narrator of **The Philosopher's Pupil** declares that "Many men are violent (the sealed doors of houses conceal how many)" (74). In her most dramatic and direct gesture "on behalf of the downtrodden group" to which she did and did not belong, Murdoch unseals many a door in the private sphere to reveal the prevalence of the abuse of power—an abuse she most consistently links to "'too many men.'"

Notes

1. Comparing *The Flight from the Enchanter* to *Under the Net,* Frank Baldanza describes the former as "considerably more complex in plot, characterization, and meaning [. . .] it is the first distinctively original work that bears the full mark of the author's peculiar genius" (*Iris Murdoch* 43).

2. In *Women in the House of Fiction,* Lorna Sage notes that like Elizabeth Gaskell and George Eliot, "Murdoch puts the woman question to one side" (74). Sage's linking Eliot and Murdoch is particularly interesting in light of John Bayley's comment that "Iris never cared for the novels of George Eliot [. . .]" (117). Exploring the very considerable connection between Eliot and Murdoch, however, waits for another essay.

3. Poignantly, Peter Conradi notes that Murdoch's "most recent work-in-progress, as yet unfinished, is a weighty study of Heidegger" ("Preface," *Existentialists and Mystics* xxi).

4. In her study of Murdoch's fiction, Hilda Spear argues she does not write of the "domesticities of family life" (122). Not knowing what Spear means by "domesticities," I would still argue against this reading of Murdoch whose focus on family life and its horrors easily wins her her laureateship.

Works Cited

Baldanza, Frank. *Iris Murdoch.* New York: Twayne, 1974.

Bayley, John. *Elegy for Iris.* New York: St. Martin's, 1999.

Bellamy, Michael O. "An Interview with Iris Murdoch." *Contemporary Literature* 18 (Spring 1977): 129-40.

Bove, Cheryl. "New Directions: Iris Murdoch's Latest Women." *Critical Essays on Iris Murdoch.* Ed. Lindsey Tucker. New York: G. K. Hall, 1992. 188-98.

Chevalier, Jean-Louis. "Closing Debate." *Rencontres avec Iris Murdoch.* Caen: Centre de Recherches de Litterature et Linguistique des Pays de Langue Anglaise, 1978. 73-93.

Conradi, Peter. *Iris Murdoch: A Life.* New York: Norton, 2001.

Dipple, Elizabeth. *Iris Murdoch: Work for the Spirit.* Chicago: U of Chicago P, 1982.

Hale, Sheila, and A. S. Byatt. "Women Writers Now: Their Approach and Apprenticeship." *Harpers and Queen* Oct. 1976: 178-91.

Heusel, Barbara Stevens. *Patterned Aimlessness: Iris Murdoch's Novels of the 1970s and 1980s.* Athens: U of Georgia P, 1995.

Johnson, Deborah. *Iris Murdoch.* Bloomington: Indiana UP, 1987.

Kenyon, Olga. *Women Novelists Today: A Survey of English Writing in the Seventies and Eighties.* New York: St. Martin's, 1988.

Murdoch, Iris. "Against Dryness." *Encounter* 16 (Jan. 1961): 16-20.

———. *A Fairly Honourable Defeat.* Harmondsworth: Penguin, 1972.

———. *A Severed Head.* Harmondsworth: Penguin, 1963.

———. *A Word Child.* Harmondsworth: Penguin, 1976.

———. *Bruno's Dream.* Harmondsworth: Penguin, 1970.

———. *Existentialists and Mystics: Writings on Philosophy and Literature.* Ed. Peter Conradi. New York: Allen Lane, Penguin, 1998.

———. *Jackson's Dilemma.* New York: Viking Penguin, 1996.

———. *Nuns and Soldiers.* New York: Penguin, 1982.

———. *The Book and the Brotherhood.* New York: Penguin, 1988.

———. *The Flight from the Enchanter.* London: Triad/Panther, 1976.

———. *The Green Knight.* New York: Viking Penguin, 1994.

———. *The Philosopher's Pupil.* New York: Viking Penguin, 1984.

———. *The Sacred and Profane Love Machine.* Harmondsworth: Penguin, 1976.

———. *The Sandcastle.* London: Triad/Granada, 1979.

———. *The Sea, The Sea.* Harmondsworth: Penguin, 1980.

———. *The Time of the Angels.* London: Triad/Granada, 1978.

Sage, Lorna. *Women in the House of Fiction: Post-War Women Novelists.* New York: Routledge, 1992.

Spear, Hilda D. *Iris Murdoch.* New York: St. Martin's, 1995.

Widmer, Kingsley. "The Wages of Intellectuality . . . and the Fictional Wagers of Iris Murdoch." *Twentieth-Century Women Novelists.* Ed. Thomas F. Staley. Totowa, NJ: Barnes & Noble, 1982.

FURTHER READING

Bibliography

Soule, George. "Iris Murdoch." In *Four British Women Novelists: Anita Brookner, Margaret Drabble, Iris Murdoch, Barbara Pym: An Annotated and Critical Secondary Bibliography,* pp. 141-422. Lanham, Md.: The Scarecrow Press, Inc., 1998.

> An extensive secondary bibliography of Murdoch criticism, with sections for "General Studies" and each of Murdoch's novels.

Criticism

Alexander, Flora. "Iris Murdoch's Moral Comedy." In *The Comic Tradition in Irish Women Writers,* edited by Theresa O'Connor, pp. 99-107. Gainesville: University Press of Florida, 1996.

> Describes the ways in which Murdoch's treatment of comedy is uncharacteristic of traditional Irish female writing.

Antonaccio, Maria. "Iris Murdoch's Secular Theology of Culture." *Literature and Theology* 18, no. 3 (September 2004): 271-91.

> Maintains that in her novels and works of philosophy, Murdoch provides a compelling justification for religious life in a secular world in two ways: first, by defending the significance of individual consciousness; and second, by salvaging an idea of the religious depth of morality.

Bove, Cheryl K. *Understanding Iris Murdoch.* Columbia: University of South Carolina Press, 1993, 216 p.

> Book-length study that includes plot summaries and interpretations of all of Murdoch's works, including her major philosophical writings.

Denham, A. E. "Envisioning the Good: Iris Murdoch's Moral Psychology." *Modern Fiction Studies* 47, no. 3 (fall 2001): 602-29.

> Elucidates some key features of Murdoch's "meta-ethics" and "moral psychology," arguing that although Murdoch's fiction should not be read as literary representations of her philosophical ideas, the novel form "manifests a way of thinking about moral experience that her philosophical writings both recommend and vindicate."

Heusel, Barbara Stevens. *Iris Murdoch's Paradoxical Novels: Thirty Years of Critical Reception.* Rochester, N.Y.: Camden House, 2001, 185 p.

> Traces and assesses the critical response to Murdoch's twenty-six novels during the last thirty years of the twentieth century.

Howard, Catherine E. "'Only Connect': Logical Aesthetic of Fragmentation in *A Word Child.*" *Twentieth Century Literature* 38, no. 1 (spring 1992): 54-65.

> Argues that Murdoch's novel *A Word Child,* like E. M. Forester's *Howard's End,* is primarily concerned with the idea that "the preservation of hope and love is the key to a meaningful existence."

Kerr, Fergus. "Back to Plato with Iris Murdoch." In *Immortal Longings: Versions of Transcending Humanity,* pp. 68-88. Notre Dame, Ind.: University of Notre Dame Press, 1997.

> Discusses the central importance of Plato in Murdoch's philosophy, specifically seen in her belief that goodness exists in the world and is a state that human beings can achieve through knowledge and intuition, and through unselfish love.

Levenson, Michael. "Iris Murdoch: The Philosophic Fifties and *The Bell.*" *Modern Fiction Studies* 47, no. 3 (fall 2001): 558-79.

> Attempts to "establish the integrity of Murdoch's early philosophy," developed during the 1950s when she was a tutor in philosophy at St. Anne's College, Oxford, and to situate Murdoch's 1958 novel, *The Bell,* "within her emerging metaphysical perspective."

Rice, Thomas Jackson. "Death and Love in Iris Murdoch's *The Time of Angels.*" *Critique* 36, no. 2 (winter 1995): 130-44.

> Examines the metaphysical conception at the center of *The Time of Angels,* arguing that the novel works on the levels of both fiction and philosophy because "there is no line of separation, ultimately, between the 'story' of the novel and the 'idea' that drives it."

Turner, Jack. "Iris Murdoch and the Good Psychoanalyst." *Twentieth Century Literature* 40, no. 3 (fall 1994): 300-17.

Argues that the character of Thomas in *The Good Apprentice* serves a central purpose for Murdoch in the novel, namely to discredit Freudian psycho- analysis. Turner also discusses the theme of "losing and finding" a father and the nature of Murdoch's authorial will or control over her subject matter.

Additional coverage of Murdoch's life and career is contained in the following sources published by Thomson Gale: *British Writers Supplement,* **Vol. 1;** *Concise Dictionary of British Literary Biography: 1960 to Present*; *Contemporary Authors,* **Vols. 13-16R 179;** *Contemporary Authors New Revision Series,* **Vols. 8, 43, 68, 103, 142;** *Contemporary British Dramatists*; *Contemporary Literary Criticism,* **Vols. 1, 2, 3, 4, 6, 8, 11, 15, 22, 31, 51;** *Contemporary Novelists,* **Ed. 7;** *Contemporary Women Dramatists*; *Dictionary of Literary Biography,* **Vols. 14, 194, 233;** *DISCovering Authors: British Edition*; *DISCovering Authors: Canadian Edition*; *DISCovering Authors Modules: Most-studied Authors* **and** *Novelists*; *DISCovering Authors 3.0*; *Encyclopedia of World Literature in the 20th Century,* **Ed. 3;** *Literature Resource Center*; *Major 20th-Century Writers,* **Eds. 1, 2;** *Major 21st-Century Writers*; *Novels for Students,* **Vol. 18;** *Reference Guide to English Literature,* **Ed. 2;** *Twayne's Companion to Contemporary Literature in English,* **Ed. 1;** *Twayne's English Authors*; **and** *World Literature and Its Times,* **Ed. 4.**

Christopher Okigbo
1930-1967

(Full name Christopher Ifenayichukwu Okigbo) Nigerian poet.

The following entry presents an overview of Okigbo's life and works. For additional information on his career, see *CLC*, Volumes 25 and 84.

INTRODUCTION

Okigbo is a key figure in the development of African literature in the twentieth century. He has won praise for his explorations of culture and ritual, innovative use of rhythm and song, deft treatment of language and form, and imaginative blending of African culture with such non-African influences as Christianity and Western poetics. Okigbo derived his aesthetic sensibilities from art, music, classical and modern poetry, and his interaction with the young artists of his native Nigeria. Because of his interest in art in broadly human terms, Okigbo became an important figure in international literature while drawing the attention of the literary world to the post-colonial experience in Nigeria and across Africa.

BIOGRAPHICAL INFORMATION

Okigbo was born August 16, 1930 (although some biographers place his birth in 1932). He was born in Ojoto, Nigeria, to Anna Onugwalobi Okigbo and James Okoye Okigbo, a traveling teacher and headmaster commissioned by a local Roman Catholic mission. Okigbo's childhood was strongly shaped both by his time living at mission-schools throughout Nigeria and by his native village of Ojoto. This blending of indigenous and Western worldviews would become a central element in Okigbo's poetry. Another significant influence on Okigbo's writing was the storytelling of the family's housekeeper, Eunice, who cared for the children after Okigbo's mother died in 1936. The Okigbo family moved to Ekwulobia in 1936, where Christopher began primary school and first encountered the teacher he would later refer to as "Kepkanly" in the poems of *Heavensgate* (1962). After completing his primary schooling, Okigbo passed the rigorous entrance exams and entered Umuahia Government College in 1945. While there he developed an interest in Western sports such as cricket, football, tennis, and boxing. From Umuahia, Okigbo gained admission to the elite University College, Ibadan, where he studied classics and graduated with a Bachelor of Arts degree in 1956. For the next four years Okigbo held various jobs, including a teaching position at Fiditi Grammar School, where he promoted the study of poetry and assisted several of the school's athletic teams. It was during this time that Okigbo wrote and published his earliest poems, including "Debtor's Lane," published in the *Horn* literary journal, and "Song of the Forest."

Between 1960 and 1962 Okigbo worked as a librarian for the University of Nigeria, at both the Nsukka and Enugu campuses. During this time he immersed himself in Nigeria's emerging literary circles, communicating with academics and students alike. It was also during this period that Okigbo completed the poem "Lament of the Lavender Mist" (published in the journal *Black Orpheus* in 1962) and finished the final drafts of *Heavensgate* and *Limits* (1962). After he resigned his library post in 1962, Okigbo became the representative for Cambridge University Press in West Africa. This position allowed him to pursue his love of literature, make contacts within the international literary community, and travel throughout the region. Also in 1962, Okigbo was appointed as the West African editor for the intellectual journal *Transition,* where he eventually published several of his poems. In 1963 Okigbo married a teacher named Sefi. Their daughter, Ibrahimat, was born in 1964. Despite these attachments, Okigbo continued to live in Ibadan apart from his wife and daughter. In 1966, after a military coup, a massacre of the eastern Nigerians began. The ensuing mass exodus of Igbos and other easterners led Okigbo to write his last and most admired set of poems, *Path of Thunder: Poems Prophesying War.* These were published posthumously in *Labyrinths, with Path of Thunder* (1971). When the tension in Nigeria erupted into full-scale civil war, Okigbo joined the Biafran Army and was commissioned a major. He was shot and killed at the Nsukka front two months after the war started in August 1967.

MAJOR WORKS

Okigbo produced a relatively small body of work. During his lifetime he published only two collections of poetry: *Heavensgate* and *Limits.* Two other works, *Poems: Four Canzones* (1968) and *Labyrinths, with Path of Thunder,* were published after his death. Despite the limited size of Okigbo's canon, each work is recognized as a substantial contribution to African and world literature. Critics note as well that each volume is indispensable to an appreciation of Okigbo's broader poetic vision; individual poems and entire collections are seen as interdependent pieces of a greater whole, rather than as isolated works.

Heavensgate is a poem sequence of five sections which critics have praised for its musicality and craftsmanship. The work is also noted for breaking with the sentimental Nigerian poetry of the day and establishing a more personal and highly symbolic style of verse. The sequence covers a variety of themes, including love, sexuality, Christianity, childhood, and native religion. The central figure of the poems is the archetypal prodigal who returns to the Nigerian deity Idoto and sets off on a great quest. As the speaker confronts the central issues of the sequence, his response is often ritualistic, demonstrated through prayer, mourning, supplication, and cleansing. Many commentators consider *Heavensgate* to be an account of Okigbo's inner life and his struggle to reconcile the imagery and substance of two different faiths.

Okigbo's second major work, *Limits*, is divided into two sections: first, a sequence of four poems entitled "Siren Limits," and second, a six-part section entitled "Fragments out of the Deluge." "Siren Limits" begins with the protagonist of *Heavensgate* having cleansed himself in order to return to the Queen, a figure who simultaneously refers to Idoto and to various other female archetypes that appear throughout Okigbo's work. Other poems in the section trace themes of success and disillusionment related to the protagonist's personal and spiritual quest. In contrast, "Fragments out of the Deluge" deals primarily with the social and political climate of Okigbo's time. Drawing on mythic and historical imagery, the poems explore life in Okigbo's native country, focusing especially on the consequences of colonial exploitation and cultural suppression.

Okigbo composed portions of *Poems: Four Canzones* as early as 1957, and he published some of the poems in the journal *Black Orpheus* in 1962. The collection was not published in its entirety until 1968. Combining early pieces with others from the prime of his career, *Poems: Four Canzones* both traces the development of Okigbo's verse and highlights the interdependence of his canon. One of the early poems, "Debtor's Lane," demonstrates the influence of T. S. Eliot and other modernist writers on Okigbo. Another early canzone, "Song of the Forest," introduces the author's preoccupation with the prodigal, a theme that dominates *Heavensgate* and *Limits* and runs throughout his work. "Lament of the Flutes," composed in 1960, explores the recurring motifs of childhood and homecoming, and "Lament of the Lavender Mist" returns to the theme of love, both

human and divine. Stylistically, "Lament of the Lavender Mist" resembles Okigbo's early work in its disjunctive use of imagery and sound, and in its use of literary references.

Labyrinths, with Path of Thunder, published posthumously, contains new versions of poems that had previously appeared in different journals during Okigbo's lifetime, along with previously unpublished poems and notes by the author on the content and style of his verse. The work returns to Okigbo's common themes, such as the juxtaposition of Western and native mythologies and the tension between the internal world of the poet and external reality; it also includes Okigbo's most direct and impassioned response to contemporary events, in the sequence *Path of Thunder: Poems Prophesying War.* This work, in addition to being one of Okigbo's final poetic endeavors, is also widely regarded as the pinnacle of his literary career.

CRITICAL RECEPTION

Okigbo was widely praised throughout his career. However, his use of myth, ritual, personal experience, and dense symbolism has often divided critics over the meaning and importance of his poetry. Some have maintained that the poems reflect the human quest for the divine, while others have viewed them as a veiled attack on Christianity. Still others have interpreted the poems exploring the cultural and political alienation of Nigerians during the colonial period as literary artifacts of Okigbo's social and political views. Despite this lack of consensus, most scholars have maintained that Okigbo's greatest contribution to world literature is the innovation he brought to African poetry. Most African verse of the time restricted itself to patriotic themes and conventional modes of expression. Okigbo's work, by contrast, deals with complex personal subject matter. Many critics have noted that Okigbo's style shows influences by Western artists. Specifically, Okigbo employs stylistic elements and images from the work of Ezra Pound, and he often cited an affinity for other notable modernist writers. Critics have also connected the musicality of Okigbo's verse not only to the symphonic structure of Pound's *Cantos* but also to the work of such composers as Maurice Ravel and Claude Debussy. The blending of these disparate Western elements with Okigbo's cultural and national perspective further differentiate his poetry from those of his contemporaries. While Okigbo participated in the tradition of Western literature, he also employed its devices and symbolism for his inquiry into African identity.

While most current commentators focus largely on the richness of Okigbo's poetic and cultural contributions, some recent critics have stressed his prophetic role.

This mode of examination is most often utilized in discussions of *Labyrinths, with Path of Thunder,* because of the book's style of imagery and its powerful voice. Others critics have focused their observations on the formal construction of Okigbo's work, stressing its reliance on musical patterns in both sound and phrase. Catherine Acholonu has asserted the central significance of music in Okigbo's verse, arguing that the "musicality of language, the recurrent patterns and variations upon the same theme, the accumulating images of infrastructure and dramatized experience function as carriers of the poet's vision. Through music, the poet attains a state of abstraction in his pursuit of the artistic ideal of purity, of the perfect identification of matter with form." Others have speculated on how Okigbo's poetry might have developed had his life not been cut short. Chukwuma Azuonye has stated that "*Path of Thunder* is not a fulfillment but a promise of the revolutionary direction of the unrealized future of Okigbo's poetry. Had he survived to realize that future, it is conceivable that he would have shed the remnants of obscurity in imagery and allusion, which, despite his new poetic manifesto, can be found still lingering in this essentially transitional piece."

PRINCIPAL WORKS

Heavensgate (poetry) 1962
*Limits (poetry) 1962
†Poems: Four Canzones (poetry) 1968
Labyrinths, with Path of Thunder (poetry) 1971
Collected Poems (poetry) 1986

*This work was published in two parts in the journal *Transition* in 1962 and as a book in 1964.

†Portions of this work were published in the journal *Black Orpheus* in 1962.

CRITICISM

Modupe Olaogun (essay date 1991)

SOURCE: Olaogun, Modupe. "Graphology & Meaning in the Poetry of Christopher Okigbo." *African Literature Today* 17 (1991): 108-30.

[*In the following essay, Olaogun argues that the graphology—the physical appearance of the text on the page—of Okigbo's poetry serves as both a source of "obscurity" and a means of "unraveling" the complexities present in the works.*]

I

Graphology refers to the physical appearance of the text on the page. Here graphology is given the kind of interpretative potential that would be ascribed to phonology, lexis and syntax in linguistic analysis. The category is taken to include 'orthography, punctuation, and anything else that is concerned with showing how a language uses its graphic resources to carry its grammatical and lexical patterns'.[1]

Graphology has often been disregarded or subordinated to phonology in much analysis of processes of signification, the argument usually being that it is merely a way of representing speech. But, as Angus McIntosh demonstrates in a seminal study of graphology,

> an organised written system of language has a status equivalent to any spoken 'opposite number' it may have; it simply manifests *language* in another substance - one which appeals to the eye rather than to the ear. In other words it is not a mere second-degree system in the way implied by Aristotle in *De Interpretatione* when he says that written words are the symbols of spoken words . . . [W]ritten language and spoken language both symbolise mental experience but . . . written language, by virtue of its graphological system, *also* symbolises spoken language.[2]

Indeed, one need only look at the Chinese ideographs to demonstrate McIntosh's point. In the scribal tradition, the emblematic poems of George Herbert and Dylan Thomas,[3] or, more strikingly, the calligraphic poetry of Guillaume Apollinaire,[4] as well as the 'concrete' poetry of Ian Finlay, Emmett Williams and Nichols[5] also readily prove McIntosh's point.

Taking a different route, Jacques Derrida in his reappraisal of the rhetoric of philosophy also reinstates writing to a position of equal, if not greater, respectability *vis-à-vis* speech. Derrida's strategy is a vigorous questioning of the assumption of 'the Western metaphysics of presence', which grounds itself in the myth of origin and consequently pursues an ultimate, transcendental signified. This erstwhile logocentric tradition, Derrida proves, had bestowed on speech a supreme value based upon its supposedly inherent capability to embody intention, hence its unique privilege to ideal objectivity. In contrast, writing is presumed to bear the taint of mediation or, at best, to be a lifeless token of expressive, contentfilled speech. In Derrida's deconstructive project, which entails the exposure of the illusion of a determinate meaning predicated upon presence, the term 'writing' is applied not simply to the graphic notation of language but also to the more insidious inscriptions of language that are generated by a complex historical-intertextual process within which an utterance or a text is located. The active ingredient in Derrida's appreciation of language is a feature which he terms 'differance'.

According to Derrida, 'differance' is evoked not so much as a word or a concept but as 'the *strategic* note or connection . . . which indicates the closure of presence'.[6] Stated differently, 'differance' indicates the lack of immediate and total accessibility to meaning by virtue of the fact that language entails a canny and interminable interplay of deferral and difference.

The implications of Derrida's arguments cannot be fully investigated here,[7] but their point of interest for the present study derives from the exposure of the constructed nature of the prioritization of speech as repository of meaning. Also, Derrida's investigation demonstrates the active, rather than passive, interaction of texts in the sense of a critical dialogue of a text with itself as well as with other texts. The former marks the text's self-deconstructive propensity and the latter its intertextuality.

Concomitant with Derrida's demystificatory project is a relocation of meaning not in immanent and immutable terms, but in more human and sceptical terms. But, for all its breakthrough in the discussion of the rhetoric of language, Derrida's deconstructive theory, with its overwrought attention to the 'textness' of the text, has been seen as a ruse for escaping the actuality of the world and its political urgencies. Edward Said's corresponding appreciation of the text's public nature, its political circumstantiality or 'worldliness',[8] reaffirms the text's cardinal relations to palpable politics. The present focus on graphology is not riveted to just the 'textness' of the text but anchors the text within its circumstantiality.

The study does not preclude references to the other levels of language. The various levels, after all, do often collaborate in the making and meaning of poetry. The interrelationship of the various levels will be seen, for example, in the harmony between phonology and graphology in much rhymed poetry. The placing of the rhyme at the end of a line is an announcement through graphology of the phonological significance of the line. It is also impossible to think of a strict dichotomy between graphology and syntax in the complex inversion that is characteristic of the poetry of Gerard Manley Hopkins, Wole Soyinka and most characteristically, Okigbo. The semantic aspect comes in when it is realized that any poetic arrangement is ultimately a mode of meaning, or a physical purveyor for a more generalized or abstract kind of meaning.

Often a poet manipulates a text graphologically to make it easily distinguishable as poetry: traditionally, poetry has a 'characteristic' lineation which has no equivalent in prose. Within the genre of poetry are various kinds with different styles of lineation. In the sonnet, for example, variations in the thought-pattern are mediated through lineation: in the Petrarchan type, the situation or problem is stated in the octave, with the resolution taking place in the sestet. The ballad has stanzas whose lines are metrically regulated to achieve a musical tempo. Free verse, without the traditional accoutrements of rhyme and uniform metre, achieves through graphology similar and other important effects. By merely 'playing' with the line poets evoke symbolic shapes for the ideas they try to convey. George Herbert's supplications in 'Easter-Wings' float on the poem's visual wings. Dylan Thomas draws attention to the complementarity of the two parts of 'Vision and Prayer' through their shapes. The graphological architecture of this poem is suggestive of the mortise and tenon. The shapes could, however, also be seen as diamonds, hour-glasses and wings.[9] Through graphology, Dylan Thomas heightens the ambiguity of his poem.

The line, too, serves as a punctuation mark for some poets. By isolating a word or a word group, the poet draws attention to it. The line becomes a warning system to the reader about the significance of the word or word group, as in the poem titled 'Luo Plains' by Wole Soyinka:

> Plague
> Of comet tails, of bled horizons
> Where egrets hone a sky-lane for
> Worlds to turn on pennants
>
> Lakemists
> On her shadeless dugs, parched
> At waterhole. Veils. Molten silver
> Down cloudflues of alchemist sun . . .
> A lake's grey salve at dawn?
>
> That dawn
> Her eyes were tipped with sunset spears
> Seasons' quills upon her parchment, yet
> The hidden lake of her
>
> Forgives!
>
> For she has milked a cycle of
> Red sunset spears, sucked reeds of poison
> To a cowherd's flute. The plains
> Are swift again on migrant wings
> And the cactus
> Flowers the eagle sentinel[10]

A violent concourse of expressive and archetypal phenomena, the scene captured by this poem breaks forth in the impressionistic description. The confluence of forceful words and their arrangement produces a picture of grand, yet raw, energy. The staccato appearance of some of the words fits the general purpose of recording impressions. The lexical items 'plague' and 'lakemists', which are segments of larger grammatical units, are given special focus by being linearly isolated from their post-modifiers—one a genitival-prepositional phrase, the other a prepositional-locative. The nominal group, 'That dawn', is linearly amplified to take a central place in the poem: it becomes the theme from the third stanza to the end. The dawn is both setting and, in its archetypal role as the sun's consort, accomplice in the sexual violence which dominates the poem: 'Her eyes were tipped with sunset spears / Seasons' quills upon her parchment'; 'For she has milked a cycle of / Red sunset spears, sucked reeds of poison'. The cycle of relentless craving and pain is sustained by the singular act of forgiveness. This gesture of extenuation is underscored graphologically by isolating the word 'forgives' and putting an exclamation mark after it. The verb, separated from its grammatical subject by enjambment, is so placed that it calls attention to itself.

Through the use of the more conventional punctuation marks various lyrical effects are achieved by poets. Rather than be seen as sheer eccentricity, Emily Dickinson's dashes seem to be devised as a means of preventing the reader from racing through the lyrics without pondering the words. Dickinson, in addition, imbues words with majesty through the capitalization of the initial letters.

Also through the employment of punctuation, Atukwei Okai is able to bring to the reader's ears the *tomtom-from* which throbs in the background of his poetry. The drum rises to a frenzied crescendo in his invocation of each historical or literary figure, and continues to pulsate as he assumes his lament, in 'Lorgorligi Logarithms':

> jawa apronti, ARE YOU THERE?!
> ayikwei armah, WHERE ARE YOU?!
> atta britwum, ARE YOU THERE?![11]

In Okigbo's poetry, tonality, laconicism, ambiguity, symbolism and lyricism are among the chief effects of the exploitation of graphology. An attempt to achieve some or all of these effects in one breath often leads to obscurity, but sometimes it simply heightens the density of the poetry.

II

Okigbo's concern for the graphological shape of his poetry is perhaps suggested by his acknowledgement, on more than one occasion, of his debt to Ben Obumselu, then of the University of Ibadan, 'for criticisms which led to improvements in phrase and structure'.[12] The poems themselves are strong evidence of this concern. From the early poems, including *Four Canzones,*[13] to *Path of Thunder,*[14] there is a technical adventurousness, climaxed in the *Transition* **"Distances"**,[15] which contains visually striking architectonic shapes. The Heinemann **"Distances"**,[16] as well as many of the 'revised versions' of the other poems, shows considerable trimming at the grapho-syntactic level.

Perhaps Okigbo's famous declaration that he was a poets' poet[17] was meant to suggest that he aimed at utilizing to the fullest, and going beyond, the licence ordi-

narily granted to poets. His predominant choice of free verse would seem appropriate because it offered the least restrictions, especially graphologically. Okigbo grew up in the ferment of the influence of T. S. Eliot, Ezra Pound and Dylan Thomas—poets who had immediate recognition for their inventiveness. This inventiveness cannot be fully investigated here, but suffice it to mention the salient features of the trio's poetry: grammatical deviation, syntactic inversion, allusiveness, verbal terseness and tonality. Like these poets and others before him, Okigbo honed his poems until the gem remained. Graphology bore the brunt of this sculpturing.

One of Okigbo's earliest poems is **"Song of the Forest"**, published as part of the *Four Canzones.* Ostensibly based on Virgil's *Tityrus,*[18] the derivation is not one of literal correspondence or subservience and, indeed, Virgil's poem is a model in a very broad sense. Omolara Leslie has already indicated Okigbo's formal departure in terms of the pointed brevity of the poem and also his transposition of the pastoral to a modern Nigerian scene in which a city-dweller feels an acute sense of alienation from rural life. Leslie tacitly attributes the formal simplicity of **"Song of the Forest"** to Virgil's example in the eclogue.[19] However, **"Song of the Forest"** also shares with some of the other earliest poems, without bringing in Virgil,[20] a graphological and syntactic simplicity that makes them easy reading.

"Song of the Forest" 'translates' Virgil on Okigbo's terms. It begins characteristically with the capitalization of the first two words:

> YOU LOAF, child of the forest,

The capitalized words gain focus typographically and rhetorically as a nominative of address. Commas are used, quite conventionally, as a device for appositional elaboration and, more strikingly, for tonality. Through well-measured pauses the commas produce a majestic melody:

> YOU LOAF, child of the forest,
> beneath a village umbrella,
> plucking from tender string a
>   Song of the forest.
> Me, away from home, run-
> away, must leave the borders of our home
> land, fruitful fields,
>   must leave our homeland.
>
> But you, child of the forest,
> loaf beneath an umbrella,
> teaching the woods to sing a
>   song of the forest.

The commas are integral to the depiction of the dramatis personae of the poem. The two 'characters' are contrasted pronominally. Through appositional elaboration the one emerges as a denizen and the other as a fugitive. The commas make the syntax easy to follow. The lexical items are generally everyday, not arcane. One of such everyday words, 'runaway', is exploited graphologically—through hyphenation—to direct the interpretation of the poem along more ambiguous lines. Because it is compound, and located at the end of the line, 'runaway' presumably has a basis for being split. By separating the suffix 'away' from the root 'run' (5th and 6th lines), the suffix is given an independent status, and consequently acquires a similarity with the first 'away' in the 5th line. This intensifies the adverbial quality of the preposition 'away', and places the focus on the uneventful situation of the fugitive rather than on the act of escape.

Although published together with **"Song of the Forest"** in the *Four Canzones*, both **"Lament of the Flutes"** (1960) and **"Lament of the Lavender Mist"** (1961) are remarkably different from the first poem. By this time Okigbo tended to be less lavish with words, resorting more frequently to ellipses, and designating the connective 'and' by a sign. In addition, he breaks off sentences with dashes and paradoxically employs these dashes as a means of connecting fragmented units or of forcing connections between independent clauses or thought units.

"Lament of the Flutes" traces memories of some catalytic experiences in the poet's development. Apprehension about the reliability of the apparatus of recall is pre-empted in the elliptical marks which take over soon after the poem begins:

> TIDEWASH . . . Memories
> fold-over-fold free-furrow,
> mingling old tunes with new.
> Tidewash . . .

The elliptical marks convey the vagueness and fragmentary nature of memory, just as words serve as a regulatory device:

> Ride me
> memories, astride on firm
> saddle.

Elliptical marks accompany the refrain until the end of the poem when they are dropped to affirm the transformation in the poet's sensibility. The tentativeness and dilatoriness found in the refrain at the beginning:

> Sing to the rustic flute:
> Sing a new note . . .

gives way to a more positive assertion as the poet's probing progresses to a finale:

> Shall I offer to *Idoto*
> my sandhouse and bones,
> then write no more on snow-patch?

> Sing to the rustic flute.
> Sing a new note.

Nearly every kind of punctuation mark employed in **"Lament of the Flutes"** will be found in **"Lament of the Lavender Mist"**, but the latter poem is much more complex. The poem's complexity is jointly accounted for by collocational deviation and graphology. The poem begins as follows:

>   (i)
>
> BLACK dolls
> Returning from the foam:
> Two faces of a coin
> That meet afar off . . .
>
> Sea smiles at distance
>   with lips of foam
> Sea walks like rainbow
>   beyond them.

The style established by these lines is very much sustained throughout the poem. The salient aspects of that style are: a propensity for separating grammatical elements which are often proximate in discursive formations; ellipsis; and a profuse use of dashes. Take, for instance, the construction beginning 'And voice' ending 'wakes us . . .', which, considered as a sentence, displays a number of interruptive elements. The line, 'Air, sun, blood . . .' bears no discursive continuity with the construction, yet its appearance in that particular spot will have to be accounted for. Generally, dashes serve as an elaborative and a parenthetic device, and it is not difficult to discern these traditional roles of dashes. However, within the entire graphological layout of the poem the dashes and ellipses appear to derange the syntax, as illustrated by the sequence,

> And voice
> Returning from a dream,
> Descends, rejoices—
> Air, sun, blood . . .
>   And wakes us . . .
>
> DOLLS . . .
> Forms
> Of memory,
> To be worshipped
> Adored
> By innocence:
> Creatures of the Mind's eye
> Barren—
> Of memory—
> Remembrance of things past.
>
>   [Okigbo's ellipses]

The poem presents what Annemarie Heywood describes in a study of *Labyrinths* as a 'building up of compulsive series of significances'.[21] Through a configuration of the 'significances' which she identifies in *Labyrinths*,

Heywood is able to determine that Okigbo's poetry is 'ritual' in the sense of being 'in itself a ritual instrument'. It is indeed possible to sort out the various themes, motifs and so on in Okigbo's poems and reconfigure these to arrive at some kind of overall significance of the poetry. However, this structural remoulding of the poetry underplays, or even disregards altogether, whatever significance is generated by the space relations governing the various configurations.

"Lament of the Lavender Mist" (1961) prefigures later poems, particularly *Limits* and *Path of Thunder*, as prophetic poetry. The graphological evidence of the poem supports this reading. First, the poem evokes phases from precreation to apocalypse. Secondly, it recalls and projects aspects of cultural history. The inchoate, precreative state is captured in such surrealistic images as 'Sea walks like rainbow / beyond them', and in more straightforward descriptions and allusive phrases such as 'abyss', 'the wind and the waves' and 'Echoes of the waters of the beginning'. The apocalypse is hinted at in 'Shadows of the fires of the end'. Between the polar stages of birth and death the poem enacts the intervening phases, mostly initiatory and exploratory. These are engendered by the act of worship and through the protagonist's metaphysical experience with the female figure, the 'Lady of the lavender-mist'.

As Okigbo explores the events of the individual's life cycle from birth to death in the poem, so does he proclaim on public events. The black dolls are cultural icons of childhood and of the incarnative/image-making propensity. The historical pith of the dolls is projected not simply through the cultural specificity implied by 'black' but, by virtue of its allusion to Leon Damas's poem 'Limbe', the phrase evokes the context which generated Damas's journey back to his childhood and the reaffirmation of his original cultural values.[22] Okigbo's poem is more a reappraisal of African cultural and historical experience. The re-vision in **"Lament of the Lavender Mist"** is graphically realized through the repetition of dolls and in the modulated form, 'Of masks, black masks, idols'. The reverberation is effected through the elliptical marks and dashes—punctuation marks which will ordinarily be perceived as anacoluthic (interruptive) agents. An exception, Dan Izevbaye remarks of ellipsis in Okigbo's poetry that it is 'an invitation to conjecture and deduction'.[23] No doubt, the ellipses in Okigbo's poetry proclaim semantic openness; however, they frame meaning in a less chancy and schematic manner than might be implied in Izevbaye's suggestion. In **"Lament of the Masks"** the ellipses kindle circumspection even as they invite interpretative openness. The poem invites circumspection of the 'forms of memory' presented by the black dolls:

> BLACK dolls
> Returning from the foam:

> Two faces of a coin
> That meet afar off . . .

and

> And voice
> Returning from a dream,
> Descends, rejoices—
> Air, sun, blood . . .
>   And wakes us . . .
> DOLLS . . .

[Okigbo's ellipses]

Like the inspired medium which arouses worshippers and bereaved relatives in the ceremony of souls,[24] or the charged voice of the Old Testament prophets, 'voice' descends in Okigbo's poem and memory is awakened. The pre-vocal barrenness associated with mind gives way to remembrance; and mind, released from the prison of abstraction, opens up to extraordinary perceptions. The protagonist wakes up into the 'abyss of wonders'; he encounters the multiform lady of the lavender-mist, who as earth mother is supremely constituted in **"Dance of the Painted Maidens"**.[25] In the latter poem exact phrases identified with creation and apocalypse in **"Lament of the Lavender Mist"**, namely 'waters of the beginning' and 'fires of the end', define the earth mother. The metaphysical 'Lady' is the instrument by which the protagonist undergoes the vital initiations, the passages through the various stages of life's cycle from birth to death.

As vision and pre-vision of public events, perhaps the poem's most remarkable line is: 'Eagles in space and earth and sky'. This line recurs in both *Limits* and *Path of Thunder.* By examining its recurrence or reverberations it will be demonstrated how the line is generated into a leitmotif of public prophecy in Okigbo's poetry.

In *Limits* the metaphor of the eagles occurs in the poem titled **"Fragments out of the Deluge"**, specifically in sections VIII and X. **"Limits VIII"** presents the sunbird iterating from the oilbean tree a vision of a fleet of eagles omniously parading their strength and splendour. The eagles, ostentatious and vexatious, are identified with the bronze metal. They bedazzle the landscape with their strength. **"Limits X"** projects the eagle metaphor again as it recounts an outrage committed by an invading fleet. The invaders had spitefully desolated the community by murdering its gods and the prophetic sunbird.

The sunbird overlooking the landscape from the sacred oilbean tree in **"Limits VIII"** is easily placed as a priest-prophet. Read against the events of the day the eagles in the sunbird's utterance may be matched with the power-brokers of Nigeria's first republic. Historical interpolations imposed by the tense of, and the kind of details in, **"Limits X"** identify the set of eagles here as the colonizers, but Okigbo's metaphor fuses into one archetypal image both sets of participants in the two historical references.

In *Path of Thunder* the metaphor of eagles is resonant in these lines:

> Statuettes of legendary heroes - iron birds
>
>   **("Thunder Can Break", *Labyrinths*,** p. 63)

> Magic birds with the miracle of lightning flash on
>   their feathers . . .
>
>   **("Come Thunder",** ibid., p. 66)

> AND THE HORN may now paw the air howling goodbye
>   . . .

> For the Eagles are now in sight:
> Shadows in the horizon—

> THE ROBBERS are here in black sudden steps of show-
>   ers, of caterpillars—

> THE EAGLES have come again,
> The eagles rain down on us—
>
>   **("Elegy for Alto",** ibid., p. 71)

The most prominent occurrence of the eagle metaphor is in **"Elegy for Alto"**, where eagles are explicitly made to stand for politicians. The politicians, who are called robbers, are identified here with iron, symbol of inexorable strength and, in classical mythology, of ultimate degeneracy.

If Okigbo's poetry were to be read backwards, from *Path of Thunder* to **"Lament of the Lavender Mist"**, the line 'Eagles in space and earth and sky' would be more readily recognizable as an important prognostic leitmotif in his mytho-history. The linguistic accuracy of **"Lament of the Lavender Mist"** comes from Okigbo's archetypal apprehension of both individual and cultural history, as well as his assured mythopoeic dispensation of language. But, whereas **"Lament of the Lavender Mist"** functions as prophecy through its intuitive apprehension of cycles of individual and cultural history, *Path of Thunder* defines prophecy in terms of forecast and forewarning. The latter is consequently far less recondite grapho-syntactically.

The most striking feature of *Path of Thunder*, explicitly subtitled 'poems prophesying war', is the extendedness of the utterance units in contrast to the highly compressed form of **"Lament of the Lavender Mist"**. Words come forth more freely; verbs are not frequently suppressed; and there is less collocational confusion. The proximity of clause elements aids intelligibility. The themes are repeated within and across the poems

which make up *Path of Thunder*. Again there is a profuse use of elliptical marks and dashes, with the former bearing reverberative echoes and the latter being generally elaborative or anacoluthic (i.e. interruptive), for instance:

> The General is up . . . the General is up . . . com-
>   mandments . . .
> the General is up the General is up the General is
>   up—
> condolences from our twin-beaks and feathers of con-
>   dolence

and

> thunder fells the trees cut a path
> thunder smashes them all—condolences . . .

> THUNDER that has struck the elephant
> the same thunder should wear a plume—condolences
>
>   **("Elegy for Slit-drum",** *Labyrinths*, pp. 68-70)

Nearly every one of the poems in *Path of Thunder* ends in ellipses, the poems solemnly trailing into apprehensive silence. Silence is Okigbo's metaphorical exploration of 'the music to which all imperishable cries must aspire'.[26] *Path of Thunder* in fact shares with the poems in the sequence titled *Silences*[27] a deep anguish that words seem unable to give adequate shape.

The foregoing reveals the close relationship of **"Lament of the Lavender Mist"** to *Limits* and *Path of Thunder* despite the pervasive tendency to overlook this seminal poem in discussions of Okigbo's poetry; or to sketchily identify it, when it finds rare mention, with Okigbo's more self-exploratory poems in *Labyrinths*.

The poems which Okigbo published with Heinemann as a volume titled *Labyrinths* are compositionally placed between the *Canzones* and *Path of Thunder*. Generally, the poems in *Labyrinths* have some affinity with **"Lament of the Lavender Mist"**—in their tendency to be cryptic. The fact that the poems are often very allusive, coupled with the complex inversions and a ruthless economy through a suppression of verbs and other graphic resources, accounts for the difficulty associated with reading these poems. The problems identified here are perhaps as intense as those created by Okigbo's 'revisions' of the poems which eventually make up this volume. To illustrate both sets of difficulties I shall examine **"Distances"**, which presents the most striking variants, each of which I shall denote by their means of publication, respectively, as *Transition* **"Distances"** and Heinemann **"Distances"**. Of Okigbo's poems it is also **"Distances"** which I find to be the most compelling—by virtue of its extraordinary construction of the perennial subject, death; in Heinemann **"Distances"** Okigbo's lyrical genius attains its peak.

Transition **"Distances"** presents an attempt at a conflation of shape and meaning while Heinemann **"Distances"** shows a dependence on ordinary lineation and the sheer collocational force of words to project meaning. Like George Herbert, Okigbo constructed graphological shapes which emulate architectural structures in *Transition* **"Distances IV"**:

And at the archway	T
a triangular lintel	HE
of alabaster	ONL
enclosed in a square	YWAY
inscribed in a circle	TOGOT
with a hollow centre	HROUGH
above the archway	THEMARB
yawning shutterless	LEARCHWA
like celestial pincers	YTOTHECAT
like a vast countenance	ATONICPING
	PONGOFTHEEV
	ANESCENTHALO

    the only way to go
    through the marble archway
    to the catatonic pingpong
    of the evanescent halo . . .

and beyond the archway
like pentecostal orbs
resplendent far distant
in the intangible void
an immense crucifix
of phosphorescent mantles:

          AFTER
          WEHAD
THENONLYTHEFORMSWEREFORMEDANDALLTHEFORMSWERE
          AFTER
          OURFO
          RMING

    after we had formed
    then only the forms were formed
    and all the forms were formed
    after our forming . . .
       (*Transition*, vol. 4, no. 16, 1964, pp. 11-12)

In Heinemann **"Distances"**, Okigbo is content with ordinary lineation and does away with the emblematic use of graphology. *Transition* **"Distances IV"** is actually verbally similar to Heinemann **"Distances IV"**, the basic difference being the absence of the iconic shapes which are constructed of words taken from the italicized lines of the poem.

The entire *Transition* **"Distances"** shows a very important structural difference from the Heinemann **"Distances"** in the former's use of the connective 'and' to provide narrative continuity. This connective is replaced by the function word 'for' or sometimes expunged altogether in several structurally confluent positions in Heinemann **"Distances"**, as indicated by the following excerpts:

I

For [*And*] in the inflorescence of the white chamber,

II

For [*And*] the wind, eternal suitor of dead leaves, unrolled his bandages to the finest swimmer . . .

[*And*] It was an evening without flesh or skeleton;

III

[*And*] In the scattered line of pilgrims

VI

[*for*] the goat still knows [*will know*] its fodder
[*and*] the leopards [*leopard*] on its trail . . .
For [*And*] it is the same blood
through the same orifices

    [My italics and interpolations—to indicate *Transition* version]

Also as a means of maintaining structural continuity in *Transition* **"Distances"**, there is consistency in the denotation of the white chamber as the physical location where the experience takes place. But in Heinemann **"Distances"** the white chamber gives way to Shibboleth in section III. Finally, five lines which begin section VI of *Transition* **"Distances"** are excised in Heinemann **"Distances"**:

    And in the intimacy
    of the evanescent halo,
    the symbol, forsaken
    in a cloud of incense,

    delivers herself of her bandages . . .

These lines, which begin with the ubiquitous 'and', provide a double-edged form of continuity between this section and the rest of the poem, dwelling as they do on the ambience of the phantasmic experience. They evoke symbols of death's realm and of the initiate's experience.

The implications of all these structural differences will lead to a suggestion that, rather than be seen as versions of each other, *Transition* **"Distances"** and Heinemann **"Distances"** are indeed two separate poems. To elaborate, in *Transition* **"Distances"** the word 'and' functions variously in the manner of the connective temporal adverbials 'then', 'thereupon', 'next', 'afterwards', 'in addition'. In Heinemann **"Distances"** the word 'for', also conjunctive, is understood to function as an explanative: 'wherefore', 'since', 'because'. The word 'and' projects a sequential manner of revelation and it is an invitation to a paratactic apprehension of experience. On the other hand the situations introduced by the word 'for' need not be diachronically related to the situations described by their grammatical antecedents. In fact, Heinemann **"Distances"** reinforces a complex synchronicity in the apprehension of the ethereal experiences delineated by this poem. Whereas the strophes in *Transition* **"Distances"** are more laterally connected to each other, the strophes in Heinemann **"Distances"** are technically more independent of one another but in fact interact both laterally and vertically. Heinemann **"Distances"** is more liable to greater structural looseness and multivalency. Okigbo's achievement in this respect is comparable to that of Guillaume Apollinaire, who substituted graphically evocative shapes and disruptive structures for linear and discursive forms to project his concept of 'simultaneity'. By his practice Apollinaire was inviting an active engagement of the reader with the process of synthesis involved in poetic representation.[28]

The reference to Shibboleth in section III of Heinemann **"Distances"** retains the poem within the context of purgative death. But paradoxically it widens and inscribes this context through the mytho-religious archetype. On the other hand, the white chamber employed throughout *Transition* **"Distances"** is imbued with associative freedom although that freedom is also circumscribed by the identification of 'white' and 'chamber' with the ubiquitous female figure who tortures and redeems the poem's protagonist.

Overall *Transition* **"Distances"** tends towards structural explicitness. As already demonstrated above, the particular structural connective employed in the poem proclaims a paratactic style. The poem's graphic icons may also be seen as a demystificatory scheme. For one thing the vision is very abstract, but it presents geometrical shapes which are quite definite. And for all their superfluity the shapes do incarnate this very abstract vision. The two graphic shapes represent symbols which are identified with religion and geometry; the one is a speculative or metaphysical field, the other traces very precise and definite outlines. But the speculativeness of the one is belied by the forceful, palpable position it occupies in human activity; while the imaginative disposition of the other is not occluded by its precision. The tension between these two symbolic polar values is what this section of the poem is about. All through the section images of three-dimensional experience jostle with fourth-dimensional reality, the palpable with the ultra-fine. The vision is, after all, death's portal and the transitional nature of the experience is suggested in the fusion of the two symbolic representational modes.

The potential for greater ambiguities in Heinemann **"Distances"** will be acknowledged. Without the emblematic shapes, the poem is tighter and more brief. The lines which provide the bricks for the architectonics in *Transition* **"Distances"** are, after all, italicized in both poems. The italicization constitutes in itself a form

of highlight, so that the emblematic shapes might be taken as an over-representation. Conversely, intensity rather than a mid or *sotto voce* effect might have been intended, taking into account the musical terms on which the poem invites appreciation, from the implicit analogy with music in section I:

> For in the inflorescence of the white
> chamber, a voice, from very far away,
> chanted, and the chamber descanted, the birthday of
> earth,
> paddled me home through some dark
> labyrinth, from laughter to the dream.

> (from Heinemann **"Distances"**)

In fact, read as a musical score, Heinemann **"Distances IV"** does not have the strongly contrapuntal suggestiveness of *Transition* **"Distances IV"**. However, the rest of Heinemann **"Distances"** shows a more assured cadence than does *Transition* **"Distances"**. As illustration, the lines above are more finely and elegantly modulated than the following, which constitute the equivalent in *Transition* **"Distances"**:

> And in the inflorescence of the white chamber,
> a voice, from very far away, chanted, and the chamber
> descanted
> the birthday of earth, paddling me home through
> some dark labyrinth, from laughter to the dream.

The greater tonality of Heinemann **"Distances"** can be related to the greater relaxation towards the subject of death which this poem conveys overall. This effect is partly a product of the semantic import of the structural connective 'for', which has been partially commented on. This word is suggestive of 'the already and always': 'since' 'because'. It is attended by knowledge and retrospection. Thus, 'the goat still knows its fodder, / the leopards on its trail' rather than the *Transition's* 'the goat will know its fodder / and the leopard on its trail'. The situations which advance the protagonist to death are then welcomed with greater assurance and faith. The end of *Transition* **"Distances"**,[29] with its largely unvarying rhythm, dulls the arrival of the protagonist while the finale of Heinemann **"Distances"** bespeaks a triumphal but solemn arrival through its superb, varied measure:

> And at this chaste instant of delineated anguish,
> the same voice, importunate, aglow with the god-
> dess—

> unquenchable, yellow, darkening homeward
> like a cry of wolf above crumbling houses—

> strips the dream naked,
> bares the entrails;

> and in the orangery of immense corridors,
> I wash my feet in your pure head, O maid,

and walk along your feverish, solitary shores,

seeking, among your variegated teeth,
the tuberose putrescent laughter;

I have fed out of the drum
I have drunk out of the cymbal

I have entered your bridal
chamber; and lo,

I am sole witness to my homecoming.

The foregoing, while unravelling the graphological features of **"Distances"**, has also put in a different perspective the troublesome issue of the different editions of Okigbo's poetry. In discussions of the so-called different 'versions', there has tended to be an appeal for ultimate resolution in Okigbo's prefatorial comments in Heinemann *Labyrinths* that the poems in that collection were a 'final' version. But suppose the first published editions of Okigbo's poems were actually 'intended' and the subsequent 'revisions' a peace-offering to critics? Considering the fact that Okigbo had a penchant for rewriting/rereading his poems, how can we be sure that he would not have undertaken another rewriting/ rereading had he lived? This point will, however, not obscure the truth that Okigbo did develop his skills. *Path of Thunder,* as already demonstrated, is generally easier to read and more lyrical than a number of Okigbo's earlier poems. Similarly, Heinemann *Labyrinths* is divested of the Latinisms and the enigmatic lines which were common in the earlier Mbari version. The Latinisms of Mbari *Labyrinths* portray Okigbo as being, like Ezra Pound, eclectic. In addition, in Mbari *Labyrinths* there are some private orthographic inventions denoting private references which are spliced with Latinisms. These are simply vexatious for their unnecessary attempt to mystify; indeed, they have been mistaken for the expression of some grand revelation by at least one critic.[30]

The allusive nature of Okigbo's poetry cannot be glossed over. It accounts in part for the reflexivity of the poetry. Another contributory factor to this reflexivity is Okigbo's situation at the juncture between orality and writing. How does this reflexive aspect of the graphology of Okigbo's poetry call attention to the larger context of writing?

One prevalent attitude to the allusions, echoes and other forms of linkages to other texts in Okigbo's poetry has been to regard such as material evidence of Okigbo's derivativeness. A pithy statement by the semiotician, Roland Barthes, might serve as a riposte to this kind of perfunctory source-hunting. According to Barthes, 'to search for the "sources of" and "influence upon" a work is to satisfy the myth of filiation'.[31] Upon close examination it will be revealed that this attitude posits a cer-

tain ultimate origin of ideas, linguistic formulations, and so on. The parallel to this ultimate origin will be the transcendental signified which Derrida identifies as the chimera of the 'metaphysics of presence'. Barthes's formulation which follows upon his observation is worth quoting, for pointing yet again to the possibility of a proto-writing antedating both writing and speech:

> The quotations from which a text is constructed are anonymous, irrecoverable, and yet *already read*: they are quotations without quotation marks.

[Barthes's emphasis]

An appreciation of this feature of the intertext, and of the intertextuality of Okigbo's poetry, may prevent the sometimes misleading interpretation attendant upon a monistic construal of Okigbo's poetic resources. In this respect, an article by Catherine Acholonu appears to be a reductionist reading of Okigbo's poetry which ignores all signposts against such reductionism. In the article titled '*Ogbanje*: a motif and theme in the poetry of Christopher Okigbo', Acholonu suggests that 'Okigbo's life-style was a classical [*sic*] example of what the Igbo people refer to as *ogbanje*.' The *ogbanje,* as Acholonu indicates, are the semi-human and semi-spirit people of Igbo mythology, 'who are fated to die young and if they grow into adulthood . . . [die] at a momentous period of their lives'. Acholonu deduces from Okigbo's reference to the images of the drowning virgins and Gilgamesh an indication of Okigbo's own *ogbanje* status. The introductory lines of *Heavensgate* and **"The Passage"** (two poems in *Labyrinths*) are inferred by Acholonu to be a proleptic mourning of Okigbo's death. Acholonu also identifies the female figure(s) that feature(s) in Okigbo's poetry as 'a water spirit' with whom Okigbo has a 'love affair' and equates the silent sisters of Okigbo's *Silences* to the 'seven *ogbanje* girls' of folklore, 'who brandish their beauty to attract suitors, while concealing the fatality of their existence'.[32] Also, there is a widely held view that Okigbo owes those of his lines which carry themes of reincarnation to Wordsworth's 'Ode: Intimations of Immortality'.[33] Let us at this point examine in greater detail the self-reflexivity and intertextuality of Okigbo's poetry.

Beginning with the suggestion that Okigbo's poetry is reflexive of his destiny as an *ogbanje,* what is the relation of the poet Okigbo to the subject generally denoted by 'I' in the poetry? What are the shared aspects of this subject and the situation of the set conjured by such figures as the drowning virgins and Gilgamesh?

Indeed a common link between the drowning virgins, Gilgamesh and the protagonist of Okigbo's poetry may be their death, but the point to be made embraces not just the essence, but also the significance, of this death. Through an extensive build-up of the sacrificial image which describes Okigbo's protagonist he is actually made to share this much with Gilgamesh. But just as the virgins dream of death (and pursue it as a means to martyrdom) so does Okigbo's protagonist show an ardent fascination with death, so that death here is a form of adventure. The *ogbanje,* on the other hand, dies as a matter of course: no adventure motivates him/her; no mission of redemption urges him/her. He/she is, therefore, precluded from the anguish and elation that must attend the desired death of Okigbo's protagonist.

Neither **Heavensgate** nor **"The Passage"** can be taken so extemporaneously as a proleptic mourning of Okigbo's death. The following lines can hardly be taken as a vision of 'darkness, gloom and chaos':

> DARK WATERS of the beginning.
>
> Rays, violet, and short, piercing the gloom,
> foreshadow the fire that is dreamed of.

Contrary to the claim that the picture painted here is a gloomy portent of a young man's fated death, the vision suggests a supersession of gloom by light. The idea projected by these lines has an intertext to which others similar to it belong, for instance, the Biblical account of creation. These lines or modifications of them are also used in connection with the 'Lady of the lavender-mist' and the 'earth mother' of **"Dance of the Painted Maidens"**. This intertextual reference certainly carries some significance. **Heavensgate** is expressly about the subject's confrontation with Idoto, a female figure comparable to both the 'earth mother' and the 'Lady of the lavender-mist'. Idoto, identified as the village stream, also bears a connotative relation to the 'maid' of **"Distances VI"**, whose 'pure head' provides the channel whereby the subject's ultimate deliverance is realized. Wherever these four functionally related figures feature, the theme is one of redemptive yearning on the subject's part. The figures are subsequently celebrated in archetypally powerful terms, as for example in the lines quoted above.

The number seven features in **"Dance of the Painted Maidens"** in the lines, 'From the seven quarters of the globe, / Past the seven seas past the seven / Distant deserts, bearing beads of coral and / kolanuts fit for a queen'. The context of this poem, which is a celebratory welcome of the earth mother by her handmaidens, puts the figure seven in an eminently positive connotation. It is inconceivable that the number would be consigned to absolute evil. In fact, seven functions in Okigbo's poetry as a symbol of consummate energy.[34]

Let us briefly examine **"Lament of the Drums"** and its evocation of the figure seven. The immediately relevant lines are:

> We are tuned for a feast-of-seven-souls . . .
>
> (*Labyrinths*, p. 45; Okigbo's ellipsis)

> But distant seven winds invite us and our cannons
> To limber our membranes for a dance of elephants
> . . .
>
> (Ibid., p. 46; Okigbo's ellipsis)

> The distant seven cannons invite us
> To a sonorous
> Ishthar's lament for Tammuz
>
> (Ibid., p. 49)

"Lament of the Drums" features an anthropomorphized chorus of drums who begin their 'lament' by invoking their constitutive elements, basically flora and fauna which imprint the drums' strength and efficacy. The drums announce their pressing task, contained in the lines quoted above. Certainly the drums' lament recalls that of the 'silent sisters', in the profound anguish for the tragic events which occasion their lament. But there is nothing to suggest that the number seven specifically denotes the 'silent sisters'. The activities of both the drums and the sisters cannot be simply termed evil. The prescient disposition of both choruses is employed for a positive (and optimistic) engagement with the tragic events of their lament. Thus, after outpouring their grief, the 'Crier' and the 'Chorus' intimate an exultant vision in **"Lament of the Silent Sisters"**:

> I hear painted harmonies
> From the mushrooms of the sky—
>
> Silences are melodies
> Heard in retrospect:
>
> And how does one say NO in thunder?
>
> (*Labyrinths*, p. 59)

In **"Lament of the Drums"** Palinurus is metaphorically counterpoised with Tammuz to indicate the complexity of the grief. Of Palinurus the drums intone:

> *Tears of grace, not of sorrow, broken*
> *In two, protest your inviolable image.*

But no exultant tone surges through **"Ishthar's lament for Tammuz"**, in which the focus is the pain of deprivation (brought about by death) rather than death's tansformative aspect:

> *The wailing is for the fields of men*:
>
> The drums' lament is:
> They grow not . . .
>
> [Okigbo's ellipses]

If the sheer matter of death provides a link between Palinurus, Tammuz and the *ogbanje*, the question again is, what kind of death? Because the *ogbanje* is caught in a relentless cycle of death, it might be suggested that death is the *ogbanje's* destiny. The major part of Palinurus's and Tammuz's identity is that their death constitutes an aperture for society's new beginning.

It cannot be presumed, as is frequently the case, that a one-to-one correspondence exists between the central subject of Okigbo's poetry and the poet Okigbo. The most overtly self-reflexive section of Okigbo's poetry is *Path of Thunder,* where the subject is dramatized as follows:

> If I don't learn to shut my mouth I'll soon go to hell
> I, Okigbo, town-crier, together with my iron-bell.

("Hurrah for Thunder", *Labyrinths,* **p. 67)**

> the mythmaker accompanies us (the Egret had come
>   and gone)
> Okigbo accompanies us the oracle enkindles us
> the Hornbill is there again (the Hornbill has had a
>   bath)
> Okigbo accompanies us the rattles enlighten us—

("Elegy for Slit-drum", *Labyrinths,* **p. 69)**

The explicit reference—'I Okigbo, town-crier'—in these poems is invariably welcomed by explicators of Okigbo's poetry as the infallible revelation of the identity of the 'I' as the real Okigbo. This hazy equation leads to the kind of logically confusing statement presented by the following:

> In *Path of Thunder,* Okigbo witnesses the actualization of the death and destruction he has so long prophesied and clamoured for . . . Okigbo the town crier discards his 'iron bell' and makes way for the *ogbanje,* who bids the world 'a howling farewell' and prays to be allowed to perish with his dying folk, and the poem ends with his voluntary martyrdom.[35]

The poet Okigbo did die shortly after writing this poem and no one will deny the poem's premonitory hint. However, the passage is logically confusing. To clarify the confusions we need to examine more closely the relationship between the graphic symbol, 'Okigbo', and its referent(s). Graphic substitutes for 'Okigbo' include 'I', 'town-crier', 'mythmaker' and 'Hornbill'. All of these nominals do not exhibit the same deep-structure status. 'Town-crier', 'mythmaker' and 'Hornbill' are metaphorical in varying degrees, and in this respect contrast with 'I', which is in turn imbued with self-ness—an awareness of possession of a personal individuality (to paraphrase *Webster's New Collegiate Dictionary,* 1973). The metaphorical fluidity of the nominals, with the exception of 'I', makes it possible to enlist other nominals from Okigbo's entire poetry with which they bear functional similarity, namely, 'wagtail', 'sunbird'. The 'I' equally enlists another epithet, 'prodigal' (from *Labyrinths*), and the string of associations can grow indefinitely. Because it is the functional or attributive role of these various substitutive nominals

which is being engaged, the correspondence is not *in toto*. The metaphorical substitutes are temporally mediated. For instance, the prodigal image, which is implied in **"Song of the Forest"**, is prominent in *Labyrinths,* and then fades off in *Path of Thunder*. Similarly, **"Limits X"** records the killing of 'the Sunbird', but it is clear that the victim here is not the 'Okigbo' of the poem. Also, it is known that the real Okigbo was employed in different occupations but not as an actual town-crier. The 'I, Okigbo, town-crier' is thus a mythical construct. Its relation to the real Okigbo is conceptual rather than actual. The 'I' serves as a construct of continuity to enforce this conceptual relation.

The reference 'I, Okigbo, town-crier' indeed serves as an index to a reading of Okigbo's poetry as 'metapoetry', that is, 'poetry that includes within itself a commentary on its own poetic and/or linguistic identity'.[36] An awareness of this metapoetic feature should provoke a more self-conscious and critical disposition to the analysis of the poetry. 'If our knowledge of this world is now seen to be mediated through language,' thus reasons one narratologist, 'then literary fiction (*worlds constructed entirely of language*) becomes a useful model for learning about the construction of "reality" itself.'[37] Quite so; my emphasis.

The foregoing has not sought to be an inclusive commentary on the graphology of Okigbo's poetry, but, by concentrating on salient aspects of the graphological patterns, it has attempted to lay bare some of the veiled meanings of that poetry. Through a close attention to the graphology of the earlier poetry, for instance, we discover Okigbo's prognostic leitmotif and find a striking link between the early poem, **"Lament of the Lavender Mist"**, and *Path of Thunder* which has not hitherto been acknowledged. The problematic of the various 'versions' of Okigbo's poetry has also been re-examined; through an exploration of the implications of the graphological differences of the two 'versions' of **"Distances"** we are led to a startling discovery, that these two so-called versions are more accurately described as two separate poems. The graphology has also been demonstrated to be very revealing of the self-reflexivity and intertextuality of the poetry—features whose recognition prevents the pitfalls of a monistic search for filiation. Okigbo's exploitation of the graphological possibilities of poetry has produced very dense, poignantly lyrical and tonal poetry. Occasionally the poignancy flags but this does not overall detract from the striking achievement of the poetry. Graphology is one of the pre-eminent hallmarks of Okigbo's style.

Notes

1. M. A. K. Halliday, A. McIntosh and P. Stevens, *The Linguistic Sciences and Language Teaching,* London, Longmans, 1964, p. 50.

2. Angus McIntosh, '"Graphology" and Meaning,' *Archivum Linguisticum,* vol. 13, no. 2, 1962, p. 108.

3. Notable among the emblematic poems of George Herbert (early seventeenth-century English poet) are 'The Altar' and 'Easter-Wings', both of which may be found in *The Poetical Works of George Herbert,* London, James Nisbet, 1865, pp. 27 and 49. Dylan Thomas's more elaborate iconic poem is titled 'Vision and Prayer' and may be found in *Dylan Thomas: The Poems,* ed. Daniel Jones, London, J. M. Dent, 1974, pp. 180-5). 'Vision and Prayer' was first published in 1945.

4. Guillaume Apollinaire (French poet, 1880-1918) developed the term '*calligraphie*' for his innovative, visually striking poetry, which aimed at provoking instant and multidimensional awareness of the object. He applied the term 'simultaneity' to this practice in his poetry. His outstanding collection in the mode is titled *Calligrammes* (completed in 1912-13), Berkeley, University of California Press, 1980. Apollinaire's original calligraphy is retained in this text.

5. For examples of the 'concrete' poetry of Finlay, Williams and Nichols, see the entry 'concrete poetry' in *Twentieth-Century Poetry and Poetics,* ed. Gary Gedes, Toronto, Oxford University Press, 1973.

6. Jacques Derrida, 'Difference', in *Speech and Phenomena and Other Essays on Husserl's Theory of Signs,* trans. David B. Allison, Evanston, Northwestern University Press, 1973, p. 131.

7. Evaluations of Derrida's theory of deconstruction, and its subsequent application by other critics, can be found, among others, in Christopher Norris, *Deconstruction: Theory and Practice,* London, Methuen, 1982; *The Deconstructive Turn: Essays in the Rhetoric of Philosophy,* London and New York, Methuen, 1983; David Carroll, *Paraesthetics,* New York, Methuen, 1987.

8. See Edward Said, 'The Text, the World, the Critic', in *Textual Strategies: Perspectives in Post-Structuralist Criticism,* Ithaca, Cornell University Press, 1979, pp. 161-88.

9. See William York Tindall, *A Reader's Guide to Dylan Thomas,* New York, Farrar, Strauss and Cudahy, 1962, pp. 239ff.

10. Wole Soyinka, *Idanre and Other Poems,* London, Methuen, 1967, p. 13.

11. Atukwei Okai, *Lorgorligi Logarithms and Other Poems,* Accra, Ghana Publishing Corporation, 1974, p. 13.

12. See Christopher Okigbo, 'Distances', *Transition,* vol. 4, no. 16, 1964, p. 9; 'Lament of the Masks',

in *W. B. Yeats, 1865-1965: Centenary Essays,* ed. D. E. S. Maxwell and S. B. Bushrui, Ibadan, Ibadan University Press, 1965, p. xv.

13. Christopher Okigbo, *Four Canzones, Black Orpheus,* vol. 11, 1962, pp. 5-9. *Four Canzones* is reproduced in *Collected Poems,* London, Heinemann, 1986.

14. *Path of Thunder* was posthumously published with the volume *Labyrinths* by Heinemann, London, in 1971. The volume was simultaneously published in the United States by Africana Publishing Corporation and has lately been reproduced with other poems in Christopher Okigbo, *Collected Poems,* op. cit.

15. Christopher Okigbo, 'Distances', *Transition,* vol. 4, no. 16, 1964, pp. 9-13.

16. 'Distances', *Labyrinths,* op. cit.

17. When asked on one occasion what he conceived as his audience, Okigbo replied that he 'was writing for other poets all over the world'. See Okigbo's interview with Lewis Nkosi, in *African Writers Talking,* ed. Dennis Duerden and Cosmo Pieterse, London, Heinemann, 1972, p. 135.

18. Okigbo states beneath the title of 'Song of the Forest' that it is based on Virgil's *Tityrus.*

19. Omolara Leslie [Molara Ogundipe-Leslie], 'The poetry of Christopher Okigbo: its evolution and significance', in *Critical Perspectives on Christopher Okigbo,* ed. Donatus Nwoga, Washington, DC, Three Continents Press, 1984, pp. 291-2.

20. See, for example, 'On the New Year' and 'Debtors' Lane', in 'Four Canzones', op. cit.

21. Annemarie Heywood, 'The ritual and the plot: the critic and Okigbo's *Labyrinths*', in *Critical Perspectives on Christopher Okigbo,* op. cit., p. 209. Heywood's article was first published in 1978.

22. O. R. Dathorne rightly indicates that Okigbo has transformed Damas's dolls but does not demonstrate how. See 'Ritual and ceremony in Okigbo's poetry', in *Critical Perspectives On Christopher Okigbo,* op. cit., p. 264. Damas's 'Limbe' (first published in 1937) may be found in *Pigments,* Paris, Présence Africaine, 1972, pp. 43-5.

23. Dan Izevbaye, 'From reality to the dream: the poetry of Christopher Okigbo', in *Critical Perspectives on Christopher Okigbo,* op. cit., p. 327.

24. The ceremony of souls is a soul-cleansing ceremony whereby the living confront the dead to enable each party to proceed with living or afterlife responsibilities. A very poignant dramatization of the practice and concept is provided by George Lamming in *Season of Adventure,* London, Allison and Busby, 1979; first published 1960.

25. Christopher Okigbo, 'Dance of the Painted Maidens', *Collected Poems,* op. cit., pp. 83-6.

26. See Okigbo's 'Introduction to *Labyrinths*', *Labyrinths,* London, Heinemann, 1971, p. xii. The first 'version' of *Labyrinths,* published by Mbari (Ibadan), 1962, did not contain an introduction.

27. *Silences* is one of the sequences which make up Heinemann *Labyrinths.*

28. See note 5 above. See also the 'Introduction' by S. I. Lockerbie, *Calligrammes,* op. cit., pp. 1-20.

29. The following lines usher the protagonist into the final redemptive stage in *Transition* 'Distances':

> And at this chaste instant
> of delineated anguish,
> the same voice, importunate,
> aglow with the goddess—
> unquenchable, yellow,
> darkening homeward
> like a cry of wolf
> above crumbling houses—
> strips the dream naked,
> bares its entrails;

The unvarying rhythm, the monotone, does not project the tension and the thrill of this penultimate instant.

30. For instance, one critic, Wole Ogundele, in a peculiar interpretation assumes one of such *mélanges* to be speaking of 'that Elysian past when harmony between man, nature, and god obtained'. The lines quoted by Ogundele, which include '*etru bo pi alo a she e anando we aquandem . . .*' have been revealed to be a conflation of a childhood corruption of 'Little Bo Peep' and phrases from Catholic liturgy, as well as an account of Okigbo's boyhood imitation of birds' songs. See Wole Ogundele, 'From the labyrinth to the temple: the structure of Okigbo's religious experience', *Okike,* vol. 24, 1983, pp. 61-2. Compare O. R. Dathorne, 'Ritual and ceremony in Okigbo's poetry', in *Critical Perspectives on Christopher Okigbo,* op. cit., p. 263.

31. Roland Barthes, 'From work to text', in *Textual Strategies: Perspectives in Post-Structuralist Criticism,* op. cit., p. 77.

32. Catherine Acholonu, '*Ogbanje*: A motif and a theme in the poetry of Christopher Okigbo', *African Literature Today,* no. 16, 1988, pp. 103-11.

33. This effete view has recently been revived, for instance, by Robert Fraser, *West African Poetry: A Critical History,* Cambridge, Cambridge University Press, 1986, p. 133; Catherine Acholonu, op. cit., p. 107. The relevant lines in Okigbo's poetry are 'The man embodies the child / The child embodies the man.' Wordsworth's famous epigram begins with the line, 'The Child is father of the Man.' Wordsworth's line could easily pass for a translation of a Yoruba truism, 'Omo ju Baba', literally 'The child is greater / older than its father.' This expression appears to 'have always been' because it is attributed to no one. But to suggest any kind of vertical passage of the Yoruba expression to Wordsworth is to succumb to an unfruitful solipsism. Okigbo's lines record a paradox that any culture might have recognized long ago from observations of cycles of regeneration. They belong to an intertext of pithy expressions of cycles of regeneration.

34. Although Okigbo is sometimes almost exclusively situated within the Igbo mythic tradition, his word-lore was not woven from Igbo mythology alone. For instance, Okigbo lived and worked among the Yoruba, in the cities of Ibadan, Fiditi and Lagos, where he composed a substantial part of his poetry. In Yoruba linguistic cosmology seven is evoked as a figure of expansivity and climactic activity. Okigbo acknowledges both explicitly and implicitly several other cultures which had provided materials for his poetry.

35. Catherine Acholonu, op. cit., p. 110.

36. This operational definition is an adaptation of Linda Hutcheon's definition of 'metafiction' in *Narcissistic Narrative: The Metafictional Paradox,* Waterloo, Wilfrid Laurier University Press, 1980, p. 1.

37. Patricia Waugh, *Metafiction: The Theory and Practice of Self-Conscious Fiction,* London and New York, Methuen, 1984, p. 3.

Catherine O. Acholonu (essay date 1991)

SOURCE: Acholonu, Catherine O. "From Rhetoric to Occultism: The Word as Music & Drama in Okigbo's *Labyrinths.*" *African Literature Today* 17 (1991): 131-40.

[*In the following essay, Acholonu argues that Okigbo achieves "the artistic ideal of purity" and the "perfect identification of matter with form" through the musicality of his language.*]

For Baudelaire, Rimbaud and Mallarmé, the flag-bearers of the French symbolist movement, the purist goal of poetry was the state of music. Paul Valéry maintains that all art aims ultimately at attaining purity, that kind of unity and wholesomeness which is attainable only through music.252[1] In Christopher Okigbo's **Labyrinths** music and drama play a vital role in the poet's attainment of his ultimate goal of fulfilment. The musicality of language, the recurrent patterns and variations upon the same theme, the accumulating images of infrastructure and dramatized experience, function as carriers of the poet's vision. Through music, the poet attains a state of abstraction in his pursuit of the artistic ideal of purity, of the perfect identification of matter with form.[2]

In *Labyrinths* there are two main personalities through whose voices the poet's vision becomes apparent. These are the persona 'I' and the chorus. Through these personalities or characters, the audience is brought nearer to the inner world of the poem. The reader or audience is made to believe in the action and spectacle of the poem because it is what the persona 'I' and the chorus see. In this sense, Okigbo's poetry is a poetry of experience in the Nietzschean sense of 'a poem which originates in song and passes temporarily through drama in order to articulate the song and refer us back to the song for meaning'.[3]

Labyrinths starts as the 'broken monody' or dirge of a young bird whose language is characterized by uncertainty:

> On one leg standing
> in silence at the passage
> the young bird at the passage[4]
>
> (p. 4)

The persona is standing before the shrine of mother Idoto, praying for purification. *Heavensgate* is a death-in-life poem, its characters are living dead encountered by the persona in the erring early period of his existential journey. All the tunes heard in the language of *Heavensgate* are more echoes of the poet's unworthy past, a past characterized by illusion:

> where the players of loft pipe organs
> rehearse old lovely fragments, alone
> for we are listening in cornfields
>   among the windplayers,
> listening to the wind leaning over
>   its loveliest fragment
>
> (p. 5)

and by 'errors of the rendering' (p. 8) such as the song of Jadum, a half-demented village minstrel, 'from Rockland'.

As the Newcomer emerges with a new life and a new identity, the persona begins to identify with his native religion and his native culture, while the sound of the bells of the angelus begin to recede:

> softly sing the bells of exile
> the angelus
> softly sings my guardian angel
>
> (p. 17)

and are replaced by the thundering drums and cannons that accompany the ascending spirit in the palm grove:

> Thundering drums and cannons
> in palm grove
> the spirit is in ascent.
>
> (p. 16)

The first signs of the dramatic lyric are seen as early as *Heavensgate,* as the persona introduces his characters and even puts words into their mouths:

> So comes John the Baptist
> with bowl of salt water
> preaching the gambit:
> life without sin, without/life;
>
> (p. 6)

Jadum, the mad minstrel, comes with words of advice and caution from Rockland. He sings to shepherds with a flute on his lip:

> Do not wander in speargrass
> After the lights
> Probing liars in stockings,
> To roast
> The viper alive . . .
>
> (p 8)

Then comes Upandru saying:

> Screen your bedchamber thoughts
> with sun-glasses,
> who could jump your eye,
> your mind-window,
>
> (p. 9)

to which the persona of the poem makes a reply, creating an occasion for verbal exchange or *dialogue* thus:

> And I said:
> The prophet only the poet.
> And he said: Logistics.
> (Which is what poetry is) . . .
> And he said to the ram: Disarm.
> And I said:
> Except by rooting,
> Who could pluck yam tubers from their base?
>
> (p. 9)

Another element of drama which is found in *Labyrinths* is *action,* with or without dialogue. Physical action or movement can be observed from the persona's encounter with the watermaid:

> BRIGHT
> with the armpit-dazzle of a lioness,
> she answers,
>
> wearing white light about her;

and the waves escort her,

Downward . . .
the waves distill her;
gold crop
sinking ungathered.

(p. 11)

In the **"Newcomer"** we see a sure-footed protagonist standing above the bridgehead as large as life, so real, so vivid; and we can hear the rippling of the waters as they flow by:

I AM standing above the noontide,
Above the bridgehead;

Listening to the laughter of waters

I am standing above the noontide
    with my head above it;

Under my feet float the waters
Tide blows them under . . .

(p. 19)

The use of the present tense—'I am standing', 'listening', 'blows'—in this episode helps to strengthen the dramatic element; the element of uncertainty which had earlier characterized the language of the hero now gives way to more surety and self-confidence.

The combination of the dramatic and the musical in poetry results in a genre known as the dramatic lyric or the lyrical drama as the case may be. The lyrical drama or the dramatic lyric 'began with those poets of the neoclassic age who, in trying—as a counterpoint to the satirical and didactic poetry of the time—to be lyrical, found it necessary to give their lyrical poems a dramatic setting, to draw their feelings and reflections out of the observation of a scene remarkable for its beauty and picturesqueness'.[5] The music is the music of the poet's soul, the music of evolution and continuity; the drama, a drama of the poet's experience. The quest hero in this journey is an observer who seeks out incidents and establishes among them a sequence, however illogical, with the power of his experiences. Also the references to biographical elements such as the poet's personal experiences and personal relationships help to strengthen the message of the poem and lend it a validity which otherwise might have been lost as a result of the vagueness of the events and the illogicality of their sequence. The question of validity is a rhetorical question. In a dramatic lyric a new validity is created, a new logic out of non-logic, for it is not just the description of optical perceptions as they are in true life, or as they appear to the narrator, which is significant, rather, it is the re-creation of these observed objects. They assume a new life, a new significance, through the poet's imagination, through the music of the poet's soul. The dramatic element is a sign that the experience is really taking place, that the object is seen and felt—

I am standing above the noontide . . .
Under my feet float the waters . . .

(p. 19)

—and not just remembered as an abstract idea or point of view. The experience has more validity because it is dramatized as an event, a palpable experience, rather than formulated as an abstraction. The poet's perspective, even though extraordinary, and his imagery, even though farfetched, are made palpable by the musicality of his rendering. Every living being on earth responds to music, there is music in growth, in movement, in stillness, even in silence. This is what Okigbo refers to as the 'music of the firmament' (p. 41).

Labyrinths is made musical not only through the usual musical elements of verse such as rhythm, metre, onomatopoeia, consonance, assonance, etc., but also through the adaptation of its structure to such musical structural patterns as leitmotif, symphonic form (movements), orchestration, the musicality of recurrent patterns, of accumulating images, of infra-structure and dramatized experience. These function as rhetorical devices, as objective correlative carriers of the poet's vision, unifying his diverse experiences and the different variations of the same themes by the force of the voice and personality of the persona 'I'.

Labyrinths was originally conceived as a musical experience; it is, like classical music, made up of movements. In addition, it is a drama whose performance is to be accompanied by traditional Igbo musical instruments like the drums (*ekwe*), the flutes (*oja*), *ubo* (the Igbo equivalent of the guitar) and the *ogene*. Okigbo's distribution of the musical accompaniments for his poetry is most elaborate in his early publications, especially in the **Four Canzones,** published in *Black Orpheus*, no. 11. But, even though these arrangements are not clearly spelt out in **Labyrinths,** the musical quality of these poems is in no way minimized. The first thing that strikes a reader of **Labyrinths** is the measured cadence of syllables, lines and stanzas, and the resultant rhythm and melody, as in the following stanzas:

1. A Before you, mother Idoto,
        naked I stand;
      before your watery presence,
        a prodigal

   B leaning on an oilbean,
        lost in your legend.

   A Under your power wait I
        on barefoot,
      watchman for the watchword
        at *Heavensgate*;

B　out of the depths my cry:
　　　give ear and hearken . . .

　　　　　　　　　　　　(p. 3)

2. A　And to the Distant—but
　　　　how shall we go?
　　　The robbers will strip us of
　　　　our tendons!

　B　For we sense
　　　With dog-nose a Babylonian
　　　　capture,
　　　The martyrdom
　　　Blended into that chaliced
　　　　vintage;

　B　And savour
　　　The incense and in high
　　　　buskin,
　　　Like a web
　　　Of voices all rent by jav-
　　　　elins.

　A　But distant seven winds in-
　　　　vite us and our cannons
　　　To limber our membranes
　　　　for a dance of elephants
　　　　. . .

　　　　　　　　　　　　(p. 46)

The graphological arrangement and punctuation of these lines equally enhance the musical effect. Other musical patterns prevalent in *Labyrinths* are onomatopoeia, consonance, assonance, metre and pitch. All these together give the effect of orchestration, as in the lament of the drums:

　　—So, like a dead letter unanswered
　　　Our rococo
　　　Choir of insects is null
　　　Cacophony . . .

　　—But the antiphony, still clamorous
　　　In tremolo,
　　　Like an afternoon, for shadows;

　　　　　　　　　　　　(p. 49)

It is necessary to note that these lines are supposed to sound like the beating of the Igbo drum; they echo and re-echo with a sonorous invitation to Isthar's lament for Tammuz. Words like rococo, cacophony, tremolo, antiphony, clamorous are onomatopoeic, but also they are well chosen for their consonance (rhyming of consonants) and assonance (rhyming of vowels). But the reader of *Labyrinths* must learn to recognize where

sheer rhetoric and artistic embellishments end and where occultism begins. In fact very often rhetoric and occultism run concurrently in Okigbo's poetry. Through the activity of the imagination, the poet fuses 'opposite and discordant qualities', of creation and destruction, life and death, just and unjust, the idea and the image, and thus establishes the paradox of his creative or Promethean ego as the vehicle of tragedy in the Nietzschean sense. By the original title of his book *The Birth of Tragedy Out of the Spirit of Music,* Nietzsche declares tragedy to be, 'not the illustration of an idea of the world, of an objective order of values, but a birth, a natural growth from the unarticulated life-surge, from what he calls the "Primordial Unity" or "Primordial Pain", of which music is an expression'[6]—Okigbo's 'music of the firmament'.

Okigbo's first attempt at achieving this primordial unity can be seen in **"Siren Limits",** as the creative artist 'feeling for audience' is seen 'straining thin among the echoes':

　　Into the soul
　　The selves extended their branches
　　Into the moments of each living hour . . .
　　And out of the solitude
　　Voice and soul with selves unite
　　Riding the echoes . . .
　　And crowned with one self
　　The name displays its foliage

　　　　　　　　　　　　(p. 24)

Anozie has remarked that 'the poet's "soul" which is said to disintegrate into "moments of each living hour" seems to have been installed as the One or the Primeval Being (Supreme Being) itself. "Selves", as used above, by virtue of its plurality, may be said to be already fragmentalized. Each fragment is perhaps one ideal Self?'[7]

This Promethean or creative realization of the poet's ego strengthens him for a larger task yet to follow. The triumph of the creative ego equals the discovery of a new voice, a new language, a new vision—'the name displays its foliage':

　　Horsemen of the apocalypse
　　And crowned with one self
　　The name displays its foliage

　　　　　　　　　　　　(p. 24)

It is very significant that this point marks a milestone in the poet's development. This new voice that 'displays its foliage' in **"Siren Limits II"** is already put into action in **"Siren Limits III",** the very next poem. For the very first time, musical leitmotifs occur in *Labyrinths* in the form of refrain:

　　and the mortar is not yet dry . . .
　　and the mortar is not yet dry . . .

　　　　　　　　　　　　(p. 25)

The music is becoming louder and the voice stronger, in fact the poet finds it difficult to control the current of sound issuing from his soul:

> And the voice that is reborn transpires
> Not thro' pores in the flesh
>   but the soul's back-bone
>
> (p. 25)

The protagonist now nears the destination of his journey; the speed is increased especially for the hero's second self who is nearing his end:[8]

> Hurry on down—
>   Thro' the high-arched gate—
> Hurry on down
>   little stream to the lake;
> Hurry on down
>   Thro' the cinder market
> Hurry on down
>   in the wake of the dream . . .
>
> (p. 26)

This second self which, like Gilgamesh's Enkidu, represents the limitations of mortal man, is eventually destroyed in **"Fragments out of the Deluge"** and the hero is thus finally freed of all earthly limitations.

In *Silences* this new-found voice burgeons into a new life with a new vitality and insistence. In the **"Lament of the Silent Sisters"** music and drama actually spring into life. The dramatic lyric of *Labyrinths* suddenly metamorphoses into lyrical drama, a performance whose characters are the silent sisters—the crier and chorus. Theirs is a triumphant dirge that unifies life and death, through memories, through the silent music of the soul:

> CRIER:
>
> > I hear sounds as, they say,
> > A worshipper hears the flutes
>
> CHORUS:
>
> > The music sounds so in the soul
> > I can hear nothing else
>
> CRIER:
>
> > I hear painted harmonies
> > From the mushroom of the sky
>
> CHORUS:
>
> > Silences are melodies
> > Heard in retrospect: . . .
>
> (p. 43)

The Crier represents the narrative voice of the persona of *Labyrinths*; the Chorus represents the gods. As such the chorus lends wisdom and sacredness to the language of *Labyrinths.* Through them, the lyric is trans-

formed into a dramatic evocation of the psychic union of the 'I' of the poem (the narrator) with the infinite power that nurtures all creation.

In *Silences* Okigbo's language becomes incantatory due to the fusion of music with actual drama, something akin to what Rimbaud refers to as 'Alchimie du Verbe' and what Anozie refers to as 'incantatory lyricism'.[9] The 'I' of the lyricist, the 'we' and 'our' of the crier and chorus, sound from the abyss of being. It is an invocative 'I' and is further made potent by the 'plastic music of words reaching out now into the silence of the night, now into the mountain cataracts; now conjuring up twisted forms mirrored from the sea, now invoking a panorama of vague but symbolic images'.[10] The following incantatory images are from the **"Lament of the Silent Sisters"**:

> For as in sea-fever globules of fresh anguish.
>   immense golden eggs empty of albumen
>   sink into our balcony . . .
>
> Where is there for us an anchorage;
> A shank for a sheet, a double arch
>
>   scented shadows above the underrush
>
> (p. 39)

> So, one dips one's tongue in the ocean, and begins
> To cry to the mushroom of the sky
>
> (p. 40)

> And there will be a continual going to the well
> Until they smash their calabashes
>
> (p. 40)

> Unseen shadows like long-fingered winds
> Pluck from our strings
>
> (p. 41)

> Wild winds cry out against us . . .
> We shall wear the green habit of kolanuts . . .
> The kingfisher gathers his ropes in the distance
> The salt water gathers them inward
>
> (p. 42)

In traditional African religion, religious practice is evocative; as in the religion of the Negro spiritual, faith is expressed through the invocation of a god. In this ritual, which is a form of occultism or magic, three main vehicles abound. These are: dance, drum (flute, or other musical instruments) and the spoken word, which is recited or sung. The dance is a form of dramatic performance, the drum a musical instrument and the incantation is still music. Thus, whichever way we approach it, we still arrive at the two poles of drama and music which are essential in the practice of the African cult. Mbiti has observed that 'Music, singing and dancing reach deep into the innermost parts of the African peoples, and many things come to the surface under musical inspiration which otherwise may not be really revealed.'[11] And Janheinz Jahn observes that 'drums and other percussion instruments are indispensable for the practice of an African cult . . . particular gods are invoked by particular drum-beat formulas. These formulas are the *nommo* names with which the gods are invoked.'[12] Jahn describes the African culture as 'a culture in which invocatory poetry is simply word magic: not the written word but the word which is sung and danced'.[13] This is the evolutional point in Okigbo's poetry. In *Silences* the written word gets transformed into cultic language. The 'swan song' and 'jubilee dance' of the silent sisters, the lament of the drums, all these are essential ingredients to transform the written word into magic, which is still a prerogative of the poet. He invokes, by the power of this magic word, the goddess of the sea, the hidden face of the dream who becomes one with Idoto, the watermaid, the poet's mother Anna, the lioness, the silent sisters and even the drums (which incidentally are female drums: Okigbo refers to them as mother and daughter drums in his introduction to *Labyrinths*). The song of the silent sisters is a lament, a song of death (swan song).

> This is our swan song
> This is our senses' stillness . . .
> This is our swan song
> This is the sigh of our spirits
>
> (p. 41)

(The swan is a death bird in European mythology; its equivalent in Igbo is the owl or *ajo nnunu*). Their dance is a dance of death, a 'jubilee-dance above the carrion' (p. 39).

This female essence which is destructive is also creative. It destroys the hero's second self so that his immortal soul might surface with greater creative power. She is the poet's muse, and through her he gains the power of prophecy; thus in the **"Lament of the Silent Sisters"** and in the **"Lament of the Drums"** we see glimpses of future events such as war:

> What cast-iron steps cascading down the valley
>   all forged into thunder of tanks
> And detonators cannoned into splintered flames
>   in this jubilee dance of fire-flies
>
> (p. 40)

betrayal:

> And bearded Judas
> Resplendent among the dancers
>
> (p. 43)

and oppression:

> For the far removed there is wailing:
> For the far removed;
> For the Distant . . .
>
> The wailing is for the fields of crop:
>
> The drums' lament is:
> They grow not . . .
>
> The wailing is for the fields of men:
>
> For the barren wedded ones
> For perishing children
>
> The wailing is for the Great River
>
> Her pot-bellied watchers
> Despoil her . . .
>
> (p. 50)

Thus the poet's use of cultic language can be said to be positive rather than negative, useful rather than harmful.

The climax of this ecstatic experience of the poet is in **"Distances"**, where the poet, having lost all consciousness, compares this new state to that of 'sensual anaesthesia':

> From flesh into phantom
>
> (p. 53)

> And the eye lost its light
> and the light lost its shadow
>
> (p. 54)

From now on the poet no longer 'describes' images and scenery that are symbolic of the idea; rather, he formulates the idea itself: this new vision of Primeval Unity, in a visionary language devoid of rhetorical embellishments. This new language is precise; it is mathematical and architectural rather than merely rhetorical:

> And at the archway
> a triangular lintel
> of solid alabaster
> enclosed in a square
> inscribed in a circle
> with a hollow centre
> above the archway
> yawning shutterless . . .
>
> (p. 57)

Through ritual and invocation, through music and drama, Okigbo, the poet from a lineage of priests of the water cult (Idoto worship), roots his poetry in African traditional cultic religion, where word magic is not simply the written word but the word which is chanted and danced to musical accompaniments; the word which links man with God; through which the creative process is accomplished:

> In the beginning there was the word
> And the word was with God
> And the word was God . . .
> Through him all things were made . . .[14]

Language ceases to be mere rhetoric and assumes a cultic stance. The dramatic hero who has now become one with the Supreme Being experiences what Coleridge refers to as the 'synthetic and magical' power of the imagination made manifest through the spoken word. Symbolism deepens into occultism—the 'Alchimie du Verbe'.

Finally, in **Path of Thunder,** the soothsayer—priest of the water cult—emerges from the cocoon of the creative artist, takes up his iron bell and moves through the streets as town-crier, prophesying impending war.

Notes

1. Paul Valéry, 'Pure Poetry', *The Art of Poetry,* trans. Denise Folliot, New York, 1958, pp. 184-5.

2. See Wayne C. Booth, *The Rhetoric of Fiction,* Chicago, University of Chicago Press, 1961, p. 95.

3. Robert Langbaum, *Poetry of Experience,* Harmondsworth, Penguin, 1974, p. 228.

4. Christopher Okigbo, *Labyrinths,* London, Heinemann, 1971. All further quotations are from this edition.

5. Langbaum, op. cit., p. 32.

6. Ibid., p. 226.

7. Sunday Anozie, *Christopher Okigbo,* London, Evans, 1972, p. 75.

8. C. O. Acholonu, 'From Ritual to Politics: Christopher Okigbo and the Loadstone Myth', paper presented at the Unical International Conference on Literature and the Teaching of English, 1-6 May 1984.

9. Anozie, op. cit., p. 103.

10. Ibid., pp. 102-3.

11. John Mbiti, *African Religions and Philosophy,* London, Heinemann, 1980, p. 67.

12. Janheinz Jahn, *A History of Neo-African Literature,* London, Faber, n.d., p. 159.

13. Ibid.

14. St. John, I:1.

Chukwuma Azuonye (essay date 1994)

SOURCE: Azuonye, Chukwuma. "'I, Okigbo, Town-Crier': The Transition from Mythopoeic Symbolism to a Revolutionary Aesthetic in *Path of Thunder.*" In *The Gong and the Flute: African Literary Development and Celebration,* edited by Kalu Ogbaa, pp. 19-36. Westport, Conn.: Greenwood Press, 1994.

[*In the following essay, Azuonye offers a detailed analysis of* Path of Thunder *in order to highlight Okigbo's transition from "the mythopoeic symbolism" of his early works to "a largely unfulfilled revolutionary aesthetic" in his final works.*]

There is a clear pattern in the development of the poetry of Christopher Okigbo. As has been shown in my earlier essays,[1] there are probably two major phases in this development. The first phase, stretching from *Four Canzones*[2] to "Distances,"[3] was dominated by a symbolist aesthetic of the kind ritually re-enacted in *Heavensgate III.*[4] Here, the poet-hero, in the romantic solitude of a beach, plants the "secret" of his muse in beach sand, completely unconcerned about "name or audience." This ritual symbolism of covering up a unique vision of reality in utter disregard of overt statements epitomizes the symbolist attitude. Okigbo's poetry up to "Distances" presents various dramatic moments of this ultra-romantic attitude. **"Lament of the Masks"**[5] marks a turning point in the development of the poems. In this poem, dedicated to W. B. Yeats, on the occasion of the centenary of his birth, Okigbo now assumes, as it were, the mantle of prophecy, having evolved a new person after the attainment of full individuation at the close of **"Distances."**[6] No longer the songbird singing "tongue-tied . . . among the branches," he speaks of "thunder," "cannons," and "battle" and gives clear promise of more open statements about his crisis-ridden country.

The roots of the development described above were already present in **"Fragments out of the Deluge,"** *Silences,*[7] and the closing strophe of **"Distances."** Even in *Heavensgate,* the **"Initiation"** poems move from the intensely esoteric explorations of subconscious reality through the archetypal pictographs of the cross, the triangle, the square, the rhombus, and the rectangle (the full implications of which I have ventured to discuss elsewhere),[8] to open invectives, first, against

> the moron,
> fanatics and priests and popes,
> organizing secretaries and party managers
> and, subsequently, against
> brothers and deacons,
> liberal politicians,
> selfish selfseekers—all who are good
> doing nothing at all.

Later, within the overriding oracular symbolism of **"Fragments out of the Deluge,"** we have a thorough-going tirade against cultural alienation, philistinism, Christian vandalism, and sentimental literary fads such as "negritude." In *Silences,* we can see in the "Who can say No in thunder" passages presentiments of war arising from the despoiling of the "Great River" (Nigeria) by "her pot-bellied watchers." And, amid the beatific experience of mystical union with the goddess, in **"Distances,"** we are confronted with "the taste of ash in the air's marrow." It is, however, in **"Lament of the Masks"** that the tendency toward direct and open political statements clearly declares itself. The mythical mask of the early sequences now begins to tear asunder and we get a faint glimpse of the face behind the mask, a man who, in many ways, would be identified with the Yeats of the later years. In *Path of Thunder,*[9] the mask falls off completely and the poet reveals himself and unequivocally declares his revolutionary options.

This essay will examine, through a detailed analysis of the six poems which make up *Path of Thunder,* the highlights of the remarkable transition from the mythopoeic symbolism of the early phase to a largely unfulfilled revolutionary aesthetic of the second phase. The examination invites a look back into the future of Okigbo's poetic career which was prematurely cut short by the civil war. Nevertheless, it is hoped that by doing this, we rationalize the poet's direct involvement in action and appreciate certain moot tendencies wrapped up in the myth and symbolism of the earlier phase. A good starting point in this investigation seems to be the second strophe of *Path of Thunder,* **"Elegy of the Wind,"** which is by far the most coherent and categorical statement of the main principles of the revolutionary aesthetic of the unfulfilled second phase. Here, the poet describes himself as "Man of iron throat"—a man forced by the prevailing circumstances to "make broadcast with eunuch-horn of seven valves."[10] Then he declares:

> I will follow the wind to the clearing,
> And with muffled steps seemingly out of breath break
> the silence the myth of her gate.

The allusions contained in these declarations must be clear to anyone who is familiar with Okigbo's poetry preceding *Path of Thunder.* The "wind" of the title of the elegy and of the lines quoted above is clearly the political turbulence and upheavals of the middle sixties in Nigeria: it is one and the same with Harold Macmillian's "wind of change" blowing through Africa, but which in the mid-sixties had become a vicious harbinger of "mere anarchy." Okigbo, in the ivory tower of the earlier phase of his poetry, had charted the movements of the wind at "various stations of his cross,"[11] in his progression from *Four Canzones* to **"Distances."** The symbolist poetry of these earlier sequences had been as good as silence. We should notice how this is suggested in the unpunctuated collection, "the silence the myth of her gate." What the new situation of crisis

requires is poetry of action. The poet, so to speak, must now take to the soapbox with a microphone: he must speak directly to the people. The idea of making broadcasts: the poet of action explores the same area as the broadcaster. He is like the traditional spokesman, the oral artist, who interprets communal experience and forewarns of dangers ahead. He speaks directly to the masses in the public square, "the clearing." But the erstwhile ivory poet is unused to this mode of communication. That is why he approaches "the clearing" with anxiety and caution: "with muffled steps seemingly out of breath." Later, in the third strophe of the sequence, we see him in person, unmasked, like the town-crier, warning the nation of its follies, despite his awareness of the risks of taking such a course of action:

> If I don't learn to shut my mouth I will soon go to
> hell,
> I, Okigbo, town-crier, together with my iron bell.[12]

And in the fourth strophe, **"Elegy for Slit-drum,"** in which we are drawn into a dance of condolences, there is, paradoxically, public rejoicing in the new solidarity between the poet and the masses, for the masses need the oracular insights of the mythmaker in their moments of doubts and uncertainties, as in the fabulous darkness which provides the backdrop to **"Elegy of the Wind"**:

> The mythmaker accompanies us (the Egret had come
> and gone)
> Okigbo accompanies us the oracle enkindles us
> the Hornbill is there again (the Hornbill has had a
> bath)
> Okigbo accompanies us the rattles enlighten us—

The poet of action enjoys this approchement with, and acknowledgment by, the masses that recognize him and rejoice in the insights that they receive from him in times of trouble. It is in the poetry of action alone that the poet can make active, for the benefit of the masses, the special knowledge which he, as the medium of the goddess, is alone privileged to receive.

Every poet who begins his career as a "mythmaker," like Okigbo, comes to this kind of knowledge at a certain point in his career. Yeats, faced with "responsibilities"[13] similar to that which now faces Okigbo, repudiates his earlier poetry as a "coat / Covered with embroideries / Out of old mythologies"[14] and then he realizes "There is more enterprise in walking naked." Poetry of action is "naked poetry," one that does not rely on the tapestry of myth for its effects but on the sincerity and force of the poet's direct questionings and doubts. That is why Okigbo now wants to break "the silence the myth of her gate." In **"Elegy of the Wind,"** therefore, we have a new poetic manifesto, a revision of the old mode, such as every serious, committed poet makes in the face of violence and anarchy. The realization that the old oracular mode will not now suffice to meet the challenges of the times is clearly stated: "I have lived the oracle dry on the cradle of a new generation." Breaking with the restriction of the old mode, the poet must now embrace larger causes and deal openly with issues of wider dimension:

> O Wind, swell my sails; and may my banner run the course of wider waters.

There is, here, a Shellyian Paradox[15] in the image of destructive wind which is also the activator of the poet's dead thoughts, the destroyer which is also the preserver, quickening a new birth and scattering the poet's insights throughout the universe.

I have begun this analysis with the second strophe of **Path of Thunder** because the declarations contained in it assure us of the poet's purpose in the sequence and enable us to take the reading we shall record in the rest of this chapter, a reading which involves a closer socio-political interpretation of the images and symbols in the sequence than would be possible in any analysis of Okigbo's poetry: "the myth of her gate" or "the oracle" of the past mode. The declarations of purpose seem clear enough and the new mode already beginning to assert itself ("the chant, already all wings") is here before us actively following "the thunder clouds." All these seem to us clearly stated, but to reassure ourselves lest we fall into grievous error, it is perhaps necessary for us to attend more closely to these declarations through a paraphrase of the elegy; and perhaps, it may also be necessary for us to go further to show how these declarations are consistently made all through **Path of Thunder** and how they develop from statements of artistic purpose made elsewhere, not only in **Labyrinths** but also in the preceding and intervening poems.[16]

"Elegy of the Wind"

It might be stated right away that **"Elegy of the Wind"** is informed by the poet's visions and revisions, his fears and expectations, and his doubts and questionings as he considers what his proper role should be in the "new generation," on the "cradle" of which he finds himself. It is, in essence, a record of his past efforts and failures and an anticipation of the new active role he must now fulfill with all its dangers and challenges.

First, in the opening stanza, he invokes the heavenly muse, "White light . . . the milky way"; perhaps once again, but in a different situation, he finds himself a suppliant at Heavensgate. The first time he is discovered in this attitude of ritual supplication before Idoto, in the overture to **Heavensgate,** he is "the young bird at the passage," a child, "lost in the legend" of the mother-goddess of the stream whose worship he had abandoned in the pursuit of strange gods. There, "at *Heavensgate,*" he is "watchman for the watchword," waiting under her power, for the goddess to inspire and make him worthy. Now, he has attained manhood, and after his excruciating experiences, he feels he can take the initiative: "let me clasp you to my waist." The phallic overtones are unmistakable; and here, as in the opening strophe of the **"Watermaid"** monologues in **Heavensgate III,** images of sexual union combine with those of plant growth to suggest the exfoliation of art. The same attitudes enacted in that first strophe of the **"Watermaid"** sequence are repeated here. I have elsewhere dealt with this at length.[17] The unique poetic vision of the poet is a secret akin to the secret which burdens King Midas's barber and which he can declare only at the pain of death or suffering of some sort. Even where the poet invents a clever means of unburdening himself of the secret without telling it into any ear, burying it in beach sand, he does not escape the consequences. King Midas's barber suffers death; Okigbo's prodigal is wounded, when the secret breaks into blossom. The same twilight setting is here again invoked and the poet boldly conjures "the burden of the centuries" (the insights and archetypal modes of perception which he has shared with other poets over the centuries) to break into plumule, disregarding the dangers:

> And may my muted tones of twilight
> Break your iron gate, the burden of several centuries,
> into twin tremulous cotyledons

Here is a passionate plea for liberation from the strictures of mythic imagining. In the second stanza, we have the declaration of his intention to come out in the open, speaking with microphonic audacity, making public statements. Then follows, in stanzas three, four, and five, a look back into the future. Stanza three recapitulates and alludes to the kind of growth recorded in **Limits II,** where the "shrub among the poplars," after the unification in solitude of voice and soul with the selves, becomes the "green cloud above the forest," the crown of its own glory. It had been a unique and spectacular rise for which there is cause for pride:

> For I have lived the sapling sprung from the bed
> of the old vegetation;
> Have shouldered my way through a mass of ancient
> nights to chlorophyll

Next, in the following stanza, he summarizes his progress as a suppliant, beginning from **Heavensgate** to his first close encounters with the maid in her bedchamber, in **"Distances":**

> Or leaned upon a withered branch
> A blind beggar leaning on a porch.

These two lines which form stanza four are difficult to interpret. But the first line seems to refer to the poet's posture "at Heavensgate," where he is discovered, early in his prodigal state, "leaning on an oilbean," before mother Idoto. The second, on the other hand, probably refers to the later encounters of the poet as the importunate hero in the bedchamber of his muse, the intractable maid. The lines, however, clearly summarize the progress of the poet: his psychological journey from innocence to experience. *Path of Thunder* then is a sequence in which the poet accepts the responsibilities which come with experience and in which he rejects "the errors of the rendering" in the oracular first phase of his career. The rejection of the "errors" of the earlier phase is explicitly stated in the fifth stanza:

> I have lived the oracle dry on the cradle of a new generation. . . .
> The autocycle leans on a porch, the branch dissolves into embers,

Here, the inadequacy of the old mode to deal with the challenges of the "new generation" is announced, and the collapse of these modes described. The "autocycle" leaning "on a porch" may refer to the vehicle which the poet now abandons, and the dissolution of "the branch" may refer to the final dissolution of the poet's principal poetic figure—the female figure (the *anima*) which dominates his adventures in the unconscious[18] throughout the first phase of his poetic career. This dissolution of the *anima* figure signifies maturity or individuation through the unification of the opposite tendencies in the poet's psyche and the arrival at a "still-point"—the "motion into stillness" of the sixth stanza, a stanza replete with images of regeneration, manhood, and the pains of maturation. Here the poet, having abandoned his old mode of operation (stanza five), emerges like a phoenix from the ashes of his past and attains full poetic manhood with all its responsibilities and pains, the latter symbolized by the pains of circumcision—the traditional symbol of manhood in African rites of passage. But some aspects of "the child" linger in manhood, just as there are some aspects of manhood in childhood:

> The man embodies the child
> The child embodies the man

We are here confronted with a familiar cyclical pattern in African mythology, a pattern well illustrated by the eternal cycle of "returning to the world" as child (*ilo uwa*) and "returning to the spirit sphere" as man (*ila mmuo*) in Igbo mythology. The man "returning to the spirit sphere" at death will be reborn in the land of spirit as a child, and the child "returning to the world" at birth is a man reborn from the spirit sphere. But apart from this reference to the cyclical interrelationship between the man and the child in Igbo mythology, the idea of the man embodying the child and the child embodying the man is reminiscent of one of the key archetypes in Jungian psychology, namely the child as a symbol of the fully individuated self.[19] We are thus here presented with an image of the fully individuated self

who, amid a painful initiation rite, contemplates the bloodshed and suffering of his full involvement in the adult responsibilities ahead of him.

But the bloodshed and suffering notwithstanding, the poet is undeterred. He relishes his emergence from the ivory tower into "wider" social responsibilities:

> O wind, swell my sails; and may my banner run
> the course of wider waters.
>
> (stanza seven)

Meanwhile, he reflects on the limitations imposed on his full realization of the wider responsibilities by the opposing forces of innocence ("the child") and of experience ("the man") in him, the former making it difficult for him to reach out for "the high shelf on the wall" (possibly high political office) while the latter draws him toward "the narrow neck of a calabash" (possibly narrow ideological commitments).[20] But amid these reflections, he is suddenly overwhelmed by the winds of the prophecy—"the chant, already full wings"—which it is his duty to transmit to the nation. This chant, of course, is **"Come Thunder,"** the third poem in *Path of Thunder,* in which the poet forewarns of the dangers inherent in the political crises of the period before the January 1966 military coup in Nigeria. We shall return to this poem presently; but first, let us look at the antecedent to **"Elegy of the Wind,"** namely **"Thunder Can Break,"** the first poem in *Path of Thunder,* which forms the background to the manifesto presented in the **"Elegy of the Wind."**

"Thunder Can Break"

"Thunder Can Break," as the title implies, is a warning. It sums up in succinct images and symbols the implications of armed revolution of January 1966 in Nigeria and its inescapable consequences. **"Thunder"** is, of course, a traditional symbol for divine wrath and justice. Only the innocent can escape the wrath of **"Thunder"** (the Igbo god, Amadioha or Kamalu): it is the only hope of the ordinary man against the tyranny of his rulers. Thus, for example, amid the festive excesses of the decadent civilian regime in Achebe's *A Man of the People,* Odili declares: "I wished for a miracle, for a voice of Thunder, to hush this ridiculous festival and tell the poor contemptible people one or two truths. But of course it would be quite useless. They were not only ignorant but cynical." (p. 2) Nevertheless, at the end of *A Man of the People,* Odili's wish is answered in the form of the military coup which topples the civilian government whose members patronize such ridiculous festivals. The coup at the end of *A Man of the People* which has been described as "a terrifyingly accurate prophecy" is essentially the same as the coup (the "miracl . . . of Thunder") which toppled the ridiculous Balewa regime in January 1966. It is the same "Miracle of Thunder" that is celebrated in **"Thunder Can Break"**:

> This day belongs to a miracle of Thunder;
> Iron has carried the forum
> With token gestures. Thunder has spoken
> Left no signature broken
> Barbicans alone tell one table the winds scatter

Two kinds of "thunder" are here implied: the man-made thunder of cannons and guns and the thunder of divine wrath, the former being the instrument of the latter in this particular context. The idea of describing the "thunder" of January 15, 1966, as a miracle arises from the general feeling, before the coup, that the Balewa regime was far too entrenched to be toppled, an illusion of a kind from which inept but oppressive regimes everywhere in the world suffer from time to time. But "the voice of the people is the voice of God," and no matter how deeply entrenched an evil regime may be, it is bound to collapse one day before the wrath of thunder.

"Thunder Can Break" beings with an image of a "fanfare of drums" and of "wooden bells," an image suggestive of celebration:

> Fanfare of drums, wooden bells: iron chapter;
> And our dividing airs are gathered home.

The occasion is the dawn of a great new chapter of national history, an "iron chapter" which is expected to bring about an end to the "dividing airs" (or the perennial disunity) of the nation. The key idea here is "iron chapter," the military force of cohesion for which the celebration is being staged. The word "iron" appears to be used in, at least, three distinct but related senses. First of all, it seems to signify armed revolution; second, it seems to allude to the name of the man, General Ironsi (nicknamed "Ironsides"), who emerged as Head of State as a consequence of the coup; and, third, it would appear that there is a pun here on the idea of "iron" in "irony," for it is, indeed, an "ironic chapter" of Nigerian history. There is something ironic about the coup, not only because of the sudden popularity of an unelected potentially totalitarian regime but also because of the contradictions between the hopes of the masses and the actions of the new military rulers which soon emerged. In **"Thunder Can Break,"** the poet is particularly concerned with the supreme irony of the January coup—first, the assumption of "the forum" by Ironsi (Iron), a man who does not share the revolutionary ideals of the coup leaders, and, second, the unjustifiable imprisonment of the coup leaders, the instruments of thunder: "For barricaded in iron handiwork a miracle caged."[21] The poet then appeals to the Ironsi regime to release the imprisoned heroes:

> Bring them out we say, bring them out
> Faces and hands and feet,
> The stories behind the myth, the plot
> Which the ritual enacts.[22]

Quite literally, there is a call here for the heroes of the coup to be released unharmed so that the general public can see and honor them. There is no doubt in the poet's mind that the heroic act of the coup leaders has already earned them a place in history and popular myth. The general public is entitled to share in the stories of their heroic exploits and to understand more fully the manner in which the revolution was accomplished.

The poem then ends on a note of warning: The new regime is still suffering from the disease of the ousted civilian regime (symbolized by the elephant); its "obduracy" in refusing to heed the commonweal may call down thunder on it:

> Thunder can break—Earth, bind me fast—
> Obduracy, the disease of elephant.

This warning is repeated in **"Hurrah for Thunder"** (the fourth poem in the sequence), where the new military regime is accused of tending toward the repetition of the excesses of the "fallen elephant" (the ousted civilian government):

> Alas! the elephant has fallen—
> Hurrah for thunder—
> But already the hunters are talking about pumpkins:
> If they share the meat let them remember thunder.

Okigbo's personal and ideological involvement on the side of the leaders of the coup of January 15, 1966, is now well known, and his later role and death in action on the side of Biafra in the civil war are perhaps better known. He is obviously partisan here, defending the course of the young majors whom he had supported in the belief that they were an instrument of divine wrath but who had now fallen into the hands of a new elephantine iron force likely to repeat the follies of the past and plunge the nation into war. It is this situation that gives rise to his decision, in **"Elegy of the Wind,"** to "follow the winds to the clearing" and "make broadcast with eunuch-horn of seven-valves" of "what is past, is passing, and to come."

This prophetic role attains its full maturity in **"Come Thunder,"** the third poem in the sequence. Discarding all obscurantic mythical and oracular imagery, the poet speaks directly to his people:

> Now that the triumphant march has entered the last
> street corners
> Remember, O dancers, the thunder among the clouds.
> But that the laughter, broken in two, hangs
> tremulous between the teeth,
> Remember, O dancers, the lightning beyond the
> earth. . . .
> The smell of blood already floats in the lavender-mist
> of the afternoon.
> The death sentence lies in ambush along the
> corridors of power;
> And a great fearful thing already tugs at the cables of
> the open air,
> A nebula immense and immeasurable, a night of

deep waters—
An iron dream unnamed and unprintable, a path of
  stone.

This, clearly, is the new Okigbo—a new voice in the
"new generation" of **"Elegy of the Wind."** Its appeal is
direct and its imagery seems to derive from the oral tradition. Chants of the same tone, imagery, and rhetorical
vigor can be found in the repertoire of many an African
contemporary oral poet in like situations.

"HURRAH FOR THUNDER"

In the next movement, **"Hurrah for Thunder,"** the image of "the elephant" as the symbol of the brutal destructiveness of Nigeria's first republic is further developed:

> The elephant, tetrarch of the jungle:
> With a wave of the hand
> He could pull down four trees to the ground;
> His four mortar legs pounded the earth:
> Wherever they treaded
> The grass was forbidden to be there.

Here, "the jungle" is unmistakably Nigeria of the turbulent early sixties and the "four trees" are decidedly the
four regions—East, West, Midwest, and the North—
whose unity and progress were ruthlessly devastated by
the elephantine forces which dominated the center. Perhaps, more specifically for Okigbo, these destructive elephantine forces were represented by "the tetrarch of
the jungle" (the Sardauna of Sokoto, who was killed in
the January 1966 coup) and the dominant Hausa-Fulani
elite (which has now metamorphosed into the "Kaduna
Mafia"). **"Hurrah for Thunder,"** as its title and overriding tone of cynical celebration imply, is an approval
of the coup of January 1966—the thunder—which
brought about the fall of the brute forces:

> Whatever happened to the elephant—
> Hurrah for thunder—
>   . . . . .
> Alas! the elephant has fallen—
> Hurrah for thunder—

But there is no facile approval here. As has been pointed
out, hardly is "the miracle of thunder" fully realized
than there are suggestions that the new military leadership ("the hunters") may be succumbing to the temptation to "share" the resources (the meat) of the nation
among its members as the ousted civilian leadership
did. Okigbo's position on this is clear and simply stated:
it was the scramble for the sharing of the national cake
that brought down the thunder on the civilian government; if the new military leaders indulge in the same
kind of excesses, they too will be visited by thunder.
What is needed under the new dispensation is not the
sharing of meat but fair play, responsibility, and the fitting of the right pegs in the right holes. Token gestures
and promises alone will not do in the circumstances:

> The eye that looks down will surely see the nose;
> The finger that fits should be used to pick the nose;
> Today—for tomorrow, today becomes yesterday:
> How many million promises can ever fill a bas-
>   ket. . . .

In the midst of these homiletic reflections, the poet suddenly realizes the danger of his outspokenness:

> If I don't learn to shut my mouth I'll soon go to hell,
> I, Okigbo, town-crier, together with my iron bell.

But, of course, he does not shut his mouth and even
goes further to match his words with action for which
he ultimately pays the supreme sacrifice, while fighting
for Biafra in the Nigerian civil war.

What happens in **"Elegy for Slit-drum"** is hard to pin
down; but here, there are close references to events immediately arising from the coup of January 1966 and
clear presentiments of the outbreak of war. To begin
with, the poet reveals his dissatisfaction with the myopic and indecisive conduct of the regime of General
Ironsi:

> The General is up . . . the General is up . . . Com-
>   mandments . . .
> the General is up the General is up the General is
>   up—
> Condolences for our twin-beaks and feathers of con-
>   dolences:
> the General is near the throne
> an iron mask covers his face
> the General has carried the day
> the mortars are far away. . . .
> Condolences to appease the fever of a wake among
> tumbled tombs

Okigbo's misgiving about the performance of General
Ironsi is that, despite the popular reception of his regime throughout the country, his policy of appeasement
toward the North as if to mollify its elite over the loss
of its leaders (The Sardauna and Balewa) was a position of weakness which undermined the force of his de-
crees. By harping repeatedly on the idea of "condolences," the poet forces the reader to perceive the
irrelevance of the General's insistence on continued appeasement in the face of the numerous challenges before him. At this point, he begins to entertain doubts as
to the propriety of the fate of the elephant which he had
earlier celebrated in **"Hurrah for Thunder":**

> the elephant has fallen
> the mortars have won the day
> the elephant has fallen
> does he deserve his fate
> the elephant has fallen
> can we remember the date—

But these doubts and questionings are soon resolved in
favor of the revolution. The destruction of the elephant
is seen as a blast on "Britain's last stand"—a frontal

onslaught on neo-colonialism which, for the poet, has "cut a path" in a jungle situation. Then comes a picture of the pre-revolution jungle situation of the first republic, a state of fulsome anarchy which was unfortunately repeated in the second republic (1979-83):

> the elephant ravages the jungle
> the jungle is peopled with snakes
> the snake says to the squirrel
> I will swallow you
> the mongoose says to the snake
> I will mangle you
> the elephant says to the mongoose
> I will strangle you

Having painted this picture of the savagery of the first republic, Okigbo returns to his defense of the revolutionary significance of the January 1966 coup and its leaders. In the two lines which carry the central image of the sequence, he presents the coup leaders as thunder which has cut a path through the fabulous darkness of the jungle:

> Thunder fells the trees cut a path
> thunder smashes them all

The picture is especially that of Nzeogwu. The poet cannot see why Nzeogwu and other heroes of what he regards as a revolution should not be honored rather than punished:

> Thunder that has struck the elephant
> The same thunder should wear a plume

The same argument is pursued in the image of the road-marker and the road:

> a roadmarker makes a road
> the road becomes a throne
> can we cane him for felling a tree.

Something has clearly gone wrong. The heroes of the coup who made the road by felling the trees that constituted an obstacle have now been relegated to the background by someone else (General Ironsi), who, it is suggested, sees the road as a throne. Once again the poet warns that "the same thunder" that has struck the elephant "can make a bruise" in this kind of situation.

At the end of **"Elegy for Slit-drum,"** Okigbo's ideological position with regard to the events of 1966 stands out clearly. His death, if nothing else, is proof that when he has come to accept a cause, he does so with unflagging commitment and can unabashedly defend it both in his poetry and in real life. The entire sequence, *Path of Thunder,* merely gives a hint of what would have matured into the most robust, modern committed poetry from the black world.

"Elegy for Alto"

The closing movement of *Path of Thunder,* **"Elegy for Alto,"** is ironically also Okigbo's swan song—his fare-

well to poetry and, indeed, to life. In retrospect, the opening lines sound ominously accurate:

> And the Horn may now paw the air howling good-bye. . . .
> For the Eagles are now in sight:
> Shadows in the horizon

There is, here, a clear anticipation of war as in the other images which dominate the poem: "giant hidden steps of howitzers, of detonators," "Bayonets and cannons" with which the Eagles descend, and "iron dances of mortars, of generators." In the end, the poet takes his leave:

> An old star departs, leaves us here on the shore
> Gazing heavenward for a new star approaching;
> The new star appears, foreshadows its going
> Before a going and coming that goes on forever . . .

So much is wrapped up here in what is essentially an adaptation of lines from other sources that the interpretations will certainly be many and varied. The lines may refer to the cyclical pattern of Okigbo's own poetry and the succession of Okigbo by a new generation of poets who share his mythopoeic imagination; they may also refer to the idea of progressive revelation in which every poet-prophet represents a point of illumination in a process of progressive illumination that goes on forever. But negative interpretations of the pattern are also possible.

Conclusion

Although the poems that make up *Path of Thunder* were written separately (like everything else in Okigbo's poetic output) they are organically related and, in the form in which they are published in *Labyrinths,* they even evince a coherent logic. We may summarize the plot as follows:

First Movement (**"Thunder Can Break"**): There is general rejoicing. A revolution (the "miracle of Thunder") has taken place. A new (iron/military) leadership has emerged. But the leaders of the revolution have been imprisoned, despite public clamor to see and honor them. The poet pleads for the release of the jailed heroes ("miracle caged") and warns against the dangers of obduracy in flaunting the weal of the masses.

Second Movement (**"Elegy of the Wind"**): The new situation demands neither silence nor muffled oracular statements of the poet but open public statements and direct participation in public affairs. The poet, therefore, declares his resolve to abandon the old mode of oracular communication and to address his public more directly on wider issues.

Third Movement (**"Come Thunder"**): In his first public prophecy, the poet draws attention to the danger of war breaking out in the midst of a general atmosphere of euphoria.

Fourth Movement (**"Hurrah for Thunder"**): The poet returns to the "miracle of thunder" presented in the first movement. He celebrates the destruction of the elephant (brute, destructive force) by thunder (a revolution representing divine wrath). But he goes on to warn the new regime about relapsing into the excesses of the old order, a relapse which, if it happens, must be visited by thunder.

Fifth Movement (**"Elegy for Slit-drums"**): The failures of the new military government are decried; but the poet reasserts his belief that, despite these failures, the military coup that had brought the government into power was the right action to break what amounted to a law of the jungle in the country. In the end, the poet renews his plea for honoring rather than punishing the heroes of the coup.

Sixth Movement (**"Elegy for Alto"**): The poet takes his leave amid visions of war and general violence.

As has been pointed out, Okigbo's **Path of Thunder** occupies a position in the poet's corpus similar to that occupied by the "responsibilities" poems of the final phase of the works of most great poets, such as Blake, Eliot, and Yeats. This involves the abandonment of earlier obscure symbolism for mere direct statement of faith and ideology. A definitive statement of the exact complexion of Okigbo's ideology and the relation of his ideology to his role in the Nigerian crisis and civil war is yet to be attempted. The present chapter has merely sketched out the framework for such inquiry.[23] **Path of Thunder** is not a fulfillment but a promise of the revolutionary direction of the unrealized future of Okigbo's poetry. Had he survived to realize that future, it is conceivable that he would have shed the remnants of obscurity in imagery and allusion, which, despite his new poetic manifesto, can be found still lingering in this essentially transitional piece.

Notes

1. See Chukwuma Azuonye, "The Secret of the Watermaid: Dramatization of the Symbolist Process in *Heavensgate III*," unpublished paper, Nsukka, 1973; "Memories, Initiations and Geometrical Symbolism in Okigbo's Poetry," English Departmental Seminar Paper, University of Ibadan, May 1979; "The Organic Unity of Christopher Okigbo's Poetry," English Departmental Seminar Paper, University of Ibadan, March 1980; and "Christopher Okigbo and the Psychological Theories of Carl Gustav Jung," *Journal of African and Comparative Literature* no. 1 (March 1981), 30-51.

2. *Black Orpheus* II, 1962.

3. In *Labyrinths with Path of Thunder,* London: Heinemann African Writers Series, 1971.

4. *Ibid.*

5. In *W. B. Yeats: 1865-1965: Centenary Essays* (Ibadan: Ibadan University Press, 1965).

6. In *Labyrinths, op. cit.*

7. *Ibid.*

8. Chukwuma Azuonye, "Memories, Initiations and Geometrical Symbolism," *op. cit.*

9. Labyrinths, *op. cit.*

10. The precise meaning of "eunuch horn with seven valves" has not been ascertained. But, apart from its other possible meanings, Okigbo may be using "eunuch" here by analogy to the adjectival use of "virgin" to suggest a horn that has never been put to use before.

11. The phrase is from Okigbo's Introduction to *Labyrinths, op. cit.*

12. Okigbo is here the traditional town-crier calling attention to his message by the beating of the "iron bell," actually the Igbo metal gong, *ogene*. The use of *bell* here instead of *gong* is, however, probably deliberate. It forces the reader to call to mind a modern, urban type of the towncrier, the evangelist who parades the streets, often before daybreak, crying forth his homilies and warnings about the imminent destruction of the utterly sinful world.

13. Cf. W. B. Yeats, "Responsibilities" poems (1914) in his *Collected Poems* (London: Macmillan, 1933, 1950, etc.).

14. See W. B. Yeats, "A Coat," in *Poems of W. B. Yeats,* selected with an Introduction and Notes by A. Norman Jeffares (London: Macmillan, 1963), p. 58.

15. See Shelley's "Ode to the West Wind," in *The Poems of Percy Bysshe Shelley* (London: Collins, 1966), p. 514.

16. These include "Lament of the Masks," *op. cit.,* and *Dance of the Painted Maidens, In Verse and Voice: A Festival of Commonwealth Poetry,* ed. Douglas Cleverdon (London: Poetry Book Society, 1965).

17. Chukwuma Azuonye, "The Secret of the Watermaid," *op. cit.*

18. See Chukwuma Azuonye, "The Secret of the Watermaid," *op. cit.*

19. *Ibid.*

20. In an obituary on Christopher Okigbo published in *Black Orpheus,* shortly after the end of the civil war, the impression is given that Okigbo wasted

his life in pursuit of narrow sectional or ethnic interests. The same argument runs through Ali Mazrui's unfortunately ill-informed so-called novel of ideas, *The Trial of Christopher Okigbo* (London: Heinemann, 1971). Anyone who met Okigbo in his lifetime would recollect that he was one of the most de-tribalized Nigerians, the last person to sacrifice his life on the altar of sectionalism or ethnicism. Okigbo's self-sacrifice can be understood better if it is seen from the point of view of ideological commitment or of the kind of romantic fascination for new experiences which, in other countries, has led many sensitive young artists like him to the same kind of adventure.

21. The "miracle caged" here may refer specifically to the leader of the revolution, Major Chukwuma Nzeogwu.

22. There are close echoes in these lines of the mythic pattern described by John Speirs in his "A Survey of Medieval Verse," in Boris Ford, ed., *The Age of Chaucer* (London: Pelican Books), p. 39: "The young god slays and supplants the old; yet he *is* the old renewed, become young again". In the original ritual—for *a myth is the story of a ritual, the story the ritual enacts*—the old divine king and the young king who supplanted him evidently impersonated one and the same god. "The implications of this mythic pattern become clearer when, in "Thunder Can Break" Okigbo perceives certain genotypal relationships between the new military regime and the ousted civilian regime in their predilection to scramble for the national cake.

23. See also Ime Ikiddeh, "Iron, Thunder and Elephants: A Study of Okigbo's *Path of Thunder*," in *New Horn* I, ii (1974), p. 46, and Sunday Anozie, *Christopher Okigbo: Creative Rhetoric* (London: Evans Brothers, 1972), for earlier contributions to the discussion of the text.

Romanus N. Egudu (essay date 2003)

SOURCE: Egudu, Romanus N. "G. M. Hopkins's 'The Wreck of the Deutschland' and Christopher Okigbo's 'Lament of the Silent Sisters': A Comparative Study." *Comparative Literature Studies* 40, no. 1 (2003): 26-36.

[*In the following essay, Egudu compares Okigbo's "Lament of the Silent Sisters" to Gerard Manley Hopkins's "The Wreck of the Deutschland."*]

It should be expected that African writers who have inherited the English language as a colonial legacy, and who are therefore using this language as their creative medium, will manifest in their work some evidence of their contact not only with the language but also with some English writers. For example, the work of some African novelists reflects the influence of some English and European novels; the drama of some African playwrights points to some links with English and even Greek dramatic tradition; and similarly some African poets have reflected in their work the influence of certain English and European poets, as well as such literary movements as romanticism, symbolism, and surrealism. And all this is without prejudice to the natural and essential influence which African traditional oral literature has on these same African writers.

But the specific nature of the foreign influences and the degree of their impact vary greatly from writer to writer in accordance with their imaginative and creative capabilities. In other words, what should be of interest to the critic of African literature in this regard is, perhaps, not simply the mere fact of the English/European influence, but more importantly the use the African writer has made of that influence, that is, without compromising his/her creative originality and emotional as well as cultural identity. And Nigerian Christopher Okigbo's contact with Gerard Manley Hopkins appears to be a fruitful case for this kind of investigation.

Christopher Okigbo (d. 1967), a renowned poet, had, with reference to his poem **"Lament of the Silent Sisters,"** said that "the **'Silent Sisters'** are [. . .] sometimes like the drowning Franciscan nuns of Hopkins's 'The Wreck of the Deutschland'."[1] On the surface this statement implies that there are significant points of convergence between Okigbo's poem and Hopkins's, and that possibly Okigbo imitated Hopkins in some ways, since he was almost a century younger than Hopkins.

On the issue of literary influence, Hopkins himself had written to Robert Bridges, saying, "I must read something of Greek and Latin letters and lately I sent you a sonnet, on the Heraclitean Fire, in which a great deal of early Greek philosophical thought was distilled; but the liquor of the distillation did not taste very Greek, did it? The effect of studying masterpieces is to make me admire and do otherwise. So it must be on every original artist to some degree, on me to a marked degree."[2] Against the backdrop of this statement, it may be worthwhile to see the nature and degree of the effect on Okigbo of his reading of Hopkins's poem, or in other words, to investigate the areas and extent of convergence and/or divergence between the two works under study.

In the first instance, there is the event of a shipwreck in both poems. It is literal and historical (though it later becomes metaphorical and anagogical) in Hopkins's poem, for it is dedicated "To the happy memory of five Franciscan nuns, exiles by the Falck Laws, drowned between midnight and morning of Dec. 7th, 1875."[3] And in the poem itself we are informed that

> On Saturday sailed from Bremen,
> American-outward-bound,
> Take settler and seamen, tell men and with women,
> Two hundred souls in the round—
>
> (stanza 12).

We next learn that "Into the snows she sweeps, / Hurling the haven behind, / The Deutschland, on Sunday," a day on which the "air is unkind," the "sea flint-flake" and "black-backed," and the "wind" sits "Eastnortheast in cursed quarter," with "Wiry white-fiery and whirlwind-swivelled snow" spinning and sending the ship to the "widow-making unchilding unfathering deeps" (stanza 13).

The depiction of the ship's tragic journey continues with the same historical factuality and emotional intensity in subsequent stanzas. After "she struck—not a reef or rock / But the combs of a smother of sand" and "night drew her / Dead to the Kentish Knock," and after "she beat the bank down with her bows and the ride of her keel; / The breakers rolled on her beam with ruinous shock." At that point, nothing could save her, for "the whorl and wheel / Idle for ever" in vain in their bid to "waft her or wind her with" the obvious tools, "canvass and compass" (stanza 14). As for the crew and the passengers, "the deck / [Crushed them] or water [drowned them] or rolled / With the sea-romp over the wreck" (stanza 17).

Commenting on the syntax of these preceding lines from stanza 17, W. A. M. Peters says, "It might sound strange that the deck 'crushed' the victims of the waves as if it were falling on top of them with its 'crushing' weight and not the other way about. To Hopkins the deck displayed an activity and actively took part in the ruin of the crew and the passengers as much as the storm-winds and the waves and the falling snow."[4] Peters seems to have adopted a too narrow interpretation of the word "crush." The word implies the coming in contact with force of two entities, one stronger or harder than the other. Irrespective of which one of them is under or above, it is the stronger or harder one that crushes the other. If, for example, the victims had fallen on a heap of sand or a padded spot, they would not have been crushed; for neither sand nor pad could crush them. Furthermore, since it is an aspect of the nature or essence of the hard "deck" to destroy a weaker substance, it seems that Hopkins has used that particular syntactic arrangement to bring out and emphasize the "inscape," the innate destructiveness, of the deck.

Turning to Okigbo's poem, we find that the shipwreck is entirely metaphoric; the ship is the Nigerian society of the early 1960's which foundered in a political storm.

The poet himself had said that the poem was inspired "by the Western Nigerian Crisis of 1962" (xii)—a crisis in which there was a conflict between the leaders of a major political party, the Action Group, and which became so serious that the Federal Government declared a state of emergency in the Region and sent troops there to maintain law and order.[5] This situation is portrayed in the poem by a storm image, with "breakers in sea-fever," in which "compass or cross / makes a difference: certainly makes / not an escape ladder," and against which the "silent sisters" (the masses who are the passengers of the ship of society) are forced to look for safety, "Where is there for us an anchorage; / A shank for a sheet, a double arch—?" (Part I). Furthermore, one of the "drowning" "sisters," the "Crier," moans,

> I see many colours in the salt teeth of foam
> Which is no where to face under the half-light
>
> . . . . .
>
> Wild winds cry out against us
> We shall swallow our heart in our stomach
> More wrinkles on the salt face of glass.
>
> (Part I)

She ends with a rhetorical question: "Will the water gather us in her sibylline chamber?" (Part IV). If this "water" as a sorceress, like Sibyl, with a mysterious prophetic power, has any prophecy for the people, it is only that of a civil war, which engulfed the whole country from 1967 to 1970, and in which incidentally the poet, Okigbo, lost his life in combatant action. But "water" is not always impartial in its destruction in Okigbo's poem. As the "silent sisters" lament the social crisis that is eating them up, some members of the same society are exploiting the situation for their selfish benefit. It is these latter who "comb the afternoon the scavengers / For scented shadows above the underrush" (Part I).

It is striking how differently the same expressions are employed and how the same objects are differently, yet effectively, presented in both poems. For example, while the "compass" is seen as necessary in Hopkins's poem for directing the "wafting" of the ship, it is shown in Okigbo's poem to be incapable of becoming "an escape ladder." Also while the "breakers rolled" on the ship's "beam with ruinous shock" in Hopkins's poem, the same "breakers" are assigned no specific role beyond their being part of the "sea fever"—the general stormy chaos—in Okigbo's poem.

Perhaps the word "cross" constitutes the strongest point of verbal convergence and semantic divergence between Hopkins and Okigbo. In stanza 24 Hopkins says, "The cross to her she calls Christ to her." The "tall nun," who does the calling, equates the "cross" with "Christ," who is the savior of the world and is the only gateway to Heaven, according to the Christian belief. That is why, just a line before, she "was calling 'O Christ, Christ, come quickly'" not to prevent the wreck but rather to receive her soul and those of the other victims for safe-keeping in eternity. Thus the "cross" is not here to serve a material rescue purpose, but a metaphysical, spiritual one.

In Okigbo's poem, Hopkins's line is reproduced almost verbatim: "The cross to us we still call to us" (Part I). The use of the direct-speech form here is in consonance with the mode of "narration" employed throughout the poem, in which the victims are the "reporters" of events. This is unlike the situation in Hopkins's poem where the indirect-speech form is pervasively used because it is the poet that does the narrating/reporting. It is also remarkable that Okigbo's line follows closely the syntactic order of Hopkins's, even though the word "Christ" is omitted.

But the omission of "Christ" from Okigbo's line is not simply a matter of stylistic option. It was noted above that to the "silent sisters" the "cross" (like the "compass") is "not an escape ladder." To collocate these two and divest the "cross" of its divine significance as the representation of Christ and the Christian faith, is to reduce it to the material level of a mere tool expected in vain, like the "compass," to guide the victims out of the waves and the storm. In view of this presentation of the "cross" as undependable, the calling of "the cross to us" made by the "silent sisters" can only be understood in ironic terms; they have no faith in what they are calling to themselves. This ironic twist is intensified by the continuous futility signified by the word "still" injected into the borrowed line.

We also find the word "thunder" used in both poems for different reasons and in different senses. In stanza 34 of his poem, Hopkins describes Christ as the "Midnumbered he in three of the thunder-throne," with the implication that "thunder" is a metaphor for the omnipotence of God or the Blessed Trinity (which is the same thing) as the King of the universe. "Thunder" is here a protective and benevolent force, and that is why, through her faith in Christ and her solicitation for his intervention, the "tall nun" firmly embraces it. And she is not disappointed, for James Finn Cotter points out that in stanza 21, "Christ is depicted as sitting in judgment, not as a stern judge but as a lover awaiting the arrival of his beloved and faithful ones."[6]

But it is not so in Okigbo's poem where "thunder" stands for something evil and dreadful—a socio-political upheaval approximating to the magnitude and terror of a war. Early in the poem, the "silent sisters" wonder in utter bewilderment, "How does one say NO in thunder" (Part I). In Part II, we learn of the "cast-iron steps cascading down the valley / all forged into thunder of tanks; / And detonators cannoned into splintered flames." Here "thunder" becomes a metaphor for

war. And nine lines to the end of the final part (V) of the poem, the same rhetorical question, with the same obvious implication of impossibility, is repeated, "And how does one say NO in thunder?" "Thunder" is for Okigbo a force to be resisted and opposed, not desirable or adorable like in Hopkins's poem.

With regard to this word "thunder," Okigbo has another literary ancestor, Herman Melville, besides Hopkins. We are informed by the poet himself that the "motif 'NO in thunder,'" which features in his poem, is taken "from one of Melville's letters to Hawthorne" (xii). The particular letter, which is not specified by Okigbo, is the one Melville wrote on April 16, 1851, in which he said, *inter alia,*

> We think that in no recorded mind has the intense feeling of the visable truth ever entered more deeply than into this man's. By visable truth, we mean the apprehension of the absolute condition of present things as they strike the eye of the man who fears them not, though they do their worst to him. [. . .] There is the grand truth about Nathaniel Hawthorne. He says No! in thunder; but the Devil himself cannot make him say yes.[7]

Melville wrote this letter after reading the copy of Hawthorne's *The House of the Seven Gables,*[8] which the author had earlier given him. The novel is a virulent attack on the hypocritical and oppressive Puritan aristocratic regime in New England in those days. It was a regime in which, according to the novel (3), "clergymen, judges, statesmen—the wisest, calmest, holiest persons of their day—stood in the inner circle round about the gallows, loudest to applaud the work of blood, latest to confess themselves miserably deceived." A member of this "idle aristocracy," Colonel Pyncheon, "had joined in the general cry, to purge the land from witchcraft," but "there was an invidious acrimony in the zeal with which he had sought the condemnation of Matthew Maule," who was old and belonged to the lower class in the society. This poor old man, when he was about to be executed, "with the halter about his neck," pointed his finger at Colonel Pyncheon and cursed him, saying, "God will give him blood to drink." And this curse has been transmitted from generation to generation in the Pyncheon family, as one of them, Hepzibah, has occasion to confess (182), "Alas, Cousin Jaffrey, this hard and grasping spirit has run in our blood these two hundred years. You are but doing over again, in another shape, what your ancestor before you did, and sending down to our posterity the curse inherited from him!" Hawthorne's bold and acrid criticism of this evil hegemony, and Maule's courageous cursing of the "Puritan magnate," which is his final fight against the oppressive system, demonstrate that they have said "No in thunder" in their different ways.

The frightful "absolute condition of present things" which "do their worst" to people, as mentioned by Melville and as experienced and opposed by Hawthorne and his character, Maule, is echoed by the crushing situation in which Okigbo's "silent sisters" find themselves. But their response to their predicament is contrary to that of Hawthorne and Maule, for while the latter are courageous enough to refuse to passively yield to oppressive forces, the former succumb with trepidation to them. Thus Okigbo has lifted the expression "No in thunder" wholly from Melville's letter, where it is used in a positive light, and planted it in his poem where the effect is negative.

The idea of delight in tragedy, which we find in Okigbo's poem, appears to have been borrowed from Hopkins. In stanza 18, Hopkins wonders how in the face of the tragedy of the nuns there could be an impulse of joy within him: "Never-eldering revel and river of youth, / What can it be, this glee? the good you have there of your own?" It has been observed, with reference to these lines, that "the poet rejoices in the fortitude and faith of the 'tall nun,' her ability to read 'the unshapeable shock night.'"[9] But it is more than mere "rejoicing" on the part of the poet, for he is himself surprised that his "heart" (the addressee in that stanza), which is the "mother of being in me" and which has been "touched in your bower of bone" by the tragedy, should generate in him "revel" or "glee" instead of "tears." In other words, Hopkins (or his heart) has intuitively captured the ultimate meaning of the "tall nun's" suffering, which is its being a veritable avenue to the eternal bliss awaiting her.

This "glee" is at once echoed and negated in Okigbo's poem. In Part I, the "silent sisters" are stunned by "this jubilee-dance above the carrion," which in Part II becomes "this jubilee-dance of fireflies." The similarity between the word "glee" in Hopkins's poem and the word "jubilee" in Okigbo's at the phonological and semantic levels is quite clear, but the character of the people rejoicing and their reason for doing so in Okigbo's poem are very different from what they are in that of Hopkins. Earlier on we saw "scavengers" chasing "shadows" as their ship of nation is sinking. It is the same "scavengers" who are engaged in the "jubilee-dance" over the "carrion" (corpse) of their country. They are the politicians who, like "fireflies," deceive the masses with the false light of their dubious lives.

Furthermore, Okigbo's depiction of some natural phenomena comes close to that of Hopkins but again strikes into a different path. For example, while Hopkins describes the waves as "the sea-romp over the wreck" (stanza 17), Okigbo depicts them as "wrinkles on the salt face of glass" (Part IV). Also "seas" are "endragoned" in Hopkins's poem (stanza 27), but "the salt water" is inhabited by "inconstant dolphins" in that of Okigbo (Part IV). And the "foam" of the sea, which is disastrous in both poems, is presented as "the cobbled foam-fleece" by Hopkins (stanza 16), but by Okigbo as toothed—"the salt teeth of foam" (Part IV). Finally in this regard, the "wind," which is the agent of the wreck

in the two poems, is seen by Hopkins as "sitting [. . .] in cursed quarter" (stanza 13), but by Okigbo as "wild" (Part IV). And though each poet's imagery in all these cases is different from that of the other, both poets have effectively portrayed what a critic describes, with reference to Hopkins's poem, as the "forces of chaos present in the storm," the "monstrous nature of the storm," and the "malignancy of the water."[10]

Thus far, what has been said about Hopkins with regard to his attitude to his literary ancestry is very much applicable to Okigbo: "Hopkins leaned toward Milton, Keats, the Bible, Whitman. He took what he wanted from them and wrote in his own style."[11] The shadow of "The Wreck of the Deutschland" is noticeable almost everywhere in **"Lament of the Silent Sisters,"** but in substance and style Okigbo's poem is nothing other than itself—a purely different creation. This is as it should be with a poet such as Okigbo, with his high-level originality and artistry; for according to one critic, "every good poet can be like another only in accidentals; each poet is essentially his own species [. . .] and any likeness with others cannot be but superficial."[12] Incidentally, this observation has been made about Hopkins in relation to those poets considered to be his mentors.

As noted above, Okigbo did say that his "silent sisters" are "sometimes like the drowning Franciscan nuns" of Hopkins's poem. But beyond the bare fact of their being in a dreadful situation, there appears to be no essential likeness between the two groups of women. And this divergence is remarkably glaring in their responses to the catastrophe they face. In Hopkins's poem, in the thick of the crisis, the "tall nun," representative of the other nuns and victims, rose superior to the situation and took command over the storm and the others' wailing, "a lioness arose breasting the babble, / A prophetess towered in the tumult, a virginal tongue told" (stanza 17). A combination of bravery, vision, purity, and physical height enabled the nun to rise like a "tower" or belfry, from where her "virginal tongue told" (reported) the event and, like a bell, tolled,[13] signalling not doom but faith and salvation; for, as we learn in stanza 19, "she that weather sees one thing [. . .] / Has one fetch in her: she rears herself to divine / Ears." And hers was the voice that "rode over the storm's brawling" both literally and, especially, metaphorically; for her faith in Christ, to whom she repeatedly called, as earlier noted, quite overpowered the storm by saving the victims' souls.

Furthermore, we learn in stanza 29 that hers "was a heart right," and hers the "single eye" that "read the unshapeable shock night." Her unshaken and unshakeable faith had enabled her to correctly interpret the suffering she and the others were going through. She therefore understood that "the stress felt" does not "spring" out of God's "bliss" and that "the stroke dealt" does not "swing" from "heaven," but that this stress or stroke has a healing and saving function; "guilt is hushed" and "hearts are flushed" by it (stanza 6). The nun knew that the "why" of their suffering is salvation, and that is why she "christens her wild-worst / Best" (stanza 24), thus indicating her whole-hearted acceptance of the suffering. And this is in accord with the belief that the "merit" in true Christian suffering "is not in not feeling pain but in accepting it."[14]

Hopkins firmly believes and hopes that because of the "tall nun's" strong faith and steadfastness, God would save her and all the other victims of the wreck, so that ultimately the "shipwrack" would become a "harvest," and the "tempest" the conveyor of the "grain" for Him (stanza 31). Thus in the end the drowning of the nuns is not a tragedy in the ordinary sense of the word, but God's "glory of this nun" with all the others in the "heaven-haven" of eternity. It is therefore no wonder that the response of the "tall nun" to the shipwreck with the agony involved has been that of relentless hope in God. Indeed suffering as an indispensable means of salvation is a central theme not only in "The Wreck of the Deutschland" but also in Hopkins's entire poetry, as has been demonstrated in detail elsewhere.[15]

The case of Okigbo's "sisters" is very different; their response to their problem is most antithetical to that of the nuns, being utterly one of negativity, futility, and disillusion. The "sisters" see themselves in a negative light; they are like the "immense golden eggs empty of albumen" which, according to them, "sink into our balcony" (Part I). In their own words again, they are "DUMB-BELLS outside the gates / In hollow seascapes without memory" (Part III). Theirs is constant stifled wailing, with no positive action or thought: "We carry in our worlds that flourish / Our worlds that have failed" (Part III). And instead of plucking up heart in the face of their crisis, they decide to lose it: "We shall swallow our heart in our stomach" (a literal translation of the vernacular (Igbo) expression of inertia and despair) (Part IV).

This despair of theirs is compounded by their ironic thought of "crying" to heaven after expressing a total lack of faith in the "cross," which shows how mentally confused they are: "So, one dips one's tongue in ocean, and begins / To cry to the mushroom of the sky" (Part II). And they sum up their "dumbness," "silences," and whimpering into a "swan song": "This is our swan song / This is our senses' stillness," and it is also "the sigh of our spirits" (Part III). The "sisters," like the swan, are singing their death-song, for the sea-water will "gather" (swallow) them and everything around, excepting the "crew"—the leadership—who are the wreckers of the nation. In their condition of hopelessness, these "sisters" realistically represent those masses who were impoverished and starving while the politicians and other corruptly rich members of the same society were wallowing in false wealth and health: there was truly a failed world within a flourishing one. Thus

the response of these "sisters" to their social wreck is totally contrary to that of Hopkins's nuns.

In his essay on Philip Massinger, T. S. Eliot says, among other things, that "mature poets steal" as against "imitating"; they make what they take "into something better, or at least something different"; they "weld" what they steal "into a whole of feeling which is unique, utterly different from that from which it was torn"; and they usually borrow from "authors remote in time, or alien in language, or diverse in interest."[16] Applying these parameters to Okigbo, one can rightly say that he has effectively "stolen" something from Hopkins, and that the way he has used his "theft" demonstrates his artistic maturity, uniqueness, and excellence. It can also be rightly said that whatever of Hopkins is found in Okigbo has been changed "into something rich and strange" (to borrow from Shakespeare).

This transformation has resulted from Okigbo's special imaginative ability to create a totally different aesthetic environment in his work for the images, ideas, and expressions he has borrowed from Hopkins—an ability he has also demonstrated in respect of his borrowings from Ezra Pound.[17] Thus Okigbo has, as it were, used Hopkins to demonstrate the validity of Hopkins's poetic principle; he has "admired" Hopkins, and the result is that he has done "otherwise."

Notes

1. Christopher Okigbo, *Labyrinths, with Path of Thunder* (London: Heinemann, 1971) xii. Subsequent references are to this edition and are indicated in the body of the essay.

2. Claude Colleer Abbott, ed., *The Letters of Gerard Manley Hopkins to Robert Bridges* (London: Oxford UP, 1955) 291.

3. W. H. Gardner and N. H. Mackenzie, eds., *The Poems of Gerard Manley Hopkins,* 4th edition, revised and enlarged (London: Oxford UP, 1970) 51. All the lines/stanzas of "The Wreck of the Deutschland" quoted in this essay are from this edition.

4. W. A. M. Peters, S.J., *Gerard Manley Hopkins: A Critical Essay towards the Understanding of his Poetry* (London: Oxford UP, 1948) 12.

5. See Michael Crowder, *The Story of Nigeria* (London: Faber, 1966) 317-318.

6. James Finn Cotter, "Orion Behind the Lattices: Stanza 21 of 'The Wreck of the Deutschland,'"*The Hopkins Quarterly* 26.1-2 (1999): 24.

7. See Harrison Hayford and Hershel Parker, eds., *Moby-Dick: An Authoritative Text, Reviews and Letters by Melville, Analogues and Sources, and Criticism* (New York: W. W. Norton, 1967) 555.

8. (New York: Bantam Books, 1981). The novel was first published in 1851.

9. Gardner and Mackenzie, 260.

10. Peter Milward, S.J., "Biblical Imagery of Water in 'The Wreck of the Deutschland,'"*The Hopkins Quarterly* 1.3 (1974): 115-116.

11. Arthur MacGillivray, S.J., "Hopkins and Creative Writing," *Immortal Diamond: Studies in Gerard Manley Hopkins,* ed. Norman Weyand, S.J. (New York: Oxtagon, 1969) 58.

12. Peters, xvii.

13. See Peters, 58 for a discussion of the ambiguity of "told" in this context.

14. See Elizabeth Isichei, *Entirely for God: The Life of Michael Iwene Tansi* (London: Macmillan, 1980) 57. The statement is attributed to one Brother Michael Okoye.

15. R. N. Egudu, "Gerard Manley Hopkins and the Christian Apostleship," *The Hopkins Quarterly* 3.1 (1976): 3-18.

16. T. S. Eliot, *Selected Essays* (New York: Harcourt, Brace & World, 1964) 182.

17. Okigbo has borrowed Pound's line "as the mortar is not yet dry" (Canto VIII) from a building situation and planted it in a creative-writing one in his poem, "Siren Limits" (*Labyrinths* 25), where it assumes a different meaning and generates a contrary emotion. See R. N. Egudu, "Ezra Pound in African Poetry: Christopher Okigbo," *Comparative Literature Studies* 8.2 (1971): 143-154.

FURTHER READING

Criticism

Cooke, Michael G. "Christopher Okigbo and Robert Hayden: From Mould to Stars." *World Literature Written in English* 30, no. 2 (autumn 1990): 131-44.

Explores the similarity in imagery, outlook, themes, and techniques in the poetry of Okigbo and Robert Hayden.

Echeruo, Michael J. C. "Christopher Okigbo, *Poetry* Magazine, and the 'Lament of the Silent Sisters.'" *Research in African Literatures* 35, no. 3 (fall 2004): 8-19.

Discusses the revision history of "Lament of the Silent Sisters."

Knipp, Thomas R. "Okigbo and *Labyrinths*: The Death of a Poet and the Life of a Poem." *Research in African Literatures* 26, no. 4 (winter 1995): 197-205.

Reviews five selected studies of Okigbo's *Labyrinths*, then offers his own reading of the work.

Okafor, Dubem. *The Dance of Death: Nigerian History and Christopher Okigbo's Poetry,* Trenton, N.J.: Africa World Press, Inc., 1998, 297 p.

Study of Okigbo that follows the "man and his works" school of critical enquiry.

Okunoye, Oyeniyi. "Captives of Empire: Early Ibadan Poets and Poetry." *Journal of Commonwealth Literature* 34, no. 2 (1999): 105-16.

Focuses on the development of an "influential Ibadan literary tradition," facilitated by the impact of such writers as Okigbo, J. P. Clark, and Wole Soyinka.

Wieland, James. "Fire from Heaven: Myth and the Poetry of Christopher Okigbo and Nissim Ezekiel." In *The Ensphering Mind: History, Myth, and Fictions in the Poetry of Allen Curnow, Nissim Ezekiel, A. D. Hope, A. M. Klein, Christopher Okigbo, and Derek Walcott*, pp. 189-218. Washington, D.C.: Three Continents Press, Inc., 1988.

Explores the mythic scope and focus of Okigbo's body of poetry.

How to Use This Index

The main references

> **Calvino, Italo**
> 1923-1985 .... CLC **5, 8, 11, 22, 33, 39,**
> **73; SSC 3, 48**

list all author entries in the following Gale Literary Criticism series:

AAL = *Asian American Literature*
BG = *The Beat Generation: A Gale Critical Companion*
BLC = *Black Literature Criticism*
BLCS = *Black Literature Criticism Supplement*
CLC = *Contemporary Literary Criticism*
CLR = *Children's Literature Review*
CMLC = *Classical and Medieval Literature Criticism*
DC = *Drama Criticism*
HLC = *Hispanic Literature Criticism*
HLCS = *Hispanic Literature Criticism Supplement*
HR = *Harlem Renaissance: A Gale Critical Companion*
LC = *Literature Criticism from 1400 to 1800*
NCLC = *Nineteenth-Century Literature Criticism*
NNAL = *Native North American Literature*
PC = *Poetry Criticism*
SSC = *Short Story Criticism*
TCLC = *Twentieth-Century Literary Criticism*
WLC = *World Literature Criticism, 1500 to the Present*
WLCS = *World Literature Criticism Supplement*

The cross-references

> See also CA 85-88, 116; CANR 23, 61;
> DAM NOV; DLB 196; EW 13; MTCW 1, 2;
> RGSF 2; RGWL 2; SFW 4; SSFS 12

list all author entries in the following Gale biographical and literary sources:

AAYA = *Authors & Artists for Young Adults*
AFAW = *African American Writers*
AFW = *African Writers*
AITN = *Authors in the News*
AMW = *American Writers*
AMWR = *American Writers Retrospective Supplement*
AMWS = *American Writers Supplement*
ANW = *American Nature Writers*
AW = *Ancient Writers*
BEST = *Bestsellers*
BPFB = *Beacham's Encyclopedia of Popular Fiction: Biography and Resources*
BRW = *British Writers*
BRWS = *British Writers Supplement*
BW = *Black Writers*
BYA = *Beacham's Guide to Literature for Young Adults*
CA = *Contemporary Authors*
CAAS = *Contemporary Authors Autobiography Series*
CABS = *Contemporary Authors Bibliographical Series*
CAD = *Contemporary American Dramatists*
CANR = *Contemporary Authors New Revision Series*
CAP = *Contemporary Authors Permanent Series*
CBD = *Contemporary British Dramatists*
CCA = *Contemporary Canadian Authors*
CD = *Contemporary Dramatists*
CDALB = *Concise Dictionary of American Literary Biography*
CDALBS = *Concise Dictionary of American Literary Biography Supplement*
CDBLB = *Concise Dictionary of British Literary Biography*

CMW = *St. James Guide to Crime & Mystery Writers*
CN = *Contemporary Novelists*
CP = *Contemporary Poets*
CPW = *Contemporary Popular Writers*
CSW = *Contemporary Southern Writers*
CWD = *Contemporary Women Dramatists*
CWP = *Contemporary Women Poets*
CWRI = *St. James Guide to Children's Writers*
CWW = *Contemporary World Writers*
DA = *DISCovering Authors*
DA3 = *DISCovering Authors 3.0*
DAB = *DISCovering Authors: British Edition*
DAC = *DISCovering Authors: Canadian Edition*
DAM = *DISCovering Authors: Modules*
   DRAM: *Dramatists Module;* ***MST:*** *Most-studied Authors Module;*
   MULT: *Multicultural Authors Module;* ***NOV:*** *Novelists Module;*
   POET: *Poets Module;* ***POP:*** *Popular Fiction and Genre Authors Module*
DFS = *Drama for Students*
DLB = *Dictionary of Literary Biography*
DLBD = *Dictionary of Literary Biography Documentary Series*
DLBY = *Dictionary of Literary Biography Yearbook*
DNFS = *Literature of Developing Nations for Students*
EFS = *Epics for Students*
EXPN = *Exploring Novels*
EXPP = *Exploring Poetry*
EXPS = *Exploring Short Stories*
EW = *European Writers*
FANT = *St. James Guide to Fantasy Writers*
FW = *Feminist Writers*
GFL = *Guide to French Literature,* Beginnings to 1789, 1798 to the Present
GLL = *Gay and Lesbian Literature*
HGG = *St. James Guide to Horror, Ghost & Gothic Writers*
HW = *Hispanic Writers*
IDFW = *International Dictionary of Films and Filmmakers: Writers and Production Artists*
IDTP = *International Dictionary of Theatre: Playwrights*
LAIT = *Literature and Its Times*
LAW = *Latin American Writers*
JRDA = *Junior DISCovering Authors*
MAICYA = *Major Authors and Illustrators for Children and Young Adults*
MAICYAS = *Major Authors and Illustrators for Children and Young Adults Supplement*
MAWW = *Modern American Women Writers*
MJW = *Modern Japanese Writers*
MTCW = *Major 20th-Century Writers*
NCFS = *Nonfiction Classics for Students*
NFS = *Novels for Students*
PAB = *Poets: American and British*
PFS = *Poetry for Students*
RGAL = *Reference Guide to American Literature*
RGEL = *Reference Guide to English Literature*
RGSF = *Reference Guide to Short Fiction*
RGWL = *Reference Guide to World Literature*
RHW = *Twentieth-Century Romance and Historical Writers*
SAAS = *Something about the Author Autobiography Series*
SATA = *Something about the Author*
SFW = *St. James Guide to Science Fiction Writers*
SSFS = *Short Stories for Students*
TCWW = *Twentieth-Century Western Writers*
WLIT = *World Literature and Its Times*
WP = *World Poets*
YABC = *Yesterday's Authors of Books for Children*
YAW = *St. James Guide to Young Adult Writers*

Literary Criticism Series
Cumulative Author Index

Benary-Isbert, Margot 1889-1979 .... **CLC 12**
See also CA 5-8R; 89-92; CANR 4, 72;
CLR 12; MAICYA 1, 2; SATA 2; SATA-
Obit 21

Benavente (y Martinez), Jacinto
1866-1954 .... **DC 26; HLCS 1; TCLC 3**
See also CA 106; 131; CANR 81; DAM
DRAM, MULT; EWL 3; GLL 2; HW 1,
2; MTCW 1, 2

Benchley, Peter (Bradford) 1940- .. **CLC 4, 8**
See also AAYA 14; AITN 2; BPFB 1; CA
17-20R; CANR 12, 35, 66, 115; CPW;
DAM NOV, POP; HGG; MTCW 1, 2;
SATA 3, 89

Benchley, Robert (Charles)
1889-1945 .... **TCLC 1, 55**
See also CA 105; 153; DLB 11; RGAL 4

Benda, Julien 1867-1956 .... **TCLC 60**
See also CA 120; 154; GFL 1789 to the
Present

Benedict, Ruth (Fulton)
1887-1948 .... **TCLC 60**
See also CA 158; DLB 246

Benedikt, Michael 1935- .... **CLC 4, 14**
See also CA 13-16R; CANR 7; CP 7; DLB
5

Benet, Juan 1927-1993 .... **CLC 28**
See also CA 143; EWL 3

Benet, Stephen Vincent 1898-1943 ..... **PC 64;**
SSC 10, 86; TCLC 7
See also AMWS 11; CA 104; 152; DA3;
DAM POET; DLB 4, 48, 102, 249, 284;
DLBY 1997; EWL 3; HGG; MTCW 1;
RGAL 4; RGSF 2; SUFW; WP; YABC 1

Benet, William Rose 1886-1950 ..... **TCLC 28**
See also CA 118; 152; DAM POET; DLB
45; RGAL 4

Benford, Gregory (Albert) 1941- ..... **CLC 52**
See also BPFB 1; CA 69-72, 175; CAAE
175; CAAS 27; CANR 12, 24, 49, 95,
134; CSW; DLBY 1982; SCFW 2; SFW
4

Bengtsson, Frans (Gunnar)
1894-1954 .... **TCLC 48**
See also CA 170; EWL 3

Benjamin, David
See Slavitt, David R(ytman)

Benjamin, Lois
See Gould, Lois

Benjamin, Walter 1892-1940 .... **TCLC 39**
See also CA 164; DLB 242; EW 11; EWL
3

Ben Jelloun, Tahar 1944-
See Jelloun, Tahar ben
See also CA 135; CWW 2; EWL 3; RGWL
3; WLIT 2

Benn, Gottfried 1886-1956 .. **PC 35; TCLC 3**
See also CA 106; 153; DLB 56; EWL 3;
RGWL 2, 3

Bennett, Alan 1934- .... **CLC 45, 77**
See also BRWS 8; CA 103; CANR 35, 55,
106; CBD; CD 5; DAB; DAM MST;
MTCW 1, 2

Bennett, (Enoch) Arnold
1867-1931 .... **TCLC 5, 20**
See also BRW 6; CA 106; 155; CDBLB
1890-1914; DLB 10, 34, 98, 135; EWL 3;
MTCW 2

Bennett, Elizabeth
See Mitchell, Margaret (Munnerlyn)

Bennett, George Harold 1930-
See Bennett, Hal
See also BW 1; CA 97-100; CANR 87

Bennett, Gwendolyn B. 1902-1981 .... **HR 2**
See also BW 1; CA 125; DLB 51; WP

Bennett, Hal .... **CLC 5**
See Bennett, George Harold
See also DLB 33

Bennett, Jay 1912- .... **CLC 35**
See also AAYA 10; CA 69-72; CANR 11,
42, 79; JRDA; SAAS 4; SATA 41, 87;
SATA-Brief 27; WYA; YAW

Bennett, Louise (Simone) 1919- .... **BLC 1;**
CLC 28
See also BW 2, 3; CA 151; CDWLB 3; CP
7; DAM MULT; DLB 117; EWL 3

Benson, A. C. 1862-1925 .... **TCLC 123**
See also DLB 98

Benson, E(dward) F(rederic)
1867-1940 .... **TCLC 27**
See also CA 114; 157; DLB 135, 153;
HGG; SUFW 1

Benson, Jackson J. 1930- .... **CLC 34**
See also CA 25-28R; DLB 111

Benson, Sally 1900-1972 .... **CLC 17**
See also CA 19-20; 37-40R; CAP 1; SATA
1, 35; SATA-Obit 27

Benson, Stella 1892-1933 .... **TCLC 17**
See also CA 117; 154, 155; DLB 36, 162;
FANT; TEA

Bentham, Jeremy 1748-1832 .... **NCLC 38**
See also DLB 107, 158, 252

Bentley, E(dmund) C(lerihew)
1875-1956 .... **TCLC 12**
See also CA 108; DLB 70; MSW

Bentley, Eric (Russell) 1916- .... **CLC 24**
See also CA 5-8R; CAD; CANR 6, 67;
CBD; CD 5; INT CANR-6

ben Uzair, Salem
See Horne, Richard Henry Hengist

Beranger, Pierre Jean de
1780-1857 .... **NCLC 34**

Berdyaev, Nicolas
See Berdyaev, Nikolai (Aleksandrovich)

Berdyaev, Nikolai (Aleksandrovich)
1874-1948 .... **TCLC 67**
See also CA 120; 157

Berdyayev, Nikolai (Aleksandrovich)
See Berdyaev, Nikolai (Aleksandrovich)

Berendt, John (Lawrence) 1939- ...... **CLC 86**
See also CA 146; CANR 75, 93; DA3;
MTCW 1

Beresford, J(ohn) D(avys)
1873-1947 .... **TCLC 81**
See also CA 112; 155; DLB 162, 178, 197;
SFW 4; SUFW 1

Bergelson, David (Rafailovich)
1884-1952 .... **TCLC 81**
See Bergelson, Dovid
See also CA 220

Bergelson, Dovid
See Bergelson, David (Rafailovich)
See also EWL 3

Berger, Colonel
See Malraux, (Georges-)Andre

Berger, John (Peter) 1926- .... **CLC 2, 19**
See also BRWS 4; CA 81-84; CANR 51,
78, 117; CN 7; DLB 14, 207

Berger, Melvin H. 1927- .... **CLC 12**
See also CA 5-8R; CANR 4; CLR 32;
SAAS 2; SATA 5, 88; SATA-Essay 124

Berger, Thomas (Louis) 1924- .. **CLC 3, 5, 8,**
11, 18, 38
See also BPFB 1; CA 1-4R; CANR 5, 28,
51, 128; CN 7; DAM NOV; DLB 2;
DLBY 1980; EWL 3; FANT; INT CANR-
28; MTCW 1, 2; RHW; TCWW 2

Bergman, (Ernst) Ingmar 1918- ...... **CLC 16,**
72, 219
See also CA 81-84; CANR 33, 70; CWW
2; DLB 257; MTCW 2

Bergson, Henri(-Louis) 1859-1941 . **TCLC 32**
See also CA 164; EW 8; EWL 3; GFL 1789
to the Present

Bergstein, Eleanor 1938- .... **CLC 4**
See also CA 53-56; CANR 5

Berkeley, George 1685-1753 .... **LC 65**
See also DLB 31, 101, 252

Berkoff, Steven 1937- .... **CLC 56**
See also CA 104; CANR 72; CBD; CD 5

Berlin, Isaiah 1909-1997 .... **TCLC 105**
See also CA 85-88; 162

Bermant, Chaim (Icyk) 1929-1998 ... **CLC 40**
See also CA 57-60; CANR 6, 31, 57, 105;
CN 7

Bern, Victoria
See Fisher, M(ary) F(rances) K(ennedy)

Bernanos, (Paul Louis) Georges
1888-1948 .... **TCLC 3**
See also CA 104; 130; CANR 94; DLB 72;
EWL 3; GFL 1789 to the Present; RGWL
2, 3

Bernard, April 1956- .... **CLC 59**
See also CA 131

Bernard of Clairvaux 1090-1153 .. **CMLC 71**
See also DLB 208

Berne, Victoria
See Fisher, M(ary) F(rances) K(ennedy)

Bernhard, Thomas 1931-1989 ..... **CLC 3, 32,**
61; DC 14; TCLC 165
See also CA 85-88; 127; CANR 32, 57; CD-
WLB 2; DLB 85, 124; EWL 3; MTCW 1;
RGWL 2, 3

Bernhardt, Sarah (Henriette Rosine)
1844-1923 .... **TCLC 75**
See also CA 157

Bernstein, Charles 1950- .... **CLC 142,**
See also CA 129; CAAS 24; CANR 90; CP
7; DLB 169

Bernstein, Ingrid
See Kirsch, Sarah

Beroul fl. c. 1150- .... **CMLC 75**

Berriault, Gina 1926-1999 .... **CLC 54, 109;**
SSC 30
See also CA 116; 129; 185; CANR 66; DLB
130; SSFS 7,11

Berrigan, Daniel 1921- .... **CLC 4**
See also CA 33-36R, 187; CAAE 187;
CAAS 1; CANR 11, 43, 78; CP 7; DLB 5

Berrigan, Edmund Joseph Michael, Jr.
1934-1983
See Berrigan, Ted
See also CA 61-64; 110; CANR 14, 102

Berrigan, Ted .... **CLC 37**
See Berrigan, Edmund Joseph Michael, Jr.
See also DLB 5, 169; WP

Berry, Charles Edward Anderson 1931-
See Berry, Chuck
See also CA 115

Berry, Chuck .... **CLC 17**
See Berry, Charles Edward Anderson

Berry, Jonas
See Ashbery, John (Lawrence)
See also GLL 1

Berry, Wendell (Erdman) 1934- ... **CLC 4, 6,**
8, 27, 46; PC 28
See also AITN 1; AMWS 10; ANW; CA
73-76; CANR 50, 73, 101, 132; CP 7;
CSW; DAM POET; DLB 5, 6, 234, 275;
MTCW 1

Berryman, John 1914-1972 ... **CLC 1, 2, 3, 4,**
6, 8, 10, 13, 25, 62; PC 64
See also AMW; CA 13-16; 33-36R; CABS
2; CANR 35; CAP 1; CDALB 1941-1968;
DAM POET; DLB 48; EWL 3; MTCW 1,
2; PAB; RGAL 4; WP

Bertolucci, Bernardo 1940- ...... **CLC 16, 157**
See also CA 106; CANR 125

Berton, Pierre (Francis Demarigny)
1920-2004 .... **CLC 104**
See also CA 1-4R; CANR 2, 56; CPW;
DLB 68; SATA 99

Bertrand, Aloysius 1807-1841 .... **NCLC 31**
See Bertrand, Louis oAloysiusc

Bertrand, Louis oAloysiusc
See Bertrand, Aloysius
See also DLB 217

Bertran de Born c. 1140-1215 .... **CMLC 5**

Besant, Annie (Wood) 1847-1933 ..... **TCLC 9**
See also CA 105; 185

Bessie, Alvah 1904-1985 .... **CLC 23**
See also CA 5-8R; 116; CANR 2, 80; DLB 26

Bestuzhev, Aleksandr Aleksandrovich
1797-1837 .... **NCLC 131**
See also DLB 198

Bethlen, T. D.
See Silverberg, Robert

Beti, Mongo .... **BLC 1; CLC 27**
See Biyidi, Alexandre
See also AFW; CANR 79; DAM MULT; EWL 3; WLIT 2

Betjeman, John 1906-1984 ...... **CLC 2, 6, 10, 34, 43**
See also BRW 7; CA 9-12R; 112; CANR 33, 56; CDBLB 1945-1960; DA3; DAB; DAM MST, POET; DLB 20; DLBY 1984; EWL 3; MTCW 1, 2

Bettelheim, Bruno 1903-1990 .... **CLC 79; TCLC 143**
See also CA 81-84; 131; CANR 23, 61; DA3; MTCW 1, 2

Betti, Ugo 1892-1953 .... **TCLC 5**
See also CA 104; 155; EWL 3; RGWL 2, 3

Betts, Doris (Waugh) 1932- ..... **CLC 3, 6, 28; SSC 45**
See also CA 13-16R; CANR 9, 66, 77; CN 7; CSW; DLB 218; DLBY 1982; INT CANR-9; RGAL 4

Bevan, Alistair
See Roberts, Keith (John Kingston)

Bey, Pilaff
See Douglas, (George) Norman

Bialik, Chaim Nachman
1873-1934 .... **TCLC 25**
See also CA 170; EWL 3

Bickerstaff, Isaac
See Swift, Jonathan

Bidart, Frank 1939- .... **CLC 33**
See also CA 140; CANR 106; CP 7

Bienek, Horst 1930- .... **CLC 7, 11**
See also CA 73-76; DLB 75

Bierce, Ambrose (Gwinett)
1842-1914(?) ..... **SSC 9, 72; TCLC 1, 7, 44; WLC**
See also AAYA 55; AMW; BYA 11; CA 104; 139; CANR 78; CDALB 1865-1917; DA; DA3; DAC; DAM MST; DLB 11, 12, 23, 71, 74, 186; EWL 3; EXPS; HGG; LAIT 2; RGAL 4; RGSF 2; SSFS 9; SUFW 1

Biggers, Earl Derr 1884-1933 .... **TCLC 65**
See also CA 108; 153; DLB 306

Billiken, Bud
See Motley, Willard (Francis)

Billings, Josh
See Shaw, Henry Wheeler

Billington, (Lady) Rachel (Mary)
1942- .... **CLC 43**
See also AITN 2; CA 33-36R; CANR 44; CN 7

Binchy, Maeve 1940- .... **CLC 153**
See also BEST 90:1; BPFB 1; CA 127; 134; CANR 50, 96, 134; CN 7; CPW; DA3; DAM POP; INT CA-134; MTCW 1; RHW

Binyon, T(imothy) J(ohn) 1936- .... **CLC 34**
See also CA 111; CANR 28

Bion 335B.C.-245B.C. .... **CMLC 39**

Bioy Casares, Adolfo 1914-1999 ... **CLC 4, 8, 13, 88; HLC 1; SSC 17**
See Casares, Adolfo Bioy; Miranda, Javier; Sacastru, Martin
See also CA 29-32R; 177; CANR 19, 43, 66; CWW 2; DAM MULT; DLB 113; EWL 3; HW 1, 2; LAW; MTCW 1, 2

Birch, Allison .... **CLC 65**

Bird, Cordwainer
See Ellison, Harlan (Jay)

Bird, Robert Montgomery
1806-1854 .... **NCLC 1**
See also DLB 202; RGAL 4

Birkerts, Sven 1951- .... **CLC 116**
See also CA 128; 133, 176; CAAE 176; CAAS 29; INT CA-133

Birney, (Alfred) Earle 1904-1995 .. **CLC 1, 4, 6, 11; PC 52**
See also CA 1-4R; CANR 5, 20; CP 7; DAC; DAM MST, POET; DLB 88; MTCW 1; PFS 8; RGEL 2

Biruni, al 973-1048(?) .... **CMLC 28**

Bishop, Elizabeth 1911-1979 ..... **CLC 1, 4, 9, 13, 15, 32; PC 3, 34; TCLC 121**
See also AMWR 2; AMWS 1; CA 5-8R; 89-92; CABS 2; CANR 26, 61, 108; CDALB 1968-1988; DA; DA3; DAC; DAM MST, POET; DLB 5, 169; EWL 3; GLL 2; MAWW; MTCW 1, 2; PAB; PFS 6, 12; RGAL 4; SATA-Obit 24; TUS; WP

Bishop, John 1935- .... **CLC 10**
See also CA 105

Bishop, John Peale 1892-1944 ..... **TCLC 103**
See also CA 107; 155; DLB 4, 9, 45; RGAL 4

Bissett, Bill 1939- .... **CLC 18; PC 14**
See also CA 69-72; CAAS 19; CANR 15; CCA 1; CP 7; DLB 53; MTCW 1

Bissoondath, Neil (Devindra)
1955- .... **CLC 120**
See also CA 136; CANR 123; CN 7; DAC

Bitov, Andrei (Georgievich) 1937- ... **CLC 57**
See also CA 142; DLB 302

Biyidi, Alexandre 1932-
See Beti, Mongo
See also BW 1, 3; CA 114; 124; CANR 81; DA3; MTCW 1, 2

Bjarme, Brynjolf
See Ibsen, Henrik (Johan)

Bjoernson, Bjoernstjerne (Martinius)
1832-1910 .... **TCLC 7, 37**
See also CA 104

Black, Robert
See Holdstock, Robert P.

Blackburn, Paul 1926-1971 .... **CLC 9, 43**
See also BG 2; CA 81-84; 33-36R; CANR 34; DLB 16; DLBY 1981

Black Elk 1863-1950 .... **NNAL; TCLC 33**
See also CA 144; DAM MULT; MTCW 1; WP

Black Hawk 1767-1838 .... **NNAL**

Black Hobart
See Sanders, (James) Ed(ward)

Blacklin, Malcolm
See Chambers, Aidan

Blackmore, R(ichard) D(oddridge)
1825-1900 .... **TCLC 27**
See also CA 120; DLB 18; RGEL 2

Blackmur, R(ichard) P(almer)
1904-1965 .... **CLC 2, 24**
See also AMWS 2; CA 11-12; 25-28R; CANR 71; CAP 1; DLB 63; EWL 3

Black Tarantula
See Acker, Kathy

Blackwood, Algernon (Henry)
1869-1951 .... **TCLC 5**
See also CA 105; 150; DLB 153, 156, 178; HGG; SUFW 1

Blackwood, Caroline 1931-1996 .... **CLC 6, 9, 100**
See also BRWS 9; CA 85-88; 151; CANR 32, 61, 65; CN 7; DLB 14, 207; HGG; MTCW 1

Blade, Alexander
See Hamilton, Edmond; Silverberg, Robert

Blaga, Lucian 1895-1961 .... **CLC 75**
See also CA 157; DLB 220; EWL 3

Blair, Eric (Arthur) 1903-1950 .... **TCLC 123**
See Orwell, George
See also CA 104; 132; DA; DA3; DAB; DAC; DAM MST, NOV; MTCW 1, 2; SATA 29

Blair, Hugh 1718-1800 .... **NCLC 75**

Blais, Marie-Claire 1939- .... **CLC 2, 4, 6, 13, 22**
See also CA 21-24R; CAAS 4; CANR 38, 75, 93; CWW 2; DAC; DAM MST; DLB 53; EWL 3; FW; MTCW 1, 2; TWA

Blaise, Clark 1940- .... **CLC 29**
See also AITN 2; CA 53-56; CAAS 3; CANR 5, 66, 106; CN 7; DLB 53; RGSF 2

Blake, Fairley
See De Voto, Bernard (Augustine)

Blake, Nicholas
See Day Lewis, C(ecil)
See also DLB 77; MSW

Blake, Sterling
See Benford, Gregory (Albert)

Blake, William 1757-1827 . **NCLC 13, 37, 57, 127; PC 12, 63; WLC**
See also AAYA 47; BRW 3; BRWR 1; CD-BLB 1789-1832; CLR 52; DA; DA3; DAB; DAC; DAM MST, POET; DLB 93, 163; EXPP; LATS 1:1; LMFS 1; MAI-CYA 1, 2; PAB; PFS 2, 12; SATA 30; TEA; WCH; WLIT 3; WP

Blanchot, Maurice 1907-2003 .... **CLC 135**
See also CA 117; 144; 213; DLB 72, 296; EWL 3

Blasco Ibanez, Vicente 1867-1928 . **TCLC 12**
See also BPFB 1; CA 110; 131; CANR 81; DA3; DAM NOV; EW 8; EWL 3; HW 1, 2; MTCW 1

Blatty, William Peter 1928- .... **CLC 2**
See also CA 5-8R; CANR 9, 124; DAM POP; HGG

Bleeck, Oliver
See Thomas, Ross (Elmore)

Blessing, Lee 1949- .... **CLC 54**
See also CAD; CD 5

Blight, Rose
See Greer, Germaine

Blish, James (Benjamin) 1921-1975 . **CLC 14**
See also BPFB 1; CA 1-4R; 57-60; CANR 3; DLB 8; MTCW 1; SATA 66; SCFW 2; SFW 4

Bliss, Frederick
See Card, Orson Scott

Bliss, Reginald
See Wells, H(erbert) G(eorge)

Blixen, Karen (Christentze Dinesen)
1885-1962
See Dinesen, Isak
See also CA 25-28; CANR 22, 50; CAP 2; DA3; DLB 214; LMFS 1; MTCW 1, 2; SATA 44; SSFS 20

Bloch, Robert (Albert) 1917-1994 .... **CLC 33**
See also AAYA 29; CA 5-8R, 179; 146; CAAE 179; CAAS 20; CANR 5, 78; DA3; DLB 44; HGG; INT CANR-5; MTCW 1; SATA 12; SATA-Obit 82; SFW 4; SUFW 1, 2

Blok, Alexander (Alexandrovich)
1880-1921 .... **PC 21; TCLC 5**
See also CA 104; 183; DLB 295; EW 9; EWL 3; LMFS 2; RGWL 2, 3

Blom, Jan
See Breytenbach, Breyten

Bloom, Harold 1930- .... **CLC 24, 103**
See also CA 13-16R; CANR 39, 75, 92, 133; DLB 67; EWL 3; MTCW 1; RGAL 4

Bloomfield, Aurelius
See Bourne, Randolph S(illiman)

Bloomfield, Robert 1766-1823 ..... **NCLC 145**
See also DLB 93

Blount, Roy (Alton), Jr. 1941- .... **CLC 38**
See also CA 53-56; CANR 10, 28, 61, 125; CSW; INT CANR-28; MTCW 1, 2

Blowsnake, Sam 1875-(?) .... **NNAL**

Bloy, Leon 1846-1917 .... **TCLC 22**
See also CA 121; 183; DLB 123; GFL 1789 to the Present

Blue Cloud, Peter (Aroniawenrate) 1933- .... **NNAL**
See also CA 117; CANR 40; DAM MULT

Bluggage, Oranthy
See Alcott, Louisa May

Blume, Judy (Sussman) 1938- .... **CLC 12, 30**
See also AAYA 3, 26; BYA 1, 8, 12; CA 29-32R; CANR 13, 37, 66, 124; CLR 2, 15, 69; CPW; DA3; DAM NOV, POP; DLB 52; JRDA; MAICYA 1, 2; MAICYAS 1; MTCW 1, 2; SATA 2, 31, 79, 142; WYA; YAW

Blunden, Edmund (Charles) 1896-1974 .... **CLC 2, 56; PC 66**
See also BRW 6; CA 17-18; 45-48; CANR 54; CAP 2; DLB 20, 100, 155; MTCW 1; PAB

Bly, Robert (Elwood) 1926- .... **CLC 1, 2, 5, 10, 15, 38, 128; PC 39**
See also AMWS 4; CA 5-8R; CANR 41, 73, 125; CP 7; DA3; DAM POET; DLB 5; EWL 3; MTCW 1, 2; PFS 6, 17; RGAL 4

Boas, Franz 1858-1942 .... **TCLC 56**
See also CA 115; 181

Bobette
See Simenon, Georges (Jacques Christian)

Boccaccio, Giovanni 1313-1375 ... **CMLC 13, 57; SSC 10**
See also EW 2; RGSF 2; RGWL 2, 3; TWA

Bochco, Steven 1943- .... **CLC 35**
See also AAYA 11; CA 124; 138

Bode, Sigmund
See O'Doherty, Brian

Bodel, Jean 1167(?)-1210 .... **CMLC 28**

Bodenheim, Maxwell 1892-1954 .... **TCLC 44**
See also CA 110; 187; DLB 9, 45; RGAL 4

Bodenheimer, Maxwell
See Bodenheim, Maxwell

Bodker, Cecil 1927-
See Bodker, Cecil

Bodker, Cecil 1927- .... **CLC 21**
See also CA 73-76; CANR 13, 44, 111; CLR 23; MAICYA 1, 2; SATA 14, 133

Boell, Heinrich (Theodor) 1917-1985 ..... **CLC 2, 3, 6, 9, 11, 15, 27, 32, 72; SSC 23; WLC**
See Boll, Heinrich
See also CA 21-24R; 116; CANR 24; DA; DA3; DAB; DAC; DAM MST, NOV; DLB 69; DLBY 1985; MTCW 1, 2; SSFS 20; TWA

Boerne, Alfred
See Doeblin, Alfred

Boethius c. 480-c. 524 .... **CMLC 15**
See also DLB 115; RGWL 2, 3

Boff, Leonardo (Genezio Darci) 1938- .... **CLC 70; HLC 1**
See also CA 150; DAM MULT; HW 2

Bogan, Louise 1897-1970 .... **CLC 4, 39, 46, 93; PC 12**
See also AMWS 3; CA 73-76; 25-28R; CANR 33, 82; DAM POET; DLB 45, 169; EWL 3; MAWW; MTCW 1, 2; PFS 21; RGAL 4

Bogarde, Dirk
See Van Den Bogarde, Derek Jules Gaspard Ulric Niven
See also DLB 14

Bogosian, Eric 1953- .... **CLC 45, 141**
See also CA 138; CAD; CANR 102; CD 5

Bograd, Larry 1953- .... **CLC 35**
See also CA 93-96; CANR 57; SAAS 21; SATA 33, 89; WYA

Boiardo, Matteo Maria 1441-1494 .... **LC 6**

Boileau-Despreaux, Nicolas 1636-1711 . **LC 3**
See also DLB 268; EW 3; GFL Beginnings to 1789; RGWL 2, 3

Boissard, Maurice
See Leautaud, Paul

Bojer, Johan 1872-1959 .... **TCLC 64**
See also CA 189; EWL 3

Bok, Edward W(illiam) 1863-1930 .... **TCLC 101**
See also CA 217; DLB 91; DLBD 16

Boker, George Henry 1823-1890 . **NCLC 125**
See also RGAL 4

Boland, Eavan (Aisling) 1944- .. **CLC 40, 67, 113; PC 58**
See also BRWS 5; CA 143, 207; CAAE 207; CANR 61; CP 7; CWP; DAM POET; DLB 40; FW; MTCW 2; PFS 12

Boll, Heinrich
See Boell, Heinrich (Theodor)
See also BPFB 1; CDWLB 2; EW 13; EWL 3; RGSF 2; RGWL 2, 3

Bolt, Lee
See Faust, Frederick (Schiller)

Bolt, Robert (Oxton) 1924-1995 .... **CLC 14**
See also CA 17-20R; 147; CANR 35, 67; CBD; DAM DRAM; DFS 2; DLB 13, 233; EWL 3; LAIT 1; MTCW 1

Bombal, Maria Luisa 1910-1980 .... **HLCS 1; SSC 37**
See also CA 127; CANR 72; EWL 3; HW 1; LAW; RGSF 2

Bombet, Louis-Alexandre-Cesar
See Stendhal

Bomkauf
See Kaufman, Bob (Garnell)

Bonaventura .... **NCLC 35**
See also DLB 90

Bonaventure, Saint c. 1217-1274 .. **CMLC 79**
See also DLB 115

Bond, Edward 1934- .... **CLC 4, 6, 13, 23**
See also AAYA 50; BRWS 1; CA 25-28R; CANR 38, 67, 106; CBD; CD 5; DAM DRAM; DFS 3, 8; DLB 13; EWL 3; MTCW 1

Bonham, Frank 1914-1989 .... **CLC 12**
See also AAYA 1; BYA 1, 3; CA 9-12R; CANR 4, 36; JRDA; MAICYA 1, 2; SAAS 3; SATA 1, 49; SATA-Obit 62; TCWW 2; YAW

Bonnefoy, Yves 1923- . **CLC 9, 15, 58; PC 58**
See also CA 85-88; CANR 33, 75, 97; CWW 2; DAM MST, POET; DLB 258; EWL 3; GFL 1789 to the Present; MTCW 1, 2

Bonner, Marita .... **HR 2**
See Occomy, Marita (Odette) Bonner

Bonnin, Gertrude 1876-1938 .... **NNAL**
See Zitkala-Sa
See also CA 150; DAM MULT

Bontemps, Arna(ud Wendell) 1902-1973 ..... **BLC 1; CLC 1, 18; HR 2**
See also BW 1; CA 1-4R; 41-44R; CANR 4, 35; CLR 6; CWRI 5; DA3; DAM MULT, NOV, POET; DLB 48, 51; JRDA; MAICYA 1, 2; MTCW 1, 2; SATA 2, 44; SATA-Obit 24; WCH; WP

Boot, William
See Stoppard, Tom

Booth, Martin 1944-2004 .... **CLC 13**
See also CA 93-96, 188; 223; CAAE 188; CAAS 2; CANR 92

Booth, Philip 1925- .... **CLC 23**
See also CA 5-8R; CANR 5, 88; CP 7; DLBY 1982

Booth, Wayne C(layson) 1921- .... **CLC 24**
See also CA 1-4R; CAAS 5; CANR 3, 43, 117; DLB 67

Borchert, Wolfgang 1921-1947 .... **TCLC 5**
See also CA 104; 188; DLB 69, 124; EWL 3

Borel, Petrus 1809-1859 .... **NCLC 41**
See also DLB 119; GFL 1789 to the Present

Borges, Jorge Luis 1899-1986 ... **CLC 1, 2, 3, 4, 6, 8, 9, 10, 13, 19, 44, 48, 83; HLC 1; PC 22, 32; SSC 4, 41; TCLC 109; WLC**
See also AAYA 26; BPFB 1; CA 21-24R; CANR 19, 33, 75, 105, 133; CDWLB 3; DA; DA3; DAB; DAC; DAM MST, MULT; DLB 113, 283; DLBY 1986; DNFS 1, 2; EWL 3; HW 1, 2; LAW; LMFS 2; MSW; MTCW 1, 2; RGSF 2; RGWL 2, 3; SFW 4; SSFS 17; TWA; WLIT 1

Borowski, Tadeusz 1922-1951 .... **SSC 48; TCLC 9**
See also CA 106; 154; CDWLB 4; DLB 215; EWL 3; RGSF 2; RGWL 3; SSFS 13

Borrow, George (Henry) 1803-1881 .... **NCLC 9**
See also DLB 21, 55, 166

Bosch (Gavino), Juan 1909-2001 ..... **HLCS 1**
See also CA 151; 204; DAM MST, MULT; DLB 145; HW 1, 2

Bosman, Herman Charles 1905-1951 .... **TCLC 49**
See Malan, Herman
See also CA 160; DLB 225; RGSF 2

Bosschere, Jean de 1878(?)-1953 ... **TCLC 19**
See also CA 115; 186

Boswell, James 1740-1795 ... **LC 4, 50; WLC**
See also BRW 3; CDBLB 1660-1789; DA; DAB; DAC; DAM MST; DLB 104, 142; TEA; WLIT 3

Bottomley, Gordon 1874-1948 ..... **TCLC 107**
See also CA 120; 192; DLB 10

Bottoms, David 1949- .... **CLC 53**
See also CA 105; CANR 22; CSW; DLB 120; DLBY 1983

Boucicault, Dion 1820-1890 .... **NCLC 41**

Boucolon, Maryse
See Conde, Maryse

Bourdieu, Pierre 1930-2002 .... **CLC 198**
See also CA 130; 204

Bourget, Paul (Charles Joseph) 1852-1935 .... **TCLC 12**
See also CA 107; 196; DLB 123; GFL 1789 to the Present

Bourjaily, Vance (Nye) 1922- .... **CLC 8, 62**
See also CA 1-4R; CAAS 1; CANR 2, 72; CN 7; DLB 2, 143

Bourne, Randolph S(illiman) 1886-1918 .... **TCLC 16**
See also AMW; CA 117; 155; DLB 63

Burroughs, Edgar Rice 1875-1950 . **TCLC 2, 32**
See also AAYA 11; BPFB 1; BYA 4, 9; CA 104; 132; CANR 131; DA3; DAM NOV; DLB 8; FANT; MTCW 1, 2; RGAL 4; SATA 41; SCFW 2; SFW 4; TUS; YAW

Burroughs, William S(eward) 1914-1997 .. **CLC 1, 2, 5, 15, 22, 42, 75, 109; TCLC 121; WLC**
See Lee, William; Lee, Willy
See also AAYA 60; AITN 2; AMWS 3; BG 2; BPFB 1; CA 9-12R; 160; CANR 20, 52, 104; CN 7; CPW; DA; DA3; DAB; DAC; DAM MST, NOV, POP; DLB 2, 8, 16, 152, 237; DLBY 1981, 1997; EWL 3; HGG; LMFS 2; MTCW 1, 2; RGAL 4; SFW 4

Burton, Sir Richard F(rancis) 1821-1890 .... **NCLC 42**
See also DLB 55, 166, 184

Burton, Robert 1577-1640 .... **LC 74**
See also DLB 151; RGEL 2

Buruma, Ian 1951- .... **CLC 163**
See also CA 128; CANR 65

Busch, Frederick 1941- ... **CLC 7, 10, 18, 47, 166**
See also CA 33-36R; CAAS 1; CANR 45, 73, 92; CN 7; DLB 6, 218

Bush, Barney (Furman) 1946- .... **NNAL**
See also CA 145

Bush, Ronald 1946- .... **CLC 34**
See also CA 136

Bustos, F(rancisco)
See Borges, Jorge Luis

Bustos Domecq, H(onorio)
See Bioy Casares, Adolfo; Borges, Jorge Luis

Butler, Octavia E(stelle) 1947- .. **BLCS; CLC 38, 121**
See also AAYA 18, 48; AFAW 2; AMWS 13; BPFB 1; BW 2, 3; CA 73-76; CANR 12, 24, 38, 73; CLR 65; CPW; DA3; DAM MULT, POP; DLB 33; LATS 1:2; MTCW 1, 2; NFS 8; SATA 84; SCFW 2; SFW 4; SSFS 6; YAW

Butler, Robert Olen, (Jr.) 1945- ...... **CLC 81, 162**
See also AMWS 12; BPFB 1; CA 112; CANR 66; CSW; DAM POP; DLB 173; INT CA-112; MTCW 1; SSFS 11

Butler, Samuel 1612-1680 .... **LC 16, 43**
See also DLB 101, 126; RGEL 2

Butler, Samuel 1835-1902 .... **TCLC 1, 33; WLC**
See also BRWS 2; CA 143; CDBLB 1890-1914; DA; DA3; DAB; DAC; DAM MST, NOV; DLB 18, 57, 174; RGEL 2; SFW 4; TEA

Butler, Walter C.
See Faust, Frederick (Schiller)

Butor, Michel (Marie Francois) 1926- .... **CLC 1, 3, 8, 11, 15, 161**
See also CA 9-12R; CANR 33, 66; CWW 2; DLB 83; EW 13; EWL 3; GFL 1789 to the Present; MTCW 1, 2

Butts, Mary 1890(?)-1937 .... **TCLC 77**
See also CA 148; DLB 240

Buxton, Ralph
See Silverstein, Alvin; Silverstein, Virginia B(arbara Opshelor)

Buzo, Alex
See Buzo, Alexander (John)
See also DLB 289

Buzo, Alexander (John) 1944- .... **CLC 61**
See also CA 97-100; CANR 17, 39, 69; CD 5

Buzzati, Dino 1906-1972 .... **CLC 36**
See also CA 160; 33-36R; DLB 177; RGWL 2, 3; SFW 4

Byars, Betsy (Cromer) 1928- .... **CLC 35**
See also AAYA 19; BYA 3; CA 33-36R, 183; CAAE 183; CANR 18, 36, 57, 102; CLR 1, 16, 72; DLB 52; INT CANR-18; JRDA; MAICYA 1, 2; MAICYAS 1; MTCW 1; SAAS 1; SATA 4, 46, 80; SATA-Essay 108; WYA; YAW

Byatt, A(ntonia) S(usan Drabble) 1936- .... **CLC 19, 65, 136**
See also BPFB 1; BRWC 2; BRWS 4; CA 13-16R; CANR 13, 33, 50, 75, 96, 133; DA3; DAM NOV, POP; DLB 14, 194; EWL 3; MTCW 1, 2; RGSF 2; RHW; TEA

Byrd, Willam II 1674-1744 .... **LC 112**
See also DLB 24, 140; RGAL 4

Byrne, David 1952- .... **CLC 26**
See also CA 127

Byrne, John Keyes 1926-
See Leonard, Hugh
See also CA 102; CANR 78; INT CA-102

Byron, George Gordon (Noel) 1788-1824 ..... **DC 24; NCLC 2, 12, 109, 149; PC 16; WLC**
See also BRW 4; BRWC 2; CDBLB 1789-1832; DA; DA3; DAB; DAC; DAM MST, POET; DLB 96, 110; EXPP; LMFS 1; PAB; PFS 1, 14; RGEL 2; TEA; WLIT 3; WP

Byron, Robert 1905-1941 .... **TCLC 67**
See also CA 160; DLB 195

C. 3. 3.
See Wilde, Oscar (Fingal O'Flahertie Wills)

Caballero, Fernan 1796-1877 .... **NCLC 10**

Cabell, Branch
See Cabell, James Branch

Cabell, James Branch 1879-1958 .... **TCLC 6**
See also CA 105; 152; DLB 9, 78; FANT; MTCW 1; RGAL 4; SUFW 1

Cabeza de Vaca, Alvar Nunez 1490-1557(?) .... **LC 61**

Cable, George Washington 1844-1925 .... **SSC 4; TCLC 4**
See also CA 104; 155; DLB 12, 74; DLBD 13; RGAL 4; TUS

Cabral de Melo Neto, Joao 1920-1999 .... **CLC 76**
See Melo Neto, Joao Cabral de
See also CA 151; DAM MULT; DLB 307; LAW; LAWS 1

Cabrera Infante, G(uillermo) 1929- . **CLC 5, 25, 45, 120; HLC 1; SSC 39**
See also CA 85-88; CANR 29, 65, 110; CDWLB 3; CWW 2; DA3; DAM MULT; DLB 113; EWL 3; HW 1, 2; LAW; LAWS 1; MTCW 1, 2; RGSF 2; WLIT 1

Cade, Toni
See Bambara, Toni Cade

Cadmus and Harmonia
See Buchan, John

Caedmon fl. 658-680 .... **CMLC 7**
See also DLB 146

Caeiro, Alberto
See Pessoa, Fernando (Antonio Nogueira)

Caesar, Julius .... **CMLC 47**
See Julius Caesar
See also AW 1; RGWL 2, 3

Cage, John (Milton, Jr.) 1912-1992 .... **CLC 41; PC 58**
See also CA 13-16R; 169; CANR 9, 78; DLB 193; INT CANR-9

Cahan, Abraham 1860-1951 .... **TCLC 71**
See also CA 108; 154; DLB 9, 25, 28; RGAL 4

Cain, G.
See Cabrera Infante, G(uillermo)

Cain, Guillermo
See Cabrera Infante, G(uillermo)

Cain, James M(allahan) 1892-1977 .. **CLC 3, 11, 28**
See also AITN 1; BPFB 1; CA 17-20R; 73-76; CANR 8, 34, 61; CMW 4; DLB 226; EWL 3; MSW; MTCW 1; RGAL 4

Caine, Hall 1853-1931 .... **TCLC 97**
See also RHW

Caine, Mark
See Raphael, Frederic (Michael)

Calasso, Roberto 1941- .... **CLC 81**
See also CA 143; CANR 89

Calderon de la Barca, Pedro 1600-1681 .... **DC 3; HLCS 1; LC 23**
See also EW 2; RGWL 2, 3; TWA

Caldwell, Erskine (Preston) 1903-1987 .... **CLC 1, 8, 14, 50, 60; SSC 19; TCLC 117**
See also AITN 1; AMW; BPFB 1; CA 1-4R; 121; CAAS 1; CANR 2, 33; DA3; DAM NOV; DLB 9, 86; EWL 3; MTCW 1, 2; RGAL 4; RGSF 2; TUS

Caldwell, (Janet Miriam) Taylor (Holland) 1900-1985 .... **CLC 2, 28, 39**
See also BPFB 1; CA 5-8R; 116; CANR 5; DA3; DAM NOV, POP; DLBD 17; RHW

Calhoun, John Caldwell 1782-1850 .... **NCLC 15**
See also DLB 3, 248

Calisher, Hortense 1911- ..... **CLC 2, 4, 8, 38, 134; SSC 15**
See also CA 1-4R; CANR 1, 22, 117; CN 7; DA3; DAM NOV; DLB 2, 218; INT CANR-22; MTCW 1, 2; RGAL 4; RGSF 2

Callaghan, Morley Edward 1903-1990 ..... **CLC 3, 14, 41, 65; TCLC 145**
See also CA 9-12R; 132; CANR 33, 73; DAC; DAM MST; DLB 68; EWL 3; MTCW 1, 2; RGEL 2; RGSF 2; SSFS 19

Callimachus c. 305B.C.-c. 240B.C. .... **CMLC 18**
See also AW 1; DLB 176; RGWL 2, 3

Calvin, Jean
See Calvin, John
See also GFL Beginnings to 1789

Calvin, John 1509-1564 .... **LC 37**
See Calvin, Jean

Calvino, Italo 1923-1985 .... **CLC 5, 8, 11, 22, 33, 39, 73; SSC 3, 48**
See also AAYA 58; CA 85-88; 116; CANR 23, 61, 132; DAM NOV; DLB 196; EW 13; EWL 3; MTCW 1, 2; RGSF 2; RGWL 2, 3; SFW 4; SSFS 12

Camara Laye
See Laye, Camara
See also EWL 3

Camden, William 1551-1623 .... **LC 77**
See also DLB 172

Cameron, Carey 1952- .... **CLC 59**
See also CA 135

Cameron, Peter 1959- .... **CLC 44**
See also AMWS 12; CA 125; CANR 50, 117; DLB 234; GLL 2

Camoens, Luis Vaz de 1524(?)-1580
See Camoes, Luis de
See also EW 2

Camoes, Luis de 1524(?)-1580 . **HLCS 1; LC 62; PC 31**
See Camoens, Luis Vaz de
See also DLB 287; RGWL 2, 3

Campana, Dino 1885-1932 .... **TCLC 20**
See also CA 117; DLB 114; EWL 3

Campanella, Tommaso 1568-1639 .... **LC 32**
See also RGWL 2, 3

Campbell, John W(ood, Jr.) 1910-1971 .... **CLC 32**
See also CA 21-22; 29-32R; CANR 34; CAP 2; DLB 8; MTCW 1; SCFW; SFW 4

Campbell, Joseph 1904-1987 .... **CLC 69; TCLC 140**
See also AAYA 3; BEST 89:2; CA 1-4R; 124; CANR 3, 28, 61, 107; DA3; MTCW 1, 2

Campbell, Maria 1940- .... **CLC 85; NNAL**
See also CA 102; CANR 54; CCA 1; DAC

Campbell, (John) Ramsey 1946- ..... **CLC 42; SSC 19**
See also AAYA 51; CA 57-60, 228; CAAE 228; CANR 7, 102; DLB 261; HGG; INT CANR-7; SUFW 1, 2

Campbell, (Ignatius) Roy (Dunnachie) 1901-1957 .... **TCLC 5**
See also AFW; CA 104; 155; DLB 20, 225; EWL 3; MTCW 2; RGEL 2

Campbell, Thomas 1777-1844 .... **NCLC 19**
See also DLB 93, 144; RGEL 2

Campbell, Wilfred .... **TCLC 9**
See Campbell, William

Campbell, William 1858(?)-1918
See Campbell, Wilfred
See also CA 106; DLB 92

Campion, Jane 1954- .... **CLC 95**
See also AAYA 33; CA 138; CANR 87

Campion, Thomas 1567-1620 .... **LC 78**
See also CDBLB Before 1660; DAM POET; DLB 58, 172; RGEL 2

Camus, Albert 1913-1960 ...... **CLC 1, 2, 4, 9, 11, 14, 32, 63, 69, 124; DC 2; SSC 9, 76; WLC**
See also AAYA 36; AFW; BPFB 1; CA 89-92; CANR 131; DA; DA3; DAB; DAC; DAM DRAM, MST, NOV; DLB 72; EW 13; EWL 3; EXPN; EXPS; GFL 1789 to the Present; LATS 1:2; LMFS 2; MTCW 1, 2; NFS 6, 16; RGSF 2; RGWL 2, 3; SSFS 4; TWA

Canby, Vincent 1924-2000 .... **CLC 13**
See also CA 81-84; 191

Cancale
See Desnos, Robert

Canetti, Elias 1905-1994 .. **CLC 3, 14, 25, 75, 86; TCLC 157**
See also CA 21-24R; 146; CANR 23, 61, 79; CDWLB 2; CWW 2; DA3; DLB 85, 124; EW 12; EWL 3; MTCW 1, 2; RGWL 2, 3; TWA

Canfield, Dorothea F.
See Fisher, Dorothy (Frances) Canfield

Canfield, Dorothea Frances
See Fisher, Dorothy (Frances) Canfield

Canfield, Dorothy
See Fisher, Dorothy (Frances) Canfield

Canin, Ethan 1960- .... **CLC 55; SSC 70**
See also CA 131; 135

Cankar, Ivan 1876-1918 .... **TCLC 105**
See also CDWLB 4; DLB 147; EWL 3

Cannon, Curt
See Hunter, Evan

Cao, Lan 1961- .... **CLC 109**
See also CA 165

Cape, Judith
See Page, P(atricia) K(athleen)
See also CCA 1

Capek, Karel 1890-1938 .... **DC 1; SSC 36; TCLC 6, 37; WLC**
See also CA 104; 140; CDWLB 4; DA; DA3; DAB; DAC; DAM DRAM, MST, NOV; DFS 7, 11; DLB 215; EW 10; EWL 3; MTCW 1; RGSF 2; RGWL 2, 3; SCFW 2; SFW 4

Capote, Truman 1924-1984 . **CLC 1, 3, 8, 13, 19, 34, 38, 58; SSC 2, 47; TCLC 164; WLC**
See also AMWS 3; BPFB 1; CA 5-8R; 113; CANR 18, 62; CDALB 1941-1968; CPW; DA; DA3; DAB; DAC; DAM MST, NOV, POP; DLB 2, 185, 227; DLBY 1980,

1984; EWL 3; EXPS; GLL 1; LAIT 3; MTCW 1, 2; NCFS 2; RGAL 4; RGSF 2; SATA 91; SSFS 2; TUS

Capra, Frank 1897-1991 .... **CLC 16**
See also AAYA 52; CA 61-64; 135

Caputo, Philip 1941- .... **CLC 32**
See also AAYA 60; CA 73-76; CANR 40, 135; YAW

Caragiale, Ion Luca 1852-1912 ...... **TCLC 76**
See also CA 157

Card, Orson Scott 1951- .... **CLC 44, 47, 50**
See also AAYA 11, 42; BPFB 1; BYA 5, 8; CA 102; CANR 27, 47, 73, 102, 106, 133; CPW; DA3; DAM POP; FANT; INT CANR-27; MTCW 1, 2; NFS 5; SATA 83, 127; SCFW 2; SFW 4; SUFW 2; YAW

Cardenal, Ernesto 1925- .... **CLC 31, 161; HLC 1; PC 22**
See also CA 49-52; CANR 2, 32, 66; CWW 2; DAM MULT, POET; DLB 290; EWL 3; HW 1, 2; LAWS 1; MTCW 1, 2; RGWL 2, 3

Cardinal, Marie 1929-2001 .... **CLC 189**
See also CA 177; CWW 2; DLB 83; FW

Cardozo, Benjamin N(athan) 1870-1938 .... **TCLC 65**
See also CA 117; 164

Carducci, Giosue (Alessandro Giuseppe) 1835-1907 .... **PC 46; TCLC 32**
See also CA 163; EW 7; RGWL 2, 3

Carew, Thomas 1595(?)-1640 . **LC 13; PC 29**
See also BRW 2; DLB 126; PAB; RGEL 2

Carey, Ernestine Gilbreth 1908- ...... **CLC 17**
See also CA 5-8R; CANR 71; SATA 2

Carey, Peter 1943- .... **CLC 40, 55, 96, 183**
See also CA 123; 127; CANR 53, 76, 117; CN 7; DLB 289; EWL 3; INT CA-127; MTCW 1, 2; RGSF 2; SATA 94

Carleton, William 1794-1869 .... **NCLC 3**
See also DLB 159; RGEL 2; RGSF 2

Carlisle, Henry (Coffin) 1926- .... **CLC 33**
See also CA 13-16R; CANR 15, 85

Carlsen, Chris
See Holdstock, Robert P.

Carlson, Ron(ald F.) 1947- .... **CLC 54**
See also CA 105; 189; CAAE 189; CANR 27; DLB 244

Carlyle, Thomas 1795-1881 ..... **NCLC 22, 70**
See also BRW 4; CDBLB 1789-1832; DA; DAB; DAC; DAM MST; DLB 55, 144, 254; RGEL 2; TEA

Carman, (William) Bliss 1861-1929 ... **PC 34; TCLC 7**
See also CA 104; 152; DAC; DLB 92; RGEL 2

Carnegie, Dale 1888-1955 .... **TCLC 53**
See also CA 218

Carossa, Hans 1878-1956 .... **TCLC 48**
See also CA 170; DLB 66; EWL 3

Carpenter, Don(ald Richard) 1931-1995 .... **CLC 41**
See also CA 45-48; 149; CANR 1, 71

Carpenter, Edward 1844-1929 .... **TCLC 88**
See also CA 163; GLL 1

Carpenter, John (Howard) 1948- ... **CLC 161**
See also AAYA 2; CA 134; SATA 58

Carpenter, Johnny
See Carpenter, John (Howard)

Carpentier (y Valmont), Alejo 1904-1980 . **CLC 8, 11, 38, 110; HLC 1; SSC 35**
See also CA 65-68; 97-100; CANR 11, 70; CDWLB 3; DAM MULT; DLB 113; EWL 3; HW 1, 2; LAW; LMFS 2; RGSF 2; RGWL 2, 3; WLIT 1

Carr, Caleb 1955- .... **CLC 86**
See also CA 147; CANR 73, 134; DA3

Carr, Emily 1871-1945 .... **TCLC 32**
See also CA 159; DLB 68; FW; GLL 2

Carr, John Dickson 1906-1977 .... **CLC 3**
See Fairbairn, Roger
See also CA 49-52; 69-72; CANR 3, 33, 60; CMW 4; DLB 306; MSW; MTCW 1, 2

Carr, Philippa
See Hibbert, Eleanor Alice Burford

Carr, Virginia Spencer 1929- .... **CLC 34**
See also CA 61-64; DLB 111

Carrere, Emmanuel 1957- .... **CLC 89**
See also CA 200

Carrier, Roch 1937- .... **CLC 13, 78**
See also CA 130; CANR 61; CCA 1; DAC; DAM MST; DLB 53; SATA 105

Carroll, James Dennis
See Carroll, Jim

Carroll, James P. 1943(?)- .... **CLC 38**
See also CA 81-84; CANR 73; MTCW 1

Carroll, Jim 1951- .... **CLC 35, 143**
See also AAYA 17; CA 45-48; CANR 42, 115; NCFS 5

Carroll, Lewis .... **NCLC 2, 53, 139; PC 18; WLC**
See Dodgson, Charles L(utwidge)
See also AAYA 39; BRW 5; BYA 5, 13; CD-BLB 1832-1890; CLR 2, 18; DLB 18, 163, 178; DLBY 1998; EXPN; EXPP; FANT; JRDA; LAIT 1; NFS 7; PFS 11; RGEL 2; SUFW 1; TEA; WCH

Carroll, Paul Vincent 1900-1968 ...... **CLC 10**
See also CA 9-12R; 25-28R; DLB 10; EWL 3; RGEL 2

Carruth, Hayden 1921- ..... **CLC 4, 7, 10, 18, 84; PC 10**
See also CA 9-12R; CANR 4, 38, 59, 110; CP 7; DLB 5, 165; INT CANR-4; MTCW 1, 2; SATA 47

Carson, Anne 1950- .... **CLC 185; PC 64**
See also AMWS 12; CA 203; DLB 193; PFS 18

Carson, Ciaran 1948- .... **CLC 201**
See also CA 153; CA-Brief 112; CANR 113; CP 7

Carson, Rachel
See Carson, Rachel Louise
See also AAYA 49; DLB 275

Carson, Rachel Louise 1907-1964 .... **CLC 71**
See Carson, Rachel
See also AMWS 9; ANW; CA 77-80; CANR 35; DA3; DAM POP; FW; LAIT 4; MTCW 1, 2; NCFS 1; SATA 23

Carter, Angela (Olive) 1940-1992 ..... **CLC 5, 41, 76; SSC 13, 85; TCLC 139**
See also BRWS 3; CA 53-56; 136; CANR 12, 36, 61, 106; DA3; DLB 14, 207, 261; EXPS; FANT; FW; MTCW 1, 2; RGSF 2; SATA 66; SATA-Obit 70; SFW 4; SSFS 4, 12; SUFW 2; WLIT 4

Carter, Nick
See Smith, Martin Cruz

Carver, Raymond 1938-1988 ..... **CLC 22, 36, 53, 55, 126; PC 54; SSC 8, 51**
See also AAYA 44; AMWS 3; BPFB 1; CA 33-36R; 126; CANR 17, 34, 61, 103; CPW; DA3; DAM NOV; DLB 130; DLBY 1984, 1988; EWL 3; MTCW 1, 2; PFS 17; RGAL 4; RGSF 2; SSFS 3, 6, 12, 13; TCWW 2; TUS

Cary, Elizabeth, Lady Falkland 1585-1639 .... **LC 30**

Cary, (Arthur) Joyce (Lunel) 1888-1957 .... **TCLC 1, 29**
See also BRW 7; CA 104; 164; CDBLB 1914-1945; DLB 15, 100; EWL 3; MTCW 2; RGEL 2; TEA

Casal, Julian del 1863-1893 .... **NCLC 131**
See also DLB 283; LAW

Casanova de Seingalt, Giovanni Jacopo
    1725-1798 .... LC 13
Casares, Adolfo Bioy
    See Bioy Casares, Adolfo
    See also RGSF 2
Casas, Bartolome de las 1474-1566
    See Las Casas, Bartolome de
    See also WLIT 1
Casely-Hayford, J(oseph) E(phraim)
    1866-1903 .... BLC 1; TCLC 24
    See also BW 2; CA 123; 152; DAM MULT
Casey, John (Dudley) 1939- .... CLC 59
    See also BEST 90:2; CA 69-72; CANR 23,
    100
Casey, Michael 1947- .... CLC 2
    See also CA 65-68; CANR 109; DLB 5
Casey, Patrick
    See Thurman, Wallace (Henry)
Casey, Warren (Peter) 1935-1988 .... CLC 12
    See also CA 101; 127; INT CA-101
Casona, Alejandro .... CLC 49
    See Alvarez, Alejandro Rodriguez
    See also EWL 3
Cassavetes, John 1929-1989 .... CLC 20
    See also CA 85-88; 127; CANR 82
Cassian, Nina 1924- .... PC 17
    See also CWP; CWW 2
Cassill, R(onald) V(erlin)
    1919-2002 .... CLC 4, 23
    See also CA 9-12R; 208; CAAS 1; CANR
    7, 45; CN 7; DLB 6, 218; DLBY 2002
Cassiodorus, Flavius Magnus c. 490(?)-c.
    583(?) .... CMLC 43
Cassirer, Ernst 1874-1945 .... TCLC 61
    See also CA 157
Cassity, (Allen) Turner 1929- .... CLC 6, 42
    See also CA 17-20R; 223; CAAE 223;
    CAAS 8; CANR 11; CSW; DLB 105
Castaneda, Carlos (Cesar Aranha)
    1931(?)-1998 .... CLC 12, 119
    See also CA 25-28R; CANR 32, 66, 105;
    DNFS 1; HW 1; MTCW 1
Castedo, Elena 1937- .... CLC 65
    See also CA 132
Castedo-Ellerman, Elena
    See Castedo, Elena
Castellanos, Rosario 1925-1974 .... CLC 66;
    HLC 1; SSC 39, 68
    See also CA 131; 53-56; CANR 58; CD-
    WLB 3; DAM MULT; DLB 113, 290;
    EWL 3; FW; HW 1; LAW; MTCW 1;
    RGSF 2; RGWL 2, 3
Castelvetro, Lodovico 1505-1571 .... LC 12
Castiglione, Baldassare 1478-1529 ...... LC 12
    See Castiglione, Baldesar
    See also LMFS 1; RGWL 2, 3
Castiglione, Baldesar
    See Castiglione, Baldassare
    See also EW 2
Castillo, Ana (Hernandez Del)
    1953- .... CLC 151
    See also AAYA 42; CA 131; CANR 51, 86,
    128; CWP; DLB 122, 227; DNFS 2; FW;
    HW 1; LLW 1; PFS 21
Castle, Robert
    See Hamilton, Edmond
Castro (Ruz), Fidel 1926(?)- .... HLC 1
    See also CA 110; 129; CANR 81; DAM
    MULT; HW 2
Castro, Guillen de 1569-1631 .... LC 19
Castro, Rosalia de 1837-1885 ... NCLC 3, 78;
    PC 41
    See also DAM MULT
Cather, Willa (Sibert) 1873-1947 . SSC 2, 50;
    TCLC 1, 11, 31, 99, 132, 152; WLC
    See also AAYA 24; AMW; AMWC 1;
    AMWR 1; BPFB 1; CA 104; 128; CDALB
    1865-1917; CLR 98; DA; DA3; DAB;
    DAC; DAM MST, NOV; DLB 9, 54, 78,

256; DLBD 1; EWL 3; EXPN; EXPS;
    LAIT 3; LATS 1:1; MAWW; MTCW 1,
    2; NFS 2, 19; RGAL 4; RGSF 2; RHW;
    SATA 30; SSFS 2, 7, 16; TCWW 2; TUS
Catherine II
    See Catherine the Great
    See also DLB 150
Catherine the Great 1729-1796 .... LC 69
    See Catherine II
Cato, Marcus Porcius
    234B.C.-149B.C. .... CMLC 21
    See Cato the Elder
Cato, Marcus Porcius, the Elder
    See Cato, Marcus Porcius
Cato the Elder
    See Cato, Marcus Porcius
    See also DLB 211
Catton, (Charles) Bruce 1899-1978 . CLC 35
    See also AITN 1; CA 5-8R; 81-84; CANR
    7, 74; DLB 17; SATA 2; SATA-Obit 24
Catullus c. 84B.C.-54B.C. .... CMLC 18
    See also AW 2; CDWLB 1; DLB 211;
    RGWL 2, 3
Cauldwell, Frank
    See King, Francis (Henry)
Caunitz, William J. 1933-1996 .... CLC 34
    See also BEST 89:3; CA 125; 130; 152;
    CANR 73; INT CA-130
Causley, Charles (Stanley)
    1917-2003 .... CLC 7
    See also CA 9-12R; 223; CANR 5, 35, 94;
    CLR 30; CWRI 5; DLB 27; MTCW 1;
    SATA 3, 66; SATA-Obit 149
Caute, (John) David 1936- .... CLC 29
    See also CA 1-4R; CAAS 4; CANR 1, 33,
    64, 120; CBD; CD 5; CN 7; DAM NOV;
    DLB 14, 231
Cavafy, C(onstantine) P(eter) .... PC 36;
    TCLC 2, 7
    See Kavafis, Konstantinos Petrou
    See also CA 148; DA3; DAM POET; EW
    8; EWL 3; MTCW 1; PFS 19; RGWL 2,
    3; WP
Cavalcanti, Guido c. 1250-c.
    1300 .... CMLC 54
    See also RGWL 2, 3
Cavallo, Evelyn
    See Spark, Muriel (Sarah)
Cavanna, Betty .... CLC 12
    See Harrison, Elizabeth (Allen) Cavanna
    See also JRDA; MAICYA 1; SAAS 4;
    SATA 1, 30
Cavendish, Margaret Lucas
    1623-1673 .... LC 30
    See also DLB 131, 252, 281; RGEL 2
Caxton, William 1421(?)-1491(?) .... LC 17
    See also DLB 170
Cayer, D. M.
    See Duffy, Maureen
Cayrol, Jean 1911- .... CLC 11
    See also CA 89-92; DLB 83; EWL 3
Cela (y Trulock), Camilo Jose
    See Cela, Camilo Jose
    See also CWW 2
Cela, Camilo Jose 1916-2002 .... CLC 4, 13,
    59, 122; HLC 1; SSC 71
    See Cela (y Trulock), Camilo Jose
    See also BEST 90:2; CA 21-24R; 206;
    CAAS 10; CANR 21, 32, 76; DAM
    MULT; DLBY 1989; EW 13; EWL 3; HW
    1; MTCW 1, 2; RGSF 2; RGWL 2, 3
Celan, Paul .... CLC 10, 19, 53, 82; PC 10
    See Antschel, Paul
    See also CDWLB 2; DLB 69; EWL 3;
    RGWL 2, 3

Celine, Louis-Ferdinand ... CLC 1, 3, 4, 7, 9,
    15, 47, 124
    See Destouches, Louis-Ferdinand
    See also DLB 72; EW 11; EWL 3; GFL
    1789 to the Present; RGWL 2, 3
Cellini, Benvenuto 1500-1571 .... LC 7
Cendrars, Blaise .... CLC 18, 106
    See Sauser-Hall, Frederic
    See also DLB 258; EWL 3; GFL 1789 to
    the Present; RGWL 2, 3; WP
Centlivre, Susanna 1669(?)-1723 .... DC 25;
    LC 65
    See also DLB 84; RGEL 2
Cernuda (y Bidon), Luis
    1902-1963 .... CLC 54; PC 62
    See also CA 131; 89-92; DAM POET; DLB
    134; EWL 3; GLL 1; HW 1; RGWL 2, 3
Cervantes, Lorna Dee 1954- ..... HLCS 1; PC
    35
    See also CA 131; CANR 80; CWP; DLB
    82; EXPP; HW 1; LLW 1
Cervantes (Saavedra), Miguel de
    1547-1616 .... HLCS; LC 6, 23, 93; SSC
    12; WLC
    See also AAYA 56; BYA 1, 14; DA; DAB;
    DAC; DAM MST, NOV; EW 2; LAIT 1;
    LATS 1:1; LMFS 1; NFS 8; RGSF 2;
    RGWL 2, 3; TWA
Cesaire, Aime (Fernand) 1913- .... BLC 1;
    CLC 19, 32, 112; DC 22; PC 25
    See also BW 2, 3; CA 65-68; CANR 24,
    43, 81; CWW 2; DA3; DAM MULT,
    POET; EWL 3; GFL 1789 to the Present;
    MTCW 1, 2; WP
Chabon, Michael 1963- ... CLC 55, 149; SSC
    59
    See also AAYA 45; AMWS 11; CA 139;
    CANR 57, 96, 127; DLB 278; SATA 145
Chabrol, Claude 1930- .... CLC 16
    See also CA 110
Chairil Anwar
    See Anwar, Chairil
    See also EWL 3
Challans, Mary 1905-1983
    See Renault, Mary
    See also CA 81-84; 111; CANR 74; DA3;
    MTCW 2; SATA 23; SATA-Obit 36; TEA
Challis, George
    See Faust, Frederick (Schiller)
    See also TCWW 2
Chambers, Aidan 1934- .... CLC 35
    See also AAYA 27; CA 25-28R; CANR 12,
    31, 58, 116; JRDA; MAICYA 1, 2; SAAS
    12; SATA 1, 69, 108; WYA; YAW
Chambers, James 1948-
    See Cliff, Jimmy
    See also CA 124
Chambers, Jessie
    See Lawrence, D(avid) H(erbert Richards)
    See also GLL 1
Chambers, Robert W(illiam)
    1865-1933 .... TCLC 41
    See also CA 165; DLB 202; HGG; SATA
    107; SUFW 1
Chambers, (David) Whittaker
    1901-1961 .... TCLC 129
    See also CA 89-92; DLB 303
Chamisso, Adelbert von
    1781-1838 .... NCLC 82
    See also DLB 90; RGWL 2, 3; SUFW 1
Chance, James T.
    See Carpenter, John (Howard)
Chance, John T.
    See Carpenter, John (Howard)
Chandler, Raymond (Thornton)
    1888-1959 .... SSC 23; TCLC 1, 7
    See also AAYA 25; AMWC 2; AMWS 4;
    BPFB 1; CA 104; 129; CANR 60, 107;
    CDALB 1929-1941; CMW 4; DA3; DLB
    226, 253; DLBD 6; EWL 3; MSW;
    MTCW 1, 2; NFS 17; RGAL 4; TUS

34, 98, 156; EWL 3; EXPN; EXPS; LAIT 2; LATS 1:1; LMFS 1; MTCW 1, 2; NFS 2, 16; RGEL 2; RGSF 2; SATA 27; SSFS 1, 12; TEA; WLIT 4

Conrad, Robert Arnold
See Hart, Moss

Conroy, (Donald) Pat(rick) 1945- ... **CLC 30, 74**
See also AAYA 8, 52; AITN 1; BPFB 1; CA 85-88; CANR 24, 53, 129; CPW; CSW; DA3; DAM NOV, POP; DLB 6; LAIT 5; MTCW 1, 2

Constant (de Rebecque), (Henri) Benjamin 1767-1830 .... **NCLC 6**
See also DLB 119; EW 4; GFL 1789 to the Present

Conway, Jill K(er) 1934- .... **CLC 152**
See also CA 130; CANR 94

Conybeare, Charles Augustus
See Eliot, T(homas) S(tearns)

Cook, Michael 1933-1994 .... **CLC 58**
See also CA 93-96; CANR 68; DLB 53

Cook, Robin 1940- .... **CLC 14**
See also AAYA 32; BEST 90:2; BPFB 1; CA 108; 111; CANR 41, 90, 109; CPW; DA3; DAM POP; HGG; INT CA-111

Cook, Roy
See Silverberg, Robert

Cooke, Elizabeth 1948- .... **CLC 55**
See also CA 129

Cooke, John Esten 1830-1886 .... **NCLC 5**
See also DLB 3, 248; RGAL 4

Cooke, John Estes
See Baum, L(yman) Frank

Cooke, M. E.
See Creasey, John

Cooke, Margaret
See Creasey, John

Cooke, Rose Terry 1827-1892 ...... **NCLC 110**
See also DLB 12, 74

Cook-Lynn, Elizabeth 1930- .... **CLC 93; NNAL**
See also CA 133; DAM MULT; DLB 175

Cooney, Ray .... **CLC 62**
See also CBD

Cooper, Anthony Ashley 1671-1713 .. **LC 107**
See also DLB 101

Cooper, Dennis 1953- .... **CLC 203**
See also CA 133; CANR 72, 86; GLL 1; St. James Guide to Horror, Ghost, and Gothic Writers.

Cooper, Douglas 1960- .... **CLC 86**

Cooper, Henry St. John
See Creasey, John

Cooper, J(oan) California (?)- .... **CLC 56**
See also AAYA 12; BW 1; CA 125; CANR 55; DAM MULT; DLB 212

Cooper, James Fenimore
1789-1851 .... **NCLC 1, 27, 54**
See also AAYA 22; AMW; BPFB 1; CDALB 1640-1865; DA3; DLB 3, 183, 250, 254; LAIT 1; NFS 9; RGAL 4; SATA 19; TUS; WCH

Cooper, Susan Fenimore
1813-1894 .... **NCLC 129**
See also ANW; DLB 239, 254

Coover, Robert (Lowell) 1932- ...... **CLC 3, 7, 15, 32, 46, 87, 161; SSC 15**
See also AMWS 5; BPFB 1; CA 45-48; CANR 3, 37, 58, 115; CN 7; DAM NOV; DLB 2, 227; DLBY 1981; EWL 3; MTCW 1, 2; RGAL 4; RGSF 2

Copeland, Stewart (Armstrong)
1952- .... **CLC 26**

Copernicus, Nicolaus 1473-1543 .... **LC 45**

Coppard, A(lfred) E(dgar)
1878-1957 .... **SSC 21; TCLC 5**
See also BRWS 8; CA 114; 167; DLB 162; EWL 3; HGG; RGEL 2; RGSF 2; SUFW 1; YABC 1

Coppee, Francois 1842-1908 .... **TCLC 25**
See also CA 170; DLB 217

Coppola, Francis Ford 1939- ... **CLC 16, 126**
See also AAYA 39; CA 77-80; CANR 40, 78; DLB 44

Copway, George 1818-1869 .... **NNAL**
See also DAM MULT; DLB 175, 183

Corbiere, Tristan 1845-1875 .... **NCLC 43**
See also DLB 217; GFL 1789 to the Present

Corcoran, Barbara (Asenath)
1911- .... **CLC 17**
See also AAYA 14; CA 21-24R, 191; CAAE 191; CAAS 2; CANR 11, 28, 48; CLR 50; DLB 52; JRDA; MAICYA 2; MAIC-YAS 1; RHW; SAAS 20; SATA 3, 77; SATA-Essay 125

Cordelier, Maurice
See Giraudoux, Jean(-Hippolyte)

Corelli, Marie .... **TCLC 51**
See Mackay, Mary
See also DLB 34, 156; RGEL 2; SUFW 1

Corinna c. 225B.C.-c. 305B.C. ...... **CMLC 72**

Corman, Cid .... **CLC 9**
See Corman, Sidney
See also CAAS 2; DLB 5, 193

Corman, Sidney 1924-2004
See Corman, Cid
See also CA 85-88; 225; CANR 44; CP 7; DAM POET

Cormier, Robert (Edmund)
1925-2000 .... **CLC 12, 30**
See also AAYA 3, 19; BYA 1, 2, 6, 8, 9; CA 1-4R; CANR 5, 23, 76, 93; CDALB 1968-1988; CLR 12, 55; DA; DAB; DAC; DAM MST, NOV; DLB 52; EXPN; INT CANR-23; JRDA; LAIT 5; MAICYA 1, 2; MTCW 1, 2; NFS 2, 18; SATA 10, 45, 83; SATA-Obit 122; WYA; YAW

Corn, Alfred (DeWitt III) 1943- .... **CLC 33**
See also CA 179; CAAE 179; CAAS 25; CANR 44; CP 7; CSW; DLB 120, 282; DLBY 1980

Corneille, Pierre 1606-1684 ... **DC 21; LC 28**
See also DAB; DAM MST; DLB 268; EW 3; GFL Beginnings to 1789; RGWL 2, 3; TWA

Cornwell, David (John Moore)
1931- .... **CLC 9, 15**
See le Carre, John
See also CA 5-8R; CANR 13, 33, 59, 107, 132; DA3; DAM POP; MTCW 1, 2

Cornwell, Patricia (Daniels) 1956- . **CLC 155**
See also AAYA 16, 56; BPFB 1; CA 134; CANR 53, 131; CMW 4; CPW; CSW; DAM POP; DLB 306; MSW; MTCW 1

Corso, (Nunzio) Gregory 1930-2001 . **CLC 1, 11; PC 33**
See also AMWS 12; BG 2; CA 5-8R; 193; CANR 41, 76, 132; CP 7; DA3; DLB 5, 16, 237; LMFS 2; MTCW 1, 2; WP

Cortazar, Julio 1914-1984 ... **CLC 2, 3, 5, 10, 13, 15, 33, 34, 92; HLC 1; SSC 7, 76**
See also BPFB 1; CA 21-24R; CANR 12, 32, 81; CDWLB 3; DA3; DAM MULT, NOV; DLB 113; EWL 3; EXPS; HW 1, 2; LAW; MTCW 1, 2; RGSF 2; RGWL 2, 3; SSFS 3, 20; TWA; WLIT 1

Cortes, Hernan 1485-1547 .... **LC 31**

Corvinus, Jakob
See Raabe, Wilhelm (Karl)

Corwin, Cecil
See Kornbluth, C(yril) M.

Cosic, Dobrica 1921- .... **CLC 14**
See also CA 122; 138; CDWLB 4; CWW 2; DLB 181; EWL 3

Costain, Thomas B(ertram)
1885-1965 .... **CLC 30**
See also BYA 3; CA 5-8R; 25-28R; DLB 9; RHW

Costantini, Humberto 1924(?)-1987 . **CLC 49**
See also CA 131; 122; EWL 3; HW 1

Costello, Elvis 1954- .... **CLC 21**
See also CA 204

Costenoble, Philostene
See Ghelderode, Michel de

Cotes, Cecil V.
See Duncan, Sara Jeannette

Cotter, Joseph Seamon Sr.
1861-1949 .... **BLC 1; TCLC 28**
See also BW 1; CA 124; DAM MULT; DLB 50

Couch, Arthur Thomas Quiller
See Quiller-Couch, Sir Arthur (Thomas)

Coulton, James
See Hansen, Joseph

Couperus, Louis (Marie Anne)
1863-1923 .... **TCLC 15**
See also CA 115; EWL 3; RGWL 2, 3

Coupland, Douglas 1961- .... **CLC 85, 133**
See also AAYA 34; CA 142; CANR 57, 90, 130; CCA 1; CPW; DAC; DAM POP

Court, Wesli
See Turco, Lewis (Putnam)

Courtenay, Bryce 1933- .... **CLC 59**
See also CA 138; CPW

Courtney, Robert
See Ellison, Harlan (Jay)

Cousteau, Jacques-Yves 1910-1997 .. **CLC 30**
See also CA 65-68; 159; CANR 15, 67; MTCW 1; SATA 38, 98

Coventry, Francis 1725-1754 .... **LC 46**

Coverdale, Miles c. 1487-1569 .... **LC 77**
See also DLB 167

Cowan, Peter (Walkinshaw)
1914-2002 .... **SSC 28**
See also CA 21-24R; CANR 9, 25, 50, 83; CN 7; DLB 260; RGSF 2

Coward, Noel (Peirce) 1899-1973 . **CLC 1, 9, 29, 51**
See also AITN 1; BRWS 2; CA 17-18; 41-44R; CANR 35, 132; CAP 2; CDBLB 1914-1945; DA3; DAM DRAM; DFS 3, 6; DLB 10, 245; EWL 3; IDFW 3, 4; MTCW 1, 2; RGEL 2; TEA

Cowley, Abraham 1618-1667 .... **LC 43**
See also BRW 2; DLB 131, 151; PAB; RGEL 2

Cowley, Malcolm 1898-1989 .... **CLC 39**
See also AMWS 2; CA 5-8R; 128; CANR 3, 55; DLB 4, 48; DLBY 1981, 1989; EWL 3; MTCW 1, 2

Cowper, William 1731-1800 ..... **NCLC 8, 94; PC 40**
See also BRW 3; DA3; DAM POET; DLB 104, 109; RGEL 2

Cox, William Trevor 1928-
See Trevor, William
See also CA 9-12R; CANR 4, 37, 55, 76, 102; DAM NOV; INT CANR-37; MTCW 1, 2; TEA

Coyne, P. J.
See Masters, Hilary

Cozzens, James Gould 1903-1978 . **CLC 1, 4, 11, 92**
See also AMW; BPFB 1; CA 9-12R; 81-84; CANR 19; CDALB 1941-1968; DLB 9, 294; DLBD 2; DLBY 1984, 1997; EWL 3; MTCW 1, 2; RGAL 4

Crabbe, George 1754-1832 .... **NCLC 26, 121**
See also BRW 3; DLB 93; RGEL 2

Crace, Jim 1946- .... **CLC 157; SSC 61**
See also CA 128; 135; CANR 55, 70, 123; CN 7; DLB 231; INT CA-135

Craddock, Charles Egbert
See Murfree, Mary Noailles

Craig, A. A.
See Anderson, Poul (William)

Dawson, (Guy) Fielding (Lewis)
   1930-2002 .... **CLC 6**
   See also CA 85-88; 202; CANR 108; DLB
   130; DLBY 2002
Dawson, Peter
   See Faust, Frederick (Schiller)
   See also TCWW 2, 2
Day, Clarence (Shepard, Jr.)
   1874-1935 .... **TCLC 25**
   See also CA 108; 199; DLB 11
Day, John 1574(?)-1640(?) .... **LC 70**
   See also DLB 62, 170; RGEL 2
Day, Thomas 1748-1789 .... **LC 1**
   See also DLB 39; YABC 1
Day Lewis, C(ecil) 1904-1972 . **CLC 1, 6, 10;**
      PC 11
   See Blake, Nicholas
   See also BRWS 3; CA 13-16; 33-36R;
   CANR 34; CAP 1; CWRI 5; DAM POET;
   DLB 15, 20; EWL 3; MTCW 1, 2; RGEL
   2
Dazai Osamu .... **SSC 41; TCLC 11**
   See Tsushima, Shuji
   See also CA 164; DLB 182; EWL 3; MJW;
   RGSF 2; RGWL 2, 3; TWA
de Andrade, Carlos Drummond
   See Drummond de Andrade, Carlos
de Andrade, Mario 1892(?)-1945
   See Andrade, Mario de
   See also CA 178; HW 2
Deane, Norman
   See Creasey, John
Deane, Seamus (Francis) 1940- ...... **CLC 122**
   See also CA 118; CANR 42
de Beauvoir, Simone (Lucie Ernestine Marie
      Bertrand)
   See Beauvoir, Simone (Lucie Ernestine
   Marie Bertrand) de
de Beer, P.
   See Bosman, Herman Charles
de Botton, Alain 1969- .... **CLC 203**
   See also CA 159; CANR 96
de Brissac, Malcolm
   See Dickinson, Peter (Malcolm de Brissac)
de Campos, Alvaro
   See Pessoa, Fernando (Antonio Nogueira)
de Chardin, Pierre Teilhard
   See Teilhard de Chardin, (Marie Joseph)
   Pierre
de Crenne, Hélisenne c. 1510-c.
   1560 .... **LC 113**
Dee, John 1527-1608 .... **LC 20**
   See also DLB 136, 213
Deer, Sandra 1940- .... **CLC 45**
   See also CA 186
De Ferrari, Gabriella 1941- .... **CLC 65**
   See also CA 146
de Filippo, Eduardo 1900-1984 ... **TCLC 127**
   See also CA 132; 114; EWL 3; MTCW 1;
   RGWL 2, 3
Defoe, Daniel 1660(?)-1731 .... **LC 1, 42, 108;**
      WLC
   See also AAYA 27; BRW 3; BRWR 1; BYA
   4; CDBLB 1660-1789; CLR 61; DA;
   DA3; DAB; DAC; DAM MST, NOV;
   DLB 39, 95, 101; JRDA; LAIT 1; LMFS
   1; MAICYA 1, 2; NFS 9, 13; RGEL 2;
   SATA 22; TEA; WCH; WLIT 3
de Gourmont, Remy(-Marie-Charles)
   See Gourmont, Remy(-Marie-Charles) de
de Gournay, Marie le Jars
   1566-1645 .... **LC 98**
   See also FW
de Hartog, Jan 1914-2002 .... **CLC 19**
   See also CA 1-4R; 210; CANR 1; DFS 12
de Hostos, E. M.
   See Hostos (y Bonilla), Eugenio Maria de
de Hostos, Eugenio M.
   See Hostos (y Bonilla), Eugenio Maria de

Deighton, Len .... **CLC 4, 7, 22, 46**
   See Deighton, Leonard Cyril
   See also AAYA 6; BEST 89:2; BPFB 1; CD-
   BLB 1960 to Present; CMW 4; CN 7;
   CPW; DLB 87
Deighton, Leonard Cyril 1929-
   See Deighton, Len
   See also AAYA 57; CA 9-12R; CANR 19,
   33, 68; DA3; DAM NOV, POP; MTCW
   1, 2
Dekker, Thomas 1572(?)-1632 ..... **DC 12; LC**
      22
   See also CDBLB Before 1660; DAM
   DRAM; DLB 62, 172; LMFS 1; RGEL 2
de Laclos, Pierre Ambroise Franois
   See Laclos, Pierre Ambroise Francois
Delacroix, (Ferdinand-Victor-)Eugene
   1798-1863 .... **NCLC 133**
   See also EW 5
Delafield, E. M. .... **TCLC 61**
   See Dashwood, Edmee Elizabeth Monica
   de la Pasture
   See also DLB 34; RHW
de la Mare, Walter (John)
   1873-1956 . **SSC 14; TCLC 4, 53; WLC**
   See also CA 163; CDBLB 1914-1945; CLR
   23; CWRI 5; DA3; DAB; DAC; DAM
   MST, POET; DLB 19, 153, 162, 255, 284;
   EWL 3; EXPP; HGG; MAICYA 1, 2;
   MTCW 1; RGEL 2; RGSF 2; SATA 16;
   SUFW 1; TEA; WCH
de Lamartine, Alphonse (Marie Louis Prat)
   See Lamartine, Alphonse (Marie Louis Prat)
   de
Delaney, Franey
   See O'Hara, John (Henry)
Delaney, Shelagh 1939- .... **CLC 29**
   See also CA 17-20R; CANR 30, 67; CBD;
   CD 5; CDBLB 1960 to Present; CWD;
   DAM DRAM; DFS 7; DLB 13; MTCW 1
Delany, Martin Robison
   1812-1885 .... **NCLC 93**
   See also DLB 50; RGAL 4
Delany, Mary (Granville Pendarves)
   1700-1788 .... **LC 12**
Delany, Samuel R(ay), Jr. 1942- .... **BLC 1;**
      CLC 8, 14, 38, 141
   See also AAYA 24; AFAW 2; BPFB 1; BW
   2, 3; CA 81-84; CANR 27, 43, 115, 116;
   CN 7; DAM MULT; DLB 8, 33; FANT;
   MTCW 1, 2; RGAL 4; SATA 92; SCFW;
   SFW 4; SUFW 2
De la Ramee, Marie Louise (Ouida)
   1839-1908
   See Ouida
   See also CA 204; SATA 20
de la Roche, Mazo 1879-1961 .... **CLC 14**
   See also CA 85-88; CANR 30; DLB 68;
   RGEL 2; RHW; SATA 64
De La Salle, Innocent
   See Hartmann, Sadakichi
de Laureamont, Comte
   See Lautreamont
Delbanco, Nicholas (Franklin)
   1942- .... **CLC 6, 13, 167**
   See also CA 17-20R, 189; CAAE 189;
   CAAS 2; CANR 29, 55, 116; DLB 6, 234
del Castillo, Michel 1933- .... **CLC 38**
   See also CA 109; CANR 77
Deledda, Grazia (Cosima)
   1875(?)-1936 .... **TCLC 23**
   See also CA 123; 205; DLB 264; EWL 3;
   RGWL 2, 3
Deleuze, Gilles 1925-1995 .... **TCLC 116**
   See also DLB 296
Delgado, Abelardo (Lalo) B(arrientos)
   1930-2004 .... **HLC 1**
   See also CA 131; CAAS 15; CANR 90;
   DAM MST, MULT; DLB 82; HW 1, 2

Delibes, Miguel .... **CLC 8, 18**
   See Delibes Setien, Miguel
   See also EWL 3
Delibes Setien, Miguel 1920-
   See Delibes, Miguel
   See also CA 45-48; CANR 1, 32; CWW 2;
   HW 1; MTCW 1
DeLillo, Don 1936- ..... **CLC 8, 10, 13, 27, 39,**
      54, 76, 143, 210, 213
   See also AMWC 2; AMWS 6; BEST 89:1;
   BPFB 1; CA 81-84; CANR 21, 76, 92,
   133; CN 7; CPW; DA3; DAM NOV, POP;
   DLB 6, 173; EWL 3; MTCW 1, 2; RGAL
   4; TUS
de Lisser, H. G.
   See De Lisser, H(erbert) G(eorge)
   See also DLB 117
De Lisser, H(erbert) G(eorge)
   1878-1944 .... **TCLC 12**
   See de Lisser, H. G.
   See also BW 2; CA 109; 152
Deloire, Pierre
   See Peguy, Charles (Pierre)
Deloney, Thomas 1543(?)-1600 .... **LC 41**
   See also DLB 167; RGEL 2
Deloria, Ella (Cara) 1889-1971(?) ..... **NNAL**
   See also CA 152; DAM MULT; DLB 175
Deloria, Vine (Victor), Jr. 1933- ...... **CLC 21,**
      122; NNAL
   See also CA 53-56; CANR 5, 20, 48, 98;
   DAM MULT; DLB 175; MTCW 1; SATA
   21
del Valle-Inclan, Ramon (Maria)
   See Valle-Inclan, Ramon (Maria) del
Del Vecchio, John M(ichael) 1947- .. **CLC 29**
   See also CA 110; DLBD 9
de Man, Paul (Adolph Michel)
   1919-1983 .... **CLC 55**
   See also CA 128; 111; CANR 61; DLB 67;
   MTCW 1, 2
DeMarinis, Rick 1934- .... **CLC 54**
   See also CA 57-60, 184; CAAE 184; CAAS
   24; CANR 9, 25, 50; DLB 218
de Maupassant, (Henri Rene Albert) Guy
   See Maupassant, (Henri Rene Albert) Guy
   de
Dembry, R. Emmet
   See Murfree, Mary Noailles
Demby, William 1922- .... **BLC 1; CLC 53**
   See also BW 1, 3; CA 81-84; CANR 81;
   DAM MULT; DLB 33
de Menton, Francisco
   See Chin, Frank (Chew, Jr.)
Demetrius of Phalerum c.
   307B.C.- .... **CMLC 34**
Demijohn, Thom
   See Disch, Thomas M(ichael)
De Mille, James 1833-1880 .... **NCLC 123**
   See also DLB 99, 251
Deming, Richard 1915-1983
   See Queen, Ellery
   See also CA 9-12R; CANR 3, 94; SATA 24
Democritus c. 460B.C.-c. 370B.C. . **CMLC 47**
de Montaigne, Michel (Eyquem)
   See Montaigne, Michel (Eyquem) de
de Montherlant, Henry (Milon)
   See Montherlant, Henry (Milon) de
Demosthenes 384B.C.-322B.C. ...... **CMLC 13**
   See also AW 1; DLB 176; RGWL 2, 3
de Musset, (Louis Charles) Alfred
   See Musset, (Louis Charles) Alfred de
de Natale, Francine
   See Malzberg, Barry N(athaniel)
de Navarre, Marguerite 1492-1549 ... **LC 61;**
      SSC 85
   See Marguerite d'Angouleme; Marguerite
   de Navarre
Denby, Edwin (Orr) 1903-1983 .... **CLC 48**
   See also CA 138; 110

de Nerval, Gerard
See Nerval, Gerard de
Denham, John 1615-1669 .... **LC 73**
See also DLB 58, 126; RGEL 2
Denis, Julio
See Cortazar, Julio
Denmark, Harrison
See Zelazny, Roger (Joseph)
Dennis, John 1658-1734 .... **LC 11**
See also DLB 101; RGEL 2
Dennis, Nigel (Forbes) 1912-1989 ...... **CLC 8**
See also CA 25-28R; 129; DLB 13, 15, 233;
EWL 3; MTCW 1
Dent, Lester 1904-1959 .... **TCLC 72**
See also CA 112; 161; CMW 4; DLB 306;
SFW 4
De Palma, Brian (Russell) 1940- ...... **CLC 20**
See also CA 109
De Quincey, Thomas 1785-1859 ..... **NCLC 4,
87**
See also BRW 4; CDBLB 1789-1832; DLB
110, 144; RGEL 2
Deren, Eleanora 1908(?)-1961
See Deren, Maya
See also CA 192; 111
Deren, Maya .... **CLC 16, 102**
See Deren, Eleanora
Derleth, August (William)
1909-1971 .... **CLC 31**
See also BPFB 1; BYA 9, 10; CA 1-4R; 29-
32R; CANR 4; CMW 4; DLB 9; DLBD
17; HGG; SATA 5; SUFW 1
Der Nister 1884-1950 .... **TCLC 56**
See Nister, Der
Der Stricker c. 1190-c. 1250 .... **CMLC 75**
de Routisie, Albert
See Aragon, Louis
Derrida, Jacques 1930-2004 .... **CLC 24, 87**
See also CA 124; 127; CANR 76, 98, 133;
DLB 242; EWL 3; LMFS 2; MTCW 1;
TWA
Derry Down Derry
See Lear, Edward
Dersonnes, Jacques
See Simenon, Georges (Jacques Christian)
Desai, Anita 1937- .... **CLC 19, 37, 97, 175**
See also BRWS 5; CA 81-84; CANR 33,
53, 95, 133; CN 7; CWRI 5; DA3; DAB;
DAM NOV; DLB 271; DNFS 2; EWL 3;
FW; MTCW 1, 2; SATA 63, 126
Desai, Kiran 1971- .... **CLC 119**
See also BYA 16; CA 171; CANR 127
de Saint-Luc, Jean
See Glassco, John
de Saint Roman, Arnaud
See Aragon, Louis
Desbordes-Valmore, Marceline
1786-1859 .... **NCLC 97**
See also DLB 217
Descartes, Rene 1596-1650 .... **LC 20, 35**
See also DLB 268; EW 3; GFL Beginnings
to 1789
Deschamps, Eustache 1340(?)-1404 .. **LC 103**
See also DLB 208
De Sica, Vittorio 1901(?)-1974 .... **CLC 20**
See also CA 117
Desnos, Robert 1900-1945 .... **TCLC 22**
See also CA 121; 151; CANR 107; DLB
258; EWL 3; LMFS 2
Des Roches, Catherine 1542-1587 ..... **LC 117**
Destouches, Louis-Ferdinand
1894-1961 .... **CLC 9, 15**
See Celine, Louis-Ferdinand
See also CA 85-88; CANR 28; MTCW 1
de Tolignac, Gaston
See Griffith, D(avid Lewelyn) W(ark)

Deutsch, Babette 1895-1982 .... **CLC 18**
See also BYA 3; CA 1-4R; 108; CANR 4,
79; DLB 45; SATA 1; SATA-Obit 33
Devenant, William 1606-1649 .... **LC 13**
Devkota, Laxmiprasad 1909-1959 . **TCLC 23**
See also CA 123
De Voto, Bernard (Augustine)
1897-1955 .... **TCLC 29**
See also CA 113; 160; DLB 9, 256
De Vries, Peter 1910-1993 ..... **CLC 1, 2, 3, 7,
10, 28, 46**
See also CA 17-20R; 142; CANR 41; DAM
NOV; DLB 6; DLBY 1982; MTCW 1, 2
Dewey, John 1859-1952 .... **TCLC 95**
See also CA 114; 170; DLB 246, 270;
RGAL 4
Dexter, John
See Bradley, Marion Zimmer
See also GLL 1
Dexter, Martin
See Faust, Frederick (Schiller)
See also TCWW 2
Dexter, Pete 1943- .... **CLC 34, 55**
See also BEST 89:2; CA 127; 131; CANR
129; CPW; DAM POP; INT CA-131;
MTCW 1
Diamano, Silmang
See Senghor, Leopold Sedar
Diamond, Neil 1941- .... **CLC 30**
See also CA 108
Diaz del Castillo, Bernal
1496-1584 .... **HLCS 1; LC 31**
See also LAW
di Bassetto, Corno
See Shaw, George Bernard
Dick, Philip K(indred) 1928-1982 ... **CLC 10,
30, 72; SSC 57**
See also AAYA 24; BPFB 1; BYA 11; CA
49-52; 106; CANR 2, 16, 132; CPW;
DA3; DAM NOV, POP; DLB 8; MTCW
1, 2; NFS 5; SCFW; SFW 4
Dickens, Charles (John Huffam)
1812-1870 .... **NCLC 3, 8, 18, 26, 37, 50,
86, 105, 113, 161; SSC 17, 49; WLC**
See also AAYA 23; BRW 5; BRWC 1, 2;
BYA 1, 2, 3, 13, 14; CDBLB 1832-1890;
CLR 95; CMW 4; DA; DA3; DAB; DAC;
DAM MST, NOV; DLB 21, 55, 70, 159,
166; EXPN; HGG; JRDA; LAIT 1, 2;
LATS 1:1; LMFS 1; MAICYA 1, 2; NFS
4, 5, 10, 14, 20; RGEL 2; RGSF 2; SATA
15; SUFW 1; TEA; WCH; WLIT 4; WYA
Dickey, James (Lafayette)
1923-1997 .... **CLC 1, 2, 4, 7, 10, 15, 47,
109; PC 40; TCLC 151**
See also AAYA 50; AITN 1, 2; AMWS 4;
BPFB 1; CA 9-12R; 156; CABS 2; CANR
10, 48, 61, 105; CDALB 1968-1988; CP
7; CPW; CSW; DA3; DAM NOV, POET,
POP; DLB 5, 193; DLBD 7; DLBY 1982,
1993, 1996, 1997, 1998; EWL 3; INT
CANR-10; MTCW 1, 2; NFS 9; PFS 6,
11; RGAL 4; TUS
Dickey, William 1928-1994 .... **CLC 3, 28**
See also CA 9-12R; 145; CANR 24, 79;
DLB 5
Dickinson, Charles 1951- .... **CLC 49**
See also CA 128
Dickinson, Emily (Elizabeth)
1830-1886 ... **NCLC 21, 77; PC 1; WLC**
See also AAYA 22; AMW; AMWR 1;
CDALB 1865-1917; DA; DA3; DAB;
DAC; DAM MST, POET; DLB 1, 243;
EXPP; MAWW; PAB; PFS 1, 2, 3, 4, 5,
6, 8, 10, 11, 13, 16; RGAL 4; SATA 29;
TUS; WP; WYA
Dickinson, Mrs. Herbert Ward
See Phelps, Elizabeth Stuart

Dickinson, Peter (Malcolm de Brissac)
1927- .... **CLC 12, 35**
See also AAYA 9, 49; BYA 5; CA 41-44R;
CANR 31, 58, 88, 134; CLR 29; CMW 4;
DLB 87, 161, 276; JRDA; MAICYA 1, 2;
SATA 5, 62, 95, 150; SFW 4; WYA; YAW
Dickson, Carr
See Carr, John Dickson
Dickson, Carter
See Carr, John Dickson
Diderot, Denis 1713-1784 .... **LC 26**
See also EW 4; GFL Beginnings to 1789;
LMFS 1; RGWL 2, 3
Didion, Joan 1934- . **CLC 1, 3, 8, 14, 32, 129**
See also AITN 1; AMWS 4; CA 5-8R;
CANR 14, 52, 76, 125; CDALB 1968-
1988; CN 7; DA3; DAM NOV; DLB 2,
173, 185; DLBY 1981, 1986; EWL 3;
MAWW; MTCW 1, 2; NFS 3; RGAL 4;
TCWW 2; TUS
di Donato, Pietro 1911-1992 .... **TCLC 159**
See also CA 101; 136; DLB 9
Dietrich, Robert
See Hunt, E(verette) Howard, (Jr.)
Difusa, Pati
See Almodovar, Pedro
Dillard, Annie 1945- .... **CLC 9, 60, 115**
See also AAYA 6, 43; AMWS 6; ANW; CA
49-52; CANR 3, 43, 62, 90, 125; DA3;
DAM NOV; DLB 275, 278; DLBY 1980;
LAIT 4, 5; MTCW 1, 2; NCFS 1; RGAL
4; SATA 10, 140; TUS
Dillard, R(ichard) H(enry) W(ilde)
1937- .... **CLC 5**
See also CA 21-24R; CAAS 7; CANR 10;
CP 7; CSW; DLB 5, 244
Dillon, Eilis 1920-1994 .... **CLC 17**
See also CA 9-12R, 182; 147; CAAE 182;
CAAS 3; CANR 4, 38, 78; CLR 26; MAI-
CYA 1, 2; MAICYAS 1; SATA 2, 74;
SATA-Essay 105; SATA-Obit 83; YAW
Dimont, Penelope
See Mortimer, Penelope (Ruth)
Dinesen, Isak ...... **CLC 10, 29, 95; SSC 7, 75**
See Blixen, Karen (Christentze Dinesen)
See also EW 10; EWL 3; EXPS; FW; HGG;
LAIT 3; MTCW 1; NCFS 2; NFS 9;
RGSF 2; RGWL 2, 3; SSFS 3, 6, 13;
WLIT 2
Ding Ling .... **CLC 68**
See Chiang, Pin-chin
See also RGWL 3
Diphusa, Patty
See Almodovar, Pedro
Disch, Thomas M(ichael) 1940- ... **CLC 7, 36**
See Disch, Tom
See also AAYA 17; BPFB 1; CA 21-24R;
CAAS 4; CANR 17, 36, 54, 89; CLR 18;
CP 7; DA3; DLB 8; HGG; MAICYA 1, 2;
MTCW 1, 2; SAAS 15; SATA 92; SCFW;
SFW 4; SUFW 2
Disch, Tom
See Disch, Thomas M(ichael)
See also DLB 282
d'Isly, Georges
See Simenon, Georges (Jacques Christian)
Disraeli, Benjamin 1804-1881 ... **NCLC 2, 39,
79**
See also BRW 4; DLB 21, 55; RGEL 2
Ditcum, Steve
See Crumb, R(obert)
Dixon, Paige
See Corcoran, Barbara (Asenath)
Dixon, Stephen 1936- .... **CLC 52; SSC 16**
See also AMWS 12; CA 89-92; CANR 17,
40, 54, 91; CN 7; DLB 130
Dixon, Thomas 1864-1946 .... **TCLC 163**
See also RHW

Doyle, Conan
See Doyle, Sir Arthur Conan

Doyle, John
See Graves, Robert (von Ranke)

Doyle, Roddy 1958(?)- .... **CLC 81, 178**
See also AAYA 14; BRWS 5; CA 143;
CANR 73, 128; CN 7; DA3; DLB 194

Doyle, Sir A. Conan
See Doyle, Sir Arthur Conan

Dr. A
See Asimov, Isaac; Silverstein, Alvin; Silverstein, Virginia B(arbara Opshelor)

Drabble, Margaret 1939- ...... **CLC 2, 3, 5, 8,
10, 22, 53, 129**
See also BRWS 4; CA 13-16R; CANR 18,
35, 63, 112, 131; CDBLB 1960 to Present;
CN 7; CPW; DA3; DAB; DAC; DAM
MST, NOV, POP; DLB 14, 155, 231;
EWL 3; FW; MTCW 1, 2; RGEL 2; SATA
48; TEA

Drakulic, Slavenka 1949- .... **CLC 173**
See also CA 144; CANR 92

Drakulic-Ilic, Slavenka
See Drakulic, Slavenka

Drapier, M. B.
See Swift, Jonathan

Drayham, James
See Mencken, H(enry) L(ouis)

Drayton, Michael 1563-1631 .... **LC 8**
See also DAM POET; DLB 121; RGEL 2

Dreadstone, Carl
See Campbell, (John) Ramsey

Dreiser, Theodore (Herman Albert)
1871-1945 .... **SSC 30; TCLC 10, 18, 35,
83; WLC**
See also AMW; AMWC 2; AMWR 2; BYA
15, 16; CA 106; 132; CDALB 1865-1917;
DA; DA3; DAC; DAM MST, NOV; DLB
9, 12, 102, 137; DLBD 1; EWL 3; LAIT
2; LMFS 2; MTCW 1, 2; NFS 8, 17;
RGAL 4; TUS

Drexler, Rosalyn 1926- .... **CLC 2, 6**
See also CA 81-84; CAD; CANR 68, 124;
CD 5; CWD

Dreyer, Carl Theodor 1889-1968 ...... **CLC 16**
See also CA 116

Drieu la Rochelle, Pierre(-Eugene)
1893-1945 .... **TCLC 21**
See also CA 117; DLB 72; EWL 3; GFL
1789 to the Present

Drinkwater, John 1882-1937 .... **TCLC 57**
See also CA 109; 149; DLB 10, 19, 149;
RGEL 2

Drop Shot
See Cable, George Washington

Droste-Hulshoff, Annette Freiin von
1797-1848 .... **NCLC 3, 133**
See also CDWLB 2; DLB 133; RGSF 2;
RGWL 2, 3

Drummond, Walter
See Silverberg, Robert

Drummond, William Henry
1854-1907 .... **TCLC 25**
See also CA 160; DLB 92

Drummond de Andrade, Carlos
1902-1987 .... **CLC 18; TCLC 139**
See Andrade, Carlos Drummond de
See also CA 132; 123; DLB 307; LAW

Drummond of Hawthornden, William
1585-1649 .... **LC 83**
See also DLB 121, 213; RGEL 2

Drury, Allen (Stuart) 1918-1998 .... **CLC 37**
See also CA 57-60; 170; CANR 18, 52; CN
7; INT CANR-18

Druse, Eleanor
See King, Stephen (Edwin)

Dryden, John 1631-1700 ..... **DC 3; LC 3, 21,
115; PC 25; WLC**
See also BRW 2; CDBLB 1660-1789; DA;
DAB; DAC; DAM DRAM, MST, POET;
DLB 80, 101, 131; EXPP; IDTP; LMFS
1; RGEL 2; TEA; WLIT 3

du Bellay, Joachim 1524-1560 .... **LC 92**
See also GFL Beginnings to 1789; RGWL
2, 3

Duberman, Martin (Bauml) 1930- ..... **CLC 8**
See also CA 1-4R; CAD; CANR 2, 63; CD
5

Dubie, Norman (Evans) 1945- .... **CLC 36**
See also CA 69-72; CANR 12, 115; CP 7;
DLB 120; PFS 12

Du Bois, W(illiam) E(dward) B(urghardt)
1868-1963 ..... **BLC 1; CLC 1, 2, 13, 64,
96; HR 2; TCLC 169; WLC**
See also AAYA 40; AFAW 1, 2; AMWC 1;
AMWS 2; BW 1, 3; CA 85-88; CANR
34, 82, 132; CDALB 1865-1917; DA;
DA3; DAC; DAM MST, MULT, NOV;
DLB 47, 50, 91, 246, 284; EWL 3; EXPP;
LAIT 2; LMFS 2; MTCW 1, 2; NCFS 1;
PFS 13; RGAL 4; SATA 42

Dubus, Andre 1936-1999 ..... **CLC 13, 36, 97;
SSC 15**
See also AMWS 7; CA 21-24R; 177; CANR
17; CN 7; CSW; DLB 130; INT CANR-
17; RGAL 4; SSFS 10

Duca Minimo
See D'Annunzio, Gabriele

Ducharme, Rejean 1941- .... **CLC 74**
See also CA 165; DLB 60

du Chatelet, Emilie 1706-1749 .... **LC 96**

Duchen, Claire .... **CLC 65**

Duclos, Charles Pinot- 1704-1772 .... **LC 1**
See also GFL Beginnings to 1789

Dudek, Louis 1918-2001 .... **CLC 11, 19**
See also CA 45-48; 215; CAAS 14; CANR
1; CP 7; DLB 88

Duerrenmatt, Friedrich 1921-1990 ... **CLC 1,
4, 8, 11, 15, 43, 102**
See Durrenmatt, Friedrich
See also CA 17-20R; CANR 33; CMW 4;
DAM DRAM; DLB 69, 124; MTCW 1, 2

Duffy, Bruce 1953(?)- .... **CLC 50**
See also CA 172

Duffy, Maureen 1933- .... **CLC 37**
See also CA 25-28R; CANR 33, 68; CBD;
CN 7; CP 7; CWD; CWP; DFS 15; DLB
14; FW; MTCW 1

Du Fu
See Tu Fu
See also RGWL 2, 3

Dugan, Alan 1923-2003 .... **CLC 2, 6**
See also CA 81-84; 220; CANR 119; CP 7;
DLB 5; PFS 10

du Gard, Roger Martin
See Martin du Gard, Roger

Duhamel, Georges 1884-1966 .... **CLC 8**
See also CA 81-84; 25-28R; CANR 35;
DLB 65; EWL 3; GFL 1789 to the
Present; MTCW 1

Dujardin, Edouard (Emile Louis)
1861-1949 .... **TCLC 13**
See also CA 109; DLB 123

Duke, Raoul
See Thompson, Hunter S(tockton)

Dulles, John Foster 1888-1959 .... **TCLC 72**
See also CA 115; 149

Dumas, Alexandre (pere)
1802-1870 .... **NCLC 11, 71; WLC**
See also AAYA 22; BYA 3; DA; DA3;
DAB; DAC; DAM MST, NOV; DLB 119,
192; EW 6; GFL 1789 to the Present;
LAIT 1, 2; NFS 14, 19; RGWL 2, 3;
SATA 18; TWA; WCH

Dumas, Alexandre (fils) 1824-1895 ...... **DC 1;
NCLC 9**
See also DLB 192; GFL 1789 to the Present;
RGWL 2, 3

Dumas, Claudine
See Malzberg, Barry N(athaniel)

Dumas, Henry L. 1934-1968 .... **CLC 6, 62**
See also BW 1; CA 85-88; DLB 41; RGAL
4

du Maurier, Daphne 1907-1989 .. **CLC 6, 11,
59; SSC 18**
See also AAYA 37; BPFB 1; BRWS 3; CA
5-8R; 128; CANR 6, 55; CMW 4; CPW;
DA3; DAB; DAC; DAM MST, POP;
DLB 191; HGG; LAIT 3; MSW; MTCW
1, 2; NFS 12; RGEL 2; RGSF 2; RHW;
SATA 27; SATA-Obit 60; SSFS 14, 16;
TEA

Du Maurier, George 1834-1896 ..... **NCLC 86**
See also DLB 153, 178; RGEL 2

Dunbar, Paul Laurence 1872-1906 .. **BLC 1;
PC 5; SSC 8; TCLC 2, 12; WLC**
See also AFAW 1, 2; AMWS 2; BW 1, 3;
CA 104; 124; CANR 79; CDALB 1865-
1917; DA; DA3; DAC; DAM MST,
MULT, POET; DLB 50, 54, 78; EXPP;
RGAL 4; SATA 34

Dunbar, William 1460(?)-1520(?) .... **LC 20;
PC 67**
See also BRWS 8; DLB 132, 146; RGEL 2

Dunbar-Nelson, Alice .... **HR 2**
See Nelson, Alice Ruth Moore Dunbar

Duncan, Dora Angela
See Duncan, Isadora

Duncan, Isadora 1877(?)-1927 .... **TCLC 68**
See also CA 118; 149

Duncan, Lois 1934- .... **CLC 26**
See also AAYA 4, 34; BYA 6, 8; CA 1-4R;
CANR 2, 23, 36, 111; CLR 29; JRDA;
MAICYA 1, 2; MAICYAS 1; SAAS 2;
SATA 1, 36, 75, 133, 141; SATA-Essay
141; WYA; YAW

Duncan, Robert (Edward)
1919-1988 .... **CLC 1, 2, 4, 7, 15, 41, 55;
PC 2**
See also BG 2; CA 9-12R; 124; CANR 28,
62; DAM POET; DLB 5, 16, 193; EWL
3; MTCW 1, 2; PFS 13; RGAL 4; WP

Duncan, Sara Jeannette
1861-1922 .... **TCLC 60**
See also CA 157; DLB 92

Dunlap, William 1766-1839 .... **NCLC 2**
See also DLB 30, 37, 59; RGAL 4

Dunn, Douglas (Eaglesham) 1942- .... **CLC 6,
40**
See also BRWS 10; CA 45-48; CANR 2,
33, 126; CP 7; DLB 40; MTCW 1

Dunn, Katherine (Karen) 1945- .... **CLC 71**
See also CA 33-36R; CANR 72; HGG;
MTCW 1

Dunn, Stephen (Elliott) 1939- .. **CLC 36, 206**
See also AMWS 11; CA 33-36R; CANR
12, 48, 53, 105; CP 7; DLB 105; PFS 21

Dunne, Finley Peter 1867-1936 ...... **TCLC 28**
See also CA 108; 178; DLB 11, 23; RGAL
4

Dunne, John Gregory 1932-2003 ..... **CLC 28**
See also CA 25-28R; 222; CANR 14, 50;
CN 7; DLBY 1980

Dunsany, Lord .... **TCLC 2, 59**
See Dunsany, Edward John Moreton Drax
Plunkett
See also DLB 77, 153, 156, 255; FANT;
IDTP; RGEL 2; SFW 4; SUFW 1

**Dunsany, Edward John Moreton Drax
Plunkett** 1878-1957
See Dunsany, Lord
See also CA 104; 148; DLB 10; MTCW 1

Ekelof, (Bengt) Gunnar 1907-1968
  See Ekeloef, (Bengt) Gunnar
  See also DLB 259; EW 12; EWL 3
Ekelund, Vilhelm 1880-1949 .... **TCLC 75**
  See also CA 189; EWL 3
Ekwensi, C. O. D.
  See Ekwensi, Cyprian (Odiatu Duaka)
Ekwensi, Cyprian (Odiatu Duaka)
  1921- .... **BLC 1; CLC 4**
  See also AFW; BW 2, 3; CA 29-32R;
  CANR 18, 42, 74, 125; CDWLB 3; CN
  7; CWRI 5; DAM MULT; DLB 117; EWL
  3; MTCW 1, 2; RGEL 2; SATA 66; WLIT
  2
Elaine .... **TCLC 18**
  See Leverson, Ada Esther
El Crummo
  See Crumb, R(obert)
Elder, Lonne III 1931-1996 ..... **BLC 1; DC 8**
  See also BW 1, 3; CA 81-84; 152; CAD;
  CANR 25; DAM MULT; DLB 7, 38, 44
Eleanor of Aquitaine 1122-1204 ... **CMLC 39**
Elia
  See Lamb, Charles
Eliade, Mircea 1907-1986 .... **CLC 19**
  See also CA 65-68; 119; CANR 30, 62; CD-
  WLB 4; DLB 220; EWL 3; MTCW 1;
  RGWL 3; SFW 4
Eliot, A. D.
  See Jewett, (Theodora) Sarah Orne
Eliot, Alice
  See Jewett, (Theodora) Sarah Orne
Eliot, Dan
  See Silverberg, Robert
Eliot, George 1819-1880 ...... **NCLC 4, 13, 23,**
  41, 49, 89, 118; PC 20; SSC 72; WLC
  See Evans, Mary Ann
  See also BRW 5; BRWC 1, 2; BRWR 2;
  CDBLB 1832-1890; CN 7; CPW; DA;
  DA3; DAB; DAC; DAM MST, NOV;
  DLB 21, 35, 55; LATS 1:1; LMFS 1; NFS
  17; RGEL 2; RGSF 2; SSFS 8; TEA;
  WLIT 3
Eliot, John 1604-1690 .... **LC 5**
  See also DLB 24
Eliot, T(homas) S(tearns)
  1888-1965 ...... **CLC 1, 2, 3, 6, 9, 10, 13,**
  15, 24, 34, 41, 55, 57, 113; PC 5, 31;
  WLC
  See also AAYA 28; AMW; AMWC 1;
  AMWR 1; BRW 7; BRWR 2; CA 5-8R;
  25-28R; CANR 41; CDALB 1929-1941;
  DA; DA3; DAB; DAC; DAM DRAM,
  MST, POET; DFS 4, 13; DLB 7, 10, 45,
  63, 245; DLBY 1988; EWL 3; EXPP;
  LAIT 3; LATS 1:1; LMFS 2; MTCW 1,
  2; NCFS 5; PAB; PFS 1, 7, 20; RGAL 4;
  RGEL 2; TUS; WLIT 4; WP
Elizabeth 1866-1941 .... **TCLC 41**
Elizabeth I .... **LC 118**
  See also DLB 136
Elkin, Stanley L(awrence)
  1930-1995 .. **CLC 4, 6, 9, 14, 27, 51, 91;**
  SSC 12
  See also AMWS 6; BPFB 1; CA 9-12R;
  148; CANR 8, 46; CN 7; CPW; DAM
  NOV, POP; DLB 2, 28, 218, 278; DLBY
  1980; EWL 3; INT CANR-8; MTCW 1,
  2; RGAL 4
Elledge, Scott .... **CLC 34**
Elliott, Don
  See Silverberg, Robert
Elliott, George P(aul) 1918-1980 .... **CLC 2**
  See also CA 1-4R; 97-100; CANR 2; DLB
  244
Elliott, Janice 1931-1995 .... **CLC 47**
  See also CA 13-16R; CANR 8, 29, 84; CN
  7; DLB 14; SATA 119

Elliott, Sumner Locke 1917-1991 ..... **CLC 38**
  See also CA 5-8R; 134; CANR 2, 21; DLB
  289
Elliott, William
  See Bradbury, Ray (Douglas)
Ellis, A. E. .... **CLC 7**
Ellis, Alice Thomas .... **CLC 40**
  See Haycraft, Anna (Margaret)
  See also DLB 194; MTCW 1
Ellis, Bret Easton 1964- ...... **CLC 39, 71, 117**
  See also AAYA 2, 43; CA 118; 123; CANR
  51, 74, 126; CN 7; CPW; DA3; DAM
  POP; DLB 292; HGG; INT CA-123;
  MTCW 1; NFS 11
Ellis, (Henry) Havelock
  1859-1939 .... **TCLC 14**
  See also CA 109; 169; DLB 190
Ellis, Landon
  See Ellison, Harlan (Jay)
Ellis, Trey 1962- .... **CLC 55**
  See also CA 146; CANR 92
Ellison, Harlan (Jay) 1934- ... **CLC 1, 13, 42,**
  139; SSC 14
  See also AAYA 29; BPFB 1; BYA 14; CA
  5-8R; CANR 5, 46, 115; CPW; DAM
  POP; DLB 8; HGG; INT CANR-5;
  MTCW 1, 2; SCFW 2; SFW 4; SSFS 13,
  14, 15; SUFW 1, 2
Ellison, Ralph (Waldo) 1914-1994 .... **BLC 1;**
  CLC 1, 3, 11, 54, 86, 114; SSC 26, 79;
  WLC
  See also AAYA 19; AFAW 1, 2; AMWC;
  AMWR 2; AMWS 2; BPFB 1; BW 1, 3;
  BYA 2; CA 9-12R; 145; CANR 24, 53;
  CDALB 1941-1968; CSW; DA; DA3;
  DAB; DAC; DAM MST, MULT, NOV;
  DLB 2, 76, 227; DLBY 1994; EWL 3;
  EXPN; EXPS; LAIT 4; MTCW 1, 2;
  NCFS 3; NFS 2; RGAL 4; RGSF 2; SSFS
  1, 11; YAW
Ellmann, Lucy (Elizabeth) 1956- ..... **CLC 61**
  See also CA 128
Ellmann, Richard (David)
  1918-1987 .... **CLC 50**
  See also BEST 89:2; CA 1-4R; 122; CANR
  2, 28, 61; DLB 103; DLBY 1987; MTCW
  1, 2
Elman, Richard (Martin)
  1934-1997 .... **CLC 19**
  See also CA 17-20R; 163; CAAS 3; CANR
  47
Elron
  See Hubbard, L(afayette) Ron(ald)
El Saadawi, Nawal 1931- .... **CLC 196**
  See al'Sadaawi, Nawal; Sa'adawi, al-
  Nawal; Saadawi, Nawal El; Sa'dawi,
  Nawal al-
  See also CA 118; CAAS 11; CANR 44, 92
Eluard, Paul .... **PC 38; TCLC 7, 41**
  See Grindel, Eugene
  See also EWL 3; GFL 1789 to the Present;
  RGWL 2, 3
Ensler, Eve 1953- .... **CLC 212**
  See also CA 172; CANR 126
Elyot, Thomas 1490(?)-1546 .... **LC 11**
  See also DLB 136; RGEL 2
Elytis, Odysseus 1911-1996 .... **CLC 15, 49,**
  100; PC 21
  See Alepoudelis, Odysseus
  See also CA 102; 151; CANR 94; CWW 2;
  DAM POET; EW 13; EWL 3; MTCW 1,
  2; RGWL 2, 3
Emecheta, (Florence Onye) Buchi
  1944- ...... **BLC 2; CLC 14, 48, 128, 214**
  See also AFW; BW 2, 3; CA 81-84; CANR
  27, 81, 126; CDWLB 3; CN 7; CWRI 5;
  DA3; DAM MULT; DLB 117; EWL 3;
  FW; MTCW 1, 2; NFS 12, 14; SATA 66;
  WLIT 2

Emerson, Mary Moody
  1774-1863 .... **NCLC 66**
Emerson, Ralph Waldo 1803-1882 . **NCLC 1,**
  38, 98; PC 18; WLC
  See also AAYA 60; AMW; ANW; CDALB
  1640-1865; DA; DA3; DAB; DAC; DAM
  MST, POET; DLB 1, 59, 73, 183, 223,
  270; EXPP; LAIT 2; LMFS 1; NCFS 3;
  PFS 4, 17; RGAL 4; TUS; WP
Eminescu, Mihail 1850-1889 .. **NCLC 33, 131**
Empedocles 5th cent. B.C.- .... **CMLC 50**
  See also DLB 176
Empson, William 1906-1984 ... **CLC 3, 8, 19,**
  33, 34
  See also BRWS 2; CA 17-20R; 112; CANR
  31, 61; DLB 20; EWL 3; MTCW 1, 2;
  RGEL 2
Enchi, Fumiko (Ueda) 1905-1986 ..... **CLC 31**
  See Enchi Fumiko
  See also CA 129; 121; FW; MJW
Enchi Fumiko
  See Enchi, Fumiko (Ueda)
  See also DLB 182; EWL 3
Ende, Michael (Andreas Helmuth)
  1929-1995 .... **CLC 31**
  See also BYA 5; CA 118; 124; 149; CANR
  36, 110; CLR 14; DLB 75; MAICYA 1,
  2; MAICYAS 1; SATA 61, 130; SATA-
  Brief 42; SATA-Obit 86
Endo, Shusaku 1923-1996 ..... **CLC 7, 14, 19,**
  54, 99; SSC 48; TCLC 152
  See Endo Shusaku
  See also CA 29-32R; 153; CANR 21, 54,
  131; DA3; DAM NOV; MTCW 1, 2;
  RGSF 2; RGWL 2, 3
Endo Shusaku
  See Endo, Shusaku
  See also CWW 2; DLB 182; EWL 3
Engel, Marian 1933-1985 .... **CLC 36; TCLC**
  137
  See also CA 25-28R; CANR 12; DLB 53;
  FW; INT CANR-12
Engelhardt, Frederick
  See Hubbard, L(afayette) Ron(ald)
Engels, Friedrich 1820-1895 .. **NCLC 85, 114**
  See also DLB 129; LATS 1:1
Enright, D(ennis) J(oseph)
  1920-2002 .... **CLC 4, 8, 31**
  See also CA 1-4R; 211; CANR 1, 42, 83;
  CP 7; DLB 27; EWL 3; SATA 25; SATA-
  Obit 140
Enzensberger, Hans Magnus
  1929- .... **CLC 43; PC 28**
  See also CA 116; 119; CANR 103; CWW
  2; EWL 3
Ephron, Nora 1941- .... **CLC 17, 31**
  See also AAYA 35; AITN 2; CA 65-68;
  CANR 12, 39, 83
Epicurus 341B.C.-270B.C. .... **CMLC 21**
  See also DLB 176
Epsilon
  See Betjeman, John
Epstein, Daniel Mark 1948- .... **CLC 7**
  See also CA 49-52; CANR 2, 53, 90
Epstein, Jacob 1956- .... **CLC 19**
  See also CA 114
Epstein, Jean 1897-1953 .... **TCLC 92**
Epstein, Joseph 1937- .... **CLC 39, 204**
  See also AMWS 14; CA 112; 119; CANR
  50, 65, 117
Epstein, Leslie 1938- .... **CLC 27**
  See also AMWS 12; CA 73-76, 215; CAAE
  215; CAAS 12; CANR 23, 69; DLB 299
Equiano, Olaudah 1745(?)-1797 . **BLC 2; LC**
  16
  See also AFAW 1, 2; CDWLB 3; DAM
  MULT; DLB 37, 50; WLIT 2

Fast, Howard (Melvin) 1914-2003 .. **CLC 23, 131**
See also AAYA 16; BPFB 1; CA 1-4R, 181; 214; CAAE 181; CAAS 18; CANR 1, 33, 54, 75, 98; CMW 4; CN 7; CPW; DAM NOV; DLB 9; INT CANR-33; LATS 1:1; MTCW 1; RHW; SATA 7; SATA-Essay 107; TCWW 2; YAW

Faulcon, Robert
See Holdstock, Robert P.

Faulkner, William (Cuthbert) 1897-1962 .... **CLC 1, 3, 6, 8, 9, 11, 14, 18, 28, 52, 68; SSC 1, 35, 42; TCLC 141; WLC**
See also AAYA 7; AMW; AMWR 1; BPFB 1; BYA 5, 15; CA 81-84; CANR 33; CDALB 1929-1941; DA; DA3; DAB; DAC; DAM MST, NOV; DLB 9, 11, 44, 102; DLBD 2; DLBY 1986, 1997; EWL 3; EXPN; EXPS; LAIT 2; LATS 1:1; LMFS 2; MTCW 1, 2; NFS 4, 8, 13; RGAL 4; RGSF 2; SSFS 2, 5, 6, 12; TUS

Fauset, Jessie Redmon 1882(?)-1961 .. **BLC 2; CLC 19, 54; HR 2**
See also AFAW 2; BW 1; CA 109; CANR 83; DAM MULT; DLB 51; FW; LMFS 2; MAWW

Faust, Frederick (Schiller) 1892-1944(?) .... **TCLC 49**
See also Austin, Frank; Brand, Max; Challis, George; Dawson, Peter; Dexter, Martin; Evans, Evan; Frederick, John; Frost, Frederick; Manning, David; Silver, Nicholas
See also CA 108; 152; DAM POP; DLB 256; TUS

Faust, Irvin 1924- .... **CLC 8**
See also CA 33-36R; CANR 28, 67; CN 7; DLB 2, 28, 218, 278; DLBY 1980

Faustino, Domingo 1811-1888 ...... **NCLC 123**

Fawkes, Guy
See Benchley, Robert (Charles)

Fearing, Kenneth (Flexner) 1902-1961 .... **CLC 51**
See also CA 93-96; CANR 59; CMW 4; DLB 9; RGAL 4

Fecamps, Elise
See Creasey, John

Federman, Raymond 1928- .... **CLC 6, 47**
See also CA 17-20R, 208; CAAE 208; CAAS 8; CANR 10, 43, 83, 108; CN 7; DLBY 1980

Federspiel, J(uerg) F. 1931- .... **CLC 42**
See also CA 146

Feiffer, Jules (Ralph) 1929- ...... **CLC 2, 8, 64**
See also AAYA 3; CA 17-20R; CAD; CANR 30, 59, 129; CD 5; DAM DRAM; DLB 7, 44; INT CANR-30; MTCW 1; SATA 8, 61, 111

Feige, Hermann Albert Otto Maximilian
See Traven, B.

Feinberg, David B. 1956-1994 .... **CLC 59**
See also CA 135; 147

Feinstein, Elaine 1930- .... **CLC 36**
See also CA 69-72; CAAS 1; CANR 31, 68, 121; CN 7; CP 7; CWP; DLB 14, 40; MTCW 1

Feke, Gilbert David .... **CLC 65**

Feldman, Irving (Mordecai) 1928- ..... **CLC 7**
See also CA 1-4R; CANR 1; CP 7; DLB 169

Felix-Tchicaya, Gerald
See Tchicaya, Gerald Felix

Fellini, Federico 1920-1993 .... **CLC 16, 85**
See also CA 65-68; 143; CANR 33

Felltham, Owen 1602(?)-1668 .... **LC 92**
See also DLB 126, 151

Felsen, Henry Gregor 1916-1995 ..... **CLC 17**
See also CA 1-4R; 180; CANR 1; SAAS 2; SATA 1

Felski, Rita .... **CLC 65**

Fenno, Jack
See Calisher, Hortense

Fenollosa, Ernest (Francisco) 1853-1908 .... **TCLC 91**

Fenton, James Martin 1949- .... **CLC 32, 209**
See also CA 102; CANR 108; CP 7; DLB 40; PFS 11

Ferber, Edna 1887-1968 .... **CLC 18, 93**
See also AITN 1; CA 5-8R; 25-28R; CANR 68, 105; DLB 9, 28, 86, 266; MTCW 1, 2; RGAL 4; RHW; SATA 7; TCWW 2

Ferdowsi, Abu'l Qasem 940-1020 . **CMLC 43**
See also RGWL 2, 3

Ferguson, Helen
See Kavan, Anna

Ferguson, Niall 1964- .... **CLC 134**
See also CA 190

Ferguson, Samuel 1810-1886 .... **NCLC 33**
See also DLB 32; RGEL 2

Fergusson, Robert 1750-1774 .... **LC 29**
See also DLB 109; RGEL 2

Ferling, Lawrence
See Ferlinghetti, Lawrence (Monsanto)

Ferlinghetti, Lawrence (Monsanto) 1919(?)- .... **CLC 2, 6, 10, 27, 111; PC 1**
See also CA 5-8R; CANR 3, 41, 73, 125; CDALB 1941-1968; CP 7; DA3; DAM POET; DLB 5, 16; MTCW 1, 2; RGAL 4; WP

Fern, Fanny
See Parton, Sara Payson Willis

Fernandez, Vicente Garcia Huidobro
See Huidobro Fernandez, Vicente Garcia

Fernandez-Armesto, Felipe .... **CLC 70**

Fernandez de Lizardi, Jose Joaquin
See Lizardi, Jose Joaquin Fernandez de

Ferre, Rosario 1938- ...... **CLC 139; HLCS 1; SSC 36**
See also CA 131; CANR 55, 81, 134; CWW 2; DLB 145; EWL 3; HW 1, 2; LAWS 1; MTCW 1; WLIT 1

Ferrer, Gabriel (Francisco Victor) Miro
See Miro (Ferrer), Gabriel (Francisco Victor)

Ferrier, Susan (Edmonstone) 1782-1854 .... **NCLC 8**
See also DLB 116; RGEL 2

Ferrigno, Robert 1948(?)- .... **CLC 65**
See also CA 140; CANR 125

Ferron, Jacques 1921-1985 .... **CLC 94**
See also CA 117; 129; CCA 1; DAC; DLB 60; EWL 3

Feuchtwanger, Lion 1884-1958 .... **TCLC 3**
See also CA 104; 187; DLB 66; EWL 3

Feuerbach, Ludwig 1804-1872 ..... **NCLC 139**
See also DLB 133

Feuillet, Octave 1821-1890 .... **NCLC 45**
See also DLB 192

Feydeau, Georges (Leon Jules Marie) 1862-1921 .... **TCLC 22**
See also CA 113; 152; CANR 84; DAM DRAM; DLB 192; EWL 3; GFL 1789 to the Present; RGWL 2, 3

Fichte, Johann Gottlieb 1762-1814 .... **NCLC 62**
See also DLB 90

Ficino, Marsilio 1433-1499 .... **LC 12**
See also LMFS 1

Fiedeler, Hans
See Doeblin, Alfred

Fiedler, Leslie A(aron) 1917-2003 ..... **CLC 4, 13, 24**
See also AMWS 13; CA 9-12R; 212; CANR 7, 63; CN 7; DLB 28, 67; EWL 3; MTCW 1, 2; RGAL 4; TUS

Field, Andrew 1938- .... **CLC 44**
See also CA 97-100; CANR 25

Field, Eugene 1850-1895 .... **NCLC 3**
See also DLB 23, 42, 140; DLBD 13; MAICYA 1, 2; RGAL 4; SATA 16

Field, Gans T.
See Wellman, Manly Wade

Field, Michael 1915-1971 .... **TCLC 43**
See also CA 29-32R

Field, Peter
See Hobson, Laura Z(ametkin)
See also TCWW 2

Fielding, Helen 1958- .... **CLC 146**
See also CA 172; CANR 127; DLB 231

Fielding, Henry 1707-1754 .... **LC 1, 46, 85; WLC**
See also BRW 3; BRWR 1; CDBLB 1660-1789; DA; DA3; DAB; DAC; DAM DRAM, MST, NOV; DLB 39, 84, 101; NFS 18; RGEL 2; TEA; WLIT 3

Fielding, Sarah 1710-1768 .... **LC 1, 44**
See also DLB 39; RGEL 2; TEA

Fields, W. C. 1880-1946 .... **TCLC 80**
See also DLB 44

Fierstein, Harvey (Forbes) 1954- ...... **CLC 33**
See also CA 123; 129; CAD; CD 5; CPW; DA3; DAM DRAM, POP; DFS 6; DLB 266; GLL

Figes, Eva 1932- .... **CLC 31**
See also CA 53-56; CANR 4, 44, 83; CN 7; DLB 14, 271; FW

Filippo, Eduardo de
See de Filippo, Eduardo

Finch, Anne 1661-1720 .... **LC 3; PC 21**
See also BRWS 9; DLB 95

Finch, Robert (Duer Claydon) 1900-1995 .... **CLC 18**
See also CA 57-60; CANR 9, 24, 49; CP 7; DLB 88

Findley, Timothy (Irving Frederick) 1930-2002 .... **CLC 27, 102**
See also CA 25-28R; 206; CANR 12, 42, 69, 109; CCA 1; CN 7; DAC; DAM MST; DLB 53; FANT; RHW

Fink, William
See Mencken, H(enry) L(ouis)

Firbank, Louis 1942-
See Reed, Lou
See also CA 117

Firbank, (Arthur Annesley) Ronald 1886-1926 .... **TCLC 1**
See also BRWS 2; CA 104; 177; DLB 36; EWL 3; RGEL 2

Fish, Stanley
See Fish, Stanley Eugene

Fish, Stanley E.
See Fish, Stanley Eugene

Fish, Stanley Eugene 1938- .... **CLC 142**
See also CA 112; 132; CANR 90; DLB 67

Fisher, Dorothy (Frances) Canfield 1879-1958 .... **TCLC 87**
See also CA 114; 136; CANR 80; CLR 71,; CWRI 5; DLB 9, 102, 284; MAICYA 1, 2; YABC 1

Fisher, M(ary) F(rances) K(ennedy) 1908-1992 .... **CLC 76, 87**
See also CA 77-80; 138; CANR 44; MTCW 1

Fisher, Roy 1930- .... **CLC 25**
See also CA 81-84; CAAS 10; CANR 16; CP 7; DLB 40

Fouque, Friedrich (Heinrich Karl) de la
Motte 1777-1843 .... **NCLC 2**
See also DLB 90; RGWL 2, 3; SUFW 1

Fourier, Charles 1772-1837 .... **NCLC 51**

Fournier, Henri-Alban 1886-1914
See Alain-Fournier
See also CA 104; 179

Fournier, Pierre 1916- .... **CLC 11**
See Gascar, Pierre
See also CA 89-92; CANR 16, 40

Fowles, John (Robert) 1926- . **CLC 1, 2, 3, 4,**
6, 9, 10, 15, 33, 87; SSC 33
See also BPFB 1; BRWS 1; CA 5-8R;
CANR 25, 71, 103; CDBLB 1960 to
Present; CN 7; DA3; DAB; DAC; DAM
MST; DLB 14, 139, 207; EWL 3; HGG;
MTCW 1, 2; RGEL 2; RHW; SATA 22;
TEA; WLIT 4

Fox, Paula 1923- .... **CLC 2, 8, 121**
See also AAYA 3, 37; BYA 3, 8; CA 73-76;
CANR 20, 36, 62, 105; CLR 1, 44, 96;
DLB 52; JRDA; MAICYA 1, 2; MTCW
1; NFS 12; SATA 17, 60, 120; WYA;
YAW

Fox, William Price (Jr.) 1926- .... **CLC 22**
See also CA 17-20R; CAAS 19; CANR 11;
CSW; DLB 2; DLBY 1981

Foxe, John 1517(?)-1587 .... **LC 14**
See also DLB 132

Frame, Janet ... **CLC 2, 3, 6, 22, 66, 96; SSC**
29
See Clutha, Janet Paterson Frame
See also CN 7; CWP; EWL 3; RGEL 2;
RGSF 2; TWA

France, Anatole .... **TCLC 9**
See Thibault, Jacques Anatole Francois
See also DLB 123; EWL 3; GFL 1789 to
the Present; MTCW 1; RGWL 2, 3;
SUFW 1

Francis, Claude .... **CLC 50**
See also CA 192

Francis, Richard Stanley 1920- ... **CLC 2, 22,**
42, 102
See also AAYA 5, 21; BEST 89:3; BPFB 1;
CA 5-8R; CANR 9, 42, 68, 100; CDBLB
1960 to Present; CMW 4; CN 7; DA3;
DAM POP; DLB 87; INT CANR-9;
MSW; MTCW 1, 2

Francis, Robert (Churchill)
1901-1987 .... **CLC 15; PC 34**
See also AMWS 9; CA 1-4R; 123; CANR
1; EXPP; PFS 12

Francis, Lord Jeffrey
See Jeffrey, Francis
See also DLB 107

Frank, Anne(lies Marie)
1929-1945 .... **TCLC 17; WLC**
See also AAYA 12; BYA 1; CA 113; 133;
CANR 68; CLR 101; DA; DA3; DAB;
DAC; DAM MST; LAIT 4; MAICYA 2;
MAICYAS 1; MTCW 1, 2; NCFS 2;
SATA 87; SATA-Brief 42; WYA; YAW

Frank, Bruno 1887-1945 .... **TCLC 81**
See also CA 189; DLB 118; EWL 3

Frank, Elizabeth 1945- .... **CLC 39**
See also CA 121; 126; CANR 78; INT CA-
126

Frankl, Viktor E(mil) 1905-1997 ...... **CLC 93**
See also CA 65-68; 161

Franklin, Benjamin
See Hasek, Jaroslav (Matej Frantisek)

Franklin, Benjamin 1706-1790 .... **LC 25;**
WLCS
See also AMW; CDALB 1640-1865; DA;
DA3; DAB; DAC; DAM MST; DLB 24,
43, 73, 183; LAIT 1; RGAL 4; TUS

Franklin, (Stella Maria Sarah) Miles
(Lampe) 1879-1954 .... **TCLC 7**
See also CA 104; 164; DLB 230; FW;
MTCW 2; RGEL 2; TWA

Franzen, Jonathan 1959- .... **CLC 202**
See also CA 129; CANR 105

Fraser, Antonia (Pakenham) 1932- . **CLC 32,**
107
See also AAYA 57; CA 85-88; CANR 44,
65, 119; CMW; DLB 276; MTCW 1, 2;
SATA-Brief 32

Fraser, George MacDonald 1925- ...... **CLC 7**
See also AAYA 48; CA 45-48, 180; CAAE
180; CANR 2, 48, 74; MTCW 1; RHW

Fraser, Sylvia 1935- .... **CLC 64**
See also CA 45-48; CANR 1, 16, 60; CCA
1

Frayn, Michael 1933- . **CLC 3, 7, 31, 47, 176**
See also BRWC 2; BRWS 7; CA 5-8R;
CANR 30, 69, 114, 133; CBD; CD 5; CN
7; DAM DRAM, NOV; DLB 13, 14, 194,
245; FANT; MTCW 1, 2; SFW 4

Fraze, Candida (Merrill) 1945- .... **CLC 50**
See also CA 126

Frazer, Andrew
See Marlowe, Stephen

Frazer, J(ames) G(eorge)
1854-1941 .... **TCLC 32**
See also BRWS 3; CA 118; NCFS 5

Frazer, Robert Caine
See Creasey, John

Frazer, Sir James George
See Frazer, J(ames) G(eorge)

Frazier, Charles 1950- .... **CLC 109**
See also AAYA 34; CA 161; CANR 126;
CSW; DLB 292

Frazier, Ian 1951- .... **CLC 46**
See also CA 130; CANR 54, 93

Frederic, Harold 1856-1898 .... **NCLC 10**
See also AMW; DLB 12, 23; DLBD 13;
RGAL 4

Frederick, John
See Faust, Frederick (Schiller)
See also TCWW 2

Frederick the Great 1712-1786 .... **LC 14**

Fredro, Aleksander 1793-1876 .... **NCLC 8**

Freeling, Nicolas 1927-2003 .... **CLC 38**
See also CA 49-52; 218; CAAS 12; CANR
1, 17, 50, 84; CMW 4; CN 7; DLB 87

Freeman, Douglas Southall
1886-1953 .... **TCLC 11**
See also CA 109; 195; DLB 17; DLBD 17

Freeman, Judith 1946- .... **CLC 55**
See also CA 148; CANR 120; DLB 256

Freeman, Mary E(leanor) Wilkins
1852-1930 .... **SSC 1, 47; TCLC 9**
See also CA 106; 177; DLB 12, 78, 221;
EXPS; FW; HGG; MAWW; RGAL 4;
RGSF 2; SSFS 4, 8; SUFW 1; TUS

Freeman, R(ichard) Austin
1862-1943 .... **TCLC 21**
See also CA 113; CANR 84; CMW 4; DLB
70

French, Albert 1943- .... **CLC 86**
See also BW 3; CA 167

French, Antonia
See Kureishi, Hanif

French, Marilyn 1929- .. **CLC 10, 18, 60, 177**
See also BPFB 1; CA 69-72; CANR 3, 31,
134; CN 7; CPW; DAM DRAM, NOV,
POP; FW; INT CANR-31; MTCW 1, 2

French, Paul
See Asimov, Isaac

Freneau, Philip Morin 1752-1832 .. **NCLC 1,**
111
See also AMWS 2; DLB 37, 43; RGAL 4

Freud, Sigmund 1856-1939 .... **TCLC 52**
See also CA 115; 133; CANR 69; DLB 296;
EW 8; EWL 3; LATS 1:1; MTCW 1, 2;
NCFS 3; TWA

Freytag, Gustav 1816-1895 .... **NCLC 109**
See also DLB 129

Friedan, Betty (Naomi) 1921- .... **CLC 74**
See also CA 65-68; CANR 18, 45, 74; DLB
246; FW; MTCW 1, 2; NCFS 5

Friedlander, Saul 1932- .... **CLC 90**
See also CA 117; 130; CANR 72

Friedman, B(ernard) H(arper)
1926- .... **CLC 7**
See also CA 1-4R; CANR 3, 48

Friedman, Bruce Jay 1930- ...... **CLC 3, 5, 56**
See also CA 9-12R; CAD; CANR 25, 52,
101; CD 7; CN 7; DLB 2, 28, 244; INT
CANR-25; SSFS 18

Friel, Brian 1929- .... **CLC 5, 42, 59, 115; DC**
8; SSC 76
See also BRWS 5; CA 21-24R; CANR 33,
69, 131; CBD; CD 5; DFS 11; DLB 13;
EWL 3; MTCW 1; RGEL 2; TEA

Friis-Baastad, Babbis Ellinor
1921-1970 .... **CLC 12**
See also CA 17-20R; 134; SATA 7

Frisch, Max (Rudolf) 1911-1991 ... **CLC 3, 9,**
14, 18, 32, 44; TCLC 121
See also CA 85-88; 134; CANR 32, 74; CD-
WLB 2; DAM DRAM, NOV; DLB 69,
124; EW 13; EWL 3; MTCW 1, 2; RGWL
2, 3

Fromentin, Eugene (Samuel Auguste)
1820-1876 .... **NCLC 10, 125**
See also DLB 123; GFL 1789 to the Present

Frost, Frederick
See Faust, Frederick (Schiller)
See also TCWW 2

Frost, Robert (Lee) 1874-1963 .. **CLC 1, 3, 4,**
9, 10, 13, 15, 26, 34, 44; PC 1, 39;
WLC
See also AAYA 21; AMW; AMWR 1; CA
89-92; CANR 33; CDALB 1917-1929;
CLR 67; DA; DA3; DAB; DAC; DAM
MST, POET; DLB 54, 284; DLBD 7;
EWL 3; EXPP; MTCW 1, 2; PAB; PFS 1,
2, 3, 4, 5, 6, 7, 10, 13; RGAL 4; SATA
14; TUS; WP; WYA

Froude, James Anthony
1818-1894 .... **NCLC 43**
See also DLB 18, 57, 144

Froy, Herald
See Waterhouse, Keith (Spencer)

Fry, Christopher 1907- .... **CLC 2, 10, 14**
See also BRWS 3; CA 17-20R; CAAS 23;
CANR 9, 30, 74, 132; CBD; CD 5; CP 7;
DAM DRAM; DLB 13; EWL 3; MTCW
1, 2; RGEL 2; SATA 66; TEA

Frye, (Herman) Northrop
1912-1991 .... **CLC 24, 70; TCLC 165**
See also CA 5-8R; 133; CANR 8, 37; DLB
67, 68, 246; EWL 3; MTCW 1, 2; RGAL
4; TWA

Fuchs, Daniel 1909-1993 .... **CLC 8, 22**
See also CA 81-84; 142; CAAS 5; CANR
40; DLB 9, 26, 28; DLBY 1993

Fuchs, Daniel 1934- .... **CLC 34**
See also CA 37-40R; CANR 14, 48

Fuentes, Carlos 1928- .. **CLC 3, 8, 10, 13, 22,**
41, 60, 113; HLC 1; SSC 24; WLC
See also AAYA 4, 45; AITN 2; BPFB 1;
CA 69-72; CANR 10, 32, 68, 104; CD-
WLB 3; CWW 2; DA; DA3; DAB; DAC;
DAM MST, MULT, NOV; DLB 113;
DNFS 2; EWL 3; HW 1, 2; LAIT 3; LATS
1:2; LAW; LAWS 1; LMFS 2; MTCW 1,
2; NFS 8; RGSF 2; RGWL 2, 3; TWA;
WLIT 1

Fuentes, Gregorio Lopez y
See Lopez y Fuentes, Gregorio

Fuertes, Gloria 1918-1998 .... **PC 27**
See also CA 178, 180; DLB 108; HW 2;
SATA 115

Fugard, (Harold) Athol 1932- . **CLC 5, 9, 14, 25, 40, 80, 211; DC 3**
See also AAYA 17; AFW; CA 85-88; CANR 32, 54, 118; CD 5; DAM DRAM; DFS 3, 6, 10; DLB 225; DNFS 1, 2; EWL 3; LATS 1:2; MTCW 1; RGEL 2; WLIT 2

Fugard, Sheila 1932- .... **CLC 48**
See also CA 125

Fukuyama, Francis 1952- .... **CLC 131**
See also CA 140; CANR 72, 125

Fuller, Charles (H.), (Jr.) 1939- .... **BLC 2; CLC 25; DC 1**
See also BW 2; CA 108; 112; CAD; CANR 87; CD 5; DAM DRAM, MULT; DFS 8; DLB 38, 266; EWL 3; INT CA-112; MTCW 1

Fuller, Henry Blake 1857-1929 .... **TCLC 103**
See also CA 108; 177; DLB 12; RGAL 4

Fuller, John (Leopold) 1937- .... **CLC 62**
See also CA 21-24R; CANR 9, 44; CP 7; DLB 40

Fuller, Margaret
See Ossoli, Sarah Margaret (Fuller)
See also AMWS 2; DLB 183, 223, 239

Fuller, Roy (Broadbent) 1912-1991 ... **CLC 4, 28**
See also BRWS 7; CA 5-8R; 135; CAAS 10; CANR 53, 83; CWRI 5; DLB 15, 20; EWL 3; RGEL 2; SATA 87

Fuller, Sarah Margaret
See Ossoli, Sarah Margaret (Fuller)

Fuller, Sarah Margaret
See Ossoli, Sarah Margaret (Fuller)
See also DLB 1, 59, 73

Fuller, Thomas 1608-1661 .... **LC 111**
See also DLB 151

Fulton, Alice 1952- .... **CLC 52**
See also CA 116; CANR 57, 88; CP 7; CWP; DLB 193

Furphy, Joseph 1843-1912 .... **TCLC 25**
See Collins, Tom
See also CA 163; DLB 230; EWL 3; RGEL 2

Fuson, Robert H(enderson) 1927- .... **CLC 70**
See also CA 89-92; CANR 103

Fussell, Paul 1924- .... **CLC 74**
See also BEST 90:1; CA 17-20R; CANR 8, 21, 35, 69, 135; INT CANR-21; MTCW 1, 2

Futabatei, Shimei 1864-1909 .... **TCLC 44**
See Futabatei Shimei
See also CA 162; MJW

Futabatei Shimei
See Futabatei, Shimei
See also DLB 180; EWL 3

Futrelle, Jacques 1875-1912 .... **TCLC 19**
See also CA 113; 155; CMW 4

Gaboriau, Emile 1835-1873 .... **NCLC 14**
See also CMW 4; MSW

Gadda, Carlo Emilio 1893-1973 ...... **CLC 11; TCLC 144**
See also CA 89-92; DLB 177; EWL 3

Gaddis, William 1922-1998 ... **CLC 1, 3, 6, 8, 10, 19, 43, 86**
See also AMWS 4; BPFB 1; CA 17-20R; 172; CANR 21, 48; CN 7; DLB 2, 278; EWL 3; MTCW 1, 2; RGAL 4

Gaelique, Moruen le
See Jacob, (Cyprien-)Max

Gage, Walter
See Inge, William (Motter)

Gaiman, Neil (Richard) 1960- .... **CLC 195**
See also AAYA 19, 42; CA 133; CANR 81, 129; DLB 261; HGG; SATA 85, 146; SFW 4; SUFW 2

Gaines, Ernest J(ames) 1933- .. **BLC 2; CLC 3, 11, 18, 86, 181; SSC 68**
See also AAYA 18; AFAW 1, 2; AITN 1; BPFB 2; BW 2, 3; BYA 6; CA 9-12R; CANR 6, 24, 42, 75, 126; CDALB 1968-1988; CLR 62; CN 7; CSW; DA3; DAM MULT; DLB 2, 33, 152; DLBY 1980; EWL 3; EXPN; LAIT 5; LATS 1:2; MTCW 1, 2; NFS 5, 7, 16; RGAL 4; RGSF 2; RHW; SATA 86; SSFS 5; YAW

Gaitskill, Mary (Lawrence) 1954- .... **CLC 69**
See also CA 128; CANR 61; DLB 244

Gaius Suetonius Tranquillus
See Suetonius

Galdos, Benito Perez
See Perez Galdos, Benito
See also EW 7

Gale, Zona 1874-1938 .... **TCLC 7**
See also CA 105; 153; CANR 84; DAM DRAM; DFS 17; DLB 9, 78, 228; RGAL 4

Galeano, Eduardo (Hughes) 1940- . **CLC 72; HLCS 1**
See also CA 29-32R; CANR 13, 32, 100; HW 1

Galiano, Juan Valera y Alcala
See Valera y Alcala-Galiano, Juan

Galilei, Galileo 1564-1642 .... **LC 45**

Gallagher, Tess 1943- .... **CLC 18, 63; PC 9**
See also CA 106; CP 7; CWP; DAM POET; DLB 120, 212, 244; PFS 16

Gallant, Mavis 1922- ..... **CLC 7, 18, 38, 172; SSC 5, 78**
See also CA 69-72; CANR 29, 69, 117; CCA 1; CN 7; DAC; DAM MST; DLB 53; EWL 3; MTCW 1, 2; RGEL 2; RGSF 2

Gallant, Roy A(rthur) 1924- .... **CLC 17**
See also CA 5-8R; CANR 4, 29, 54, 117; CLR 30; MAICYA 1, 2; SATA 4, 68, 110

Gallico, Paul (William) 1897-1976 ..... **CLC 2**
See also AITN 1; CA 5-8R; 69-72; CANR 23; DLB 9, 171; FANT; MAICYA 1, 2; SATA 13

Gallo, Max Louis 1932- .... **CLC 95**
See also CA 85-88

Gallois, Lucien
See Desnos, Robert

Gallup, Ralph
See Whitemore, Hugh (John)

Galsworthy, John 1867-1933 .... **SSC 22; TCLC 1, 45; WLC**
See also BRW 6; CA 104; 141; CANR 75; CDBLB 1890-1914; DA; DA3; DAB; DAC; DAM DRAM, MST, NOV; DLB 10, 34, 98, 162; DLBD 16; EWL 3; MTCW 1; RGEL 2; SSFS 3; TEA

Galt, John 1779-1839 .... **NCLC 1, 110**
See also DLB 99, 116, 159; RGEL 2; RGSF 2

Galvin, James 1951- .... **CLC 38**
See also CA 108; CANR 26

Gamboa, Federico 1864-1939 .... **TCLC 36**
See also CA 167; HW 2; LAW

Gandhi, M. K.
See Gandhi, Mohandas Karamchand

Gandhi, Mahatma
See Gandhi, Mohandas Karamchand

Gandhi, Mohandas Karamchand 1869-1948 .... **TCLC 59**
See also CA 121; 132; DA3; DAM MULT; MTCW 1, 2

Gann, Ernest Kellogg 1910-1991 ..... **CLC 23**
See also AITN 1; BPFB 2; CA 1-4R; 136; CANR 1, 83; RHW

Gao Xingjian 1940- .... **CLC 167**
See Xingjian, Gao

Garber, Eric 1943(?)-
See Holleran, Andrew
See also CANR 89

Garcia, Cristina 1958- .... **CLC 76**
See also AMWS 11; CA 141; CANR 73, 130; DLB 292; DNFS 1; EWL 3; HW 2; LLW 1

Garcia Lorca, Federico 1898-1936 ...... **DC 2; HLC 2; PC 3; TCLC 1, 7, 49; WLC**
See Lorca, Federico Garcia
See also AAYA 46; CA 104; 131; CANR 81; DA; DA3; DAB; DAC; DAM DRAM, MST, MULT, POET; DFS 4, 10; DLB 108; EWL 3; HW 1, 2; LATS 1:2; MTCW 1, 2; TWA

Garcia Marquez, Gabriel (Jose) 1928- .... **CLC 2, 3, 8, 10, 15, 27, 47, 55, 68, 170; HLC 1; SSC 8, 83; WLC**
See also AAYA 3, 33; BEST 89:1, 90:4; BPFB 2; BYA 12, 16; CA 33-36R; CANR 10, 28, 50, 75, 82, 128; CDWLB 3; CPW; CWW 2; DA; DA3; DAB; DAC; DAM MST, MULT, NOV, POP; DLB 113; DNFS 1, 2; EWL 3; EXPN; EXPS; HW 1, 2; LAIT 2; LATS 1:2; LAW; LAWS 1; LMFS 2; MTCW 1, 2; NCFS 3; NFS 1, 5, 10; RGSF 2; RGWL 2, 3; SSFS 1, 6, 16; TWA; WLIT 1

Garcilaso de la Vega, El Inca 1503-1536 .... **HLCS 1**
See also LAW

Gard, Janice
See Latham, Jean Lee

Gard, Roger Martin du
See Martin du Gard, Roger

Gardam, Jane (Mary) 1928- .... **CLC 43**
See also CA 49-52; CANR 2, 18, 33, 54, 106; CLR 12; DLB 14, 161, 231; MAICYA 1, 2; MTCW 1; SAAS 9; SATA 39, 76, 130; SATA-Brief 28; YAW

Gardner, Herb(ert George) 1934-2003 .... **CLC 44**
See also CA 149; 220; CAD; CANR 119; CD 5; DFS 18, 20

Gardner, John (Champlin), Jr. 1933-1982 ...... **CLC 2, 3, 5, 7, 8, 10, 18, 28, 34; SSC 7**
See also AAYA 45; AITN 1; AMWS 6; BPFB 2; CA 65-68; 107; CANR 33, 73; CDALBS; CPW; DA3; DAM NOV, POP; DLB 2; DLBY 1982; EWL 3; FANT; LATS 1:2; MTCW 1; NFS 3; RGAL 4; RGSF 2; SATA 40; SATA-Obit 31; SSFS 8

Gardner, John (Edmund) 1926- .... **CLC 30**
See also CA 103; CANR 15, 69, 127; CMW 4; CPW; DAM POP; MTCW 1

Gardner, Miriam
See Bradley, Marion Zimmer
See also GLL 1

Gardner, Noel
See Kuttner, Henry

Gardons, S. S.
See Snodgrass, W(illiam) D(e Witt)

Garfield, Leon 1921-1996 .... **CLC 12**
See also AAYA 8; BYA 1, 3; CA 17-20R; 152; CANR 38, 41, 78; CLR 21; DLB 161; JRDA; MAICYA 1, 2; MAICYAS 1; SATA 1, 32, 76; SATA-Obit 90; TEA; WYA; YAW

Garland, (Hannibal) Hamlin 1860-1940 .... **SSC 18; TCLC 3**
See also CA 104; DLB 12, 71, 78, 186; RGAL 4; RGSF 2; TCWW 2

Garneau, (Hector de) Saint-Denys 1912-1943 .... **TCLC 13**
See also CA 111; DLB 88

Harper, Frances E. W.
See Harper, Frances Ellen Watkins
Harper, Frances E. Watkins
See Harper, Frances Ellen Watkins
Harper, Frances Ellen
See Harper, Frances Ellen Watkins
Harper, Frances Ellen Watkins
1825-1911 ..... **BLC 2; PC 21; TCLC 14**
See also AFAW 1, 2; BW 1, 3; CA 111; 125;
CANR 79; DAM MULT, POET; DLB 50,
221; MAWW; RGAL 4
Harper, Michael S(teven) 1938- ... **CLC 7, 22**
See also AFAW 2; BW 1; CA 33-36R, 224;
CAAE 224; CANR 24, 108; CP 7; DLB
41; RGAL 4
Harper, Mrs. F. E. W.
See Harper, Frances Ellen Watkins
Harpur, Charles 1813-1868 .... **NCLC 114**
See also DLB 230; RGEL 2
Harris, Christie
See Harris, Christie (Lucy) Irwin
Harris, Christie (Lucy) Irwin
1907-2002 .... **CLC 12**
See also CA 5-8R; CANR 6, 83; CLR 47;
DLB 88; JRDA; MAICYA 1, 2; SAAS 10;
SATA 6, 74; SATA-Essay 116
Harris, Frank 1856-1931 .... **TCLC 24**
See also CA 109; 150; CANR 80; DLB 156,
197; RGEL 2
Harris, George Washington
1814-1869 .... **NCLC 23**
See also DLB 3, 11, 248; RGAL 4
Harris, Joel Chandler 1848-1908 ..... **SSC 19;
TCLC 2**
See also CA 104; 137; CANR 80; CLR 49;
DLB 11, 23, 42, 78, 91; LAIT 2; MAI-
CYA 1, 2; RGSF 2; SATA 100; WCH;
YABC 1
**Harris, John (Wyndham Parkes Lucas)
Beynon** 1903-1969
See Wyndham, John
See also CA 102; 89-92; CANR 84; SATA
118; SFW 4
Harris, MacDonald .... **CLC 9**
See Heiney, Donald (William)
Harris, Mark 1922- .... **CLC 19**
See also CA 5-8R; CAAS 3; CANR 2, 55,
83; CN 7; DLB 2; DLBY 1980
Harris, Norman .... **CLC 65**
Harris, (Theodore) Wilson 1921- .... **CLC 25,
159**
See also BRWS 5; BW 2, 3; CA 65-68;
CAAS 16; CANR 11, 27, 69, 114; CD-
WLB 3; CN 7; CP 7; DLB 117; EWL 3;
MTCW 1; RGEL 2
Harrison, Barbara Grizzuti
1934-2002 .... **CLC 144**
See also CA 77-80; 205; CANR 15, 48; INT
CANR-15
Harrison, Elizabeth (Allen) Cavanna
1909-2001
See Cavanna, Betty
See also CA 9-12R; 200; CANR 6, 27, 85,
104, 121; MAICYA 2; SATA 142; YAW
Harrison, Harry (Max) 1925- .... **CLC 42**
See also CA 1-4R; CANR 5, 21, 84; DLB
8; SATA 4; SCFW 2; SFW 4
Harrison, James (Thomas) 1937- ...... **CLC 6,
14, 33, 66, 143; SSC 19**
See Harrison, Jim
See also CA 13-16R; CANR 8, 51, 79; CN
7; CP 7; DLBY 1982; INT CANR-8
Harrison, Jim
See Harrison, James (Thomas)
See also AMWS 8; RGAL 4; TCWW 2;
TUS
Harrison, Kathryn 1961- .... **CLC 70, 151**
See also CA 144; CANR 68, 122

Harrison, Tony 1937- .... **CLC 43, 129**
See also BRWS 5; CA 65-68; CANR 44,
98; CBD; CD 5; CP 7; DLB 40, 245;
MTCW 1; RGEL 2
Harriss, Will(ard Irvin) 1922- .... **CLC 34**
See also CA 111
Hart, Ellis
See Ellison, Harlan (Jay)
Hart, Josephine 1942(?)- .... **CLC 70**
See also CA 138; CANR 70; CPW; DAM
POP
Hart, Moss 1904-1961 .... **CLC 66**
See also CA 109; 89-92; CANR 84; DAM
DRAM; DFS 1; DLB 7, 266; RGAL 4
Harte, (Francis) Bret(t)
1836(?)-1902 ... **SSC 8, 59; TCLC 1, 25;
WLC**
See also AMWS 2; CA 104; 140; CANR
80; CDALB 1865-1917; DA; DA3; DAC;
DAM MST; DLB 12, 64, 74, 79, 186;
EXPS; LAIT 2; RGAL 4; RGSF 2; SATA
26; SSFS 3; TUS
Hartley, L(eslie) P(oles) 1895-1972 ... **CLC 2,
22**
See also BRWS 7; CA 45-48; 37-40R;
CANR 33; DLB 15, 139; EWL 3; HGG;
MTCW 1, 2; RGEL 2; RGSF 2; SUFW 1
Hartman, Geoffrey H. 1929- .... **CLC 27**
See also CA 117; 125; CANR 79; DLB 67
Hartmann, Sadakichi 1869-1944 ... **TCLC 73**
See also CA 157; DLB 54
Hartmann von Aue c. 1170-c.
1210 .... **CMLC 15**
See also CDWLB 2; DLB 138; RGWL 2, 3
Hartog, Jan de
See de Hartog, Jan
Haruf, Kent 1943- .... **CLC 34**
See also AAYA 44; CA 149; CANR 91, 131
Harvey, Caroline
See Trollope, Joanna
Harvey, Gabriel 1550(?)-1631 .... **LC 88**
See also DLB 167, 213, 281
Harwood, Ronald 1934- .... **CLC 32**
See also CA 1-4R; CANR 4, 55; CBD; CD
5; DAM DRAM, MST; DLB 13
Hasegawa Tatsunosuke
See Futabatei, Shimei
Hasek, Jaroslav (Matej Frantisek)
1883-1923 .... **SSC 69; TCLC 4**
See also CA 104; 129; CDWLB 4; DLB
215; EW 9; EWL 3; MTCW 1, 2; RGSF
2; RGWL 2, 3
Hass, Robert 1941- ... **CLC 18, 39, 99; PC 16**
See also AMWS 6; CA 111; CANR 30, 50,
71; CP 7; DLB 105, 206; EWL 3; RGAL
4; SATA 94
Hastings, Hudson
See Kuttner, Henry
Hastings, Selina .... **CLC 44**
Hathorne, John 1641-1717 .... **LC 38**
Hatteras, Amelia
See Mencken, H(enry) L(ouis)
Hatteras, Owen .... **TCLC 18**
See Mencken, H(enry) L(ouis); Nathan,
George Jean
Hauptmann, Gerhart (Johann Robert)
1862-1946 .... **SSC 37; TCLC 4**
See also CA 104; 153; CDWLB 2; DAM
DRAM; DLB 66, 118; EW 8; EWL 3;
RGSF 2; RGWL 2, 3; TWA
Havel, Vaclav 1936- ..... **CLC 25, 58, 65, 123;
DC 6**
See also CA 104; CANR 36, 63, 124; CD-
WLB 4; CWW 2; DA3; DAM DRAM;
DFS 10; DLB 232; EWL 3; LMFS 2;
MTCW 1, 2; RGWL 3
Haviaras, Stratis .... **CLC 33**
See Chaviaras, Strates

Hawes, Stephen 1475(?)-1529(?) .... **LC 17**
See also DLB 132; RGEL 2
Hawkes, John (Clendennin Burne, Jr.)
1925-1998 .. **CLC 1, 2, 3, 4, 7, 9, 14, 15,
27, 49**
See also BPFB 2; CA 1-4R; 167; CANR 2,
47, 64; CN 7; DLB 2, 7, 227; DLBY
1980, 1998; EWL 3; MTCW 1, 2; RGAL
4
Hawking, S. W.
See Hawking, Stephen W(illiam)
Hawking, Stephen W(illiam) 1942- . **CLC 63,
105**
See also AAYA 13; BEST 89:1; CA 126;
129; CANR 48, 115; CPW; DA3; MTCW
2
Hawkins, Anthony Hope
See Hope, Anthony
Hawthorne, Julian 1846-1934 .... **TCLC 25**
See also CA 165; HGG
Hawthorne, Nathaniel 1804-1864 ... **NCLC 2,
10, 17, 23, 39, 79, 95, 158; SSC 3, 29,
39; WLC**
See also AAYA 18; AMW; AMWC 1;
AMWR 1; BPFB 2; BYA 3; CDALB
1640-1865; DA; DA3; DAB; DAC; DAM
MST, NOV; DLB 1, 74, 183, 223, 269;
EXPN; EXPS; HGG; LAIT 1; NFS 1, 20;
RGAL 4; RGSF 2; SSFS 1, 7, 11, 15;
SUFW 1; TUS; WCH; YABC 2
Hawthorne, Sophia Peabody
1809-1871 .... **NCLC 150**
See also DLB 183, 239
Haxton, Josephine Ayres 1921-
See Douglas, Ellen
See also CA 115; CANR 41, 83
Hayaseca y Eizaguirre, Jorge
See Echegaray (y Eizaguirre), Jose (Maria
Waldo)
Hayashi, Fumiko 1904-1951 .... **TCLC 27**
See Hayashi Fumiko
See also CA 161
Hayashi Fumiko
See Hayashi, Fumiko
See also DLB 180; EWL 3
Haycraft, Anna (Margaret) 1932-
See Ellis, Alice Thomas
See also CA 122; CANR 85, 90; MTCW 2
Hayden, Robert E(arl) 1913-1980 ..... **BLC 2;
CLC 5, 9, 14, 37; PC 6**
See also AFAW 1, 2; AMWS 2; BW 1, 3;
CA 69-72; 97-100; CABS 2; CANR 24,
75, 82; CDALB 1941-1968; DA; DAC;
DAM MST, MULT, POET; DLB 5, 76;
EWL 3; EXPP; MTCW 1, 2; PFS 1;
RGAL 4; SATA 19; SATA-Obit 26; WP
Haydon, Benjamin Robert
1786-1846 .... **NCLC 146**
See also DLB 110
Hayek, F(riedrich) A(ugust von)
1899-1992 .... **TCLC 109**
See also CA 93-96; 137; CANR 20; MTCW
1, 2
Hayford, J(oseph) E(phraim) Casely
See Casely-Hayford, J(oseph) E(phraim)
Hayman, Ronald 1932- .... **CLC 44**
See also CA 25-28R; CANR 18, 50, 88; CD
5; DLB 155
Hayne, Paul Hamilton 1830-1886 . **NCLC 94**
See also DLB 3, 64, 79, 248; RGAL 4
Hays, Mary 1760-1843 .... **NCLC 114**
See also DLB 142, 158; RGEL 2
Haywood, Eliza (Fowler)
1693(?)-1756 .... **LC 1, 44**
See also DLB 39; RGEL 2
Hazlitt, William 1778-1830 ...... **NCLC 29, 82**
See also BRW 4; DLB 110, 158; RGEL 2;
TEA

Herring, Guilles
See Somerville, Edith Oenone
Herriot, James 1916-1995 .... **CLC 12**
See Wight, James Alfred
See also AAYA 1, 54; BPFB 2; CA 148;
CANR 40; CLR 80; CPW; DAM POP;
LAIT 3; MAICYA 2; MAICYAS 1;
MTCW 2; SATA 86, 135; TEA; YAW

Herris, Violet
See Hunt, Violet
Herrmann, Dorothy 1941- .... **CLC 44**
See also CA 107

Herrmann, Taffy
See Herrmann, Dorothy
Hersey, John (Richard) 1914-1993 .... **CLC 1,**
2, 7, 9, 40, 81, 97
See also AAYA 29; BPFB 2; CA 17-20R;
140; CANR 33; CDALBS; CPW; DAM
POP; DLB 6, 185, 278, 299; MTCW 1, 2;
SATA 25; SATA-Obit 76; TUS

Herzen, Aleksandr Ivanovich
1812-1870 .... **NCLC 10, 61**
See Herzen, Alexander
Herzen, Alexander
See Herzen, Aleksandr Ivanovich
See also DLB 277
Herzl, Theodor 1860-1904 .... **TCLC 36**
See also CA 168
Herzog, Werner 1942- .... **CLC 16**
See also CA 89-92
Hesiod c. 8th cent. B.C.- .... **CMLC 5**
See also AW 1; DLB 176; RGWL 2, 3
Hesse, Hermann 1877-1962 ... **CLC 1, 2, 3, 6,**
11, 17, 25, 69; SSC 9, 49; TCLC 148;
WLC
See also AAYA 43; BPFB 2; CA 17-18;
CAP 2; CDWLB 2; DA; DA3; DAB;
DAC; DAM MST, NOV; DLB 66; EW 9;
EWL 3; EXPN; LAIT 1; MTCW 1, 2;
NFS 6, 15; RGWL 2, 3; SATA 50; TWA

Hewes, Cady
See De Voto, Bernard (Augustine)
Heyen, William 1940- .... **CLC 13, 18**
See also CA 33-36R, 220; CAAE 220;
CAAS 9; CANR 98; CP 7; DLB 5
Heyerdahl, Thor 1914-2002 .... **CLC 26**
See also CA 5-8R; 207; CANR 5, 22, 66,
73; LAIT 4; MTCW 1, 2; SATA 2, 52
Heym, Georg (Theodor Franz Arthur)
1887-1912 .... **TCLC 9**
See also CA 106; 181
Heym, Stefan 1913-2001 .... **CLC 41**
See also CA 9-12R; 203; CANR 4; CWW
2; DLB 69; EWL 3
Heyse, Paul (Johann Ludwig von)
1830-1914 .... **TCLC 8**
See also CA 104; 209; DLB 129
Heyward, (Edwin) DuBose
1885-1940 .... **HR 2; TCLC 59**
See also CA 108; 157; DLB 7, 9, 45, 249;
SATA 21
Heywood, John 1497(?)-1580(?) .... **LC 65**
See also DLB 136; RGEL 2
Heywood, Thomas 1573(?)-1641 .... **LC 111**
See also DLB 62; DAM DRAM; LMFS 1;
RGEL 2; TWA
Hibbert, Eleanor Alice Burford
1906-1993 .... **CLC 7**
See Holt, Victoria
See also BEST 90:4; CA 17-20R; 140;
CANR 9, 28, 59; CMW 4; CPW; DAM
POP; MTCW 2; RHW; SATA 2; SATA-
Obit 74
Hichens, Robert (Smythe)
1864-1950 .... **TCLC 64**
See also CA 162; DLB 153; HGG; RHW;
SUFW

Higgins, Aidan 1927- .... **SSC 68**
See also CA 9-12R; CANR 70, 115; CN 7;
DLB 14
Higgins, George V(incent)
1939-1999 .... **CLC 4, 7, 10, 18**
See also BPFB 2; CA 77-80; 186; CAAS 5;
CANR 17, 51, 89, 96; CMW 4; CN 7;
DLB 2; DLBY 1981, 1998; INT CANR-
17; MSW; MTCW 1
Higginson, Thomas Wentworth
1823-1911 .... **TCLC 36**
See also CA 162; DLB 1, 64, 243
Higgonet, Margaret ed. .... **CLC 65**
Highet, Helen
See MacInnes, Helen (Clark)
Highsmith, (Mary) Patricia
1921-1995 .... **CLC 2, 4, 14, 42, 102**
See Morgan, Claire
See also AAYA 48; BRWS 5; CA 1-4R; 147;
CANR 1, 20, 48, 62, 108; CMW 4; CPW;
DA3; DAM NOV, POP; DLB 306; MSW;
MTCW 1, 2
Highwater, Jamake (Mamake)
1942(?)-2001 .... **CLC 12**
See also AAYA 7; BPFB 2; BYA 4; CA 65-
68; 199; CAAS 7; CANR 10, 34, 84; CLR
17; CWRI 5; DLB 52; DLBY 1985;
JRDA; MAICYA 1, 2; SATA 32, 69;
SATA-Brief 30
Highway, Tomson 1951- ...... **CLC 92; NNAL**
See also CA 151; CANR 75; CCA 1; CD 5;
DAC; DAM MULT; DFS 2; MTCW 2
Hijuelos, Oscar 1951- .... **CLC 65; HLC 1**
See also AAYA 25; AMWS 8; BEST 90:1;
CA 123; CANR 50, 75, 125; CPW; DA3;
DAM MULT, POP; DLB 145; HW 1, 2;
LLW 1; MTCW 2; NFS 17; RGAL 4;
WLIT 1
Hikmet, Nazim 1902(?)-1963 .... **CLC 40**
See also CA 141; 93-96; EWL 3
Hildegard von Bingen 1098-1179 . **CMLC 20**
See also DLB 148
Hildesheimer, Wolfgang 1916-1991 .. **CLC 49**
See also CA 101; 135; DLB 69, 124; EWL
3
Hill, Geoffrey (William) 1932- ...... **CLC 5, 8,**
18, 45
See also BRWS 5; CA 81-84; CANR 21,
89; CDBLB 1960 to Present; CP 7; DAM
POET; DLB 40; EWL 3; MTCW 1; RGEL
2
Hill, George Roy 1921-2002 .... **CLC 26**
See also CA 110; 122; 213
Hill, John
See Koontz, Dean R(ay)
Hill, Susan (Elizabeth) 1942- ...... **CLC 4, 113**
See also CA 33-36R; CANR 29, 69, 129;
CN 7; DAB; DAM MST, NOV; DLB 14,
139; HGG; MTCW 1; RHW
Hillard, Asa G. III .... **CLC 70**
Hillerman, Tony 1925- .... **CLC 62, 170**
See also AAYA 40; BEST 89:1; BPFB 2;
CA 29-32R; CANR 21, 42, 65, 97, 134;
CMW 4; CPW; DA3; DAM POP; DLB
206; DLB; MSW; RGAL 4; SATA 6;
TCWW 2; YAW
Hillesum, Etty 1914-1943 .... **TCLC 49**
See also CA 137
Hilliard, Noel (Harvey) 1929-1996 ... **CLC 15**
See also CA 9-12R; CANR 7, 69; CN 7
Hillis, Rick 1956- .... **CLC 66**
See also CA 134
Hilton, James 1900-1954 .... **TCLC 21**
See also CA 108; 169; DLB 34, 77; FANT;
SATA 34
Hilton, Walter (?)-1396 .... **CMLC 58**
See also DLB 146; RGEL 2

Himes, Chester (Bomar) 1909-1984 .. **BLC 2;**
CLC 2, 4, 7, 18, 58, 108; TCLC 139
See also AFAW 2; BPFB 2; BW 2; CA 25-
28R; 114; CANR 22, 89; CMW 4; DAM
MULT; DLB 2, 76, 143, 226; EWL 3;
MSW; MTCW 1, 2; RGAL 4
Himmelfarb, Gertrude 1922- .... **CLC 202**
See also CA 49-52; CANR 28, 66, 102;
Hinde, Thomas .... **CLC 6, 11**
See Chitty, Thomas Willes
See also EWL 3
Hine, (William) Daryl 1936- .... **CLC 15**
See also CA 1-4R; CAAS 15; CANR 1, 20;
CP 7; DLB 60
Hinkson, Katharine Tynan
See Tynan, Katharine
Hinojosa(-Smith), Rolando (R.)
1929- .... **HLC 1**
See Hinojosa-Smith, Rolando
See also CA 131; CAAS 16; CANR 62;
DAM MULT; DLB 82; HW 1, 2; LLW 1;
MTCW 2; RGAL 4
Hinton, S(usan) E(loise) 1950- .. **CLC 30, 111**
See also AAYA 2, 33; BPFB 2; BYA 2, 3;
CA 81-84; CANR 32, 62, 92, 133;
CDALBS; CLR 3, 23; CPW; DA; DA3;
DAB; DAC; DAM MST, NOV; JRDA;
LAIT 5; MAICYA 1, 2; MTCW 1, 2; NFS
5, 9, 15, 16; SATA 19, 58, 115; WYA;
YAW
Hippius, Zinaida (Nikolaevna) .... **TCLC 9**
See Gippius, Zinaida (Nikolaevna)
See also DLB 295; EWL 3
Hiraoka, Kimitake 1925-1970
See Mishima, Yukio
See also CA 97-100; 29-32R; DA3; DAM
DRAM; GLL 1; MTCW 1, 2
Hirsch, E(ric) D(onald), Jr. 1928- .... **CLC 79**
See also CA 25-28R; CANR 27, 51; DLB
67; INT CANR-27; MTCW 1
Hirsch, Edward 1950- .... **CLC 31, 50**
See also CA 104; CANR 20, 42, 102; CP 7;
DLB 120
Hitchcock, Alfred (Joseph)
1899-1980 .... **CLC 16**
See also AAYA 22; CA 159; 97-100; SATA
27; SATA-Obit 24
Hitchens, Christopher (Eric)
1949- .... **CLC 157**
See also CA 152; CANR 89
Hitler, Adolf 1889-1945 .... **TCLC 53**
See also CA 117; 147
Hoagland, Edward 1932- .... **CLC 28**
See also ANW; CA 1-4R; CANR 2, 31, 57,
107; CN 7; DLB 6; SATA 51; TCWW 2
Hoban, Russell (Conwell) 1925- ... **CLC 7, 25**
See also BPFB 2; CA 5-8R; CANR 23, 37,
66, 114; CLR 3, 69; CN 7; CWRI 5; DAM
NOV; DLB 52; FANT; MAICYA 1, 2;
MTCW 1, 2; SATA 1, 40, 78, 136; SFW
4; SUFW 2
Hobbes, Thomas 1588-1679 .... **LC 36**
See also DLB 151, 252, 281; RGEL 2
Hobbs, Perry
See Blackmur, R(ichard) P(almer)
Hobson, Laura Z(ametkin)
1900-1986 .... **CLC 7, 25**
See Field, Peter
See also BPFB 2; CA 17-20R; 118; CANR
55; DLB 28; SATA 52
Hoccleve, Thomas c. 1368-c. 1437 ...... **LC 75**
See also DLB 146; RGEL 2
Hoch, Edward D(entinger) 1930-
See Queen, Ellery
See also CA 29-32R; CANR 11, 27, 51, 97;
CMW 4; DLB 306; SFW 4

Ivask, Ivar Vidrik 1927-1992 .... **CLC 14**
See also CA 37-40R; 139; CANR 24

Ives, Morgan
See Bradley, Marion Zimmer
See also GLL 1

Izumi Shikibu c. 973-c. 1034 .... **CMLC 33**

J. R. S.
See Gogarty, Oliver St. John

Jabran, Kahlil
See Gibran, Kahlil

Jabran, Khalil
See Gibran, Kahlil

Jackson, Daniel
See Wingrove, David (John)

Jackson, Helen Hunt 1830-1885 .... **NCLC 90**
See also DLB 42, 47, 186, 189; RGAL 4

Jackson, Jesse 1908-1983 .... **CLC 12**
See also BW 1; CA 25-28R; 109; CANR
27; CLR 28; CWRI 5; MAICYA 1, 2;
SATA 2, 29; SATA-Obit 48

Jackson, Laura (Riding) 1901-1991 .... **PC 44**
See Riding, Laura
See also CA 65-68; 135; CANR 28, 89;
DLB 48

Jackson, Sam
See Trumbo, Dalton

Jackson, Sara
See Wingrove, David (John)

Jackson, Shirley 1919-1965 . **CLC 11, 60, 87;**
SSC 9, 39; WLC
See also AAYA 9; AMWS 9; BPFB 2; CA
1-4R; 25-28R; CANR 4, 52; CDALB
1941-1968; DA; DA3; DAC; DAM MST;
DLB 6, 234; EXPS; HGG; LAIT 4;
MTCW 2; RGAL 4; RGSF 2; SATA 2;
SSFS 1; SUFW 1, 2

Jacob, (Cyprien-)Max 1876-1944 .... **TCLC 6**
See also CA 104; 193; DLB 258; EWL 3;
GFL 1789 to the Present; GLL 2; RGWL
2, 3

Jacobs, Harriet A(nn)
1813(?)-1897 .... **NCLC 67**
See also AFAW 1, 2; DLB 239; FW; LAIT
2; RGAL 4

Jacobs, Jim 1942- .... **CLC 12**
See also CA 97-100; INT CA-97-100

Jacobs, W(illiam) W(ymark)
1863-1943 .... **SSC 73; TCLC 22**
See also CA 121; 167; DLB 135; EXPS;
HGG; RGEL 2; RGSF 2; SSFS 2; SUFW
1

Jacobsen, Jens Peter 1847-1885 .... **NCLC 34**

Jacobsen, Josephine (Winder)
1908-2003 .... **CLC 48, 102; PC 62**
See also CA 33-36R; 218; CAAS 18; CANR
23, 48; CCA 1; CP 7; DLB 244

Jacobson, Dan 1929- .... **CLC 4, 14**
See also AFW; CA 1-4R; CANR 2, 25, 66;
CN 7; DLB 14, 207, 225; EWL 3; MTCW
1; RGSF 2

Jacqueline
See Carpentier (y Valmont), Alejo

Jacques de Vitry c. 1160-1240 ...... **CMLC 63**
See also DLB 208

Jagger, Mick 1944- .... **CLC 17**

Jahiz, al- c. 780-c. 869 .... **CMLC 25**

Jakes, John (William) 1932- .... **CLC 29**
See also AAYA 32; BEST 89:4; BPFB 2;
CA 57-60, 214; CAAE 214; CANR 10,
43, 66, 111; CPW; CSW; DA3; DAM
NOV, POP; DLB 278; DLBY 1983;
FANT; INT CANR-10; MTCW 1, 2;
RHW; SATA 62; SFW 4; TCWW 2

James I 1394-1437 .... **LC 20**
See also RGEL 2

James, Andrew
See Kirkup, James

James, C(yril) L(ionel) R(obert)
1901-1989 .... **BLCS; CLC 33**
See also BW 2; CA 117; 125; 128; CANR
62; DLB 125; MTCW 1

James, Daniel (Lewis) 1911-1988
See Santiago, Danny
See also CA 174; 125

James, Dynely
See Mayne, William (James Carter)

James, Henry Sr. 1811-1882 .... **NCLC 53**

James, Henry 1843-1916 .... **SSC 8, 32, 47;**
TCLC 2, 11, 24, 40, 47, 64, 171; WLC
See also AMW; AMWC 1; AMWR 1; BPFB
2; BRW 6; CA 104; 132; CDALB 1865-
1917; DA; DA3; DAB; DAC; DAM MST,
NOV; DLB 12, 71, 74, 189; DLBD 13;
EWL 3; EXPS; HGG; LAIT 2; MTCW 1,
2; NFS 12, 16, 19; RGAL 4; RGEL 2;
RGSF 2; SSFS 9; SUFW 1; TUS

James, M. R.
See James, Montague (Rhodes)
See also DLB 156, 201

James, Montague (Rhodes)
1862-1936 .... **SSC 16; TCLC 6**
See James, M. R.
See also CA 104; 203; HGG; RGEL 2;
RGSF 2; SUFW 1

James, P. D. .... **CLC 18, 46, 122**
See White, Phyllis Dorothy James
See also BEST 90:2; BPFB 2; BRWS 4;
CDBLB 1960 to Present; DLB 87, 276;
DLBD 17; MSW

James, Philip
See Moorcock, Michael (John)

James, Samuel
See Stephens, James

James, Seumas
See Stephens, James

James, Stephen
See Stephens, James

James, William 1842-1910 .... **TCLC 15, 32**
See also AMW; CA 109; 193; DLB 270,
284; NCFS 5; RGAL 4

Jameson, Anna 1794-1860 .... **NCLC 43**
See also DLB 99, 166

Jameson, Fredric (R.) 1934- .... **CLC 142**
See also CA 196; DLB 67; LMFS 2

James VI of Scotland 1566-1625 .... **LC 109**
See also DLB 151, 172

Jami, Nur al-Din 'Abd al-Rahman
1414-1492 .... **LC 9**

Jammes, Francis 1868-1938 .... **TCLC 75**
See also CA 198; EWL 3; GFL 1789 to the
Present

Jandl, Ernst 1925-2000 .... **CLC 34**
See also CA 200; EWL 3

Janowitz, Tama 1957- .... **CLC 43, 145**
See also CA 106; CANR 52, 89, 129; CN
7; CPW; DAM POP; DLB 292

Japrisot, Sebastien 1931- .... **CLC 90**
See Rossi, Jean-Baptiste
See also CMW 4; NFS 18

Jarrell, Randall 1914-1965 .... **CLC 1, 2, 6, 9,**
13, 49; PC 41
See also AMW; BYA 5; CA 5-8R; 25-28R;
CABS 2; CANR 6, 34; CDALB 1941-
1968; CLR 6; CWRI 5; DAM POET;
DLB 48, 52; EWL 3; EXPP; MAICYA 1,
2; MTCW 1, 2; PAB; PFS 2; RGAL 4;
SATA 7

Jarry, Alfred 1873-1907 .... **SSC 20; TCLC 2,**
14, 147
See also CA 104; 153; DA3; DAM DRAM;
DFS 8; DLB 192, 258; EW 9; EWL 3;
GFL 1789 to the Present; RGWL 2, 3;
TWA

Jarvis, E. K.
See Ellison, Harlan (Jay)

Jawien, Andrzej
See John Paul II, Pope

Jaynes, Roderick
See Coen, Ethan

Jeake, Samuel, Jr.
See Aiken, Conrad (Potter)

Jean Paul 1763-1825 .... **NCLC 7**

Jefferies, (John) Richard
1848-1887 .... **NCLC 47**
See also DLB 98, 141; RGEL 2; SATA 16;
SFW 4

Jeffers, (John) Robinson 1887-1962 .. **CLC 2,**
3, 11, 15, 54; PC 17; WLC
See also AMWS 2; CA 85-88; CANR 35;
CDALB 1917-1929; DA; DAC; DAM
MST, POET; DLB 45, 212; EWL 3;
MTCW 1, 2; PAB; PFS 3, 4; RGAL 4

Jefferson, Janet
See Mencken, H(enry) L(ouis)

Jefferson, Thomas 1743-1826 . **NCLC 11, 103**
See also AAYA 54; ANW; CDALB 1640-
1865; DA3; DLB 31, 183; LAIT 1; RGAL
4

Jeffrey, Francis 1773-1850 .... **NCLC 33**
See Francis, Lord Jeffrey

Jelakowitch, Ivan
See Heijermans, Herman

Jelinek, Elfriede 1946- .... **CLC 169**
See also CA 154; DLB 85; FW

Jellicoe, (Patricia) Ann 1927- .... **CLC 27**
See also CA 85-88; CBD; CD 5; CWD;
CWRI 5; DLB 13, 233; FW

Jelloun, Tahar ben 1944- .... **CLC 180**
See Ben Jelloun, Tahar
See also CA 162; CANR 100

Jemyma
See Holley, Marietta

Jen, Gish .... **AAL; CLC 70, 198**
See Jen, Lillian
See also AMWC 2

Jen, Lillian 1956(?)-
See Jen, Gish
See also CA 135; CANR 89, 130

Jenkins, (John) Robin 1912- .... **CLC 52**
See also CA 1-4R; CANR 1, 135; CN 7;
DLB 14, 271

Jennings, Elizabeth (Joan)
1926-2001 .... **CLC 5, 14, 131**
See also BRWS 5; CA 61-64; 200; CAAS
5; CANR 8, 39, 66, 127; CP 7; CWP;
DLB 27; EWL 3; MTCW 1; SATA 66

Jennings, Waylon 1937- .... **CLC 21**

Jensen, Johannes V(ilhelm)
1873-1950 .... **TCLC 41**
See also CA 170; DLB 214; EWL 3; RGWL
3

Jensen, Laura (Linnea) 1948- .... **CLC 37**
See also CA 103

Jerome, Saint 345-420 .... **CMLC 30**
See also RGWL 3

Jerome, Jerome K(lapka)
1859-1927 .... **TCLC 23**
See also CA 119; 177; DLB 10, 34, 135;
RGEL 2

Jerrold, Douglas William
1803-1857 .... **NCLC 2**
See also DLB 158, 159; RGEL 2

Jewett, (Theodora) Sarah Orne
1849-1909 .... **SSC 6, 44; TCLC 1, 22**
See also AMW; AMWC 2; AMWR 2; CA
108; 127; CANR 71; DLB 12, 74, 221;
EXPS; FW; MAWW; NFS 15; RGAL 4;
RGSF 2; SATA 15; SSFS 4

Jewsbury, Geraldine (Endsor)
1812-1880 .... **NCLC 22**
See also DLB 21

Kazantzakis, Nikos 1883(?)-1957 .... **TCLC 2, 5, 33**
See also BPFB 2; CA 105; 132; DA3; EW 9; EWL 3; MTCW 1, 2; RGWL 2, 3

Kazin, Alfred 1915-1998 ..... **CLC 34, 38, 119**
See also AMWS 8; CA 1-4R; CAAS 7; CANR 1, 45, 79; DLB 67; EWL 3

Keane, Mary Nesta (Skrine) 1904-1996
See Keane, Molly
See also CA 108; 114; 151; CN 7; RHW

Keane, Molly .... **CLC 31**
See Keane, Mary Nesta (Skrine)
See also INT CA-114

Keates, Jonathan 1946(?)- .... **CLC 34**
See also CA 163; CANR 126

Keaton, Buster 1895-1966 .... **CLC 20**
See also CA 194

Keats, John 1795-1821 ...... **NCLC 8, 73, 121; PC 1; WLC**
See also AAYA 58; BRW 4; BRWR 1; CD-BLB 1789-1832; DA; DA3; DAB; DAC; DAM MST, POET; DLB 96, 110; EXPP; LMFS 1; PAB; PFS 1, 2, 3, 9, 17; RGEL 2; TEA; WLIT 3; WP

Keble, John 1792-1866 .... **NCLC 87**
See also DLB 32, 55; RGEL 2

Keene, Donald 1922- .... **CLC 34**
See also CA 1-4R; CANR 5, 119

Keillor, Garrison .... **CLC 40, 115**
See Keillor, Gary (Edward)
See also AAYA 2; BEST 89:3; BPFB 2; DLBY 1987; EWL 3; SATA 58; TUS

Keillor, Gary (Edward) 1942-
See Keillor, Garrison
See also CA 111; 117; CANR 36, 59, 124; CPW; DA3; DAM POP; MTCW 1, 2

Keith, Carlos
See Lewton, Val

Keith, Michael
See Hubbard, L(afayette) Ron(ald)

Keller, Gottfried 1819-1890 .... **NCLC 2; SSC 26**
See also CDWLB 2; DLB 129; EW; RGSF 2; RGWL 2, 3

Keller, Nora Okja 1965- .... **CLC 109**
See also CA 187

Kellerman, Jonathan 1949- .... **CLC 44**
See also AAYA 35; BEST 90:1; CA 106; CANR 29, 51; CMW 4; CPW; DA3; DAM POP; INT CANR-29

Kelley, William Melvin 1937- .... **CLC 22**
See also BW 1; CA 77-80; CANR 27, 83; CN 7; DLB 33; EWL 3

Kellogg, Marjorie 1922- .... **CLC 2**
See also CA 81-84

Kellow, Kathleen
See Hibbert, Eleanor Alice Burford

Kelly, M(ilton) T(errence) 1947- ...... **CLC 55**
See also CA 97-100; CAAS 22; CANR 19, 43, 84; CN 7

Kelly, Robert 1935- .... **SSC 50**
See also CA 17-20R; CAAS 19; CANR 47; CP 7; DLB 5, 130, 165

Kelman, James 1946- .... **CLC 58, 86**
See also BRWS 5; CA 148; CANR 85, 130; CN 7; DLB 194; RGSF 2; WLIT 4

Kemal, Yasar
See Kemal, Yashar
See also CWW 2; EWL 3

Kemal, Yashar 1923(?)- .... **CLC 14, 29**
See also CA 89-92; CANR 44

Kemble, Fanny 1809-1893 .... **NCLC 18**
See also DLB 32

Kemelman, Harry 1908-1996 .... **CLC 2**
See also AITN 1; BPFB 2; CA 9-12R; 155; CANR 6, 71; CMW 4; DLB 28

Kempe, Margery 1373(?)-1440(?) .. **LC 6, 56**
See also DLB 146; RGEL 2

Kempis, Thomas a 1380-1471 .... **LC 11**

Kendall, Henry 1839-1882 .... **NCLC 12**
See also DLB 230

Keneally, Thomas (Michael) 1935- ... **CLC 5, 8, 10, 14, 19, 27, 43, 117**
See also BRWS 4; CA 85-88; CANR 10, 50, 74, 130; CN 7; CPW; DA3; DAM NOV; DLB 289, 299; EWL 3; MTCW 1, 2; NFS 17; RGEL 2; RHW

Kennedy, A(lison) L(ouise) 1965- ... **CLC 188**
See also CA 168, 213; CAAE 213; CANR 108; CD 5; CN 7; DLB 271; RGSF 2

Kennedy, Adrienne (Lita) 1931- .... **BLC 2; CLC 66; DC 5**
See also AFAW 2; BW 2, 3; CA 103; CAAS 20; CABS 3; CANR 26, 53, 82; CD 5; DAM MULT; DFS 9; DLB 38; FW

Kennedy, John Pendleton 1795-1870 .... **NCLC 2**
See also DLB 3, 248, 254; RGAL 4

Kennedy, Joseph Charles 1929-
See Kennedy, X. J.
See also CA 1-4R, 201; CAAE 201; CANR 4, 30, 40; CP 7; CWRI 5; MAICYA 2; MAICYAS 1; SATA 14, 86, 130; SATA-Essay 130

Kennedy, William 1928- ... **CLC 6, 28, 34, 53**
See also AAYA 1; AMWS 7; BPFB 2; CA 85-88; CANR 14, 31, 76, 134; CN 7; DA3; DAM NOV; DLB 143; DLBY 1985; EWL 3; INT CANR-31; MTCW 1, 2; SATA 57

Kennedy, X. J. .... **CLC 8, 42**
See Kennedy, Joseph Charles
See also CAAS 9; CLR 27; DLB 5; SAAS 22

Kenny, Maurice (Francis) 1929- ..... **CLC 87; NNAL**
See also CA 144; CAAS 22; DAM MULT; DLB 175

Kent, Kelvin
See Kuttner, Henry

Kenton, Maxwell
See Southern, Terry

Kenyon, Jane 1947-1995 .... **PC 57**
See also AMWS 7; CA 118; 148; CANR 44, 69; CP 7; CWP; DLB 120; PFS 9, 17; RGAL 4

Kenyon, Robert O.
See Kuttner, Henry

Kepler, Johannes 1571-1630 .... **LC 45**

Ker, Jill
See Conway, Jill K(er)

Kerkow, H. C.
See Lewton, Val

Kerouac, Jack 1922-1969 ...... **CLC 1, 2, 3, 5, 14, 29, 61; TCLC 117; WLC**
See Kerouac, Jean-Louis Lebris de
See also AAYA 25; AMWC 1; AMWS 3; BG 3; BPFB 2; CDALB 1941-1968; CPW; DLB 2, 16, 237; DLBD 3; DLBY 1995; EWL 3; GLL 1; LATS 1:2; LMFS 2; MTCW 2; NFS 8; RGAL 4; TUS; WP

Kerouac, Jean-Louis Lebris de 1922-1969
See Kerouac, Jack
See also AITN 1; CA 5-8R; 25-28R; CANR 26, 54, 95; DA; DA3; DAB; DAC; DAM MST, NOV, POET, POP; MTCW 1, 2

Kerr, (Bridget) Jean (Collins) 1923(?)-2003 .... **CLC 22**
See also CA 5-8R; 212; CANR 7; INT CANR-7

Kerr, M. E. .... **CLC 12, 35**
See Meaker, Marijane (Agnes)
See also AAYA 2, 23; BYA 1, 7, 8; CLR 29; SAAS 1; WYA

Kerr, Robert .... **CLC 55**

Kerrigan, (Thomas) Anthony 1918- .. **CLC 4, 6**
See also CA 49-52; CAAS 11; CANR 4

Kerry, Lois
See Duncan, Lois

Kesey, Ken (Elton) 1935-2001 ... **CLC 1, 3, 6, 11, 46, 64, 184; WLC**
See also AAYA 25; BG 3; BPFB 2; CA 1-4R; 204; CANR 22, 38, 66, 124; CDALB 1968-1988; CN 7; CPW; DA; DA3; DAB; DAC; DAM MST, NOV, POP; DLB 2, 16, 206; EWL 3; EXPN; LAIT 4; MTCW 1, 2; NFS 2; RGAL 4; SATA 66; SATA-Obit 131; TUS; YAW

Kesselring, Joseph (Otto) 1902-1967 .... **CLC 45**
See also CA 150; DAM DRAM, MST; DFS 20

Kessler, Jascha (Frederick) 1929- ...... **CLC 4**
See also CA 17-20R; CANR 8, 48, 111

Kettelkamp, Larry (Dale) 1933- .... **CLC 12**
See also CA 29-32R; CANR 16; SAAS 3; SATA 2

Key, Ellen (Karolina Sofia) 1849-1926 .... **TCLC 65**
See also DLB 259

Keyber, Conny
See Fielding, Henry

Keyes, Daniel 1927- .... **CLC 80**
See also AAYA 23; BYA 11; CA 17-20R, 181; CAAE 181; CANR 10, 26, 54, 74; DA; DA3; DAC; DAM MST, NOV; EXPN; LAIT 4; MTCW 2; NFS 2; SATA 37; SFW 4

Keynes, John Maynard 1883-1946 .... **TCLC 64**
See also CA 114; 162, 163; DLBD 10; MTCW 2

Khanshendel, Chiron
See Rose, Wendy

Khayyam, Omar 1048-1131 ... **CMLC 11; PC 8**
See Omar Khayyam
See also DA3; DAM POET

Kherdian, David 1931- .... **CLC 6, 9**
See also AAYA 42; CA 21-24R, 192; CAAE 192; CAAS 2; CANR 39, 78; CLR 24; JRDA; LAIT 3; MAICYA 1, 2; SATA 16, 74; SATA-Essay 125

Khlebnikov, Velimir .... **TCLC 20**
See Khlebnikov, Viktor Vladimirovich
See also DLB 295; EW 10; EWL 3; RGWL 2, 3

Khlebnikov, Viktor Vladimirovich 1885-1922
See Khlebnikov, Velimir
See also CA 117; 217

Khodasevich, Vladislav (Felitsianovich) 1886-1939 .... **TCLC 15**
See also CA 115; EWL 3

Kielland, Alexander Lange 1849-1906 .... **TCLC 5**
See also CA 104

Kiely, Benedict 1919- ... **CLC 23, 43; SSC 58**
See also CA 1-4R; CANR 2, 84; CN 7; DLB 15

Kienzle, William X(avier) 1928-2001 .... **CLC 25**
See also CA 93-96; 203; CAAS 1; CANR 9, 31, 59, 111; CMW 4; DA3; DAM POP; INT CANR-31; MSW; MTCW 1, 2

Kierkegaard, Soren 1813-1855 ..... **NCLC 34, 78, 125**
See also DLB 300; EW 6; LMFS 2; RGWL 3; TWA

Kieslowski, Krzysztof 1941-1996 .... **CLC 120**
See also CA 147; 151

Killens, John Oliver 1916-1987 .... **CLC 10**
See also BW 2; CA 77-80; 123; CAAS 2; CANR 26; DLB 33; EWL 3

Killigrew, Anne 1660-1685 .... **LC 4, 73**
See also DLB 131

Killigrew, Thomas 1612-1683 .... **LC 57**
See also DLB 58; RGEL 2

Kim
See Simenon, Georges (Jacques Christian)

Kincaid, Jamaica 1949- ...... **BLC 2; CLC 43, 68, 137; SSC 72**
See also AAYA 13, 56; AFAW 2; AMWS 7; BRWS 7; BW 2, 3; CA 125; CANR 47, 59, 95, 133; CDALBS; CDWLB 3; CLR 63; CN 7; DA3; DAM MULT, NOV; DLB 157, 227; DNFS 1; EWL 3; EXPS; FW; LATS 1:2; LMFS 2; MTCW 2; NCFS 1; NFS 3; SSFS 5, 7; TUS; WWE 1; YAW

King, Francis (Henry) 1923- .... **CLC 8, 53, 145**
See also CA 1-4R; CANR 1, 33, 86; CN 7; DAM NOV; DLB 15, 139; MTCW 1

King, Kennedy
See Brown, George Douglas

King, Martin Luther, Jr. 1929-1968 . **BLC 2; CLC 83; WLCS**
See also BW 2, 3; CA 25-28; CANR 27, 44; CAP 2; DA; DA3; DAB; DAC; DAM MST, MULT; LAIT 5; LATS 1:2; MTCW 1, 2; SATA 14

King, Stephen (Edwin) 1947- .... **CLC 12, 26, 37, 61, 113; SSC 17, 55**
See also AAYA 1, 17; AMWS 5; BEST 90:1; BPFB 2; CA 61-64; CANR 1, 30, 52, 76, 119, 134; CPW; DA3; DAM NOV, POP; DLB 143; DLBY 1980; HGG; JRDA; LAIT 5; MTCW 1, 2; RGAL 4; SATA 9, 55; SUFW 1, 2; WYAS 1; YAW

King, Steve
See King, Stephen (Edwin)

King, Thomas 1943- .... **CLC 89, 171; NNAL**
See also CA 144; CANR 95; CCA 1; CN 7; DAC; DAM MULT; DLB 175; SATA 96

Kingman, Lee .... **CLC 17**
See Natti, (Mary) Lee
See also CWRI 5; SAAS 3; SATA 1, 67

Kingsley, Charles 1819-1875 .... **NCLC 35**
See also CLR 77; DLB 21, 32, 163, 178, 190; FANT; MAICYA 2; MAICYAS 1; RGEL 2; WCH; YABC 2

Kingsley, Henry 1830-1876 .... **NCLC 107**
See also DLB 21, 230; RGEL 2

Kingsley, Sidney 1906-1995 .... **CLC 44**
See also CA 85-88; 147; CAD; DFS 14, 19; DLB 7; RGAL 4

Kingsolver, Barbara 1955- . **CLC 55, 81, 130**
See also AAYA 15; AMWS 7; CA 129; 134; CANR 60, 96, 133; CDALBS; CPW; CSW; DA3; DAM POP; DLB 206; INT CA-134; LAIT 5; MTCW 2; NFS 5, 10, 12; RGAL 4

Kingston, Maxine (Ting Ting) Hong 1940- .... **AAL; CLC 12, 19, 58, 121; WLCS**
See also AAYA 8, 55; AMWS 5; BPFB 2; CA 69-72; CANR 13, 38, 74, 87, 128; CDALBS; CN 7; DA3; DAM MULT, NOV; DLB 173, 212; DLBY 1980; EWL 3; FW; INT CANR-13; LAIT 5; MAWW; MTCW 1, 2; NFS 6; RGAL 4; SATA 53; SSFS 3

Kinnell, Galway 1927- ..... **CLC 1, 2, 3, 5, 13, 29, 129; PC 26**
See also AMWS 3; CA 9-12R; CANR 10, 34, 66, 116; CP 7; DLB 5; DLBY 1987; EWL 3; INT CANR-34; MTCW 1, 2; PAB; PFS 9; RGAL 4; WP

Kinsella, Thomas 1928- .... **CLC 4, 19, 138**
See also BRWS 5; CA 17-20R; CANR 15, 122; CP 7; DLB 27; EWL 3; MTCW 1, 2; RGEL 2; TEA

Kinsella, W(illiam) P(atrick) 1935- . **CLC 27, 43, 166**
See also AAYA 7, 60; BPFB 2; CA 97-100, 222; CAAE 222; CAAS 7; CANR 21, 35, 66, 75, 129; CN 7; CPW; DAC; DAM NOV, POP; FANT; INT CANR-21; LAIT 5; MTCW 1, 2; NFS 15; RGSF 2

Kinsey, Alfred C(harles) 1894-1956 .... **TCLC 91**
See also CA 115; 170; MTCW 2

Kipling, (Joseph) Rudyard 1865-1936 . **PC 3; SSC 5, 54; TCLC 8, 17, 167; WLC**
See also AAYA 32; BRW 6; BRWC 1, 2; BYA 4; CA 105; 120; CANR 33; CDBLB 1890-1914; CLR 39, 65; CWRI 5; DA; DA3; DAB; DAC; DAM MST, POET; DLB 19, 34, 141, 156; EWL 3; EXPS; FANT; LAIT 3; LMFS 1; MAICYA 1, 2; MTCW 1, 2; RGEL 2; RGSF 2; SATA 100; SFW 4; SSFS 8; SUFW 1; TEA; WCH; WLIT 4; YABC 2

Kircher, Athanasius 1602-1680 .... **LC 121**
See also DLB 164

Kirk, Russell (Amos) 1918-1994 .. **TCLC 119**
See also AITN 1; CA 1-4R; 145; CAAS 9; CANR 1, 20, 60; HGG; INT CANR-20; MTCW 1

Kirkham, Dinah
See Card, Orson Scott

Kirkland, Caroline M. 1801-1864 . **NCLC 85**
See also DLB 3, 73, 74, 250, 254; DLBD 13

Kirkup, James 1918- .... **CLC 1**
See also CA 1-4R; CAAS 4; CANR 2; CP 7; DLB 27; SATA 12

Kirkwood, James 1930(?)-1989 .... **CLC 9**
See also AITN 2; CA 1-4R; 128; CANR 6, 40; GLL 2

Kirsch, Sarah 1935- .... **CLC 176**
See also CA 178; CWW 2; DLB 75; EWL 3

Kirshner, Sidney
See Kingsley, Sidney

Kis, Danilo 1935-1989 .... **CLC 57**
See also CA 109; 118; 129; CANR 61; CDWLB 4; DLB 181; EWL 3; MTCW 1; RGSF 2; RGWL 2, 3

Kissinger, Henry A(lfred) 1923- ..... **CLC 137**
See also CA 1-4R; CANR 2, 33, 66, 109; MTCW 1

Kivi, Aleksis 1834-1872 .... **NCLC 30**

Kizer, Carolyn (Ashley) 1925- ... **CLC 15, 39, 80; PC 66**
See also CA 65-68; CAAS 5; CANR 24, 70, 134; CP 7; CWP; DAM POET; DLB 5, 169; EWL 3; MTCW 2; PFS 18

Klabund 1890-1928 .... **TCLC 44**
See also CA 162; DLB 66

Klappert, Peter 1942- .... **CLC 57**
See also CA 33-36R; CSW; DLB 5

Klein, A(braham) M(oses) 1909-1972 .... **CLC 19**
See also CA 101; 37-40R; DAB; DAC; DAM MST; DLB 68; EWL 3; RGEL 2

Klein, Joe
See Klein, Joseph

Klein, Joseph 1946- .... **CLC 154**
See also CA 85-88; CANR 55

Klein, Norma 1938-1989 .... **CLC 30**
See also AAYA 2, 35; BPFB 2; BYA 6, 7, 8; CA 41-44R; 128; CANR 15, 37; CLR 2, 19; INT CANR-15; JRDA; MAICYA 1, 2; SAAS 1; SATA 7, 57; WYA; YAW

Klein, T(heodore) E(ibon) D(onald) 1947- .... **CLC 34**
See also CA 119; CANR 44, 75; HGG

Kleist, Heinrich von 1777-1811 ...... **NCLC 2, 37; SSC 22**
See also CDWLB 2; DAM DRAM; DLB 90; EW 5; RGSF 2; RGWL 2, 3

Klima, Ivan 1931- .... **CLC 56, 172**
See also CA 25-28R; CANR 17, 50, 91; CDWLB 4; CWW 2; DAM NOV; DLB 232; EWL 3; RGWL 3

Klimentev, Andrei Platonovich
See Klimentov, Andrei Platonovich

Klimentov, Andrei Platonovich 1899-1951 .... **SSC 42; TCLC 14**
See Platonov, Andrei Platonovich; Platonov, Andrey Platonovich
See also CA 108

Klinger, Friedrich Maximilian von 1752-1831 .... **NCLC 1**
See also DLB 94

Klingsor the Magician
See Hartmann, Sadakichi

Klopstock, Friedrich Gottlieb 1724-1803 .... **NCLC 11**
See also DLB 97; EW 4; RGWL 2, 3

Kluge, Alexander 1932- .... **SSC 61**
See also CA 81-84; DLB 75

Knapp, Caroline 1959-2002 .... **CLC 99**
See also CA 154; 207

Knebel, Fletcher 1911-1993 .... **CLC 14**
See also AITN 1; CA 1-4R; 140; CAAS 3; CANR 1, 36; SATA 36; SATA-Obit 75

Knickerbocker, Diedrich
See Irving, Washington

Knight, Etheridge 1931-1991 ... **BLC 2; CLC 40; PC 14**
See also BW 1, 3; CA 21-24R; 133; CANR 23, 82; DAM POET; DLB 41; MTCW 2; RGAL 4

Knight, Sarah Kemble 1666-1727 .... **LC 7**
See also DLB 24, 200

Knister, Raymond 1899-1932 .... **TCLC 56**
See also CA 186; DLB 68; RGEL 2

Knowles, John 1926-2001 ... **CLC 1, 4, 10, 26**
See also AAYA 10; AMWS 12; BPFB 2; BYA 3; CA 17-20R; 203; CANR 40, 74, 76, 132; CDALB 1968-1988; CLR 98; CN 7; DA; DAC; DAM MST, NOV; DLB 6; EXPN; MTCW 1, 2; NFS 2; RGAL 4; SATA 8, 89; SATA-Obit 134; YAW

Knox, Calvin M.
See Silverberg, Robert

Knox, John c. 1505-1572 .... **LC 37**
See also DLB 132

Knye, Cassandra
See Disch, Thomas M(ichael)

Koch, C(hristopher) J(ohn) 1932- .... **CLC 42**
See also CA 127; CANR 84; CN 7; DLB 289

Koch, Christopher
See Koch, C(hristopher) J(ohn)

Koch, Kenneth (Jay) 1925-2002 .... **CLC 5, 8, 44**
See also CA 1-4R; 207; CAD; CANR 6, 36, 57, 97, 131; CD 5; CP 7; DAM POET; DLB 5; INT CANR-36; MTCW 2; PFS 20; SATA 65; WP

Kochanowski, Jan 1530-1584 .... **LC 10**
See also RGWL 2, 3

Kock, Charles Paul de 1794-1871 . **NCLC 16**

Koda Rohan
See Koda Shigeyuki

Koda Rohan
See Koda Shigeyuki
See also DLB 180

Koda Shigeyuki 1867-1947 .... **TCLC 22**
See Koda Rohan
See also CA 121; 183

Lee, Vernon .... **SSC 33; TCLC 5**
See Paget, Violet
See also DLB 57, 153, 156, 174, 178; GLL
1; SUFW 1

Lee, William
See Burroughs, William S(eward)
See also GLL 1

Lee, Willy
See Burroughs, William S(eward)
See also GLL 1

Lee-Hamilton, Eugene (Jacob)
1845-1907 .... **TCLC 22**
See also CA 117

Leet, Judith 1935- .... **CLC 11**
See also CA 187

Le Fanu, Joseph Sheridan
1814-1873 .... **NCLC 9, 58; SSC 14, 84**
See also CMW 4; DA3; DAM POP; DLB
21, 70, 159, 178; HGG; RGEL 2; RGSF
2; SUFW 1

Leffland, Ella 1931- .... **CLC 19**
See also CA 29-32R; CANR 35, 78, 82;
DLBY 1984; INT CANR-35; SATA 65

Leger, Alexis
See Leger, (Marie-Rene Auguste) Alexis
Saint-Leger

Leger, (Marie-Rene Auguste) Alexis
Saint-Leger 1887-1975 .. **CLC 4, 11, 46;**
PC 23
See Perse, Saint-John; Saint-John Perse
See also CA 13-16R; 61-64; CANR 43;
DAM POET; MTCW 1

Leger, Saintleger
See Leger, (Marie-Rene Auguste) Alexis
Saint-Leger

Le Guin, Ursula K(roeber) 1929- ..... **CLC 8,**
13, 22, 45, 71, 136; SSC 12, 69
See also AAYA 9, 27; AITN 1; BPFB 2;
BYA 5, 8, 11, 14; CA 21-24R; CANR 9,
32, 52, 74, 132; CDALB 1968-1988; CLR
3, 28, 91; CN 7; CPW; DA3; DAB; DAC;
DAM MST, POP; DLB 8, 52, 256, 275;
EXPS; FANT; FW; INT CANR-32;
JRDA; LAIT 5; MAICYA 1, 2; MTCW 1,
2; NFS 6, 9; SATA 4, 52, 99, 149; SCFW;
SFW 4; SSFS 2; SUFW 1, 2; WYA; YAW

Lehmann, Rosamond (Nina)
1901-1990 .... **CLC 5**
See also CA 77-80; 131; CANR 8, 73; DLB
15; MTCW 2; RGEL 2; RHW

Leiber, Fritz (Reuter, Jr.)
1910-1992 .... **CLC 25**
See also BPFB 2; CA 45-48; 139; CANR 2,
40, 86; DLB 8; FANT; HGG; MTCW 1,
2; SATA 45; SATA-Obit 73; SCFW 2;
SFW 4; SUFW 1, 2

Leibniz, Gottfried Wilhelm von
1646-1716 .... **LC 35**
See also DLB 168

Leimbach, Martha 1963-
See Leimbach, Marti
See also CA 130

Leimbach, Marti .... **CLC 65**
See Leimbach, Martha

Leino, Eino .... **TCLC 24**
See Lonnbohm, Armas Eino Leopold
See also EWL 3

Leiris, Michel (Julien) 1901-1990 ..... **CLC 61**
See also CA 119; 128; 132; EWL 3; GFL
1789 to the Present

Leithauser, Brad 1953- .... **CLC 27**
See also CA 107; CANR 27, 81; CP 7; DLB
120, 282

le Jars de Gournay, Marie
See de Gournay, Marie le Jars

Lelchuk, Alan 1938- .... **CLC 5**
See also CA 45-48; CAAS 20; CANR 1,
70; CN 7

Lem, Stanislaw 1921- ...... **CLC 8, 15, 40, 149**
See also CA 105; CAAS 1; CANR 32;
CWW 2; MTCW 1; SCFW 2; SFW 4

Lemann, Nancy (Elise) 1956- .... **CLC 39**
See also CA 118; 136; CANR 121

Lemonnier, (Antoine Louis) Camille
1844-1913 .... **TCLC 22**
See also CA 121

Lenau, Nikolaus 1802-1850 .... **NCLC 16**

L'Engle, Madeleine (Camp Franklin)
1918- .... **CLC 12**
See also AAYA 28; AITN 2; BPFB 2; BYA
2, 4, 5, 7; CA 1-4R; CANR 3, 21, 39, 66,
107; CLR 1, 14, 57; CPW; CWRI 5; DA3;
DAM POP; DLB 52; JRDA; MAICYA 1,
2; MTCW 1, 2; SAAS 15; SATA 1, 27,
75, 128; SFW 4; WYA; YAW

Lengyel, Jozsef 1896-1975 .... **CLC 7**
See also CA 85-88; 57-60; CANR 71;
RGSF 2

Lenin 1870-1924
See Lenin, V. I.
See also CA 121; 168

Lenin, V. I. .... **TCLC 67**
See Lenin

Lennon, John (Ono) 1940-1980 .. **CLC 12, 35**
See also CA 102; SATA 114

Lennox, Charlotte Ramsay
1729(?)-1804 .... **NCLC 23, 134**
See also DLB 39; RGEL 2

Lentricchia, Frank, (Jr.) 1940- .... **CLC 34**
See also CA 25-28R; CANR 19, 106; DLB
246

Lenz, Gunter .... **CLC 65**

Lenz, Jakob Michael Reinhold
1751-1792 .... **LC 100**
See also DLB 94; RGWL 2, 3

Lenz, Siegfried 1926- .... **CLC 27; SSC 33**
See also CA 89-92; CANR 80; CWW 2;
DLB 75; EWL 3; RGSF 2; RGWL 2, 3

Leon, David
See Jacob, (Cyprien-)Max

Leonard, Elmore (John, Jr.) 1925- . **CLC 28,**
34, 71, 120
See also AAYA 22, 59; AITN 1; BEST 89:1,
90:4; BPFB 2; CA 81-84; CANR 12, 28,
53, 76, 96, 133; CMW 4; CN 7; CPW;
DA3; DAM POP; DLB 173, 226; INT
CANR-28; MSW; MTCW 1, 2; RGAL 4;
TCWW 2

Leonard, Hugh .... **CLC 19**
See Byrne, John Keyes
See also CBD; CD 5; DFS 13; DLB 13

Leonov, Leonid (Maximovich)
1899-1994 .... **CLC 92**
See Leonov, Leonid Maksimovich
See also CA 129; CANR 74, 76; DAM
NOV; EWL 3; MTCW 1, 2

Leonov, Leonid Maksimovich
See Leonov, Leonid (Maximovich)
See also DLB 272

Leopardi, (Conte) Giacomo
1798-1837 .... **NCLC 22, 129; PC 37**
See also EW 5; RGWL 2, 3; WP

Le Reveler
See Artaud, Antonin (Marie Joseph)

Lerman, Eleanor 1952- .... **CLC 9**
See also CA 85-88; CANR 69, 124

Lerman, Rhoda 1936- .... **CLC 56**
See also CA 49-52; CANR 70

Lermontov, Mikhail Iur'evich
See Lermontov, Mikhail Yuryevich
See also DLB 205

Lermontov, Mikhail Yuryevich
1814-1841 .... **NCLC 5, 47, 126; PC 18**
See Lermontov, Mikhail Iur'evich
See also EW 6; RGWL 2, 3; TWA

Leroux, Gaston 1868-1927 .... **TCLC 25**
See also CA 108; 136; CANR 69; CMW 4;
NFS 20; SATA 65

Lesage, Alain-Rene 1668-1747 .... **LC 2, 28**
See also EW 3; GFL Beginnings to 1789;
RGWL 2, 3

Leskov, N(ikolai) S(emenovich) 1831-1895
See Leskov, Nikolai (Semyonovich)

Leskov, Nikolai (Semyonovich)
1831-1895 .... **NCLC 25; SSC 34**
See Leskov, Nikolai Semenovich

Leskov, Nikolai Semenovich
See Leskov, Nikolai (Semyonovich)
See also DLB 238

Lesser, Milton
See Marlowe, Stephen

Lessing, Doris (May) 1919- ... **CLC 1, 2, 3, 6,**
10, 15, 22, 40, 94, 170; SSC 6, 61;
WLCS
See also AAYA 57; AFW; BRWS 1; CA
9-12R; CAAS 14; CANR 33, 54, 76, 122;
CD 5; CDBLB 1960 to Present; CN 7;
DA; DA3; DAB; DAC; DAM MST, NOV;
DFS 20; DLB 15, 139; DLBY 1985; EWL
3; EXPS; FW; LAIT 4; MTCW 1, 2;
RGEL 2; RGSF 2; SFW 4; SSFS 1, 12,
20; TEA; WLIT 2, 4

Lessing, Gotthold Ephraim
1729-1781 .... **DC 26; LC 8**
See also CDWLB 2; DLB 97; EW 4; RGWL
2, 3

Lester, Richard 1932- .... **CLC 20**

Levenson, Jay .... **CLC 70**

Lever, Charles (James)
1806-1872 .... **NCLC 23**
See also DLB 21; RGEL 2

Leverson, Ada Esther
1862(?)-1933(?) .... **TCLC 18**
See Elaine
See also CA 117; 202; DLB 153; RGEL 2

Levertov, Denise 1923-1997 .. **CLC 1, 2, 3, 5,**
8, 15, 28, 66; PC 11
See also AMWS 3; CA 1-4R; 178; 163;
CAAE 178; CAAS 19; CANR 3, 29, 50,
108; CDALBS; CP 7; CWP; DAM POET;
DLB 5, 165; EWL 3; EXPP; FW; INT
CANR-29; MTCW 1, 2; PAB; PFS 7, 17;
RGAL 4; TUS; WP

Levi, Carlo 1902-1975 .... **TCLC 125**
See also CA 65-68; 53-56; CANR 10; EWL
3; RGWL 2, 3

Levi, Jonathan .... **CLC 76**
See also CA 197

Levi, Peter (Chad Tigar)
1931-2000 .... **CLC 41**
See also CA 5-8R; 187; CANR 34, 80; CP
7; DLB 40

Levi, Primo 1919-1987 ...... **CLC 37, 50; SSC**
12; TCLC 109
See also CA 13-16R; 122; CANR 12, 33,
61, 70, 132; DLB 177, 299; EWL 3;
MTCW 1, 2; RGWL 2, 3

Levin, Ira 1929- .... **CLC 3, 6**
See also CA 21-24R; CANR 17, 44, 74;
CMW 4; CN 7; CPW; DA3; DAM POP;
HGG; MTCW 1, 2; SATA 66; SFW 4

Levin, Meyer 1905-1981 .... **CLC 7**
See also AITN 1; CA 9-12R; 104; CANR
15; DAM POP; DLB 9, 28; DLBY 1981;
SATA 21; SATA-Obit 27

Levine, Norman 1924- .... **CLC 54**
See also CA 73-76; CAAS 23; CANR 14,
70; DLB 88

Levine, Philip 1928- .. **CLC 2, 4, 5, 9, 14, 33,**
118; PC 22
See also AMWS 5; CA 9-12R; CANR 9,
37, 52, 116; CP 7; DAM POET; DLB 5;
EWL 3; PFS 8

Luke, Peter (Ambrose Cyprian)
1919-1995 .... **CLC 38**
See also CA 81-84; 147; CANR 72; CBD;
CD 5; DLB 13
Lunar, Dennis
See Mungo, Raymond
Lurie, Alison 1926- ..... **CLC 4, 5, 18, 39, 175**
See also BPFB 2; CA 1-4R; CANR 2, 17,
50, 88; CN 7; DLB 2; MTCW 1; SATA
46, 112
Lustig, Arnost 1926- .... **CLC 56**
See also AAYA 3; CA 69-72; CANR 47,
102; CWW 2; DLB 232, 299; EWL 3;
SATA 56
Luther, Martin 1483-1546 .... **LC 9, 37**
See also CDWLB 2; DLB 179; EW 2;
RGWL 2, 3
Luxemburg, Rosa 1870(?)-1919 ..... **TCLC 63**
See also CA 118
Luzi, Mario 1914- .... **CLC 13**
See also CA 61-64; CANR 9, 70; CWW 2;
DLB 128; EWL 3
L'vov, Arkady .... **CLC 59**
Lydgate, John c. 1370-1450(?) .... **LC 81**
See also BRW 1; DLB 146; RGEL 2
Lyly, John 1554(?)-1606 .... **DC 7; LC 41**
See also BRW 1; DAM DRAM; DLB 62,
167; RGEL 2
L'Ymagier
See Gourmont, Remy(-Marie-Charles) de
Lynch, B. Suarez
See Borges, Jorge Luis
Lynch, David (Keith) 1946- ..... **CLC 66, 162**
See also AAYA 55; CA 124; 129; CANR
111
Lynch, James
See Andreyev, Leonid (Nikolaevich)
Lyndsay, Sir David 1485-1555 .... **LC 20**
See also RGEL 2
Lynn, Kenneth S(chuyler)
1923-2001 .... **CLC 50**
See also CA 1-4R; 196; CANR 3, 27, 65
Lynx
See West, Rebecca
Lyons, Marcus
See Blish, James (Benjamin)
Lyotard, Jean-Francois
1924-1998 .... **TCLC 103**
See also DLB 242; EWL 3
Lyre, Pinchbeck
See Sassoon, Siegfried (Lorraine)
Lytle, Andrew (Nelson) 1902-1995 ... **CLC 22**
See also CA 9-12R; 150; CANR 70; CN 7;
CSW; DLB 6; DLBY 1995; RGAL 4;
RHW
Lyttelton, George 1709-1773 .... **LC 10**
See also RGEL 2
Lytton of Knebworth, Baron
See Bulwer-Lytton, Edward (George Earle
Lytton)
Maas, Peter 1929-2001 .... **CLC 29**
See also CA 93-96; 201; INT CA-93-96;
MTCW 2
Macaulay, Catherine 1731-1791 .... **LC 64**
See also DLB 104
Macaulay, (Emilie) Rose
1881(?)-1958 .... **TCLC 7, 44**
See also CA 104; DLB 36; EWL 3; RGEL
2; RHW
Macaulay, Thomas Babington
1800-1859 .... **NCLC 42**
See also BRW 4; CDBLB 1832-1890; DLB
32, 55; RGEL 2
MacBeth, George (Mann)
1932-1992 .... **CLC 2, 5, 9**
See also CA 25-28R; 136; CANR 61, 66;
DLB 40; MTCW 1; PFS 8; SATA 4;
SATA-Obit 70

MacCaig, Norman (Alexander)
1910-1996 .... **CLC 36**
See also BRWS 6; CA 9-12R; CANR 3, 34;
CP 7; DAB; DAM POET; DLB 27; EWL
3; RGEL 2
MacCarthy, Sir (Charles Otto) Desmond
1877-1952 .... **TCLC 36**
See also CA 167
MacDiarmid, Hugh ..... **CLC 2, 4, 11, 19, 63;
PC 9**
See Grieve, C(hristopher) M(urray)
See also CDBLB 1945-1960; DLB 20;
EWL 3; RGEL 2
MacDonald, Anson
See Heinlein, Robert A(nson)
Macdonald, Cynthia 1928- .... **CLC 13, 19**
See also CA 49-52; CANR 4, 44; DLB 105
MacDonald, George 1824-1905 .... **TCLC 9,
113**
See also AAYA 57; BYA 5; CA 106; 137;
CANR 80; CLR 67; DLB 18, 163, 178;
FANT; MAICYA 1, 2; RGEL 2; SATA 33,
100; SFW 4; SUFW; WCH
Macdonald, John
See Millar, Kenneth
MacDonald, John D(ann)
1916-1986 .... **CLC 3, 27, 44**
See also BPFB 2; CA 1-4R; 121; CANR 1,
19, 60; CMW 4; CPW; DAM NOV, POP;
DLB 8, 306; DLBY 1986; MSW; MTCW
1, 2; SFW 4
Macdonald, John Ross
See Millar, Kenneth
Macdonald, Ross ...... **CLC 1, 2, 3, 14, 34, 41**
See Millar, Kenneth
See also AMWS 4; BPFB 2; DLBD 6;
MSW; RGAL 4
MacDougal, John
See Blish, James (Benjamin)
MacDougal, John
See Blish, James (Benjamin)
MacDowell, John
See Parks, Tim(othy Harold)
MacEwen, Gwendolyn (Margaret)
1941-1987 .... **CLC 13, 55**
See also CA 9-12R; 124; CANR 7, 22; DLB
53, 251; SATA 50; SATA-Obit 55
Macha, Karel Hynek 1810-1846 .... **NCLC 46**
Machado (y Ruiz), Antonio
1875-1939 .... **TCLC 3**
See also CA 104; 174; DLB 108; EW 9;
EWL 3; HW 2; RGWL 2, 3
Machado de Assis, Joaquim Maria
1839-1908 .... **BLC 2; HLCS 2; SSC 24;
TCLC 10**
See also CA 107; 153; CANR 91; DLB 307;
LAW; RGSF 2; RGWL 2, 3; TWA; WLIT
1
Machaut, Guillaume de c.
1300-1377 .... **CMLC 64**
See also DLB 208
Machen, Arthur .... **SSC 20; TCLC 4**
See Jones, Arthur Llewellyn
See also CA 179; DLB 156, 178; RGEL 2;
SUFW 1
Machiavelli, Niccolo 1469-1527 ... **DC 16; LC
8, 36; WLCS**
See also AAYA 58; DA; DAB; DAC; DAM
MST; EW 2; LAIT 1; LMFS 1; NFS 9;
RGWL 2, 3; TWA
MacInnes, Colin 1914-1976 .... **CLC 4, 23**
See also CA 69-72; 65-68; CANR 21; DLB
14; MTCW 1, 2; RGEL 2; RHW
MacInnes, Helen (Clark)
1907-1985 .... **CLC 27, 39**
See also BPFB 2; CA 1-4R; 117; CANR 1,
28, 58; CMW 4; CPW; DAM POP; DLB
87; MSW; MTCW 1, 2; SATA 22; SATA-
Obit 44

Mackay, Mary 1855-1924
See Corelli, Marie
See also CA 118; 177; FANT; RHW
Mackay, Shena 1944- .... **CLC 195**
See also CA 104; CANR 88; DLB 231
Mackenzie, Compton (Edward Montague)
1883-1972 .... **CLC 18; TCLC 116**
See also CA 21-22; 37-40R; CAP 2; DLB
34, 100; RGEL 2
Mackenzie, Henry 1745-1831 .... **NCLC 41**
See also DLB 39; RGEL 2
Mackey, Nathaniel (Ernest) 1947- .... **PC 49**
See also CA 153; CANR 114; CP 7; DLB
169
MacKinnon, Catharine A. 1946- .... **CLC 181**
See also CA 128; 132; CANR 73; FW;
MTCW 2
Mackintosh, Elizabeth 1896(?)-1952
See Tey, Josephine
See also CA 110; CMW 4
MacLaren, James
See Grieve, C(hristopher) M(urray)
Mac Laverty, Bernard 1942- .... **CLC 31**
See also CA 116; 118; CANR 43, 88; CN
7; DLB 267; INT CA-118; RGSF 2
MacLean, Alistair (Stuart)
1922(?)-1987 .... **CLC 3, 13, 50, 63**
See also CA 57-60; 121; CANR 28, 61;
CMW 4; CPW; DAM POP; DLB 276;
MTCW 1; SATA 23; SATA-Obit 50;
TCWW 2
Maclean, Norman (Fitzroy)
1902-1990 .... **CLC 78; SSC 13**
See also AMWS 14; CA 102; 132; CANR
49; CPW; DAM POP; DLB 206; TCWW
2
MacLeish, Archibald 1892-1982 ... **CLC 3, 8,
14, 68; PC 47**
See also AMW; CA 9-12R; 106; CAD;
CANR 33, 63; CDALBS; DAM POET;
DFS 15; DLB 4, 7, 45; DLBY 1982; EWL
3; EXPP; MTCW 1, 2; PAB; PFS 5;
RGAL 4; TUS
MacLennan, (John) Hugh
1907-1990 .... **CLC 2, 14, 92**
See also CA 5-8R; 142; CANR 33; DAC;
DAM MST; DLB 68; EWL 3; MTCW 1,
2; RGEL 2; TWA
MacLeod, Alistair 1936- .... **CLC 56, 165**
See also CA 123; CCA 1; DAC; DAM
MST; DLB 60; MTCW 2; RGSF 2
Macleod, Fiona
See Sharp, William
See also RGEL 2; SUFW
MacNeice, (Frederick) Louis
1907-1963 .... **CLC 1, 4, 10, 53; PC 61**
See also BRW 7; CA 85-88; CANR 61;
DAB; DAM POET; DLB 10, 20; EWL 3;
MTCW 1, 2; RGEL 2
MacNeill, Dand
See Fraser, George MacDonald
Macpherson, James 1736-1796 .... **LC 29**
See Ossian
See also BRWS 8; DLB 109; RGEL 2
Macpherson, (Jean) Jay 1931- .... **CLC 14**
See also CA 5-8R; CANR 90; CP 7; CWP;
DLB 53
Macrobius fl. 430- .... **CMLC 48**
MacShane, Frank 1927-1999 .... **CLC 39**
See also CA 9-12R; 186; CANR 3, 33; DLB
111
Macumber, Mari
See Sandoz, Mari(e Susette)
Madach, Imre 1823-1864 .... **NCLC 19**
Madden, (Jerry) David 1933- .... **CLC 5, 15**
See also CA 1-4R; CAAS 3; CANR 4, 45;
CN 7; CSW; DLB 6; MTCW 1
Maddern, Al(an)
See Ellison, Harlan (Jay)

Madhubuti, Haki R. 1942- ... **BLC 2; CLC 6, 73; PC 5**
See Lee, Don L.
See also BW 2, 3; CA 73-76; CANR 24, 51, 73; CP 7; CSW; DAM MULT, POET; DLB 5, 41; DLBD 8; EWL 3; MTCW 2; RGAL 4

Madison, James 1751-1836 .... **NCLC 126**
See also DLB 37

Maepenn, Hugh
See Kuttner, Henry

Maepenn, K. H.
See Kuttner, Henry

Maeterlinck, Maurice 1862-1949 ..... **TCLC 3**
See also CA 104; 136; CANR 80; DAM DRAM; DLB 192; EW 8; EWL 3; GFL 1789 to the Present; LMFS 2; RGWL 2, 3; SATA 66; TWA

Maginn, William 1794-1842 .... **NCLC 8**
See also DLB 110, 159

Mahapatra, Jayanta 1928- .... **CLC 33**
See also CA 73-76; CAAS 9; CANR 15, 33, 66, 87; CP 7; DAM MULT

Mahfouz, Naguib (Abdel Aziz Al-Sabilgi) 1911(?)- .... **CLC 153; SSC 66**
See Mahfuz, Najib (Abdel Aziz al-Sabilgi)
See also AAYA 49; BEST 89:2; CA 128; CANR 55, 101; DA3; DAM NOV; MTCW 1, 2; RGWL 2, 3; SSFS 9

Mahfuz, Najib (Abdel Aziz al-Sabilgi) .... **CLC 52, 55**
See Mahfouz, Naguib (Abdel Aziz Al-Sabilgi)
See also AFW; CWW 2; DLBY 1988; EWL 3; RGSF 2; WLIT 2

Mahon, Derek 1941- .... **CLC 27; PC 60**
See also BRWS 6; CA 113; 128; CANR 88; CP 7; DLB 40; EWL 3

Maiakovskii, Vladimir
See Mayakovski, Vladimir (Vladimirovich)
See also IDTP; RGWL 2, 3

Mailer, Norman (Kingsley) 1923- . **CLC 1, 2, 3, 4, 5, 8, 11, 14, 28, 39, 74, 111**
See also AAYA 31; AITN 2; AMW; AMWC 2; AMWR 2; BPFB 2; CA 9-12R; CABS 1; CANR 28, 74, 77, 130; CDALB 1968-1988; CN 7; CPW; DA; DA3; DAB; DAC; DAM MST, NOV, POP; DLB 2, 16, 28, 185, 278; DLBD 3; DLBY 1980, 1983; EWL 3; MTCW 1, 2; NFS 10; RGAL 4; TUS

Maillet, Antonine 1929- .... **CLC 54, 118**
See also CA 115; 120; CANR 46, 74, 77, 134; CCA 1; CWW 2; DAC; DLB 60; INT CA-120; MTCW 2

Maimonides 1135-1204 .... **CMLC 76**
See also DLB 115

Mais, Roger 1905-1955 .... **TCLC 8**
See also BW 1, 3; CA 105; 124; CANR 82; CDWLB 3; DLB 125; EWL 3; MTCW 1; RGEL 2

Maistre, Joseph 1753-1821 .... **NCLC 37**
See also GFL 1789 to the Present

Maitland, Frederic William 1850-1906 .... **TCLC 65**

Maitland, Sara (Louise) 1950- .... **CLC 49**
See also CA 69-72; CANR 13, 59; DLB 271; FW

Major, Clarence 1936- ... **BLC 2; CLC 3, 19, 48**
See also AFAW 2; BW 2, 3; CA 21-24R; CAAS 6; CANR 13, 25, 53, 82; CN 7; CP 7; CSW; DAM MULT; DLB 33; EWL 3; MSW

Major, Kevin (Gerald) 1949- .... **CLC 26**
See also AAYA 16; CA 97-100; CANR 21, 38, 112; CLR 11; DAC; DLB 60; INT CANR-21; JRDA; MAICYA 1, 2; MAICYAS 1; SATA 32, 82, 134; WYA; YAW

Maki, James
See Ozu, Yasujiro

Makine, Andrei 1957- .... **CLC 198**
See also CA 176; CANR 103

Malabaila, Damiano
See Levi, Primo

Malamud, Bernard 1914-1986 .. **CLC 1, 2, 3, 5, 8, 9, 11, 18, 27, 44, 78, 85; SSC 15; TCLC 129; WLC**
See also AAYA 16; AMWS 1; BPFB 2; BYA 15; CA 5-8R; 118; CABS 1; CANR 28, 62, 114; CDALB 1941-1968; CPW; DA; DA3; DAB; DAC; DAM MST, NOV, POP; DLB 2, 28, 152; DLBY 1980, 1986; EWL 3; EXPS; LAIT 4; LATS 1:1; MTCW 1, 2; NFS 4, 9; RGAL 4; RGSF 2; SSFS 8, 13, 16; TUS

Malan, Herman
See Bosman, Herman Charles; Bosman, Herman Charles

Malaparte, Curzio 1898-1957 .... **TCLC 52**
See also DLB 264

Malcolm, Dan
See Silverberg, Robert

Malcolm, Janet 1934- .... **CLC 201**
See also CA 123; CANR 89; NCFS 1

Malcolm X ...... **BLC 2; CLC 82, 117; WLCS**
See Little, Malcolm
See also LAIT 5; NCFS 3

Malherbe, Francois de 1555-1628 .... **LC 5**
See also GFL Beginnings to 1789

Mallarme, Stephane 1842-1898 ...... **NCLC 4, 41; PC 4**
See also DAM POET; DLB 217; EW 7; GFL 1789 to the Present; LMFS 2; RGWL 2, 3; TWA

Mallet-Joris, Francoise 1930- .... **CLC 11**
See also CA 65-68; CANR 17; CWW 2; DLB 83; EWL 3; GFL 1789 to the Present

Malley, Ern
See McAuley, James Phillip

Mallon, Thomas 1951- .... **CLC 172**
See also CA 110; CANR 29, 57, 92

Mallowan, Agatha Christie
See Christie, Agatha (Mary Clarissa)

Maloff, Saul 1922- .... **CLC 5**
See also CA 33-36R

Malone, Louis
See MacNeice, (Frederick) Louis

Malone, Michael (Christopher) 1942- .... **CLC 43**
See also CA 77-80; CANR 14, 32, 57, 114

Malory, Sir Thomas 1410(?)-1471(?) . **LC 11, 88; WLCS**
See also BRW 1; BRWR 2; CDBLB Before 1660; DA; DAB; DAC; DAM MST; DLB 146; EFS 2; RGEL 2; SATA 59; SATA-Brief 33; TEA; WLIT 3

Malouf, (George Joseph) David 1934- .... **CLC 28, 86**
See also CA 124; CANR 50, 76; CN 7; CP 7; DLB 289; EWL 3; MTCW 2

Malraux, (Georges-)Andre 1901-1976 .... **CLC 1, 4, 9, 13, 15, 57**
See also BPFB 2; CA 21-22; 69-72; CANR 34, 58; CAP 2; DA3; DAM NOV; DLB 72; EW 12; EWL 3; GFL 1789 to the Present; MTCW 1, 2; RGWL 2, 3; TWA

Malthus, Thomas Robert 1766-1834 .... **NCLC 145**
See also DLB 107, 158; RGEL 2

Malzberg, Barry N(athaniel) 1939- ... **CLC 7**
See also CA 61-64; CAAS 4; CANR 16; CMW 4; DLB 8; SFW 4

Mamet, David (Alan) 1947- .. **CLC 9, 15, 34, 46, 91, 166; DC 4, 24**
See also AAYA 3, 60; AMWS 14; CA 81-84; CABS 3; CANR 15, 41, 67, 72, 129; CD 5; DA3; DAM DRAM; DFS 2, 3, 6, 12, 15; DLB 7; EWL 3; IDFW 4; MTCW 1, 2; RGAL 4

Mamoulian, Rouben (Zachary) 1897-1987 .... **CLC 16**
See also CA 25-28R; 124; CANR 85

Mandelshtam, Osip
See Mandelstam, Osip (Emilievich)
See also EW 10; EWL 3; RGWL 2, 3

Mandelstam, Osip (Emilievich) 1891(?)-1943(?) .... **PC 14; TCLC 2, 6**
See Mandelshtam, Osip
See also CA 104; 150; MTCW 2; TWA

Mander, (Mary) Jane 1877-1949 ... **TCLC 31**
See also CA 162; RGEL 2

Mandeville, Bernard 1670-1733 .... **LC 82**
See also DLB 101

Mandeville, Sir John fl. 1350- ...... **CMLC 19**
See also DLB 146

Mandiargues, Andre Pieyre de .... **CLC 41**
See Pieyre de Mandiargues, Andre
See also DLB 83

Mandrake, Ethel Belle
See Thurman, Wallace (Henry)

Mangan, James Clarence 1803-1849 .... **NCLC 27**
See also RGEL 2

Maniere, J.-E.
See Giraudoux, Jean(-Hippolyte)

Mankiewicz, Herman (Jacob) 1897-1953 .... **TCLC 85**
See also CA 120; 169; DLB 26; IDFW 3, 4

Manley, (Mary) Delariviere 1672(?)-1724 .... **LC 1, 42**
See also DLB 39, 80; RGEL 2

Mann, Abel
See Creasey, John

Mann, Emily 1952- .... **DC 7**
See also CA 130; CAD; CANR 55; CD 5; CWD; DLB 266

Mann, (Luiz) Heinrich 1871-1950 ... **TCLC 9**
See also CA 106; 164; 181; DLB 66, 118; EW 8; EWL 3; RGWL 2, 3

Mann, (Paul) Thomas 1875-1955 . **SSC 5, 80, 82; TCLC 2, 8, 14, 21, 35, 44, 60, 168; WLC**
See also BPFB 2; CA 104; 128; CANR 133; CDWLB 2; DA; DA3; DAB; DAC; DAM MST, NOV; DLB 66; EW 9; EWL 3; GLL 1; LATS 1:1; LMFS 1; MTCW 1, 2; NFS 17; RGSF 2; RGWL 2, 3; SSFS 4, 9; TWA

Mannheim, Karl 1893-1947 .... **TCLC 65**
See also CA 204

Manning, David
See Faust, Frederick (Schiller)
See also TCWW 2

Manning, Frederic 1882-1935 .... **TCLC 25**
See also CA 124; 216; DLB 260

Manning, Olivia 1915-1980 .... **CLC 5, 19**
See also CA 5-8R; 101; CANR 29; EWL 3; FW; MTCW 1; RGEL 2

Mano, D. Keith 1942- .... **CLC 2, 10**
See also CA 25-28R; CAAS 6; CANR 26, 57; DLB 6

Mansfield, Katherine .... **SSC 9, 23, 38, 81; TCLC 2, 8, 39, 164; WLC**
See Beauchamp, Kathleen Mansfield
See also BPFB 2; BRW 7; DAB; DLB 162; EWL 3; EXPS; FW; GLL 1; RGEL 2; RGSF 2; SSFS 2, 8, 10, 11; WWE 1

Manso, Peter 1940- .... **CLC 39**
See also CA 29-32R; CANR 44

Mantecon, Juan Jimenez
See Jimenez (Mantecon), Juan Ramon

Mantel, Hilary (Mary) 1952- .... **CLC 144**
See also CA 125; CANR 54, 101; CN 7; DLB 271; RHW

Manton, Peter
See Creasey, John

Man Without a Spleen, A
See Chekhov, Anton (Pavlovich)

Melville, Herman 1819-1891 ..... **NCLC 3, 12, 29, 45, 49, 91, 93, 123, 157; SSC 1, 17, 46; WLC**
See also AAYA 25; AMW; AMWR 1; CDALB 1640-1865; DA; DA3; DAB; DAC; DAM MST, NOV; DLB 3, 74, 250, 254; EXPN; EXPS; LAIT 1, 2; NFS 7, 9; RGAL 4; RGSF 2; SATA 59; SSFS 3; TUS

Members, Mark
See Powell, Anthony (Dymoke)

Membreno, Alejandro .... **CLC 59**

Menand, Louis 1952- .... **CLC 208**
See also CA 200

Menander c. 342B.C.-c. 293B.C. .... **CMLC 9, 51; DC 3**
See also AW 1; CDWLB 1; DAM DRAM; DLB 176; LMFS 1; RGWL 2, 3

Menchu, Rigoberta 1959- .. **CLC 160; HLCS 2**
See also CA 175; DNFS 1; WLIT 1

Mencken, H(enry) L(ouis)
1880-1956 .... **TCLC 13**
See also AMW; CA 105; 125; CDALB 1917-1929; DLB 11, 29, 63, 137, 222; EWL 3; MTCW 1, 2; NCFS 4; RGAL 4; TUS

Mendelsohn, Jane 1965- .... **CLC 99**
See also CA 154; CANR 94

Menton, Francisco de
See Chin, Frank (Chew, Jr.)

Mercer, David 1928-1980 .... **CLC 5**
See also CA 9-12R; 102; CANR 23; CBD; DAM DRAM; DLB 13; MTCW 1; RGEL 2

Merchant, Paul
See Ellison, Harlan (Jay)

Meredith, George 1828-1909 .. **PC 60; TCLC 17, 43**
See also CA 117; 153; CANR 80; CDBLB 1832-1890; DAM POET; DLB 18, 35, 57, 159; RGEL 2; TEA

Meredith, William (Morris) 1919- .... **CLC 4, 13, 22, 55; PC 28**
See also CA 9-12R; CAAS 14; CANR 6, 40, 129; CP 7; DAM POET; DLB 5

Merezhkovsky, Dmitrii Sergeevich
See Merezhkovsky, Dmitry Sergeyevich
See also DLB 295

Merezhkovsky, Dmitry Sergeevich
See Merezhkovsky, Dmitry Sergeyevich
See also EWL 3

Merezhkovsky, Dmitry Sergeyevich
1865-1941 .... **TCLC 29**
See Merezhkovsky, Dmitrii Sergeevich; Merezhkovsky, Dmitry Sergeevich
See also CA 169

Merimee, Prosper 1803-1870 ... **NCLC 6, 65; SSC 7, 77**
See also DLB 119, 192; EW 6; EXPS; GFL 1789 to the Present; RGSF 2; RGWL 2, 3; SSFS 8; SUFW

Merkin, Daphne 1954- .... **CLC 44**
See also CA 123

Merleau-Ponty, Maurice
1908-1961 .... **TCLC 156**
See also CA 114; 89-92; DLB 296; GFL 1789 to the Present

Merlin, Arthur
See Blish, James (Benjamin)

Mernissi, Fatima 1940- .... **CLC 171**
See also CA 152; FW

Merrill, James (Ingram) 1926-1995 .. **CLC 2, 3, 6, 8, 13, 18, 34, 91; PC 28**
See also AMWS 3; CA 13-16R; 147; CANR 10, 49, 63, 108; DA3; DAM POET; DLB 5, 165; DLBY 1985; EWL 3; INT CANR-10; MTCW 1, 2; PAB; RGAL 4

Merriman, Alex
See Silverberg, Robert

Merriman, Brian 1747-1805 .... **NCLC 70**

Merritt, E. B.
See Waddington, Miriam

Merton, Thomas (James)
1915-1968 . **CLC 1, 3, 11, 34, 83; PC 10**
See also AMWS 8; CA 5-8R; 25-28R; CANR 22, 53, 111, 131; DA3; DLB 48; DLBY 1981; MTCW 1, 2

Merwin, W(illiam) S(tanley) 1927- ... **CLC 1, 2, 3, 5, 8, 13, 18, 45, 88; PC 45**
See also AMWS 3; CA 13-16R; CANR 15, 51, 112; CP 7; DA3; DAM POET; DLB 5, 169; EWL 3; INT CANR-15; MTCW 1, 2; PAB; PFS 5, 15; RGAL 4

Metastasio, Pietro 1698-1782 .... **LC 115**
See also RGWL 2, 3

Metcalf, John 1938- .... **CLC 37; SSC 43**
See also CA 113; CN 7; DLB 60; RGSF 2; TWA

Metcalf, Suzanne
See Baum, L(yman) Frank

Mew, Charlotte (Mary) 1870-1928 .. **TCLC 8**
See also CA 105; 189; DLB 19, 135; RGEL 2

Mewshaw, Michael 1943- .... **CLC 9**
See also CA 53-56; CANR 7, 47; DLBY 1980

Meyer, Conrad Ferdinand
1825-1898 .... **NCLC 81; SSC 30**
See also DLB 129; EW; RGWL 2, 3

Meyer, Gustav 1868-1932
See Meyrink, Gustav
See also CA 117; 190

Meyer, June
See Jordan, June (Meyer)

Meyer, Lynn
See Slavitt, David R(ytman)

Meyers, Jeffrey 1939- .... **CLC 39**
See also CA 73-76, 186; CAAE 186; CANR 54, 102; DLB 111

Meynell, Alice (Christina Gertrude Thompson) 1847-1922 .... **TCLC 6**
See also CA 104; 177; DLB 19, 98; RGEL 2

Meyrink, Gustav .... **TCLC 21**
See Meyer, Gustav
See also DLB 81; EWL 3

Michaels, Leonard 1933-2003 ..... **CLC 6, 25; SSC 16**
See also CA 61-64; 216; CANR 21, 62, 119; CN 7; DLB 130; MTCW 1

Michaux, Henri 1899-1984 .... **CLC 8, 19**
See also CA 85-88; 114; DLB 258; EWL 3; GFL 1789 to the Present; RGWL 2, 3

Micheaux, Oscar (Devereaux)
1884-1951 .... **TCLC 76**
See also BW 3; CA 174; DLB 50; TCWW 2

Michelangelo 1475-1564 .... **LC 12**
See also AAYA 43

Michelet, Jules 1798-1874 .... **NCLC 31**
See also EW 5; GFL 1789 to the Present

Michels, Robert 1876-1936 .... **TCLC 88**
See also CA 212

Michener, James A(lbert)
1907(?)-1997 .. **CLC 1, 5, 11, 29, 60, 109**
See also AAYA 27; AITN 1; BEST 90:1; BPFB 2; CA 5-8R; 161; CANR 21, 45, 68; CN 7; CPW; DA3; DAM NOV, POP; DLB 6; MTCW 1, 2; RHW

Mickiewicz, Adam 1798-1855 . **NCLC 3, 101; PC 38**
See also EW 5; RGWL 2, 3

Middleton, (John) Christopher
1926- .... **CLC 13**
See also CA 13-16R; CANR 29, 54, 117; CP 7; DLB 40

Middleton, Richard (Barham)
1882-1911 .... **TCLC 56**
See also CA 187; DLB 156; HGG

Middleton, Stanley 1919- .... **CLC 7, 38**
See also CA 25-28R; CAAS 23; CANR 21, 46, 81; CN 7; DLB 14

Middleton, Thomas 1580-1627 ...... **DC 5; LC 33**
See also BRW 2; DAM DRAM, MST; DFS 18; DLB 58; RGEL 2

Migueis, Jose Rodrigues 1901-1980 . **CLC 10**
See also DLB 287

Mikszath, Kalman 1847-1910 .... **TCLC 31**
See also CA 170

Miles, Jack .... **CLC 100**
See also CA 200

Miles, John Russiano
See Miles, Jack

Miles, Josephine (Louise)
1911-1985 .... **CLC 1, 2, 14, 34, 39**
See also CA 1-4R; 116; CANR 2, 55; DAM POET; DLB 48

Militant
See Sandburg, Carl (August)

Mill, Harriet (Hardy) Taylor
1807-1858 .... **NCLC 102**
See also FW

Mill, John Stuart 1806-1873 .... **NCLC 11, 58**
See also CDBLB 1832-1890; DLB 55, 190, 262; FW 1; RGEL 2; TEA

Millar, Kenneth 1915-1983 .... **CLC 14**
See Macdonald, Ross
See also CA 9-12R; 110; CANR 16, 63, 107; CMW 4; CPW; DA3; DAM POP; DLB 2, 226; DLBD 6; DLBY 1983; MTCW 1, 2

Millay, E. Vincent
See Millay, Edna St. Vincent

Millay, Edna St. Vincent 1892-1950 ..... **PC 6, 61; TCLC 4, 49, 169; WLCS**
See Boyd, Nancy
See also AMW; CA 104; 130; CDALB 1917-1929; DA; DA3; DAB; DAC; DAM MST, POET; DLB 45, 249; EWL 3; EXPP; MAWW; MTCW 1, 2; PAB; PFS 3, 17; RGAL 4; TUS; WP

Miller, Arthur 1915- ...... **CLC 1, 2, 6, 10, 15, 26, 47, 78, 179; DC 1; WLC**
See also AAYA 15; AITN 1; AMW; AMWC 1; CA 1-4R; CABS 3; CAD; CANR 2, 30, 54, 76, 132; CD 5; CDALB 1941-1968; DA; DA3; DAB; DAC; DAM DRAM, MST; DFS 1, 3, 8; DLB 7, 266; EWL 3; LAIT 1, 4; LATS 1:2; MTCW 1, 2; RGAL 4; TUS; WYAS 1

Miller, Henry (Valentine)
1891-1980 .... **CLC 1, 2, 4, 9, 14, 43, 84; WLC**
See also AMW; BPFB 2; CA 9-12R; 97-100; CANR 33, 64; CDALB 1929-1941; DA; DA3; DAB; DAC; DAM MST, NOV; DLB 4, 9; DLBY 1980; EWL 3; MTCW 1, 2; RGAL 4; TUS

Miller, Hugh 1802-1856 .... **NCLC 143**
See also DLB 190

Miller, Jason 1939(?)-2001 .... **CLC 2**
See also AITN 1; CA 73-76; 197; CAD; CANR 130; DFS 12; DLB 7

Miller, Sue 1943- .... **CLC 44**
See also AMWS 12; BEST 90:3; CA 139; CANR 59, 91, 128; DA3; DAM POP; DLB 143

Miller, Walter M(ichael, Jr.)
1923-1996 .... **CLC 4, 30**
See also BPFB 2; CA 85-88; CANR 108; DLB 8; SCFW; SFW 4

Millett, Kate 1934- .... **CLC 67**
See also AITN 1; CA 73-76; CANR 32, 53, 76, 110; DA3; DLB 246; FW; GLL 1; MTCW 1, 2

Millhauser, Steven (Lewis) 1943- .... **CLC 21, 54, 109; SSC 57**
See also CA 110; 111; CANR 63, 114, 133; CN 7; DA3; DLB 2; FANT; INT CA-111; MTCW 2

Millin, Sarah Gertrude 1889-1968 ... **CLC 49**
See also CA 102; 93-96; DLB 225; EWL 3

Milne, A(lan) A(lexander)
1882-1956 .... **TCLC 6, 88**
See also BRWS 5; CA 104; 133; CLR 1, 26; CMW 4; CWRI 5; DA3; DAB; DAC; DAM MST; DLB 10, 77, 100, 160; FANT; MAICYA 1, 2; MTCW 1, 2; RGEL 2; SATA 100; WCH; YABC 1

Milner, Ron(ald) 1938-2004 ..... **BLC 3; CLC 56**
See also AITN 1; BW 1; CA 73-76; CAD; CANR 24, 81; CD 5; DAM MULT; DLB 38; MTCW 1

Milnes, Richard Monckton
1809-1885 .... **NCLC 61**
See also DLB 32, 184

Milosz, Czeslaw 1911- ...... **CLC 5, 11, 22, 31, 56, 82; PC 8; WLCS**
See also CA 81-84; CANR 23, 51, 91, 126; CDWLB 4; CWW 2; DA3; DAM MST, POET; DLB 215; EW 13; EWL 3; MTCW 1, 2; PFS 16; RGWL 2, 3

Milton, John 1608-1674 ..... **LC 9, 43, 92; PC 19, 29; WLC**
See also BRW 2; BRWR 2; CDBLB 1660-1789; DA; DA3; DAB; DAC; DAM MST, POET; DLB 131, 151, 281; EFS 1; EXPP; LAIT 1; PAB; PFS 3, 17; RGEL 2; TEA; WLIT 3; WP

Min, Anchee 1957- .... **CLC 86**
See also CA 146; CANR 94

Minehaha, Cornelius
See Wedekind, (Benjamin) Frank(lin)

Miner, Valerie 1947- .... **CLC 40**
See also CA 97-100; CANR 59; FW; GLL 2

Minimo, Duca
See D'Annunzio, Gabriele

Minot, Susan 1956- .... **CLC 44, 159**
See also AMWS 6; CA 134; CANR 118; CN 7

Minus, Ed 1938- .... **CLC 39**
See also CA 185

Mirabai 1498(?)-1550(?) .... **PC 48**

Miranda, Javier
See Bioy Casares, Adolfo
See also CWW 2

Mirbeau, Octave 1848-1917 .... **TCLC 55**
See also CA 216; DLB 123, 192; GFL 1789 to the Present

Mirikitani, Janice 1942- .... **AAL**
See also CA 211; RGAL 4

Mirk, John (?)-c. 1414 .... **LC 105**
See also DLB 146

Miro (Ferrer), Gabriel (Francisco Victor)
1879-1930 .... **TCLC 5**
See also CA 104; 185; EWL 3

Misharin, Alexandr .... **CLC 59**

Mishima, Yukio .... **CLC 2, 4, 6, 9, 27; DC 1; SSC 4, TCLC 161**
See Hiraoka, Kimitake
See also AAYA 50; BPFB 2; GLL 1; MJW; MTCW 2; RGSF 2; RGWL 2, 3; SSFS 5, 12

Mistral, Frederic 1830-1914 .... **TCLC 51**
See also CA 122; 213; GFL 1789 to the Present

Mistral, Gabriela
See Godoy Alcayaga, Lucila
See also DLB 283; DNFS 1; EWL 3; LAW; RGWL 2, 3; WP

Mistry, Rohinton 1952- ... **CLC 71, 196; SSC 73**
See also BRWS 10; CA 141; CANR 86, 114; CCA 1; CN 7; DAC; SSFS 6

Mitchell, Clyde
See Ellison, Harlan (Jay)

Mitchell, Emerson Blackhorse Barney
1945- .... **NNAL**
See also CA 45-48

Mitchell, James Leslie 1901-1935
See Gibbon, Lewis Grassic
See also CA 104; 188; DLB 15

Mitchell, Joni 1943- .... **CLC 12**
See also CA 112; CCA 1

Mitchell, Joseph (Quincy)
1908-1996 .... **CLC 98**
See also CA 77-80; 152; CANR 69; CN 7; CSW; DLB 185; DLBY 1996

Mitchell, Margaret (Munnerlyn)
1900-1949 .... **TCLC 11**
See also AAYA 23; BPFB 2; BYA 1; CA 109; 125; CANR 55, 94; CDALBS; DA3; DAM NOV, POP; DLB 9; LAIT 2; MTCW 1, 2; NFS 9; RGAL 4; RHW; TUS; WYAS 1; YAW

Mitchell, Peggy
See Mitchell, Margaret (Munnerlyn)

Mitchell, S(ilas) Weir 1829-1914 .... **TCLC 36**
See also CA 165; DLB 202; RGAL 4

Mitchell, W(illiam) O(rmond)
1914-1998 .... **CLC 25**
See also CA 77-80; 165; CANR 15, 43; CN 7; DAC; DAM MST; DLB 88

Mitchell, William (Lendrum)
1879-1936 .... **TCLC 81**
See also CA 213

Mitford, Mary Russell 1787-1855 ... **NCLC 4**
See also DLB 110, 116; RGEL 2

Mitford, Nancy 1904-1973 .... **CLC 44**
See also BRWS 10; CA 9-12R; DLB 191; RGEL 2

Miyamoto, (Chujo) Yuriko
1899-1951 .... **TCLC 37**
See Miyamoto Yuriko
See also CA 170, 174

Miyamoto Yuriko
See Miyamoto, (Chujo) Yuriko
See also DLB 180

Miyazawa, Kenji 1896-1933 .... **TCLC 76**
See Miyazawa Kenji
See also CA 157; RGWL 3

Miyazawa Kenji
See Miyazawa, Kenji
See also EWL 3

Mizoguchi, Kenji 1898-1956 .... **TCLC 72**
See also CA 167

Mo, Timothy (Peter) 1950(?)- ... **CLC 46, 134**
See also CA 117; CANR 128; CN 7; DLB 194; MTCW 1; WLIT 4; WWE 1

Modarressi, Taghi (M.) 1931-1997 ... **CLC 44**
See also CA 121; 134; INT CA-134

Modiano, Patrick (Jean) 1945- .... **CLC 18**
See also CA 85-88; CANR 17, 40, 115; CWW 2; DLB 83, 299; EWL 3

Mofolo, Thomas (Mokopu)
1875(?)-1948 .... **BLC 3; TCLC 22**
See also AFW; CA 121; 153; CANR 83; DAM MULT; DLB 225; EWL 3; MTCW 2; WLIT 2

Mohr, Nicholasa 1938- .... **CLC 12; HLC 2**
See also AAYA 8, 46; CA 49-52; CANR 1, 32, 64; CLR 22; DAM MULT; DLB 145; HW 1, 2; JRDA; LAIT 5; LLW 1; MAICYA 2; MAICYAS 1; RGAL 4; SAAS 8; SATA 8, 97; SATA-Essay 113; WYA; YAW

Moi, Toril 1953- .... **CLC 172**
See also CA 154; CANR 102; FW

Mojtabai, A(nn) G(race) 1938- ..... **CLC 5, 9, 15, 29**
See also CA 85-88; CANR 88

Moliere 1622-1673 ..... **DC 13; LC 10, 28, 64; WLC**
See also DA; DA3; DAB; DAC; DAM DRAM, MST; DFS 13, 18, 20; DLB 268; EW 3; GFL Beginnings to 1789; LATS 1:1; RGWL 2, 3; TWA

Molin, Charles
See Mayne, William (James Carter)

Molnar, Ferenc 1878-1952 .... **TCLC 20**
See also CA 109; 153; CANR 83; CDWLB 4; DAM DRAM; DLB 215; EWL 3; RGWL 2, 3

Momaday, N(avarre) Scott 1934- ...... **CLC 2, 19, 85, 95, 160; NNAL; PC 25; WLCS**
See also AAYA 11; AMWS 4; ANW; BPFB 2; BYA 12; CA 25-28R; CANR 14, 34, 68, 134; CDALBS; CN 7; CPW; DA; DA3; DAB; DAC; DAM MST, MULT, NOV, POP; DLB 143, 175, 256; EWL 3; EXPP; INT CANR-14; LAIT 4; LATS 1:2; MTCW 1, 2; NFS 10; PFS 2, 11; RGAL 4; SATA 48; SATA-Brief 30; WP; YAW

Monette, Paul 1945-1995 .... **CLC 82**
See also AMWS 10; CA 139; 147; CN 7; GLL 1

Monroe, Harriet 1860-1936 .... **TCLC 12**
See also CA 109; 204; DLB 54, 91

Monroe, Lyle
See Heinlein, Robert A(nson)

Montagu, Elizabeth 1720-1800 .... **NCLC 7, 117**
See also FW

Montagu, Mary (Pierrepont) Wortley
1689-1762 .... **LC 9, 57; PC 16**
See also DLB 95, 101; RGEL 2

Montagu, W. H.
See Coleridge, Samuel Taylor

Montague, John (Patrick) 1929- ..... **CLC 13, 46**
See also CA 9-12R; CANR 9, 69, 121; CP 7; DLB 40; EWL 3; MTCW 1; PFS 12; RGEL 2

Montaigne, Michel (Eyquem) de
1533-1592 .... **LC 8, 105; WLC**
See also DA; DAB; DAC; DAM MST; EW 2; GFL Beginnings to 1789; LMFS 1; RGWL 2, 3; TWA

Montale, Eugenio 1896-1981 ... **CLC 7, 9, 18; PC 13**
See also CA 17-20R; 104; CANR 30; DLB 114; EW 11; EWL 3; MTCW 1; RGWL 2, 3; TWA

Montesquieu, Charles-Louis de Secondat
1689-1755 .... **LC 7, 69**
See also EW 3; GFL Beginnings to 1789; TWA

Montessori, Maria 1870-1952 ...... **TCLC 103**
See also CA 115; 147

Montgomery, (Robert) Bruce 1921(?)-1978
See Crispin, Edmund
See also CA 179; 104; CMW 4

Montgomery, L(ucy) M(aud)
1874-1942 .... **TCLC 51, 140**
See also AAYA 12; BYA 1; CA 108; 137; CLR 8, 91; DA3; DAC; DAM MST; DLB 92; DLBD 14; JRDA; MAICYA 1, 2; MTCW 2; RGEL 2; SATA 100; TWA; WCH; WYA; YABC 1

Montgomery, Marion H., Jr. 1925- ... **CLC 7**
See also AITN 1; CA 1-4R; CANR 3, 48; CSW; DLB 6

Montgomery, Max
See Davenport, Guy (Mattison, Jr.)

Montherlant, Henry (Milon) de
1896-1972 .... **CLC 8, 19**
See also CA 85-88; 37-40R; DAM DRAM;
DLB 72; EW 11; EWL 3; GFL 1789 to
the Present; MTCW 1

Monty Python
See Chapman, Graham; Cleese, John
(Marwood); Gilliam, Terry (Vance); Idle,
Eric; Jones, Terence Graham Parry; Palin,
Michael (Edward)
See also AAYA 7

Moodie, Susanna (Strickland)
1803-1885 .... **NCLC 14, 113**
See also DLB 99

Moody, Hiram (F. III) 1961-
See Moody, Rick
See also CA 138; CANR 64, 112

Moody, Minerva
See Alcott, Louisa May

Moody, Rick .... **CLC 147**
See Moody, Hiram (F. III)

Moody, William Vaughan
1869-1910 .... **TCLC 105**
See also CA 110; 178; DLB 7, 54; RGAL 4

Mooney, Edward 1951-
See Mooney, Ted
See also CA 130

Mooney, Ted .... **CLC 25**
See Mooney, Edward

Moorcock, Michael (John) 1939- ...... **CLC 5,**
27, 58
See Bradbury, Edward P.
See also AAYA 26; CA 45-48; CAAS 5;
CANR 2, 17, 38, 64, 122; CN 7; DLB 14,
231, 261; FANT; MTCW 1, 2; SATA 93;
SCFW 2; SFW 4; SUFW 1, 2

Moore, Brian 1921-1999 ... **CLC 1, 3, 5, 7, 8,**
19, 32, 90
See Bryan, Michael
See also BRWS 9; CA 1-4R; 174; CANR 1,
25, 42, 63; CCA 1; CN 7; DAB; DAC;
DAM MST; DLB 251; EWL 3; FANT;
MTCW 1, 2; RGEL 2

Moore, Edward
See Muir, Edwin
See also RGEL 2

Moore, G. E. 1873-1958 .... **TCLC 89**
See also DLB 262

Moore, George Augustus
1852-1933 .... **SSC 19; TCLC 7**
See also BRW 6; CA 104; 177; DLB 10,
18, 57, 135; EWL 3; RGEL 2; RGSF 2

Moore, Lorrie .... **CLC 39, 45, 68**
See Moore, Marie Lorena
See also AMWS 10; DLB 234; SSFS 19

Moore, Marianne (Craig)
1887-1972 .... **CLC 1, 2, 4, 8, 10, 13, 19,**
47; PC 4, 49; WLCS
See also AMW; CA 1-4R; 33-36R; CANR
3, 61; CDALB 1929-1941; DA; DA3;
DAB; DAC; DAM MST, POET; DLB 45;
DLBD 7; EWL 3; EXPP; MAWW;
MTCW 1, 2; PAB; PFS 14, 17; RGAL 4;
SATA 20; TUS; WP

Moore, Marie Lorena 1957- .... **CLC 165**
See Moore, Lorrie
See also CA 116; CANR 39, 83; CN 7; DLB
234

Moore, Thomas 1779-1852 .... **NCLC 6, 110**
See also DLB 96, 144; RGEL 2

Moorhouse, Frank 1938- .... **SSC 40**
See also CA 118; CANR 92; CN 7; DLB
289; RGSF 2

Mora, Pat(ricia) 1942- .... **HLC 2**
See also AMWS 13; CA 129; CANR 57,
81, 112; CLR 58; DAM MULT; DLB 209;
HW 1, 2; LLW 1; MAICYA 2; SATA 92,
134

Moraga, Cherrie 1952- ...... **CLC 126; DC 22**
See also CA 131; CANR 66; DAM MULT;
DLB 82, 249; FW; GLL 1; HW 1, 2; LLW
1

Morand, Paul 1888-1976 .... **CLC 41; SSC 22**
See also CA 184; 69-72; DLB 65; EWL 3

Morante, Elsa 1918-1985 .... **CLC 8, 47**
See also CA 85-88; 117; CANR 35; DLB
177; EWL 3; MTCW 1, 2; RGWL 2, 3

Moravia, Alberto . **CLC 2, 7, 11, 27, 46; SSC**
26
See Pincherle, Alberto
See also DLB 177; EW 12; EWL 3; MTCW
2; RGSF 2; RGWL 2, 3

More, Hannah 1745-1833 ...... **NCLC 27, 141**
See also DLB 107, 109, 116, 158; RGEL 2

More, Henry 1614-1687 .... **LC 9**
See also DLB 126, 252

More, Sir Thomas 1478(?)-1535 .... **LC 10, 32**
See also BRWC 1; BRWS 7; DLB 136, 281;
LMFS 1; RGEL 2; TEA

Moreas, Jean .... **TCLC 18**
See Papadiamantopoulos, Johannes
See also GFL 1789 to the Present

Moreton, Andrew Esq.
See Defoe, Daniel

Morgan, Berry 1919-2002 .... **CLC 6**
See also CA 49-52; 208; DLB 6

Morgan, Claire
See Highsmith, (Mary) Patricia
See also GLL 1

Morgan, Edwin (George) 1920- .... **CLC 31**
See also BRWS 9; CA 5-8R; CANR 3, 43,
90; CP 7; DLB 27

Morgan, (George) Frederick
1922-2004 .... **CLC 23**
See also CA 17-20R; 224; CANR 21; CP 7

Morgan, Harriet
See Mencken, H(enry) L(ouis)

Morgan, Jane
See Cooper, James Fenimore

Morgan, Janet 1945- .... **CLC 39**
See also CA 65-68

Morgan, Lady 1776(?)-1859 .... **NCLC 29**
See also DLB 116, 158; RGEL 2

Morgan, Robin (Evonne) 1941- .... **CLC 2**
See also CA 69-72; CANR 29, 68; FW;
GLL 2; MTCW 1; SATA 80

Morgan, Scott
See Kuttner, Henry

Morgan, Seth 1949(?)-1990 .... **CLC 65**
See also CA 185; 132

Morgenstern, Christian (Otto Josef
Wolfgang) 1871-1914 .... **TCLC 8**
See also CA 105; 191; EWL 3

Morgenstern, S.
See Goldman, William (W.)

Mori, Rintaro
See Mori Ogai
See also CA 110

Mori, Toshio 1910-1980 .... **SSC 83**
See also AAL; CA 116; DLB 312; RGSF 2

Moricz, Zsigmond 1879-1942 .... **TCLC 33**
See also CA 165; DLB 215; EWL 3

Morike, Eduard (Friedrich)
1804-1875 .... **NCLC 10**
See also DLB 133; RGWL 2, 3

Mori Ogai 1862-1922 .... **TCLC 14**
See Ogai
See also CA 164; DLB 180; EWL 3; RGWL
3; TWA

Moritz, Karl Philipp 1756-1793 .... **LC 2**
See also DLB 94

Morland, Peter Henry
See Faust, Frederick (Schiller)

Morley, Christopher (Darlington)
1890-1957 .... **TCLC 87**
See also CA 112; 213; DLB 9; RGAL 4

Morren, Theophil
See Hofmannsthal, Hugo von

Morris, Bill 1952- .... **CLC 76**
See also CA 225

Morris, Julian
See West, Morris L(anglo)

Morris, Steveland Judkins 1950(?)-
See Wonder, Stevie
See also CA 111

Morris, William 1834-1896 . **NCLC 4; PC 55**
See also BRW 5; CDBLB 1832-1890; DLB
18, 35, 57, 156, 178, 184; FANT; RGEL
2; SFW 4; SUFW

Morris, Wright 1910-1998 .. **CLC 1, 3, 7, 18,**
37; TCLC 107
See also AMW; CA 9-12R; 167; CANR 21,
81; CN 7; DLB 2, 206, 218; DLBY 1981;
EWL 3; MTCW 1, 2; RGAL 4; TCWW 2

Morrison, Arthur 1863-1945 .... **SSC 40;**
TCLC 72
See also CA 120; 157; CMW 4; DLB 70,
135, 197; RGEL 2

Morrison, Chloe Anthony Wofford
See Morrison, Toni

Morrison, James Douglas 1943-1971
See Morrison, Jim
See also CA 73-76; CANR 40

Morrison, Jim .... **CLC 17**
See Morrison, James Douglas

Morrison, Toni 1931- ..... **BLC 3; CLC 4, 10,**
22, 55, 81, 87, 173, 194
See also AAYA 1, 22; AFAW 1, 2; AMWC
1; AMWS 3; BPFB 2; BW 2, 3; CA 29-
32R; CANR 27, 42, 67, 113, 124; CDALB
1968-1988; CLR 99; CN 7; CPW; DA;
DA3; DAB; DAC; DAM MST, MULT,
NOV, POP; DLB 6, 33, 143; DLBY 1981;
EWL 3; EXPN; FW; LAIT 2, 4; LATS
1:2; LMFS 2; MAWW; MTCW 1, 2; NFS
1, 6, 8, 14; RGAL 4; RHW; SATA 57,
144; SSFS 5; TUS; YAW

Morrison, Van 1945- .... **CLC 21**
See also CA 116; 168

Morrissy, Mary 1957- .... **CLC 99**
See also CA 205; DLB 267

Mortimer, John (Clifford) 1923- ..... **CLC 28,**
43
See also CA 13-16R; CANR 21, 69, 109;
CD 5; CDBLB 1960 to Present; CMW 4;
CN 7; CPW; DA3; DAM DRAM, POP;
DLB 13, 245, 271; INT CANR-21; MSW;
MTCW 1, 2; RGEL 2

Mortimer, Penelope (Ruth)
1918-1999 .... **CLC 5**
See also CA 57-60; 187; CANR 45, 88; CN
7

Mortimer, Sir John
See Mortimer, John (Clifford)

Morton, Anthony
See Creasey, John

Morton, Thomas 1579(?)-1647(?) .... **LC 72**
See also DLB 24; RGEL 2

Mosca, Gaetano 1858-1941 .... **TCLC 75**

Moses, Daniel David 1952- .... **NNAL**
See also CA 186

Mosher, Howard Frank 1943- .... **CLC 62**
See also CA 139; CANR 65, 115

Mosley, Nicholas 1923- .... **CLC 43, 70**
See also CA 69-72; CANR 41, 60, 108; CN
7; DLB 14, 207

Mosley, Walter 1952- .... **BLCS; CLC 97, 184**
See also AAYA 57; AMWS 13; BPFB 2;
BW 2; CA 142; CANR 57, 92; CMW 4;
CPW; DA3; DAM MULT, POP; DLB
306; MSW; MTCW 2

Moss, Howard 1922-1987 . **CLC 7, 14, 45, 50**
See also CA 1-4R; 123; CANR 1, 44; DAM
POET; DLB 5

Naidu, Sarojini 1879-1949 .... **TCLC 80**
See also EWL 3; RGEL 2

Naipaul, Shiva(dhar Srinivasa)
1945-1985 .... **CLC 32, 39; TCLC 153**
See also CA 110; 112; 116; CANR 33;
DA3; DAM NOV; DLB 157; DLBY 1985;
EWL 3; MTCW 1, 2

Naipaul, V(idiadhar) S(urajprasad)
1932- .... **CLC 4, 7, 9, 13, 18, 37, 105,
199; SSC 38**
See also BPFB 2; BRWS 1; CA 1-4R;
CANR 1, 33, 51, 91, 126; CDBLB 1960
to Present; CDWLB 3; CN 7; DA3; DAB;
DAC; DAM MST, NOV; DLB 125, 204,
207; DLBY 1985, 2001; EWL 3; LATS
1:2; MTCW 1, 2; RGEL 2; RGSF 2;
TWA; WLIT 4; WWE 1

Nakos, Lilika 1903(?)-1989 .... **CLC 29**

Napoleon
See Yamamoto, Hisaye

Narayan, R(asipuram) K(rishnaswami)
1906-2001 .... **CLC 7, 28, 47, 121, 211;
SSC 25**
See also BPFB 2; CA 81-84; 196; CANR
33, 61, 112; CN 7; DA3; DAM NOV;
DNFS 1; EWL 3; MTCW 1, 2; RGEL 2;
RGSF 2; SATA 62; SSFS 5; WWE 1

Nash, (Fredric) Ogden 1902-1971 . **CLC 23;
PC 21; TCLC 109**
See also CA 13-14; 29-32R; CANR 34, 61;
CAP 1; DAM POET; DLB 11; MAICYA
1, 2; MTCW 1, 2; RGAL 4; SATA 2, 46;
WP

Nashe, Thomas 1567-1601(?) .... **LC 41, 89**
See also DLB 167; RGEL 2

Nathan, Daniel
See Dannay, Frederic

Nathan, George Jean 1882-1958 .... **TCLC 18**
See Hatteras, Owen
See also CA 114; 169; DLB 137

Natsume, Kinnosuke
See Natsume, Soseki

Natsume, Soseki 1867-1916 .... **TCLC 2, 10**
See Natsume Soseki; Soseki
See also CA 104; 195; RGWL 2, 3; TWA

Natsume Soseki
See Natsume, Soseki
See also DLB 180; EWL 3

Natti, (Mary) Lee 1919-
See Kingman, Lee
See also CA 5-8R; CANR 2

Navarre, Marguerite de
See de Navarre, Marguerite

Naylor, Gloria 1950- ..... **BLC 3; CLC 28, 52,
156; WLCS**
See also AAYA 6, 39; AFAW 1, 2; AMWS
8; BW 2, 3; CA 107; CANR 27, 51, 74,
130; CN 7; CPW; DA; DA3; DAC; DAM
MST, MULT, NOV, POP; DLB 173; EWL
3; FW; MTCW 1, 2; NFS 4, 7; RGAL 4;
TUS

Neal, John 1793-1876 .... **NCLC 161**
See also DLB 1, 59, 243; FW; RGAL 4

Neff, Debra .... **CLC 59**

Neihardt, John Gneisenau
1881-1973 .... **CLC 32**
See also CA 13-14; CANR 65; CAP 1; DLB
9, 54, 256; LAIT 2

Nekrasov, Nikolai Alekseevich
1821-1878 .... **NCLC 11**
See also DLB 277

Nelligan, Emile 1879-1941 .... **TCLC 14**
See also CA 114; 204; DLB 92; EWL 3

Nelson, Willie 1933- .... **CLC 17**
See also CA 107; CANR 114

Nemerov, Howard (Stanley)
1920-1991 .... **CLC 2, 6, 9, 36; PC 24;
TCLC 124**
See also AMW; CA 1-4R; 134; CABS 2;
CANR 1, 27, 53; DAM POET; DLB 5, 6;
DLBY 1983; EWL 3; INT CANR-27;
MTCW 1, 2; PFS 10, 14; RGAL 4

Neruda, Pablo 1904-1973 .. **CLC 1, 2, 5, 7, 9,
28, 62; HLC 2; PC 4, 64; WLC**
See also CA 19-20; 45-48; CANR 131; CAP
2; DA; DA3; DAB; DAC; DAM MST,
MULT, POET; DLB 283; DNFS 2; EWL
3; HW 1; LAW; MTCW 1, 2; PFS 11;
RGWL 2, 3; TWA; WLIT 1; WP

Nerval, Gerard de 1808-1855 ... **NCLC 1, 67;
PC 13; SSC 18**
See also DLB 217; EW 6; GFL 1789 to the
Present; RGSF 2; RGWL 2, 3

Nervo, (Jose) Amado (Ruiz de)
1870-1919 .... **HLCS 2; TCLC 11**
See also CA 109; 131; DLB 290; EWL 3;
HW 1; LAW

Nesbit, Malcolm
See Chester, Alfred

Nessi, Pio Baroja y
See Baroja (y Nessi), Pio

Nestroy, Johann 1801-1862 .... **NCLC 42**
See also DLB 133; RGWL 2, 3

Netterville, Luke
See O'Grady, Standish (James)

Neufeld, John (Arthur) 1938- .... **CLC 17**
See also AAYA 11; CA 25-28R; CANR 11,
37, 56; CLR 52; MAICYA 1, 2; SAAS 3;
SATA 6, 81, 131; SATA-Essay 131; YAW

Neumann, Alfred 1895-1952 .... **TCLC 100**
See also CA 183; DLB 56

Neumann, Ferenc
See Molnar, Ferenc

Neville, Emily Cheney 1919- .... **CLC 12**
See also BYA 2; CA 5-8R; CANR 3, 37,
85; JRDA; MAICYA 1, 2; SAAS 2; SATA
1; YAW

Newbound, Bernard Slade 1930-
See Slade, Bernard
See also CA 81-84; CANR 49; CD 5; DAM
DRAM

Newby, P(ercy) H(oward)
1918-1997 .... **CLC 2, 13**
See also CA 5-8R; 161; CANR 32, 67; CN
7; DAM NOV; DLB 15; MTCW 1; RGEL
2

Newcastle
See Cavendish, Margaret Lucas

Newlove, Donald 1928- .... **CLC 6**
See also CA 29-32R; CANR 25

Newlove, John (Herbert) 1938- .... **CLC 14**
See also CA 21-24R; CANR 9, 25; CP 7

Newman, Charles 1938- .... **CLC 2, 8**
See also CA 21-24R; CANR 84; CN 7

Newman, Edwin (Harold) 1919- ...... **CLC 14**
See also AITN 1; CA 69-72; CANR 5

Newman, John Henry 1801-1890 . **NCLC 38,
99**
See also BRWS 7; DLB 18, 32, 55; RGEL
2

Newton, (Sir) Isaac 1642-1727 ...... **LC 35, 53**
See also DLB 252

Newton, Suzanne 1936- .... **CLC 35**
See also BYA 7; CA 41-44R; CANR 14;
JRDA; SATA 5, 77

New York Dept. of Ed. .... **CLC 70**

Nexo, Martin Andersen
1869-1954 .... **TCLC 43**
See also CA 202; DLB 214; EWL 3

Nezval, Vitezslav 1900-1958 .... **TCLC 44**
See also CA 123; CDWLB 4; DLB 215;
EWL 3

Ng, Fae Myenne 1957(?)- .... **CLC 81**
See also BYA 11; CA 146

Ngema, Mbongeni 1955- .... **CLC 57**
See also BW 2; CA 143; CANR 84; CD 5

Ngugi, James T(hiong'o) .. **CLC 3, 7, 13, 182**
See Ngugi wa Thiong'o

Ngugi wa Thiong'o
See Ngugi wa Thiong'o
See also DLB 125; EWL 3

Ngugi wa Thiong'o 1938- ... **BLC 3; CLC 36,
182**
See Ngugi, James T(hiong'o); Ngugi wa
Thiong'o
See also AFW; BRWS 8; BW 2; CA 81-84;
CANR 27, 58; CDWLB 3; DAM MULT,
NOV; DNFS 2; MTCW 1, 2; RGEL 2;
WWE 1

Niatum, Duane 1938- .... **NNAL**
See also CA 41-44R; CANR 21, 45, 83;
DLB 175

Nichol, B(arrie) P(hillip) 1944-1988 . **CLC 18**
See also CA 53-56; DLB 53; SATA 66

Nicholas of Cusa 1401-1464 .... **LC 80**
See also DLB 115

Nichols, John (Treadwell) 1940- .... **CLC 38**
See also AMWS 13; CA 9-12R, 190; CAAE
190; CAAS 2; CANR 6, 70, 121; DLBY
1982; LATS 1:2; TCWW 2

Nichols, Leigh
See Koontz, Dean R(ay)

Nichols, Peter (Richard) 1927- .... **CLC 5, 36,
65**
See also CA 104; CANR 33, 86; CBD; CD
5; DLB 13, 245; MTCW 1

Nicholson, Linda ed. .... **CLC 65**

Ni Chuilleanain, Eilean 1942- .... **PC 34**
See also CA 126; CANR 53, 83; CP 7;
CWP; DLB 40

Nicolas, F. R. E.
See Freeling, Nicolas

Niedecker, Lorine 1903-1970 ..... **CLC 10, 42;
PC 42**
See also CA 25-28; CAP 2; DAM POET;
DLB 48

Nietzsche, Friedrich (Wilhelm)
1844-1900 .... **TCLC 10, 18, 55**
See also CA 107; 121; CDWLB 2; DLB
129; EW 7; RGWL 2, 3; TWA

Nievo, Ippolito 1831-1861 .... **NCLC 22**

Nightingale, Anne Redmon 1943-
See Redmon, Anne
See also CA 103

Nightingale, Florence 1820-1910 ... **TCLC 85**
See also CA 188; DLB 166

Nijo Yoshimoto 1320-1388 .... **CMLC 49**
See also DLB 203

Nik. T. O.
See Annensky, Innokenty (Fyodorovich)

Nin, Anais 1903-1977 ..... **CLC 1, 4, 8, 11, 14,
60, 127; SSC 10**
See also AITN 2; AMWS 10; BPFB 2; CA
13-16R; 69-72; CANR 22, 53; DAM
NOV, POP; DLB 2, 4, 152; EWL 3; GLL
2; MAWW; MTCW 1, 2; RGAL 4; RGSF
2

Nisbet, Robert A(lexander)
1913-1996 .... **TCLC 117**
See also CA 25-28R; 153; CANR 17; INT
CANR-17

Nishida, Kitaro 1870-1945 .... **TCLC 83**

Nishiwaki, Junzaburo
See Nishiwaki, Junzaburo
See also CA 194

Nishiwaki, Junzaburo 1894-1982 .... **PC 15**
See Nishiwaki, Junzaburo; Nishiwaki
Junzaburo
See also CA 194; 107; MJW; RGWL 3

Nishiwaki Junzaburo
See Nishiwaki, Junzaburo
See also EWL 3

Oe, Kenzaburo 1935- .. **CLC 10, 36, 86, 187;**
SSC 20
See Oe Kenzaburo
See also CA 97-100; CANR 36, 50, 74, 126;
DA3; DAM NOV; DLB 182; DLBY 1994;
LATS 1:2; MJW; MTCW 1, 2; RGSF 2;
RGWL 2, 3

Oe Kenzaburo
See Oe, Kenzaburo
See also CWW 2; EWL 3

O'Faolain, Julia 1932- .... **CLC 6, 19, 47, 108**
See also CA 81-84; CAAS 2; CANR 12,
61; CN 7; DLB 14, 231; FW; MTCW 1;
RHW

O'Faolain, Sean 1900-1991 ...... **CLC 1, 7, 14,**
32, 70; SSC 13; TCLC 143
See also CA 61-64; 134; CANR 12, 66;
DLB 15, 162; MTCW 1, 2; RGEL 2;
RGSF 2

O'Flaherty, Liam 1896-1984 .... **CLC 5, 34;**
SSC 6
See also CA 101; 113; CANR 35; DLB 36,
162; DLBY 1984; MTCW 1, 2; RGEL 2;
RGSF 2; SSFS 5, 20

Ogai
See Mori Ogai
See also MJW

Ogilvy, Gavin
See Barrie, J(ames) M(atthew)

O'Grady, Standish (James)
1846-1928 .... **TCLC 5**
See also CA 104; 157

O'Grady, Timothy 1951- .... **CLC 59**
See also CA 138

O'Hara, Frank 1926-1966 .... **CLC 2, 5, 13,**
78; PC 45
See also CA 9-12R; 25-28R; CANR 33;
DA3; DAM POET; DLB 5, 16, 193; EWL
3; MTCW 1, 2; PFS 8; 12; RGAL 4; WP

O'Hara, John (Henry) 1905-1970 . **CLC 1, 2,**
3, 6, 11, 42; SSC 15
See also AMW; BPFB 3; CA 5-8R; 25-28R;
CANR 31, 60; CDALB 1929-1941; DAM
NOV; DLB 9, 86; DLBD 2; EWL 3;
MTCW 1, 2; NFS 11; RGAL 4; RGSF 2

O Hehir, Diana 1922- .... **CLC 41**
See also CA 93-96

Ohiyesa
See Eastman, Charles A(lexander)

Okada, John 1923-1971 .... **AAL**
See also BYA 14; CA 212

Okigbo, Christopher (Ifenayichukwu)
1932-1967 .. **BLC 3; CLC 25, 84; PC 7;**
TCLC 171
See also AFW; BW 1, 3; CA 77-80; CANR
74; CDWLB 3; DAM MULT, POET; DLB
125; EWL 3; MTCW 1, 2; RGEL 2

Okri, Ben 1959- .... **CLC 87**
See also AFW; BRWS 5; BW 2, 3; CA 130;
138; CANR 65, 128; CN 7; DLB 157,
231; EWL 3; INT CA-138; MTCW 2;
RGSF 2; SSFS 20; WLIT 2; WWE 1

Olds, Sharon 1942- .. **CLC 32, 39, 85; PC 22**
See also AMWS 10; CA 101; CANR 18,
41, 66, 98, 135; CP 7; CPW; CWP; DAM
POET; DLB 120; MTCW 2; PFS 17

Oldstyle, Jonathan
See Irving, Washington

Olesha, Iurii
See Olesha, Yuri (Karlovich)
See also RGWL 2

Olesha, Iurii Karlovich
See Olesha, Yuri (Karlovich)
See also DLB 272

Olesha, Yuri (Karlovich) 1899-1960 . **CLC 8;**
SSC 69; TCLC 136
See Olesha, Iurii; Olesha, Iurii Karlovich;
Olesha, Yury Karlovich
See also CA 85-88; EW 11; RGWL 3

Olesha, Yury Karlovich
See Olesha, Yuri (Karlovich)
See also EWL 3

Oliphant, Mrs.
See Oliphant, Margaret (Oliphant Wilson)
See also SUFW

Oliphant, Laurence 1829(?)-1888 .. **NCLC 47**
See also DLB 18, 166

Oliphant, Margaret (Oliphant Wilson)
1828-1897 .... **NCLC 11, 61; SSC 25**
See Oliphant, Mrs.
See also BRWS 10; DLB 18, 159, 190;
HGG; RGEL 2; RGSF 2

Oliver, Mary 1935- .... **CLC 19, 34, 98**
See also AMWS 7; CA 21-24R; CANR 9,
43, 84, 92; CP 7; CWP; DLB 5, 193;
EWL 3; PFS 15

Olivier, Laurence (Kerr) 1907-1989 . **CLC 20**
See also CA 111; 150; 129

Olsen, Tillie 1912- ... **CLC 4, 13, 114; SSC 11**
See also AAYA 51; AMWS 13; BYA 11;
CA 1-4R; CANR 1, 43, 74, 132;
CDALBS; CN 7; DA; DA3; DAB; DAC;
DAM MST; DLB 28, 206; DLBY 1980;
EWL 3; EXPS; FW; MTCW 1, 2; RGAL
4; RGSF 2; SSFS 1; TUS

Olson, Charles (John) 1910-1970 .. **CLC 1, 2,**
5, 6, 9, 11, 29; PC 19
See also AMWS 2; CA 13-16; 25-28R;
CABS 2; CANR 35, 61; CAP 1; DAM
POET; DLB 5, 16, 193; EWL 3; MTCW
1, 2; RGAL 4; WP

Olson, Toby 1937- .... **CLC 28**
See also CA 65-68; CANR 9, 31, 84; CP 7

Olyesha, Yuri
See Olesha, Yuri (Karlovich)

Olympiodorus of Thebes c. 375-c.
430 .... **CMLC 59**

Omar Khayyam
See Khayyam, Omar
See also RGWL 2, 3

Ondaatje, (Philip) Michael 1943- .... **CLC 14,**
29, 51, 76, 180; PC 28
See also CA 77-80; CANR 42, 74, 109, 133;
CN 7; CP 7; DA3; DAB; DAC; DAM
MST; DLB 60; EWL 3; LATS 1:2; LMFS
2; MTCW 2; PFS 8, 19; TWA; WWE 1

Oneal, Elizabeth 1934-
See Oneal, Zibby
See also CA 106; CANR 28, 84; MAICYA
1, 2; SATA 30, 82; YAW

Oneal, Zibby .... **CLC 30**
See Oneal, Elizabeth
See also AAYA 5, 41; BYA 13; CLR 13;
JRDA; WYA

O'Neill, Eugene (Gladstone)
1888-1953 ... **DC 20; TCLC 1, 6, 27, 49;**
WLC
See also AAYA 54; AITN 1; AMW; AMWC
1; CA 110; 132; CAD; CANR 131;
CDALB 1929-1941; DA; DA3; DAB;
DAC; DAM DRAM, MST; DFS 2, 4, 5,
6, 9, 11, 12, 16, 20; DLB 7; EWL 3; LAIT
3; LMFS 2; MTCW 1, 2; RGAL 4; TUS

Onetti, Juan Carlos 1909-1994 ... **CLC 7, 10;**
HLCS 2; SSC 23; TCLC 131
See also CA 85-88; 145; CANR 32, 63; CD-
WLB 3; CWW 2; DAM MULT, NOV;
DLB 113; EWL 3; HW 1, 2; LAW;
MTCW 1, 2; RGSF 2

O Nuallain, Brian 1911-1966
See O'Brien, Flann
See also CA 21-22; 25-28R; CAP 2; DLB
231; FANT; TEA

Ophuls, Max 1902-1957 .... **TCLC 79**
See also CA 113

Opie, Amelia 1769-1853 .... **NCLC 65**
See also DLB 116, 159; RGEL 2

Oppen, George 1908-1984 ..... **CLC 7, 13, 34;**
PC 35; TCLC 107
See also CA 13-16R; 113; CANR 8, 82;
DLB 5, 165

Oppenheim, E(dward) Phillips
1866-1946 .... **TCLC 45**
See also CA 111; 202; CMW 4; DLB 70

Opuls, Max
See Ophuls, Max

Orage, A(lfred) R(ichard)
1873-1934 .... **TCLC 157**
See also CA 122

Origen c. 185-c. 254 .... **CMLC 19**

Orlovitz, Gil 1918-1973 .... **CLC 22**
See also CA 77-80; 45-48; DLB 2, 5

O'Rourke, P(atrick) J(ake) 1947- .. **CLC 209**
See also CA 77-80; CANR 13, 41, 67, 111;
CPW; DLB 185; DAM POP

Orris
See Ingelow, Jean

Ortega y Gasset, Jose 1883-1955 ...... **HLC 2;**
TCLC 9
See also CA 106; 130; DAM MULT; EW 9;
EWL 3; HW 1, 2; MTCW 1, 2

Ortese, Anna Maria 1914-1998 .... **CLC 89**
See also DLB 177; EWL 3

Ortiz, Simon J(oseph) 1941- ... **CLC 45, 208;**
NNAL; PC 17
See also AMWS 4; CA 134; CANR 69, 118;
CP 7; DAM MULT, POET; DLB 120,
175, 256; EXPP; PFS 4, 16; RGAL 4

Orton, Joe .... **CLC 4, 13, 43; DC 3; TCLC**
157
See Orton, John Kingsley
See also BRWS 5; CBD; CDBLB 1960 to
Present; DFS 3, 6; DLB 13; GLL 1;
MTCW 2; RGEL 2; TEA; WLIT 4

Orton, John Kingsley 1933-1967
See Orton, Joe
See also CA 85-88; CANR 35, 66; DAM
DRAM; MTCW 1, 2

Orwell, George . **SSC 68; TCLC 2, 6, 15, 31,**
51, 128, 129; WLC
See Blair, Eric (Arthur)
See also BPFB 3; BRW 7; BYA 5; CDBLB
1945-1960; CLR 68; DAB; DLB 15, 98,
195, 255; EWL 3; EXPN; LAIT 4, 5;
LATS 1:1; NFS 3, 7; RGEL 2; SCFW 2;
SFW 4; SSFS 4; TEA; WLIT 4; YAW

Osborne, David
See Silverberg, Robert

Osborne, George
See Silverberg, Robert

Osborne, John (James) 1929-1994 .... **CLC 1,**
2, 5, 11, 45; TCLC 153; WLC
See also BRWS 1; CA 13-16R; 147; CANR
21, 56; CDBLB 1945-1960; DA; DAB;
DAC; DAM DRAM, MST; DFS 4, 19;
DLB 13; EWL 3; MTCW 1, 2; RGEL 2

Osborne, Lawrence 1958- .... **CLC 50**
See also CA 189

Osbourne, Lloyd 1868-1947 .... **TCLC 93**

Osgood, Frances Sargent
1811-1850 .... **NCLC 141**
See also DLB 250

Oshima, Nagisa 1932- .... **CLC 20**
See also CA 116; 121; CANR 78

Oskison, John Milton
1874-1947 .... **NNAL; TCLC 35**
See also CA 144; CANR 84; DAM MULT;
DLB 175

Ossian c. 3rd cent. - .... **CMLC 28**
See Macpherson, James

Ossoli, Sarah Margaret (Fuller)
1810-1850 .... **NCLC 5, 50**
See Fuller, Margaret; Fuller, Sarah Margaret
See also CDALB 1640-1865; FW; LMFS 1;
SATA 25

Pixerecourt, (Rene Charles) Guilbert de
1773-1844 .... **NCLC 39**
See also DLB 192; GFL 1789 to the Present
Plaatje, Sol(omon) T(shekisho)
1878-1932 .... **BLCS; TCLC 73**
See also BW 2, 3; CA 141; CANR 79; DLB
125, 225
Plaidy, Jean
See Hibbert, Eleanor Alice Burford
Planche, James Robinson
1796-1880 .... **NCLC 42**
See also RGEL 2
Plant, Robert 1948- .... **CLC 12**
Plante, David (Robert) 1940- . **CLC 7, 23, 38**
See also CA 37-40R; CANR 12, 36, 58, 82;
CN 7; DAM NOV; DLBY 1983; INT
CANR-12; MTCW 1
Plath, Sylvia 1932-1963 ..... **CLC 1, 2, 3, 5, 9,
11, 14, 17, 50, 51, 62, 111; PC 1, 37;
WLC**
See also AAYA 13; AMWR 2; AMWS 1;
BPFB 3; CA 19-20; CANR 34, 101; CAP
2; CDALB 1941-1968; DA; DA3; DAB;
DAC; DAM MST, POET; DLB 5, 6, 152;
EWL 3; EXPN; EXPP; FW; LAIT 4;
MAWW; MTCW 1, 2; NFS 1; PAB; PFS
1, 15; RGAL 4; SATA 96; TUS; WP;
YAW
Plato c. 428B.C.-347B.C. .... **CMLC 8, 75;
WLCS**
See also AW 1; CDWLB 1; DA; DA3;
DAB; DAC; DAM MST; DLB 176; LAIT
1; LATS 1:1; RGWL 2, 3
Platonov, Andrei
See Klimentov, Andrei Platonovich
Platonov, Andrei Platonovich
See Klimentov, Andrei Platonovich
See also DLB 272
Platonov, Andrey Platonovich
See Klimentov, Andrei Platonovich
See also EWL 3
Platt, Kin 1911- .... **CLC 26**
See also AAYA 11; CA 17-20R; CANR 11;
JRDA; SAAS 17; SATA 21, 86; WYA
Plautus c. 254B.C.-c. 184B.C. ...... **CMLC 24;
DC 6**
See also AW 1; CDWLB 1; DLB 211;
RGWL 2, 3
Plick et Plock
See Simenon, Georges (Jacques Christian)
Plieksans, Janis
See Rainis, Janis
Plimpton, George (Ames)
1927-2003 .... **CLC 36**
See also AITN 1; CA 21-24R; 224; CANR
32, 70, 103, 133; DLB 185, 241; MTCW
1, 2; SATA 10; SATA-Obit 150
Pliny the Elder c. 23-79 .... **CMLC 23**
See also DLB 211
Pliny the Younger c. 61-c. 112 ...... **CMLC 62**
See also AW 2; DLB 211
Plomer, William Charles Franklin
1903-1973 .... **CLC 4, 8**
See also AFW; CA 21-22; CANR 34; CAP
2; DLB 20, 162, 191, 225; EWL 3;
MTCW 1; RGEL 2; RGSF 2; SATA 24
Plotinus 204-270 .... **CMLC 46**
See also CDWLB 1; DLB 176
Plowman, Piers
See Kavanagh, Patrick (Joseph)
Plum, J.
See Wodehouse, P(elham) G(renville)
Plumly, Stanley (Ross) 1939- .... **CLC 33**
See also CA 108; 110; CANR 97; CP 7;
DLB 5, 193; INT CA-110
Plumpe, Friedrich Wilhelm
1888-1931 .... **TCLC 53**
See also CA 112

Plutarch c. 46-c. 120 .... **CMLC 60**
See also AW 2; CDWLB 1; DLB 176;
RGWL 2, 3; TWA
Po Chu-i 772-846 .... **CMLC 24**
Podhoretz, Norman 1930- .... **CLC 189**
See also AMWS 8; CA 9-12R; CANR 7,
78, 135
Poe, Edgar Allan 1809-1849 ..... **NCLC 1, 16,
55, 78, 94, 97, 117; PC 1, 54; SSC 1,
22, 34, 35, 54; WLC**
See also AAYA 14; AMW; AMWC 1;
AMWR 2; BPFB 3; BYA 5, 11; CDALB
1640-1865; CMW 4; DA; DA3; DAB;
DAC; DAM MST, POET; DLB 3, 59, 73,
74, 248, 254; EXPP; EXPS; HGG; LAIT
2; LATS 1:1; LMFS 1; MSW; PAB; PFS
1, 3, 9; RGAL 4; RGSF 2; SATA 23;
SCFW 2; SFW 4; SSFS 2, 4, 7, 8, 16;
SUFW; TUS; WP; WYA
Poet of Titchfield Street, The
See Pound, Ezra (Weston Loomis)
Pohl, Frederik 1919- .... **CLC 18; SSC 25**
See also AAYA 24; CA 61-64, 188; CAAE
188; CAAS 1; CANR 11, 37, 81; CN 7;
DLB 8; INT CANR-11; MTCW 1, 2;
SATA 24; SCFW 2; SFW 4
Poirier, Louis 1910-
See Gracq, Julien
See also CA 122; 126
Poitier, Sidney 1927- .... **CLC 26**
See also AAYA 60; BW 1; CA 117; CANR
94
Pokagon, Simon 1830-1899 .... **NNAL**
See also DAM MULT
Polanski, Roman 1933- .... **CLC 16, 178**
See also CA 77-80
Poliakoff, Stephen 1952- .... **CLC 38**
See also CA 106; CANR 116; CBD; CD 5;
DLB 13
Police, The
See Copeland, Stewart (Armstrong); Sum-
mers, Andrew James
Polidori, John William 1795-1821 . **NCLC 51**
See also DLB 116; HGG
Pollitt, Katha 1949- .... **CLC 28, 122**
See also CA 120; 122; CANR 66, 108;
MTCW 1, 2
Poliziano, Angelo 1454-1494 .... **LC 120**
See also WLIT 7
Pollock, (Mary) Sharon 1936- .... **CLC 50**
See also CA 141; CANR 132; CD 5; CWD;
DAC; DAM DRAM, MST; DFS 3; DLB
60; FW
Pollock, Sharon 1936- .... **DC 20**
Polo, Marco 1254-1324 .... **CMLC 15**
Polonsky, Abraham (Lincoln)
1910-1999 .... **CLC 92**
See also CA 104; 187; DLB 26; INT CA-
104
Polybius c. 200B.C.-c. 118B.C. ...... **CMLC 17**
See also AW 1; DLB 176; RGWL 2, 3
Pomerance, Bernard 1940- .... **CLC 13**
See also CA 101; CAD; CANR 49, 134;
CD 5; DAM DRAM; DFS 9; LAIT 2
Ponge, Francis 1899-1988 .... **CLC 6, 18**
See also CA 85-88; 126; CANR 40, 86;
DAM POET; DLBY 2002; EWL 3; GFL
1789 to the Present; RGWL 2, 3
Poniatowska, Elena 1933- ..... **CLC 140; HLC 2**
See also CA 101; CANR 32, 66, 107; CD-
WLB 3; CWW 2; DAM MULT; DLB 113;
EWL 3; HW 1, 2; LAWS 1; WLIT 1
Pontoppidan, Henrik 1857-1943 .... **TCLC 29**
See also CA 170; DLB 300
Ponty, Maurice Merleau
See Merleau-Ponty, Maurice
Poole, Josephine .... **CLC 17**
See Helyar, Jane Penelope Josephine
See also SAAS 2; SATA 5

Popa, Vasko 1922-1991 . **CLC 19; TCLC 167**
See also CA 112; 148; CDWLB 4; DLB
181; EWL 3; RGWL 2, 3
Pope, Alexander 1688-1744 ...... **LC 3, 58, 60,
64; PC 26; WLC**
See also BRW 3; BRWC 1; BRWR 1; CD-
BLB 1660-1789; DA; DA3; DAB; DAC;
DAM MST, POET; DLB 95, 101, 213;
EXPP; PAB; PFS 12; RGEL 2; WLIT 3;
WP
Popov, Evgenii Anatol'evich
See Popov, Yevgeny
See also DLB 285
Popov, Yevgeny .... **CLC 59**
See Popov, Evgenii Anatol'evich
Poquelin, Jean-Baptiste
See Moliere
Porete, Marguerite c. 1250-1310 .. **CMLC 73**
See also DLB 208
Porphyry c. 233-c. 305 .... **CMLC 71**
Porter, Connie (Rose) 1959(?)- .... **CLC 70**
See also BW 2, 3; CA 142; CANR 90, 109;
SATA 81, 129
Porter, Gene(va Grace) Stratton ... **TCLC 21**
See Stratton-Porter, Gene(va Grace)
See also BPFB 3; CA 112; CWRI 5; RHW
Porter, Katherine Anne 1890-1980 ... **CLC 1,
3, 7, 10, 13, 15, 27, 101; SSC 4, 31, 43**
See also AAYA 42; AITN 2; AMW; BPFB
3; CA 1-4R; 101; CANR 1, 65; CDALBS;
DA; DA3; DAB; DAC; DAM MST, NOV;
DLB 4, 9, 102; DLBD 12; DLBY 1980;
EWL 3; EXPS; LAIT 3; MAWW; MTCW
1, 2; NFS 14; RGAL 4; RGSF 2; SATA
39; SATA-Obit 23; SSFS 1, 8, 11, 16;
TUS
Porter, Peter (Neville Frederick)
1929- .... **CLC 5, 13, 33**
See also CA 85-88; CP 7; DLB 40, 289;
WWE 1
Porter, William Sydney 1862-1910
See Henry, O.
See also CA 104; 131; CDALB 1865-1917;
DA; DA3; DAB; DAC; DAM MST; DLB
12, 78, 79; MTCW 1, 2; TUS; YABC 2
Portillo (y Pacheco), Jose Lopez
See Lopez Portillo (y Pacheco), Jose
Portillo Trambley, Estela
1927-1998 .... **HLC 2; TCLC 163**
See Trambley, Estela Portillo
See also CANR 32; DAM MULT; DLB
209; HW 1
Posey, Alexander (Lawrence)
1873-1908 .... **NNAL**
See also CA 144; CANR 80; DAM MULT;
DLB 175
Posse, Abel .... **CLC 70**
Post, Melville Davisson
1869-1930 .... **TCLC 39**
See also CA 110; 202; CMW 4
Potok, Chaim 1929-2002 ... **CLC 2, 7, 14, 26,
112**
See also AAYA 15, 50; AITN 1, 2; BPFB 3;
BYA 1; CA 17-20R; 208; CANR 19, 35,
64, 98; CLR 92; CN 7; DA3; DAM NOV;
DLB 28, 152; EXPN; INT CANR-19;
LAIT 4; MTCW 1, 2; NFS 4; SATA 33,
106; SATA-Obit 134; TUS; YAW
Potok, Herbert Harold -2002
See Potok, Chaim
Potok, Herman Harold
See Potok, Chaim
Potter, Dennis (Christopher George)
1935-1994 .... **CLC 58, 86, 123**
See also BRWS 10; CA 107; 145; CANR
33, 61; CBD; DLB 233; MTCW 1

Pyle, Ernie .... **TCLC 75**
See Pyle, Ernest Taylor
See also DLB 29; MTCW 2

Pyle, Howard 1853-1911 .... **TCLC 81**
See also AAYA 57; BYA 2, 4; CA 109; 137;
CLR 22; DLB 42, 188; DLBD 13; LAIT
1; MAICYA 1, 2; SATA 16, 100; WCH;
YAW

Pym, Barbara (Mary Crampton)
1913-1980 .... **CLC 13, 19, 37, 111**
See also BPFB 3; BRWS 2; CA 13-14; 97-
100; CANR 13, 34; CAP 1; DLB 14, 207;
DLBY 1987; EWL 3; MTCW 1, 2; RGEL
2; TEA

Pynchon, Thomas (Ruggles, Jr.)
1937- ...... **CLC 2, 3, 6, 9, 11, 18, 33, 62,
72, 123, 192, 213; SSC 14, 84; WLC**
See also AMWS 2; BEST 90:2; BPFB 3;
CA 17-20R; CANR 22, 46, 73; CN 7;
CPW 1; DA; DA3; DAB; DAC; DAM
MST, NOV, POP; DLB 2, 173; EWL 3;
MTCW 1, 2; RGAL 4; SFW 4; TUS

Pythagoras c. 582B.C.-c. 507B.C. . **CMLC 22**
See also DLB 176

Q
See Quiller-Couch, Sir Arthur (Thomas)

Qian, Chongzhu
See Ch'ien, Chung-shu

Qian, Sima 145B.C.-c. 89B.C. .... **CMLC 72**

Qian Zhongshu
See Ch'ien, Chung-shu
See also CWW 2

Qroll
See Dagerman, Stig (Halvard)

Quarles, Francis 1592-1644 .... **LC 117**
See also DLB 126; RGEL 2

Quarrington, Paul (Lewis) 1953- ..... **CLC 65**
See also CA 129; CANR 62, 95

Quasimodo, Salvatore 1901-1968 .... **CLC 10;
PC 47**
See also CA 13-16; 25-28R; CAP 1; DLB
114; EW 12; EWL 3; MTCW 1; RGWL
2, 3

Quatermass, Martin
See Carpenter, John (Howard)

Quay, Stephen 1947- .... **CLC 95**
See also CA 189

Quay, Timothy 1947- .... **CLC 95**
See also CA 189

Queen, Ellery .... **CLC 3, 11**
See Dannay, Frederic; Davidson, Avram
(James); Deming, Richard; Fairman, Paul
W.; Flora, Fletcher; Hoch, Edward
D(entinger); Kane, Henry; Lee, Manfred
B(ennington); Marlowe, Stephen; Powell,
(Oval) Talmage; Sheldon, Walter J(ames);
Sturgeon, Theodore (Hamilton); Tracy,
Don(ald Fiske); Vance, John Holbrook
See also BPFB 3; CMW 4; MSW; RGAL 4

Queen, Ellery, Jr.
See Dannay, Frederic; Lee, Manfred
B(ennington)

Queneau, Raymond 1903-1976 ..... **CLC 2, 5,
10, 42**
See also CA 77-80; 69-72; CANR 32; DLB
72, 258; EW 12; EWL 3; GFL 1789 to
the Present; MTCW 1, 2; RGWL 2, 3

Quevedo, Francisco de 1580-1645 .... **LC 23**

Quiller-Couch, Sir Arthur (Thomas)
1863-1944 .... **TCLC 53**
See also CA 118; 166; DLB 135, 153, 190;
HGG; RGEL 2; SUFW 1

Quin, Ann (Marie) 1936-1973 .... **CLC 6**
See also CA 9-12R; 45-48; DLB 14, 231

Quincey, Thomas de
See De Quincey, Thomas

Quindlen, Anna 1953- .... **CLC 191**
See also AAYA 35; CA 138; CANR 73, 126;
DA3; DLB 292; MTCW 2

Quinn, Martin
See Smith, Martin Cruz

Quinn, Peter 1947- .... **CLC 91**
See also CA 197

Quinn, Simon
See Smith, Martin Cruz

Quintana, Leroy V. 1944- ...... **HLC 2; PC 36**
See also CA 131; CANR 65; DAM MULT;
DLB 82; HW 1, 2

Quintilian c. 35-40-c. 96. .... **CMLC 77**
See also AW 2; DLB 211; RGWL 2, 3

Quiroga, Horacio (Sylvestre)
1878-1937 .... **HLC 2; TCLC 20**
See also CA 117; 131; DAM MULT; EWL
3; HW 1; LAW; MTCW 1; RGSF 2;
WLIT 1

Quoirez, Francoise 1935- .... **CLC 9**
See Sagan, Francoise
See also CA 49-52; CANR 6, 39, 73;
MTCW 1, 2; TWA

Raabe, Wilhelm (Karl) 1831-1910 . **TCLC 45**
See also CA 167; DLB 129

Rabe, David (William) 1940- .. **CLC 4, 8, 33,
200; DC 16**
See also CA 85-88; CABS 3; CAD; CANR
59, 129; CD 5; DAM DRAM; DFS 3, 8,
13; DLB 7, 228; EWL 3

Rabelais, Francois 1494-1553 .... **LC 5, 60;
WLC**
See also DA; DAB; DAC; DAM MST; EW
2; GFL Beginnings to 1789; LMFS 1;
RGWL 2, 3; TWA

Rabinovitch, Sholem 1859-1916
See Aleichem, Sholom
See also CA 104

Rabinyan, Dorit 1972- .... **CLC 119**
See also CA 170

Rachilde
See Vallette, Marguerite Eymery; Vallette,
Marguerite Eymery
See also EWL 3

Racine, Jean 1639-1699 .... **LC 28, 113**
See also DA3; DAB; DAM MST; DLB 268;
EW 3; GFL Beginnings to 1789; LMFS
1; RGWL 2, 3; TWA

Radcliffe, Ann (Ward) 1764-1823 ... **NCLC 6,
55, 106**
See also DLB 39, 178; HGG; LMFS 1;
RGEL 2; SUFW; WLIT 3

Radclyffe-Hall, Marguerite
See Hall, (Marguerite) Radclyffe

Radiguet, Raymond 1903-1923 ...... **TCLC 29**
See also CA 162; DLB 65; EWL 3; GFL
1789 to the Present; RGWL 2, 3

Radnoti, Miklos 1909-1944 .... **TCLC 16**
See also CA 118; 212; CDWLB 4; DLB
215; EWL 3; RGWL 2, 3

Rado, James 1939- .... **CLC 17**
See also CA 105

Radvanyi, Netty 1900-1983
See Seghers, Anna
See also CA 85-88; 110; CANR 82

Rae, Ben
See Griffiths, Trevor

Raeburn, John (Hay) 1941- .... **CLC 34**
See also CA 57-60

Ragni, Gerome 1942-1991 .... **CLC 17**
See also CA 105; 134

Rahv, Philip .... **CLC 24**
See Greenberg, Ivan
See also DLB 137

Raimund, Ferdinand Jakob
1790-1836 .... **NCLC 69**
See also DLB 90

Raine, Craig (Anthony) 1944- .. **CLC 32, 103**
See also CA 108; CANR 29, 51, 103; CP 7;
DLB 40; PFS 7

Raine, Kathleen (Jessie) 1908-2003 .. **CLC 7,
45**
See also CA 85-88; 218; CANR 46, 109;
CP 7; DLB 20; EWL 3; MTCW 1; RGEL
2

Rainis, Janis 1865-1929 .... **TCLC 29**
See also CA 170; CDWLB 4; DLB 220;
EWL 3

Rakosi, Carl .... **CLC 47**
See Rawley, Callman
See also CA 228; CAAS 5; CP 7; DLB 193

Ralegh, Sir Walter
See Raleigh, Sir Walter
See also BRW 1; RGEL 2; WP

Raleigh, Richard
See Lovecraft, H(oward) P(hillips)

Raleigh, Sir Walter 1554(?)-1618 .... **LC 31,
39; PC 31**
See Ralegh, Sir Walter
See also CDBLB Before 1660; DLB 172;
EXPP; PFS 14; TEA

Rallentando, H. P.
See Sayers, Dorothy L(eigh)

Ramal, Walter
See de la Mare, Walter (John)

Ramana Maharshi 1879-1950 .... **TCLC 84**

Ramoacn y Cajal, Santiago
1852-1934 .... **TCLC 93**

Ramon, Juan
See Jimenez (Mantecon), Juan Ramon

Ramos, Graciliano 1892-1953 .... **TCLC 32**
See also CA 167; DLB 307; EWL 3; HW 2;
LAW; WLIT 1

Rampersad, Arnold 1941- .... **CLC 44**
See also BW 2, 3; CA 127; 133; CANR 81;
DLB 111; INT CA-133

Rampling, Anne
See Rice, Anne
See also GLL 2

Ramsay, Allan 1686(?)-1758 .... **LC 29**
See also DLB 95; RGEL 2

Ramsay, Jay
See Campbell, (John) Ramsey

Ramuz, Charles-Ferdinand
1878-1947 .... **TCLC 33**
See also CA 165; EWL 3

Rand, Ayn 1905-1982 ...... **CLC 3, 30, 44, 79;
WLC**
See also AAYA 10; AMWS 4; BPFB 3;
BYA 12; CA 13-16R; 105; CANR 27, 73;
CDALBS; CPW; DA; DA3; DAC; DAM
MST, NOV, POP; DLB 227, 279; MTCW
1, 2; NFS 10, 16; RGAL 4; SFW 4; TUS;
YAW

Randall, Dudley (Felker) 1914-2000 . **BLC 3;
CLC 1, 135**
See also BW 1, 3; CA 25-28R; 189; CANR
23, 82; DAM MULT; DLB 41; PFS 5

Randall, Robert
See Silverberg, Robert

Ranger, Ken
See Creasey, John

Rank, Otto 1884-1939 .... **TCLC 115**

Ransom, John Crowe 1888-1974 .. **CLC 2, 4,
5, 11, 24; PC 61**
See also AMW; CA 5-8R; 49-52; CANR 6,
34; CDALBS; DA3; DAM POET; DLB
45, 63; EWL 3; EXPP; MTCW 1, 2;
RGAL 4; TUS

Rao, Raja 1909- .... **CLC 25, 56**
See also CA 73-76; CANR 51; CN 7; DAM
NOV; EWL 3; MTCW 1, 2; RGEL 2;
RGSF 2

Raphael, Frederic (Michael) 1931- ... **CLC 2,
14**
See also CA 1-4R; CANR 1, 86; CN 7;
DLB 14

Ratcliffe, James P.
See Mencken, H(enry) L(ouis)

Rathbone, Julian 1935- .... **CLC 41**
See also CA 101; CANR 34, 73

Rattigan, Terence (Mervyn)
1911-1977 .... **CLC 7; DC 18**
See also BRWS 7; CA 85-88; 73-76; CBD;
CDBLB 1945-1960; DAM DRAM; DFS
8; DLB 13; IDFW 3, 4; MTCW 1, 2;
RGEL 2

Ratushinskaya, Irina 1954- .... **CLC 54**
See also CA 129; CANR 68; CWW 2

Raven, Simon (Arthur Noel)
1927-2001 .... **CLC 14**
See also CA 81-84; 197; CANR 86; CN 7;
DLB 271

Ravenna, Michael
See Welty, Eudora (Alice)

Rawley, Callman 1903-2004
See Rakosi, Carl
See also CA 21-24R; CANR 12, 32, 91

Rawlings, Marjorie Kinnan
1896-1953 .... **TCLC 4**
See also AAYA 20; AMWS 10; ANW;
BPFB 3; BYA 3; CA 104; 137; CANR 74;
CLR 63; DLB 9, 22, 102; DLBD 17;
JRDA; MAICYA 1, 2; MTCW 1; RGAL
4; SATA 100; WCH; YABC 1; YAW

Ray, Satyajit 1921-1992 .... **CLC 16, 76**
See also CA 114; 137; DAM MULT

Read, Herbert Edward 1893-1968 ..... **CLC 4**
See also BRW 6; CA 85-88; 25-28R; DLB
20, 149; EWL 3; PAB; RGEL 2

Read, Piers Paul 1941- .... **CLC 4, 10, 25**
See also CA 21-24R; CANR 38, 86; CN 7;
DLB 14; SATA 21

Reade, Charles 1814-1884 .... **NCLC 2, 74**
See also DLB 21; RGEL 2

Reade, Hamish
See Gray, Simon (James Holliday)

Reading, Peter 1946- .... **CLC 47**
See also BRWS 8; CA 103; CANR 46, 96;
CP 7; DLB 40

Reaney, James 1926- .... **CLC 13**
See also CA 41-44R; CAAS 15; CANR 42;
CD 5; CP 7; DAC; DAM MST; DLB 68;
RGEL 2; SATA 43

Rebreanu, Liviu 1885-1944 .... **TCLC 28**
See also CA 165; DLB 220; EWL 3

Rechy, John (Francisco) 1934- ...... **CLC 1, 7,**
14, 18, 107; HLC 2
See also CA 5-8R; 195; CAAE 195; CAAS
4; CANR 6, 32, 64; CN 7; DAM MULT;
DLB 122, 278; DLBY 1982; HW 1, 2;
INT CANR-6; LLW 1; RGAL 4

Redcam, Tom 1870-1933 .... **TCLC 25**

Reddin, Keith .... **CLC 67**
See also CAD

Redgrove, Peter (William)
1932-2003 .... **CLC 6, 41**
See also BRWS 6; CA 1-4R; 217; CANR 3,
39, 77; CP 7; DLB 40

Redmon, Anne .... **CLC 22**
See Nightingale, Anne Redmon
See also DLBY 1986

Reed, Eliot
See Ambler, Eric

Reed, Ishmael 1938- ..... **BLC 3; CLC 2, 3, 5,**
6, 13, 32, 60, 174; PC 68
See also AFAW 1, 2; AMWS 10; BPFB 3;
BW 2, 3; CA 21-24R; CANR 25, 48, 74,
128; CN 7; CP 7; CSW; DA3; DAM
MULT; DLB 2, 5, 33, 169, 227; DLBD 8;
EWL 3; LMFS 2; MSW; MTCW 1, 2;
PFS 6; RGAL 4; TCWW 2

Reed, John (Silas) 1887-1920 .... **TCLC 9**
See also CA 106; 195; TUS

Reed, Lou .... **CLC 21**
See Firbank, Louis

Reese, Lizette Woodworth 1856-1935 . **PC 29**
See also CA 180; DLB 54

Reeve, Clara 1729-1807 .... **NCLC 19**
See also DLB 39; RGEL 2

Reich, Wilhelm 1897-1957 .... **TCLC 57**
See also CA 199

Reid, Christopher (John) 1949- .... **CLC 33**
See also CA 140; CANR 89; CP 7; DLB
40; EWL 3

Reid, Desmond
See Moorcock, Michael (John)

Reid Banks, Lynne 1929-
See Banks, Lynne Reid
See also AAYA 49; CA 1-4R; CANR 6, 22,
38, 87; CLR 24; CN 7; JRDA; MAICYA
1, 2; SATA 22, 75, 111; YAW

Reilly, William K.
See Creasey, John

Reiner, Max
See Caldwell, (Janet Miriam) Taylor
(Holland)

Reis, Ricardo
See Pessoa, Fernando (Antonio Nogueira)

Reizenstein, Elmer Leopold
See Rice, Elmer (Leopold)
See also EWL 3

Remarque, Erich Maria 1898-1970 . **CLC 21**
See also AAYA 27; BPFB 3; CA 77-80; 29-
32R; CDWLB 2; DA; DA3; DAB; DAC;
DAM MST, NOV; DLB 56; EWL 3;
EXPN; LAIT 3; MTCW 1, 2; NFS 4;
RGWL 2, 3

Remington, Frederic 1861-1909 ..... **TCLC 89**
See also CA 108; 169; DLB 12, 186, 188;
SATA 41

Remizov, A.
See Remizov, Aleksei (Mikhailovich)

Remizov, A. M.
See Remizov, Aleksei (Mikhailovich)

Remizov, Aleksei (Mikhailovich)
1877-1957 .... **TCLC 27**
See Remizov, Alexey Mikhaylovich
See also CA 125; 133; DLB 295

Remizov, Alexey Mikhaylovich
See Remizov, Aleksei (Mikhailovich)
See also EWL 3

Renan, Joseph Ernest 1823-1892 . **NCLC 26,**
145
See also GFL 1789 to the Present

Renard, Jules(-Pierre) 1864-1910 .. **TCLC 17**
See also CA 117; 202; GFL 1789 to the
Present

Renault, Mary .... **CLC 3, 11, 17**
See Challans, Mary
See also BPFB 3; BYA 2; DLBY 1983;
EWL 3; GLL 1; LAIT 1; MTCW 2; RGEL
2; RHW

Rendell, Ruth (Barbara) 1930- .. **CLC 28, 48**
See Vine, Barbara
See also BPFB 3; BRWS 9; CA 109; CANR
32, 52, 74, 127; CN 7; CPW; DAM POP;
DLB 87, 276; INT CANR-32; MSW;
MTCW 1, 2

Renoir, Jean 1894-1979 .... **CLC 20**
See also CA 129; 85-88

Resnais, Alain 1922- .... **CLC 16**

Revard, Carter (Curtis) 1931- .... **NNAL**
See also CA 144; CANR 81; PFS 5

Reverdy, Pierre 1889-1960 .... **CLC 53**
See also CA 97-100; 89-92; DLB 258; EWL
3; GFL 1789 to the Present

Rexroth, Kenneth 1905-1982 .... **CLC 1, 2, 6,**
11, 22, 49, 112; PC 20
See also BG 3; CA 5-8R; 107; CANR 14,
34, 63; CDALB 1941-1968; DAM POET;
DLB 16, 48, 165, 212; DLBY 1982; EWL
3; INT CANR-14; MTCW 1, 2; RGAL 4

Reyes, Alfonso 1889-1959 .... **HLCS 2; TCLC**
33
See also CA 131; EWL 3; HW 1; LAW

Reyes y Basoalto, Ricardo Eliecer Neftali
See Neruda, Pablo

Reymont, Wladyslaw (Stanislaw)
1868(?)-1925 .... **TCLC 5**
See also CA 104; EWL 3

Reynolds, John Hamilton
1794-1852 .... **NCLC 146**
See also DLB 96

Reynolds, Jonathan 1942- .... **CLC 6, 38**
See also CA 65-68; CANR 28

Reynolds, Joshua 1723-1792 .... **LC 15**
See also DLB 104

Reynolds, Michael S(hane)
1937-2000 .... **CLC 44**
See also CA 65-68; 189; CANR 9, 89, 97

Reznikoff, Charles 1894-1976 .... **CLC 9**
See also AMWS 14; CA 33-36; 61-64; CAP
2; DLB 28, 45; WP

Rezzori (d'Arezzo), Gregor von
1914-1998 .... **CLC 25**
See also CA 122; 136; 167

Rhine, Richard
See Silverstein, Alvin; Silverstein, Virginia
B(arbara Opshelor)

Rhodes, Eugene Manlove
1869-1934 .... **TCLC 53**
See also CA 198; DLB 256

R'hoone, Lord
See Balzac, Honore de

Rhys, Jean 1890-1979 .... **CLC 2, 4, 6, 14, 19,**
51, 124; SSC 21, 76
See also BRWS 2; CA 25-28R; 85-88;
CANR 35, 62; CDBLB 1945-1960; CD-
WLB 3; DA3; DAM NOV; DLB 36, 117,
162; DNFS 2; EWL 3; LATS 1:1; MTCW
1, 2; RGEL 2; RGSF 2; RHW; TEA;
WWE 1

Ribeiro, Darcy 1922-1997 .... **CLC 34**
See also CA 33-36R; 156; EWL 3

Ribeiro, Joao Ubaldo (Osorio Pimentel)
1941- .... **CLC 10, 67**
See also CA 81-84; CWW 2; EWL 3

Ribman, Ronald (Burt) 1932- .... **CLC 7**
See also CA 21-24R; CAD; CANR 46, 80;
CD 5

Ricci, Nino (Pio) 1959- .... **CLC 70**
See also CA 137; CANR 130; CCA 1

Rice, Anne 1941- .... **CLC 41, 128**
See Rampling, Anne
See also AAYA 9, 53; AMWS 7; BEST
89:2; BPFB 3; CA 65-68; CANR 12, 36,
53, 74, 100, 133; CN 7; CPW; CSW;
DA3; DAM POP; DLB 292; GLL 2;
HGG; MTCW 2; SUFW 2; YAW

Rice, Elmer (Leopold) 1892-1967 ...... **CLC 7,**
49
See Reizenstein, Elmer Leopold
See also CA 21-22; 25-28R; CAP 2; DAM
DRAM; DFS 12; DLB 4, 7; MTCW 1, 2;
RGAL 4

Rice, Tim(othy Miles Bindon)
1944- .... **CLC 21**
See also CA 103; CANR 46; DFS 7

Rich, Adrienne (Cecile) 1929- ... **CLC 3, 6, 7,**
11, 18, 36, 73, 76, 125; PC 5
See also AMWR 2; AMWS 1; CA 9-12R;
CANR 20, 53, 74, 128; CDALBS; CP 7;
CSW; CWP; DA3; DAM POET; DLB 5,
67; EWL 3; EXPP; FW; MAWW; MTCW
1, 2; PAB; PFS 15; RGAL 4; WP

Rich, Barbara
See Graves, Robert (von Ranke)

Rich, Robert
See Trumbo, Dalton

Richard, Keith .... **CLC 17**
See Richards, Keith

Richards, David Adams 1950- .... **CLC 59**
See also CA 93-96; CANR 60, 110; DAC;
DLB 53

Roy, Arundhati 1960(?)- .... **CLC 109; 210**
See also CA 163; CANR 90, 126; DLBY 1997; EWL 3; LATS 1:2; WWE 1

Roy, Gabrielle 1909-1983 .... **CLC 10, 14**
See also CA 53-56; 110; CANR 5, 61; CCA 1; DAB; DAC; DAM MST; DLB 68; EWL 3; MTCW 1; RGWL 2, 3; SATA 104

Royko, Mike 1932-1997 .... **CLC 109**
See also CA 89-92; 157; CANR 26, 111; CPW

Rozanov, Vasilii Vasil'evich
See Rozanov, Vassili
See also DLB 295

Rozanov, Vasily Vasilyevich
See Rozanov, Vassili
See also EWL 3

Rozanov, Vassili 1856-1919 .... **TCLC 104**
See Rozanov, Vasilii Vasil'evich; Rozanov, Vasily Vasilyevich

Rozewicz, Tadeusz 1921- ...... **CLC 9, 23, 139**
See also CA 108; CANR 36, 66; CWW 2; DA3; DAM POET; DLB 232; EWL 3; MTCW 1, 2; RGWL 3

Ruark, Gibbons 1941- .... **CLC 3**
See also CA 33-36R; CAAS 23; CANR 14, 31, 57; DLB 120

Rubens, Bernice (Ruth) 1923-2004 . **CLC 19, 31**
See also CA 25-28R; CANR 33, 65, 128; CN 7; DLB 14, 207; MTCW 1

Rubin, Harold
See Robbins, Harold

Rudkin, (James) David 1936- .... **CLC 14**
See also CA 89-92; CBD; CD 5; DLB 13

Rudnik, Raphael 1933- .... **CLC 7**
See also CA 29-32R

Ruffian, M.
See Hasek, Jaroslav (Matej Frantisek)

Ruiz, Jose Martinez .... **CLC 11**
See Martinez Ruiz, Jose

Ruiz, Juan c. 1283-c. 1350 .... **CMLC 66**

Rukeyser, Muriel 1913-1980 . **CLC 6, 10, 15, 27; PC 12**
See also AMWS 6; CA 5-8R; 93-96; CANR 26, 60; DA3; DAM POET; DLB 48; EWL 3; FW; GLL 2; MTCW 1, 2; PFS 10; RGAL 4; SATA-Obit 22

Rule, Jane (Vance) 1931- .... **CLC 27**
See also CA 25-28R; CAAS 18; CANR 12, 87; CN 7; DLB 60; FW

Rulfo, Juan 1918-1986 .. **CLC 8, 80; HLC 2; SSC 25**
See also CA 85-88; 118; CANR 26; CD-WLB 3; DAM MULT; DLB 113; EWL 3; HW 1, 2; LAW; MTCW 1, 2; RGSF 2; RGWL 2, 3; WLIT 1

Rumi, Jalal al-Din 1207-1273 ...... **CMLC 20; PC 45**
See also RGWL 2, 3; WP

Runeberg, Johan 1804-1877 .... **NCLC 41**

Runyon, (Alfred) Damon 1884(?)-1946 .... **TCLC 10**
See also CA 107; 165; DLB 11, 86, 171; MTCW 2; RGAL 4

Rush, Norman 1933- .... **CLC 44**
See also CA 121; 126; CANR 130; INT CA-126

Rushdie, (Ahmed) Salman 1947- .... **CLC 23, 31, 55, 100, 191; SSC 83; WLCS**
See also BEST 89:3; BPFB 3; BRWS 4; CA 108; 111; CANR 33, 56, 108, 133; CN 7; CPW 1; DA3; DAB; DAC; DAM MST, NOV, POP; DLB 194; EWL 3; FANT; INT CA-111; LATS 1:2; LMFS 2; MTCW 1, 2; RGEL 2; RGSF 2; TEA; WLIT 4; WWE 1

Rushforth, Peter (Scott) 1945- .... **CLC 19**
See also CA 101

Ruskin, John 1819-1900 .... **TCLC 63**
See also BRW 5; BYA 5; CA 114; 129; CD-BLB 1832-1890; DLB 55, 163, 190; RGEL 2; SATA 24; TEA; WCH

Russ, Joanna 1937- .... **CLC 15**
See also BPFB 3; CA 5-28R; CANR 11, 31, 65; CN 7; DLB 8; FW; GLL 1; MTCW 1; SCFW 2; SFW 4

Russ, Richard Patrick
See O'Brian, Patrick

Russell, George William 1867-1935
See A.E.; Baker, Jean H.
See also BRWS 8; CA 104; 153; CDBLB 1890-1914; DAM POET; EWL 3; RGEL 2

Russell, Jeffrey Burton 1934- .... **CLC 70**
See also CA 25-28R; CANR 11, 28, 52

Russell, (Henry) Ken(neth Alfred) 1927- .... **CLC 16**
See also CA 105

Russell, William Martin 1947-
See Russell, Willy
See also CA 164; CANR 107

Russell, Willy .... **CLC 60**
See Russell, William Martin
See also CBD; CD 5; DLB 233

Russo, Richard 1949- .... **CLC 181**
See also AMWS 12; CA 127; 133; CANR 87, 114

Rutherford, Mark .... **TCLC 25**
See White, William Hale
See also DLB 18; RGEL 2

Ruyslinck, Ward .... **CLC 14**
See Belser, Reimond Karel Maria de

Ryan, Cornelius (John) 1920-1974 ..... **CLC 7**
See also CA 69-72; 53-56; CANR 38

Ryan, Michael 1946- .... **CLC 65**
See also CA 49-52; CANR 109; DLBY 1982

Ryan, Tim
See Dent, Lester

Rybakov, Anatoli (Naumovich) 1911-1998 .... **CLC 23, 53**
See Rybakov, Anatolii (Naumovich)
See also CA 126; 135; 172; SATA 79; SATA-Obit 108

Rybakov, Anatolii (Naumovich)
See Rybakov, Anatoli (Naumovich)
See also DLB 302

Ryder, Jonathan
See Ludlum, Robert

Ryga, George 1932-1987 .... **CLC 14**
See also CA 101; 124; CANR 43, 90; CCA 1; DAC; DAM MST; DLB 60

S. H.
See Hartmann, Sadakichi

S. S.
See Sassoon, Siegfried (Lorraine)

Sa'adawi, al- Nawal
See El Saadawi, Nawal
See also AFW; EWL 3

Saadawi, Nawal El
See El Saadawi, Nawal
See also WLIT 2

Saba, Umberto 1883-1957 .... **TCLC 33**
See also CA 144; CANR 79; DLB 114; EWL 3; RGWL 2, 3

Sabatini, Rafael 1875-1950 .... **TCLC 47**
See also BPFB 3; CA 162; RHW

Sabato, Ernesto (R.) 1911- .... **CLC 10, 23; HLC 2**
See also CA 97-100; CANR 32, 65; CD-WLB 3; CWW 2; DAM MULT; DLB 145; EWL 3; HW 1, 2; LAW; MTCW 1, 2

Sa-Carneiro, Mario de 1890-1916 . **TCLC 83**
See also DLB 287; EWL 3

Sacastru, Martin
See Bioy Casares, Adolfo
See also CWW 2

Sacher-Masoch, Leopold von 1836(?)-1895 .... **NCLC 31**

Sachs, Hans 1494-1576 .... **LC 95**
See also CDWLB 2; DLB 179; RGWL 2, 3

Sachs, Marilyn (Stickle) 1927- .... **CLC 35**
See also AAYA 2; BYA 6; CA 17-20R; CANR 13, 47; CLR 2; JRDA; MAICYA 1, 2; SAAS 2; SATA 3, 68; SATA-Essay 110; WYA; YAW

Sachs, Nelly 1891-1970 .... **CLC 14, 98**
See also CA 17-18; 25-28R; CANR 87; CAP 2; EWL 3; MTCW 2; PFS 20; RGWL 2, 3

Sackler, Howard (Oliver) 1929-1982 .... **CLC 14**
See also CA 61-64; 108; CAD; CANR 30; DFS 15; DLB 7

Sacks, Oliver (Wolf) 1933- .... **CLC 67, 202**
See also CA 53-56; CANR 28, 50, 76; CPW; DA3; INT CANR-28; MTCW 1, 2

Sackville, Thomas 1536-1608 .... **LC 98**
See also DAM DRAM; DLB 62, 132; RGEL 2

Sadakichi
See Hartmann, Sadakichi

Sa'dawi, Nawal al-
See El Saadawi, Nawal
See also CWW 2

Sade, Donatien Alphonse Francois 1740-1814 .... **NCLC 3, 47**
See also EW 4; GFL Beginnings to 1789; RGWL 2, 3

Sade, Marquis de
See Sade, Donatien Alphonse Francois

Sadoff, Ira 1945- .... **CLC 9**
See also CA 53-56; CANR 5, 21, 109; DLB 120

Saetone
See Camus, Albert

Safire, William 1929- .... **CLC 10**
See also CA 17-20R; CANR 31, 54, 91

Sagan, Carl (Edward) 1934-1996 .... **CLC 30, 112**
See also AAYA 2; CA 25-28R; 155; CANR 11, 36, 74; CPW; DA3; MTCW 1, 2; SATA 58; SATA-Obit 94

Sagan, Francoise .... **CLC 3, 6, 9, 17, 36**
See Quoirez, Francoise
See also CWW 2; DLB 83; EWL 3; GFL 1789 to the Present; MTCW 2

Sahgal, Nayantara (Pandit) 1927- .... **CLC 41**
See also CA 9-12R; CANR 11, 88; CN 7

Said, Edward W. 1935-2003 .... **CLC 123**
See also CA 21-24R; 220; CANR 45, 74, 107, 131; DLB 67; MTCW 2

Saigyō 1118-1190 .... **CMLC 77**
See also DLB 203; RGWL 3

Saint, H(arry) F. 1941- .... **CLC 50**
See also CA 127

St. Aubin de Teran, Lisa 1953-
See Teran, Lisa St. Aubin de
See also CA 118; 126; CN 7; INT CA-126

Saint Birgitta of Sweden c. 1303-1373 .... **CMLC 24**

Sainte-Beuve, Charles Augustin 1804-1869 .... **NCLC 5**
See also DLB 217; EW 6; GFL 1789 to the Present

Saint-Exupery, Antoine (Jean Baptiste Marie Roger) de 1900-1944 .... **TCLC 2, 56, 169; WLC**
See also BPFB 3; BYA 3; CA 108; 132; CLR 10; DA3; DAM NOV; DLB 72; EW 12; EWL 3; GFL 1789 to the Present; LAIT 3; MAICYA 1, 2; MTCW 1, 2; RGWL 2, 3; SATA 20; TWA

St. John, David
See Hunt, E(verette) Howard, (Jr.)

St. John, J. Hector
See Crevecoeur, Michel Guillaume Jean de
Saint-John Perse
See Leger, (Marie-Rene Auguste) Alexis Saint-Leger
See also EW 10; EWL 3; GFL 1789 to the Present; RGWL 2
Saintsbury, George (Edward Bateman)
1845-1933 .... **TCLC 31**
See also CA 160; DLB 57, 149
Sait Faik .... **TCLC 23**
See also Abasiyanik, Sait Faik
Saki .... **SSC 12; TCLC 3**
See Munro, H(ector) H(ugh)
See also BRWS 6; BYA 11; LAIT 2; MTCW 2; RGEL 2; SSFS 1; SUFW
Sala, George Augustus 1828-1895 . **NCLC 46**
Saladin 1138-1193 .... **CMLC 38**
Salama, Hannu 1936- .... **CLC 18**
See also EWL 3
Salamanca, J(ack) R(ichard) 1922- .. **CLC 4, 15**
See also CA 25-28R, 193; CAAE 193
Salas, Floyd Francis 1931- .... **HLC 2**
See also CA 119; CAAS 27; CANR 44, 75, 93; DAM MULT; DLB 82; HW 1, 2; MTCW 2
Sale, J. Kirkpatrick
See Sale, Kirkpatrick
Sale, Kirkpatrick 1937- .... **CLC 68**
See also CA 13-16R; CANR 10
Salinas, Luis Omar 1937- ... **CLC 90; HLC 2**
See also AMWS 13; CA 131; CANR 81; DAM MULT; DLB 82; HW 1, 2
Salinas (y Serrano), Pedro
1891(?)-1951 .... **TCLC 17**
See also CA 117; DLB 134; EWL 3
Salinger, J(erome) D(avid) 1919- .. **CLC 1, 3, 8, 12, 55, 56, 138; SSC 2, 28, 65; WLC**
See also AAYA 2, 36; AMW; AMWC 1; BPFB 3; CA 5-8R; CANR 39, 129; CDALB 1941-1968; CLR 18; CN 7; CPW 1; DA; DA3; DAB; DAC; DAM MST, NOV, POP; DLB 2, 102, 173; EWL 3; EXPN; LAIT 4; MAICYA 1, 2; MTCW 1, 2; NFS 1; RGAL 4; RGSF 2; SATA 67; SSFS 17; TUS; WYA; YAW
Salisbury, John
See Caute, (John) David
Sallust c. 86B.C.-35B.C. .... **CMLC 68**
See also AW 2; CDWLB 1; DLB 211; RGWL 2, 3
Salter, James 1925- .. **CLC 7, 52, 59; SSC 58**
See also AMWS 9; CA 73-76; CANR 107; DLB 130
Saltus, Edgar (Everton) 1855-1921 . **TCLC 8**
See also CA 105; DLB 202; RGAL 4
Saltykov, Mikhail Evgrafovich
1826-1889 .... **NCLC 16**
See also DLB 238:
Saltykov-Shchedrin, N.
See Saltykov, Mikhail Evgrafovich
Samarakis, Andonis
See Samarakis, Antonis
See also EWL 3
Samarakis, Antonis 1919-2003 .... **CLC 5**
See Samarakis, Andonis
See also CA 25-28R; 224; CAAS 16; CANR 36
Sanchez, Florencio 1875-1910 .... **TCLC 37**
See also CA 153; DLB 305; EWL 3; HW 1; LAW
Sanchez, Luis Rafael 1936- .... **CLC 23**
See also CA 128; DLB 305; EWL 3; HW 1; WLIT 1

Sanchez, Sonia 1934- .... **BLC 3; CLC 5, 116; PC 9**
See also BW 2, 3; CA 33-36R; CANR 24, 49, 74, 115; CLR 18; CP 7; CSW; CWP; DA3; DAM MULT; DLB 41; DLBD 8; EWL 3; MAICYA 1, 2; MTCW 1, 2; SATA 22, 136; WP
Sancho, Ignatius 1729-1780 .... **LC 84**
Sand, George 1804-1876 ..... **NCLC 2, 42, 57; WLC**
See also DA; DA3; DAB; DAC; DAM MST, NOV; DLB 119, 192; EW 6; FW; GFL 1789 to the Present; RGWL 2, 3; TWA
Sandburg, Carl (August) 1878-1967 . **CLC 1, 4, 10, 15, 35; PC 2, 41; WLC**
See also AAYA 24; AMW; BYA 1, 3; CA 5-8R; 25-28R; CANR 35; CDALB 1865-1917; CLR 67; DA; DA3; DAB; DAC; DAM MST, POET; DLB 17, 54, 284; EWL 3; EXPP; LAIT 2; MAICYA 1, 2; MTCW 1, 2; PAB; PFS 3, 6, 12; RGAL 4; SATA 8; TUS; WCH; WP; WYA
Sandburg, Charles
See Sandburg, Carl (August)
Sandburg, Charles A.
See Sandburg, Carl (August)
Sanders, (James) Ed(ward) 1939- .... **CLC 53**
See Sanders, Edward
See also BG 3; CA 13-16R; CAAS 21; CANR 13, 44, 78; CP 7; DAM POET; DLB 16, 244
Sanders, Edward
See Sanders, (James) Ed(ward)
See also DLB 244
Sanders, Lawrence 1920-1998 .... **CLC 41**
See also BEST 89:4; BPFB 3; CA 81-84; 165; CANR 33, 62; CMW 4; CPW; DA3; DAM POP; MTCW 1
Sanders, Noah
See Blount, Roy (Alton), Jr.
Sanders, Winston P.
See Anderson, Poul (William)
Sandoz, Mari(e Susette) 1900-1966 .. **CLC 28**
See also CA 1-4R; 25-28R; CANR 17, 64; DLB 9, 212; LAIT 2; MTCW 1, 2; SATA 5; TCWW 2
Sandys, George 1578-1644 .... **LC 80**
See also DLB 24, 121
Saner, Reg(inald Anthony) 1931- .... **CLC 9**
See also CA 65-68; CP 7
Sankara 788-820 .... **CMLC 32**
Sannazaro, Jacopo 1456(?)-1530 .... **LC 8**
See also RGWL 2, 3
Sansom, William 1912-1976 . **CLC 2, 6; SSC 21**
See also CA 5-8R; 65-68; CANR 42; DAM NOV; DLB 139; EWL 3; MTCW 1; RGEL 2; RGSF 2
Santayana, George 1863-1952 .... **TCLC 40**
See also AMW; CA 115; 194; DLB 54, 71, 246, 270; DLBD 13; EWL 3; RGAL 4; TUS
Santiago, Danny .... **CLC 33**
See James, Daniel (Lewis)
See also DLB 122
Santillana, Íñigo López de Mendoza, Marqués de 1398-1458 .... **LC 111**
See also DLB 286
Santmyer, Helen Hooven
1895-1986 .... **CLC 33; TCLC 133**
See also CA 1-4R; 118; CANR 15, 33; DLBY 1984; MTCW 1; RHW
Santoka, Taneda 1882-1940 .... **TCLC 72**
Santos, Bienvenido N(uqui)
1911-1996 ... **AAL; CLC 22; TCLC 156**
See also CA 101; 151; CANR 19, 46; DAM MULT; EWL; RGAL 4; SSFS 19

Sapir, Edward 1884-1939 .... **TCLC 108**
See also CA 211; DLB 92
Sapper .... **TCLC 44**
See McNeile, Herman Cyril
Sapphire
See Sapphire, Brenda
Sapphire, Brenda 1950- .... **CLC 99**
Sappho fl. 6th cent. B.C.- ... **CMLC 3, 67; PC 5**
See also CDWLB 1; DA3; DAM POET; DLB 176; PFS 20; RGWL 2, 3; WP
Saramago, Jose 1922- ..... **CLC 119; HLCS 1**
See also CA 153; CANR 96; CWW 2; DLB 287; EWL 3; LATS 1:2
Sarduy, Severo 1937-1993 .... **CLC 6, 97; HLCS 2; TCLC 167**
See also CA 89-92; 142; CANR 58, 81; CWW 2; DLB 113; EWL 3; HW 1, 2; LAW
Sargeson, Frank 1903-1982 .... **CLC 31**
See also CA 25-28R; 106; CANR 38, 79; EWL 3; GLL 2; RGEL 2; RGSF 2; SSFS 20
Sarmiento, Domingo Faustino
1811-1888 .... **HLCS 2**
See also LAW; WLIT 1
Sarmiento, Felix Ruben Garcia
See Dario, Ruben
Saro-Wiwa, Ken(ule Beeson)
1941-1995 .... **CLC 114**
See also BW 2; CA 142; 150; CANR 60; DLB 157
Saroyan, William 1908-1981 ... **CLC 1, 8, 10, 29, 34, 56; SSC 21; TCLC 137; WLC**
See also CA 5-8R; 103; CAD; CANR 30; CDALBS; DA; DA3; DAB; DAC; DAM DRAM, MST, NOV; DFS 17; DLB 7, 9, 86; DLBY 1981; EWL 3; LAIT 4; MTCW 1, 2; RGAL 4; RGSF 2; SATA 23; SATA-Obit 24; SSFS 14; TUS
Sarraute, Nathalie 1900-1999 .... **CLC 1, 2, 4, 8, 10, 31, 80; TCLC 145**
See also BPFB 3; CA 9-12R; 187; CANR 23, 66, 134; CWW 2; DLB 83; EW 12; EWL 3; GFL 1789 to the Present; MTCW 1, 2; RGWL 2, 3
Sarton, (Eleanor) May 1912-1995 ..... **CLC 4, 14, 49, 91; PC 39; TCLC 120**
See also AMWS 8; CA 1-4R; 149; CANR 1, 34, 55, 116; CN 7; CP 7; DAM POET; DLB 48; DLBY 1981; EWL 3; FW; INT CANR-34; MTCW 1, 2; RGAL 4; SATA 36; SATA-Obit 86; TUS
Sartre, Jean-Paul 1905-1980 . **CLC 1, 4, 7, 9, 13, 18, 24, 44, 50, 52; DC 3; SSC 32; WLC**
See also CA 9-12R; 97-100; CANR 21; DA; DA3; DAB; DAC; DAM DRAM, MST, NOV; DFS 5; DLB 72, 296; EW 12; EWL 3; GFL 1789 to the Present; LMFS 2; MTCW 1, 2; RGSF 2; RGWL 2, 3; SSFS 9; TWA
Sassoon, Siegfried (Lorraine)
1886-1967 .... **CLC 36, 130; PC 12**
See also BRW 6; CA 104; 25-28R; CANR 36; DAB; DAM MST, NOV, POET; DLB 20, 191; DLBD 18; EWL 3; MTCW 1, 2; PAB; RGEL 2; TEA
Satterfield, Charles
See Pohl, Frederik
Satyremont
See Peret, Benjamin
Saul, John (W. III) 1942- .... **CLC 46**
See also AAYA 10; BEST 90:4; CA 81-84; CANR 16, 40, 81; CPW; DAM NOV, POP; HGG; SATA 98
Saunders, Caleb
See Heinlein, Robert A(nson)
Saura (Atares), Carlos 1932-1998 .... **CLC 20**
See also CA 114; 131; CANR 79; HW 1

Sauser, Frederic Louis
    See Sauser-Hall, Frederic
Sauser-Hall, Frederic 1887-1961 ...... **CLC 18**
    See Cendrars, Blaise
    See also CA 102; 93-96; CANR 36, 62;
    MTCW 1
Saussure, Ferdinand de
    1857-1913 .... **TCLC 49**
    See also DLB 242
Savage, Catharine
    See Brosman, Catharine Savage
Savage, Richard 1697(?)-1743 .... **LC 96**
    See also DLB 95; RGEL 2
Savage, Thomas 1915-2003 .... **CLC 40**
    See also CA 126; 132; 218; CAAS 15; CN
    7; INT CA-132; SATA-Obit 147; TCWW
    2
Savan, Glenn 1953-2003 .... **CLC 50**
    See also CA 225
Sax, Robert
    See Johnson, Robert
Saxo Grammaticus c. 1150-c.
    1222 .... **CMLC 58**
Saxton, Robert
    See Johnson, Robert
Sayers, Dorothy L(eigh) 1893-1957 . **SSC 71;**
    TCLC 2, 15
    See also BPFB 3; BRWS 3; CA 104; 119;
    CANR 60; CDBLB 1914-1945; CMW 4;
    DAM POP; DLB 10, 36, 77, 100; MSW;
    MTCW 1, 2; RGEL 2; SSFS 12; TEA
Sayers, Valerie 1952- .... **CLC 50, 122**
    See also CA 134; CANR 61; CSW
Sayles, John (Thomas) 1950- .... **CLC 7, 10,**
    14, 198
    See also CA 57-60; CANR 41, 84; DLB 44
Scammell, Michael 1935- .... **CLC 34**
    See also CA 156
Scannell, Vernon 1922- .... **CLC 49**
    See also CA 5-8R; CANR 8, 24, 57; CP 7;
    CWRI 5; DLB 27; SATA 59
Scarlett, Susan
    See Streatfeild, (Mary) Noel
Scarron, Paul 1610-1660 .... **LC 116**
    See also GFL Beginnings to 1789; RGWL
    2, 3
Scarron 1847-1910
    See Mikszath, Kalman
Schaeffer, Susan Fromberg 1941- ..... **CLC 6,**
    11, 22
    See also CA 49-52; CANR 18, 65; CN 7;
    DLB 28, 299; MTCW 1, 2; SATA 22
Schama, Simon (Michael) 1945- ...... **CLC 150**
    See also BEST 89:4; CA 105; CANR 39,
    91
Schary, Jill
    See Robinson, Jill
Schell, Jonathan 1943- .... **CLC 35**
    See also CA 73-76; CANR 12, 117
Schelling, Friedrich Wilhelm Joseph von
    1775-1854 .... **NCLC 30**
    See also DLB 90
Scherer, Jean-Marie Maurice 1920-
    See Rohmer, Eric
    See also CA 110
Schevill, James (Erwin) 1920- .... **CLC 7**
    See also CA 5-8R; CAAS 12; CAD; CD 5
Schiller, Friedrich von 1759-1805 ...... **DC 12;**
    NCLC 39, 69
    See also CDWLB 2; DAM DRAM; DLB
    94; EW 5; RGWL 2, 3; TWA
Schisgal, Murray (Joseph) 1926- .... **CLC 6**
    See also CA 21-24R; CAD; CANR 48, 86;
    CD 5
Schlee, Ann 1934- .... **CLC 35**
    See also CA 101; CANR 29, 88; SATA 44;
    SATA-Brief 36

Schlegel, August Wilhelm von
    1767-1845 .... **NCLC 15, 142**
    See also DLB 94; RGWL 2, 3
Schlegel, Friedrich 1772-1829 .... **NCLC 45**
    See also DLB 90; EW 5; RGWL 2, 3; TWA
Schlegel, Johann Elias (von)
    1719(?)-1749 .... **LC 5**
Schleiermacher, Friedrich
    1768-1834 .... **NCLC 107**
    See also DLB 90
Schlesinger, Arthur M(eier), Jr.
    1917- .... **CLC 84**
    See also AITN 1; CA 1-4R; CANR 1, 28,
    58, 105; DLB 17; INT CANR-28; MTCW
    1, 2; SATA 61
Schlink, Bernhard 1944- .... **CLC 174**
    See also CA 163; CANR 116
Schmidt, Arno (Otto) 1914-1979 ...... **CLC 56**
    See also CA 128; 109; DLB 69; EWL 3
Schmitz, Aron Hector 1861-1928
    See Svevo, Italo
    See also CA 104; 122; MTCW 1
Schnackenberg, Gjertrud (Cecelia)
    1953- .... **CLC 40; PC 45**
    See also CA 116; CANR 100; CP 7; CWP;
    DLB 120, 282; PFS 13
Schneider, Leonard Alfred 1925-1966
    See Bruce, Lenny
    See also CA 89-92
Schnitzler, Arthur 1862-1931 ..... **DC 17; SSC**
    15, 61; TCLC 4
    See also CA 104; CDWLB 2; DLB 81, 118;
    EW 8; EWL 3; RGSF 2; RGWL 2, 3
Schoenberg, Arnold Franz Walter
    1874-1951 .... **TCLC 75**
    See also CA 109; 188
Schonberg, Arnold
    See Schoenberg, Arnold Franz Walter
Schopenhauer, Arthur 1788-1860 . **NCLC 51,**
    157
    See also DLB 90; EW 5
Schor, Sandra (M.) 1932(?)-1990 ..... **CLC 65**
    See also CA 132
Schorer, Mark 1908-1977 .... **CLC 9**
    See also CA 5-8R; 73-76; CANR 7; DLB
    103
Schrader, Paul (Joseph) 1946- . **CLC 26, 212**
    See also CA 37-40R; CANR 41; DLB 44
Schreber, Daniel 1842-1911 .... **TCLC 123**
Schreiner, Olive (Emilie Albertina)
    1855-1920 .... **TCLC 9**
    See also AFW; BRWS 2; CA 105; 154;
    DLB 18, 156, 190, 225; EWL 3; FW;
    RGEL 2; TWA; WLIT 2; WWE 1
Schulberg, Budd (Wilson) 1914- .. **CLC 7, 48**
    See also BPFB 3; CA 25-28R; CANR 19,
    87; CN 7; DLB 6, 26, 28; DLBY 1981,
    2001
Schulman, Arnold
    See Trumbo, Dalton
Schulz, Bruno 1892-1942 .. **SSC 13; TCLC 5,**
    51
    See also CA 115; 123; CANR 86; CDWLB
    4; DLB 215; EWL 3; MTCW 2; RGSF 2;
    RGWL 2, 3
Schulz, Charles M(onroe)
    1922-2000 .... **CLC 12**
    See also AAYA 39; CA 9-12R; 187; CANR
    6, 132; INT CANR-6; SATA 10; SATA-
    Obit 118
Schumacher, E(rnst) F(riedrich)
    1911-1977 .... **CLC 80**
    See also CA 81-84; 73-76; CANR 34, 85
Schumann, Robert 1810-1856 ...... **NCLC 143**
Schuyler, George Samuel 1895-1977 .... **HR 3**
    See also BW 2; CA 81-84; 73-76; CANR
    42; DLB 29, 51

Schuyler, James Marcus 1923-1991 .. **CLC 5,**
    23
    See also CA 101; 134; DAM POET; DLB
    5, 169; EWL 3; INT CA-101; WP
Schwartz, Delmore (David)
    1913-1966 ... **CLC 2, 4, 10, 45, 87; PC 8**
    See also AMWS 2; CA 17-18; 25-28R;
    CANR 35; CAP 2; DLB 28, 48; EWL 3;
    MTCW 1, 2; PAB; RGAL 4; TUS
Schwartz, Ernst
    See Ozu, Yasujiro
Schwartz, John Burnham 1965- .... **CLC 59**
    See also CA 132; CANR 116
Schwartz, Lynne Sharon 1939- .... **CLC 31**
    See also CA 103; CANR 44, 89; DLB 218;
    MTCW 2
Schwartz, Muriel A.
    See Eliot, T(homas) S(tearns)
Schwarz-Bart, Andre 1928- .... **CLC 2, 4**
    See also CA 89-92; CANR 109; DLB 299
Schwarz-Bart, Simone 1938- . **BLCS; CLC 7**
    See also BW 2; CA 97-100; CANR 117;
    EWL 3
Schwerner, Armand 1927-1999 .... **PC 42**
    See also CA 9-12R; 179; CANR 50, 85; CP
    7; DLB 165
Schwitters, Kurt (Hermann Edward Karl
    Julius) 1887-1948 .... **TCLC 95**
    See also CA 158
Schwob, Marcel (Mayer Andre)
    1867-1905 .... **TCLC 20**
    See also CA 117; 168; DLB 123; GFL 1789
    to the Present
Sciascia, Leonardo 1921-1989 .. **CLC 8, 9, 41**
    See also CA 85-88; 130; CANR 35; DLB
    177; EWL 3; MTCW 1; RGWL 2, 3
Scoppettone, Sandra 1936- .... **CLC 26**
    See Early, Jack
    See also AAYA 11; BYA 8; CA 5-8R;
    CANR 41, 73; GLL 1; MAICYA 2; MAI-
    CYAS 1; SATA 9, 92; WYA; YAW
Scorsese, Martin 1942- .... **CLC 20, 89, 207**
    See also AAYA 38; CA 110, 114; CANR
    46, 85
Scotland, Jay
    See Jakes, John (William)
Scott, Duncan Campbell
    1862-1947 .... **TCLC 6**
    See also CA 104; 153; DAC; DLB 92;
    RGEL 2
Scott, Evelyn 1893-1963 .... **CLC 43**
    See also CA 104; 112; CANR 64; DLB 9,
    48; RHW
Scott, F(rancis) R(eginald)
    1899-1985 .... **CLC 22**
    See also CA 101; 114; CANR 87; DLB 88;
    INT CA-101; RGEL 2
Scott, Frank
    See Scott, F(rancis) R(eginald)
Scott, Joan .... **CLC 65**
Scott, Joanna 1960- .... **CLC 50**
    See also CA 126; CANR 53, 92
Scott, Paul (Mark) 1920-1978 ...... **CLC 9, 60**
    See also BRWS 1; CA 81-84; 77-80; CANR
    33; DLB 14, 207; EWL 3; MTCW 1;
    RGEL 2; RHW; WWE 1
Scott, Ridley 1937- .... **CLC 183**
    See also AAYA 13, 43
Scott, Sarah 1723-1795 .... **LC 44**
    See also DLB 39
Scott, Sir Walter 1771-1832 .... **NCLC 15, 69,**
    110; PC 13; SSC 32; WLC
    See also AAYA 22; BRW 4; BYA 2; CD-
    BLB 1789-1832; DA; DAB; DAC; DAM
    MST, NOV, POET; DLB 93, 107, 116,
    144, 159; HGG; LAIT 1; RGEL 2; RGSF
    2; SSFS 10; SUFW 1; TEA; WLIT 3;
    YABC 2

Sharp, William 1855-1905 .... **TCLC 39**
  See Macleod, Fiona
  See also CA 160; DLB 156; RGEL 2
Sharpe, Thomas Ridley 1928-
  See Sharpe, Tom
  See also CA 114; 122; CANR 85; INT CA-122
Sharpe, Tom .... **CLC 36**
  See Sharpe, Thomas Ridley
  See also CN 7; DLB 14, 231
Shatrov, Mikhail .... **CLC 59**
Shaw, Bernard
  See Shaw, George Bernard
  See also DLB 190
Shaw, G. Bernard
  See Shaw, George Bernard
Shaw, George Bernard 1856-1950 ..... **DC 23; TCLC 3, 9, 21, 45; WLC**
  See Shaw, Bernard
  See also BRW 6; BRWC 1; BRWR 2; CA 104; 128; CDBLB 1914-1945; DA; DA3; DAB; DAC; DAM DRAM, MST; DFS 1, 3, 6, 11, 19; DLB 10, 57; EWL 3; LAIT 3; LATS 1:1; MTCW 1, 2; RGEL 2; TEA; WLIT 4
Shaw, Henry Wheeler 1818-1885 .. **NCLC 15**
  See also DLB 11; RGAL 4
Shaw, Irwin 1913-1984 .... **CLC 7, 23, 34**
  See also AITN 1; BPFB 3; CA 13-16R; 112; CANR 21; CDALB 1941-1968; CPW; DAM DRAM, POP; DLB 6, 102; DLBY 1984; MTCW 1, 21
Shaw, Robert 1927-1978 .... **CLC 5**
  See also AITN 1; CA 1-4R; 81-84; CANR 4; DLB 13, 14
Shaw, T. E.
  See Lawrence, T(homas) E(dward)
Shawn, Wallace 1943- .... **CLC 41**
  See also CA 112; CAD; CD 5; DLB 266
Shchedrin, N.
  See Saltykov, Mikhail Evgrafovich
Shea, Lisa 1953- .... **CLC 86**
  See also CA 147
Sheed, Wilfrid (John Joseph) 1930- . **CLC 2, 4, 10, 53**
  See also CA 65-68; CANR 30, 66; CN 7; DLB 6; MTCW 1, 2
Sheehy, Gail 1937- .... **CLC 171**
  See also CA 49-52; CANR 1, 33, 55, 92; CPW; MTCW 1
Sheldon, Alice Hastings Bradley 1915(?)-1987
  See Tiptree, James, Jr.
  See also CA 108; 122; CANR 34; INT CA-108; MTCW 1
Sheldon, John
  See Bloch, Robert (Albert)
Sheldon, Walter J(ames) 1917-1996
  See Queen, Ellery
  See also AITN 1; CA 25-28R; CANR 10
Shelley, Mary Wollstonecraft (Godwin) 1797-1851 ...... **NCLC 14, 59, 103; WLC**
  See also AAYA 20; BPFB 3; BRW 3; BRWC 2; BRWS 3; BYA 5; CDBLB 1789-1832; DA; DA3; DAB; DAC; DAM MST, NOV; DLB 110, 116, 159, 178; EXPN; HGG; LAIT 1; LMFS 1, 2; NFS 1; RGEL 2; SATA 29; SCFW; SFW 4; TEA; WLIT 3
Shelley, Percy Bysshe 1792-1822 .. **NCLC 18, 93, 143; PC 14, 67; WLC**
  See also BRW 4; BRWR 1; CDBLB 1789-1832; DA; DA3; DAB; DAC; DAM MST, POET; DLB 96, 110, 158; EXPP; LMFS 1; PAB; PFS 2; RGEL 2; TEA; WLIT 3; WP
Shepard, Jim 1956- .... **CLC 36**
  See also CA 137; CANR 59, 104; SATA 90

Shepard, Lucius 1947- .... **CLC 34**
  See also CA 128; 141; CANR 81, 124; HGG; SCFW 2; SFW 4; SUFW 2
Shepard, Sam 1943- .... **CLC 4, 6, 17, 34, 41, 44, 169; DC 5**
  See also AAYA 1, 58; AMWS 3; CA 69-72; CABS 3; CAD; CANR 22, 120; CD 5; DA3; DAM DRAM; DFS 3, 6, 7, 14; DLB 7, 212; EWL 3; IDFW 3, 4; MTCW 1, 2; RGAL 4
Shepherd, Michael
  See Ludlum, Robert
Sherburne, Zoa (Lillian Morin) 1912-1995 .... **CLC 30**
  See also AAYA 13; CA 1-4R; 176; CANR 3, 37; MAICYA 1, 2; SAAS 18; SATA 3; YAW
Sheridan, Frances 1724-1766 .... **LC 7**
  See also DLB 39, 84
Sheridan, Richard Brinsley 1751-1816 .... **DC 1; NCLC 5, 91; WLC**
  See also BRW 3; CDBLB 1660-1789; DA; DAB; DAC; DAM DRAM, MST; DFS 15; DLB 89; WLIT 3
Sherman, Jonathan Marc .... **CLC 55**
Sherman, Martin 1941(?)- .... **CLC 19**
  See also CA 116; 123; CAD; CANR 86; CD 5; DFS 20; DLB 228; GLL 1; IDTP
Sherwin, Judith Johnson
  See Johnson, Judith (Emlyn)
  See also CANR 85; CP 7; CWP
Sherwood, Frances 1940- .... **CLC 81**
  See also CA 146, 220; CAAE 220
Sherwood, Robert E(mmet) 1896-1955 .... **TCLC 3**
  See also CA 104; 153; CANR 86; DAM DRAM; DFS 11, 15, 17; DLB 7, 26, 249; IDFW 3, 4; RGAL 4
Shestov, Lev 1866-1938 .... **TCLC 56**
Shevchenko, Taras 1814-1861 .... **NCLC 54**
Shiel, M(atthew) P(hipps) 1865-1947 .... **TCLC 8**
  See Holmes, Gordon
  See also CA 106; 160; DLB 153; HGG; MTCW 2; SFW 4; SUFW
Shields, Carol (Ann) 1935-2003 ...... **CLC 91, 113, 193**
  See also AMWS 7; CA 81-84; 218; CANR 51, 74, 98, 133; CCA 1; CN 7; CPW; DA3; DAC; MTCW 2
Shields, David (Jonathan) 1956- ...... **CLC 97**
  See also CA 124; CANR 48, 99, 112
Shiga, Naoya 1883-1971 ..... **CLC 33; SSC 23**
  See Shiga Naoya
  See also CA 101; 33-36R; MJW; RGWL 3
Shiga Naoya
  See Shiga, Naoya
  See also DLB 180; EWL 3; RGWL 3
Shilts, Randy 1951-1994 .... **CLC 85**
  See also AAYA 19; CA 115; 127; 144; CANR 45; DA3; GLL 1; INT CA-127; MTCW 2
Shimazaki, Haruki 1872-1943
  See Shimazaki Toson
  See also CA 105; 134; CANR 84; RGWL 3
Shimazaki Toson .... **TCLC 5**
  See Shimazaki, Haruki
  See also DLB 180; EWL 3
Shirley, James 1596-1666 .... **DC 25; LC 96**
  See also DLB 58; RGEL 2
Sholokhov, Mikhail (Aleksandrovich) 1905-1984 .... **CLC 7, 15**
  See also CA 101; 112; DLB 272; EWL 3; MTCW 1, 2; RGWL 2, 3; SATA-Obit 36
Shone, Patric
  See Hanley, James
Showalter, Elaine 1941- .... **CLC 169**
  See also CA 57-60; CANR 58, 106; DLB 67; FW; GLL 2

Shreve, Susan
  See Shreve, Susan Richards
Shreve, Susan Richards 1939- .... **CLC 23**
  See also CA 49-52; CAAS 5; CANR 5, 38, 69, 100; MAICYA 1, 2; SATA 46, 95, 152; SATA-Brief 41
Shue, Larry 1946-1985 .... **CLC 52**
  See also CA 145; 117; DAM DRAM; DFS 7
Shu-Jen, Chou 1881-1936
  See Lu Hsun
  See also CA 104
Shulman, Alix Kates 1932- .... **CLC 2, 10**
  See also CA 29-32R; CANR 43; FW; SATA 7
Shuster, Joe 1914-1992 .... **CLC 21**
  See also AAYA 50
Shute, Nevil .... **CLC 30**
  See Norway, Nevil Shute
  See also BPFB 3; DLB 255; NFS 9; RHW; SFW 4
Shuttle, Penelope (Diane) 1947- .... **CLC 7**
  See also CA 93-96; CANR 39, 84, 92, 108; CP 7; CWP; DLB 14, 40
Shvarts, Elena 1948- .... **PC 50**
  See also CA 147
Sidhwa, Bapsy (N.) 1938- .... **CLC 168**
  See also CA 108; CANR 25, 57; CN 7; FW
Sidney, Mary 1561-1621 .... **LC 19, 39**
  See Sidney Herbert, Mary
Sidney, Sir Philip 1554-1586 . **LC 19, 39; PC 32**
  See also BRW 1; BRWR 2; CDBLB Before 1660; DA; DA3; DAB; DAC; DAM MST, POET; DLB 167; EXPP; PAB; RGEL 2; TEA; WP
Sidney Herbert, Mary
  See Sidney, Mary
  See also DLB 167
Siegel, Jerome 1914-1996 .... **CLC 21**
  See Siegel, Jerry
  See also CA 116; 169; 151
Siegel, Jerry
  See Siegel, Jerome
  See also AAYA 50
Sienkiewicz, Henryk (Adam Alexander Pius) 1846-1916 .... **TCLC 3**
  See also CA 104; 134; CANR 84; EWL 3; RGSF 2; RGWL 2, 3
Sierra, Gregorio Martinez
  See Martinez Sierra, Gregorio
Sierra, Maria (de la O'LeJarraga) Martinez
  See Martinez Sierra, Maria (de la O'LeJarraga)
Sigal, Clancy 1926- .... **CLC 7**
  See also CA 1-4R; CANR 85; CN 7
Siger of Brabant 1240(?)-1284(?) . **CMLC 69**
  See also DLB 115
Sigourney, Lydia H.
  See Sigourney, Lydia Howard (Huntley)
  See also DLB 73, 183
Sigourney, Lydia Howard (Huntley) 1791-1865 .... **NCLC 21, 87**
  See Sigourney, Lydia H.; Sigourney, Lydia Huntley
  See also DLB 1
Sigourney, Lydia Huntley
  See Sigourney, Lydia Howard (Huntley)
  See also DLB 42, 239, 243
Siguenza y Gongora, Carlos de 1645-1700 .... **HLCS 2; LC 8**
  See also LAW
Sigurjonsson, Johann
  See Sigurjonsson, Johann
Sigurjonsson, Johann 1880-1919 ... **TCLC 27**
  See also CA 170; DLB 293; EWL 3
Sikelianos, Angelos 1884-1951 .... **PC 29; TCLC 39**
  See also EWL 3; RGWL 2, 3

Silkin, Jon 1930-1997 .... **CLC 2, 6, 43**
See also CA 5-8R; CAAS 5; CANR 89; CP 7; DLB 27

Silko, Leslie (Marmon) 1948- .... **CLC 23, 74, 114, 211; NNAL; SSC 37, 66; WLCS**
See also AAYA 14; AMWS 4; ANW; BYA 12; CA 115; 122; CANR 45, 65, 118; CN 7; CP 7; CPW 1; CWP; DA; DA3; DAC; DAM MST, MULT, POP; DLB 143, 175, 256, 275; EWL 3; EXPP; EXPS; LAIT 4; MTCW 2; NFS 4; PFS 9, 16; RGAL 4; RGSF 2; SSFS 4, 8, 10, 11

Sillanpaa, Frans Eemil 1888-1964 ... **CLC 19**
See also CA 129; 93-96; EWL 3; MTCW 1

Sillitoe, Alan 1928- .. **CLC 1, 3, 6, 10, 19, 57, 148**
See also AITN 1; BRWS 5; CA 9-12R, 191; CAAE 191; CAAS 2; CANR 8, 26, 55; CDBLB 1960 to Present; CN 7; DLB 14, 139; EWL 3; MTCW 1, 2; RGEL 2; RGSF 2; SATA 61

Silone, Ignazio 1900-1978 .... **CLC 4**
See also CA 25-28; 81-84; CANR 34; CAP 2; DLB 264; EW 12; EWL 3; MTCW 1; RGSF 2; RGWL 2, 3

Silone, Ignazione
See Silone, Ignazio

Silver, Joan Micklin 1935- .... **CLC 20**
See also CA 114; 121; INT CA-121

Silver, Nicholas
See Faust, Frederick (Schiller)
See also TCWW 2

Silverberg, Robert 1935- .... **CLC 7, 140**
See also AAYA 24; BPFB 3; BYA 7, 9; CA 1-4R, 186; CAAE 186; CAAS 3; CANR 1, 20, 36, 85; CLR 59; CN 7; CPW; DAM POP; DLB 8; INT CANR-20; MAICYA 1, 2; MTCW 1, 2; SATA 13, 91; SATA-Essay 104; SCFW 2; SFW 4; SUFW 2

Silverstein, Alvin 1933- .... **CLC 17**
See also CA 49-52; CANR 2; CLR 25; JRDA; MAICYA 1, 2; SATA 8, 69, 124

Silverstein, Shel(don Allan) 1932-1999 .... **PC 49**
See also AAYA 40; BW 3; CA 107; 179; CANR 47, 74, 81; CLR 5, 96; CWRI 5; JRDA; MAICYA 1, 2; MTCW 2; SATA 33, 92; SATA-Brief 27; SATA-Obit 116

Silverstein, Virginia B(arbara Opshelor) 1937- .... **CLC 17**
See also CA 49-52; CANR 2; CLR 25; JRDA; MAICYA 1, 2; SATA 8, 69, 124

Sim, Georges
See Simenon, Georges (Jacques Christian)

Simak, Clifford D(onald) 1904-1988 . **CLC 1, 55**
See also CA 1-4R; 125; CANR 1, 35; DLB 8; MTCW 1; SATA-Obit 56; SFW 4

Simenon, Georges (Jacques Christian) 1903-1989 .... **CLC 1, 2, 3, 8, 18, 47**
See also BPFB 3; CA 85-88; 129; CANR 35; CMW 4; DA3; DAM POP; DLB 72; DLBY 1989; EW 12; EWL 3; GFL 1789 to the Present; MSW; MTCW 1, 2; RGWL 2, 3

Simic, Charles 1938- .... **CLC 6, 9, 22, 49, 68, 130**
See also AMWS 8; CA 29-32R; CAAS 4; CANR 12, 33, 52, 61, 96; CP 7; DA3; DAM POET; DLB 105; MTCW 2; PFS 7; RGAL 4; WP

Simmel, Georg 1858-1918 .... **TCLC 64**
See also CA 157; DLB 296

Simmons, Charles (Paul) 1924- .... **CLC 57**
See also CA 89-92; INT CA-89-92

Simmons, Dan 1948- .... **CLC 44**
See also AAYA 16, 54; CA 138; CANR 53, 81, 126; CPW; DAM POP; HGG; SUFW 2

Simmons, James (Stewart Alexander) 1933- .... **CLC 43**
See also CA 105; CAAS 21; CP 7; DLB 40

Simms, William Gilmore 1806-1870 .... **NCLC 3**
See also DLB 3, 30, 59, 73, 248, 254; RGAL 4

Simon, Carly 1945- .... **CLC 26**
See also CA 105

Simon, Claude (Eugene Henri) 1913-1984 .... **CLC 4, 9, 15, 39**
See also CA 89-92; CANR 33, 117; CWW 2; DAM NOV; DLB 83; EW 13; EWL 3; GFL 1789 to the Present; MTCW 1

Simon, Myles
See Follett, Ken(neth Martin)

Simon, (Marvin) Neil 1927- ... **CLC 6, 11, 31, 39, 70; DC 14**
See also AAYA 32; AITN 1; AMWS 4; CA 21-24R; CANR 26, 54, 87, 126; CD 5; DA3; DAM DRAM; DFS 2, 6, 12, 18; DLB 7, 266; LAIT 4; MTCW 1, 2; RGAL 4; TUS

Simon, Paul (Frederick) 1941(?)- ..... **CLC 17**
See also CA 116; 153

Simonon, Paul 1956(?)- .... **CLC 30**

Simonson, Rick ed. .... **CLC 70**

Simpson, Harriette
See Arnow, Harriette (Louisa) Simpson

Simpson, Louis (Aston Marantz) 1923- .... **CLC 4, 7, 9, 32, 149**
See also AMWS 9; CA 1-4R; CAAS 4; CANR 1, 61; CP 7; DAM POET; DLB 5; MTCW 1, 2; PFS 7, 11, 14; RGAL 4

Simpson, Mona (Elizabeth) 1957- ... **CLC 44, 146**
See also CA 122; 135; CANR 68, 103; CN 7; EWL 3

Simpson, N(orman) F(rederick) 1919- .... **CLC 29**
See also CA 13-16R; CBD; DLB 13; RGEL 2

Sinclair, Andrew (Annandale) 1935- . **CLC 2, 14**
See also CA 9-12R; CAAS 5; CANR 14, 38, 91; CN 7; DLB 14; FANT; MTCW 1

Sinclair, Emil
See Hesse, Hermann

Sinclair, Iain 1943- .... **CLC 76**
See also CA 132; CANR 81; CP 7; HGG

Sinclair, Iain MacGregor
See Sinclair, Iain

Sinclair, Irene
See Griffith, D(avid Lewelyn) W(ark)

Sinclair, Mary Amelia St. Clair 1865(?)-1946
See Sinclair, May
See also CA 104; HGG; RHW

Sinclair, May .... **TCLC 3, 11**
See Sinclair, Mary Amelia St. Clair
See also CA 166; DLB 36, 135; EWL 3; RGEL 2; SUFW

Sinclair, Roy
See Griffith, D(avid Lewelyn) W(ark)

Sinclair, Upton (Beall) 1878-1968 ..... **CLC 1, 11, 15, 63; TCLC 160; WLC**
See also AMWS 5; BPFB 3; BYA 2; CA 5-8R; 25-28R; CANR 7; CDALB 1929-1941; DA; DA3; DAB; DAC; DAM MST, NOV; DLB 9; EWL 3; INT CANR-7; LAIT 3; MTCW 1, 2; NFS 6; RGAL 4; SATA 9; TUS; YAW

Singe, (Edmund) J(ohn) M(illington) 1871-1909 .... **WLC**

Singer, Isaac
See Singer, Isaac Bashevis

Singer, Isaac Bashevis 1904-1991 .. **CLC 1, 3, 6, 9, 11, 15, 23, 38, 69, 111; SSC 3, 53, 80; WLC**
See also AAYA 32; AITN 1, 2; AMW; AMWR 2; BPFB 3; BYA 1, 4; CA 1-4R; 134; CANR 1, 39, 106; CDALB 1941-1968; CLR 1; CWRI 5; DA; DA3; DAB; DAC; DAM MST, NOV; DLB 6, 28, 52, 278; DLBY 1991; EWL 3; EXPS; HGG; JRDA; LAIT 3; MAICYA 1, 2; MTCW 1, 2; RGAL 4; RGSF 2; SATA 3, 27; SATA-Obit 68; SSFS 2, 12, 16; TUS; TWA

Singer, Israel Joshua 1893-1944 .... **TCLC 33**
See also CA 169; EWL 3

Singh, Khushwant 1915- .... **CLC 11**
See also CA 9-12R; CAAS 9; CANR 6, 84; CN 7; EWL 3; RGEL 2

Singleton, Ann
See Benedict, Ruth (Fulton)

Singleton, John 1968(?)- .... **CLC 156**
See also AAYA 50; BW 2, 3; CA 138; CANR 67, 82; DAM MULT

Siniavski, Andrei
See Sinyavsky, Andrei (Donatevich)
See also CWW 2

Sinjohn, John
See Galsworthy, John

Sinyavsky, Andrei (Donatevich) 1925-1997 .... **CLC 8**
See Siniavskii, Andrei; Sinyavsky, Andrey Donatovich; Tertz, Abram
See also CA 85-88; 159

Sinyavsky, Andrey Donatovich
See Sinyavsky, Andrei (Donatevich)
See also EWL 3

Sirin, V.
See Nabokov, Vladimir (Vladimirovich)

Sissman, L(ouis) E(dward) 1928-1976 .... **CLC 9, 18**
See also CA 21-24R; 65-68; CANR 13; DLB 5

Sisson, C(harles) H(ubert) 1914-2003 .... **CLC 8**
See also CA 1-4R; 220; CAAS 3; CANR 3, 48, 84; CP 7; DLB 27

Sitting Bull 1831(?)-1890 .... **NNAL**
See also DA3; DAM MULT

Sitwell, Dame Edith 1887-1964 ..... **CLC 2, 9, 67; PC 3**
See also BRW 7; CA 9-12R; CANR 35; CDBLB 1945-1960; DAM POET; DLB 20; EWL 3; MTCW 1, 2; RGEL 2; TEA

Siwaarmill, H. P.
See Sharp, William

Sjoewall, Maj 1935- .... **CLC 7**
See Sjowall, Maj
See also CA 65-68; CANR 73

Sjowall, Maj
See Sjoewall, Maj
See also BPFB 3; CMW 4; MSW

Skelton, John 1460(?)-1529 ..... **LC 71; PC 25**
See also BRW 1; DLB 136; RGEL 2

Skelton, Robin 1925-1997 .... **CLC 13**
See Zuk, Georges
See also AITN 2; CA 5-8R; 160; CAAS 5; CANR 28, 89; CCA 1; CP 7; DLB 27, 53

Skolimowski, Jerzy 1938- .... **CLC 20**
See also CA 128

Skram, Amalie (Bertha) 1847-1905 .... **TCLC 25**
See also CA 165

Skvorecky, Josef (Vaclav) 1924- ...... **CLC 15, 39, 69, 152**
See also CA 61-64; CAAS 1; CANR 10, 34, 63, 108; CDWLB 4; CWW 2; DA3; DAC; DAM NOV; DLB 232; EWL 3; MTCW 1, 2

Sorokin, Vladimir Georgievich
 See Sorokin, Vladimir
 See also DLB 285
Sorrentino, Gilbert 1929- .. **CLC 3, 7, 14, 22, 40**
 See also CA 77-80; CANR 14, 33, 115; CN 7; CP 7; DLB 5, 173; DLBY 1980; INT CANR-14
Soseki
 See Natsume, Soseki
 See also MJW
Soto, Gary 1952- ... **CLC 32, 80; HLC 2; PC 28**
 See also AAYA 10, 37; BYA 11; CA 119; 125; CANR 50, 74, 107; CLR 38; CP 7; DAM MULT; DLB 82; EWL 3; EXPP; HW 1, 2; INT CA-125; JRDA; LLW 1; MAICYA 2; MAICYAS 1; MTCW 2; PFS 7; RGAL 4; SATA 80, 120; WYA; YAW
Soupault, Philippe 1897-1990 .... **CLC 68**
 See also CA 116; 147; 131; EWL 3; GFL 1789 to the Present; LMFS 2
Souster, (Holmes) Raymond 1921- .... **CLC 5, 14**
 See also CA 13-16R; CAAS 14; CANR 13, 29, 53; CP 7; DA3; DAC; DAM POET; DLB 88; RGEL 2; SATA 63
Southern, Terry 1924(?)-1995 .... **CLC 7**
 See also AMWS 11; BPFB 3; CA 1-4R; 150; CANR 1, 55, 107; CN 7; DLB 2; IDFW 3, 4
Southerne, Thomas 1660-1746 .... **LC 99**
 See also DLB 80; RGEL 2
Southey, Robert 1774-1843 .... **NCLC 8, 97**
 See also BRW 4; DLB 93, 107, 142; RGEL 2; SATA 54
Southwell, Robert 1561(?)-1595 .... **LC 108**
 See also DLB 167; RGEL 2; TEA
Southworth, Emma Dorothy Eliza Nevitte 1819-1899 .... **NCLC 26**
 See also DLB 239
Souza, Ernest
 See Scott, Evelyn
Soyinka, Wole 1934- .. **BLC 3; CLC 3, 5, 14, 36, 44, 179; DC 2; WLC**
 See also AFW; BW 2, 3; CA 13-16R; CANR 27, 39, 82; CD 5; CDWLB 3; CN 7; CP 7; DA; DA3; DAB; DAC; DAM DRAM, MST, MULT; DFS 10; DLB 125; EWL 3; MTCW 1, 2; RGEL 2; TWA; WLIT 2; WWE 1
Spackman, W(illiam) M(ode) 1905-1990 .... **CLC 46**
 See also CA 81-84; 132
Spacks, Barry (Bernard) 1931- .... **CLC 14**
 See also CA 154; CANR 33, 109; CP 7; DLB 105
Spanidou, Irini 1946- .... **CLC 44**
 See also CA 185
Spark, Muriel (Sarah) 1918- ..... **CLC 2, 3, 5, 8, 13, 18, 40, 94; SSC 10**
 See also BRWS 1; CA 5-8R; CANR 12, 36, 76, 89, 131; CDBLB 1945-1960; CN 7; CP 7; DA3; DAB; DAC; DAM MST, NOV; DLB 15, 139; EWL 3; FW; INT CANR-12; LAIT 4; MTCW 1, 2; RGEL 2; TEA; WLIT 4; YAW
Spaulding, Douglas
 See Bradbury, Ray (Douglas)
Spaulding, Leonard
 See Bradbury, Ray (Douglas)
Speght, Rachel 1597-c. 1630 .... **LC 97**
 See also DLB 126
Spelman, Elizabeth .... **CLC 65**
Spence, J. A. D.
 See Eliot, T(homas) S(tearns)
Spencer, Anne 1882-1975 .... **HR 3**
 See also BW 2; CA 161; DLB 51, 54

Spencer, Elizabeth 1921- .... **CLC 22; SSC 57**
 See also CA 13-16R; CANR 32, 65, 87; CN 7; CSW; DLB 6, 218; EWL 3; MTCW 1; RGAL 4; SATA 14
Spencer, Leonard G.
 See Silverberg, Robert
Spencer, Scott 1945- .... **CLC 30**
 See also CA 113; CANR 51; DLBY 1986
Spender, Stephen (Harold) 1909-1995 .... **CLC 1, 2, 5, 10, 41, 91**
 See also BRWS 2; CA 9-12R; 149; CANR 31, 54; CDBLB 1945-1960; CP 7; DA3; DAM POET; DLB 20; EWL 3; MTCW 1, 2; PAB; RGEL 2; TEA
Spengler, Oswald (Arnold Gottfried) 1880-1936 .... **TCLC 25**
 See also CA 118; 189
Spenser, Edmund 1552(?)-1599 ...... **LC 5, 39, 117; PC 8, 42; WLC**
 See also AAYA 60; BRW 1; CDBLB Before 1660; DA; DA3; DAB; DAC; DAM MST, POET; DLB 167; EFS 2; EXPP; PAB; RGEL 2; TEA; WLIT 3; WP
Spicer, Jack 1925-1965 .... **CLC 8, 18, 72**
 See also BG 3; CA 85-88; DAM POET; DLB 5, 16, 193; GLL 1; WP
Spiegelman, Art 1948- .... **CLC 76, 178**
 See also AAYA 10, 46; CA 125; CANR 41, 55, 74, 124; DLB 299; MTCW 2; SATA 109; YAW
Spielberg, Peter 1929- .... **CLC 6**
 See also CA 5-8R; CANR 4, 48; DLBY 1981
Spielberg, Steven 1947- .... **CLC 20, 188**
 See also AAYA 8, 24; CA 77-80; CANR 32; SATA 32
Spillane, Frank Morrison 1918-
 See Spillane, Mickey
 See also CA 25-28R; CANR 28, 63, 125; DA3; MTCW 1, 2; SATA 66
Spillane, Mickey .... **CLC 3, 13**
 See Spillane, Frank Morrison
 See also BPFB 3; CMW 4; DLB 226; MSW; MTCW 2
Spinoza, Benedictus de 1632-1677 .. **LC 9, 58**
Spinrad, Norman (Richard) 1940- ... **CLC 46**
 See also BPFB 3; CA 37-40R; CAAS 19; CANR 20, 91; DLB 8; INT CANR-20; SFW 4
Spitteler, Carl (Friedrich Georg) 1845-1924 .... **TCLC 12**
 See also CA 109; DLB 129; EWL 3
Spivack, Kathleen (Romola Drucker) 1938- .... **CLC 6**
 See also CA 49-52
Spoto, Donald 1941- .... **CLC 39**
 See also CA 65-68; CANR 11, 57, 93
Springsteen, Bruce (F.) 1949- .... **CLC 17**
 See also CA 111
Spurling, (Susan) Hilary 1940- .... **CLC 34**
 See also CA 104; CANR 25, 52, 94
Spyker, John Howland
 See Elman, Richard (Martin)
Squared, A.
 See Abbott, Edwin A.
Squires, (James) Radcliffe 1917-1993 .... **CLC 51**
 See also CA 1-4R; 140; CANR 6, 21
Srivastava, Dhanpat Rai 1880(?)-1936
 See Premchand
 See also CA 118; 197
Stacy, Donald
 See Pohl, Frederik
Stael
 See Stael-Holstein, Anne Louise Germaine Necker
 See also EW 5; RGWL 2, 3

Stael, Germaine de
 See Stael-Holstein, Anne Louise Germaine Necker
 See also DLB 119, 192; FW; GFL 1789 to the Present; TWA
Stael-Holstein, Anne Louise Germaine Necker 1766-1817 .... **NCLC 3, 91**
 See Stael; Stael, Germaine de
Stafford, Jean 1915-1979 .. **CLC 4, 7, 19, 68; SSC 26, 86**
 See also CA 1-4R; 85-88; CANR 3, 65; DLB 2, 173; MTCW 1, 2; RGAL 4; RGSF 2; SATA-Obit 22; TCWW 2; TUS
Stafford, William (Edgar) 1914-1993 .... **CLC 4, 7, 29**
 See also AMWS 11; CA 5-8R; 142; CAAS 3; CANR 5, 22; DAM POET; DLB 5, 206; EXPP; INT CANR-22; PFS 2, 8, 16; RGAL 4; WP
Stagnelius, Eric Johan 1793-1823 . **NCLC 61**
Staines, Trevor
 See Brunner, John (Kilian Houston)
Stairs, Gordon
 See Austin, Mary (Hunter)
 See also TCWW 2
Stalin, Joseph 1879-1953 .... **TCLC 92**
Stampa, Gaspara c. 1524-1554 .... **PC 43; LC 114**
 See also RGWL 2, 3
Stampflinger, K. A.
 See Benjamin, Walter
Stancykowna
 See Szymborska, Wislawa
Standing Bear, Luther 1868(?)-1939(?) .... **NNAL**
 See also CA 113; 144; DAM MULT
Stanislavsky, Konstantin 1863-1938 .... **TCLC 167**
 See also CA 118
Stannard, Martin 1947- .... **CLC 44**
 See also CA 142; DLB 155
Stanton, Elizabeth Cady 1815-1902 .... **TCLC 73**
 See also CA 171; DLB 79; FW
Stanton, Maura 1946- .... **CLC 9**
 See also CA 89-92; CANR 15, 123; DLB 120
Stanton, Schuyler
 See Baum, L(yman) Frank
Stapledon, (William) Olaf 1886-1950 .... **TCLC 22**
 See also CA 111; 162; DLB 15, 255; SFW 4
Starbuck, George (Edwin) 1931-1996 .... **CLC 53**
 See also CA 21-24R; 153; CANR 23; DAM POET
Stark, Richard
 See Westlake, Donald E(dwin)
Staunton, Schuyler
 See Baum, L(yman) Frank
Stead, Christina (Ellen) 1902-1983 ... **CLC 2, 5, 8, 32, 80**
 See also BRWS 4; CA 13-16R; 109; CANR 33, 40; DLB 260; EWL 3; FW; MTCW 1, 2; RGEL 2; RGSF 2; WWE 1
Stead, William Thomas 1849-1912 .... **TCLC 48**
 See also CA 167
Stebnitsky, M.
 See Leskov, Nikolai (Semyonovich)
Steele, Sir Richard 1672-1729 .... **LC 18**
 See also BRW 3; CDBLB 1660-1789; DLB 84, 101; RGEL 2; WLIT 3
Steele, Timothy (Reid) 1948- .... **CLC 45**
 See also CA 93-96; CANR 16, 50, 92; CP 7; DLB 120, 282

Steffens, (Joseph) Lincoln
1866-1936 .... **TCLC 20**
See also CA 117; 198; DLB 303

Stegner, Wallace (Earle) 1909-1993 .. **CLC 9,
49, 81; SSC 27**
See also AITN 1; AMWS 4; ANW; BEST
90:3; BPFB 3; CA 1-4R; 141; CAAS 9;
CANR 1, 21, 46; DAM NOV; DLB 9,
206, 275; DLBY 1993; EWL 3; MTCW
1, 2; RGAL 4; TCWW 2; TUS

Stein, Gertrude 1874-1946 .... **DC 19; PC 18;
SSC 42; TCLC 1, 6, 28, 48; WLC**
See also AMW; AMWC 2; CA 104; 132;
CANR 108; CDALB 1917-1929; DA;
DA3; DAB; DAC; DAM MST, NOV,
POET; DLB 4, 54, 86, 228; DLBD 15;
EWL 3; EXPS; GLL 1; MAWW; MTCW
1, 2; NCFS 4; RGAL 4; RGSF 2; SSFS 5;
TUS; WP

Steinbeck, John (Ernst) 1902-1968 ... **CLC 1,
5, 9, 13, 21, 34, 45, 75, 124; SSC 11, 37,
77; TCLC 135; WLC**
See also AAYA 12; AMW; BPFB 3; BYA 2,
3, 13; CA 1-4R; 25-28R; CANR 1, 35;
CDALB 1929-1941; DA; DA3; DAB;
DAC; DAM DRAM, MST, NOV; DLB 7,
9, 212, 275, 309; DLBD 2; EWL 3;
EXPS; LAIT 3; MTCW 1, 2; NFS 1, 5, 7,
17, 19; RGAL 4; RGSF 2; RHW; SATA
9; SSFS 3, 6; TCWW 2; TUS; WYA;
YABC

Steinem, Gloria 1934- .... **CLC 63**
See also CA 53-56; CANR 28, 51; DLB
246; FW; MTCW 1, 2

Steiner, George 1929- .... **CLC 24**
See also CA 73-76; CANR 31, 67, 108;
DAM NOV; DLB 67, 299; EWL 3;
MTCW 1, 2; SATA 62

Steiner, K. Leslie
See Delany, Samuel R(ay), Jr.

Steiner, Rudolf 1861-1925 .... **TCLC 13**
See also CA 107

Stendhal 1783-1842 .. **NCLC 23, 46; SSC 27;
WLC**
See also DA; DA3; DAB; DAC; DAM
MST, NOV; DLB 119; EW 5; GFL 1789
to the Present; RGWL 2, 3; TWA

Stephen, Adeline Virginia
See Woolf, (Adeline) Virginia

Stephen, Sir Leslie 1832-1904 .... **TCLC 23**
See also BRW 5; CA 123; DLB 57, 144,
190

Stephen, Sir Leslie
See Stephen, Sir Leslie

Stephen, Virginia
See Woolf, (Adeline) Virginia

Stephens, James 1882(?)-1950 .... **SSC 50;
TCLC 4**
See also CA 104; 192; DLB 19, 153, 162;
EWL 3; FANT; RGEL 2; SUFW

Stephens, Reed
See Donaldson, Stephen R(eeder)

Steptoe, Lydia
See Barnes, Djuna
See also GLL 1

Sterchi, Beat 1949- .... **CLC 65**
See also CA 203

Sterling, Brett
See Bradbury, Ray (Douglas); Hamilton,
Edmond

Sterling, Bruce 1954- .... **CLC 72**
See also CA 119; CANR 44, 135; SCFW 2;
SFW 4

Sterling, George 1869-1926 .... **TCLC 20**
See also CA 117; 165; DLB 54

Stern, Gerald 1925- .... **CLC 40, 100**
See also AMWS 9; CA 81-84; CANR 28,
94; CP 7; DLB 105; RGAL 4

Stern, Richard (Gustave) 1928- ... **CLC 4, 39**
See also CA 1-4R; CANR 1, 25, 52, 120;
CN 7; DLB 218; DLBY 1987; INT
CANR-25

Sternberg, Josef von 1894-1969 .... **CLC 20**
See also CA 81-84

Sterne, Laurence 1713-1768 .... **LC 2, 48;
WLC**
See also BRW 3; BRWC 1; CDBLB 1660-
1789; DA; DAB; DAC; DAM MST, NOV;
DLB 39; RGEL 2; TEA

Sternheim, (William Adolf) Carl
1878-1942 .... **TCLC 8**
See also CA 105; 193; DLB 56, 118; EWL
3; RGWL 2, 3

Stevens, Mark 1951- .... **CLC 34**
See also CA 122

Stevens, Wallace 1879-1955 . **PC 6; TCLC 3,
12, 45; WLC**
See also AMW; AMWR 1; CA 104; 124;
CDALB 1929-1941; DA; DA3; DAB;
DAC; DAM MST, POET; DLB 54; EWL
3; EXPP; MTCW 1, 2; PAB; PFS 13, 16;
RGAL 4; TUS; WP

Stevenson, Anne (Katharine) 1933- .. **CLC 7,
33**
See also BRWS 6; CA 17-20R; CAAS 9;
CANR 9, 33, 123; CP 7; CWP; DLB 40;
MTCW 1; RHW

Stevenson, Robert Louis (Balfour)
1850-1894 ...... **NCLC 5, 14, 63; SSC 11,
51; WLC**
See also AAYA 24; BPFB 3; BRW 5;
BRWC 1; BRWR 1; BYA 1, 2, 4, 13; CD-
BLB 1890-1914; CLR 10, 11; DA; DA3;
DAB; DAC; DAM MST, NOV; DLB 18,
57, 141, 156, 174; DLBD 13; HGG;
JRDA; LAIT 1, 3; MAICYA 1, 2; NFS
11, 20; RGEL 2; RGSF 2; SATA 100;
SUFW; TEA; WCH; WLIT 4; WYA;
YABC 2; YAW

Stewart, J(ohn) I(nnes) M(ackintosh)
1906-1994 .... **CLC 7, 14, 32**
See Innes, Michael
See also CA 85-88; 147; CAAS 3; CANR
47; CMW 4; MTCW 1, 2

Stewart, Mary (Florence Elinor)
1916- .... **CLC 7, 35, 117**
See also AAYA 29; BPFB 3; CA 1-4R;
CANR 1, 59, 130; CMW 4; CPW; DAB;
FANT; RHW; SATA 12; YAW

Stewart, Mary Rainbow
See Stewart, Mary (Florence Elinor)

Stifle, June
See Campbell, Maria

Stifter, Adalbert 1805-1868 .. **NCLC 41; SSC
28**
See also CDWLB 2; DLB 133; RGSF 2;
RGWL 2, 3

Still, James 1906-2001 .... **CLC 49**
See also CA 65-68; 195; CAAS 17; CANR
10, 26; CSW; DLB 9; DLBY 01; SATA
29; SATA-Obit 127

Sting 1951-
See Sumner, Gordon Matthew
See also CA 167

Stirling, Arthur
See Sinclair, Upton (Beall)

Stitt, Milan 1941- .... **CLC 29**
See also CA 69-72

Stockton, Francis Richard 1834-1902
See Stockton, Frank R.
See also CA 108; 137; MAICYA 1, 2; SATA
44; SFW 4

Stockton, Frank R. .... **TCLC 47**
See Stockton, Francis Richard
See also BYA 4, 13; DLB 42, 74; DLBD
13; EXPS; SATA-Brief 32; SSFS 3;
SUFW; WCH

Stoddard, Charles
See Kuttner, Henry

Stoker, Abraham 1847-1912
See Stoker, Bram
See also CA 105; 150; DA; DA3; DAC;
DAM MST, NOV; HGG; SATA 29

Stoker, Bram .. **SSC 62; TCLC 8, 144; WLC**
See Stoker, Abraham
See also AAYA 23; BPFB 3; BRWS 3; BYA
5; CDBLB 1890-1914; DAB; DLB 304;
LATS 1:1; NFS 18; RGEL 2; SUFW;
TEA; WLIT 4

Stolz, Mary (Slattery) 1920- .... **CLC 12**
See also AAYA 8; AITN 1; CA 5-8R;
CANR 13, 41, 112; JRDA; MAICYA 1,
2; SAAS 3; SATA 10, 71, 133; YAW

Stone, Irving 1903-1989 .... **CLC 7**
See also AITN 1; BPFB 3; CA 1-4R; 129;
CAAS 3; CANR 1, 23; CPW; DA3; DAM
POP; INT CANR-23; MTCW 1, 2; RHW;
SATA 3; SATA-Obit 64

Stone, Oliver (William) 1946- .... **CLC 73**
See also AAYA 15; CA 110; CANR 55, 125

Stone, Robert (Anthony) 1937- ... **CLC 5, 23,
42, 175**
See also AMWS 5; BPFB 3; CA 85-88;
CANR 23, 66, 95; CN 7; DLB 152; EWL
3; INT CANR-23; MTCW 1

Stone, Ruth 1915- .... **PC 53**
See also CA 45-48; CANR 2, 91; CP 7;
CSW; DLB 105; PFS 19

Stone, Zachary
See Follett, Ken(neth Martin)

Stoppard, Tom 1937- ... **CLC 1, 3, 4, 5, 8, 15,
29, 34, 63, 91; DC 6; WLC**
See also BRWC 1; BRWR 2; BRWS 1; CA
81-84; CANR 39, 67, 125; CBD; CD 5;
CDBLB 1960 to Present; DA; DA3;
DAB; DAC; DAM DRAM, MST; DFS 2,
5, 8, 11, 13, 16; DLB 13, 233; DLBY
1985; EWL 3; LATS 1:2; MTCW 1, 2;
RGEL 2; TEA; WLIT 4

Storey, David (Malcolm) 1933- . **CLC 2, 4, 5,
8**
See also BRWS 1; CA 81-84; CANR 36;
CBD; CD 5; CN 7; DAM DRAM; DLB
13, 14, 207, 245; EWL 3; MTCW 1;
RGEL 2

Storm, Hyemeyohsts 1935- ... **CLC 3; NNAL**
See also CA 81-84; CANR 45; DAM MULT

Storm, (Hans) Theodor (Woldsen)
1817-1888 .... **NCLC 1; SSC 27**
See also CDWLB 2; DLB 129; EW; RGSF
2; RGWL 2, 3

Storni, Alfonsina 1892-1938 . **HLC 2; PC 33;
TCLC 5**
See also CA 104; 131; DAM MULT; DLB
283; HW 1; LAW

Stoughton, William 1631-1701 .... **LC 38**
See also DLB 24

Stout, Rex (Todhunter) 1886-1975 ..... **CLC 3**
See also AITN 2; BPFB 3; CA 61-64;
CANR 71; CMW 4; DLB 306; MSW;
RGAL 4

Stow, (Julian) Randolph 1935- ... **CLC 23, 48**
See also CA 13-16R; CANR 33; CN 7;
DLB 260; MTCW 1; RGEL 2

Stowe, Harriet (Elizabeth) Beecher
1811-1896 .... **NCLC 3, 50, 133; WLC**
See also AAYA 53; AMWS 1; CDALB
1865-1917; DA; DA3; DAC; DAM; DAM
MST, NOV; DLB 1, 12, 42, 74, 189, 239,
243; EXPN; JRDA; LAIT 2; MAICYA 1,
2; NFS 6; RGAL 4; TUS; YABC 1

Strabo c. 64B.C.-c. 25 .... **CMLC 37**
See also DLB 176

Strachey, (Giles) Lytton
1880-1932 .... **TCLC 12**
See also BRWS 2; CA 110; 178; DLB 149;
DLBD 10; EWL 3; MTCW 2; NCFS 4

Sylvia
See Ashton-Warner, Sylvia (Constance)

Symmes, Robert Edward
See Duncan, Robert (Edward)

Symonds, John Addington
1840-1893 .... **NCLC 34**
See also DLB 57, 144

Symons, Arthur 1865-1945 .... **TCLC 11**
See also CA 107; 189; DLB 19, 57, 149;
RGEL 2

Symons, Julian (Gustave)
1912-1994 .... **CLC 2, 14, 32**
See also CA 49-52; 147; CAAS 3; CANR
3, 33, 59; CMW 4; DLB 87, 155; DLBY
1992; MSW; MTCW 1

Synge, (Edmund) J(ohn) M(illington)
1871-1909 .... **DC 2; TCLC 6, 37**
See also BRW 6; BRWR 1; CA 104; 141;
CDBLB 1890-1914; DAM DRAM; DFS
18; DLB 10, 19; EWL 3; RGEL 2; TEA;
WLIT 4

Syruc, J.
See Milosz, Czeslaw

Szirtes, George 1948- .... **CLC 46; PC 51**
See also CA 109; CANR 27, 61, 117; CP 7

Szymborska, Wislawa 1923- ... **CLC 99, 190;
PC 44**
See also CA 154; CANR 91, 133; CDWLB
4; CWP; CWW 2; DA3; DLB 232; DLBY
1996; EWL 3; MTCW 2; PFS 15; RGWL
3

T. O., Nik
See Annensky, Innokenty (Fyodorovich)

Tabori, George 1914- .... **CLC 19**
See also CA 49-52; CANR 4, 69; CBD; CD
5; DLB 245

Tacitus c. 55-c. 117 .... **CMLC 56**
See also AW 2; CDWLB 1; DLB 211;
RGWL 2, 3

Tagore, Rabindranath 1861-1941 .... **PC 8;
SSC 48; TCLC 3, 53**
See also CA 104; 120; DA3; DAM DRAM,
POET; EWL 3; MTCW 1, 2; PFS 18;
RGEL 2; RGSF 2; RGWL 2, 3; TWA

Taine, Hippolyte Adolphe
1828-1893 .... **NCLC 15**
See also EW 7; GFL 1789 to the Present

Talayesva, Don C. 1890-(?) .... **NNAL**

Talese, Gay 1932- .... **CLC 37**
See also AITN 1; CA 1-4R; CANR 9, 58;
DLB 185; INT CANR-9; MTCW 1, 2

Tallent, Elizabeth (Ann) 1954- .... **CLC 45**
See also CA 117; CANR 72; DLB 130

Tallmountain, Mary 1918-1997 .... **NNAL**
See also CA 146; 161; DLB 193

Tally, Ted 1952- .... **CLC 42**
See also CA 120; 124; CAD; CANR 125;
CD 5; INT CA-124

Talvik, Heiti 1904-1947 .... **TCLC 87**
See also EWL 3

Tamayo y Baus, Manuel
1829-1898 .... **NCLC 1**

Tammsaare, A(nton) H(ansen)
1878-1940 .... **TCLC 27**
See also CA 164; CDWLB 4; DLB 220;
EWL 3

Tam'si, Tchicaya U
See Tchicaya, Gerald Felix

Tan, Amy (Ruth) 1952- . **AAL; CLC 59, 120,
151**
See also AAYA 9, 48; AMWS 10; BEST
89:3; BPFB 3; CA 136; CANR 54, 105,
132; CDALBS; CN 7; CPW 1; DA3;
DAM MULT, NOV, POP; DLB 173;
EXPN; FW; LAIT 3, 5; MTCW 2; NFS
1, 13, 16; RGAL 4; SATA 75; SSFS 9;
YAW

Tandem, Felix
See Spitteler, Carl (Friedrich Georg)

Tanizaki, Jun'ichiro 1886-1965 ... **CLC 8, 14,
28; SSC 21**
See Tanizaki Jun'ichiro
See also CA 93-96; 25-28R; MJW; MTCW
2; RGSF 2; RGWL 2

Tanizaki Jun'ichiro
See Tanizaki, Jun'ichiro
See also DLB 180; EWL 3

Tannen, Deborah F. 1945- .... **CLC 206**
See also CA 118; CANR 95

Tanner, William
See Amis, Kingsley (William)

Tao Lao
See Storni, Alfonsina

Tapahonso, Luci 1953- .... **NNAL; PC 65**
See also CA 145; CANR 72, 127; DLB 175

Tarantino, Quentin (Jerome)
1963- .... **CLC 125**
See also AAYA 58; CA 171; CANR 125

Tarassoff, Lev
See Troyat, Henri

Tarbell, Ida M(inerva) 1857-1944 . **TCLC 40**
See also CA 122; 181; DLB 47

Tarkington, (Newton) Booth
1869-1946 .... **TCLC 9**
See also BPFB 3; BYA 3; CA 110; 143;
CWRI 5; DLB 9, 102; MTCW 2; RGAL
4; SATA 17

Tarkovskii, Andrei Arsen'evich
See Tarkovsky, Andrei (Arsenyevich)

Tarkovsky, Andrei (Arsenyevich)
1932-1986 .... **CLC 75**
See also CA 127

Tartt, Donna 1963- .... **CLC 76**
See also AAYA 56; CA 142

Tasso, Torquato 1544-1595 .... **LC 5, 94**
See also EFS 2; EW 2; RGWL 2, 3

Tate, (John Orley) Allen 1899-1979 .. **CLC 2,
4, 6, 9, 11, 14, 24; PC 50**
See also AMW; CA 5-8R; 85-88; CANR
32, 108; DLB 4, 45, 63; DLBD 17; EWL
3; MTCW 1, 2; RGAL 4; RHW

Tate, Ellalice
See Hibbert, Eleanor Alice Burford

Tate, James (Vincent) 1943- ..... **CLC 2, 6, 25**
See also CA 21-24R; CANR 29, 57, 114;
CP 7; DLB 5, 169; EWL 3; PFS 10, 15;
RGAL 4; WP

Tate, Nahum 1652(?)-1715 .... **LC 109**
See also DLB 80; RGEL 2

Tauler, Johannes c. 1300-1361 ...... **CMLC 37**
See also DLB 179; LMFS 1

Tavel, Ronald 1940- .... **CLC 6**
See also CA 21-24R; CAD; CANR 33; CD
5

Taviani, Paolo 1931- .... **CLC 70**
See also CA 153

Taylor, Bayard 1825-1878 .... **NCLC 89**
See also DLB 3, 189, 250, 254; RGAL 4

Taylor, C(ecil) P(hilip) 1929-1981 .... **CLC 27**
See also CA 25-28R; 105; CANR 47; CBD

Taylor, Edward 1642(?)-1729 . **LC 11; PC 63**
See also AMW; DA; DAB; DAC; DAM
MST, POET; DLB 24; EXPP; RGAL 4;
TUS

Taylor, Eleanor Ross 1920- .... **CLC 5**
See also CA 81-84; CANR 70

Taylor, Elizabeth 1932-1975 ..... **CLC 2, 4, 29**
See also CA 13-16R; CANR 9, 70; DLB
139; MTCW 1; RGEL 2; SATA 13

Taylor, Frederick Winslow
1856-1915 .... **TCLC 76**
See also CA 188

Taylor, Henry (Splawn) 1942- .... **CLC 44**
See also CA 33-36R; CAAS 7; CANR 31;
CP 7; DLB 5; PFS 10

Taylor, Kamala (Purnaiya) 1924-2004
See Markandaya, Kamala
See also CA 77-80; 227; NFS 13

Taylor, Mildred D(elois) 1943- .... **CLC 21**
See also AAYA 10, 47; BW 1; BYA 3, 8;
CA 85-88; CANR 25, 115; CLR 9, 59,
90; CSW; DLB 52; JRDA; LAIT 3; MAI-
CYA 1, 2; SAAS 5; SATA 135; WYA;
YAW

Taylor, Peter (Hillsman) 1917-1994 .. **CLC 1,
4, 18, 37, 44, 50, 71; SSC 10, 84**
See also AMWS 5; BPFB 3; CA 13-16R;
147; CANR 9, 50; CSW; DLB 218, 278;
DLBY 1981, 1994; EWL 3; EXPS; INT
CANR-9; MTCW 1, 2; RGSF 2; SSFS 9;
TUS

Taylor, Robert Lewis 1912-1998 .... **CLC 14**
See also CA 1-4R; 170; CANR 3, 64; SATA
10

Tchekhov, Anton
See Chekhov, Anton (Pavlovich)

Tchicaya, Gerald Felix 1931-1988 .. **CLC 101**
See Tchicaya U Tam'si
See also CA 129; 125; CANR 81

Tchicaya U Tam'si
See Tchicaya, Gerald Felix
See also EWL 3

Teasdale, Sara 1884-1933 .... **PC 31; TCLC 4**
See also CA 104; 163; DLB 45; GLL 1;
PFS 14; RGAL 4; SATA 32; TUS

Tecumseh 1768-1813 .... **NNAL**
See also DAM MULT

Tegner, Esaias 1782-1846 .... **NCLC 2**

Fujiwara no Teika 1162-1241 .... **CMLC 73**
See also DLB 203

Teilhard de Chardin, (Marie Joseph) Pierre
1881-1955 .... **TCLC 9**
See also CA 105; 210; GFL 1789 to the
Present

Temple, Ann
See Mortimer, Penelope (Ruth)

Tennant, Emma (Christina) 1937- .. **CLC 13,
52**
See also BRWS 9; CA 65-68; CAAS 9;
CANR 10, 38, 59, 88; CN 7; DLB 14;
EWL 3; SFW 4

Tenneshaw, S. M.
See Silverberg, Robert

Tenney, Tabitha Gilman
1762-1837 .... **NCLC 122**
See also DLB 37, 200

Tennyson, Alfred 1809-1892 ... **NCLC 30, 65,
115; PC 6; WLC**
See also AAYA 50; BRW 4; CDBLB 1832-
1890; DA; DA3; DAB; DAC; DAM MST,
POET; DLB 32; EXPP; PAB; PFS 1, 2, 4,
11, 15, 19; RGEL 2; TEA; WLIT 4; WP

Teran, Lisa St. Aubin de .... **CLC 36**
See St. Aubin de Teran, Lisa

Terence c. 184B.C.-c. 159B.C. ...... **CMLC 14;
DC 7**
See also AW 1; CDWLB 1; DLB 211;
RGWL 2, 3; TWA

Teresa de Jesus, St. 1515-1582 .... **LC 18**

Terkel, Louis 1912-
See Terkel, Studs
See also CA 57-60; CANR 18, 45, 67, 132;
DA3; MTCW 1, 2

Terkel, Studs .... **CLC 38**
See Terkel, Louis
See also AAYA 32; AITN 1; MTCW 2; TUS

Terry, C. V.
See Slaughter, Frank G(ill)

Terry, Megan 1932- .... **CLC 19; DC 13**
See also CA 77-80; CABS 3; CAD; CANR
43; CD 5; CWD; DFS 18; DLB 7, 249;
GLL 2

Tertullian c. 155-c. 245 .... **CMLC 29**

Tertz, Abram
See Sinyavsky, Andrei (Donatevich)
See also RGSF 2

Vaihinger, Hans 1852-1933 .... **TCLC 71**
　See also CA 116; 166
Valdez, Luis (Miguel) 1940- ..... **CLC 84; DC 10; HLC 2**
　See also CA 101; CAD; CANR 32, 81; CD 5; DAM MULT; DFS 5; DLB 122; EWL 3; HW 1; LAIT 4; LLW 1
Valenzuela, Luisa 1938- .... **CLC 31, 104; HLCS 2; SSC 14, 82**
　See also CA 101; CANR 32, 65, 123; CD-WLB 3; CWW 2; DAM MULT; DLB 113; EWL 3; FW; HW 1, 2; LAW; RGSF 2; RGWL 3
Valera y Alcala-Galiano, Juan 1824-1905 .... **TCLC 10**
　See also CA 106
Valerius Maximus fl. 20- .... **CMLC 64**
　See also DLB 211
Valery, (Ambroise) Paul (Toussaint Jules) 1871-1945 .... **PC 9; TCLC 4, 15**
　See also CA 104; 122; DA3; DAM POET; DLB 258; EW 8; EWL 3; GFL 1789 to the Present; MTCW 1, 2; RGWL 2, 3; TWA
Valle-Inclan, Ramon (Maria) del 1866-1936 .... **HLC 2; TCLC 5**
　See also CA 106; 153; CANR 80; DAM MULT; DLB 134; EW 8; EWL 3; HW 2; RGSF 2; RGWL 2, 3
Vallejo, Antonio Buero
　See Buero Vallejo, Antonio
Vallejo, Cesar (Abraham) 1892-1938 .... **HLC 2; TCLC 3, 56**
　See also CA 105; 153; DAM MULT; DLB 290; EWL 3; HW 1; LAW; RGWL 2, 3
Valles, Jules 1832-1885 .... **NCLC 71**
　See also DLB 123; GFL 1789 to the Present
Vallette, Marguerite Eymery 1860-1953 .... **TCLC 67**
　See Rachilde
　See also CA 182; DLB 123, 192
Valle Y Pena, Ramon del
　See Valle-Inclan, Ramon (Maria) del
Van Ash, Cay 1918-1994 .... **CLC 34**
　See also CA 220
Vanbrugh, Sir John 1664-1726 .... **LC 21**
　See also BRW 2; DAM DRAM; DLB 80; IDTP; RGEL 2
Van Campen, Karl
　See Campbell, John W(ood, Jr.)
Vance, Gerald
　See Silverberg, Robert
Vance, Jack .... **CLC 35**
　See Vance, John Holbrook
　See also DLB 8; FANT; SCFW 2; SFW 4; SUFW 1, 2
Vance, John Holbrook 1916-
　See Queen, Ellery; Vance, Jack
　See also CA 29-32R; CANR 17, 65; CMW 4; MTCW 1
Van Den Bogarde, Derek Jules Gaspard Ulric Niven 1921-1999 .... **CLC 14**
　See Bogarde, Dirk
　See also CA 77-80; 179
Vandenburgh, Jane .... **CLC 59**
　See also CA 168
Vanderhaeghe, Guy 1951- .... **CLC 41**
　See also BPFB 3; CA 113; CANR 72
van der Post, Laurens (Jan) 1906-1996 .... **CLC 5**
　See also AFW; CA 5-8R; 155; CANR 35; CN 7; DLB 204; RGEL 2
van de Wetering, Janwillem 1931- ... **CLC 47**
　See also CA 49-52; CANR 4, 62, 90; CMW 4
Van Dine, S. S. .... **TCLC 23**
　See Wright, Willard Huntington
　See also DLB 306; MSW

Van Doren, Carl (Clinton) 1885-1950 .... **TCLC 18**
　See also CA 111; 168
Van Doren, Mark 1894-1972 .... **CLC 6, 10**
　See also CA 1-4R; 37-40R; CANR 3; DLB 45, 284; MTCW 1, 2; RGAL 4
Van Druten, John (William) 1901-1957 .... **TCLC 2**
　See also CA 104; 161; DLB 10; RGAL 4
Van Duyn, Mona (Jane) 1921- ...... **CLC 3, 7, 63, 116**
　See also CA 9-12R; CANR 7, 38, 60, 116; CP 7; CWP; DAM POET; DLB 5; PFS 20
Van Dyne, Edith
　See Baum, L(yman) Frank
van Itallie, Jean-Claude 1936- .... **CLC 3**
　See also CA 45-48; CAAS 2; CAD; CANR 1, 48; CD 5; DLB 7
Van Loot, Cornelius Obenchain
　See Roberts, Kenneth (Lewis)
van Ostaijen, Paul 1896-1928 .... **TCLC 33**
　See also CA 163
Van Peebles, Melvin 1932- .... **CLC 2, 20**
　See also BW 2, 3; CA 85-88; CANR 27, 67, 82; DAM MULT
van Schendel, Arthur(-Francois-Emile) 1874-1946 .... **TCLC 56**
　See also EWL 3
Vansittart, Peter 1920- .... **CLC 42**
　See also CA 1-4R; CANR 3, 49, 90; CN 7; RHW
Van Vechten, Carl 1880-1964 ... **CLC 33; HR 3**
　See also AMWS 2; CA 183; 89-92; DLB 4, 9, 51; RGAL 4
van Vogt, A(lfred) E(lton) 1912-2000 . **CLC 1**
　See also BPFB 3; BYA 13, 14; CA 21-24R; 190; CANR 28; DLB 8, 251; SATA 14; SATA-Obit 124; SCFW; SFW 4
Vara, Madeleine
　See Jackson, Laura (Riding)
Varda, Agnes 1928- .... **CLC 16**
　See also CA 116; 122
Vargas Llosa, (Jorge) Mario (Pedro) 1939- .... **CLC 3, 6, 9, 10, 15, 31, 42, 85, 181; HLC 2**
　See Llosa, (Jorge) Mario (Pedro) Vargas
　See also BPFB 3; CA 73-76; CANR 18, 32, 42, 67, 116; CDWLB 3; CWW 2; DA; DA3; DAB; DAC; DAM MST, MULT, NOV; DLB 145; DNFS 2; EWL 3; HW 1, 2; LAIT 5; LATS 1:2; LAW; LAWS 1; MTCW 1, 2; RGWL 2; SSFS 14; TWA; WLIT 1
Varnhagen von Ense, Rahel 1771-1833 .... **NCLC 130**
　See also DLB 90
Vasari, Giorgio 1511-1574 .... **LC 114**
Vasiliu, George
　See Bacovia, George
Vasiliu, Gheorghe
　See Bacovia, George
　See also CA 123; 189
Vassa, Gustavus
　See Equiano, Olaudah
Vassilikos, Vassilis 1933- .... **CLC 4, 8**
　See also CA 81-84; CANR 75; EWL 3
Vaughan, Henry 1621-1695 .... **LC 27**
　See also BRW 2; DLB 131; PAB; RGEL 2
Vaughn, Stephanie .... **CLC 62**
Vazov, Ivan (Minchov) 1850-1921 . **TCLC 25**
　See also CA 121; 167; CDWLB 4; DLB 147
Veblen, Thorstein B(unde) 1857-1929 .... **TCLC 31**
　See also AMWS 1; CA 115; 165; DLB 246

Vega, Lope de 1562-1635 ... **HLCS 2; LC 23, 119**
　See also EW 2; RGWL 2, 3
Vendler, Helen (Hennessy) 1933- ... **CLC 138**
　See also CA 41-44R; CANR 25, 72; MTCW 1, 2
Venison, Alfred
　See Pound, Ezra (Weston Loomis)
Ventsel, Elena Sergeevna 1907-2002
　See Grekova, I.
　See also CA 154
Verdi, Marie de
　See Mencken, H(enry) L(ouis)
Verdu, Matilde
　See Cela, Camilo Jose
Verga, Giovanni (Carmelo) 1840-1922 .... **SSC 21; TCLC 3**
　See also CA 104; 123; CANR 101; EW 7; EWL 3; RGSF 2; RGWL 2, 3
Vergil 70B.C.-19B.C. ... **CMLC 9, 40; PC 12; WLCS**
　See Virgil
　See also AW 2; DA; DA3; DAB; DAC; DAM MST, POET; EFS 1; LMFS 1
Vergil, Polydore c. 1470-1555 .... **LC 108**
　See also DLB 132
Verhaeren, Emile (Adolphe Gustave) 1855-1916 .... **TCLC 12**
　See also CA 109; EWL 3; GFL 1789 to the Present
Verlaine, Paul (Marie) 1844-1896 .. **NCLC 2, 51; PC 2, 32**
　See also DAM POET; DLB 217; EW 7; GFL 1789 to the Present; LMFS 2; RGWL 2, 3; TWA
Verne, Jules (Gabriel) 1828-1905 ... **TCLC 6, 52**
　See also AAYA 16; BYA 4; CA 110; 131; CLR 88; DA3; DLB 123; GFL 1789 to the Present; JRDA; LAIT 2; LMFS 2; MAICYA 1, 2; RGWL 2, 3; SATA 21; SCFW; SFW 4; TWA; WCH
Verus, Marcus Annius
　See Aurelius, Marcus
Very, Jones 1813-1880 .... **NCLC 9**
　See also DLB 1, 243; RGAL 4
Vesaas, Tarjei 1897-1970 .... **CLC 48**
　See also CA 190; 29-32R; DLB 297; EW 11; EWL 3; RGWL 3
Vialis, Gaston
　See Simenon, Georges (Jacques Christian)
Vian, Boris 1920-1959(?) .... **TCLC 9**
　See also CA 106; 164; CANR 111; DLB 72; EWL 3; GFL 1789 to the Present; MTCW 2; RGWL 2, 3
Viaud, (Louis Marie) Julien 1850-1923
　See Loti, Pierre
　See also CA 107
Vicar, Henry
　See Felsen, Henry Gregor
Vicente, Gil 1465-c. 1536 .... **LC 99**
　See also DLB 287; RGWL 2, 3
Vicker, Angus
　See Felsen, Henry Gregor
Vidal, (Eugene Luther) Gore 1925- .. **CLC 2, 4, 6, 8, 10, 22, 33, 72, 142**
　See Box, Edgar
　See also AITN 1; AMWS 4; BEST 90:2; BPFB 3; CA 5-8R; CAD; CANR 13, 45, 65, 100, 132; CD 5; CDALBS; CN 7; CPW; DA3; DAM NOV, POP; DFS 2; DLB 6, 152; EWL 3; INT CANR-13; MTCW 1, 2; RGAL 4; RHW; TUS
Viereck, Peter (Robert Edwin) 1916- .... **CLC 4; PC 27**
　See also CA 1-4R; CANR 1, 47; CP 7; DLB 5; PFS 9, 14

Walker, Alice (Malsenior) 1944- .... **BLC 3; CLC 5, 6, 9, 19, 27, 46, 58, 103, 167; PC 30; SSC 5; WLCS**
See also AAYA 3, 33; AFAW 1, 2; AMWS 3; BEST 89:4; BPFB 3; BW 2, 3; CA 37-40R; CANR 9, 27, 49, 66, 82, 131; CDALB 1968-1988; CN 7; CPW; CSW; DA; DA3; DAB; DAC; DAM MST, MULT, NOV, POET, POP; DLB 6, 33, 143; EWL 3; EXPN; EXPS; FW; INT CANR-27; LAIT 3; MAWW; MTCW 1, 2; NFS 5; RGAL 4; RGSF 2; SATA 31; SSFS 2, 11; TUS; YAW

Walker, David Harry 1911-1992 ...... **CLC 14**
See also CA 1-4R; 137; CANR 1; CWRI 5; SATA 8; SATA-Obit 71

Walker, Edward Joseph 1934-2004
See Walker, Ted
See also CA 21-24R; 226; CANR 12, 28, 53; CP 7

Walker, George F. 1947- .... **CLC 44, 61**
See also CA 103; CANR 21, 43, 59; CD 5; DAB; DAC; DAM MST; DLB 60

Walker, Joseph A. 1935- .... **CLC 19**
See also BW 1, 3; CA 89-92; CAD; CANR 26; CD 5; DAM DRAM, MST; DFS 12; DLB 38

Walker, Margaret (Abigail) 1915-1998 .... **BLC; CLC 1, 6; PC 20; TCLC 129**
See also AFAW 1, 2; BW 2, 3; CA 73-76; 172; CANR 26, 54, 76; CN 7; CP 7; CSW; DAM MULT; DLB 76, 152; EXPP; FW; MTCW 1, 2; RGAL 4; RHW

Walker, Ted .... **CLC 13**
See Walker, Edward Joseph
See also DLB 40

Wallace, David Foster 1962- ... **CLC 50, 114; SSC 68**
See also AAYA 50; AMWS 10; CA 132; CANR 59, 133; DA3; MTCW 2

Wallace, Dexter
See Masters, Edgar Lee

Wallace, (Richard Horatio) Edgar 1875-1932 .... **TCLC 57**
See also CA 115; 218; CMW 4; DLB 70; MSW; RGEL 2

Wallace, Irving 1916-1990 .... **CLC 7, 13**
See also AITN 1; BPFB 3; CA 1-4R; 132; CAAS 1; CANR 1, 27; CPW; DAM NOV, POP; INT CANR-27; MTCW 1, 2

Wallant, Edward Lewis 1926-1962 ... **CLC 5, 10**
See also CA 1-4R; CANR 22; DLB 2, 28, 143, 299; EWL 3; MTCW 1, 2; RGAL 4

Wallas, Graham 1858-1932 .... **TCLC 91**

Waller, Edmund 1606-1687 .... **LC 86**
See also BRW 2; DAM POET; DLB 126; PAB; RGEL 2

Walley, Byron
See Card, Orson Scott

Walpole, Horace 1717-1797 .... **LC 2, 49**
See also BRW 3; DLB 39, 104, 213; HGG; LMFS 1; RGEL 2; SUFW 1; TEA

Walpole, Hugh (Seymour) 1884-1941 .... **TCLC 5**
See also CA 104; 165; DLB 34; HGG; MTCW 2; RGEL 2; RHW

Walrond, Eric (Derwent) 1898-1966 .... **HR 3**
See also BW 1; CA 125; DLB 51

Walser, Martin 1927- .... **CLC 27, 183**
See also CA 57-60; CANR 8, 46; CWW 2; DLB 75, 124; EWL 3

Walser, Robert 1878-1956 ..... **SSC 20; TCLC 18**
See also CA 118; 165; CANR 100; DLB 66; EWL 3

Walsh, Gillian Paton
See Paton Walsh, Gillian

Walsh, Jill Paton .... **CLC 35**
See Paton Walsh, Gillian
See also CLR 2, 65; WYA

Walter, Villiam Christian
See Andersen, Hans Christian

Walters, Anna L(ee) 1946- .... **NNAL**
See also CA 73-76

Walther von der Vogelweide c. 1170-1228 .... **CMLC 56**

Walton, Izaak 1593-1683 .... **LC 72**
See also BRW 2; CDBLB Before 1660; DLB 151, 213; RGEL 2

Wambaugh, Joseph (Aloysius), Jr. 1937- .... **CLC 3, 18**
See also AITN 1; BEST 89:3; BPFB 3; CA 33-36R; CANR 42, 65, 115; CMW 4; CPW 1; DA3; DAM NOV, POP; DLB 6; DLBY 1983; MSW; MTCW 1, 2

Wang Wei 699(?)-761(?) .... **PC 18**
See also TWA

Warburton, William 1698-1779 .... **LC 97**
See also DLB 104

Ward, Arthur Henry Sarsfield 1883-1959
See Rohmer, Sax
See also CA 108; 173; CMW 4; HGG

Ward, Douglas Turner 1930- .... **CLC 19**
See also BW 1; CA 81-84; CAD; CANR 27; CD 5; DLB 7, 38

Ward, E. D.
See Lucas, E(dward) V(errall)

Ward, Mrs. Humphry 1851-1920
See Ward, Mary Augusta
See also RGEL 2

Ward, Mary Augusta 1851-1920 ... **TCLC 55**
See Ward, Mrs. Humphry
See also DLB 18

Ward, Nathaniel 1578(?)-1652 .... **LC 114**
See also DLB 24

Ward, Peter
See Faust, Frederick (Schiller)

Warhol, Andy 1928(?)-1987 .... **CLC 20**
See also AAYA 12; BEST 89:4; CA 89-92; 121; CANR 34

Warner, Francis (Robert le Plastrier) 1937- .... **CLC 14**
See also CA 53-56; CANR 11

Warner, Marina 1946- .... **CLC 59**
See also CA 65-68; CANR 21, 55, 118; CN 7; DLB 194

Warner, Rex (Ernest) 1905-1986 ...... **CLC 45**
See also CA 89-92; 119; DLB 15; RGEL 2; RHW

Warner, Susan (Bogert) 1819-1885 .... **NCLC 31, 146**
See also DLB 3, 42, 239, 250, 254

Warner, Sylvia (Constance) Ashton
See Ashton-Warner, Sylvia (Constance)

Warner, Sylvia Townsend 1893-1978 .. **CLC 7, 19; SSC 23; TCLC 131**
See also BRWS 7; CA 61-64; 77-80; CANR 16, 60, 104; DLB 34, 139; EWL 3; FANT; FW; MTCW 1, 2; RGEL 2; RGSF 2; RHW

Warren, Mercy Otis 1728-1814 ..... **NCLC 13**
See also DLB 31, 200; RGAL 4; TUS

Warren, Robert Penn 1905-1989 .. **CLC 1, 4, 6, 8, 10, 13, 18, 39, 53, 59; PC 37; SSC 4, 58; WLC**
See also AITN 1; AMW; AMWC 2; BPFB 3; BYA 1; CA 13-16R; 129; CANR 10, 47; CDALB 1968-1988; DA; DA3; DAB; DAC; DAM MST, NOV, POET; DLB 2, 48, 152; DLBY 1980, 1989; EWL 3; INT CANR-10; MTCW 1, 2; NFS 13; RGAL 4; RGSF 2; RHW; SATA 46; SATA-Obit 63; SSFS 8; TUS

Warrigal, Jack
See Furphy, Joseph

Warshofsky, Isaac
See Singer, Isaac Bashevis

Warton, Joseph 1722-1800 .... **NCLC 118**
See also DLB 104, 109; RGEL 2

Warton, Thomas 1728-1790 .... **LC 15, 82**
See also DAM POET; DLB 104, 109; RGEL 2

Waruk, Kona
See Harris, (Theodore) Wilson

Warung, Price .... **TCLC 45**
See Astley, William
See also DLB 230; RGEL 2

Warwick, Jarvis
See Garner, Hugh
See also CCA 1

Washington, Alex
See Harris, Mark

Washington, Booker T(aliaferro) 1856-1915 .... **BLC 3; TCLC 10**
See also BW 1; CA 114; 125; DA3; DAM MULT; LAIT 2; RGAL 4; SATA 28

Washington, George 1732-1799 .... **LC 25**
See also DLB 31

Wassermann, (Karl) Jakob 1873-1934 .... **TCLC 6**
See also CA 104; 163; DLB 66; EWL 3

Wasserstein, Wendy 1950- ... **CLC 32, 59, 90, 183; DC 4**
See also CA 121; 129; CABS 3; CAD; CANR 53, 75, 128; CD 5; CWD; DA3; DAM DRAM; DFS 5, 17; DLB 228; EWL 3; FW; INT CA-129; MTCW 2; SATA 94

Waterhouse, Keith (Spencer) 1929- . **CLC 47**
See also CA 5-8R; CANR 38, 67, 109; CBD; CN 7; DLB 13, 15; MTCW 1, 2

Waters, Frank (Joseph) 1902-1995 .. **CLC 88**
See also CA 5-8R; 149; CAAS 13; CANR 3, 18, 63, 121; DLB 212; DLBY 1986; RGAL 4; TCWW 2

Waters, Mary C. .... **CLC 70**

Waters, Roger 1944- .... **CLC 35**

Watkins, Frances Ellen
See Harper, Frances Ellen Watkins

Watkins, Gerrold
See Malzberg, Barry N(athaniel)

Watkins, Gloria Jean 1952(?)- .... **CLC 94**
See also BW 2; CA 143; CANR 87, 126; DLB 246; MTCW 2; SATA 115

Watkins, Paul 1964- .... **CLC 55**
See also CA 132; CANR 62, 98

Watkins, Vernon Phillips 1906-1967 .... **CLC 43**
See also CA 9-10; 25-28R; CAP 1; DLB 20; EWL 3; RGEL 2

Watson, Irving S.
See Mencken, H(enry) L(ouis)

Watson, John H.
See Farmer, Philip Jose

Watson, Richard F.
See Silverberg, Robert

Watts, Ephraim
See Horne, Richard Henry Hengist

Watts, Isaac 1674-1748 .... **LC 98**
See also DLB 95; RGEL 2; SATA 52

Waugh, Auberon (Alexander) 1939-2001 .... **CLC 7**
See also CA 45-48; 192; CANR 6, 22, 92; DLB 14, 194

Waugh, Evelyn (Arthur St. John) 1903-1966 .. **CLC 1, 3, 8, 13, 19, 27, 44, 107; SSC 41; WLC**
See also BPFB 3; BRW 7; CA 85-88; 25-28R; CANR 22; CDBLB 1914-1945; DA; DA3; DAB; DAC; DAM MST, NOV, POP; DLB 15, 162, 195; EWL 3; MTCW 1, 2; NFS 13, 17; RGEL 2; RGSF 2; TEA; WLIT 4

Waugh, Harriet 1944- .... **CLC 6**
See also CA 85-88; CANR 22
Ways, C. R.
See Blount, Roy (Alton), Jr.
Waystaff, Simon
See Swift, Jonathan
Webb, Beatrice (Martha Potter)
1858-1943 .... **TCLC 22**
See also CA 117; 162; DLB 190; FW
Webb, Charles (Richard) 1939- .... **CLC 7**
See also CA 25-28R; CANR 114
Webb, Frank J. .... **NCLC 143**
See also DLB 50
Webb, James H(enry), Jr. 1946- ...... **CLC 22**
See also CA 81-84
Webb, Mary Gladys (Meredith)
1881-1927 .... **TCLC 24**
See also CA 182; 123; DLB 34; FW
Webb, Mrs. Sidney
See Webb, Beatrice (Martha Potter)
Webb, Phyllis 1927- .... **CLC 18**
See also CA 104; CANR 23; CCA 1; CP 7;
CWP; DLB 53
Webb, Sidney (James) 1859-1947 .. **TCLC 22**
See also CA 117; 163; DLB 190
Webber, Andrew Lloyd .... **CLC 21**
See Lloyd Webber, Andrew
See also DFS 7
Weber, Lenora Mattingly
1895-1971 .... **CLC 12**
See also CA 19-20; 29-32R; CAP 1; SATA
2; SATA-Obit 26
Weber, Max 1864-1920 .... **TCLC 69**
See also CA 109; 189; DLB 296
Webster, John 1580(?)-1634(?) ...... **DC 2; LC
33, 84; WLC**
See also BRW 2; CDBLB Before 1660; DA;
DAB; DAC; DAM DRAM, MST; DFS
17, 19; DLB 58; IDTP; RGEL 2; WLIT 3
Webster, Noah 1758-1843 .... **NCLC 30**
See also DLB 1, 37, 42, 43, 73, 243
Wedekind, (Benjamin) Frank(lin)
1864-1918 .... **TCLC 7**
See also CA 104; 153; CANR 121, 122;
CDWLB 2; DAM DRAM; DLB 118; EW
8; EWL 3; LMFS 2; RGWL 2, 3
Wehr, Demaris .... **CLC 65**
Weidman, Jerome 1913-1998 .... **CLC 7**
See also AITN 2; CA 1-4R; 171; CAD;
CANR 1; DLB 28
Weil, Simone (Adolphine)
1909-1943 .... **TCLC 23**
See also CA 117; 159; EW 12; EWL 3; FW;
GFL 1789 to the Present; MTCW 2
Weininger, Otto 1880-1903 .... **TCLC 84**
Weinstein, Nathan
See West, Nathanael
Weinstein, Nathan von Wallenstein
See West, Nathanael
Weir, Peter (Lindsay) 1944- .... **CLC 20**
See also CA 113; 123
Weiss, Peter (Ulrich) 1916-1982 .. **CLC 3, 15,
51; TCLC 152**
See also CA 45-48; 106; CANR 3; DAM
DRAM; DFS 3; DLB 69, 124; EWL 3;
RGWL 2, 3
Weiss, Theodore (Russell)
1916-2003 .... **CLC 3, 8, 14**
See also CA 9-12R; 189; 216; CAAE 189;
CAAS 2; CANR 46, 94; CP 7; DLB 5
Welch, (Maurice) Denton
1915-1948 .... **TCLC 22**
See also BRWS 8, 9; CA 121; 148; RGEL
2

Welch, James (Phillip) 1940-2003 ..... **CLC 6,
14, 52; NNAL; PC 62**
See also CA 85-88; 219; CANR 42, 66, 107;
CN 7; CP 7; CPW; DAM MULT, POP;
DLB 175, 256; LATS 1:1; RGAL 4;
TCWW 2
Weldon, Fay 1931- . **CLC 6, 9, 11, 19, 36, 59,
122**
See also BRWS 4; CA 21-24R; CANR 16,
46, 63, 97; CDBLB 1960 to Present; CN
7; CPW; DAM POP; DLB 14, 194; EWL
3; FW; HGG; INT CANR-16; MTCW 1,
2; RGEL 2; RGSF 2
Wellek, Rene 1903-1995 .... **CLC 28**
See also CA 5-8R; 150; CAAS 7; CANR 8;
DLB 63; EWL 3; INT CANR-8
Weller, Michael 1942- .... **CLC 10, 53**
See also CA 85-88; CAD; CD 5
Weller, Paul 1958- .... **CLC 26**
Wellershoff, Dieter 1925- .... **CLC 46**
See also CA 89-92; CANR 16, 37
Welles, (George) Orson 1915-1985 .. **CLC 20,
80**
See also AAYA 40; CA 93-96; 117
Wellman, John McDowell 1945-
See Wellman, Mac
See also CA 166; CD 5
Wellman, Mac .... **CLC 65**
See Wellman, John McDowell; Wellman,
John McDowell
See also CAD; RGAL 4
Wellman, Manly Wade 1903-1986 ... **CLC 49**
See also CA 1-4R; 118; CANR 6, 16, 44;
FANT; SATA 6; SATA-Obit 47; SFW 4;
SUFW
Wells, Carolyn 1869(?)-1942 .... **TCLC 35**
See also CA 113; 185; CMW 4; DLB 11
Wells, H(erbert) G(eorge) 1866-1946 . **SSC 6,
70; TCLC 6, 12, 19, 133; WLC**
See also AAYA 18; BPFB 3; BRW 6; CA
110; 121; CDBLB 1914-1945; CLR 64;
DA; DA3; DAB; DAC; DAM MST, NOV;
DLB 34, 70, 156, 178; EWL 3; EXPS;
HGG; LAIT 3; LMFS 2; MTCW 1, 2;
NFS 17, 20; RGEL 2; RGSF 2; SATA 20;
SCFW; SFW 4; SSFS 3; SUFW; TEA;
WCH; WLIT 4; YAW
Wells, Rosemary 1943- .... **CLC 12**
See also AAYA 13; BYA 7, 8; CA 85-88;
CANR 48, 120; CLR 16, 69; CWRI 5;
MAICYA 1, 2; SAAS 1; SATA 18, 69,
114; YAW
Wells-Barnett, Ida B(ell)
1862-1931 .... **TCLC 125**
See also CA 182; DLB 23, 221
Welsh, Irvine 1958- .... **CLC 144**
See also CA 173; DLB 271
Welty, Eudora (Alice) 1909-2001 .. **CLC 1, 2,
5, 14, 22, 33, 105; SSC 1, 27, 51; WLC**
See also AAYA 48; AMW; AMWR 1; BPFB
3; CA 9-12R; 199; CABS 1; CANR 32,
65, 128; CDALB 1941-1968; CN 7; CSW;
DA; DA3; DAB; DAC; DAM MST, NOV;
DLB 2, 102, 143; DLBD 12; DLBY 1987,
2001; EWL 3; EXPS; HGG; LAIT 3;
MAWW; MTCW 1, 2; NFS 13, 15; RGAL
4; RGSF 2; RHW; SSFS 2, 10; TUS
Wen I-to 1899-1946 .... **TCLC 28**
See also EWL 3
Wentworth, Robert
See Hamilton, Edmond
Werfel, Franz (Viktor) 1890-1945 ... **TCLC 8**
See also CA 104; 161; DLB 81, 124; EWL
3; RGWL 2, 3
Wergeland, Henrik Arnold
1808-1845 .... **NCLC 5**
Wersba, Barbara 1932- .... **CLC 30**
See also AAYA 2, 30; BYA 6, 12, 13; CA
29-32R, 182; CAAE 182; CANR 16, 38;

CLR 3, 78; DLB 52; JRDA; MAICYA 1,
2; SAAS 2; SATA 1, 58; SATA-Essay 103;
WYA; YAW
Wertmueller, Lina 1928- .... **CLC 16**
See also CA 97-100; CANR 39, 78
Wescott, Glenway 1901-1987 .. **CLC 13; SSC
35**
See also CA 13-16R; 121; CANR 23, 70;
DLB 4, 9, 102; RGAL 4
Wesker, Arnold 1932- .... **CLC 3, 5, 42**
See also CA 1-4R; CAAS 7; CANR 1, 33;
CBD; CD 5; CDBLB 1960 to Present;
DAB; DAM DRAM; DLB 13; EWL 3;
MTCW 1; RGEL 2; TEA
Wesley, John 1703-1791 .... **LC 88**
See also DLB 104
Wesley, Richard (Errol) 1945- .... **CLC 7**
See also BW 1; CA 57-60; CAD; CANR
27; CD 5; DLB 38
Wessel, Johan Herman 1742-1785 .... **LC 7**
See also DLB 300
West, Anthony (Panther)
1914-1987 .... **CLC 50**
See also CA 45-48; 124; CANR 3, 19; DLB
15
West, C. P.
See Wodehouse, P(elham) G(renville)
West, Cornel (Ronald) 1953- .... **BLCS; CLC
134**
See also CA 144; CANR 91; DLB 246
West, Delno C(loyde), Jr. 1936- .... **CLC 70**
See also CA 57-60
West, Dorothy 1907-1998 .. **HR 3; TCLC 108**
See also BW 2; CA 143; 169; DLB 76
West, (Mary) Jessamyn 1902-1984 ... **CLC 7,
17**
See also CA 9-12R; 112; CANR 27; DLB
6; DLBY 1984; MTCW 1, 2; RGAL 4;
RHW; SATA-Obit 37; TCWW 2; TUS;
YAW
West, Morris
See West, Morris L(anglo)
See also DLB 289
West, Morris L(anglo) 1916-1999 ..... **CLC 6,
33**
See West, Morris
See also BPFB 3; CA 5-8R; 187; CANR
24, 49, 64; CN 7; CPW; MTCW 1, 2
West, Nathanael 1903-1940 ... **SSC 16; TCLC
1, 14, 44**
See also AMW; AMWR 2; BPFB 3; CA
104; 125; CDALB 1929-1941; DA3; DLB
4, 9, 28; EWL 3; MTCW 1, 2; NFS 16;
RGAL 4; TUS
West, Owen
See Koontz, Dean R(ay)
West, Paul 1930- .... **CLC 7, 14, 96**
See also CA 13-16R; CAAS 7; CANR 22,
53, 76, 89; CN 7; DLB 14; INT CANR-
22; MTCW 2
West, Rebecca 1892-1983 ... **CLC 7, 9, 31, 50**
See also BPFB 3; BRWS 3; CA 5-8R; 109;
CANR 19; DLB 36; DLBY 1983; EWL
3; FW; MTCW 1, 2; NCFS 4; RGEL 2;
TEA
Westall, Robert (Atkinson)
1929-1993 .... **CLC 17**
See also AAYA 12; BYA 2, 6, 7, 8, 9, 15;
CA 69-72; 141; CANR 18, 68; CLR 13;
FANT; JRDA; MAICYA 1, 2; MAICYAS
1; SAAS 2; SATA 23, 69; SATA-Obit 75;
WYA; YAW
Westermarck, Edward 1862-1939 . **TCLC 87**
Westlake, Donald E(dwin) 1933- . **CLC 7, 33**
See also BPFB 3; CA 17-20R; CAAS 13;
CANR 16, 44, 65, 94; CMW 4; CPW;
DAM POP; INT CANR-16; MSW;
MTCW 2

Literary Criticism Series
Cumulative Topic Index

This index lists all topic entries in Gale's *Children's Literature Review* (CLR), *Classical and Medieval Literature Criticism* (CMLC), *Contemporary Literary Criticism* (CLC), *Drama Criticism* (DC), *Literature Criticism from 1400 to 1800* (LC), *Nineteenth-Century Literature Criticism* (NCLC), *Short Story Criticism* (SSC), and *Twentieth-Century Literary Criticism* (TCLC). The index also lists topic entries in the Gale Critical Companion Collection, which includes the following publications: *The Beat Generation* (BG), and *Harlem Renaissance* (HR).

TCLC Cumulative Nationality Index

AMERICAN

Abbey, Edward **160**
Adams, Andy **56**
Adams, Brooks **80**
Adams, Henry (Brooks) **4, 52**
Addams, Jane **76**
Agee, James (Rufus) **1, 19**
Aldrich, Bess (Genevra) Streeter **125**
Allen, Fred **87**
Anderson, Maxwell **2, 144**
Anderson, Sherwood **1, 10, 24, 123**
Anthony, Susan B(rownell) **84**
Atherton, Gertrude (Franklin Horn) **2**
Austin, Mary (Hunter) **25**
Baker, Ray Stannard **47**
Baker, Carlos (Heard) **119**
Bambara, Toni Cade **116**
Barry, Philip **11**
Baum, L(yman) Frank **7, 132**
Beard, Charles A(ustin) **15**
Becker, Carl (Lotus) **63**
Belasco, David **3**
Bell, James Madison **43**
Benchley, Robert (Charles) **1, 55**
Benedict, Ruth (Fulton) **60**
Benét, Stephen Vincent **7**
Benét, William Rose **28**
Bettelheim, Bruno **143**
Bierce, Ambrose (Gwinett) **1, 7, 44**
Biggers, Earl Derr **65**
Bishop, Elizabeth **121**
Bishop, John Peale **103**
Black Elk **33**
Boas, Franz **56**
Bodenheim, Maxwell **44**
Bok, Edward W. **101**
Bourne, Randolph S(illiman) **16**
Boyd, James **115**
Boyd, Thomas (Alexander) **111**
Bradford, Gamaliel **36**
Brautigan, Richard **133**
Brennan, Christopher John **17**
Brennan, Maeve **124**
Brodkey, Harold (Roy) **123**
Bromfield, Louis (Brucker) **11**
Broun, Heywood **104**
Bryan, William Jennings **99**
Burroughs, Edgar Rice **2, 32**
Burroughs, William S(eward) **121**
Cabell, James Branch **6**
Cable, George Washington **4**
Cahan, Abraham **71**
Caldwell, Erskine (Preston) **117**
Campbell, Joseph **140**
Capote, Truman **164**
Cardozo, Benjamin N(athan) **65**
Carnegie, Dale **53**
Cather, Willa (Sibert) **1, 11, 31, 99, 132, 152**
Chambers, Robert W(illiam) **41**
Chambers, (David) Whittaker **129**
Chandler, Raymond (Thornton) **1, 7**
Chapman, John Jay **7**

Chase, Mary Ellen **124**
Chesnutt, Charles W(addell) **5, 39**
Childress, Alice **116**
Chopin, Katherine **5, 14, 127**
Cobb, Irvin S(hrewsbury) **77**
Coffin, Robert P(eter) Tristram **95**
Cohan, George M(ichael) **60**
Comstock, Anthony **13**
Cotter, Joseph Seamon Sr. **28**
Cram, Ralph Adams **45**
Crane, (Harold) Hart **2, 5, 80**
Crane, Stephen (Townley) **11, 17, 32**
Crawford, F(rancis) Marion **10**
Crothers, Rachel **19**
Cullen, Countée **4, 37**
Cummings, E. E. **137**
Darrow, Clarence (Seward) **81**
Davis, Rebecca (Blaine) Harding **6**
Davis, Richard Harding **24**
Day, Clarence (Shepard Jr.) **25**
Dent, Lester **72**
De Voto, Bernard (Augustine) **29**
Dewey, John **95**
Dickey, James **151**
Dixon, Thomas, Jr. **163**
di Donato, Pietro **159**
Dreiser, Theodore (Herman Albert) **10, 18, 35, 83**
Du Bois, W. E. B. **169**
Dulles, John Foster **72**
Dunbar, Paul Laurence **2, 12**
Duncan, Isadora **68**
Dunne, Finley Peter **28**
Eastman, Charles A(lexander) **55**
Eddy, Mary (Ann Morse) Baker **71**
Einstein, Albert **65**
Erskine, John **84**
Faulkner, William **141**
Faust, Frederick (Schiller) **49**
Fenollosa, Ernest (Francisco) **91**
Fields, W. C. **80**
Fisher, Dorothy (Frances) Canfield **87**
Fisher, Rudolph **11**
Fisher, Vardis **140**
Fitzgerald, F(rancis) Scott (Key) **1, 6, 14, 28, 55, 157**
Fitzgerald, Zelda (Sayre) **52**
Fletcher, John Gould **35**
Foote, Mary Hallock **108**
Ford, Henry **73**
Forten, Charlotte L. **16**
Freeman, Douglas Southall **11**
Freeman, Mary E(leanor) Wilkins **9**
Fuller, Henry Blake **103**
Futrelle, Jacques **19**
Gale, Zona **7**
Garland, (Hannibal) Hamlin **3**
Gilman, Charlotte (Anna) Perkins (Stetson) **9, 37, 117**
Ginsberg, Allen **120**
Glasgow, Ellen (Anderson Gholson) **2, 7**
Glaspell, Susan **55**
Goldman, Emma **13**

Green, Anna Katharine **63**
Grey, Zane **6**
Griffith, D(avid Lewelyn) W(ark) **68**
Griggs, Sutton (Elbert) **77**
Guest, Edgar A(lbert) **95**
Guiney, Louise Imogen **41**
Haley, Alex **147**
Hall, James Norman **23**
Handy, W(illiam) C(hristopher) **97**
Harper, Frances Ellen Watkins **14**
Harris, Joel Chandler **2**
Harte, (Francis) Bret(t) **1, 25**
Hartmann, Sadakichi **73**
Hatteras, Owen **18**
Hawthorne, Julian **25**
Hearn, (Patricio) Lafcadio (Tessima Carlos) **9**
Hecht, Ben **101**
Heller, Joseph **131, 151**
Hellman, Lillian (Florence) **119**
Hemingway, Ernest (Miller) **115**
Henry, O. **1, 19**
Hergesheimer, Joseph **11**
Heyward, (Edwin) DuBose **59**
Higginson, Thomas Wentworth **36**
Himes, Chester **139**
Holley, Marietta **99**
Holly, Buddy **65**
Holmes, Oliver Wendell Jr. **77**
Hopkins, Pauline Elizabeth **28**
Horney, Karen (Clementine Theodore Danielsen) **71**
Howard, Robert E(rvin) **8**
Howe, Julia Ward **21**
Howells, William Dean **7, 17, 41**
Huneker, James Gibbons **65**
Hurston, Zora Neale **121, 131**
Ince, Thomas H. **89**
James, Henry **2, 11, 24, 40, 47, 64, 171**
James, William **15, 32**
Jewett, (Theodora) Sarah Orne **1, 22**
Johnson, James Weldon **3, 19**
Johnson, Robert **69**
Kerouac, Jack **117**
Kinsey, Alfred C(harles) **91**
Kirk, Russell (Amos) **119**
Kornbluth, C(yril) M. **8**
Korzybski, Alfred (Habdank Skarbek) **61**
Kubrick, Stanley **112**
Kuttner, Henry **10**
Lardner, Ring(gold) W(ilmer) **2, 14**
Lewis, (Harry) Sinclair **4, 13, 23, 39**
Lewisohn, Ludwig **19**
Lewton, Val **76**
Lindsay, (Nicholas) Vachel **17**
Locke, Alain (Le Roy) **43**
Lockridge, Ross (Franklin) Jr. **111**
London, Jack **9, 15, 39**
Lovecraft, H(oward) P(hillips) **4, 22**
Lowell, Amy **1, 8**
Malamud, Bernard **129**
Mankiewicz, Herman (Jacob) **85**
March, William **96**
Markham, Edwin **47**

DUTCH

Bok, Edward W. **101**
Couperus, Louis (Marie Anne) **15**
Heijermans, Herman **24**
Hillesum, Etty **49**
van Schendel, Arthur(-Francois-Émile) **56**

ENGLISH

Abbott, Edwin **139**
Abercrombie, Lascelles **141**
Alexander, Samuel **77**
Barbellion, W. N. P. **24**
Baring, Maurice **8**
Baring-Gould, Sabine **88**
Beerbohm, (Henry) Max(imilian) **1, 24**
Bell, Gertrude (Margaret Lowthian) **67**
Belloc, (Joseph) Hilaire (Pierre Sebastien
  Rene Swanton) **7, 18**
Bennett, (Enoch) Arnold **5, 20**
Benson, A.C. **123**
Benson, E(dward) F(rederic) **27**
Benson, Stella **17**
Bentley, E(dmund) C(lerihew) **12**
Beresford, J(ohn) D(avys) **81**
Besant, Annie (Wood) **9**
Blackmore, R(ichard) D(oddridge) **27**
Blackwood, Algernon (Henry) **5**
Bottomley, Gordon **107**
Bowen, Elizabeth **148**
Braddon, Mary Elizabeth **111**
Bramah, Ernest **72**
Bridges, Robert (Seymour) **1**
Brooke, Rupert (Chawner) **2, 7**
Buchanan, Robert **107**
Burke, Thomas **63**
Butler, Samuel **1, 33**
Butts, Mary **77**
Byron, Robert **67**
Caine, Hall **97**
Carpenter, Edward **88**
Carter, Angela **139**
Chesterton, G(ilbert) K(eith) **1, 6, 64**
Childers, (Robert) Erskine **65**
Churchill, Winston (Leonard Spencer) **113**
Clark, Kenneth Mackenzie **147**
Coleridge, Mary E(lizabeth) **73**
Collier, John **127**
Collingwood, R(obin) G(eorge) **67**
Conrad, Joseph **1, 6, 13, 25, 43, 57**
Coppard, A(lfred) E(dgar) **5**
Corelli, Marie **51**
Crofts, Freeman Wills **55**
Crowley, Aleister **7**
Dale, Colin **18**
Davies, William Henry **5**
Delafield, E. M. **61**
de la Mare, Walter (John) **4, 53**
Dobson, Austin **79**
Doughty, Charles M(ontagu) **27**
Douglas, Keith (Castellain) **40**
Dowson, Ernest (Christopher) **4**
Doyle, Arthur Conan **7**
Drinkwater, John **57**
Dunsany **2, 59**
Eddison, E(ric) R(ucker) **15**
Elaine **18**
Elizabeth **41**
Ellis, (Henry) Havelock **14**
Firbank, (Arthur Annesley) Ronald **1**
Flecker, (Herman) James Elroy **43**
Ford, Ford Madox **1, 15, 39, 57**
Forester, C(ecil) S(cott) **152**
Forster, E(dward) M(organ) **125**
Freeman, R(ichard) Austin **21**
Galsworthy, John **1, 45**
Gilbert, W(illiam) S(chwenck) **3**
Gill, Eric **85**
Gissing, George (Robert) **3, 24, 47**
Glyn, Elinor **72**
Gosse, Edmund (William) **28**
Grahame, Kenneth **64, 136**

Granville-Barker, Harley **2**
Gray, John (Henry) **19**
Gurney, Ivor (Bertie) **33**
Haggard, H(enry) Rider **11**
Hall, (Marguerite) Radclyffe **12**
Hardy, Thomas **4, 10, 18, 32, 48, 53, 72,
  143, 153**
Henley, William Ernest **8**
Hilton, James **21**
Hodgson, William Hope **13**
Hope, Anthony **83**
Housman, A(lfred) E(dward) **1, 10**
Housman, Laurence **7**
Hudson, W(illiam) H(enry) **29**
Hulme, T(homas) E(rnest) **21**
Hunt, Violet **53**
Jacobs, W(illiam) W(ymark) **22**
James, Montague (Rhodes) **6**
Jerome, Jerome K(lapka) **23**
Johnson, Lionel (Pigot) **19**
Kaye-Smith, Sheila **20**
Keynes, John Maynard **64**
Kipling, (Joseph) Rudyard **8, 17, 167**
Laski, Harold J(oseph) **79**
Lawrence, D(avid) H(erbert Richards) **2, 9,
  16, 33, 48, 61, 93**
Lawrence, T(homas) E(dward) **18**
Lee, Vernon **5**
Lee-Hamilton, Eugene (Jacob) **22**
Leverson, Ada **18**
Lindsay, David **15**
Lowndes, Marie Adelaide (Belloc) **12**
Lowry, (Clarence) Malcolm **6, 40**
Lucas, E(dward) V(errall) **73**
Macaulay, (Emilie) Rose **7, 44**
MacCarthy, (Charles Otto) Desmond **36**
Mackenzie, Compton (Edward Montague)
  116
Maitland, Frederic William **65**
Manning, Frederic **25**
Marsh, Edward **99**
McTaggart, John McTaggart Ellis **105**
Meredith, George **17, 43**
Mew, Charlotte (Mary) **8**
Meynell, Alice (Christina Gertrude
  Thompson) **6**
Middleton, Richard (Barham) **56**
Milne, A(lan) A(lexander) **6, 88**
Moore, G. E. **89**
Morrison, Arthur **72**
Muggeridge, Thomas (Malcom) **120**
Murdoch, Iris **171**
Murry, John Middleton **16**
Myers, L(eopold) H(amilton) **59**
Nightingale, Florence **85**
Naipaul, Shiva(dhar) (Srinivasa) **153**
Noyes, Alfred **7**
Oppenheim, E(dward) Phillips **45**
Orage, Alfred Richard **157**
Orton, Joe **157**
Orwell, George **2, 6, 15, 31, 51, 128, 129**
Osborne, John **153**
Owen, Wilfred (Edward Salter) **5, 27**
Pankhurst, Emmeline (Goulden) **100**
Pinero, Arthur Wing **32**
Powys, T(heodore) F(rancis) **9**
Quiller-Couch, Arthur (Thomas) **53**
Richardson, Dorothy Miller **3**
Rolfe, Frederick (William Serafino Austin
  Lewis Mary) **12**
Rosenberg, Isaac **12**
Ruskin, John **20**
Sabatini, Rafael **47**
Saintsbury, George (Edward Bateman) **31**
Sapper **44**
Sayers, Dorothy L(eigh) **2, 15**
Shiel, M(atthew) P(hipps) **8**
Sinclair, May **3, 11**
Stapledon, (William) Olaf **22**
Stead, William Thomas **48**
Stephen, Leslie **23**
Strachey, (Giles) Lytton **12**

Summers, (Alphonsus Joseph-Mary
  Augustus) Montague **16**
Sutro, Alfred **6**
Swinburne, Algernon Charles **8, 36**
Symons, Arthur **11**
Thomas, (Philip) Edward **10**
Thompson, Francis (Joseph) **4**
Tolkien, J. R. R. **137**
Tomlinson, H(enry) M(ajor) **71**
Trotter, Wilfred **97**
Upward, Allen **85**
Van Druten, John (William) **2**
Wakefield, Herbert (Russell) **120**
Wallace, (Richard Horatio) Edgar **57**
Wallas, Graham **91**
Walpole, Hugh (Seymour) **5**
Ward, Mary Augusta **55**
Warner, Sylvia Townsend **131**
Warung, Price **45**
Webb, Mary Gladys (Meredith) **24**
Webb, Sidney (James) **22**
Welch, (Maurice) Denton **22**
Wells, H(erbert) G(eorge) **6, 12, 19, 133**
Whitehead, Alfred North **97**
Williams, Charles (Walter Stansby) **1, 11**
Wodehouse, P(elham) G(renville) **108**
Woolf, (Adeline) Virginia **1, 5, 20, 43, 56,
  101, 128**
Yonge, Charlotte (Mary) **48**
Zangwill, Israel **16**

ESTONIAN

Talvik, Heiti **87**
Tammsaare, A(nton) H(ansen) **27**

FINNISH

Leino, Eino **24**
Soedergran, Edith (Irene) **31**
Westermarck, Edward **87**

FRENCH

Alain **41**
Apollinaire, Guillaume **3, 8, 51**
Arp, Jean **115**
Artaud, Antonin (Marie Joseph) **3, 36**
Bachelard, Gaston **128**
Barbusse, Henri **5**
Barrès, (Auguste-)Maurice **47**
Barthes, Roland **135**
Bataille, Georges **155**
Benda, Julien **60**
Bergson, Henri(-Louis) **32**
Bernanos, (Paul Louis) Georges **3**
Bernhardt, Sarah (Henriette Rosine) **75**
Bloy, Léon **22**
Bourget, Paul (Charles Joseph) **12**
Claudel, Paul (Louis Charles Marie) **2, 10**
Cocteau, Jean (Maurice Eugene Clement)
  119
Colette, (Sidonie-Gabrielle) **1, 5, 16**
Coppee, Francois **25**
Crevel, Rene **112**
Daumal, Rene **14**
Deleuze, Gilles **116**
Desnos, Robert **22**
Drieu la Rochelle, Pierre(-Eugène) **21**
Dujardin, Edouard (Emile Louis) **13**
Durkheim, Emile **55**
Epstein, Jean **92**
Fargue, Leon-Paul **11**
Feydeau, Georges (Léon Jules Marie) **22**
Fondane, Benjamin **159**
Genet, Jean **128**
Gide, André (Paul Guillaume) **5, 12, 36**
Giono, Jean **124**
Giraudoux, Jean(-Hippolyte) **2, 7**
Gourmont, Remy(-Marie-Charles) de **17**
Halévy, Elie **104**
Huysmans, Joris-Karl **7, 69**
Jacob, (Cyprien-)Max **6**
Jammes, Francis **75**

Suzuki, Daisetz Teitaro **109**
Yokomitsu, Riichi **47**
Yosano Akiko **59**

LATVIAN

Berlin, Isaiah **105**
Rainis, Jānis **29**

LEBANESE

Gibran, Kahlil **1, 9**

LESOTHAN

Mofolo, Thomas (Mokopu) **22**

LITHUANIAN

Kreve (Mickevicius), Vincas **27**

MEXICAN

Azuela, Mariano **3**
Gamboa, Federico **36**
Garro, Elena **153**
Gonzalez Martinez, Enrique **72**
Ibargüengoitia, Jorge **148**
Nervo, (Jose) Amado (Ruiz de) **11**
Reyes, Alfonso **33**
Romero, José Rubén **14**
Villaurrutia, Xavier **80**

NEPALI

Devkota, Laxmiprasad **23**

NEW ZEALANDER

Mander, (Mary) Jane **31**
Mansfield, Katherine **2, 8, 39, 164**

NICARAGUAN

Darío, Rubén **4**

NIGERIAN

Okigbo, Christopher **171**

NORWEGIAN

Bjoernson, Bjoernstjerne (Martinius) **7, 37**
Bojer, Johan **64**
Grieg, (Johan) Nordahl (Brun) **10**
Hamsun, Knut **151**
Ibsen, Henrik (Johan) **2, 8, 16, 37, 52**
Kielland, Alexander Lange **5**
Lie, Jonas (Lauritz Idemil) **5**
Obstfelder, Sigbjoern **23**
Skram, Amalie (Bertha) **25**
Undset, Sigrid **3**

PAKISTANI

Iqbal, Muhammad **28**

PERUVIAN

Arguedas, José María **147**
Palma, Ricardo **29**
Vallejo, César (Abraham) **3, 56**

POLISH

Asch, Sholem **3**
Borowski, Tadeusz **9**
Conrad, Joseph **1, 6, 13, 25, 43, 57**
Herbert, Zbigniew **168**
Peretz, Isaac Loeb **16**
Prus, Boleslaw **48**
Przybyszewski, Stanislaw **36**
Reymont, Wladyslaw (Stanislaw) **5**
Schulz, Bruno **5, 51**
Sienkiewicz, Henryk (Adam Alexander Pius) **3**
Singer, Israel Joshua **33**
Witkiewicz, Stanislaw Ignacy **8**

PORTUGUESE

Pessoa, Fernando (António Nogueira) **27**
Sa-Carniero, Mario de **83**

PUERTO RICAN

Hostos (y Bonilla), Eugenio Maria de **24**

ROMANIAN

Bacovia, George **24**
Caragiale, Ion Luca **76**
Rebreanu, Liviu **28**

RUSSIAN

Aldanov, Mark (Alexandrovich) **23**
Andreyev, Leonid (Nikolaevich) **3**
Annensky, Innokenty (Fyodorovich) **14**
Artsybashev, Mikhail (Petrovich) **31**
Babel, Isaak (Emmanuilovich) **2, 13, 171**
Bagritsky, Eduard **60**
Bakhtin, Mikhail **160**
Balmont, Konstantin (Dmitriyevich) **11**
Bely, Andrey **7**
Berdyaev, Nikolai (Aleksandrovich) **67**
Bergelson, David **81**
Blok, Alexander (Alexandrovich) **5**
Bryusov, Valery Yakovlevich **10**
Bulgakov, Mikhail (Afanas'evich) **2, 16, 159**
Bulgya, Alexander Alexandrovich **53**
Bunin, Ivan Alexeyevich **6**
Chekhov, Anton (Pavlovich) **3, 10, 31, 55, 96, 163**
Der Nister **56**
Eisenstein, Sergei (Mikhailovich) **57**
Esenin, Sergei (Alexandrovich) **4**
Fadeyev, Alexander **53**
Gladkov, Fyodor (Vasilyevich) **27**
Gumilev, Nikolai (Stepanovich) **60**
Gurdjieff, G(eorgei) I(vanovich) **71**
Guro, Elena **56**
Hippius, Zinaida **9**
Ilf, Ilya **21**
Ivanov, Vyacheslav Ivanovich **33**
Kandinsky, Wassily **92**
Khlebnikov, Velimir **20**
Khodasevich, Vladislav (Felitsianovich) **15**
Klimentov, Andrei Platonovich **14**
Korolenko, Vladimir Galaktionovich **22**
Kropotkin, Peter (Aleksieevich) **36**
Kuprin, Aleksander Ivanovich **5**
Kuzmin, Mikhail **40**
Lenin, V. I. **67**
Mandelstam, Osip (Emilievich) **2, 6**
Mayakovski, Vladimir (Vladimirovich) **4, 18**
Merezhkovsky, Dmitry Sergeyevich **29**
Nabokov, Vladimir (Vladimirovich) **108**
Olesha, Yuri **136**
Pavlov, Ivan Petrovich **91**
Petrov, Evgeny **21**
Pilnyak, Boris **23**
Prishvin, Mikhail **75**
Remizov, Aleksei (Mikhailovich) **27**
Rozanov, Vassili **104**
Shestov, Lev **56**
Sologub, Fyodor **9**
Stalin, Joseph **92**
Stanislavsky, Konstantin **167**
Tolstoy, Alexey Nikolaevich **18**
Tolstoy, Leo (Nikolaevich) **4, 11, 17, 28, 44, 79**
Trotsky, Leon **22**
Tsvetaeva (Efron), Marina (Ivanovna) **7, 35**
Zabolotsky, Nikolai Alekseevich **52**
Zamyatin, Evgeny Ivanovich **8, 37**
Zhdanov, Andrei Alexandrovich **18**
Zoshchenko, Mikhail (Mikhailovich) **15**

SCOTTISH

Barrie, J(ames) M(atthew) **2, 164**
Brown, George Douglas **28**
Buchan, John **41**

Cunninghame Graham, Robert (Gallnigad) Bontine **19**
Davidson, John **24**
Doyle, Arthur Conan **7**
Frazer, J(ames) G(eorge) **32**
Lang, Andrew **16**
MacDonald, George **9, 113**
Muir, Edwin **2, 87**
Murray, James Augustus Henry **117**
Sharp, William **39**
Tey, Josephine **14**

SLOVENIAN

Cankar, Ivan **105**

SOUTH AFRICAN

Bosman, Herman Charles **49**
Campbell, (Ignatius) Roy (Dunnachie) **5**
La Guma, Alex **140**
Mqhayi, S(amuel) E(dward) K(rune Loliwe) **25**
Paton, Alan **165**
Plaatje, Sol(omon) T(shekisho) **73**
Schreiner, Olive (Emilie Albertina) **9**
Smith, Pauline (Urmson) **25**
Vilakazi, Benedict Wallet **37**

SPANISH

Alas (y Urena), Leopoldo (Enrique Garcia) **29**
Aleixandre, Vicente **113**
Barea, Arturo **14**
Baroja (y Nessi), Pio **8**
Benavente (y Martinez), Jacinto **3**
Blasco Ibáñez, Vicente **12**
Echegaray (y Eizaguirre), Jose (Maria Waldo) **4**
García Lorca, Federico **1, 7, 49**
Jiménez (Mantecón), Juan Ramón **4**
Machado (y Ruiz), Antonio **3**
Martinez Sierra, Gregorio **6**
Martinez Sierra, Maria (de la O'LeJarraga) **6**
Miro (Ferrer), Gabriel (Francisco Victor) **5**
Onetti, Juan Carlos **131**
Ortega y Gasset, José **9**
Pereda (y Sanchez de Porrua), Jose Maria de **16**
Pérez Galdós, Benito **27**
Ramoacn y Cajal, Santiago **93**
Salinas (y Serrano), Pedro **17**
Sender, Ramón **136**
Unamuno (y Jugo), Miguel de **2, 9, 148**
Valera y Alcala-Galiano, Juan **10**
Valle-Inclán, Ramón (Maria) del **5**

SWEDISH

Bengtsson, Frans (Gunnar) **48**
Dagerman, Stig (Halvard) **17**
Ekelund, Vilhelm **75**
Heidenstam, (Carl Gustaf) Verner von **5**
Key, Ellen (Karolina Sofia) **65**
Lagerkvist, Pär **144**
Lagerloef, Selma (Ottiliana Lovisa) **4, 36**
Söderberg, Hjalmar **39**
Strindberg, (Johan) August **1, 8, 21, 47**
Weiss, Peter **152**

SWISS

Canetti, Elias **157**
Frisch, Max (Rudolf) **121**
Hesse, Herman **148**
Ramuz, Charles-Ferdinand **33**
Rod, Edouard **52**
Saussure, Ferdinand de **49**
Spitteler, Carl (Friedrich Georg) **12**
Walser, Robert **18**

SYRIAN

Gibran, Kahlil **1, 9**

TCLC-171 Title Index